ART

A HISTORY OF PAINTING · SCULPTURE · ARCHITECTURE

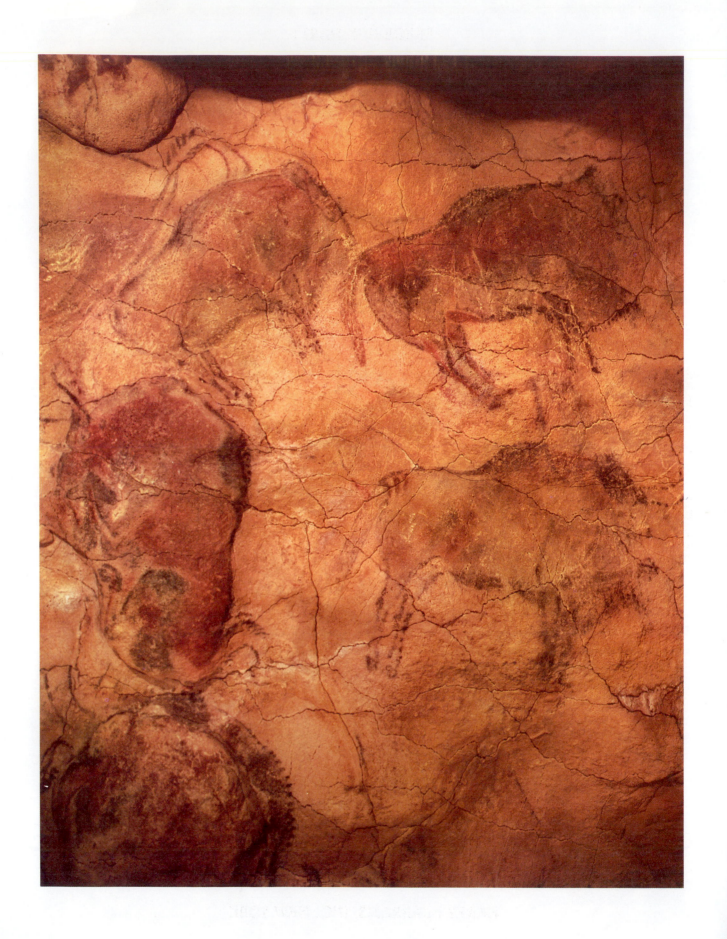

FREDERICK HARTT

ART

A
HISTORY
OF
PAINTING
SCULPTURE
ARCHITECTURE

VOLUME ONE

FOURTH EDITION

PRENTICE HALL, INC., ENGLEWOOD CLIFFS, NEW JERSEY

AND

HARRY N. ABRAMS, INC., NEW YORK

To Meyer Schapiro

Scholar, teacher, counselor, friend

Project Managers: Sheila Franklin Lieber and Julia Moore

Editor: Ellyn Childs Allison

Designers: Dirk Luykx and Ellen Nygaard Ford

Picture Research, Rights and Reproductions: Lauren Boucher assisted by Colin Scott

Frontispiece: *Bison,* cave painting, Altamira, Spain (figure 1-6)

Library of Congress Cataloging-in-Publication Data
Hartt, Frederick.
Art : a history of painting, sculpture, architecture / Frederick
Hartt. — 4th ed.
p.   cm.
Includes bibliographical references and indexes.
ISBN 0–13–052416–6 (v. 1 : pbk.). — ISBN 0–13–052424–7 (v. 2 : pbk.)
1. Art — History.   I. Title.
N5300.H283   1992
709 — dc20   92–5809
                                                                CIP

Fourth Edition 1993
Copyright © 1989, 1993 Harry N. Abrams, Inc.
Published in 1993 by Harry N. Abrams, Incorporated, New York
A Times Mirror Company
Printed and bound in Japan

CONTENTS

PREFACE

Art is the only thing that can go on mattering
once it has stopped hurting.

Elizabeth Bowen

The purpose of this book is to give students of all ages something that really will go on mattering, once the blue books have been handed in and the painfully memorized names and dates have receded into dimmer levels of consciousness. To this end I have tried to put together a usable account of the whole history of the artistic production of men and women—an activity that ranks as the highest of all human achievements (so I maintain), surpassing even the most startling cures of modern medicine and the little machine hurtling past the last planets and out into interstellar space. Obviously no teacher can use all the material assembled here. But I respect teachers enough to give them their choice of what to include and what to leave out and students enough to want them to have a book that they can keep and continue to explore on their own, whether or not they ever take another course in the history of art.

The fourth edition is the product of many months of thought and labor. One hundred more illustrations have been reproduced in color. In order to keep the book within manageable proportions, the number of images remains about the same, although the addition of forty-eight pages has facilitated the enlargement of a great number of illustrations. The reader will note several substitutions in accordance with altered criteria of importance. In the third edition, to my great satisfaction, it was possible to make this book truly global by the addition of chapters on the arts of the three great civilizations of East Asia—India, China, and Japan. These chapters have benefited immensely by the criticism and suggestions of Marsha Weidner. For practical reasons it was necessary to place the chapters at the end of the book. In the fourth edition they have been brought to their most useful position, between the Middle Ages and the Renaissance in the West.

No single scholar can claim specialized knowledge of all periods in the history of art, and I have sought and welcomed criticism, especially of those chapters that lie outside my fields of study. But a committee book runs the same dangers as a committee course. Throughout the book, the interest of the reader has required unity of viewpoint. All the text, therefore, is the work of the same author, since it has luckily been possible for me to see and study in person the vast majority of the monuments and works of art treated here, from whatever region or period.

In the third edition, a pioneer attempt was made to give women something approaching their just position in the history of art. In the present edition, the number of women artists has been somewhat increased. But the reader should understand that the task is not as easy as it might seem. What can one say about women artists in periods when women were systematically excluded from all forms of artistic production except, let us say, embroidery? And what can one write about women as artistic leaders in later periods when they were still permitted only marginal participation? In those chapters in which women either do not appear at all or turn up in minor roles, an attempt is made to explain why. I hope the reader will also understand that what I say in the Introduction about women in art, and what I undertake in other chapters, has been carried out with enthusiasm and conviction. Time alone will tell whether it is sufficient.

The teacher-student relationship is one of the deepest and most productive of all human bonds. How can I forget what my own long career has owed to the teachers, graduate and undergraduate, who gave me my start? Fifty-nine years ago, as a college sophomore, I registered for a class with Meyer Schapiro, and the whole course of my life was transformed. Not only did he introduce me to the fields of medieval and modern art, in which his knowledge is vast, but he opened my eyes to the meaning of art-historical studies and to methods of art-historical thought and investigation. I am grateful to other magnificent teachers, now no longer living, especially to Walter W. S. Cook, Walter Friedlaender, Karl Lehmann, Millard Meiss, Richard Offner, Erwin Panofsky, George Rowley, and Rudolf Wittkower, and to Richard Krautheimer, abundantly alive and active at ninety-four. The faith, advice, and inspiration of Bernard Berenson stood me in good stead in many a difficult moment. I owe much to the generosity of Katherine S. Dreier, who in 1935 opened to me her pioneer collection of modern art, and to the rigorous discipline of the sculptor Robert Aitken, who taught me what a line means.

At this moment I think also with warmth and happiness of all my students since I began teaching in 1939—of those seas of faces in the big survey courses at Smith College, Washington University, the University of Pennsylvania, and the University of Virginia, as well as of the advanced and graduate groups, many of whose members have themselves been teaching for a quarter of a century and are now in a position to give me valued criticism and advice.

I am greatly indebted to professional colleagues who read chapters of the manuscript pertaining to their special fields, offered valuable criticism once the book was in print, or otherwise contributed to the first three editions, especially Malcolm Bell III, Miles Chappell, Kenneth J. Conant, John J. Dobbins, Marvin Eisenberg, Karl Kilinski II, Fred S. Kleiner, Keith P. F. Moxey, Marion Roberts, Martin S. Stanford, David Winter, Jeryldene Wood, and John J. Yiannias; and to Samuel Y. Edgerton, Jr., Scott Redford, and Fred T. Smith, who gave me many useful suggestions for the present edition.

I deeply appreciate the confidence of the late Harry N. Abrams for having entrusted me with the task of writing this book and am grateful to the unforgettable Milton S. Fox for starting me off on it. My thanks also go to Margaret L. Kaplan for her able direction of the first two editions, to John P. O'Neill and Margaret Donovan for their painstaking editorship of the first and second respectively, to Sheila Franklin Lieber for coping with the innumerable problems of the third and fourth, to Ellyn Childs Allison for her keen eye and sensitive care in editing them, and to Barbara Lyons and her staff, who—with infinite labor—assembled the illustrative material for all four editions, and especially to Lauren Boucher, who has solved increasingly difficult photographic problems for the present edition. Dirk Luykx brought his great ability to the redesign of the second edition, to the many adjustments in the layout of the third, and to the fresh design for the fourth.

Frederick Hartt
Fall 1991

PUBLISHER'S NOTE   Frederick Hartt died suddenly on October 31, 1991, just as he was finishing the revisions for this fourth edition. Harry N. Abrams, Inc., Professor Hartt's publisher for thirty-nine years, notes his passing with great regret and profound respect and thanks Nan Rosenthal for her wise counsel and assistance at a critical time, enabling us to publish the fourth edition of *Art: A History of Painting, Sculpture, Architecture* when Professor Hartt intended it.

INTRODUCTION

What is art? That question would have been answered differently in almost every epoch of history. Our word *art* comes from a Latin term meaning "skill, way, or method," and the most advanced technical procedures are still today characterized as "state of the art." In ancient times and during the Middle Ages all kinds of trades and professions were known as arts. The liberal arts of the medieval curriculum included music but neither painting, sculpture, nor architecture, which were numbered among the "mechanical" arts, since they involved making objects by hand. At least since the fifteenth century, the term *art* has taken on as its principal characteristic in most societies the element of aesthetic appreciation as distinguished from mere utility. Even if its primary purpose is shelter, a great building, for example, is surely a work of art.

The word *aesthetic* derives from a Greek term for "perceive," and perception will occupy us a little farther on. What is perceived aesthetically is "beauty," according to the *Oxford Dictionary*, and beauty is defined as the quality of giving pleasure to the senses. Yet underlying concepts can be experienced as beautiful even when they can be perceived only in their results. Moreover there are paintings, sculptures, plays, novels, films intended to produce terror or revulsion by the vivid representation of tragic or painful subjects. The same goes for certain moments in music, when loud or dissonant sounds, hardly distinguishable from noise, are essential for the full realization of the composer's purpose. These are undeniably works of art in the modern meaning of the term, even though beauty conceived as pleasure is largely excluded—that is, unless we are willing to count the pleasure we feel in admiring the author's ability to present reality or the not especially admirable pleasure a horror film gives to an audience seated in perfect safety.

Clearly something essential has been overlooked in the *Oxford* definition of beauty. To be sure, throughout history beauty has been analyzed on a far loftier plane than mere sensory pleasure, beginning in Greek philosophy with treatments

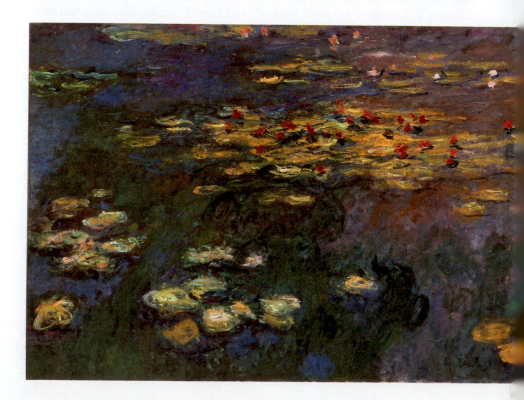

THE NATURE OF ART

of a divine order of which the beauty we perceive is a dim earthly reflection. Leonbattista Alberti, architect and the first Renaissance writer on art, defined beauty to be "a harmony of all the parts, in whatsoever subject it appears, fitted together with such proportion and connection, that nothing could be added, diminished, or altered but for the worse." This definition tells us a great deal about the mathematically based art of Alberti's time, with every emphasis on ideal and finite beauty. As fate would have it, Alberti's own buildings were never completed as he wished, yet to our eyes are beautiful. So are Gothic cathedrals, built over long periods of time in different styles and according to different systems. And if one of Claude Monet's huge *Nymphéas (Water Lilies)* (fig. 1) were cut off a bit at either end, how many would consider it less beautiful? Is there not a beauty in thin veils of color or sudden bursts of tone which has nothing to do with proportion? See, for example, the pen-and-wash drawing by Claude Lorrain *On the Slopes of the Janiculum* (fig. 2).

Later writers on the philosophy of art—especially in the eighteenth century and since, culminating in the self-proclaimed "science" of aesthetics—have considered beauty from many different standpoints, constructing elaborate philosophical systems, often on the basis of limited knowledge of art and its history. Is there not some distinguishing quality in the very nature of a work of visual, literary, or musical art that can embrace both the beautiful and the repellent, so often equally important to the greatest works of art? The question may perhaps be answered in the light of a concept developed many years ago by the early-twentieth-century American philosopher of education John Dewey in his book *Art as Experience*. Without necessarily subscribing to all of Dewey's doctrines, one can assent to his basic belief that all of human experience, beautiful and ugly, pleasurable and painful, even humorous and absurd, can be distilled by the artist, crystallized in a work of art, and preserved to be experienced by the observer as long as that work

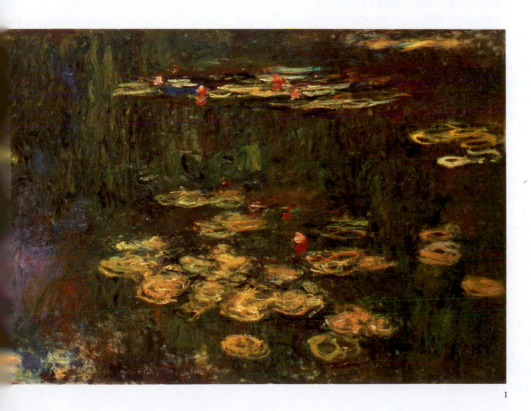

1. CLAUDE MONET. *Nymphéas (Water Lilies)*. c. 1920. Oil on canvas, 6'8½" × 19'9¼" (2.04 × 5.79 m). Museum of Art, Carnegie Institute, Pittsburgh. Purchased through the generosity of Mrs. Alan M. Scaife

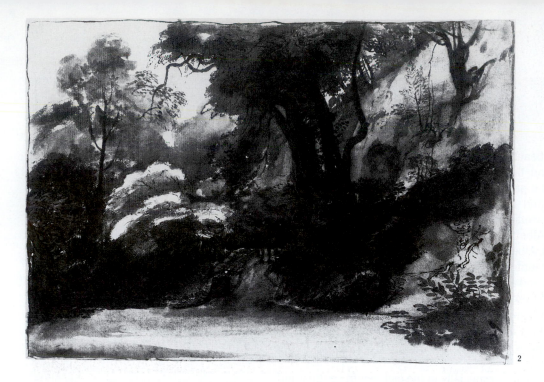

2

lasts. It is this ability to embrace human experience of all sorts and transmit it to the observer that distinguishes the work of art.

Purpose

If all of human experience can be embodied in works of art, we have then to ask, "Whose experience?" Today we would be tempted to reply, "Obviously the artist's first of all." But in many periods of history the work of art discloses nothing of the artist's existence but is shaped by the requirements of the time in which he or she lived. It may have been ordered by a patron for a specific purpose. If a building or part of a building or a ceremonial image, the work undoubtedly had a role to play in the social or religious life of the artist's time, and nothing of the artist's personality can be determined, aside from his knowledge, taste, and skill. Can we appreciate such works without knowing anything of their purpose, standing as we do at a totally different moment in history?

Perhaps we can. There are many works of prehistoric art—like the animals painted or carved in prehistoric times on cave walls and ceilings—that we cannot interpret accurately in the complete absence of reliable knowledge, but to our eyes they remain beautiful and convincing. This may be because we can easily relate them to our own experience of animals. And there are others, such as the colossal Easter Island sculptures (fig. 3), that are impressive to us even if foreign to every kind of experience we can possibly know. Simply as forms, masses, lines, we find them interesting. Yet how much more articulate and intelligent our response to works of art can be if we know their purpose in the individual or corporate experience of their makers. We can take a part of a building that strikes us as beautiful, study how it was originally devised to fit a specific practical use, then watch it develop under changing pressures, sometimes to the point of total transformation. Or we can watch a type of religious image arise, change, become transfigured, or disappear, according to demands wholly outside the artist's control. Such knowledge can generate in us a deeper understanding and eventually an enriched appreciation of the works of art we study. If we learn to share the artist's experience, insofar as the historical records and the works of art themselves make it accessible to us, then our own life experience can expand and grow. We may end up appreciating the beauty and meaning of a work of art we did not even like at first.

Today people generally make works of art because they want to. In fact, everyone who opens this book has made works of art as a child, and many continue to do so.

2. CLAUDE LORRAIN. *On the Slopes of the Janiculum*. 17th century. Pen and ink, with bister wash shading, 8⅝ × 12½″ (22 × 32 cm). Accademia Nazionale dei Lincei, Rome; on loan from the Gabinetto Nazionale delle Stampe, Rome

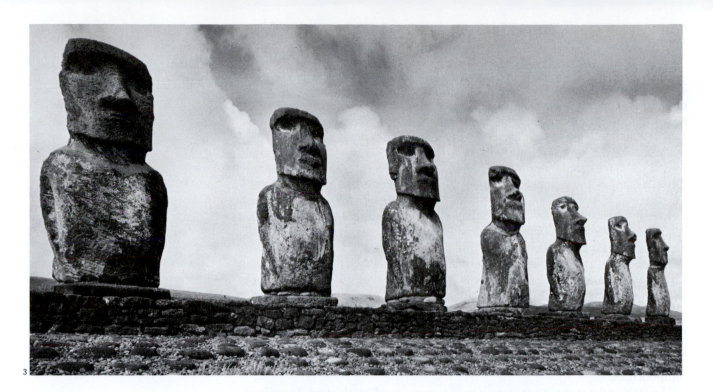

3. Stone images. 17th century or earlier. Height 30′ (9.15 m); weight approx. 16 tons each. Easter Island, South Pacific

People enjoy the excitement of creation and the feeling of achievement, not to speak of the triumph of translating their sensory impressions of the visible world into a personal language of lines, surfaces, forms, and colors. This was not always so. Throughout most of history artists worked characteristically on commission. No matter how much they enjoyed their work, and how much of themselves they poured into it, they never thought of undertaking a major work without the support of a patron and the security of a contract. In most periods of history artists in any field had a clear and definable place in society—sometimes modest, sometimes very important—and their creations thus tended to reflect to a large degree the desires of their patrons and the forces in their human environment.

In earlier periods in history factors of aesthetic enjoyment and social prestige were equally important. Great monarchs or religious leaders enjoyed hiring talented artists not only to build palaces or cathedrals but also to paint pictures, to carve statues, to illustrate manuscripts, or to make jewels—partly because they enjoyed the beautiful forms and colors, but partly also to allegorize their power and prestige, or to set forth the doctrines of their faith in a form designed to impress their subjects or their followers. Today the desires that prompt patrons to buy works of art are still only partly aesthetic. Collectors and buyers for museums and business corporations do really experience a deep pleasure in surrounding themselves with beautiful things. But there are other purposes in collecting. Patrons want to have the best or the latest (often, sadly enough, equated with the best) in order to acquire or retain social status. Inevitably, the thought of eventual salability to collectors can, and often does, play a formative role in determining aspects of an artist's style. It takes a courageous artist to go on turning out works of art that will not sell, so patronage is a strong force even today.

Unless we are to study the history of art as a chronological series of scientific specimens, quality is the leading determinant. It certainly was in the selection of works of art for this book. However much they may tell us about the society they were made for, works below a certain level of quality tend to be omitted from books or consigned to museum storerooms. Conversely, an exhibition of paintings organized to illustrate the life of bourgeois France in the last three decades of the nineteenth century would attract few visitors unless they happened to notice the names of the universally beloved Impressionist and Post-Impressionist painters.

If our appreciation of art is subject to alterations brought about by time and experience, what then is quality? What makes a work of art good? Are there standards of artistic value? These essential questions, perpetually asked anew, elude satisfactory answer on a verbal plane. One can only give examples, and even these are sure to be contradictory. The nineteenth-century American poet Emily Dickinson was once asked how she knew when a piece of verse was really poetry. "When it takes the top of your head off," she replied. But what if a work of art that ought to take the top of your head off refuses to do so? Demonstrably, the same work that moves some viewers is unrewarding to others. Moreover, time and repeated viewing can change the attitude of even an experienced person. A work of art one enjoys at a certain period in life may lose its charm ten years later. Conversely, study, prolonged contemplation, or the mere passage of time may render more accessible a once-forbidding work of art. And even observers of long experience can disagree in matters of quality.

The twentieth century, blessed by unprecedented methods of reproduction of works of art, has given readers a new access to the widest variety of styles and periods. Incidentally, André Malraux in his book *The Museum Without Walls* pointed out the dangers of this very opportunity in reducing works of art of every size and character to approximately the same dimensions and texture. There is, of course, no substitute for the direct experience of the real work of art, sometimes overwhelming in its intensity no matter how many times the student has seen reproductions.

The ideal of the twentieth century is to like every "good" work of art. There is an obvious advantage in such an attitude—one gains that many more wonderful experiences. Yet there are inborn differences between people that no amount of experience can ever change. If after reading many books and seeing many works of art ineradicable personal preferences and even blind spots still remain, the student should by no means be ashamed of them. Barriers of temperament are natural and should be expected. But—and this is all-important—such admissions should come *after*, not before, a wholehearted attempt to accept the most disparate works of art on their own grounds; one must not merely condemn them because they are unfamiliar. The world of art is wide and rich; there is room in it for everyone who wants to learn, to experience, above all to *see*.

Destruction and Preservation

Art is an endangered species. It is tragic to think of the countless works of art, many certainly of the greatest beauty and importance, that have been destroyed by natural causes or by human action. Exposure to water and to frost will eventually corrode any work of art, including architecture. If stone and brick buildings are kept in a reasonable state of repair, however, they and their contents may last indefinitely. But repair inevitably includes replacement of weathered stones, some of which may have been richly carved. Eventually, large parts of such a building can only be considered copies, whose accuracy depends on the conscience, skill, and technological equipment of the restorers. The floods to which Florence has been subjected periodically throughout its history have devastated scores of altarpieces and wall paintings. After surviving for millennia in excellent condition masterpieces of Egyptian tomb painting are now threatened by the rise in the water table due to the building of the Aswan dam.

The same humanity that creates works of art also destroys them. Wars and other social upheavals are by no means the only causes of destruction. Human greed is responsible for the disappearance of all the colossal ancient statues in gold and ivory, for the scraping of gold backgrounds from Russian icons, even for the burning of marble statues to produce lime. As a result only a very few surviving works of Greek sculpture bear any claim to the names of the great masters recorded by ancient writers. The demise of paganism left the great temples of Greece and Rome without a purpose, thus obvious sources for marble columns to be used in Christian churches, and soon most other public buildings also disappeared. Entire quarters of eighteenth-century London have fallen to the wrecker, as have innumerable historic buildings everywhere, especially in the United States. Not only in the highly publicized incidents but in many cases that never reach public attention hundreds of works of art, many of them world-renowned masterpieces, are stolen every year from museums, private collections, and religious buildings. Less than 10 percent are ever recovered. Deranged persons have defaced works of the importance of Michelangelo's *Pietà* and Rembrandt's *Night Watch*. Industrial pollution is corroding Greek temples, Gothic cathedrals, and the entire city of Venice.

Changes in taste have also been destructive. Countless works of art, many of great importance, have either perished or been substantially altered because the next generation did not like them. For instance, all the stained glass from the side aisles of Reims Cathedral was smashed to provide more light for the coronation ceremonies of King Louis XV of France. Even more unhappily, strict interpretation of the Second Commandment and other religious prohibitions has resulted in enormous destruction, especially of Greek, Roman, early Byzantine, medieval English, and Netherlandish art, even when the very groups doing the hacking and burning nonetheless encouraged the production of secular art, such as plant and animal ornament, portraiture, landscapes, or still lifes. Ignorant or misguided restoration has taken its toll, altering faces, repainting drapery, removing irreplaceable glazes. In the last twenty years great monuments of medieval, Renaissance, and Baroque architecture, especially in England and Italy, have been disfigured by glass and metal doors and enclosures.

The light that illuminates this dismal picture is that from the excellent teams of conservators of painting, sculpture, and architecture, aided by scientists and often subsidized by governments, who battle for the rescue of endangered works and the protection of historic buildings. In the United States private organizations have done heroic but, alas, often unsuccessful work in historic preservation. It is impossible to overestimate either the crucial importance or the magnitude of the task.

Women in Art

Throughout history women's contribution to the visual arts has been significant, yet the art-historical record has not sufficiently reflected that fact. The very terms "old master" and "masterpiece" imply that the creators were men. Even when women managed against great odds to pursue successful artistic careers, their work, while valued in its day, has often been lost, destroyed, or attributed to other artists, and the details of their lives have gone unrecorded. The woman who aspired to status as artist beyond amateur could encounter male opposition at every juncture, whether in the form of a husband, fellow artist, critic, patron, or government official. There were numerous occasions from the sixteenth to the eighteenth centuries when incredulous experts required women to paint in their presence to prove that their pictures were not painted for them by men.

Part of the explanation of women's exclusion from artistic endeavors, as well as from many others, such as politics and business, is to be sought in their virtually complete lack of economic autonomy and the tolls exacted by childbirth and domestic responsibilities. A case in point is Marietta Robusti, daughter of the famous Venetian Mannerist painter known as Tintoretto. After years as an apprentice in her father's studio, she gained international recognition as a portraitist and was called to the Spanish royal court of Philip II. Her father forbade her to go and found her a husband instead. She died four years later in childbirth. Her father, on the other hand, lived to the age of seventy-six. The extreme brevity of the careers of many brilliant women artists has meant that few of their works remain. Such is the case of the talented and highly original sculptor Properzia de' Rossi, who died of illness at an early age, or the French painter Marie Guillemine Benoist, who was forced to abandon her art because her husband's official appointment made it impossible for her to continue to participate in the state-sponsored exhibitions that had been opened to women under the revolutionary government. A notable exception to these truncated careers is that of a sixteenth-century painter from Bologna, Lavinia Fontana, who painted for several decades in spite of familial duties (with which her husband helped), received papal commissions, and was elected to the Roman Academy.

More commonly, women were not granted membership in the guilds, workshops, studios, and academies where artists were trained. Moreover, they were systematically banned from studying from the nude model in periods when such study was the very foundation of all art involving human representation, which was regarded as the highest form art could attain. As recently as 1931–1934, when I attended drawing and sculpture classes at the Art School of the National Academy of Design in New York City, women and men were required to work in separate life classes, and, although men were permitted to view nude female models, no male model could be shown entirely nude to women. With few exceptions, the traditionally "feminine" arts—miniatures, pastels, portraits, still lifes, and crafts—have been undervalued in cultures that place the greatest stock in the heroics of history painting and monumental sculpture.

Furthermore, a woman tied to domesticity and constant pregnancy would have endured considerable physical hardship in the arduous activities of carpenters or stonemasons, the crafts that traditionally produced professional architects, or of stonecutters, the trade that produced sculptors. Even painting, in the Renaissance, involved strenuous activity high on scaffolding, carrying sacks of sand and lime and pots of water. The only women artists recorded in antiquity painted portraits, which could be done in comfortable surroundings. Alas, their work is all lost. But in the Middle Ages nuns in convents, like monks in monasteries, were considered expert painters of illuminated manuscripts. Five splendid examples known to have been painted by women are included in this book, for the first time in any general text. Then in the sixteenth and seventeenth centuries, painters' daughters (such as Lavinia Fontana, Elisabetta Sirani, Artemisia Gentileschi, and Marietta Robusti) began to produce works of real artistic merit, thanks in part to the training acquired in their fathers' studios, and the occasional woman painter or sculptor appeared independently. But even as late as the eighteenth century women were still mostly limited to portrait painting, though often with excellent results (fig. 4).

The widespread use of the pointing machine eventually relegated stonecutting to expert workmen, and once the procedure of sculpture, now restricted to modeling, became less physically demanding, numbers of women sculptors appeared—in the mid- and late-nineteenth century. Today, women cut stone directly, on the same basis as men. And when architecture began to be taught in schools rather than springing spontaneously from woodworking or stoneworking shops, women became practitioners of the art, although the profession is still male-dominated.

Since the early 1970s, feminist art historians have produced a literature of enormous value, on which I have heavily relied, that has begun to redress the marginal role ascribed to women in the history of art. Although the serious study of women artists is still in its infancy, this literature has helped to reevaluate and, in many cases, rediscover the achievements of women artists of the past. At the same time these authors have examined other gender-related issues that permeate the entire discipline of art history. For it is not simply men and women artists but the entire art apparatus—audiences, institutions, patrons, critics—that has helped to shape attitudes toward women in the visual arts. Although a book like this one is not the place to go into such questions systematically, here and there in the following pages they will be raised.

In periods when women artists are infrequent or absent I have tried to explain why. When they begin to turn up in numbers, they take their place with the men in these pages. Since the final work of art often owes a great deal to the desires of the patron who commissioned it, consideration has also been given to women patrons, who were in general imaginative and original, and who strongly influenced the male artists who worked for them—even by means of direct instruction.

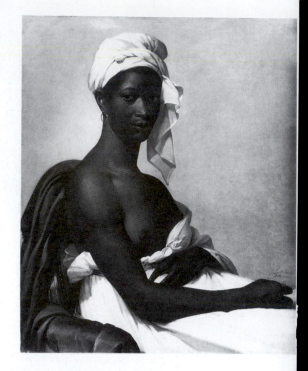

4. MARIE GUILLEMINE BENOIST. *Portrait of a Negress.* 1800. Oil on canvas, 31⅞ × 25⅝″ (81 × 65.1 cm). Musée du Louvre, Paris

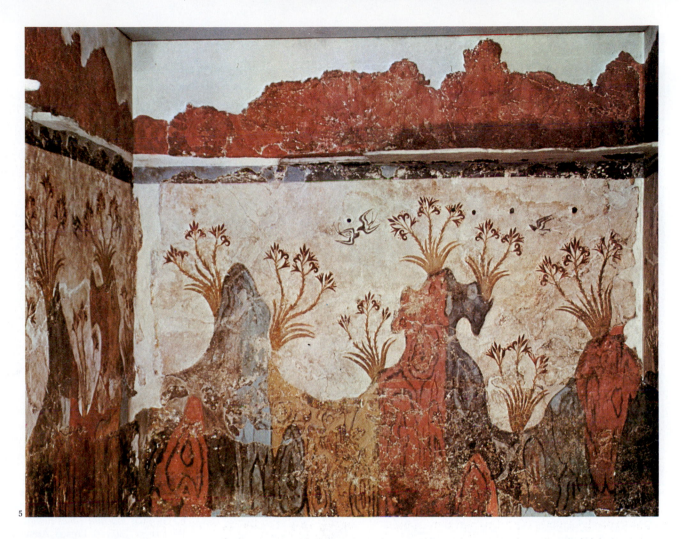

5. *Rocky Landscape with Red Lilies and Swallows,* fresco from Building D in the town of Akrotiri, Santorini (ancient Thera), Cyclades, including areas of modern reconstruction. Before 1500 B.C. National Archaeological Museum, Athens

Style

PERCEPTION AND REPRESENTATION   How has the artist perceived and recorded the visible world—trees, let us say—in widely separated periods in the history of art? The earliest known European landscape, a wall painting from the Greek island of Santorini, known in ancient times as Thera (fig. 5), dates from about 1500 B.C. and shows natural forms reduced to what look like flat cutouts. The contours and a few inner shapes of rocks, plants, and birds are drawn in outline (as in most very early art or indeed the art of children or of present-day untrained adults) and simply colored in, accurately enough, however, for identification. Doubtless the occupants of the room felt they were in the midst of a "real" landscape, wrapped around them on three walls, but few today would agree, despite the charm of the murals as decoration and the bouncing vitality of the outlines.

In a work (fig. 6) painted shortly after A.D. 1300 by the Italian artist Giotto, rocks and plants are beautifully modeled in light and shade and do seem to exist in three dimensions, yet they are anything but real to our eyes compared with the figures who stand in front of them. Accounts written by one of Giotto's followers indicate that he advised painting one rock accurately and letting that stand for a mountain or one branch for a tree. Nonetheless we know that Giotto's contemporaries thought that his paintings carried out according to this principle looked very real.

A little more than a hundred years later the Netherlandish painter Jan van Eyck presented in a panel from the *Ghent Altarpiece* (fig. 7) a view of rocky outcroppings and vegetation similar in structure to that of Giotto's fresco, but in a manner anyone

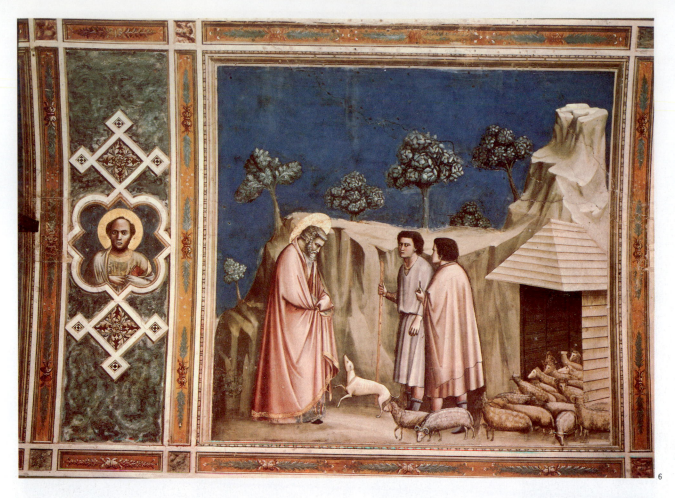

6. Giotto. *Joachim Takes Refuge in the Wilderness.* 1305–6. Fresco. Arena Chapel, Padua, Italy

today would easily call realistic. Van Eyck's amazingly sharp perception enabled him to render every object, from the smallest pebble in the foreground to the loftiest cloud in the sky, with an accuracy few photographs can rival. Every tree appears entire and in natural scale, down to the last leaf, and in believable light and shade. Yet is the picture as real as it seems at first sight? Do we encounter in real experience figures looking like this, all turned toward us and lined up on a rocky ledge that is sharply tilted so we can see every object clearly?

A radically different and very modern form of perception is seen in such Impressionist paintings of the late nineteenth century as Pierre Auguste Renoir's *Les Grands Boulevards* (fig. 8), in which all contours and indeed all details disappear, being blurred or lost as the artist seeks to seize with rapid brushstrokes a fleeting view of city life in bright sunlight and in constant motion. Trees and their component branches and foliage are now mere touches of the brush. This was the uncalculated, accidental way in which Renoir and his fellow Impressionists viewed the world, striving in their pictures for the speed and immediacy no snapshot photograph could then achieve and at the same time for a brilliance of color inaccessible to photography until many decades later. Today most viewers accept this image quite happily, but not in Renoir's day, when the Impressionists were violently attacked in print for being so unreal!

Finally, in the twentieth century, painters fully trained in both realist and Impressionist methods transformed the image of trees into a pattern almost as unreal to our eyes as that of the Santorini murals, even though it is often rendered with a freedom of brushwork that owes much to the Impressionists. To the Dutch painter Piet Mondrian, his *Red Tree* (fig. 9), overpowering in its fiery red against a blue sky, translates what may have been the color of sunset light into an expression of the ultimate reality of subjective emotional experience.

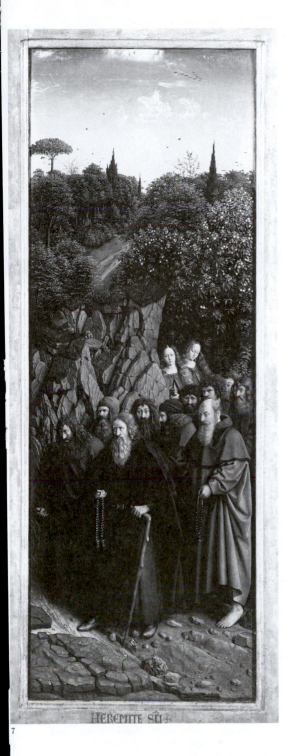

Optically, there can have been very little difference in the images of trees transmitted to the retinas of Mondrian, Renoir, van Eyck, Giotto, and the unknown painter of Santorini. The startling difference in the results is due to the differing sets of conventions, inherited or self-imposed, according to which each artist selected, reinforced, and recombined those aspects of the visual image that seemed important. Reality, in the long run, is as elusive and subjective a concept as beauty, yet just as compelling for the artist and for us.

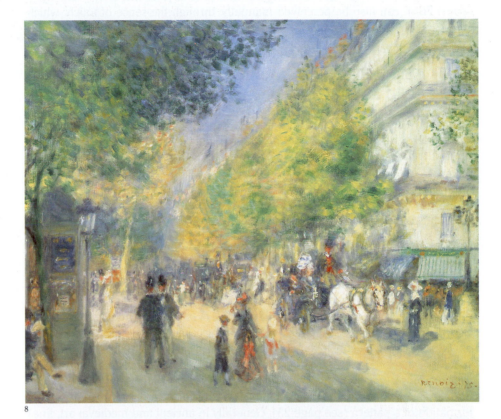

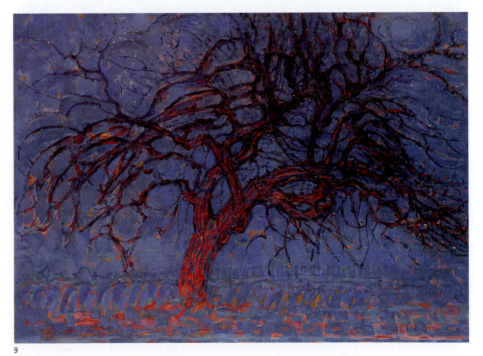

7. HUBERT (?) and JAN VAN EYCK. *Hermit Saints,* detail of the *Ghent Altarpiece* (open). Completed 1432. Oil on panel. Cathedral of St. Bavo, Ghent, Belgium

8. PIERRE AUGUSTE RENOIR. *Les Grands Boulevards.* 1875. Oil on canvas, 20½ × 25″ (52 × 63.5 cm). The Philadelphia Museum of Art; The Henry P. McIlhenny Collection in Memory of Frances P. McIlhenny

9. PIET MONDRIAN. *Red Tree.* 1908. Oil on canvas, 27½ × 39″ (69.5 × 99 cm). Collection Haags Gemeentemuseum, The Hague

THE VOCABULARY OF ART

Form. The *form* of an object is its shape, usually considered in three dimensions. (The word *form* is also used in music and literature, and in the visual arts as well, to mean the interrelationship of all the parts of a work.) Visual form is perceived first of all through binocular vision, by means of which each eye sees the object from a slightly different point of view, enabling the mind to create a three-dimensional image. The reader has only to test this proposition by closing one eye and noting the difficulty in perceiving accurately the shapes of objects and their positions in space. Form can also be perceived manually, through the sense of touch, which sends messages to the brain; by its very nature sculpture appeals to this sense. Painting, generally on flat or nearly flat surfaces, can only suggest the "3-D" effect that is the birthright of sculpture. The elements used in painting to indicate form are line, light and shade, and color, each of which as we will see can also play other important parts in the effect of the work of art. The much-used expression *formalist* really means "concerned with style," of which form is only one aspect, and is thus technically a misnomer.

The words *volume* and *mass* are also used almost interchangeably to indicate three-dimensionality, but without the connotation of shape, which is essential to the word *form*. *Volume* can even indicate the spatial content of an interior. The impact of mass on the observer is greatly enhanced by scale, which is an absolute factor in works of art—hence the difficulty in experiencing from small illustrations the breathtaking effect of colossal buildings such as Egyptian or Indian temples or Gothic cathedrals.

Line. *Line* can be seen as an edge or contour, of one shape against another or against distance, by means of which form can be deduced. A line can also be drawn, like the lines of a diagram or those that make up a printed letter of the alphabet. This kind of line can not only convey a great deal of factual information but can also clearly delineate form, as in Greek vase paintings (fig. 10). A line can be tremendously strong; think of the high wire on which daring acrobats perform across great spaces, or the cord that can restrict a person's movements as effectively as a prison cell, or the jagged line of a key, a slight variation in which can render a lock unopenable. Lines can be independent, or several lines can cooperate in the formation of a pattern (see page 25). Generally in ancient and medieval art, lines are drawn firmly and appear unbroken, but sometimes a very lively effect is obtained by preserving in a sketchy line the actual motion of the artist's hand carrying the drawing instrument, whose trajectory eventually gives rise to form (fig. 11). Finally, line can suggest the direction of motion ("line of fire," for example), seen typically in such instances as the "sweep" or "fall" of folds of cloth (*drapery* is the technical term; fig. 12).

Light and Shade. *Light* falling on an object leaves a *shade* on the side opposite to the source of light (see fig. 16); this shade is distinct from the *shadow* cast by the object on other objects or surfaces (see fig. 15). The shade may be hard and clear-cut or soft and indistinct, according to the degree of diffusion of the light that causes it. The relationship of light and shade suggests form but can be deceptive, since shade varies not only according to projections but to the position of the source of light. The same work of sculpture can look entirely different in photographs taken in different lights. Light and shade are also often used very effectively in strong contrast to produce effects of emotion (see fig. 2).

Color. *Color* is subject to more precise and complex scientific analysis than any of the other elements that make up the visual experience of art. For this book the most useful terms are those describing the effects of the various ways the artist employs *hue* (red, blue, yellow, etc.), *saturation* (intensity of a single color), and *value* (proportion of color to black and white). Colors can be described in terms such as

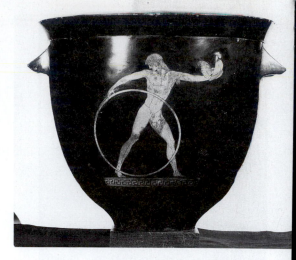

10. THE BERLIN PAINTER. *Ganymede,* painting in the Attic (Athenian) style on a bell-shaped krater found in Etruria, Italy. Early 5th century B.C. Height approx. 13" (33 cm). Musée du Louvre, Paris

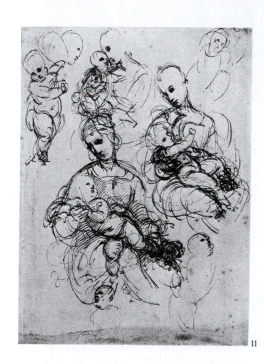

11. RAPHAEL. *Studies of the Madonna and Child.* c. 1505–8. Pen and ink, 10 × 7¼" (25.5 × 18.5 cm). British Museum, London

12. *Virgin of Paris,* from St.-Aignan. Early 14th century. Stone. Notre-Dame, Paris

13. *Laestrygonians Hurling Rocks at the Fleet of Odysseus,* Second Style wall painting from a villa on the Esquiline Hill, Rome. Middle 1st century B.C. Musei Vaticani, Rome

14. LIANG KAI. *Hui Neng, the Sixth Chan Patriarch, Chopping Bamboo at the Moment of Enlightenment.* Southern Song dynasty, late 12th century–early 13th century. Hanging scroll; ink on paper, height 29¼" (74.5 cm). National Museum, Tokyo

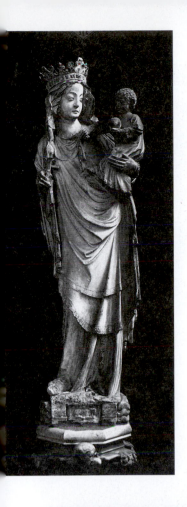

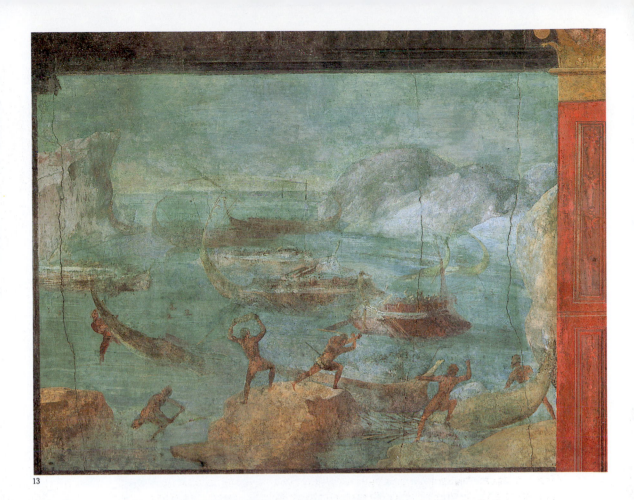

13

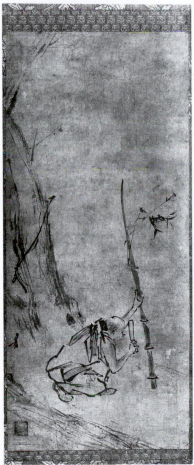

14

brilliant, soft, harmonious, dissonant, harsh, delicate, strident, dull, and in a host of other ways. Blue and its adjacent colors in the familiar color circle, green and violet, are generally felt as cool, and through association with the sky and distant landscape appear to recede from us. Yellow and red, with their intermediate neighbor orange, are warm and seem nearer. In most early painting, color is applied as a flat tone from outline to outline (see figs. 5, 10). Broken color, in contrast, utilizes brushwork to produce rich effects of light (see fig. 8). Modeling in variations of warm and cool colors suggests form, but color, modeled or not, evokes by itself more immediate emotion than any element available to the artist, to such a degree that extremely saturated color, such as bright red or yellow, would be felt as unbearable if applied to all four walls and the ceiling of a room.

Surface. The physical *surface* of any work of art is potentially eloquent. A painted surface has a *texture* (a word from the Latin for "weave"), which can sometimes be consistent and unaltered; such is the case with many ancient murals (see fig. 5), where the surface declares the clean white plaster of the wall, or with Greek vases (see fig. 10), where red clay slip is set against glossy black. Or it can be enriched as we have seen, in the rendering of light and shade and color, by countless brush-strokes so as to form a vibrant web of tone, as in Roman painting (fig. 13). In the painting of China and Japan surface is of extreme importance and is often left largely untouched, as a foil to deft and varied strokes of an ink-laden brush, which convey inner experience and convert silk or paper into limitless space (fig. 14). In mosaic—the art of producing an image by means of cubes of colored stone or glass—the handling of the surface is especially important. In the Middle Ages these facets were set at constantly changing angles to the light so as to sparkle.

Depending on the inherent properties of the material, sculpture in stone can sometimes be smooth and polished to reflect light (as in fig. 15). Or the crisp details of a marble surface can be filed away so that the crystalline structure of the stone can retain light and blur shadow, or it can be left very rough and unfinished,

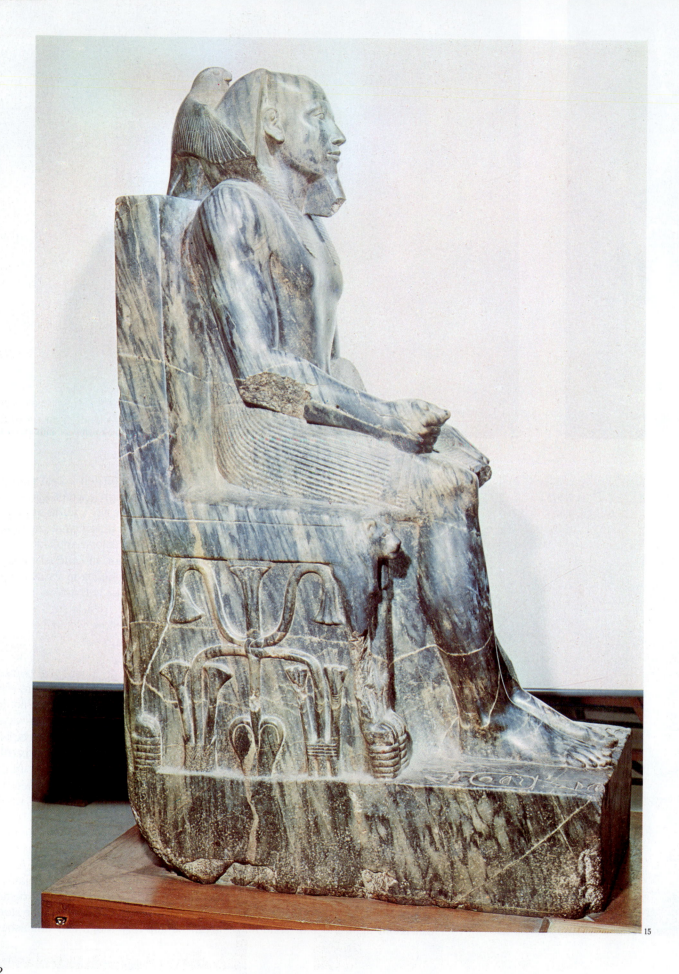

15

15. *King Chephren*, from Giza, Egypt. c. 2530 B.C. Diorite, height 66⅛" (1.68 m). Egyptian Museum, Cairo

16. AUGUSTE RODIN. *The Kiss.* 1886. Marble, over life size. Musée Rodin, Paris

17. AUGUSTE RODIN. *Monument to Balzac.* 1897–98. Bronze (cast 1954), height 9'3" (2.82 m). Collection, The Museum of Modern Art, New York. Presented in memory of Curt Valentin by his friends

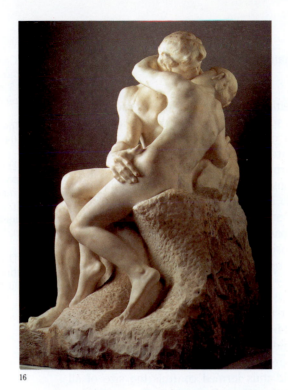

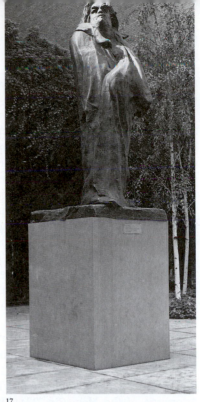

16

17

showing the tool marks; both techniques are seen side by side in the marble work of the nineteenth-century French sculptor Auguste Rodin, a contemporary of the Impressionists (fig. 16). Sculpture cast in bronze has generally been smoothed by tools after casting to produce a polished surface reflecting light. The tool marks scratched in the original clay model from which the molds were made can be left unaltered or even reinforced by cutting with a sharp metal implement into the final bronze surface. Rodin, however, often allowed the bronze to preserve all the freshness of the soft clay without any attempt to smooth away the marks of the fingers (fig. 17). Such surfaces may be compared with the free brushwork of the Impressionists.

Opposites in architectural surface are the inert, quiet stone of the oldest Egyptian monuments (fig. 18), left untreated to bring out the essential inner power of the stone, and the bewildering shimmer of later Islamic buildings (fig. 19), carved into

18. Valley Temple of Chephren, Giza, Egypt. c. 2530 B.C.

19. The Queen's Chamber, the Alhambra, Granada, Spain. c. 1354–91

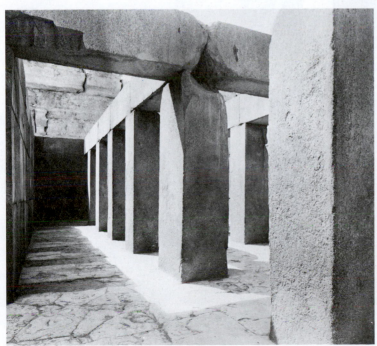

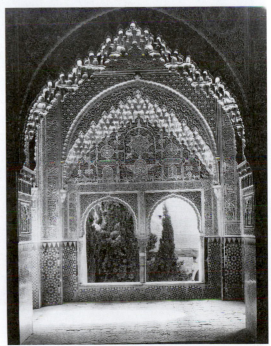

18

19

a lacework that seems to defy the very nature of stone, dissolving it in countless sparkles of light and shade.

Space.   *Space* may be defined as extent, either between points or limits, or without known limits, as in outer or interplanetary space. Since space encourages, limits, or directs human existence and motion, it constitutes one of the most powerful elements in art just as it does in life. An architect can set boundaries for space in actuality, as a painter or sculptor can through representation. The space of the Pantheon (fig. 20)—a Roman temple consisting of a hemispherical dome on a circular interior whose height is equal to its radius and therefore to that of the dome—has a liberating effect the minute one steps inside, almost like a view into the sky (itself often called a dome). The space would seem to rotate constantly if it were not held fast by a single niche opposite the entrance. In sharp contrast the interior of the French abbey church of Vézelay (fig. 21)—long, relatively low, and cut into segments by heavy, striped arches—seems to constrict and gradually drive the observer inward.

A painter or sculptor can represent space by means of *linear perspective*. This is a system in which spatial depth is indicated by means of receding parallel lines that meet at a vanishing point on the horizon and cross all lines parallel to the surface of the image, as seen in Leonardo da Vinci's preparatory drawing for a painting of the Adoration of the Magi (fig. 22). The grid thus formed controls the size of all represented objects according to their positions in its diminishing squares, so that

20. GIOVANNI PAOLO PANNINI. *Interior of the Pantheon.* c. 1750. Oil on canvas, 50½ × 39″ (128.5 × 99 cm). National Gallery of Art, Washington, D.C. Samuel H. Kress Collection

21. Interior, Ste.-Madeleine, Vézelay, France. c. 1104–32

22. LEONARDO DA VINCI. *Architectural Perspective and Background Figures,* for the *Adoration of the Magi.* c. 1481. Pen and ink, wash, and white, 6½ × 11½″ (16.5 × 29.5 cm). Gabinetto dei Disegni e Stampe, Galleria degli Uffizi, Florence

23. Decorative page from the *Book of Durrow.* Northumbria, England. Second half of 7th century. Illumination. Trinity College, Dublin

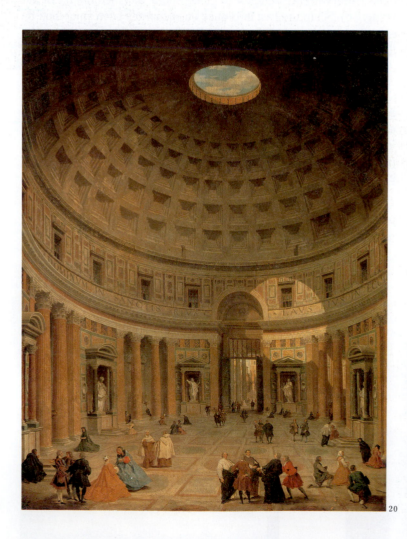

20

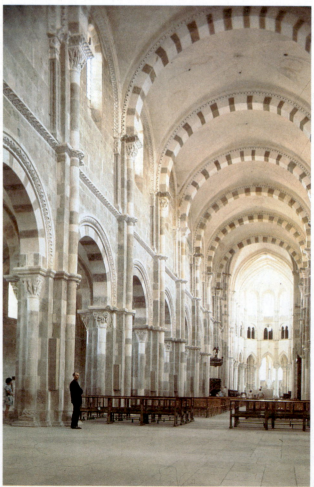

21

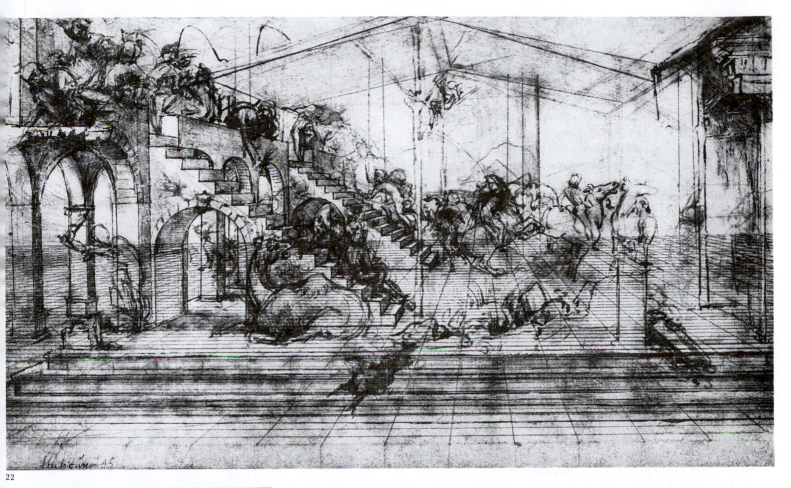

22

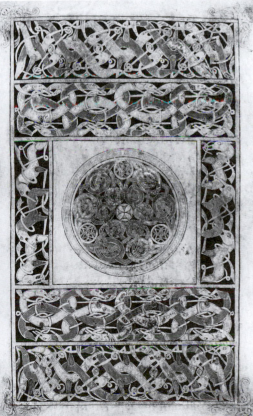

they too diminish in an orderly fashion as they recede from the eye. Although diminution takes place just the same indoors and outdoors, a consistent system of linear perspective obviously demands a man-made enclosing structure, composed of regularly recurring elements, such as a colonnade or a checkered floor. Perspective can also be *atmospheric,* that is, objects can lose their clarity according to their distance from us, because of the always increasing amount of moisture-laden atmosphere that intervenes (see fig. 13). In early art, space is generally represented diagrammatically, by superimposing distant objects above those nearby. Space can even be suggested, though not represented, by means of flat, continuous backgrounds without defined limits (see figs. 5, 6).

Pattern.   Most of the previously mentioned elements—line, light and shade, color, surface—can be combined to form a *pattern* if the individual sections (known as *motifs* or *motives*) recur with some regularity, either exactly or in recognizable variations. Brilliant examples of pattern raised to a high pitch of complexity are Islamic buildings, an example of which we have just seen, and the Hiberno-Saxon illuminated manuscripts of the early Middle Ages (fig. 23). Generally pattern is considered to operate only in two dimensions, so form and space have been excluded. Pattern is particularly important in decoration of walls, floors, and ceilings as well as in decorative objects such as rugs and ceramics.

Composition.   All of the elements we have been discussing, or any selection from them, can be combined to form a *composition,* understood as a general embracing order, if the artist has determined their coherence consistently. The artist may have made a preliminary sketch, as in Leonardo's drawing, showing where the various sections would go, or they may have fallen into place as the artist worked. Types of composition can be enumerated almost indefinitely, according to the artist's decision to emphasize one element or another or to the kind of system the artist devises to bring all the motifs together. A great many different types will appear in the following pages.

Style.   Finally, in any work of art, visual, musical, dramatic, or literary, the total aesthetic character, as distinguished from the *content* or meaning (see page 29), is known as *style*. In other words, style is the way in which the artist has treated the visual elements we have been considering (or such corresponding elements as words, phrases, sentences in literature; tones, melodies, harmonies in music). The process of carefully considering all elements of style is known as *stylistic analysis*. Names, such as primitive, archaic, classic, realistic, abstract, have been developed for styles and are capitalized if they correspond to specific countries, historical periods (Middle Ages, Renaissance), or movements (Impressionism, Cubism). Such names are useful as hooks on which to hang works of art in our minds so that we can find them again. But they can be dangerous if we consider them as entities in themselves. Indeed, if we try to force our observations of works of art into grooves predetermined by names of styles, we may find ourselves shaping our conceptions of various elements in order to make them fit the names, or even ignoring incongruous elements altogether. In many periods, such as Egyptian, a common style was imposed upon all works of art with only occasional exceptions. Nonetheless quite different styles, sometimes many of them, can flourish at the same time and place, and even make war upon each other. Throughout this book an effort has been made to bring out the special style of each work of art and to place it in relation to the complex and perhaps even contradictory stylistic tendencies of the period in which it was produced.

Iconography

In almost every society, up to and including the present, what we call *iconography* (from two Greek words meaning "image" and "write"), that is, the subject matter of art, is of primary importance.

   In the past, iconography was generally related predominantly to religion or politics or both and was therefore likely to be systematic. In a religious building the subjects of wall paintings, stained-glass windows, or sculpture were usually worked out by the patron, often with the help of a learned adviser, so as to narrate in the proper sequence scenes from the lives of sacred beings or to present important doctrines in visible form through an array of images with a properly determined order and placing, and even with the appropriate colors. The artist was usually presented with such a program and required to execute it. Sometimes, as in the wall paintings in the interiors of Byzantine churches, the subjects, the ways of representing them, and the places in churches in which they could be painted were codified down to the smallest detail and keyed delicately to the tightly organized Liturgy, which left nothing to the discretion of the individual priest except the language of the sermon. Even in those periods in history when powerful artistic personalities worked in close relationship with the patrons and advisers, artists were seldom free to choose their subjects at will.

   In regard to secular subjects as well, when patrons wished to commemorate their historic deeds they were almost certain to direct the artist as to how these should be represented. Only extremely learned artists, in certain relatively late periods of historic development, might be in a position to make crucial decisions regarding secular iconography on their own, and even then only with the general approval of the patron. Often in regard to both religious and secular subjects artists worked with the aid of iconographic handbooks compiled for the purpose and in use for centuries.

Also, although we have little documentary evidence, the desires of the secular or religious patron for an effect—aiming at such qualities as grandeur, magnificence, austerity, or grace—were necessarily taken into consideration by the artist and therefore determined the prevailing mood of a work of art. Both religious and secular works of art were sometimes refused as unsuitable to the purpose for which they had been commissioned; often the artist was required to change certain crucial aspects that offended the patron. A study of the subjects of contemporary art—in those cases in which subjects are still recognizable—might well suggest patterns of social preference that have influenced artists without their being fully aware of them.

Patronage, in exercising an influence on iconography, may also affect style. For example, until the Renaissance Christianity held the representation of the nude human body in horror, save when the soul appears naked before God for judgment or when a saint is stripped (shamed) before martyrdom. It is not likely, therefore, that an art thoroughly dominated by the more rigorous forms of Christianity, as in certain periods during the Middle Ages, could show much comprehension of or interest in the movement of the clothed figure, which can only be understood through study of the nude body. Similarly, a culture such as ancient Greece that placed a high valuation on the total human being, including physical enjoyment and athletic prowess, and displayed nude images, including those of their deities, in places of great prominence was likely to reject instinctively those colors and ornaments that might eclipse the beauty of the body.

The study of iconography can also assist us in understanding what one might call the magical aspects of works of art, for the process of representation has always seemed to be somewhat magical. Totems and symbols in tribal societies warded off evil spirits and propitiated favorable ones. Even today certain peoples defend themselves by force against the taking of photographs, which might drain off some of their strength. Armed police still prevent anyone from taking pictures of the parliament building in New Delhi, which thousands walk past every day seeing all that the camera could record. In many societies the injury of an image of a hated person is deemed to aid in bringing about that person's illness or death. Enemies are still burned in effigy, and a national flag is so potent a symbol that laws are proposed to protect it from disrespect.

When ancient city-states were defeated in battle the conquerors often destroyed or carried off the statues from the enemies' temples in order to deprive them of their gods and therefore their power. The instances of miracle-working images in the history of Christianity are innumerable and still occur. Many today feel a power emanating from a great work of art. A picture may be said to "fill a room," though it occupies only a small space on the wall, or a building to "dominate a town" when it is only one of many on the skyline, because of the supernatural power we still instinctively attribute to images.

Finally, the very existence or nonexistence of works of art has been until relatively recent times due first of all to their subjects. The patron wanted a statue or a picture of a god, a saint, an event, or a person, not primarily because of its beauty but for a specific iconographic purpose. Even in seventeenth-century Holland, in the early days of the open art market, artists often chose certain subjects for their easy salability. The converse is often true. Taken literally, the Second Commandment severely limited if it did not indeed rule out entirely the creation of religious images by the Hebrews, the Muslims, and the Calvinists and, as we have seen, often brought about their destruction in large numbers.

The iconographic purpose of art, especially in the representation of events or ideas but also in the depiction of people and nature, has given the work of art its occasionally strong affinity with religion. Artists can be so moved by religious meditation, or by the contemplation of human beauty or human suffering, or by communion with nature, that they can create compelling works of art offering a strong parallel to religious experience. The religious art of the past generally offers

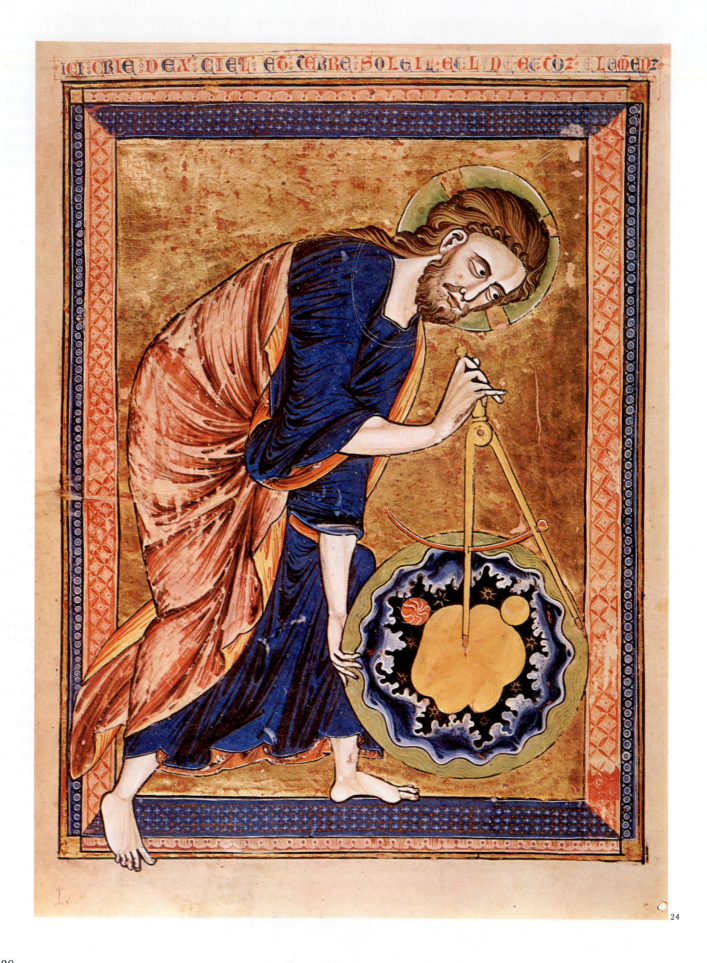

24

us the most persuasive access to religious ideas. So effective can be religious art that many agnostic scholars find themselves unconsciously dealing with religious images as reverently as if they were believers.

The links between art and religion are observed at their strongest in the creative act itself, which mystifies even the artist. However carefully the process of creation can be documented in preparatory sketches and models for the finished work of art, it still eludes our understanding. In the Judeo-Christian-Islamic tradition, and in many other religions as well, God (or the gods) plays the role of an artist. God is the creator of the universe and of all living beings. Even those who profess no belief in a personal god nonetheless often speak of creative power or creative energy as inherent in the natural world. In medieval art God is often represented as an artist, sometimes specifically as an architect (fig. 24), tracing with a gigantic compass a system and an order upon the earth, which was previously "without form, and void." Conversely, in certain periods artists themselves have been considered to be endowed with divine or quasi-divine powers. Certain artists have been considered saints: soon after his death Raphael was called "divine"; Michelangelo was often so addressed during his lifetime. The emotion art lovers sometimes feel in the presence of works of art is clearly akin to religious experience. An individual can become carried away and unable to move while standing before the stained-glass windows of Chartres Cathedral or the *David* by Michelangelo.

Of course, many works of art in the past, and many more today, were made for purposes that have a merely peripheral iconographic intent. We enjoy a well-painted realistic picture of a pleasant landscape partly because it is a pleasant landscape, with no iconographic purpose save the love of nature or the thought of an enjoyable vacation, and partly because it possesses in itself agreeable shapes and colors. Furthermore, a jewel, an arch or columns, or a passage of nonrepresentational ornament may be felt as beautiful entirely in and of itself. In most societies, however, such works have been limited to decoration or personal embellishment. Only when nonrepresentational images have been endowed with strong symbolic significance, as those in Christian art (the Cross, the initial letters in illuminated manuscripts), have they been raised to a considerably higher level and permitted to assume prominent positions (except, of course, in architecture, where certain basic forms exist primarily through constructional necessity and often symbolize nothing). Only in the twentieth century have people created works of art with no immediately recognizable subjects, the so-called abstractions.

Above, beyond, and within iconography lies the sphere of *content*. While content is not so easy to define as iconography, which can almost always be set down in neat verbal equivalents, it relies on iconography as the blood relies on the veins through which it flows. Like all supremely important matters, content is elusive. Better to try an illustration. Let us imagine two equally competent representations (from a technical point of view, that is), both depicting the same religious subject, such as the Nativity of Christ or his Crucifixion. Each one shows all the prescribed figures, each personage dressed according to expectations and performing just the right actions, the settings and props fitting the narrative exactly. Iconographically, both images could be described in the selfsame words. Yet one leaves us cold despite its illustrational accuracy while the other moves us to tears. The difference is one of content, which we might try to express as the psychological message or effect of a work of art. It is the content of works of art, almost as much as their style, and in certain cases even more, that affects the observer and relates the painter, the sculptor, the architect (for buildings can excite deep emotions) to the poet, the dramatist, the novelist, the composer—indeed to the actor, the musician, the dancer. In a mysterious and still inexplicable fusion, content is at times hardly separable from style, giving it life and meaning. Iconography can be dictated to the artist by his patron; content is the sign of the artist's full allegiance and inspiration. Like style, content is miraculously implicit in the very act of creation.

24. *God as Architect,* from a *Bible Moralisée.* Reims, France. Middle 13th century. Illumination. Österreichische Nationalbibliothek, Vienna

The History of Art

Any form of human activity has its history. The history of art, like the purpose of art, is inevitably bound up with many other aspects of history, and it is therefore generally organized according to the broad cultural divisions of history as a whole. But individual styles have their own inner cycles of change, not only from one period to the next but within any given period, or even within the work of a single artist. Iconography and purpose can be studied with little reference to the appearance of the work of art, but stylistic change, like style itself, is the special province of the study of art history. The individual work of art can and must be considered in relation to its position in a pattern of historical development if we wish to understand it fully. Long ago it occurred to people to wonder whether there might be laws governing stylistic change which, if discovered, could render more intelligible the transformations we see taking place as time is unrolled before us. Of necessity we refer to a succession of such transformations as an evolution, but without necessarily implying the superiority of one stage over another.

The earliest explanations of stylistic development can be classified as *evolutionary in a technical sense*. We possess no complete ancient account of the theory of artistic development, but the Greeks appear to have assumed a steady progression from easy to constantly more difficult stages of technical achievement. This kind of thinking, which parallels progress in representation with that in the acquisition of any other kind of technical skill, is easy enough to understand but tends to downgrade the importance of early stages in any evolutionary sequence. Implicit also in such thinking is the idea of a summit of perfection beyond which no artist can ascend, and from which the way leads only downward, unless every now and then a later artist can recapture the lost glories of a supposed Golden Age.

The metaphor of technical evolution has great weaknesses when confronted with the historical facts. Artistic evolution is not always orderly. In ancient Egypt, for example, after an initial phase lasting for about two centuries, a complete system of conventions for representing the human figure was devised shortly after the beginning of the third millennium B.C. and changed very little for nearly three thousand years thereafter. Certainly, one cannot speak of evolution from simple to complex, or indeed of any evolution at all. Even more difficult to explain in evolutionary terms is the sudden decline in interest in the naturalistic representation of the human figure and the surrounding world in late Roman art (fig. 25) as compared with the subtle, complex, and complete early Roman systems of representation (fig. 26). It looks as if the evolutionary clock had been turned backward from the complex to the simple.

A new pattern of art-historical thinking, which can be characterized as *evolutionary in a biographical sense*, is stated in the writings of the sixteenth-century Italian architect, painter, and decorator Giorgio Vasari, who has often been called the first art historian. He compared the development of art to the life of a human being, saying that the arts, "like human bodies, have their birth, their growing up, their growing old and their dying." Vasari dodged any uncomfortable predictions about the growing old and dying of art after his time, but his successors were not always so wise. Much of the theoretical and historical writing on art during the seventeenth century looks backward nostalgically to the perfection of the High Renaissance.

Imperceptibly, the ideas of Charles Darwin in the nineteenth century began to affect the thought of art historians, and a third tendency, seldom clearly expressed but often implicit in the methods and evaluations of late-nineteenth- and early-twentieth-century writers, began to make itself felt. This theory explained stylistic change according to an inherent process that we might call *evolutionary in a biological sense*. Ambitious histories were written setting forth the art of entire nations or civilizations, as were monographs analyzing the careers of individual artists, in an orderly manner proceeding from early to late works as if from elementary to more advanced stages, less of technical achievement than of visual

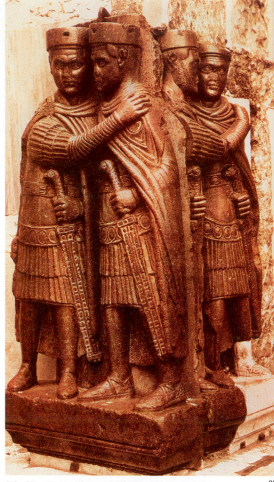

25. *The Tetrarchs.* c. 305. Porphyry, height approx. 51″ (1.3 m). Façade of S. Marco, Venice

25

perception. In the early twentieth century the Swiss art historian Heinrich Wölfflin formulated sets of opposed categories according to which the progression from a "classic" phase to a "baroque" one could be understood as a natural law applicable to the artistic development of all major periods and countries. The analysis was brilliant but highly selective, ignoring styles and periods that did not fit the theory. The biological-evolutionary metaphor underlies much art-historical writing and thinking even today and is evident in the frequent use of the word *evolution,* generally in a Darwinian spirit.

A fourth major tendency of art-historical interpretation, which might be described as *evolutionary in a dialectical sense,* developed in Germany through the essentially mystical doctrines of the early-nineteenth-century German philosopher Georg Wilhelm Friedrich Hegel, who adopted from Plato the idea of a world-soul, in accordance with whose laws history proceeds by means of a sort of pendulum-swing from one situation (*thesis*) to its opposite (*antithesis*), union between which results in a new and higher situation (*synthesis*), which in turn becomes the start of a new triple swing. Attractive to those who could not accept the Darwinian theory of continuous progress in one direction, the Hegelian model was adopted by the art historian Erwin Panofsky, who spoke of history as a "spatial spiral," constantly returning to the same place but always on a higher level. But what happens to the law if Panofsky's spatial spiral goes downward, as at the end of the Roman Empire? .

Although Karl Marx and his followers rejected the mysticism of Hegel, they adopted his concept of an inherent, dialectical law of history. More recently Neo-Marxist art historians, and others who have no connection with Marxism, have assumed a fifth model, of *evolution in a sociological sense.* Many have written about separate periods or events in the history of art along sociological lines, demonstrating what appear to be strong interconnections between forms and methods of representation in art and the demands of the societies for which these works were produced. Often, however, sociological explanations fail to hold up under close examination. How does one explain, for example, the simultaneous existence of two or more quite different—even mutually antagonistic—styles, representative examples of which were bought or commissioned by persons of the same social class or even by the same person?

Stylistic tendencies or preferences are, in fact, often explicable by widely differing interpretations (the notion of cause and effect in the history of art is always dangerous), sometimes not responsive to any clear-cut explanation. Three of the five theories discussed above—the technical, biological, and sociological—are still useful in different ways and at different moments in the history of art. But Vasari's biographical premise is generally renounced as a fallacious kind of reasoning by analogy. None of the five can be rigorously and consistently applied throughout the history of art. In fact, any deterministic theory that claims to account for styles and their evolution according to a system everywhere applicable will always trip over the maverick case.

Despite its above-mentioned shortcomings, there is something seductive about the Greek theory of technical evolution. This can be shown to correspond, for example, to the learning history of a given individual, who builds new experiences into patterns created by earlier ones, and may be said to evolve from stage to stage of always greater relative difficulty. The stopping point in such a cycle might correspond to the gradual weakening of the ability to learn, and it varies widely among individuals. Certain artists never cease developing; others reach their peak at a certain moment and repeat themselves endlessly thereafter. From the achievements of one artist, the next takes over, and the developmental process continues. The element of competition also plays its part, as in the Gothic period, when cathedral builders were trying to outdo each other in height and lightness of structure, or in the Impressionist period, when painters often worked side by side, competing in their attempt to seize the most fugitive aspects of sunlight and color (see page 18 and fig. 8). Such an orderly development of refinements on the

26. *L'Arringatore (The Orator),* portrait of Aulus Metellus, from Sanguineto, near Lake Trasimeno, Italy. c. 90–70 B.C. Bronze, height 71″ (1.81 m). Museo Archeologico, Florence

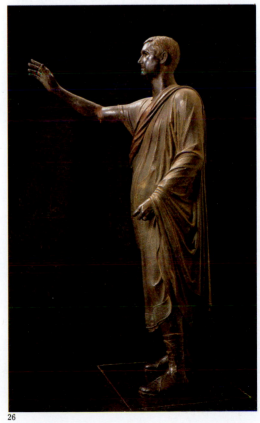

26

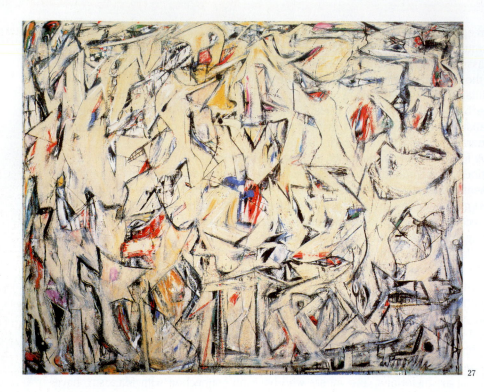

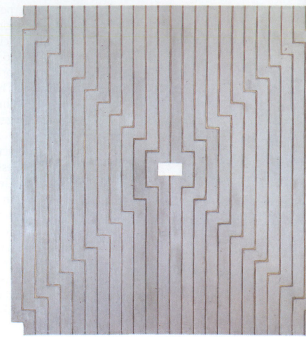

27

original idea motivating a school of artists can also be made to correspond to the biological-evolutionary theory, showing (as it seems) a certain inherent momentum.

We must face a sixth and totally unpredictable principle dictating change, which might be termed *evolution by mutation*. In art as in any other aspect of human life, changes of style may result from sheer boredom. Especially in our restless era, when a given style has been around to the point of saturation, artists and public alike thirst for something new. A startling case in point is that of Abstract Expressionism, based on emotional violence and the intense, rich, seemingly disordered application of paint (fig. 27), which found its hegemony in the 1950s disputed almost overnight by Pop Art and by color-field and hard-edge painting (fig. 28), with its severe, often ruled lines and mechanized appearance. Mutations may even occur from time to time through purely accidental discoveries, a factor that has yet to be thoroughly explored. On investigation, apparent artistic accidents may turn out to be in reality the result of subconscious tendencies long brewing in an artist's mind, which almost any striking external event could bring into full play.

In the seventies and eighties of this century many art historians have become increasingly dissatisfied with existing method, and a number of new approaches have been recommended, often with great vehemence and intolerance, resulting at times in bitter intradepartmental warfare. This ferment is a part of a wide picture of conflict and disagreement throughout humanistic studies. Proponents of the sharply differing doctrines that comprise the "new art history" have yet to agree on a consistent method and put it into practice. In my opinion important results are being achieved by second-generation feminists who—now that the struggle for the inclusion of women artists in the accepted canon has been launched—are forcing a reexamination of long-cherished viewpoints and terminology in historically male-dominated thinking and writing about the history of art, and are seeking to determine what is feminine in the art of women. Neo-Marxists have produced striking evidence to account with precision for the subject matter of Impressionist pictures and its treatment, but, alas, not for Impressionist style. Some have gone so far as to decry any emphasis on artistic quality and on the "aesthetic emotion" itself, which would have the effect of regarding art as a mere illustration of anthropology,

27. WILLEM DE KOONING. *Excavation*. 1950. Oil on canvas, 6'8⅛ × 8'4½" (2.03 × 2.54 m). The Art Institute of Chicago. Gift of Mr. and Mrs. Noah Goldowsky and Edgar Kaufmann Jr.; and Mr. and Mrs. Frank G. Logan Prize Fund, 1952

28. FRANK STELLA. *Avicenna*. 1960. Aluminum paint on canvas, 6'2½" × 6' (1.89 × 1.83 m). The Menil Collection, Houston, Texas

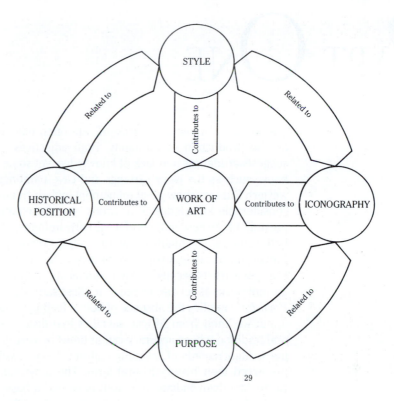

29. The Total Work of Art

or social history, or whatever, and of destroying most students' principal reason for reading a book like this one. Nothing could be more anti-historical than such attempts, which subvert everything that written records tell us about mankind's reasons for creating and looking at works of art.

In my view, any art-historical method can be useful that takes into account all the relevant circumstances, distorting none, and does not lose sight of the work of art itself. It is to be hoped that once the achievements and the shortcomings of the various contending viewpoints become clear that struggle will simmer down, and critics and scholars will come to recognize that what we are all concerned with is the history of art, not the art of history.

The Total Work of Art

The four major factors we have been considering—purpose, style, iconography, and historical position—are involved in the formation of any work of art, and all four should be considered in our study. The total work of art consists of the sum, or more exactly the product, of these four factors. At the risk of oversimplification, we may diagram the total work of art as a series of circles, one for each element, arranged around a larger circle (fig. 29), all contributing to the work of art at the center, and all related to each other. In the effort to interpret any given work of art we can start anywhere in the larger circle and move in any direction, including across it, as long as we realize that those elements that are separated for the purpose of diagrammatic clarity are in reality fused into a transcendent whole, with blurred and shifting boundaries.

The only certainty in art-historical studies is that as we try to penetrate deeply into the work of art, to understand it fully, and to conjecture why and how it came to be as it is, we must examine in each individual instance all the factors available to us that might have been brought to bear on the act of creation and regard with healthy skepticism any all-embracing theory that might tend to place a limitation on the still largely mysterious and totally unpredictable forces of human creativity.

PART ONE

The words *primitive* and *prehistoric* are often used to denote early phases in the artistic production of humanity. Both adjectives can be misleading. *Primitive* suggests crudeness and lack of knowledge, yet some of the oldest works of art we know, such as the ivory carvings and cave paintings of the first true humans in western Europe, show great refinement in their treatment of polished surfaces and considerable knowledge of methods of representation, while much later works, presumably by descendants of these early humans, sometimes betray loss of skill in both respects. The highly formalized objects made by African and North American Indian cultures close to our own time have been valued by some twentieth-century European artists because of their supposed primitivism; nonetheless, the few really ancient works as yet discovered from these same cultures are strikingly naturalistic. *Prehistoric* implies the absence of both a feeling for the past and a desire to record it, but we know from African societies that history was carefully preserved in an oral tradition whose accuracy can at times be corroborated when checked against the written records of invading cultures. Very possibly the earliest humans also preserved their history in oral form. The unwritten legends of the Eskimo and North American Indians may well have had a basis in historic fact.

The first section of this book brings together the arts of certain societies that flourished in a wide variety of geographic and climatic environments, and some that still do. These cultures all lacked the ability to compile permanent records, although the contemporary ones adopted writing from European invaders. But their arts have other important characteristics in common. One extremely important trait is the identification of representation with magical or religious power, so that the object of art itself comes into existence as the embodiment of an attempt to control or to propitiate, through ritual, natural beings or natural forces. Fantasy and magic generally operate outside the control of reason. Measure, the basis of order in art as in life, can exist only with writing, and measure is conspicuously absent from all preliterate art forms except only those which, like weaving or the building of wood-frame houses, are by their very nature dependent on a considerable number of material elements of approximately identical size, subject to distribution and repetition. Without the rational overlay governing the art of most subsequent periods, basic human impulses find expression in rhythmic form. In a magical art the motion of the hand holding the tool takes on the quality of a dance, and visual patterns that of choreography. No wonder that works of art produced for magical purposes and based on antirational principles should have been considered "barbaric" by historic societies whose culture was based on writing or that such works should have been codified as evolutionary stages in human development by the encyclopedic science of the mid-nineteenth century.

A second universal trait of these arts until very recent times is the lack of concern for the representation of the space in which we all must move, or even the ground on which we stand. The surface the artist works on is the only space and the only ground (see fig. 1–6). Animals, birds, fish, and to a lesser extent human beings, are widely represented, usually in conformity with transmitted stereotypes; plants appear only quite late, and then are ornamentalized. Landscape elements (save for isolated depictions such as the volcano of Çatal Hüyük, see fig. 1–18) never demand representation, and the immense spaces surrounding mankind, which must have appeared mysterious and challenging, are not even suggested.

Some of the arts described in this section precede chronologically the more developed phases of civilization; others persist side by side with them right up to

Art Before Writing

the present time. Interestingly enough, the humans of the late nineteenth century and twentieth century, who have conquered physical space to such an extraordinary degree, and who have transcended representation by photography, the cinema and television, and even writing by means of electronic communication and records, have been the first to find the art of early people artistically exciting. This may be in part because the modern period has also discovered the irrational basis of much of humanity's inner life through the researches of psychology and thus has found preliterate art emotionally accessible. But as we continue our study of art through later periods, even in the most highly literate cultures, it will become apparent that the irrational and impulsive nature of humanity lies fairly close to the surface and, at moments of intense individual or collective experience, can again determine essential aspects of the work of art.

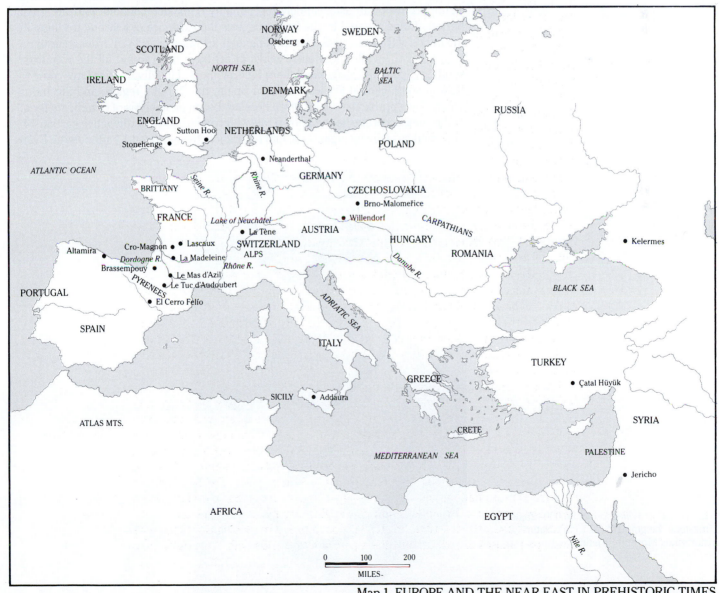

Map 1. EUROPE AND THE NEAR EAST IN PREHISTORIC TIMES

CHAPTER ONE

We do not know when or how human beings took the significant step of making objects for their own interest and enjoyment rather than for pure utility; probably we shall never know. But we do have extensive evidence, almost all of it discovered within the past hundred years, regarding human artistic production at a very early stage. Such subhuman groups as the Neanderthal did not make works of art. The first artists were the ancestors of modern Europeans, the Cro-Magnon people, who roamed over Europe, equipped with stone tools and weapons, during the last glacial period, when the Alpine region, northeastern Europe, and most of the British Isles were covered deep in glacial ice. So much of the world's water was frozen in polar ice caps and continental glaciers that coastlines were very different from their present shape, and the southern portions of the British Isles were connected with each other and the Continent. Vegetation was subarctic; most of western Europe was a tundra, and forests were limited to the Mediterranean region. In this inhospitable environment early humans, vastly outnumbered by the animals on which they depended for food, lived in caves or in temporary settlements of shelters made from mud and branches.

There seem to be no early stages in the evolution of Paleolithic art; the earliest examples are of an astonishingly high quality. This fact, coupled with the great period of time covered by the finds, suggests the existence of a strong tradition in the hands of trained artists, transmitting their knowledge and skill from generation to generation. While these early works of art have been found all the way from southern Spain and Sicily to southern Siberia, most of the discoveries have come to light in south-central France, northern Spain, the Danube region, and the Indus Valley. The approximate dates given here are based on analysis of organic material at the sites, according to the known rate of disintegration of radioactive carbon 14, absorbed by all living organisms, into nonradioactive nitrogen 14 after death. Even

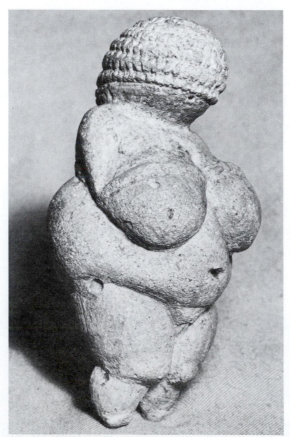

1-1. *"Venus" of Willendorf.* c. 30,000–25,000 B.C. Limestone, height 4⅜″ (11.1 cm). Natur-historisches Museum, Vienna

1-1

more surprising than the immense age of the earliest finds is the extraordinary duration of the cave culture, some twenty thousand years. It is evident that the species to which we belong—*Homo sapiens*—was from its very beginnings endowed with a high degree of artistic talent and that this talent was exercised over a period lasting at least four times as long as all of recorded history. This is a discovery of the greatest intellectual, even spiritual, importance. On the basis of the works rediscovered by chance or by plan we can safely say that artistic ability is not, like science or any form of learning, something achieved through millennia of struggle, but is an inborn essential of human nature. Prehistoric art, therefore, has now told us much, not only about early humanity but about ourselves.

Paleolithic Art (Old Stone Age), 30,000–10,000 B.C.

SCULPTURE   The tiny female statuette jocularly known as Venus (fig. 1–1), found near Willendorf in Lower Austria, is datable between 30,000 and 25,000 B.C. It is one of the earliest known representations. Grotesque as it may at first appear, the *"Venus" of Willendorf* is, on careful analysis, a superb work of art. The lack of any delineation of the face, the rudimentary arms crossed on the enormous bosom, and the almost equally enlarged belly and genitals indicate that the statuette was not intended as a naturalistic representation but as a fertility symbol; as such, it is compelling. From the modern point of view, the statue harmonizes spherical and spheroid volumes with such power and poise that it has influenced twentieth-century abstract sculpture. One of the finest of these tiny carvings is the delicate ivory head of a woman from the cave called Grotte du Pape at Brassempouy in southwestern France (fig. 1–2). As in the *"Venus" of Willendorf,* the hair is delineated as a grid suggesting an elaborate hairdo, which hangs down on the sides to

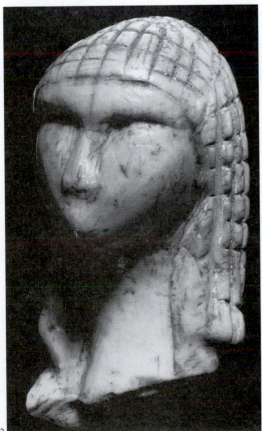

1-2

1-2. *Woman's Head,* from Grotte du Pape, Brassempouy (Landes), France. c. 22,000 B.C. Ivory, height 1¼″ (3 cm). Musée des Antiquités Nationales, St.-Germain-en-Laye, France

1-3. *Bison,* from La Madeleine (Tarn), France. c. 12,000
B.C. Antler, length 4″ (10 cm). Musée des Antiquités
Nationales, St.-Germain-en-Laye, France

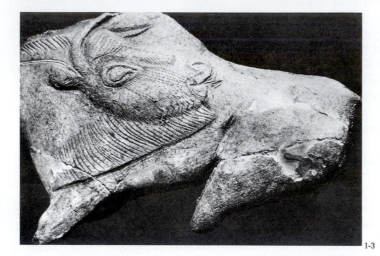

1-3

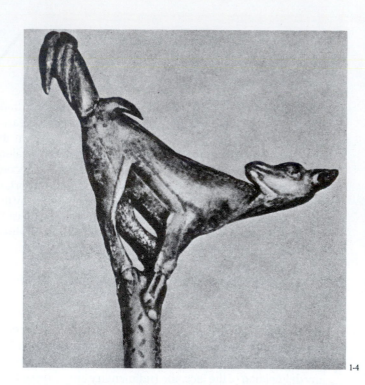

1-4

1-4. *Chamois,* from Le Mas d'Azil (Ariège),
France. Antler, length 11⅝″ (30 cm). Collection
Péquart, St.-Brieuc, France

flank a slender neck. The pointed face is divided only by nose and eyebrows; the mouth and eyes may originally have been painted on.

As compared with these stylized images of human beings, the earliest represented animals are strikingly naturalistic. A little bison (fig. 1–3) carved about 12,000 B.C. from a piece of antler was found at La Madeleine in south-central France. The legs are only partially preserved, but the head, turned to look backward, is convincingly alive, with its open mouth, wide eye, mane, and furry ruff indicated by firm, sure incisions. The projections are so slight that the relief approaches the nature of drawing. Another brilliant example of animal art is the little spear-thrower (fig. 1–4), from Le Mas d'Azil in southwestern France, representing a chamois in a similar pose of alarm, its head turned backward and its feet brought almost together in a precarious perch on the end of the implement.

CAVE ART   The most impressive creations of Paleolithic humans are the large-scale paintings, engravings, and even sculptures, almost exclusively representing animals, that decorate the walls and ceilings of limestone caves in southwestern France and northern Spain (see figs. 1–6 to 1–8). Their purpose is still obscure. By analogy with the experience of surviving tribal cultures, it has been suggested that these paintings are an attempt to gain magical control, by means of representation, of the animals early humans hunted for food. This interpretation has been strongly questioned. Judging from the bones found in the inhabited caves, the principal food of the cave dwellers was reindeer meat. But the chief animals represented, in order of frequency, were the horse, the bison, the mammoth, the ibex, the aurochs, and at long last several species of deer. Most of the paintings are found at a distance from the portions of the caves (near the entrances) where early humanity lived, worked, cooked, and ate (as at Lascaux in France, fig. 1–5). Often the painted chambers are accessible only by crawling through long, tortuous passages or by crossing underground streams. This placing, together with the enormous size and compelling grandeur of some of these paintings, suggests that the remote chambers were sanctuaries for magical or religious rituals to which we have as yet no clue.

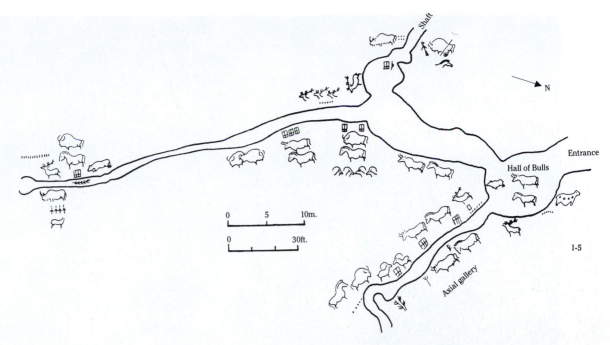

1-5

1-5. Diagrammatic plan showing the layout of caves at Lascaux (Dordogne), France

Evidence indicates that the chambers were used continuously for thousands of years, and microscopic analysis by the American scholar Alexander Marshack has shown that the paintings were repainted periodically, many times in fact, in layer after layer. Abstract signs and symbols, which may be the ancestors of writing, appear consistently throughout all the painted caves and also on many of the bone implements found in them. One day these symbols may yield to interpretation; possibly they will provide the answer to the mysterious questions of the meaning and purpose of these magnificent paintings.

In the absence of natural light, the paintings could only have been done with the aid of stone lamps filled with animal fat and burning wicks of woven moss fibers or hair. The colors were derived from easily found minerals and include red, yellow, black, brown, and violet, but no green or blue. The vehicle could not have been fat, which would not penetrate the chronically damp, porous walls; a water vehicle could amalgamate with the moisture and carry the color into the structure of the limestone. No brushes have been found, so in all probability the broad black outlines were applied by means of mats of moss or hair or even by chunks or sticks of raw color. The surfaces appear to have been covered by paint blown from a tube; color-stained tubes of bone have been found in the caves.

The paintings have always been described as "lifelike," and so they are, but they are also in some respects standardized. The animals were invariably represented from the side, and generally as standing in an alert position, the legs tense and apart, the off legs convincingly more distant from the observer, the tail partially extended. Rarer running poses show front and rear legs extended in pairs, like the legs of rocking horses. No vegetation appears, nor even a groundline. The animals float as if by magic on the rock surface. Their liveliness is achieved by the energy of the broad, rhythmic outline, set down with full arm movements so that it pulsates around the sprayed areas of soft color.

The cave of Altamira in Spain, now dated between 15,000 and 10,000 B.C., was the first to be discovered a century ago but was not at once accepted as authentic. Today it is considered the finest. The famous bison on the ceiling of Altamira (fig. 1–6), vividly alert, are as powerful as representations of animals can be. Although artists of periods later in human history analyzed both surface and anatomical structure more extensively, the majesty of the Altamira animals has never been surpassed. The cave of Lascaux in France, dating from about 15,000 B.C. and discovered in 1940, is a close competitor to Altamira. It is one of a large number of

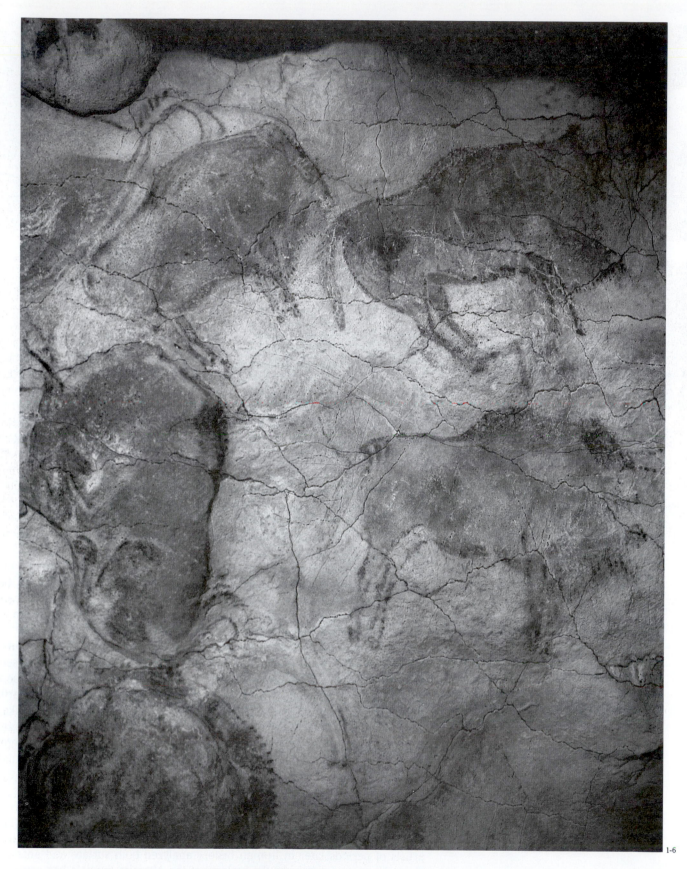

1-6

1-6. *Bison.* c. 15,000–10,000 B.C. Cave painting. Altamira, Spain. (Reproduced in color on page 2.)

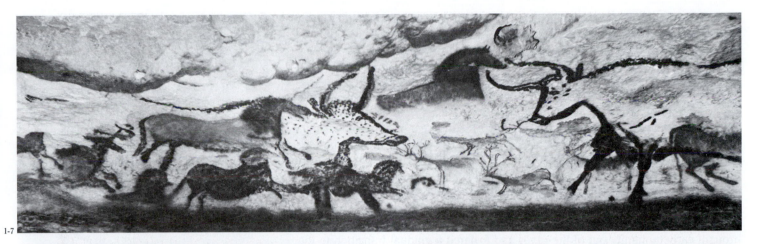

1-7

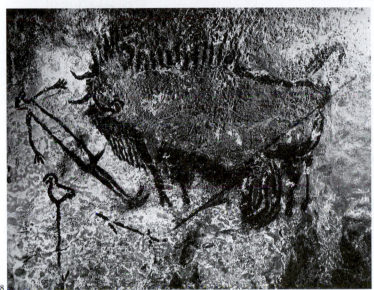

1-8

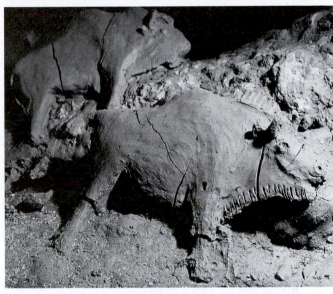

1-9

1-7. Cave painting in the Hall of Bulls, Lascaux (Dordogne), France. c. 15,000–10,000 B.C.

1-8. *Wounded Bison Attacking a Man.* c. 15,000–10,000 B.C. Cave painting, length of bison 43″ (1.09 m). Lascaux

1-9. *Two Bison,* from the cave at Le Tuc d'Audoubert (Ariège), France. c. 15,000 B.C. Clay low relief, length 24″ (61 cm) each

painted caves in the Dordogne region. The low ceiling of the so-called Hall of Bulls at Lascaux (fig. 1–7) is covered with bulls and horses, often partly superimposed, painted with such vitality that they fairly thunder off the rock surfaces at us. In another chamber is the tragic painting of a bison pierced by a spear (fig. 1–8), dragging his intestines as he turns to gore a man who is represented schematically as compared to the naturalistic treatment of the animals.

Some images are in relief, some almost completely in the round, such as the tense, seemingly still throbbing bison modeled in clay (fig. 1–9) about 15,000 B.C. on the sloping ground of a cave at Le Tuc d'Audoubert in southern France, filled with the same organic power as the paintings. The strokes of some sort of flat tool, possibly an animal's shoulder blade, with which the clay was applied can still be clearly seen.

Our understanding of cave paintings cannot help being different from that of the people who painted them so many thousands of years ago. Until we learn to decipher the signs and symbols appearing in the caves we have no real clue as to what may have been going through the minds of the painters, or for that matter even whether they were men or women. But we can perhaps reach them across the intervening millennia through our common humanity. To our eyes the attitudes and sometimes even the expressions of the painted animals are so intense, and the outlines painted or modeled with such force and freedom, that it would be amazing if these early artists did not experience deep creative pleasure in what they were doing, regardless of any purpose the pictures might have been intended to serve. In fact Louis-René Nougier has suggested that to the cave artists *artistic* creation may have seemed identical with *actual* creation, and that by their activity in paint they were somehow making these animals who moved through their forest world. "Prehistoric art," Nougier wrote, "is essentially action." This concept of action identifies, then, the artist's movements of arm and hand with those of the animals the artist reproduces. The fact that the individual images were so often painted right over one another would in itself show that the moment of creation, whether religious, magical, or some mysterious combination of both, was more important than the final image and its survival.

Mesolithic Art (Middle Stone Age), c. 10,000–8000 B.C.

The disappearance of the great glaciers and the consequent rise in temperature brought early humanity out of the caves and fostered a gradual transition to the farming society of the Neolithic period (New Stone Age). This intermediate stage, known as the Mesolithic (Middle Stone Age), is far less rewarding artistically than the Paleolithic. Paintings were made on the walls of open shelters on rocky cliff faces. More than sixty sites have been located in eastern Spain, but the small-scale paintings of animals lack not only the size but also the vigor of the cave paintings, and were usually done in a single tone of red. An example from El Cerro Felío (fig. 1–10) shows a group of male and female hunters, greatly schematized but nonetheless pursuing at remarkable speed an antelope that seems to have eluded their spears and arrows. Mesolithic rock paintings of a somewhat similar style are scattered from Scandinavia to South Africa. By far the most striking works of art from the Mesolithic period are the brilliant series of outline drawings of human figures and animals discovered in 1952 on the walls of a small cave at Addaura, just outside Palermo, Sicily (fig. 1–11). The figures, depicted in a variety of attitudes, may be engaged in a ritual dance, perhaps including acts of torture; the vigor and freedom of their movements remind one of certain twentieth-century works, notably those of Henri Matisse.

Neolithic Art (New Stone Age), c. 8000–3000 B.C.

With the recession of the last glaciers, the climate grew irregularly but inexorably warmer, and humanity, all the way from the British Isles to the Indus Valley, was able to set up a new existence free from the limitations of the caves. Wild grains and legumes now flourished throughout a wide area and were eventually domesticated. So, one by one, were various species of animals. Although stone remained the principal material for weapons and tools, here and there humans discovered how to smelt certain metals. Pottery, often richly decorated, began to replace utensils of wood or stone, and weaving became highly developed. Objects made of nonindigenous materials indicate the existence of travel and commerce. Although they were still hunters, people were no longer utterly dependent on wild animals, and representations of animals consequently lost the intimate naturalism so impressive in Paleolithic art. More lasting settlements grew up, some of a considerable size, and the beginnings of architecture made their appearance, these early examples being generally constructed of perishable materials such as timber, wicker, and thatch. The many Neolithic town sites excavated throughout central Europe and northern Italy have yielded much information about a wide variety of early cultures; only in the Middle East, however, have there appeared ruins of masonry structures, which can be considered the ancestors of architecture as we know it. From the evidence available, what may have been Paleolithic religious life is scarcely distinguishable from magic, but in the Neolithic period structures appear that can only be described as sanctuaries, implying the existence of an organized religion, with a priestly class making new demands on art.

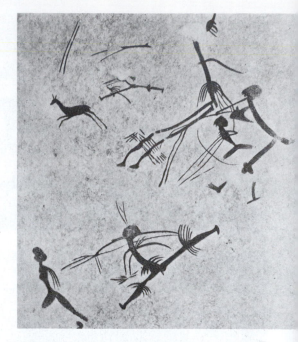

1-10. *Hunting Scene*. Watercolor copy of a cave painting at El Cerro Felío (near Alacón), Spain

1-11. *Ritual Dance*. c. 15,000–10,000 B.C. Drawing in the cave at Addaura, Sicily. Height of figures 10″ (25.4 cm)

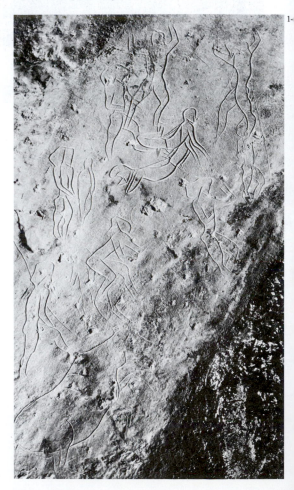

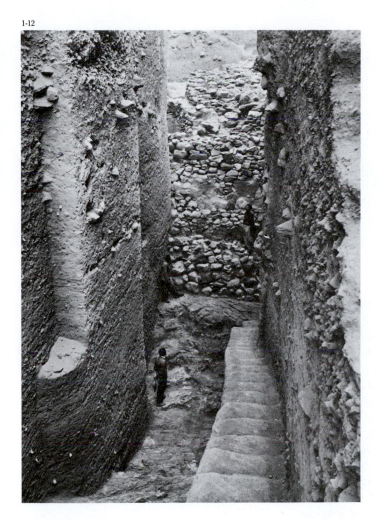

1-12. Fortifications, Jericho, Jordan. c. 7500 B.C.

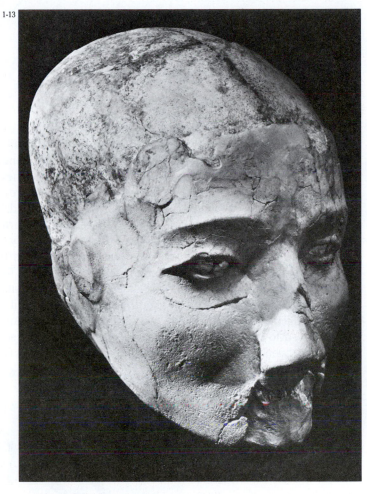

1-13. Plastered skull. c. 7000–6000 B.C. Jericho

JERICHO   The earliest masonry town yet known is the still only partially excavated city of Jericho in southern Palestine (now Jordan). About 8000 B.C. the settlement was composed of oval mud-brick houses on stone foundations. By about 7500 B.C. it was surrounded by a rough stone wall whose preserved portions reach a height of twelve feet and was further defended by a moat cut in the rock and by at least one stone tower thirty feet high (fig. 1–12), the earliest surviving fortifications in stone. Even more impressive are the human skulls found here (fig. 1–13). Their features had been reconstructed in modeled plaster. These skulls originally belonged to bodies buried beneath the plaster floors of the houses and were doubtless intended to serve as homes for ancestral spirits, to be propitiated by the living. The soft modeling is delicately observed; when painted, these heads must have been alarmingly vivid, the more so since seashells were inserted in the eye sockets and painted to resemble eyes.

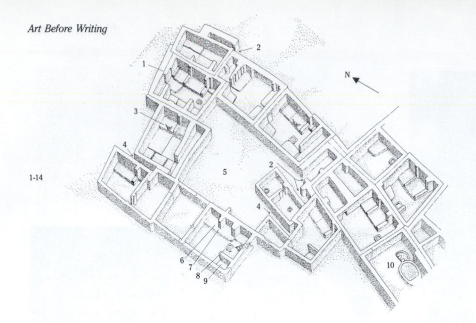

1-14. Reconstruction of houses, Çatal Hüyük, Turkey (after J. Mellaart). 6500–5700 B.C.
1. Shrine   2. Access to the roof   3. Bull's-head effigy   4. Passage to the roof   5. Open court
6. Platform   7. Buttress   8. Hearth
9. Entrance shaft   10. Bread oven

ÇATAL HÜYÜK   From 1961 to 1963, excavations in the mound of Çatal Hüyük on the plain of Anatolia, in central Turkey, disclosed a small portion of a city that, according to carbon-14 dating, enjoyed a life of some eight hundred years, from 6500 to 5700 B.C. The city was destroyed and rebuilt twelve times, the successive layers of mud brick revealing a high level of Neolithic culture, whose artifacts included woven rugs with bold decorative patterns (not preserved, but simulated in wall paintings) and polished mirrors made from obsidian, a hard volcanic stone. Oddly enough, the inhabitants had not yet discovered pottery and made their receptacles from stone or wood and from wicker. The houses (fig. 1–14) were clustered together without streets in a manner not unlike that of the pueblos of the American Southwest, with a common outer wall for defense, and they could be entered only by means of ladders. The furniture was built-in; it consisted of low plastered couches under which the bones of the dead were buried after having been exposed to vultures to remove the flesh. A remarkable series of religious artifacts has been found, including statues of a mother goddess (fig. 1–15) whose

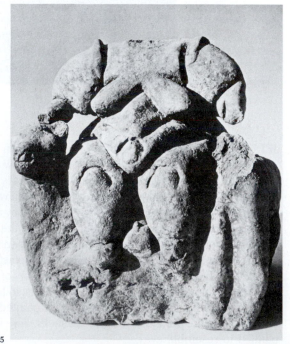

1-15. *Goddess Giving Birth,* from Çatal Hüyük. c. 6500–5700 B.C. Baked clay, height 8″ (20 cm). Archaeological Museum, Ankara, Turkey

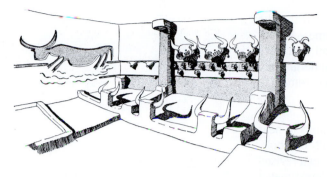

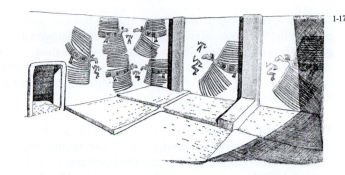

1-16. Reconstructed view of a shrine with bull horn and skull decoration, Çatal Hüyük (after J. Mellaart). c. 6500–5700 B.C.

1-17. Reconstructed view of a shrine with wall paintings of vultures, Çatal Hüyük (after J. Mellaart). c. 6500–5700 B.C.

immense breasts and belly recall the *"Venus" of Willendorf*. The head appearing between her knees clearly symbolizes childbirth. The existence of commerce with other still-to-be-discovered centers is suggested by the fact that some objects were made of materials that could only have come from great distances.

Alongside the rooms intended for lay habitation, shrines are occasionally found with couches doubtless meant for the priesthood. These shrines enclose symbols of magical potency and—even in reconstruction—of awesome grandeur. Some shrines were adorned by rows of paired wild-bull horns mounted on the floor, facing entire bull skulls fixed to the wall above (fig. 1–16). These were probably male symbols. A stylized but very aggressive silhouette painting of a bull appears on a flanking wall. Other shrines (fig. 1–17) were apparently dedicated to death, symbolized by wall paintings of huge vultures devouring tiny, headless humans depicted in the poses in which corpses were buried. Schematized and flattened though they are, these birds, whose wings spread diagonally across whole walls as if wheeling through the air, must have struck terror into the hearts of the inhabitants. On one wall was found the earliest known landscape painting (fig. 1–18), showing Çatal Hüyük itself, represented as a series of rough squares surmounted by an erupting volcano.

All excavations bring up surprises of some kind, but the urban civilization of Çatal Hüyük, with its far-flung connections, was totally unexpected at so early a date. Yet after the abandonment of the town it seems to have had little or no influence on later cultures, and should not be confused with the great Mesopotamian civilizations that flourished millennia later, far to the south. Only the bull deities, if that is what they were, may have been picked up by Egypt, Mesopotamia, and Crete. But after all, the bull is a natural symbol of magical strength and potency. Everything that could be salvaged from the excavations was removed to the

1-18. Landscape painting (copy), from Çatal Hüyük. c. 6150 B.C.

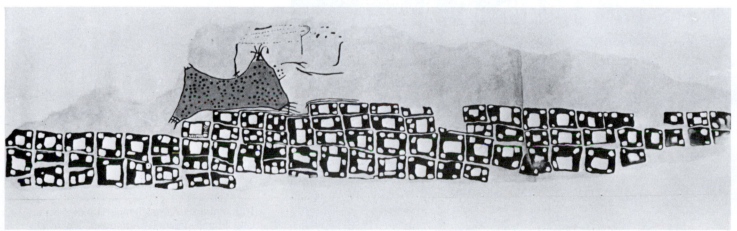

1-18

National Archaeological Museum at Ankara, but it is especially sad to relate that the only partially uncovered ruins have now been destroyed a thirteenth time—and for good. The sun and wind have reduced them to dust, and winds and rain have carried the dust away. At least three-quarters of Çatal Hüyük is still underground. Who knows what later excavations may yield, or what other early centers remain to be discovered.

MEGALITHIC ARCHITECTURE   A number of sites, generally on islands or near the seacoast, preserve impressive remains of monuments made partially or wholly of giant stones (*megaliths*). The accepted dating of these buildings has been revised in the light of the discovery that the carbon-14 method consistently underestimated by as much as eight hundred years the age of California bristlecone pine trees, in some of whose cross sections more than eight thousand rings have been counted, one for each year of life. The ancient civilization on the Mediterranean island of Malta, for example, which lasted about eight hundred years, has now been dated before 3000 B.C. A hard limestone was used for the exterior walls of the temples. A double vinescroll ornament of unexpected rhythmic grace, the earliest known appearance of a motif that later became universal in classical decoration, is carved in low relief on the entrance slab of one of the temples at Tarxien (fig. 1–19). The interiors of tombs and temples generally follow a trefoil plan; the stones are *corbeled* (projected one beyond the other) to form a sloping wall that probably supported a wooden roof.

Long famous are the megaliths of Brittany, giant single stones known as *menhirs,* which march across the countryside for miles, and the *dolmens* or *trilithons* (two vertical stones supporting a horizontal one: the basic unit of *post-and-lintel* construction), which were probably intended as graves to be surrounded by mounds. A number of *cromlechs,* ritual stone circles, are preserved in England, the grandest of which is Stonehenge on the Salisbury Plain (figs. 1–20, 1–21). Now datable about 2000 B.C., this is the third and most ambitious circle built on the site. The central circle, of "bluestones" from the Prescelly Mountains 134 miles distant, is surrounded by an outer circle of Wiltshire flinty sandstone from a source twenty-four miles away, dragged by hundreds of men. Claims of extraordinary astronomical

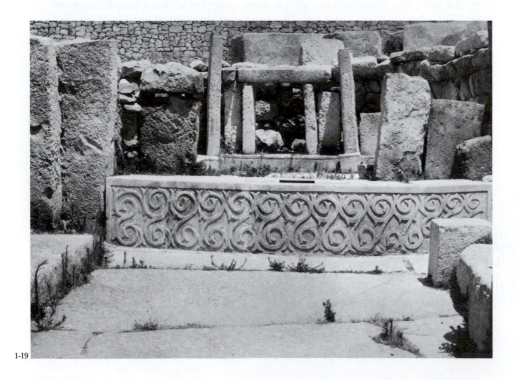

1-19

1-19. Entrance slab of Temple, Tarxien, Malta. Late 3d millennium B.C. Limestone low relief

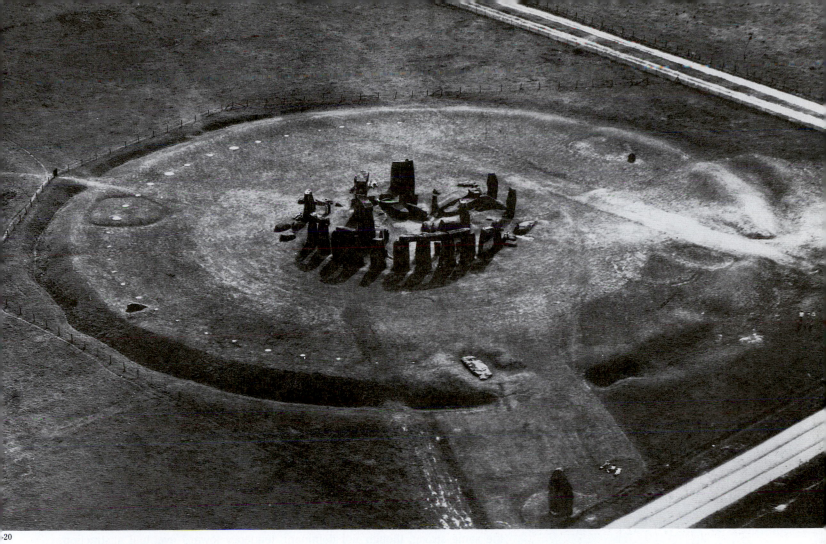

1-20. Aerial view of Stonehenge, Salisbury Plain (Wiltshire), England. c. 2000 B.C. Diameter of circle 97′ (29.6 m)

competence on behalf of these Stone Age builders, surpassing even that of the later Greeks, have been challenged, but it is clear that the stones were arranged to coincide at least roughly with sunrise at the summer solstice. The impression of rude majesty they impart is tempered somewhat by the observation of considerable subtleties: the stones, weighing as much as fifty tons, were *dressed* (trimmed) to taper upward and even endowed with a slight swelling known later to the Greeks as *entasis,* and then lifted into position, and their lintels were curved according to their places in the circle.

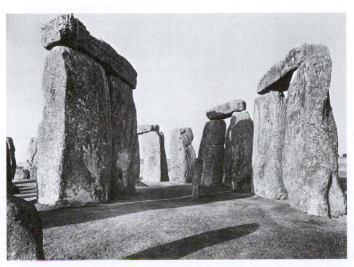

1-21. Trilithon (left) and portion of the outer circle of upright stones and lintels, Stonehenge. Height of trilithon approx. 21′ (6.4 m)

1-21

47

CHAPTER TWO

Inevitably, the bulk of this book is concerned with the long and continuous artistic traditions of European and Asiatic societies and of their descendants in North America. The preliterate arts introduced in Chapter One were indeed produced by the direct ancestors of modern Europeans and of the European settlers of North America. But there exists a vast field of ancient and recent artistic production by societies in Africa, North America, and the islands of the Pacific that have had only the most limited—and generally unfortunate—contacts with European and Asiatic cultures; this art must be studied in and for itself, not only to do justice to the societies that produced it but for its intrinsic aesthetic interest. In contrast to historic states, which are almost invariably multiracial, with few exceptions these societies were and are based on ethnic unity rather than clearly defined territorial frontiers, predominantly agricultural with only small urban centers, and ruled by chieftains or other monarchs. These ethnic groups may thus realistically be described as *tribes* even when their numbers are so great that the word *nation* has also been used to characterize them.

In tribal cultures there is obviously no direct development from preliterate to literate art; there is rather the sudden overlay of a comparatively late phase of the art of white people imposed, along with the other values of a white society, upon red, brown, or black preliterate groups, often by force. Much the same process took place much earlier, when the Celtic and Germanic societies of northern Europe were conquered by the Romans. Yet the artistic traditions of these subject or displaced tribes have continued to flourish up to our own time, even when adulterated by European ingredients. The frequent use of magical imagery and an essential spacelessness unite these arts with those of early humanity. There is also the same strong, though not dominant, tendency toward eventual abstraction, through the constant repetition of traditional ideas and forms that probably began as naturalistic. Mysteriously, across many thousands of miles of land and ocean, the more recent tribal arts have elevated the mask to a special importance approached in Europe only by the role it assumed in ancient Greek drama. In ritual or in death, confronting the forces of the supernatural or personifying them, individuals must transfigure their identity by means of artificial faces or even entire heads, sometimes serene, more frequently awesome. On these masks enormous skill and every resource of the artist are lavished for overwhelming effect. Tribal arts also share the concepts of utilitarianism and impermanence. Despite the high respect often accorded to artists, once their creations became worn or damaged in use these objects shared the fate of old cars rather than antique furniture in Western society. With the exception of a few masonry villages in the American Southwest and a few now-ruined cities in certain portions of Africa, habitations were built of impermanent materials and have largely vanished. In consequence, the past of tribal art remains largely unknown and its history cannot be written. The great beauty of the rare antiquities in permanent materials raises the disturbing possibility that what we have lost from precolonial eras may be superior to anything we have left.

The arts of early humanity had been dormant and forgotten for thousands of years and were rediscovered only within the past century, even the past few decades, while tribal arts were being produced in quantity when Europeans arrived on the scene, and in fact still are. By a fascinating historical irony, these tradition-bound arts were found by the more sophisticated European observers to be fresh and free from tradition, meaning of course from the customs and conventions of European society. Thus the arts of "primitive" peoples have had an enormous influence on those of Europe and of Europeanized American societies. Primitive became fashionable, and the forms and colors of black African, "South

Sea" island, and North and South American Indian artists remain essential ingredients in the culture of the industrialized world.

Black African Art

Below the Sahara Desert stretches a vast region of Africa, including uplands, open steppes, and tropical rain forests, the home of an incredible number and variety of artistically productive black cultures, especially in the tightly organized West African kingdoms bordering on the Gulf of Guinea, within which the Yoruba people, centering on present-day Nigeria, are at once the most productive and the most talented.

European contacts with the arts of black Africa have undergone at least four distinct phases. At first, artifacts were brought home as curiosities by early explorers, traders, and colonists. To this activity we often owe the continued existence of wooden objects, doomed to a short life in African society and climate. Then, with the growth of anthropological studies in the nineteenth century, the objects were exhibited as specimens in museums of natural history. Next, at the turn of the present century, great exhibitions were given in major European centers, and the aesthetic properties of African art were discovered as a powerful source of inspiration by adventurous European artists. Since then, archaeological excavation, still all too rare and limited, has discovered a few works of courtly art of astonishing beauty and great antiquity, antedating any contacts with Europeans, and systematic study has separated and interpreted the recent works in accordance with the results of anthropological, linguistic, and religious investigations, not to speak of the study of the closely interrelated arts of oral literature, music, and the dance, at which Africans traditionally excel.

ANCIENT ARTS   The earliest known examples of African art are the striking Neolithic rock engravings and paintings of humans and animals, most of which were discovered in great numbers in 1956 and the immediately following years in what are today the deserts of southern Algeria but were then flourishing regions. These may have been done by ancestors of the present tribes of black Africa at some time between the fifth millennium and 1200 B.C. Small heads and fragments of other sculptures in clay from central Nigeria, collectively labeled as products of the Nok culture and datable between 500 B.C. and A.D. 200, constitute our earliest certain examples of black African art.

The discovery in 1910 of a fine series of naturalistic heads and masks in clay at Ife in Nigeria changed our view of African art considerably, but the accidental unearthing of eleven superb bronze heads and masks in the same area in 1938 came as a total surprise. Ife artists had been thoroughly familiar with the *lost-wax process* of casting. They modeled their heads in clay, spread them with a thin layer of beeswax, and then covered them with a heavy layer of clay. When this mold hardened it was heated, the wax ran out, and molten metal was poured in, thus assuming the shape and thickness of the original wax layer. When cool, the mold was broken off the hardened bronze, and the clay emptied out from the interior. Invented by Bronze Age peoples, this method was known throughout the Mediterranean world in antiquity. No contacts have been traced between the Ife civilization, which flourished between the eleventh and thirteenth centuries A.D., and the Mediterranean; it is now generally accepted that the Ife artists discovered the lost-wax method independently.

These portrait heads are of striking nobility and beauty, which would be called

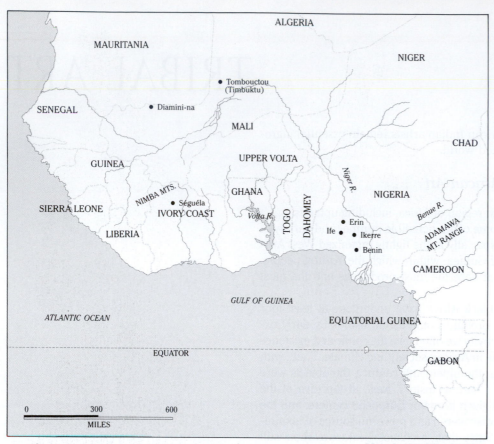

Map 2. WEST AFRICA

classic by any society fortunate enough to have produced them. The calm and majestic head surmounted by a diadem of feathers and an erect, plaited ornament (fig. 2–1) was once identified as that of the mythical Olokun, wife of the second *oni* (divine king) of Ife, but is now recognized as probably the portrait of an oni himself. The broad, smooth surfaces of the skin are striated with parallel grooves representing tribal scars and are perforated around the mouth and jawbone with holes possibly intended for the insertion of a beaded veil (a black glass bead has been found in one) still used today to protect the hearers from the powerful effects of the words uttered by this exalted personage. Probably these heads were made to surmount wooden bodies, but this is not certain.

Sixteenth-century Portuguese explorers were the first Europeans to visit the nearby Nigerian kingdom of Benin, known for its slave trade and for human sacrifice. Its art, however, was not widely recognized until the town of Benin was destroyed by the British in 1897 and a large number of splendid bronze objects from the royal palace were taken to England. Among them was the elegant and serene head, dating from the early sixteenth century, now identified as that of a queen mother (fig. 2–2). She wears a high, beaded collar and a beautiful horn-shaped headdress consisting of a net woven of beads. The queen mother was a powerful figure in African society; in monumental wood sculpture of the Yoruba, senior queens often stand behind the kings, towering over them. The refined workmanship of the very thin bronze-casting is derived, according to oral tradition, from the older Ife culture, but a certain stylization has softened the overwhelming sense of reality of the Ife heads.

Handsome leopards of ivory studded with brass disks (fig. 2–3), symbols of royal power, and many grand bronze reliefs from the palace—like the sixteenth- or seventeenth-century one representing a king mounted sidesaddle on a tiny and unidentifiable mount between two children who hold the reins (fig. 2–4), while two larger attendants at either side shade the king's head with palm branches—show other possibilities of the Benin style. Strong, cylindrical volumes are generally opposed to surfaces enriched by parallel grooves, striations, and ornament incised

2-1. *Portrait of the Oni of Ife,* from Nigeria. c. 11th–13th centuries A.D. Clay and bronze, height to top of ornament approx. 36″ (91 cm). British Museum, London

2-2. *Queen Mother,* from Benin, Nigeria. Early 16th century A.D. Bronze, life size. British Museum, London

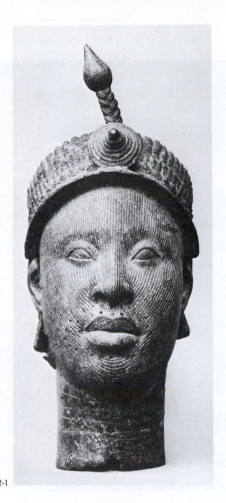

2-1

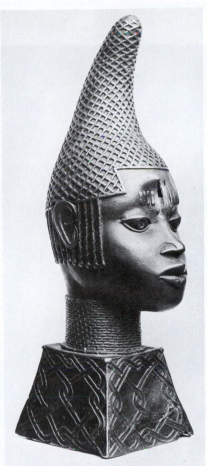

2-2

on the surface after casting. As was characteristic of Ife art as well (judging from a surviving small, full-length statue), there was a triple system of proportions—large for the head, half that scale for the body and arms, and half again for the legs. A triple or double scale (large head, torso and arms, small legs), in individual variations, is found throughout African wood sculpture.

ARCHITECTURE   In the inaccessibility of stone for building, most black African architecture was not built to last. Only occasional circular enclosures, tombs, and monuments survive, and the firing of brick seems not to have been discovered. As in Mesolithic and Neolithic Europe, buildings were and still are constructed largely, often entirely, of organic materials. Reverence for the inner nature of branches, trunks, and thatch is what gives black African architecture and, as we shall see, African wood sculpture as well, its wonderful organic quality. The tree is lovingly shaped in the hand with an adz, a tool resembling an ax but with the blade running at right angles to the handle like that of a hoe and inclined toward the user. Saws and planes are unknown, so there are no boards. No edge is even, no angle straight, no vertical plumb, no surface true, nor need they be. Sun-dried mud walls support and conform to vast thatched roofs, often conical and beautifully layered, which, in principle, are colossal baskets. Freed from the strictures of measure, a building resembles a work of nature, whose deities are revered by African religion, and like a work of nature the building dies. Pictures, as known to European and Asiatic cultures, do not exist in black African culture, but the mud walls are often ornamented in brilliantly colored patterns or low reliefs, which sometimes include representations of surprising elements from imposed European culture, such as motor vehicles.

Buildings constructed on these principles have reached astonishing dimensions. Royal palaces often consist of numbers of huge, conical houses, sometimes with arc-shaped, arcaded verandas, linked by long corridors forming courtyards. Ac-

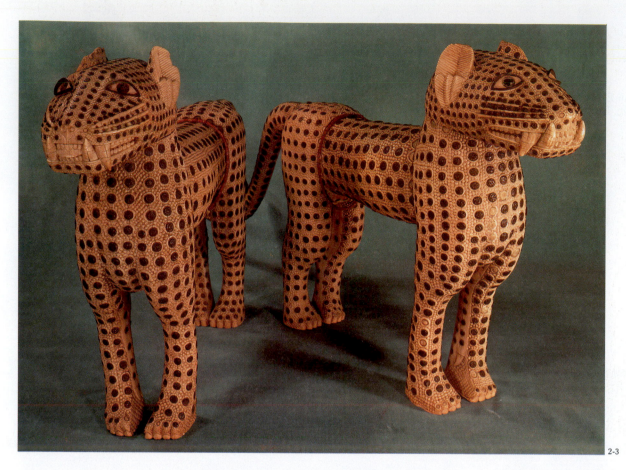

2-3

2-3. *Leopards,* from Benin. c. 16th–17th centuries A.D. Ivory with brass inlay, length 32⅝″ (82.87 cm). British Museum, London

counts and drawings by early European visitors record audience halls two hundred feet in length, with roofs whose height was governed only by that of the multiple tree-trunks used for supports. Rarely, mud bricks are cemented together to rise to the height of two or even three stories. In some areas round clay buildings, nicknamed "bomb houses," are constructed like pots but with a hole at the top for light and ventilation and are fired on the spot. Other unfired brick houses crowd up cliffs in the Dogon area of the bend in the Niger River like North American pueblos. There is apparently no limit to the imaginative freedom and variety of these clay buildings, particularly when the minarets of mosques had to be accounted for. One of the most pleasing of these is the Mosque at Séguéla on the Ivory Coast (fig. 2–5), constructed on a wooden framework whose beams protrude and resembling nothing so much as a free-form pincushion bristling with pins.

RECENT REPRESENTATIONAL ART More than two hundred separate tribal cultures spread across the vast area of sub-Saharan Africa produced and still produce a wide variety of separate styles that doubtless perpetuate, in stylized form, the elements of older and now-lost works, since the art of sculpture, like all crafts, was handed down from father to son. A few examples must suffice to suggest the superb artistic and expressive qualities of these carvings. Figural reliefs continue some aspects of the ornamentalized Benin tradition into the twentieth century. The wood doors carved for the palace of the *oba* (king) Ogoga of Ikerre in Nigeria (fig. 2–6) by OLOWE (died 1938), considered the greatest known Yoruba sculptor, are works of art of a high order. The curved contours of the unequal panels, culminating in pivots to revolve in stone sockets, preserve the organic shapes of the trunks from which they were cut, and the panels are divided at random intervals into five irregularly spaced registers in which is narrated the visit of a British official. The oba on his throne, with his senior wife behind him,

2-4. *Mounted King with Attendants,* from Benin. c. A.D. 1550–1680. Bronze relief plaque, height 19½″ (49.53 cm). The Metropolitan Museum of Art, New York. The Michael Rockefeller Memorial Collection. Gift of Nelson A. Rockefeller

2-5. Mosque, Séguéla, Ivory Coast

2-6. OLOWE. Carved doors, from Ikerre, Nigeria. Yoruba culture, c. A.D. 1910–14. Wood, height 7′ (2.17 cm). British Museum, London

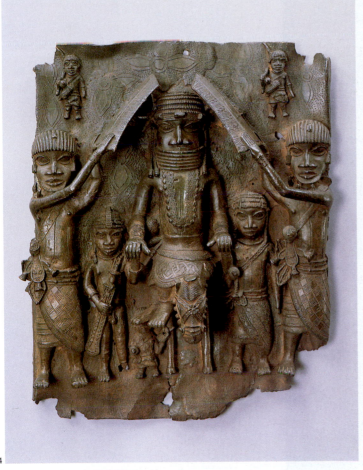

2-4

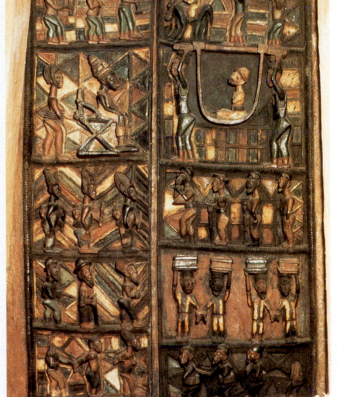

2-6

2-5

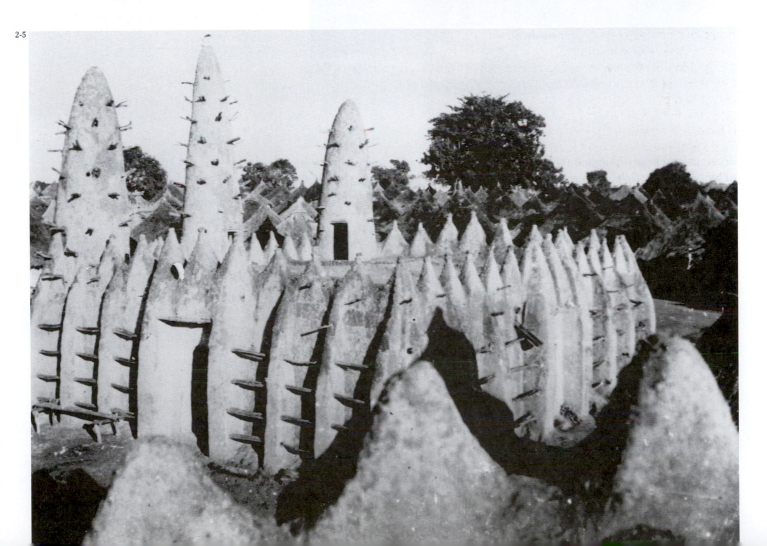

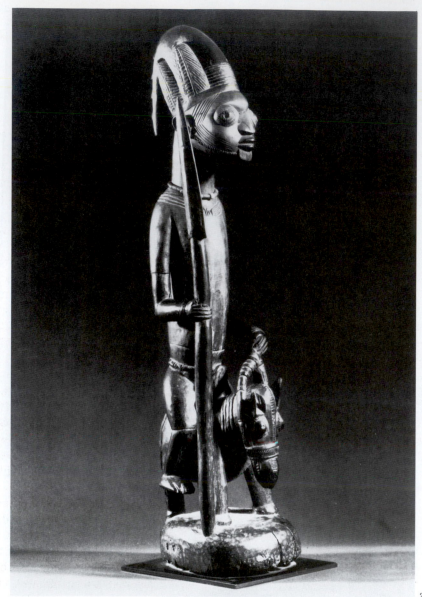

2-7. Maku. *Mounted Warrior,* from Erin, Nigeria. Yoruba culture, early 20th century A.D. Wood, height 38½″ (98 cm). Courtesy of The Center for African Art, New York

2-7

accompanied by his retinue on the left and the official carried in a litter among his entourage on the right, are projected in sharply undercut high relief, as are all the figures. As always in wood sculpture, the basic work is done with an adz, the fine strokes with knives. In spite of the absence of any specific indication of space, two different worlds are suggested in the contrast between the rich and vibrant zigzag patterning of the backgrounds at the left and the more reserved—in one case missing—ornamentation at the right. The doors are part of a four-year sculptural campaign at Ogoga's palace (1910–14), including monumental veranda posts carved into figural groups. Olowe's work is still to be seen in other palaces, proudly enumerated by his wives in the course of an ode from which a few lines may be quoted:

> *Olowe, my excellent husband.*
> *Outstanding leader in war....*
> *One with a mighty sword.*
> *Handsome among his friends.*
> *Outstanding among his peers.*
> *One who carves the hard wood of the troko tree as if it were*
>   *as soft as a calabash.*

One who achieves fame with the proceeds of his carvings. . . .
Olowe, you are great,
The awesome one who moves like a stream
That flows at its own pace and wherever it wills.

Could there be a more moving sign of both the significance of the artist and the importance of words in a society?

Another of the eminent Yoruba sculptors of recent times was MAKU, from the village of Erin, who died about 1927, to be succeeded by his son Toibo. Like Olowe, Maku created a number of monumental wood sculptures for veranda supports, the best known of which are in shrines. A smaller work, a mounted warrior (fig. 2–7), in beautiful condition, shows Maku's style at its best. In its tall, elastic curves—even the long-bladed spear appears curved—the group preserves not only the shape but the vitality of the trunk from which it was carved. Broad, smooth surfaces show clearly the strokes of the adz, in contrast with the fine striations of hair, mustache and beard, headdress, and ornaments executed with the knife. It is the angles and straight lines of the traditional rendering of such works that were of great value to the Cubists in Paris in the first decade of the twentieth century. The unidentifiable mount attracts little interest and is rendered in a scale even smaller than that of the warrior's legs.

RECENT CEREMONIAL ART   Every aspect of daily life in equatorial Africa is governed by ceremonials, intended to propitiate both the gods and the spirits of the dead, some of whom have been deified. The traditional guardian figures of wood covered with copper or sheet brass (fig. 2–8), from the Kota tribe of Gabon in West Africa, were originally set over urns containing ancestral skulls to ward off evil spirits. Their clear-cut, tense geometric forms and strong magical content aided greatly in the development of abstract art in Europe.

The majestic ceremonial masks should always be imagined as being actually worn by participants in complex rituals of fertility or death, rituals accompanied by dances and by music of astonishing rhythmic intricacy. The *kanaga* masks (fig. 2–9), used in the *dama* feasts of a secret religious society of the Dogon people in the Republic of Mali, are considered so sacred and so charged with magical powers that between feasts they are kept hidden. Women and children, not yet initiated, may not go near them for fear of being harmed. The masks embody a complete world system, expressed in the outstretched wings of the cosmic bird (accidentally resembling a so-called Cross of Lorraine) and its sharp beak above the wearer's face. Even the motion of the raffia skirts and arm-fringes should be pictured as part of the total experience when one sees such works of art in glass cases or hung on walls today.

An intensely expressive group of fertility masks called *nimba* (fig. 2–10) are carried in procession by the Baga people of Guinea at planting and harvest times. The wearer's head fits in the hollow of the torso, his eyes looking out between the flat and pendulous breasts, and the whole structure is supported on four leglike struts going over his shoulders and chest. Little of the wearer save his arms appears above the attached raffia skirt. The head, with its staring eyes and monstrous nose outlined by raised dots like nail heads, would bob and sway with the dancer's ritual motions. No twentieth-century European or American sculpture has ever surpassed the grandeur and severity of these almost architectural forms.

Blacks who survived the horrors of the slave ships could bring no ritual objects with them, but they did not leave their creativity in their bereaved villages in Africa. Black folk-arts of great interest grew up in areas of the American South and continue to flourish. And black artists in the twentieth century have not only taken their rightful place among the communities of painters, sculptors, and architects of American metropolitan centers but have often returned to Africa to study their heritage, which has deeply influenced their work today.

2-8. Guardian figure, from Gabon. Kota culture, 19th–20th centuries A.D. Wood covered with sheet copper, height 30″ (76.3 cm). Musée d'Ethnographie, Geneva. Gift of Dr. Graz, 1929

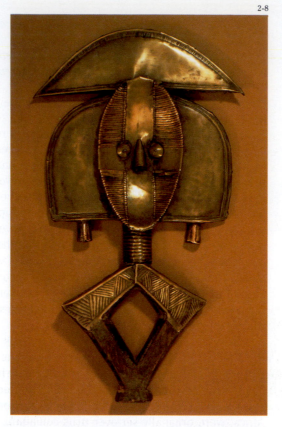

2-9. Dogon dancers wearing *kanaga* masks during a *dama*, Diamini-na, Mali

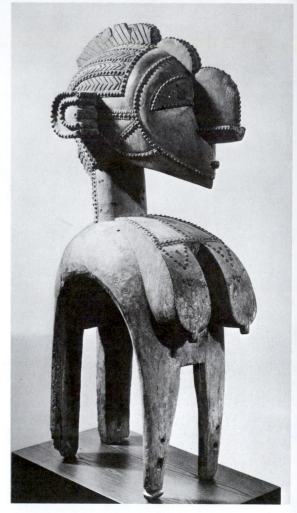

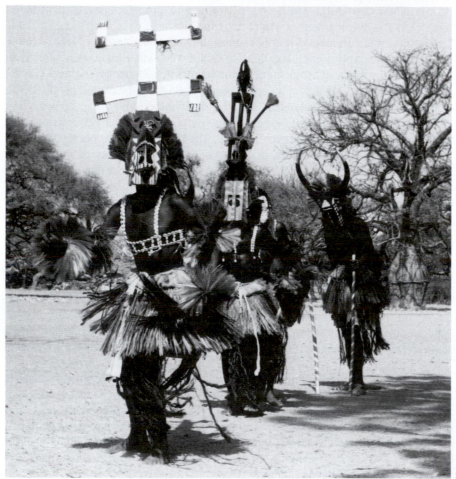

2-10. Fertility mask (*nimba*) with carrying yoke, from the Guinea Coast. Baga culture. Wood, height 52″ (1.32 m). Private collection, New York

2-11. War shield, from the Sepik River region, New Guinea. Late 19th century–early 20th century A.D. Wood, height 61⅜″ (1.56 m). University Museum of Archaeology and Ethnology, Cambridge, England

2-9

Oceanic Art

A strikingly different but equally wide range of aesthetic and emotional values was exploited by the mixed Mongoloid and melanotic (dark-skinned) peoples from Asia, who as early as the second millennium B.C., in adventurous voyages with no idea of where or even whether they would find land, settled the innumerable islands that dot the western Pacific Ocean. The separate tribes that flourished in the rain forests of the coastal areas, the river valleys, and the mountainous uplands of New Guinea were often headhunters (the enemy's strength was supposed to reside in his head, and these were often painted), sometimes ritual cannibals. Their surviving artifacts, usually carved in wood and painted, and therefore of quite recent date, were designed to satisfy practical and ceremonial necessities. Human and animal figures of compelling physical presence coexist with shapes that, at first sight, appear entirely abstract. But the dizzying effect on the modern observer, and presumably on the enemy, of the swirling curves and floating ovoids that decorate a war shield from the Sepik River region of northern New Guinea, the richest artistic region of the island (fig. 2–11), is stabilized by the realization that the shield resembles a gigantic mask, with nose, eyes, and ornamentalized teeth, bearing on its brow a smaller and even more frightening face. Such objects were, of course, never intended to be seen apart from the context of tribal life, some of the intensity of which engulfs us in the huge "soul boat" from New Ireland (fig. 2–12) containing wooden sculptures whose meaning is problematic but which probably represent a dead chieftain and his relatives. The work, discovered in 1903, is unique, possibly because all the other "soul boats" were actually sent to sea, perpetuating an earlier rite in which the bodies themselves were thus treated. The fierce and jagged shapes of the stylized figures, the bird heads that crown them, and the great boat itself with its fins and its open, toothy mouth and lashing tongue compete in power and drama with the finest Northwest Coast American Indian works.

Still unexplained, although possibly ancestral figures, are the colossal stone images on Easter Island (see Introduction fig. 3) that stand in long rows, suggesting the menhirs of Brittany, and lead along avenues to the volcanic craters from whose

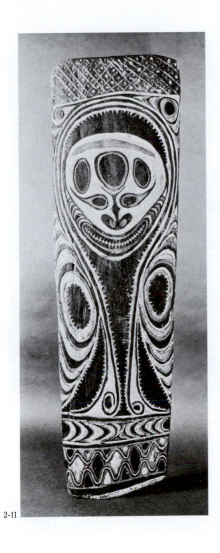

2-11

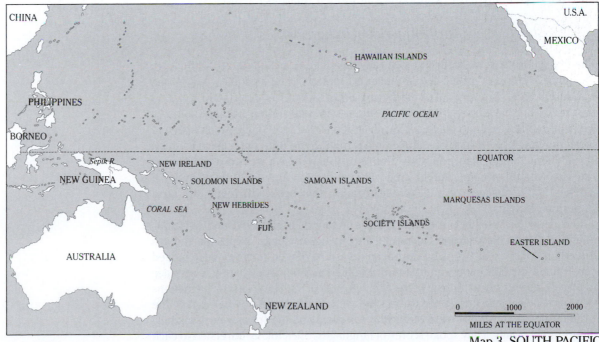

Map 3. SOUTH PACIFIC

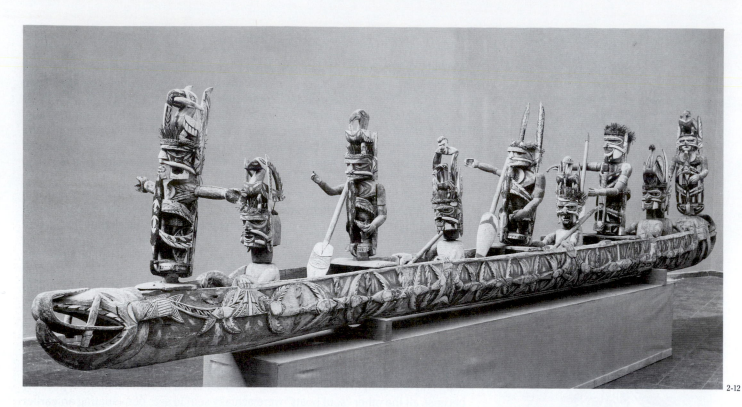

2-12

2-12. "Soul boat," from New Ireland. c. A.D. 1903. Wood, length 19' (5.79 m). Linden-Museum, Stuttgart, Germany

soft lava they were carved. As early as the seventeenth century the first European explorers noted that the inhabitants had lost track of the meaning of the statues and had pushed many of them into the sea. The backs of the heads are entirely absent, the bodies barely suggested, so that the images are really a succession of staring masks, overpowering largely because of their gigantic scale, which unites them with the now-desolate but once-fertile landscape. Their empty eye-sockets were originally filled with painted shells, which must have made their effect still more uncanny. How they were ever transported and set up is as much of a mystery as their purpose. Many have been found still in their quarries.

North American Indian Art

The first Europeans in North America may have been closer to the truth than we recognize when they called the inhabitants "Indians"; these peoples had in fact wandered from Asia, by way of the Bering Strait, about 30,000–10,000 B.C., and they may even have brought Asiatic traditions with them. Many of these nomadic tribes of hunters were still technologically in the Old or the Middle Stone Age, and some remained so, in spite of enforced mass migrations, until the present century. To call them "Native Americans" is a double misnomer: there was no such entity as America when they came, and anyone whoever born in America is by definition a native. In the absence of a better designation this book will retain the term "American Indians."

Our conception of the American Indians is founded on an old and fallacious image of the "naked savage," nomadic and living in tepees. While the Indians driven onto the Great Plains by European invasions of their territory were indeed constrained by their environment to hunt buffalo and move constantly from place to place, this was not at all true of the tribal groups of the Southwest or the nations that once populated the northeast and the central heartland of what is now the United States. These last were ethnically complex, and the tribes were strikingly different physically. They spoke scores of languages, often totally unrelated to each

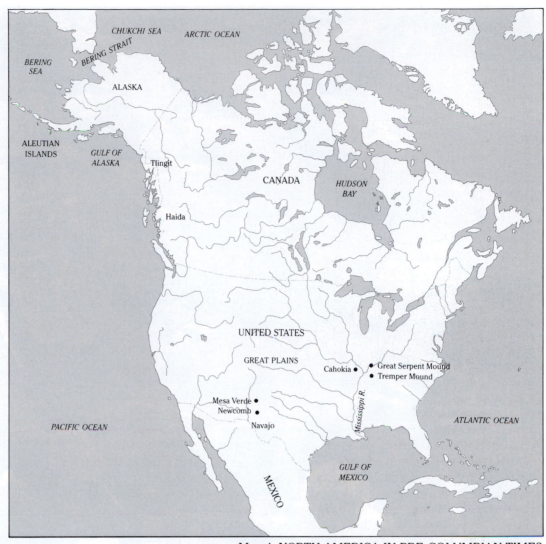

Map 4. NORTH AMERICA IN PRE-COLUMBIAN TIMES

other. During the glacial era they hunted and gathered food, like Paleolithic humanity in Europe. But from about 7000 B.C. they lived in villages, and from about 1000 B.C. to A.D. 1700 they existed by farming and inhabited groups of villages composing considerable towns along the great rivers in the center of the North American continent. Excavations have shown that these Indians maintained a widespread commerce, for materials from thousands of miles away have turned up at their burial sites. Their buildings were constructed of vertical logs, plastered with mud, like those of northern Europe.

The principal Indian architectural monuments were the famous mounds, found all the way from Florida to Wisconsin. There were once more than 10,000 mounds in the Ohio Valley alone, some as much as one hundred feet high. Depending on the particular culture, these mounds were employed for religious purposes, for burials, for the residences of rulers and nobles, or for temples. Some were built in the shapes of gigantic animals or birds, with wings spread (reminding us of Çatal Hüyük!), others were cones or domes, and the latest built were formed like truncated pyramids. The largest of these, at Cahokia just outside East Saint Louis, Illinois, has a greater volume than the greatest of the Egyptian pyramids. Astonishingly, these millions of tons of earth were all brought up by hand, in baskets or cloths, then tamped down. Most of the mounds have perished, victims of the spade, the bulldozer, the reservoir, or the highway, but many thousands have been preserved. They are almost impossible to photograph effectively, and their full

Mississippi Valley, still utilizing their temple and palace mounds, were massacred by the thousands at the hands of the Spanish explorer Hernando de Soto and his men.

The Indians of the Southwest built masonry villages in the broad cave mouths of cliffs, the grandest of which is the famous Cliff Palace at Mesa Verde in Colorado (fig. 2–19), dating from about A.D. 1150. Again we are reminded, perhaps accidentally, of Çatal Hüyük because there are no streets and the houses were entered from each other, in tiers, by means of ladders. Descendants of the Anasazi Indians who built these stupendous structures live today in adobe pueblos constructed along exactly the same principle. Sand paintings, intended to have a healing effect, are still produced today in the Southwest, but do not outlive the moment of their creation (fig. 2–15). Exclusively as works of art, such sand paintings were of great importance to the "Action Painters" of the 1950s in New York. In recent years, so great has become the interest in and demand for carvings of such superb quality as the Haida bear mask illustrated in fig. 2–16 that some Northwest Coast tribes have set up programs to train native artists in the ancient, sometimes almost forgotten, techniques. Widely appreciated, collected, and exhibited, too, are Indian blankets, whose lively, flickering designs are produced by the complex interactions of basic geometric shapes (fig. 2–17). So indeed are the painted tepees and shields, the pottery, baskets, and beaded clothing, blazing with color and bursting with vitality of conception and design.

2-17. Wearing blanket. Navajo culture, A.D. 1855–65. Handspun Saxony and Bayeta wool yarn, 61 × 43″ (1.55 × 1.10 m). Collection of The Newark Museum, Newark, New Jersey. Gift of Miss Louisa MacDougall 1926

2-18. Bear screen. Tlingit culture (Northwest Coast), A.D. 1840. Carved and painted wood, 15 × 9′ (4.57 × 2.74 m). The Denver Art Museum, Denver, Colorado

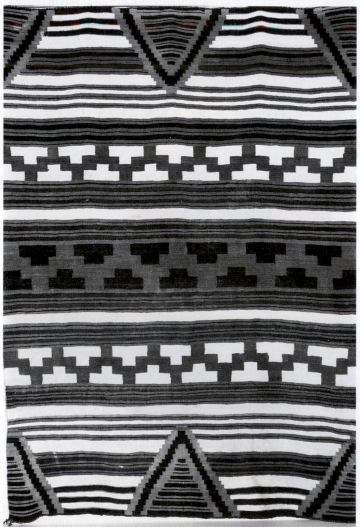

2-17

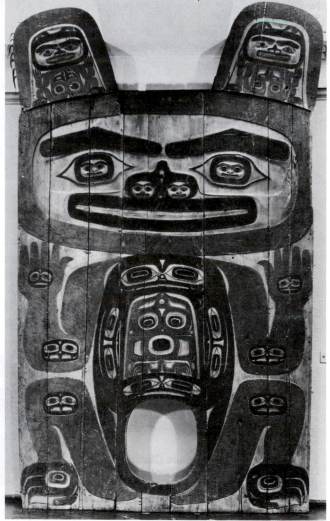

2-18

2-19. Cliff Palace, Mesa Verde,
Colorado. Anasazi culture,
C. A.D. 1150

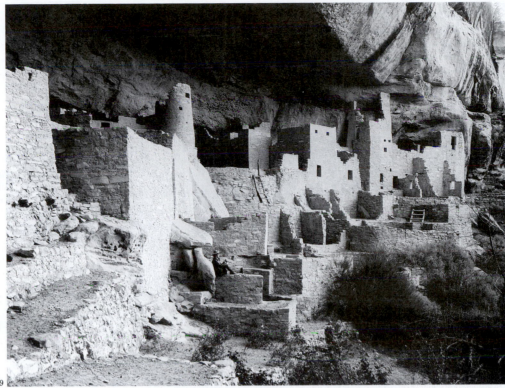

2-19

Perhaps the most powerful of more recent Indian works are the ceremonial animal sculptures of the Northwest Coast, which owe their origin to beliefs according to which humans descend from animal ancestry. On the death of the holder of such an ancestral title a massive feast known as a *potlatch* is given, at which the host gives splendid gifts to the chief guests, who are then obligated to reciprocate by an even more magnificent potlatch and even more lavish gifts. These events are memorialized in the towering wood sculptures of the Tlingit—doorjambs, totem poles, gables, house partitions—of which one of the grandest is a colossal bear screen (fig. 2–18). An effect of great mass is obtained by surrounding broad areas with incised rectangular contours having slightly rounded corners, all under stern formal control. Limbs and paws outstretched, the larger bear discloses smaller ones—in his stomach, his ears, his body joints, even his eyes, ears, and mouth—like the Scythian panther from southern Russia (see fig. 12–2). At the other end of the scale a Haida bear mask (see fig. 2–16) with little bears in its ears, made of painted wood, is provided with eyes and teeth of brilliant, veined blue abalone shell, suggesting to modern eyes that we are looking past and through the staring animal into distant sky.

The fate of the American Indians at the hands of their white conquerors ranks with that of the African slaves as one of the darkest chapters in American history; neither chapter has yet come to a close. The reservations onto which many Indian tribes have been pushed have destroyed their civilization and substituted little. Only in the Southwest does American Indian culture still function with anything approaching its former vitality. Nonetheless, while few white Americans realize it, some descendants of the builders of the midwestern mounds and the far western cliff dwellings (see fig. 2–19) have been working for decades in the construction of the steel frames of present-day American skyscrapers, where their immense skill and their legendary courage and self-control are invaluable in building the most characteristic structures of the modern world.

TIME LINE I

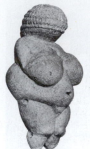

"Venus" of Willendorf

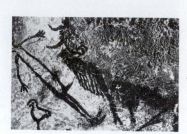

Wounded Bison

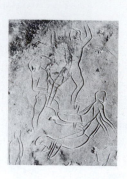

Ritual Dance, Addaura (detail)

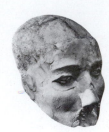

Plastered Skull, Jericho

ENVIRONMENT	HUMAN ACTIVITY
30,000 B.C. *Upper Paleolithic Period* Alternate cold and mild phases Northwest Spain is western boundary of Eurasian Ice Sheet	"Blade" cultures develop in Eurasia and Africa
20,000 East Asians of Mongoloid physical type migrate to North and South America Expansion of Paleolithic man into north Europe and Asia *Mesolithic Period*	Stone toolmaking becomes commonplace Increased specialization of stone tools Invention of bow and arrow, spear-thrower, and chisel
10,000 Postglacial period; birch forests and parkland appear in north Europe and Asia Hunters in North America migrate south and east; lakeshore settlements in Europe	Hunting-fishing-fowling cultures prevail Increase in tool repertory; development of bone harpoon, fish traps, heavy adzes and axes Domestication of the dog
8,000 *Neolithic Period* Steady rise in average temperatures Rise in sea levels Increased foresting of land	Jericho develops farming Irrigation, plant cultivation, and animal husbandry gain sophistication Pottery; ground and polished tools Start of mining and quarrying
4,000 Climatic optimum: worldwide warm spell	Diffusion of farming to Crete, Sicily, south Italy
2,000 Stabilization of climatic conditions East Asians of Mongoloid and melanotic physical	Bronze Age; Tigris-Euphrates civilizations flourish
1,000 type settle Oceania	Metallurgy spreads from Near East to Egypt, Mediterranean; Iron Age
A.D. 1100 Viking settlement in northern Newfoundland	In Africa, Ife independently invent lost-wax bronze-casting technique
1500 Drought in American Southwest forces Anasazi to abandon cliff settlements; Navajo and Apache move into the area, followed by the Spanish	Portuguese explorers visit Benin
1700 Introduction of the horse and horse-mounted nomadism on American Great Plains	
1900	Battle of Wounded Knee, S. Dakota, ends American Indian armed resistance to white settlement

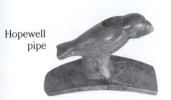

Hopewell
pipe

Cliff Palace,
Mesa Verde

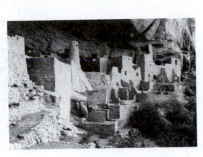

Oni of
Ife

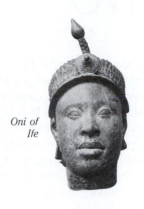

Leopard
from Benin

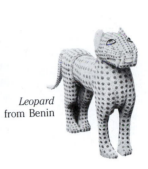

PAINTING, SCULPTURE, ARCHITECTURE

"Venus" of Willendorf

Woman's Head from Grotte du Pape

Painted caves at Lascaux; *Bison,* La Madeleine
Bison, Altamira

Ritual Dance, Addaura

Stone fortifications, Jericho
Houses, Çatal Hüyük

Rock art, northern Africa
Temple, Tarxien, Malta; Stonehenge

Great Serpent Mound, Ohio
Hopewell pipe
Portrait of the Oni of Ife
Cliff Palace, Mesa Verde
Queen Mother and bronze reliefs from Benin

War shield from Sepik River; "soul boat" from New Ireland
Tlingit screen; Navajo wearing blanket

CHAPTERS

Art in the Stone Age Paleolithic Art	30,000 B.C.
	20,000
Mesolithic Art	10,000
Neolithic Art	8,000 B.C.
	4,000
	2,000
Tribal Art	1,000
	A.D. 1100
	1500
	1700
	1900

Part Two

For many thousands of years, Neolithic humans were able to produce and preserve food and thus develop permanent settlements, yet they depended entirely on memory for records, communications, and the preservation of history, religion, and literature. No matter how highly developed, memory is notoriously fickle. With the sole, astounding exception of the Inca in South America, no large-scale systematic enterprise, whether political, economic, or religious, was possible in the absence of reliable and enduring records. Nor were measure or any other sort of calculation possible. How humans first hit on the idea of setting down information in visible form, thus arriving at a system of writing, we do not know, but this essential change seems to have taken place a little more than five thousand years ago, in Mesopotamia and Egypt, on both sides of the land bridge connecting Asia and Africa. In both of these civilizations the earliest writing was pictographic, but soon the little images became codified and developed connections with syllables and words independent of their original derivation. Egypt, which possessed both quantities of hard stone and swamps from whose reeds a paper-like material called papyrus was fabricated, long retained the pictorial shapes the Greeks named *hieroglyphs* ("sacred writing," because its use was a prerogative of the priesthood). Mesopotamia, however, relied on soft clay as a writing surface, and there the pictographs were rapidly codified into groups of impressions made with the wedge-shaped end of a reed stylus—a form of writing we call *cuneiform* (from the Latin word for "wedge").

Records and communications facilitated commerce and systematic agriculture as well as the development of governmental authority. Cities grew to considerable size. Monarchies arose and extended their sway to ever wider regions by the subjugation of neighboring states. By the middle of the second millennium B.C., three powerful and prosperous empires had developed: in Egypt, in Mesopotamia, and in the islands of the Aegean Sea. (Parallel in time, but in total isolation, important cultures flourished in Mesoamerica.) The end of the second millennium, however, was a time of great upheaval for the ancient world, and none of the major powers escaped unscathed. From the ensuing chaos arose the glorious, if partial and short-lived, democratic experiment of the Greek city-states. But despite the enormous influence of Greek culture on the future, the separate Greek political systems could not resist the march to power of Rome. By the end of the first millennium B.C., all the states of the Mediterranean world and many of the still tribal polities of northern, central, and eastern Europe were either absorbed or on the road to absorption by the Roman Empire. Political unification prepared the ancient world for religious unification as well, and the religions surviving from the ancient states proved no match for the universal claims of Christianity or, a few centuries later, of Islam.

Along with writing and the new attitudes and systems it made possible, there arose entirely new modes of intellectual activity based on writing and aimed at the intellectual and physical control of the environment and of humanity itself. History and epic and religious poetry were put in writing in Egypt, Mesopotamia, and the kingdoms of Israel and Judah. The sciences of zoology, botany, anatomy, and medicine made remarkable progress. Numbers, considered apart from enumerated objects, became transferable to any object, or became subject to consideration in and for themselves. Arithmetic and geometry, including principles still valid and methods still taught, were discovered. Optics, perspective, and astronomy made remarkable beginnings, and scientific calendars were devised. Speculation and abstract reasoning followed observation, and under the Greeks and Romans the

THE ANCIENT WORLD

major branches of philosophy were established. New scientific attitudes began, step by dangerous step, to replace mythological systems with a cosmology based on scientific method.

The Hebrew alphabet was in use well before the ninth century B.C., the probable date of the oldest component of the Book of Genesis. The adoption by the Greeks of the Phoenician alphabet about 750 B.C. facilitated the codification of language and the establishment of regular grammar and syntax. Recorded literature included not only the preliterate oral poetry of the Greeks, which could at last be set down, but newly composed dramas and lyrics and a systematic attempt at accurate history. Fortunately Greek, Latin, and Hebrew have always remained alive or at least accessible, but in the case of the twin colossi of the pre-Greek world, Egypt and Mesopotamia, not only their languages but even their systems of writing had seemed hopelessly lost. Only a combination of lucky accident and tireless investigation in the nineteenth century has enabled us at last to read the writing in which their civilizations were crystallized, and thus to reconstruct a remarkable proportion of their history and religion. These writings have also helped us to understand the purpose and meaning of thousands of works of art.

Ancient music, now almost entirely lost, was based on scales, some of which are still in use today; it apparently reached great heights. But along with the earliest steps in the evolution of science, and before any presently known achievements of philosophy, literature, and music, the mental attitudes born of writing made possible entirely new purposes, standards, and practices for the visual arts. For the first time, in Egypt and Mesopotamia, emphasis in figural art was transferred from animals to humans, individually or in groups, described with accuracy and analyzed with understanding, and set upon a continuous groundline or within an increasingly complex spatial environment. Compositions could be measured and controlled. Empirical Neolithic building methods gave way to a rational architecture composed of regular and regularly recurring modular units and spaces, often mathematically interrelated, and constructed with so accurate an understanding of physical stresses that, if they had been kept in repair, most ancient masonry structures would be standing today. Not only buildings but whole cities were laid out according to regular plans and provided with systematic water supply and drainage.

In all fields of human endeavor, reason is the triumphant discovery of the ancient world. The best works of ancient art, founded upon reason, are of a quality that has seldom since been equaled and never surpassed. Indeed, none of the other great conquests of the ancient world in any field—practical, intellectual, or spiritual—could have been achieved without reason. Professionals in all fields, whose activities were based on systematic exploitation of every facet and consequence of the reasoning process, were highly regarded in all ancient civilizations, and as we shall see, especially in Egypt and Greece, they sometimes attained high positions. As far as we can tell, from pictures and from literary evidence, these professionals were always male, except for an occasional woman poet (such as the matchless Sappho, in Greece in the sixth century B.C.) and a handful of later Greek portrait painters. This situation was entirely due to the social restrictions placed on women. In Egypt women could become dancers, but this was not a highly regarded profession. In recompense, however, powerful female patrons, such as the Egyptian queen Hatshepsut or the Roman empress Livia, must have imposed their own ideas of style on some of the greatest monuments of the ancient world.

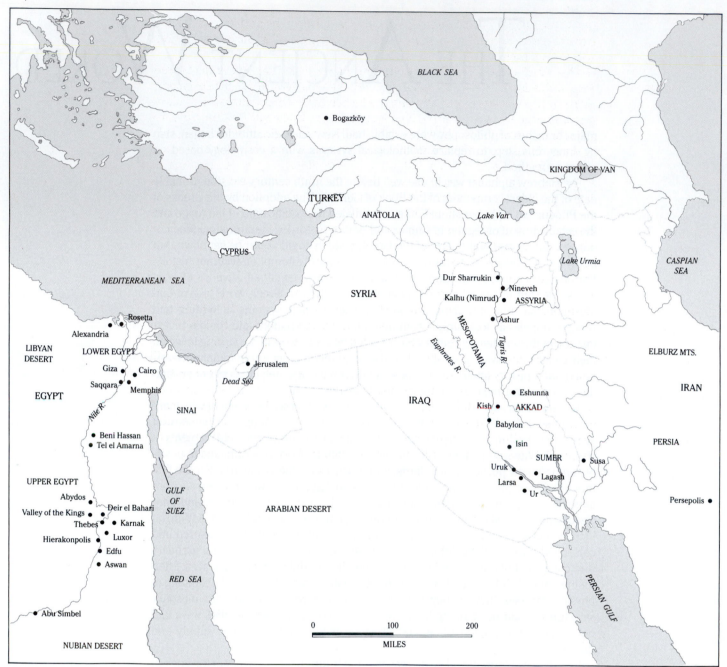

Map 5. EGYPT AND THE NEAR EAST IN ANCIENT TIMES

Ancient humanity was still haunted from every side by the irrational, embodied and given legal force in the form of state religions, the violation of whose codes could bring death, as it did to even a figure as universally admired as the philosopher Socrates in Athens in the fifth century B.C. The hidden purposes of ancient deities could be divined only by specially gifted persons (priests or oracles), and their favor was won by sacrifices. Dangerous as these irrational forces might become if not propitiated, it was still to them that some of the most impressive structures of antiquity, with all their works of art, were consecrated. We might even say that in the ancient world, with the shining exception of the monotheist Hebrews, *irrational* content (devotion to unpredictable and vengeful divinities, sometimes part animal and often free from any commitment to morality in their own behavior) provided the animating spirit within the *rationally* organized works we now respect. At some moment, especially in conventions imposed by religious purposes but systematically carried out, rational and irrational can be said to coalesce. It is from this very equipoise between reason and unreason that ancient art derives much of its excitement.

The social upheavals following the dissolution of the ancient empires were responsible for the destruction of much of humanity's early artistic achievements. Tragic as are our losses—most of the productions of ancient visual art and literature and all of ancient music but for a few tantalizing fragments—archaeology has won back countless works of art from what had seemed impenetrable darkness. To the High Renaissance of the sixteenth century in Italy, archaeology was a humanist scholar's impracticable dream, but in the eighteenth century it became a reality, and whole buried cities were dug up. Since then archaeology has developed a scientific theory and a rigorous methodology. In most countries this science has also inspired a determined and often successful attempt at legal control of excavation, whose validity has been recognized internationally by resolutions of the United Nations. The majority of the works of art illustrated in this section, "The Ancient World," were either once buried under the continually rising level of the earth or sunk in the sea. They owe their resurrection to archaeology. The discoveries continue. In recent years, many splendid works of art have come to light, including the two powerful bronze statues illustrated in figs. 7–37 and 7–38.

Alas, not all excavation has been disinterested. Temples and tombs have been robbed of their treasures for private gain, and many of the results of such depredations, often involving the ruin of what was left in place or underground, fill museums in every country. It is an experience of unforgettable sadness to visit, for example, the majestic rock-cut temples at Longmen in northern China and witness the pitiful remnants of beheaded figures, or the scars left by statues clumsily hacked from their bases. But in spite of violence and cupidity, what is left of ancient art, no matter how scarred or brutally torn from its original setting, remains a supreme intellectual and spiritual heritage—and inspiration—for us today.

CHAPTER THREE

The antiquity and continuity of Egyptian civilization were legendary, even to the Greeks and Romans. In fact, the period of roughly three thousand years during which Egyptian culture and Egyptian art persisted, unchanged in many essential respects, is longer by a third than the entire time that has elapsed since the identity of Egypt was submerged in the larger unity of the Roman Empire. Although the rival cultures of the Near East, especially Mesopotamia, had a somewhat earlier start, and even influenced to a limited extent some of the early manifestations of Egyptian art, the Mesopotamian region did not enjoy natural barriers like those that protected Egypt. Consequently, group after group of invaders overwhelmed, destroyed, or absorbed preceding invaders throughout Mesopotamia's stormy history. Moreover, with few observable outside influences, the Egyptians rapidly developed their own highly original forms of architecture, sculpture, and painting earlier than any comparable arts in Mesopotamia, and it is Egyptian rather than Mesopotamian art that provided norms for the entire ancient world. It seems preferable, therefore, to commence our story of the ancient world with Egypt.

The dominating reality of Egyptian life has always been the gigantic vitality of the Nile River. For nearly a quarter of its four thousand miles, it flows through Egyptian territory (see Map 5, page 68). The Nile Valley, nowhere more than twelve and a half miles wide, forms a winding green ribbon between the barren rocky or sandy wastes of the Libyan Desert to the west and the Arabian Desert to the east. During the fourth millennium B.C., the valley was inhabited by a long-headed, brown-skinned ethnic group, apparently of African origin, while the Nile Delta to the north was the home of a round-skulled people originally from Asia. Remains of Neolithic cultures, including a rich variety of decorated ceramics, abound in both regions.

At many periods of Egyptian history emigration from the south brought black-skinned people from Nubia into Egypt, often as mercenary soldiers; the Twenty-fifth Dynasty of Egyptian rulers was a family of Nubian conquerors. Late in Egyptian history Phoenicians, Greeks, and Romans ruled Egypt and left their mark. The chronology of Egyptian history is still far from clear, and most dates are approximate and disputed. But, according to an account set down by a Hellenized Egyptian called Manetho in the second century B.C., the separate kingdoms of Upper (southern) and Lower (northern) Egypt were united by a powerful Upper Egyptian monarch called Menes, founder of the first of those dynasties into which Manetho divided Egyptian history. Menes has been identified by modern scholars as Narmer, the king depicted on the slate tablet in fig. 3–2. His tremendous achievement—establishing the first large-scale, unified state known to history—took place either shortly before or shortly after 3000 B.C.

The inscriptions that abound on all Egyptian monuments were written in a form of picture writing known as hieroglyphic (examples appear in many illustrations; see figs. 3–10, 3–23, 3–27, 3–36). Although, for millennia afterward, hieroglyphic was known in Europe and admired for its beauty, it was never understood. In fact, it became the subject for the most fantastic theorizing. Then, in one of the greatest discoveries in the history of archaeology, the Rosetta Stone, a fragmentary inscribed slab, was found near the town of Rosetta in the Nile Delta by French scholars who accompanied the armies of General Napoleon Bonaparte in his invasion of Egypt in 1799. The slab contained texts in three scripts: Greek (which everyone knew), demotic (a late, popular form of Egyptian writing), and hieroglyphic. Although it was immediately guessed that the text was the same in all three scripts, not until 1821 did the young French scholar Jean-François Champollion (1790–1832) succeed in deciphering the other two. Ancient Egyptian turned out to be the direct ancestor of Coptic, an extinct language spoken by the Egyptians in Early Christian times and thus known to scholars. Champollion, and his many successors, now had the key for the deciphering of countless inscriptions and manuscripts, a practice that continues to the present day. Egyptian history, economics, social structure, literature, and religion were open to study, and much can be read in translation.

The Egyptian king, or *pharaoh* as he is known in the Old Testament (from an Egyptian word originally meaning "great house"), was considered divine. He participated, therefore, in the rule of universal law that governed the natural life of the entire valley. The sun rose over the eastern cliffs in the morning and set over the western cliffs in the evening. All day the sun sent down its vivifying rays until it was devoured by the night, but one could be perfectly sure that next morning it would be resurrected. In the same way the Egyptians faced death with the certainty that, like the sun, they would live again. Every autumn the river overflowed, spreading over the land the fertile silt brought from central Africa. Even in the almost total absence of rainfall, abundant crops could be produced. The unchanging order of the natural world was personified by a complex and often changing pantheon of nature deities engaged in a continuous mythological drama rhythmically repeated according to the cycles of nature. By these deities the pharaoh was believed to have been generated, and to them he would return after a life spent maintaining in the state an order similar to that which they had ordained for the Nile Valley—beyond which, at the start of Egyptian civilization at least, little was known and nothing mattered.

The Egyptians built their houses, their cities, and even their palaces of simple materials such as palm trunks, papyrus bundles, Nile mud, and sun-dried bricks. Little is left of the palaces beyond an occasional foundation or fragments of a floor or painted ceiling, and almost nothing of the dwellings of ordinary people. Surviving evidence, however, has permitted the reconstruction of typical upper-class dwellings, which must have been quite comfortable, constructed around a central pool, with shaded clerestory windows high up under the roof to break the heat of the sun and circulate the air (see pages 88–89). But tombs and temples were soon to be constructed of stone, of which there was an abundance in the desert—sandstone, limestone, granite, conglomerate, and diorite, to name only a few. The Egyptians devoted their major artistic efforts to the gods and to the afterlife, not only in architecture but also in sculpture—both of which were often of colossal dimensions, meant to rival the immensity of the landscape and the sky—and in those delightful decorative reliefs and paintings from which we derive most of our knowledge of Egyptian life. As we will see throughout our survey of their art, with rare exceptions the Egyptians' desire for permanence, stability, and order runs through every aspect of their temples, their tombs, their sculpture, and their painting, determining down to the last detail how every structure should be organized and carried out and even how the human figure should be posed and proportioned.

The Archaic Period and the Old Kingdom (c. 3500–2185 B.C.)

A striking illustration of the difference between preliterate, predynastic Egypt and the subsequent tightly organized civilization that was to prove so amazingly durable can be seen by comparing the earliest known example of an Egyptian mural painting (fig. 3–1), made about 3500 B.C., with almost any subsequent works of Egyptian figurative art. The painting comes from the plaster wall of a tomb chamber at Hierakonpolis, a city in Upper Egypt about fifty miles south of Thebes. Not essentially different from Neolithic rock paintings found in southern Algeria and eastern Spain, the random composition shows three Nile boats, possibly carrying

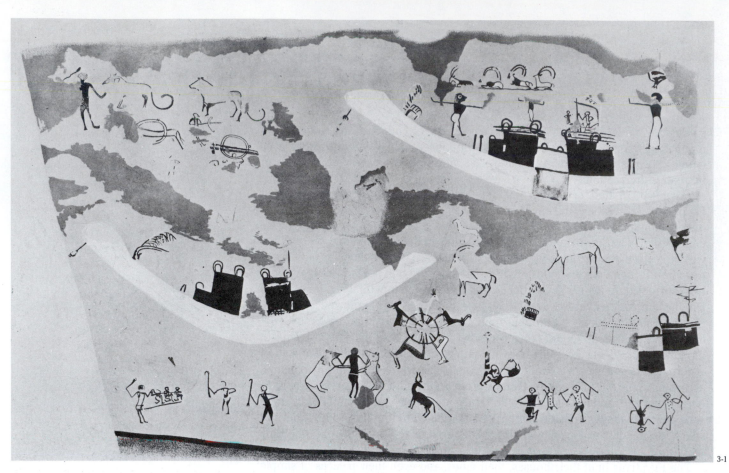

3-1. *People, Boats, and Animals,* wall painting from Hierakonpolis, Upper Egypt. c. 3500 B.C. Egyptian Museum, Cairo

coffins, attended by tiny figures with raised arms who may represent mourning women. Antelope and other animals are scattered about, and men fight animals and each other.

THE STONE PALETTES Within a relatively short time after this improvised mural with its diagrammatic figures—perhaps as little as a century or two— Egyptian art had changed totally, reflecting the character of the monarchy, which had impressed itself on all aspects of Egyptian life. The most striking examples of this newborn Egyptian art are the stone "palettes" carved on both sides with images in low relief and on one side hollowed into a slight depression. The exact purpose of these palettes is unknown, but since they were found in the lowest levels of religious buildings excavated at Abydos and Hierakonpolis, it is doubtful that they had a purely practical purpose. It has been surmised that they were used to mix the paint applied to the eyes of divine images in order to provide the gods with sight. The finest of these palettes is that of King Narmer (fig. 3–2), whose capital was at Thinis in Upper Egypt. In this work a sense of total order prevails. The king appears in his own right, standing firmly on a definite groundline; adorned with a bull's tail and wearing the crown of Upper Egypt, he grasps his enemy by the forelock with his left hand while his uplifted right hand brandishes a mace. Cow heads (sign of the goddess Hathor) representing the four corners of the heavens flank an abbreviated symbol of a palace bearing the king's name. Behind the king walks a servant bearing his sandals; the king is unshod as if to indicate the sanctity of the moment (as later with Moses on Mount Sinai). A hawk, symbol of the sky-god Horus, protector of the pharaohs, holds a rope attached to a head growing from the same soil as the papyrus plants of Lower Egypt. Below the king's feet his foes flee in terror.

The other side of the palette (fig. 3–3) is divided into three registers beneath the cow heads at the top. The king, now wearing the crown of Lower Egypt, strides

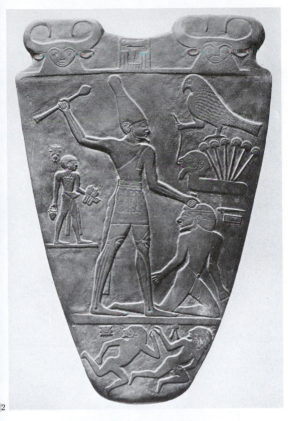

3-2. *Palette of King Narmer* (front view), from Hierakonpolis, Upper Egypt. c. 3200–2980 B.C. Slate, height 25" (63.5 cm). Egyptian Museum, Cairo

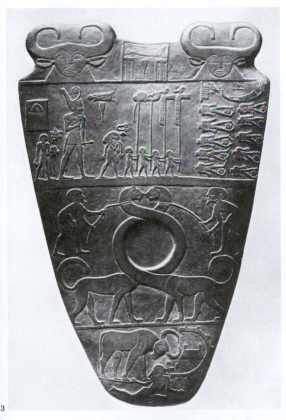

3-3. *Palette of King Narmer* (back view)

forth, followed by the sandal bearer and preceded by warriors carrying standards, in order to inspect ten decapitated bodies, their heads placed between their legs. As if to emphasize the king's immense strength, his leg and arm muscles are sharply demarcated. In the central register two felines resembling panthers, perhaps representing the eastern and western heavens, led by divinities from barbaric regions to the east and west of Egypt, entwine their fantastically prolonged necks to embrace the sun disk, hollowed out to form a cup for the paint. (The meanings of these early images are often far from certain; the animals can also be interpreted as symbols of Upper and Lower Egypt.) Below, a bull symbolizing the king gores a prostrate enemy before his captured citadel, its walls and towers represented in plan—the earliest architectural plan known. The naturalism and sense of order that appear for the first time in these reliefs are no more striking than their introduction of a set of conventions that controlled Egyptian representations of the figure for the next three thousand years. Apparently in order to provide the observer with complete information, the eyes and shoulders are shown frontally while the head, legs, and hips are represented in profile. The weight is evenly divided between both legs, with the far leg advanced. Exceptions are made only when both hands are engaged in the same action, as in the agricultural occupations depicted in wall paintings; then the near shoulder is folded around so that it, too, appears in profile.

THE TOMB AND THE AFTERLIFE The Old Kingdom began in earnest with the Third Dynasty and the removal of the capital to Memphis, in Lower Egypt. Now appear for the first time in monumental form those amazing manifestations of the belief in existence beyond death that dominated Egyptian life and thought. Each human had a mysterious double, the *ka* or life force, that survived his or her death but still required a body; hence the development of the art of mummification. In case the mummy were to disintegrate, the ka could still find a home in the statue of the deceased, which sat or stood within the tomb in a special chamber provided with a false door to the other world and with a peephole through which incense from the funeral rites could penetrate to its nostrils. The deceased was surrounded with the delights of this world to ensure enjoyment of them in the next: the tomb was filled with food, furniture, household implements, a considerable treasure, and sometimes even with mummified dogs and cats. The coffin, in the shape of the mummy, could be made of wood and merely painted with ornamental inscriptions and with the face of the deceased or, in the case of the pharaoh, made of solid gold. The walls of the tomb were adorned with paintings or painted reliefs depicting in exhaustive detail the deceased's life on earth as well as the funeral banquet at which the deceased was represented alive and enjoying the viands. Once the ceremonies were over and the tomb sealed, all this beauty was, of course, doomed to eternal darkness and oblivion. But not quite all, because the royal tombs were systematically plundered even during the Old Kingdom, perhaps by the very hands that had placed the precious objects in their chambers—an odd commentary on the discrepancy between belief and practice.

The characteristic external form of the Egyptian tomb, doubtless descended from the burial mounds common to many early cultures, is called *mastaba* (Arabic for "bench"), a solid, rectangular mass of masonry and mud brick with sloping sides, on one of which was the entrance to a shaft leading diagonally to interconnected tomb chambers excavated from the rocky ground of the western desert (fig. 3–4). The location was important: the tombs had to be placed both out of reach of the annual floods that inundated the entire Nile Valley and to the west of the city, where the sun sank nightly into the desert, for that was the direction from which the deceased began their journeys into the other world.

The Step-Pyramid at Saqqara. The earliest colossal stone structure we know, the step-pyramid of King Zoser at Saqqara (fig. 3–5), to the west of Memphis, was

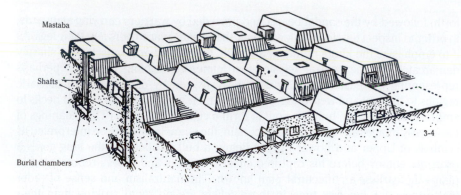

Mastaba

Shafts

Burial chambers

3-4. Group of mastabas (reconstruction after A. Badawy)

originally planned about 2750 B.C. as such a mastaba. However, it occurred to the royal architect IMHOTEP, the first artist whose name has come down to us, to set six mastabas of constant height but diminishing area one upon the other to form a majestic staircase ascending to the heavens. His creation, rising from the desert, is still a work of overwhelming grandeur, and Imhotep was revered by posterity as a god. The funerary temple, on the north side of the pyramid, was far more impressive when its complex series of surrounding courtyards and temples, whose outer walls measure approximately 1,800 by 900 feet, was intact (fig. 3–6). All of Imhotep's forms were derived from wooden palace architecture—including the tent roof sustained by poles, seen at left in fig. 3–5, which he imitated with the utmost elegance in clear golden-white limestone. The surrounding walls, now partly reconstructed, were divided into projecting and recessed members, each paneled. The processional entrance hall, recently partly rebuilt largely from its original stones, had a ceiling made of cylindrical stones in imitation of palm logs, supported by slender columns reflecting in their channeled surfaces the forms of plants, probably palm branches lashed together since the capitals appear to be formalized palm leaves (fig. 3–7). These are the earliest known columns, and apparently Imhotep did not entirely trust them to bear so great a weight because he attached them to projecting walls that do most of the work. But the essentials of the classical column—shaft, capital, and base—are already here.

3-5. IMHOTEP. Funerary Complex of King Zoser with step-pyramid, Saqqara. C. 2750 B.C.

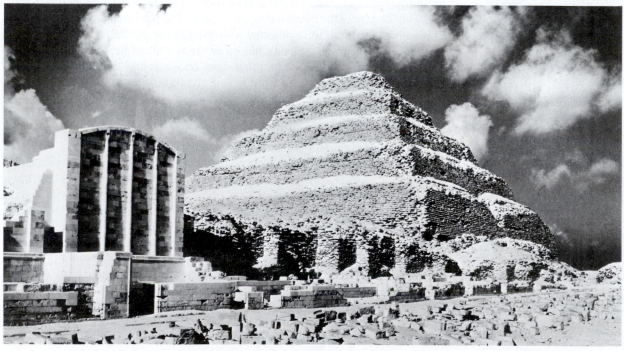

3-7. Reconstructed view of the entrance hall and colonnade, Funerary Complex of King Zoser, Saqqara (after Jean Philippe Lauer)

3-6. Model of the Funerary Complex of King Zoser, Saqqara

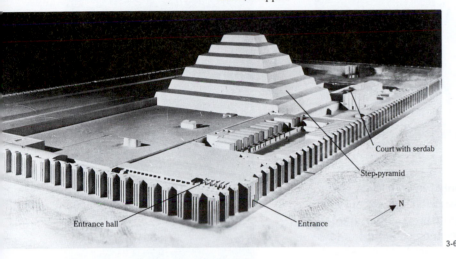

Court with serdab

Step-pyramid

N

Entrance hall

Entrance

3-6

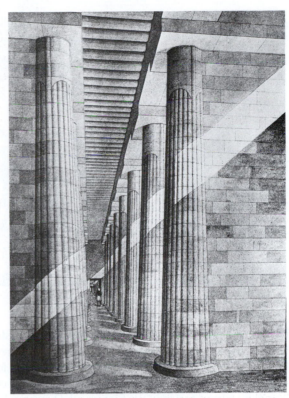

3-7

3-8. *King Zoser.* c. 2750 B.C. Limestone with traces of paint, height 55″ (1.4 m). Egyptian Museum, Cairo

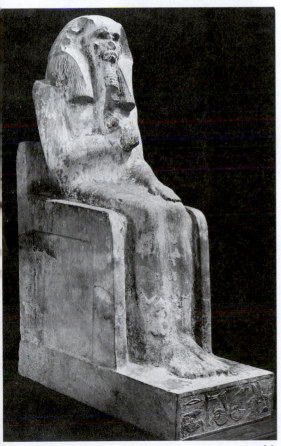

3-8

Similar plant forms of the greatest elegance appear throughout the architecture of the courtyards, in which stood statues of the king and his family, including a colossus, the earliest known, of which only fragments survive. But one splendid seated life-size statue of Zoser in limestone, still another first (the earliest known royal portrait in the round) among the achievements of this extraordinary reign, has survived relatively intact. In its majestic pose (fig. 3–8) we have the prototype of all subsequent seated statues for the rest of Egyptian history. It bears the name of Imhotep on its base. The statue was originally placed in the *serdab,* or sealed statue chamber, built against the north wall of the step-pyramid, with two peepholes through which the king could look forth to the sky. The statue's appearance may have been less solemn when the rock-crystal eyes, gouged out long ago by tomb robbers, and the original surface paint were intact. The king wears the "divine" false beard, and his massive wig is partly concealed by the royal linen covering. He is swathed in a long mantle descending almost to his feet. The statue is absolutely frontal, utterly immobile, and perfectly calm. Like all Egyptian statues, it was drawn upon three faces of the block of stone and carved inward until the three sides of the figure merged into one another; its nobility of form arises from the perfect discipline of this procedure, recommended for sculptors as late as the Italian Renaissance.

Later stages of the carving process are illustrated in a Sixth Dynasty relief from Saqqara (fig. 3–9) in which we see two sculptors finishing a statue with mallet and bronze chisel, then polishing it with stone tools. Interestingly enough, while the sculptors are represented with shoulders frontal or folded round according to the necessities of the action, the statue does not conform to the conventions governing living figures, and remains in profile throughout. Immense dignity, if not the majesty of the divine monarch, is shared by court officials such as Hesira (fig. 3–10), holding symbols of his authority as well as writing instruments, in a wooden relief from his tomb at Saqqara. Although slenderer than King Narmer, he stands

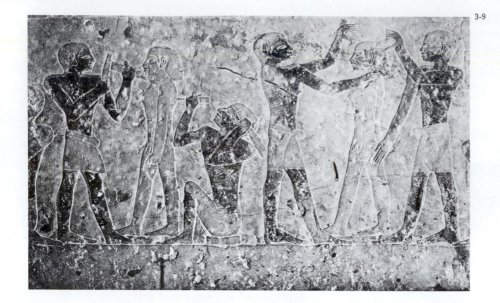

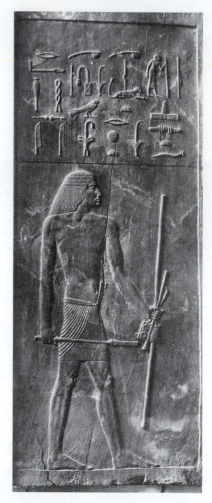

before us in the same manner, with weight evenly distributed on both feet. Convention also invariably and inexplicably gives relief figures two left hands, except when the right hand is holding something, and two left feet (or two right, in the rare instances when they move from right to left). This convention continues in force except for a brief period in the Eighteenth Dynasty when the feet, but not the hands, are shown as in nature (see fig. 3–23); immediately thereafter the old convention returns. The present impression of beautifully controlled surfaces of wood given by the *Hesira* relief would be sharply different if it still retained its original bright paint, but it must always have shown the grace, authority, and firm handling of muscular shapes characteristic of Old Kingdom art.

The Pyramids of Giza. The grandest monuments of the Old Kingdom, and the universal wonder of mankind ever since, are the great pyramids of Giza (fig. 3–11), a few miles to the north of Saqqara. They were built by three kings of the Fourth Dynasty who are generally known by their Greek names: Cheops, Chephren, and Mycerinus (Egyptian: Khufu, Khafre, and Menkure). It is still unclear whether the perfect shape, with its four isosceles-triangular sides (fig. 3–12), evolved from the step-pyramids at Saqqara and elsewhere, or whether it had special religious significance. The earliest of the Giza pyramids, that of Cheops, is also the largest, originally 480 feet high, more than twice the height of the step-pyramid of Zoser. Whether seen from modern Cairo some eight miles distant or across the rocky ledges and sands of the desert or towering close at hand, these amazing structures convey an impression of unimaginable size and mass. Originally, they also had the characteristic Old Kingdom perfection of form, but this, alas, has vanished since the smooth, finely dressed limestone surface was stripped from the underlying blocks for use in the buildings of Cairo. Only a small portion at the top of Chephren's pyramid remains. No elaborate courtyards were ever contemplated. Each pyramid had a small temple directly before it, united by a causeway with a second or valley temple at the edge of cultivation (fig. 3–13); the valley temple was accessible from the Nile by canal or, during the floods, directly by boat. Flanking the great pyramids were extensive and carefully planned groups of smaller pyramids for members of the royal family and mastabas for court officials. The great pyramids were oriented directly north and south, and the pyramids of Cheops and Chephren were constructed along a common diagonal axis.

The accounts by Greek and Roman writers of forced labor used to build the pyramids are probably legendary. The concept of large firms of contractors and

3-9. *Sculptors at Work,* from Saqqara. c. 2340–2170 B.C. Painted stone relief. Egyptian Museum, Cairo

3-10. *Hesira,* from Saqqara. c. 2750 B.C. Wood relief, height 45″ (1.14 m). Egyptian Museum, Cairo

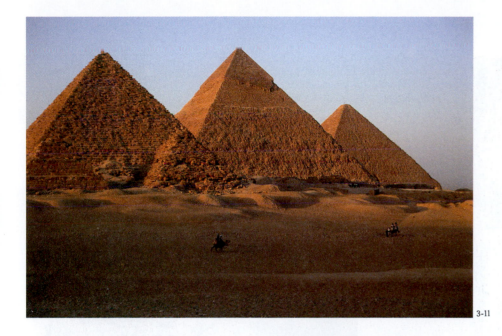

3-11

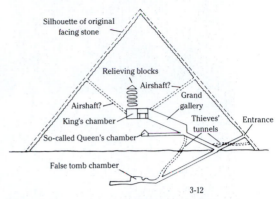

3-11. Right to left: Pyramids of Cheops or Khufu (c. 2570 B.C.), Chephren or Khafre (c. 2530 B.C.), and Mycerinus or Menkure (c. 2500 B.C.), Giza. Height of Cheops pyramid approx. 480' (146 m)

3-12. North-south section of the Pyramid of Cheops, Giza (after L. Borchardt)

Silhouette of original facing stone

Relieving blocks

Airshaft?

Airshaft?

Grand gallery

King's chamber

Thieves' tunnels

Entrance

So-called Queen's chamber

False tomb chamber

3-12

3-13

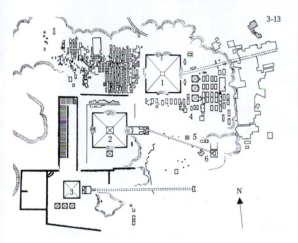

N

3-14

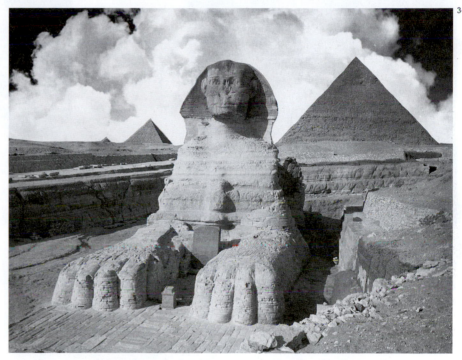

3-13. Plan of the funerary district at Giza
1. Pyramid of Cheops   2. Pyramid of Chephren   3. Pyramid of Mycerinus
4. Pyramids and tombs of lesser nobles
5. Great Sphinx   6. Valley Temple of Chephren

3-14. Great Sphinx, Giza. c. 2530 B.C. Sandstone, height 65' (19.8 m)

paid labor is more consistent with what we know of Egyptian society, and remains have been found of a considerable settlement that grew up at the edge of the valley to house workers, supervisors, and planners. Brick ramps were built up; on these the limestone blocks, transported by boat from quarries on the other side of the Nile, could be dragged, probably on timber rollers (the wheel was as yet unknown).

Only the valley temple of Chephren can now be seen (see Introduction fig. 18); in contrast to Imhotep's architecture at Saqqara, all its forms derive their beauty from the very nature of stone. The walls are built of pink granite blocks, the shafts and lintels are granite monoliths, and the floor is paved with irregularly shaped slabs of alabaster. All the masonry is fitted together without mortar and with perfect accuracy, creating an impression of austere harmony. Alongside the valley temple rises the Great Sphinx (fig. 3–14), carved from the living sandstone; it is not only the earliest colossus to be preserved but also by far the largest to survive. In spite of

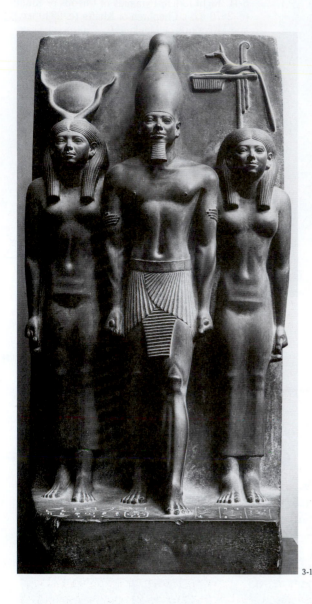

3-15

3-15. *King Mycerinus between Two Goddesses,* from the Valley Temple of Mycerinus, Giza. c. 2520 B.C. Gray-green schist, height 37⅜″ (95 cm). Egyptian Museum, Cairo

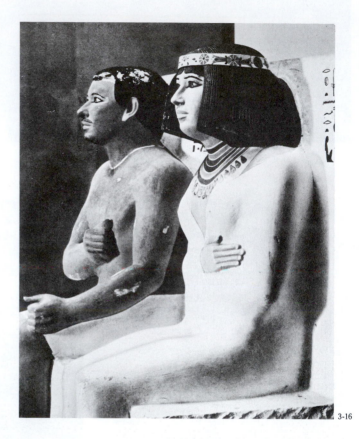

3-16

3-16. *Prince Rahotep and His Wife Nofret.* c. 2610 B.C. Painted limestone, height 47¼″ (1.2 m). Egyptian Museum, Cairo

later damage by Muslims that has almost destroyed the face, this immense lion with the head of Chephren is possibly the most imposing symbol of royal power ever created.

OLD KINGDOM STATUES   A statue of Chephren (see Introduction fig. 15), which once stood in his valley temple, is luckily almost undamaged. Immobile, grand, unchanging, the pose of the figure derives eventually from that of Zoser (see fig. 3–8). Seated on a lion throne, the king is clad only in a richly pleated kilt and a linen head-covering, horizontally pleated over the shoulders, that completely conceals the customary wig. The lines of this massive headdress are perfectly aligned with the wings of the hawk-god Horus, spread in protection behind the king's head. The broad, simple treatment of the shapes, the grand proportioning of the elements, and the smooth movement of the unbroken surfaces of diorite all culminate in the noble features of the king, whose serene expression bespeaks calm, total, un-challengeable control. In lesser works the systematic method of the Egyptian artists sometimes results in uniformity and mediocrity, but in the hands of the finest Old Kingdom sculptors the method itself exemplifies Egyptian beliefs regarding the divinity of the king and is the visual counterpart of the unalterable law governing earth and sky, life and death. By common consent, the *Chephren* is both one of the supreme examples of ancient sculpture and one of the great works of art of all time.

3-17. *Bust of Prince Ankhhaf,* from Giza. c. 2550 B.C. Painted limestone, height 22⅛″ (56 cm). Courtesy, Museum of Fine Arts, Boston

3-18. *Kaaper (Sheikh el Beled),* from Saqqara. c. 2400 B.C. Wood, height 43″ (1.09 m). Egyptian Museum, Cairo

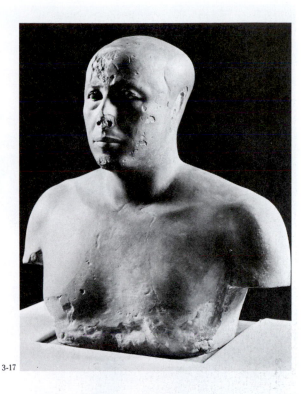

3-17

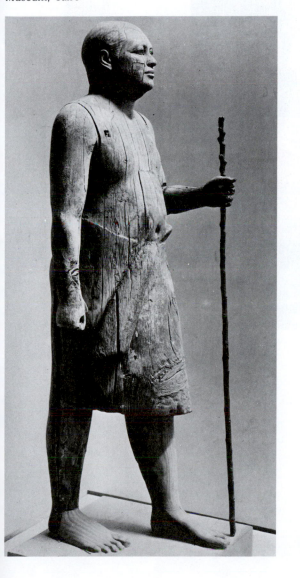

Somewhat less impersonal than the *Chephren* is the superb group statue showing King Mycerinus, wearing a kilt and the crown of Upper Egypt, flanked by the cow-goddess Hathor and a local deity (fig. 3–15). Each of the goddesses has an arm around Mycerinus as if to demonstrate his habitual intimacy with divinities. The work is carved from gray-green schist, and although the sculptor has not maintained quite the exalted dignity so impressive in the *Chephren,* he has delightfully contrasted the broad-shouldered, athletic figure of the king with the trim, youthful, sensuously beautiful forms of the female divinities, fully revealed by their clinging garments. Interestingly enough, while the king stands with legs apart, weight evenly distributed on both feet as in the *Hesira* relief, Hathor takes only a timid step forward and the local goddess keeps her feet together as if rooted to the spot.

While the royal statues are clearly individualized portraits, Old Kingdom naturalism is held in check by the need to emphasize the majesty and divinity of the pharaoh. But even in the more vividly lifelike statues of princes and officials, the dignity, simplicity, and balance characteristic of the Old Kingdom are consistently maintained. *Prince Rahotep and His Wife Nofret* (fig. 3–16) is carved from limestone, softer and easier to work than diorite or schist. The pair retain most of their original coating of paint. Rahotep is brown, his wife yellow ocher—the colors used by the Egyptians to distinguish male from female, probably to show that men braved the fierce sun from which delicate female skin was protected. The coloring, combined with the inlaid eyes of rock crystal, Rahotep's little mustache, and Nofret's plump cheeks, gives the pair an uncanny air of actuality that, to modern eyes, contrasts strangely with their ceremonial poses. On a far loftier plane is the painted limestone bust of Prince Ankhhaf (fig. 3–17), son-in-law of Cheops. The aging forms of body and face are clearly indicated, but the whole is pervaded with a mood of pensive melancholy that makes the observer wonder about its origin and meaning. This beautiful psychological portrait is unique in its subtlety among the more forthright Old Kingdom figures.

The Fifth Dynasty wooden statue of Kaaper (fig. 3–18), originally painted, betrays a lower-class allegiance; its uncompromising realism, not sparing the fat belly and smug expression of the subject, has earned the statue the modern

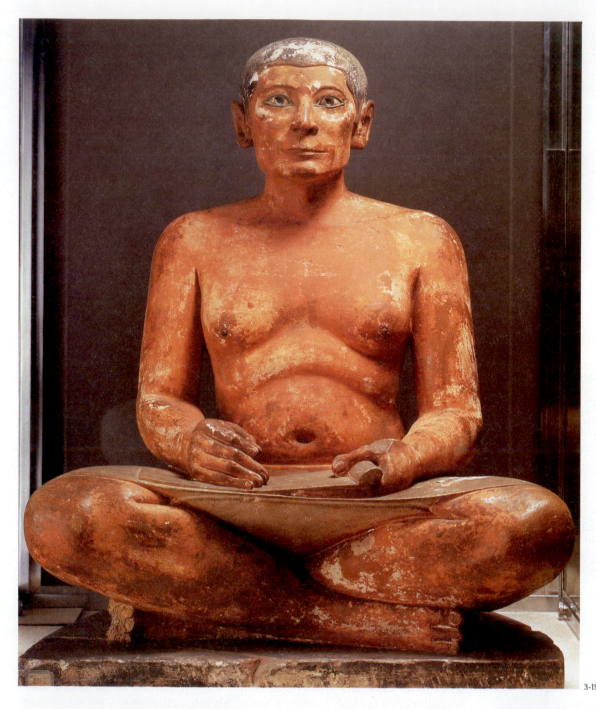

3-19

3-19. *Seated Scribe*, from Saqqara. c. 2400 B.C. Painted limestone, height 21″ (53 cm). Musée du Louvre, Paris

nickname of *Sheikh el Beled* (Arabic for "headman of the village"), but the artist has not sacrificed any of the firmness and control typical of the best Old Kingdom work or indeed the serene dignity of the formalized pose. Another brilliant Fifth Dynasty portrait is the painted limestone *Seated Scribe* (fig. 3–19), doubtless portraying a bureaucrat, alert and ready to write on his papyrus scroll. The engaging figure is just as intensely real—not sparing the scrawny neck and sagging pectorals—and just as rigid as *Kaaper*.

RELIEF SCULPTURE AND PAINTING   Our understanding of life in Old Kingdom Egypt is illustrated with a completeness beyond any expectations by the innumerable scenes—carved in low relief on the limestone blocks of tomb chambers and then painted, or painted directly without underlying relief—that describe in exhaustive detail the existence the deceased enjoyed in this world and hoped would be perpetuated in the next. Only such scenes are represented; the paintings do not tell stories. Within the conventional structure of Egyptian style, these scenes describe in rich detail all the elements of what we know to be taking place, not just the incident as we might see it from one vantage point. Usually the walls are divided into registers, each with a firm and continuous groundline and no indication of distant space. For example, in a relief representing a high official, *Ti Watching a Hippopotamus Hunt* (fig. 3–21), the owner of the tomb is represented at least twice the size of the lesser figures, and he merely contemplates, but does not participate in, the events of daily existence. Yet, since the scenes line the walls of the tomb chambers on all sides, they surround us with the illusion of an enveloping space in which we walk among the humans, animals, birds, and plants of 4,400 years ago. In this case the background consists of vertical grooves to indicate the stems of a papyrus swamp. Ti stands in his boat, posed according to the principles of relief representation we have already seen, holding his staff of office, while men in a neighboring boat spear the hippopotamuses. Toward the top of the relief are scattered papyrus flowers, among which wild animals lurk and birds fly or nest in an amazing variety of beautifully rendered poses. There is none of the random waywardness of the Hierakonpolis mural (see fig. 3–1). An exact sense of order prevails—even the spears of the huntsmen are drawn parallel to one line of the triangle formed by Ti's kilt. Among the many incidents that line the tomb is a touching scene (fig. 3–20) in which cattle are being led across a river and a terrified calf, too small to ford the stream, turns its head as it is carried over and cries to its anxious mother. The water is convincingly suggested by parallel vertical zigzags, over which the legs of humans and animals are painted, not carved.

The celebrated *Geese of Medum* (fig. 3–22), actually a strip from a continuous series of wall paintings, shows the extent to which the Old Kingdom could carry both its naturalism and its strong sense of form, so fused that the formalization characteristic of almost all Egyptian art seems to be derived effortlessly from the motion of these delightful birds, rather than from outside, as is so often the case with representations of human beings.

Luckily, a few unfinished tomb designs are preserved, left in that state because the deceased, for some unknown reason, had to be buried in haste. An unfinished passage from the later tomb of the pharaoh Horemheb (fig. 3–23), in the Eigh-

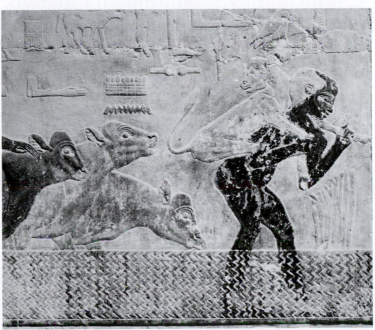

3-20. *Cattle Fording a River,* detail of a relief from the Tomb of Ti, Saqqara. c. 2400 B.C. Painted limestone

3-20

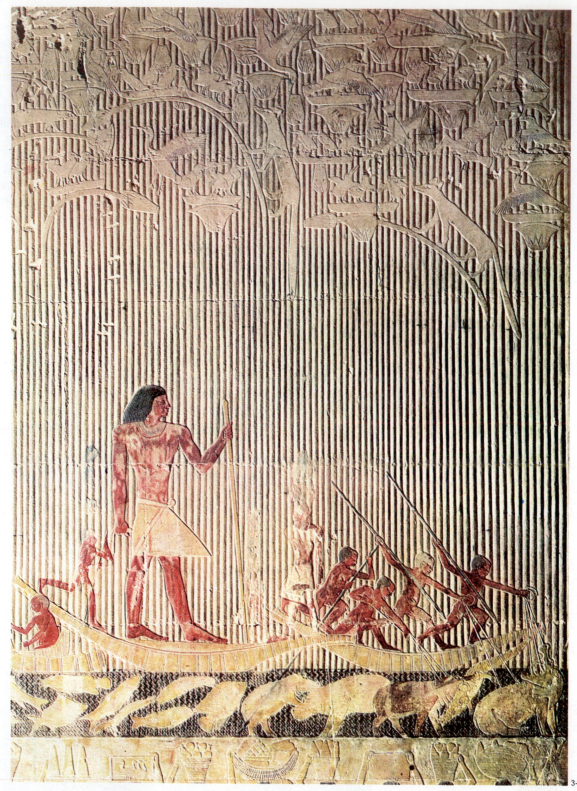

3-21

3-21. *Ti Watching a Hippopotamus Hunt,* from the Tomb of Ti, Saqqara. c. 2400 B.C. Painted limestone relief, height approx. 45″ (1.14 m)

3-22. *Geese of Medum* (detail of a fresco). c. 2600 B.C. Egyptian Museum, Cairo

3-23. Preparatory drawing and relief from the Tomb of Horemheb, Valley of the Kings (west of Thebes, Egypt). c. 1334–1306 B.C.

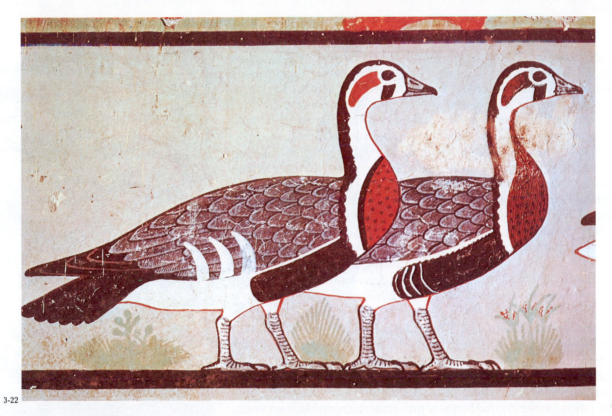

3-22

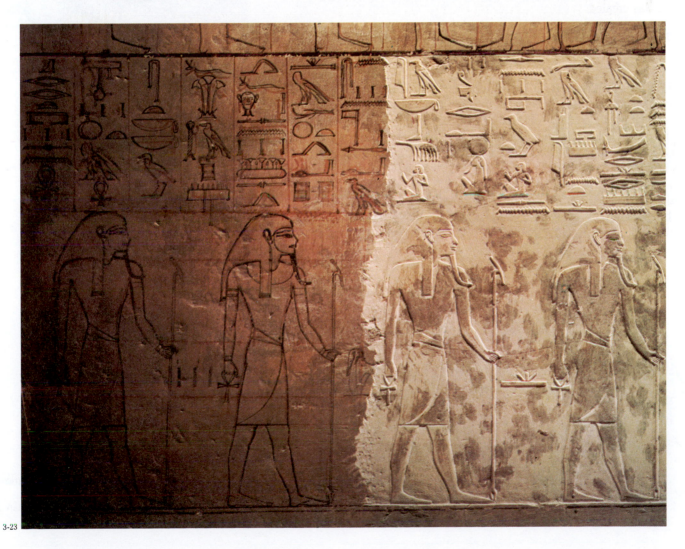

3-23

teenth Dynasty, shows us how the reliefs were made. First, as we see in the two figures at left, the painter did his preparatory drawing on the stone, according to a fixed system of proportions represented by ruled lines. But the artist was clearly very sensitive to nuances of contour and changed his outline two or three times before he was satisfied. (Such changes of mind are known as *pentimenti,* from the Italian word for "repentance.") Then, either he or a specialized stone carver cut out the shallow relief according to the drawing, down to a uniform background level. Finally, the painter returned to color the figures and objects. Even more revealing is a scene from the tomb of Neferirkara (fig. 3–24), from the Fifth Dynasty, in which only the preliminary drawing was ever done. Presumably the finished birds would have been drawn and painted with the same precision as the *Geese of Medum,* but the present airy grace of the descending pigeons comes not only from the astonishing variety of their poses but from the lightness of the brush drawing as well.

Although it was in Old Kingdom Egypt that people first learned to be fully human, our ideas of Old Kingdom art and life are entirely formed on the funerary art through which the Egyptians faced eternity. Their houses, palaces, and temples have mostly vanished, leaving hardly a clue. In the very nature of things, the beautiful system that sustained and gave meaning to the life of the Old Kingdom could not last forever. Perhaps the cost of the great funerary temples and pyramids was too heavy to bear. A king who is also a god must be able to act the part. At any rate, the weak kings of the Seventh and Eighth dynasties could not meet these demands, and their reigns were followed by a period of great social disorder during which the real power passed into the hands of provincial rulers and little art worthy of notice was created.

The Middle Kingdom, c. 2040–1650 B.C., and the Empire (New Kingdom), c. 1550–1070 B.C.

MIDDLE KINGDOM ARCHITECTURE   In a prolonged struggle, the kings of the Eleventh Dynasty regained power from provincial rulers and reunited the country, whose capital oscillated between Memphis in Lower Egypt and Thebes in Upper Egypt. Power no longer depended upon the divine authority of the pharaoh but on military force. Tombs often contained remarkable miniature groups in wood, representing every kind of daily activity, including the all-important military ones. A company of forty Nubian mercenaries (fig. 3–25) advancing toward us is a brutal indication of the changed conditions of the Middle Kingdom. Some small stone-faced brick pyramids were built, and numerous tombs whose chambers and columned halls were cut directly into the rock, but the most impressive architec-

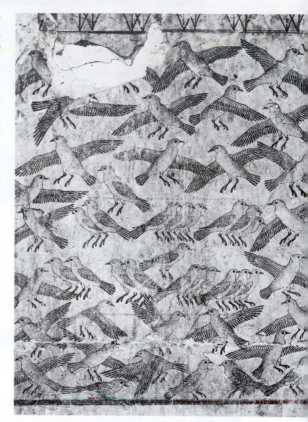

3-24. *Birds in Flight,* preparatory drawing from the Tomb of Neferirkara, Saqqara. c. 2480–2340 B.C. Limestone

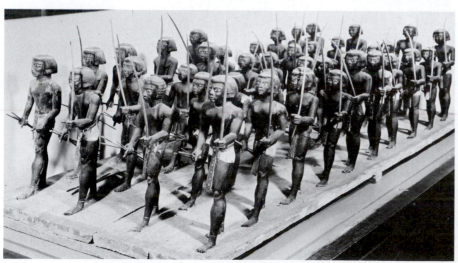

3-25

3-25. Model of a troop of Nubian mercenaries, from a tomb at Asyūt, Egypt. c. 2040 B.C. Painted wood, height 15¾″ (40 cm). Egyptian Museum, Cairo

tural work we know from this period is the funerary temple of Mentuhotep III at Deir el Bahari, across the Nile from Thebes. From what remains of the building, alongside which Queen Hatshepsut was later to build her even more ambitious temple, we can reconstruct its original appearance (see fig. 3–31, background). From a grove of geometrically aligned trees a long ramp led to a terrace supported by a row of square piers; from there one entered a second colonnade through a canted doorway and moved into a courtyard from the center of which rose a massive block with canted sides like a huge mastaba outlined against the cliffs of the western mountain. According to some scholars, the tomb may have been topped with a small pyramid, as in this reconstruction. The scale, as compared to Old Kingdom tombs, is almost human.

MIDDLE KINGDOM SCULPTURE   Some royal portraits reveal with devastating frankness the chronic anxiety in which, according to literary accounts, Middle Kingdom monarchs lived, tormented by the military struggles needed to maintain their rule. Especially intense are the brooding portraits of Sesostris III (fig. 3–26), whose careworn face shows none of the serene confidence of the Old Kingdom. Against such a background, the exquisite seated statue of Princess Sennuwy, posed like a pharaoh (fig. 3–27), comes as a delightful surprise. This masterpiece in polished granite shows in its slender forms and softly flowing surfaces a style as sensuous as that of the best Old Kingdom female figures but endowed with a wholly new elegance and grace. As in the standing pharaonic statues, her legs are joined to the block on which she sits by a thin wall of granite, thus preventing the piercing of the block, which seems to have run counter to Egyptian aesthetic principles.

At the close of the Twelfth Dynasty ensued a new period of political chaos, during which Lower Egypt was invaded by Asiatic rulers known as the Hyksos, or

3-26. *King Sesostris III,* from Medamud. c. 1878–1843 B.C. Granite, height 11″ (28 cm). Egyptian Museum, Cairo

3-27. *Princess Sennuwy,* from Kerma, Sudan. c. 1950 B.C. Granite, height 67½″ (1.71 m). Courtesy, Museum of Fine Arts, Boston

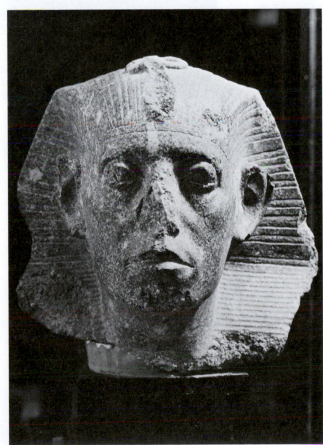

3-26

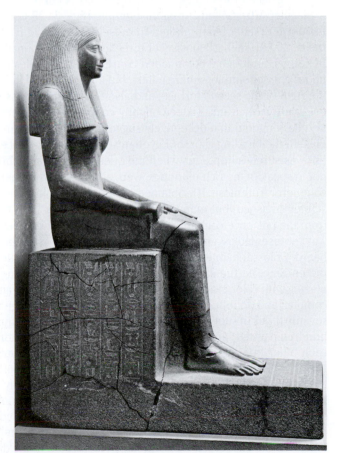

3-27

shepherd-kings. These conquerors imported two commodities soon to be triumphantly adopted by the Egyptians—the horse and the wheel. After a century of foreign rule, pharaohs from Upper Egypt for the third time regained power, and the Eighteenth Dynasty saw not only the expulsion of the Hyksos and the reunification of the country, with its capital at Thebes, but also the extension of Egyptian power over neighboring lands as well—Syria, Palestine, Libya, and Nubia, an area more than 2,000 miles in length.

ARCHITECTURE OF THE EMPIRE   The next five centuries, variously known as the Empire or the New Kingdom, constitute a period of unprecedented imperial power and wealth, celebrated by enormous architectural projects, largely in the surroundings of the Theban metropolis—at modern Karnak and Luxor on the east bank of the Nile and Deir el Bahari on the west. Amon, the local deity of Thebes, was promoted to the ruling position among the gods in recognition of his services to the Empire and was identified with Ra, the sun-god, thus becoming Amon-Ra. The new temples were often decorated with statues, reliefs, and paintings representing the power and historic exploits of the pharaohs.

The Funerary Temple of Queen Hatshepsut.   Among the earliest of these ambitious builders of the Empire was Queen Hatshepsut, the first great female ruler of whom we have any record. Daughter of Tuthmosis I, half-sister and wife of his weak successor, Tuthmosis II, she ruled first as queen consort and after her husband's death supposedly as regent for her stepson Tuthmosis III. In fact, she assumed power as pharaoh and governed peacefully for twenty years (c. 1501–1481 B.C.). A limestone statue of this brilliant monarch (fig. 3–28), clad in her kingly headcloth and kilt, reminds us of the slenderness and delicacy of the statue of Sennuwy more than four hundred years earlier, yet radiates an air of majesty and quiet power. The upper surface of the block on which she sits is curved, as if to suggest a throne.

Hatshepsut's immense funerary temple (figs. 3–29 to 3–31), alongside and to the north of that of Mentuhotep III at Deir el Bahari, directly across the Nile from the capital at Thebes, consists of three ascending colonnaded terraces, connected by ramps, and a final colonnaded court, now largely destroyed. The outer colonnades employ simple, square pillars, but the columns of the sanctuary of Anubis, at the right of the second terrace, and also the inner columns of the sanctuaries, are delicately faceted into sixteen slightly concave sides, a form invented during the Middle Kingdom that deceptively suggests the fluted columns of later Greek temples. In the blinding glare of Egyptian sunlight the present effect looks a bit bleak, but was surely sumptuous when the queen's full array of brightly painted statues, not to speak of the rich plantings, were all in place. Alas, her successor, the mighty conqueror Tuthmosis III, obtained his revenge for his long wait by having all the statues smashed, but many have been put together from the fragments, salvaged from the pits once containing trees into which they had been thrown. Hatshepsut was represented as a divine king, with red or yellow skin, blue eyebrows, and false beard. Colossal painted statues of the queen in dark granite knelt at either side of the entrance to the sanctuary, and a row of huge standing statues in limestone, blazing with color, stood before the pillars of the upper terrace, crowning the entire complex and doubtless visible for miles. All in all the queen was shown more than seventy times in superhuman scale; in addition, her head appeared on more than a hundred painted sandstone sphinxes and on twenty-two more in red granite facing each other in a double rank up the center of the lower terrace.

All that is still left in place of this brilliant display of color are the open halls on the right side of the middle terrace, which contain generally well-preserved reliefs narrating in great detail scenes from Hatshepsut's life, beginning with her supposed divine origin as a daughter of Amon. The terraces were filled with rows of fragrant myrrh trees, highly prized as a source of incense, and the reliefs include representations of the expedition dispatched by Hatshepsut to the distant land of Punt, in

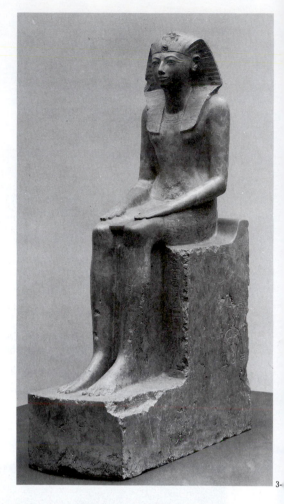

3-28. *Queen Hatshepsut.* c. 1495 B.C. Limestone, height approx. 6′5″ (1.96 m). The Metropolitan Museum of Art, New York. Rogers Fund and contribution from Edward S. Harkness, 1929

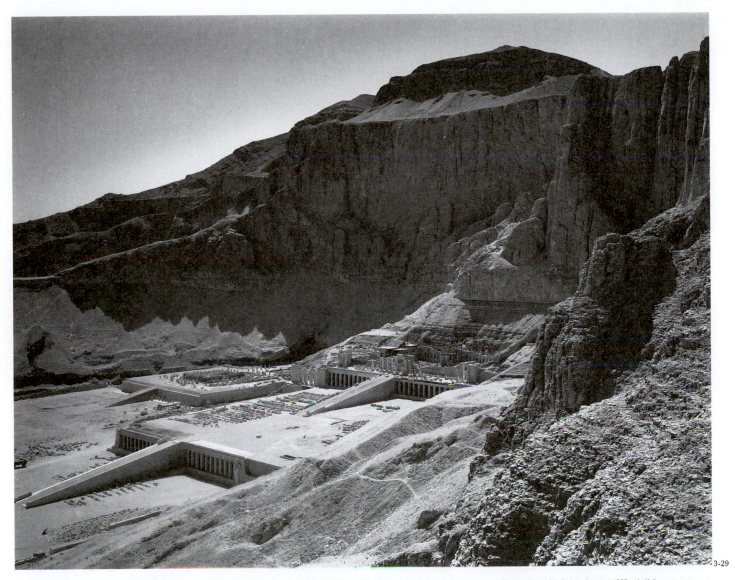

3-29. SENMUT. Funerary Temple of Queen Hatshepsut, Deir el Bahari (base and ramp of Funerary Temple of Mentuhotep III visible at extreme left). C. 1480 B.C.

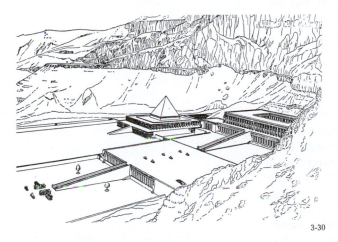

3-30. Reconstructed view of the Funerary Temple of Queen Hatshepsut (Funerary Temple of Mentuhotep III, with pyramid, visible at left), Deir el Bahari (after F. Lange and M. Hirmer)

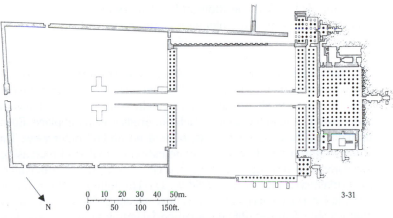

3-31. Plan of Funerary Temple of Queen Hatshepsut (after H. Ricke and M. Hirmer)

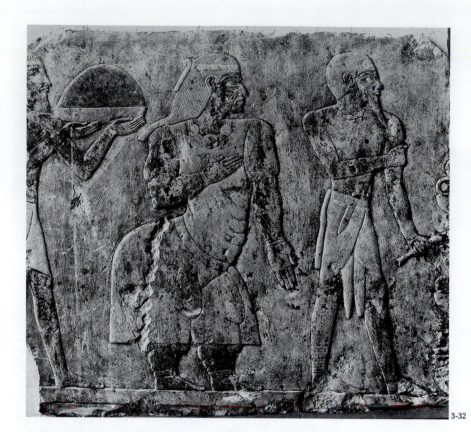

3-32

3-32. *King and Queen of Punt,* from Funerary Temple of Queen Hatshepsut, Deir el Bahari. c. 1480 B.C. Painted relief. Egyptian Museum, Cairo

modern Somalia near the coast of the Red Sea, to acquire these precious trees. People, dwellings, plants, animals, and birds all appear, and the ruler of Punt is shown next to his magnificently corpulent queen (fig. 3–32), whose fat piles up in rolls on her swaybacked body, long arms, and stubby legs. There are also a number of tiny portraits of Hatshepsut's architect and chief minister, SENMUT, usually shown kneeling at the entrances to various sanctuaries. Senmut may also have been the queen's lover; his tomb, left unfinished at her death, was carved from solid rock underneath the temple. A worthy successor to Imhotep of the Old Kingdom, Senmut planned the uppermost courtyard to abut the mass of the cliff into which the sanctuary chamber of Amon is cut, since the sun-bark disappeared over the mountain daily. Thus the thousand-foot mass of the living rock of the western mountain, with which the colonnades of the courtyards work in majestic harmony, substitutes for a man-made pyramid.

The Temples at Luxor and Karnak.   A powerful priesthood in Thebes administered the royal temples of the god Amon, his wife Mut, and their son Khonsu at Luxor and at Karnak. These were originally connected by an avenue of sphinxes more than a mile in length, of which hundreds are still in place. Egyptian temples, unlike those of the later Greeks, offered no unified outer view. They were built along a central axis to enclose a succession of spaces of increasing sanctity and exclusiveness, starting with the entrance gateway, which was flanked by slanting stone masses called *pylons* (see fig. 3–35). Through the gateway the worshiper was admitted to a spacious colonnaded court (see fig. 3–34). Then came one of the most characteristic features of Egyptian imperial temples, the *hypostyle hall,* a lofty room whose stone roof was supported by immense columns. The central section of this structure (see fig. 3–37) was usually elevated above the sides and was lighted and ventilated by a row of upper windows known as a *clerestory.* This feature was adopted in Roman architecture as well and was then used constantly throughout

3-33. Plan of the Temple of Amon-Mut-Khonsu, Luxor (after N. de Garis Davies). Begun c. 1390 B.C. 1. Sanctuaries 2. Hypostyle hall 3. Colonnaded court 4. Entrance hall (addition by Amenhotep III) 5. Colonnaded court (addition by Ramses II) 6. Pylons (addition by Ramses II)

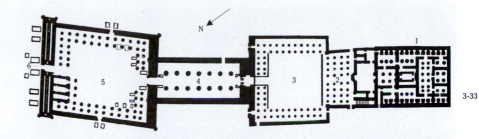

3-33

3-34. Colonnaded court of Amenhotep III, Temple of Amon-Mut-Khonsu, Luxor (view into the hypostyle hall). After 1390 B.C.

the Middle Ages in Europe and the Near East. The strong Egyptian sunlight and great heat were controlled by stone grilles in the clerestory windows. Clerestory, grilles, and all were derived from wooden counterparts in Egyptian houses. After the hypostyle hall came the smaller, even more secret, and much darker sanctuaries containing cult statues and the "bark of Amon" (sacred boat), reserved for the priesthood and their rituals.

The Temple of Amon-Mut-Khonsu at Luxor was built by Amenhotep III on this standard principle in the early fourteenth century B.C., but he soon added an impressive entrance hall (fig. 3–33). Later Ramses II added a second courtyard and a new set of entrance pylons in front (fig. 3–35), deflecting the axis on account of the curve of the nearby Nile. The immensity and rather bulbous shapes of Amenhotep's thirty-foot columns (fig. 3–34) are far removed from the elegance, purity, and hardness of Imhotep's forms, but the problems themselves required new solutions. The unknown architect at Luxor built freestanding columns of local sandstone rather than of the fine limestone available at Saqqara, and he shaped them according to the conventionalized forms of bundles of papyrus reeds, tradi-

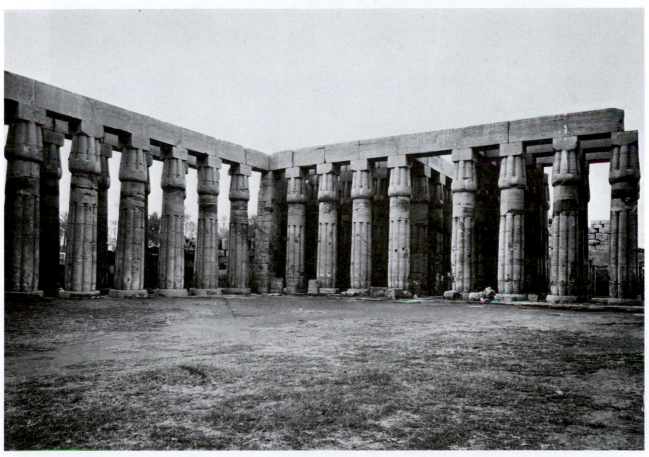

3-34

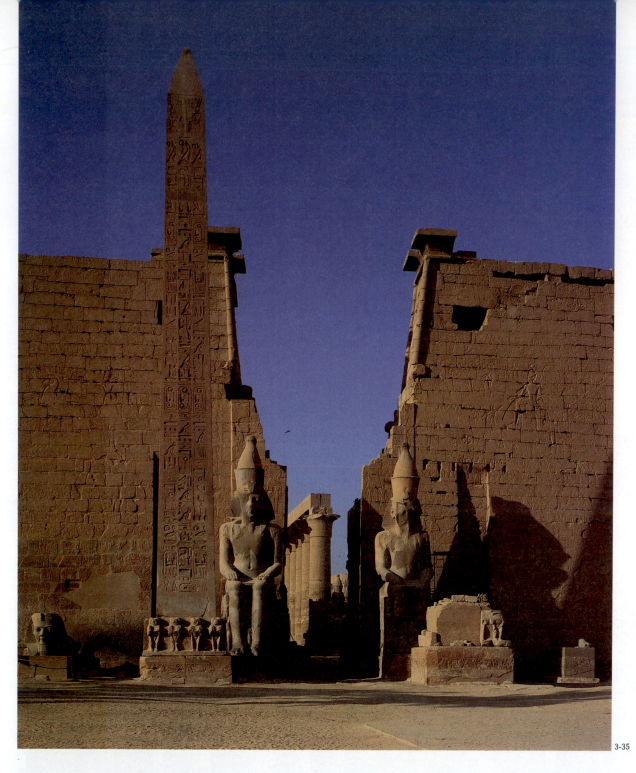

3-35

3-35. Pylons of Ramses II, Temple of Amon-Mut-Khonsu, Luxor. c. 1260 B.C.

tional supports for the more ephemeral architecture of the vanished Egyptian houses and palaces. The columns sustain huge undecorated sandstone lintels that surround the courtyard and continue in the hypostyle hall, where they supported a now-fallen roof of stone slabs. Light came from the clerestory over low walls, so that the center of the hall remained mysteriously dim. The grand proportions of the columns, which seem to continue in all directions, always blocking any clear view, create an effect of majestic solemnity.

The even larger and far more complex temple at Karnak was one of the most extensive sanctuaries of the ancient world, with a perimeter wall about a mile and a half in circumference. The partially ruined temple was constructed piecemeal by so many pharaohs that the overall effect is confusing, yet many of the surviving

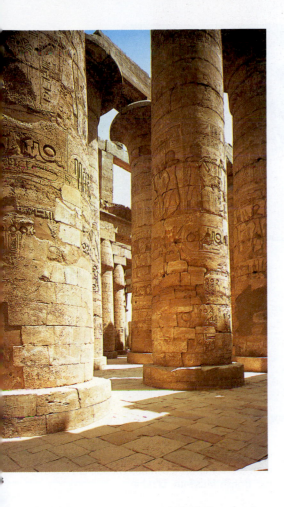

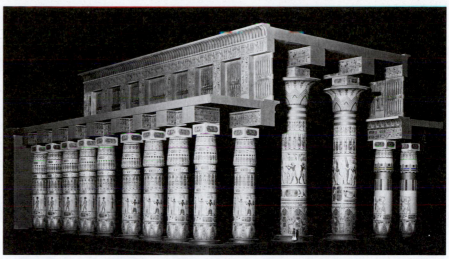

3-37

portions are very beautiful. The hypostyle hall (figs. 3–36, 3–37) built by Seti I and Ramses II in the Nineteenth Dynasty was filled with columns so massive that diagonal views are impossible from the central axis. Wherever one looks, the vista is blocked by these immense shapes, decorated by bands of incised hieroglyphics and painted reliefs.

TOMB DECORATIONS   Scores of tombs survive from the period of the Empire. Pharaohs and aristocracy alike gave up building monumental tombs, which could not be defended against robbers. The dead were buried deep in rock-cut chambers in mountain valleys, and the entrances carefully hidden. Even the royal tombs in the Valley of the Kings, west of Thebes, were invariably discovered and plundered, but the wall decorations remain. In the splendid Eighteenth Dynasty painted tomb of Nebamun at Thebes (fig. 3–38), the deceased is shown fowling. Accompanied by

3-36. View into the hypostyle hall, Temple of Amon-Ra, Karnak. c. 1290 B.C. (begun by Seti I and completed by Ramses II)

3-37. Model of the hypostyle hall, Temple of Amon-Ra, Karnak. c. 1290 B.C. The Metropolitan Museum of Art, New York. Purchase, 1890, Levi Hale Willard Bequest

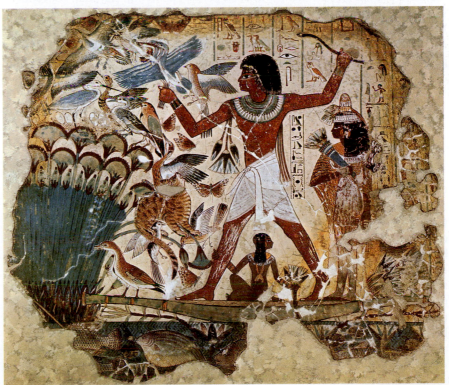

3-38. *Nebamun Hunting Birds,* fragment of a wall painting from the Tomb of Nebamun, Thebes. c. 1400 B.C. British Museum, London

3-38

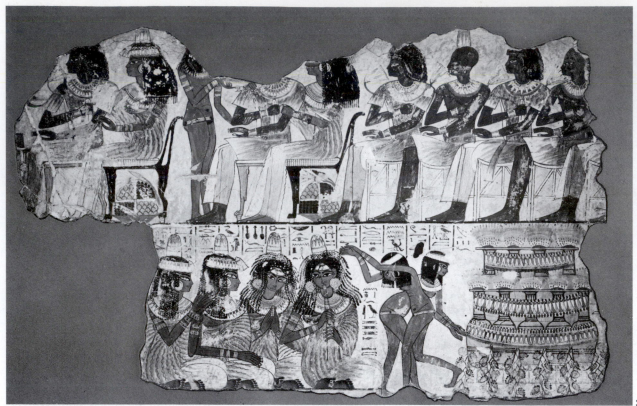

3-39

his hunting cat, he plays havoc among the brilliantly drawn and painted birds of a papyrus swamp. A fragment from this same tomb (fig. 3–39) shows an entrancing banquet scene, at which both the revelers and the musicians wear cones of perfumed unguents on their heads. Delightful female dancers, clad only in jeweled collars and tiny golden belts, clap their hands as they move with exquisite lightness and grace. While most of the figures are shown from the side, two of the crouching musicians unexpectedly face directly outward, and all the crouching figures point the soles of their feet toward us. In such poses, apparently, Egyptian conventions were useless and therefore thrown aside. In the subtle, delicate style of Eighteenth Dynasty tomb decorations there can also be great pathos, as in the relief of the *Blind Harper* (fig. 3–40) from the tomb of Patenemhab at Saqqara, in which the harper gently strums his octave of strings. His song is inscribed on the wall beside him:

> *Pass the day happily, O priest.*
> *. . . have music and singing before you,*
> *Cast all ill behind you and think only of joy,*
> *Until the day comes when you moor your boat in the land that*
>   *loves silence.*

Characteristic of the arrangement of scenes in superimposed strips is the Nineteenth Dynasty tomb of Sen-nedjem at Deir el Medineh, adjoining the funerary temple of Mentuhotep III (fig. 3–41). At the end of the chamber the deceased crosses to the other world in the boat of the dead to be received by the gods, and below are shown the harvest of his grainfields and the rows of his fruit trees. On the right the gods themselves are aligned above his funeral feast. As in the tomb of Ti, scenes like these in registers continuing around the chamber create a special kind of space that, once one accepts the conventions of Egyptian art, becomes surprisingly real and convincing when one actually stands in the chamber, surrounded by the paintings on all sides.

AKHENATEN Just when everything about Egyptian life and art seemed to be safely settled for an indefinite period, an unexpected reformer appeared who tried

3-39. *Banquet Scene,* fragment of a wall painting from the Tomb of Nebamun, Thebes. c. 1400 B.C. British Museum, London

3-40. *Blind Harper,* relief from the Tomb of Patenemhab, Saqqara. Middle 16th century–late 14th century B.C. Rijksmuseum van Oudheden, Leiden, the Netherlands

3-41. Wall paintings from the Tomb of Sen-nedjem, Deir el Medineh (Thebes). 13th century B.C.

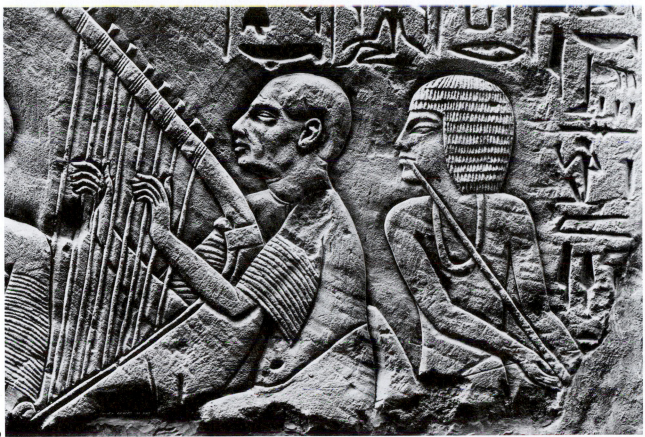

3-40

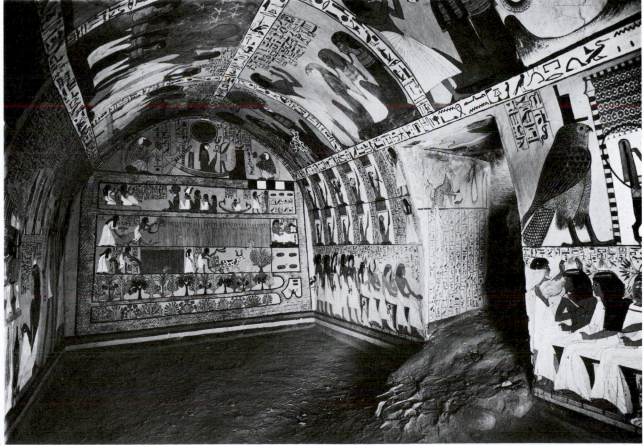

3-41

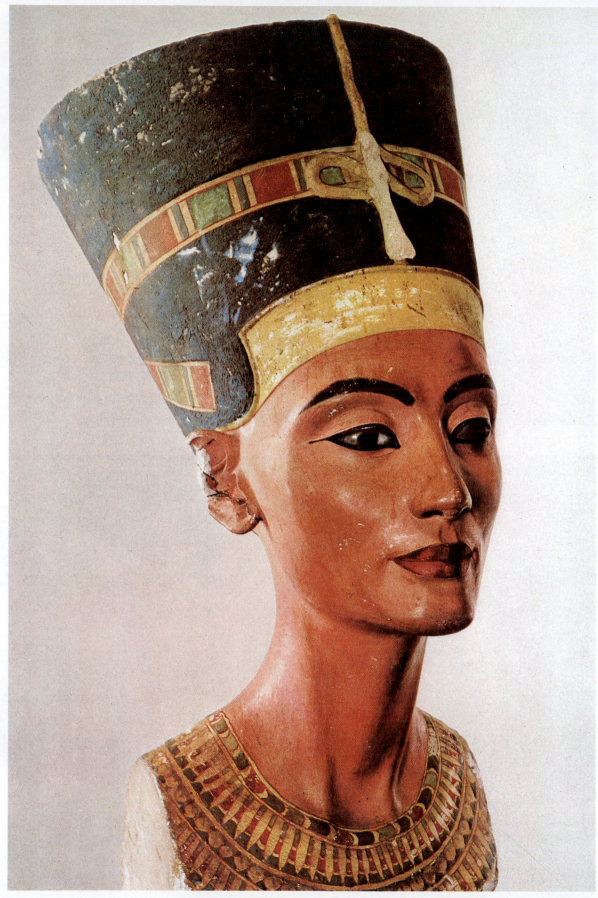

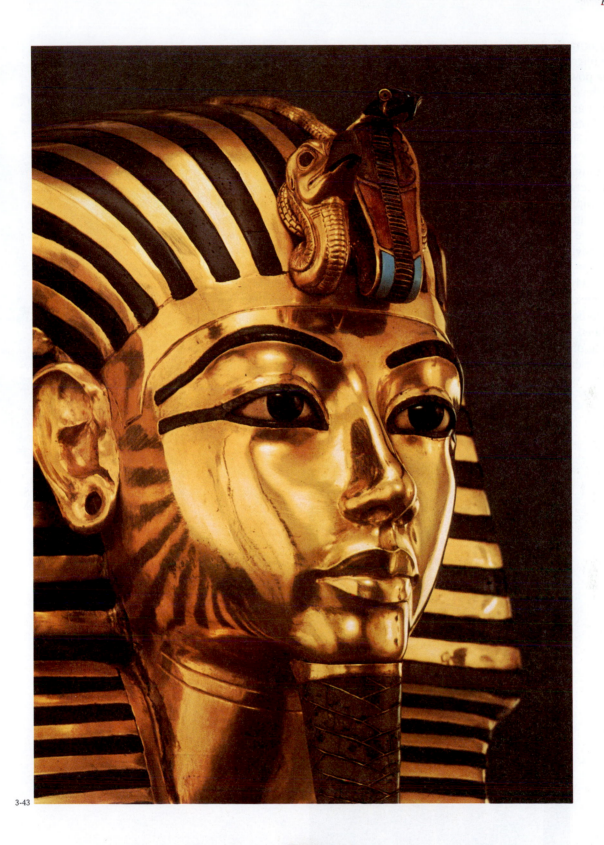

3-43

3-42. *Queen Nefertiti*. c. 1365 B.C. Painted limestone, height 19″ (48.3 cm). Staatliche Museen zu Berlin—Preussischer Kulturbesitz

3-43. Mask of King Tutankhamen, from the Tomb of Tutankhamen, Valley of the Kings (west of Thebes). c. 1355–1342 B.C. Gold inlaid with blue glass, lapis lazuli, turquoise, carnelian, and feldspar, height 21¼″ (54 cm). Egyptian Museum, Cairo

his best to unravel the entire fabric, and indeed succeeded for a limited time. During the reign of Amenhotep III, who married a brilliant commoner, probably a Nubian, the powerful Queen Tiy, there arose at the imperial court a new cult that worshiped the disk of the sun, called the Aten. The son of Amenhotep and Tiy, first their co-ruler and then their successor (ruled 1379–1362 B.C.), changed his name from Amenhotep IV to Akhenaten in honor of the new solar god, of whom he declared himself to be the sole earthly representative. This extraordinary religion, a kind of early monotheism, required the closing of the temples of Amon-Ra and the disinheriting of the priesthood, which had become the true ruling class of Egyptian society. Although Akhenaten built a new Temple of Aten at Karnak, he moved the capital from Thebes to an entirely new site, dedicated to Aten and named Akhetaten, at a spot now called Tell el Amarna. The insubstantial secular buildings of the Egyptians usually vanished, like those of Çatal Hüyük, under new structures, leaving few traces, but when Akhenaten died his successors were so anxious to wipe out the memory of the heretic that they destroyed Akhenaten's new city immediately. The plans and even painted floors from the palace and from the houses of state officials have, however, been excavated, and the entire contents of a sculptor's studio were discovered, including casts from life, models for sculpture, and unfinished works.

Something of the character of this royal visionary who neglected the military necessities of empire to promulgate his new religion can be seen from strange

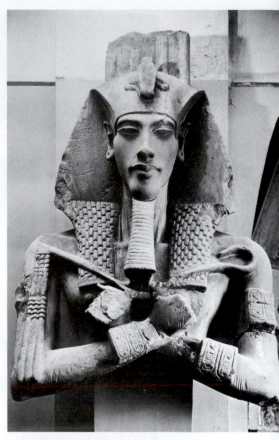

3-44. *King Akhenaten*, from the Temple of Aten, Karnak (fragment). c. 1360 B.C. Sandstone, height 60¼″ (1.53 m). Egyptian Museum, Cairo

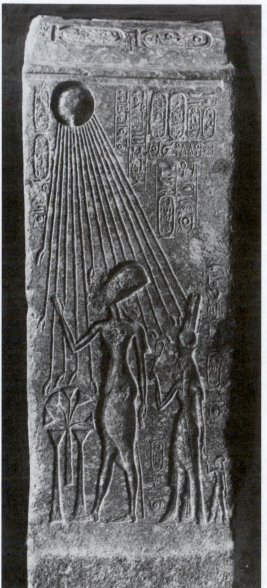

3-45. *King Akhenaten and His Family Sacrificing to Aten*, from Tell el Amarna. c. 1360 B.C. Limestone relief. Egyptian Museum, Cairo

3-45

statues and reliefs of him and others, which have been found in considerable numbers because they were used as building blocks by later pharaohs. One colossal pillar statue from the Temple of Aten at Karnak (fig. 3–44) shows his slack-jawed, heavy-lipped features and dreamy gaze and, instead of the athletic male ideal of all other pharaohs, an exaggeratedly feminine body with swelling breasts— probably because the king in his new messianic role was to embody both paternal and maternal principles, as did the god Aten. An incised relief (this method, which freed the sculptor from the necessity of reducing the entire background, was characteristic of large-scale Empire reliefs) shows the king sacrificing to Aten (fig. 3–45), whose rays terminate in hands that bestow life to the earth, represented by papyrus plants. He is followed by the queen, Nefertiti, whose figure is shaped just like his, though in smaller scale, and by a still smaller daughter.

The famous painted limestone bust of Nefertiti (fig. 3–42), a work of consummate elegance and grace, shows the queen at the height of her beauty, wearing the crown of Upper and Lower Egypt and decked with the usual ceremonial necklaces. Every plane of her strong cheekbones, perfect nose, firm chin, and full lips, and every line of the heavy makeup applied to her eyebrows, eyes, and mouth move with an arresting combination of smoothness and tension. The slender, long-necked ideal is irresistible to twentieth-century eyes, attuned to contemporary fashion. But entranced viewers of this masterpiece, less often of the original than the countless reproductions on sale everywhere, seldom realize that this bust was never intended for public view. It is a model for official portraits of the queen and was found in the studio of the sculptor who made it. It comes as a shock to note that he never finished the left eye (the eye is completed in all the copies). If we were to see this same lovely head poised above the flat-chested, full-bellied figure visible in all representations of Akhenaten's surprising family, we might be less charmed. Nonetheless, there is something undeniably personal about this astonishing model. We would perhaps be justified in considering it a testament of admiration on the part of a great if unknown artist to the beauty but also to the intelligence and supreme calm of an extraordinary woman.

TUTANKHAMEN   Through a happy accident of history, even more is preserved to show the brief life and activities of Akhenaten's successor, Tutankhamen, who died between eighteen and twenty years of age. The young king may have been Akhenaten's younger half brother, therefore the son of the great Queen Tiy. Originally Tutankhaten, his new name was forced upon him by the revived priesthood of Amon. His is the only royal tomb that has been found intact; it had been obscured and protected by debris from a later tomb. When discovered in 1922, the chambers contained a dazzling array of beautiful objects, displaying the taste of the imperial court for delicacy and grace. The king's many coffins, one inside the other, were found intact. The innermost, of solid gold, weighs 243 pounds! The cover of the coffin has a breathtaking portrait of the boy king in solid gold, with the ceremonial beard, the eyebrows, and lashes all inlaid in lapis lazuli. But even more beautiful, if possible, is the gold mask that covered the face of the actual mummy (fig. 3–43). The dead king wears the usual divine beard, and over his forehead appear the heads of the vulture-goddess of Upper Egypt and the serpent-goddess of Lower Egypt. While the brilliant blue stripes on the headdress are glass paste, the other inlays come from semiprecious stones, such as lapis lazuli, turquoise, carnelian, and feldspar. His clearly negroid features recall those of his mother. To the effect of splendor produced by the intrinsic value of the materials is added an impression of the greatest poetic sensitivity and gentleness. The wide eyes of the young king seem to be looking through and beyond us; no other work of art from antiquity brings us so close to the personality of a deceased monarch. Among the thousands of objects from the tomb, one of the most beautiful is the carved wood throne, covered with gold and inlaid with faience, glass paste, semiprecious stones, and silver. The charming relief on the back (fig. 3–46) shows the disk of Aten shining on the king,

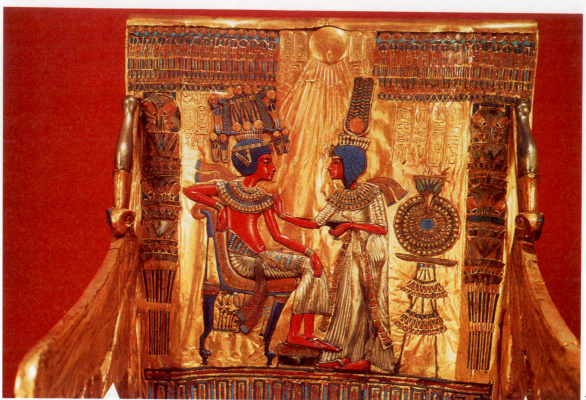

3-46

who is seated on a delicately carved chair while his queen, Ankhesenamen, who may have been his sister, lightly touches his shoulder as she presents him with a beautiful bowl.

LATER PHARAOHS Succeeding monarchs, particularly the Ramesside pharaohs, were anxious to reestablish symbols of imperial might along with the neglected cult of Amon. Ramses II had himself portrayed in immense statues characteristic of the megalomania of his dynasty, not only between the columns of his forecourt for the Temple of Amon-Mut-Khonsu at Luxor, but in the four colossal seated figures that flank the entrance to his majestic tomb at Abu Simbel (fig. 3–47). These have become universally known in recent years through the successful campaign to cut the entire tomb from the rock, statues and all, and raise it to a new position above the rising waters of the Nile, dammed at Aswan.

Even under the Greek rulers of Egypt in the last centuries B.C., the principles of Egyptian architecture, sculpture, and painting continued virtually unchanged. If some of the conviction may have gone out of Egyptian art, the late works, such as the Temple of Horus at Edfu, south of Luxor, are often impressive. This is the best preserved of all major Egyptian temples, still retaining the stone roof over its great hall. Its traditional pylons, terminated by simple, crisp moldings, are punctuated by recessed shafts for flagpoles and decorated with beautifully incised reliefs showing the (Greek!) pharaoh before Horus.

We cannot leave the Egyptians without a word about another of their inventions, the illuminated manuscript. These illustrated books were written and painted on rolls of papyrus, a surface made from the thin-shaved pith of the papyrus plant, glued together to form a continuous sheet. The most important of these are the so-called Books of the Dead, collections of prayers for the protection of the deceased during their perilous adventures in the other world. The best-known scene in every

3-46. Throne of King Tutankhamen and his queen, Ankhesenamen, from the Tomb of Tutankhamen, Valley of the Kings (west of Thebes). c. 1355–1342 B.C. Carved wood covered with gold and inlaid with faience, glass paste, semiprecious stones, and silver; height of throne 41″ (1.04 m). Egyptian Museum, Cairo

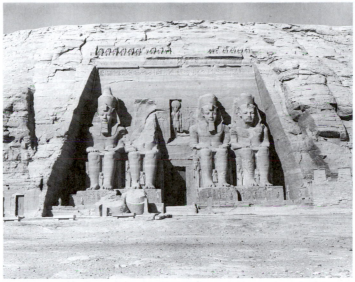

3-47. Entrance façade, rock temple of Abu Simbel, Nubia (now relocated). c. 1290–1225 B.C. Height of figures approx. 60′ (18.29 m)

3-47

Book of the Dead is the dramatic moment (fig. 3–48) when, below a lineup of enthroned gods, the heart of the dead person (who is the little human-headed hawk just above the heart toward the left) is weighed against a feather. Luckily, it has just balanced, or the deceased would have been thrown to the crocodile-hyena-hippopotamus hungrily waiting at the right.

While the great architectural and figurative achievements of the Egyptians are often considered preparations for those of the Greeks, the Books of the Dead prefigure the illuminated manuscripts that form such an important part of medieval culture, and the weighing of the deceased's heart is a forerunner of the Christian Last Judgment. But we would do better to enjoy the beauties of Egyptian art for themselves. This, indeed, is just what the peoples of other ancient cultures did, for the road that Egyptian artists, despite the severe conventions within which they were obliged to work, opened up for the understanding of nature and its re-creation in visible form was the one soon to be followed by every ancient civilization. Often, as we will see in studying Minoan and early Greek art, the debt is obvious. And, at times, as in the early years of the Roman Empire, Egyptian art was nostalgically imitated. It was also revived, almost as a fashion, in the eighteenth and early nineteenth centuries, when the first excavations took place.

3-48. *Last Judgment before Osiris,* from the *Book of the Dead,* found at the Theban Necropolis. c. 1310 B.C. Painted papyrus, 17¾ × 35¾″ (45 × 91 cm). British Museum, London

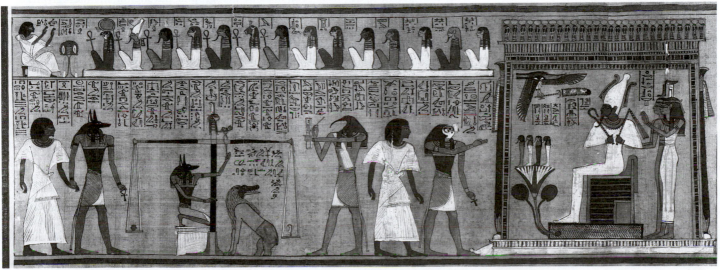

3-48

CHAPTER FOUR

Roughly parallel with the civilization of Egypt, another, in some ways equally great, historic culture was developing in the region of the Near East known as Mesopotamia, from the Greek word meaning "land between the rivers" (see Map 5, page 68). Traversed by the almost parallel courses of the Tigris to the northeast and the Euphrates to the southwest, this fertile valley was as attractive to ancient peoples as that of the Nile. But unity, stability, and permanence, the three foundation stones of Egyptian culture, were denied by nature to Mesopotamia. The narrow ribbon of the Nile Valley was protected from all but the best-organized invaders by the natural barriers of the Libyan and Arabian deserts, and the placid Nile itself formed an ideal means of communication between all parts of the Egyptian realm, facilitating unified control. The broad valley of the two turbulent rivers of Mesopotamia, on the contrary, was open to invasion from all directions and had no easy means of internal communication. Consequently, the natural shape for human communities to assume was that of a city-state in the middle of supporting territory rather than a unified nation. Mesopotamian cities were under frequent and repeated siege from their neighbors or from foreign invaders and thus had to be heavily fortified. Nevertheless, Mesopotamian texts tell us of the continual destruction of these cities and of the removal of their power to other centers.

The climate itself, as compared with the rainless warmth that favored Egypt, watered only by its friendly river, was often hostile. As the recent wars in this region have made us all aware, Mesopotamia is subject to sharp contrasts of heat and cold, flood and drought, as well as to violent storms that echo in the realm of nature the endemic conflicts between human communities. Not surprisingly, little attention seems to have been paid by Mesopotamian cultures to the afterlife, so important to the Egyptians. Security in *this* life, which except for intermediate periods of disorder was taken for granted throughout Egypt's long history, could be achieved in Mesopotamia only by strenuous and concerted efforts and was at best unpredictable. Propitiation of the deities who personified the mysterious and often menacing forces of nature was essential. At the opening of recorded history, the city-state was organized around the service of a local deity, who could intervene for its protection in the councils of heaven. The central temple controlled much economic activity, and shops and offices were grouped around it. Writing, laboriously taught in the earliest recorded schools, was accomplished by means of pressing the sharpened end of a reed into clay tablets to make cuneiform ("wedge-shaped") marks. Originally pictographs, these soon became ideographs, paralleling the hieroglyphs of Egypt. The tablets, which have been found by the thousands in Mesopotamian excavations, permit the economic and social life in the early theocracies to be reconstructed down to the minutest details.

Elected rulers rapidly assumed authority in their own right as kings and aspired to the control of neighboring states and eventually of the entire region, even of those outlying areas that produced the raw materials required by the economy of the state. Mesopotamian history is, in consequence, a bewilderingly complex succession of conquests and defeats, of rises and falls, of city-states and eventually of hastily conquered empires with universal pretensions that melted away after a century or so of power, sometimes after only a few decades. Any attempt, therefore, to give an orderly outline of Mesopotamian history is sure to be an oversimplification. As in Egypt, the basic ethnic structure of Mesopotamian civilization was not unified. One people, the Sumerians, apparently entered the region from the mountains to the north, but their exact origin is as mysterious as their language, which is not inflected and bears no relation to any other that we know. The Sumerians in turn were conquered by the Akkadians, Semitic invaders from the west, but eventually Sumerian culture was adopted by the conquerors. Regardless of the ethnic origin of any Mesopotamian peoples, however, certain essentials characterize Mesopotamian cities for about three thousand years.

First, the central temple was invariably raised on a platform above the level of the surrounding town. Generally, the temple consisted of a series of superimposed solid structures forming a broadly based tower or artificial mountain known as a *ziggurat,* on the summit of which propitiatory ceremonies to the gods of nature took place. These ziggurats, the one best known to us being, of course, the Tower of Babel (Babylon), represented an immense communal effort and were visible for great distances across the Mesopotamian plain. They clearly symbolized humanity's attempt to reach the celestial deities—an ambition which, during heavy weather with low-hanging clouds, may often have appeared to succeed. One should recall that according to the Greeks the gods dwelt on Mount Olympus, and that Moses went to the top of Mount Sinai for his conversations with the Almighty. Even in the later period of empires, the royal palace in Mesopotamia always contained a ziggurat.

Second, there were no local supplies of stone, so architecture in the manner of the Egyptian pyramids, tombs, and temples was out of the question. Mud brick, sometimes reinforced by timber, was the basic material for all Mesopotamian buildings, as it had been for the ephemeral dwellings of the Egyptians. Although Mesopotamian structures were sometimes faced with fired brick, most of them survive only in ground plan or in foundations, when these could be built of imported stone. Even sculpture, forced to rely on materials brought from a distance, was limited to modest dimensions, save for the ambitious palace decorations of the Assyrians, who lived in a northern region closer to a supply of stone. Under such circumstances neither architecture nor sculpture could be expected to function on the exalted level that it did in Egyptian art, with its endless sources of material and its continuous artistic tradition—but Mesopotamia did achieve some brilliant creations of its own.

Third, probably because of the extremes of Mesopotamian climate and the violence of Mesopotamian history, no wall paintings survive in condition remotely comparable to those of Egypt.

Sumer (c. 3500–2340 B.C.)

The earliest preserved ziggurat was built in the land of Sumer at Uruk (biblical Erech, modern Warka) on the banks of the Euphrates in southern Mesopotamia between 3500 and 3000 B.C. and was dedicated to the sky-god Anu (figs. 4–1, 4–2). It is older than any known Egyptian monument. The building owes its partial preservation to having been enclosed in a far later Hellenistic sanctuary. The mound was so oriented as to direct its corners toward the four points of the compass and was sheathed by sloping brick walls so as to form a gigantic oblong platform, standing some forty feet above the level of the surrounding plain. On this terrace stood a small whitewashed brick temple (nicknamed the White Temple), only the lower portions of which remain. Curiously enough, the entrances do not face the steep stairway ascending the mound, and the altar is tucked into a corner of the interior, possibly for protection from wind. The buttressed walls were reinforced by timber, but it is not known just how the building was roofed. Since the Sumerian name for such temples means "waiting room," the enclosure may well have provided a setting in which the company of worshipers could await the descent of the deity.

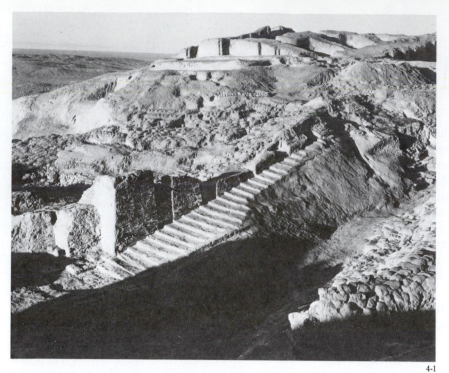

4-1. The White Temple on its ziggurat, Uruk (present-day Warka), Iraq. c. 3500–3000 B.C.

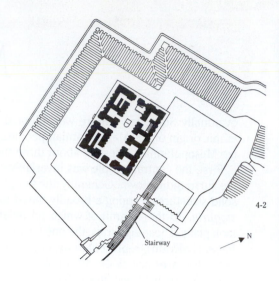

4-2. Plan of the White Temple on its ziggurat, Uruk (after H. Frankfort)

4-3. Reconstructed view of the Ziggurat, Ur (after H. Frankfort)

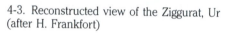

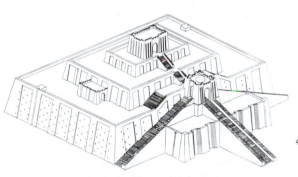

4-4. Ziggurat, Ur (present-day El Muqeiyar), Iraq. c. 2100 B.C.

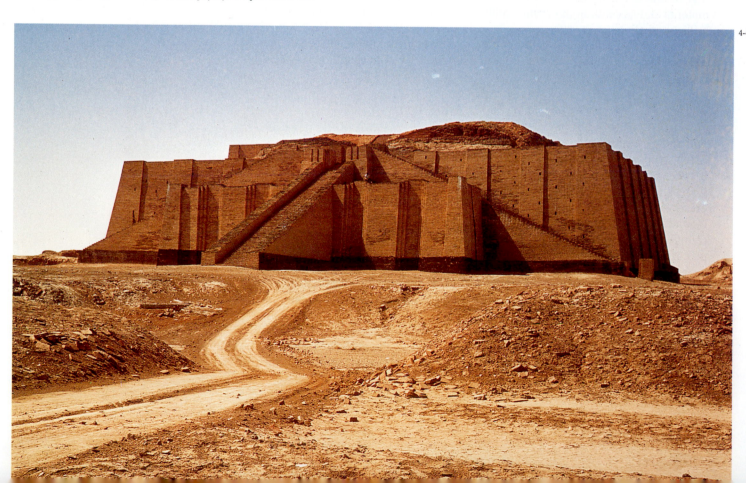

The better preserved and considerably larger ziggurat at Ur (fig. 4–4), near the confluence of the Tigris and the Euphrates, was built much later, during the so-called Neo-Sumerian period (see pages 107–8), when the Sumerians temporarily regained power after the collapse of the Akkadian Empire, about 2100 B.C. Three stairways, each of a hundred steps, converge at the top of the first platform; others ascended a second and then a third level, on which stood the temple (fig. 4–3). The remaining masses of brickwork, recently somewhat restored, dominate the plain for many miles. The original monument, perhaps planted with trees and other vegetation, must have made a majestic setting for religious ceremonials. The Iraqi government built an airport adjacent to the ziggurat, but great care in Allied bombing during the 1991 Gulf War seems to have preserved it from major damage.

Two pieces of sculpture from Uruk, dating from the period of the White Temple, give us some insight into the character of these ceremonies. A superb alabaster vase (fig. 4–5) some three feet in height was probably intended to hold libations in honor of E-anna, the goddess of fertility and love. The cylindrical surface of the vase, only slightly swelling toward the top, is divided into four bands of low relief celebrating her cult. In the lowest, date palms alternate with stalks of barley, in the next ewes with rams. The third tier shows naked worshipers bringing baskets of fruit and other offerings, and the fourth the crowned goddess receiving a worshiper whose basket is brimming with fruit. (Nakedness survives in the Christian tradition that all will be naked before God at the Last Judgment; see fig. 14–11.) Some of the strength of the composition derives from the alternation, from one level to the next, of the directions in which the bands of figures are moving; some derives from the sturdy proportions and simple carving of the stocky figures. Their representation is governed by conventions not unlike those of Egyptian art: the torso seen in three-quarters view, the legs and heads in profile.

E-anna herself may be the subject of the beautiful *Female Head* (fig. 4–6) carved from white marble. It was probably intended to surmount a wooden statue. Originally, the eyes were filled with colored material, most likely shell and lapis lazuli held in by bitumen, which would have made the magical stare even more

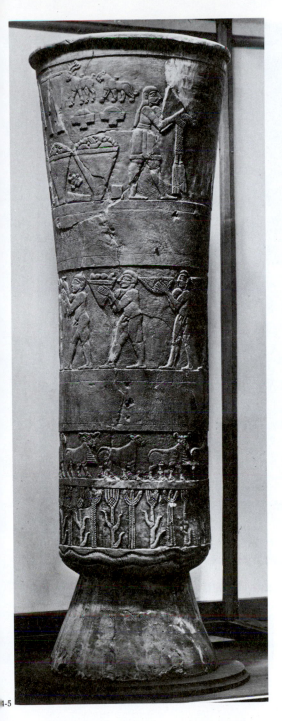

4-5. Sculptured vase, from Uruk, c. 3500–3000 B.C. Alabaster, height 36″ (91 cm). Iraq Museum, Baghdad

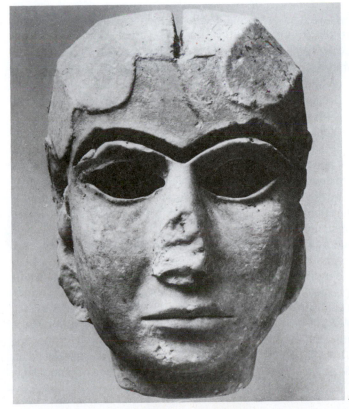

4-6. *Female Head*, from Uruk. c. 3500–3000 B.C. White marble, height approx. 8″ (20 cm). Iraq Museum, Baghdad

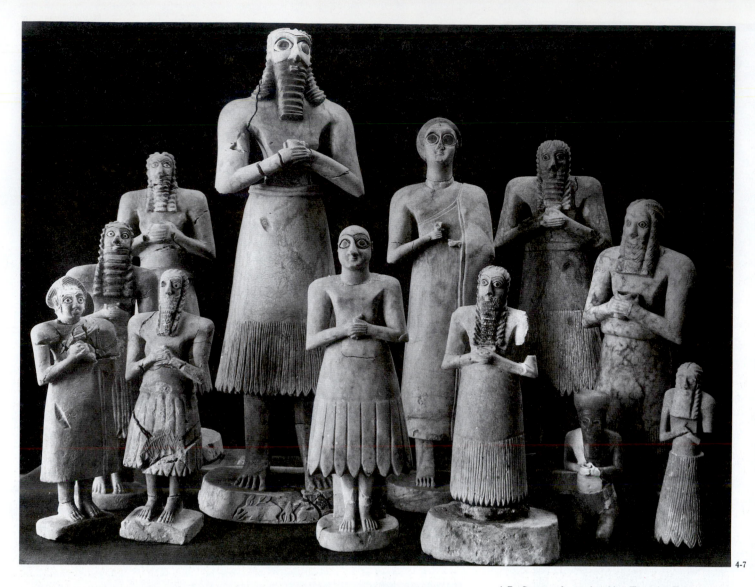

4-7. Statues from the Abu Temple, Eshnunna (present-day Tell Asmar), Iraq. c. 2700–2500 B.C. Marble with shell and black limestone inlay, height of tallest figure approx. 30″ (76.2 cm). Iraq Museum, Baghdad, and The Oriental Institute, University of Chicago

intense. The eyebrows were probably inlaid with bitumen and the hair plated with gold. Even in its present stripped condition, the contrast between the enormous eyes and the sensitively modeled surfaces of the delicate mouth and chin renders the head unforgettable. A much later assemblage of small marble statues (fig. 4–7) from the sanctuary of Abu, god of vegetation, at Tell Asmar shows the hypnotic effect of these great, staring eyes in Sumerian religious sculpture when the shell and lapis lazuli inlays (in this case, shell and black limestone) are still preserved. Grouped before the altar, the statues seem to be solemnly awaiting the divine presence. It is thought that the largest figures represent the god, whose emblem is inscribed on its base, and his spouse, but more probably they are meant to be the king and queen, since their hands are presenting offerings like those of some of the smaller figures. Their cylindrical shape, characteristic of Mesopotamian figures, is far removed from the cubic mass of Egyptian statues, which preserve the shape of the original block of stone.

Some of the splendor of a Sumerian court can be imagined from the gorgeous harp found in the tomb of Puabi, queen of Ur. The strings and wooden portions have been restored, but the gold-covered posts and a bull's-head ornament, with a human beard of lapis lazuli, are original; so are the four narrative scenes on the sound box, inlaid in gold, lapis lazuli, and shell (fig. 4–8). The uppermost scene on the sound box, showing a naked man wrestling two bearded bulls, all of whom stare out at us vacantly, and the lowest, a scorpion-man attended by a goat bearing libation cups, come from the epic of Gilgamesh, the half-historical, half-legendary hero. But the two incidents between are, alas, not so easy to trace. In one a table heaped with a boar's head and a sheep's head and leg is carried by a solicitous wolf with a carving knife tucked into its belt, followed by a lion bearing a wine jug and cup; in the other a donkey plays a bull-harp while a bear beats time and a jackal brandishes a rattle and beats a drum. Possibly these human-handed beasts come from some Sumerian legend yet unknown, but they suggest with perhaps illusory ease the tradition of animal fables known to us in every era from the days of Aesop to those of *Peter Rabbit*.

That such representations may contain a far deeper meaning than we tend to give them is suggested by the splendid goat, made of wood overlaid with gold and lapis lazuli, also found in the royal graves at Ur (fig. 4–9). We know from contemporary representations on the stone seals used to imprint clay tablets that this is the kind of offering stand customarily set before the male fertility god Tammuz. The he-goat, proverbial symbol of masculinity, stands proudly erect before a gold tree, forelegs bent, eyes glaring outward with great intensity. The artist has executed every lock and every leaf with crispness and elegance. Descendants of such symbolic animals persist in heraldry even into modern times and are still endowed with allegorical significance.

4-8. Inlay panel from the sound box of a harp, from Ur. c. 2600 B.C. Gold, lapis lazuli, shell, and bitumen, 12¼ × 4½″ (31.1 × 11.4 cm). The University Museum, University of Pennsylvania, Philadelphia

4-9. *He-Goat and Tree,* offering stand from Ur. c. 2600 B.C. Wood overlaid with gold and lapis lazuli, height 20″ (50.8 cm). The University Museum, University of Pennsylvania, Philadelphia

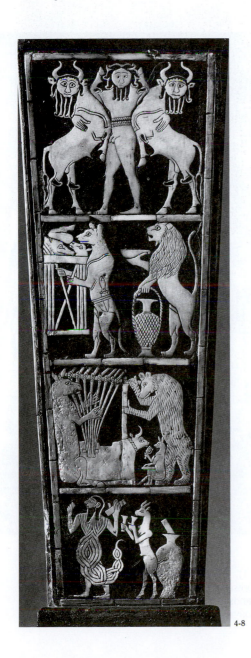

4-8

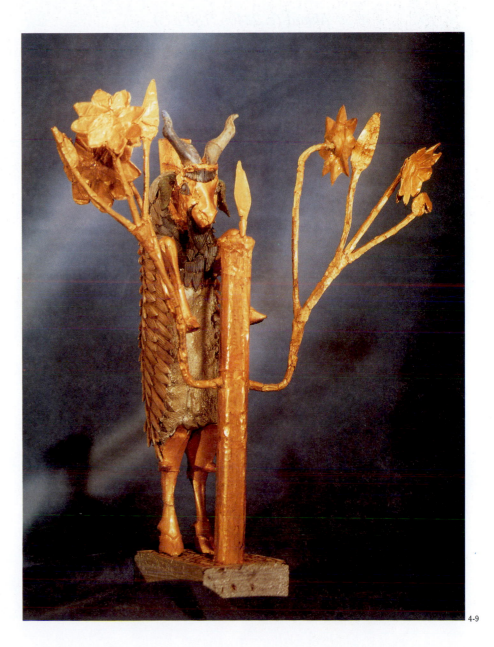

4-9

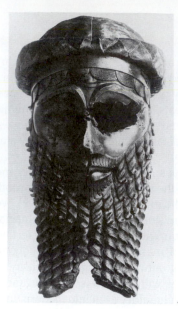

4-10. *Head of an Akkadian Ruler,* from Nineveh
(present-day Kuyunjik), Iraq. c. 2300–2200 B.C.
Bronze, height 14⅜″ (36.5 cm). Iraq Museum,
Baghdad

4-10

Akkad (c. 2340–2180 B.C.)

Endemic warfare between the Sumerian city-states was to be followed by something far worse, the virtual collapse of the Sumerian social order under the weight
of entirely new conceptions of divine monarchy, like that of Old Kingdom Egypt but
maintained wholly by force of arms. A Semitic ruler, Sargon I, usurped the throne of
Kish and then ruled for fifty-six years from neighboring Akkad, whose site has not
yet been discovered. Sargon founded a dynasty of five kings who aspired to world
conquest and in fact controlled the Middle East from the Mediterranean Sea to the
Persian Gulf. The magnificent bronze *Head of an Akkadian Ruler* (fig. 4–10) is so
great a work of art that it makes us regret that so little survives from the days of
these Akkadian monarchs except for the literary texts in which their power and
majesty were extolled. Even in the absence of the eyes, gouged out long ago, the
head is overwhelming. The hair, braided and bound to form a kind of diadem, is
gathered in a chignon on the neck. The face is half hidden in a beard whose two
superimposed tiers of curls, each made up of spirals moving in the opposite
direction to those in the tier below, exert an almost dizzying effect on the beholder
by their blend of formal grandeur and linear delicacy. The great, flaring eyebrows
plunge in convergence upon an aquiline nose below which the sensual lips are held
quietly in a superb double curve of arrogant power not to be approached again
until Greek and Roman sculpture. The identity of this monarch is unknown, but it is
hard to believe that the great Sargon looked much different.

The only other work of art of first importance remaining from Akkadian rule also
exudes an emotional violence that makes Sumerian art look bland in contrast. The
sandstone *Stela of King Naram Sin* (fig. 4–11), Sargon's grandson, shows him
protected by the luminaries of heaven and about to dispatch the last of his enemies.
The king stands proudly beside the sacred mountain, mace in hand. One crumpled
enemy attempts in agony to pluck the spear from his throat, another pleads for his
life, two others hang over the edge of a cliff down which still another falls headlong.
Meanwhile, up the ascending levels of the landscape stride the victorious soldiers
of the king. The tremendous drama of this relief, the strength of the projection of
the sculptural figures, and the freedom with which they move at various heights
within the landscape space give the stele a unique position in Mesopotamian art.

Akkad, which lived by the sword, perished by it as well. A powerful people called
the Guti invaded Mesopotamia from the mountainous regions to the northeast,
conquered the Akkadian Empire, and destroyed its capital, only to vanish into
history without positive achievements. Ironically, the proud *Stela of King Naram Sin*
was carried off as booty.

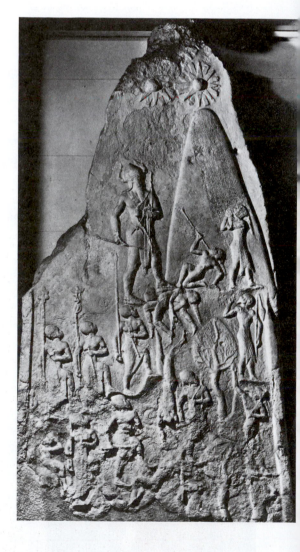

4-11. *Stela of King Naram Sin,* from Susa
(present-day Shush), Iran. c. 2300–2200 B.C.
Sandstone, height 6′6″ (1.98 m). Musée du
Louvre, Paris

Neo-Sumer and Babylon (c. 2125–1750 B.C.); the Hittites (c. 1640–1200 B.C.)

Only the city-state of Lagash mysteriously escaped the general devastation wrought by the Guti, and its ruler, Gudea, interpreted this deliverance as a sign of divine favor. In gratitude he dedicated a number of votive statues of himself, all carved either from diorite or from dolerite, imported stones of great hardness, as gifts to temples in his small realm. All the Gudea statues radiate a sense of calm, even of wisdom. Holding a plan of a building on his lap, Gudea sits quietly with hands folded (fig. 4–12). Only the tension of the toes and the arm muscles betrays his inner feelings kept in check by control of the will. The surviving heads (fig. 4–13), often crowned with what appears to be a lambskin cap, show this same beautiful composure, expressed artistically in the broad curves of the brows and the smooth volumes of the cheeks and chin, handled with firmness and accuracy. While less dramatic than the *Head of an Akkadian Ruler,* the modest Gudea portraits achieve real nobility of form and content.

Remarkably enough, Gudea was able to win control by peaceful means over a considerable region of the former Akkadian Empire. In 2111, Urnammu, governor of Ur, usurped the monarchy of Sumer and Akkad and built the great ziggurat at Ur (see fig. 4–4). Little else of artistic merit survives from his reign, after which

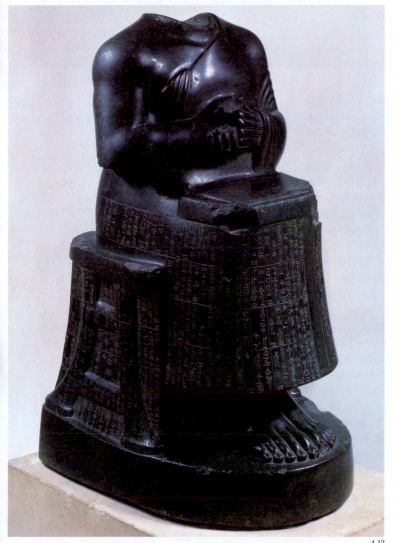

4-12. Seated statue of Gudea with architectural plan, from Lagash (present-day Tello). c. 2150 B.C. Diorite, height 29″ (74 cm). Musée du Louvre, Paris

4-12

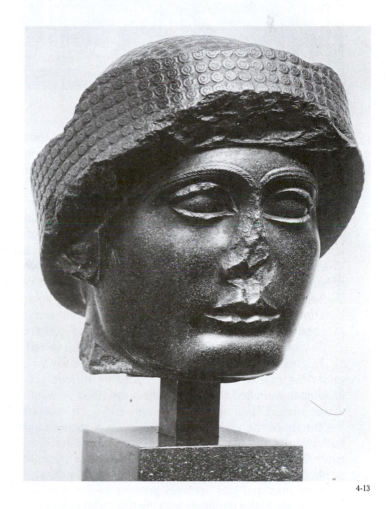

4-13

4-13. *Head of Gudea,* from Lagash. c. 2150 B.C. Diorite, height 9″ (23 cm). Courtesy, Museum of Fine Arts, Boston

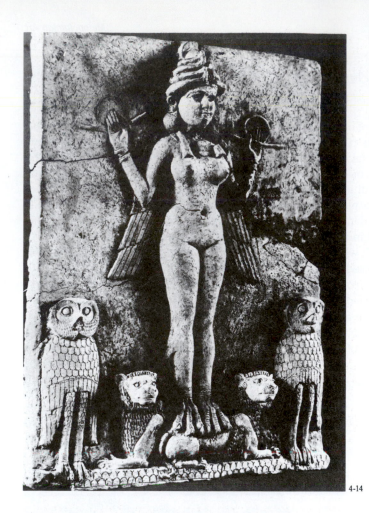

4-14

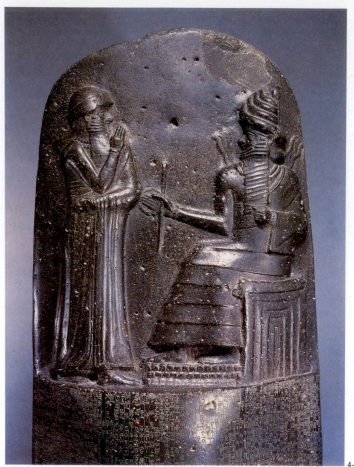

4-15

Mesopotamia reverted to its former chaotic pattern of conflicting city-states. From the brief Isin-Larsa period (2025–1763 B.C.), so called from the ascendancy of the cities bearing these names, dates a terra-cotta relief of extraordinary power and beauty, the first voluptuous female nude known from antiquity (fig. 4–14). This creature, at once alluring and frightening, represents the goddess of death, the baleful Lilith, possibly the screech owl of Isaiah 34:14. Adorned only with gigantic earrings and the characteristic four-tiered headdress of a deity, she smilingly upholds, behind her head, a looped cord—either the symbol of human life or the instrument with which she brings it to an end. Her great wings are partially spread behind her full-breasted, round-hipped body. Instead of feet she has terrible feathered talons; flanked by staring owls, she perches upon the rumps of two lions back-to-back. Originally, her body was painted red, one owl black and the other red, and the manes of the lions black. The setting is established by the pattern of scales along the base, a conventionalization of the sacred mountain.

The great king Hammurabi (1792–1750 B.C.) briefly brought all of Mesopotamia under the rule of Babylon and reduced its various and often conflicting legal systems to a unified code; this code is inscribed on a tall stela of black basalt at whose summit Hammurabi, in a simple and noble relief (fig. 4–15), stands before the throne of the god Shamash, again on a sacred mountain indicated by the customary scale pattern. Wearing the same four-tiered headdress as Lilith and with triple flames emerging from his shoulders, this magnificent being extends his symbols of power, a rod and a ring. At first sight prosaic, this elemental colloquy between man and god becomes grander as one watches; like Moses on Mount Sinai, the king talks familiarly with the deity who sanctifies his laws. The cylindrical figures typical of early Mesopotamian art are conventionalized in pose, as indeed they are throughout pre-Greek art, so that the torso is shown frontally while the hips and legs, insofar as they can be seen within the enveloping drapery, are

4-14. *The Goddess Lilith.* c. 2025–1763 B.C. Terra-cotta relief, height 19⅝″ (50 cm). Collection Colonel Norman Colville, United Kingdom

4-15. Upper portion of the stela inscribed with the Law Code of Hammurabi. c. 1792–1750 B.C. Basalt, height of relief 28″ (71.1 cm); height of stela 7′ (2.13 m). Musée du Louvre, Paris

4-16. The Lion Gate, Boğazköy, Turkey. Hittite, c. 1400 B.C.

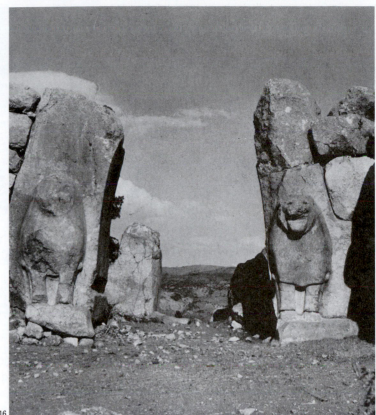

4-16

depicted in profile. For the first time, however, the eyes are not frontal; the gaze between man and god is unswerving.

About 1595 B.C., the Babylonian kingdom was conquered by the Hittites, a people from Anatolia. The sturdy, virile art of the Hittites is seldom of a quality to compete with the best of Mesopotamian art, but the rude and massive lions (c. 1400 B.C.) that flank the entrance to the gigantic stone walls of the Hittite citadel near modern Boğazköy (fig. 4–16) are the ancestors of the winged beasts that guard the portals of the palaces of the Assyrian kings. It is interesting that after the death of Tutankhamen, the Hittites were so powerful in the Middle East that Ankhesenamen, the distraught widow of the young pharaoh, besought the Hittite king Suppiluliuma I for the hand of one of his sons in marriage as protection.

Assyria (c. 1000–612 B.C.)

In the welter of warring peoples—including the Elamites, Kassites, and Mitannians—who disputed with each other for the succession to Babylonian and Hittite power, a single warlike nation called the Assyrians, after their original home at Ashur on the Tigris River in northern Mesopotamia, was both skillful and ruthless enough to gain eventual ascendancy over the entire region. In fact, for a considerable period their power extended to the west over Syria, the Sinai Peninsula, and into Lower Egypt, where they destroyed Memphis, and to the north into the mountains of Armenia. The Assyrians gloried in what from their voluminous historical records and their art seems to have been very nearly continuous warfare, mercilessly destroying populations and cities before they in turn were vanquished and their own cities razed to the ground.

THE PALACE OF SARGON II   Only one of the great Assyrian royal residences is known in some detail, the eighth-century palace of King Sargon II at Dur Sharrukin, the modern Khorsabad, which has been systematically excavated (fig. 4–17). This massive structure was built into the perimeter of a citadel some five hundred feet square, which was in turn incorporated into the city wall. The entire complex

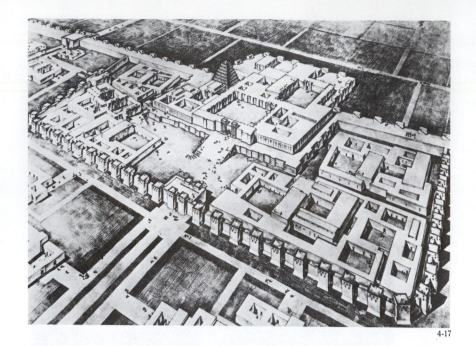

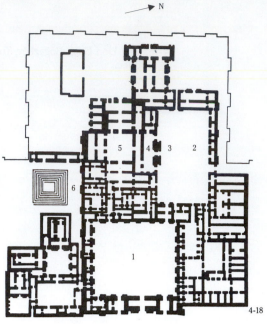

4-18

was laid out as symmetrically as possible (fig. 4–18). Above a network of courtyards on either side surrounded by administrative buildings, barracks, and warehouses rose a platform the height of the city wall. On this eminence stood the palace proper, protruding from the wall into the surrounding plain, so that the king and the court could survey the countryside from its ramparts. It was defended by its own towers. The entire complex was dominated by a lofty ziggurat, descendant of those at Uruk and at Ur (see figs. 4–1, 4–4) and doubtless intended for a similar purpose. It was, however, much more carefully formalized. Its successive stages—there may have been seven of these, each painted a different color—were not separate platforms; the structure was ascended counterclockwise by a continuous ramp, a square spiral as it were, so that worshipers always had the paneled wall on their left while on their right they looked out over ever-widening views of the plain.

Like all Mesopotamian buildings, the palace of Sargon II was mostly built of mud brick (although certain crucial portions were faced by baked and glazed brick), which accounts for the ease of its demolition by the next wave of invaders.

4-17. Reconstructed view of the Citadel of King Sargon II, Dur Sharrukin (present-day Khorsabad), Iraq (after Charles Altman). c. 742–706 B.C.

4-18. Plan of the Palace in the Citadel of King Sargon II, Dur Sharrukin 1. Central courtyard, accessible from Citadel 2. Courtyard of the Ambassadors, lined with relief sculpture 3. Gate shown in fig. 4-19 4. Throne room, lined with mural paintings 5. Royal apartments 6. Ziggurat

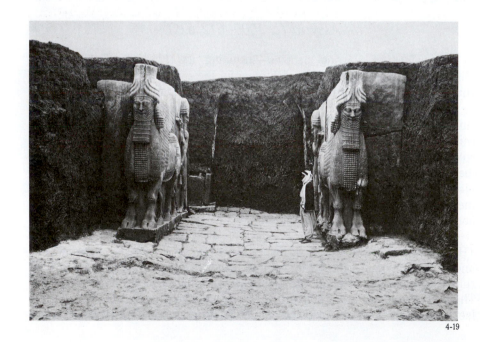

4-19. Gate, Palace of King Sargon II, Dur Sharrukin (during excavation)

Considerable use seems to have been made of arches and barrel vaults. Luckily, the Assyrians had access to stone for sculpture, and they were able to flank the entrances to the brightly painted throne room with colossal limestone guardians, in the tradition of the Hittite lions (see fig. 4–16). Two of these majestic creatures are shown still in place in fig. 4–19. They were monstrous beings with the bodies of bulls (one recalls the royal bulls of archaic Egyptian palettes, see fig. 3–3), grand, diagonally elevated wings, and human heads with long curly beards and many-tiered divine headdresses, doubtless symbols of the supernatural powers of the king. Built into the gates and visible only from two sides, they were really a kind of relief sculpture rather than statues in the round. So that the viewer might see four legs from any point of view the sculptors generously gave these creatures five.

THE PALACES OF NIMRUD AND NINEVEH   Emissaries of friendly rulers could approach the Assyrian monarch only through a succession of halls lined with continuous wall reliefs intended to overawe the visitors not only with the king's intimacy with the gods but also with his military exploits and personal courage. These historical reliefs are ancestors of the lengthy political narratives of Roman imperial sculpture (see figs. 9–47, 9–48). In strips often superimposed in the manner of Egyptian tomb reliefs, the Assyrians can be seen fighting battles that they always win and cheerfully burning cities, dismantling the fortifications, and massacring the inhabitants. The reliefs were drawn on the surface of alabaster slabs and the background was then cut away to give just a slight projection, as in Egyptian relief. Yet the contours are so bold and so strongly ornamentalized and the proportions are so chunky that they convey an impression of massive volume instead of Egyptian delicacy and elegance. The innumerable scenes of unrelieved mayhem can become monotonous, especially because the quality of the reliefs, which were apparently turned out at some speed, is not uniformly high. But there were great sculptors in the group who could find in their narrative subjects inspiration for an epic breadth of vision entirely new in art. Sometimes the scenes have an unconscious humor, as in *Elamite Fugitives Crossing a River* (fig. 4–20), from the palace of Ashurnasirpal II at Nimrud. Two Assyrian bowmen shoot from the bank at two fully clothed Elamites who cling to inflated goatskins and at a third who has to rely entirely on his own strength to stay afloat as they swim toward the walls of their little city, defended by Elamite warriors on the tops of the towers. In the manner of Egyptian reliefs and paintings, the swimmers have two left hands. The undulating shapes of the swimmers and the ornamentalized trees on the bank create the strong and effective pattern characteristic of the best Assyrian reliefs.

4-20. *Elamite Fugitives Crossing a River*, from the Palace of King Ashurnasirpal II, Nimrud (ancient Kalakh), Iraq. c. 883–859 B.C. Alabaster relief, height approx. 39″ (99 cm). British Museum, London

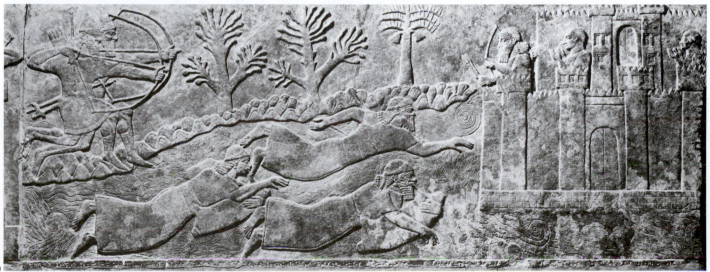

4-20

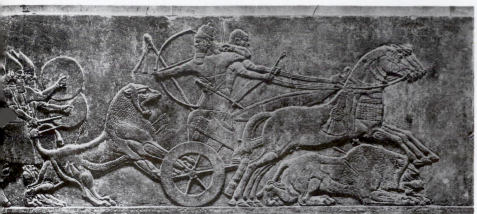
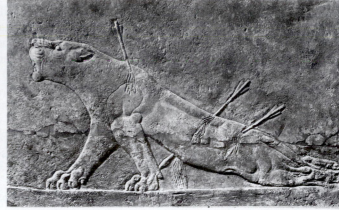

4-21 4-22

Strangely enough, while human expressions remain impassive under any conditions, those of animals are represented with a depth of understanding that turns the conflicts between men and beasts into the grandest action scenes in Mesopotamian art—in fact, into some of the most powerful in the entire history of art. Lions were released from their cages, after having been goaded into fury, so that the king could display his strength and courage by shooting down the maddened beasts from his chariot. The best sculptors seem to have been employed for these heroic reliefs, which unleash an astonishing explosion of forces—the swift flight of the horses, the resolute power of the monarch, the snarling rage of the tormented beasts. Not since predynastic Egypt have the muscles of humans and animals been shown swelling with such tremendous tension as in the relief depicting Ashurnasirpal engaged in his cruel sport (fig. 4–21). Almost unbearable in its tragic intensity is the detail of the *Dying Lioness* from the palace of Ashurbanipal at Nineveh (fig. 4–22). Pierced by three arrows, bleeding profusely, and howling in impotent defeat, the poor beast drags her paralyzed hindquarters desperately along. After these horrors the relief of a flock of gazelles from the same palace (fig. 4–23) is totally unexpected in its airy

4-21. *King Ashurnasirpal II Killing Lions,* from the Palace of King Ashurnasirpal II, Nimrud. c. 883–859 B.C. Alabaster relief, 39 × 100″ (99.1 × 254 cm). British Museum, London

4-22. *Dying Lioness* (detail of *The Great Lion Hunt*), from the Palace of King Ashurbanipal, Nineveh. c. 668–627 B.C. Alabaster relief, height 13¾″ (35 cm). British Museum, London

4-23. *Herd of Fleeing Gazelles,* detail of an alabaster relief from the Palace of King Ashurbanipal, Nineveh. c. 668–627 B.C. Height 20⅞″ (53 cm). British Museum, London

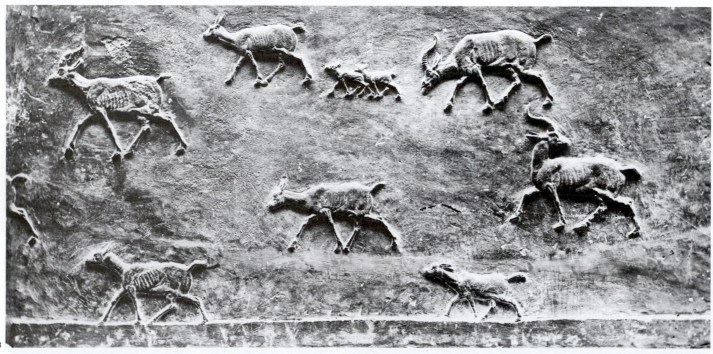

4-23

grace. One turns his head in fear, the others plod along, the little ones struggling to keep up, as they flee their archenemy, man. Equally surprising is the device of scattering the animals lightly about the surface of the slab to suggest open space.

Neo-Babylonia (605–539 B.C.)

The collapse of Assyria in 612 B.C. was brought about by invasions of Scythians from the east and Medes from the north. Order was restored by Nebuchadnezzar II, ruling from Babylon in the south, which had never lost its cultural importance even under Assyrian domination. In the scanty remains of Neo-Babylonian stone sculpture an attempt can be discerned to emulate the style of Sargon I, some seventeen hundred years earlier, but the brief revival of Babylonian glory is best known for its architectural remains. For two hundred years or so Babylon had possessed the Hanging Gardens, one of the wonders of the ancient world, a series of four brick terraces rising above the Euphrates, whose waters were piped up to irrigate a splendid profusion of flowering trees, shrubs, and herbs. Nebuchadnezzar added a splendid palace with a ziggurat, which was the biblical Tower of Babel, and built eight monumental arched gates in the fortified city walls. One gate (fig. 4–24), connected with the inner city by a processional way and dedicated to the goddess Ishtar, was faced with glazed brick. Excavated early in this century, it is installed,

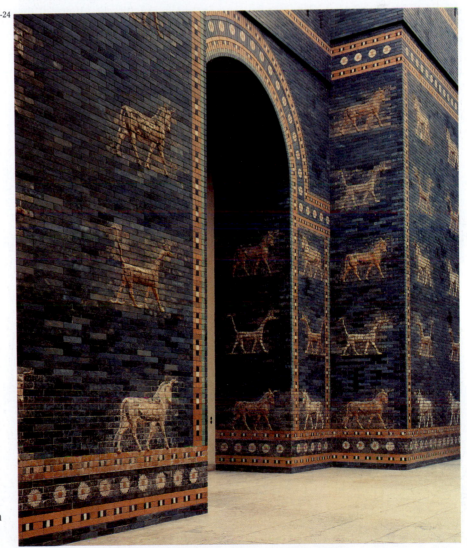

4-24

4-24. The Ishtar Gate (restored), from Babylon, Iraq. c. 575 B.C. Glazed brick. Staatliche Museen zu Berlin—Preussischer Kulturbesitz: Vorderasiatisches Museum

113

with missing portions liberally supplied, in Berlin, the only place in the world where one can gain any idea of the scale and brilliance of the ephemeral brick architecture of ancient Mesopotamia. The clear, bright blue of the background glaze sets off the geometric ornament in white and gold and the widely spaced, stylized bulls and dragons in raised relief. They are composed of many separately molded and glazed bricks and form a happy postlude to the repetitive slaughters of the bloodthirsty Assyrians. Nebuchadnezzar's gorgeous Babylon must have deserved the boastful title he gave it—"navel of the world."

Persia (539–331 B.C.)

We obtain a one-sided account of the Persian Empire from the Greeks, to whom the Persians appeared as a juggernaut threatening to crush the cherished independence of the Greek city-states. The tidy administration of the Persians may have come as a relief to the weary peoples of the Near East. Out of the mountainous regions of what is today Iran, northeast of Mesopotamia, came the nomadic Persians under Cyrus the Great; under his successors Darius I and Xerxes I they conquered an empire that was centered on Mesopotamia but included also Syria, Asia Minor, and Egypt on one side and parts of India on the other. Although they set themselves up as kings of Babylon they styled themselves, and quite rightly, kings of the world. Only the Greeks prevented them from extending their rule into Europe, and the Greeks, under Alexander the Great, eventually brought about their downfall. Their orderly and decent government made cruelties like those of the Assyrians unnecessary. The Persian Empire, more than twice as extensive as any of its predecessors, was divided into provinces called satrapies, administered by governors, or satraps, responsible directly to the king. The capital moved about, but its great palace was at Persepolis, near the edge of the mountains above the Persian Gulf, to the east of Mesopotamia.

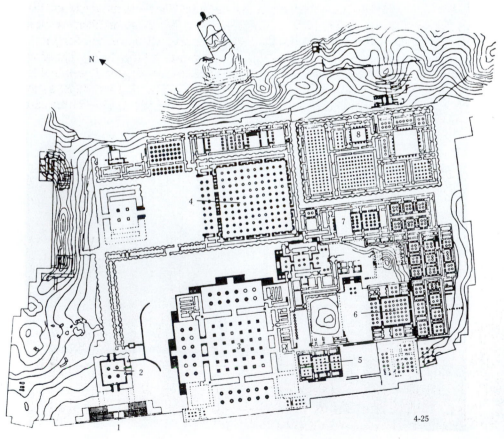

4-25. Plan of the Palace Complex of Darius and Xerxes, Persepolis, Iran 1. Great entrance stairway 2. Gatehouse of Xerxes 3. Apadana (Audience Hall) of Darius and Xerxes 4. Hundred-Column Hall (Throne Hall of Xerxes) 5. Tachara (Palace) of Darius 6. Palace, probably rebuilt by Artaxerxes III 7. Hadish (Palace) of Xerxes 8. Tripylon (Council Hall)

4-26. Apadana (Audience Hall), Palace Complex of Darius and Xerxes, Persepolis. c. 500 B.C.

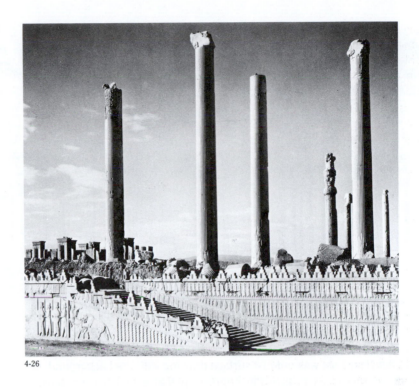

4-26

4-27. *Darius and Xerxes Giving Audience.* c. 490 B.C. Limestone relief, height 8′4″ (2.54 m). Palace Complex of Darius and Xerxes, Persepolis

There Darius commenced his residence, continued and completed by his son Xerxes about 500 B.C.; it was an orderly and systematic complex of buildings and courts surrounded by the inevitable, and now-vanished, mud-brick wall (fig. 4–25). Persian art, perhaps not as imaginative as some that preceded it, included many elements borrowed from the subject peoples; in fact, many of the artisans were Babylonians, and others were Greeks from Asia Minor. The Persians worshiped the god of light, Ahuramazda, at outdoor fire altars for which no architecture was needed, so there were no ziggurats. But the palace was built, like that of Sargon II, on a huge platform, this time of stone, quite well preserved (fig. 4–26). The king had no need to terrify his visitors, so the relief sculpture showed interminable superimposed rows of neatly uniformed bodyguards mounting the steps, as in reality they did, and the great king himself giving audience (fig. 4–27). For the first

4-27

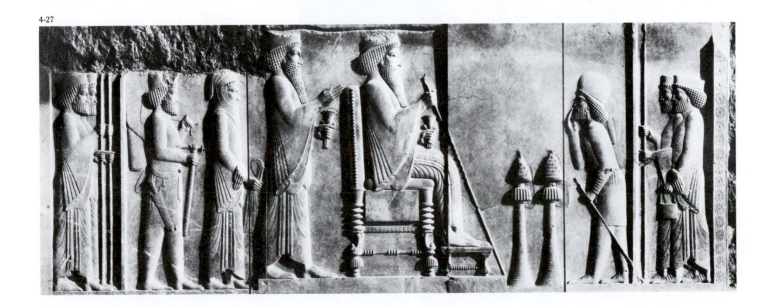

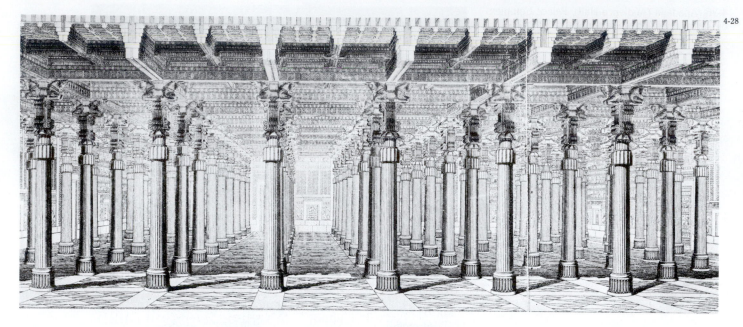

4-28. Hundred-Column Hall (Throne Hall of Xerxes), Palace Complex of Darius and Xerxes, Persepolis (reconstruction by C. Chipiez). c. 500 B.C.

time, relief in the Near East was not just surface drawing with the background cut away, but was so carved as to give the impression that actual figures, having cylindrical volume, move on a shallow stage. This idea was derived from Greek art, and the sculptors may have been Ionian Greeks. The statue-like figures are shown in true profile, although the eyes are still frontal. The prim rows of curls in hair and beard are obviously derived from Akkadian and Assyrian forebears, but the drap-

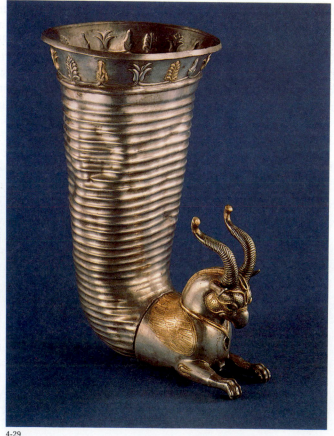

4-29

4-29. Rhyton, from the Oxus Treasury, Armenia. Silver, height 10″ (25 cm). c. 500–400 B.C. British Museum, London

4-30. Painted beaker, from Susa. c. 5000–4000 B.C. Height 11¼" (28.5 cm). Musée du Louvre, Paris

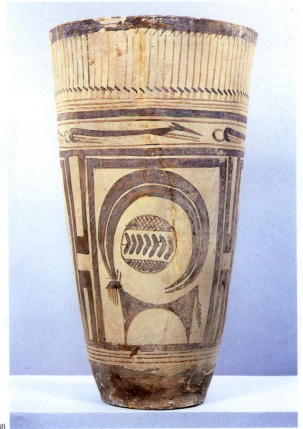

4-30

ery folds now have edges that ripple in long, descending cataracts as in Archaic Greek sculpture (see fig. 7–10), and the garments clearly show underlying limbs, as in Old Kingdom Egyptian sculpture (see fig. 3–15). In a civilization such as that of the Persians, individualization was not encouraged, but there is a crisp, fresh elegance of drawing and carving that gives Persian decorative sculpture great distinction. It was doubtless even more striking with its original brilliant colors and gilding.

Persian rooms were characteristically square, and the great hall of Xerxes must have been one of the most impressive in the ancient world (fig. 4–28). Its hundred stone columns, each forty feet high (several are still standing) and brightly painted, were delicately fluted and terminated in paired bulls that acted as brackets and helped to support the gigantic beams of imported wood, also painted. No such interior had, of course, existed in the Mesopotamian world, where columns were unknown. Quite possibly the Persians drew their idea partly from the columned porticoes of Ionian Greek temples, partly from the columned temple halls of the Egyptians. The notion of a forest of columns, with no dominant axis in any direction, may have been the origin of the typical plan of many Islamic mosques several centuries later (see figs. 11–6, 11–10).

The gold and silver rhytons or libation vessels (fig. 4–29), with their hybrid animal forms, show the Persian love of elegance, grace, and rational organization of elements. The linear rhythms of the animals themselves still suggest those of prehistoric pottery from Susa, not far from Persepolis, three millennia earlier (fig. 4–30), not to speak of many characteristic elements of later Mesopotamian cultures, but the alternating palmette and floral ornament on the upper border is already characteristically Greek. Sadly enough, it is upon the Greeks that the responsibility rests for the destruction of the palace, burned by Alexander after a long and violent banquet.

TIME LINE II

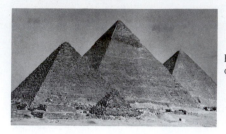

Pyramids of Giza

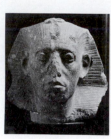

Sesostris III

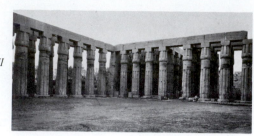

Court of Amonhotep III, Temple of Luxor

HISTORY	CULTURE
5000 B.C. Sumerians settle in Mesopotamia	
	Pictographic writing, Sumer, c. 3500
	Wheeled carts, Sumer, c. 3500–3000
	Sailboats, Egypt, after 3500
3000 Upper and Lower Egypt united, c. 3100	Potter's wheel, Sumer, c. 3250
Protodynastic period, Sumer, c. 3000–2340	Hieroglyphic writing, Egypt, c. 3000
	Cuneiform writing, Sumer, c. 2900
	First bronze tools and weapons, Sumer
First Intermediate Period, Egypt, 2155–2040	Divine kingship of pharaoh, Egypt
Dynasty III of Ur	Theocratic socialism, Sumer
Middle Kingdom, Egypt, c. 2040–1785	
2000	Bronze tools and weapons, Egypt
1800 B.C. Hammurabi brings Mesopotamia under	Mathematics and astronomy flourish in Babylon
Babylonian rule, 1792–1750	Code of Hammurabi, c. 1760
Hyksos invade and control Upper Egypt,	Hyksos bring horses and wheeled vehicles to Egypt
c. 1650–1550	Hittites introduce iron tools and weapons
Hittites conquer Babylon	
Expulsion of Hyksos, expansion of Egyptian	
1400 Empire, 1550–1070, especially under	Monotheism of Akhenaten, temples of Amon-Ra
Amenhotep I, Hatshepsut, Amenhotep III, Seti I,	closed, c. 1360; Tutankhamen restores old
Ramses II	religion
Assyrian Empire, 1000–612	
600 Nebuchadnezzar II of Babylon, r. 604–539,	Hebrews accept monotheism
Neo-Babylonian period	
Persian Empire founded by Cyrus the Great,	Zoroaster (born c. 628)
r. 559–529	

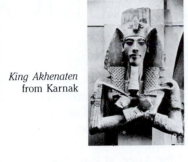

King Akhenaten
from Karnak

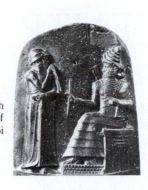

Stele with
Code of
Hammurabi

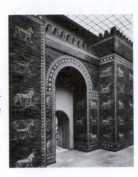

Ishtar
Gate

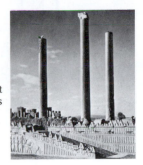

Palace at
Persepolis

PAINTING, SCULPTURE, ARCHITECTURE

Painted beaker from Susa

Ziggurat, White Temple, and sculptured head and vase, Uruk
Wall painting from Hierakonpolis
Palette of King Narmer

Step-pyramid, Funerary Complex, and statue of *King Zoser*
Statues from Abu Temple at Eshnunna (Tell Asmar)
Pyramids, Valley Temples, and Great Sphinx, Giza
Sculpture portraits of *Akkadian Ruler* and *Gudea*
Ziggurat at Ur

Head of *Sesostris III; Princess Sennuwy*
Stela with the Code of Hammurabi

Funerary Temple of Queen Hatshepsut

Paintings from tombs of Nebamun and Sen-nedjem, Thebes
Lion Gate at Boğazköy
Temple of Amon-Mut-Khonsu, Luxor
King Akhenaten; Queen Nefertiti
Reliefs, Palace of Ashurnasirpal II, Nimrud
Ishtar Gate, Babylon

Palace of Darius and Xerxes at Persepolis

PARALLEL SOCIETIES

5000 B.C.

Sumerian
Predynastic Egyptian
Old Kingdom in Egypt

3000

Akkadian
Neo-Sumerian
Cycladic
Middle Kingdom in Egypt   2000
Babylonian   1800 B.C.
Minoan

Mycenean
Empire or New Kingdom in   1400
   Egypt

Hittite

Assyrian
Neo-Babylonian
Archaic Greek   600
Persian
Etruscan

CHAPTER FIVE

IN MEXICO, CENTRAL AMERICA

Those cultures that flourished in what is known as Mesoamerica (central and southeastern Mexico, Guatemala, Belize, and Honduras) and in the northern reaches of the Andes Mountains and parallel coastlands in South America (Columbia, Ecuador, Peru, and Bolivia) before the arrival of the Europeans in the sixteenth century are certainly to be counted among the great civilizations of the ancient world. In most respects it can be said that the Maya and the Aztec, at least, had reached a stage of development roughly comparable to that of ancient Mesopotamia, and so had the Inca, save only for their lack of writing. These pre-Columbian civilizations run parallel in time with the Western European cultures of Greece, Rome, and the Middle Ages, with which they had not the remotest contact. In large part classifiable as Neolithic, these civilizations were created by peoples related to the North American Indians, but who went far beyond them in the creation of organized states—sometimes capable of dominating vast areas—large cities, and masonry architecture. Before the Spaniards tore it down, house by house, in the protracted siege of 1520–21, the lake city of Tenochtitlán, whose ruins are buried under the modern Mexico City, boasted a regular plan with wide, straight streets, a luxurious palace, towering temples, naturalistic sculpture (fig. 5–1), a marketplace the invaders considered superior to anything in either Rome or Constantinople, fine residences united by a network of canals, and causeways connecting it with the mainland. The last Aztec monarch, Motecuhzoma II, whose capital it was, showed the Spaniards with pride his botanical garden, which had a specimen of every identifiable plant that grew in his empire, and his subjects had even developed a system of universal education. Astonishingly enough, although wheels were used for children's toys, none of the pre-Columbian cultures knew the use of the wheel for vehicles, and the Mesoamericans had no draft animals, so all burdens were carried or dragged by humans.

We can speculate that all the early Americans arrived from Asia by way of a land bridge formed at the Bering Strait during the last glacial period and cut off when the glaciers receded and the water level rose. After settling in North, Central, and South America, these peoples must have independently originated much of what Asiatic, North African, and European peoples were simultaneously inventing. Until about 3000 B.C. the early Americans remained technologically in the Old Stone Age. The first mature pottery and clay statuettes can be dated about 1500 B.C. Metals and the techniques of working them were discovered fairly late, about A.D. 1000; most of the great works of architecture and sculpture were executed with stone tools. Obsidian, a kind of volcanic glass, in use today for the finest surgical instruments, was employed for many cutting tools.

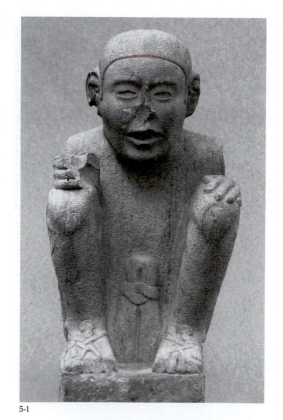

5-1

5-1. *Seated Standard-Bearer,* from Tenochtitlán (Mexico City), Mexico. Aztec culture, 15th century A.D. Sandstone, height 31⅝" (80.3 cm). The Metropolitan Museum of Art, New York. Harris Brisbane Dick Fund, 1962

Mesoamerican Art

The small bands of Spanish adventurers, who with the aid of gunpowder defeated and subjugated the Aztec hegemony and the Inca Empire, but only partially the Mayan states, were astonished at the high level of urban culture they found. Throughout the kaleidoscopic and constantly shifting history of the city-states and principalities of the region, monumental architecture was founded on measure and rule, carried out with stretched cord, right angle, level, and plumb line, and enriched by monumental sculpture and painting. Archaeologists have applied the term *Classic* to characterize the period of highest development of Mesoamerican civilizations, from about A.D. 200 to 900.

Throughout the perhaps three-thousand-year duration of Mesoamerican culture, religion was central, so fused with the social order as to create theocratic states embracing every phase of human existence. The temple complex is therefore at the core of every Mesoamerican town or city. In all periods and societies a farming class brought produce to towns dominated by an aristocratic priestly caste, under rulers who had divine status and powers. Throughout Mesoamerica dressed-masonry architecture, writing, and learning were restricted to these dominant classes; peasants and ordinary city dwellers, who included what must have been a large proportion of construction workers, lived in thatched houses built of rough masonry. In this respect they were comparable to the peasants of Europe up until the Renaissance or even later.

The rites of early American nature worship required hilltops, and when these were unavailable, mounds were built, as in the North American Midwest (see fig. 2–13). Eventually these were formalized into the familiar pyramids that dominate the civic centers of all Mesoamerican cities. Sometimes these contained tombs, but they were universally intended primarily as temples, like the ziggurats of Mesopotamia.

THE OLMEC   The still-mysterious pre-Classic Olmec culture, which flourished on the Gulf Coast of central Mexico from about 1500 B.C. to about A.D. 300, appears to have laid the foundation of the Mesoamerican social organization, including human sacrifice, even of children. Cannibalized human bones have been found at Olmec centers. With the Olmec the masonry-faced temple mound, in one case reaching the height of one hundred feet, and surrounding or intervening court-yards established the characteristic layout of later Mesoamerican urban complexes. The Olmec produced a strikingly naturalistic figure sculpture in the round, including stone images of a lifelike wrestler and a series of colossal heads, now believed to be portraits of rulers, flanking temple sites. An example from San Lorenzo has been provided with a close-fitting helmet, under which the brows are knitted in a frown; the prominent lips are partly open, as if in speech, and the large eyes stare (fig. 5–2). The ten-ton mass of basalt has thus been transformed into the appearance of living flesh with astonishing power and intensity.

TEOTIHUACÁN   The Aztec were aware that they were latecomers to the Mexican highland and that they had had predecessors there in a golden-age era before human sacrifice became "necessary." These earlier peoples, about whom very little is yet known, built cities the most impressive of which was Teotihuacán, whose broad avenue of temples, dating from A.D. 50 to 200, has been excavated; one section of the temple group, the so-called Ciudadela ("citadel") laid out in a rectangle around the central temple of the feathered-serpent god Quetzalcóatl, is illustrated (fig. 5–3). By about the beginning of the Christian era, the mounds at Teotihuacán had reached the form of carefully constructed step-pyramids, ascended by a central steep flight of stairs, and doubtless crowned by temples. The

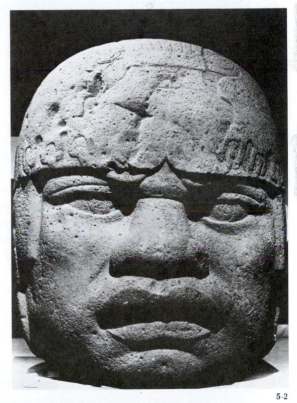

5-2

5-2. Colossal head, from San Lorenzo (Veracruz), Mexico. Olmec culture, c. 1500 B.C.–c. A.D. 300. Basalt, height 70⅞″ (1.8 m). Museo de Antropología, Jalapa, Mexico

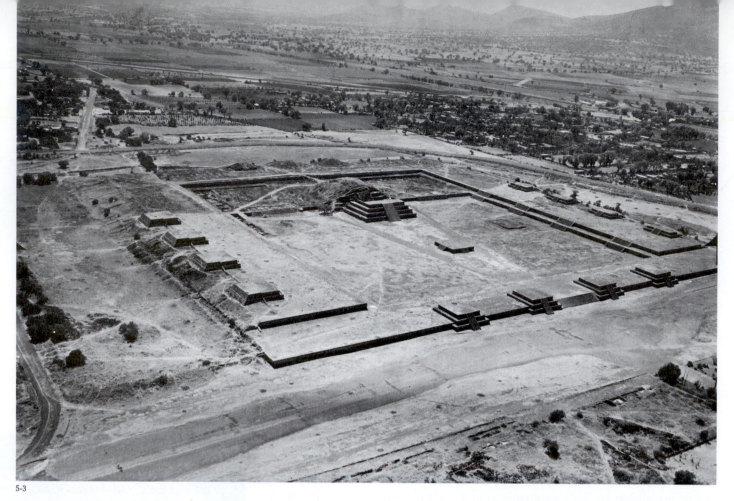

5-3

5-3. Ciudadela court, Teotihuacán, Mexico (view from the west). A.D. 50–200

5-4. *Water Goddess*, from Teotihuacán. Before A.D. 600. Basalt, height 10′6″ (3.2 m). Museo Nacional de Antropología, Mexico City

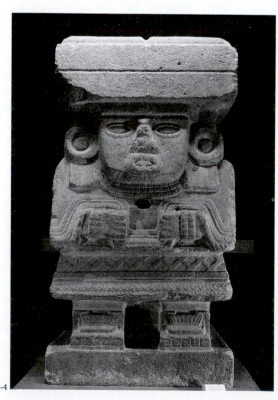

parallel in purpose, though not in form, with Mesopotamian ziggurats (see figs. 4–1, 4–4) is compelling. The American structures were, however, not built of mud brick but according to an elaborate system of inner stone piers and fin walls, filled in with earth and rubble and faced with well-cut stone masonry. Not only in sheer craftsmanship but also in the feeling for mass and proportion and in the disposition of spaces, these pyramids of Teotihuacán are majestic works of architecture. With the single exception of the richly decorated temple of Quetzalcóatl, the various levels of the buildings are ornamented only with simple paneling, which accentuates their cubic grandeur. The entire city was laid out on a rigorous gridiron plan; judging from the excavated remains, Teotihuacán at its zenith, about A.D. 600, was one of the largest cities anywhere in the world, counting some two hundred thousand inhabitants. It was mysteriously destroyed about 750, but nearly a thousand years after its abandonment the Aztec still considered the site sacred, and applied the names by which its avenues and temples are known.

A rare example of monumental sculpture in the round from Teotihuacán is the colossal *Water Goddess,* dating before 600 (fig. 5–4). The immense size (10½ feet high) and blocky appearance of the image may be explained by its probable function as a caryatid figure upholding a central wooden roof-beam. Not only in execution but in basic conception the work is a relief. Ears, limbs, and extremities are drawn upon and carved into the flat surfaces of the block with stone tools that permitted little or no undercutting and are shown frontally so that fingers and toes may be counted. The rectilinearity of the block mass controls every aspect of the representation. The eyes stare blankly forward and in the open mouth may be seen a protruding tongue. The chest contains a cavity in which, apparently, was placed a stone heart. In the dimness of an ancient interior the total effect of the towering yet squat deity must have been awesome.

5-4

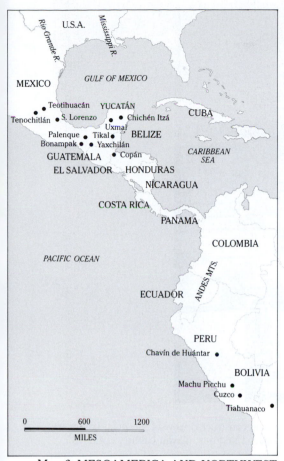

Map 6. MESOAMERICA AND NORTHWEST SOUTH AMERICA IN PRE-COLUMBIAN TIMES

THE MAYA From an artistic as well as intellectual standpoint, the civilization of the Maya in eastern Mexico, Guatemala, Belize, and Honduras, roughly contemporary with that of Teotihuacán in central Mexico, was the greatest of all the pre-Columbian cultures. The Maya, who engaged in widespread commerce, possessed a complex system of hieroglyphic writing; about 80 to 90 percent of known Mayan hieroglyphs have been deciphered, but hundreds of inscriptions, particularly on pottery, remain to be read. Combined with elaborate arithmetical calculation, based on units of twenty rather than ten in our style, and accurate plotting of the eclipses and the movements of the planets, the hieroglyphs permitted the exact recording of time, by means of a calendar so precise that their historical events can be dated down to the day according to our system. Contending that the the Mayan pictorial manuscripts were devoted to devil-worship, the Franciscan missionary bishop Diego de Landa burned in a massive auto-da-fé in 1561 all he could lay his hands on, thereby destroying at one blow the richest source for possible knowledge of Mayan history and culture. His journal records the terrible grief of the Maya at this destruction. The manuscripts were written on a kind of paper made from the bark of the fig tree, folded into lengths like screens; only four examples survive. Fortunately some of the information the destroyed manuscripts must have contained was preserved in accounts by Maya who had learned Latin characters.

While their massive temples were intended mostly for exterior use, the Maya knew and employed the post-and-lintel system, the corbel arch, and the corbel vault (see Glossary). The essential of Mayan religious life, conducted in ceremonies before crowds gathered in the great plazas below, was sacrifice—whether of food, or valuables, or blood, or human hearts—in small temples at the apex of the pyramids, to various aspects of nature deities, some benevolent, some destructive, around whom one of the most complex and poetic mythologies and cosmogonies in human history was woven. To obtain the favors of these divinities or to appease them, even to obtain a kind of mystic union with them, and to assure the continued life of the universe they controlled as well as that of the individual Mayan society, rulers and their families offered their own blood, the women from their tongues, through which a spiked cord was drawn, the ruler from his perforated penis. In later periods the blood was smeared upon the image of the god and even upon the priest. Sacrificial rituals were preceded by fasting and abstinence, accompanied by incense, and followed by feasting at which drunkenness, on beverages fermented from maize or pulque, was universal. Narcotics and hallucinogens, and group dancing of extraordinary precision, described by the Spanish conquerors, formed part of the religious ritual. In times of necessity such as drought, or for great historic events such as dynastic installations, as well as at recurring twenty-year intervals, and especially at the "new fire" ceremony celebrating the fifty-two-year recurrence of the intersection of the Mayan solar calendar of 365 days with their ritual one of 260 days, humans were sacrificed, including women and children. As time went on these sacrifices became more and more frequent, and wars were fought exclusively to obtain victims—the Mayan rulers did not sacrifice their own. Often, the victims were painted the sacred, heavenly color blue and stretched out on an altar at the apex of the pyramid, where a priest cut out the still-beating heart with a flint knife. The body was then tossed down the steep steps to waiting priests of lower rank, who skinned it, except for hands and feet, whereupon the celebrant shed his vestments, dressed himself in the skin—thus assuming the form of the deity into whom the victim had been transformed—and danced along with the worshipers. Hands and feet were eaten by the nobility as part of the religious rite. The victim might also be attached to a stake in the courtyard and his heart shot full of arrows. Victims were also beheaded. The rain-god was appeased by throwing live victims into a vast, quarry-like well, along with precious ornaments; many wonderful gold and jade objects have been retrieved from one such well at Chichén Itzá.

At every Mayan religious center, a ball game was played in which the rubber ball passing back and forth overhead symbolized the course of the sun through the

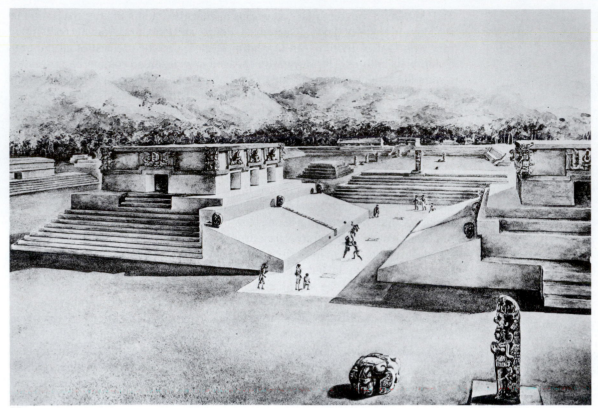

5-5

5-5. Reconstructed view of the main ball court, Copán, Honduras. Mayan culture, c. A.D. 735

heavens. The players were not permitted to touch the hard rubber ball with their hands, only with their elbows, knees, or hips; a goal was scored by bouncing the ball off parrot-headed sculptures on the sloping walls. Enthusiastic spectators took sides, betting even their possessions on the outcome. Death by decapitation awaited the losers. The reconstruction of a twice-rebuilt ball court at Copán, in Honduras (fig. 5–5), as it appeared in its final version of A.D. 735, shows the Mayan genius for the deployment of architectural masses, often unrelieved, crowned here with a corbel-vaulted story richly ornamented with the relief sculpture at which the Maya excelled.

The pyramid with central staircase, as seen at Teotihuacán, was recapitulated in countless regional variations of size, shape, and proportion throughout Meso-america; its form became sharply steeper and higher in the Mayan civilization, in examples spread throughout the cities in their territory. One of the most splendid — only recently being won back from the dense invading forest—is Tikal, in Guate-mala, which at its height may have sheltered as many as seventy-five thousand inhabitants in irregular groups of houses connected by causeways to the religious center. This is dominated by two lofty pyramids on opposite sides of a central plaza. Temple I, some 144 feet in height, rises over the tomb of the ruler Ah Cacau (ruled A.D. 682–c. 721/31). Its steep, almost tower-like structure is formed of nine shallow levels interlocking with five vertical divisions, centering on a precipitous central staircase to form a majestic structure in which opposed architectural forces are concentrated in compact form (fig. 5–6). It should be kept in mind that the outer surfaces of the pyramid were largely devoured by the forest and nine-tenths of those we see are accurate modern reconstruction.

An especially impressive Mayan building is the Palace in the powerful city-state of Palenque, in Chiapas, Mexico, commenced about A.D. 650 and remodeled and extended at intervals for the next 150 years (fig. 5–7). Provided with lavatories that discharged into a stream passing underneath, steam baths, ample courtyards, and

5-6. Temple I (Temple of the Giant Jaguar), Tikal (El Petén), Guatemala. Mayan culture, early 8th century A.D. Height approx. 144′ (43.89 m)

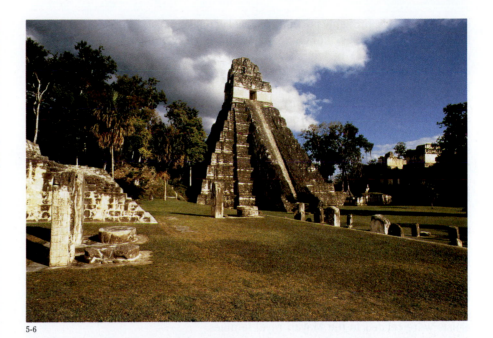

5-6

enclosures separating the ruling family from the courtiers, the Palace must have been remarkably comfortable. The upper walls incline to produce corbel vaults, and the stone roofs originally culminated in the tall, usually perforated structures called roof-combs. The absolutely unique feature of the Palace is a tower built as an observatory about 721 in four slightly diminishing levels, each pierced on all four sides by openings of increasing width, demarcated by doubled cornices and crowned with a hipped roof. As at Tikal, the partially ruined masonry, including almost the entire fourth story of the tower, has been heavily reconstructed.

Below the so-called Temple of the Inscriptions at Palenque was found the burial chamber of Lord Pacal ("Shield"), who brought his kingdom to greatness and may have enjoyed an astonishing reign from 615 to 683, one of the longest of any known monarchs. Among the magnificent objects found in this tomb are two beautiful life-

5-7

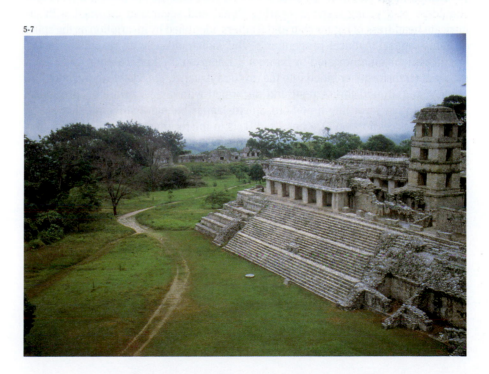

5-7. West stairway and Building D, Palace, Palenque (Chiapas), Mexico. Mayan culture, c. A.D. 650–800

size stucco heads, probably portraits of Pacal when young and his wife, believed to have come from statues, though no statues have been found. The forehead of the male head (fig. 5–8) had been flattened by the device Mayan children were required to wear, creating a flange that prolongs the curve of the aquiline nose. The hair, into which flowers are woven, is brought up from the back into a plumelike arc, and cut in the front into bangs across the forehead. The gliding movement of surfaces around the full lips, broad cheekbones, and heavy-lidded eyes enhances the dreamy expression on the man's face, as is characteristic of many Mayan heads, sometimes in sharp contrast with the ornamentalized bodies encased in stiff ceremonial garb.

Interestingly enough, although in daily life most Mayan men were nude except for a loincloth, and although the flexibility of the human body and the poses it can assume were sensitively observed in painting and in relief sculpture, rarely in pre-Columbian monumental art do we find any human figures in the round free from the massive ornamental network of ceremonial costumes, and even then they are not standing or moving. Human images in relief are usually restricted in projection by the surfaces of the slabs on which they were first drawn, then carved, or more precisely, incised, lowering the background to a uniform level. Artists' signatures abound, on sculptured reliefs and on pottery. It has been speculated that these artists were related to the Mayan royal families.

Among the sculptured friezes, *stelae* (standing slabs), and lintels of the Maya perhaps the most beautiful are the series of lintels found in covered ceremonial pavilions facing the public plaza at Yaxchilán, in Chiapas. A densely packed relief, one of a series of three lintels decorating the structure that contained the throne of Lord Shield-Jaguar (ruled A.D. 681–742), shows a visionary event which had already taken place in the year 709 (fig. 5–9). Lady Xoc, a principal consort of Lord Shield-Jaguar and perhaps a priestess, has just finished the bloodletting ceremony, which is depicted in the neighboring lintel. Holding in her left hand a basket containing bloodletting instruments, she kneels before a basin in which with her right hand she has set fire to blood-soaked scrolls of paper and the spiked cord which was drawn through her tongue. The smoke rises in curving but angular shapes of the greatest intricacy and beauty, which resolve themselves into two serpent's heads. One grimaces at the level of Xoc's arm, the other towers above her astonished head, and from its wide-stretched jaws emerge the powerful head and shoulders of a young warrior, bearing shield and spear and crowned with an intricate headdress of jaguar skin and feathers, identified by inscription as the spirit of Penis-Jaguar, mythical progenitor of the Jaguar dynasty at Yaxchilán. In the interpretation communicated by Samuel Y. Edgerton, Jr., to the author, Lady Xoc's ritual acts transform her blood into the mystic substance *k'ul,* visible in the hooklike curve rising around the serpent and decorated with glyphs meaning "precious." The inscription recording how Lord Shield-Jaguar beheld a similar vision at the time of his accession, on October 23, 681, is in mirror image. Another inscription places the represented scene in the middle of the plaza at Yaxchilán. Even the perforated ornament in Lady Xoc's splendid garment is symbolic; each hole is at once the birth canal and the entrance into the gullet of the great reptile Itzamná, the earth at death, all controlled by the Mayan ruler symbolized by the knot at the center. The relief gains its intense effect from the tension between vivid realism in the profiles, dense angular pattern in the hieroglyphic inscriptions, and mystical vision in the curves of the smoke and the apocalyptic apparition.

Mayan wall painting was done in *fresco* (see Glossary)—that is, on wet plaster, which apparently dried slowly enough in the humid atmosphere to permit the covering of large surfaces. No brushes have been found, but a representation of a hand holding a tubular brush with a finely drawn point is known. Characteristically, unmodeled figures stand or move against a flat background, depending for effect on the subtlety and descriptive power of their dark contours. The greatest treasure of Mayan mural painting is the series of frescoes lining the three rooms of a small

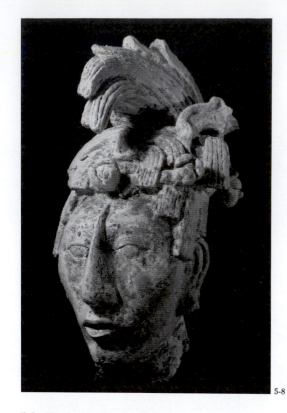

5-8

5-8. *Head of a Man* (possibly a portrait of Lord Pacal), from the crypt in the Temple of the Inscriptions, Palenque. Mayan culture, 7th century A.D. Stucco, height 16⅞″ (43 cm). Museo Nacional de Antropología, Mexico City

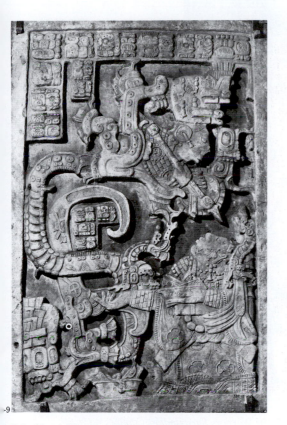

5-9. Lintel 25, from Building 23, Yaxchilán (Chiapas), Mexico. Mayan culture, c. A.D. 726. Stone, height 51¼″ (1.3 m). British Museum, London

structure discovered in 1946 at Bonampak, to the south of Yaxchilán, by the anthropologist Giles Healey. According to the hieroglyphic inscriptions, this was built and decorated to celebrate the events of August 2, A.D. 792, and the following days, in which the ruler Chaan Muan ("Sky Owl") captured warriors of a neighboring state for sacrifice to celebrate his succession to power, pronounced sentence upon them, and presided over the sacrifice. The now considerably abraded judgment scene (fig. 5–10) takes place on seven steps before a temple or palace. In order to understand the reconstruction, which appears to be in one plane, we should keep in mind that the figures in the lowest register, divided by the door, stand directly on a dais that runs around the room, cut only by the central door that extends below the level of the illustration. Along a line running at the level of the lintel the upper three steps and their figures are tilted toward us on the corbeled ceiling. The figures are therefore not in registers as in Egyptian tomb painting but actually stand in ascending levels; on the upper three steps the figures overlap from one step to the next, those in the topmost row silhouetted against a sky-blue background. Dressed in a jaguar vest and anklets and crowned with immense plumes, Chaan Muan stands on the topmost step holding a spear on which a jaguar tail has been impaled, flanked by attendants, three of whom are dressed in jaguar skins, wearing headdresses of jaguar, crocodile, or bird heads. To our right stands his principal wife, Lady Rabbit, holding a fan (the original fresco shows only four pleats), and a lesser wife. A darker-skinned prisoner sprawls dead on the second step, a wound showing where his heart has been cut out, with a severed head resting partly on his foot. Other dark prisoners crouch with outstretched arms before the stern Chaan Muan, gazing with horrified expressions at the drops of blood falling from their hands. Slightly less than life size, the figures presuppose a certain distance between them and the spectator. The vivid illusionistic effect of the frescoes, tilted toward the observer or wrapped around him, is completed by the realism of the poses and characterizations and expressions, even the varying profiles and skin colors of the guards; two or three are quite fat. Unfortunately the reconstruction loses a great deal of the bite and power of the original painting.

Even when the Mayan civilization fell under the domination of the Toltec, a warrior nation from central Mexico, the originality of Mayan architecture was maintained. The Maya-Toltec center of Chichén Itzá, one of the most powerful states of the Yucatán Peninsula, is filled with structures whose massive grandeur, imaginative architectural innovations, and delicate relief carving create an impression of the greatest variety and richness. The Caracol (a name that means "winding staircase"), actually a cylindrical, tower-like building at the top of three earlier ascending platforms, is one of the grandest (fig. 5–11). Built about the year A.D. 840 and used and remodeled for about four hundred years thereafter, the tower functioned as an observatory; the windows and shafts leading to them from the two concentric circles of the corbel-vaulted interior are so oriented as to indicate south and west, equinoxes and summer solstice. Masks appear over the projecting cornice above each of the four entrances.

The institution of human sacrifice, intended to ensure the perpetuation of the Mayan states, had the reverse effect. The warfare essential to procure victims constantly increased in intensity at the expense of the agricultural lands, which were already woefully insufficient for the support of expanding populations. Moreover, so did the campaigns to build always grander monuments for sacrificial rites. Scholars have speculated as to whether unrecorded worker rebellions against these campaigns might not have taken place; at any rate before the year 900, in every one of the magnificent centers of Classic Maya artistic achievement—Palenque, Yaxchilán, Piedras Negras, Tikal, Copán, Quirigua, Bonampak, and more—all buildings, sculpture, painting, and hieroglyphic writing ceased. New excavations at the great Mayan site of Dos Pilas in Guatemala have shown that the surrounding farmland was dotted with graves and full of spearheads, while an immense rampart surrounded the city, formed in large part of cut stones torn from the pyramids

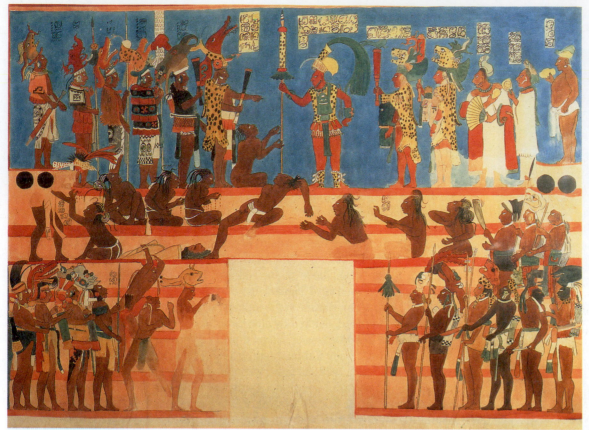

5-10

and temples. Apparently the populations simply fled the great centers and moved deeper into the jungle, where they still remain.

It is easy to allow our horror at the cruelty of their ceremonies to blind us to the brilliance of the Mayan achievements and the beauty of their art. We would do well to remember that the Spanish, whose intense religiosity gave rise to the spirituality

5-10. *Warriors Surrounding Captives on a Terraced Platform*, mural in a temple at Bonampak (Chiapas), Mexico. Mayan culture, late 8th century A.D. Watercolor copy by Antonio Tejeda. Peabody Museum of Archaeology and Ethnology, Harvard University, Cambridge, Massachusetts

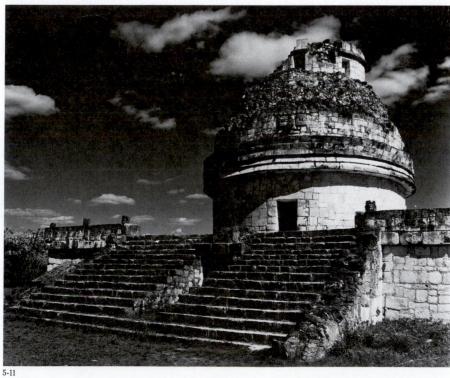

5-11

5-11. The Caracol (observatory), Chichén Itzá (Yucatán), Mexico. Maya-Toltec culture, 11th century A.D.

of the Counter-Reformation mystics, the music of Tomás Luis de Victoria, and the painting of El Greco, could slaughter entire civilian populations and burn thousands of heretics at the stake in the name of Jesus.

The ruins of a huge pyramid temple, rebuilt five times, have been found under the central plaza of Mexico City. Life-size, in-the-round stone sculptures, such as the striking *Seated Standard Bearer*, now in the Metropolitan Museum of Art, New York (see fig. 5–1), adorned this sacred complex (the figure's right hand once held a tall wooden flagpole). Nevertheless, Aztec carvings never reached the artistic level of the great Mayan creations, nor indeed did their limited knowledge of writing. The Spaniards were horrified not only by the long lines of prisoners awaiting sacrifice but by the blood-caked temples. Spanish conquest of the Aztec, aided by the neighboring states who resented their cruelty, took only a few years, but although the Maya were in a state of sharp decline after the collapse of their great civilization some five hundred years earlier, they resisted the Spanish invaders for nearly two hundred years; remote areas were never subdued. Mayan languages are widely spoken today, and some Mayan beliefs, assimilated into Christianity, are still preserved. Incense is still burned in some of the ancient temples.

Andean Art

The Andean region formed a totally distinct area of pre-Columbian culture, whose origins are gradually being traced by archaeological means, since the Incas had no writing. The Spaniards arriving in Peru in 1533 found an even more recent empire than the Aztec hegemony in Mexico. The vast Inca realm was held together by an extraordinary system of oral communication; messages were delivered by runners in short and frequent relays, making it possible for a message to travel one hundred and fifty miles in a day—as compared with the twelve to fifteen days required by the later Spanish system of post-horses. The Spaniards were astonished to find themselves everywhere expected. In the absence of writing, the Incas made relief models of areas of their mountainous empire to aid them in moving subject peoples from one region to another in order to forestall revolt. The region was divided into three strips: an arid coastal area cut by green river valleys, the western slopes of the lofty mountains containing temperate plateau areas, and the humid jungles of the eastern slopes. In Andean architecture we find many of the familiar features we have encountered in Mesoamerica—platforms, step-pyramids, gridiron cities. Mining was extensively practiced, and the smelting, casting, beating, and chasing of metals were done with the utmost skill.

The important religious and political center of Chavín de Huantar, in northern Peru, with its complex of temple platforms and labyrinthine stone-lined corridors, has given its name to the still imperfectly understood Chavín cult. One of the most fascinating Andean reliefs is the *Raimondi Monolith* (fig. 5–12), datable between 1000 and 600 B.C. and known by the name of its discoverer in 1874. Andean carvings were generally incised on stone but not further carved save for reduction of the background. They do not show complete human figures, as do those of the Maya, but encase human elements in fantastic patterns of enormous complexity, including parts of animals. This great slab was probably a ceiling decoration, intended to be read in either direction and requiring close concentration in order to decipher the represented forms. At first sight one distinguishes in the lower third of the relief a chunky deity with claws on his feet; his short arms and massive hands extend to hold two richly carved scepters. His face is a mask, displaying a grinning mouth full of square teeth, and saucer-shaped depressions for nostrils and eyes. The upper two-thirds of the relief are filled with a towering headdress from which feathers sprout on either side, composed of superimposed masks, each issuing from the jaws of the one above. The intensity of the complex pattern with its constantly shifting accents is almost hypnotic.

Few remains of Andean buildings can compete in splendor with those of the

5-12

5-12. *Raimondi Monolith*, from Chavín de Huantar (Ancash), Peru. Chavín culture, 1000–600 B.C. Diorite, height 6′6″ (1.95 m). Museo Nacional de Antropología y Arqueología, Lima

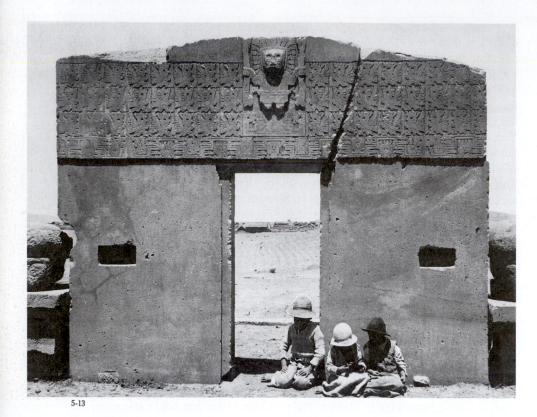

5-13

5-13. Gateway of the Sun, Tiahuanaco, Bolivia. Tiahuanacan culture, A.D. 500–900. Height 9′ (2.74 m)

5-14. *"Laughing Man,"* stirrup-spout jar. Moche culture, c. A.D. 500. Museo Nacional de Antropología y Arqueología, Lima

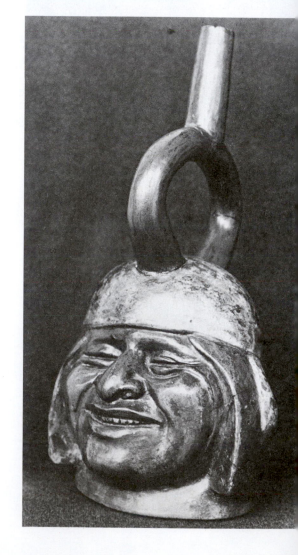

Mesoamerican cultures. The great ceremonial center of Tiahuanaco, located in the lofty plateau region surrounding Lake Titicaca, a site now in northern Bolivia, was one of the richest, but it has been ransacked over the centuries to the point of no return; its probable dates fall somewhere between the sixth and the ninth centuries A.D. The best-preserved monument, the so-called Gateway of the Sun (fig. 5–13), a monolith about nine feet high, is a majestic creation in its own right. The jambs appear to support a huge lintel—actually a part of the same block—decorated with three superimposed strips of incised images above a lower border of a meander pattern suggesting those common in ancient Greece and throughout the decorative art of China. In the center, over the doorway, is a sharply stylized frontal relief showing the sun-god holding a massive scepter in each hand in the manner of the deity in the *Raimondi Monolith*. From his masklike countenance emerge gigantic rays. On closer inspection, the strips of ornaments on either side of the god resolve themselves into registers of eight sharply flattened running figures, thus forty-eight in all, each holding two arrows and wearing a feather crown. Those in the upper and lower rows have human heads in profile directed straight forward, while the upturned heads of those in the central row display open bird beaks. All have staring eyes, some round, some square, and all these minions of the sun-god are propelled by wings lifted behind them. Into the openings in the meander pattern are inserted other sun-masks in wigwag style, now up, now down. As in the *Raimondi Monolith* the combination of powerful vertical and horizontal rhythms with an elusive balance between apparently floral but actually animal representations produces an almost dizzying effect.

At the opposite pole from this very nearly abstract art, with its probable religious significance and ritual purpose, the Moche culture of northern Peru, at roughly the same period as the *Raimondi* relief, produced a strikingly naturalistic pottery intended for daily use, immense numbers of which have been found at burial sites. Characteristic is the stirrup-shaped top, which serves as both handle and spout. Often the entire pot was turned into an image of a human head. Moche potters experimented with different types of facial expressions until they were able to produce natural and spontaneous ones, an example of which is shown in the so-

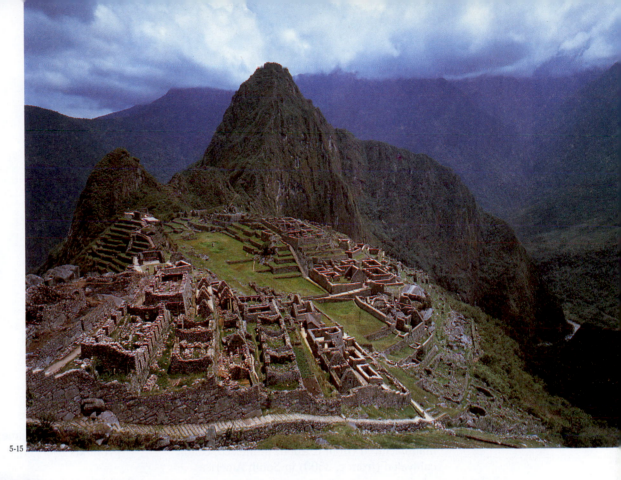

5-15. Aerial view of Machu Picchu, Peru. Inca culture, c. A.D. 1500

5-16. Female figurine in the Quimbaya style, from Colombia. Cast gold, height 9″ (23 cm). The University Museum, University of Pennsylvania, Philadelphia

5-15

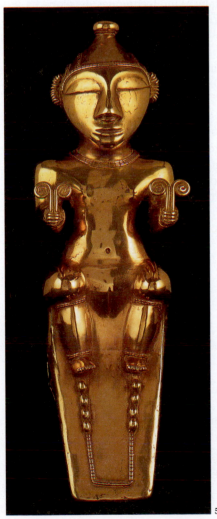

5-16

called *Laughing Man* (fig. 5–14), from the fifth or sixth century A.D., whose animated expression may not actually be laughter, but whose mouth is open showing the teeth and whose eyes are almost closed by the wrinkling of the cheeks.

Although the Spanish invaders melted down most of the goldwork they found, Andean gold objects have been discovered in enormous profusion in the waters of the sacred lakes of Colombia into which they had been thrown from rafts over the centuries by young sovereigns, naked but covered with gold dust, as sacrifices to the water deity. In spite of the explorations of archaeologists and the depredations of robbers, untold numbers must still lie in the depths of these lakes. Under the circumstances even approximate dating is impossible, but several different styles have been distinguished. A beautiful seated female figurine (fig. 5–16) of the Quimbaya style, holding what is apparently a flower in either hand, can only suggest the magnificence of these recovered treasures. Some are in beaten gold, some drawn like wire; some, like this little statue, are cast. The artist has been careful to preserve a smooth movement of surface in order to suggest the softness of the female nude and to exploit the refulgence of the precious material.

The grandest productions of the short-lived Inca Empire, which governed an enormous Andean area from its capital at Cuzco in southern Peru, are its cities, built of masonry that has been sculptured to fit, stone against stone, so that literally the blade of a knife cannot be inserted between them. The fortress town of Machu Picchu, most of whose buildings are datable about A.D. 1500, is probably the most fantastic of all early American cities known to us (fig. 5–15). Its extensive ruins stand on a crag that towers among other crags about two thousand feet above a misty valley, every terrace and every house in perfect harmony with the masses of the rock.

The culture of the Spanish Renaissance put an immediate end to indigenous art of the ancient American civilizations in the sixteenth century and imposed its own European styles on the conquered inhabitants, along with its language and religion. Renaissance and Baroque churches and palaces were subsequently constructed, often on the ruins of temples and pyramids, and decorated with paintings and sculpture, by the descendants of the original early American builders.

TIME LINE III

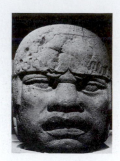

Colossal Olmec head

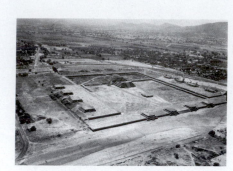

Ciudadela court, Teotihuacán

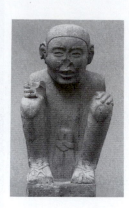

Seated Standard-Bearer

HISTORY

1200 B.C.	Maize in cultivation (from c. 6000), pottery manufactured (from c. 2000) in Mexico; cotton cultivated (from c. 3500) in South America
1000	
A.D. 1	City of Teotihuacán founded, c. A.D. 1–50 Intensified farming, population increase in the Petén, Guatemala (lowland Maya area), c. 100–300
200	Proliferation of Mayan city-states, c. 290–790
600	Lord Pacal rules Palenque (615–83)
	Teotihuacán burned, c. 750; Toltec establish capital city at Tula, Mexico Mysterious collapse of Mayan cities in lowland rain-forest area
900	
	Manco Capac founds Inca dynasty at Cuzco, c. 1200 Itzá settle in the Yucatán, c. 1250 Aztec settle in Valley of Mexico, c. 1350
	Siege of Tenochtitlán by Cortez, 1520–21 Pizarro arrives in Peru, 1533
1550	

CULTURE

Olmec invent ball game; build large temple pyramids

Sophisticated metalworking techniques developed in northern Peru

Hieroglyphic writing, arithmetical calendar system developed in Oaxaca and Veracruz regions of Mesoamerica, c. 100

Colombian artisans refine lost-wax–casting technique to produce superb gold sculpture

Maya refine calendrical system, concept of zero, historical record-keeping in ideographic-phonetic script; develop productive system of raised-field agriculture

Aztec refine productive system of raised-field agriculture

Inca build 2,000-mile roadway linking their empire north-south

PRE-COLUMBIAN MEXICO, CENTRAL AMERICA, SOUTH AMERICA

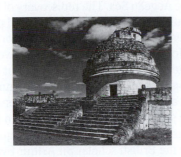

The Caracol,
Chichén Itzá

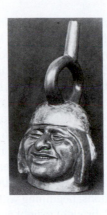

"Laughing Man"

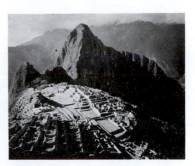

Machu Picchu

PAINTING, SCULPTURE, ARCHITECTURE

Colossal head, San Lorenzo

Raimondi Monolith, Chavín de Huantar

Ciudadela, Teotihuacán
Water Goddess, from Teotihuacán

"Laughing Man" stirrup-spout jar, from northern Peru

Temple I, Tikal
Lintel 25, Yaxchilán
Gateway of the Sun, Tiahuanaco
Fresco, Bonampak

Caracol, Chichén-Itzá
Machu Picchu

PARALLEL SOCIETIES

Olmec	1200 B.C.
Chavín	1000
Mound Builders (eastern N. America)	
	A.D. 1
Classic period of Mesoamerican civilization, 200–900	200
Moche	
	600
Classic Mayan and Teotihuacán Tiahuanacan	
Postclassic period of Mesoamerican civilization, 900–1521	900
Cliff Dwellers (southwest N. America)	
Toltec	
Inca	
	1550

CHAPTER SIX

6-1. Cycladic idol, from Amorgos. 2500–1100 B.C. Marble, height 30" (76.2 cm). The Ashmolean Museum, Oxford, England

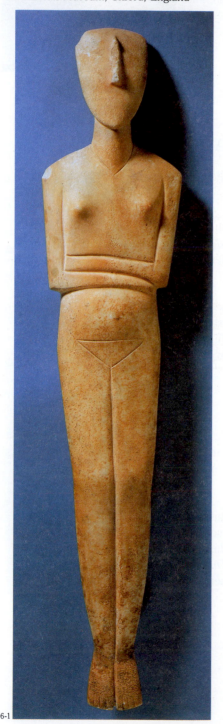

6-1

Somewhat later than the first manifestations of the splendid cultures that flourished in the Nile Valley and in Mesopotamia, a third artistically productive civilization arose in the islands and rocky peninsulas of the Aegean Sea. The rediscovery of this vanished civilization, like that of the cave paintings and of Sumer, Akkad, and pre-Columbian America, has been an achievement of the past hundred years or so. Nineteenth-century scholarship had taken it for granted that the cities and events described in the poems of Homer were largely if not entirely mythical, but the excavations of the German amateur archaeologist Heinrich Schliemann, beginning at the site of Troy in 1870 and continuing later at Mycenae and other centers on the Greek mainland, made clear that the Homeric stories must have had a basis in fact and that the cities mentioned in the poems had indeed existed. Subsequent excavations, beginning with those initiated by the British scholar Sir Arthur Evans in 1900, brought to light a completely unsuspected group of buildings on the island of Crete, containing works of art of surprising originality and freshness of imagination. It has now become clear that there were two distinct cultures. One was centered on Crete and has been called Minoan, after Minos, the legendary Cretan king; the other is known as Helladic, after Hellas, the Greek mainland. The final phase of Helladic culture, and its most interesting artistically, is known as Mycenaean, from its principal center at Mycenae.

Minoan civilization is almost as much of a mystery as that of preliterate humans. The Minoan and Helladic peoples spoke different tongues, and Minoan scripts are still undecipherable. Their language, apparently non–Indo-European, is completely unknown. However, a late form of Aegean writing, found both in Crete and on the mainland, was first deciphered in 1953 and turned out to be a pre-Homeric form of Greek. The now-legible documents, of a purely practical nature and without literary interest, suggest that Minoan civilization eventually succumbed to Mycenaean overlords. Thus our slight knowledge of Aegean history, social structure, and religious beliefs must be gleaned largely from the study of Aegean buildings and other works of art and from the mythology of the later Greeks— however much distorted by the later poetic tradition that culminated in Homer— which seems to have been woven, in part at least, from surviving memories of the Aegean world. Even *Minos* may only be a generic Cretan name for "king."

Approximate dates for Minoan art have been ascertained largely by the systematic excavation of pottery. Minoan and Helladic artifacts have now been traced as far back as 3000 B.C., and some even earlier, but the great artistic periods of both civilizations belong to the second millennium B.C., roughly between the years 1900 and 1100—a period contemporary with the Empire in Egypt and with the Babylonian period in Mesopotamia. About 1400 B.C. Minoan civilization perished in a catastrophe whose nature is still not certain but which may have been related to the volcanic eruption that destroyed Thera (modern Santorini). Mycenaean culture survived only another three centuries before succumbing to the combined effects of internal dissent and attacks by other Greek invaders.

Cycladic Art

Even before the rise of the Minoan and Helladic civilizations, there had been another artistically creative culture in the Aegean. Called Cycladic, from the islands where its remains are found, this late Neolithic culture flourished in the third millennium B.C. and has left no trace of writing.

The Cycladic tombs have yielded many stone sculptures, ranging from statuettes to images about half life size. The meaning of these figures is not known, but the female ones with their folded arms (fig. 6–1) seem to be descendants of Neolithic mother goddesses elsewhere (see fig. 1–15). Interestingly enough, their whole character has changed; they are no longer abundantly maternal but touchingly slight and virginal, with delicate proportions, gently swelling and subsiding shapes, and subtle contours. The simplicity and understatement of these Cycladic figures have made them particularly attractive to contemporary artists. It should be borne in mind, however, that the flattened faces originally displayed other features than the sharply projecting noses that now remain. Traces of pigment make clear that eyes and mouths, as well as other details, were originally painted on. Of equal interest are the less frequently found male musicians, such as the *Lyre Player* (fig. 6–2), perhaps intended to commemorate a funerary celebration or even to evoke music in the afterlife. The musicians are almost tubular in their stylization, and the forms of body, lyre, and chair enclose beautifully shaped open spaces that prefigure those of some twentieth-century sculpture.

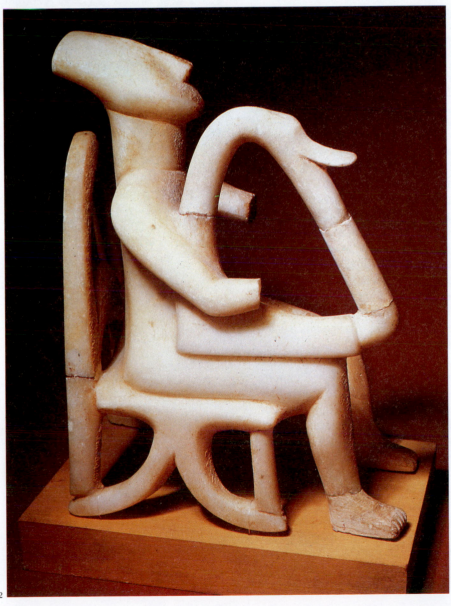

6-2

6-2. *Lyre Player,* from Amorgos. c. 2000 B.C. Marble, height 8½″ (23 cm). National Archaeological Museum, Athens

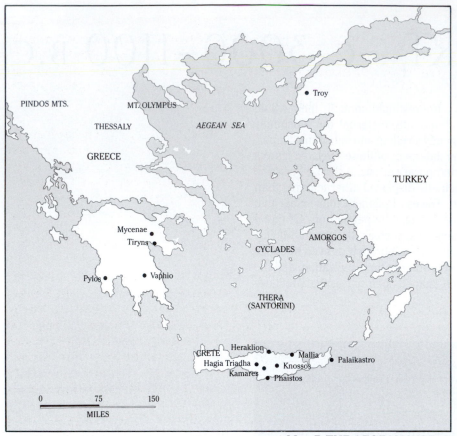

Map 7. THE AEGEAN WORLD

Minoan Art

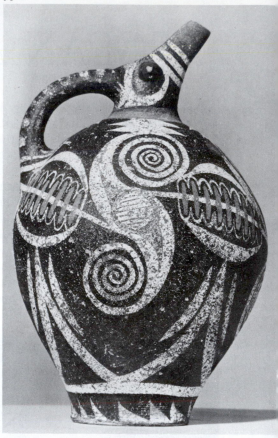

6-3. Beaked jug in the Kamares style, from Phaistos, Crete. c. 1800 B.C. Height 10⅝" (27 cm). Archaeological Museum, Heraklion, Crete

POTTERY Baked clay pots, produced in abundance by almost all Mesopotamian and Mediterranean peoples for household use, were worthless after breakage and were tossed on the dump heap. Yet pottery fragments are virtually indestructible, and the lowest layers of potsherds in any heap are naturally the earliest, the next later, and so on. Because the shapes and methods of manufacture of these pots and the style of their decoration changed from one period to the next, sometimes quite rapidly, it has been possible for archaeologists to establish a relative chronology for the development of style by recording the potsherds according to the layers in which they were found. Often the Minoan and, later, the Greek pots are supremely beautiful as works of art, in both shape and decoration, and their style is strongly related to that of wall painting and other arts. Thus their chronology is applicable to other works of art as well. Sometimes, also, the circumstances of a find link a dated group of pots to the building in or near which it was discovered.

Since we know so little of their writing, we cannot yet say whether the Minoans themselves accurately recorded dates and specific events. But luckily they were great seafarers and traders. Their pots have turned up in Egyptian sites whose dates can be determined by numerous inscriptions, and the chronology based on the potsherds can thus often be anchored to firm historical knowledge. Approximate dates have, therefore, been assigned to the early, middle, and late periods into which Minoan art has been divided.

Not until the Middle Minoan period, about the nineteenth century B.C., does the art of the potter achieve truly great artistic stature, but objects of the quality of the beaked Kamares-style jug from Phaistos (fig. 6–3) would be welcomed as master-pieces in any period. The curvilinear shapes have an extraordinary vitality and are different in style from anything we have previously seen, except perhaps for the carved decorations of the temple at Tarxien (see fig. 1–19). Palmlike shapes in soft white quiver against a black ground among curling and uncurling spirals and counterspirals, all beautifully related to the shape of the vessel itself. In Late

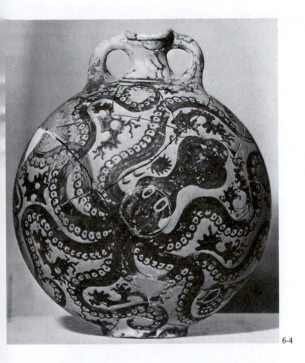

6-4. *Octopus Vase,* from Palaikastro, Crete. c. 1500 B.C. Height 11″ (28 cm). Archaeological Museum, Heraklion

6-5. Plan of the Palace at Knossos, Crete, including areas of reconstruction (after J. D. S. Pendlebury). c. 1600–1400 B.C.   A. Central court   B. East wing   C. Theater area (?)
1. West porch   2. Corridor of the Procession
3. South propylon (inner gate)   4. Storeroom
5. Palace shrine   6. Throne room   7. Pillar hall   8. Grand staircase   9. Light well   10. Hall of the Double Axes (main reception room)
11. "Queen's Megaron"

Minoan, about 1500 B.C., the swirling shapes take on naturalistic forms. The entire front of a vase from Palaikastro (fig. 6–4), for example, is embraced by the tentacles of an octopus, writing in menacing profusion. The abstract shapes on the first vase have become naturalistic, but the principle of dynamic curvilinear decoration is the same and reappears in the wall paintings as well.

THE PALACES   In Middle Minoan times, after about 2000 B.C., the inhabitants of Crete, previously at a rather modest stage of Neolithic development as compared with their contemporaries in Egypt and Mesopotamia, adopted metals and a system of writing, and rapidly developed an urban, mercantile civilization. The Minoans seem to have depended for protection entirely on their command of the sea; not a trace of fortification has ever been found. This reliance may well have proved their undoing. Immense palaces were built at Knossos and Mallia on the north coast of the island, at Phaistos on the south, and elsewhere. Devastated about 1700 B.C., these first palaces were soon repaired or rebuilt. The most extensive and artistically important is the vast palace at Knossos, about which we know more than about any other palace before Persepolis. Although Knossos was again laid waste between 1450 and 1400 B.C., it has been largely—perhaps even excessively and not always correctly—reconstructed from the ruins. A stroll through it affords an insight into the delightful existence of these mysterious people, who seem to have concerned themselves little with religion and not at all with the hereafter (they left no temples, only small hilltop shrines, and few monumental tombs) but entirely with the pleasures of the here and now. From the plan (fig. 6–5) and from the surviving and reconstructed portions, it is clear that the palace could never have presented the imposing, symmetrical, and ordered appearance of Mesopotamian royal residences. Built around a not perfectly oblong central courtyard, the hundreds of rooms and connecting corridors climb gently up the slopes of the hill in such a haphazard manner as to give color to the Greek legend of the Cretan labyrinth, at the center of which King Minos was supposed to have stabled the dreaded Minotaur, half man, half bull.

Clearly, the Minoan monarchs felt no need to impress visitors with royal might and cruelty. Entrances are unobtrusive; the apartments sprout terraces, open galleries (fig. 6–6), and vistas at random; even the decorated rooms intended for

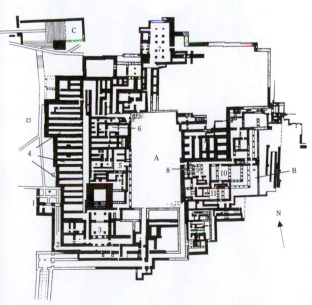

6-5

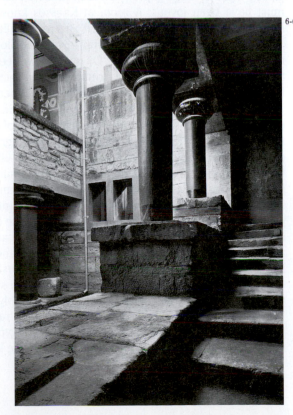

6-6. Lower section of the grand staircase and light well, east wing, Palace at Knossos (reconstructed)

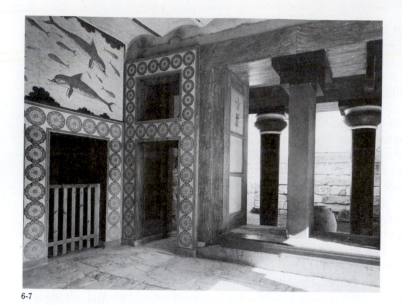

6-7

6-7. "Queen's Megaron," Palace at Knossos (reconstructed). c. 1600–1400 B.C.

6-9. *Bull Dance*, fresco from the Palace at Knossos. c. 1500 B.C. Height including upper border approx. 24½" (62.2 cm). Archaeological Museum, Heraklion

6-10. *Bird in a Landscape*, fragment of a fresco from the Palace at Knossos. c. 1600–1400 B.C. Archaeological Museum, Heraklion

6-8. *Boxers (The Young Princes)*, fragment of a fresco from Building B in the town of Akrotiri, Santorini (ancient Thera), Cyclades. Before 1500 B.C. National Archaeological Museum, Athens

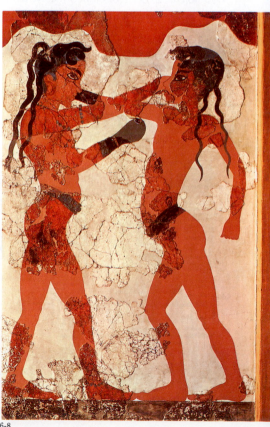

6-8

the royal family are small, with low ceilings and a general air of bright and happy intimacy. The walls are of massive stone masonry; some supports are square piers recalling those in the valley temple of Chephren (see Introduction fig. 18), but wooden columns were frequently used. These are now lost, but their form can be reconstructed through representations in wall paintings, from their bases, which are square stone slabs with a socket for the column, and from their cushion-shaped stone capitals, distant ancestors of the Doric capitals of the Greeks (see figs. 7–13, 7–16). Strangely enough, the columns tapered downward, a feature that further increased the feeling of lowness and intimacy in the rooms.

PAINTING   The mural decorations, painted on wet plaster like the frescoes of fourteenth-century Italy, have survived only in tiny fragments, which have been pieced together; large gaps are filled by modern restorations. The painted interiors must have been joyous. A room at Knossos known incorrectly as the Queen's Megaron (*megaron* means "great hall"; fig. 6–7) is illuminated softly by a light-well. The doorways are ornamented with formalized floral designs, the columns and capitals are painted red and blue. On one wall we seem to look straight into the sea, as if through the glass of an aquarium; between rocks indicated by typical Minoan free curves, fish swim around two huge and contented dolphins.

In murals as in ceramics, unfettered rhythmic contours—astonishing when compared with the stratified compositions typical of Egypt and Mesopotamia—are the chief delight of Minoan painting. In the still-enigmatic *Bull Dance* from Knossos (fig. 6–9), these pulsating contours are extremely effective. Unlike the murderous bulls in Egyptian and Mesopotamian art, this resilient creature seems almost to have been trained for his role. He and his attendants are engaged not in mutual slaughter but in some kind of ritual dance. One almost nude girl dancer (painted yellow as in Egyptian art) grasps with impunity the bull's horns; a second extends her arms from the sidelines; and the boy (red-brown) vaults over the bull with the agility of an acrobat. The forward lunge of the bull and the arching movement of the boy are enhanced by the sideward and upward thrust of the conventionalized rocks of the border. It is believed that the bull ritual we see in this fresco actually took place in the great court of the palace itself, suitably barricaded and sealed off.

The naturalism of Minoan frescoes, such as the fragment from Knossos showing a bird in a landscape (fig. 6–10), recalls that of Egyptian paintings, which Minoan merchants must have seen on their visits to the Nile Valley. But the spirit of Minoan

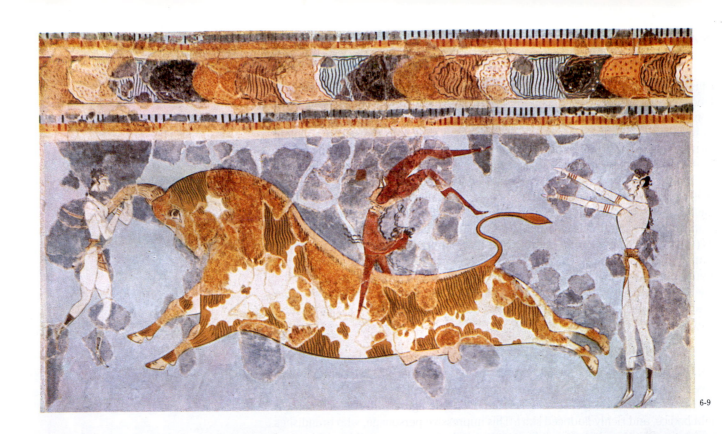

6-9

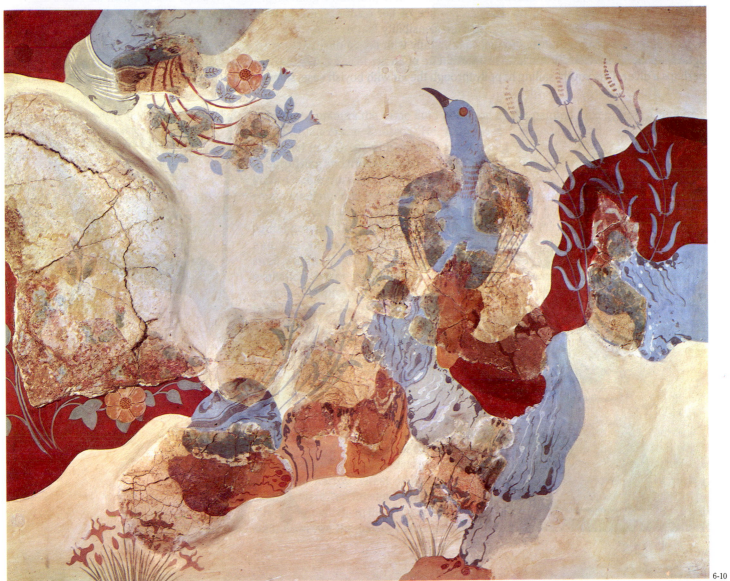

6-10

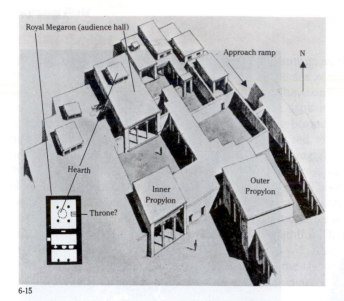

6-15

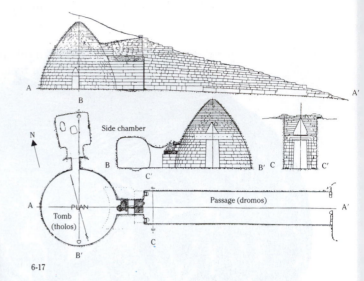

6-15. Reconstructed view of the Citadel of Tiryns, Greece (after G. Karo and British School at Athens). 13th century B.C.

6-17

6-17. Plan of the "Treasury of Atreus," Mycenae (after A. W. Lawrence). 13th century B.C.

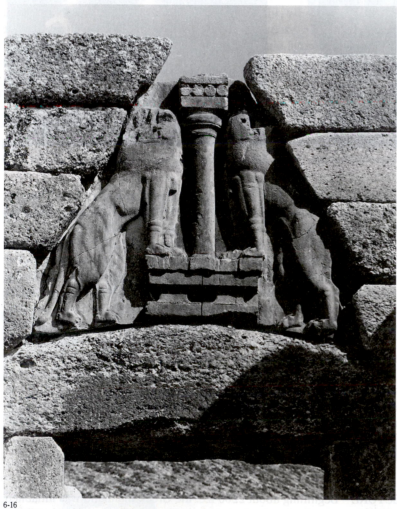

6-16

6-16. The Lion Gate, Mycenae, Greece (detail). c. 1250 B.C. Limestone high relief, height approx. 9'6" (2.9 m)

potamia. We gain entrance to the palace proper in the thirteenth-century-B.C. citadel of Tiryns (fig. 6–15) through a *propylon,* or columned gateway. Before us rises the columned façade of the royal audience hall, or *megaron,* whose roof was supported within by four columns around a circular hearth. Traces of rich painted decoration have been found on the plastered floor, and there were numerous wall

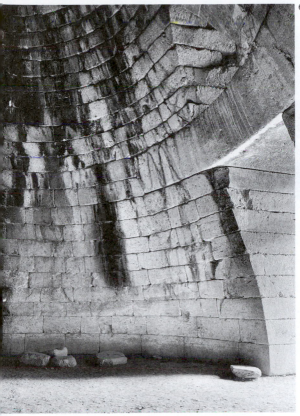

6-18. Interior, "Treasury of Atreus," Mycenae

paintings. The relative positions of propylon and megaron foretell those of the Athenian Propylaia, or entrance gate to the Acropolis (see fig. 7–60), and the Parthenon in Classical times.

The formidable walls of the citadel at Mycenae, also built of cyclopean masonry, were entered through a trilithon (three-stone) gate recalling the megalithic architecture of the Late Stone Age. The triangle framed by the lintel and the progressively projecting blocks above is occupied by one of the few pieces of monumental sculpture surviving from Aegean times, a massive high relief showing two muscular lions (alas, now headless) placing their front paws upon the base of a typical Minoan tapering column (fig. 6–16). Clearly the column had a religious significance that required it to be flanked and protected by the royal beasts.

By far the most accomplished and ambitious of these cyclopean constructions is the so-called Treasury of Atreus at Mycenae (fig. 6–17), actually a thirteenth-century royal tomb, some 43 feet in height and 47½ in diameter. Although all the rich decoration, possibly in precious metals, that once enlivened the interior and the entrance has been plundered, the effect of the simple masonry vault is majestic in the extreme (fig. 6–18). It is a corbel vault, with superimposed courses of masonry projecting one beyond the other. The blocks are trimmed off inside to form a colossal beehive shape of remarkable precision and accuracy. This is the largest unobstructed interior space known to us before that of the Pantheon in imperial Rome (see Introduction fig. 20).

GOLDWORK, IVORY, AND PAINTING Schliemann's excavations of the royal graves at Mycenae in 1876 yielded a dazzling array of objects in gold, silver, and other metals, some ceremonial, some intended for daily use. A number of masks in beaten gold (fig. 6–19) were probably intended to cover the faces of deceased

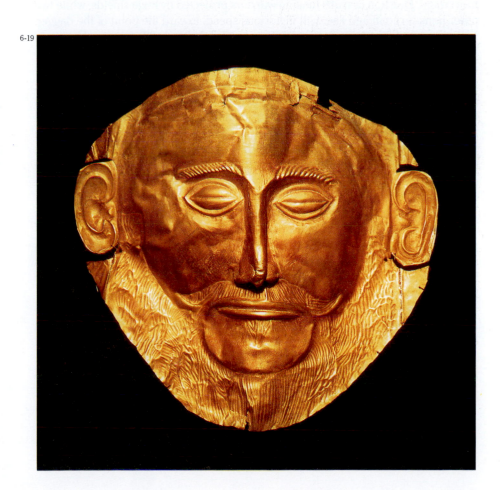

6-19. Funeral mask, from the royal tombs, Mycenae. c. 1500 B.C. Beaten gold, height approx. 12″ (30.5 cm). National Archaeological Museum, Athens

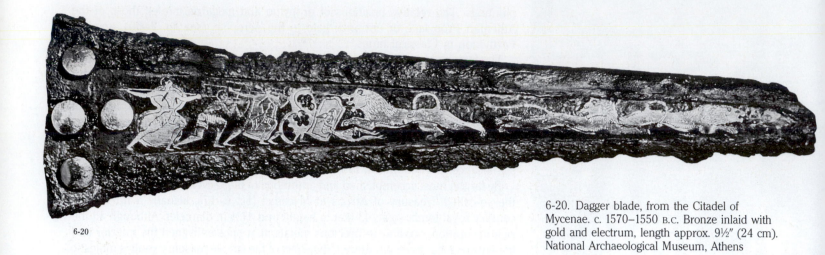

6-20

6-20. Dagger blade, from the Citadel of
Mycenae. c. 1570–1550 B.C. Bronze inlaid with
gold and electrum, length approx. 9½″ (24 cm).
National Archaeological Museum, Athens

kings. Although hardly to be compared with the refinement of the gold mask of
Tutankhamen (see fig. 3–43), their solemn honesty is nonetheless impressive.

The Mycenaean warrior-kings attached great importance to their weapons, and
superb examples have been found. A bronze dagger blade inlaid with gold and
electrum, a natural alloy of silver and gold (fig. 6–20), shows a spirited battle of
men against lions, surpassing anything we have thus far seen in swiftness of
movement. One lion assaults lunging warriors protected by huge shields, while two
other lions turn tail and flee with inglorious speed, toward the point of the dagger.

Even more beautiful are two golden cups (figs. 6–21, 6–22) found at Vaphio in
Laconia and datable to about 1500 B.C. These works, to be ranked among the
masterpieces of ancient art, are covered with continuous reliefs of extraordinary
vivacity and power showing the capture of bulls. While the style is clearly Minoan,
recalling the movement and expressive intensity of the *Harvester Vase,* these violent
bulls are far removed from the graceful creature that appeared in the Knossos
fresco. Various methods of entrapment are shown, ranging from lassoing the
fetlock with a rope, held by a characteristically wasp-waisted, muscular young man,
to capture by nets and enticement by a friendly cow. The cups pulsate with the
movement of the powerful bodies and flying hooves; the motion subsides only in
the romantic tête-à-tête of the bull and the cow.

A little ivory group of unknown purpose (fig. 6–23) has recently been found near
a sanctuary at Mycenae. It shows three deities, possibly Demeter, the earth-
goddess, her daughter Persephone, and the young god Iakchos, although this is
pure conjecture. The affectionate grouping of the figures, with arms over shoulders
and free, playful poses, combined with the fluid movement of the skirts, renders
this one of the most poetic works of Aegean art.

Under the attacks of another group of Greek invaders from the north, the
Dorians, the rich and powerful Mycenaean civilization was overwhelmed and
destroyed about 1100 B.C., to be succeeded by a period often known as the Dark
Ages. The darkness was deepened by obscurity and neglect. As far as we know, the
great achievements of Aegean art were without influence on their Greek successors
and remained unknown until our own times.

6-21, 6-22. *Vaphio Cups,* from Laconia, Greece.
c. 1500 B.C. Gold, height approx. 3½″ (9 cm).
National Archaeological Museum, Athens

6-23. *Three Deities,* from Mycenae. c. 1500–1400
B.C. Ivory, height 3″ (7.6 cm). National
Archaeological Museum, Athens

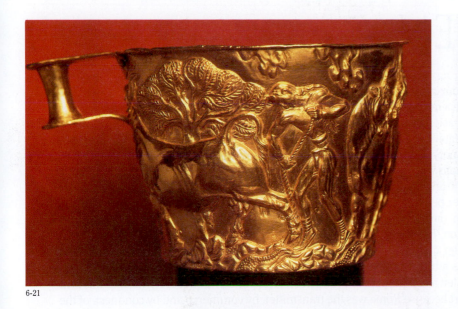

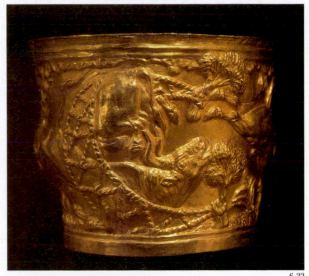

6-21

6-22

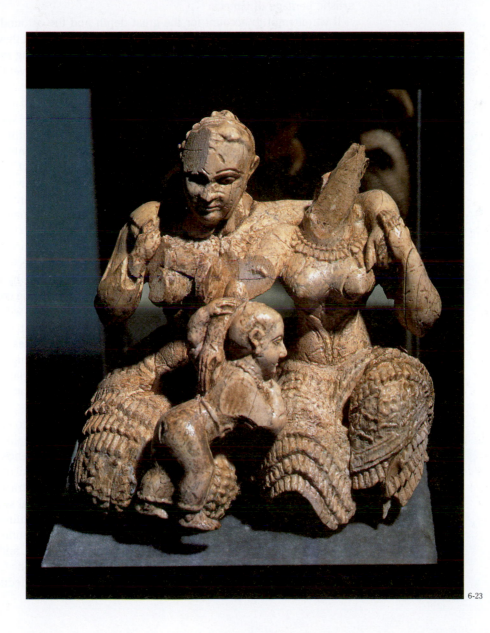

6-23

CHAPTER SEVEN

Of the four great historic arts we have considered up to this point, that of Egypt alone left a measurable influence on later periods, and even Egyptian influence was only occasionally fruitful or decisive. Splendid though they were, the arts of Mesopotamia and of the Aegean world vanished almost entirely from human sight and memory until very nearly our own times. And, of course, the pre-Columbian civilizations were totally unknown and unsuspected in either Europe or Asia. When we turn to ancient Greece, however, we are dealing for the first time with an art that has never been entirely forgotten. Greek art, like Greek culture in general, influenced in one way or another the art of every subsequent period of Western civilization, including the present, sometimes to an overwhelming degree. Even when later cultures felt they must revolt against Greek influence, each revolt in itself was a tribute to the greatness of Greek achievement. The only other culture that has left a comparable impression on later periods is that of Rome, and this is in large part because Rome was the transmitter, by commerce and by conquest, of the artistic heritage of Greece.

If we attempt to account for the great depth and the astounding durability of Greek influence, we will probably come to the conclusion that they are both due to the primacy of Greek civilization and Greek art in developing rational norms for every aspect of the arts, as distinguished from the rigid conventions imposed by Egyptian society upon Egyptian art. The Greeks derived these norms from human nature and behavior, accessible to Greek thinkers, writers, and artists through their unprecedented powers of observation, inquiry, and analysis. "Man is the measure of all things," said the Greek philosopher Protagoras in the fifth century B.C., and while Protagoras' own subjectivity aroused considerable controversy in his lifetime, his celebrated remark may still be taken as typical of the Greek attitude toward life and toward art. The dignity and beauty of the individual human being and the rich texture of physical and psychological interplay among human beings constitute at once the subject, the goal, and the final determinant of Greek artistic and literary creation.

Both land and climate stimulated the unprecedented concentration of Greek culture on the quality of human life and on physical and intellectual activity. Greece is a land of mountainous peninsulas and islands, separated by narrow, fjordlike straits and bays, with scanty arable land. It is subject to strong contrasts of winter cold and summer heat and to fierce and unpredictable sea winds. Horizons are limited by mountains and rocky islands. Under a sunlight whose intensity is credible only to those who have experienced it, the land takes on a golden color against a sea and sky of piercing blue. Day gives way to night almost without intervening twilight—or did, until air pollution masked the clarity of Greek light. Against such a background and in such light, forms and relationships are clear and sharp.

In such an environment it was neither easy nor necessary to establish cooperative relationships between communities, separated by mountain walls or by arms of the sea. A living had to be wrested by force and by intelligence from rocky land and treacherous water. The beautiful but often hostile Greek surroundings fostered an athletic and inquiring attitude toward existence that contrasted strongly with Egyptian passivity and that precluded submission to universal systems of government. Farming was not easy in the rocky soil; grain crops required great expenditure of effort, and the olive tree and the vine needed careful tending. In addition to the limited agricultural class, a trading class eventually arose, and finally a manufacturing class engaged in the production of such characteristic Greek artifacts as pottery and metalwork, which were exported to the entire Mediterranean world.

GREEK ART

Like the Minoans before them, the Greeks were excellent sailors; like the Mycenaeans, they were valiant soldiers. Greek systems of government were experimental and constantly changing. It is no accident that so many English words for governmental forms derive from Greek—*democracy, autocracy, tyranny, aristocracy, oligarchy,* and *monarchy,* to name only a few. Even *politics* comes from the Greek *polis,* the word for the independent city-state with its surrounding territory, which was the basic unit of Greek society. All six of the forms of government just mentioned were practiced at one time or another by the Greek city-states on the mainland, the islands, Asia Minor, Sicily, and southern Italy, often in rapid succession or alternation. But even when popular liberties were sacrificed for a period to a tyrant or to an oligarchic group, the Greek ideal was always that of self-government. The tragedy of Greek history lies in the inability of the Greek city-states to subordinate individual sovereignty to any ideal of a permanent federation that could embrace the whole Greek world and put a stop to the endemic warfare that sapped the energies of the separate states and eventually brought about their subjugation. Until the time of Alexander the Great, who borrowed the idea from the Near Eastern cultures he conquered, the notion of a god-king on the Egyptian or Mesopotamian model was wholly absent from Greek history. We can find a special significance in the fact that, while the Egyptians and Mesopotamians recounted their history in terms of royal reigns or of dynasties, the Greeks measured time in Olympiads, the four-year span between the Olympic Games, an athletic festival celebrated throughout ancient Greek history. Athletics (a Greek word) could hardly have been a better symbol of the value placed by Greek culture on the individual, for the Olympics were not team games in our sense, any more than they are today, but individual contests of physical skill and strength. They had no counterpart elsewhere in the ancient world.

The Greeks peopled their cosmos (a Greek word) with gods who, like themselves, lived in a state of constant rivalry and even conflict, often possessed ungovernable appetites on a glorified human scale, took sides in human wars, and even coupled with human beings to produce a race of demigods known as heroes. Only in their greater power and knowledge and in their immortality did the gods differ from humans. Just as no single mortal ruled the Greek world, so no god was truly omnipotent, not even Zeus, the king of the gods (see fig. 7–33).

The Greeks were strongly aware of their achievements, and not least of their history, as a record of individual human actions rather than merely of events. Their art is the first to *have* a real history in our familiar sense of an internal development. Egyptian art seems to spring into existence fully formed and can hardly be said to have developed after its initial splendid creations. And certain basic forms and ideas run throughout Mesopotamian art from the Sumerians to the Persians. But Greek art shows a steady evolution from simple to always more complex phases, some of which are for convenience labeled Archaic, Classical, and Hellenistic. Although this development was not steady, nor uniform at all geographic points, it is strikingly visible and has often been compared with that of European art from the late Middle Ages through the Renaissance and the Baroque periods. From start to finish, the entire evolution of Greek art took only about seven centuries, or less than one-quarter of the long period during which Egyptian art continued relatively unchanged. The Age of Pericles, often considered the peak of Greek artistic achievement, lasted only a few decades.

Despite the anthropocentric nature of Greek culture, the Greeks were under no illusions about the limitations or indeed the inevitable downfall of human ambitions. One of their favorite literary forms, which they invented and in whose

portraits of women, and also a large picture of an old woman at Naples, and a portrait of herself, executed with the help of a mirror. No artist worked more rapidly than she did, and her pictures had such merit that they sold for higher prices than those of Sopolis and Dionysios, well-known contemporary painters, whose works fill our picture galleries. Olympias was also a painter; of her we know only that Autoboulos was her pupil.

We have, of course, no more evidence of the work of these women painters than of their male contemporaries, but we can glean from this passage that women painted even in Archaic times, that their work was highly valued, that they had male pupils, but that their work was limited almost entirely to portraits—only a single painting of a mythological or historical subject is recorded (see pages 198–99). At least one representation of a woman actually painting a vase is known, and it is wholly possible that a considerable proportion of unsigned Greek vases were painted by women.

Another serious loss is that of color in architecture and sculpture. Under the influence of marble statues and capitals from which the original coloring leached out centuries ago, we tend to think of Greek art—and Greek costumes, too—as white. Nothing could be further from the truth. In early periods the coloring applied to the statues was quite bright, even garish, judging from traces of the original paint still remaining here and there. In the Classical period, coloring was undoubtedly more restrained but was certainly used to suggest actual life, especially in eyes, lips, and hair. Garments were colored, and certain details were added in gold or other metals in all periods. Limestone or sandstone temples in regions such as Sicily and southern Italy in which marble was not available were coated with fine plaster tinted to resemble marble. In all temples, including the marble ones, capitals and other architectural details were brightly painted. Wall decorations from the Hellenistic era survive to indicate that the interiors of prosperous homes were also ornamented in color (see fig. 7–107). If the well-known Greek sense of harmony and of the fitness of things gives us any basis for speculation, then Greek color must have been harmoniously adjusted and must have formed an essential ingredient in the total effect of works of architecture and sculpture. We must attempt to restore this effect in our imaginations if we are to understand the work of art as the artist intended it. Only the pots, which as we have seen (page 136) are unlikely ever to be totally destroyed, survive in vast numbers and with their coloring intact. In Greek ceramics the color is generally limited to red terra-cotta; black and white slip, baked on; and an occasional touch of violet. But even the pots, made for practical, everyday purposes, were intended to be seen not, as now too often, in superimposed rows in museum cases, but as small, movable accents in richly colored interiors.

The Geometric and Orientalizing Styles (800–600 B.C.)

The three centuries from about 1100 to about 800 B.C. are still an era of mystery and confusion, often called—by analogy with the later one following the breakup of the Roman Empire—the Dark Ages. The title is intended to suggest not only the dimness of our present knowledge of this era but also the fact that what little has been unearthed about it indicates a fairly low stage of cultural development—indeed, a sharp decline from the splendor of Mycenaean art and civilization. At the beginning of this period tribes from the north, probably the Danube basin, moved south into the areas formerly ruled by Mycenaeans, settling largely in the Peloponnesos, the cluster of peninsulas that makes up southern Greece. Later Greeks called these people Dorians; Sparta, always the most conservative and warlike of the Greek city-states, prided itself on its Dorian origin. Some of the older peoples of Mycenaean derivation fled to the islands of the Aegean and to Asia Minor, where they founded such important centers as Ephesus and Miletus. These tribes, known

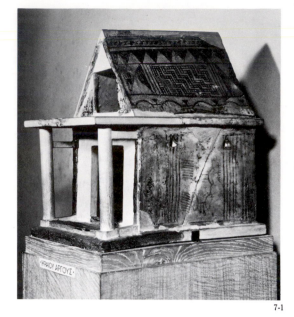

7-1

7-1. Model of a temple, from the Heraion near Argos. Middle 8th century B.C. Terra-cotta, length approx. 14½″ (37 cm). National Archaeological Museum, Athens

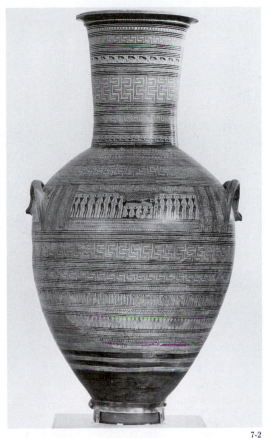

7-2. Amphora painted in the Geometric style, from the Dipylon Cemetery, Athens. c. 750 B.C. Height 61″ (1.55 m). National Archaeological Museum, Athens

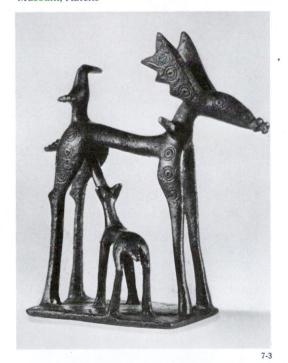

7-3. *Deer Nursing a Fawn*, from Thebes, Greece. 8th century B.C. Bronze, height 2⅞″ (7.3 cm). Courtesy, Museum of Fine Arts, Boston

as Ionians, were, however, not wholly driven out of Greece by the invaders. Some were able to preserve their identity, notably the inhabitants of the peninsula of Attica, with its most important center at Athens.

Understandably enough, architectural remains from this earliest period of Greek art are extremely scanty, although some foundations of temples have been uncovered. But we possess precious evidence as to the modest external appearance of such buildings from two small terra-cotta models (fig. 7–1) and fragments of another, which can be dated about the middle of the eighth century B.C. by comparison with contemporary pottery. Basically, these temples appear to be direct descendants of the Mycenaean megaron type, such as that at Tiryns (see fig. 6–15). A single oblong room, sometimes square-ended, sometimes terminating in an *apse* (semicircular end), was roofed with a gable and preceded by a columned portico. Probably the walls were of rubble or mud brick and the columns of wood; the roof may even have been woven from thatch. These are humble buildings indeed, yet they are the obvious prototypes of the Greek temples of a more splendid era (see figs. 7–19, 7–50).

The finest remains of eighth-century Greek art are certainly the pots, covered with the abundant ornament that gives the period its name, *Geometric*. Some of them are truly majestic, especially the huge *amphora* (jar for oil or wine; fig. 7–2) from the Dipylon Cemetery in Athens. This type of jar was placed over graves and perforated at the bottom so that offerings of oil or wine could seep through. The shape, with powerful body and lofty neck, slender handles, and slightly flaring lip, is of the greatest elegance. In contrast to the free-floating organic shapes of Minoan pottery, even the tiniest element is accessible to human reason and arranged in rational sequence. The surface is divided into almost innumerable bands of constantly varying width, ornamented with slender black lines describing against the terra-cotta background geometric figures—dots, diamonds, lozenges, and three different versions of the meander or "Greek fret" motif so common in later Greek decoration, some bands apparently moving from right to left, some from left to right, some readable either way. A single band on the neck shows simplified and very graceful antelope grazing, moving from left to right. At the level of the handles, the frets seem to be parted, as it were, and forced to run vertically to make way for a funerary scene. The deceased, represented schematically and frontally on his bier, is flanked by identical wasp-waisted mourners with their arms elevated, looking like abstract versions of Aegean figures. Across the grand volume of the jar the slender lines of geometric ornament seem to shimmer in contrast to the strong black of the expanding and contracting figures.

A large number of statuettes in terra-cotta and in bronze remain from the Geometric period. A delightful example is the tiny bronze *Deer Nursing a Fawn* (fig. 7–3), hardly more naturalistic than the figures on the amphora from the Dipylon Cemetery but just as intense in pattern and feeling. From none of the works of visual art, however, could we possibly guess that during this same crucial eighth century were composed the two great Homeric epics, the *Iliad* and the *Odyssey*, which seem to us in retrospect the very foundation stones of European literature. The discrepancy between these elaborate narratives—which display in a highly developed phase every facet of the skill of the oral epic poet—and the stylized images of Geometric painting and sculpture does not, however, constitute a unique instance as we follow the relations between the arts throughout history.

It is perhaps significant that words and meanings in ancient Greece developed earlier and more rapidly than visual images. But the pictorial arts did not remain long behind. Seventh-century vases show a considerable loosening of the tight Geometric style. At Eleusis, a massive amphora (fig. 7–4), almost as tall as the Dipylon vase, is a striking example of the Proto-Attic style, so called because it precedes the full development of vase painting in Athens in the sixth and fifth centuries. The relatively inert Geometric ornament of the eighth century, which only suggested motion, has now "come alive" and depicts motion. The very shape of the vase has changed. The bottom is narrower, so that the body seems to swell, and the neck flares more sharply. The handles have grown enormously and are composed of cutout shapes, largely crosses and palmettes. The greatly reduced ornament, consisting largely of intertwined black and white bands, is extremely active. The main fields of the vase are now taken over by figures. Visible on the side of the body shown in the illustration are two fierce, snake-haired Gorgon sisters, confronted by Athena (whose figure is only partially preserved); in the panel above is a fight between a lion and a boar. The most terrible scene is enacted on the neck, where Odysseus and two companions force a burning stake into the one eye of the Cyclops Polyphemos. The action of the figures seems reinforced by the centralized floral ornaments scattered freely throughout the background. These derive from Near Eastern sources and have given rise to the term *Orientalizing* for this second phase of Greek art.

Some sculpture in stone survives. Although less than life size, the limestone *"Lady of Auxerre"* (fig. 7–5), so called because she once stood in a museum in that French city, is impressive in her combination of linear precision and a rude massiveness that suggests at all points the original contour of the block. Her tight costume forms a pillowy shaft that conceals her legs, and it is decorated with a delicately incised meander pattern. About her bosom the costume tightens to reveal firm and abundant breasts. Her huge head is surmounted by a wiglike mass of hair, falling in four great locks on either side and so bound at intervals that they appear to be separated into little cushions. Her remaining eye and her mouth, with its delicate smile, are executed with a sensitivity that renders the relative clumsiness of hands and feet more surprising. Although this statue offers only a slight challenge to the then already two-thousand-year-old Egyptian tradition of figure sculpture, it is still a powerful work.

The Archaic Period (600–480 B.C.)

The term *Archaic,* from a Greek word meaning "early," is applied to the unexpectedly vigorous and inventive period in which the main lines of the arts in Greece were rapidly established. Enormous developments were made in a very brief span of time. Although it is a matter of personal taste, many prefer the incisive strength and brilliance of Archaic art, perhaps even because of its stylizations, to the richer, fuller, and more harmonious Classical phase that succeeded it. What is undeniable is that the sixth century B.C. is one of the great creative periods in world art. Beginning modestly, temple building achieved structures of the greatest originality, on an increasingly grand scale. Architecture was adorned with sculpture at many crucial points and was sometimes almost enveloped by it. Painting, as we know from countless thousands of painted vases, kept abreast of the other arts and perhaps—although we shall never know, since the wall paintings are forever lost—outstripped them. Since we have chosen Protagoras' famous saying, "Man is the measure of all things," as a text for our consideration of Greek art, it is perhaps best to start with the evolution of the human figure in Greek sculpture and then to consider how the figure was used as a measure for the other arts.

FREESTANDING SCULPTURE   Greece is a land dominated by stone, and fortunately much of it is usable for sculpture. The Greek islands, notably Paros, and Mount Hymettos and Mount Pentelikon near Athens yielded marble of superb luminosity and clarity, far more beautiful than Egyptian limestone. Greek marble was not only easier to carve but more appropriate to the representation of human flesh than either the speckled granite or the dark diorite utilized by the Egyptians for monumental statues. And the Greeks' possession of iron gave them tools more effective than the softer bronze implements relied upon by the Egyptians. Iron points, claw chisels, and drills—essentially the same instruments used by sculptors ever since—made it possible for the sculptor to bring out all the expressive beauty

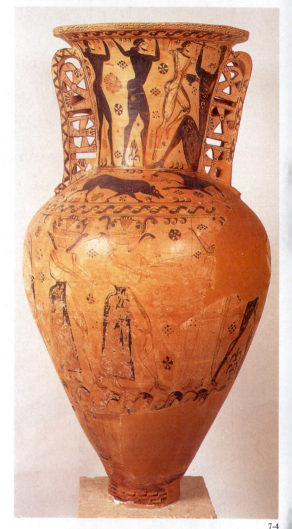

7-4. Amphora painted in the Proto-Attic style, with *Odysseus Blinding Polyphemos* (above) and *Fighting Animals* and *Gorgons* (below). Middle 7th century B.C. Height 56″ (1.42 m). Archaeological Museum, Eleusis

7-5. Female figure, called *Lady of Auxerre.* c. 650 B.C. Limestone, height 24½″ (62 cm). Musée du Louvre, Paris

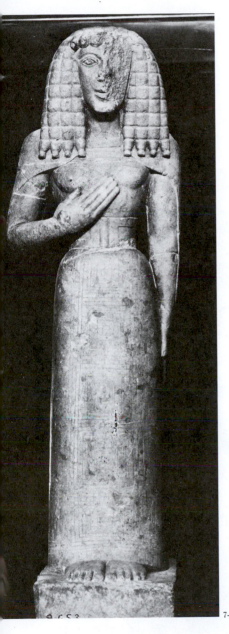

7-5

7-6. *Kouros of Sounion.* c. 600 B.C. Marble, height approx. 10′ (3.05 m). National Archaeological Museum, Athens

7-7. *Anavyssos Kouros.* c. 525 B.C. Marble, height 6′4″ (1.93 m). National Archaeological Museum, Athens

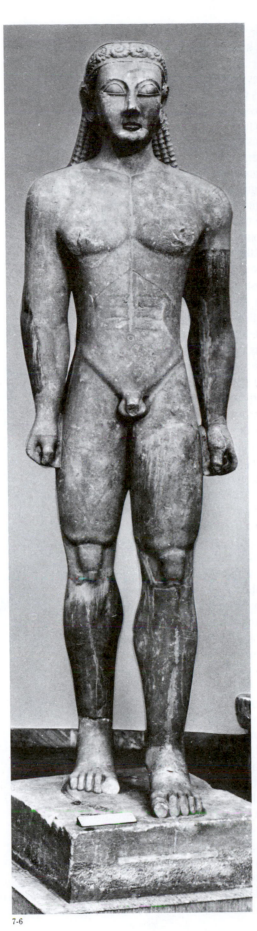

7-6

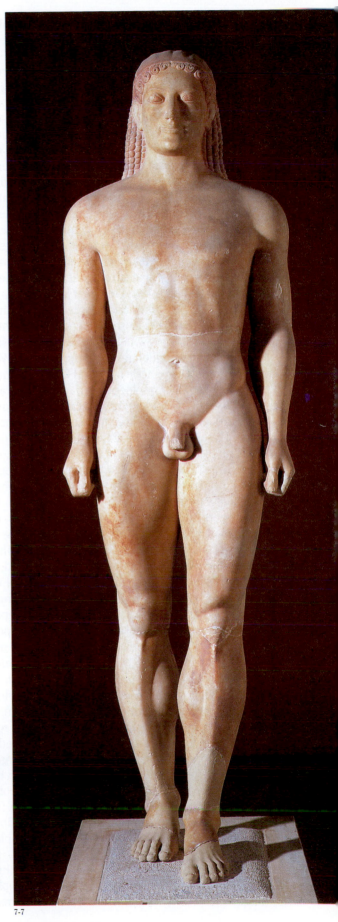

7-7

of the marble, which he could then smooth by the time-honored methods of abrasion, and finally wax in order to bring the surface to the highest degree of perfection.

An impressive series of standing marble figures remains from the sixth century. For want of more precise terms the male statue is generally called *kouros* ("youth"; even today a Greek barbershop is known as a *koureion*), the female *kore* ("maiden"). Some statues were signed by their sculptors, others inscribed with the name of a donor. Some were dedicated to various deities; some were placed over graves. Votive and commemorative statues they certainly were, but not portraits in the sense of likenesses. Apparently, we should regard these statues as idealizations.

Strangely enough to modern eyes, the male figures are always totally nude, the female always fully clothed, but these conventions of male nudity and female modesty correspond to the fact that, while nude male athletes were seen daily in the *palaestra* (public open-air gymnasium), women never appeared unclothed. Moreover, men were completely free to go where they wished, while women, as we have seen, were generally restricted to their quarters.

The largest and grandest, and one of the earliest, of the kouros figures—a statue almost ten feet high—was found at Sounion near Athens and is datable about 600 B.C. (fig. 7–6). It shows undeniable Egyptian influence in the rigid stance of the figure, with the arms close to the sides and the left leg advanced. Given Greek commercial relations with Egypt, such influence is easier to account for than the as yet unexplained suddenness of its appearance. We still do not know why the Greeks began carving large-scale figures at the end of the seventh century B.C. At first sight the figure, for all its grandeur, seems much less advanced from the point of view of naturalism than Old Kingdom statues dating from two thousand years earlier. But there are telltale differences that suggest the enormous development soon to take place. First, although the Egyptian sculptor thought of his stone figures as free-standing (see the drawings of sculptors at work, fig. 3–9), in practice he invariably left a smooth wall of uncut stone between the legs and arms and the body (see fig. 3–15). Apparently, he was trying to avoid fracture in carving with soft bronze tools, on which enormous pressure had to be exerted. Such inert passages of stone must have been intolerable to the Greek artist as restrictions on the mobility and freedom of his figure, and he reduced them to the smallest possible bridges of stone between hand and flank. (He also did away with the kilt of the Egyptian statue to display the male figure in total nudity.) Second, while the weight of an Egyptian figure rests largely on the right (rear) leg, that of the kouros statue is always evenly distributed, so that the figure seems to be striding rather than standing. Finally, the total calm of the Egyptian figure, which never seems to have known the meaning of strain, gives way to an alert look and, where possible, to a strong suggestion of tension, as in the muscles around the kneecap and especially in the torso, whose abdominal muscle is cut into channels as yet neither clearly understood nor accurately counted. The preternaturally large and magnificent head of the *Kouros of Sounion,* while divided into stylized parts in conformity with a lingering Geometric taste, shows the characteristic Greek tension in every line.

In the *Anavyssos Kouros* (fig. 7–7), done only some sixty to eighty years later and placed over the grave of a fallen warrior called Kroisos, the stylistic revolution hinted at in the Sounion *Kouros* has been largely achieved. At every point the muscles seem to swell with actual life. Although the full curves of breast, arm, and thigh muscles may as yet be imperfectly controlled, the pride of the figure in its youthful masculine strength is unprecedented. The sharp divisions between the muscles have relaxed; forms and surfaces now flow easily into each other. Even the lines of the still-stylized locks are no longer absolutely straight but flow in recognition of the fact that hair is soft.

A somewhat more mature, bearded figure, the *Calf-Bearer* (fig. 7–8), of about 570 B.C., shows the transition between the two phases. The sharp divisions of the muscles have softened, and the channels in the abdominal muscle are correctly

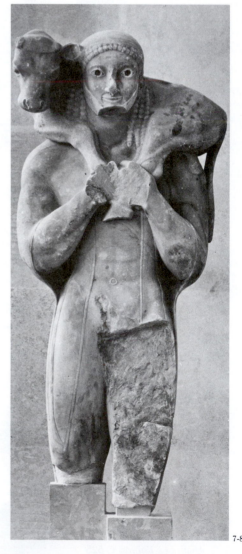

7-8. *Calf-Bearer,* from the Acropolis, Athens. c. 570 B.C. Marble, height 66″ (1.68 m). Acropolis Museum, Athens

placed and counted. The now largely destroyed legs originally had the characteristic kouros pose. The meaning of the famous "Archaic smile" that lifts the corners of the mouth still eludes us, but this expression is characteristic of Archaic art, even in battle or in death, throughout the sixth century, after which it soon disapppears. While still proclaiming the original surface of the block, the head of the calf the man bears as an offering is modeled with great sensitivity.

A superb funerary stela carved as a memorial portrait of the Athenian warrior Aristion (fig. 7–9) shows the rich possibilities opened up by Archaic artists. The sculptor ARISTOKLES, who signed this work, was able to control gradations of low relief with great delicacy so as to suggest the varying distance of the left and right legs and arms from the viewer's eye and the fullness of the torso inside its leather body-armor. Aristokles' attention to visual effects freed the warrior completely from the Egyptian convention of two left hands and two left feet, and he seems to have delighted in contrasting the smoothly flowing surfaces of the body, neck, and limbs with the delicate folds and rippling edges of the *chiton* (garment worn next to the skin), which escape from beneath the armor and cling gently to the upper arm and the strong thigh. He was at pains even to indicate the exact extent of the leather greaves, which protect the shinbones but not the calves.

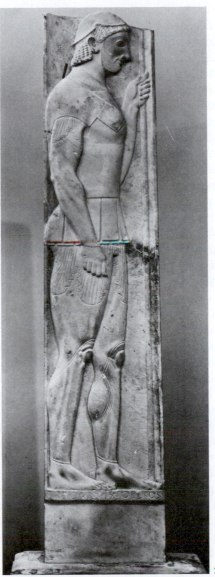

7-9. ARISTOKLES. *Stela of Aristion.* c. 525 B.C.
Marble, height (without base) 8′ (2.44 m).
National Archaeological Museum, Athens

7-9

One of the earliest of the kore figures was found in the Temple of Hera on the island of Samos (fig. 7–10) and is majestic enough to have been a statue of a goddess. About contemporary with the *Calf-Bearer,* the figure shows a striking change from the *"Lady of Auxerre"* (see fig. 7–5); the block, as is customary in Samian work, has here become a cylinder. When the missing head was intact, the hair fell over the back. The missing left hand probably held a gift. The *himation* (cloak), looped at the waist, is thrown around the torso and gathered lightly with the fingers of the right hand. The forms of the bosom are at once concealed and revealed by the streaming spiral folds, which contrast strongly with the tiny vertical pleats of the chiton. The profile of the figure, often compared to a column, has much in common with the elastic silhouette of an early amphora (see figs. 7–2, 7–4), expanding and contracting, elegant and restrained.

Another sixth-century masterpiece is the *Peplos Kore* from Athens (fig. 7–11), so named because the figure wears the *peplos,* a simple woolen garment. The statue is somewhat blocky in its general mass and beautifully reticent in its details. The severe peplos falls simply over the noble bosom and hangs lightly just above the narrow girdle about the waist. The missing left forearm was originally extended, and thus freed entirely from the mass of the body, with a daring we have never before witnessed in stone sculpture. In fact, it had to be made of a separate piece of marble and inserted into a socket, where a piece of it may still be seen. The right arm hangs along the body, the contours beautifully played off against the subtle curve of the hip and thigh, which the heel of the hand barely touches, eliminating the necessity for a connecting bridge. To modern eyes the broad face looks unexpectedly happy, almost whimsical in its expression, and the soft painted red locks, three on each side, flow gently over the shoulders, setting off the full forms of the body. The *Peplos Kore* is datable about 530 B.C. The climax of the Archaic style can be seen in the enchanting kore nicknamed *La Delicata* (fig. 7–12), of just a few years later. The corners of the large and heavy-lidded eyes are lifted slightly, and the "smile" has begun to fade; indeed, the face looks pensive. The folds and rippling edges of the rich Ionian himation, together with the three locks on either side, almost drown the basic forms of the figure in the exuberance of their ornamental rhythms. Traces of the original coloring are preserved, especially in the hair and eyes and in the border of the peplos, adding to the delight of one of the richest of all the kore figures. Both arms were "pieced," as can be seen from the round sockets, and have disappeared. By about the beginning of the fifth century this practice was abandoned, and entire figures were carved from a single block no matter how great the extension of the limbs. The next steps in the evolution of both male and female figures belong to another era.

ARCHITECTURE AND ARCHITECTURAL SCULPTURE   Great as were the new developments in Greek sculpture in the sixth century, they were at least equaled, perhaps even surpassed, by the achievements of Greek architects. These were not in the realm of private building, for houses remained modest until Hellenistic times. Neither kings nor tyrants, nor least of all, of course, democratic officials, built palaces like those of Mesopotamia, which as we have seen incorporated temples into their far-flung complexes.

The principal public building of the Greeks was the temple. Generally in a sanctuary dedicated to one or several deities, some temples were in lowland sites, others set upon a commanding height, like the Acropolis at Athens. But the Greek temple was not intended for public worship, which took place before altars in the open air. Its primary purposes were to house the image of the god and to preserve the offerings brought by the faithful. At first of modest dimensions and never of a size remotely comparable to that of its Egyptian counterpart, it was impressive only in its exterior. Its appearance was dominated by the colonnaded portico, or *peristyle,* which surrounded all larger temples and existed in the form of porches even in very small ones (see figs. 7–16, 7–62). In a Greek polis a portico provided

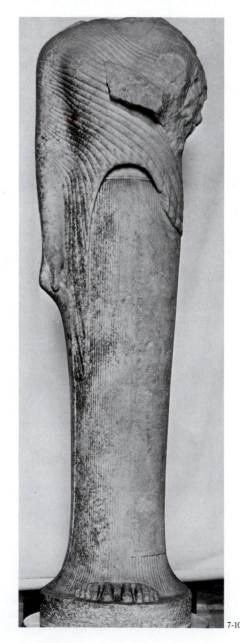

7-10. *Hera,* from Samos. c. 565 B.C. Marble, height 6′4″ (1.93 m). Musée du Louvre, Paris

7-10

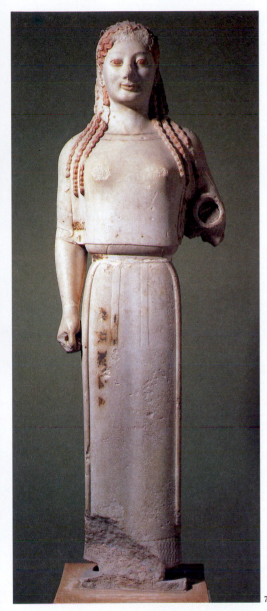

7-11. *Peplos Kore*, from Athens. c. 530 B.C. Marble, height 48″ (1.22 m). Acropolis Museum, Athens

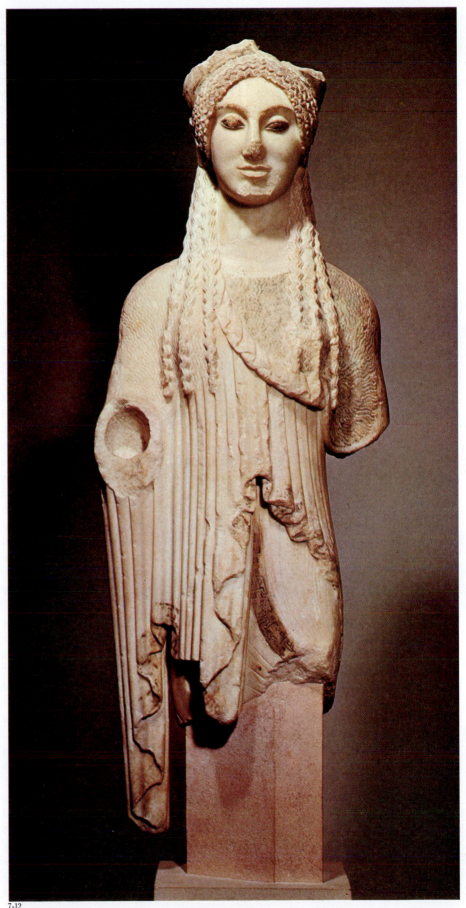

7-12. *Kore*, also called *La Delicata*, from the Acropolis, Athens. c. 525 B.C. Marble, height 36″ (91 cm). Acropolis Museum, Athens

shelter from sun or rain and a freely accessible public place in which to discuss political or philosophical principles, conduct business, or just stroll. In fact, in Hellenistic times independent porticoes known as *stoas* were built for just these purposes. They were walled on three sides and open on the fourth, and were sometimes hundreds of feet long (see figs. 7–87 and 7–88 for a plan and reconstruction of the stoa in the *agora,* or marketplace, at Assos). The walls of early colonnaded temples were built of mud brick and the columns of wood. In the course of time stone was substituted for these perishable materials, but the shapes of wooden columns and wooden beams continued to be followed in their stone successors, just as the architecture of Imhotep at Saqqara (see fig. 3–7) perpetuated palm-trunk and reed-bundle construction.

Clearly differentiated systems known as orders governed all the forms of any Greek temple. The orders may be thought of as languages, each with its own vocabulary and rules of grammar and syntax, or as scales in music. At first there were only two orders, named for the two major ethnic divisions of the Greeks, the Doric and the Ionic. In the fifth century the Corinthian appeared (fig. 7–13); this order was seldom used by the Greeks but became a favorite among the Romans, who added two orders of their own, the Tuscan and the Composite. In Hellenistic times individual variants of the Greek orders appeared here and there, but these are occasional exceptions that prove the universal rule.

The *column* and the *entablature,* the basic components of the Greek orders, are simply more elaborate versions of post-and-lintel construction. The column was divided into *shaft, capital,* and *base* (Greek Doric columns had no base; one was added in the Roman version), the entablature into *architrave, frieze,* and *cornice.* The capital (from the Latin word for "head") was intended to transfer the weight of the entablature onto the shaft. The Doric capital consisted of a square slab known as the *abacus* above a smooth, round, cushion-shaped member called the *echinus.* The Ionic capital, more elaborate, had a richly ornamented abacus and echinus separated by a double-scroll–shaped member, the *volute.* The Doric architrave (Greek: "principal beam") was a single unmolded stone beam, and the frieze was divided between *triglyphs* and *metopes.* The triglyph (Greek: "three grooves") was a block with two complete vertical grooves in the center and a half groove at each side. The triglyphs derived from the joist-ends of wooden buildings; the metopes were the slabs between the beams. The Ionic architrave was divided into three flat strips called *fasciae,* each projecting slightly beyond the one below. The Ionic frieze had no special architectural character but could be ornamented or sculptured. The temple was usually roofed by a low gable whose open triangular ends, backed by slabs of stone, were called *pediments.*

Ancient writers considered the Doric order masculine and robust, the Ionic feminine and elegant. In every Doric or Ionic temple the basic elements were the same. The columns were made of cylindrical blocks, called *drums,* turned on a lathe. These were held together by metal dowels and were *fluted,* that is, channeled by shallow vertical grooves, after being erected. The earliest Doric columns had twenty-four flutes, which increased their apparent verticality and slenderness. Doric flutes met in a sharp edge; Ionic flutes were separated by a narrow strip of stone. Whatever may have been their purpose, the flutes have the effect of increasing the clarity of progression from light to shade in easily distinguishable stages around a shaft. The flutes may possibly be related to the polygonal columns occasionally used in Egypt.

Unlike Egyptian polygonal and convexly fluted columns, which were always straight, and Aegean columns, which tapered downward, Greek columns tapered noticeably toward the capital. Egyptian cylindrical columns, generally based on plant forms, showed a considerable bulge near the bottom (see fig. 3–34); Greek columns, instead, had a slight swell, known as the *entasis,* suggesting the tonus of a muscle. They were, moreover, governed by the proportions of contemporary human sculptured figures. As the Greek figure grew slenderer and the head propor-

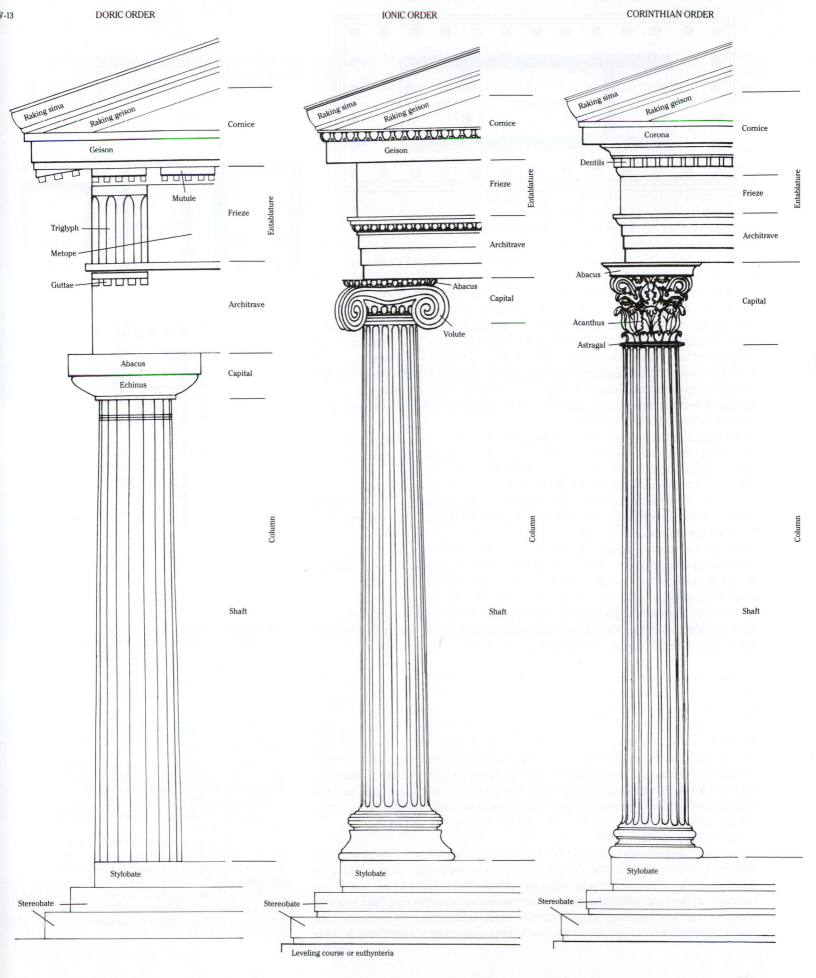

DORIC ORDER

Raking sima

Raking geison

Cornice

Geison

Mutule

Frieze

Triglyph

Metope

Guttae

Architrave

Abacus

Echinus

Capital

Entablature

Column

Shaft

Stylobate

Stereobate

IONIC ORDER

Raking sima

Raking geison

Cornice

Geison

Frieze

Architrave

Abacus

Volute

Capital

Entablature

Column

Shaft

Stylobate

Stereobate

Leveling course or euthynteria

CORINTHIAN ORDER

Raking sima

Raking geison

Corona

Cornice

Dentils

Frieze

Architrave

Abacus

Capital

Acanthus

Astragal

Entablature

Column

Shaft

Stylobate

Stereobate

159

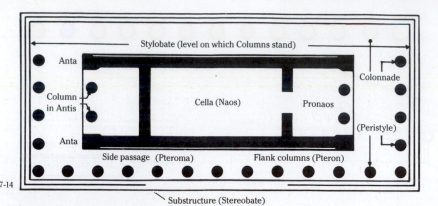

7-14

7-14. Plan of a typical Greek peripteral temple
(after I. H. Grinnell)

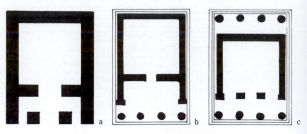

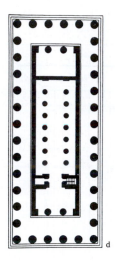

tionately smaller, so the column diminished in bulk and its capital in size. On occasion the column could even be substituted by a human figure carrying the architrave (see figs. 7–19, 7–65)—without the slightest sign of strain.

Like the parts of the orders, the structural elements of the temples (fig. 7–14) and also the disposition of those elements in typical plans (fig. 7–15) were controlled by rules as stringent as those of grammar and music. Small temples often consisted only of a *cella* (the central rectangular structure housing the image of the deity), whose side walls were prolonged forward to carry the entablature and pediment directly and to frame two columns; such a temple was called *in antis*. If the portico ran across its entire front, the temple was *prostyle;* if it had front and rear porticoes, it was *amphiprostyle;* if the colonnade, known as a *peristyle,* ran around all four sides, the temple was *peripteral;* if the portico was two columns deep all around, the temple was *dipteral.*

Yet just as sonnets written in the same language or fugues composed according to the same rules will vary infinitely according to the ideas and talents of the poet or the musician, there are a surprising number of individual variations within what appear to be the stern limitations of Greek architectural orders and types. As we have already seen, there was a rapid change in the proportion of the columns corresponding to those of contemporary sculptured figures. The tapering and entasis also changed. The earliest examples show the sharp taper and a very muscular bulge, with sharply projecting capitals, suggesting physical strain in carrying the weight of the entablature. In later columns, along with the increase in height, both taper and entasis rapidly decrease and the projection of the capital sharply diminishes, until the lofty columns of the Parthenon in the middle of the fifth century appear to carry their load effortlessly. The changes in style and taste from temple to temple, subtle though they may at first appear, are distinct enough to enable one to recognize individual temples of either Doric or Ionic order at a glance.

The corner columns invariably caused difficulties. Since there was always one triglyph above each Doric column and another above each *intercolumniation* (space between two columns), either half a metope would be left over at the corner of the building or the corner triglyph would not be over a column. This discrepancy was solved by delicate adjustments of distances, so that a two-faced triglyph always appeared at the corner, with adjacent metopes slightly extended, and the corner column was brought a little closer to its neighbors. In the Ionic order, since the capitals had two scrolled and two flat sides, the problem was again how to turn the corner. This was solved by giving the corner capital two adjacent flat sides, with a volute coming out on an angle for both, and two inner scrolled sides (compare fig. 7–13 with figs. 7–62, 7–69).

But these adjustments were by no means all. Architects also toyed with the effects of varying proportions. Early temples were nearly three times as long as wide, while the Classical formula of the fifth century provided that the number of columns on the long side of a temple should be twice the number of those at either end plus one. The relatively simple interiors were lighted only by the large door. Numerous methods of supporting the roof-beams were experimented with in early

7-15. Six typical Greek plans for temples and other public structures. (Plans are not to scale)

a. Treasury of the Siphnians, Delphi (fig. 7-19), a small single-roomed structure *in antis,* having a portico in front formed by extensions (*antae*) of the long walls, with two columns between them; many early temples had this simple plan

b. Temple B, Selinus, Sicily, a *prostyle* temple, having a columned portico across the entire front of the building

c. Temple of Athena Nike, Acropolis, Athens (fig. 7-62), an *amphiprostyle* temple, having a columned portico at both front and back

d. Temple of Hera II, Paestum (fig. 7-40), a *peripteral* temple, having a row of freestanding columns on all four sides

e. Temple of Apollo, Didyma (fig. 7-92), a *dipteral* temple, having a double row of freestanding columns surrounding the cella and porticoes

f. Tholos, Epidauros (fig. 7-72), a building with a circular plan ultimately derived from Mycenaean huts and tholos tombs (see fig. 6-17)

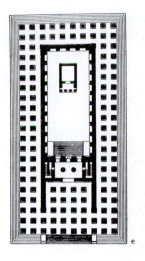

7-15

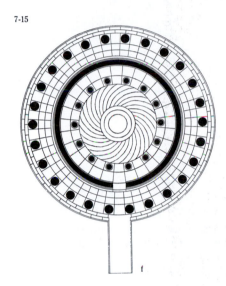

temples, including projecting spur walls like those at Saqqara (see fig. 3–7), and even a row of columns down the center, which had the disadvantage of obscuring the statue of the deity. The sixth- and fifth-century solution was generally two rows of superimposed orders of small columns, each repeating in miniature the proportions of the external peristyle (see fig. 7–41). Roof-beams in early temples were still of wood, and tiles of terra-cotta; in the sixth and fifth centuries marble was often used for roof tiles.

Sculpture could be placed almost anywhere in Egyptian temples; huge statues could sit or stand before or inside the temples; walls, columns, and pylons were alive with rows of figures carved in the shallowest relief, mingled with hieroglyphics, and painted. From the very start the Greeks made a clear-cut distinction between those sections of a temple that could be ornamented with sculpture and those that could not. Walls and columns were inviolable, save in the rare instances when a sculptured figure could become a bearing member (see figs. 7–19, 7–65). But into the empty spaces of a Greek temple, sculpture could logically be inserted. Triglyphs were blocks of some size; the intervening metopes made splendid fields for relief sculpture. Naturally, the reliefs had to be of a certain depth in order to compete with the surrounding architectural elements, and there had to be some continuity in content among the metopes running round a large building. An Ionic frieze was also an obvious place for a continuous strip of relief ornament. The corners of the pediments afforded the possibility of silhouetting sculptures (*acroteria*) against the sky. And above all, the empty pediments, which needed nothing but flat, vertical slabs to exclude wind and rain, provided spaces that could be filled with sculptured figures of a certain depth, eventually statues in the round. In those regions of Greece that enjoyed good stone for carving, and in those temples that could afford sculptural work, an unprecedented new art of architectural sculpture arose, never surpassed—or even equaled—in Europe until the Gothic cathedrals of the twelfth and thirteenth centuries (see Chapter Fifteen). For the first time in history, the architectural creations of humanity were in perfect balance with the human figure itself.

The earliest well-preserved Greek temple is not in Greece itself but in the Greek colony of Poseidonia, now called Paestum, on the western coast of Italy about fifty miles southeast of Naples. This limestone building, erroneously called the "Basilica" in the eighteenth century but probably dedicated to Hera, queen of the gods, has lost its cella walls but still retains its complete peristyle (fig. 7–16). The temple

7-16

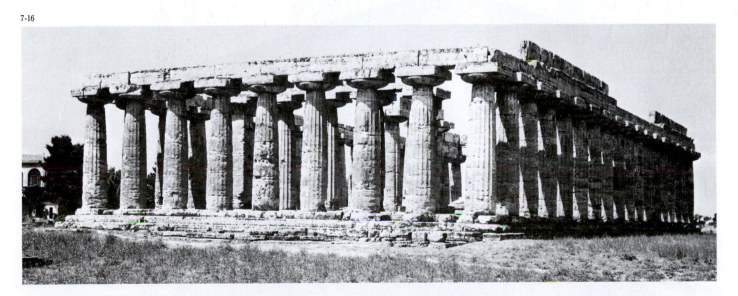

7-16. Temple of Hera I, called the Basilica, Paestum (ancient Poseidonia), Italy. Middle 6th century B.C.

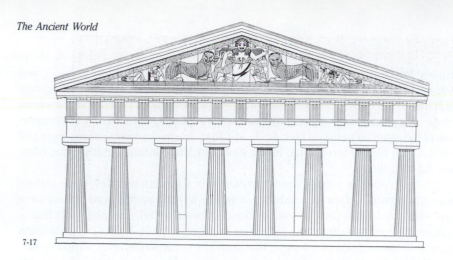

7-17

7-17. Reconstructed view of the west façade, Temple of Artemis, Corfu (after G. Rodenwaldt). Early 6th century B.C.

is unusual in having nine columns across the ends; most others show an even number. The bulky, closely spaced columns with their strong entasis and widespread capitals appear to labor to support the massive entablature. Although the temple has no sculpture, it gives us an idea of how the slightly earlier Temple of Artemis on the Greek island of Corfu must originally have looked (reconstruction in fig. 7–17). Considerable fragments of one of its limestone pediments remain (fig. 7–18). This pediment was carved in high relief, approaching sculpture in the round. The central figure, so huge that she must kneel on her right knee in order to fit, is the Gorgon Medusa, grinning hideously and sticking out her tongue. She was probably placed there to ward off evil spirits, and is aided in her task by the two symmetrical leopards that crouch on either side (one thinks of the heraldic lions of Mycenae; see fig. 6–16). On her left, as an odd anachronism and in smaller scale, appear the head and torso of the boy Chrysaor, who sprang from her neck when Perseus struck off her head; to her right is Pegasus, the winged horse, born in the same way and at the same moment. The modeling strongly suggests that of the *Calf-Bearer* (see fig. 7–8). In the empty corners of the pediment were placed smaller, battling figures of gods and giants. So symmetrical a grouping, with fillers at the corners, looks tentative when we compare it to the closely unified pediments that were created later. Nonetheless, the contrast between large and small masses of smooth stone is delightful, and so is Medusa's writhing belt, formed of live, intertwined, and very angry snakes.

7-18. *Medusa and Chrysaor, between Leopards,* from the west pediment of the Temple of Artemis, Corfu. c. 600–580 B.C. Limestone high relief, height 9′2″ (2.79 m). Archaeological Museum, Corfu

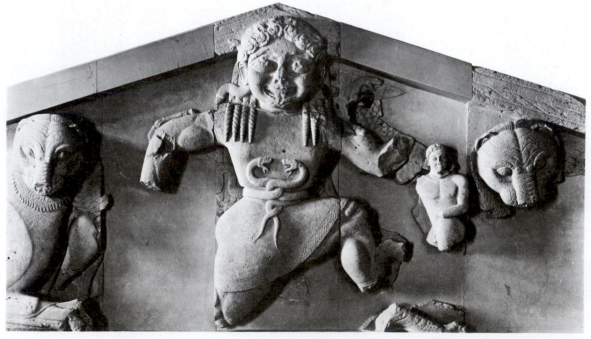

7-18

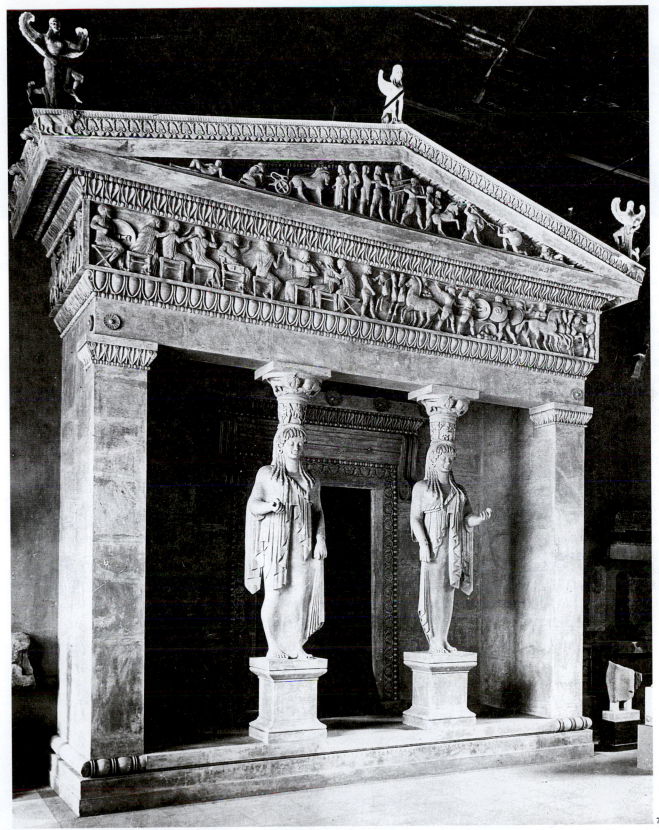

7-19

7-19. West façade, Treasury of the Siphnians, Sanctuary of Apollo, Delphi (partially reconstructed). c. 530 B.C. Marble. Archaeological Museum, Delphi

A more refined and elegant, as well as more active and complex, use of sculpture appears in the little marble treasury built at the sanctuary of Apollo at Delphi about 530 B.C. by the inhabitants of the Greek island of Siphnos to hold their gifts. The Treasury of the Siphnians has been partially reconstructed from fragments (fig. 7–19, and see plan in fig. 7–15). Here columns are replaced by two graceful kore

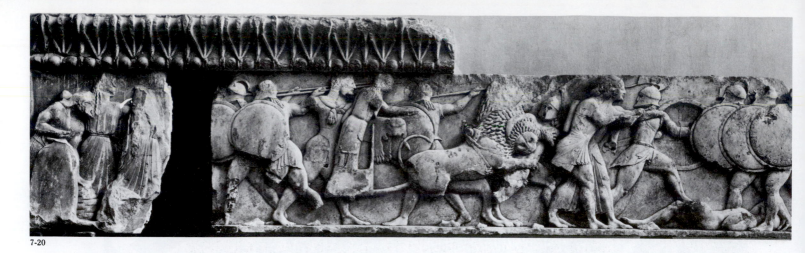

7-20

figures, known as *caryatids,* strongly resembling *La Delicata* (see fig. 7–12), on whose heads capitals are balanced to distribute effortlessly the weight of entablature and pediment. In Greek and south Italian villages women can still be seen carrying jars of wine, water, or oil in just this manner, with a scarf wrapped around the bottom of the jar playing the role of the capital. The frieze is a continuous relief, largely depicting battle scenes. The *Battle of Gods and Giants* (fig. 7–20) shows that the sculptor had a completely new conception of space. No longer does he have to place one figure above another as in Egyptian art to indicate distance. All stand or move on the same ground level and overlap in depth. Although none of the figures are in the round—they are all more or less flattened, in keeping with the character of a relief—those in the foreground are sharply undercut. The projection diminishes so that the figures farthest from the eye are only slightly raised from the background. This relief, for the first time in the history of art as far as we know, strives to achieve the optical illusion of space receding horizontally inward from the foreground. This recession is limited to a maximum of three figures (or four horses), but it is revolutionary nonetheless. The pediment contains, again for the first time, actual groups of almost freestanding statues, carved in more or less the same scale, in poses progressively adjusted to the downward slope of the pediment. The intense activity of the reliefs is kept in check only by the severity of the unrelieved wall surfaces below.

The climax of Archaic sculpture, at the threshold of the Classical period, is the temple of the local goddess Aphaia on the island of Aegina in the Gulf of Athens.

7-20. *Battle of Gods and Giants,* fragment from the north frieze of the Treasury of the Siphnians, Delphi. c. 530 B.C. Marble, height 26″ (66 cm). Archaeological Museum, Delphi

7-21. *Oriental Archer,* from the west pediment of the Temple of Aphaia, Aegina. c. 500 B.C. Marble, height 41″ (1.04 m). Staatliche Antikensammlungen und Glyptothek, Munich

7-22. *Archer,* from the east pediment of the Temple of Aphaia, Aegina. c. 490 B.C. Marble, height 31″ (79 cm). Staatliche Antikensammlungen und Glyptothek, Munich

7-21

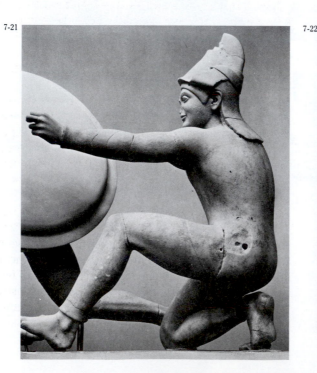

7-22

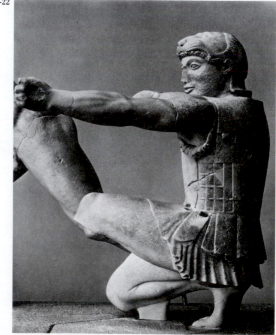

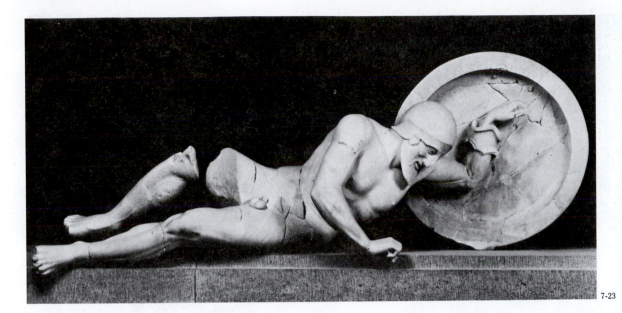

7-23

7-23. *Dying Warrior,* from the east pediment of the Temple of Aphaia, Aegina. c. 490 B.C. Marble, 24 × 72″ (61 × 182.9 cm). Staatliche Antikensammlungen und Glyptothek, Munich

The building was constructed about 500 B.C. of limestone stuccoed to resemble marble. Portions of the temple still stand. The marble pedimental statues, removed to Munich, were excessively restored in the nineteenth century, but these restorations have recently been carefully removed. These statues are superb, full of the same vitality visible in the reliefs from the Treasury of the Siphnians yet simpler and more successfully balanced. It is interesting to compare the *Oriental Archer* (fig. 7–21), so called because of his Phrygian cap, from the western pediment, carved about 500 B.C., with the *Archer* from the east pediment carved some five or ten years later (fig. 7–22). Nobly poised though the earlier statue is, it is somewhat schematic; one does not really feel the play of muscles. The masses of the later figure are held in position entirely by its beautifully understood muscular movement and tension, which must have been even more effective when the missing bronze bow was intact. The *Dying Warrior* (fig. 7–23) embodies at long last the heroic grandeur of the Homeric epics in the simple, clear-cut masses of the figure and in its celebration of self-possession and calm even at the moment of violent death. The latest statues at Aegina have, in fact, brought us to the beginning of the Classical period in content and in style.

VASE PAINTING   Painting was always considered one of the greatest of the arts by Greek writers, and a splendid tradition of painting on walls and on movable panels surely flourished during the late Archaic period. Yet so little survives that we cannot even form a clear idea of what we have lost. Nonetheless, a few echoes of this vanished art persist in far-off Etruscan tomb paintings in central Italy (see fig. 8–11). Given their well-defined, continuous outlines and flat areas of color, not unlike those of Egyptian painting, and considering also the strict limitations of Archaic sculptures with their smooth surfaces and strong, active contours, we can arrive at some notion of what the style of Archaic monumental painting must have been. Its quality, however, can only be guessed at; in this we are assisted by the beauty of the vast number of sixth-century painted vases still preserved.

The Archaic period saw the climax of Greek vase painting, which reached a high level of artistic perfection, rivaling sculpture and architecture, and which brought art of high quality into every prosperous household. Even more than contemporary sculpture, Archaic vase painting shows the flexibility of the new art, whose brilliant design is based on action and movement. How highly the Greeks themselves valued their vases is shown by the fact that so many of them were signed by the painter. Some were also signed by the potter. Through comparison with signed vases, unsigned pieces can be attributed to individual artists on account of similarities in style. In this way the development of personal styles can sometimes be

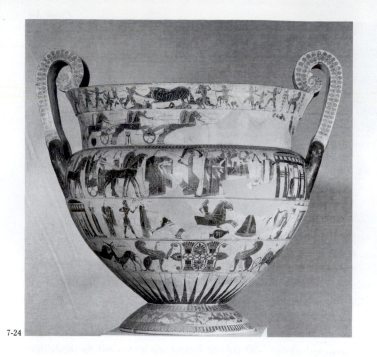

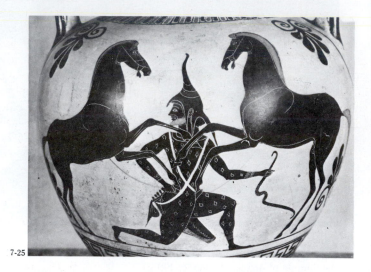

followed for decades. This is the first moment in the history of art when such distinctions can be made and such evolutions traced. It is a very important consideration because the art we are analyzing is, after all, one whose very principles of design are based on the interaction of individual human beings — in contrast to the mere alignment of standardized types so common in Egyptian and Mesopotamian art.

Vases were made for both local use and export in several Greek cities, especially Corinth and Athens. In the seventh century, Corinthian vases made of pale, yellowish clay were most popular, but in the early Archaic period the orange-red pots of Athens took the lead. The miniature style of the Corinthian painters could no longer compete with the strength, grace, and intellectual clarity of the Athenians'.

Many of the finest Greek vases are preserved because they found their way to Etruria, whose inhabitants prized them highly and buried them in the tombs of the dead. The best Attic (Athenian) vases are masterpieces of drawing and design, operating within a very restricted range of colors. The natural color of the clay was sometimes heightened by a brighter clay slip painted on for the background. The most important tone was black, used for figures and for the body of the vase. Gone is the cluttered decoration of the earlier periods. Within the contours of the black figures, details were drawn in lines incised by a metal tool. The glossy black was also a clay slip, its color achieved by controlling the air intake during the delicate and complex firing process.

One of the most ambitious sixth-century vases, known as the *François Vase* (fig. 7–24), of about 570 B.C., was found in an Etruscan tomb at Chiusi, in central Italy. It is a *krater,* a type of vase intended for mixing water and wine, the customary Greek beverage, and was proudly signed by the painter KLEITIAS and the potter ERGOTIMOS. The grand, volute-shaped handles grow like plants out of the body of the vase before curling over to rest upon its lip. The vase is still divided into registers like the Dipylon amphora (see fig. 7–2), but geometric ornament has been reduced to a single row of sharp rays above its foot; the handles are decorated with palmettes. The other registers are devoted to a lively narration of incidents from the stories of the heroes Theseus and Achilles. The figures still show the tiny waists, knees, and ankles and the full calves, buttocks, and chests that are standard in the Geometric style, but they now move with a vigor similar to that of the sculptures on the Corfu pediment (see fig. 7–18), and both men and animals have begun to

7-24. KLEITIAS and ERGOTIMOS. *François Vase,* volute krater painted in the Attic style, found at Chiusi, Italy. c. 570 B.C. Height approx. 26″ (66 cm). Museo Archeologico, Florence

7-25. PSIAX. *Oriental between Two Horses,* detail of an amphora painted in the Attic style, found at Vulci, Italy. c. 520–510 B.C. Height of amphora 14½″ (37 cm). British Museum, London

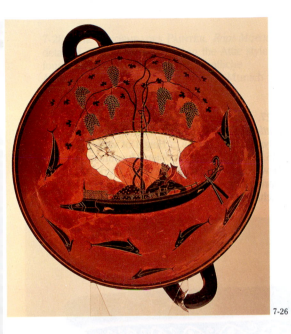

7-26

7-26. EXEKIAS. *Dionysos in a Ship,* interior of a kylix painted in the Attic style, found at Vulci. c. 540 B.C. Diameter 12″ (30.5 cm). Staatliche Antikensammlungen und Glyptothek, Munich

overlap in depth in a manner foreshadowing the deployment of figures in the frieze of the Treasury of the Siphnians (see fig. 7–20).

A splendid example of Archaic design based on organic movement is the *Oriental between Two Horses* (fig. 7–25) by the painter PSIAX, dating from about 520–510 B.C. The Oriental, who may be a horse trainer, grasps his bow by the top in his left hand and moves rapidly forward with knees sharply bent, in the style of the Medusa at Corfu—apparently an Archaic convention for running, which also appears in pre-Columbian art (see fig. 5–13), and turns his head to look backward over his right shoulder. The forcefulness of the movement and the angularity of the bent limbs recall the almost contemporary *Oriental Archer* (see fig. 7–21) from Aegina. On either side horses rear in a heraldic grouping, their slender legs overlapping the archer's body, their bodies seeming to swell with the expansion of the amphora itself. The incised lines, at once delicate and firm, are left in the red of the background.

One of the most delightful of all Archaic vase paintings is on the interior of a *kylix,* or wine cup, painted by EXEKIAS about 540 B.C. (fig. 7–26). Dionysos, god of wine, reclines in a ship from whose mast he has caused a grape-laden vine to spring in order to terrify some pirates who had captured him, and whom he then transformed into dolphins. The almost dizzying effect of the free, circular composition is, appropriately enough, not unusual in decorations for the insides of wine cups. In this case the feeling of movement is heightened by the bellying sail (originally all white) and by the seven dolphins circling hopelessly about the vessel. The entire scene, with all its suggestions of wind and sea, is carried off without the actual depiction of even a single wave.

Toward the end of the sixth century, vase painters discovered that their compositions would be more effective and their figures more lifelike if left in the red color of the terra-cotta, with the black transferred to the background, just as in pediments or friezes where the figures shone in white or softly colored marble against a darker background of red or blue. At first the change was tentative; some vases even show red figures on one side, black on the other. But once it was generally accepted the change was lasting. One of the earliest red-figure vases, and certainly one of the finest Greek vases in existence, is a combined kylix-krater (or "calyx-krater"; fig. 7–27) by EUPHRONIOS datable about 515 B.C. The principal scene depicts a rarely illustrated passage from the *Iliad,* narrating how the body of the Trojan warrior Sarpedon, son of Zeus, was removed from the field of battle by the twin brothers Hypnos and Thanatos (Sleep and Death) under the supervision of Hermes, so that it could be washed in preparation for a hero's grave. The extraordinary combination of great sculptural force, equaling that of the statues at Aegina, with extreme tenderness of feeling is completely unexpected. The blend is achieved by a line that surpasses almost anything in Greek vase painting in its tensile strength and descriptive delicacy. From the beautiful analysis of the muscular body of Sarpedon to the knife-sharp wing feathers of Hypnos and Thanatos, even to the slight curl at the tips of the fingers and toes, the movement is carried out with perfect consistency and control. The very inscriptions, usually naming adjacent figures, are not allowed to float freely against the black, but move in such a way as to carry out the inner forces of the composition. *Thanatos,* for example, is written backward to lead the eye toward the central figure of Hermes.

But vase painting did not always remain on the plane of high tragedy; the very fact that so many vases were destined to hold wine tended to promote a certain freedom in both subject and treatment, often crossing the boundaries of what we would term pornography. Among the followers of the great Euphronios, two sensitive masters have been distinguished—one called the KLEOPHRADES PAINTER because his work is so often found on vases signed by the potter of that name, the other called the BERLIN PAINTER, from the location of his principal work. How free the actual execution of red-figure vases can be is seen in the former's treatment of a rapt blond *maenad* (female follower of Dionysos) in fig. 7–28. The deft, sure, linear

The Classical Period—The Severe Style (480–450 B.C.) and Its Consequences

In the early decades of the fifth century B.C., the individualism of the Greek city-states was put to its severest test in a protracted struggle against Mesopotamian autocracy in the form of the Persian Empire, first under Darius I and then under his son Xerxes I. Persia had succeeded in subjugating all the Greek cities of Asia Minor and then insisted on extending her domination to European Greece. The resistance to the Persian threat brought about one of the rare instances of near unity among the rival Greek states. In 480 B.C. Xerxes conquered Attica, occupied Athens (which had been evacuated by its citizens), and laid waste the city. Yet in this selfsame year the Greeks managed to trap and destroy the Persian fleet at Salamis, and after another defeat on land in 479, Xerxes was forced to retire. Although the struggle continued sporadically in northern Greece, the Greek states were temporarily safe. Athens, which had led the resistance, embarked on a period of unprecedented prosperity and power.

The new development of the Classical style in the years immediately following Salamis shows above all an increased awareness of the role of individual character in determining human destiny, and it incorporates the ideal of ennobled humanity in a bodily structure of previously unimagined strength, resilience, and harmony. This development was no accident, any more than it was an accident that the Classical belief in the autonomy of the individual was revived in the early Renaissance in fifteenth-century Florence under very similar circumstances. We need only set the new images of heroic, self-controlled, and complete individuals that followed (especially figs. 7–33, 7–34) against the standardized soldiers of Persian autocracy in order to realize the extent of the revolution that came to fulfillment in Greek art of the Classical period.

FREESTANDING AND RELIEF SCULPTURE   The brief and significant generation between the close of the Archaic period and the height of Classical art in the Age of Pericles shows a remarkable transformation not only in style but also in general tone. The term Severe Style suggests the moral ideals of dignity and self-control that characterize the art of the time and mirror the short-lived Greek resolve to repel the Persian invader. Complex draperies constructed of many delicate, flattened, linear folds give way to simple, tubular masses. The face is now constructed of square or rounded forms rather than the pointed features of the Archaic period: the square, broad nose joins the brows in a single plane, the mouth is short, the lips full, the eyes wide open, the chin and jaw rounded and firm. Most important of all, the Archaic smile has given way to an utter and deliberate calm, as if the figure were wearing a mask. (It should be remembered that actors in Greek drama did indeed wear masks, but with set expressions for comedy or tragedy.)

We may well commence our consideration of this period with the earliest of the rare Greek life-size bronzes to come down to us, the superb *Charioteer of Delphi* (fig. 7–30), dedicated by Polyzalos, tyrant of the Greek city-state of Gela in Sicily, to celebrate his victory in the chariot race at the Delphic Games just before 470 B.C. Originally the charioteer stood in a bronze chariot and controlled four bronze horses with their bridles; only fragments of the horses survive. The dignity and calm of the figure remind us that the metaphor of a charioteer was later used by Plato to symbolize man's control of the contrary forces in his soul. The bronze, originally polished, is relieved in the face by inlaid copper lips and eyelashes and by eyes made of glass paste. (We should mentally restore such features whenever they are missing in Greek and Roman bronzes.) The charioteer stands with a resiliency new to Greek sculpture; the folds of his long chiton drape easily across the chest and fall from the high belt in full, tubular shapes as cloth actually does. The figure has at once the verticality and strength of a fluted Doric column and the possibility for action of any nude athlete.

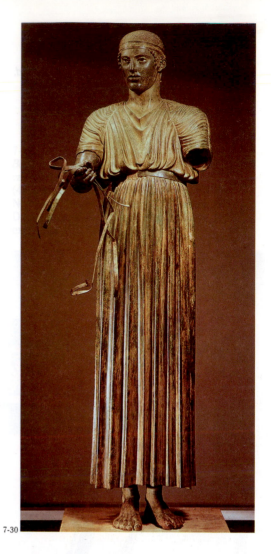

7-30

7-30. *Charioteer of Delphi,* from the Sanctuary of Apollo, Delphi. c. 470 B.C. Bronze, height 71″ (1.8 m). Archaeological Museum, Delphi

7-31. *Kritios Boy,* from the Acropolis, Athens. c. 480 B.C. Marble, height 34″ (86.4 cm). Acropolis Museum, Athens

7-32. *Blond Youth,* from the Acropolis, Athens. c. 480 B.C. Marble, height 9⅝″ (24.4 cm). Acropolis Museum, Athens

7-33. *Zeus,* found in the sea off Cape Artemision (Euboea), Greece. c. 460 B.C. Bronze, height 6′10″ (2.08 m). National Archaeological Museum, Athens

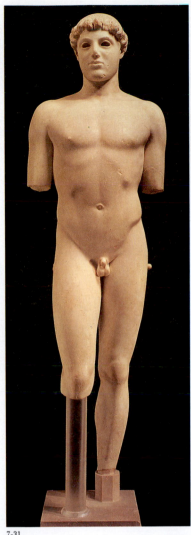

7-31

A slightly earlier statue (fig. 7–31), called the *Kritios Boy* because it embodies what is thought to have been the style of the sculptor Kritios, should be compared with the Archaic kouros figures (see figs. 7–6, 7–7) to bring out the scope of the transformation in Greek sculpture. Although the kouros figures are also standing, they appear frozen in a pose derived from walking, with the weight evenly distributed on both legs. In the *Kritios Boy,* the figure stands *at rest,* as people actually do, with the weight placed on one leg while the other remains free. In consequence the left hip, on which the weight rests, is slightly higher than the right. In recompense, the right shoulder should be higher than the left, but the sculptor does not seem to have noticed this. He has discovered that in a resting figure the masses respond to stresses just as in a moving one, and that rest in a living being is not equivalent to inertia, as in Egyptian sculpture, or to the unreal symmetry of the Archaic, but to a balanced composure of stresses. The fullness, richness, and warmth of the human body, hinted at for the first time in the *Anavyssos Kouros* (see fig. 7–7), are now fully realized, as the forms blend effortlessly into each other. The firm beauty of the features and facial proportions preferred by the Severe Style is seen at its grandest in the *Blond Youth* (fig. 7–32), also dating from about 480 B.C., so called because traces of blond coloring could once be seen in the hair. The irises of the characteristically heavy-lidded eyes still retain considerable color, and the typical pensive, serene expression of the Severe Style is beautifully realized. The hair is still ornamentalized and worn almost like a cap (was it oiled and curled?), although occasionally a lock breaks free.

Fortunately, a single original bronze action-statue of the Severe Style has come to light, a glorious, over-life-size figure of the nude Zeus (fig. 7–33), found in the

7-32

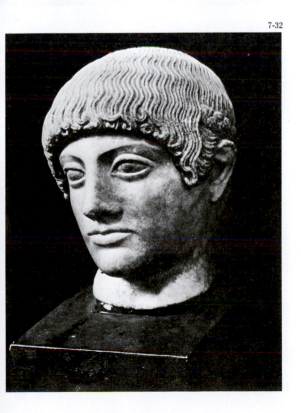

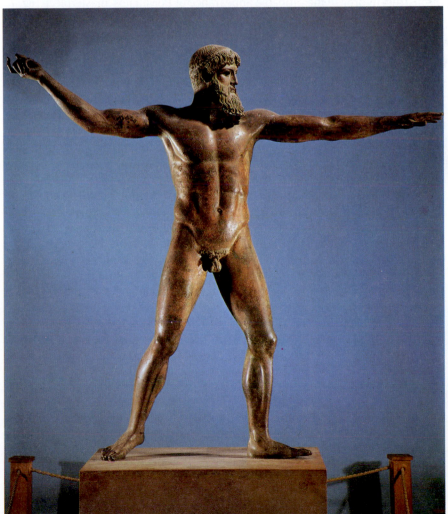

7-33

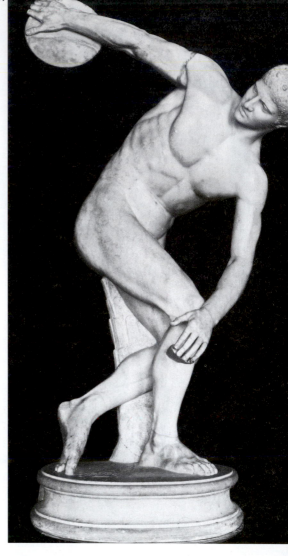

sea off Cape Artemision. The subject is often considered to be Poseidon, god of the sea, but if the trident (three-tined spear) wielded by Poseidon were to be placed in the figure's right hand it would obscure the face; more likely the figure represents Zeus hurling a thunderbolt. In no other remaining example can we see the magnificence of the Greek athletic ideal in the very person of the ruler of the gods. While the hair, bound in by a braid, and the beard and eyebrows are still stylized, the muscles of the body and the limbs vibrate with a new intensity. From about this time on increasing naturalism makes it possible to represent the pubic hair.

The leading sculptors of the period immediately following, especially Myron and Polykleitos, were trained in the Severe Style, of which their work is an immediate outgrowth. Both were chiefly concerned with athletic subjects, which enabled them to exemplify the Classical principles of rhythmic organization derived from the poses of powerful nude male figures. In his bronze *Diskobolos (Discus-Thrower),* of about 450 B.C., which we know only through Roman copies in marble (fig. 7–34), MYRON chose the moment when the athlete bent forward, in a pose of great tension and compression, before turning to hurl his discus. The composition, operating in one plane like the *Zeus of Artemision,* is built on the transitory equipoise of the two intersecting arcs formed by the arms and the torso. Like all Classical figural groupings, this one dissolves the moment the action is over; its beauty lies in the lasting grandeur of a geometrical composition abstracted from a fleeting moment of action. The new dynamics of the Severe Style have been concentrated into a single image of extraordinary power.

The ultimate development of the kouros type can be seen in the *Doryphoros (Spear-Bearer)* by POLYKLEITOS, executed probably between 450 and 440 B.C. Again the lost bronze original is accessible only through a number of Roman copies and ancient literary descriptions. A remarkably successful attempt was made in 1935 to reconstruct in bronze the probable appearance of Polykleitos' masterpiece (fig. 7–35). The problem of the standing figure, posed in the *Kritios Boy* (see fig. 7–31), has now been completely solved. The right leg bears the full weight of the body, so that the hip is thrust outward; the left leg is free; the tilt of the pelvis is answered by a tilt of the shoulders in the opposite direction; and the whole body rises effortlessly in a single long S-curve from the feet to the head, culminating in the glance directed slightly to the figure's right. Regardless of the fact that the figure is at rest—as never before—the dynamism of the pose transforms it into an easy walk and is expressed in the musculature by means of the differentiation of flexed and relaxed shapes, producing a rich interplay of changing curves throughout the powerful masses of torso and limbs. A fragmentary Roman copy in black basalt (fig. 7–36) shows what must have been the effect in dark bronze of the superb muscular structure of the torso, with its characteristic prominent external oblique muscles and sharply defined, U-shaped pelvic groove. Polykleitos wrote a treatise to explain his meticulous system of proportions as exemplified by this statue, but the book is lost and his system still imperfectly understood. Polykleitos called both the *Doryphoros* and the book his "Canon" (measuring rod or standard). The Greek interest in arithmetic and geometry manifested in the theories of Greek philosophers—especially Pythagoras, who saw the universe as operating on mathematical systems—was expressed in all the arts, including music. We should keep in mind that the Greek systems of human proportion, like that of Polykleitos, derive from their love of mathematical relationships; such relationships run through Greek architecture as well, down to the last detail. Significantly, Greek mathematics (Euclid is still in use in one form or another) extended to plane and solid geometry but no further.

Our knowledge of Classical sculpture has been dramatically enriched by the discovery in 1972 of two nude, bearded bronze *Warriors* (figs. 7–37, 7–38), each well over six feet tall, in the sandy bottom of the Ionian Sea about a quarter of a mile from the village of Riace on the shore of Calabria, the toe of the Italian boot. The statues, thickly encrusted with salt and corrosion, were taken in 1975 to Florence for a lengthy cleaning process. Only in 1980 were they placed on exhibition in their

7-34. MYRON. *Diskobolos (Discus-Thrower).* c. 450 B.C. Roman marble copy of bronze original, life size. Museo Nazionale Romano, Rome

7-35. POLYKLEITOS. *Doryphoros (Spear-Bearer).* c. 450–440 B.C. Bronze reconstruction. Universität, Munich

7-36. POLYKLEITOS. *Doryphoros* (fragment). Roman copy in black basalt of bronze original. Galleria degli Uffizi, Florence

7-37, 7-38. *Two Warriors,* found in the sea off Riace, Italy. c. 460–450 B.C. Bronze, height approx. 6′8″ (2.03 m) each. Museo Archeologico, Reggio Calabria, Italy

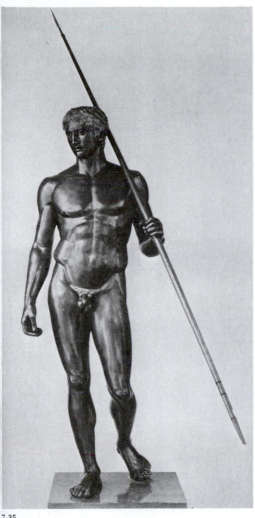

full splendor of gleaming bronze muscles. Immediately they were recognized as works of great importance by scholars and public alike, and created a sensation—in fact, a near riot—when they were eventually removed from Florence for exhibition in Rome at the Quirinal Palace, the official residence of the president of the Italian Republic. Each figure originally held a sword or spear in the right hand and had a shield strapped to the left forearm, but these have disappeared along with the helmet that once covered one of the heads. The statues are otherwise astonishingly complete, down to bronze eyelashes, copper lips and nipples, eyes made of ivory and glass paste, and in one case fierce-looking teeth plated with silver. The massive, muscular bodies quiver with life, and the unknown sculptor has been attentive even to the veins appearing through the skin in the groin, in the inner elbows, and on the lower legs, ankles, and feet. The extraordinary power of these figures, their simple, limited poses, and the combination of great naturalism in some details (the veins) with persistent ornamentalism in others (the hair and beard), coupled with the exceptionally high quality of conception and execution, have convinced most but not all specialists that these are indeed Greek works of the middle of the fifth century. Presumably they were tossed overboard to lighten ship by some small vessel caught in a storm near the treacherous Straits of Messina. More important, no one has yet even made a guess as to where they came from or what purpose these fearless warriors were intended to serve.

7-35

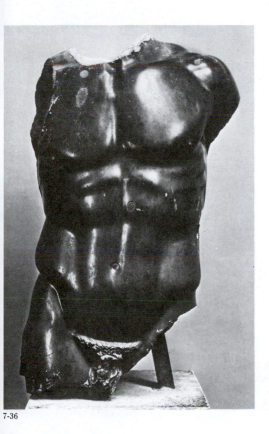

7-36

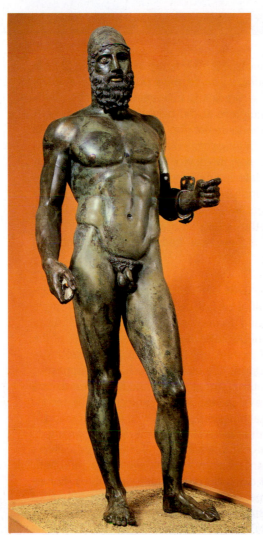

7-37

7-38

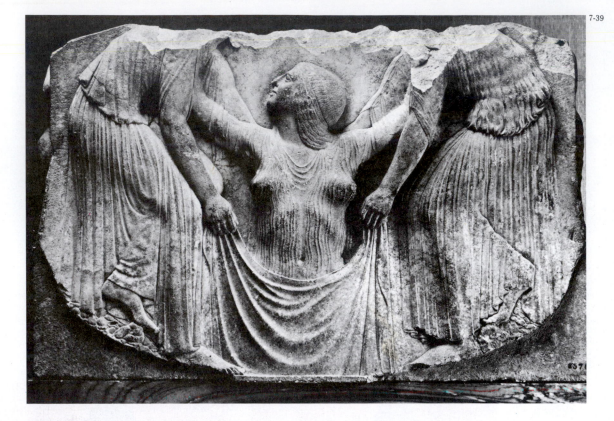

An exquisite example of the treatment of the female figure in the Severe Style is the group of low reliefs known as the *Ludovisi Throne;* more probably, these reliefs once formed an altar. Perhaps made in a Greek city in southern Italy, the reliefs nonetheless show early fifth-century sculpture at the height of its perfection. A relief that probably represents the *Birth of Aphrodite* (fig. 7–39) delineates full and graceful female figures visible through clinging garments that seem almost transparent. As Aphrodite was born from the sea, the device of sheer garments (often known as "wet drapery") seems appropriate; in any case it was used consistently in fifth-century sculpture to reveal the roundness of female forms even when fully clothed and completely dry. Experiments by the archaeologist Margarete Bieber showed that the kinds of cloth used by the Greeks do not fall in such folds when draped around the body (see fig. 7–44), so these "wet" folds are a convention, but a very beautiful one.

ARCHITECTURE AND ARCHITECTURAL SCULPTURE   The greatest architectural and sculptural project of the first half of the fifth century was the Doric Temple of Zeus at Olympia, whose construction and decoration may be dated 470–456 B.C. The temple was the principal building of the sanctuary at Olympia, center of the quadrennial games that provided one of the few unifying threads in the chaotic life of the endemically warring Greek city-states. The temple, which has disappeared but for the *stylobate* (platform on which the columns stand) and the lowest drums of the columns, has been carefully excavated, and its appearance can be reconstructed with accuracy. It was built of local limestone, coated with a plaster made of marble dust, but the sculpture and roof tiles were of Parian marble. The architect, LIBON OF ELIS, designed a peristyle six columns wide and thirteen long. Libon's columns were slenderer and more elegant than any we have seen so far, and both their entasis and the projection of their capitals were slighter and subtler. Something of the grandeur of the original appearance of his building may be felt in the probably contemporary and somewhat smaller Temple of Hera, formerly known as the Temple of Poseidon, at Paestum (fig. 7–40, and see plan in fig. 7–15), despite its

7-39. *Birth of Aphrodite,* from the *Ludovisi Throne.* Early 5th century B.C. Marble low relief, width 56″ (1.42 m). Museo Nazionale Romano, Rome

7-40. Temple of Hera II, Paestum (ancient Poseidonia), Italy. c. 460 B.C.

7-41. Interior, Temple of Hera II, Paestum

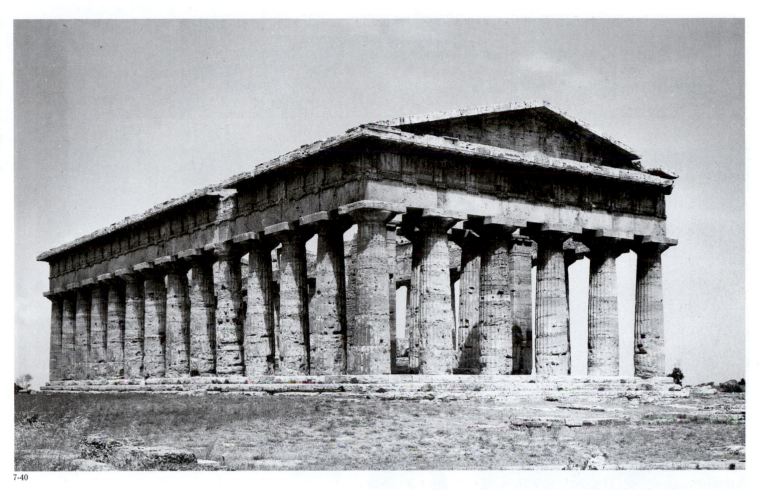

7-40

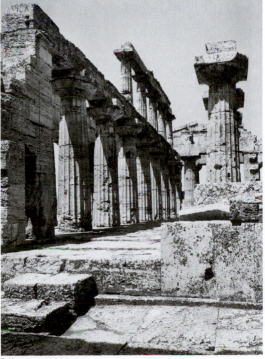

7-41

more massive proportions and closer spacing of columns due to local taste. Both interiors utilized the double row of superimposed columns initiated at the Temple of Aphaia at Aegina. Even in its unroofed state, the effect of the double row in the Temple of Hera II is very handsome (fig. 7–41).

The sculpture at Olympia, much of which is preserved, ranks among the ablest Greek architectural sculpture. Neither the name of the sculptor nor the city of his origin is known, but a single leading master and a host of assistants must have been at work to produce so rich a cycle of sculpture in so short a time. The mythological subjects were chosen to symbolize the civilizing effect of the Olympic Games, held under divine protection. The two pedimental groups are fairly well preserved, but since the exact order and location of the statues are not clear, several conflicting attempts at reconstruction have been made. The west pediment deals with the *Battle of Lapiths and Centaurs* (fig. 7–42), a frequent subject in Greek art. The centaurs, half man and half horse, descend on the wedding feast of the Lapith king Peirithoös, and there they taste wine for the first time. Under its influence they attempt to carry off the Lapith women, whom Peirithoös and his friend Theseus strive to rescue. Apollo, god of light and, therefore, of order and reason, presides over the subjugation of the centaurs. The scene is possibly an allegory of the effect of the Olympian sanctuary on the struggles between Greek states, since all such hostilities had to be laid aside before contestants could enter its sacred gates.

However the statues were arranged, the poses were carefully calculated for the raking cornices, and the pedimental composition was more closely unified than any of its predecessors. The stupendous figure of Apollo (fig. 7–43), standing erect and with his right arm outstretched, commands the centaurs to desist in their depredations. In spite of heavy damage to the statue of a Lapith woman, her pose may be mentally reconstructed. She struggles in the embrace of a centaur's forelegs,

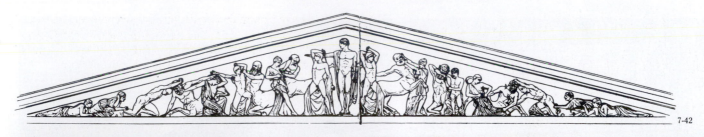

7-42

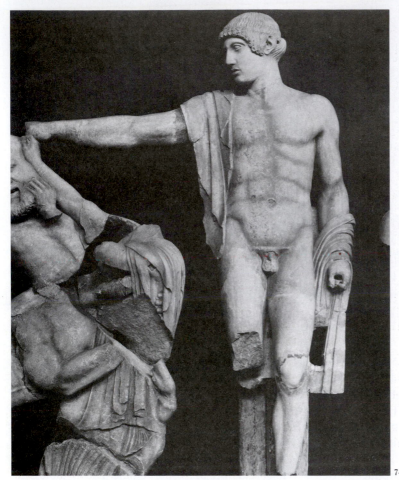

7-43

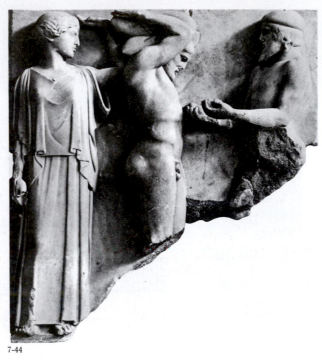

7-44

pushing him off with her hands. While the stern Apollo figure shows—naturally enough, given his commanding role in the action—none of the relaxation of the *Doryphoros* (see fig. 7–35), the structure and definition of the musculature are in keeping with the principles of the Severe Style. So indeed is the beautiful face, with its nose descending in a straight line from the forehead, its full jaw and rounded chin, and the caplike mass of ornamentalized hair. Despite their freedom of movement, the drapery folds are proportioned to harmonize with the fluting of the columns below.

The metopes of the outer peristyle were left blank, but as observers ascended the ramp before the temple they could see between the outer columns the frieze above the two columns of the inner portico in antis at either end of the cella, each end having six metopes representing the Labors of Herakles. The high reliefs, almost statues in the round, were kept austerely simple, their broad, full masses contrasting with the flat slab behind. One of the finest (fig. 7–44) shows the giant Atlas bringing back to Herakles (who has temporarily relieved him in his task of supporting the heavens) the Golden Apples of the Hesperides. The goddess Athena gently assists the hero. Garbed in her simple Doric peplos, she is one of the grandest

7-42. *Battle of Lapiths and Centaurs,* reconstruction drawing (after G. Treu) of the west pediment of the Temple of Zeus, Olympia. c. 470–456 B.C.

7-43. *Apollo with a Centaur and a Lapith Woman,* fragment from the west pediment of the Temple of Zeus, Olympia. c. 470–456 B.C. Marble, height of Apollo approx. 10′2″ (3.1 m). Archaeological Museum, Olympia

7-44. *Atlas Bringing Herakles the Golden Apples,* fragment from a metope of the Temple of Zeus, Olympia. c. 470–456 B.C. Marble high relief, height 63″ (1.6 m). Archaeological Museum, Olympia

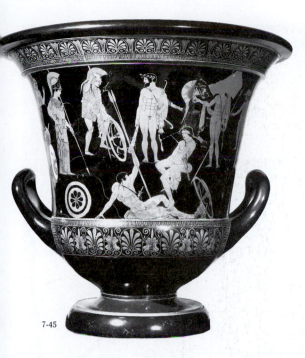

7-45

7-45. THE NIOBID PAINTER. Painting in the Attic style of an unidentified subject on a calyx-krater found at Orvieto, Italy. c. 455–450 B.C. Height 21¼″ (54 cm). Musée du Louvre, Paris

7-46. *Banqueting Scene*, fresco from the Diver Tomb at Paestum (ancient Poseidonia), Italy. c. 470 B.C. Museo Archeologico Nazionale, Paestum

female figures of the century, and Herakles is sculptured with a reticence and dignity typical of the Severe Style. Some of the breadth of treatment of the Aegina sculptures remains here, but with a new roundness of shape and smoothness of transition from one form to the next.

PAINTING   Vase painting continued throughout the Classical period, but a sharp decline in quality is notable, as if the painters had lost interest, perhaps because of the sudden increase in scope offered by the great commissions for wall paintings. One of the leading vase painters of the Severe Style is known as the NIOBID PAINTER, after a vase depicting the slaughter of the children of Niobe by Apollo. He is less important in his own right than because his paintings may tell us something about the vanished works of mural art, particularly those of Polygnotos, the most celebrated painter of the age and, in many ways, a pictorial counterpart of Polykleitos. According to ancient literary descriptions, Polygnotos gave his figures the nobility we have found in the sculpture of the Severe Style and of Polykleitos, as well as a new quality of emotional expression. He was also able to paint transparent or translucent draperies, through which could be seen the forms of the body (like those in the *Ludovisi Throne;* see fig. 7–39). While he did not use shading, and was thus constrained to rely on line to indicate form, Polygnotos was in one respect a great innovator: he scattered his figures at various points in space, freeing them for the first time from the groundline to which they had previously been confined. He also indicated such landscape elements as rocks and trees. One of the finest works by the Niobid Painter, a calyx-krater found at Orvieto in central Italy and dating from about 455–450 B.C., shows on one side a still unidentified subject that includes both Herakles and Athena and possibly Theseus (fig. 7–45). The noble, relaxed figures remind us of the sculpture of the Severe Style, and they correspond to the descriptions of Polygnotos' art. Even more striking is the free placing of figures at various points to indicate depth. Each is standing on a separate patch of ground, and all are united by a single wavy line running from one to the next. Another indication of the new interest in actual visual experience, freeing the painter from age-old conventions, is that, for the first time in art, the eyes of profile figures are drawn in profile rather than in full face.

There the story would have stopped had it not been for the extraordinary discovery in 1968 of a painted Greek tomb, datable about 470 B.C., in a cemetery outside the city of Paestum. The boxlike tomb was formed of six slabs of stone—for the ends, sides, top, and bottom—and all but the bottom slab were painted in *fresco,* that is, pigment on wet plaster. A layer of coarse plaster was first spread over the slab, and preparatory drawings were made on that. Then smooth plaster was laid on, which had to be painted rapidly so that the colors would amalgamate with the

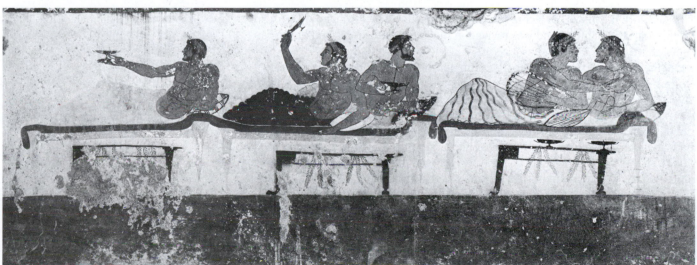

7-46

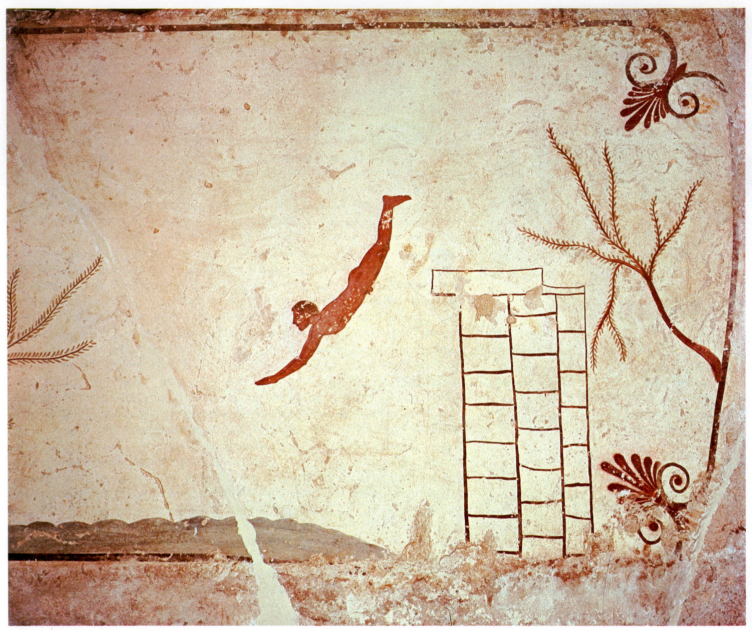

7-47

plaster before it dried. This technique was later used widely throughout Etruscan and Roman wall painting and was revived in the later Middle Ages and the Italian Renaissance.

On the four side slabs of the Paestum tomb were painted nude men at a symposium, reclining on couches as was customary, their legs wrapped in cloth covers. A solitary bearded adult at the left extends his kylix so that the youth adorned with side-whiskers on the next couch may flick the remains of his wine into it, while reclining against an adult who turns to gaze at the youth and adult on the last couch, forgetful of their musical instruments and interested only in each other (fig. 7–46). On the inside of the lid appears an unexampled scene—a nude figure in early manhood diving from a kind of springboard into the sea (fig. 7–47). This may represent a scene from real life, or perhaps its significance is allegorical— the soul plunging into the waters of the Beyond, in which it is purified of the corruption of the body. There are neither texts nor images to support either interpretation, but an allegory of the future life would seem probable for an image on the interior of a tomb. Whatever their significance, all the figures show a new

7-47. *The Diver,* fresco from the Diver Tomb at Paestum. c. 470 B.C. Museo Archeologico Nazionale, Paestum suppleness of line, used to describe the fullness of muscular forms as well as a wide range of expressions; between the contours the solid areas of brown flesh tones contain no hint of shading. The eye is shown, as in the work of the Niobid Painter, in profile rather than full face. Schematic landscape elements appear, also for the first time in Greek painting; two trees are represented, as well as the waves of the sea. All this is in keeping with what we read about Polygnotos' paintings.

If a provincial master, decorating the tomb of an unknown youth with images destined for eternal darkness, could draw and paint like this, what must have been the lost masterpieces of Athens?

The Classical Period—The Age of Pericles (450–400 B.C.)

The culmination of the Classical period in architecture and sculpture in Athens coincided with the greatest extent of Athenian military and political power and with the peak of Athenian prosperity—also, unexpectedly, with the height of democratic participation in the affairs of the Athenian polis. This was no accident; the vision and vitality of a single statesman, Pericles, brought Athens to her new political hegemony, and it was Pericles who commissioned the monuments for which Athens is eternally renowned. And with the inevitability of an Athenian tragedy, it was the long and disastrous war begun by Pericles that brought about the defeat of Athens in 404 B.C. and the end of her political power. Had Pericles not died in 429 the end might well have been different. Nevertheless, in some twenty dizzying years Pericles and the great architects and sculptors who worked under his direction created a series of monuments that have been the envy of the civilized world ever since, perhaps because they first proclaimed the new ideal of a transfigured humanity, raised to a plane of superhuman dignity and freedom. The sublime style of the Age of Pericles, as this transitory period should properly be called, was in many respects never equaled and can be paralleled only by the even briefer period of the early sixteenth century in central Italy, the High Renaissance, also dominated and inspired by a single political genius, Pope Julius II. It is instructive to remember that with Egypt and Sumeria we thought in millennia and with Archaic Greece in centuries, while with Classical Greece we must think in decades.

THE ACROPOLIS AT ATHENS AND ITS MONUMENTS   The massive limestone rock dominating Athens had been in Mycenaean times the site of the royal palace, and in the Archaic period it contained the principal sanctuaries of the city. When the Persians attacked in 480 B.C., they succeeded in capturing the fortress and in setting fire to the scaffolding around a great new temple to Athena, patron deity of Athens, which was then rising on the highest point of the Acropolis. When the Athenians returned to their city the following year, they vowed to leave the Acropolis in its devastated condition as a memorial to barbarian sacrilege. Nonetheless, they utilized marble fragments, including unfluted drums from the first Parthenon and many Archaic statues, as materials for new fortifications. By 449 B.C. the Athenians seem to have repented of their vow, for in that year they embarked on one of the most ambitious building programs in history. Money was, apparently, no object. But it could not be provided by the rudimentary system of taxation then in effect. Pericles' solution was simple. After the victories of 480–479 B.C., Athens had led an alliance of Ionian states, known as the Delian League because its meeting place and treasury were on the island of Delos, against the Persian invaders. For years Athens had kept the smaller states in line, and imperceptibly and inevitably the Delian League had been transformed into a veritable Athenian empire. States that attempted to secede were treated as rebels and severely punished. Ostensibly for greater security, the treasury was moved to Athens in 454 B.C. Before many years passed, its contents were used for the rebuilding of the Acropolis and its monuments, not to speak of other splendid buildings in Athens. Pericles was sharply criticized, but the work went on with astonishing rapidity.

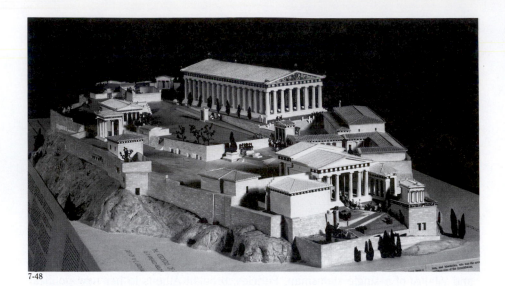

7-48. Model of the Acropolis, Athens, about 405 B.C. (view from the northwest). The Royal Ontario Museum, Toronto, and J. Walter Graham

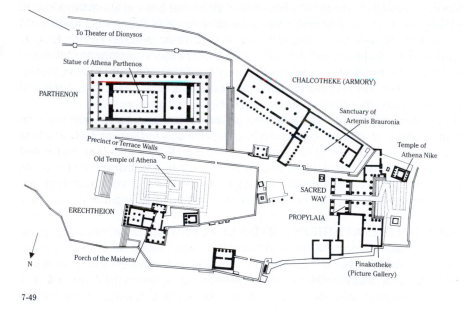

To Theater of Dionysos

Statue of Athena Parthenos

CHALCOTHEKE (ARMORY)

PARTHENON

Sanctuary of Artemis Brauronia

Precinct or Terrace Walls

Temple of Athena Nike

Old Temple of Athena

SACRED WAY

ERECHTHEION

PROPYLAIA

N

Porch of the Maidens

Pinakotheke (Picture Gallery)

7-49. Plan of the Acropolis, Athens

Given the Greek ideals of harmony and order, one might have expected the newly rebuilt center of Athenian civic pride and state religion to have been organized on rational principles at least as highly developed as those that were so successful in Egyptian temples and in Mesopotamian palaces. Nothing could be further from the truth. Only an imperial autocracy, apparently, could impose a sense of order on all the disparate elements of such a traditional center. In fact, no Greek sanctuary before the Hellenistic period was organized along symmetrical lines, or for that matter along any rational principles save those of ready accessibility. The greatest of all Greek sanctuaries, that of Zeus at Olympia, was at any moment in its history a jumble of temples large and small, shrines, altars, colonnades, and throngs of statues, each erected without the slightest consideration for its neighbors. The Temple of Zeus itself was not even centrally placed.

The Parthenon: Architecture. When Pericles rebuilt the Acropolis, he erected the temples on ancient, sacred sites, and where he could he utilized foundations remaining from older buildings, with the result that the Parthenon, the principal structure on the Acropolis and by general acclaim the supreme monument of Greek architecture, could never have been seen in ancient times in any harmonious relation to neighboring buildings. It was once thought that the view of the Parthenon from the Sacred Way, which passed through the entrance gate (see page 187), would have been partially blocked by several intervening constructions. In fact, the small, columned structure visible in the model (fig. 7–48) directly in front and to the west of the Parthenon is a propylon or gateway, and its actual form and size are still in doubt. Even more important, archaeological investigations by John J. Dobbins and Robin F. Rhodes have shown that the projecting wing of the Sanctuary of Artemis Brauronia, whose eastern wall is shared by the Chalkotheke ("bronze storeroom": armory), as seen on both model and plan (fig. 7–49), constitutes the final architectural phase of the sanctuary, built after the construction of the Parthenon. So even if the projecting wing blocked the view at some later date, it did not when the Parthenon was built. The initial view of the Parthenon, to worshiper and casual visitor alike, from the northwest corner, would have been as clear and open as it is now. The great structure, seen in all its cubic majesty from front and side at once, would have seemed to grow naturally from its rocky pedestal. The slight leaning of the outer columns inward, which lessens nearer and nearer to the center of the west front, has the effect of increasing the apparent height of the building above us as we approach from the considerably lower entrance gate, and we may presume that this is just what the architects intended, turning the stubborn irregularity of the site into an instrument to enhance the grandeur of the temple. Phidias' colossal bronze statue of Athena Promachos—cast from the melted-down weapons of the defeated Persians, armed with gilded helmet, breastplate, shield, and spear, and visible to ships far out at sea—would have seemed to flank and protect this sanctuary of the patron deity of the Athenians.

From a modern point of view the other aspects of the Parthenon were not quite so happily situated. The south colonnade was too close to the rampart to afford comfortable visibility, but even this fact would have had the advantage of directing the glance of anyone skirting the temple to the south upward toward the frieze around the cella wall. The north colonnade was favored by a broad, open area, but the space before the east front, the principal entrance, was too restricted to afford what we would call a good view. Clearly the Greeks were able to conceive to their satisfaction a mental image of a building in its entirety even from angular or fragmentary views. But the crystalline architectural shapes of the Periclean buildings, even in their present ruinous condition, tower in unexampled majesty above the city and the narrow plain; as if set down on the great rock by a divine hand, they vie with the surrounding mountains, without recognizing the limitations of nature, except here and there to exploit them.

Most of the smaller structures of the Acropolis are known today only through excavations, and the statues that once adorned it are lost without a trace. But the Parthenon was preserved for centuries as a religious building. It was converted successively into a Byzantine church, a Catholic church, and a mosque, in which latter phase it sported a minaret. Although the interior had been repeatedly remodeled, the exterior remained intact with all its sculptures in place until 1687. The Turks, at that time at war with the Venetians, were using the temple as a powder magazine. A Venetian mortar shell struck the building, and the resultant explosion blew out its center. The Venetians carried the destruction a step further in an ill-fated attempt to plunder some of the pedimental statues, which fell to the rocky ground in the process of removal and were dashed to pieces. In 1801–3 Thomas Bruce, Lord Elgin, a British diplomat, saved most of what remained of the sculptures from possible destruction in the disordered conditions then prevailing in Athens by removing many statues and reliefs to London. In the present century the north colonnade has been carefully set up again, almost entirely with the original drums, and work has begun on the south colonnade.

Pericles is believed to have placed the Athenian sculptor PHIDIAS in general

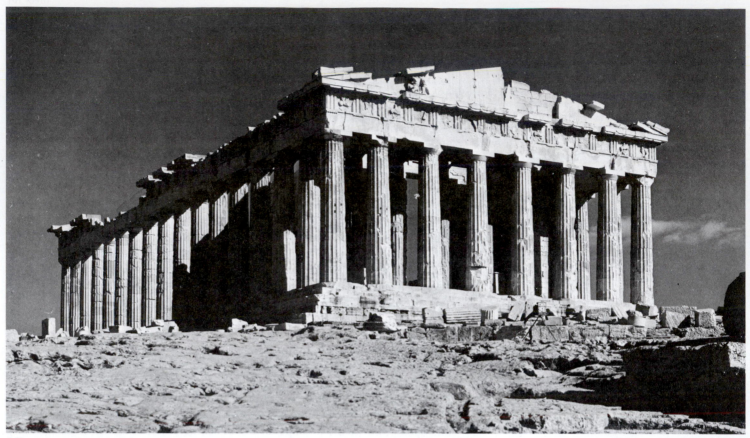

7-50

charge of all of his artistic undertakings. It is noteworthy that he did not choose either of the great sculptors of the single athletic figure, Myron and Polykleitos, who were in their prime. The principal designer of the Parthenon appears to have been the architect IKTINOS, working in a still·imperfectly understood partnership with KALLIKRATES. Construction began in 447 B.C. and was finished in the extraordinarily brief time of nine years, save for the sculpture, which was all in place by 432 B.C. Iktinos utilized and extended the foundations of the older temple of Athena for his new structure, which was not called the Parthenon (*parthenos,* meaning "virgin," referring to Athena) until much later; originally, the title was applied only to the treasury. While the dimensions of the "great temple," as the inscriptions call it, are not much larger than those of the Temple of Zeus at Olympia, it must have looked far larger. It is a regular Doric temple (figs. 7–50, 7–51), but differs from most of its predecessors in having eight rather than six columns across the front, and seventeen rather than thirteen along each side. The columns are far taller in proportion to their thickness than earlier Doric columns, and this greater slenderness is matched by a decrease in entasis and in the projection of the capitals, as well as in the mass and weight of the entablature. A glance at the Temple of Hera I at Paestum (see fig. 7–16) shows how much Greek architecture evolved in little more than a century. The wonderful sense of unity, harmony, and organic grace experienced by visitors to the Parthenon derives largely from the infinite number of refinements in the traditional elements of the Doric order. For example, the stylobate is curved upward several inches in the center to avoid the appearance of sagging, the columns lean progressively inward as we approach the corners (see page 181 for a suggested explanation), and the intercolumniations are progressively narrower toward the ends. Few of these refinements are immediately visible, but a great many have been measured, and even the most minute ones play their part in the total effect of the building. The whole structure, even the roof tiles, was built of Pentelic marble.

7-50. IKTINOS and KALLIKRATES. The Parthenon, Acropolis, Athens (view from the northwest). c. 447–438 B.C.

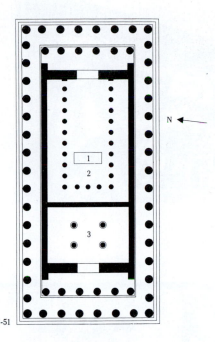

7-51. Plan of the Parthenon, Acropolis, Athens
1. Reflecting pool   2. Statue of Athena Parthenos
3. Treasury

7-52. JACQUES CARREY. *Contest between Athena and Poseidon for the Land of Attica,* drawing of the north half of the west pediment of the Parthenon, Acropolis, Athens. A.D. 1673. Bibliothèque Nationale, Paris

The Parthenon: Sculpture.   The decoration of the Parthenon was by far the most ambitious sculptural program ever undertaken by the ancient Greeks. The east and west pediments were filled with over-life-size statues; the ninety-two metopes were sculptured in high relief; and a continuous frieze in the Ionic manner, uninterrupted by triglyphs, ran right round the building along the top of the cella wall for a total length of 550 feet. The backgrounds of the pediments were painted bright blue, those of the metopes and friezes red. Many ornaments were added in metal. Hair and eyes were painted, and the capitals were decorated with ornament in bright colors. The whole building must have shone with color.

The interior of the cella, entered only from the east, was intended to house the colossal statue of Athena by Phidias. We do not know what the ceiling was like, but it was certainly supported by two superimposed Doric colonnades like those still in place in the Temple of Aphaia at Aegina and the Temple of Hera II at Paestum (see fig. 7–40). No access existed between the cella and the treasury, which was entered from the west and was apparently the principal treasury of the city. Its ceiling was supported by four Ionic columns, the first in any Athenian temple.

The magnificent array of sculptures for the Parthenon was produced in only twelve years. The belief that they were all executed under the general supervision of Phidias—or at the least show aspects of his style and artistic intention—is supported by a remarkable unity of taste and feeling that runs through the entire series. But the scope of the undertaking and the speed of its execution must have required an army of artists; some of these were clearly sculptors of great ability, others were stonecutters, presumably executing ideas sketched out by the major masters in clay models or perhaps working from drawings on papyrus. That all of these preparatory studies could have been made by Phidias himself, who was then busily occupied in work on his statue of Athena, is unlikely. The surviving statues for the two pediments, in spite of the heavy damage they have sustained, are among the most majestic in the whole history of art. The east pediment represented the *Birth of Athena,* the west the *Contest between Athena and Poseidon for the Land of Attica.* From the individual statues, as well as from sketches made by JACQUES CARREY, a French traveler, when they were still in place (fig. 7–52), it is clear that the compositions were not symmetrically organized on either side of a static central

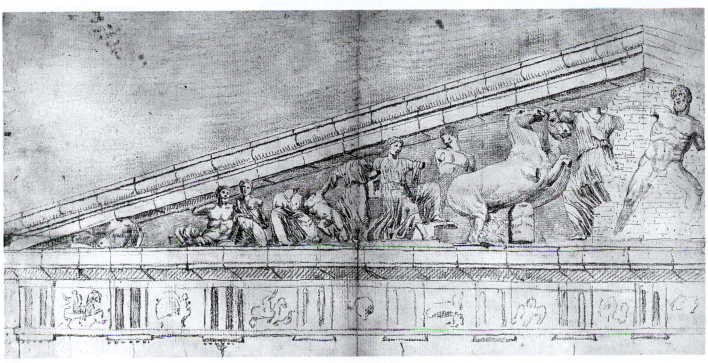

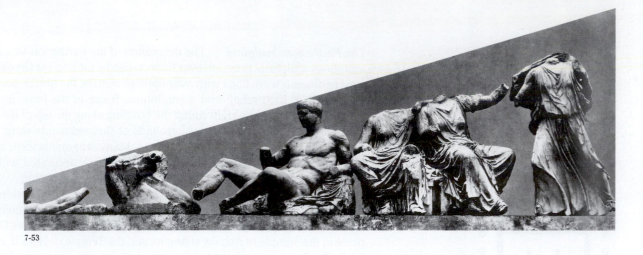

7-53

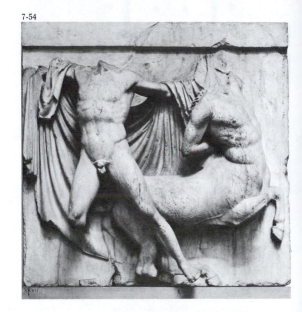

7-54

figure in the manner of the Olympia pediments (see figs. 7–42, 7–43), but were at every point based on action, which came to its climax toward the center.

Some of this movement runs through the three goddesses (fig. 7–53, right)— probably Hestia, Dione, and Aphrodite—who recline nobly in a group that sloped along with the downward movement of the raking cornice of the east pediment. Aphrodite rests her elbow and shoulders against her mother, Dione, while Hestia, closer to the center of the composition, is seated slightly apart. The intricate drapery folds cling to the figures and reveal rather than conceal the splendid masses of the bodies and limbs. As may be expected, the folds no longer show a trace of the ornamental drapery forms of the Archaic, but neither does the drapery fall into the simple, naturalistic folds of the Severe Style. It seems to be endowed with an energy of its own, and to rush around the figures in loops and even in spirals, as if communicating to the very corner of the pediment the high excitement of the central miracle, the birth of Athena from the head of Zeus. From this moment onward drapery movement becomes a vehicle for the expression of emotion, not only in Greek art but also in that of most subsequent civilizations.

The swirling lines of crumpled drapery have still another function. Like the *Diskobolos* of Myron (see fig. 7–34) on a smaller scale, indeed like any Classical composition, the Parthenon pediments crystallize for eternity a moment of dynamic action, this time the *interaction* of many figures. The essential of a Classical composition in any period may be defined as the perpetuation of the moment of equipoise between opposed forces. Once this moment has passed the composition will dissolve. The drapery lines serve as lines of energy, letting us follow the trajectory of all the interacting forces. Finally, speeding around the figures, the drapery folds allow us to grasp the fullness of their majestic volumes. But action and emotion are exercised by the poses and drapery folds alone: wherever preserved, anywhere in the sculptures of the Parthenon, the faces maintain a complete calm, as masklike as those of the Severe Style.

A splendid male figure, perhaps Herakles (fig. 7–53, left), leans back on one elbow in lordly ease in the opposite corner of the east pediment (most of the intervening figures are lost). He is as powerful as any of the nudes of the Severe Style, if less ostentatiously athletic. New and unexpected is the beautiful relaxation of the abdominal muscles below the rib cage, which seems almost to expand with an intake of breath. In consequence of the restful pose, new and smoother transitions carry the eye from one muscular or bony form to the next. No nobler embodiment of the Greek ideal of physical perfection and emotional control can be imagined.

The metopes all depicted battle scenes—Greeks against Trojans, Greeks against Amazons, gods against giants, Lapiths against centaurs. Like the pedimental compositions, and in contrast to the static figural groups of Olympia, the metopes are dynamic scenes, each crystallizing in a composition of perfect balance a single

7-54. *Lapith Fighting a Centaur,* fragment from a metope on the south side of the Parthenon, Acropolis, Athens. c. 440 B.C. Marble, height 56″ (1.42 m). British Museum, London

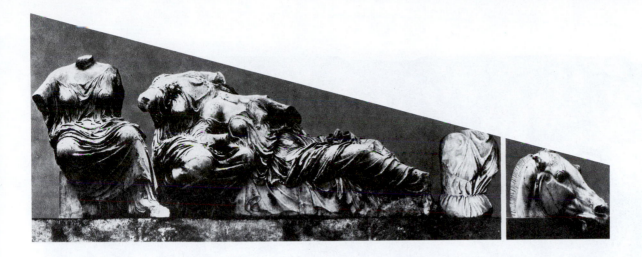

7-53. *Birth of Athena*. One possible reconstruction, using photographs of the original sculptures, of the east pediment of the Parthenon, Acropolis, Athens. Left to right across pages 184–85: Helios and the horses drawing his chariot; Herakles or Dionysos; Persephone (Kore) and Demeter; Iris; Hestia or Leto, Dione, and Aphrodite; Selene and one of the horses drawing her chariot. 438–432 B.C. Marble, over life size. British Museum, London, and (torso of Selene) Acropolis Museum, Athens

7-55. West entrance of the cella of the Parthenon, Acropolis, Athens, showing a portion of the marble frieze

moment of interaction. In the interests of legibility from the ground more than forty feet below, and in order to fit into the ninety-two restricted spaces, the narratives were mostly broken into pairs of figures in hand-to-hand combat, which "our side" does not invariably win. Incredible richness of invention characterizes the many variations on this single theme. One of the finest (fig. 7–54), in spite of the destruction of the heads, shows a Lapith in a proud action pose, charging toward his right, with his head turned over his left shoulder, as he drags a centaur backward by the hair. The tension of the composition, in which the figures are pulled together by the force of their own opposite movements, is expressed in curves of the greatest beauty; these are amplified by the broad sweep of the Lapith's cloak, which falls into crescent-shaped folds decreasing steadily in curvature as they move upward.

The frieze around the top of the cella wall (fig. 7–55) represented the Panathenaic Procession—an annual festival in which the youth of Athens marched to the Acropolis to pay homage to the city's patron deity and in which, every fourth year, a new peplos was brought to clothe her ancient wooden image in the nearby

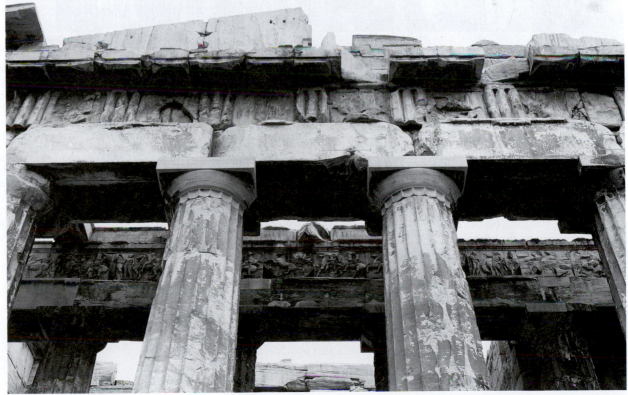

7-55

185

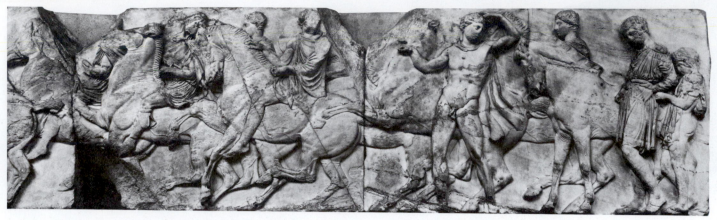

7-56

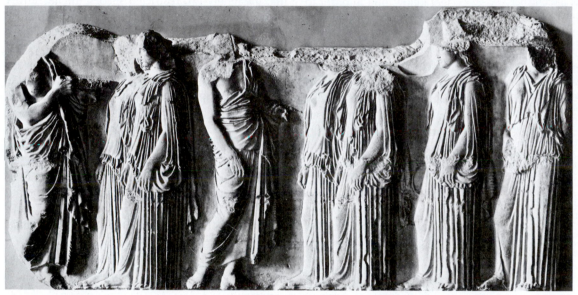

7-57

Erechtheion. The procession, of necessity, was not represented as if taking place at one moment but as a cumulative experience, because the observer moving around the building could see only one section at a time. Some of the most impressive parts of this long composition are those representing riders on horses and youths leading horses in a splendid flow of overlapping figures suggesting great depth (fig. 7–56). In order to maintain uniformity of scale throughout the frieze and yet avoid empty spaces where there were no horses, the sculptors adopted a convention, followed throughout Greek relief sculpture, of reducing the size of the horses as compared with the riders. Very beautiful is the passage (fig. 7–57) originally over the east doorway to the cella, where the procession converges from both sides of the building. The standing figures show all the new ease and grace of posture and are clothed in drapery that flows with all the new rhythmic beauty. Admittedly the frieze, in the only location permitted by the rules of the Greek orders, was not placed in the best position for perfect visibility, being some thirty feet above the stylobate and under the shadow of the peristyle ceiling. Nonetheless, it was hardly as difficult to view as some writers maintain. At most moments of the day, the strong Greek sunlight, reflected upward from the marble stylobate and (on the south side) from the cella wall, must have cast a soft, diffused light into the shadow under the marble ceiling beams and slabs. Moreover, the heads and shoulders of the figures were carved in a higher projection than the lower portions. Also, the red background set off all the figures with considerable sharpness.

7-56. *Mounted Horsemen, Horseman Crowning Himself with a Wreath, Servant Helping a Horseman Prepare to Mount,* fragment of the *Panathenaic Procession,* from the north frieze of the Parthenon, Acropolis, Athens. Marble, height 41¾″ (1.06 m). British Museum, London

7-57. *Maidens and Leaders,* fragment of the *Panathenaic Procession,* from the east frieze of the Parthenon, Acropolis, Athens. Marble, height approx. 43″ (1.09 m). Musée du Louvre, Paris

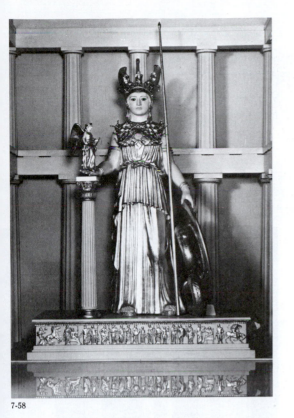

7-58

7-58. Small-scale reconstruction of the colossal statue of Athena by PHIDIAS (c. 438–432 B.C.) for the cella of the Parthenon. The Royal Ontario Museum, Toronto

7-59. PHIDIAS. *Lemnian Athena*. c. 450 B.C. Roman marble copy of the bronze original, height 17¼″ (44 cm). Museo Archeologico, Bologna

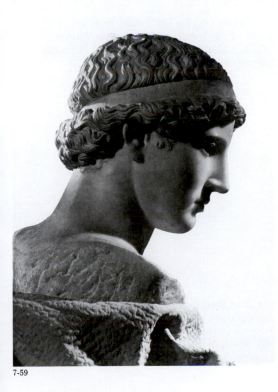

7-59

Once inside the cella the observer stood in the awesome presence of Phidias' forty-foot-high statue of Athena, dimly illuminated, since the only light in the windowless temple came from the east door and was, of course, at its strongest in the morning. From literary accounts of the statue and from tiny, ancient replicas, a small-scale model has been made (fig. 7–58). Although any reconstruction will perforce be inadequate, with this one as a basis, and with a good deal of poetic imagination, we can form some idea of what must have been the grandeur of the original. Thin plates of ivory and sheets of gold attached to plates of wood were arranged on a framework of great complexity so that it looked as though all the flesh portions were solid ivory and all the drapery solid gold. A shallow basin of water in the floor before the statue served as a humidifier to protect the ivory from shrinking and splitting in the dry climate of Athens and also, doubtless, as a pool to mirror the shining goddess and as a source of reflected light to play upward on her features. No large-scale copy remains to suggest how her face may have looked, but we do have a convincing Roman marble copy of the head of the destroyed *Lemnian Athena* by Phidias (fig. 7–59), also once on the Acropolis. Although this work was much smaller and thus more informal in pose than the hieratic *Athena Parthenos*, we can glean from its calm, clear, harmonious features at least a hint of the beauty we have lost. Athena's left hand sustained a shield above the folds of the sacred serpent, and on her extended right hand stood a golden statue of Victory six feet tall. So enormous was the *Athena Parthenos* that splendid reliefs by Phidias decorated both sides of the shield, the pedestal, and even the thickness of the soles of the goddess's sandals. According to ancient literary sources, Phidias also executed an even finer gold-and-ivory statue of the enthroned Zeus for the Temple of Zeus at Olympia. It was so tall that if Zeus had risen to his feet his head would have burst through the temple roof.

We possess not a scrap of sculpture that we can with certainty attribute to Phidias' own hand, yet the work done under his direction and possibly from his models on the Parthenon is consistent with the architecture of the building and with the literary accounts of Phidias' style. He invented new ways of combining figures on foot and on horseback into free action groups; he was responsible for a new grandeur of proportions and harmony of movement; he was the first to use drapery in order to reveal the masses of the figure, increase the impression of movement, and express the drama of the subject; he was responsible for a new dynamic harmony between figural compositions and architecture. Clearly, we are confronted by a universal genius, the first in history, the only one in the visual arts in the ancient world, and probably one of the greatest who ever lived. It is sad to record that Phidias, like so many of the great men of Athens (one recalls Themistocles, who was exiled; Socrates, who was forced to drink poison), met an ignominious end. He was imprisoned (or perhaps exiled) on trumped-up charges of impiety by jealous citizens of the very city to whose lasting glory he had contributed so much.

The Propylaia. The Acropolis was entered through a monumental gateway called the Propylaia, constructed—doubtless under Phidias' supervision—by the architect MNESIKLES from 437 to 432 B.C., while the sculptures of the Parthenon were being completed. The problems posed for the erection of a suitable gateway were not easy. One could approach the site only by means of the Sacred Way, a ramp not zigzagging steeply up the rock as it does today but ascending sharply from the west (then the city center) and turning from about 260 feet (80 meters) out, for a dramatic rise straight to the entrance. A formal entranceway was clearly needed. The solution was a central pedimented Doric portico of six columns facing west, flanked by two smaller and lower Doric porticoes at right angles (fig. 7–60, and see plan in fig. 7–49). Pedestrians could climb steps on either side, but a ramp was required for animals, and to accommodate this the central intercolumniation was widened by one triglyph and one metope—not an ideal solution, but the only one

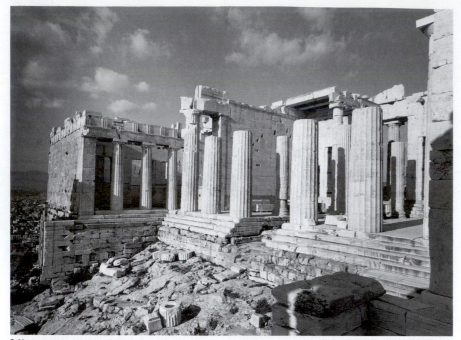

7-60

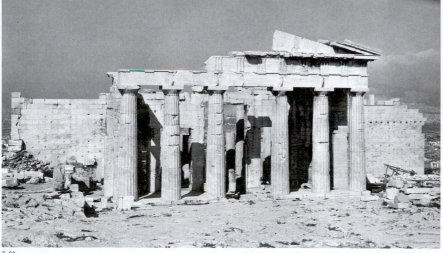

7-61

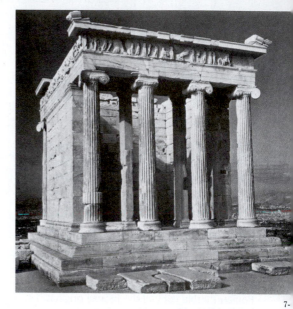

7-

7-60. MNESIKLES. The Propylaia, Acropolis, Athens (view from the southwest). c. 437–432 B.C.

7-61. The Propylaia, Acropolis, Athens (view from the east)

7-62. KALLIKRATES. Temple of Athena Nike, Acropolis, Athens (view from the east). c. 425 B.C.

7-63. *Victory Untying Her Sandal*, from the parapet of the Temple of Athena Nike, Athens. c. 410 B.C. Marble, height 42″ (1.07 m). Acropolis Museum, Athens

7-64. The Erechtheion, Acropolis, Athens (view from the east). c. 421–405 B.C.

7-65. Porch of the Maidens, the Erechtheion, Acropolis, Athens

consistent with the strict principles and limited vocabulary of the Doric order. Inside the building the roadway was lined with Ionic columns, three on each side, and the inner gateway was again a pedimented Doric portico (fig. 7–61). This inner gateway was to have been flanked by two halls, whose prospective use is not known; construction was halted by the outbreak of the Peloponnesian War, and the halls were never built. Whether seen from below as one toils up the ramps, or from the higher ground within the Acropolis, the exterior of the Propylaia is noble and graceful; the columns are similar in their lofty proportions and elegance of contour to those of the Parthenon. The small flanking structure to the north (visible at the left of fig. 7–60; on the south only the portico was built) was the Pinakotheke, a picture gallery, the earliest one on record, erected to house paintings on wood to be set around the marble walls below the windows.

The Temple of Athena Nike.   About 425 B.C., four years after the death of Pericles, the tiny Temple of Athena Nike (Victory) was constructed, presumably by Kallikrates, co-architect of the Parthenon, on the bastion flanking the Propylaia to the south in celebration of the victories of Alcibiades, which brought about a temporary lull in the catastrophic Peloponnesian War. The amphiprostyle temple has four

188

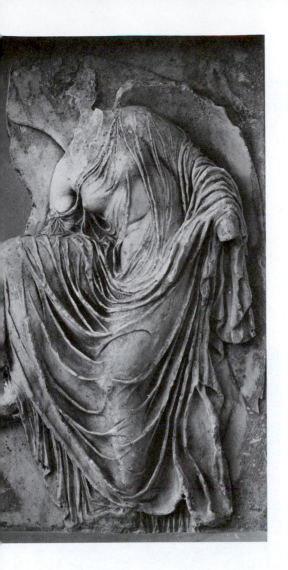

Ionic columns on each portico (fig. 7–62, and see plan in fig. 7–15). The proportions are unusually stocky, possibly so as not to contrast too strongly with the Doric columns of the Propylaia. The little structure was dismantled by the Turks and its stones used for fortifications; it was reassembled only in the nineteenth century. The finest sculptures carved for this temple originally decorated the parapet and showed personifications of Victory either separately or before Athena. These reliefs were apparently carved by masters trained initially under Phidias in the sculpture of the Parthenon. The loveliest is the exquisite *Victory Untying Her Sandal* (fig. 7–63), in which the transparent drapery of the Phidian style is transformed into a veritable cascade of folds bathing the graceful forms of the Victory. It has been suggested that the taste of the sculptor Kallimachos, credited with the invention of the Corinthian capital, is responsible for this refined, late phase of fifth-century style, which, however ingratiating its melodies may be, has certainly lost the grand cadences of Phidias.

The Erechtheion.   The final fifth-century building on the Athenian Acropolis, the Erechtheion, built from 421 to 405 B.C., was named after Erechtheus, a legendary king of Athens; it contained the ancient wooden image of Athena and possibly sheltered the spot where the sacred olive tree sprang forth at Athena's command. Rarely for a Greek temple, and presumably because of the now not entirely understood requirements of the religious rites for which it was designed, the Erechtheion is strikingly irregular. The four rooms culminate in three porches of sharply different sizes facing in three separate directions (fig. 7–64, and see plan in fig. 7–49). Yet from any view the proportions are so calculated that the effect is unexpectedly harmonious. Two porticoes are Ionic, with extremely tall, slender columns and elaborate capitals; the taller portico had four columns across, the smaller six (one column is lost). On the third portico (fig. 7–65), instead of columns, six korai uphold modified Doric capitals and an Ionic entablature, in the manner of the caryatids in the Treasury of the Siphnians at Delphi (see fig. 7–19). Despite disfiguring damage, the figures stand so calmly that the masses of marble above them seem almost to float. Anyone who has ever watched Mediterranean women carry heavy loads on their heads without the slightest apparent effort will recognize the pose.

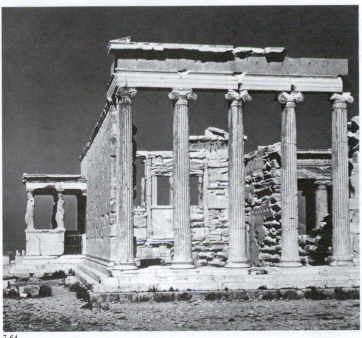

7-64

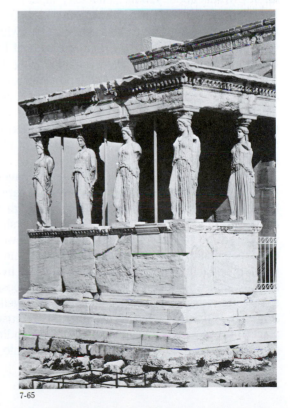

7-65

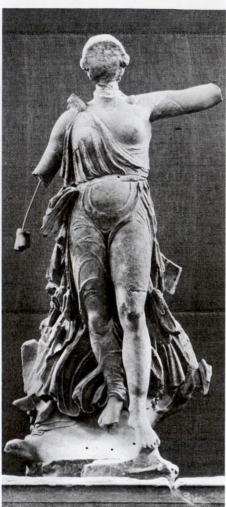

7-66

7-66. PAIONIOS. *Victory,* from Olympia. c. 420
B.C. Marble, height (including base) 7′1″
(2.16 m). Archaeological Museum, Olympia

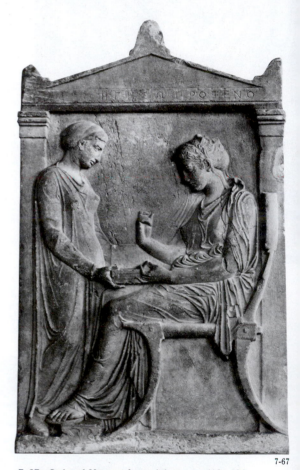

7-67

7-67. *Stela of Hegeso,* from Athens. c. 410–400
B.C. Marble, height 59″ (1.5 m). National
Archaeological Museum, Athens

MASTERPIECES FROM THE AGE OF PERICLES   Perhaps the most spectacular outgrowth of the Phidian style was PAIONIOS' *Victory* (fig. 7–66), a marble statue set up at Olympia about 420 B.C., on a lofty shaft, triangular in cross section, with its apex presented to the spectator so that in most lights it would almost disappear. The impression was thus given that the Victory—with arms and wings (now lost) extended, chiton pressed by the breeze against her full body, and her drapery billowing behind in the wind—was really flying. In contrast to the pieced arms common in the sixth century, all the projections—arms, wings, flying drapery— seem to have been carved from the same block as the body, an innovation witnessing dazzling technical skill in handling marble. In this daring experiment, leading the way to some of the tempestuous works of fourth-century and Hellenistic sculpture (see figs. 7–99, 7–103), something of Phidian grandeur was inevitably lost.

The deeper aspects of Phidian style seem to have continued to influence modest artisans, such as the sculptors of the grave stela carved in great numbers in Athens; these were often for export and uniformly of high quality. An especially touching example is the *Stela of Hegeso* (fig. 7–67), which shows the still-youthful deceased woman seated in a chair holding a piece of jewelry (painted, not carved) and accompanied by a standing girl, perhaps a daughter. The gentle melancholy of the group is not achieved by expressions—as usual in the fifth century, the faces are almost blank—but rather by the rhythm of their poses, especially the bowed heads suggesting resignation. The sculptor, who may well have been among the host of stonecutters trained on the Parthenon, has an unusual command of space. He has placed his two figures so that the back of the standing girl and the chair of Hegeso overlap the frame, causing them to emerge into our space. Yet the veil over

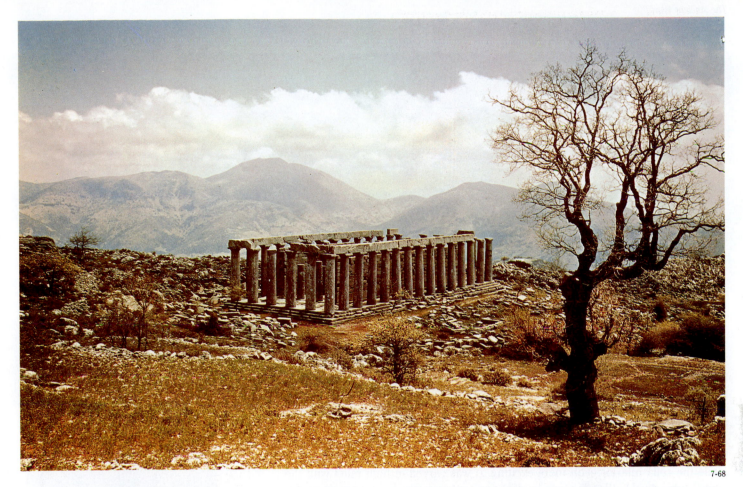

7-68. Iktinos. Temple of Apollo, Bassai.
c. 420 B.C.

Hegeso's head is so slightly projected from the marble background as to indicate an airy space within the frame.

Although the principles of the Doric and Ionic orders as applied to temples were by now firmly established, experimentation was still possible. One of the most striking variants, dating from about 420 B.C., the Temple of Apollo at Bassai in the wilds of Arcadia, has been attributed to Iktinos himself. The peripteral exterior is not exceptional (fig. 7–68); in fact, it shows fewer refinements than the Parthenon. The dramatic effect once exercised by the interior, however, is utterly new (fig. 7–69). The cella was lined with Ionic columns, engaged to the walls by projecting

7-69. Iktinos. Interior, Temple of Apollo, Bassai (reconstruction after F. Krischen)

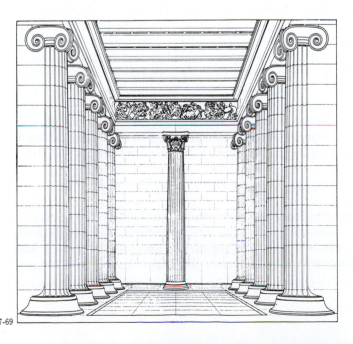

7-69

191

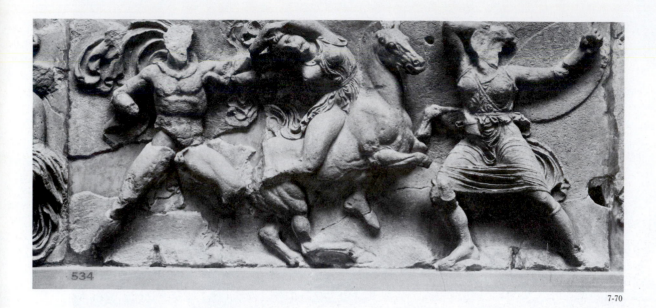

7-70

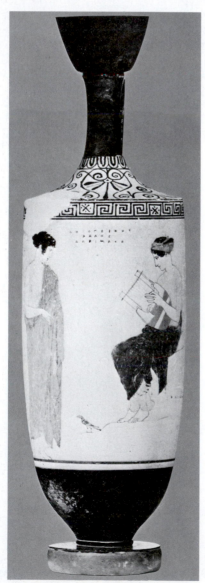

piers, supporting capitals with three equal faces. At the west end stood at least one, perhaps three, Corinthian columns, the earliest known. The abacus of a Corinthian capital (see fig. 7–72) resembles that of the Ionic, but the volutes are rudimentary; the distinguishing feature is the profusion of carved acanthus leaves (the acanthus is a Mediterranean plant of the thistle family) enveloping it, in at first one row, later two, and giving a rich and splendid appearance. The frieze above the columns made the cella interior even more exciting. It was carved in high relief with the typical subjects of battles between Lapiths and centaurs, Greeks and Amazons (fig. 7–70), but with unusually energetic poses and sharp exaggerations of movement and gesture—still in the Phidian tradition but with a touch of wildness unexpected after the equilibrium of the Parthenon metopes.

Ancient literary accounts have much to say about the advances made by painters in the second half of the fifth century, especially a new realism in depicting everyday life and a new ability in rendering the expression of intense emotion. Even more important, the masters of the period are credited with having invented the means of painting light and shade in order to give form its full roundness and set it into depth. No Classical paintings showing these new achievements have yet come to light. Their effect on vase painting seems to have been to weaken even more the firm linearity and the attachment of flat design to the vase surface, which had been the delights of Archaic vase painting, and to lure the best masters away from that limited art to more exciting new fields. Only faint hints of the new pictorial freedom can be detected in the white-ground *lekythoi* (vases made to contain oil or perfume). In these, a painted white background could be used because they were intended as funeral gifts and would never be washed. In the enchanting *Muse on Mount Helikon* (fig. 7–71) by the ACHILLES PAINTER, we can see a new softness of form and a wavering, sketchy line that suggests space and light.

Looking back at the meteoric development of Greek art in the fifth century, it is sobering to reflect that an Athenian born toward the end of the Archaic period could have watched during a long lifetime the entire evolution of the early Classical style.

The Classical Period—The Fourth Century

Toward the end of the fifth century B.C. a succession of military disasters stripped Athens of her imperial role and left the city a prey to severe social disorders. First Sparta, then Thebes exercised leadership among the Greek city-states in the first half of the fourth century, except for the Ionian cities of Asia Minor, which submit-

7-71

7-70. *Battle of Greeks and Amazons,* detail of a frieze from the cella of the Temple of Apollo, Bassai. c. 420 B.C. Marble high relief, height 25¼″ (64 cm). British Museum, London

7-71. THE ACHILLES PAINTER. *Muse on Mount Helikon,* white-ground painting in the Attic style on a lekythos. c. 440–430 B.C. Height of lekythos approx. 14½″ (37 cm). Staatliche Antikensammlungen und Glyptothek, Munich

7-72. POLYKLEITOS THE YOUNGER. Tholos (reconstructed section), Epidauros. c. 360 B.C.

7-73. Monument of Lysikrates, Athens. c. 334 B.C.

ted to Persian rule. By the middle of the century the final threat to Greek independence had appeared. Philip II, king of Macedon, ruler of a land just to the north of Greece that had previously been considered outside the sphere of Hellenic civilization, established Macedonian primacy over the Greek mainland. His son, Alexander III (the Great), in a series of lightning military ventures absorbed and then attempted to Hellenize the entire Persian Empire, carrying his domination even into India. Alexander adopted Persian dress and court customs, claimed Zeus as his father, and had himself worshiped as a god in the manner of Mesopotamian and Egyptian monarchs. Despite her diminished political power, Athens remained the center of Greek intellectual life. The foundations of Western philosophy were laid in this period in the work of Plato and Aristotle, who first submitted traditional standards to the questioning test of reason. Under the changed circumstances, the balance, integration, and control of the Classical style—so largely a product of Athenian nationalism—were sure to be dissolved in the expanded world of Alexander's conquests and were replaced by wholly new interests in space, movement, and light.

ARCHITECTURE   Clearly, the fourth century was not to be a period of ambitious building programs in mainland Greece, but some splendid new structures did make their appearance. One of the handsomest must have been the *tholos* (circular building), dating from about 360 B.C., at Epidauros. The tholos plan, derived from the round huts and tombs of Helladic times, could be devoted to a variety of purposes. For example, a fifth-century tholos in Athens served as a dining hall for the city administration. The Tholos of Epidauros, designed by POLYKLEITOS THE YOUNGER as a place for sacrifices, consisted of a cylindrical cella surrounded by an

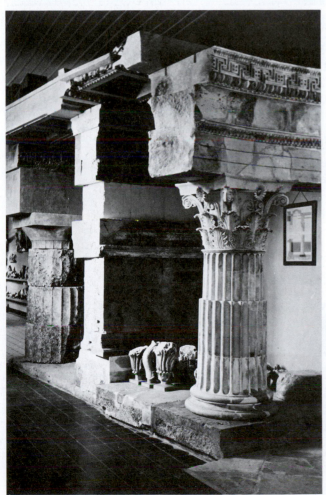

7-72

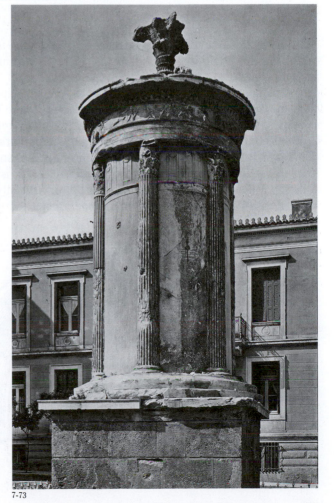

7-73

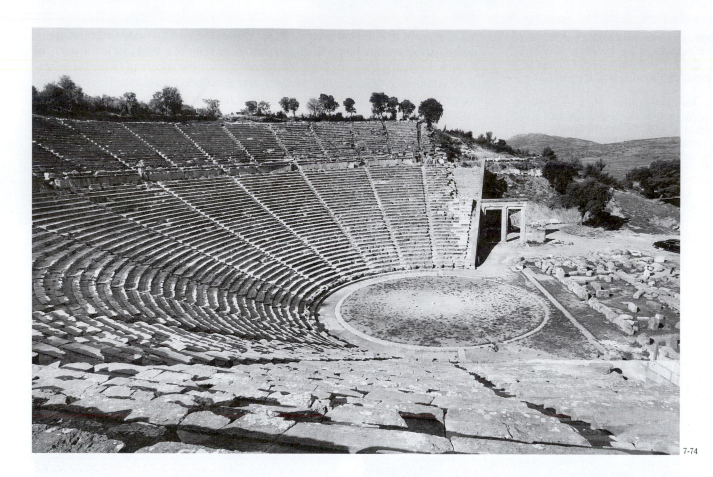

7-74

outer Doric peristyle supporting a conical roof (see plan in fig. 7–15). The inner colonnade was composed of Corinthian columns—the first such colonnade we know. Sections of this tholos have been recomposed (fig. 7–72) and show extreme elegance and refinement of carving. It will require some imagination to restore in one's mind the shafts (only capitals and bases and three intervening drums are shown) and to extend the tholos walls and the inner and outer cornices. The Corinthian capital already appears in very much the form later adopted by the Romans and revived in the Italian Renaissance, with two superimposed, staggered rows of acanthus leaves. The volutes are undercut, and so is each leaf, curving over at the tip with a jagged contour of great technical virtuosity. The earliest example we know of a Corinthian peristyle on the exterior of a building is the Monument of

7-74. POLYKLEITOS THE YOUNGER. Theater, Epidauros. C. 350 B.C.

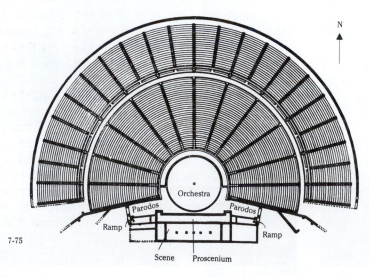

7-75

7-75. Plan of the Theater, Epidauros

7-76. Reconstruction of the Mausoleum, Halikarnassos (present-day Bodrum), Turkey. C. 353 B.C. (© 1985 by Kristian Jeppesen, Department of Classical Archaeology, University of Aarhus)

7-77. *Mausolus*, from Halikarnassos. C. 353 B.C. Marble, height 9′10″ (3 m). British Museum, London

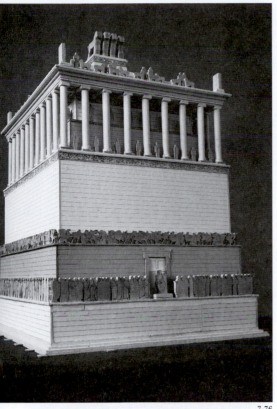

7-76

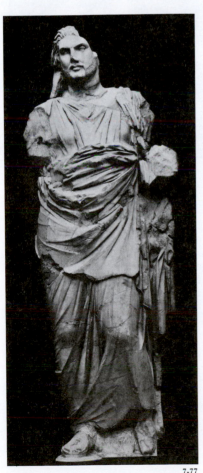

7-77

Lysikrates at Athens (fig. 7–73), a charming little structure intended to support the tripod Lysikrates won in 334 B.C., when he provided a chorus for the theater in Athens. The Corinthian columns are really only half columns, engaged to the central cylinder, which although hollow has no entrance; the conical roof, a single block of marble, supports an acanthus pedestal resembling a somewhat overblown Corinthian capital.

A new type of building that appeared in the fourth century is the monumental outdoor theater. The largest and finest of these—so considered even in antiquity—is the well-preserved theater at Epidauros, designed, like the Tholos, by Polykleitos the Younger (fig. 7–74). During the great age of Greek drama in the fifth century, theaters had consisted of mere rows of wooden benches on a hillside, grouped roughly around the *orchestra* (meaning "dancing place"), a circular area where the chorus and the actors—never more than three at a time—sang and spoke. This idea is monumentalized at Epidauros in the form of a conical formation of some fifty rows of marble benches separated by radiating aisles (fig. 7–75), still built around slightly more than half the orchestra circle. Originally, the theater had no stage; the building behind the orchestra circle supported temporary scenery. For all its simplicity, the harmony and grandeur of the space are as impressive as its acoustics. A word uttered in the orchestra circle can be clearly heard in the farthest reaches of the vast space.

The traditional elements of Greek architecture were asked to perform new functions in buildings erected outside of Greece. The most spectacular of these was the Mausoleum at Halikarnassos; the familiar name derives from its function as the tomb of Mausolus, prince of Caria in Asia Minor, who died in 353. Work began during his lifetime and continued after his death under the direction of his widow, Artemisia. The tomb, some 150 feet in height, was demolished by the Knights of Saint John in the Middle Ages and the pieces incorporated in their castle in the present-day Turkish port of Bodrum. Only fragments of sculpture and architecture have been recovered. Ancient literary descriptions, unfortunately, were incorrectly copied, so that it is now impossible to tell exactly what the building looked like (fig. 7–76 is one of several possible reconstructions). We do know that the Mausoleum had a lofty pedestal supporting a peristyle of thirty-six Ionic columns, each forty feet high, either in a single or a double row, surrounding the burial chamber. The whole was surmounted by a pyramid, in imitation of the Egyptians, culminating in a great marble chariot with four horses, presumably driven by Mausolus and Artemisia. At several still uncertain locations on the tomb, perhaps in the customary and inconvenient position at the top of the base, ran friezes representing the traditional battle subjects, carved by four of the most prominent Greek sculptors of the age.

In order really to understand the Mausoleum's sculpture preserved in the British Museum and the bare lines of the various architectural reconstructions, we must keep in mind the landscape for which the immense structure and its decorations were designed. Little is visible at the excavation today, but the site is a saddle between two hills, about three hundred feet above the port, looking down the long harbor, flanked by hills on either side, to the distant sea. The immense space is filled with light, including that reflected from the water below, and all must have come to a dramatic climax in the towering pyramid with its culminating chariot against the sky. We do not know for certain the name of the master who executed the grand statue of Mausolus (fig. 7–77)—it may have been Bryaxis—but clearly it is animated by the new dramatic spirit of the time. While this realistic portrait, one of the earliest in Greek art, lacks the sense of harmonious control of all the elements visible throughout Athenian sculpture of the fifth century, the movement of the drapery, the depth of the carving, and the intensity of the expression produce a great sense of excitement. It is instructive to compare this swaying, windblown charioteer with the serene *Charioteer of Delphi* (see fig. 7–30), of little more than a century earlier.

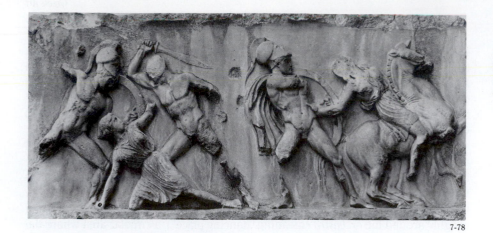

7-78. *Battle of Greeks and Amazons*, detail of a frieze from the Mausoleum, Halikarnassos. Middle 4th century B.C. Marble, height 35″ (89 cm). British Museum, London

SCULPTURE   The most eminent of the Halikarnassos sculptors was SKOPAS, born on the island of Paros but trained in Athens, known in antiquity for his ability to render movement and to convey drama. He may have been responsible for the *Battle of Greeks and Amazons* (fig. 7–78), in which the free movement of the figures in space is carried even beyond the stage of the frieze at Bassai (see fig. 7–70). In the section illustrated here, two Greek warriors are about to slay an Amazon who has fallen to her knees and cries for mercy, while a third Greek pulls an Amazon from her horse. The impression of speed is produced largely by the wide spacing of the figures, which leaves considerable areas of blank background to be traversed. Despite their mutilation, fragmentary heads attributed to Skopas from the Temple of Athena Alea at Tegea (fig. 7–79) show how he revealed new depths of passion by means of an exceptionally deep eye cavity, thus producing a powerful shadow around the eye and intensifying the expression of wildness. Even the surging rhythms of the ornaments on the helmet are used to heighten the excitement of the moment.

A complete contrast to Skopas is furnished by the Athenian PRAXITELES, whose fame was based on the grace and softness of his style. His most celebrated work in antiquity was the marble statue of Aphrodite in her sanctuary at the city of Knidos in Asia Minor, which we know only from Roman copies (fig. 7–80). This is the first nude statue of the goddess, and one of the earliest Greek statues of a female nude, which in itself indicates a sharp change in the status of women, increasingly liberated from the gynecaeum. Compared with the partially nude female figures of the fifth century, and in spite of faulty restorations (the head comes from another statue and the hands and feet are new), the copy shows a greater fullness of forms and an almost imperceptible transition from one form to the next. The result is a wholly new sense of warmth and life.

In recent years the beautiful *Hermes with the Infant Dionysos* (fig. 7–81) at Olympia has been dismissed as a Hellenistic or even Roman copy of a lost original by Praxiteles, but the quality of this statue is so much higher than that of any ancient copy known to us—a perusal of the copies illustrated in this book will reveal a certain inescapable deadness in even the best of them—that this judgment is hard to accept. The least that can be said of the *Hermes* is that no other surviving ancient work approaches its consistent pitch of refinement in the treatment of surface. Apparently, Praxiteles was one of the first to become fully aware of the crystalline and translucent nature of marble and to discover a way of exploiting its special quality by softening and veiling all transitions, abrading and polishing them until sharp edges could no longer be seen. Eyelids, for example, and the edges of lips are deliberately blurred, as is the transition from muscle to muscle in the soft and glowing torso and limbs of the god. Shadows play gently over the fluid surfaces, and light is reflected from within the crystalline structure of the marble. Even the curly locks of the god's hair are softly sketched in the marble, particularly when compared with the still clear-cut definition of hair in the fifth century. The subject

7-79

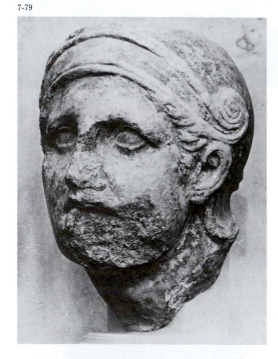

7-79. SKOPAS. *Head*, from the Temple of Athena Alea, Tegea. c. 350–340 B.C. Marble, height approx. 11¾″ (30 cm). National Archaeological Museum, Athens

itself, far from the lofty themes of the fifth century, has a quality of gentle, aesthetic dalliance. Hermes dangles a bunch of grapes to tease the infant god of wine; a dreamy half smile plays about his luminous features. In many ways this kind of attitude and treatment seem to have more in common with the nature of painting than with sculpture, and is thus often called "pictorial." Soon such pictorial ideals were to be pursued in a spectacular manner by Hellenistic and Roman sculptors, and later they were revived briefly in the Florentine Renaissance and triumphantly in the Italian Baroque.

The third great sculptor of the fourth century, LYSIPPOS, took up again, but from a new point of view, the athletic themes of Myron and Polykleitos. If one judges from the surviving Roman copies, his lost bronze *Apoxyomenos* (fig. 7–82) showed a subject visible wherever athletes gathered—a young man scraping dust and sweat from his body with an S-shaped terra-cotta instrument called a *strigil*. Again according to the Roman copies, Lysippos employed a new system of proportion in keeping with the increased slenderness, height, and grace of Greek columns after the middle of the fifth century. The head is smaller, the torso and limbs longer and lither, the divisions between the muscles less strongly marked (in common with Praxiteles) as compared with fifth-century sculpture in general. More important, the arms are raised in such a way as to make use of the space in front of the body, thereby finally breaking through the invisible frontal plane to which even such vigorous action figures as the *Diskobolos* (see fig. 7–34) and the *Zeus of Artemision* (see fig. 7–33) had been restricted. How a Lysippan bronze statue would have looked may perhaps better be seen in the wonderful figure of a youth with outstretched right arm (fig. 7–83) found in the sea off Antikythera, in the wreck of a Roman vessel presumably laden with works of Greek art. Originally, the bronze did not have the greenish patina we now admire but must have been polished to a luminous brown to suggest the deep tan of a Mediterranean youth who constantly exercised in strong sunlight. The inlaid eyes and copper lips are, luckily, still preserved. The brilliant naturalism of the work takes us across the centuries straight into a Greek palaestra.

PAINTING   For no moment in the history of art, perhaps, do we mourn the disappearance of painting so keenly as for the fourth century. According to voluminous and graphic literary accounts, painters had made almost incredible strides since the not-too-distant days when Polygnotos was content to define form with line and to fill in the areas between contours with flat color. The names of many painters are known, and their styles were described in great detail. The leading master was apparently Apelles, whose studio was visited by Alexander himself. Artists no longer chiefly painted monumental murals on commission. Instead they specialized in panel paintings done on easels in the studio, working to satisfy themselves and hoping for sales to the wealthy and powerful. Painters employed either *encaustic*, using colors dissolved in hot wax and painting while the wax was still soft, or *tempera*, mixing the colors with egg yolk. Both techniques were fairly laborious, but the effects the artists achieved were totally new. Most important, they had discovered the full meaning of light for the first time in the long story of the art of painting. They were able to indicate the source of light and follow its effects in diffusion, transparency, reflection, and cast shadow. So many of these light effects turn up as common practice in the Roman paintings done at Pompeii and Herculaneum (see figs. 9–16, 9–17) by anonymous provincial artists three centuries later that the literary accounts are more than believable. Furthermore, these effects correspond to those that the sculptors were seeking to achieve in marble and in bronze. The painters were also able to indicate depth, especially by means of foreshortening objects placed at an angle to the picture plane. Finally they were greatly interested in human character and emotion. Many portraits are described, and many dramatic scenes in which passion was represented with great success. One extremely important device discovered by fourth-century masters was *glaz-*

7-80. PRAXITELES. *Aphrodite of Knidos.* c. 350 B.C. Roman marble copy of marble original, height 6'8" (2.03 m). Musei Vaticani, Rome

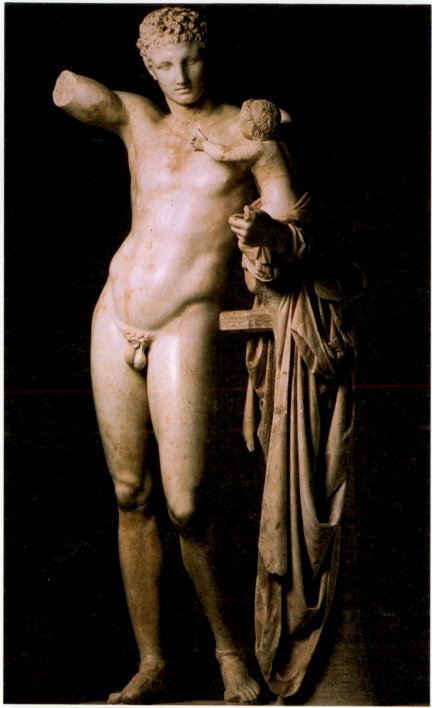

7-81

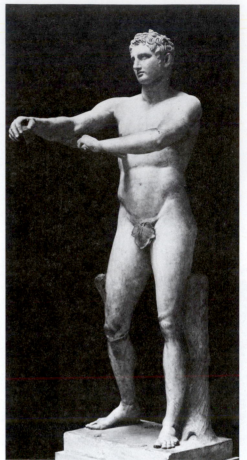

7-82

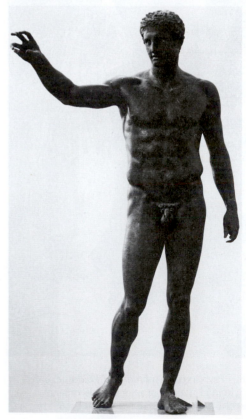

7-83

ing, or covering the surface of a painting with a quick-drying, transparent coating (which could be a varnish) in which small amounts of color had been dissolved. This gave otherwise very brilliant tones an effect of greater depth and resonance, much like the soft colors transmitted by sunlight at certain times of day.

We do at least possess occasional attempts, however halting, to reconstruct fourth-century paintings. One is a *mosaic* (a technique of building up a pictorial image by combining small pieces of hard, colored material: in Classical times stone was used) found at Pompeii. This mosaic appears to be a Roman copy of the *Victory of Alexander over Darius III* (fig. 7–84), painted about 300 B.C. for King Cassander of Macedon. The original has been attributed, without firm evidence, to a painter

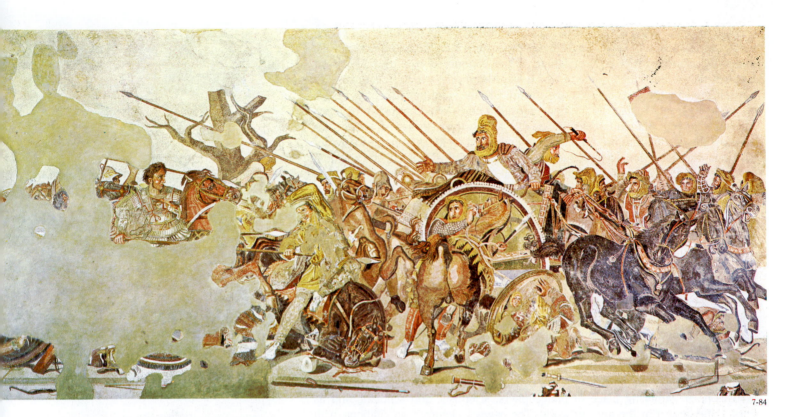

7-84

7-84. *Victory of Alexander over Darius III.* Roman mosaic copy of a painting possibly by either Philoxenos or Helen of Egypt. c. 300 B.C. Height 10′3¼″ (3.13 m). Museo Archeologico Nazionale, Naples

called PHILOXENOS, although Pliny the Elder, who died at Pompeii, believed it to have been the work of a woman, HELEN OF EGYPT. Despite the difficulty of translating a painting into such a picture-puzzle technique, and the heavy damage that has destroyed most of the left side of the mosaic copy, we can still experience the grandeur of a very noble composition. The artist has not tried to show the whole battle, but to sum up its central action in a selected grouping of figures and accessories. He (she?) has represented very effectively the impact of Alexander's cavalry on the routed army of Darius, who turns in his chariot with a gesture of intense compassion for his fallen bodyguard, run through by the Macedonian king. Tides of battle surge through what is clearly deep space within the picture, even though the background is a flat white. A sheaf of long Greek spears shows that Darius is almost surrounded, but the spears also serve as a compositional device pointing to Alexander, who can be seen over the damaged area, reining in his rearing horse. The ground is littered with weapons. Horses are represented in varying degrees of foreshortening, from front and rear. Light, as we have never seen it represented before, gleams on Alexander's armor, on the tree, the shields, and the glossy bodies of the horses and casts strong shadows on the ground. A fallen Persian is reflected in the polished surface of his shield. Anguish contorts the faces and dilates the eyes of the defeated. Certainly the great fourth-century discoveries—light, space, and emotion—appear to an extraordinary degree in this picture, which opens artistic vistas leading to modern times.

The Hellenistic Period (323–150 B.C.)

7-81. PRAXITELES. *Hermes with the Infant Dionysos,* from Olympia. c. 330–320 B.C. Marble, height 7′1″ (2.16 m). Archaeological Museum, Olympia

7-82. LYSIPPOS. *Apoxyomenos (Scraper).* c. 330 B.C. Roman marble copy of bronze original, height 6′9″ (2.06 m). Musei Vaticani, Rome

7-83. *Youth,* found in the sea off Antikythera, Greece. c. 340 B.C. Bronze, height 6′5″ (1.96 m). National Archaeological Museum, Athens

During the Archaic and Classical periods Greek culture had spread, through a steady process of colonization, as far west as the Mediterranean coast of Spain. The conquests of Alexander produced almost overnight a veritable explosion of Hellenism throughout the entire eastern Mediterranean region as well, including Egypt, and throughout all of western Asia as far as the Indus River. Ironically enough, the propelling energy for this new burst of Hellenism came from the ruler of Macedon, a country previously considered to lie on the fringe of the Greek world; yet so durable were the effects of Alexander's conquests that Greek remained the principal language spoken in Lower Egypt and in the eastern Mediterranean region, even under the Roman Empire. Everywhere in the conquered countries Alexander founded new Greek cities, some of which like Alexandria, which he named after himself, grew rapidly to enormous size; meanwhile, the older Ionian centers in Asia Minor, freed from Persian domination, enjoyed a new period of great prosperity. After Alexander's death in Babylon in 323 B.C., at only thirty-three years of age, his generals divided his empire among them and ruled as kings. Among the major divisions were Macedon itself (including Greece) under the Diadochi, the kingdom of the Seleucids in Asia Minor with its capital at Antioch in Syria, and the kingdom of the Ptolemies, who ruled Egypt as pharaohs from the new Greek capital at Alexandria. Antioch and Alexandria eventually became the first cities of the ancient world with populations of a million or more.

The riches of the eastern kingdoms contrasted sadly with the poverty and relative impotence of the Greek city-states, left with only a semblance of their former autonomy to carry on their usual fratricidal warfare, except when interrupted by one or another of the Hellenistic kingdoms. Athens was respected for its distinguished history and cultural achievements, but it had slight commercial or political importance. As the city-states declined so did their old cults; religious feeling became intensely personal, and the individual sought direct and often ecstatic contact with the gods in such Oriental religions as the worship of Cybele, the mother-goddess, or the cult of Isis, imported from Egypt. Learning flourished, not only in Athens but also in the great new cities, especially Alexandria, with its Mouseion, or gathering place of philosophers, scientists, and scholars, and its library, the largest in the ancient world. The newly Hellenized populations, with their mystery religions, provided an insatiable demand for an art that could carry the discoveries of the fourth century regarding space, light, movement, and above all emotional drama to extremes of sensuality and violence that would have shocked the Athenians of the Classical period. Yet the artists themselves were Greek, and without the discoveries of their fifth-century predecessors they could have done little.

TOWN PLANNING   Not all Greek cities grew up higgledy-piggledy like Athens, with bits of rational planning inserted here and there. But to build a planned city requires either starting from scratch, as Akhenaten did at Tell el Amarna, or tearing down a preexisting town. Seldom in Classical Greece could either of these be done. Straight streets intersecting at right angles do appear, as in those outlying sections of Miletus, a Greek city in Anatolia, in modern Turkey, planned by a local architect, Hippodamos, about 470 or 460 B.C. But the Hellenistic cities, especially the new princely capitals, required planning on a grand scale. Their straight streets intersecting at right angles, open spaces, and public buildings were necessary for all the varied activities of metropolitan life within a rational system.

A beautiful example of late Classical and early Hellenistic town planning is Priene, situated across from Miletus, on the other side of what is now a broad plain but was then an immense bay. High above the port, a perfect Hippodamian plan was superimposed about 320 B.C. on a sloping hilltop, with the result that all the straight streets tilt sharply according to the terrain (fig. 7–85), affording spectacular views of the bay and landscape and of distant Miletus. A highly irregular fortification wall, exploiting the most defensible positions, surrounded the city. Fortunately for us, Priene contained within its territory the principal sanctuary of the Ionian League of Greek cities, so the Romans deliberately neglected it and spared us later remodeling. The city has been largely excavated, and although few walls are standing more than ten feet or so in height, we can serenely walk (or climb!) the straight streets today and gain a wonderful idea of how a Hellenistic city worked. At the lower edge of the reconstruction we see the *stadium,* used for athletic events and activities. At the center is the *agora,* an open square to be found in all Greek

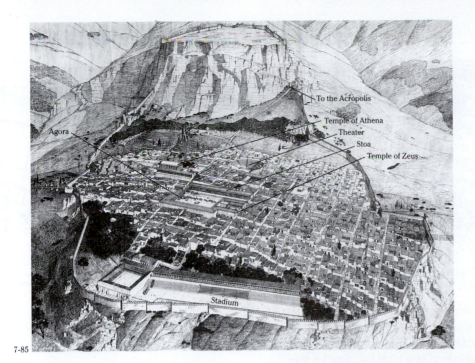

7-85. Reconstructed view of the city of Priene, Turkey (after A. Zippelius)

7-86. Model of the city of Pergamon, Turkey (view from the south). Staatliche Museen zu Berlin—Preussischer Kulturbesitz

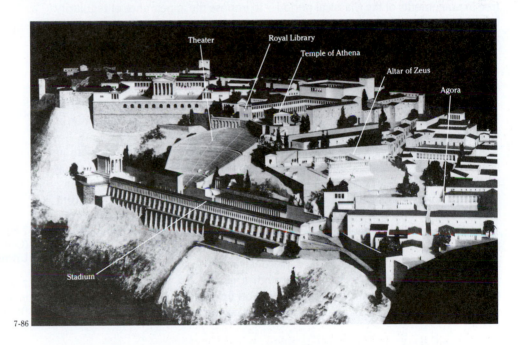

cities; surrounding the agora is that most typical of Hellenistic buildings, the *stoa*, essentially a continuous colonnade, closed by a wall behind, intended for the transaction of business or just for strolling in the shade, and generally connected with shops and markets. To the upper left, at the highest point in the city, stands the Ionic Temple of Athena, and at upper center the theater, a gem of a building, still almost intact, with a columned stage so planned that painted scenery panels could be inserted between the columns. The Acropolis, not visible in the illustration, is perched on a mighty crag soaring 1,000 feet above the port.

Town plans were designed to be as regular as possible, even when, as at Pergamon in Asia Minor, the rocky slopes of the terrain made planning extremely difficult. A restored model shows some of the principal buildings of this splendid city (fig. 7–86), even more dramatically situated than Priene. The large temple in

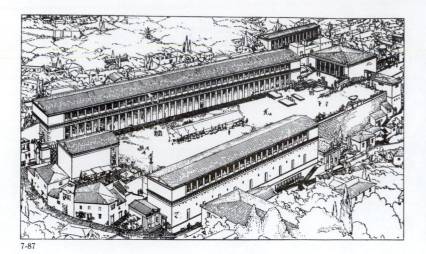

7-87

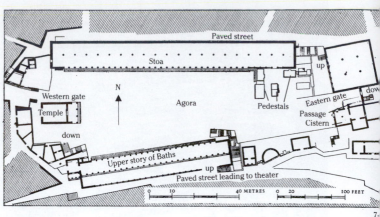

7-

the center of a square at the upper left is Roman and should be disregarded in this context. In the center is the theater, higher and narrower than that at Epidauros, because it was not built around an orchestra circle; in fact, only a semicircle was planned, and the action took place on a stage dominated by a high building for the support of scenery. Above the theater every attempt was made—in contrast to the free arrangements of the Classical period—to impose the appearance of regularity on the mountainous terrain. At the extreme right of the model is the usual agora, in the center foreground the stadium, above the right end of which rises the Altar of Zeus (see fig. 7–101), a monumental structure in itself. Higher up and just behind the theater, at right angles to one of its aisles, is the Temple of Athena; it is isolated and clearly visible from all sides in a plaza formed by a two-story stoa, not in exact alignment but handled as if it were. The second story of the stoa, towering above the exact center of the theater, gave access to the royal library, second only in importance to that of Alexandria.

An agora of the Pergamene type at Assos in Turkey (reconstruction and plan in figs. 7–87, 7–88) had handsome stoas, divergent but treated as if parallel, along both sides, a temple at one end, and at the other the *bouleuterion* (council hall). With their long, straight colonnades such complexes must have made magnificent spatial impressions. The traditional orders were still used, although Doric columns are often as tall and slender as Ionic, and Doric entablatures are correspondingly light. Usually, in two-story buildings the lower story is Doric, the upper Ionic. A superb bouleuterion of about 170 B.C. (reconstruction in fig. 7–89) at Miletus was preceded by an enclosure, entered through a Corinthian portico resembling a small temple. The courtyard was surrounded on three sides by a Doric colonnade, in the center of which was an open-air altar. The fourth side was formed by the

7-87, 7-88. Reconstructed view and plan of the Agora, Assos, Turkey (after A. W. Lawrence)

7-89. Reconstructed view of the Bouleuterion (Council House), Miletus, Turkey (after A. W. Lawrence). c. 170 B.C.

7-90. Reconstruction of the Arsinoeon (with roof in section), Samothrace (after A. W. Lawrence). Before 270 B.C.

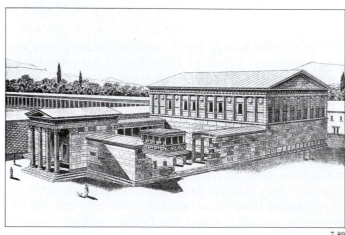

7-89

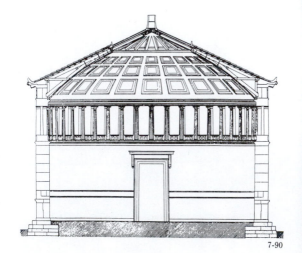

7-90

lower story of one long side of the council hall itself, whose upper story was an engaged Doric colonnade, with a pediment at either end. The Doric columns are more widely spaced than in the Classical period, with three rather than two triglyphs per column. Windows admitted light to the interior.

Large Hellenistic public buildings posed new problems for which the Greeks, thinking always in terms of post-and-lintel construction, had no organic structural solutions. Generally, interiors were roofed with wood, with sloping beams upheld in a stoa by a central row of taller columns, or sometimes in a bouleuterion by four interior columns so placed as least to obstruct the view. An ingenious device was employed at Samothrace, in a tholos called the Arsinoeon (reconstruction in fig. 7–90). Its cylindrical wall was surmounted outside by a pseudo-peristyle of square piers with Doric capitals, inside by engaged Corinthian half columns, supporting a wooden roof with a conical inner ceiling of wood, elegantly coffered (divided into recessed panels). Here is an early approach to the problem of the centralized interior without inner supports, which was solved later by the Romans through new and more imaginative construction methods (see Introduction fig. 20 and fig. 9–53) and taken up again in the great domes of the Byzantine period (see figs. 10–39, 10–40). A crown, probably of acanthus leaves, at the apex masked an aperture for ventilation, which must also have shed a soft light over the coffering.

Hellenistic temples, when compared with those of the Archaic and Classical periods, represent a strong departure from what archaeologists have liked to

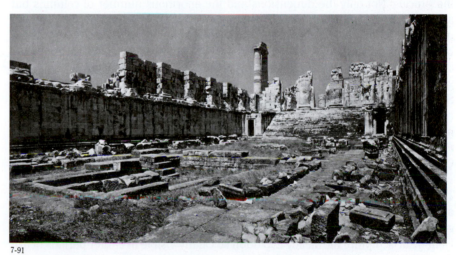

7-91

7-91. Paionios of Ephesus and Daphnis of Miletus. Temple of Apollo, Didyma, Turkey (view of inner courtyard looking east; ruins of sanctuary in foreground). c. 300 B.C.

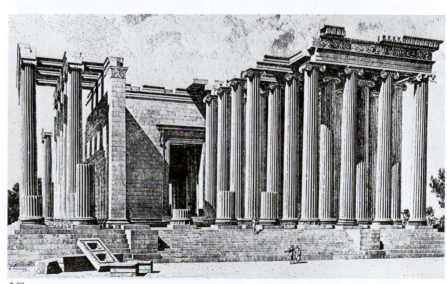

7-92. Reconstructed view of the east façade, Temple of Apollo, Didyma (after H. Knackfuss)

7-92

203

consider "good taste." Nonetheless, if we are willing to forget for a moment preferences based on Classical style and see these buildings in the context of the overriding Hellenistic concern with space and light, we must agree that they were very dramatic structures. A completely original example was the so-called Didymaion, the Temple of Apollo at Didyma, near Miletus, begun about 300 B.C. by the architects PAIONIOS OF EPHESUS and DAPHNIS OF MILETUS (figs. 7–91, 7–92, and see plan in fig. 7–15). Like a number of earlier temples in this region, the Didymaion was dipteral (with two peristyles, one inside the other). The structure was gigantic—358 feet long by 167 feet wide, with 110 columns. These were the tallest of all Greek columns, sixty-four feet in height, and there were ten across each end and two rows of twenty-one along each side; the entrance porch, with no pediment, was five columns deep. The central doorway, whose threshold was raised to make it inaccessible to the public, was used only for the promulgation of oracles, supposedly divine messages intoned by the priestess of Apollo to the crowd waiting in the shade of the towering porch. By means of a dark, barrel-vaulted passageway the few who were admitted to the sanctuary emerged not into the expected dim interior but into a giant courtyard blazing with Apollo's sunlight and lined with pilasters, whose capitals carved with griffins correspond to no conventional order, and planted with bay (laurel) trees, which were not only sacred to Apollo but whose leaves emitted a faintly intoxicating perfume in the sun. At the end of the court stood the sanctuary proper, an elegant Ionic temple approached by a flight of steps erected over a hot spring, from which arose the fumes that inspired the oracles. Not only the dimensions and the enormous number of columns but also the stages in approach to the sanctuary and the general air of mystery remind us of the great temples at Luxor and Karnak (see figs. 3–34, 3–36). The immense building was so ambitious that its construction dragged on for centuries; a number of columns are still unfluted and their capitals and bases uncarved.

SCULPTURE The sculptors of the Hellenistic age must have been almost embarrassed by the richness of their Classical heritage. Through the teaching of the innumerable followers of the great fourth-century masters—Skopas, Lysippos, and Praxiteles—Hellenistic sculptors were enabled to master the entire repertory of Classical virtuosity; they could represent anything in marble or bronze, from the vibrant warmth of nude flesh in the sunlight to the soft fluffiness of youthful hair. There are, in fact, works in which Hellenistic sculptors strove consciously to emulate their predecessors, even those of the sixth and fifth centuries, and since the great artistic conquests had already been made, it is not possible to follow in Hellenistic sculpture the steady evolution so clearly visible in earlier periods of art. Consequently, unless we have inscriptions or external evidence, Hellenistic sculpture is extremely difficult to date. Strikingly new in Hellenistic sculpture are an increased interest in naturalism and a new dimension given to drama, which violates at times all previous boundaries and standards, in keeping with the new geographic frontiers of this period and with the new spaces and light of its architecture.

Distinct schools of sculpture grew up at Athens, at Alexandria, on the island of Rhodes, and at Pergamon, to name four of the most important. It is appropriate to begin with a second-century portrait of Alexander himself (fig. 7–93), who was the motive force behind the new era and its art. The head was found at Pergamon, and it once formed part of a now-lost, larger than life-size statue of the brilliant young monarch. Although done long after his death, it is a convincing portrait of the strange hero—part visionary, part military genius—driven by the wildest ambition, stranger to no physical or emotional excess, restrained by no moral standards (he ordered his own nephew executed and murdered his closest companion in a wild debauch). The rolling eyes, the tousled hair, the furrowed brow, the already fleshy and sagging contours of cheeks and neck all betray the character of this astounding man. As in all sculptures of the Pergamene school, the master—one of

7-93

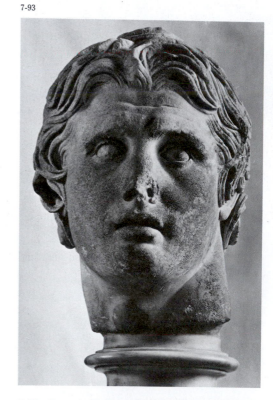

7-93. *Portrait of Alexander*, from Pergamon. 1st half of 2d century B.C. Marble, height 16⅛″ (41 cm). Archaeological Museum, Istanbul

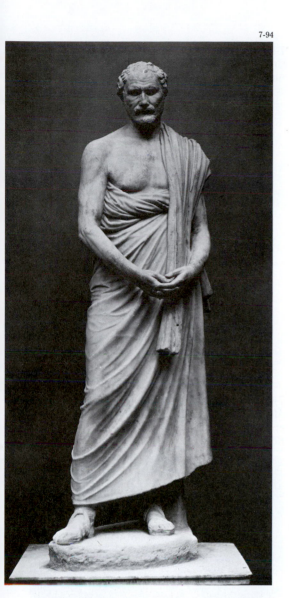

7-94

7-94. *Demosthenes*. c. 280 B.C. Roman marble copy of bronze original, height 6'7½" (2.02 m). Nationalmuseet, Copenhagen

the most gifted sculptors of his time—has maintained a carefully controlled system of exaggerated incisions and depressions in eyes, mouth, and hair in order to increase light-and-dark contrasts and to achieve a heightened emotional effect.

A different kind of portraiture—more searching, perhaps, and less dramatic but equally influential on the later art of Rome—must have characterized the lost original bronze of the archenemy of Macedon, the Athenian orator Demosthenes. This work is known from several Roman copies (fig. 7–94; the hands and forearms are an accurate modern restoration). The sculptor has embodied with great success the quiet intensity of the pensive, aging statesman, enveloped in his worn cloak; no realistic detail is spared. Hellenistic sculptors, in fact, shrank from no representations of decay or deformity in their attempt to present an intense and convincing picture of human life. A tragic example of human degradation is shown in the bronze *Seated Boxer* (fig. 7–95), probably dating from about the middle of the first century B.C., about a hundred years after Athens had lost its independence to Rome. The sculptor controlled the entire repertory of anatomical knowledge and bronze technique known to Polykleitos and Lysippos, but instead of a graceful athlete in serene command of his own destiny, he preferred to show us a muscle-bound, knotty boxer, with broken nose, cauliflower ears, swollen cheeks, and hands armed with heavy leather thongs to do as much damage as possible. Blood oozes from the still-open wounds on his face. What is left of a human soul seems almost

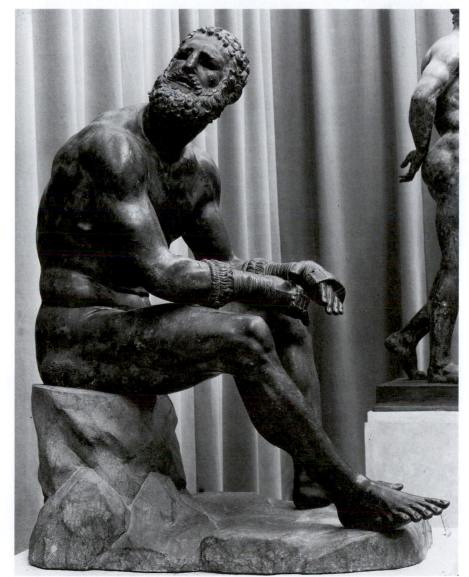

7-95. *Seated Boxer*. Middle 1st century B.C. Bronze, height 50" (1.27 m). Museo Nazionale Romano, Rome

7-95

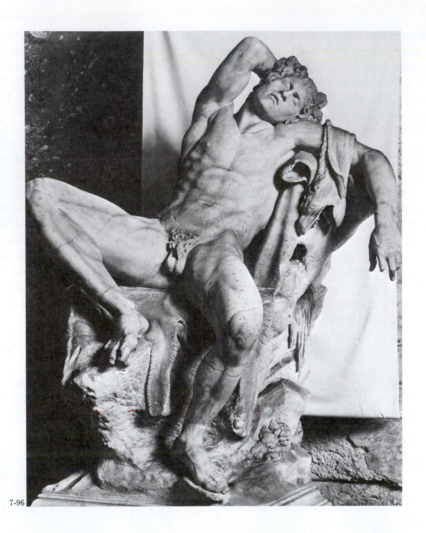

7-96

7-96. *Satyr.* c. 220 B.C. Roman marble copy of Greek original, over life size. Staatliche Antikensammlungen und Glyptothek, Munich

7-97. *Aphrodite of Cyrene*, from Cyrene, North Africa. Early 1st century B.C. Marble, height approx. 56″ (1.42 m). Museo Nazionale Romano, Rome

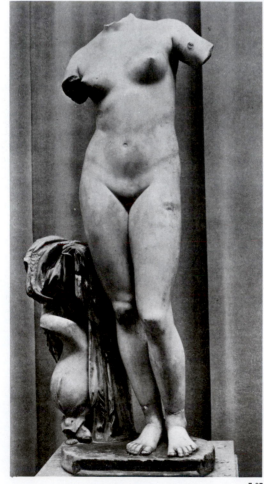

7-97

to ask for release in the expression of the stunned face, possibly even more harrowing when the inlaid eyes were preserved.

Mythology itself was seen from the point of view of the new naturalism; the satyr, a happy and irresponsible denizen of the glades in Archaic and Classical art, is shown heavy with wine (fig. 7–96) in an excellent Roman copy of a lost Hellenistic original from about the middle of the third century B.C. The sensual anatomy and the brutal face disturbed by dreams in its drunken stupor radiate the same sense of tragic imprisonment so impressive in the *Seated Boxer.* The dreamy, languorous naturalism of Praxiteles lingers on throughout the Hellenistic period, even in representations of divinities, who never radiate the impersonal grandeur of the fifth century. The *Aphrodite of Cyrene* (fig. 7–97), found in a bath in that North African Greek city, is an exquisite work of the early first century B.C. The curving surfaces and soft, warm flesh of the goddess, who has just risen from the sea (in emulation of the *Aphrodite of Knidos* of Praxiteles, see fig. 7–80), contrast with the beautiful curves of the dolphin and with the delicate folds of the garment beside her. In the *Head of a Girl* (fig. 7–98), probably of the third century, from the island of Chios, Praxitelean style is carried to its furthest extreme. The marble head was doubtless inserted in a statue made of another kind of marble, part of which was carved into drapery covering the girl's head. The upper lids melt into the brows, so soft has definition become, and the lower lids are hardly represented at all. The face is a masterpiece of pure suggestion, through luminous surfaces of marble and tremulous shadow.

In the magnificent *Nike of Samothrace* (fig. 7–99), we have an echo of Paionios' famous statue at Olympia (see fig. 7–66), but this time the unknown Hellenistic

7-99. *Nike of Samothrace.* c. 190 B.C. Marble, height 8′ (2.44 m). Musée du Louvre, Paris

7-98. *Head of a Girl,* from Chios. c. 3d century B.C. Marble, height 14⅛″ (36 cm). Courtesy, Museum of Fine Arts, Boston

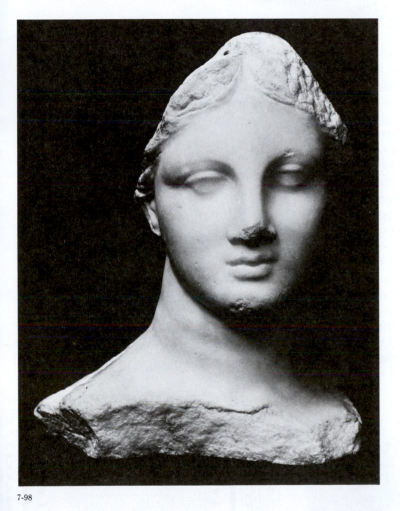

7-98

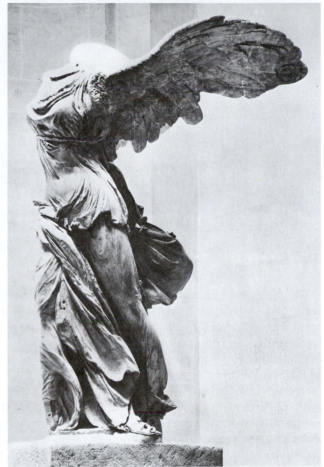

7-99

sculptor has won; his statue is far more dramatic than its Classical prototype. It was originally erected in the Sanctuary of the Great Gods at Samothrace by the Rhodians in gratitude for their naval victory over Antiochos III of Syria about 190 B.C., and it stood upon a lofty pedestal representing in marble the prow of a ship. The right hand, discovered in 1950, shows that the fingers originally held a metal victor's fillet; the head is turned partly to the left. The sea winds whip the drapery into splendid masses, producing a rich variation of light and shade. The contrast between the tempestuous movement and the power of the outstretched wings renders this one of the grandest of ancient statues.

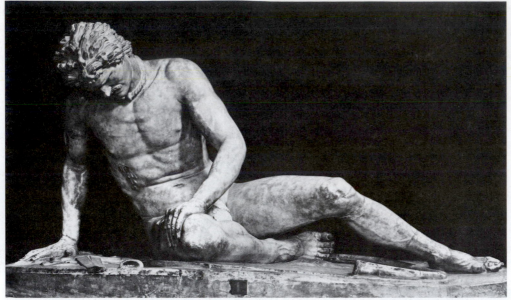

7-100

The most dramatic of all the Hellenistic schools of sculpture flourished at Pergamon, which in the third century B.C. was attacked by tribes of Gauls from the north. The victory of King Attalos I over the invaders was celebrated in a series of bronze statues and groups, known through Roman copies. A strikingly naturalistic example, the *Dying Trumpeter* (fig. 7–100), is obviously a descendant of such works as the *Dying Warrior* of Aegina (see fig. 7–23). But the beautiful reticence and geometric clarity of late Archaic sculpture should not blind us to the accomplishments of Pergamene art here in representing the collapse of the barbarian, from a wound in his side streaming blood, with a deep and unexpected sympathy of the victor for the vanquished. The most minute details of anatomy—muscles, tendons, bones, veins—are represented with a new fidelity probably gained from dissection of corpses.

The triumph of the Pergamenes is celebrated allegorically in the huge Altar of Zeus (figs. 7–101, 7–102) built between 181 and 159 B.C. and partially reconstructed in Berlin. Appropriately enough for the king of the gods, it was erected as an altar in the sky, looking over a vast landscape and out to sea (see fig. 7–86 for its position in the city). It stood on a raised platform, in the manner of a ziggurat, in the center of a court, and was accessible by a steep flight of steps. Around the altar were two peristyles, the outer one of widely spaced Ionic columns, with wings projecting on either side of the staircase. Around the entire base ran a frieze more than seven

7-100. *Dying Trumpeter,* from Pergamon, Turkey. 230–220 B.C. Roman marble copy of bronze original, life size. Museo Capitolino, Rome

7-101. Altar of Zeus, from Pergamon (west front reconstructed). c. 181–159 B.C. Staatliche Museen zu Berlin—Preussischer Kulturbesitz

7-102. Plan of the Altar of Zeus, Pergamon

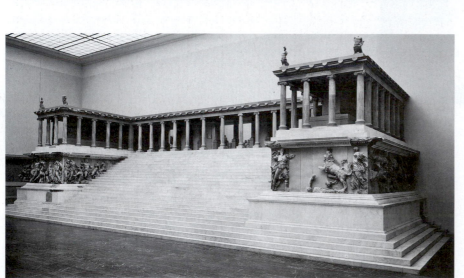

7-101

N

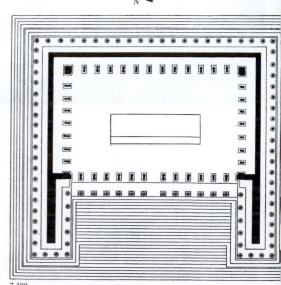

7-102

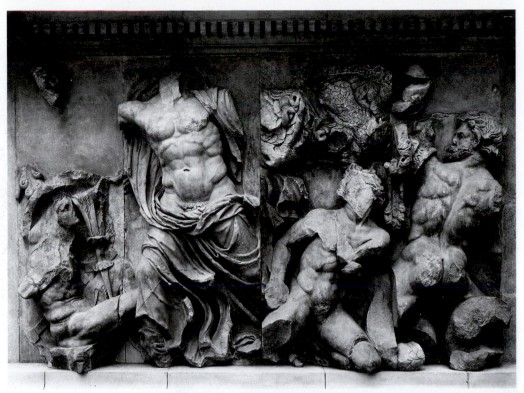

7-103. *Zeus Fighting Three Giants,* from the Altar of Zeus, Pergamon. Marble, height 7′6″ (2.29 m). Staatliche Museen zu Berlin—Preussischer Kulturbesitz

feet high, representing the *Battle of Gods and Giants* (symbolizing, of course, the triumph of the Pergamenes over the barbarian hordes), second only to the Parthenon frieze as the largest sculptural undertaking of antiquity. But the great artist who designed the frieze changed the customary place for such a decoration from the top of a high wall or entablature (Treasury of the Siphnians, Parthenon, Temple of Apollo at Bassai, and possibly the Mausoleum at Halikarnassos), where it could be read only with difficulty, to a position only just above eye level, where the larger than life-size figures, almost entirely in the round, seem to erupt from the building toward the spectator; some have even fallen out of the frieze so that they are forced to support themselves on hands and knees up the very steps that the worshiper also climbs.

No pains were spared to achieve an effect of overwhelming power and drastic immediacy. The fragile architecture is borne aloft, as it were, on the tide of battle. So dense is the crowding of intertwined, struggling figures as at times to obscure the background entirely. Figures of unparalleled musculature lunge, reel, or collapse in writhing agony (fig. 7–103). To our left Zeus has felled a giant with a thunderbolt aimed at his leg and the giant bursts into flames; to our right a giant with serpents for legs beats against the thundering wings of Zeus' eagle. Projections and hollows, large and small, were systematically exaggerated so as to increase both the expressive power of the work and the changes of light and shade as the sun moved around it. The intense light from the sky, the valley, and the sea, reflected upward from the marble steps, would have eliminated the black shadows we see in the photograph, taken in the Berlin Museum where the reliefs are lighted only from above. The sculptures must have been experienced like forces from the surrounding sky and clouds. Compared to this wild surge of violence, the battle reliefs of the fifth and fourth centuries look restrained, governed by laws of balance and measure that here are swept aside. The reliefs bear several sculptors' signatures; unfortunately, we do not know the name of the master who designed the entire work and who also may well have carved the giant head of Alexander (see fig. 7–93), which has so much in common with this relief.

By analogy with the art of the seventeenth century A.D., the style of the Altar of Zeus has often been called the Pergamene Baroque. It prevailed throughout Hellenistic times and was revived repeatedly in the art of the Roman Empire. One

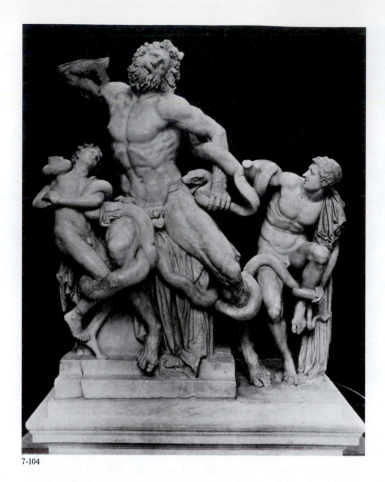

7-104

7-104. HAGESANDROS, POLYDOROS, and
ATHENODOROS. *Laocoön and His Two Sons.* 2d
century B.C.–1st century A.D. Marble, height 8′
(2.44 m). Musei Vaticani, Rome

7-105. HAGESANDROS, POLYDOROS, and
ATHENODOROS. *Head of Odysseus,* part of
Odysseus Blinding Polyphemos, from Sperlonga,
Italy. 2d century B.C.–1st century A.D. Marble, life
size. Museo Archeologico Nazionale, Sperlonga

of the most extraordinary examples of the style is the group representing *Laocoön and His Two Sons* (fig. 7–104), generally identified with the group mentioned by the Roman writer Pliny. The Trojan priest Laocoön was assailed by sea serpents sent by Poseidon and was strangled before the walls of Troy. The group is the work of three sculptors from Rhodes—HAGESANDROS, POLYDOROS, and ATHENODOROS—but we do not know when it was created. Its customary dating in the second century B.C. has been upset by an extraordinary find at Sperlonga on the coast of Italy, about halfway between Rome and Naples. Fragments of five huge sculptural groups, like the *Laocoön* depicting themes from Homer, were discovered placed around the interior of a cave that had been turned into a pleasure grotto by some wealthy Roman, only to be later systematically smashed, presumably by early Christians. One of these groups, repeating the old Homeric subject of *Odysseus Blinding Polyphemos* (see fig. 7–4), was signed by the same three Rhodian sculptors. It has been suggested that both the *Laocoön* and the Sperlonga sculptures may have been done as late as the first century A.D., possibly for the Emperor Tiberius, and should thus be considered under Roman art. Even so, the sculptors were Greek and the style, whatever its date, is a direct descendant of the Pergamene Baroque. The head of Odysseus, who was probably helping to hold the burning pike (fig. 7–105), shows strong similarities to that of Laocoön—the same cutting of the marble, the same wildly rolling eyes, and the same treatment of hair and beard. The legs of Polyphemos are those of a figure about twenty feet high. In contrast to the intense light that floods Pergamon for most of any year, the five groups must have struggled mysteriously in a dim grotto lighted only by oil lamps.

The sharp impact of the moment of dramatic action and the utter freedom from conventional restraints typical of Hellenistic sculpture may be seen again in the fragment of another group, *The Wreck of Odysseus' Ship* (fig. 7–106), which depicts in detail the stern of the vessel from which the helmsman, every muscle tense with the disaster, falls forward before our astonished eyes. Although the expert rendering of muscular strain, and even swelling veins, in the *Laocoön* may seem forced to

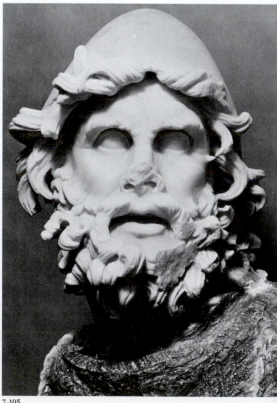

7-105

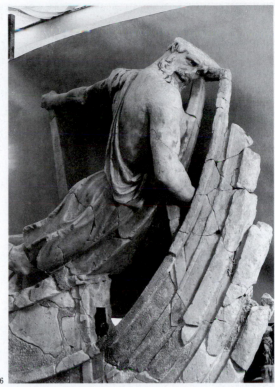

7-106. HAGESANDROS, POLYDOROS, and
ATHENODOROS. *The Wreck of Odysseus' Ship*
(detail), from Sperlonga. 2d century B.C.–1st
century A.D. Marble, life size. Museo Archeologico Nazionale, Sperlonga

7-106

us, in comparison with the Altar of Zeus, it was a revelation to the Italian Renaissance when the group was unearthed near Rome in 1506.

PAINTING AND DOMESTIC DECORATION   Unfortunately, we possess few more
original paintings from the Hellenistic period than we do fourth-century ones, but
many of the finest Roman paintings preserved at Pompeii and Herculaneum are
believed to reflect lost Hellenistic originals. A fresco of *Herakles and the Infant
Telephos* from Herculaneum (fig. 7–107) even repeats a composition carved in the
interior of the Altar of Zeus at Pergamon. The sensuous richness of the style
appears at its height in the painting of Herakles' deeply tanned body, in the
shadows on his fierce lion, and in the range of light and shade on the doe suckling
Herakles' infant son, Telephos. Hellenistic pictorial style can be clearly seen in a
number of pebble mosaics used for floors, especially the beautiful third-century
series unearthed at Pella in Macedon, the birthplace of Alexander. Even through
the difficult medium of colored pebbles, the artist has been able to show the
movement of light and shadow across the nude bodies and flying cloaks of two
youths engaged in a *Stag Hunt* (fig. 7–108). Each pebble is treated as if it were a
separate brushstroke, and the blue-gray background accentuates the play of light.
The motion is enhanced by the rhythmic surge of the vinescrolls framing the scene
and is played off against the wave pattern in the border.

A final word should be said about the Hellenistic houses lavish enough to have
such floors. Throughout Greek history up to this moment the private residence had
been meanly simple—rough stone or mud-brick walls supporting a tiled roof
around a central court whose pillars were mere wooden posts. Demosthenes writes
that in his time, the end of the fourth century, houses in Athens were becoming
larger and richer, and during the wealthy Hellenistic period every city could boast
entire streets of luxurious residences. These houses were invariably blank on the
exterior and flush with the street, but once the visitor entered the interior through a
hallway (L-shaped to keep out prying eyes), he found himself in a handsome
courtyard graced at least on the north side, and sometimes on all four, by a
peristyle, and giving access to a splendid dining room. Other rooms opened off the
court, and the houses were often two stories high. The walls were decorated with an
elaborate system of panels painted to resemble marble slabs (the so-called *in-*

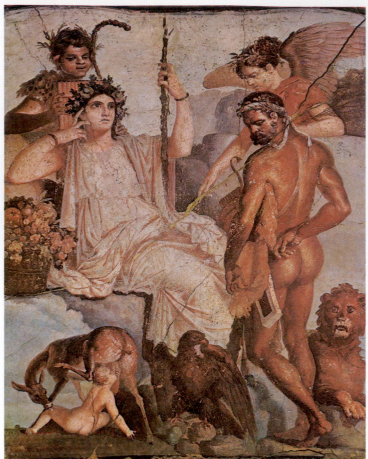

7-107

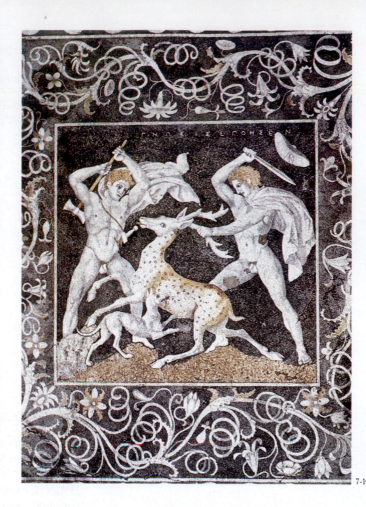

7-108

crustation style taken up later by the Romans; see fig. 9–14). Figural paintings appeared here and there, as if hanging on the wall.

Hellenistic palaces, temples, and prosperous private houses must have been sumptuously furnished with objects making lavish use of luxurious materials and precious metals. We are aided in forming a mental picture of such vanished splendors by a treasure comprising eight wine vessels of pure gold, dating from about 300 B.C., which was discovered by accident at Panagyurishte, near Plovdiv, Bulgaria. Probably intended for ritual use, these wine vessels were produced at Lampsacus (modern Lapseki), a Greek city on the Asiatic shore of the Dardanelles, the strait dividing Europe and Asia; the measurements of wine indicated on them use the units of that city. The technique, known as *repoussé* ("pressed outward"), consisted of hammering the gold plates from the reverse before they were joined together. The central object of the group is a superb amphora (fig. 7–109). The handles—produced as if by chance—are formed by sprightly, youthful centaurs whose forehooves overlap the rim and whose arms are uplifted in delight at the sight of the wine within. Traditional ornament is restricted to four bands widely scattered so as not to compete with the refulgence of the smooth, gold surfaces in the neck of the vessel and in the human and animal figures. The body of the amphora is covered with a vigorous relief, whose figures, mostly nude, enact still-unidentified mythological scenes. On the side illustrated, a nude youth carrying a staff converses with an older man, possibly Herakles. In the youth's lithe and supple figure, relaxed and resplendent, as well as in those in violent action on the other side of the vessel, the unknown craftsman has shown himself in full command of all the resources of Hellenistic monumental sculpture, reduced to the scale of an object that can be held in the hand. He has translated into surfaces of flashing gold the luminary values that are the essence of Hellenistic art in every medium and at any scale.

7-107. *Herakles and the Infant Telephos,* fresco from Herculaneum, near Naples. Roman copy of a Greek painting. 2d century B.C. Museo Archeologico Nazionale, Naples

7-108. *Stag Hunt,* from Pella. Pebble floor mosaic. 3d century B.C. Archaeological Museum, Pella

7-109. Amphora with sculptured handles, from Panagyurishte, Bulgaria. c. 300 B.C. Gold, height approx. 10″ (25 cm). National Archaeological Museum, Plovdiv, Bulgaria

212

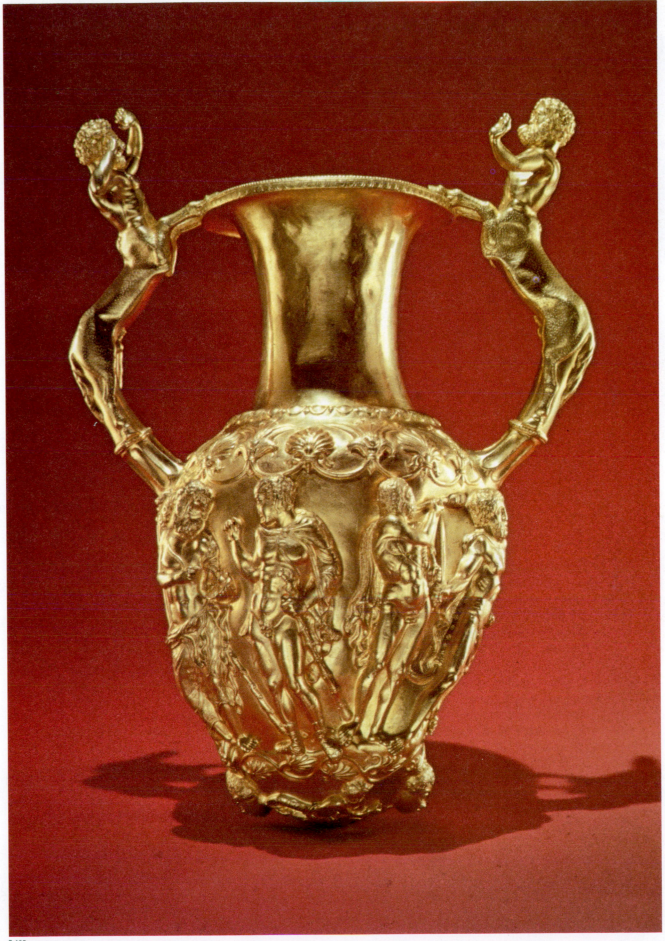

TIME LINE IV

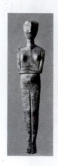

Cycladic idol from Amorgos

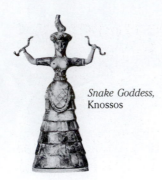

Snake Goddess, Knossos

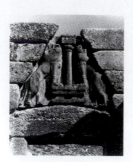

Lion Gate, Mycenae

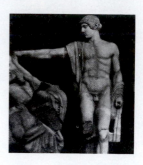

Apollo from Olympia

HISTORY

2000 B.C.	Cycladic colonies develop
1600	Minoan civilization flourishes, 1600–1400
	Volcanic explosion at Thera, c. 1400
1100	Dorians invade Greece
	Ionians resettle in Asia Minor, c. 800
600	Draconian laws in Athens
	Athenians expel Hippias and establish democracy
500	Persian Wars, 499–478; Battle of Marathon, 490; Persians destroy much of Athens, 480
	Battle of Salamis, 480; Delian League, 479–461
	Periclean Age, 460–429
450 B.C.	Peloponnesian War, 431–404
	Death of Pericles, 429
	Oligarchic revolution in Athens, 411
	Sparta defeats Athens
400	Philip of Macedon (r. 359–336) defeats allied Greeks at Battle of Chaeronea, 338
	Alexander the Great, king of Macedon (336–323) occupies Egypt and founds Alexandria, 333
	Battle of Issus, 333; Battle of Arbela, 331
	Fall of Persian Empire; death of Alexander, 323;
300	five monarchies develop out of his empire

CULTURE

Widespread worship of earth goddess as mother/mistress of animals/snake goddess

Phoenicians develop alphabet, c. 1000; Greeks adopt it, c. 750
First Olympic Games, 776
Epic poems by Homer (fl. 750–700) collected to form *Iliad* and *Odyssey,* 750–650
Coinage invented in Asia Minor adopted by Greeks

First tragedy performed at Athens by Thespis, 534
Sophocles (496–406); Euripides (d. 406)
The Persians by Aeschylus performed; Socrates (469–399); *Oresteia* by Aeschylus (458)
Hippocrates (b. 469)

The "Sophist" Protagoras in Athens, 444
Antigone by Sophocles, 440
Plato (427–347) founds Academy, 386
Trial and death of Socrates, 399
Aristotle (384–322)
Epicurus (341–270); Zeno the Stoic (336–264)

Theophrastos of Athens, botanist (fl. c. 300)

Euclid, geometrician (fl. c. 300–280)
Archimedes (287–212)
Eratosthenes of Cyrene measures the globe, c. 240

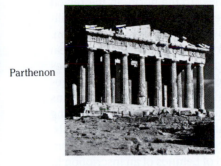

Parthenon

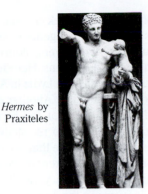

Hermes by
Praxiteles

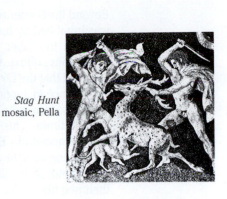

Stag Hunt
mosaic, Pella

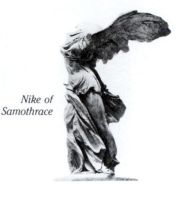

*Nike of
Samothrace*

PAINTING, SCULPTURE, ARCHITECTURE

Lyre Player, from Amorgos
Palace at Knossos
Lion Gate, Mycenae; Citadel, Tiryns

Dipylon amphora; amphora from Eleusis

Kouros of Sounion
Calf-Bearer; Hera, from Samos
Black-figure vases by Psiax and Exekias
Red-figure vases by Euphronios, Kleophrades Painter, Berlin Painter
Blond Youth; Charioteer of Delphi; Zeus of Artemision
Temple of Zeus at Olympia, with pedimental and relief sculpture
Temple of Hera II at Paestum

Diskobolos by Myron; *Doryphoros* by Polykleitos
Parthenon at Athens, with sculpture
Propylaia; Erechtheion and Temple of Athena Nike
Athena Parthenos and *Lemnian Athena* by Phidias
Victory by Paionios; *Stela of Hegeso*

Mausoleum at Halikarnassos
Tholos and Theater at Epidauros
Head by Skopas; *Apoxyomenos* by Lysippos; *Hermes* by Praxiteles
Originals of *Victory of Alexander over Darius III* and *Herakles and
    Telephos*
Alexander; Demosthenes; Dying Trumpeter; Nike of Samothrace
Altar of Zeus, Pergamon
Laocoön and *Odysseus* by Hagesandros, Polydoros, and Athenodoros

PARALLEL SOCIETIES

Neo-Sumerian	2000 B.C.
Minoan	1600
Mycenean	
Empire in Egypt	1100
Greek: Geometric and Orientalizing	
Greek: Archaic	600
Greek: Severe Style	500
Greek: Classical	
Etruscan	
Greek: Age of Pericles	450 B.C.
	400
Celtic tribes	
	300
Hellenistic	
Roman Republican	

CHAPTER EIGHT

Beyond the borders of the coastal Greek city-states of southern Italy, the hinterland was inhabited by less-developed, indigenous peoples. To the north, in the region between the Tiber and the Arno rivers, flourished an extraordinary and still-mysterious culture, that of the Etruscans. Herodotus, the Greek classical historian, reported that the Etruscans came from Lydia in Asia Minor, and there is a good deal of evidence to support his contention. Another ancient tradition, however, causes some modern scholars to believe that the Etruscans inhabited Italy from pre-historic times. This view is difficult to reconcile with the fact that the Etruscans spoke a non–Indo-European language that, as ancient authors noted, had nothing in common with the other tongues current in ancient Italy, not even with their roots. On account of this linguistic discrepancy the Etruscans were sharply isolated from their neighbors. The discovery on the Aegean island of Lemnos of an inscription in

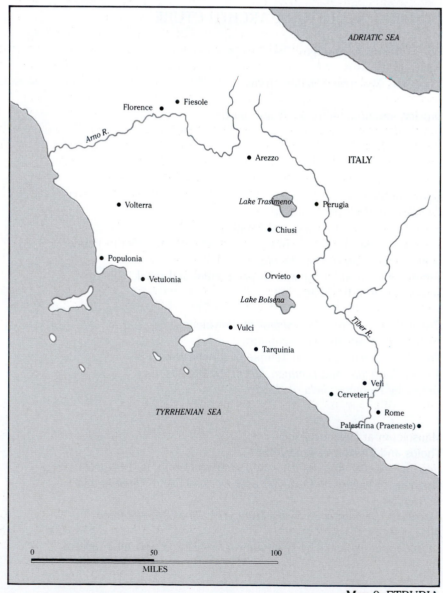

Map 9. ETRURIA

a language resembling Etruscan adds weight to the arguments for an Eastern origin.

Regardless of how the debate may eventually be settled, the fact remains that for about four hundred years this energetic people controlled much of central Italy, the region of Etruria, which has retained the name of Tuscany (from the Latin *Tuscii*, for "Etruscans") until the present day. They never formed a unified nation but rather a loose confederation of city-states, each under the rule of its own king. Many of these cities are still inhabited and flourishing, among them Veii, Tarquinii (Tarquinia), Caere (Cerveteri), Perusia (Perugia), Faesulae (Fiesole), Volaterrae (Volterra), Arretium (Arezzo), and Clusium (Chiusi). Although presently populated centers are generally impossible to excavate, requiring the demolition of countless later structures, others, since abandoned, such as Populonia and Vetulonia, have been systematically uncovered. We often know more about Etruscan cemeteries outside the city walls than about Etruscan towns.

During the sixth and fifth centuries B.C., the Etruscan states colonized an ever-expanding domain in central Italy, including Rome itself, which was ruled by a succession of Etruscan kings until the founding of the Roman Republic at the end of the sixth century. In fact, Etruscan rule spread into Campania in the south and into the plain of the Po River to the north, as far as the foothills of the Alps. Etruscan commerce in the Mediterranean vied with that of the Greeks and the Phoenicians, both of whom had reason to dread Etruscan pirates. From the fifth century onward, the expanding military power of Rome doomed the Etruscan hegemony and eventually even Etruscan independence. During the fourth century, constant warfare against the Romans attacking from the south and the Gauls from the north forced the Etruscans to develop the urban fortifications for which they were renowned. During the third century, Roman domination destroyed Etruscan power forever, and in the early first century B.C. the Etruscan cities were definitively absorbed into the Roman Republic.

Etruscan literature is lost; we know of no Etruscan philosophy or science, nor can it be claimed that the Etruscans developed an art whose originality and quality could enable it to compete with the great artistic achievements of the Egyptians, the Mesopotamians, or above all the Greeks. In many respects Etruscan art follows, about a generation behind, the progress of the Greeks, whose vases the Etruscans avidly collected. Yet many works of Etruscan sculpture and painting are very attractive in their rustic vigor, and every now and then in museums of Etruscan art we encounter a real masterpiece.

Architecture

Little Etruscan architecture is standing, even in fragmentary condition, although recent excavations have disclosed very original plans of early date. A detailed prescription for an Etruscan temple based on examples visible in his day is given by Vitruvius, a Roman architect and theoretical writer of the first century B.C. If we judge from Vitruvius (fig. 8–1), a typical Etruscan temple was roughly square in plan and placed upon a high podium of stone blocks, often tufa (a volcanic stone that was handy and easy to cut). Access was provided by a flight of steps in the front, unlike the continuous, four-sided platform of the Greek temple. The mud-brick cella occupied only the rear half of the podium; the rest was covered by an open portico; the low-pitched wooden roof had widely overhanging eaves to protect the mud-brick walls. Early columns were of wood, with stone capitals and bases; later examples were of stone throughout. Vitruvius thought that all Etruscan columns

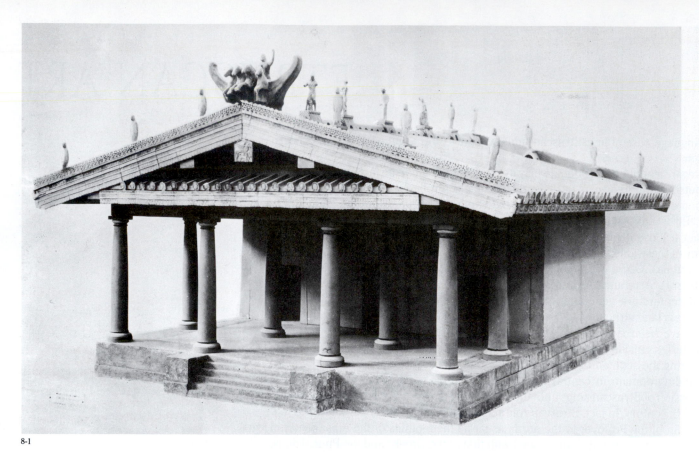

8-1

8-1. Reconstruction of a typical Etruscan temple as described by Vitruvius

8-2. Porta Marzia, Perugia. 3d or 2d century B.C.

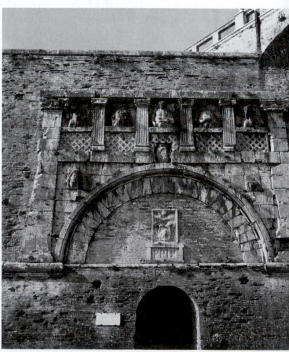

8-2

were unfluted, with molded bases and capitals close to those of the Doric order, including both echinus and abacus; he therefore postulated a fourth or Tuscan order. However, surviving examples show that the Etruscans did on occasion flute their columns and did imitate, however roughly, both Ionic and Corinthian capitals. The heavy roof-beams and protecting tiles left little room for pedimental sculpture. But the Etruscans were extremely adept at terra-cotta (baked clay) work, having learned the technique from the Greeks to the south, and their roof lines and ridgepoles often bristled with a sizable terra-cotta population.

The appearance of an Etruscan temple, with its squat proportions and crowded roof, could scarcely rival the elegance and harmony of Hellenic proportions, but the Etruscan examples were, nonetheless, the basis for the Roman experience of a temple. Several existed in Rome itself, and a very large one dedicated to Jupiter, 175 feet by 204 feet, with a triple cella and columns continuing along the sides, was dedicated in 509 B.C. on the Capitoline Hill. Although this great temple burned down in 83 B.C., it was rebuilt in 69 B.C. with lofty marble columns on the Greek model. This very circumstance tells us much about the double derivation of Roman architecture, with Greek elements grafted, so to speak, onto Etruscan trunks.

The Greeks knew the arch but used it very rarely, mostly in substructures. One of the few Greek arches above ground is in the city wall of Velia, a Greek town south of Paestum. Borrowing the idea from their Greek neighbors, the Etruscans embellished and elaborated it. Like the Babylonians, they displayed the arch proudly, at the major entrances to their cities—places that had special religious meaning. The gates of Perugia—for example, the Porta Marzia (fig. 8–2; originally open, much later filled in with brick)—are true arches, composed of trapezoidal stones called *voussoirs*, each of which presses against its neighbors so that the structure is essentially self-sustaining (see fig. 9–34). The Porta Marzia arch is flanked by pilasters of two different sizes, in rather clumsy imitation of Greek originals; nonetheless, these are important early examples of the combination of the arch with the Greek orders that later typified Roman architectural thinking.

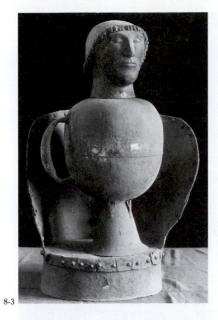

8-3

8-3. Cinerary urn, from Chiusi. 7th century B.C. Hammered bronze with terra-cotta head, height approx. 33″ (84 cm). Museo Etrusco, Chiusi

8-4. Sarcophagus, from Cerveteri. c. 520 B.C. Painted terra-cotta, length 6′7″ (2.01 m). Museo Nazionale di Villa Giulia, Rome

Sculpture

Etruscan sculpture, most of which we know from funerary examples, shows from the beginning the typical Etruscan facility in terra-cotta. The clay was modeled with the fingers and the fine details added with the use of tools, which were probably wooden. Many terra-cotta statuettes of the deceased have been found; small terra-cotta urns, made to hold incinerated remains, were widely used. A seventh-century-B.C. urn of hammered bronze from Chiusi (fig. 8–3) is surmounted by a staring terra-cotta head of great expressive power and stern simplicity of surface and detail, and the whole is set upon a bronze model of a chair. The Etruscans developed a new kind of funerary sculpture in painted terra-cotta that shows the deceased, singly or in couples, relaxing happily on the left elbow on a couch, in the pose of banqueters. The finest of these is from Cerveteri (fig. 8–4). These delightful images, whose smooth bodies, braided hair, and Archaic smiles remind us of Greek sculpture, seem to show a very happy view of the future life, in keeping with the festive paintings (see page 225) that decorate the interiors of the tomb chambers. But the most imposing Etruscan terra-cotta works were such rooftop statues as the famous *Apollo of Veii,* which still retains some of its original coloring (fig. 8–5). This figure was part of a group showing Herakles carrying off the sacred hind, with Apollo in hot pursuit. Provincial though he may appear in comparison with such contemporary Archaic Greek works as the earliest sculpture at Aegina (see fig. 7–21), the athletic god, with his grand stride and swinging drapery, whose folds are stylized into a system of geometrically related pleats, shows a freedom of motion

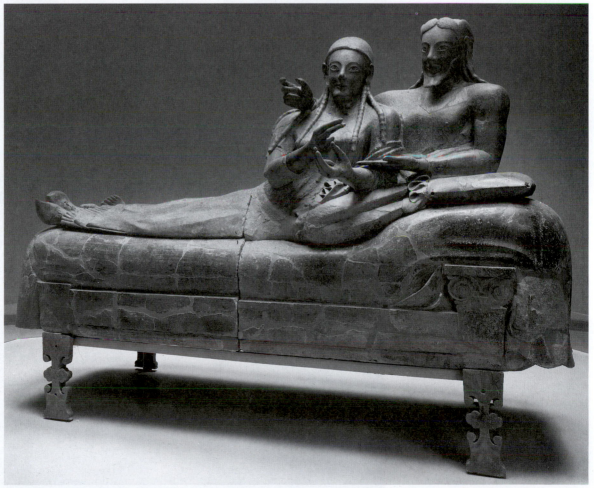

8-4

8-5

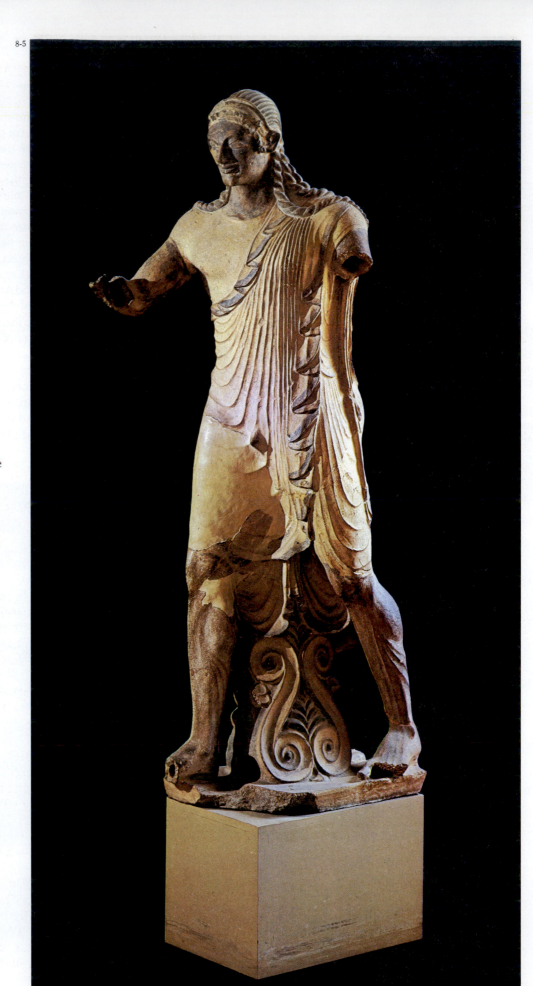

8-5. *Apollo of Veii.* c. 515–490
B.C. Painted terra-cotta, height
69″ (1.75 m). Museo Nazionale
di Villa Giulia, Rome

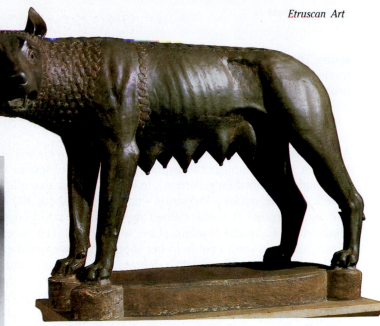

8-6. *She-Wolf.* c. 500–480 B.C. Bronze, height
33½″ (85.1 cm). Museo Capitolino, Rome

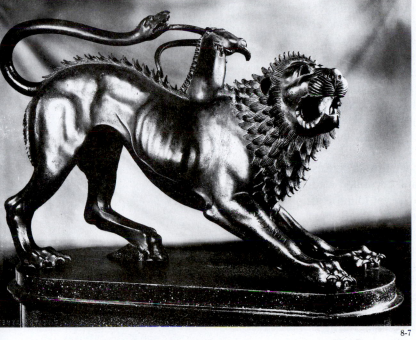

8-7. *Wounded Chimaera,* from Arezzo. Early 4th
century B.C. Bronze, height 31½″ (80 cm).
Museo Archeologico Nazionale, Florence

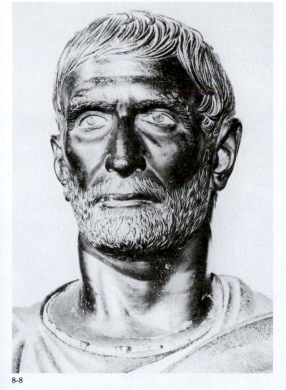

8-8. *Bearded Man (Lucius Junius Brutus).* Head,
c. 300 B.C. Bronze, height 12⅝″ (32 cm). Palazzo
dei Conservatori, Rome

that in Archaic Greek sculpture is generally restricted to reliefs; the borrowed Archaic smile and stylized folds seem almost anachronistic. This statue helps us form an idea of the terra-cotta statue of Jupiter once in the Etruscan temple on the Capitoline (see page 230), whose sculptor also came from Veii, a town eight miles north of Rome.

The fierce bronze *She-Wolf* (fig. 8–6), a symbol of the origins of Rome because a she-wolf suckled Romulus and Remus, the legendary founders of that city, is an Etruscan work of about 500 to 480 B.C., but the bronze-caster may have been a Greek. Its crisp and brilliant detail was incised in the bronze after casting. The sculptor was clearly interested in representing a fierce and defiant animal as a symbol of Rome, newly released from Etruscan tyranny, and perhaps for that reason substituted the mane of a lion, rendered in stylized Archaic curls, for the thick coat of a wolf. An equally impressive if more fantastic animal is the *Wounded Chimaera* (fig. 8–7), from the early fourth century, found at Arezzo. This three-headed beast was adopted by the Etruscans from Greek mythology, in which it was slain by the hero Bellerophon on his winged horse Pegasus. The ornamentalized locks of its lion mane and the equally stylized horns of the goat-head rising from its back derive more from sculptural tradition than from any naturalistic observation, but the ferocity of the expression and the tension of the muscles and rib cage display the power of Etruscan art at its most brilliant. A similar precision of detail and intensity of expression are still seen in the impressive portrait of a *Bearded Man* (fig. 8–8), dating from the third century, whose air of strong resolution has given it the nickname of Lucius Junius Brutus, the leader of the Roman revolt against the last Etruscan king. The head may have belonged to a lost equestrian statue. The eyes are inlaid with ivory, and the hair, beard, and strong eyebrows are treated as lines but incised in the original clay or wax before casting, not in the bronze, which suggests a new move toward visual realism.

Bronze Implements

An entirely different aspect of Etruscan taste is seen in the lovely incised images on Etruscan bronze implements, especially the backs of bronze mirrors (the fronts were highly polished for reflection). In a fairly archaic example (fig. 8–9) found at Praeneste—the modern Palestrina—dating from about 490 B.C., a remarkably chunky Aphrodite is being clothed by two nude small boys, who have been identified as Eros and Himeros (Love and Desire). Her shoes are winged, and enormous wings sprout not from her shoulders as we would expect but from her fertile loins. The line flows with a delicate ease we would hardly predict after the intensity of the preceding sculpture in bronze, an ease not only in the bodies and wings but in the ornamental border, especially the wave pattern indicating the sea from which the goddess was born.

The Etruscans commissioned many *cists,* bronze vessels intended to hold objects used in the rituals for the worship of Bacchus and Demeter, and decorated with linear images like those on the mirrors. The most elaborate cist yet found is a splendid example also from Praeneste, the so-called *Ficoroni Cist* (fig. 8–10), datable in the late fourth century B.C. The cylindrical body of the cist, topped by three bronze figures on the lid, is best seen in a photograph that unrolls the story like a scroll, reading from right to left. The Argonauts, needing fresh water, have landed in the territory of Amykos, who will permit no one to drink from his spring who cannot beat him in boxing. We see the lion-headed mouth of the spring, with a figure drinking from a kylix, then the hero Pollux practicing with a punching bag, the lofty stem of the ship Argo in the background with reclining Argonauts, but alas, no boxing match. Athena stands in the center, while Pollux vigorously binds Amykos to a tree and Victory flies overhead. At the left Pollux, now hatted again for the journey, chats affectionately with his twin, Castor, while other Argonauts fill their amphorae. The exquisite mastery of the nude body in the flowing contours is matched by the representation of rocks and even mountain peaks in the landscape background. The signature NOVIOS PLAUTIOS indicates that the artist was a Greek

8-10. NOVIOS PLAUTIOS. *The Argonauts in the Land of the Bebrykes,* frieze from the *Ficoroni Cist,* from Praeneste. Late 4th century B.C. Engraved bronze, height of cist approx. 21″ (53 cm). Museo Nazionale di Villa Giulia, Rome

8-10

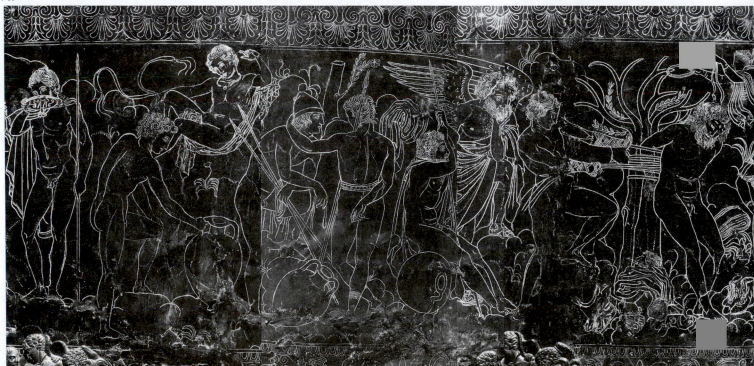

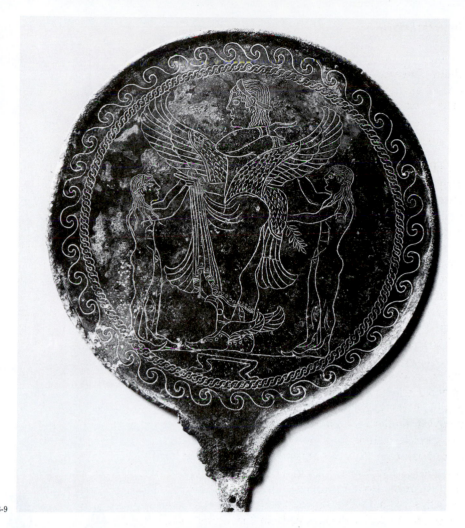

8-9. Back of a mirror, from Praeneste (present-day Palestrina). c. 490 B.C. Engraved bronze, diameter 5½″ (14 cm). British Museum, London

8-9

(not a Roman, as is often mistakenly supposed), probably a freed slave of the Roman family of the Plautii. He tells us that he made the work in Rome for a Praenestan patroness, and it has been suggested that he copied the design from a now-lost but then-famous painting of this subject by the Greek master Kydias, a work known to have been in Rome in the first century B.C. and presum-

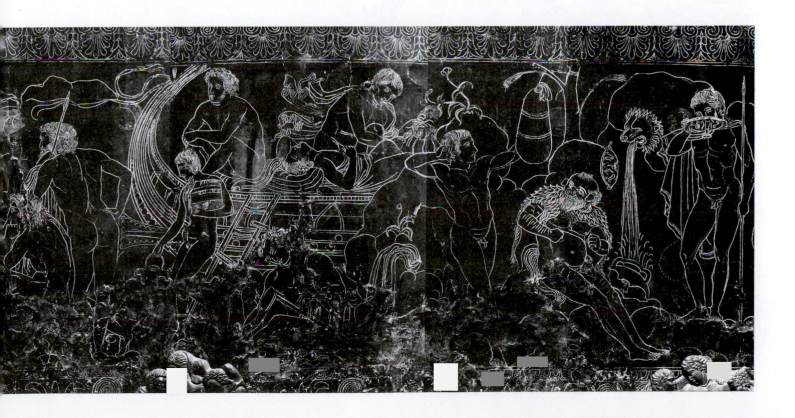

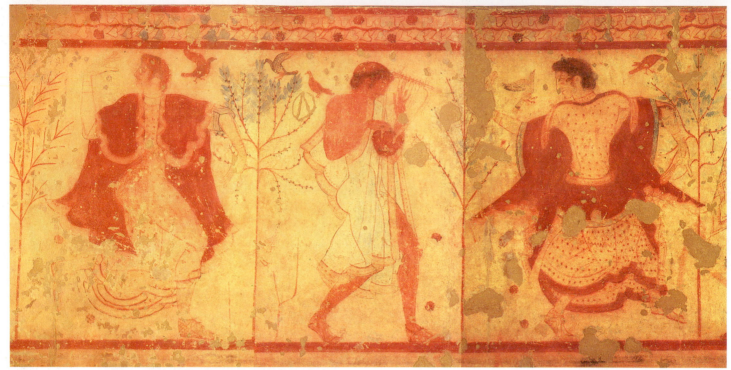

8-11

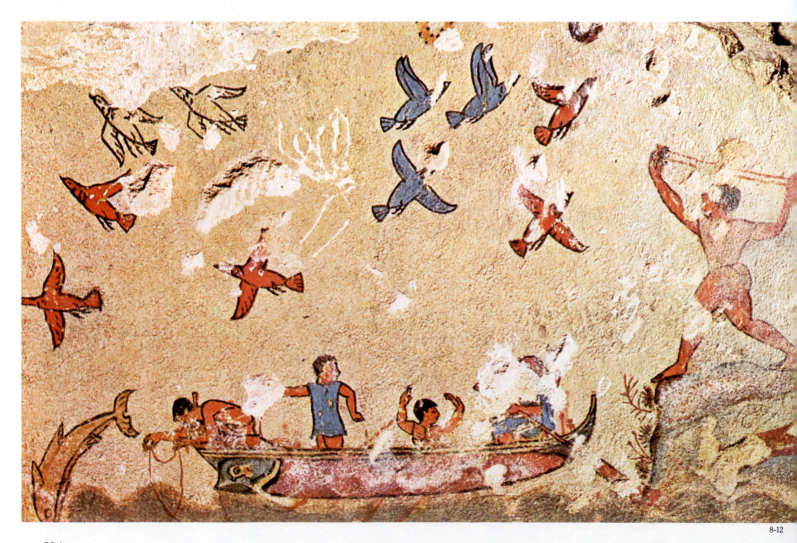

8-12

8-11. *Dancing Woman and Lyre Player,* wall painting, Tomb of the Triclinium, Tarquinia. c. 470–460 B.C.

ably earlier. This is a fascinating documentation of the complex interrelations of Greek, Etruscan, and Roman cultures.

Tombs

We know the most about the Etruscans from their innumerable tombs, of which hundreds have been explored and thousands more still lie unexcavated, a prey to tomb robbers. Most of the Greek pottery so far recovered has been found in these tombs. Typically, the Etruscan tomb was covered by a simple conical mound of earth, or tumulus, whose base was often held in place by a plain circle of masonry. Some tomb chambers were also circular with corbel vaults like that of the so-called Treasury of Atreus at Mycenae (see figs. 6–17, 6–18). More often they were rectangular, rock-cut rooms, which at Tarquinia and other cities contain some of the richest treasures of ancient wall painting we know. Early fifth-century tombs, such as the Tomb of the Triclinium at Tarquinia (fig. 8–11), were sometimes painted with scenes of daily life; at other times, the funeral feast was shown, as in Egyptian tombs. In the absence of firm knowledge of Etruscan religion, it is impossible to say whether these wall paintings were meant to comfort the deceased or to indicate the existence that awaited them in the afterlife. Their energetic contours and flat surfaces betray the influence of Greek vase painting, especially in the handling of the drapery, but even more strikingly the influence of Greek fresco painting, as attested by the Diver Tomb at Paestum (see figs. 7–46, 7–47), the single preserved fifth-century example. They also show a typically Etruscan vigor of movement, as in the depiction at Tarquinia of the dancers frolicking happily outdoors among the trees. The most spectacular of these paintings, representing hunting and fishing (fig. 8–12), shows us rather crudely contoured Etruscans trying—so far without success—to snare birds, white, red, and blue, and a plunging dolphin, which take happy refuge in the billowing waves or the endless air.

Later tombs, such as the burial chamber in the Tomb of the Reliefs at Cerveteri (fig. 8–13), project a gloomier view of the other world. The rock-cut pillars, whose capitals are derived from Greek sources, are supplied with stucco reliefs of household instruments, weapons, and even a small dog, all for the use of the deceased, but a demon of death appears at the end of the chamber, with snaky legs like those of the giants at Pergamon (see fig. 7–103), and he is accompanied by Cerberus, the three-headed dog who guarded Hades. The tomb has become an image of the underworld; the earlier joyous vitality has been forgotten.

8-12. *Hunting and Fishing,* wall painting, Tomb of Hunting and Fishing, Tarquinia. c. 510–500 B.C.

8-13

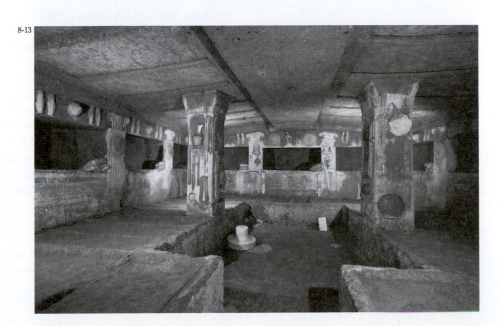

8-13. Burial chamber, Tomb of the Reliefs, Cerveteri. 3d century B.C.

CHAPTER NINE

The culminating phenomenon of ancient history was the rise of a single central Italian city-state from total obscurity to imperial rule over most of the then-known world. Far-reaching as were the effects of Alexander's rocket-like trajectory, they can scarcely be compared with the steady, inexorable expansion of Rome. At the start the Romans were chiefly concerned with maintaining their autonomy against their aggressive neighbors. In 510 B.C. they threw off the Etruscan yoke, yet in 386 B.C. the invading Gauls were strong enough to sack and burn Rome itself. Then the tides reversed; in the third century B.C. Rome, in constant warfare with her African rival Carthage, first dominated, then absorbed all of Italy, Sicily, and most of Spain. In the course of the second century B.C., she conquered the Balkan peninsula including Macedon and Greece, destroyed Carthage and annexed its territory, and expanded into Asia Minor and southern Gaul (modern France). In the first century B.C. the rest of Gaul, Syria, and Egypt fell into Roman hands; in the first century A.D. Rome conquered Britain and much of Germany; in the second, Dacia (modern Romania), Armenia, and Mesopotamia.

At the death of the emperor Trajan in A.D. 117, the Roman Empire extended from the Tigris River in Mesopotamia to the site of the Roman wall built by his successor Hadrian across Britain, close to the present Scottish border, and from the banks of the Elbe to the cataracts of the Nile. This incredible expansion, which not even the Romans could have foreseen, was partly forced upon them by their enemies, especially the Gauls and the Carthaginians, and partly engineered by well-disciplined armies and ambitious generals operating at great distances from any political control. Wherever the Romans went, they took with them their laws, their religion, their customs, and their extraordinary ability to organize. Moreover, on these lands they also imposed the Latin language, with its rigorous grammatical structure and its capacity to express complex ideas. This process of Romanization did not extend to Greece or to the Hellenized East, whose people continued to speak Greek and to preserve many elements of Greek culture. Given the universal extent of Roman power, the history of Roman art is really the history of Mediterranean and European art for half a millennium—so rich, so complex, and so many-sided that only a few of the principal types and historical phases can be treated carefully in a general account.

Quite early in the expansionist career of Rome, two developments became manifest that were destined to have profound artistic consequences. First, the almost continuous process of imperial growth led to a rapid increase in the population of Rome itself and of most of the cities under its control; this growth of population was accompanied by such inevitable problems as mass unemployment and poverty. As a result, not only the prosperous productive classes but also a numerous, idle proletariat required food, water, housing—and entertainment. The amusement devised for them, and indeed for all classes of the population including the imperial family, centered on combat to the death between humans, animals, and animals and humans. The delight taken in such mass slaughter, which did not have the religious excuse of human sacrifice, shows the darkest side of the Roman character. To their eternal credit, the Romanized Greeks resisted any importation of these bloody spectacles. New types of public buildings, including vast interior spaces, were needed on an unprecedented scale, and the traditional emphasis of Mediterranean architecture and decoration on the exterior was thus transformed. Second, the conquest of the Hellenic world—and to a more limited extent that of Egypt and Mesopotamia as well—opened Rome to the influence of cultures that far surpassed its own in their antiquity, intellectuality, and aesthetic achievement. Parallels to the Roman gods were found in Greek religion and mythology, so that

Zeus became Jupiter, Hera Juno, Athena Minerva, Aphrodite Venus, and so on. Borrowed artistic elements were superimposed on the practical inventions of the Romans, and foreign artists, especially Greek, were often employed to carry out typically Roman projects. Thus, Rome found itself in the odd position of becoming the vehicle through which Greek forms and ideas were conveyed to western and northern lands that had previously had little or no contact with Hellenism.

The Republic (509–27 B.C.)

If we judge from Roman literary accounts, we must conclude that the Romans of the early Republic were a resolutely anti-aesthetic people. Scornful of what they considered the luxurious ease of their chief competitors in Italy, the Etruscans and the Greeks, the early Romans prided themselves on their austere virtues, frugal life, and military valor. Oddly enough, at first they do not even seem to have paid much attention to town planning—in spite of the example of the Greek cities in southern Italy and Sicily, which were laid out on regular plans, and the planned Etruscan towns in the plain of the Po River. Rome itself was the last Roman city to receive a plan, which by that time could do little save rationalize the great public areas. After its destruction by the Gauls in 386 B.C., the town was rebuilt along the same disorderly lines. During the Republic and the first years of the Empire, Rome was a pell-mell collection of structures, often rebuilt to the height of several stories, with the most slipshod methods, in order to accommodate its ever-increasing population. Contemporary descriptions record vividly the discomforts and hazards of life in the metropolis, including appalling traffic problems. Public buildings, such as the great Temple of Jupiter on the Capitoline Hill (see page 230), were rebuilt from time to time, however, according to new and imported Greek principles of style. The rectilinear layout of Roman military camps, on which the Romans prided themselves and which they later adapted for their colonial cities, was borrowed from the Etruscans. From them, in fact, the Romans appear to have received their first lessons in building fortifications, bridges, aqueducts, and sewers, in which practical undertakings they took a great deal of pleasure and found—and were able to communicate—a special kind of austere beauty.

SCULPTURE   Not surprisingly, the most impressive witnesses to the formative period of Roman Republican art that have come down to us are the portraits of these sturdy Romans themselves. We have already seen the bronze Etruscan portrait from the third century, whose subject may be a Roman (see fig. 8–8). Another splendid example in bronze, the so-called *Arringatore (Orator)*, dates from the first century B.C. (see Introduction fig. 26). Found at Sanguineto near Lake Trasimeno in Etruscan territory, the statue bears an Etruscan inscription that includes the Roman name Aulus Metellus, the subject of the portrait. Whether the sculptor himself was Roman or Etruscan is almost beside the point, since the work was done at a period when the territory had already been Romanized; Aulus Metellus may have been a Roman official. The directness and force of the representation show a new and characteristically Roman attitude toward portraiture. The simple stance, with some weight on the free leg and the hand thrust forward in an oratorical gesture, has nothing to do with the tradition of organic grace that runs through even the most naturalistic poses of the Hellenistic period. The subject himself, with close-cropped hair, wrinkled forehead, and tight lips, is represented with an uncompromising directness that makes no concessions to Hellenic beauty.

The Greeks never accepted the idea of the separate portrait head or bust because

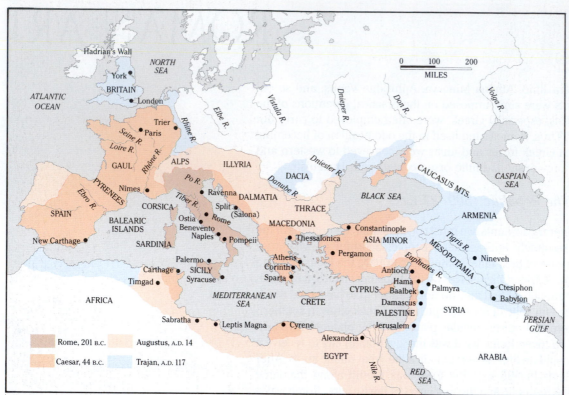

Map 10. THE ROMAN EMPIRE AT ITS GREATEST EXTENT

to them a portrait head appeared to have been decapitated. But as we have seen, such heads were in the Etruscan tradition. In Roman Republican times, exact portrait masks of the deceased were made of wax and were preserved in a wooden cabinet in the home, to be carried by relatives at later funeral ceremonies. This custom reflects a kind of ancestor worship, by means of which the old patrician families preserved their identity. The artistic result was uncompromising realism. A statue of a *Patrician Carrying Two Portrait Heads* (fig. 9–1) embodies this atavistic tradition with a brutal directness that would have horrified the Greeks and, incidentally, illustrates several stages in the early development of Roman portraiture. The heads, which show a strong family resemblance, represent wax images—that in the right hand an original of about 50–40 B.C., that in the left done about 20–15 B.C. Both show stern, bleak Romans, but the statue itself, with its elaborately draped *toga* (the outer garment worn in public by male citizens), can be dated in the early years of the Empire, about A.D. 15. By an irony of fate, the statue's original head is missing and was replaced in recent times with an unrelated one dating from about 40 B.C.

The typical Roman Republican portrait strove to render the subject with a mapmaker's fidelity to the topography of features, in keeping with the air of simplicity stoutly maintained by even the most prosperous citizen. A striking example is the portrait bust (fig. 9–2), dating from the mid-first century B.C. and possibly representing the dictator Sulla, which shows an irredeemably homely man in late middle age, whose bald forehead is creased by a frown. His cheeks are slashed by deep wrinkles, his lower lip crumpled in the middle, and above his bulging eyes one of his heavy eyebrows is punctuated by a huge wart. Apparently neither sculptor nor subject were enough disturbed by the enormous horizontal vein in the marble at the top of the forehead to spend money and labor on a flawless new piece. In contrast to such brutal Roman honesty and stinginess, an unexpectedly subtle Republican *Head of Pompey* (fig. 9–3) probably dating from about 55 B.C., although thought by some to be an early imperial copy, was almost certainly carved by a

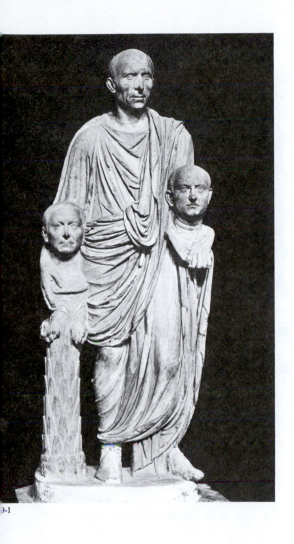

9-1

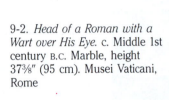

9-1. *Patrician Carrying Two Portrait Heads.* C. A.D. 15. Marble, life size. Museo Capitolino, Rome

9-2. *Head of a Roman with a Wart over His Eye.* C. Middle 1st century B.C. Marble, height 37⅜″ (95 cm). Musei Vaticani, Rome

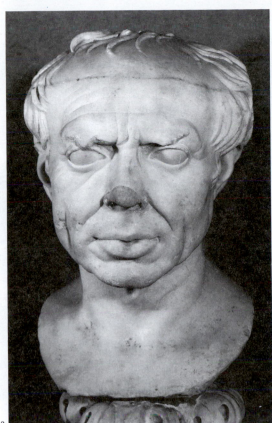

9-2

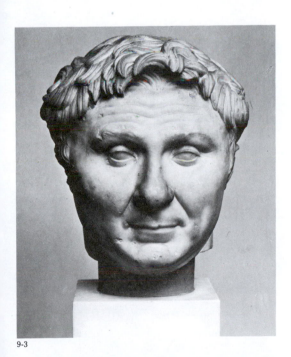

9-3

9-3. *Head of Pompey.* c. 55 B.C. Marble, height 9⅞″ (25 cm). Ny Carlsberg Glyptothek, Copenhagen

Greek sculptor. This master had at his fingertips all the traditional devices of Hellenistic art for the differentiation of the textures of the full cheeks, the wrinkled forehead, the bulbous nose, the sharp eyelids, and the short, crisply curling locks of hair, and for the manipulation of the play of light over marble surfaces. Yet if we compare this head with the *Portrait of Alexander* (see fig. 7–93)—remembering that it came from a statue—we can see that the Roman subject is treated with a psychological reserve respected by men who placed ultimate value on decisive action.

But the influence of Greek art on Roman culture was by no means limited to the importation of Greek artists; beginning with the sack of Syracuse in 212 B.C., actual works of Greek art—sculpture, painting, and minor artifacts of all sorts—arrived in Rome in great numbers. Stripped from their original settings, these works, often intended for religious or political purposes, became to the Romans only objects of adornment. In the homes of wealthy Roman patricians, extensive collections of Greek art were rapidly built up by plunder or by purchase. When no more originals were available, copies were manufactured by the thousands, often in Athens and in other Greek centers as well as in Rome, to satisfy the voracious market.

ARCHITECTURE Although Roman literature gives us admiring accounts of Greek art and artists, doubly precious to us in the absence of the original Greek works, the Romans had little to say about their own art; they seldom recorded the names and never discussed the styles of the many artists—some of them great—who carried out ambitious Roman projects. Most of the few recorded names are Greek. The profession of painter or sculptor had little social standing, and the necessity of making numerous quasi-mechanical copies must have lowered the artists' own self-esteem. In consequence no distinct artistic personalities comparable to those known to us from Greek art emerge from the thousands of preserved Roman works. In its anonymity and in its collective character, Roman art can be more easily paralleled with that of Egypt or Mesopotamia. Only in the field of

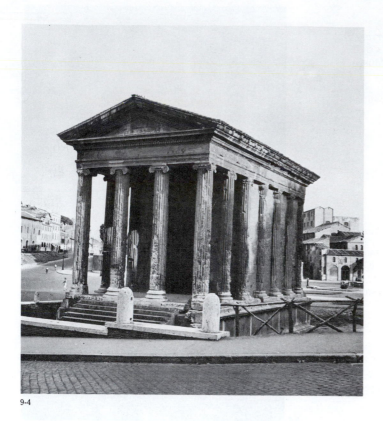

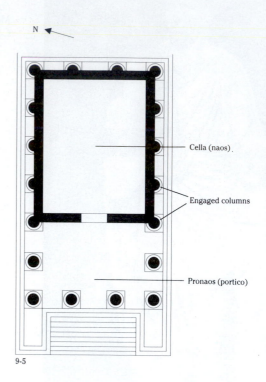

9-4

9-5

architecture—in the writings of the first-century-B.C. architect Vitruvius—do we find much interest in theory, and even here it is largely applied to the codification of an already accepted body of architectural knowledge, for much of which Vitruvius was obliged to resort to Greek terminology.

In the absence of extensive knowledge about the magnificent Temple of Jupiter Optimus Maximus, rebuilt on the Capitoline Hill in 69 B.C., with tall marble columns imitated from Greek models and bronze roof tiles covered lavishly with gold leaf, we have to rely on comparatively modest examples for an idea of Republican architecture. One of these is the well-preserved second-century build- ing known as the Temple of Fortuna Virilis (fig. 9–4; a misnomer—the building was probably dedicated to Portunus, the god of harbors), near the Tiber in Rome. Elements of Etruscan derivation are immediately visible—the *podium*, the flight of steps at the front, and the deep portico. But equally obvious is the attempt to Hellenize the building. The slender proportions were derived from Greece, as was the Ionic order (see fig. 7–62). A compromise is apparent in the way in which the peristyle was carried around the sides and back of the temple only in engaged columns rather than in the freestanding columns generally preferred by the Greeks (the plan is thus *pseudoperipteral;* fig. 9–5). Also, when compared to Hellenic architecture, there is something cold and prim about this little building; the capitals, in particular, lack the organic fluidity of Greek models.

Even more illuminating for the future of Roman architecture was the circular so- called Temple of the Sibyl (figs. 9–6, 9–7) at nearby Tivoli. Although this Co- rinthian structure may derive ultimately from Roman circular huts, some of which were religiously preserved on the Palatine Hill into imperial times, it owes its immediate formulation to the Greek tholos type (see plan in fig. 7–15). The round temple at Tivoli has one remarkable feature. Instead of the coursed masonry characteristic of almost all Greek historic architecture, the cella is built of concrete. Roman concrete was not the semiliquid substance in use today but a rougher mixture of pebbles and stone fragments with mortar, poured into wooden frames or molds. While the concrete was being formed, wedge-shaped stones (and later flat

9-4. Temple of Fortuna Virilis (Temple of Portunus), Rome. Late 2d century B.C.

9-5. Plan of the Temple of Fortuna Virilis, Rome

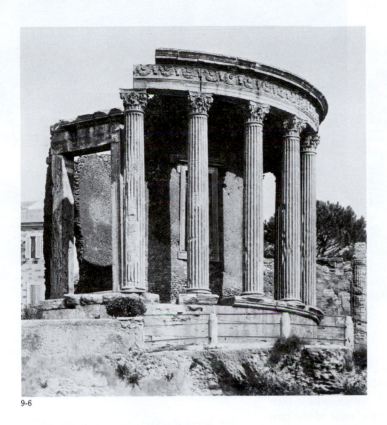

9-6

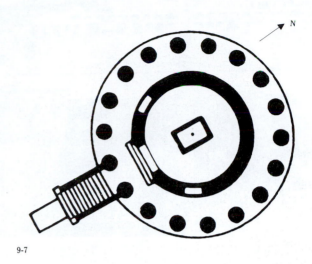

9-7

9-6. Temple of the Sibyl (Temple of Vesta?), Tivoli, Italy. Early 1st century B.C.

9-7. Plan of the Temple of the Sibyl, Tivoli

bricks) were worked into its sides, thus forming an outer skin that both protected the concrete and served to decorate the surface when it was exposed. This technique, used occasionally by the Greeks for fortifications in Asia Minor as early as the third century, was adopted by the Romans for architecture on a grand scale. They were thus freed from the limitations of the post and the lintel—which had governed architecture since before the days of the Egyptians—and were able to enclose huge areas without inner columnar supports. They could for the first time sculpture space itself, so to speak, and herein lies their greatest contribution to architecture. Rapidly in Roman architecture the column became residual, an element of decoration to be applied to the rough concrete walls, like the marble paneling or stucco with which the concrete was often veneered. Most Roman ruins, stripped of their gorgeous coverings, look grim; to gain a true idea of their original effect, we must resupply them in imagination with their missing decoration.

As early as the second century B.C., the Romans appear to have discovered how to exploit the new opportunities given to them by concrete by establishing an architecture based not on straight colonnades but on open spaces of constantly changing size and shape. They also learned how to combine their new discoveries with a dramatic conquest of landscape itself. In this respect the great civic centers built by the Hellenistic monarchs in Asia Minor were pioneers. However, Hellenistic spaces were limited by the convention of the straight colonnade, and irregular terrain could prove embarrassing, forcing an unwanted asymmetry on the architects. The flexibility of concrete construction gave Roman architects new freedom of action, and they pressed home their advantage with imaginative boldness.

A striking early example of such planning is the sanctuary of the goddess Fortuna at Praeneste—the modern Palestrina—long thought to be a work of the early first century B.C. But the date has been pushed back well into the second century by newly discovered evidence. The city on the plain was connected with the temple of the goddess some three hundred feet above by an elaborate system exploiting to the maximum the dramatic possibilities of the steep slope. A destructive air raid in World War II stripped from the Roman ruins the medieval buildings

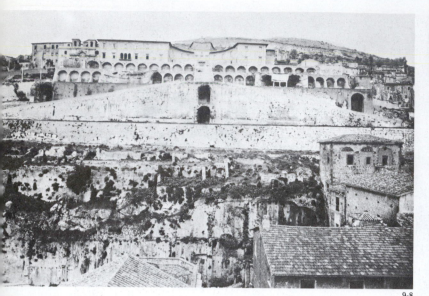

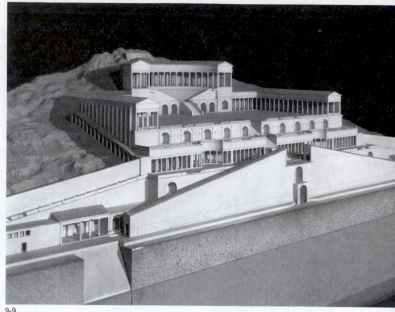

9-8   9-9

that had covered them for centuries and made visible the underlying concrete constructions (fig. 9–8). A model of the sanctuary as it originally appeared (fig. 9–9) shows that worshipers entered by means of two covered ramps, which converged on either side of a central landing, affording an immense view of the new city, the surrounding plain, and the distant sea. From this landing a steep staircase led upward to four terraces of different sizes and shapes. On the first a remarkable vaulted colonnade, punctuated by two semicircular recesses called *exedrae*, protected a continuous row of barrel-vaulted rooms (now clearly visible; see fig. 9–8). On the second, similar rooms were enclosed by an engaged colonnade—one of the earliest appearances of the arch embraced by columns and entablature, a motif that became standard in Roman imperial architecture and was revived enthusiastically in the Renaissance. The third terrace was a vast, open square, surrounded on two sides and part of a third by L-shaped colonnades reminiscent of Hellenistic stoas, terminating in pediments. Finally came a theater-like structure, apparently intended for religious festivals, surmounted by a lofty colonnaded exedra, also terminated by pediments. Almost hidden behind the exedra was the circular Temple of Fortuna. This series of ascending and interlocking masses and spaces of constantly changing character shows a new kind of architectural thinking, made possible only by the sculptural freedom afforded by concrete. Such thinking later found its grandest expression in the forums (open civic centers) that were the chief architectural glory of imperial Rome.

A vast number of Roman town houses are known, many from recent excavations in all parts of the Roman Empire but the majority from the southern Italian cities of Pompeii and Herculaneum, which were buried by the eruption of Vesuvius in A.D. 79. The excavation of these two cities, begun in the middle of the eighteenth century, disclosed not only the houses themselves but furniture, implements, and even food in a sufficiently good state of preservation to enable a detailed reconstruction of the daily life of their inhabitants. In fact, by pouring plaster into holes in the hard-packed ash, it has been possible to rediscover the long-dissolved forms of humans and animals in their death agony.

Pompeii and Herculaneum were designed according to a grid plan imitated from their Greek neighbors (for Greek city-plans, see pages 200–203), although in the case of Pompeii the plan is somewhat irregular (fig. 9–10), since a grid had to be imposed on preexisting streets. Both cities were inhabited by a mixture of Greeks and Italians, among whom the Samnites, an indigenous people related to the

9-8. Sanctuary of Fortuna, Primigenia, Praeneste (present-day Palestrina), Italy. 2d century B.C.

9-9. Reconstruction of the Sanctuary of Fortuna Primigenia, Praeneste. Museo Archeologico Nazionale, Palestrina

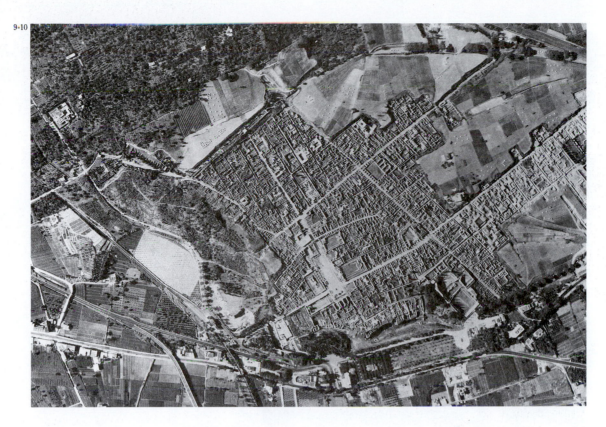

9-10. Aerial view of the city of Pompeii, Italy

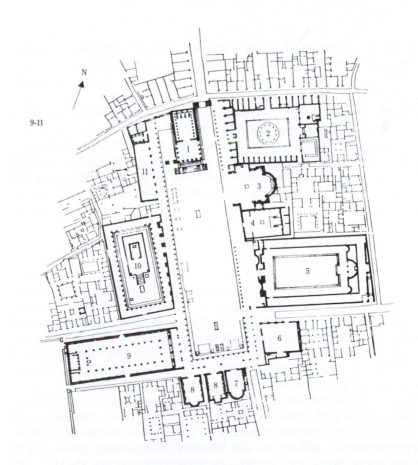

9-11. Plan of the Forum, Pompeii, under reconstruction in A.D. 79   1. Temple of Jupiter, Juno, and Minerva (Capitolium)   2. Meat market (Macellum)   3. Shrine of the city's guardian deities (Lararium)   4. Temple of Vespasian   5. Hall of the clothmakers' guild (Eumachia Building)   6. Voting Hall (Comitium)   7. Senate Chamber (Curia)   8. City office   9. Basilica   10. Temple of Apollo   11. Vegetable and grain market

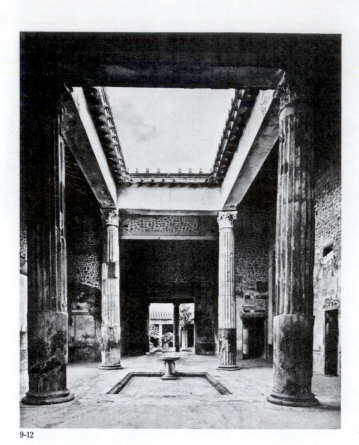

9-12. Atrium, House of the Silver Wedding, Pompeii. Early 1st century A.D.

9-12

Romans, were predominant. Both cities were brought under Roman rule by the dictator Sulla in 80 B.C. Pompeii was badly damaged by an earthquake in A.D. 62; some of its public buildings were under reconstruction, but others were still in ruins when Vesuvius buried the city for good seventeen years later. Among these were the structures surrounding the Forum (fig. 9–11). As was generally the case in Italic settlements including Rome, this central gathering place, usually barred to all but pedestrian traffic, was the result of haphazard growth. But in Pompeii the Hellenized Samnites had designed an impressive layout, which was later adopted throughout the Roman world. The design resembled the Greek agora, such as that at Assos (see fig. 7–88), but with colonnades lining both the long sides and the south end. The long, relatively narrow space was dominated by the temple of Jupiter, Juno, and Minerva (the so-called Capitoline triad) at the north end.

Toward the south end stood the Basilica, dating from about 120 B.C., the earliest known example of a type of building destined for a long and honorable history. The word is of Greek origin, but the building was developed in Italy for the same purpose as the stoa, for gatherings of businessmen and eventually for law courts. Generally a basilica was built with a long, narrow central space, or *nave* (from the Latin word for "ship"). Colonnades separated the nave from the side aisles and were customarily carried across both ends as well, forming a division before the spaces where judges held court (the apses). The side aisles often supported colonnaded *galleries* whose height was governed by the pitch of the side-aisle roofs. Light in abundance came through the windows in the galleries and from a clerestory of windows in the walls above the galleries. Until the fourth century, basilicas were always roofed with timber, protected by tiles. The nave, side aisles, and galleries should be imagined as crowded with businessmen, clients, and scribes, the apses with plaintiffs, defendants, and attorneys. (Exceptionally, the Basilica at Pompeii has neither clerestory nor apse; for a more typical example, see figs. 9–45

9-13. Plan of the House of the Faun, Pompeii. 2d century B.C.–A.D. 79 1. Shop 2. Entrance 3. Atrium with basin to catch rainwater (*impluvium*) 4. Peristyle court 5. Tablinum

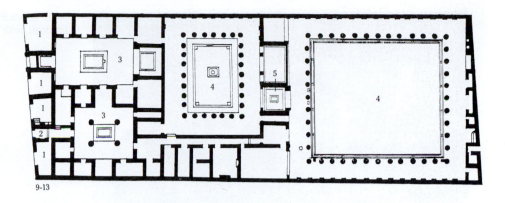

9-13

and 9–46, a plan and a reconstruction of the Basilica Ulpia in the Forum of Trajan, Rome.)

The basic plan of the private house, called by the Romans the *domus* (from which the English word *domestic* is derived), seems to have been common to the Etruscans, the Samnites, the Romans, and other Italic peoples. As often in Italian town houses even today, the street entrance was flanked by shops. A corridor led to a usually central space called the *atrium,* bordered by smaller, generally windowless rooms. The atrium roof sloped toward a central opening that let rainwater into a basin in the floor, at first of tufa or terra-cotta, later of marble, whence it drained into a cistern. At the far side of the atrium was the *tablinum,* a shrinelike room for the storage of family documents and wax portraits. By the second century B.C. every fine domus was also provided with a *peristyle court,* entered through the tablinum. In the center of the court might be a garden with fountains and statues. The family living and sleeping rooms were entered from the peristyle. The House of the Silver Wedding at Pompeii (fig. 9–12; see also the plan of the House of the Faun, fig. 9–13) is one of many such residences, more luxurious than the palaces of the kings at Pergamon. The corners of the atrium were sustained by stately Corinthian columns of marble; the open tablinum provided a delightful view of the garden in the peristyle court. Plaster casts of the holes left by roots in the earth have made it possible to identify the original flowering plants, and these have been replaced today.

The earliest known Roman apartment houses were also discovered at Pompeii. Careful examination has determined that these were formed in the later decades of the Republic, probably by real-estate operators who bought up numbers of domus houses, joined them together, and built second or even third stories on top—not to speak of rooms on balconies jutting into the street—all erected sloppily enough to justify the bitterest complaints of ancient writers regarding similar dwellings in Rome.

PAINTING Late Republican houses glowed with color. The interior walls were often decorated with painted and modeled stucco panels imitating marble incrustation. The stucco was mixed with marble dust, like that used for the exteriors of Greek temples (see page 174), and was smoothed to give the appearance of marble. Panels of rich red, tan, and green were enclosed by white frames modeled in stucco, as in a room from the House of the Centaur at Pompeii (fig. 9–14). This method has been called the First Pompeiian Style, although late examples date from just before the eruption of Vesuvius. The Second Pompeiian Style, which appears to be roughly contemporary with Julius Caesar (c. 80–15 B.C.), is far more imaginative; instead of being paneled, the wall was transformed into an architectural illusion by paintings, often of amazing skill. In a delightful little room from a

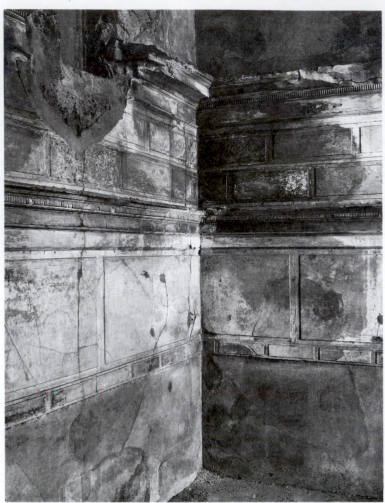

9-14

9-14. Room in the House of the Centaur, Pompeii, with First Style decoration

villa of the late first century B.C., found at Boscoreale near Naples (fig. 9–15), the walls have been simply painted away. Rich red porphyry columns, entwined with golden vinescrolls and surmounted by gilded Corinthian capitals, appear to support the architrave, to which is attached a superbly painted mask. Through this illusionistic portico we look into a sunlit garden, then out over a gilt-bronze gate framed by a marble-encrusted doorway into a view of rooftops and balconies rising in the soft, bluish air and culminating in a grand colonnade, somewhat on the principle of the view up the hillside to the sanctuary at Praeneste (see fig. 9–9). For all the apparent naturalism of the painting, which shows such details as a balcony room accessible only by a ladder, it is evident that the painter felt no responsibility to depict the entire scene as it would appear from a single viewpoint at a single moment in time. Disconcertingly, some buildings are seen from below, some from head on, and some from above. Both artist and patron were apparently content with an arrangement that stimulated without ever quite satisfying a desire to explore distant space. To our eyes the evident contradictions contribute a dream-like quality of unreality, which is enhanced by the absence of even a single person in this magical city.

The Second Pompeiian Style could also utilize the illusion of a portico as a springboard into a mythological world of the past, as in the landscapes with scenes from the *Odyssey* (see Introduction fig. 13) discovered in the nineteenth century in a villa on the Esquiline Hill in Rome and datable about the middle of the first century B.C. Although the painters may not have been Greek (there are errors in the

9-15. *Architectural View,* Second Style wall painting from a villa at Boscoreale, near Naples. c. 50–40 B.C. The Metropolitan Museum of Art, New York. Rogers Fund, 1903

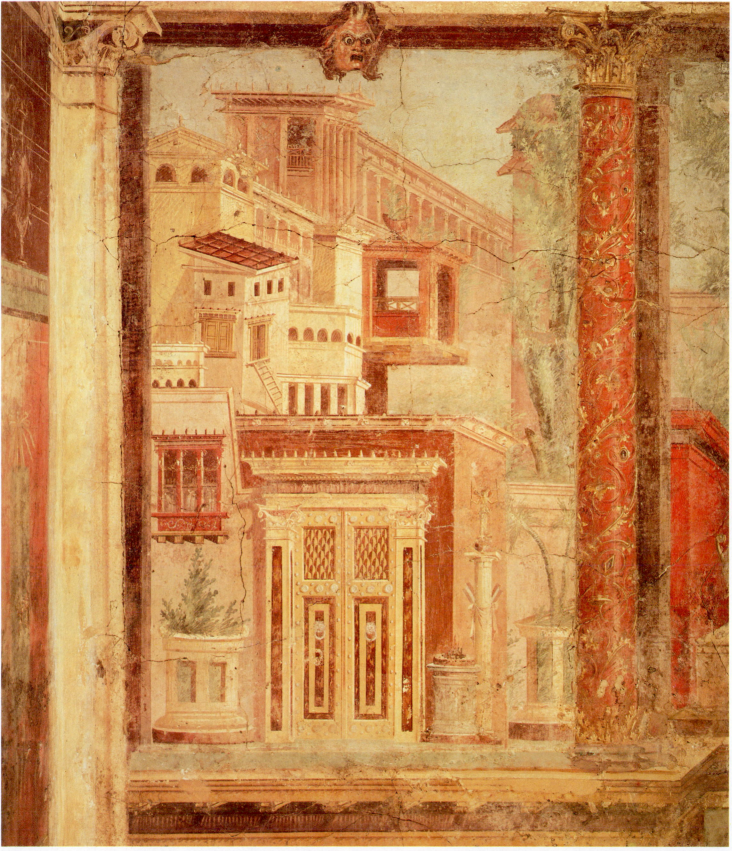

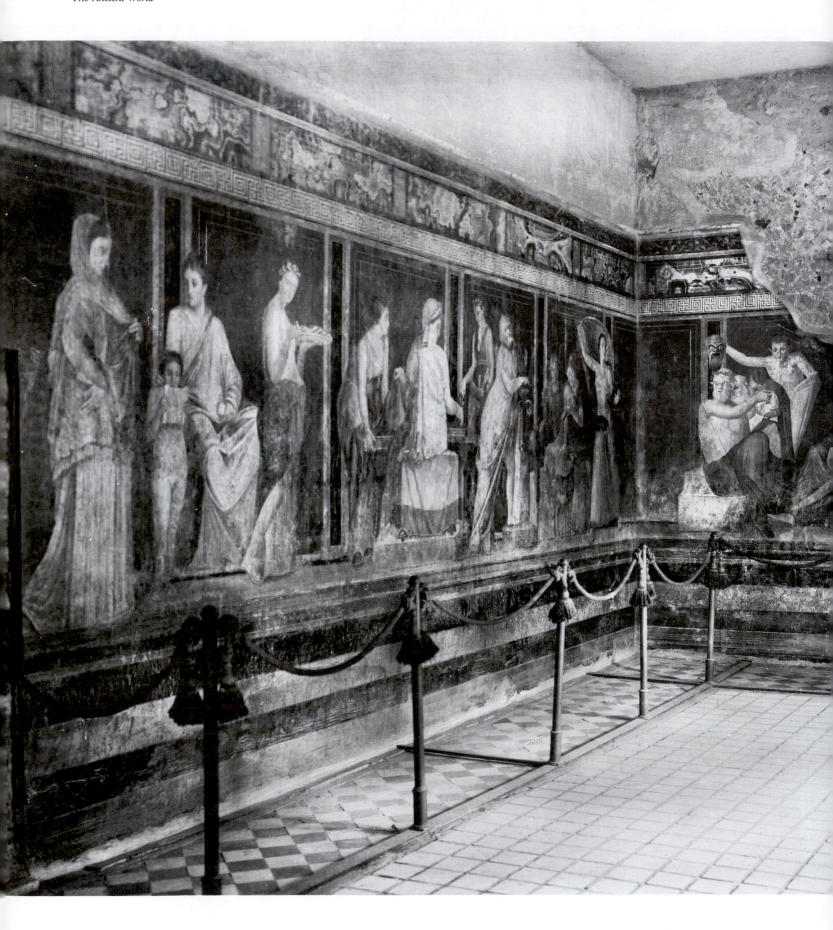

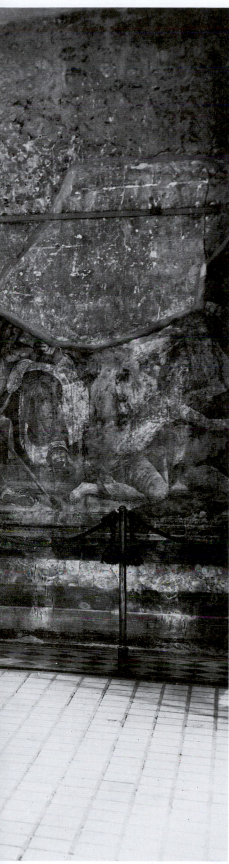

occasional Greek inscriptions), it is now believed they were working on the basis of Greek originals of the second century B.C., possibly Alexandrian or southern Italian. The square piers, bright red with gilded Corinthian capitals, form a shadowed portico through which one looks happily, as from a tower, into a far-off land of sunny rocks and blue-green sea, toward which Odysseus and his companions escape in their ships from the attacks of the fierce Laestrygonians. The landscapes were painted with ease and speed in a fluid style contrasting deliberately with the uncanny precision of the architecture.

A grand room still in place in the Villa of the Mysteries at Pompeii (fig. 9–16) shows another aspect of Second Style illusionism. The actual walls have been transformed by painted architectural elements into a sort of stage on which gods and mortals sit, move, converse, even turn their backs to us, their attitudes ranging from quiet, classical serenity to occasional and startling terror. Apparently, the subject—still not entirely understood—was drawn from the rites attending the worship of the Greek god Dionysos, one of several competing mystery cults brought to Rome from various parts of the Empire. The nobility of the broadly painted, sculptural figures, almost life size, is heightened by contrast with the brilliance of the red background panels, green borders and stage, vertical black dividing strips, and richly veined onyx attic.

Often the illusionistic skill of the Second Style painters, doubtless deriving from Hellenistic tradition, could be dazzling, as in the frequent still lifes painted on the walls of Roman houses. An example of such virtuosity repeated in the later (Fourth Style) House of Julia Felix in Pompeii (fig. 9–17) shows a corner in a kitchen, with dead birds, a plate of eggs, metal household instruments, and a towel, all arranged in a strong light from a single source, which not only reveals forms and casts shadows but conveys beautifully reflections in the polished metal. An even more

9-17

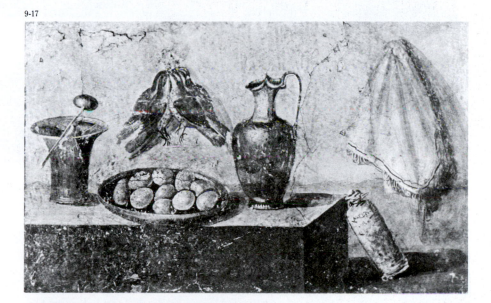

9-16. *Dionysiac Mystery Cult,* Second Style wall painting, Villa of the Mysteries, Pompeii. c. 60–50 B.C.

9-17. *Still Life,* Second Style wall painting from the early-1st-century-A.D. House of Julia Felix, Pompeii. Museo Archeologico Nazionale, Naples

9-16

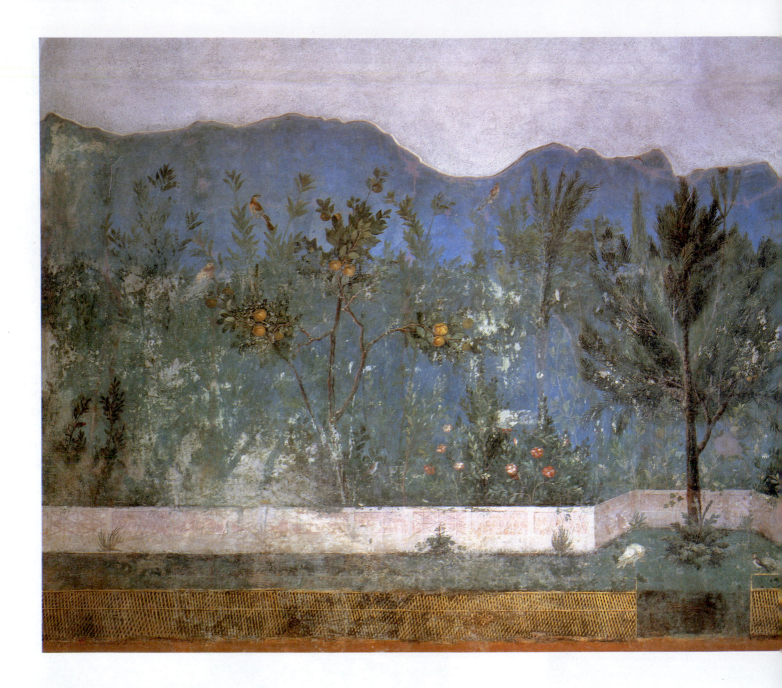

spectacular illusionistic work, in fact unparalleled in all of ancient art, is the *Garden Room* from a villa at Prima Porta, outside Rome, which once belonged to Livia, the third wife of the emperor Augustus, possibly before their marriage (fig. 9–18). All four walls disappear, in a manner attempted more modestly long before in the Minoan landscape room at Santorini (see Introduction fig. 5). A fence and a low wall are all that separate us from an exquisite garden, half cultivated, half wild, in which no earthbound creature can be seen; only fruit trees and flowering shrubs compete for the attention of the songbirds that perch here and there or float through the hazy air. Our vision roams freely around this enchanted refuge which, however, encloses us so entirely as to exclude all but the blue sky. The poetic delicacy of the conception and the consummate skill of the rapid brushwork make this a masterpiece among the world's landscape paintings.

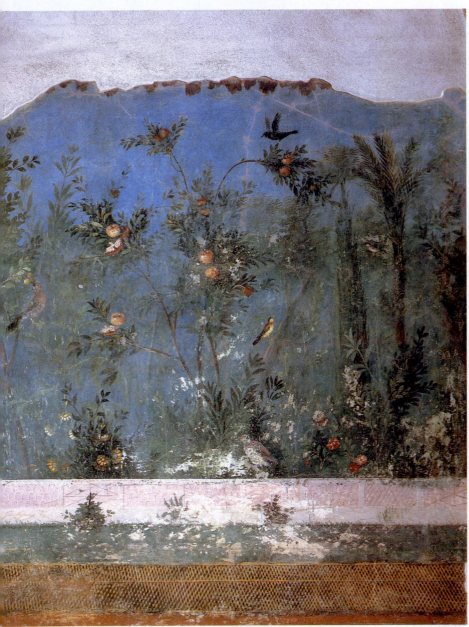

9-18. *Garden Room,* Second Style wall painting from the Villa of Livia, Prima Porta, near Rome. Late 1st century B.C. Museo Nazionale Romano, Rome

9-18

The Early Empire (27 B.C.–A.D. 96)

For more than a century, it had been apparent that the traditional political machinery of the Roman city-state—the popular assemblies, the patrician senate, and the two consuls chosen annually—was inadequate to cope with the problems posed by a vast and expanding empire and a set of freewheeling armies, often separated by weeks or even months of travel from any decree that might be issued in the capital. In several periods of bloody civil warfare, the armies competed with each other for power. Only briefly, under the dictatorships of Sulla (82–79 B.C.) and Julius Caesar (49–44 B.C.), could any form of stability be maintained. In 31 B.C. Octavian, Caesar's great-nephew and adopted son and heir, defeated Antony and Cleopatra in the Battle of Actium, sealing the fate of both the Roman Republic and the Hellenistic world. Cleopatra was the last independent Hellenistic monarch; after her

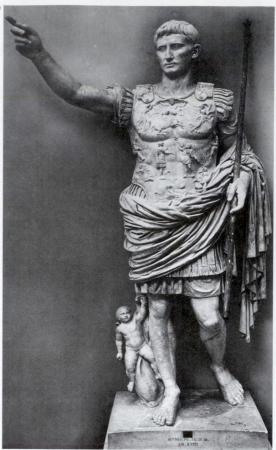

defeat Egypt became Roman. Four years later, in 27 B.C., the Roman senate voted Octavian the title of *Augustus,* and he became in effect the first legitimate Roman emperor.

Augustus ruled as emperor for forty-one years, a period of unprecedented peace and prosperity. The façade of republican government was piously maintained, but power was in fact exercised by Augustus and his successors, who controlled all military forces and appointed governors for the important provinces. The title *Imperator* meant "army commander"; nonetheless, the emperors, who rarely held office in the obsolete but well-nigh indestructible framework of the Republic, in truth governed as monarchs. Augustus' hybrid compromise survived for more than four centuries. With predictable immediacy the emperors were deified after death; Augustus erected a temple to Julius Caesar, and some of his successors demanded worship as gods while still alive, in the manner of Egyptian and Mesopotamian divine monarchs.

SCULPTURE   Now that the Romans had had time to digest their avidly devoured diet of Greek culture, they were able to profit by it and to bring forth a new art of their own. It was to be expected that its Etruscan and Greek sources would at first be plainly visible. Equally predictable was that the new art would deal less with religion and mythology, the primary concerns of the Greeks, than with transforming the often brutal facts of Roman military and political life into partly mythologized images for public consumption. In the celebrated statue of Augustus from the imperial villa at Prima Porta (fig. 9–19), the new ruler is seen as Imperator, in a grand pose easily recognizable as a blend of the *Doryphoros* (see fig. 7–35) and the *Arringatore* (see Introduction fig. 26) in equal proportions. The statue was probably a replica carved immediately after Augustus' death (otherwise, he would have been shown wearing military boots, which, as a god, he did not need), but the emperor is represented as a young man. The head is a portrait, belonging to an official type known in all parts of the Empire through its appearance on coins. Yet the features have been given a distinct Hellenic cast, idealized and ennobled. The figure stands easily, as if the oratorical gesture of the right arm grew from the very stone below the left foot. The cloak seems to have fallen accidentally in coldly Phidian folds from the shoulders to drape itself around the waist and the arm, thus revealing a relief sculptured on the armor, narrating the return by the Parthians, about 20 B.C., of the military standards captured from the Romans.

A deliberate contrast is offered by the statue of Augustus as Pontifex Maximus (the *pontifex maximus* was the Roman high priest; fig. 9–20), in which the emperor is shown about to perform a sacrificial rite, his head veiled in a fold of his toga. Unbelievably, the statue must have been made when the emperor was more than seventy years old; all signs of advancing age have been blurred by softness in the handling of the stone. The face, possibly carved much earlier, and certainly from a separate piece of marble, radiates a godlike wisdom and solemnity.

In a detailed account of the achievements of his reign, Augustus boasted that he "found Rome of brick and left it of marble." Although this claim could scarcely apply to the multistory, ramshackle tenements inhabited by the populace, Augustus energetically continued the building program initiated by Julius Caesar and constructed innumerable public buildings on his own. He desired first of all to celebrate the *Pax Augusta* ("Augustan peace") with buildings in which the new imperial power was to be dignified by the cadences of an imitated Attic style.

Chief among these monuments was the Ara Pacis (Altar of Peace; fig. 9–21), commissioned by the Senate in 13 B.C. and finished in 9 B.C. Although the monument suggests in form the Altar of Zeus at Pergamon (see fig. 7–101), it is on a far more intimate scale and is in every respect less dramatic. The altar itself is surrounded by a marble screen-wall, visible as a square block divided by delicate pilasters. These and the lower half of the wall are covered with a tracery of

9-19. *Augustus of Prima Porta.* c. A.D. 15. Probably copy of original of c. 20 B.C. Marble, height 6′6″ (2.03 m). Musei Vaticani, Rome

9-20. *Augustus as Pontifex Maximus.* 1st-century-A.D. copy of original of c. 20 B.C. Marble, height 6′9½″ (2.07 m). Museo Nazionale Romano, Rome

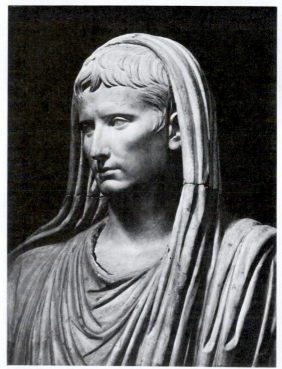

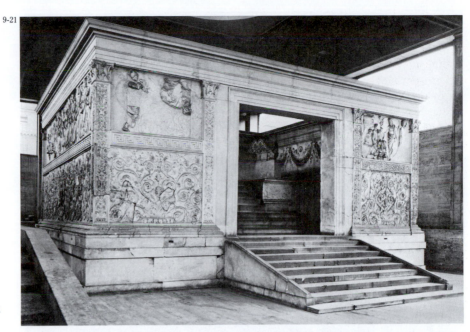

9-21. Ara Pacis. c. 13–9 B.C. Marble, width of altar approx. 35′ (10.67 m). Museum of the Ara Pacis, Rome

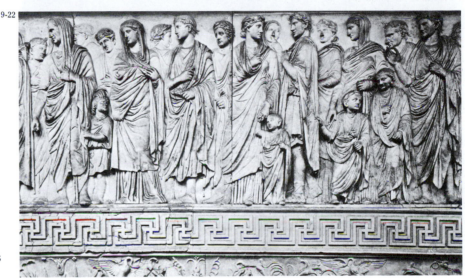

9-22. *Imperial Procession,* detail of the Ara Pacis frieze. Marble relief, height approx. 63″ (1.6 m)

vinescrolls of the utmost delicacy and elegance. Above a meander pattern are a series of reliefs, some illustrating events from Roman history and religion, some showing contemporary events. The emperor himself, his head veiled for sacrifice, leads the numerous and recognizable members of the imperial family (fig. 9–22). In the rhythmic movement of the drapery, the frieze recalls that of the Parthenon (see fig. 7–57) and was doubtless intended to. But there are instructive differences: first, the Panathenaic Procession was represented on the Parthenon as a timeless institution, while the scene on the Ara Pacis shows a specific historic event, probably that of 13 B.C., when the altar was begun; second, the figures on the Ara Pacis are far more closely massed, as undoubtedly they would have been in reality; finally, the background slab of the frieze seems to have moved away from us, allowing room for figures behind figures, with progressively reduced projections to indicate the deeper level. One of the reliefs flanking the east doorway shows Mother Earth with a personification of Tellus (Earth) accompanied by Air and Sea (fig. 9–23); all are portrayed as gracious, very Hellenic-looking goddesses, seated respec-

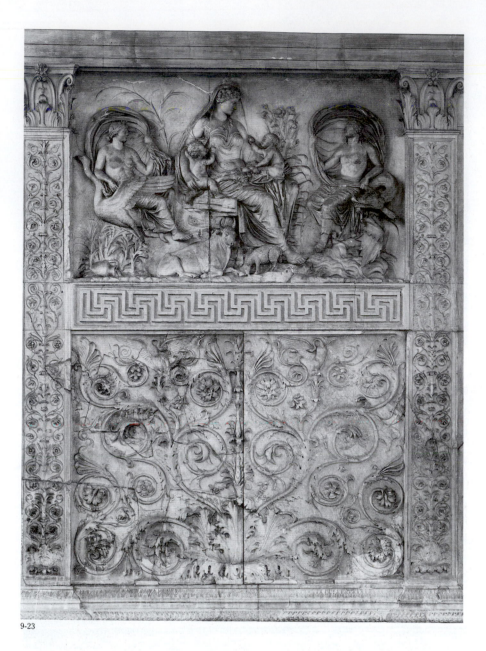

9-23

tively on a rock, on a swan, and on a sea monster. The delicately observed landscape elements come from Hellenistic sources, and the same type of billowing, parachute-like veils over the heads of Air and Water turn up again and again in later Roman and in Byzantine art to characterize personifications.

In a marvelous cameo, the *Gemma Augustea* (fig. 9–24), probably cut for Augustus' son-in-law and successor, Tiberius, the seminude emperor shares a benchlike throne with the goddess Roma, made to resemble a Greek Athena; he is attended by relatives and by allegorical figures, one of whom is about to place a laurel wreath on his head. Above Augustus is his zodiacal sign, Capricorn. In the lower zone two barbarians, male and female, crouch disconsolately while Roman soldiers erect a trophy, a pole carrying armor stripped from the barbarian; two other barbarians are pulled in by the hair. With consummate skill and grace, the artist has worked the intractable semiprecious stone into a delicate relief, exploiting the white and black levels so as to suggest the translucency of drapery and constantly suggesting space in the foreshortening of the human figures, the chariot, and the horse. In its allegorical version of history and in its exquisite refinement, this work sums up the ideals of the early Empire.

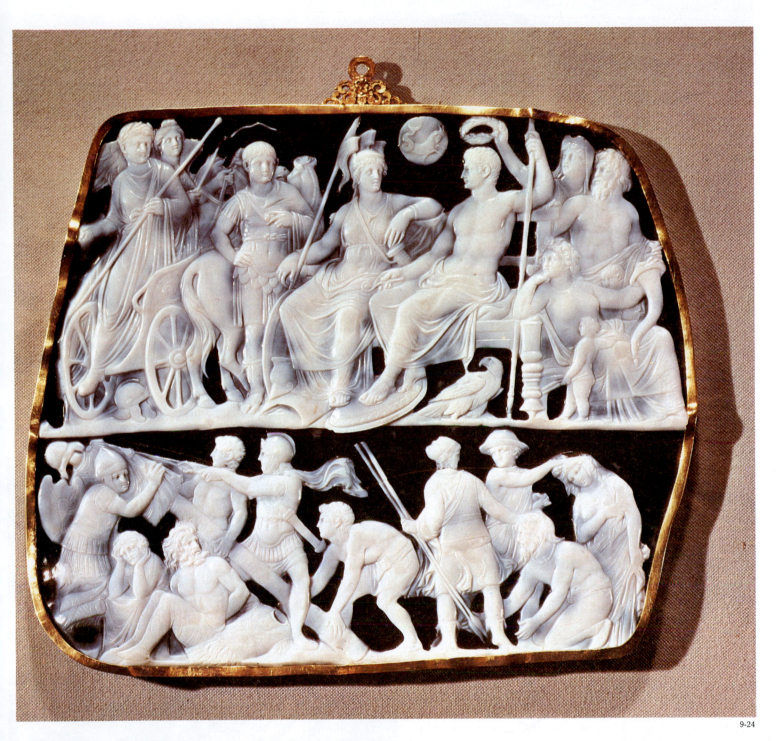

9-24

9-24. *Gemma Augustea.* Early 1st century A.D.
Onyx cameo, 7½ × 9″ (19 × 23 cm). Kunsthistorisches Museum, Vienna

AUGUSTAN AND JULIAN-CLAUDIAN ARCHITECTURE   Unfortunately, no Augustan temple survives in Rome in sufficiently good condition to enable us to
appreciate the qualities of style the emperor desired. Luckily, this gap can be partly
filled by an Augustan temple at Nîmes in southern France; nicknamed the Maison
Carrée, it was begun about A.D. 1–10 and was based on the Temple of Mars Ultor
(see below). This little structure can claim to be the best preserved of all Roman
buildings. We recognize the familiar podium, front steps with flanking postaments,

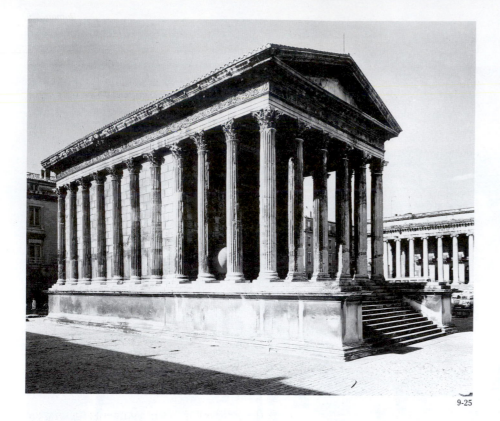

9-25. Maison Carrée, Nîmes (ancient Nemausus), France. Begun C. A.D. 1–10

9-27. The Roman (Republican) and Imperial Forums, Rome. C. A.D. 310. Reconstructed in a model of ancient Rome. Museo della Civiltà Romana, Rome   1. Temple of Capitoline Jupiter 2. Temple of Trajan   3. Basilica Ulpia 4. Market of Trajan.   5. Temple of Venus Genetrix   6. Forum of Trajan   7. Temple of Mars Ultor   8. Forum of Augustus   9. Forum of Julius Caesar   10. Senate Chamber (Curia)   11. Temple of Concord   12. Roman (Republican) Forum   13. Sacred Way (Sacra Via) 14. Basilica Julia   15. Temple of Castor and Pollux   16. Arch of Augustus   17. Temple of Vesta   18. Temple of Julius Caesar   19. Basilica Aemilia   20. Temple of Antoninus and Faustina   21. House of the Vestal Virgins 22. Temple of Romulus   23. Basilica of Maxentius and Constantine   24. Forum of Vespasian   25. Temple of Minerva   26. Forum of Nerva

9-26. Plan of the Imperial Forums, Rome. C. 46 B.C.–A.D. 117. Key to numbers is in caption 9–27

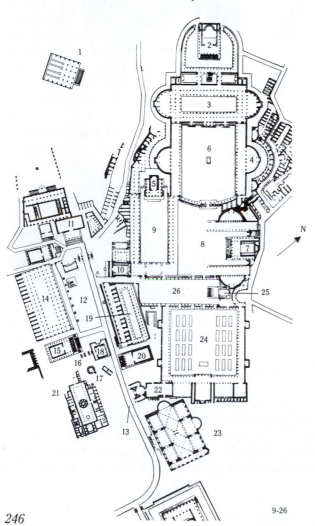

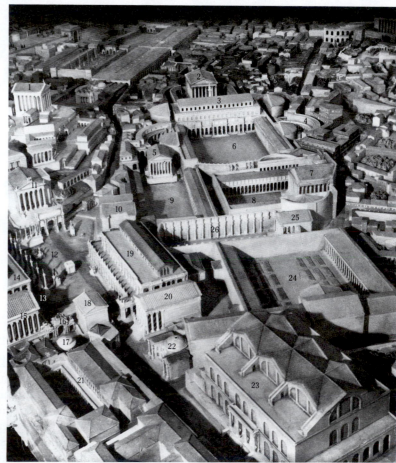

9-27

9-26

deep porch, and shallow cella of the Etrusco-Roman tradition (fig. 9–25). The temple, moreover, revives the Republican system of ornamenting the cella wall with an engaged pseudoperistyle. But the Corinthian order, henceforward the favorite in Roman buildings, is far more splendid than the austere Ionic of the Temple of Fortuna Virilis (see fig. 9–4), and its frieze, no longer blank, is enriched by the kind of delicately carved vinescroll we have seen in the Ara Pacis.

It is with all these aspects of Augustan art in mind that we should attempt to reconstruct mentally the vanished magnificence of the ruined Forum of Augustus, which met the Forum of Julius Caesar at right angles (plan in fig. 9–26, reconstruction in fig. 9–27). The Temple of Mars Ultor (Mars the Avenger), whose four standing columns give little idea of its original appearance, dominated the Forum of Augustus from the usual podium (fig. 9–28). Its back abutted an enclosing wall 115 feet high, which described an exedra on either side of the temple, cut off the view of surrounding buildings (including a slum), and protected the forum from the danger of fire. The eight lofty Corinthian columns across the front formed part of a freestanding peristyle that continued on both sides as well but ended at the enclosing wall. In front of the exedrae and along either side of the rectangular plaza in front of the temple ran a row of smaller Corinthian columns, upholding an attic story ornamented with a row of caryatid figures, mechanical copies of the maidens of the Erechtheion porch (see fig. 7–65). The white marble columns shone against back walls paneled in richly colored marbles, producing on a grand scale an effect as brilliant as that of the *Gemma Augustea*.

By no means all of Augustus' successors shared his concern with maintaining the public-spirited "image" he desired for the Julian-Claudian dynasty (the family relationships were often tenuous). Nero, last of the line, was known for the most extravagant abode of antiquity, the famous Golden House, of which only fragments remain. This residence was, in effect, a country villa in the heart of Rome, stretching from the Palatine Hill to the Esquiline Hill, with gardens that enclosed an artificial lake. The delights of the villa included a banqueting-room ceiling that showered perfumes upon guests, a statue of Nero more than one hundred feet high, and a dome that revolved so guests could follow the motions of the heavenly bodies.

The caprices of Nero should not blind us to the fact that, after the well-nigh inevitable fire of A.D. 64 (for which he has often been unjustly blamed), he promulgated a building code designed to prevent recurrences of such disasters. Streets were widened, excrescences limited, building materials controlled, and

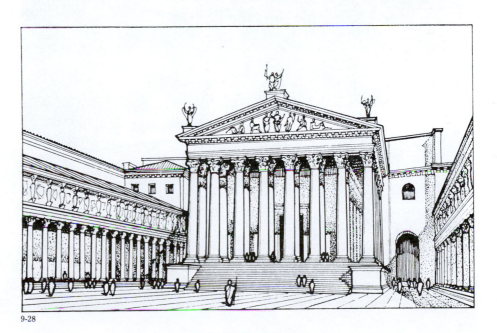

9-28. Reconstructed view of the Temple of Mars Ultor and part of the Forum of Augustus, Rome

9-28

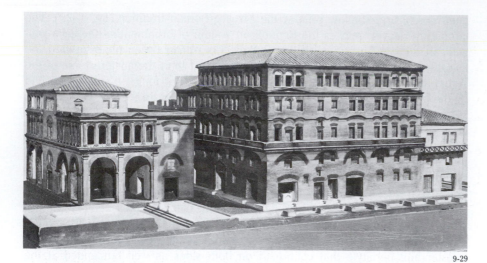

9-29

structures rebuilt in stronger form and along more rational lines. The eventual outgrowth of Nero's code was the block-shaped apartment house known as the *insula* ("island"), strikingly similar to those built in Italy almost up to our own times. These insulae were massive buildings (fig. 9–29), four or five stories in height and made of brick or stuccoed concrete. Many are partially preserved at Ostia, the port of Rome. The ground floor usually contained shops, including perhaps a tavern, and common latrines. Staircases led from a central court to the apartments. Exterior balconies were provided for some of the lower suites, which were the most desirable. Every effort was made to give these insulae a monumental character and to avoid uniformity.

An extraordinary witness to Roman ability to deal with utilitarian structures in

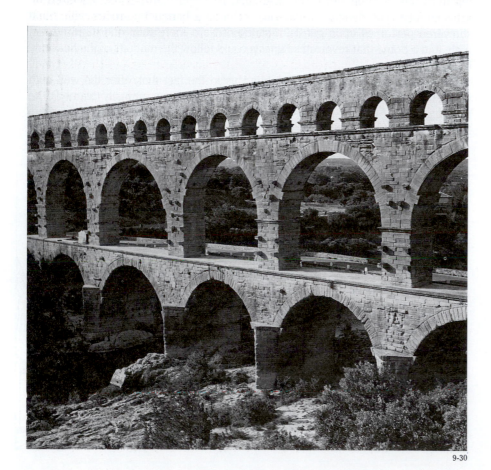

9-30. Pont du Gard, near Nîmes. Late 1st century B.C.

9-30

9-31. Porta Maggiore, Rome. C. A.D. 50

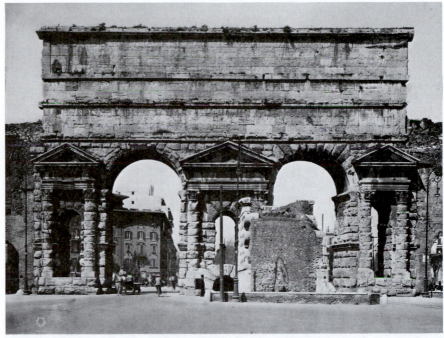

9-31

monumental terms is provided by the aqueducts erected by the Romans. These aqueducts were essential to the growing cities of the Empire; some still extend for miles in partially ruined state across the rolling plains outside Rome. One of the most daring is the Augustan aqueduct called the Pont du Gard (fig. 9–30) in southern France, constructed in the late first century B.C. by Augustus' lieutenant Agrippa to carry the water for Nîmes across a river gorge. The arches were built from unadorned, giant blocks of masonry, beautifully proportioned, in three stories; four smaller arches of the third story correspond to each single arch of the lower two. The majestic effect is, if anything, enhanced by the frankness with which the architect left blocks of stone protruding here and there as supports for scaffolding to be erected when repairs were necessary. Once an aqueduct reached a city, however, a richer treatment was appropriate, as can be seen in the Porta Maggiore at Rome (fig. 9–31), a double archway of travertine erected by Claudius, the fourth emperor of the Julian-Claudian dynasty, to carry water across two major Roman streets. The piers supporting the arches are adorned by Corinthian *aediculae* (small shrines) with pediments, but interestingly enough all the stones save those of the capitals, bases, and pediments were left untrimmed, as if to indicate the basically utilitarian nature of the enterprise and to convey a sense of rude power. This treatment, known as *rustication,* was revived extensively in the Italian Renaissance.

FLAVIAN ARCHITECTURE   Following the suicide of Nero in A.D. 68, and the year A.D. 69, in which three emperors succeeded each other, the soldier and farmer Vespasian founded the Flavian dynasty, which set about to erase the memory of the self-indulgent Nero and to reestablish Augustus' imperial system. On the site of the artificial lake of Nero's Golden House, Vespasian commenced the largest arena ever built before the enormous stadiums of the twentieth century. The Colosseum (fig. 9–32), as this building is generally known, was dedicated in A.D. 80 by Vespasian's son and successor, Titus. It belongs to a new type of structure invented by the Romans and built throughout the Empire except, significantly enough, in the Greek world now reduced to Roman provinces. Its purpose was to house the spectacles with which vast audiences, including the jobless proletariat, were amused. These buildings were known as *amphitheaters* ("double theaters") because, in order to

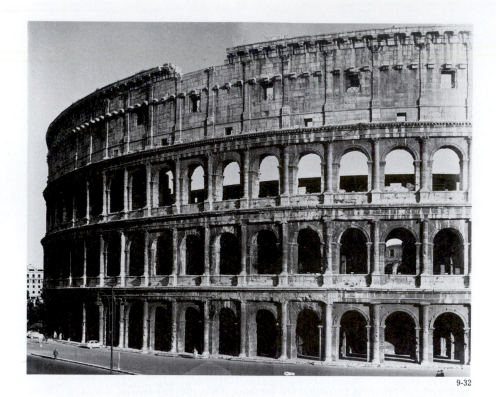

9-32

bring the greatest number of spectators as close as possible to the arena, two theaters were, in effect, placed face-to-face. The resultant shape is always elliptical, and an earlier example, the amphitheater at Pompeii, c. 80 B.C., is the first elliptical building known. While the kind of spectacle in which Roman audiences delighted—gladiatorial combats, mock naval battles, fights between wild beasts, and contests between animals and humans—hardly bears contemplation, the remains of the Colosseum enable us to see that it was one of the grandest of ancient structures. The now-vanished marble seats were supported on multilevel corridors of concrete and masonry, providing for rapid handling of as many as fifty thousand spectators, each of whom entered by a ticket numbered to correspond to a specific gate. The exterior is composed of blocks of travertine, the somewhat porous, cream-colored stone preferred also by Renaissance and Baroque architects for Roman church and palace façades. (Unhappily, these architects used the Colosseum as a quarry for their buildings.)

The arcades were decorated by columns that no longer served any structural function but acted only as a means of dividing the surface harmoniously and as a bridge between the otherwise bleak arches and the spectator. Three major orders stood one above another: Tuscan (probably used in place of Doric because the triglyphs would have been aesthetically troublesome), Ionic, and Corinthian. Above the uppermost order was a lofty wall, articulated by Corinthian pilasters; sockets at its summit were used for the insertion of masts, from which gigantic awnings were stretched across the arena to protect spectators from the sun. Windows in this fourth story alternated with applied shields of gilded bronze.

The corridors were covered with concrete, both in the familiar *barrel vault* and the *groin vault* (fig. 9–33), the latter formed by two barrel vaults intersecting at right angles, thus directing all weight to the four corners (fig. 9–34). The groin vault, like the barrel vault, was known to the Greeks, but they never used it for monumental buildings. Eventually (see page 279), the groin vault became extremely useful to the Romans as a means for covering vast spaces. The vaults of the Colosseum, now bare, were originally enriched with an elaborate surface decoration of stucco.

The Flavian emperors pulled down much of the Golden House of Nero, erecting on part of the site the now-vanished Baths of Titus, one of the earliest examples in Rome of a type of monumental building extensively built by later emperors throughout the city and the Empire (see page 279 and fig. 9–70) as a means of providing useful public services for growing populations. Having thus converted to public use much of the land Nero had enclosed for his private pleasures, the Flavians built their own extensive imperial residence on the Palatine. Now visible only in stripped condition, from which little idea of its original magnificence can be gained, the Flavian Palace contained grand-scale vaulted audience halls in which

9-33. Interior (second story), the Colosseum

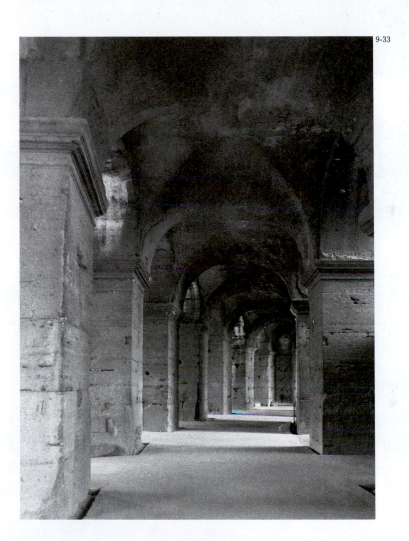

9-34. Diagram of an arch, a barrel vault, and a groin vault

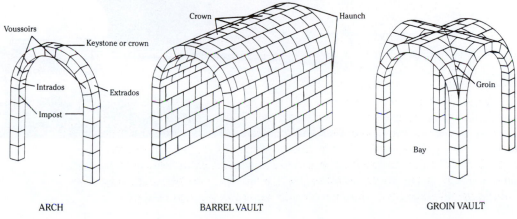

9-34   ARCH   BARREL VAULT   GROIN VAULT

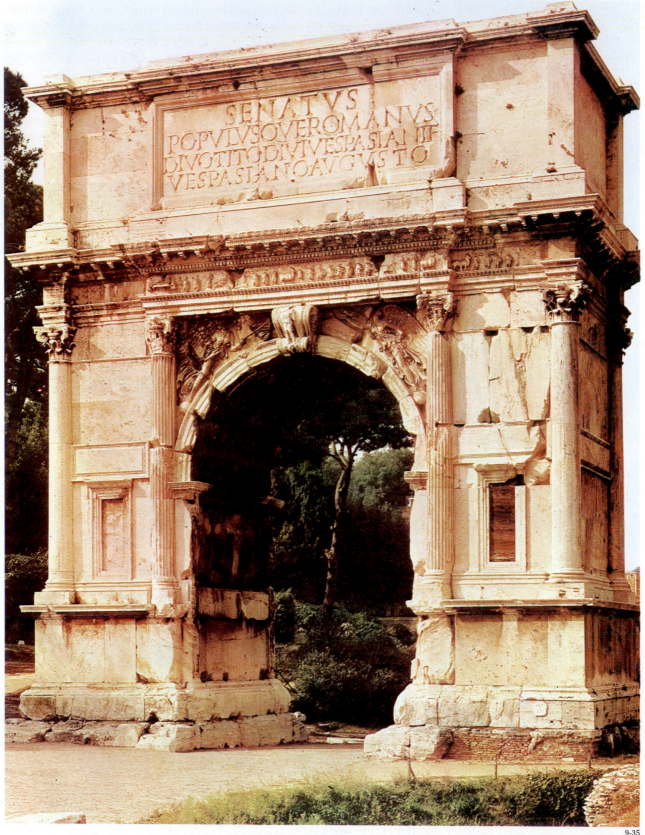

9-35

9-35. Arch of Titus, Rome. c. A.D. 81

the emperor could be seen in fitting splendor, and it was thus in a sense a public building; the Flavian Palace remained the official imperial residence until the late Empire.

To commemorate his brother Titus' capture of Jerusalem in A.D. 70 and destruction of the Temple, to be followed by the tragic Diaspora, the emperor Domitian dedicated, in A.D. 81, a white marble *triumphal arch* at the summit of the Sacred Way, the street that connected the imperial forums with the Colosseum. The Arch of Titus (fig. 9–35) was a permanent version of the kind of temporary arch customarily built by Roman commanders to celebrate their triumphal return to the capital at the head of armies bearing the spoils of war and leading fettered prisoners. By the end of the Roman Empire, some sixty-four marble triumphal arches adorned Rome, and others were scattered throughout the Empire. The Arch of Titus, built of Pentelic marble around a concrete core, is a relatively simple structure (for a more elaborate version, see the later Arch of Trajan at Benevento, fig. 9–50). A single arch between square piers is crowned with an attic story, undoubtedly once supporting a bronze, four-horse chariot driven by the emperor. The applied decorative (or "screen") architecture is formed of paired columns upholding an entablature with a sculptured frieze. Two special innovations are apparent: first, the capitals are no longer strictly Corinthian, but Composite, an even richer fifth order mentioned by Vitruvius and distinguished from the Corinthian in that the volutes have been enlarged to the scale of those in the Ionic; second, the entablature is no longer continuous, but broken so that it projects over the lateral columns, recedes close to the massive piers, and projects again over the central columns and the connecting arch. Thus screen architecture is now being molded with the same liberty as the underlying architecture of concrete, in the interests of freedom of shape and the movement of light and dark. (The unfluted columns and entablature at either side of the arch are nineteenth-century restorations.)

FLAVIAN SCULPTURE   The spectator passing along the Sacred Way in Rome was addressed by two reliefs in the inner surfaces of the piers of the Arch of Titus, one depicting the *Triumph of Titus* (fig. 9–36) and the other the *Spoils from the Temple at Jerusalem* (fig. 9–37), in which Roman legionaries are seen carrying off the trumpets, the seven-branched candlestick, and the golden table. These reliefs were, if anything, more revolutionary than the architecture. For the first time Roman historical relief came into its own. Memories of the Ara Pacis still linger, but the Attic stateliness of Augustan relief has been swept away by a new dynamism in

9-36. *Triumph of Titus,* marble relief in the passageway, Arch of Titus, Rome. c. A.D. 81. Height 6'8" (2.03 m)

9-37. *Spoils from the Temple at Jerusalem,* marble relief in the passageway, Arch of Titus, Rome. c. A.D. 81. Height 6'8" (2.03 m)

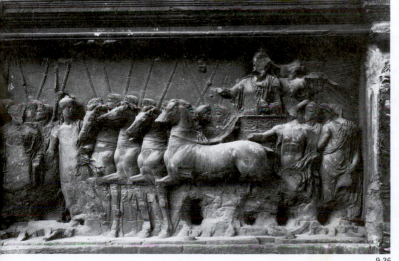

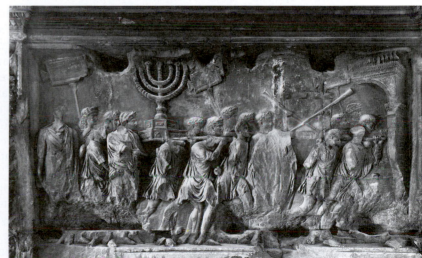

9-36   9-37

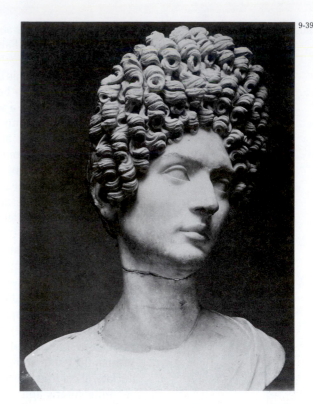

9-39. *Portrait of a Lady.* c. A.D. 90. Marble, life size. Museo Capitolino, Rome

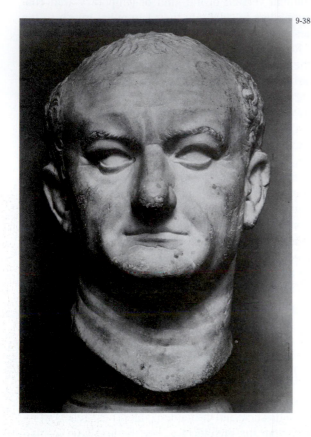

9-38

9-38. *Portrait of Vespasian.* c. A.D. 75. Marble, life size. Museo Nazionale Romano, Rome

keeping with that of the architecture. We are reminded less of the Parthenon than of Hellenistic Baroque—although these relatively small reliefs lack the grandiloquence of the Altar of Zeus at Pergamon (see fig. 7–103). The relief space is much deeper than that of the Ara Pacis, and several devices have been utilized to increase its apparent depth. At the right of the *Spoils from the Temple at Jerusalem,* an archway has been placed at an angle to the spectator so that it dissolves into the background. Even with the loss of much of the relief, it is clear that the figures exploit their newly gained space, moving freely at various levels in depth as if passing before us on a stage. Some are so sharply projected that they are almost freestanding—and thus have suffered the most damage—while others, deeper in space, are represented in slight projection. As in the varying levels in depth of the surrounding architecture, light and shade have been utilized to enrich the drama.

In Flavian portraiture this new dynamism of form and new interest in light and shade were richly explored. A superb *Portrait of Vespasian* (fig. 9–38) shows that lessons from Praxitelean and Hellenistic sculpture have been applied to bring out in marble the full play of light and dark across the weather-beaten face of the old general. The eyeballs are no longer fully carved; they are actually slightly recessed so that the shadow of the eyelids can give the impression of the colored iris. The folds of flesh are rendered with the same pride in ugliness we found in Republican portraiture (see figs. 9–2, 9–3), and the subject seems to be caught in a transitory moment between reflection and speech. A brilliant example of a standard type of Flavian female portraiture is a beautifully poised young matron (fig. 9–39), whose elegant and sensitive features are almost overpowered by a lofty Flavian coiffure of curls, probably supported on a frame. The contrast of the rich shadows in the headdress with the translucency of the features suggests the actual coloration of hair and flesh, and again a slight depression hints at the color of the eyes. The Flavian portrait style is often characterized as "coloristic," a very expressive term for the range of tonal values the heads embrace.

PAINTING AND MOSAICS   In the late Augustan period, the illusionistic achievements of the Second Style (see Introduction fig. 13 and fig. 9–15) were overlapped and eventually succeeded by paintings in the Third Pompeiian Style that show an unexpected combination of pure architectural fantasy with prim refinement, such as in a painted wall from the house of M. Lucretius Fronto at Pompeii (fig. 9–40). The lower two-thirds of the wall, painted glossy black or red, are divided by columns prolonged into spindles; against the side panels stand equally attenuated

9-40. *Architectural View* and *"Panel Paintings,"* Third Style wall painting, House of M. Lucretius Fronto, Pompeii. Middle 1st century A.D.

9-40

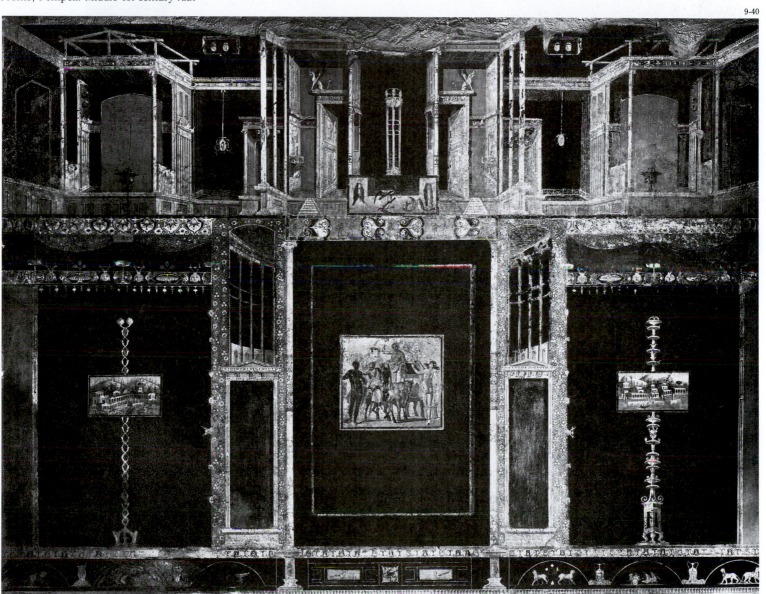

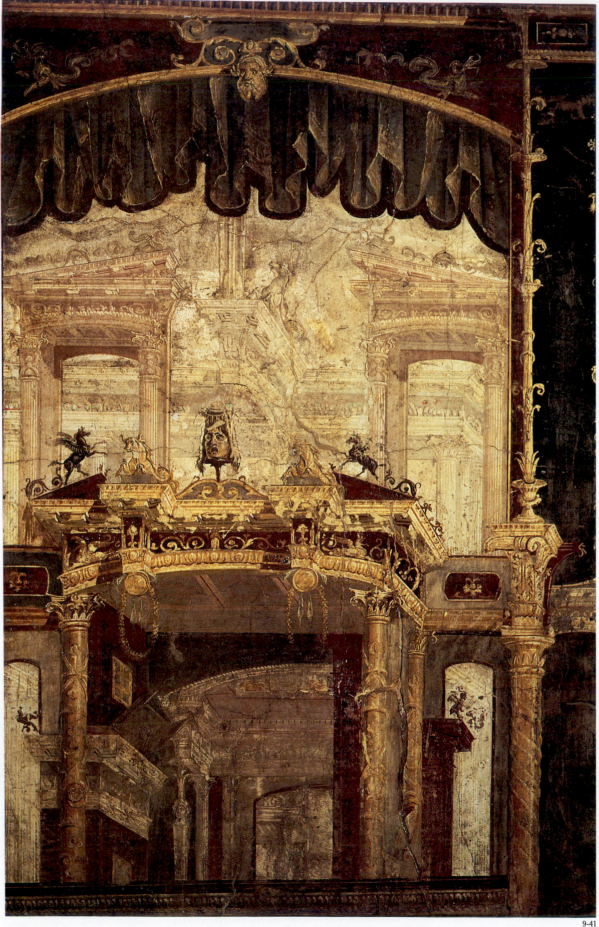

9-41

lamps, on which appear to be suspended tiny panel paintings showing views of villas by the sea, and a mythological painting is "hung" against the center panel. Above the wall one looks out into an array of fantastic structures, reduced to toylike slenderness—columns like reeds, open pergolas—all in a perspective that takes us deep into unreal space but is exactly repeated in reverse on the opposite side. Undeniably, this style shows some of the mannered elegance and grace of official Augustan art.

Most fantastic of all Pompeiian art is the Fourth Style, which flourished after the earthquake of A.D. 63 and was terminated at Pompeii and Herculaneum only by the eruption of Vesuvius in A.D. 79, a period corresponding to the last years of the reign of Nero and the first decade of the Flavian dynasty. A new and wildly imaginative manner appeared, with architectural vistas even more capricious and far more convincingly lighted and painted in an astonishing array of rich colors (fig. 9–41 shows a fine example from Herculaneum). Curtains, masks, broken pediments, and simulated bronze statues are irradiated with a sunlight as warm as that which charmed us in the Second Style. The eye penetrates into atmospheric depths crossed by always fainter architectural screens.

Especially beautiful are the Fourth Style landscapes (fig. 9–42). In these views of an imagined nature, the artists exploited every device then known in order to render sunlight and atmosphere. Rapid brushstrokes sketched in a delightful dream world of mountains and glades, shrines, Etruscan-looking temples, cattle, and lakes and bridges, all dissolved in light and air in a manner that has often been compared with nineteenth-century Impressionism. The whole subject matter of Roman landscape painting could even be modeled in stucco, with remarkably convincing effect and without any color whatever, in the reliefs often appearing on Roman ceilings. Stucco dries rapidly and requires a working speed comparable to that of the sketchy paintings so impressive in the Second, Third, and Fourth styles. A typical example, from an Augustan house near the Farnesina Palace in Rome (fig. 9–43), shows the usual shrines, trees, little figures, animals, and rocks so arranged and so treated as to suggest distance, light, and air. The painters of the Fourth Style treated even portraits with the same airy lightness and grace, as in the rapidly sketched *Portrait of Menander* (see fig. 13–7), seeming to float against its yellow wall in the House of Menander, Pompeii.

A final and extremely important field for Roman pictorial art is that of mosaic. The Hellenistic Greeks had already devised a more sensitive instrument than the pebbles used in the floor mosaics at Pella (see fig. 7–108), that is, the *tessera,* or tiny cube of colored stone, shell, and eventually glass paste, which permitted a wider range of color, sometimes extremely bright. Generally, floor mosaics were restricted to stone by the heavy wear they had to endure, as in the *Victory of Alexander over Darius III* (see fig. 7–84), but the individual cubes (also triangles and other geometrical shapes) were made as small as possible to produce the illusion of painting. A coarser, monochrome effect was also worked out for the floors of public buildings, such as baths. When the Romans began to use mosaic for wall decorations, however, a much broader spectrum of color and more delicate gradations of hue and tone became available through the use of glass. A striking example is the mosaic depicting *Neptune and Amphitrite* (fig. 9–44), part of a continuous decoration around the atrium of the house at Herculaneum of the same name. The mosaicist has been able to model flesh in sunlight with almost as fine a gradation of tone as his painter-colleague copying a Hellenistic fresco (see fig. 7–107), and set the sea-god and his sea-nymph bride in a rich and sparkling architectural framework of pale blue, deep blue, red, and yellow, reduced in complexity from those of the Fourth Pompeiian Style but brilliantly effective nonetheless. In the mosaicist's hands the individual tessera has become the equivalent of the painter's brushstroke. Roman mosaic art was to prove a marvelous instrument in the hands of Early Christian and Byzantine artists for the decoration of church interiors (see Chapter Ten).

9-41. *Architectural View,* Fourth Style wall painting from Herculaneum (near Naples). C. A.D. 63–79. Museo Archeologico Nazionale, Naples

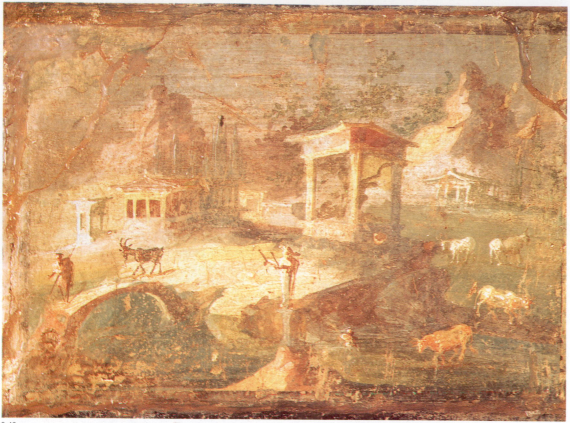

9-42

9-42. *Sacred Landscape,* Fourth Style wall painting from Pompeii. c. A.D. 63–79. Museo Archeologico Nazionale, Naples

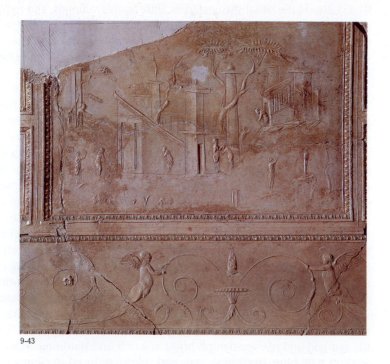

9-43

9-43. *Landscape with Figures,* from an Augustan house near the Farnesina Palace, Rome. c. 19 B.C. Stucco relief, height 18⅛″ (46 cm). Museo Nazionale Romano, Rome

The eruption of Vesuvius destroyed Pompeii and Herculaneum but preserved their art. Since modern Ercolano, complete with six-story apartment houses and modern traffic, is built above the ancient town, most of its treasures remain invisible indefinitely; only a little more than half of Pompeii has yet been excavated.

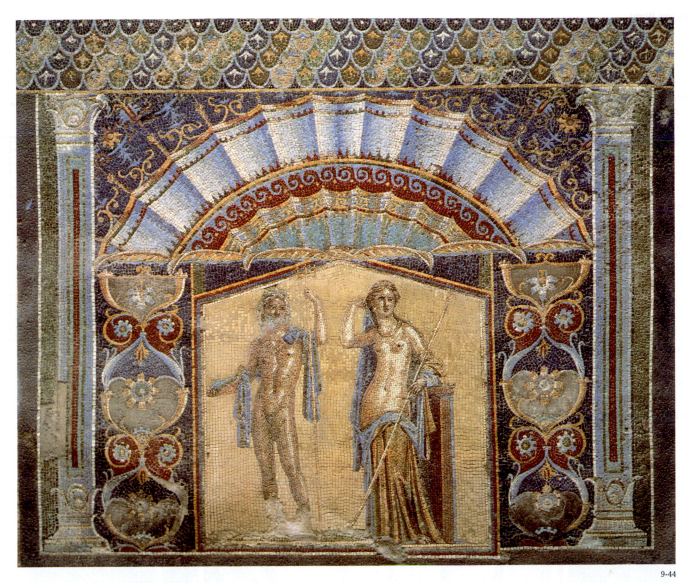

9-44

9-44. *Neptune and Amphitrite,* wall mosaic,
House of Neptune and Amphitrite, Herculaneum
(near Naples). c. A.D. 70

The Second Century (A.D. 96–192)

The assassination in A.D. 96 of the tyrannical Domitian, last of the Flavian dynasty, resulted in the rule of a new and stable succession of six emperors, the first five of whom have become known—in contrast to their immediate predecessor and several of their appalling successors—as the "good emperors."

TRAJAN   The first of these, the aged Nerva, lived only two years before he was succeeded by his adopted son, the brilliant general Trajan, born in Spain—the first non-Italian emperor. Under Trajan the Roman Empire reached its greatest expansion, and his achievements were fittingly commemorated by the dedication in A.D. 113 of the grandest of all the imperial forums (see plan in fig. 9–26, reconstruction in fig. 9–27). The Forum of Trajan, in fact, covered more ground than those of Julius Caesar, Augustus, and Nerva together. To design this project Trajan called on a Greek architect from Syria, Apollodorus of Damascus, whose imagination was equal to the grandiose ideas of his imperial patron. Apollodorus combined elements from Roman tradition with others, eventually tracing their ancestry to the bygone architecture of Egypt. The axial plan of the forum, in certain aspects, recalls strikingly the general layout of Egyptian temples, although there could have been no direct influence. A vast colonnaded plaza, similar to the Egyptian peristyle court, contained a bronze statue of the emperor on horseback. Beyond was the Basilica

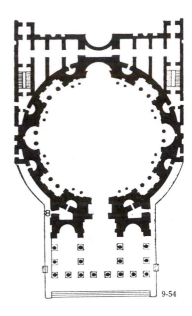

9-53. The Pantheon, Rome. c. A.D. 118–25

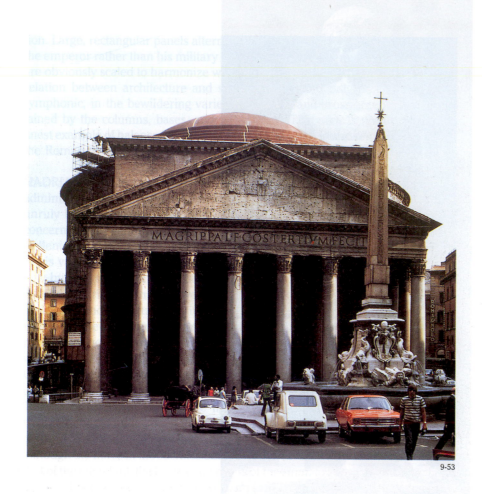

9-53.

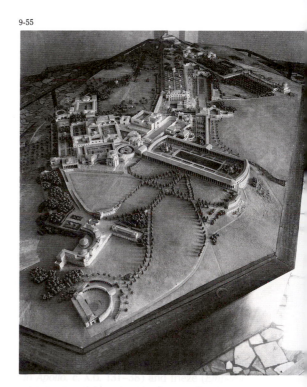

9-54. Plan of the Pantheon, Rome

9-55.

exact hemisphere of concrete 143 feet in diameter, at the top formed of lightweight materials and very slight in thickness. Farther down, the shell becomes both thicker and heavier, and it is supported not only by the walls of the cylindrical drum but by relieving arches within the walls and invisible from the interior. The height of the drum is equal to its radius, which is identical to that of the dome.

Once one enters the Pantheon its revolutionary character becomes apparent—it is one of the few truly overwhelming spatial experiences in architecture, so grand that it cannot be suggested convincingly by photographic means. We must have recourse to a painting done in the eighteenth century (see Introduction fig. 20). The original appearance of the now heavily reconstructed attic story is also made clear in this painting. The interior of the Pantheon conveys the effect of a colossal sphere, whose perfect beauty is untroubled by excrescences. The continuous entablature is upheld by paired, fluted Corinthian columns of softly colored marble in front of eight recesses, alternating with eight flat wall surfaces encrusted with colored marble from which project aediculae, once containing statues of the gods, framed by unfluted columns of polished granite. The now-bare concrete coffering of the dome was originally painted blue; each coffer contained a rosette of gilded bronze. A single great circular opening at the apex is the sole and abundant source of light, and it allows the eye to move freely out into the sky above. The effect of this vast, spherical space, whose enclosing wall is softened by the fluid colors of the marble, can only be described as sublime. No interior before or after the Pantheon has achieved quite this impression. A long tradition in ancient times associated architectural domes with the Dome of Heaven, the sky itself, a tradition also appropriate for a building dedicated to the worship of all the gods, as was the Pantheon. The breathtaking interior space of this great building arouses in us a sense of liberation analogous to what we feel when we gaze into the open sky.

9-55. Model of Hadrian's Villa, Tivoli. c. A.D. 125–35. Administrative Office, Hadrian's Villa

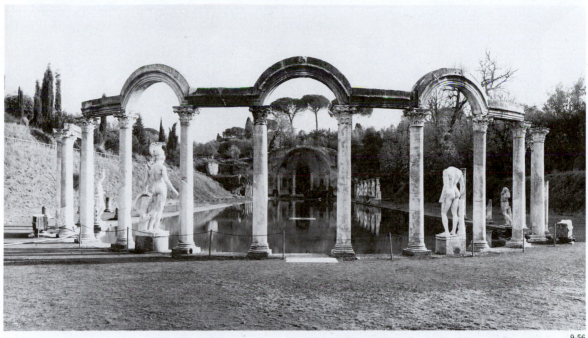

9-56

9-56. The Canopus of Alexandria, Hadrian's Villa, Tivoli (reconstructed). C. A.D. 125–35

The most imaginative architectural achievement of Hadrian's reign was the villa he constructed near Tivoli (fig. 9–55); to modern eyes it suggests nothing so much as the pleasure dome of Kubla Khan as described in Coleridge's poem. Several square miles of gently rolling countryside were adorned with a rich array of buildings and gardens. In contrast to the rigorous axial planning of the imperial forums, the constructions and spaces of Hadrian's Villa were freely scattered in groups in order to take advantage of varied levels, exposures, and vistas. Within each group, however, the buildings were arranged with close attention to harmonious and generally symmetrical relationships. The individual spaces were seldom large but almost infinitely complex, exploiting all the freedom of shape offered by Roman concrete architecture. Some interiors contained not a single straight line, only alternating convex and concave forms.

The villa had several elaborate *nymphaea* (fountain buildings), Greek and Latin libraries, a theater, baths both large and small, courtyards, plazas, and temples. A circular colonnaded pool was adorned with a central island, attainable by bridges on wheels, on which stood a tiny, self-contained abode. Many reproductions—more symbolic than accurate—of sights that Hadrian had seen on his travels throughout the Empire were constructed at the villa. These included the Grove of Academe and the Stoa Poikile ("painted porch"), both of Athens, and the Canopus of Alexandria (fig. 9–56), a long canal culminating in a temple to the Egyptian god Serapis. This temple was also a nymphaeum, and it was ornamented with Egyptian sculptures preserved today in the Vatican Museums. The end opposite the temple was colonnaded, and the entablature seems to have been bent into arches as if made of clay. When intact, Hadrian's Villa offered an unimaginable richness of forms, spaces, and colors to excite the senses and to enshrine the intellectual life of the imperial hedonist, who unfortunately died before its completion.

THE ANTONINES The uneventful reign of Hadrian's successor, Antoninus Pius, was appropriately memorialized by an undecorated column of pink marble, erected after the emperor's death in A.D. 161. The cubic base, which is all that remains, is a powerful work of art in itself. On the front face is shown the flight of the emperor and the empress to heaven; on either side is represented the cere-

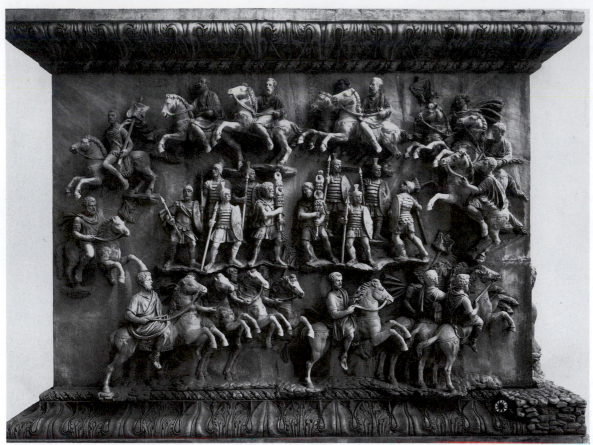

9-57

9-57. *Ceremonial Circular Gallop of the Cavalry,* from the base of the Column of Antoninus Pius. Marble relief, 8′1¼″ × 11′1⅛″ (2.47 × 3.38 m). C. A.D. 161. Musei Vaticani, Rome

monial circular gallop of the cavalry around groups of armored infantrymen holding standards at the imperial funeral (fig. 9–57). Surprisingly, the hard-won illusionistic space of the Hellenistic tradition, already compromised by the devices of Trajanic narrative style, has been completely dismissed. Although the distinction has been preserved between near figures in high relief and those farther from us in low relief, all that remains of the traditional setting is a few patches of ground under the feet of men and horses. The figures seem to float in a free space, unregulated and unenclosed, in front of the neutral marble background. What is behind is now represented as above, as if in reversion to the far-off days of Polygnotos.

The new abstract conception of space and the new carving techniques were employed in the relief sculpture on the column of Antoninus' successor, Marcus Aurelius (ruled A.D. 161–80). As emperor, Marcus Aurelius was an extraordinary blend of an efficient general, on the model of Julius Caesar and Trajan, with a Stoic philosopher. Marcus Aurelius loathed war, and he fought only defensive actions aimed at preserving the Empire from incursions of Germanic tribes, particularly in the Balkans. For him duty was man's highest goal and only reward; his own duty was to administer the Empire as a brotherhood of man under the rule of an all-pervasive God, which involved the sacrifice of his own well-being in favor of the unity of the state.

One of the most memorable works of art from Marcus Aurelius' reign is his noble equestrian statue in bronze (fig. 9–58), originally in front of the Lateran Palace in Rome, in which the emperor was born, but transferred to the Capitoline unwillingly by Michelangelo in 1536 at papal command. The statue owes its preservation to the mistaken belief that it represented Constantine, the first imperial protector of Christianity, and is the only well-preserved ancient equestrian statue in bronze to come down to us; needless to say, it has been imitated countless times from the Renaissance almost to our own day. The statue shows the emperor unarmed, his

9-58. *Equestrian Statue of Marcus Aurelius.*
c. A.D. 161–80. Bronze, over life size. Piazza del
Campidoglio, Rome

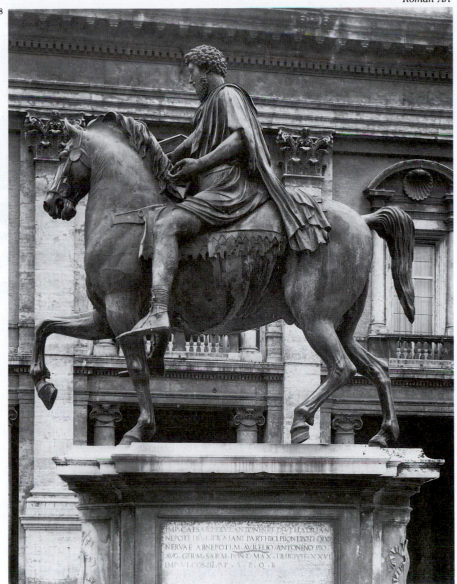

right arm outstretched in the characteristic Roman oratorical gesture (see Introduction fig. 26 and fig. 9–19) and his left guiding the now-vanished reins of his
spirited horse. As we have seen in relief sculpture, the rider here is also represented in a larger scale than the horse. The bearded emperor (the beard was a
Hadrianic innovation, in imitation of the Greeks) looks out calmly on the world; the
rich curls of his hair and beard, in contrast to the smooth parts of his face, show a
revival of Flavian colorism (see pages 254–55), which precludes the traditional
device of inserting eyes made of glass paste. The horse is superbly modeled,
revealing extensive knowledge of the proper position and function of bones,
muscles, tendons, and veins.

One of the most significant and lasting of all Roman achievements was the
foundation throughout the Empire of hundreds of towns and cities, many of which
are still inhabited, and the extensive rebuilding of Hellenistic cities in Greece and
Asia Minor. Where possible, the typical Roman town followed the foursquare
Hippodamian plan, with straight perimeter walls leading to major thoroughfares,
oriented north and south, east and west, and crossing at right angles in the center,
and minor streets also intersecting in a grid. (Such a plan was out of the question in
Rome itself, because of its haphazard prior growth on an irregular, hilly site; see fig.
9–27 for the appearance of the center.) Such self-contained, crystalline plans were,

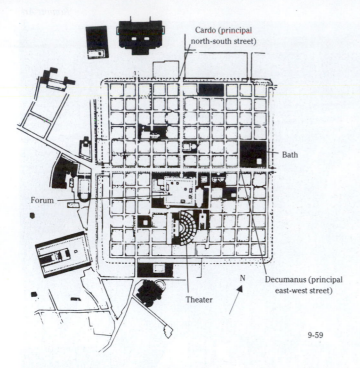

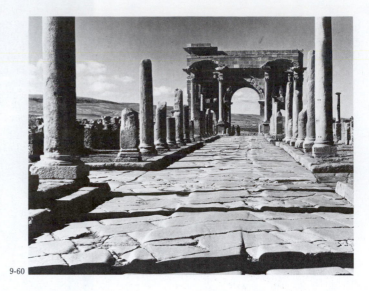

9-59

9-60

9-59. Plan of the city of Thamugadis (modern Timgad), Algeria

9-60. Colonnaded street with arched gateway, Thamugadis (modern Timgad). Late 2d century A.D.

9-61. Theater (partially reconstructed), Sabratha (ancient Abrotonum), Libya. Late 2d century A.D.

of course, fairly rigid, leaving no room for expansion. Later growth outside the square inevitably betrays the suburban sprawl all too familiar in our own world. Most cities had a central capitol dominating a forum, temples to Roman and indigenous deities, a basilica, a bath or two, a theater, and an amphitheater. The latter was rare in Greek provinces, which resisted the Roman gladiatorial combats until very late; only three amphitheaters were built in all of Asia Minor.

But these architectural undertakings were by no means uniform in style at any one moment in all parts of the Empire. For example, urban complexes and country villas in Britain, Gaul, and Germany were far less sumptuous than those designed for provinces that still cherished a Hellenistic tradition of architecture and decoration. The most dazzling provincial centers were perhaps those in Asia Minor, such as Ephesus, Miletus, Aspendus, Side, and Perge; in Syria, such as Baalbek and Palmyra; and in North Africa, especially Leptis Magna, Sbeitla, and Timgad (fig. 9–59), large portions of which are still standing. A vista (fig. 9–60) down the central colonnaded street of Timgad toward a late-second-century gateway erroneously known as the Arch of Trajan gives some inkling of the splendor of these North African and eastern Mediterranean cities in the time of Marcus Aurelius. The great central arch for horse-drawn traffic is flanked by two smaller ones for foot passengers, embraced by columns designed to culminate the colonnaded walkways rather than to relate to the central arch. These columns are united at the top by a new invention, an arched pediment, whose lower cornice is broken.

This kind of pictorial freedom in architecture can be seen at its extreme in a number of splendid eastern Mediterranean and North African gateways, façades, fountains, libraries, and above all theaters, such as that at Sabratha dating from the late second century A.D. (fig. 9–61). The relatively simple Greek and Hellenistic structures are far behind us. In the Roman theaters a high stage, here with a front composed of alternating square and semicircular recesses ornamented with carved reliefs, is dominated by a towering structure designed only for pictorial richness. With the greatest imaginative freedom three stories of Corinthian columns, now smooth, now fluted, are superimposed; some are single, some paired, some grouped in fours, some receding, some projecting for a maximum pictorial effect that goes far toward capturing in stone the fantasies imagined in paint by the Pompeiian decorators of the Fourth Style.

A spectacular Hadrianic library in the same style, the most nearly complete ancient library we possess, is that of Celsus completed about A.D. 135 at Ephesus. The façade (fig. 9–62) has been rebuilt from its original fragments and shows the

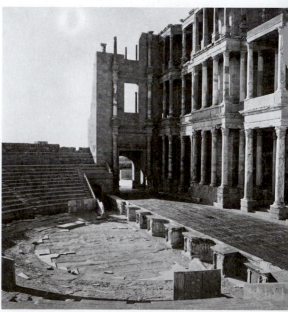

9-61

270

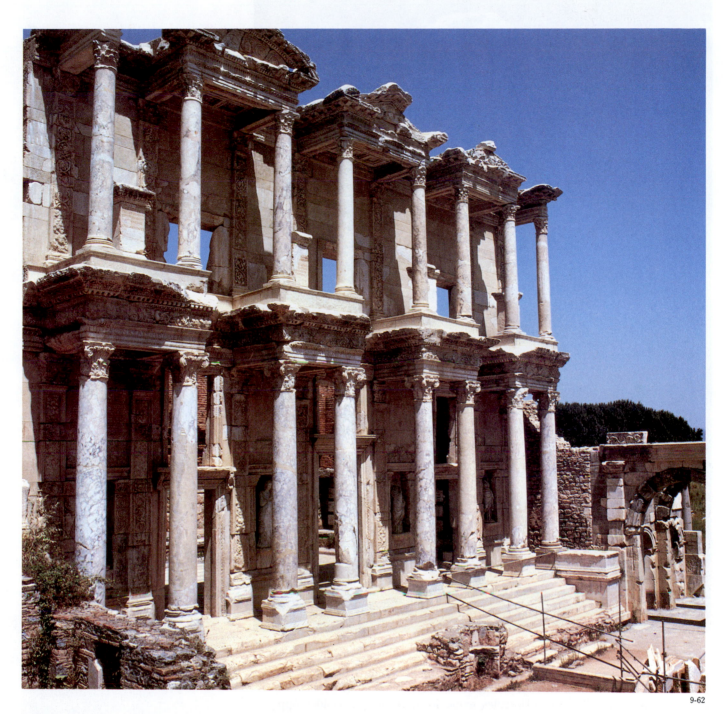

9-62.

9-62. Façade, Library of Celsus, Ephesus, Turkey. C. A.D. 135

appearance of a fine second-century structure, rich in its architectural relationships and in its sculptural ornament. The alternating arched and triangular pediments of the second story are inherited from Hellenistic art. But what one might call (borrowing a term from music) the syncopated arrangement of the columns—so that one pair straddles an opening flanked by two pairs below—is a device used in Roman architecture in Italy as early as the middle of the first century A.D. The interior, doubtless roofed with wood, was three stories high. Elegantly spaced, superimposed colonnades gave access to storage rooms for the rotuli, on which as always in pre-Christian culture the manuscripts were written.

The reigns of the five "good emperors" were followed in A.D. 180 by that of Marcus Aurelius' unworthy son and successor, Commodus, who took part in

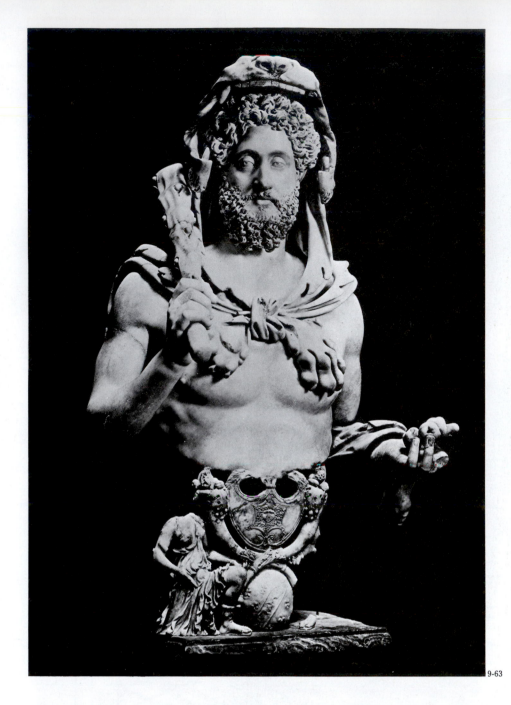

9-63. *Commodus as Hercules.* c. A.D. 192. Marble, height 42½″ (1.08 m). Palazzo dei Conservatori, Rome

9-63

gladiatorial combats, experimented with imported mystery cults, and went about dressed as Hercules, complete with lion skin and club. A celebrated bust (fig. 9–63) shows Commodus in the role of Hercules, extending nervously the Golden Apples of the Hesperides, although his unsparingly rendered effete expression and slight physique are wildly incongruous. As throughout Antonine sculpture, the locks of hair and beard, roughened and deeply undercut to suggest their color, are contrasted with the transparent pallor of the face. The eyes too are now rendered coloristically, the irises and pupils actually carved, a device that frees sculpture entirely from applied pigment and allows it to function pictorially in its own right. The serpentine complexity of the shapes, as disturbing as the portrait itself, reminds one of the nervous forms and patterns used in the sixteenth century in an Italian style known as Mannerism. In A.D. 192, members of Commodus' household conspired to have him strangled by a wrestler oddly named Narcissus. So ended the Antonine line, in a manner that prepared the way for the near chaos of the third century.

Little second-century painting remains, except a numerous series of portraits

9-64. Portrait of a Graeco-Roman Egyptian, from a mummy case found at El Faiyûm, in the Nile Valley. Third quarter of 2d century A.D. Encaustic on panel, 17⅝ × 9″ (45 × 23 cm). Staatliche Museen zu Berlin — Preussischer Kulturbesittz

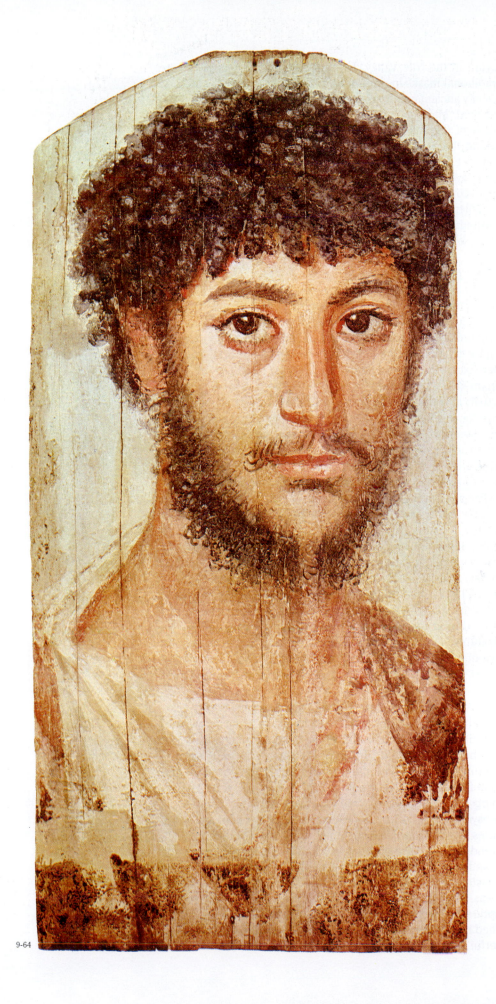

9-64

discovered at El Faiyûm in the Nile Valley. These images of the deceased were substituted for the traditional masks in mummies, which the Egyptians continued to make. They are the only ancient paintings in the encaustic, or hot-wax, technique that have been discovered. Many are strikingly expressive, rendering with great vividness the members of the multiracial society of the Roman world. As the subjects all appear young, the portraits must have been made decades before their deaths. A Graeco-Roman Egyptian (fig. 9–64) looks at us with utter candor from superbly painted brown eyes, showing that in the rendering of light on flesh and hair the painters of the second century A.D. still retained the knowledge gained from half a millennium of Hellenic tradition. These paintings also admit us to the very presence of a sensitive and graceful people, in whom are summed up the traditions of more than three thousand years of continuous civilization.

The Third Century (A.D. 192–284)

The assassination of Commodus inaugurated a period of almost unbelievable deterioration in Roman life and, consequently, in that of the entire Mediterranean and European world, culminating in a loss of Roman and even Italian preeminence and power in the Empire at large. For the next ninety-two years one brief imperial reign followed another. Except for those of Septimius Severus (ruled A.D. 193–211) and Claudius II surnamed Gothicus (ruled A.D. 268–70), each reign was terminated by violence, usually assassination by troops or by the Praetorian Guard. This bodyguard of the emperor was the single agency in the Empire still strong enough to make and unmake emperors. With provincial and uneducated soldiers serving as emperors, the vast structure of the international and intercontinental imperial state tottered virtually leaderless; only the administrative bureaucracy maintained a semblance of order. Coinage was rapidly debased; inflation followed; agriculture and trade stagnated. The sole uniting factor was the all-pervasive fear of invasion by Germanic tribes to the north and by Parthians to the east.

SCULPTURE   In imperial portraiture the penetrating frankness of the portraits of Commodus had already opened up new and unpleasant psychic vistas. Two third-century imperial portraits lead us even further into this hitherto unexplored realm. Caracalla (ruled A.D. 211–17), the brutal son and successor of the energetic Septimius Severus, appears so frighteningly his true self (fig. 9–65) that we hardly need to be told that he caused the murder of many persons, including his own brother Geta. The features, the skin, and above all the hair and eyes are still rendered with a sense of the Hellenistic heritage of colorism, handed down from Flavian and Antonine art. But the cruelty concentrated in the intense gaze and fixed frown is new and terrible.

The face of Philip the Arab (ruled A.D. 244–49), who murdered his twenty-year-old predecessor, Gordianus III, has been preserved for us in a masterpiece of characterization (fig. 9–66) even more devastating than the Caracalla portrait. The eyes peer out furtively below the endemic frown of the period; the expression is wretched and without intelligence; behind the brutish features the remnants of a debased mind cringe in fear of inevitable assassination. One recalls with nostalgia the far-off days of the godlike Augustus portrait (see fig. 9–19).

To delineate such psychological factors, a new and unsparing technique came into being; the features were constructed in broad, harsh planes; short, quick strokes of the chisel rendered the close-cropped hair and beard. The last remnants of Hellenic structure and Hellenic vision have vanished from images such as this portrait, just as the last echoes of Hellenic humanity seem to have deserted a society whose hero was the gladiator instead of the athlete.

Sarcophagus sculpture of the third century reflects the inner disorder of the period in a transformed relief style. The *Ludovisi Battle Sarcophagus* (fig. 9–67) is one of the most powerful examples. In comparison with the historical reliefs of the

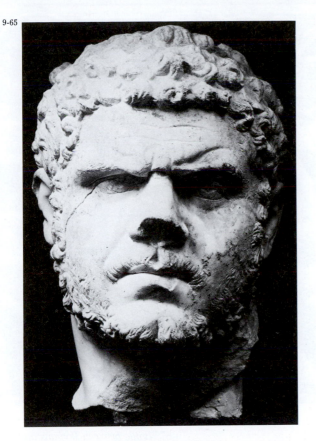

9-65. *Portrait of Caracalla.* c. A.D. 211–17.
Marble, life size. Musei Vaticani, Rome

9-66. *Philip the Arab.* c. A.D. 244–49. Marble,
life size. Musei Vaticani, Rome

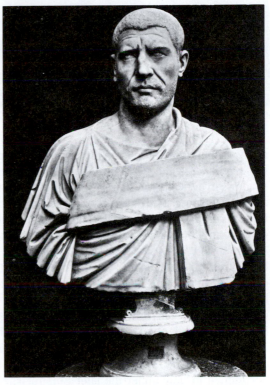

9-66

Arch of Titus and the Column of Trajan (see figs. 9–36, 9–37, 9–48), through which
the Romans move in evident command of their own destiny and triumph through
their own valor, here both Romans and barbarians seem trapped in a perpetual
conflict for which even victory offers no solution. The Romans conquer by sheer
weight, pressing down on a shapeless tangle of anguished barbarian faces and
tormented torsos and limbs. Space, mastered through centuries of Greek and
Roman effort, has been swallowed up. Neither depth nor background is represented; the wall of bodies is piled in the foreground plane like the heap of weapons
carved on the base of the Column of Trajan. And along with space the integrity of
the human body has disappeared; not a single figure in this strange composition
retains the capability of motion.

The new emotional style of third-century relief sculpture required still other

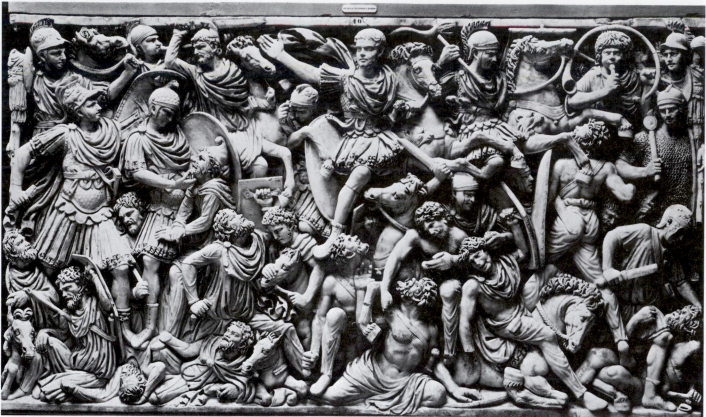

9-67

9-67. *Battle between Romans and Barbarians,* detail of the *Ludovisi Battle Sarcophagus.* c. A.D. 250. Marble, height approx. 56″ (1.42 m). Museo Nazionale Romano, Rome

methods than those employed in the bust of Philip the Arab; a direct and extensive use of the drill, for example, was necessary to reinforce with dark holes the shadows in eyes and mouths and between the writhing locks of hair. Third-century art has been described as expressionistic; the word is as inexact as is *impressionistic* for first-century landscape painting, but at least it underscores the new emphasis on raw emotion to the detriment of structure and tradition.

PAINTING AND MOSAICS   We turn almost with relief from the atmosphere of chaos and terror suggested by such sculptures to the tiny portraits on gold leaf between panels of glass, which are among the rare treasures of third-century painting. The people shown in the *Family of Vunnerius Keramus* (fig. 9–68) may not have been Christian, yet they project an image of the dignity and self-possession we ideally assign to early Christians. This gentle family's special cast of countenance and the size and depth of their eyes seem to point to a Near Eastern origin, far from uncommon in Italy under the later Empire. Their name is Greek and written in Greek letters, but in an odd hybrid of Greek and Latin grammar. The painter still retains the ability to project features in depth—note the beautifully foreshortened ears—and to render with great precision the play of diffused light on features, costumes, and jewelry. But it is above all the calm composure of the figures that affords us a glimpse into a counterculture that retained human dignity in a hostile world.

An equally intimate and even more informative view of private life in the later Roman Empire is afforded by the enchanting third-century floor mosaic unearthed in 1960 near Hama in modern Syria (fig. 9–69). The central panel measures approximately eleven by fifteen feet, and so the figures are life size. The subject is a small house orchestra completely composed of women, which might suggest the position of women as mere entertainers in the Roman world. One woman plays a lyre, another the musical bowls set out on a table, the next upholds a recorder, and a fourth plays an organ whose pipes appear to embrace three octaves. Wind is

9-68. *Family of Vunnerius Keramus.* C. A.D. 250. Painting on gold leaf sealed between glass, diameter 2⅜″ (6 cm); set into a cross, 7th century A.D. Civico Museo dell'Età Cristiana, Brescia, Italy

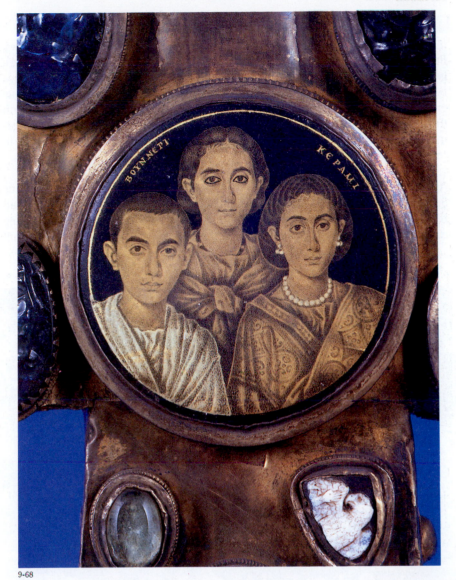

9-68

9-69

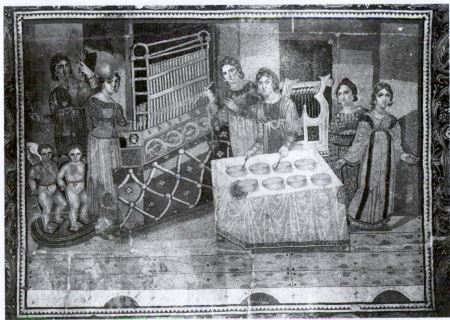

9-69. *House Orchestra,* floor mosaic from a building near Hama, Syria. 3d century A.D.

miraculously furnished by two winged *erotes* (cupids) tramping on a bellows. Percussive accents are furnished by a lady at the extreme left, while at the right a girl in a long dress performs a decorous dance. Harmony is certainly known, since both organist and bowl-player sound two notes at once. While minute tesserae enable the artist to render the play of light on the figures and the instruments with the same delicacy as in the gold-glass group portrait, the poses and the arrangements of the figures have already suffered the compression and distortion visible in relief sculpture of the period.

ARCHITECTURE   During the early part of the third century, under Septimius Severus and his immediate successors and before the crisis of imperial power had really set in, extensive building projects were undertaken in the constantly growing capital. The most ambitious of these was the Baths of Caracalla (fig. 9–70), built

9-70. Baths of Caracalla, Rome. c. A.D. 211–17

9-70

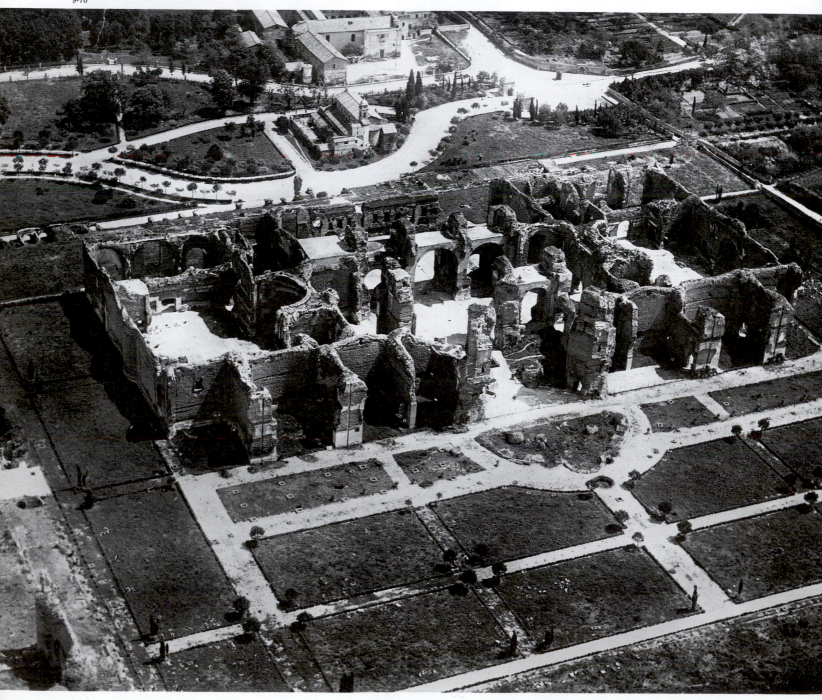

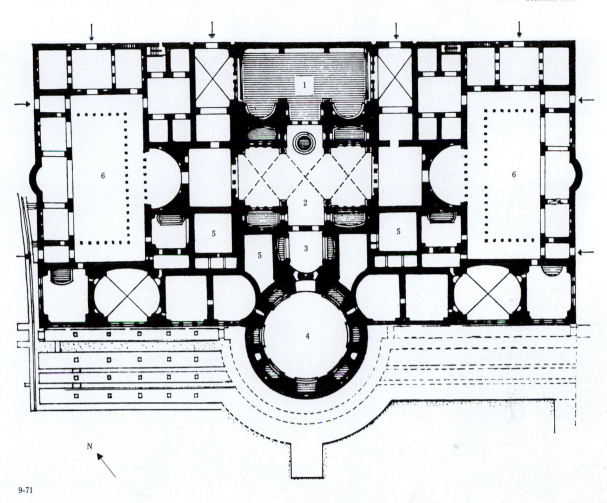

9-71

9-71. Ground plan of the Baths of Caracalla, Rome 1. Natatio (swimming pool)
2. Frigidarium (central hall with cold pools)
3. Tepidarium (hall with warm pools)
4. Caldarium (rotunda with hot pool)
5. Service rooms 6. Palaestra (gymnasium)

well to the south of the older city center. Now stripped of their marble paneling, the vast concrete ruins presently form a grandiose historical setting for opera performances. Baths, ever more luxurious, were typical constructions of the Empire; there were 952 baths in operation in Rome in the middle of the fourth century. Caracalla clearly desired to outdo in magnificence the largest baths before his time, the second-century Baths of Trajan. The compact, carefully planned central structure (fig. 9–71), more than seven hundred feet in length, was divided into interconnecting halls for hot, cold, and tepid baths (*caldarium, frigidarium,* and *tepidarium*); a swimming pool on one side; and at each end a palaestra for exercise. In the thickness of the masses of masonry were rooms for services, including the heating of the air and of the water, which arrived in its own aqueduct and was piped to the appropriate baths in terra-cotta conduits. The caldarium, whose foundations are visible in the foreground of the aerial view, was a circular, domed structure (only slightly smaller than the Pantheon), illuminated by a row of windows under the dome. Openings between the halls must have provided magnificent architectural vistas.

A reconstruction of the central frigidarium (fig. 9–72) shows a hall about two hundred feet long, roofed by groin vaults apparently supported by eight colossal Composite columns, together with their intervening blocks of entablature, but actually resting more heavily on the piers concealed behind the columns. Under galleries on either side were four small cold bathing pools. Light came from clerestory windows grouped in threes under the arches of the groin vaults (indicated on the plan by dotted Xs), which were coffered, stuccoed, painted, and gilded; the walls, floors, and columns were sheathed in colored marbles. The interior must have made an impression not only of great spatial openness but also of constantly changing light and color.

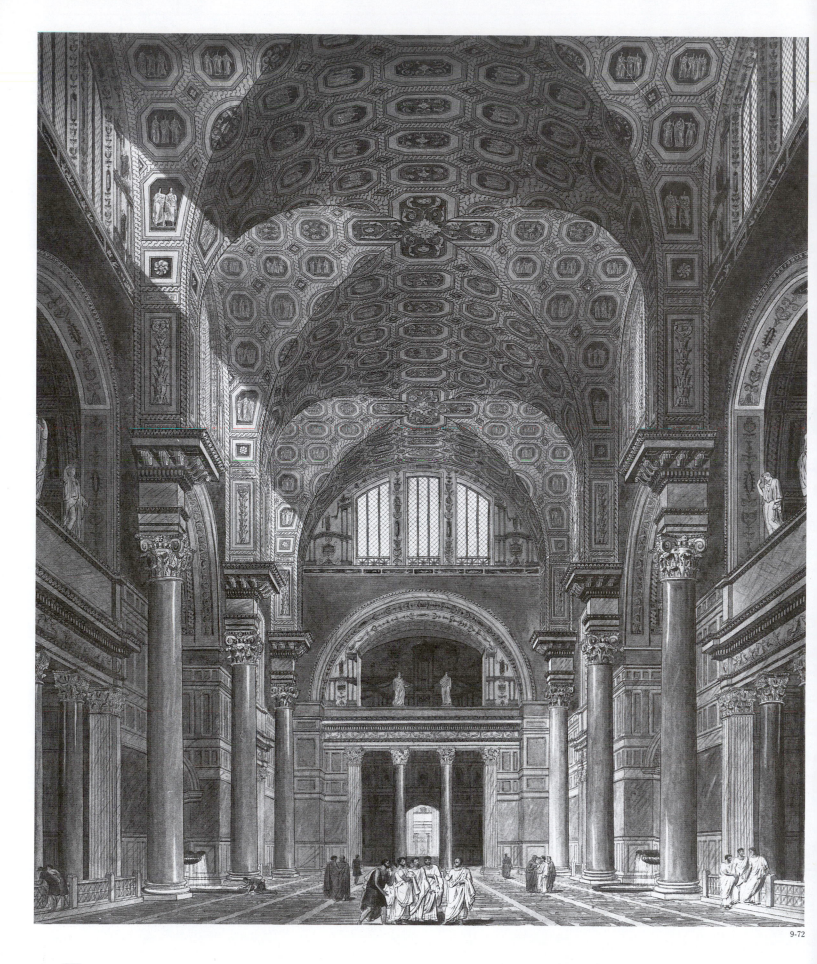

9-72

9-72. Reconstructed view through the Frigidarium (central hall) toward one of the palaestrae, Baths of Caracalla (after G. Abel Blonet)

9-73

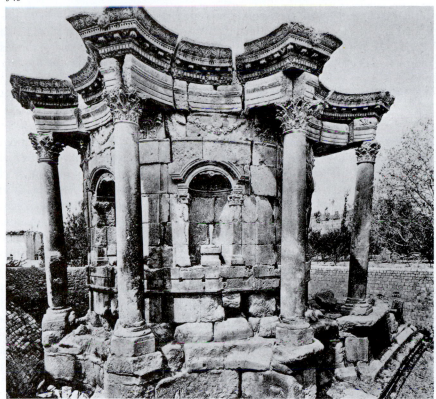

9-73. Temple of Venus, Baalbek, Lebanon. First half of 3d century A.D.

9-74

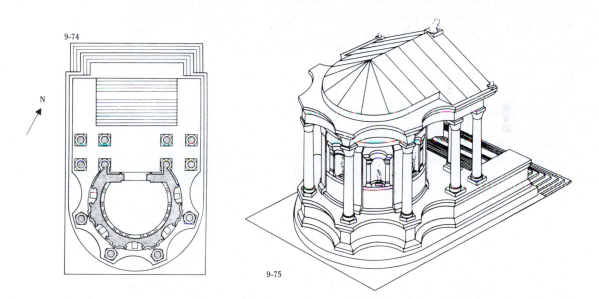

9-75

9-74. Plan of the Temple of Venus, Baalbek

9-75. Axonometric view of the Temple of Venus, Baalbek

The most extraordinary structure of the third century is the little Temple of Venus that was added to the vast second-century Roman sanctuary of the Syrian deity Baal at Baalbek (now in Lebanon; fig. 9–73). The portico is conventional enough, but the cella behind it is circular (figs. 9–74, 9–75). The peristyle is carried around it, supported on freestanding Corinthian columns. Here the architect had his most brilliant idea, making the podium and entablature curve inward from each column to touch the cella, and then outward again to the next column, producing a scalloped shape. This flow of outer concavities against inner convexity produces a free architectural fantasy as astonishing as some of the painted examples in the

Fourth Pompeiian Style. The Temple of Venus at Baalbek has often been proclaimed an ancestor of the highly imaginative architectural inventions of the Italian Baroque. At this moment, it is almost more useful to regard it as one of the last examples of such fantasy before it was terminated by the rigidity of the later Empire.

The End of the Pagan Empire (A.D. 284–323)

Under the "barracks emperors" of the third century, the government of the Empire degenerated into a situation bordering on anarchy and was frequently rent by civil war among rival claimants to imperial power. A rugged general of peasant stock from Illyria (modern Yugoslavia), the emperor Diocletian (ruled A.D. 284–305), attempted to put an end to disorder and in so doing imposed upon the Roman world a system that can only be compared with the despotism of Mesopotamian rulers. Even the shadowy authority still cherished by the Senate was set aside; personal rule was directly exercised by the emperor through an elaborate system of administrative levels, military and governmental, that functioned better in theory than in fact. Since the days of Septimius Severus, the imperial person had been considered sacred, a notion that contrasts bitterly with the ease and frequency with which individual emperors were murdered. Debasement and consequent collapse of coinage had led to economic breakdown and reversion to barter. A wealthy landowning class, precursors of the medieval nobility, had arisen throughout the Empire. Agricultural workers were increasingly attached to the land and workmen to their trades. Communications throughout the Empire had deteriorated.

The rigidity of Diocletian's system was a formal expression of an economic and political paralysis that was beyond any then-known cure. Because of the difficulty of governing the entire imperial territory from a single center—and Rome had largely given way to Milan as the seat of administration in Italy—Diocletian divided power between two theoretically coequal emperors, each known as Augustus, one ruling in the West, the other in the East. Each Augustus took on a deputy and successor with the title of Caesar. This short-lived experiment was known as the *tetrarchy* (government of four rulers), and it heralded the inevitable breakup of the Empire, whose numerous political subdivisions were already infiltrated by barbarians. Under emperors as different as Nero and Marcus Aurelius, Christianity had long been recognized as a danger to the state, in that the Christians refused to burn incense before imperial statues and to render military service. Sporadic persecutions of Christians became intense; the last was ordered by Diocletian in 303. Two years later he abdicated and retired to a palace he had built at Split (formerly Spalato, from *palatium,* or "palace").

A rapid succession of tetrarchies only perpetuated the anarchic situation that had existed before Diocletian. After a six-year struggle one tetrarch, Constantine the Great (ruled A.D. 306–37), seized sole imperial power after defeating his rival Maxentius at the Milvian Bridge over the Tiber River in 312, reportedly after a dream in which an angel appeared to him bearing the Cross and saying, "In this sign thou shalt conquer." In the Edict of Milan in 313, Constantine proclaimed toleration of Christianity, which had become the single most powerful spiritual and intellectual force in the Empire; in the same year Diocletian died in retirement. In 325 Constantine called and participated in the Council of Nicaea, which considered questions essential to the new religion. But Helleno-Roman polytheism did not rapidly die out; it was necessary in 345 to decree the death penalty for adherence to pagan cults. A short-lived attempt was made to restore paganism under Julian the Apostate (ruled A.D. 361–63), but at his death Christianity rapidly triumphed. In point of fact, however, the ancient gods were never entirely forgotten but lived a subterranean existence in folklore as well as in the literary heritage. They were to surface at unexpected moments in the Middle Ages, and on occasion they triumphed in the Renaissance.

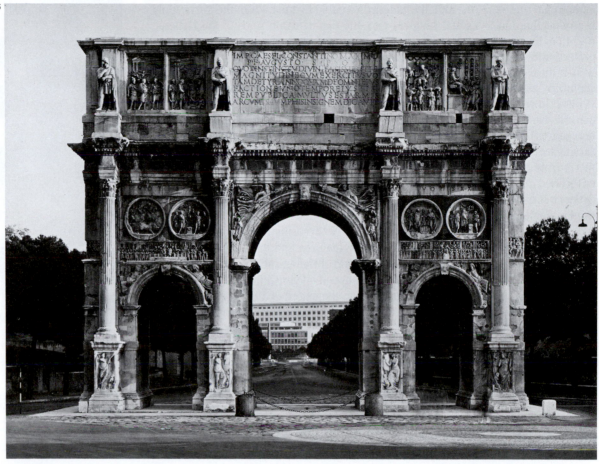

9-76

9-76. Arch of Constantine, Rome. c. A.D. 312–15

SCULPTURE An astonishing, indeed rather touching, red-brown porphyry group, about half life size (see Introduction fig. 25) and formerly attached to a column, represents four tetrarchs—we are not sure which ones, but probably Diocletian and his colleagues. Each Augustus embraces a Caesar with his right arm, and each figure firmly grasps the hilt of a sword. The style would have impressed Gudea of Lagash as archaic (see fig. 4–12). Nothing remains of the naturalistic tradition in the representation of the human body, which had evolved in Egypt, Mesopotamia, and the Hellenic world throughout more than three thousand years. The figures have been reduced to cylinders, their legs and arms to tubes, their proportions to those of dolls, and their faces to staring masks. But if freedom and beauty of face and body have been sacrificed, anxiety has not. The figures clutch each other like lost children, and an art that no longer cares to analyze features cannot forget frowns. In fact, only the individuality of their frowns differentiates these four figures.

The grand triumphal arch that Constantine erected in Rome from 312 to 315 to celebrate his assumption of sole imperial power in the West owes much of its splendor to its predecessors (fig. 9–76). The three-arched shape was used earlier in the Arch of Septimius Severus in the Roman Forum, and most of the sculpture was lifted bodily from monuments built by Trajan, Hadrian, and Marcus Aurelius, whose heads were recarved into portraits of Constantine and his generals. The sculpture contributed by Constantine's artisans (for example, the frieze seen in fig. 9–51) is startling. Tiny figures with huge heads, stiffly posed, are aligned on either side of the emperor as he addresses the people from the rostrum in the Roman Forum, whose buildings have been reduced to toys in the background. A few channels made by the drill suffice to indicate what had been the glory of Roman

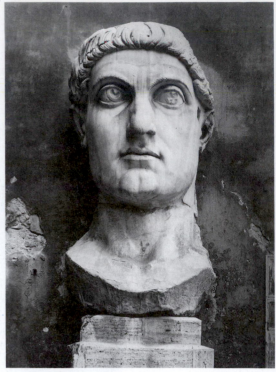

ceremonial sculpture, the melodic cadences created by the folds of the togas. Only here and there in faces and gestures can one distinguish a trace of the Hellenic tradition. Figures and architecture have been locked into an embracing structure of pattern allowing for no independent movement.

Technical inadequacy may account for part of the change; no official relief sculpture had been made in Rome for eighty years, and undoubtedly sculptors' studios, in which systematic instruction could be carried on, had broken up; only artisans were available to Constantine. But the renunciation of the classical tradition seems to have been deliberate. A new and impressive Constantinian style was rapidly formed, to be carried out by better-trained artists. One gigantic remnant is the marble head of a colossal statue of the emperor (fig. 9–77), which once was enthroned in the apse of his basilica. Head, arms, and legs were of marble, and the drapery probably of bronze plates over a masonry core. It is hard to keep from thinking of an august predecessor—the Zeus of Phidias at Olympia. Perhaps such thoughts were just what Constantine wanted. No accusation of technical decline can be leveled at this magnificent head. The features and the neck muscles are superbly modeled, showing a full understanding of Hellenistic tradition—with one significant exception: the eyes are enlarged beyond all verisimilitude. Carved with all the colorism of Antonine sculpture, even to the extent of a tiny fleck of marble left in each eye to suggest the reflection of light in the transparent cornea, they stare above and beyond us as if we could never reach their owner, as if his godlike gaze were fixed upon eternity. This enormous enlargement of the eyes as an indication of sanctity or of inspiration became a convention in Early Christian and Byzantine art. We have come a long way from the moment when marble was exploited to reflect light in fifth-century Greece to that in which it was used to represent light.

9-77. *Constantine the Great.* c. A.D. 315. Marble, height 8′ (2.44 m). Palazzo dei Conservatori, Rome

9-78. Model of the Palace of Diocletian, Split, Yugoslavia. c. A.D. 293. Museo della Civiltà Romana, Rome (reconstruction by E. Hebrard)

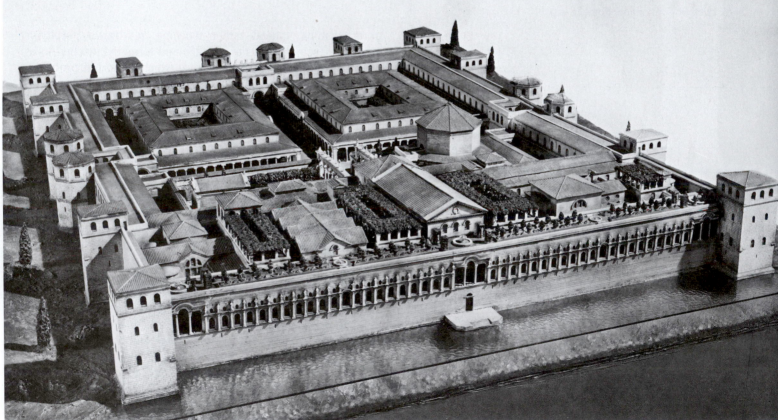

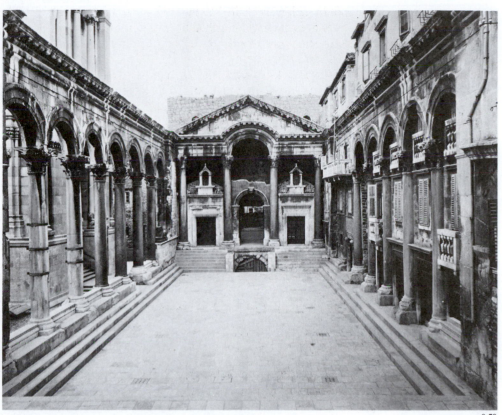

9-79. Peristyle court, Palace of Diocletian, Split

9-79

ARCHITECTURE   Two structures of great size and importance from this brief transitional period between the ancient world and the early Middle Ages still remain partially standing. One is the gigantic palace that Diocletian began to build in 293 for his retirement near his birthplace on the Dalmatian coast. Much of the present-day city of Split is built inside the palace walls, but its original appearance has been reconstructed in a model (fig. 9–78). The plan and appearance of the palace reflect the changed conditions of the Empire. A free arrangement of structures like Hadrian's Villa at Tivoli (see fig. 9–55) was no longer possible in this unstable portion of the Empire, and so close to the sea. The complex had to be defended, and it was thus laid out on the plan of a Roman camp, with the main streets intersecting in the exact center. The palace was surrounded by walls and towers except on the south side, which overhung the sea and could be approached only by boat; the imperial apartments ran along this side, with arched windows embraced by an engaged colonnade. An octagonal structure visible toward the right side of the model was designed as the emperor's mausoleum; it is in good condition and is now in use as a cathedral. A peristyle court, now forming the principal square of Split (fig. 9–79), gave access to the mausoleum on the left and the imperial apartments at the end through a sort of triumphal arch once crowned with the customary bronze group of a four-horse chariot driven by the emperor. In the center of this arch the emperor made his formal appearances to the populace. The most remarkable feature of this court is the complete change in the customary relationship of column and arch since the first century B.C. Under the central pediment the entablature is bent upward to form an arch, as we have previously seen at Hadrian's Villa (see fig. 9–56). But the monolithic Corinthian columns in gray granite along both sides of the court no longer *embrace* arches; for the first time in Roman architecture, the columns *support* the arches directly. This decisive step prepares us for the structural innovations of Early Christian architecture in the mid- and late fourth century.

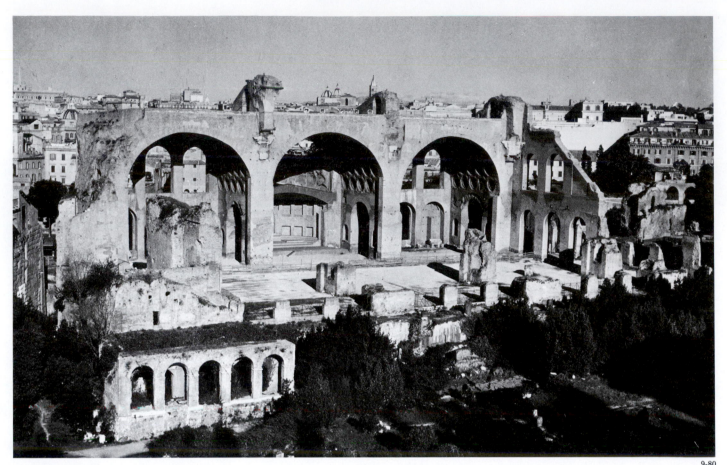

9-80

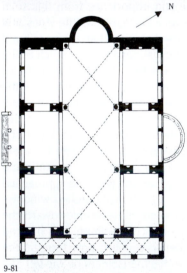

9-81

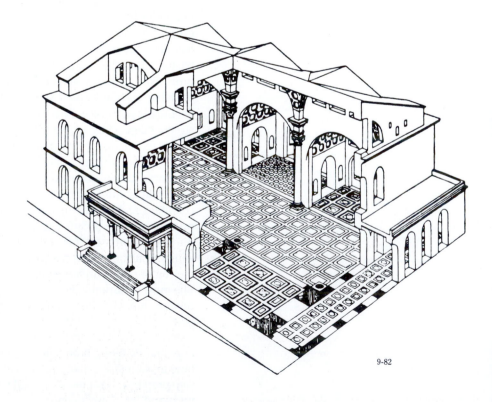

9-82

9-80. Basilica of Maxentius and Constantine, Rome. c. A.D. 306–13

9-81. Plan of the Basilica of Maxentius and Constantine, Rome

9-82. Reconstruction of the Basilica of Maxentius and Constantine, Rome (after Huelsen)

The other great pagan structure of the early fourth century is the basilica started by Maxentius in 306 and terminated under Constantine in 313 (figs. 9–80 to 9–82), a massive section of which still dominates the imperial forums in Rome. Since the basilica as an institution had been in effect transformed into a kind of imperial audience hall, it is no accident that the architect relinquished the traditional basilican plan as we have seen it in the Basilica Ulpia (see plan in fig. 9–45), with its long nave, side aisles, twin apses, and timber roof, in favor of the groin-vaulted form of hall used in the frigidaria of Roman baths, such as that of Caracalla (see fig. 9–72). The downward thrust of the heavy groin vaults upon the eight colossal Corinthian columns and the piers behind them must have been to a certain extent abutted by the massive, octagonally coffered barrel vaults of the six exedrae, the partially enclosed subsidiary spaces running off the nave on either side; these replaced the usual side aisles of a basilica. Maxentius intended the structure to be entered through a portico at the east end, providing an immediate view of the apse at the west, intended for a colossal statue of the emperor. Constantine erected a new porch on the south side to afford entrance from the Sacred Way and ran a new apse for his statue off the north side. The grandeur, simplicity, and openness of the interior seem to us so easily adaptable for religious use that it is hard at first sight to realize why the building was not adopted as a model for Early Christian churches. The answer (see page 301) tells us much about the nature of early Christianity. Equally important is the fact that this mighty ruin was universally believed in the Renaissance to have been a temple.

A strikingly austere brick basilica (fig. 9–83) of the early fourth century still stands at Trier, now in Germany but then one of the major cities of northern Gaul. Constantius, one of the tetrarchs, selected Trier as his capital in 293, and it remained the center of the whole Western Empire, even under Constantine and his successors, for more than a century until the removal of the administration to Milan in 395. In consequence Trier became the intellectual center of early Christianity; here lived and wrote figures as great as saints Jerome, Ambrose, and Augustine. The basilica is still used as a church, and it forms a remarkable link with Early

9-83

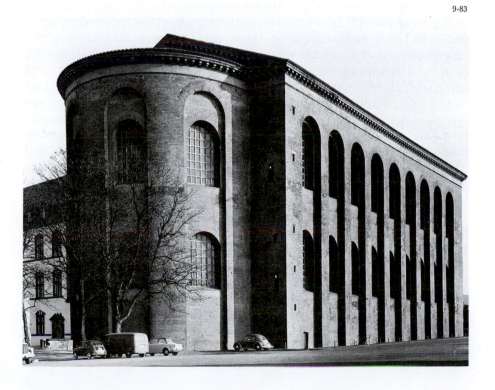

9-83. Basilica, Trier, Germany. Early 4th century A.D.

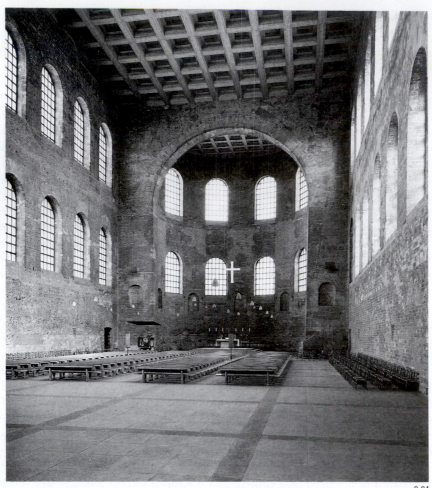

9-84

Christian architecture (fig. 9–84). The nave is an exact double square in plan, 100 by 200 Roman feet (95 by 190 modern feet), ending in a plain arch through which one looks into a semicircular apse. The equally plain walls are pierced by two superimposed stories of arched windows. One is struck by the total disappearance of all the accustomed splendors of Roman imperial architecture. Save for colored marble enframements around the insides of the windows and small mosaics in the niches below the lower windows, neither the interior nor the exterior shows ornamentation of any sort, not even columns. The exterior windows are embraced by a blind arcade recalling the arcades of the aqueducts, and wooden service galleries ran round both stories at the level of the windows. By a clever optical device, the apse is made to look deeper than it really is so as to increase the apparent size of the emperor seated there: the windowsills at both levels are about four feet lower than those in the nave, and the central windows are narrower. Terra-cotta heating ducts ran under the plain black-and-white marble floor, and both nave and apse were apparently covered with a flat, coffered ceiling as at present. The exterior was stuccoed, doubtless to protect the brick in the damp and cold climate, but the masses, shapes, and treatment were in complete harmony with those of the neighboring warehouses. The effect of the blank walls and vast spaces is majestic.

MOSAICS   In a final glance at the dying pagan tradition, we might note its survival, well into the fourth century, in floor mosaics in North Africa and in Syria, where these decorations have been discovered in great numbers. But the most

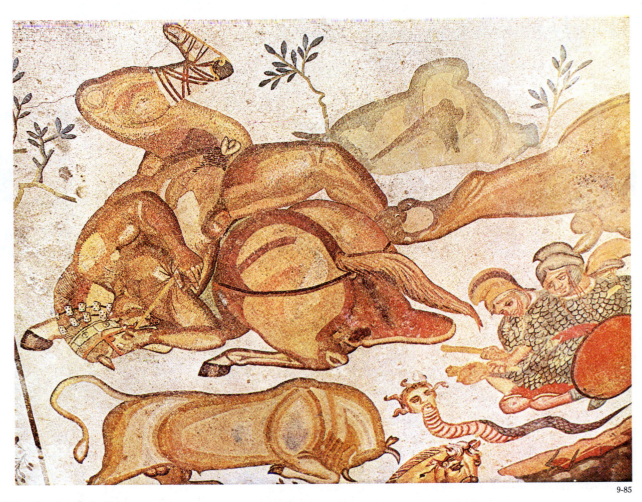

9-85. *Exploits of Hercules,* detail of a floor mosaic at the Imperial Villa, Piazza Armerina, Sicily. Early 4th century A.D.

spectacular find of all has been the villa, excavated since World War II, at Piazza Armerina in Sicily. In striking contrast to the fortified palace of Diocletian, this country residence, which may have been designed for the contemporaneous retirement of Diocletian's colleague Maximian, is composed of a series of small and flexibly shaped spaces freely arranged on the slope of a hill in a manner recalling the improvised plan of Hadrian's Villa at Tivoli. The complete series of late imperial mosaics that enliven the pavements of all the interiors of the villa at Piazza Armerina must have been done by a workshop from North Africa over a considerable span of time. Among the most striking is the group representing the *Exploits of Hercules,* seen as separate episodes scattered over a white background. A nude warrior sprawled over his dead horse, from which emerges a flood of blood and excrement, and with one leg in the air plunges his sword into his breast (fig. 9–85). The powerful masses of his muscular body recall the Pergamene style of half a millennium earlier (see figs. 7–100, 7–103). Below him an angry bull charges at nothing in particular, while two crouching soldiers clad in scale mail remonstrate with a human-headed snake. Over all the surfaces play rich changes of light, shade, and color that establish the volumes of bodies, limbs, and rock masses in depth, showing that even at this late date Hellenistic colorism was very much alive, even though rigorously simplified. In the next part of this book, we shall see this colorism employed not in the rendition of violence and bloodshed but in the depiction of hitherto unsuspected aspects of spiritual experience.

TIME LINE V

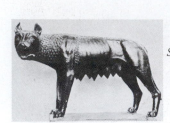
She-Wolf

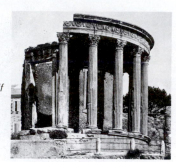
Temple of the
Sibyl, Tivoli

*Augustus of
Prima Porta*

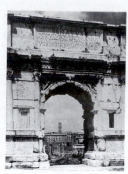
Arch of Titus

HISTORY

600 B.C.	Rome under Etruscan domination; overthrows Etruscans to establish Republic, 509
	Gauls sack Rome, 387
300	Rome extends rule to southern Italy, Sicily, Sardinia, Corsica
	Rome defeats Carthage in First Punic War, 264–241; expels Carthaginians from Spain, invades Africa, 202–201
100	Rome victorious over Macedon, 168, extends rule over Macedonia, Asia Minor, Egypt
	Sack of Athens, 86
	Sulla becomes dictator, 82–79
	First triumvirate (Pompey, Caesar, Crassus), 60
50 B.C.	Caesar assumes power, 49; assassinated, 44
	Second triumvirate, including Octavius, 43
A.D. 1	Octavius first emperor as Augustus Caesar, 27 B.C.–A.D. 14
	Principal later imperial reigns:
100	Julio-Claudians (Tiberius, Claudius, Nero), 14–68;
	Flavians (Vespasian, Titus, Domitian), 69–96
	Trajan, 98–117; Hadrian, 117–38
	Antonines (Antoninus Pius, Marcus Aurelius, Commodus), 138–80
	Septimus Severus, 193–211; Caracalla, 211–17
300	Diocletian, 284–305 (Tetrarchy, 293)
	Constantine the Great, 324–37

CULTURE

Vast quantities of Greek sculptures brought to
Rome in triumph after victory over Macedonia

Earliest water mills

Golden Age of Roman Literature: Cicero, Catullus,
Virgil, Horace, Ovid, Seneca

Vitruvius completes his ten books on architecture,
De Architectura

Jesus Christ (c. 3 B.C.–A.D. 30)

Invention of glassblowing; Pliny the Elder, *Natural
History*

Invention of paper, China

Paul (d. 65) spreads Christianity to Asia Minor,
Greece, and Italy

Tacitus (55?–after 117)

Ptolomy, astronomer (d. 160)

Galen, physician and anatomist (d. 201)

Plotinus (d. 270)

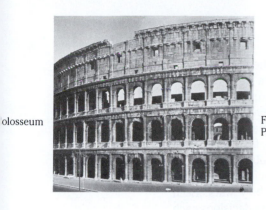

Colosseum

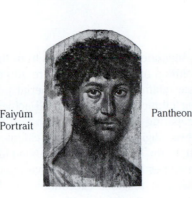

Faiyûm Portrait

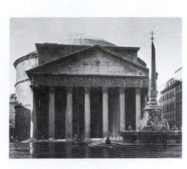

Pantheon

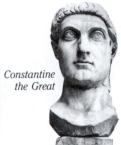

Constantine the Great

PAINTING, SCULPTURE, ARCHITECTURE

Sarcophagus, Cerveteri; *Apollo of Veii Hunting and Fishing; Dancing Woman and Lyre Player*, Tarquinia

Wounded Chimaera; Ficoroni Cist; Bearded Man
Porta Marzia, Perugia
Tomb of the Reliefs, Cerveteri
Sanctuary of Fortuna, Praeneste
Temple of Fortuna Virilis, Rome; Temple of the Sibyl, Tivoli
L'Arringatore; Head of a Roman with a Wart
Head of Pompey
Wall paintings, Villa of the Mysteries, Pompeii
Architectural View, from Boscoreale
Garden Room, Villa of Livia, Rome
Pont du Gard, near Nîmes
Statue of Augustus; *Ara Pacis*
Gemma Augustea; Maison Carrée, Nîmes; houses of Silver Wedding and Faun, Pompeii; Third, Fourth Style wall paintings, Pompeii; *Neptune and Amphitrite,* from Herculaneum
Flavian portrait sculpture; Arch of Titus; Colosseum
Forum of Trajan with Basilica Ulpia, Column, and Market
Hadrian's Villa, Tivoli; Pantheon; *Portrait of Antinoüs*
Equestrian Statue of Marcus Aurelius; Commodus
Theater at Sabratha
Family of Vunnerius Keramus
Philip the Arab; Ludovisi Battle Sarcophagus
Temple of Venus, Baalbek; Palace of Diocletian; *Tetrarchs;* mosaics at Piazza Armerina
Portrait and Arch of Constantine; Basilica of Maxentius

PARALLEL SOCIETIES

Greek Archaic	600 B.C.
Etruscan	
Gauls	
	300
Roman Republic	
	100
	50 B.C.
Roman Empire	A.D. 1
	100
Early Christian	
Han dynasty, China	
	300

PART THREE

Two overriding circumstances separated the Middle Ages from the ancient world. The first was the gradual dissolution of the Roman Empire into a wide variety of successor states. Some of these retained or revived imperial pretensions, while others frankly proclaimed their ethnic basis; however, all achieved only limited territorial jurisdiction, thus preparing the way for the modern nation-state. The second was the dominance of two religions with universal claims, first Christianity and then, in competition with it, Islam. Each religion demanded total allegiance on the part of the worshiper, sometimes to the point of active judicial and military hostility to other faiths—as seen in religious executions and holy wars. Each ordered the worshiper's ethical standards and daily life. In ultimate decisions each valued revelation above reason, that supreme goal of ancient thinkers. Each prepared the worshiper in detail for an afterlife.

Both circumstances were to have profound consequences for art. The first resulted in a far greater repertory of artistic forms, corresponding to the necessities of individual states and regions, than was possible even under the large tolerance of the Roman Empire. The second demanded a religious architecture that could handle ceremonially vast masses of people and whose interior spaces, therefore, tended to determine the character and appearance of their external forms. Equally important, the emphasis of religion on an otherworldly goal tended to weaken interest in naturalistic representation of the spaces and objects of this world. It also prohibited outright the depiction of the nude human body, the pride and glory of Helleno-Roman art, save when required by a specific religious or historical subject; even in such an instance, no beauty is discerned in the body. Explicit Scriptural support for this attitude is unfindable, but it may derive from the shame of Adam and Eve at recognizing their nakedness, prophetic denunciation of lust, and Saint Paul's distrust of all sexuality. Early in the period, therefore, representations of even the clothed human figure betray a lack of knowledge of or interest in the underlying structure of the body. As an inevitable corollary of religious antinaturalism, schemata inherited from one generation to the next were steadily substituted for the active pursuit of visual reality which, in one form or another, had occupied the attention of Mediterranean artists for more than three millennia.

At the same time, the emphasis on faith and the consequent transcendence accorded to the inner life opened up for artistic exploration rich areas of human experience hardly touched by the visually oriented art of the Helleno-Roman tradition. Formalized shapes, patterns, and color relationships, whether based on nature or wholly abstract, had been permitted only an ornamental role in ancient art. In the Middle Ages such elements took on extreme importance as vehicles for feeling and imagination. In certain aspects of Celtic and Islamic art, in fact (see Introduction fig. 23 and fig. 11–5), abstraction entirely replaces elements derived from observation. Paradoxically enough, in the service of otherworldly religions, engineering science took enormous strides in the Middle Ages. Such brilliant achievements as the lofty domes on pendentives, which crown Byzantine churches (see figs. 10–40, 10–59); the interlacing arches, which opened up new possibilities for mosques (see fig. 11–10); and the soaring ribbed vaults sustained by external buttressing that roof Gothic cathedrals (see figs. 15–14, 15–28) were feats beyond the imaginings of Roman architects.

The dividing line for both the political and the religious determinants fell within the reign of the emperor Constantine (ruled 306–37). The cumbersome tetrarchy had culminated in a chaotic civil war among the tetrarchs themselves, in which

THE MIDDLE AGES

Constantine, one of the Caesars, captured supreme power and reunited the Empire, eventually under his sole control. A major political step was his removal of the capital from western Europe (where Trier had for decades replaced Rome as the chief administrative center) to the town of Byzantium, on the shores of the Bosporus, which he rebuilt and renamed Constantinople. The direct result of this move, however, was a new and eventually permanent division of the Empire under Constantine's successors along more or less the same lines as the old tetrarchy. The Eastern Roman (or Byzantine) Empire survived for more than a thousand years, although constantly diminished by foreign inroads, until Constantinople was at last conquered by the Turks in 1453. The Western Roman Empire was repeatedly invaded during the fifth century by Germanic tribes, who twice succeeded in sacking Rome. These tribes had already eaten away at the outlying provinces and had infiltrated the very administration of the Empire; many had become Christianized. The deposition in 476 of the last Western Roman emperor, Romulus Augustulus, by the Gothic king Odoacer merely gave formal expression to what had long been a fact, the takeover by Germanic tribes of the whole of the Western Empire as a series of separate kingdoms.

Decisive for the immediate fate of long-persecuted Christianity was the battle at the Milvian Bridge in 312 between the pagan Maxentius and Constantine, who had been interested in the new religion through his mother, later canonized as Saint Helena. Constantine attributed his overwhelming victory to his vision of a floating Cross and a voice crying, "In this sign thou shalt conquer." Possibly Constantine's religious policy, beginning with his promulgation of the Edict of Milan in 313 along with his co-emperor Licinius, proclaiming complete tolerance for Christianity, would have been inevitable no matter who sat on the throne. In spite of the persecutions and widespread belief that they were indulging in obscene and perverted rites, the number of Christians in all parts of the Empire, even in the imperial administration and in the imperial family, had become too great either to persecute or to ignore. Constantine's later activities as sole emperor—for example, his presiding role at the Council of Nicaea in 325—reinforced the new importance of the Christian religion. His transfer of the capital to the most heavily Christianized region of the Empire made the supremacy of Christianity all but inevitable. Ironically, the very emperor who established the ecumenical principle still fostered the imperial cult (witness the colossal statue of himself in the former Basilica of Maxentius, see fig. 9–77), never declared Christianity the state religion, and was baptized only on his deathbed.

With imperial support, Christianity rapidly replaced Roman and other forms of polytheism as the official, indeed the only legal, religion of the entire Mediterranean world. Adherence could be enforced by the full machinery of Roman imperial government, and by almost all the successor states for many centuries. Poor at its humble beginnings, the Church was now rich. Thus began a wholly new era in human history, in which political and religious phenomena were inextricably mixed, not within national boundaries, as often in the ancient world, but on an immense scale, with worldwide claims. Even after the West had been overrun by (Christianized) barbarians, who set up their own monarchies, the title of the Roman Empire was revived in Gaul by Charlemagne in 800 and maintained in central Europe until extinguished by Napoleon in the early nineteenth century. The emperors were still called "Caesar"—the origin of the German *Kaiser* and the Slavic *czar*. Although their capital was mobile, and the emperors were almost uniformly

Germanic, their authority over lesser sovereigns was not firm until they had gone to Rome to be crowned. For the bishop of Rome had come to be recognized as pope (from the expression for "father"), supreme head of the Christian Church—in the West, at least—and however little his person might at times be respected, divine authority was considered to be in his hands. The language both of the Church and of all official documents and learned writing throughout most of the Middle Ages in the West remained Latin. In the largely Greek-speaking East, papal preeminence was not recognized, nor was there any equivalent to papal authority among the patriarchs holding sway over the regional divisions of the Eastern, or Orthodox, Church.

Gradually, under the dominance of interlocking church and state authority, a new phenomenon perhaps too easily characterized as the "medieval mind" came into being. In sharp contradistinction to the generally unfettered intellectual life of Greek and Roman antiquity, all knowledge in the Middle Ages was subordinated to the transcendent belief in divine revelation through Scripture and Church tradition. Accepted theological principles known as *dogma,* belief in which was considered necessary to salvation, were adopted at Church councils, proclaimed by popes, and refined by theological writers. Deviation was considered *heresy,* a crime punishable in theory and too often in fact by the most painful forms of death. Yet heresies arose and spread, sometimes throughout entire regions, until they were suppressed, occasionally with a ruthlessness that might have startled the pagan persecutors of the gentle early Christians. Surprisingly, the greatest of the theologians were well read in Greek and Latin literature and philosophy, and while rejecting pagan deities as demons, they systematically incorporated ancient wisdom and scientific knowledge into the structure of Christian faith. Many, indeed, maintained that there was no conflict between faith and reason. We owe most of our knowledge of classical writings to the Church's practice of copying ancient manuscripts for preservation in their libraries. Still more unexpectedly, a great deal of scientific investigation in the Islamic world permeated Christendom, partly because of the Crusades designed to rescue the Holy Land from its Arab conquerors.

A special feature of Christianity in East and West was the new institution of *monasticism.* In the troubled conditions of the later Empire, invaded and dismantled by the barbarians, and throughout the Middle Ages, thousands of men and women sought refuge in a total renunciation of worldly life, including marriage, by founding communities of single persons known as monasteries (from the Greek word for "one"). Many monks and nuns, especially in the East, were hermits, living a life of perpetual penance, meditation, and prayer in complete solitude, in caves, huts, or eventually groups of separate structures, and coming together only for corporate services. In contrast to these *eremitic* groups, there arose organized *cenobitic* orders (from the Latin word for "dining place"), who inhabited separate cells in larger structures, ate together—in silence, while listening to sacred readings—and celebrated all liturgical rites in common. Both monks and nuns were often trained as scribes, and one of their principal duties was to copy the Bible, liturgical books, and theological writings as well as those works of pagan authors considered worth preserving. The monasteries, therefore, became the main centers of learning before the year 1000. In the convents for women, the first all-female communities we know except for such tiny Roman groups as the nine Vestal Virgins, the role and authority of women were vastly enriched. Although they still needed male priests to celebrate Mass, women ruled their own convents and indeed governed whole orders of nuns, subject to the often distant authority of a bishop. Women in the convents, just as men in the monasteries, painted the illustrations for the manuscripts they copied. Thus for the first time in human history we have works of art indisputably created, and sometimes signed, by women; such works often also illustrate theological writings by women authors (see figs. 14–49, 15–48).

In the largely illiterate world outside the monasteries, cities had shrunk to a fraction of their original size or had even disappeared. Barbarian chieftains, soon Christianized, ruled as local or regional lords, with their practice of hereditary tenure of land giving rise to the concept of a "noble" class, foreign to the ancient world. (The Romans knew only the idea of "patricians," a leading class of citizens in the towns.) The *feudal system* (based on a Latin word for "oath") gradually arose and held sway throughout most of the Middle Ages. The peasant held his land from his local lord, who had sworn loyalty to a higher regional nobility, who in turn had taken an oath to a national king; over all, in theory, ruled the emperor. Marriages often generated conflicting loyalties through the inheritance of lands pledged to different overlords. And in point of fact regional nobles, throughout the Middle Ages, ruled with slight regard for royal power, just as the kings, supreme only in their own immediate territory, obeyed the emperor only when he could enforce his wishes. But imperial secular authority was held to be worldwide, corresponding to the universal spiritual authority of the pope. The system was formalized and justified in the thirteenth century by the great Italian poet and humanist Dante Alighieri in his *De Monarchia* (On Monarchy).

Not long after the year 1000 a disruptive element made its appearance within the feudal system—the rise of cities (compare Map 11, page 298, with Map 12, page 412). Often these were revived Roman centers, but sometimes important cities, such as Florence, grew up on sites that were small towns in antiquity. Owing their growth and rapidly increasing prosperity to manufacture, finance, and trading with each other and with the monarchies on a surprising scale, by land and sea, these cities were ruled by a new class of bourgeois merchants, unwilling to recognize the authority of kings and nobles, but often unable to defend their rights. In most of Italy and parts of northern Germany the cities established themselves as wholly independent republics, recalling vividly the city-states of ancient Greece. And they were often able to extend their rule over considerable regions and even disenfranchise the nobles. In the later medieval cities, whether or not they were independent, the cathedrals (churches containing the bishop's *cathedra,* or chair of authority) assumed a new importance and eventually colossal size, as symbols of civic dignity within the church-state structure. In the cities the universities rapidly replaced the monasteries as repositories of knowledge and incubators of new thought and, since any qualified male could attend, provided some social mobility within the system.

The theologians and philosophers of the Middle Ages, through the universities, necessarily had to work in harmony with Christian dogma, and they were eventually able, after many centuries of constant thought and writing, to erect a philosophical system that corresponded intellectually to the codified church and state governing their world at every level. *Scholasticism,* as the system came to be known, was perhaps the most characteristic expression of the "medieval mind." Every observable phenomenon of the natural world and human existence could be set in its proper place in this towering structure, justified by Scriptural authority, theological argument, and the reasoning of ancient philosophers. By the thirteenth century, in the *Summa* of Saint Thomas Aquinas, the system attained its peak of complexity and logical interrelationship of elements, reaching from the mysteries of heaven to the tiniest aspect of life on earth to the certitude of human destiny. Unlike the companion system of political and ecclesiastical authority, beset by all the frailties of human nature, Scholasticism worked very well indeed and proved all of its points to its own satisfaction. No one could have foreseen that free human observation and inquiry beginning in the Renaissance would eventually bring Scholasticism down, just as the example, at least, of the independent republics was to undermine both feudalism and the Empire and as the new emphasis on individual conscience was to split the Western Church.

It is sometimes maintained that Early Christian art and Byzantine art are in reality continuations of tendencies that had begun under the later pagan emperors and that they should be treated, therefore, as a final phase of ancient art. But there is a fundamental change between the conceptions of the human figure and surrounding space—and indeed the very nature and purpose of architecture, sculpture, and painting—prevalent in Greek and Roman art and those strongly evident in the new art of Christianity. This change was felt by the early Christians themselves, who used pagan buildings as quarries for materials and architectural elements and destroyed pagan statues and paintings as idolatrous and sinful, without regard for artistic value. The attitude of the early Christians toward the past contrasts strongly with that of the Romans, who protected their own earlier buildings wherever possible and cherished the statues and paintings of the Greeks. It would be more significant for us to consider the surprising developments of third-century pagan art as already partly medieval.

The earliest Christians had no practical need for art of any sort. Jesus himself, and after him the Apostles, preached and taught in houses, on hillsides, from ships, in streets and squares, and even in the Temple. Persecutions of Christians were by no means as continuous and thorough as is popularly believed. Between persecutions Christianity flourished and spread in its own quiet way. The new religion had its competitors, of course, among the mystery cults that had abounded even in the days of the Roman Republic—the religions of Dionysos, Isis, Cybele, Attis, and Mithras were the most important. But it would be a mistake to regard early Christianity as in any way comparable to these cults. True, they all promised salvation in an afterlife through the intervention of a particular divinity. But, unlike Christianity, they either culminated in orgiastic rites or included sanguinary ceremonies. For example, votaries of Mithras, the god of the favorite mystery cult of the Roman soldiery, lay on couches surrounding an altar before which a live bull was sacrificed and then drank his warm blood.

Early Christianity was nonviolent in essence. Would it had remained so! Alone save Judaism among the religions of the Roman Empire, it proclaimed a system of ethics that governed the entire behavior of the worshiper in all aspects of daily life, and alone save Judaism it possessed written authority embodied in a rich library of Scriptures, whose authenticity was generally accepted despite disagreement on specific elements and interpretations. And even Judaism, originally an ethnic religion, could not vie with the universal claims of Christianity. Thus, Christianity not only held a promise of individual salvation but also rapidly became a corporate religion, which created a counterculture inside the Roman state. Enthusiasts of the mystery cults had no objection to participating in the largely perfunctory aspects of Roman state religion, which included burning incense before the statue of the divine emperor. To the Christian such rites were anathema, and thus the very strength and pervasiveness of the Christian faith were interpreted as threats to the stability of the Empire. A tribute to the extraordinary success of early Christianity is that the two most systematic persecutions, those of Decius in 249–51 and Diocletian in 303–5, came so shortly before the Edict of Milan in 313, which marked if not the triumph of the new religion at least its liberation from fear.

During the later first and second centuries, Christian communities remained small, and believers worshiped in private houses. The basic ceremony, doubtless simple, was the communal meal, celebrating the Last Supper, which began with the breaking of bread and concluded with the drinking of wine, in ritual perpetuation of Christ's sacrifice. The ceremony included prayers, the reading of passages from the Gospels and the Epistles, discourses on the part of successors to the Apostles, and sometimes "speaking in tongues," which is today so mysterious an aspect of

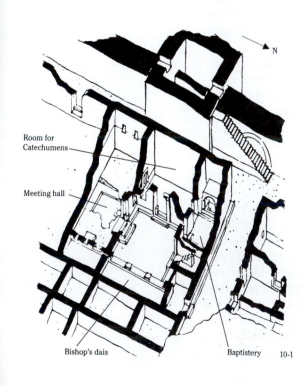

Room for Catechumens

Meeting hall

Bishop's dais

Baptistery

10-1

10-1. Reconstruction of a Christian community house, Dura-Europos, Syria. Shortly before 231

CHRISTIAN AND BYZANTINE ART

early Christianity. A dining room was essential, and the early Christians used the Roman *triclinium* (a dining room with a three-part couch extending around three sides of a table). In the crowded cities of the Eastern Empire, the triclinium was often located on an upper floor—the "upper room" mentioned in the Gospels and in Acts. Christianity was at first a religion chiefly for the lower classes, whom it sought to wean from the bloody spectacles of the arenas. Often, therefore, religious meetings took place in humble apartments in tenements, such as the insulae of Rome and Ostia (see fig. 9–29). By the third century the structure of the Mass—the word derives from the final Latin words of the rite *ite missa est,* meaning "depart, it is finished"—had become clear; it was presided over by *episkopoi* (bishops; literally, overseers), whose qualifications are listed in 1 Timothy 3. A clear distinction was maintained between the Liturgy of the Catechumens, consisting of the reading of Epistles, Gospels, and prayers and the singing of hymns (the Ordinary and Proper of the Mass, since Vatican II the Liturgy of the Word), which those under instruction could attend, and the Liturgy of the Faithful, the actual Eucharist—from a Greek word for "thanks"—or sacrifice of bread and wine (today the Canon of the Mass), to which only baptized Christians were admitted. The catechumens were required to leave before the Eucharist and could only hear but not see the Liturgy of the Faithful from an adjoining room. No altar was used, only a table brought in for the Eucharist and another table to receive offerings.

The Earliest Christian Art

THE DOMUS CHURCH   A special sort of house devoted exclusively to the observance of the Eucharist—a *domus ecclesiae* ("house of the church," from which the Italian *duomo* and the German *Dom,* both words for "cathedral," were derived)—became the first type of church building. The earliest known, dating from just before 231, was found at Dura-Europos in Syria (fig. 10–1). It is an ordinary Greek peristyle house, somewhat remodeled for Christian use, with a separate room for the catechumens, a library, and a vestry. It could not have accommodated a congregation of more than sixty and can scarcely be said to have had any pronounced architectural character; if it contained works of art, they have perished. This building had a dais for a bishop's chair, and thus it can be regarded as a cathedral. The baptistery at Dura-Europos, however, did contain very modest wall paintings. The earliest Christian churches, like early synagogues, generally were inconspicuous; their sites were selected in popular quarters near the city walls. There is, however, evidence for the erection of one substantial Christian meeting hall in Rome just before the issuance of the Edict of Milan. The existence of many others, in cities throughout the Empire before the persecution by Diocletian, is mentioned by Eusebius of Caesarea, fourth-century bishop and historian.

THE MARTYRIUM   A second kind of structure, the *martyrium,* was built over a martyr's grave or employed as a cenotaph to commemorate a martyr whose body was interred elsewhere. The earliest such structure known, dating from about 200, is a simple aedicula, or shrine, recently excavated under Saint Peter's in Rome (fig. 10–2). Inscriptions show that at that time the Christians believed it was the tomb of Peter. Whether or not this belief was founded on fact is still controversial.

CATACOMB PAINTING   The early Christians also dug *catacombs* (subterranean cemeteries). Since Christian belief in the resurrection of the body then prohibited cremation, the Christians could not use the cemeteries of lower-class Roman burial societies, where urns were kept in little niches, many tiers high. Also the Christians

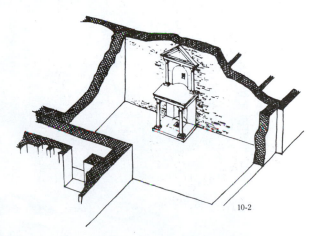

10-2. Reconstruction of the Shrine of Saint Peter, Rome. Late 2d century

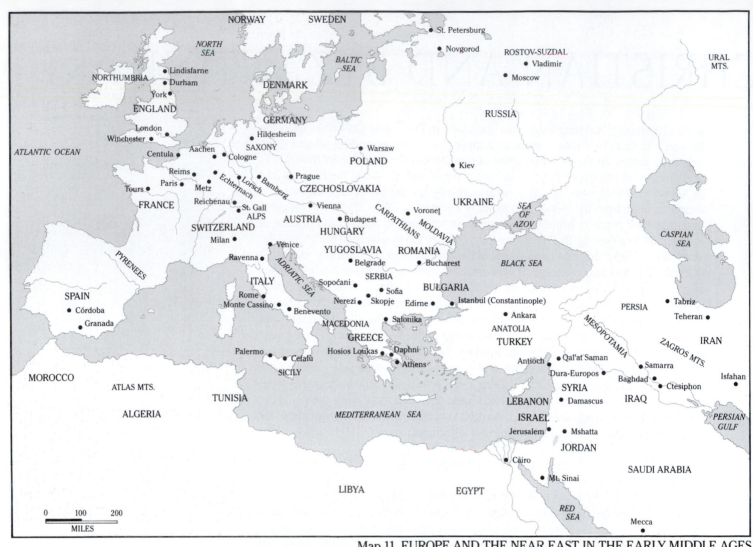

Map 11. EUROPE AND THE NEAR EAST IN THE EARLY MIDDLE AGES

10-3. *Breaking of Bread,* detail of a fresco, Catacomb of Sta. Priscilla, Rome. Late 2d century

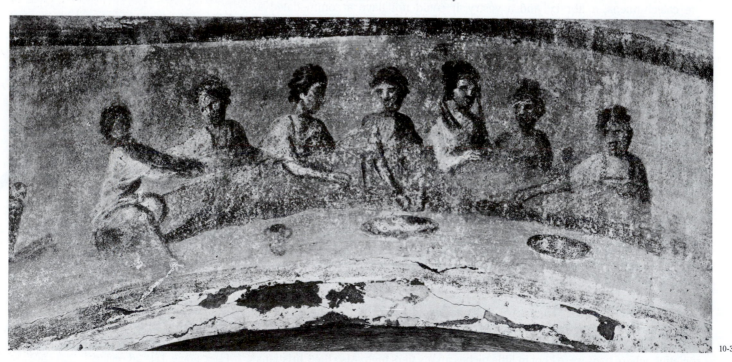

10-3

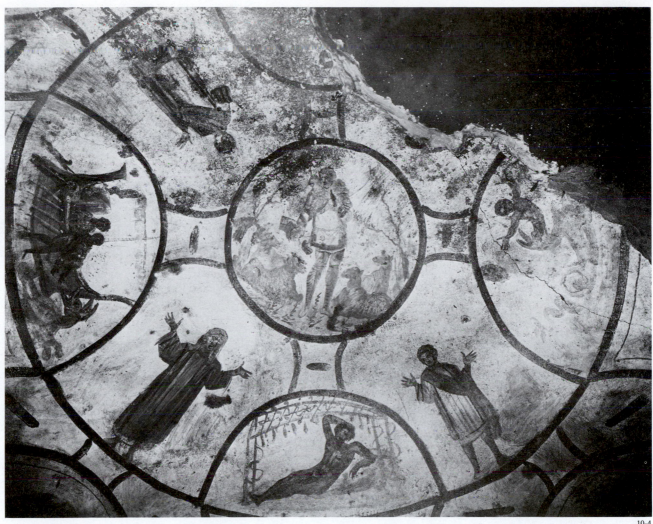

10-4. *The Good Shepherd,* ceiling fresco, Catacomb of Ss. Pietro e Marcellino, Rome. Early 4th century

felt the necessity of segregation from pagan burials. Like other Roman citizens, they could and did acquire property—as, for instance, their church buildings—and they bought land outside many cities, choosing sites where it was possible to excavate passages in the rock. Often these catacombs took advantage of local quarries as starting points. From these, tunnels were dug systematically according to plans; to conserve space, the catacombs were sometimes excavated four or five levels deep. Superimposed niches for sarcophagi, and from time to time small chapels for funeral feasts and for commemorative services, were hollowed out.

The earliest known works of Christian figurative art have been found in these chapels. These simple paintings on plaster, spread over the rock surface, were executed by modest artisans working by lamplight in the dark, dank, and probably odoriferous surroundings. Most of these paintings were on ceilings, a position that required the painter to work with his head tilted. One of the earliest, on the underside of an arch in the Catacomb of Saint Priscilla, Rome (fig. 10–3), dates from the time of the Antonine emperors in the late second century. Four men and three women are seated—diners no longer reclined—around a table on which only plates of bread and a cup are visible. The central figure is shown in the act of breaking the bread, which represents the culminating moment of the Eucharistic sacrifice. The style is a sketchy version of Roman illusionism but is adequate to convey deep excitement, transmitted from face to face by earnest glances revealing the exaltation of the participants.

A somewhat less intense ceiling fresco (fig. 10–4), probably painted in the early fourth century, in the Catacomb of Saints Peter and Marcellinus, Rome, is interest-

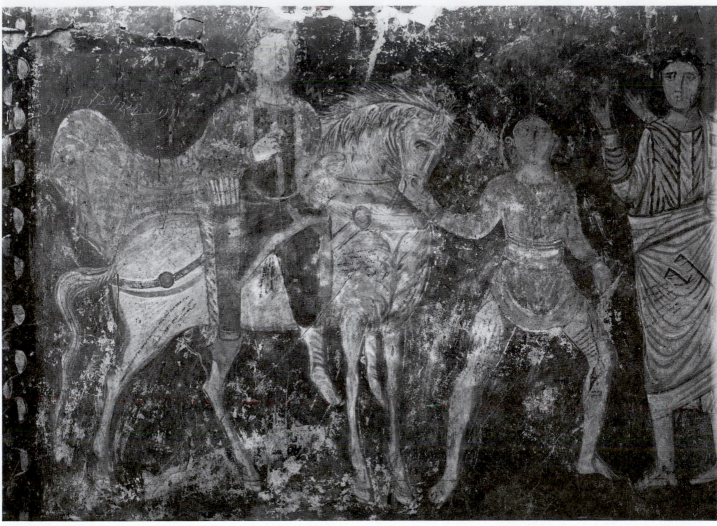

10-5

10-5. *Haman and Mordecai,* detail of a wall painting from the Synagogue, Dura-Europos. c. 250. National Museum, Damascus, Syria

ing chiefly from the symbolic standpoint. The circular design, like a miniature Pantheon dome, was doubtless intended to suggest the Dome of Heaven. Four semicircles are arranged about the central circle and are united by bands forming a Cross to show that this universal Christian symbol both embraces and reveals Heaven itself. In the central medallion, flanked by resting sheep, is the figure repeated countless times in Early Christian paintings and sarcophagus sculpture, the Good Shepherd. These are the earliest images of Christ and, of course, were not intended to inform us about his actual appearance (about which we know nothing). The youthful, beardless shepherd, with a lamb over his shoulder, is a *symbol* of Christ, who said, "I am the good shepherd; the good shepherd giveth his life for the sheep" (John 10:11). One semicircle is lost, but the remaining three tell in simple imagery the story of Jonah, tossed from his ship at the left, swallowed by the whale at the right, and at the bottom reclining below the gourd vine. Here again we are instructed by Christ's own words, "and there shall no sign be given to it, but the sign of the prophet Jonas: For as Jonas was three days and three nights in the whale's belly; so shall the Son of man be three days and three nights in the heart of the earth" (Matthew 12:39–40). Thus, as always in Christian thought, the Old Testament is interpreted in the light of the New; in the apparent death and miraculous deliverance of Jonah are prefigured the Crucifixion and Resurrection of Christ, and through faith in him, the salvation of the true believer. The "sign of the prophet

Jonas" is the Cross, between whose bars stand figures in what is known as the *orant* pose, the arms-wide gesture of prayer in Early Christian times, still used by the celebrant at certain moments in the Mass.

The only biblical wall paintings of truly monumental character that have come down to us from this early period are, however, not Christian but Jewish; they form a remarkable series and originally decorated the entire interior of a synagogue at Dura-Europos. However provincial in execution, these paintings are impressive in the solemn directness with which they set forth the biblical narratives. In *Haman and Mordecai* (fig. 10–5) these two figures move against a flat background with no indication of groundline, reminding us of the floating figures on the base of the Column of Antoninus Pius (see fig. 9–57). Mordecai stands in a Roman speaking pose, his right arm outstretched and his body enveloped in the folds of a cloak that strongly recall those of a toga. We can only surmise that Christian counterparts to this large-scale Jewish painting existed; none have yet been found.

The Age of Constantine

The Edict of Milan brought about immediate and far-reaching transformations in the life of the Church through the new relationship between church and state it established. Given the strong interest and active role of Constantine, Christianity became to all intents and purposes an official religion, inheriting the splendors of the dethroned Roman gods. Although no complete colossal statue of the emperor survives, the solemn *Colossus of Barletta* (fig. 10–6), a bronze statue probably representing one of his Byzantine successors in the fifth or sixth century, clearly indicates the majestic and superhuman authority accorded to the person of the emperor in Early Christian times. No longer divine, he was nonetheless sacred — the Unconquered Sun, the Vicar of Christ on earth.

THE EARLY CHRISTIAN BASILICA   The newly official religion, encouraged as an effective arm of imperial administration, soon took on imperial magnificence. It could no longer aim at small and intimate congregations bound together by no other ties than those of Christian love. Huge crowds of worshipers had now to be accommodated and given access to sacred places and to the sacraments of the Church. Enclosed and roofed spaces were needed in great numbers. In rapid succession and under direct imperial patronage, scores of churches rose throughout Rome and other great cities of the Empire, especially Milan and Constantinople, and at sacred sites in the Holy Land.

A model for these new buildings was needed. Although the Christians had no compunction about utilizing architectural elements taken from pagan structures, the temples themselves, even when not too small for the crowds of worshipers, were manifestly unsuitable; their very sites were regarded with abhorrence. The obvious model was the Roman basilica, or meeting hall, which existed in every inhabited Roman center. As we have seen, there was no strict uniformity of plan for these buildings. Many Roman basilicas, some quite large ones, were simple halls with no side aisles; most were entered along one long side and had apses at either end. They remained in use for their original purposes, and even if vacant they would not have entirely fitted Christian purposes. Only one apse was needed for the installation of the clergy and the enthronement of the bishop, and the entrance had to be placed at the opposite short end. Wherever possible the apse was directed toward the Holy Land, which in Europe meant toward the east. The early portable communion table was replaced by a fixed altar, which had to be visible from a considerable distance and accessible to all worshipers at Communion. The long row of columns on either side of the nave of most Roman basilicas played a double role in dramatizing the approach of the faithful to the altar and in segregating, by means of curtains hung between the columns, the catechumens from those who could participate in the Liturgy of the Faithful.

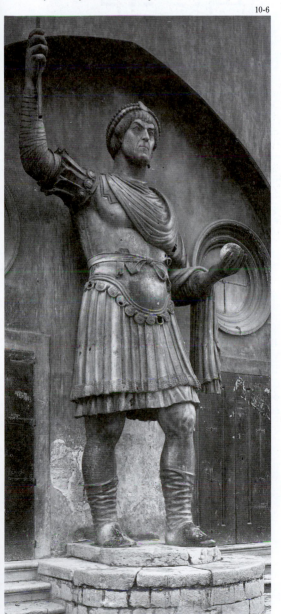

10-6. *Colossus of Barletta*. c. 5th or 6th century. Bronze, height of original part (head to knee) 11′7¾″ (3.55 m). Barletta, Italy

10-6

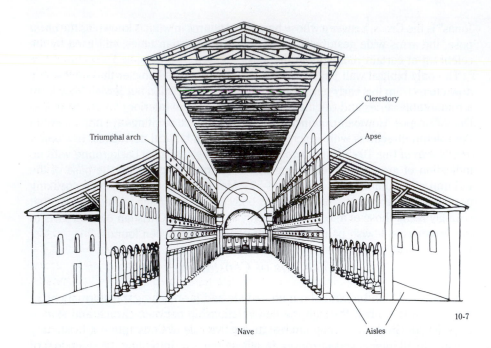

10-7

The colonnades characteristically supported a lofty wall pierced by a clerestory. The roof was usually of an open timber construction, as was the case in many ancient buildings. The large number of churches begun in the reign of Constantine required columns in great numbers and at great speed. It may be fairly doubted whether, in Constantinian Rome, it was possible either to produce so many or to order them from other regions. However, temples and other monuments of the Roman past offered an inexhaustible supply. Borrowed columns were thus uncritically installed in the new basilicas, with little or no regard for consistency of style, color, or size. Granite and marble columns, Corinthian and Ionic capitals, were placed side by side; capitals were sometimes set on columns they did not fit.

Although its inner length of 368 feet made Saint Peter's the largest of the Constantinian basilicas, in fact the largest church building in all Christendom until the construction of the French abbey church at Cluny in the eleventh century (see pages 415–17), it still did not equal the Roman Basilica Ulpia. Even though it stood intact for over a thousand years, no exact representation of its interior is known, and only a general reconstruction is possible (fig. 10–7). Saint Peter's differed from most other basilicas in its very nature as a combined basilica and martyrium. The apse enshrined what was believed to be—and may indeed have been—the tomb of Peter under a marble canopy supported by four spiral columns (later used by Gianlorenzo Bernini as a model for his colossal construction in the seventeenth century). In order to accommodate the crowds of visitors to the tomb, a large hall— the *transept*—was erected at right angles to the nave between the nave and the apse (figs. 10–8, 10–9). Before the transept came the so-called *triumphal arch,* a common feature of Early Christian basilicas. The altar, at the head of the nave, was probably movable. The columns of the basilica were either Corinthian or Composite and of many different materials, including green marble, yellow marble, red granite, and gray granite. They were closely spaced and supported a continuous, straight entablature. As in the Basilica Ulpia, Saint Peter's had double side-aisles; the colonnade separating them supported arches. The building was not completed when Constantine died in 337 nor for some time thereafter. It is not known what wall decorations were originally planned; the frescoes covering the nave walls between the colonnade and the clerestory were painted in the fifth century, but the half dome of the apse was filled with an immense pictorial composition in mosaic (see pages 306–7 and figs. 10–15, 10–16).

Initially, there was certainly no suggestion that the transept plan symbolized the

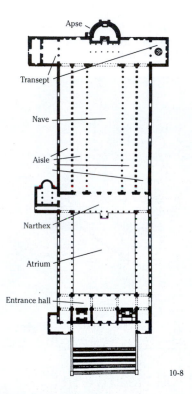

10-8

10-8. Plan of Old St. Peter's, Rome

10-9. Isometric view of Old St. Peter's, Rome. c. 400. Dotted lines indicate conjectural outline of atrium and entrance portal and, on the south side of the transept, of an imperial tomb

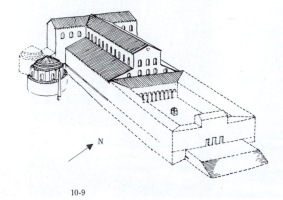

10-9

Cross, as it did in later times. The plan of Santa Sabina, erected in Rome from 422 to 432 (fig. 10–10), is more typical of Early Christian churches. It was built without a transept so that the triumphal arch embraced the apse directly. Throughout the Early Christian period, the apse was used only by the clergy, and generally it contained a marble chair for the celebrant, a feature revived since Vatican II. Arches were substituted for entablatures, as at Santa Sabina, in the course of the fifth century. None of the Constantinian basilicas survive in their original state. Saint Peter's, in fact, was demolished section by section in the Renaissance, to be replaced by a new building. The beautifully restored interior of Santa Sabina is almost the only one that still conveys the pristine appearance of an Early Christian basilica in Rome, but it is unusual in having carefully matched Corinthian columns—purloined as usual.

All Early Christian buildings were devoid of external decoration, presenting unrelieved brick walls of the utmost simplicity (as in such Roman buildings as the Basilica at Trier, fig. 9–83; see also figs. 10–20, 10–27). The pilgrim to Saint Peter's (see fig. 10–9), for example, arrived at the blank, outer wall of an atrium—in reality a large peristyle court—then proceeded to the *narthex,* or vestibule, and finally emerged into the richly colored nave with its splendid columns and bright frescoes, scores of hanging lamps, jeweled altar cloth, gold and silver vessels of the Mass, and clergy in gorgeous vestments—a far cry from the simplicity of the first centuries of Christianity. The processional principle on which the church was laid out has often been compared with the basic plan of the Egyptian temple, but it should

10-10. Interior, Sta. Sabina, Rome. 422–32

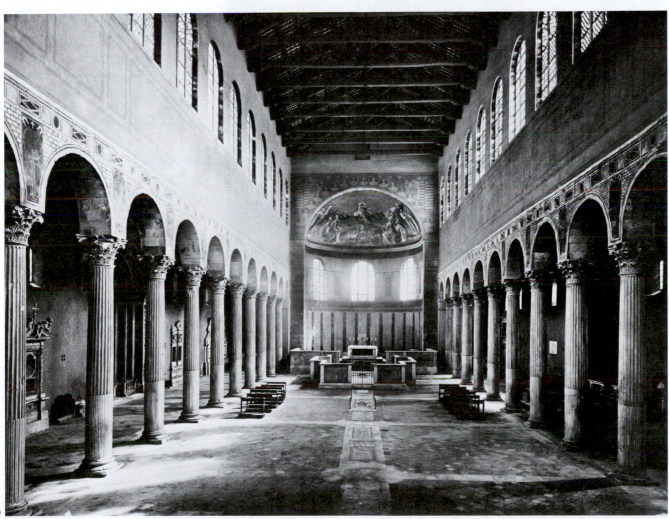

10-10

be remembered that a similar processional principle governed the alignment of spaces and structures in the Roman forum as well, especially that of Trajan (see page 259).

THE CENTRAL PLAN   A considerable number of variations could occur in the basilican plan, depending on the purpose of the building and on local traditions and requirements. An entirely different arrangement, the circular plan, was also widely used (fig. 10–11). A handsome early example is the Church of Santa Costanza (fig. 10–12), built in Rome about 350. Circular churches, unsuitable for celebrating Mass before large congregations, were almost always erected as martyria; this one was destined to contain the tomb of Princess Constantia, daughter of Constantine. Basically, of course, the circular plan is that of the Greek tholos type

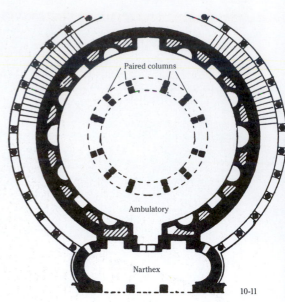

10-11. Plan of Sta. Costanza, Rome. c. 350

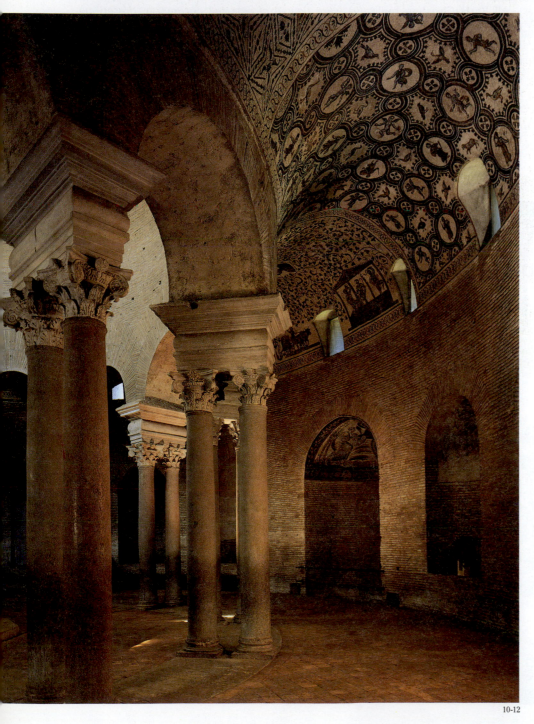

10-12. Interior, Sta. Costanza, Rome

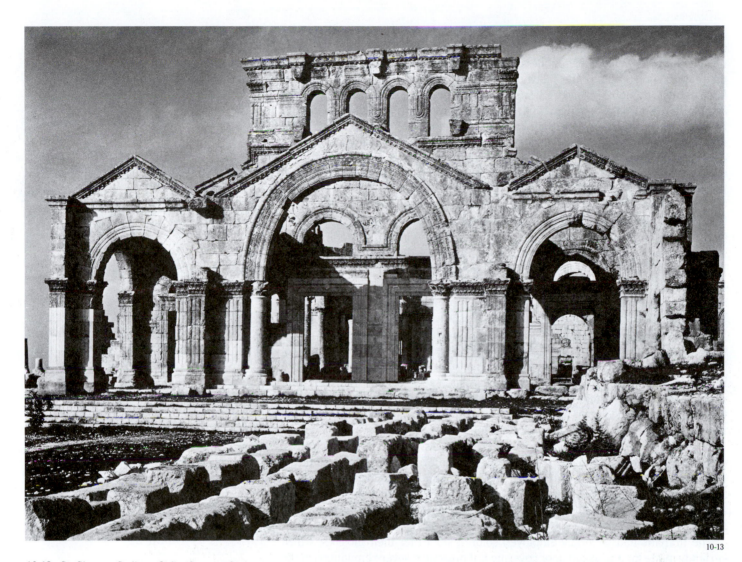

10-13

10-13. St. Simeon Stylites, Qal'at Saman, Syria.
c. 470

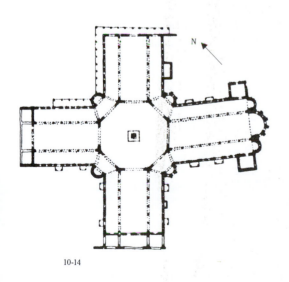

10-14

10-14. Plan of St. Simeon Stylites, Qal'at Saman

(see plan in fig. 7–15) and of its lineal descendant, the Pantheon (see fig. 9–54), but the Early Christian circular church was usually enveloped by a circular side aisle, known as the *ambulatory*, which was intended for pilgrimages and for ceremonial processions. In cross section such a church, with its elevated clerestory, would suggest a basilica, save only for the central dome. In Santa Costanza the rich mosaic decoration is still preserved in the barrel vault of the ambulatory, although that of the central portion of the church has disappeared. The coupled Composite columns in granite create an impression of outward radiation from the central space, which is enhanced by the swelling, convex frieze of the entablatures.

Any number of variations were eventually possible in the circular plan, such as its expansion into radiating apses and chapels in the sixth century (see fig. 10–28). A circular martyrium could also be combined with a basilica, as in the great church commissioned by Constantine for the Holy Sepulcher in Jerusalem. Perhaps the most spectacular fusion of a central martyrium with the basilican plan was the Church of Saint Simeon Stylites (figs. 10–13, 10–14), built about 470 at Qal'at Saman, near Aleppo, in Syria, a province that had a long tradition of highly original variations on classic norms. This consists of four distinct basilicas, three with splendid entrances and the fourth with three apses, radiating outward from a central octagon, which enshrined under an octagonal timber roof the pillar on the top of which Saint Simeon spent the last three and a half decades of his life. Syrian

305

architecture is far richer in carved elements than its Early Christian counterparts in the West. Its buildings were constructed, in the old Hellenic method, of large, rectangular blocks of stone, doubtless because of the ready availability of stone in the region. The corners of the octagon are supported by piers, flanked by sixteen freestanding, monolithic, and rather stumpy columns of granite, with acanthus capitals derived from Corinthian models; the richly molded entablature sweeps up to form arches, which lead into the four basilicas and into four small chapels fitted into the reentrant angles. The general appearance of Syrian churches is squat and massive as compared with the lofty, brick-walled basilicas of the West; the treatment of moldings and other architectural members is extremely free and imaginative.

MOSAICS   The new churches completely renounced the screen architecture so dear to the Romans and had little use for monumental sculpture. A series of life-size silver statues of Christ and the Apostles, long since disappeared, once stood below a colonnade across the apse of the Roman basilica of San Giovanni in Laterano (Saint John Lateran), but they were an exception. These churches possessed no pediments or acroteria for statues, no metopes for relief, and when friezes existed, they contained no sculpture. This art, so crucial to the Greeks and Romans, was continued in Early Christian times on a grand scale only in the imperial portraits, arches, and columns erected by the emperors in Constantinople. The Christians, on the other hand, relegated sculpture almost entirely to the more modest position of sarcophagi and ivory carvings (see pages 314–16). The wall surfaces of Early Christian churches may have been deliberately kept flat so that they might be adorned in brilliant colors with complete narrative illustrations of the new religion for the instruction of the faithful.

Where these wall decorations consisted of frescoes, as, for example, the narrative cycles in the nave of Saint Peter's, they have perished, with few exceptions. Luckily for posterity, however, Early Christian artists had another alternative, less susceptible to infiltration of water, the medium of mosaic, which Hellenistic and Roman artists had habitually used where wear or water required it, for floors and for fountains and pools.

The Romans had generally employed colored stones for their mosaics, which certainly made for a resistant floor covering but presented severe limitations in the range of available colors. Both Hellenistic and Roman floor mosaics (see figs. 7–84, 7–108, 9–85) often restrict the background to a single color plane so as to preserve the integrity of a surface intended primarily for walking. Early Christian artists, however, seem to have preferred an abstract background, at first a radiant sky-blue and later gold, for its transcendental effect in many large-scale wall mosaics. When landscape or architectural elements are required, they are either reduced to vague suggestions or else sharply schematized. Yet the techniques of pictorial representation inherited from Roman art are not forgotten but float like severed but still green branches on a tide of essentially nonintellectual religious experience.

The earliest large-scale Christian mosaic was probably the one that filled the semidome of the apse of Saint Peter's in Rome, apparently using marble tesserae (cubes) as in pagan Roman work. The original was lost in the destruction of the basilica in the sixteenth century, but its composition is preserved in a fresco copy (fig. 10–15), which shows it to have been the ancestor of many other apsidal mosaics. Christ is enthroned in the center, blessing with his right hand and holding the Gospel book with his left. He is shown with long hair and beard, as usual in East Christian art, and since one set of inscriptions is in Greek, the artist may well have come from Constantinople. The scalloped semicircle above Christ symbolizes the tabernacle, or tent, of Heaven, and on either side grow palm trees, signifying the Christian victory. Below the throne flow the four rivers of Paradise, from which stags, symbols of the human soul, are drinking (Psalm 42 in the King James Version, 41 in the Douay Version). On either side of the lower register appear two

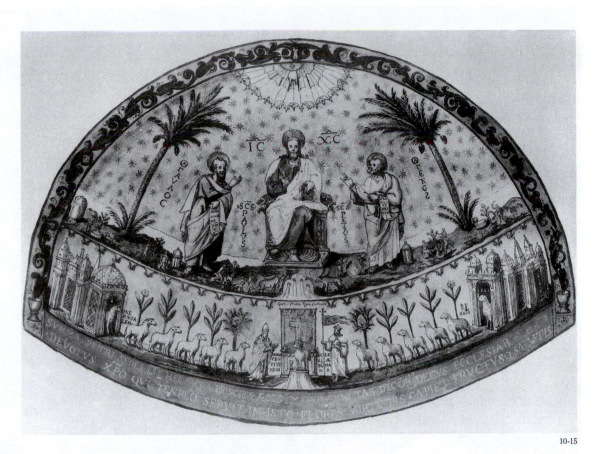

10-15

10-15. Apse mosaic, Old St. Peter's, Rome (fresco copy)

cities, labeled Jerusalem and Bethlehem, from which twelve sheep, meaning the twelve Apostles, proceed toward a central throne on which rests the Lamb of God. The two cities were reworked in the thirteenth century under Pope Innocent III, who added figures of himself and of the Roman Church and a set of inscriptions in Latin. A single, noble fragment of the original survives (fig. 10–16) and corresponds closely, even to details of the drapery folds, to the figure of Saint Paul in the fresco. The roughly matched gold-glass tesserae of the background must have been substituted in the thirteenth century for the original, doubtless a resounding deep blue as in other Early Christian mosaic backgrounds in Rome. But the figure, of exactly fitted marble tesserae like those of Roman floor mosaics, helps us to reconstruct in our imaginations the lost original mosaic, which must have been a magnificent work, and forms a precious witness to its remarkably classical style and appearance. Saint Paul's bald forehead and straight Greek nose are beautifully modeled in tone, and his hair, beard, and drapery are executed in patches of clear, bright color that preserve in the fourth century all the radiance of Pompeiian illusionism.

Later on, the early Christians used glass tesserae, which instantly opened up a whole new world of glowing colors. Moreover, they exploited gold lavishly, not only for the representation of golden objects but also for that of light and even of illuminated surfaces, and with splendid effect. Entire backgrounds came to be made of gold, on a grand scale, particularly in the Eastern Empire, and the practice was perpetuated for the next millennium and longer in the gold-leaf backgrounds characteristic of Byzantine icons and early Italian painting. The glass tesserae were pressed into soft plaster, laid a section at a time over minutely planned preparatory drawings on the wall surfaces. The tesserae were never exactly leveled off, so that each one presented a slightly varied surface to the light; thus, observers, as they move, behold a constantly changing sparkle across the surface. The technique of gold glass—gold leaf applied behind clear glass cubes—was not exact, so that the

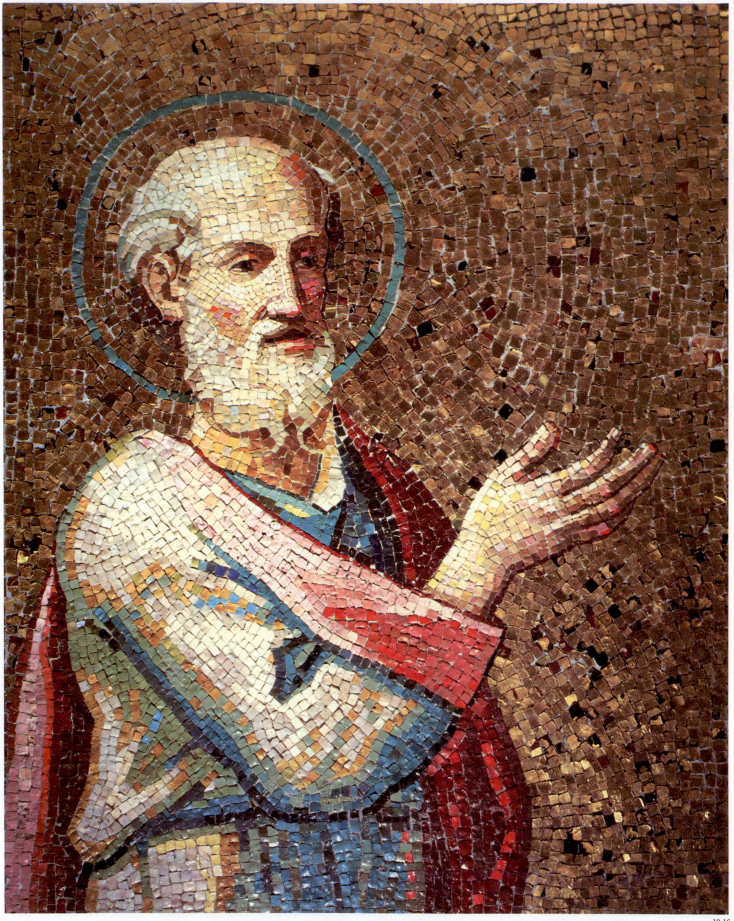

10-16

10-17

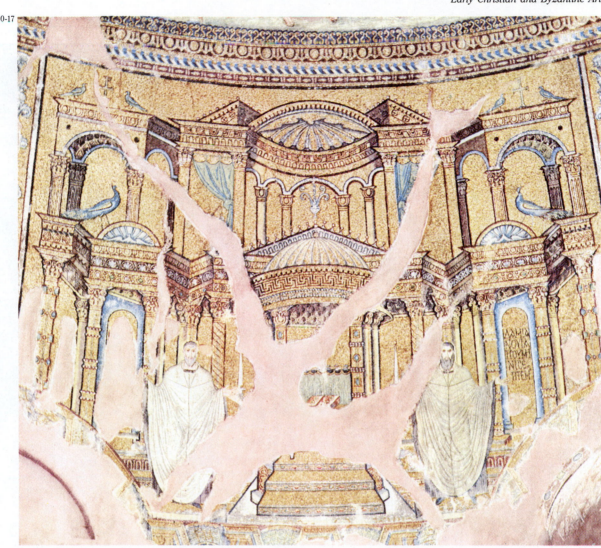

10-17. Dome mosaic, with Saint Onesiphorus and Saint Porphyrios. c. 400. Hagios Georgios, Salonika, Greece

10-16. *Saint Paul,* from the apse mosaic, Old St. Peter's, Rome

gold mosaic backgrounds have a shimmering appearance rather than the hard uniformity of more precise modern imitations.

Hagios Georgios.   One of the earliest preserved series of Early Christian mosaics (fig. 10–17 shows one section) ornaments the dome of Hagios Georgios (originally the mausoleum of the emperor Galerius, later transformed into a palace chapel) in Salonika in northeastern Greece. In imitation of the architecture of late Roman stages and other ornamental façades (see figs. 9–61, 9–62), a visionary architecture whose two stories are composed of richly interlocking columns, arches, broken pediments, niches, and coffered groin vaults, rises before us in illusionistic space. The architecture, like the background, is entirely of gold glass, but brown tesserae are used to indicate shadows; these shadows have been so subtly deployed as to convey an illusion of light reflected from below into the coffered groin vaults at either side. Shades of brilliant blue were used for curtains and to pick out such details as arches, shell niches, and the crosses at either side, the latter each accompanied by three blue-green peacocks, symbols of eternal life. Some columns are spirally fluted, others embraced here and there by collars studded with jewels. Under the dome of the tiny central tholos can just be seen an altar bearing a book with a jeweled cover (as rich, perhaps, as the one shown in fig. 13–11). Before the structure stand the martyr-saints Onesiphorus and Porphyrios in orant poses, dressed in white chasubles (the outer garment worn by the celebrant at Mass) whose soft shadows repeat the palest blue of the architecture.

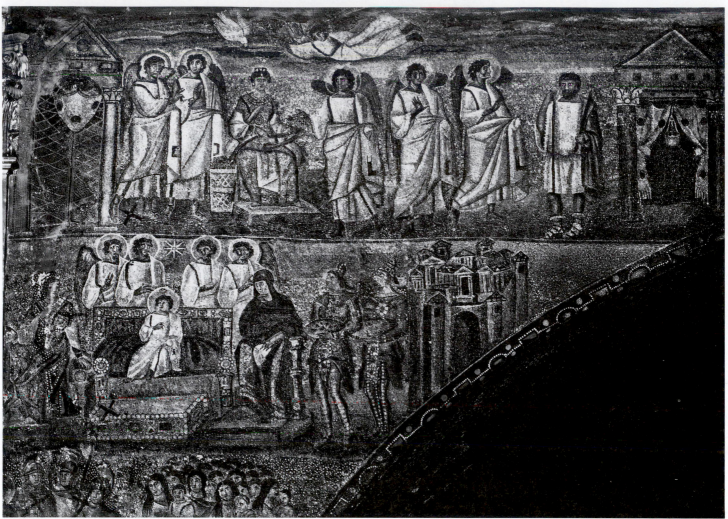

10-18

Santa Maria Maggiore.   A series of mosaics radiating imperial grandeur survives in the Roman Basilica of Santa Maria Maggiore (Saint Mary the Greater), dating from about 432–40. Instead of the architectural framework, which in Roman wall painting tied the images to the structure of the room, the triumphal arch is sheathed in mosaic. As so many Early Christian and Early Byzantine interiors show, this practice has the effect of seeming to dissolve the underlying architecture so that it is superseded by a new world of pictorial imagination. The entire left side of the arch is occupied by the first subjects drawn from Gospel narrative to be used in art, the *Annunciation* and the *Adoration of the Magi* (fig. 10–18). According to Christian doctrine, the Annunciation—the announcement to the Virgin Mary that she is to become the Mother of Christ—is the moment of the conception of his human body, brought about by the Divine Word (the Logos, or Second Person of the Trinity), conveyed by the Archangel Gabriel. Mary is seated upon a throne, robed and crowned as an Augusta (empress) of the fifth century, in all the splendor due her since the Council of Ephesus in 431 had officially proclaimed her the Theotokos (Mother of God). She is regally attended by four white-robed angels, not mentioned in the biblical text (Luke 1:26–36). She listens with one hand lifted in surprise, while Gabriel flies above her like a Roman Victory, and the white dove, which in Christian art symbolizes the Holy Spirit, descends upon her according to Gabriel's words: "The Holy Ghost shall come upon thee, and the power of the Highest shall overshadow thee." What we witness, therefore, is the moment of the Incarnation, one of the most sacred in Christian belief. The date chosen for the observance of the Annunciation was March 25, which began the Roman year; that of Christmas, nine months later, was thus automatically determined. Not until the sixteenth century in Rome and the eighteenth century in Florence and in Pisa (also in England) was New Year's Day moved to January 1, the date of the Circumcision and thus of the bestowal of the sacred name of Jesus.

At the left appears a closed gate, symbol of Mary's virginity; at the right, by a little aedicula whose hanging lamp indicates night, a majestic angel announces the momentous tidings to Joseph (Matthew 1:20). The background for both scenes is a wide plain whose horizon fades off into the sky and strips of cloud. In the lower register the Christ Child, later usually shown on Mary's lap since he was, at the time of the Three Magi's visit, only twelve days old, appears as a boy of six or seven years seated on an imperial throne and attended by four angels, while the star of Bethlehem shines over his head. Mary is barely visible, standing to Christ's right; the woman to his left may be a personification of Divine Wisdom. Christ and the angels, but oddly enough not Mary in either scene, are endowed with the golden halos used henceforward in Christian art to distinguish sacred figures. Two of the Three Kings from the East stand on one side of Christ; dressed in that fantastic Oriental garment, trousers, they present their gifts; the third king kneels at the left. Bethlehem is represented in the manner of one of the cities on the Column of Trajan as a little nugget of walls, temples, and roofs.

Twenty-seven smaller mosaics, immediately under the clerestory windows of the nave, tell stories from the Old Testament. Fig. 10–19 shows two superimposed scenes from the Book of Joshua. Above, Joshua commands the priests to bear the Ark of the Covenant across the Jordan River, which is shown piling itself "upon a

10-19

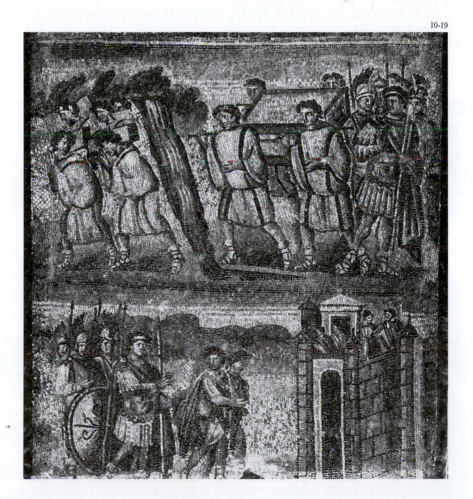

10-19. Scenes from the *Book of Joshua,* mosaic, Sta. Maria Maggiore, Rome. c. 432–40

heap" as the text states; the twelve men commanded by Joshua to bear stones from the Jordan to their lodging place have been reduced to four for the purposes of the scene. Below, Joshua sends out two spies to Jericho, this town also represented like those on the Column of Trajan. In both scenes Joshua is dressed as a Roman general, and the parallels with the Column of Trajan in poses, attitudes, and groupings are compelling. Distant space is suggested by hills of several colors, and the sky is striped with gold clouds against the blue and white tesserae. The construction of the almost cylindrical figures suggests *The Tetrarchs* (see Introduction fig. 25), but the use of color to build up these and the landscape masses is prophetic of the devices employed by Paul Cézanne in the later nineteenth century rather than of the Impressionists, of whom illusionistic Roman paintings reminded us.

The Tomb of Galla Placidia.   The finest and best-preserved ensemble of fifth-century mosaics is that which decorates the interior of the tiny mausoleum built by the empress Galla Placidia about 425–26 for members of her family at Ravenna, on the Adriatic coast of northern Italy. The administrative capital of the Western Empire had been moved in 402 by Galla Placidia's half-brother, the emperor Honorius, from Milan to Ravenna, defended from the terrible disorders of the fifth century by its surrounding marshes. In the following century the city was to reach its height under the Gothic kings and the Byzantine emperors. The customary simple brick exterior of the mausoleum (fig. 10–20), ornamented only by a blind arcade and an entablature, gives no hint of the splendors within. The walls are sheathed in smooth slabs of soft gray veined marble. The barrel vaults, the lunettes, and the walls and vault of the central lantern almost disappear under their continuous covering of mosaic. In spite of the alabaster slabs in the windows that now yellow the light, the interior is one of the most beautiful in the history of art, a refuge of serenity and peace, whose effect is impossible even to suggest in photographs. The dominant color in all the mosaics is a deep sky-blue, which in the barrel vault of the nave is studded with white, blue, and gold floral patterns in medallions that float like magic constellations in some perfect heaven.

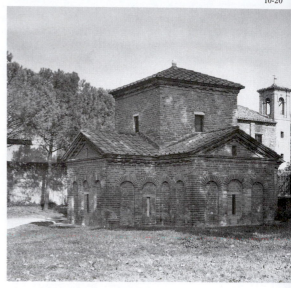

10-20. Mausoleum of Galla Placidia, Ravenna. c. 425–26

10-20

10-21. *The Good Shepherd*, mosaic, Mausoleum of Galla Placidia, Ravenna. c. 425–26

10-21

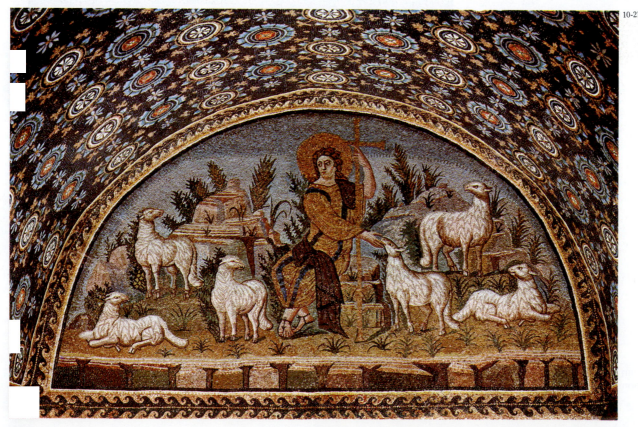

The lunette above the portal (fig. 10–21), framed by a delicate wave pattern in blue and gold, shows the Good Shepherd seated among six of his sheep in a rocky landscape, which derives from those of Roman painting. His graceful pose becomes almost a spiral as he holds the cross-staff with his left hand and with his right reaches to feed a sheep. Each rock contains a gamut of colors, ranging from gold in the lights to violet and gray in the shadows. The gold of Christ's tunic and the violet of his mantle are echoed in the distant rocks, but in softer and paler values. Rocks of about the shape shown here, but always more and more stylized, remained in the standard repertory of landscape settings throughout the millennial history of Byzantine art, after which they were taken over by early-fourteenth-century Italian painters.

THE ILLUMINATED MANUSCRIPT In addition to mural decoration, a second extremely important field for paintings was the *illumination* (illustration) of manuscripts, which were the only form of books made in Europe until the importation of printing from China in the fifteenth century. Egyptian manuscripts had been written on long rolls of papyrus (see pages 98–99 and fig. 3–48), and such rolls, known as rotuli, were adopted from the Egyptians first by the Greeks and then by the Romans. The rotulus was wound between two spindles, and only two or three vertical columns of text were visible at any one moment. Greek and Roman rotuli were illustrated only when necessity demanded, as, for example, diagrams to explain scientific matters; to avoid flaking, these illustrations were usually drawn in line and colored, if at all, with thin washes. The Hebrew Bible was written on rotuli; the scroll form of the Torah, although it is no longer on papyrus, is a still-surviving example. But the Christians were above all the People of the Book; they needed to be able to refer immediately to any verse in the Bible for authority and to move from one section to another to verify prophetical relationships and Gospel correspondences. They also required books for their increasingly formalized, complex, and uniform Liturgy.

An individual rotulus could only be wound to about thirty feet in length before becoming unmanageable; thus, each Greek or Roman literary work had to be divided into a number of rotuli, or "books"; the Bible required scores of them. Even in antiquity the difficulty of using rotuli for ready reference gave rise to the copying of key passages on thin wooden tablets, hinged together at the back. These were the ancestors of the familiar *codex* (paged volume), which became a practical reality only when parchment came into general use. This material, whose name is a corruption of Pergamon, where it was invented in the second century B.C., consisted of the carefully scraped, washed, dried, and stretched skins of young animals, especially lambs, kids, and calves. It could be dried to extreme whiteness, provided a smooth surface for writing and painting, and was durable enough to stand up under constant usage in the Liturgy.

We do not have enough early examples to be sure just when the parchment codex began to replace the rotulus, but recent investigations suggest that the change began during the first century A.D. and was complete by the fourth century. As we have seen (page 294), the copying of such manuscripts was one of the principal functions of the monasteries. Paradoxically enough, the finest early illuminated codex we know is a pagan work, the *Vatican Virgil,* dating from the fourth or perhaps the early fifth century. It should be remembered, however, that the Roman epic poet Virgil was considered by Christians throughout the Middle Ages as a prophet of the universality of Christianity, and his works were greatly respected. The *Vatican Virgil* is in fragmentary condition, and the paintings were executed by several hands of widely varying style and quality. One illuminator set forth his portion of the narrative with great vivacity, even if he lacked the refinement of the best Pompeiian painting. His *Miracle of Ascanius* (fig. 10–22; *Aeneid* II:1.680ff.) shows the cap of Ascanius, Aeneas' small son, catching fire mysteriously in the midst of the siege of Troy, the holy flames resisting all efforts to douse them.

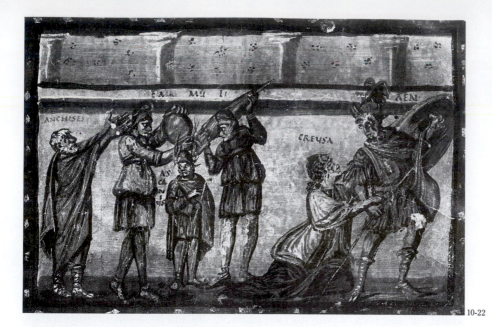

10-22. *Miracle of Ascanius,* illumination from the *Vatican Virgil.* Rome, 4th century or early 5th century. Biblioteca Apostolica Vaticana, Rome

The aged Anchises, Aeneas' father, raises his hands to the gods and is informed that this miracle is a sign that Aeneas should leave doomed Troy to found Rome. The wildly dramatic poses, especially that of Creusa, his wife, throwing herself before the departing Aeneas, recall a long tradition of Helleno-Roman sculpture (and possibly painting as well). The dismayed expression of Ascanius may appear a bit comic, but the coarse, rapid style with its strong contrasts of light and dark is very effective—on a level with catacomb painting. It is just this vivid, cursive method of narration that later formed a basis for the Christian manuscript illuminations we know from the following century.

SCULPTURE   As previously noted, little monumental sculpture was produced in the Early Christian period, and very few works survive. But marble sarcophagi were carved in great quantities. While hardly comparable in quality with the best of Helleno-Roman sculpture, the *Sarcophagus of Junius Bassus* (fig. 10–23), made for a man who died in 359, is far more accomplished than the rude contemporary reliefs on the Arch of Constantine (see fig. 9–51). Its two stories are divided into ten compartments by stumpy, spirally fluted or vine-encrusted (a reference to the wine of the Eucharist) Corinthian columns, which support niches, entablatures, and

10-24. *The Three Marys at the Sepulcher* and the *Ascension of Christ.* Late 4th century or early 5th century. Ivory panel, height 7¼″ (18 cm). Bayerisches Nationalmuseum, Munich

10-25. *Priestess of Bacchus,* leaf of a diptych. c. 390–400. Ivory, 11¾ × 5½″ (30 × 14 cm). Victoria & Albert Museum, London (Crown copyright reserved)

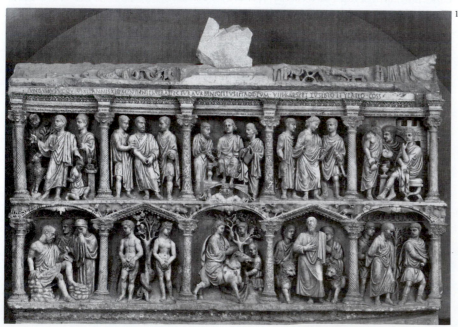

10-23. *Sarcophagus of Junius Bassus.* c. 359. Marble, 46½ × 96″ (1.18 × 2.44 m). Museo Petriano, St. Peter's, Rome

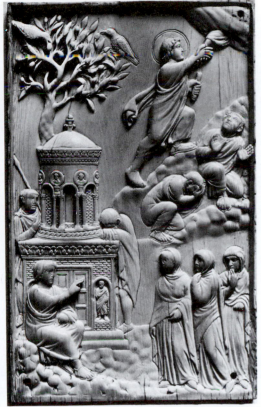

10-24

10-25

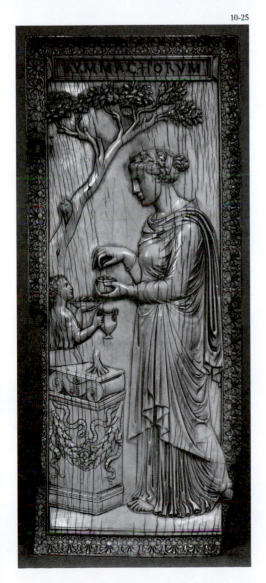

pediments drawn from the repertory of Roman stage architecture. From upper left to lower right, the scenes read as follows: the Sacrifice of Isaac, Peter Taken Prisoner, Christ Enthroned between Peter and Paul, Christ before Pilate (occupying two compartments), Job on the Dunghill, the Temptation of Adam and Eve, Christ's Entry into Jerusalem, Daniel in the Lions' Den, and Paul Led to Martyrdom. As quite generally in Early Christian art in Western Europe, Christ is shown youthful and beardless. In contrast to the dramatic style of the *Vatican Virgil,* the little figures stand or sit quietly in their fields no matter how intense the biblical narrative being enacted; they remind us, in fact, of the stately calm of the scenes on the Arch of Trajan at Benevento (see fig. 9–50). The disproportionate size of the heads, a common device in Early Christian art, allows the spectator to read the expressions, which carry the real force of the dramas, inevitably restricted by the small square fields. The little compositions serve as the coherent exposition of a single symbolic theme, the Christian victory over suffering, sin, and death. In the upper central compartment Christ appears in triumph both on Earth below and in Heaven above. Under his feet is a bearded personification of Heaven, like the personification of the Danube on the Column of Trajan (see fig. 9–48), holding a scarf over his head like those held by the personifications of Sea and Air in the Ara Pacis (see fig. 9–23). In other compartments Peter and Paul are shown fearless before their captors, as Christ was before Pilate. Adam and Eve represent the origins of death through their sin. The extreme trials of Job, Isaac, and Daniel were declared by early Christian theologians to be *types* (foreshadowings) of the Passion (suffering) and death of Christ. A properly instructed Christian could read the scenes in any order and derive the same meaning: Christ's conquest over death was predicted in the Old Testament; through Christ, man will triumph over sin and death; like Peter and Paul, man should not fear death. The figures are so heavily undercut that they are almost freestanding—the last undercut figures we will see in Western art in this book for the next 750 years. Echoes of pagan art still persist in the anatomical structure of the few legs and arms permitted to appear unclothed, and in the figures of Adam and Eve, the latter a direct descendant of fourth-century-B.C. and Hellenistic Venuses (see fig. 7–80). Soon such echoes will be heard no longer.

When necessary, the Early Christian sculptor could handle dramatic situations with simplicity and beauty in miniature, as in the numerous ivory plaques on which he carved scenes from the Old and New Testaments. One of the finest panels (fig. 10–24), dating from the late fourth or early fifth century and probably Italian, shows at the bottom right the Three Marys coming to the Sepulcher on Easter morning; the authoritative figure of the angel who tells them that the Lord is risen has been likened visually to Christ himself. At the upper right is an early form of the Ascension; Christ strides vigorously up a mountain, assisted by the hand of God the Father extended from the clouds, while two of the Apostles cower in terror. The fullness and beauty of the figures, the flow of the drapery, the power of the poses, and the intensity of the dramatic realization reveal that the most accomplished Early Christian artists remained in touch with the great Helleno-Roman repertory of form and content.

Even at this late stage, classical form in ivory carving could still convey classical content. A special field for the most delicate carving was that of the ivory *diptych* (two panels hinged together) intended for personal use; the blank inner sides could be covered with wax for writing with a stylus. An exquisite example is a leaf from the late-fourth-century diptych (fig. 10–25) celebrating the union in marriage of two families of senatorial rank, the Nicomachi and the Symmachi, who remained loyal to the old religion in spite of the edicts of the emperor Theodosius I between 380 and 393, close to the date of this diptych, recognizing Christianity as the only legal religion and allegiance to the Holy See as the seal of orthodoxy. A priestess of Bacchus is shown celebrating a sacrifice at his altar, with astonishingly classical grace and beauty. The folds of her garments fall in lines of a delicacy we have not seen since the Ara Pacis Augusti. Yet little bits of spatial and formal ambiguity betray the real date of this tiny masterpiece; the lovely priestess inside the classical frame nonetheless overlaps it in two places, and her left leg and heel are seen from behind without apparent connection with the body. Classicism is by now nostalgic; the contrapposto that was its hallmark has dissolved.

The Age of Justinian

For the Western Roman Empire the fifth century was a period of almost unmitigated disaster. In addition to the struggles between rival claimants to the imperial throne, Rome was sacked in 410 by the Visigoths, a Germanic people led by Alaric, and threatened in 452 by the Huns, a ruthless Mongol nation, under their king Attila, who died suddenly in 453. Another Germanic group, the Vandals, sacked Rome a second time, very methodically, in 455. Largely in ruins, the city was reduced to the status of a provincial town, with a greatly decreased population. By the time of the deposition of Romulus Augustulus, the last Roman emperor of the West, in 476, Italy lay devastated from constant warfare, and large areas of farmland had returned to wilderness. In 493 the Christianized Ostrogothic chieftain Theodoric captured Ravenna from the Visigoths and attempted to bring order out of the chaos. He made Ravenna the capital of his new kingdom of Italy, the first medieval monarchy, and established a splendid court there.

Soon after Theodoric's death in 526 his kingdom fell apart. A powerful new figure, Justinian I (ruled 527–65), ascended the throne of the Eastern Roman Empire—which from now on we may as well call by the name it has acquired in history, the Byzantine Empire. Although they generally spoke Greek and were in many respects the custodians of Greek culture, the Byzantine rulers maintained to the end their position as legal heirs to the Roman Empire and always referred to themselves as Romans. Justinian (who spoke Latin) dedicated his reign to restoring the stability of the Empire against the Huns, the Slavs, and the Parthians in the East and to reconquering the West, especially North Africa and Italy, from the Vandals and the Ostrogoths. In 540 the imperial forces captured Ravenna and afterward maintained it as their center of power in the West; by 555 Justinian's armies had reestablished Byzantine rule throughout Italy, driving the Ostrogoths across the Alps to a still-unknown fate. The Byzantines could not hold all of northern Italy, but before the end of the sixth century they had established the Exarchate of Ravenna, which kept Adriatic Italy and much of southern Italy in the Byzantine fold for two centuries.

Like Constantine, Justinian maintained firm imperial control over the affairs of the Church in the East, especially in regard to the establishment of dogma as well as the extirpation of heresies, which flourished like weeds in the early centuries of Christianity. During the interregnum of Visigothic and Ostrogothic overlordship of Italy, the popes had acquired a certain independence from the constantly changing and always insecure secular control. This freedom encouraged papal claims of supremacy over the other patriarchs of Christendom, who by no means universally agreed. Pope Gelasius I (492–96) went so far as to proclaim ecclesiastical superiority over imperial power, a claim renewed countless times by his successors for more than a millennium. Meantime, the chaotic conditions prevailing throughout the West strongly favored the establishment of monastic communities, which had long flourished in the East, as a refuge from secular disorder. In 529 Saint Benedict of Nursia founded the great order that bears his name and that spread throughout Western Christendom. Ruled from the Abbey of Monte Cassino in southern Italy, the Benedictine order, in fact, not only became the greatest single force directed toward the reform and discipline of monasticism, but also assumed responsibility for the transmission of the heritage of classical learning to the early Middle Ages through the preservation and copying of manuscripts—a responsibility discharged in the East by Byzantium.

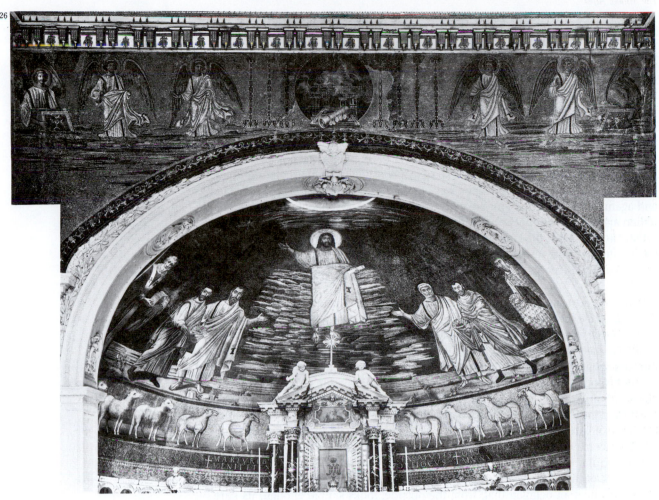

10-26. *Christ with Saints,* mosaic, Ss. Cosma e Damiano, Rome. c. 530

ROME Remarkably enough, considering that Rome had by then been reduced to a town of about fifty thousand inhabitants living under conditions of great economic and political disorder, Roman pictorial tradition was by no means dead. About 530 Pope Felix III commissioned the creation of one of the finest mosaics of the entire Middle Ages to celebrate the remodeling of a Roman temple into the Church of Saints Cosmas and Damian, two physician-martyrs. The mosaic, later reduced in size and disfigured by the addition of a plaster arch, fills the entire triumphal arch and apse (fig. 10–26), but is difficult to photograph on account of its concave surface. On either side the white-robed figures of Peter and Paul turn to look toward the spectator as they present Saints Cosmas and Damian, who in turn offer their crowns of golden oak leaves. At the extreme left, hardly visible in the photograph, Pope Felix holds forth a little model of the temple that he caused to be transformed into the church. In the center of the triumphal arch, the Lamb of God is shown upon his throne, which stands among the seven candlesticks of Revelation (1:12–20); on the footstool lies a rotulus sealed with seven seals. Four angels appear, two on either side, and at the extreme right and left another angel and an eagle, holding codices, are visible. The angel and the eagle are the symbols of the Evangelists Matthew and John (the winged lion of Mark and the winged bull of Luke have disappeared), and they are among the earliest monumental examples of a theme that reappears throughout Christian art.

The center of the mosaic is filled with a vision of overpowering splendor to which the entire composition is directed: on a pathway of sunset clouds, gold, yellow-orange, and red, against a sky of dazzling blue, the gold-robed Christ walks to us from beyond the stars, his left hand holding a scroll, his right extended in the familiar oratorical gesture of Roman tradition (see Introduction fig. 26 and fig. 9–19). As in the apse mosaic of Saint Peter's (see fig. 10–15), Christ is represented as bearded in contrast to the boyish figure in images of the Good Shepherd and on sarcophagi (see figs. 10–21, 10–23). Below the vision appear the Twelve Apostles symbolized by twelve sheep, as at Saint Peter's. In the apse mosaic of the Church of Saints Cosmas and Damian, the real world is restricted to a narrow band of green plain traversed by the shadows of the standing figures; we look above and beyond it into a heavenly realm, which replaces the time and space of our experience, just as all worldly phenomena yield to the coming of the Son of Man "in the clouds of heaven with power and great glory" (Matthew 24:30). This revelation of ultimate spiritual power may well have been a source of consolation to the shattered Rome of the sixth century. The composition was extremely influential, being copied again and again in Rome throughout the early Middle Ages, and it deeply impressed the Italian artists of the Renaissance. Throughout the long centuries to follow, mosaic art still flourished in the churches of Rome in always more simplified and stylized form until the great revival of painting at the end of the thirteenth century under Pietro Cavallini (see fig. 19–7).

RAVENNA   During the last years of the Ostrogothic kings and the first decades of Byzantine rule in Ravenna, the city was enriched by a series of new ecclesiastical monuments; even the most complex were built of local brick, and their interiors were adorned by columns and incrustations in colored marbles and gorgeous mosaics while the exteriors remained austerely simple. Although in purpose it derived from the central-plan martyrium, such as Santa Costanza (see figs. 10–11, 10–12), San Vitale at Ravenna (figs. 10–27, 10–28) was built about 525–47 on a subtle and intricate plan deriving from such Roman ancestors as the concave-and-convex structures in Hadrian's Villa at Tivoli. Concrete would seem to be called for; its absence may be explained by the difficulty of obtaining the great quantities of timber required for molds and centering during the chaotic economic and political conditions of the early Middle Ages.

San Vitale is an octagon that, from the outside, looks simple enough. Its bare brick walls, rising to the height of the second story, are broken only by arched windows and shallow buttresses. The central octagonal lantern is equally simple. The plan and interior view (fig. 10–29), however, show that only the outer walls are truly octagonal. The central space is enveloped on the ground story by an ambula-

10-27

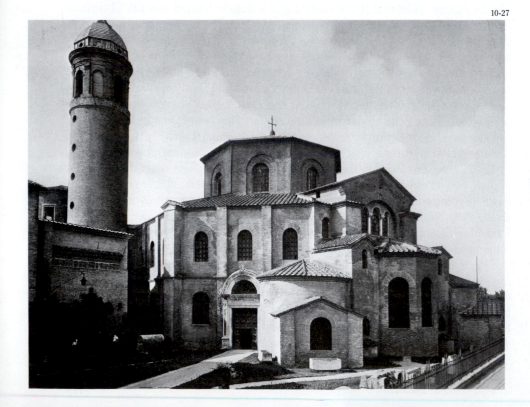

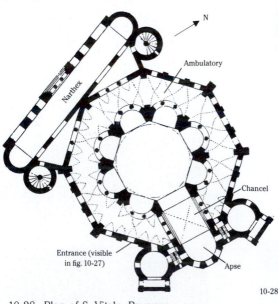

10-27. S. Vitale, Ravenna. c. 525–47

10-28

10-28. Plan of S. Vitale, Ravenna

tory and on the second by a gallery. At the eight inner corners of the ambulatory stand large piers, sustaining eight great arches, which embrace the smaller arcades of ambulatory and gallery. Instead of being flat, as we would expect, these arcades are concave with respect to the central space, expanding from it to form, as it were, seven transparent apses; the eighth is replaced by the chancel with its central altar. Even the crowning lantern is not octagonal; its corners are rounded off by tiny arches, called *squinches* (see fig. 10–38), between the windows, which cut the drum in the interior into sixteen sides. The squinches are difficult to make out through the later decoration (a clearer view, in the Katholikon at Hosios Loukas, is given in fig. 10–54).

Entering the church through the narthex, whose odd angle deflects the presbytery and apse from the east-west axis and is as yet unexplained, the worshiper proceeds through the ambulatory and then into the central octagon, with its expanding spaces, filled with light from the eight arched windows of the lantern. The impression of dazzling spatial complexity is enhanced by the colorism of the interior. The columns are of veined marble, and richly colored marble sheathes each pier up to the springing point of the smaller arches. The very capitals have been transformed (fig. 10–30); no longer is there the slightest reference to any of the classical orders with their elegant articulation of parts. These capitals resemble baskets, and their smooth, sloping sides mask a subtle transition of shape from a square at the top to a circle at the bottom; instead of acanthus leaves, sculptured in depth, they are covered with a continuous interlace of vinescrolls drawn on the surface, incised, and then painted to make them appear even more intricate. All the marble work was imported from the East, where Theodoric, who died in 526, had spent ten years as a hostage.

The entire chancel—apse, side walls, lunettes, jambs, arches, and crowning groin vault—is clothed with a continuous garment of mosaics in gold and other bright colors down to the level of the marble incrustation (fig. 10–31). Most of the subjects were drawn from the Old Testament and chosen so as to prefigure the Eucharistic sacrifice. For example, as one looks across the chancel before the altar, one sees in the lunette of the arch, below two soaring angels carrying the Cross in a golden medallion, two scenes from the story of Abraham. On the left Abraham brings to the three angels—whose appearance to him was considered by theolo-

10-29. Interior, S. Vitale, Ravenna

10-30. Marble capital with vinescroll interlace, S. Vitale, Ravenna

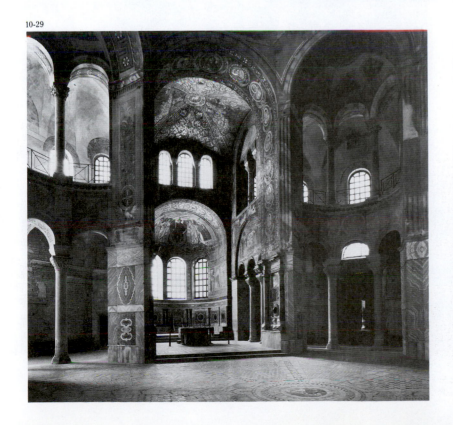

10-29

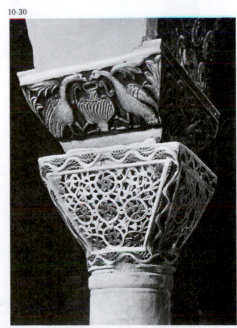

10-30

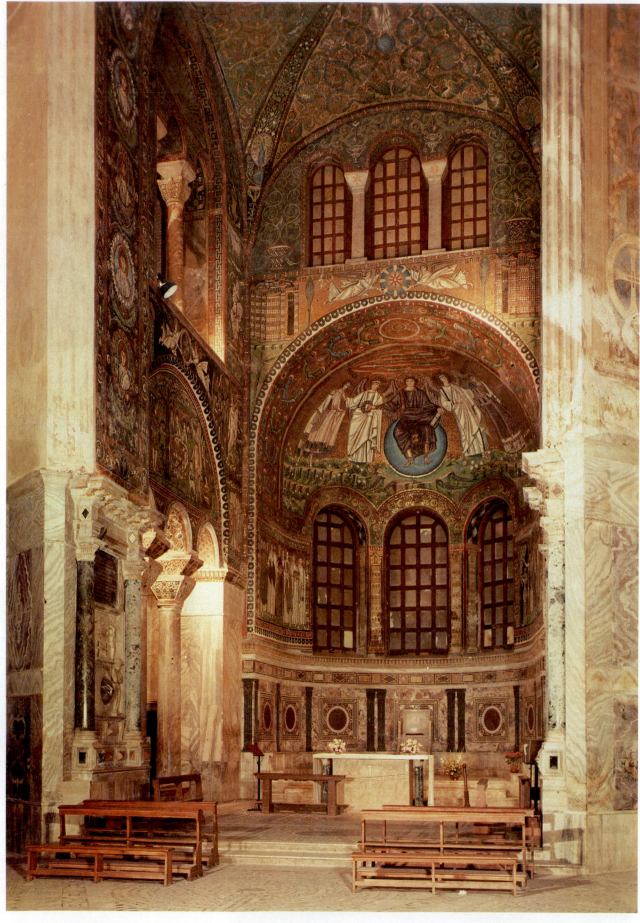

gians a revelation of the Trinity (see fig. 15–36)—a meal believed prophetic of the Eucharist. On the right he prepares to sacrifice his son Isaac, an event believed to foreshadow the sacrifice of Christ. Christ appears in Paradise in the semidome of the apse as a youthful, short-haired, and beardless figure, robed as usual in West Christian art in imperial purple and gold, and enthroned upon the orb of the heavens. The Cross, once an instrument of execution, is now the jeweled ornament of his great golden halo. From the rocky ledges below him gush the four rivers of Paradise. On either side stands a white-robed angel; one presents Saint Vitalis, to whom the church is dedicated and who holds forth hands veiled by his gold-embroidered cloak to receive from Christ a jeweled crown; the other angel introduces Bishop Ecclesius, who commenced the construction of the church, of which he holds a charming if inaccurate model. Rocks, flowers, rivers, even the figures are strongly conventionalized: no hint of bodily structure underlies the thick, tubular folds of their drapery; their feet seem hardly to rest upon the ground. In ostensible conversation with each other, these solemn figures exchange not a glance; they gaze outward, above and past us, united in inner consciousness of the surrounding glory. But none of the conditions of the real world apply any longer to this symbolic and timeless realm. Christ does not really sit upon his orb, but floats in front of it; nor does the orb rest upon the ground, but is divided from it by a strip of gold. Most of the work was completed before the Byzantine conquest in 540.

On the side walls of the chancel are two imperial mosaics. To the left of the altar is the emperor Justinian, flanked by high officials, soldiers, and priests (fig. 10–32), and, to the right, the empress Theodora (fig. 10–33) even more richly crowned than her husband, among the ladies of her court. Both figures, robed in imperial purple, stare calmly at the observer; without looking up Justinian presents a golden bowl, and Theodora a golden chalice, to Christ in the semidome above. Attempts have been made and disputed to connect these scenes with moments in the Liturgy, especially the processional offering of bread and wine at the altar. But Theodora never took part in such processions in Constantinople, going straight from the palace to the gallery reserved for women, and although she appears here before a shell-niche flanked by two different kinds of curtains and next to a small fountain, Justinian and his attendants stand on plain green, against a gold background. Clearly one symbolizes the palace, the other the outer world. Moreover, both bowl and chalice are conspicuously empty. And finally, neither Justinian nor Theodora ever saw Ravenna.

More likely the two mosaics, in keeping with the rest of the cycle, are symbolic. Emperor and empress, confirming their power, status, and new patronage of the building commenced by Theodoric, present rich liturgical gifts to Christ, just as the Three Magi are doing on the border of the empress's *pallium* (interestingly, only two are visible, both holding bowls resembling that of Justinian). If anything, these figures are more completely rigid and immobile than those of the apse mosaics, oddly enough since the faces are strongly characterized portraits, doubtless copied from models sent from Constantinople. Both Justinian and Theodora wear golden halos with red borders, like that of Saint Vitalis, startling enough considering Theodora's early life as an entertainer of easy virtue. (As empress, it should be mentioned, she carried on a determined campaign to stamp out prostitution as a degradation of women.) The emperor appears as Vicar of Christ on earth, the empress as his divinely ordained helpmeet. Haunted as Justinian was by his dreams of revived Roman glory, his anxiety-ridden countenance is quite as believable as the steady gaze of his astonishing wife. We might also recall that it was Theodora's courage fifteen years earlier that saved the day (see page 324) when Justinian was about to flee for his life before his enemies. "Purple," Theodora announced to the vacillating emperor and his generals, "makes a fine shroud." Sadly enough it did, the year after the probable date of this mosaic. Theodora died of cancer in 548, leaving Justinian desolate and, for a while, completely unnerved. In the midst of all this splendor, other portraits must be accurate as well, especially

10-31. Chancel, S. Vitale, Ravenna

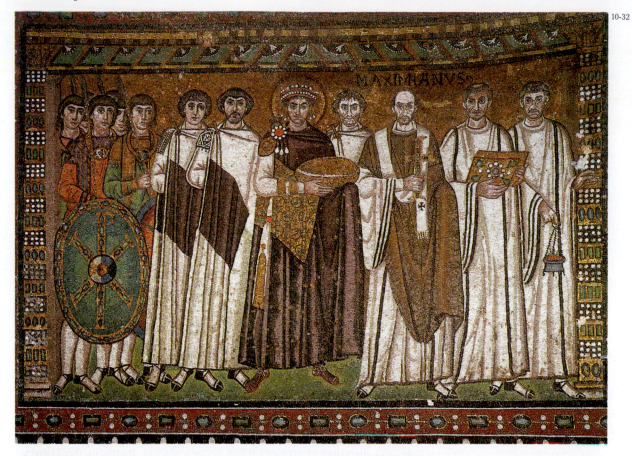

10-32

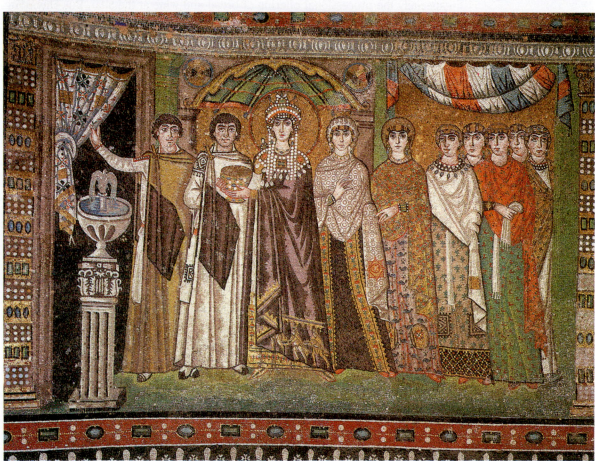

10-33

10-32. *Emperor
Justinian and
Attendants,* mosaic,
S. Vitale, Ravenna.
c. 547

10-33. *Empress
Theodora and
Attendants,* mosaic,
S. Vitale, Ravenna.
c. 547

10-34. Apse mosaic,
Sant'Apollinare in
Classe, Ravenna.
c. 533–49

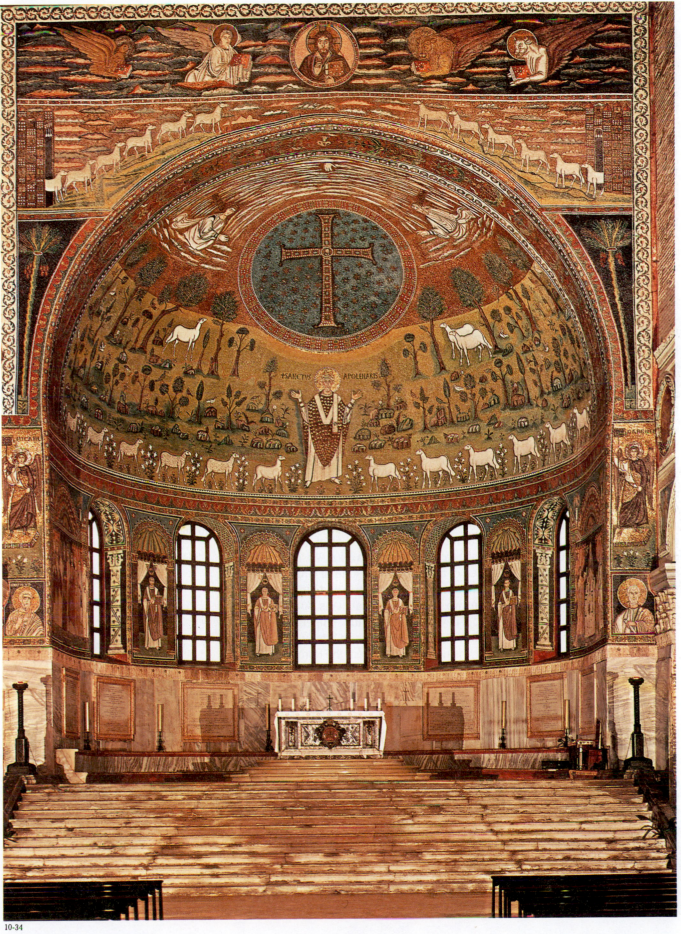

that of Bishop Maximianus, during whose episcopate the church was consecrated, which depicts even the gray stubble on his cheeks and chin. What we witness in these mosaics is the transformation of a highly developed, naturalistic art into a transcendental and symbolic one, with a new and attenuated proportion system, which still retains traces of the old Helleno-Roman illusionism in the treatment of light and surface.

A wholly symbolic representation, executed in mosaic between 533 and 549, fills the apse of Sant'Apollinare in Classe (fig. 10–34), located at the site of the old Roman port of Classis, a few miles outside Ravenna. As in the Basilica at Trier (see fig. 9–83), the exterior walls are of unadorned brick. Curtains part in the little aediculae between the windows to reveal deceased bishops of Ravenna in orant postures (several are buried in the church). The half dome is partly filled with a green pasture, at the bottom of which twelve sheep, symbolizing the Twelve Apostles, march in single file on either side of the orant Saint Apollinaris, wearing a purple chasuble ornamented with gold. Above him, against the gold background, a circle of jewels encloses a giant disk of blue sown with gold stars, on which floats a golden cross studded with gems, as if appearing to the saint in a vision. On either side of the disk Moses and Elijah, depicted to the waist only, are surrounded by clouds to indicate that they, too, are visionary apparitions. Below them among the trees three lambs look upward. These figures in the upper part of the apse symbolize the Transfiguration and portray that moment when Christ, who had climbed to a mountaintop with Peter, James, and John, was suddenly transfigured in raiment "white and glistening" (Luke 9:29) and Moses and Elijah were miraculously revealed in conversation with him. Christianity, no longer a new religion, has created its own language of symbols in which it can address the faithful with complete confidence that it will be understood. The mosaics of the triumphal arch, which show sheep emerging from Bethlehem on one side and from Jerusalem on the other before Christ flanked by the symbols of the Four Evangelists, were added in the seventh or eighth century.

CONSTANTINOPLE After a catastrophic revolt in 532, in which half the city was destroyed and Justinian nearly lost both his crown and his life, the emperor embarked on an ambitious program of rebuilding the churches of his devastated capital, including the Constantinian Basilica of Hagia Sophia (Holy Wisdom), which had burned to the ground. He dreamed of an entirely new kind of church bearing slight relation to the accepted basilican form. Instead of entrusting his bold idea to an experienced architect, he called in two noted mathematicians, ANTHEMIUS OF TRALLES and ISIDORUS OF MILETUS. They carried out the emperor's bidding faithfully; despite its many later vicissitudes, Hagia Sophia is an utterly original and successful structure, which makes surprising departures from the Roman tradition of building and—save for the imitations built by the Turks a thousand years later—remains unique.

Its plan (fig. 10–35) combines the longitudinal axis typical of a basilica (fig. 10–36) with a centralized arrangement of elements. At the corners of an area one hundred Byzantine feet square (a perfect proportion of perfect numbers) rise four piers, each seventy feet high, upholding four great arches. The arches are connected by *pendentives,* which may best be described as triangles with concave sides drawn upon the inner surface of a sphere. The upper edges of the pendentives join to form a continuous circle on which a dome may be erected (figs. 10–37, 10–38). Not only do pendentives provide a more graceful transition from a square or polygonal base to a round dome than is possible with the use of squinches, but they also permit the covering of a far greater area of floor space than is allowed by a circular base. The origin of pendentives remains unknown, but they were used for the first time on a large scale in Hagia Sophia. Henceforward, they were employed exclusively to support large domes in Byzantine architecture and later in the Renaissance, the Baroque period, and modern times. The pendentive was un-

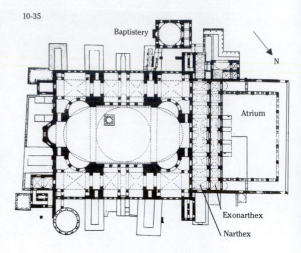

10-35. ANTHEMIUS OF TRALLES and ISIDORUS OF MILETUS. Plan of Hagia Sophia, Istanbul (after M. Trachtenberg and I. Hyman). c. 532–37

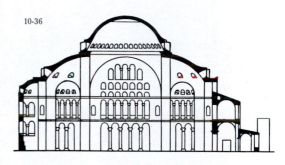

10-36. ANTHEMIUS OF TRALLES and ISIDORUS OF MILETUS. Section of Hagia Sophia, Istanbul (after Gurlitt)

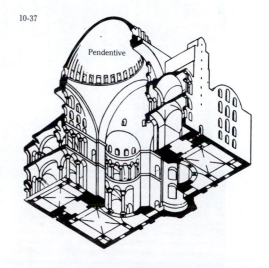

10-37. ANTHEMIUS OF TRALLES and ISIDORUS OF MILETUS. Isometric view of Hagia Sophia, Istanbul (after W. MacDonald)

doubtedly the greatest Byzantine contribution to the technique of building. The dome of Hagia Sophia is somewhat less than a hemisphere and is composed of forty ribs meeting at the center. The web of masonry connecting the ribs is slightly concave, so that the shape has been compared to that of a scallop shell (fig. 10–39). On the east and west sides the central square is prolonged by half circles, culminating in semidomes, each of which embraces three smaller semidomes, crowning three apses. Such a structure would probably have been impossible to build employing the concrete construction techniques of the Romans. Anthemius and Isidorus achieved their domes and semidomes by means of masonry constructed of bricks set edge-to-edge and only one brick deep—forming a mere shell.

The building is entered from a groin-vaulted narthex, twice the length of the central square, through a portal directly opposite the eastern apse, which sheltered the altar. The arcaded side aisles and the arcaded galleries above them are roofed by groin vaults. The cornice of the galleries marks the springing point of the pendentives and of the four arches.

Great efforts were made to support the dome. To absorb the thrust of its immense weight, and to keep it from pushing the corner arches out, huge buttresses (masses of solid masonry) were erected, clearly visible on the exterior (fig. 10–40). Beautiful as they are, the four minarets, built when the church was transformed into a mosque by the Turks after the capture of Constantinople in 1453, change considerably the appearance of the building. The reader should cover them up in the photograph in order to gain an idea of how this enormous pile of semidomes and buttresses culminating in the great central dome, towering 184 feet, originally looked.

The enclosing membrane of masonry is pierced by arched windows and by arcades in numerical arrangements, all with symbolic meaning—seven arches (the gifts of the Holy Spirit) in the galleries above five (the churches of Asia) in the side aisles, five windows above seven in the lunettes, and forty windows (the days of Lent) in the dome above five in each semidome. Since the side walls are nearly flush with their enclosing arches, the piers are hardly visible; the whole immense structure with all its shining windows and dark arches, with great domes embracing smaller ones, seems to be floating in light, an impression that must surely have been even stronger when the original decoration of gold mosaic, covered over by the Turks, delicately harmonized with the richly colored marble and porphyry of the columns and piers, and when the windows, originally more numerous than now, retained their colored glass. In fact, the chronicler Procopius wrote that the structure "seems not to rest upon solid masonry, but to cover the space with its golden dome suspended from Heaven."

The meaning of the heavenly light of Hagia Sophia can be understood only in symbolic terms. The Gospel of John (1:4–9) had defined Christ as the "light of men," shining in darkness, and Christ in the same Gospel proclaimed himself to be "the light of the world" (8:12). The Nicene Creed, adopted in 325 and still in use in Orthodox, Catholic, Anglican, and many other churches, declares universal belief in Christ as "God of God, light of light." The building itself was dedicated to Divine Wisdom, which was believed manifest in the Virgin Mary, Mother of God, in the words of the Book of Wisdom (7:26–29, omitted from Protestant Bibles):

For she is the brightness of eternal light . . . for she is more beautiful than the sun, and above all the order of the stars. Being compared with light she is found before it.

In the apse over the altar the colossal shining mosaic image of the Theotokos reminded worshipers of this mystical identification, eternal light made visible. Nor did the emperors as Vicars of Christ renounce their share of supernal splendor; one went so far as to unite pagan and Christian light by setting up a Greek nude bronze statue of the sun-god Apollo in the principal square of Constantinople, substituting

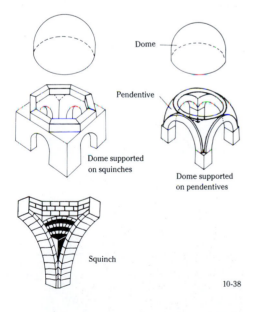

10-38. Diagram of a squinch and a pendentive

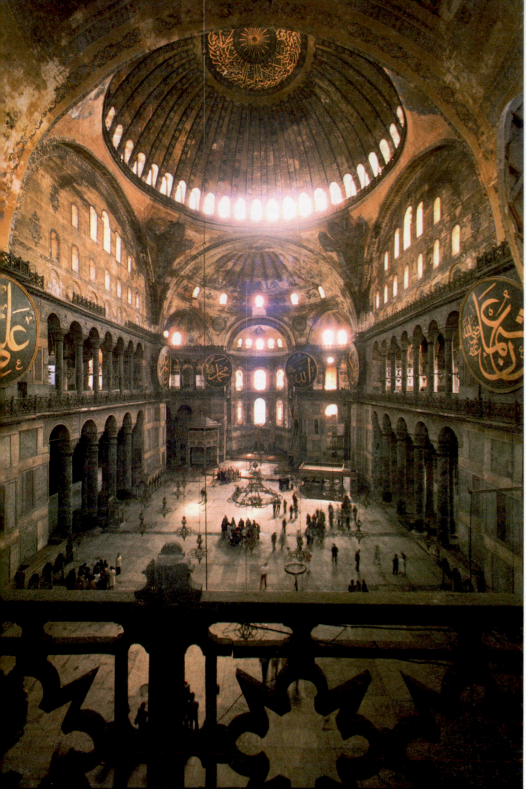

10-39. ANTHEMIUS OF TRALLES and ISIDORUS OF MILETUS. Interior, Hagia Sophia, Istanbul. c. 532–37 (Islamic medallions are later)

his own portrait for the original head, surrounded with a sunburst whose rays formed nails like those of Christ on the Cross.

The glorious impression of harmoniously blended space and light we receive in the interior today should be supplemented in imagination by visualizing the majestic processions of the Byzantine emperor and his court to the imperial enclosure at the right of the sanctuary in the south side aisle, the gleaming vestments of the patriarch and the clergy, and the incense and chanting that

10-40. ANTHEMIUS OF TRALLES and ISIDORUS OF MILETUS. Hagia Sophia, Istanbul. c. 532–37 (minarets are later)

10-41. View from the galleries, Hagia Sophia, Istanbul

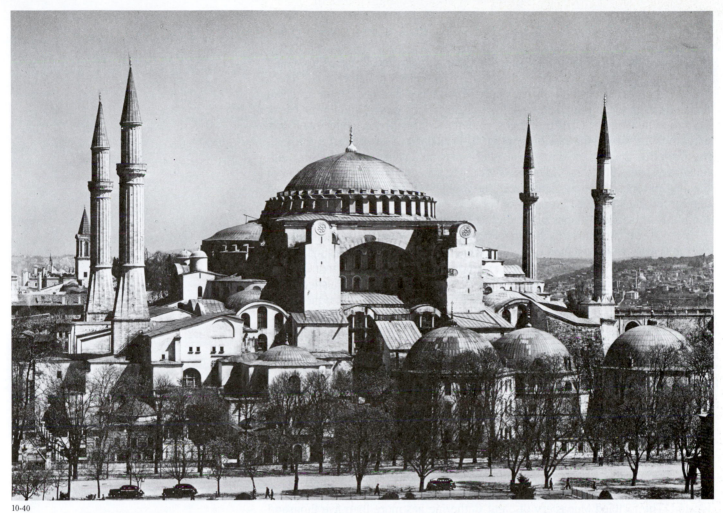

10-40

10-41

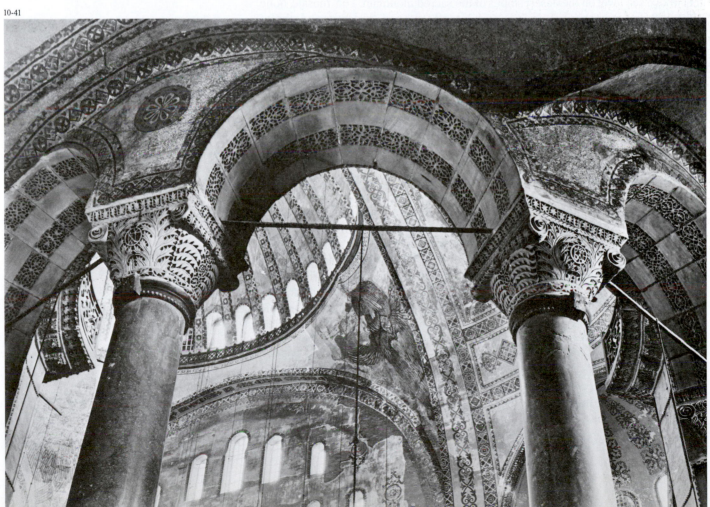

accompanied many of the rites. The congregation, restricted to the aisles, could witness only a small portion of the Liturgy, which took place, as it does to this day in Orthodox churches, behind an enclosure. The clergy emerge only at specified times, for example, for the reading of the Epistle and the Gospel and for the rite of Communion. Women and catechumens, confined to the galleries, could obtain only a fragmentary view of the vast interior (fig. 10–41), but it was a wonderful one, with the forms of the arches—curved in plan—playing against the half-seen, half-imagined spaces of the colorful nave. They could also delight in a close-up view of the new and special beauty of the Byzantine capitals—far more delicately designed and carved than those of Ravenna—out of whose undulating ornamented surfaces remnants of classical shapes protrude like half-sunken ships.

The colossal structure, by far the largest of the several major central-plan churches with which Justinian embellished his rebuilt capital, was finished in 537, after only five years' work (and a huge expenditure of money and effort). One can hardly blame Justinian for his supposed boast: "Solomon, I have vanquished thee!" However much Anthemius and Isidorus knew about conic sections, they were certainly less familiar with coefficients of safety, since their dome soon started to push its pendentives out of line and indeed collapsed in 558. The original dome was certainly lower than its replacement, completed in 563, and it perhaps continued the shape of the pendentives, forming a giant sail. The present dome has also had its mishaps, but it has been repaired, and Justinian's church has taken its place as one of the most imaginative architectural visions in the entire history of humanity.

SINAI   The otherworldly light symbolism of Justinianic art comes to its climax, appropriately enough, in a mosaic on Mount Sinai, where Moses saw the Lord in the light of the Burning Bush. This sole surviving mosaic composition commissioned by Justinian outside of Ravenna has come to general attention only very recently because of the almost inaccessible position of the church in which it is located. The fortified Monastery of Saint Catherine lies more than five thousand feet above sea level on the desert slopes of the sacred mountain. This mosaic, done after 548 and probably before 565, and recently cleaned, restored, and photographed, fills the apse of the monastery church with a representation of the *Transfiguration* (fig. 10–42), a New Testament equivalent of the luminary revelation to Moses, stated in terms of unearthly abstraction and heavenly radiance (see page 325). The Transfiguration (known as the Metamorphosis, or Transformation, in Greek) is depicted as at once sudden and eternal. The real world has shrunk to a mere strip of green at the bottom, as in the Justinian mosaic at San Vitale; all the rest of the surrounding space is gold. Blessing with his right hand, and staring over and beyond us, Christ stands at the center in an almond-shaped glory, an early appearance of the *mandorla* (the Italian word for "almond") that surrounds him in countless representations in the later Middle Ages. Seven rays of light stream from his raiment. The Apostles appear locked in the kneeling or prone positions into which the force of the miracle has thrown them, yet turn to look backward at the wondrous light with open eyes. The mandorla seems to weigh upon the back of the kneeling Peter. James and John float against the gold, while Moses and Elijah, who in the biblical text are apparitions, stand with their toes touching the green.

Faces, bodies, and drapery are reduced to hard, clear, almost geometric shapes, sometimes defined by heavy contours, showing a sharp change in style during the later years of Justinian's long reign. But if the great artist who designed the mosaic treated earthly forms as unreal, he rendered with minute precision the effects of the heavenly light, which reveals Christ's divinity to the Apostles and to Moses and Elijah. Against the four shades of sky blue into which the mandorla is gradated, Christ's glistening raiment stands forth in a pearly hue over which play magical tones of velvety white. As they cross the zones of the blue mandorla, the seven rays turn a shade lighter in each zone; they become stripes of white and cream as they traverse the gold; the rich mauves, tans, lavenders, and grays of the garments of the

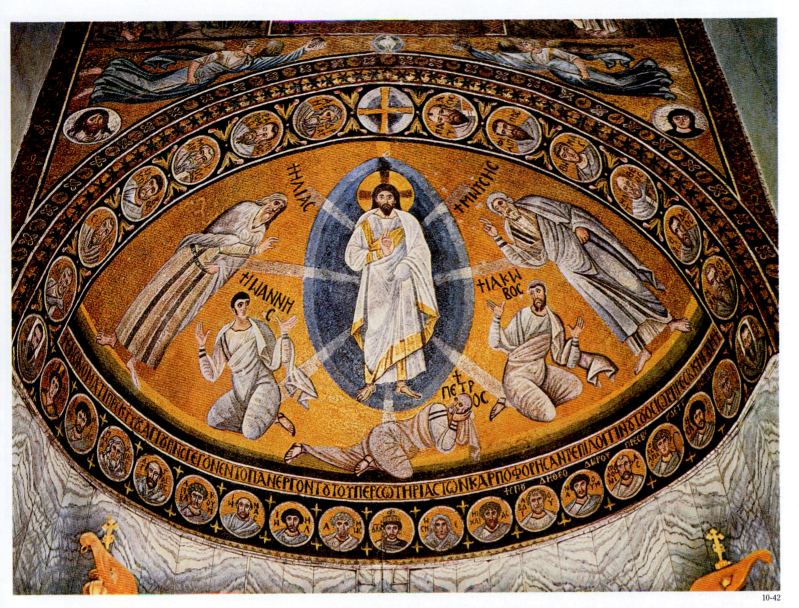

10-42

10-42. *Transfiguration,* apse mosaic, Monastery of St. Catherine, Mount Sinai, Egypt. c. 549–64

Apostles and Prophets are bleached out as the rays pass over them. No more compelling vision of the actual effects and spiritual meaning of light survives from the early Middle Ages.

The Monastery of Saint Catherine at Mount Sinai is a treasury of Byzantine panel paintings, known as *icons* ("images"). Throughout human history, as we have seen, many peoples have tended to consider images to be in some way magical (the tomb statues of the Egyptians, the images of deities of the Greeks, the emperor portraits of the Romans) and to venerate them, usually on account of the subject. However, in Christian art icons began rapidly to be endowed with miraculous powers in themselves; innumerable stories have been told throughout Christian history of the wonders performed by sacred images, and many are firmly believed to this day. As early as the sixth century, chroniclers reported accounts of suppliants kneeling before images, and the icons preserved at Saint Catherine's were doubtless intended to inspire such reverence.

Perhaps the most impressive early icon at Mount Sinai depicts a long-haired, bearded *Christ* against an architectural background reduced to the mere suggestion of a niche (fig. 10–43). His right hand is lifted in a gesture of teaching and his left holds the customary Gospel book, adorned with massive, jeweled gold covers and clasps. Probably sixth-century, although an eighth-century date has also been proposed, this may be the earliest icon of Christ to come down to us, contrasting strongly with the majestic image of the Pantocrator (All-Ruler), who in later Byzantine art appears in colossal size and majesty at the center of domes or semidomes (as once in Hagia Sophia), gazing down at the awestruck worshiper (see figs. 10–56, 10–62). The Sinai icon may be a copy of the *Christ Chalkites,* a famous icon greatly venerated by the populace and improbably believed to have been set over the entrance gate of the palace by Constantine himself. Indeed some aspects of the painting suggest knowledge of Classical Greek and Roman practice, especially the clear, sculptural modeling of the eyelids and nose, reminding us of the mosaic fragment from Saint Peter's (see fig. 10–16). Above all, however, the subject, with his pallid countenance, solemn, clear, wide-open eyes, and expression of one who has suffered—"a man of sorrows and acquainted with grief" (Isaiah 53:3)—strikes to the very heart of the observer. Instead of the terrifying images of the later mosaics the *Christ* icon conveys an impression of overpowering humanity and compassion. It is certainly one of the deepest expressions of the spirituality of Early Byzantine art.

A contrast between abstraction in the statement of form and naturalism in the rendition of light similiar to what we saw in the *Transfiguration* mosaic appears in a picture in encaustic, probably dating from the sixth century, which is at once one of the oldest-known Christian panel paintings and one of the earliest surviving examples of that favorite among all themes in the late Middle Ages and in the Renaissance, the *Virgin and Child Enthroned* (fig. 10–44). The Virgin and Child are shown royally enthroned between the warrior-saints Theodore (bearded) and George, dressed as officers of the imperial guard. Behind the throne two angels look up to an arc of blue, representing the heavens, in which appears the Hand of God (the typical method of showing God the Father in Early Christian art), from which a band of white light descends toward the figures on the throne. The Virgin appears in an almost exactly frontal pose, and the Christ Child extends his right hand in teaching while his left holds a scroll, very nearly as in the work of the Italian painter Cimabue, who was brought up in the Byzantine tradition, some seven centuries later (see fig. 19–6). The saints stand as rigidly and frontally as the imperial attendants at Ravenna (see figs. 10–32, 10–33), and the four gold halos are so aligned that they can be read, together with the Hand of God, as a cross. Even though the principal figures are so locked within this pattern that they can move only their eyes, the play of light is unexpectedly rich and the brushwork free. Variations in flesh tones, the dark circles under Mary's eyes, and the shimmer of the damasks are beautifully represented. As in the *Transfiguration,* then, illusionist vision and technique survive in the rendering of the play of light, while the grouping of the figures has been subjected to new laws of symbolic rather than naturalistic arrangement.

MANUSCRIPTS AND IVORIES   The earliest preserved Christian illuminated manuscripts seem to have been made for the imperial court. In contrast to the utilitarian character of classical books, this group of codices is written in letters of gold or silver on parchment dyed imperial purple. The finest of them is a sixth-century fragment of the Book of Genesis, now in Vienna; in reality it is a picture book, for the illustrations appear at the bottom of each leaf with just enough text to explain them written above. These little narratives move along at a lively pace on the foreground plane, like scenes on an imperial column (see fig. 9–48) without any enclosing frame or any divisions between the separate incidents, on a continuous strip of ground. No more background is represented than exactly what the story requires. For example, when Jacob tells Joseph to join his brothers where they feed the flock in Shechem (Genesis 37:13–17), there is no setting except a wayside pillar

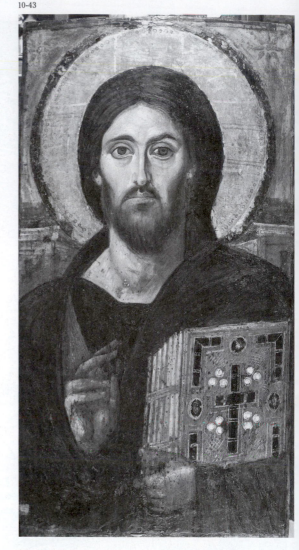

10-43. *Christ* icon, Monastery of St. Catherine, Mount Sinai. c. 6th–8th centuries. Courtesy of the Michigan-Princeton-Alexandria Expedition to Mount Sinai

10-44. *Virgin and Child Enthroned between Saint Theodore and Saint George.* c. 6th century. Panel painting, 27 × 18⅞" (69 × 48 cm). Monastery of St. Catherine, Mount Sinai

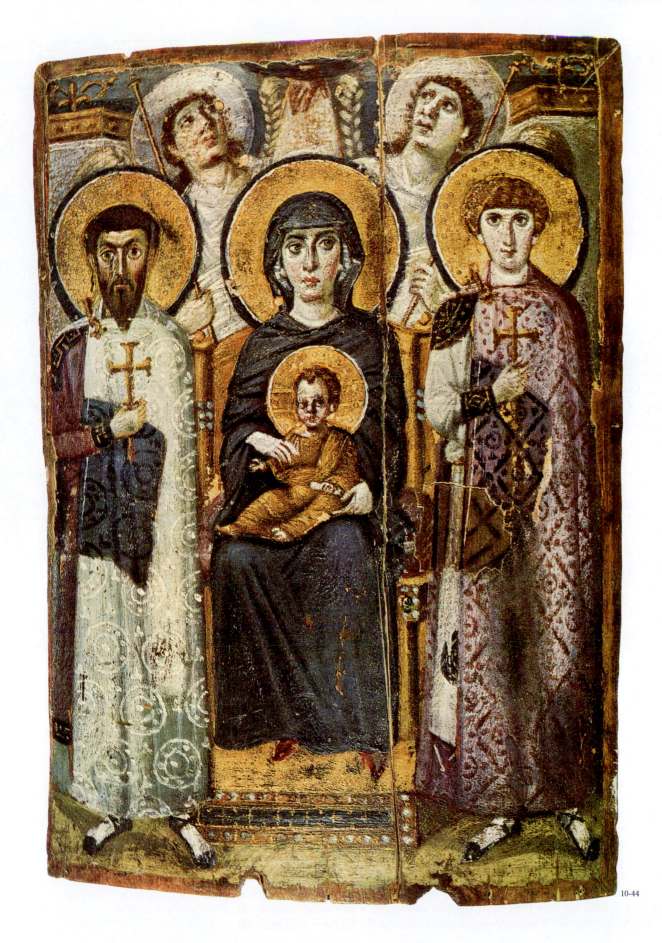

10-44

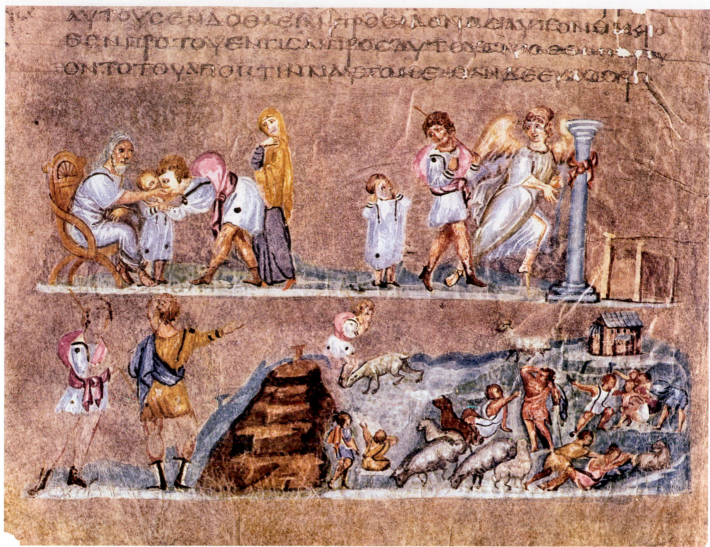

10-45

10-45. *Joseph and His Brethren,* illumination from the *Vienna Book of Genesis.* Constantinople (present-day Istanbul) or Antioch, early 6th century. Österreichische Nationalbibliothek, Vienna

to indicate the journey and a hillside when Joseph actually finds his brothers and the flock in Dothan (fig. 10–45). Otherwise, we see only the little figures themselves, shimmering in fresh and lovely colors against the parchment, which becomes by suggestion a kind of purple air. Doubtless by direction, the artist has added an element here and there. These include a touching farewell between Joseph and Benjamin, which is not in the text any more than is the angel shown accompanying Joseph on his journey.

Somewhat less luxurious is a Gospel book whose text was copied by the monk Rabula in a monastery in Syria in 586. The codex contains several full-page illustrations of great dramatic power. One of the earliest representations of the *Crucifixion* (fig. 10–46) shows Christ crucified between the two thieves; he wears a long garment—a survival of the Near Eastern tradition that nakedness was shameful (even Ionian kouroi in Archaic times were clothed). We can distinguish a Roman soldier with a sponge filled with vinegar on the end of a reed and another with the lance that pierced Christ's side, the repentant thief turning his head in a beautiful motion toward the dying Savior, Mary and John at the left, the other Marys at the right, and in the center below the Cross the soldiers playing dice for the seamless robe. Above, over the blue hills, hang the sun and moon, which were darkened at the Crucifixion. Below, in another register, can be seen the empty tomb, with the

10-46. *Crucifixion* and *The Women at the Tomb,*
illumination from the *Rabula Gospels.* Zagba on
the Euphrates, Syria, c. 586. Biblioteca
Laurenziana, Florence

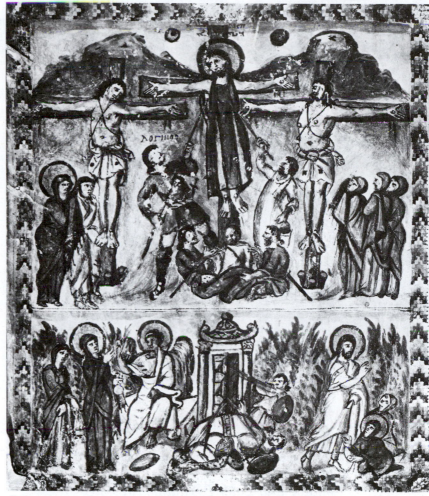

10-46

guards sleeping before it; on the left the angel tells the two Marys that Christ is
risen; on the right Christ himself appears in the garden to the Marys, prostrate
before him. Even the zigzag chevrons of the border play their part in heightening
the excitement of the narrative. The bold sketchy style recalls in some ways the
handling of the *Miracle of Ascanius* in the *Vatican Virgil* (see fig. 10–22).

A considerable number of ivory panels survive from Justinian's time, notably
diptychs, customarily given as presents to high officials on their assumption of
office. A splendid example (fig. 10–47) shows on one leaf the Virgin and Child
enthroned between two angels, and on the other Christ enthroned between Peter
and Paul; in the first the Christ Child carries a scroll to indicate his Nativity as the
fulfillment of Old Testament prophecies, and in the second the adult Christ displays
the codex of the New Testament. In the background of both, architectural space
survives only as remembered fragments, beautifully carved, yet without any real
suggestion of depth. The majestic figures seem to float before their thrones rather
than to sit upon them. Mary is a full-featured young matron; the angels who turn
their heads with such grace still retain the beauty of the Hellenic tradition. In the
strange representation of the adult Christ, shown with an unusually long beard, he
seems to have assumed the dignity we associate with God the Father. The drapery
folds, as often in Justinianic art, no longer describe the behavior of actual cloth, but
begin to develop an intense existence of their own as abstract patterns.

Justinian had overextended himself; the Byzantine forces could not continue to
hold all the territory he had reconquered. But in sections of Italy and in Asia Minor

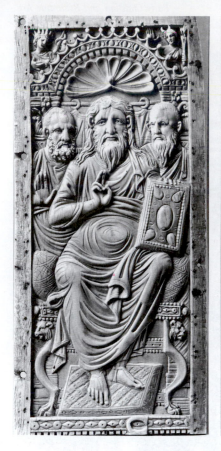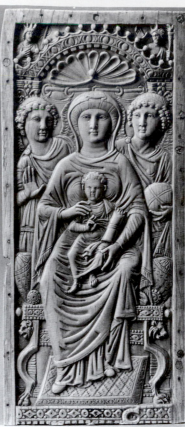

10-47. *Christ Enthroned between Saint Peter and Saint Paul* and *Virgin Enthroned between Angels.* Ivory diptych, height approx. 12″ (30.5 cm). Middle 6th century. Staatliche Museen zu Berlin—Preussischer Kulturbesitz

the Empire continued (it held sway in the Balkans for nearly nine hundred years longer), a treasure-house of classical Christian culture and a fortress against the onslaughts of Islam from the east and the Slavs and Bulgars from the north.

Middle and Later Byzantine Art

In 1944 a stroller in a dense forest of fairly young trees just west of the heavily traveled road connecting Milan with the Lake of Como came upon a small, rudely built, and totally unknown church near the village of Castelseprio; this church contained a series of small-scale frescoes of scenes from the Infancy of Christ, freely painted in an extraordinarily fresh and spontaneous style, reminiscent in some respects of the Hellenistic qualities of Pompeiian painting. In the *Appearance of the Angel to Joseph*, for example (fig. 10–48), one of the frescoes in this church, the figures, the draperies, the foliage, the rocks, and even the wayside pillar with its votive scarf must have been set down with great freedom, though on closer examination the schematic patterns in the brushwork betray that the style was not derived from observation of nature but from repeated, learned methods of rendering the effects of light. It is worthwhile noting, in this connection, that as recently as the early nineteenth century a visitor to a Greek monastery on Mount Athos watched a still-Byzantine master sketch an entire scene, full-scale, on a wall prepared for fresco in one hour without the aid of any drawing or model whatsoever. This combination of inherited compositions and techniques with great manual freedom runs through the entire course of Byzantine painting.

A controversy over the date of the Castelseprio frescoes arose soon after they became generally known at the close of World War II. Although their date remains uncertain, one early in the eighth century now seems probable. Apparently, a Greek painter was traveling through northern Italy, then controlled by the barbarian Lombards, painting wherever he could find work. Isolated though this single incident may seem, it is symptomatic of a Western need that later became endemic; when Western patrons wanted paintings or mosaics of a high quality, they often

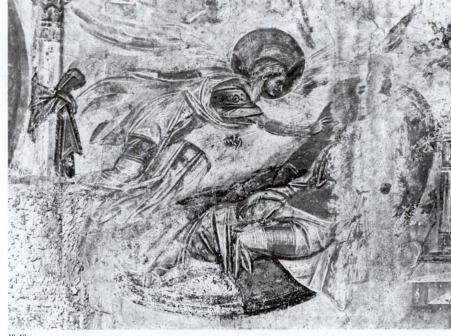

10-48

10-48. *Appearance of the Angel to Joseph,* fresco, Sta. Maria Foris Portas, Castelseprio, Italy. Early 8th century

10-49. *Virgin and Child Enthroned,* detail of the apse mosaic, Hagia Sophia, Istanbul. Dedicated 867

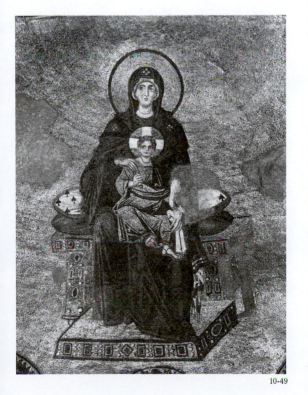

10-49

sent to Constantinople for competent artists brought up in a pictorial tradition that, from Archaic Greek times through the successors of Justinian, had remained virtually unbroken.

It is all the more tragic, therefore, that the Byzantine pictorial tradition, which for centuries constantly recharged the depleted batteries of the West, was itself menaced and for a while almost extinguished by a violent internal controversy that broke out about 726 at the court, led by the emperor himself, who deeply disapproved of the increasing attribution of miraculous powers to icons as a form of idolatry. At the height of the controversy, the possessors of images were tortured, blinded, mutilated, even executed, and representations of all sorts, including the figured mosaics that once adorned the interior of Hagia Sophia, were systematically destroyed. All the great pictorial art of the age of Justinian perished in this campaign, save only that in Byzantine Italy and in such remote fastnesses as Sinai (see figs. 10–42 to 10–44). For more than a century the struggle raged between the Iconoclasts (image breakers), who would permit only the Cross and ornament based on animal and plant forms in church decoration, and the Iconodules (image venerators), who hid their icons at great personal risk.

Although the triumph of Orthodoxy and the Iconodules was celebrated in 843, it was not until 867 that the patriarch Photios could preach a sermon in Hagia Sophia mourning the loss of the mosaics that had been scraped off the church's walls and rejoicing that the image of the Theotokos could now be restored to its former glory and that the restoration of the images of the saints would soon follow. Photios was doubtless referring to the recently re-created mosaic of the *Virgin and Child Enthroned* (fig. 10–49), which still appears in the apse of Hagia Sophia, although today in somewhat damaged condition because of the Turkish whitewash that covered it for centuries. The figures are three times life-size, but the dimensions of Hagia Sophia are so vast that the image seems tiny and is best appreciated through binoculars. It is tempting to see in the grave beauty of the Virgin's oval face and in the depth of her great eyes traces of sadness occasioned by the terrible period her devotees lived through before the triumph of Orthodoxy in 843, still celebrated as a great festival in the Eastern Church. We can certainly discern in the grace of her delicate hands, in the precision with which the drapery folds are shown as they appear along the contour, and above all in the clear definition of the masses of the body and limbs under the shimmering blue garments a new artistic ideal of refinement and definition very different from the light-mysticism of the Sinai mosaic or the entranced solemnity of the Sinai icons. The Virgin is remote, almost lost in the immensity of the golden semidome. Within a few years, however, during the latter quarter of the ninth century, many other mosaics were added to Hagia Sophia, the greatest of which was a Pantocrator in the center of the dome with angels in the pendentives. The entire ninth-century cycle has perished either in structural collapses or at the hands of the Ottoman Turks.

The last six centuries in the life of the Byzantine Empire were only intermittently peaceful. The emperors had to wage almost continuous defensive war against invasions of the Turks, Slavs, Bulgars, Avars, and Russians. Time and again invaders appeared under the very walls of Constantinople, and sieges of the capital, frequently imminent from one direction or another, were often protracted and severe. By one means or another, the Byzantines always repelled the invaders, and from time to time they regained portions of Justinian's former empire. Unexpectedly, their pagan enemies (but not the Muslims) were converted to Christianity; after some oscillation most accepted the Eastern Orthodox form. Quite as dangerous as invaders were internal dissensions, which could break out at any moment in the form of palace revolutions, often engineered by members of the emperor's family or entourage. Nonetheless, the person of the emperor was still regarded as sacred, and palace ritual was controlled by an elaborate scenario. For example, the emperor received ambassadors while seated on the Throne of Solomon, which was flanked by bronze lions and gilded trees bearing gilded birds. As the ambassadors prostrated themselves, the lions put out their tongues and roared, the birds sang (each its own tune), and the throne bearing the emperor rose nearly to the ceiling; when it descended, he was wearing a different costume. The number and riches of the palace halls, adorned with marble columns and gold mosaics, were legendary in the West. The Great Palace must have been laid out in informal groupings of chambers and buildings, somewhat on the order of Hadrian's Villa (see fig. 9–55). Possibly the Alhambra (see fig. 11–20) reflects some of the character of the Byzantine imperial palaces, whose chambers were interspersed with courtyards, fountains, and pools. When Constantinople was captured by the (Christian!) Crusaders in 1204, the Great Palace, like the rest of the city, was sacked and left a burned-out ruin. Little of its splendor remains.

THE MACEDONIAN RENAISSANCE   The Macedonian dynasty ushered in a period of intense cultural activity, especially under Constantine VII (Porphyrogenitos), a scholar and amateur painter who reigned from 913 to 959. Although their dating is still by no means certain, a group of illuminated manuscripts, whose classicism is even more impressive than that of the works of the Palace School in the Carolingian Period (see fig. 13–6), is now attributed by most scholars to the tenth century and to the personal influence of Constantine VII.

The Joshua Roll.   A wholly unique work is the *Joshua Roll* (fig. 10–50), the kind of continuously illustrated rotulus mentioned in the discussion of the Column of Trajan (see page 261). Undoubtedly the *Joshua Roll* was influenced by Roman imperial columns, two of which stood in Constantinople. The commissioning of a rotulus to depict the military campaigns of a great biblical hero may well have been prompted by a desire to commemorate allegorically the victories of the Macedonian emperors against the Muslims. In the section illustrated, two Israelite spies are sent out toward distant Jericho, then ride in search of Joshua, and finally Joshua, dressed as a Byzantine general and provided with a halo, leads his army toward the Jordan River.

Landscape elements are depicted much as they were in the *Vienna Book of Genesis* (see fig. 10–45) and in the Castelseprio frescoes, but are not restricted to the foreground plane. The illuminator has worked out an extremely effective technique for rendering foliage, rocky hillsides, and distant cities in a soft, golden brown wash, which suggests great distances and atmospheric haze. Certain details

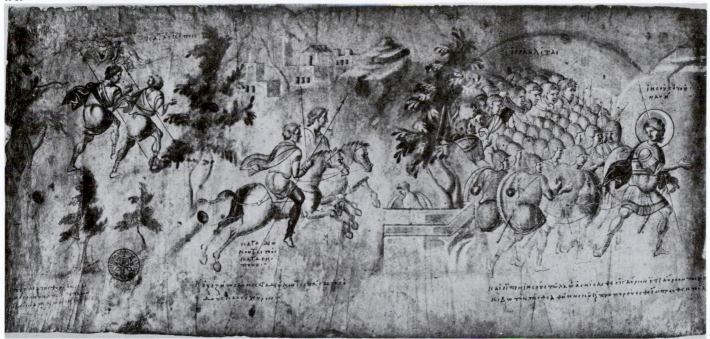

10-50. *Joshua Leading the Israelites toward the Jordan River,* detail of an illumination from the *Joshua Roll.* Constantinople (present-day Istanbul), 10th century. Biblioteca Apostolica Vaticana, Rome

(in one instance Joshua prostrates himself before the angel in the posture dictated by tenth-century court ritual) indicate that the work may not be a copy. But in all certainty the artist studied paintings of the Helleno-Roman tradition with great care. The complex, vivid action poses and the movement of the horses show a firm control of the basic principles of classical art; the rhythmic movement of the figures through landscape space is totally unexpected.

The Paris Psalter. The brilliant work of this group is the *Paris Psalter,* which contains several full-page illustrations in color, richly painted in a style so close to that of Pompeiian art (see figs. 9–16, 9–40) that it is hard to convince ourselves that we are not looking at a classical original. *David the Psalmist* (fig. 10–51) has all the appearance of an Orpheus charming the animals with his music (they are, of course, David's goats, sheep, and dog). As he plays, he is attended by a lovely Greek female figure labeled Melody; a nymph peeps shyly from behind the usual wayside column; and in the lower right-hand corner a muscular, deeply tanned, superbly painted male figure, clinging to the stump of a tree, is—of all things—the Divinity of Bethlehem! Classicism could hardly have been carried further. The scene is painted with such grace and luminosity that it is a shock to be called back to chronological reality by the stiffness and mannered quality of the drapery folds and by the parallel striations used to render light. These medieval artists could emulate classical models, possibly at the behest of the scholar-emperor, and even feel the beauty of the Hellenic style they were learning without clearly understanding the analysis of space and light that had originally given rise to it.

MONASTIC CHURCHES AND MOSAICS When the Macedonian renaissance began, Hagia Sophia and other grand-scale churches already existed in the capital, and the other large cities of the Empire were also graced with elaborate churches. These buildings were well maintained, and there was no need for more of their kind. Eleventh- and twelfth-century builders were needed for the construction of monastic buildings, intended for communities numbering a few monks, and a profusion of such churches was erected. Despite all their richness of marble paneling and mosaic decoration, therefore, these churches are by nature intimate

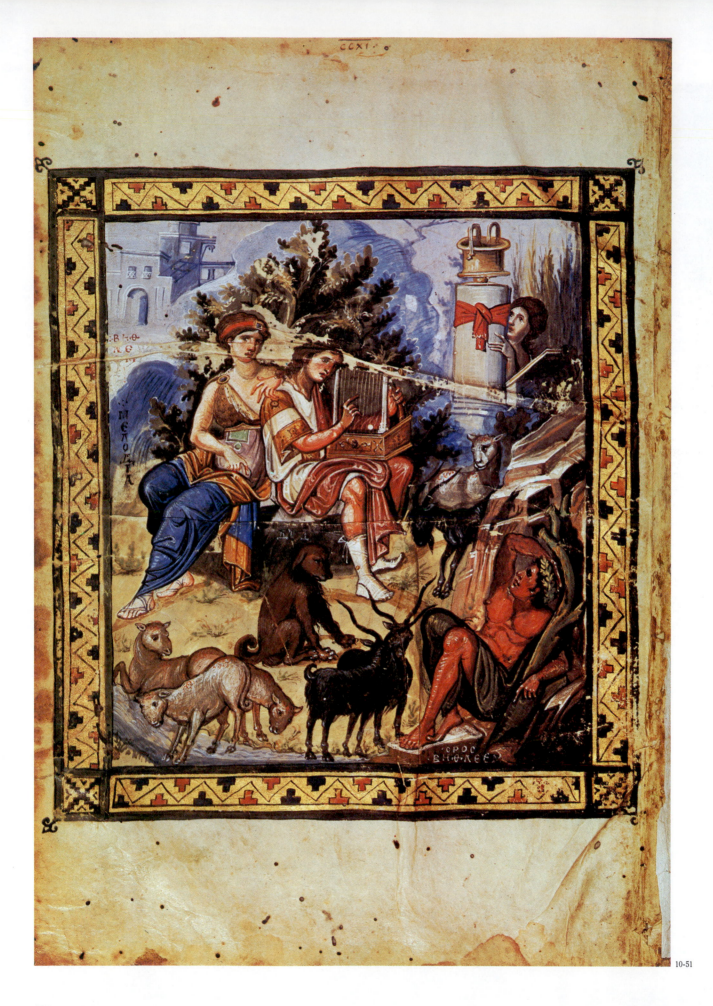

338

10-51

10-51. *David the Psalmist,* illumination from the *Paris Psalter.* c. 900. Bibliothèque Nationale, Paris

10-52. Church of the Katholikon (left) and Church of the Theotokos, Monastery of Hosios Loukas, Phocis, Greece (view from the east). Early 11th century

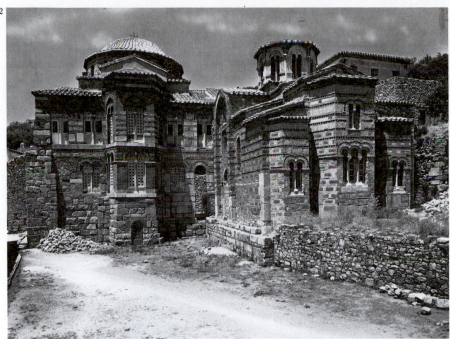
10-52

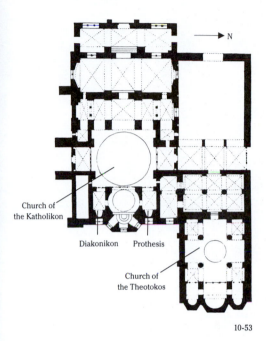

Church of the Katholikon

Diakonikon   Prothesis

Church of the Theotokos

10-53

10-53. Plan of the Katholikon and Theotokos churches, Monastery of Hosios Loukas, Phocis

in scale, designed chiefly for the celebration of the Liturgy by monks. The basic plan, which had countless individual variations, was the so-called Greek cross with four equal arms inscribed within a square and crowned by a dome. This plan maintained a central axis in that the church was prolonged on the west by a narthex and in that the east wall was broken by one or more apses.

Hosios Loukas. At the Monastery of Hosios Loukas in Phocis, between Athens and Delphi in east-central Greece, two connected monastic churches were built early in the eleventh century (fig. 10–52). Both the Katholikon and the Theotokos were laid out on Greek-cross plans (fig. 10–53); the Katholikon was provided with galleries girdling its interior. In both churches the central dome was lifted on a high drum, pierced by windows. Compared with the austerity of Early Christian exteriors, the churches at Hosios Loukas seem ornate indeed, yet the richness is one of construction, not mere decoration. Courses of stone alternate with courses of brick, set at an angle to provide even greater variety of texture. This kind of construction was used throughout Greece and the Balkans from the eleventh through the fifteenth century.

When compared with the apparently measureless space of Hagia Sophia (see fig. 10–39), the interior of the Katholikon seems at first cramped (fig. 10–54); the movement is entirely vertical, and carries the eye aloft into the dome, which is the only part of the central space lighted directly by its own windows. The light in the church is subdued, originating from windows in the galleries, in the corner spaces flanking the sanctuary, in the *prothesis* and the *diakonikon* (areas intended respectively for the preparation of the sacred elements of the Eucharist and for the storage of vessels and vestments, much like the sacristy of a Roman Catholic church), and in the arms of the transept. The dome, interestingly enough, does not spring from pendentives as at Hagia Sophia but rests on squinches as at San Vitale. In all Byzantine churches the *bema* (sanctuary) is closed off by means of an *iconostasis,* a screen bearing icons whose subjects and order are largely predetermined by tradition. Tradition also determined the order of the mosaics in a church interior. The Theotokos, enthroned or standing, adorned the semidome of the apse; the Pantocrator looked down from the center of the dome, surrounded by the heavenly hierarchy between the windows and by scenes from the life of Christ pictured in the squinches, vaults, and upper wall surfaces. Figures of standing saints decorated the lower wall surfaces. These soaring interiors, with their rich and subtle variations of spaces and lights, must always be imagined not only with their marble and mosaic

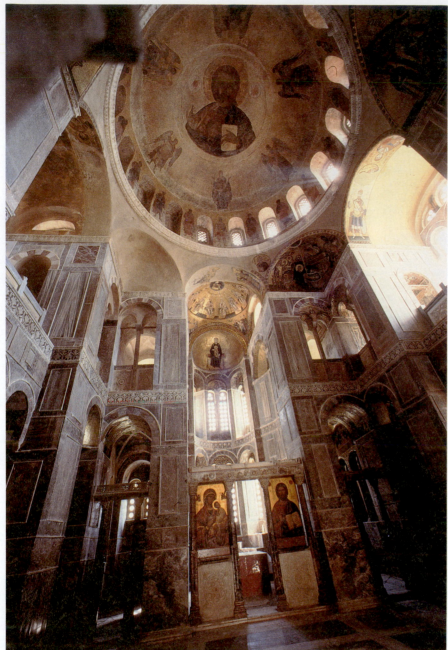

10-54

decorations but also with their Liturgy, accompanied by clouds of incense and by chanted music whose deep sonorities bear little relation to the sound of Western plainchant.

Daphni.   The finest remaining mosaics of the Middle Byzantine period are those in the Church of the Dormition at Daphni, not far from Athens, dating from about 1100. As in contemporary Ottonian and Romanesque painting in Western Europe (see Chapters Thirteen and Fourteen), the light is generalized and the drapery formalized, but at Daphni this formality is always under careful control, so that one is constantly aware of subtle balances and counterbalances of movement.

Although the *Christus patiens* (Suffering Christ) type was chosen for the *Crucifix-ion* at Daphni (fig. 10–55), the representation is timeless and symbolic; there are no soldiers, no Apostles, no thieves, only the grieving Mary and John on either side of

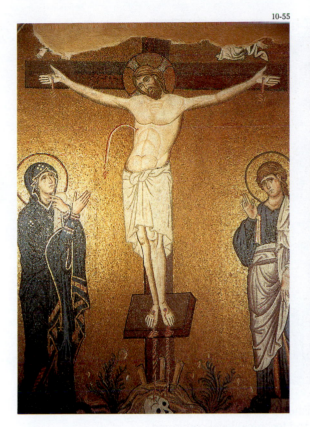

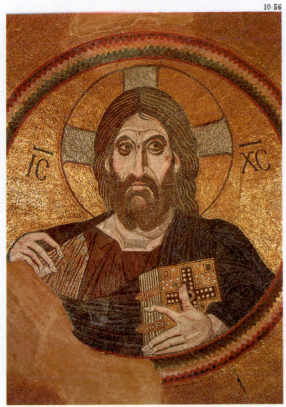

10-55. *Crucifixion,* mosaic, Church of the Dormition, Daphni, Greece. c. 1100

10-56. *Pantocrator,* dome mosaic, Church of the Dormition, Daphni. c. 1100

the Cross and, originally, mourning angels hovering above the Cross on either side. The emotion is intense, but it is held in check by a reserve comparable to that of the Classical period in Greek sculpture; in fact, the three figures have been disposed with the grand simplicity of those on a metope. Christ hangs upon the Cross, his arms describing a shallow curve that reflects in mirror image the embracing arch above, his hips toward his right in a pose repeated in most Crucifixions under Byzantine influence. His head is gently inclined toward Mary as she gazes up at him with one hand slightly extended; John, on the other hand, turns toward us. Formalized though the broad flow of the drapery masses may be in detail, it remains sculptural in feeling. As is characteristic of much Middle and Late Byzantine pictorial art, the modulations of tone are delicate in the extreme. Christ's side has been pierced, and blood accompanied by water spurts from it in a bright arc (John 19:34), symbolizing the sacraments of the Eucharist and Baptism. The streams of blood that flow from Christ's feet strike the skull at the foot of the Cross. Golgotha means "the place of a skull" in Hebrew (John 19:17). Theologians have always interpreted the skull as that of Adam. Paul had said (1 Corinthians 15:22): "For as in Adam all die, even so in Christ shall all be made alive." As if in fulfillment of Paul's promise, flowers grow from the rocks below the Cross.

From this elegiac *Crucifixion,* we turn with amazement to the awesome revelation of the *Pantocrator* (fig. 10–56) at the summit of the dome. We may possibly gain from this image some idea of the vanished mosaic that in the Macedonian renaissance adorned the center of the dome at Hagia Sophia. The light from the windows of the drum illuminates the rainbow circle in which the colossal Christ appears, his face worn and deeply lined by suffering ("Surely he hath borne our griefs, and carried our sorrows," Isaiah 53:4). The extraordinary human sensitivity of the great mosaicist at Daphni appears in the drawing of the long, aquiline nose, the flow of brows and cheekbones, the light on the half-open mouth, the streaming lines of the hair, and above all in the incomparable depth and power of the eyes. We have come far from the gentle teaching Christ of the Sinai icon (see fig. 10–43)!

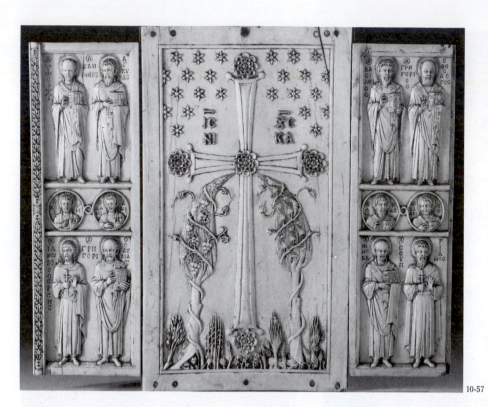

10-57

10-57. *Harbaville Triptych.* Late 10th century. Ivory, 9½×11″ (24×28 cm). Musée du Louvre, Paris

IVORY SCULPTURE Sculpture in stone all but vanished during the later periods of Byzantine art, but ivory plaques on a high artistic and technical level continued to be made in great numbers, especially those intended as aids to private devotion. These carvings preserve in miniature and in sculptural form the stately formality of the mosaics. Easily portable, they brought Byzantine style and its echoes of Greek form and harmony all over western Europe, not only through trade but by means of the Sack of Constantinople in 1204, which left little of value in the imperial city. The so-called *Harbaville Triptych* (fig. 10–57), which migrated to France, shows how the classical quality of form and spacing so beautiful in the Daphni mosaics shines through the supposed rigidity of Byzantine figure style. When the worshiper opened the leaves of the *triptych* (three panels hinged together), he found himself gazing at the court of Heaven, whose hierarchy of saints constantly relax as the eye moves upward. Actually there is considerable give in the drapery of the severely vertical bishop-saints in the lower register of the wings, a little more in the Apostles in the center, and in the warrior-saints above a clear reference to standing Greek and Roman armored figures, with one supporting, one relaxed leg. In the central scene Christ sits with ease and dignity on his throne holding the usual jeweled book, his right hand partly open in the customary gesture of discourse, between the Virgin and Saint John. In moderately high relief, the figures all stand on tiny stages against a continuous flat background, carved with the greatest skill and delicacy. The influence of this formulation of figures and space on French Gothic sculpture was incalculable (see especially the transept sculptures at Chartres, fig. 15–17).

THE EXPANSION OF BYZANTINE STYLE In the Middle and Late Byzantine periods, the artistic achievements of Greek masters were carried throughout territory stretching from Russia to Sicily.

Venice. The most ambitious of all Byzantine monuments outside the Empire is San Marco in Venice (figs. 10–58, 10–59); this republic enjoyed strong if not always cordial commercial relationships with Constantinople. The church, now the Cathedral of Venice, was commenced in 1063 as a ducal basilica connected directly with the Doges' Palace. Its plan was imitated from that of the destroyed sixth-century

10-58. Plan of S. Marco, Venice (after Bannister Fletcher)

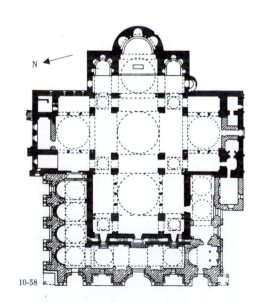

10-58

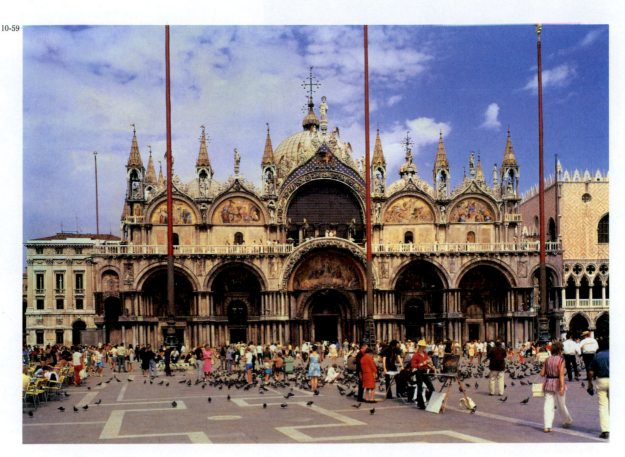

10-59. S. Marco, Venice. Begun 1063

Church of the Holy Apostles at Constantinople, built by Justinian five hundred years earlier. It is basically a Greek cross, designed on five squares, each surmounted by a dome on a high drum, crowned by a helmet-like structure of wood and copper, which imparts a verticality unknown to Early Byzantine domes. The exterior was greatly modified in the Gothic period by the addition of elaborate pinnacles and foliate ornament along the skyline, but the original Byzantine arches and unusual clustered columns are still visible. The vast interior spaces of the basilica (fig. 10–60) have much more to do with the spatial fluidity of Hagia Sophia than with the usual compressed Middle Byzantine interiors. The domes, set on pendentives rather than on the insistent squinches of the era's monastic churches, appear to have to rest exactly on their four supporting arches.

Powerful barrel vaults separate the bays and abut the thrust of the pendentives; the vaults in turn are supported on massive cubic piers, pierced by arches connecting with the galleries, which are entirely open in contrast to the arcaded galleries of Eastern churches. The nave galleries are sustained by triple arcades supported by modified Corinthian columns. The veined marble columns and the gray marble paneling of walls and piers were, of course, imported from the Byzantine East. Dim at all times, the interior shines with a soft, golden radiance shed by the continuous mosaics that line the domes, barrel vaults, and lunettes and softly veil all architectural demarcations. Mosaic artists were brought from Constantinople, but how much they accomplished is not known; presumably much of their work was destroyed in a disastrous fire in 1106. Many of the present mosaics, in Byzantine style but with Romanesque influence here and there, were done by Venetian artisans during the twelfth and thirteenth centuries; several, however, were completely replaced in the late Renaissance or in the Baroque period. Those that remain are important as witnesses to the beginning of the Venetian school of painting, which in the Renaissance became one of the two leading Italian schools.

In the earliest of the five dome mosaics, executed about 1150 in the dome above

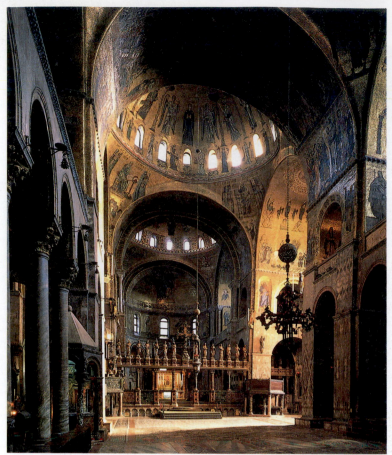

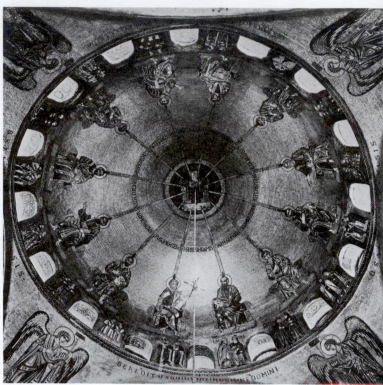

10-60   10-61

the nave, the *Pentecost* (fig. 10–61) is represented. The Descent of the Holy Spirit upon the Apostles is described in Acts as "a sound from heaven as of a rushing mighty wind." As the Apostles met "there appeared unto them cloven tongues like as of fire, and it sat upon each of them"; they then began to speak in many tongues, which were understood by people from all nations who were in the streets outside. The event is reorganized in conformity with the architecture of the dome. In the center is a throne, on which stands the dove of the Holy Spirit; from the throne rays extend to the Apostles, enthroned in a circle above the windows. Between the windows stand pairs of people from all nations. The design is like a vast wheel, but it contains a startling discrepancy: there are Twelve Apostles over sixteen windows, as if three-four time in music were being played over four-four, each measure being marked by an archangel in one of the spandrels.

Sicily.   At the other extreme of Italy, Roger II ruled as the first Norman king of Sicily from 1130 to 1154. Like other monarchs in southern and eastern Europe, he called Byzantine artists to his court to decorate a series of religious buildings and the salon of his palace. The church at Cefalù was raised to cathedral status at the request of Roger II, who intended it as his tomb-church. The team of Greek artists, who finished the mosaic decoration of the apse in 1148 (the later mosaics in the choir are by local masters), had to adapt Byzantine iconographic systems to the architectural requirements of a Western basilica and the desires of a royal patron (fig. 10–62). In the two lowest registers stand the Twelve Apostles. In the next register the beautiful Theotokos, robed in white with soft blue shadows, extends her delicate hands in orant position between four magnificent archangels, bending their heads as they hold forth scepters and orbs. Above this heavenly court, in the semidome (the church has no dome), appears the Pantocrator, as he does later at Monreale. In contrast to the austere Savior at Daphni, the Cefalù Christ seems a poet and a dreamer, sensitive and merciful. His right hand is outstretched in

10-60. Interior, S. Marco, Venice. c. 1150

10-61. *Pentecost*, dome mosaic, S. Marco, Venice. c. 1150

344

10-62

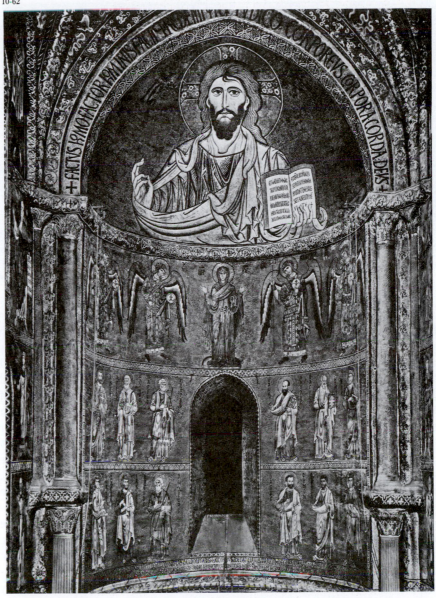

10-62. Apse mosaics, Cathedral of Cefalù, Sicily. Completed 1148

blessing; in his left, instead of a closed book as at Daphni, he upholds the Gospel of John, written in Greek and Latin, open at Chapter 8, Verse 12, for all of King Roger's Christian subjects to read: "I am the light of the world: he that followeth me shall not walk in darkness, but shall have the light of life." The light we have learned to expect in Byzantine art shimmers through the Cefalù mosaics with a delicacy that proclaims them one of the finest achievements of Byzantine art—not the radiance of revelation we saw represented at Sinai (see fig. 10–42) but the light of Paradise, a soft, uniform radiance resulting in the subtlest refinement of gradations in hue and value throughout the drapery masses, the feathers of the angels' wings, and above all in the modeling of faces and hands. Even the ornament sparkles with a new and special brilliance—the decoration above and below the arch, the jewels that stud the cross of Christ's halo, and an entrancing bit of illusionism, the mosaic acanthus capitals crowning the real colonnettes that uphold the arch. Along with the light at Cefalù, line proliferates through the countless strands of Christ's hair and beard and the crinkled folds of the drapery. On the brown tunic appear for the first time sunbursts of gold rays, fusing light and line, soon to be adopted by such Italo-Byzantine painters as Cimabue.

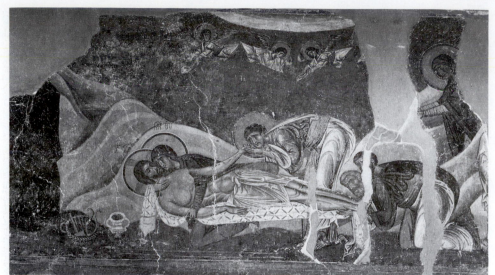

10-63

Macedonia and Serbia. An extraordinary series of frescoes (less expensive to produce than mosaics) is still preserved in churches, cathedrals, and monasteries throughout Macedonia and Serbia. At least fifteen major cycles remain, executed from the eleventh well into the fifteenth century, the last of them done barely ahead of the invading Turks. These cycles form the richest and most consistent body of mural painting left from Middle and Late Byzantine art. The finest paintings in each series were almost invariably done by artists from Constantinople or from other Greek centers; some were painted by refugees after the conquest of the capital by the Crusaders in 1204. Many of the signatures on these works are Greek, and some painters can be traced from one cycle to the next. Local, presumably monastic, artists often completed a cycle begun by an artist from Constantinople or elsewhere with frescoes of considerably less interest (usually those farthest from the eye).

An especially impressive cycle covers all of the interior walls of the beautiful little domed church of Saint Pantaleimon at Nerezi high on a mountainside overlooking the Macedonian city of Skopje; the church was completed in 1164 by a grandson of the emperor Alexius I Comnenus. The styles of several painters can be distinguished in the cycle, which is held together by an overall unity of color—especially the intense blue of the backgrounds—and by its intimacy of scale. The painter who set down the scenes of the Passion with a directness and intensity of emotion not seen in Eastern art since the days of the *Rabula Gospels* (see fig. 10–46) was undeniably a master. The *Lamentation* (fig. 10–63) shows Christ laid out for burial, his body turned toward us, his eyes closed in death. John holds Christ's left hand to his face, and the Virgin enfolds her dead son in her arms; both faces are contorted with grief. The scene must have been painted at dizzying speed; the authority of the brushstrokes and the brilliant handling of light on the drapery show that Greek painters had lost nothing of their mastery since the distant days of Castelseprio (see fig. 10–48). The expressive power shown in the Nerezi fresco leads us far in the direction of early Italian art.

The greatness of the Italian debt to Byzantine art is again indicated by the large-scale fresco cycle in the long-abandoned, recently restored Church of the Trinity at Sopoćani in Serbia. This church was one of a series of monasteries built by the Serbian kings (who wore Byzantine dress and imitated Byzantine court ritual) so that monks could celebrate the Liturgy before the royal tombs. In all of these Serbian churches the entire west wall of the interior above the doorway was given over to a vast fresco representing the Dormition of the Virgin, a nonscriptural scene in which the grieving Apostles, who surround the bier of the Virgin Mary, are

10-64. *Dormition of the Virgin,* central section of a fresco, Church of the Trinity, Sopoćani, Serbia, Yugoslavia. 1258–64

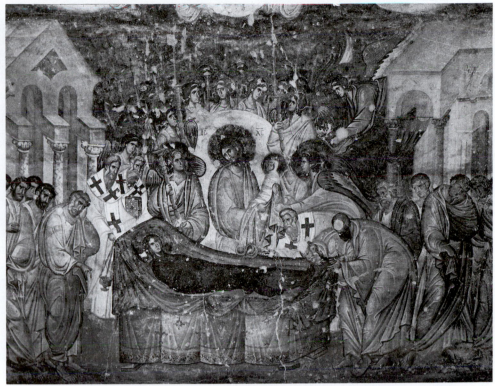

10-64

astonished by the appearance of Christ from Heaven, attended by angels, who takes her soul in his arms in the form of a tiny child. The Sopoćani frescoes must have been done between 1258 and 1264, and although the artist did not go to the same expressionistic lengths as the twelfth-century master at Nerezi, he had quite as much understanding of drama and deployed both figures and architecture with authority. Movement and emotion sweep through the scene with tremendous effect. The coloring is unexpectedly delicate; Christ and Peter, for example, are wrapped in lemon-yellow mantles, and Mary's bier is draped in alternating passages of blue and rose. The illustration (fig. 10–64) shows only the central section of the fresco, which stretches out at the sides to involve both additional grieving figures and more architecture. The new sense of drama and of scale in the Sopoćani frescoes was accompanied by increasing powers of observation; throughout this scene faces are strongly individualized. Most powerful of all is the new sense of unified modeling in light and shade, of both features and draped figures, as compared with the divided drapery shapes of Middle Byzantine art. The creation of volumes by the action of light has always been credited to Giotto and his immediate predecessor Pietro Cavallini, but it is clear from the Sopoćani frescoes that Greek painters shortly after the middle of the thirteenth century already knew how to do this, even though that light has as yet no single, identifiable source.

LATER BYZANTINE MOSAICS AND PAINTING IN CONSTANTINOPLE   In 1261 the emperor Michael VIII (Palaeologus), who had been governing in exile from Nicaea as co-emperor, returned to Constantinople and started cleaning up the devastation left by the Crusaders. To the Palaeologan period is generally attributed a very large, fragmentary, but beautiful mosaic in the south gallery of Hagia Sophia (fig. 10–65) representing the *Deësis* (Christ between the Virgin and Saint John the Baptist). The tenderness of the expressions, the grace of the poses and the linear movement, and the extraordinary sensitivity to light in the rendering of faces, hands, and hair mark a master very different from the bold dramatist at Sopoćani

10-65

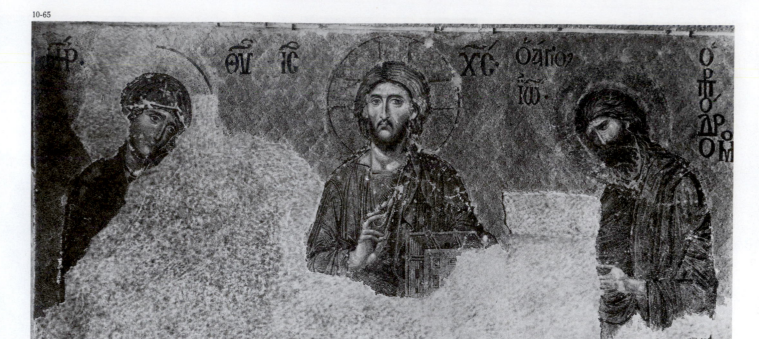

10-65. *Deësis,* south gallery mosaic, Hagia Sophia, Istanbul. Late 13th century

but, nonetheless, one who had a similar understanding of the role of light in creating volume. In the *Deësis* mosaic the diffused light, apparently from an external source, is also very different from the all-over glow of the Cefalù mosaics.

The Church of Christ in Chora. During the reign of Michael's son and successor Andronicus II, the Monastery and Church of Christ in Chora, adjacent to the imperial palace in Constantinople and now known under the Turkish name of Kariye Djami, were rebuilt, the church and its narthex decorated with mosaics, and the *parecclesion* (an adjacent funerary chapel) painted in fresco. This extensive cycle, which has been dated between 1315 and 1321, was carried out after the creation of Giotto's revolutionary works, and it is barely possible that the cubic rocks and luminous figures were influenced by his new ideas (see Introduction fig. 6). More probably the style was an independent, parallel development, since the figures float weightlessly rather than standing with Giotto's foursquare firmness.

In the startling frescoes of the parecclesion, Late Byzantine style is exemplified in its most vigorous and imaginative phase, more often visible in manuscript illumination than in monumental art. The technique of these frescoes has recently been analyzed; they were executed in the method Italian artists call *secco su fresco* ("dry on fresh"). The color was suspended in a vehicle containing an organic binding material (such as oil, egg, or wax) and laid on over the still-damp plaster. Paint thus applied forms a continuous and very hard skin. This method also allows free and rapid painting over large areas. This technique differs sharply from the "true fresco" method generally used by Italian artists during the Gothic period and the Renaissance. Probably, the *secco su fresco* technique was also used in the Macedonian and Serbian frescoes, but this has not been proved.

The fresco filling the semidome of the apse (fig. 10–66) represents the *Anastasis* (Resurrection). Although the Gospel accounts do not describe this scene, both the Apostles' Creed and the Nicene Creed declare that during the three days when Christ's body lay in the tomb he descended into Hell. Apocryphal accounts, widely believed throughout the Christian world, tell how Christ caused the gates of Hell to burst open before him, filled its darkness with light, commanded that Satan be bound until the Second Coming, and lifted Adam and Eve, followed by all the

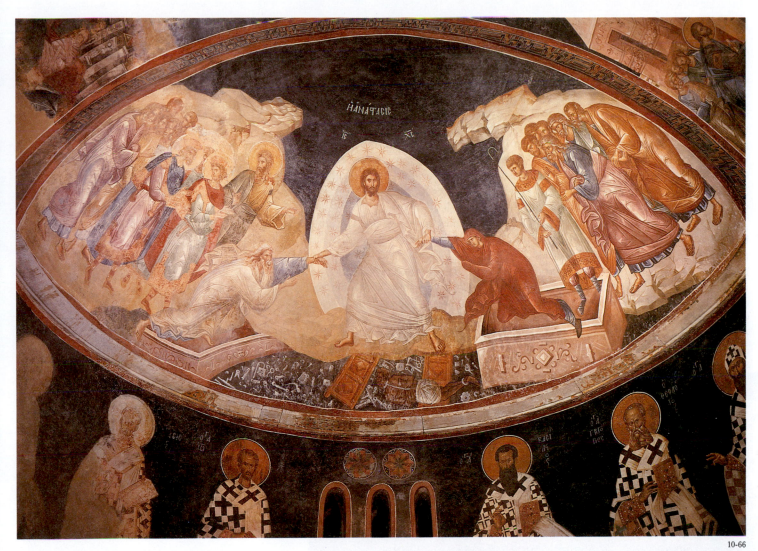

10-66. *Anastasis (Resurrection)*, apse fresco, Church of Christ in Chora (Kariye Djami), Istanbul. 1315-21

patriarchs and prophets, from the unhappy realm to which they had been doomed by Original Sin. This theme, known in Western art as the Harrowing of Hell or the Descent into Limbo, is highly appropriate for a funerary chapel, as it sets forth vividly the Christian hope for resurrection. The composition is unusual in that in order to centralize the scene in the apse the artist has shown Christ lifting Adam with one hand and Eve with the other. The unknown painter represented the subject in a style strongly related to that of the vivid frescoes of Sopoćani (see fig. 10–64) in freedom of movement, in brilliance of color, in naturalism of facial expressions, and in the effect of light in modeling volumes. As in the mosaics of Sinai (see fig. 10–42), Christ is clothed in pearly garments whose white highlights create the impression of blinding radiance. Shadow fills the tombs from which Adam and Eve are drawn up, and the side of Eve's sarcophagus opposite to the source of light in Christ remains deep in shadow. As with the contemporary frescoes of Giotto and his followers in Italy, this apparently naturalistic observation of the effects of light proceeding from a single source is in reality bound up entirely with its religious meaning. The Old Testament kings and patriarchs to the left are led by Saint John the Baptist, who accompanied Christ into Hell, and to the right the prophets are grouped behind Abel. The brilliant colors of the drapery and the creamy off-white of the rocks shine against the intense blue of the background. Satan, bound, prone, partly across the shattered gates of Hell, is surrounded by a veritable shower of locks, hasps, and bolts.

RUSSIA AND ROMANIA

Kiev. Russian religious architecture owes its origins to Byzantine models, and throughout its long and rich development it has retained the central plan for churches because of this arrangement's suitability to Orthodox liturgical requirements. In 989 Vládimir, grand prince of Kiev (who ruled a large territory comprising most of Belorussia and Ukraine), married Princess Anna, sister of the Byzantine emperor Basil II, and brought Byzantine craftsmen back with him from Constantinople to build and decorate churches in his newly converted principality as well as to instruct local artisans. In 1037 construction was begun on the magnificent Cathedral of Hagia Sophia at Kiev. This church, in Byzantine style, with five aisles surrounded on three sides by an open arcade, has thirteen domes, representing the number of Christ and the Apostles. Its mosaics date from 1043 to 1046. The apse mosaics have miraculously survived the abandonment and partial ruin of the cathedral in the sixteenth century, its rebuilding in the seventeenth century, and its partial destruction in World War II. A monumental *Theotokos* (fig. 10–67) in orant position adorns the semidome; her powerful drapery folds recall those at Hosios Loukas. She appears to stand in a golden niche, supporting its arch like one of the maidens of the Erechtheion (see fig. 7–65). Below her unfolds a scene seldom represented in Western art—the *Communion of the Apostles.* Christ officiates as priest at the central altar, distributing bread on the left and wine on the right.

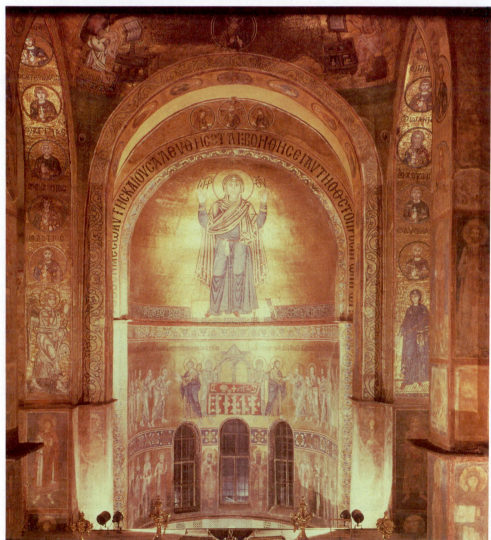

10-67

10-67. *Theotokos* and *Communion of the Apostles,* apse mosaics, Cathedral of Hagia Sophia, Kiev, Ukraine. 1043–46

10-68. Cathedral of St. Demetrius, Vladimir, Rostov-Suzdal. c. 1193–97

10-69. Barma and Postnik. Cathedral of St. Basil the Blessed, Moscow. 1554–60

10-68

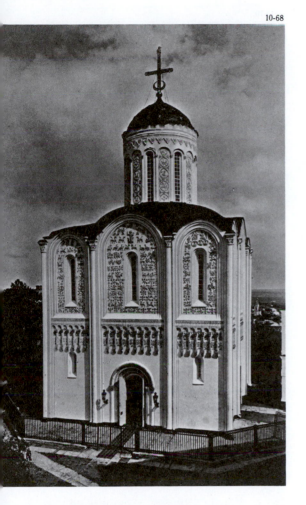

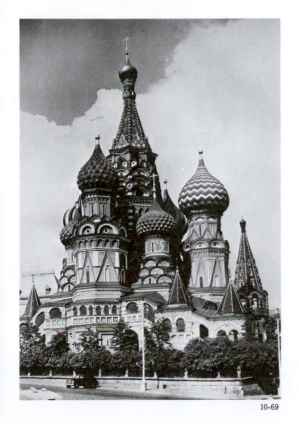

10-69

Vladimir.   Soon local tastes began to modify the Byzantine heritage; artisans imported from Western countries to carry out Russian projects added their own traditions to the amalgam. An early example of Russian hybrid style is the Cathedral of Saint Demetrius (fig. 10–68), built about 1193–97 at Vladimir in the principality of Rostov-Suzdal, far to the northeast of Kiev and beyond the sway of its *metropolitan* (archbishop). The square block of Saint Demetrius, showing traces of the inner Greek-cross plan, into whose arms the corner blocks housing prothesis, diakonikon, and galleries are fitted, and the central dome on its high drum pierced by round-arched windows are immediately recognizable as Byzantine. The screen architecture, consisting of two-story blind arcades whose arches appear along the roof line and are supported by lofty colonnettes, is also derived from Byzantine churches of the tenth and eleventh centuries. But the elaborate fabric of stone sculpture that fills the arches of the upper story and the walls of the drum with figural and ornamental reliefs of great decorative effect is derived from such Western Romanesque models as Notre-Dame-la-Grande at Poitiers (see fig. 14–17) and is wholly alien to Byzantine tradition.

Saint Basil.   The domes of many Russian churches built in the following centuries are lifted on drums so high that they look like towers; the need to protect these domes against snow and ice led to the erection of bulbous external shells, generally onion-shaped. The Kremlin at Moscow contains several such churches, some designed by Italian architects in a style combining Renaissance details with Russian architectural tradition. A final expression of pure Russian architectural fantasy, in which Byzantine elements, detached from their original meaning, were multiplied in unbelievable extravagance, is the Cathedral of Saint Basil the Blessed in Moscow (fig. 10–69). It was built for Czar Ivan IV the Terrible from 1554 to 1560 by the architects BARMA and POSTNIK in what is today called Red Square, adjacent to the Moscow Kremlin. The plan is more rational than the startling exterior might lead one to believe. A tentlike octagonal central church (a favorite shape in the sixteenth century in the region of Moscow) is surrounded by eight smaller but lofty separate churches arranged in a lozenge pattern. Each of the corner churches is octagonal and supports a towering onion dome. The architects inserted four even smaller churches, two of which are square and two heart-shaped, all four crowned by onion domes, between the corner churches. The connecting gallery and the conical bell tower, however, are seventeenth-century additions. The drums of all eight domes are ornamented with innumerable arch-shapes derived from the Byzantine blind arcade but reduced to ornaments, and with gables that become zigzags. The onion domes are fluted, twisted, or reticulated (reminding us of pineapples) and painted green and white in stripes that make a vivid contrast to the orange red of the brick.

Russian Painting.   The rich tradition of church murals and icon painting in Russia, which began perhaps as early as the tenth century with the importation of Byzantine icons, continued unabated into the nineteenth. Many of the innumerable examples are of extremely high quality, and at least two early painters are major figures, known to us by name. THEOPHANES THE GREEK, born between 1330 and 1340, had worked in Constantinople and in other Byzantine centers and brought to Russia the dramatic Palaeologan style we have seen at the Kariye Djami. In 1378 Theophanes was at work in Novgorod, and at the turn of the century in Moscow, then the center of a powerful principality. Theophanes is known to have been able to paint from memory with great rapidity and sureness, and his technique can be appreciated in his few surviving works, such as the wonderful fresco of a *Stylite* (Pillar Sitter) in the Church of Our Savior of the Transfiguration at Novgorod (fig. 10–70). The free, brilliant pictorial style of Castelseprio, with all its echoes of Helleno-Roman illusionism, still flourishes in the work of Theophanes seven centuries later. However, his brush dashes along at such speed carrying a message of religious mysticism that we are reminded of another great Greek painter, El Greco, who worked in Spain in the sixteenth century. The lightning strokes of Theophanes show a personal variant of the Byzantine tradition and vibrate at an intensity that could not be transmitted to a pupil.

In Moscow Theophanes worked in association with a younger and native Russian artist, the monk ANDREI RUBLEV, who painted a fine series of frescoes that still survives at Vladimir but who is best known for his icons. In the fourteenth and fifteenth centuries, the iconostases in Russian churches had been heightened with the addition of upper rows of images, and thus the demand for icons was very great. The style of Russian icons is usually distinguished by flat masses of only slightly modulated color, often of great brilliance, and by a keen sense of the importance of contour. Rublev was content to work within the limitations of this style, but he certainly raised it to its highest level of aesthetic and spiritual achievement. His best-known work is the so-called *Old Testament Trinity* (fig. 10–71), an icon painted in memory of the Abbot Sergius, who died in 1411. The painting is heavily damaged; gold has been scraped from the background and the drapery leaving only white *gesso* (plaster and glue), which distorts the system of highlights, but even in its present state it is a picture of haunting beauty. The scene is a traditional one in Russian icons, but Rublev did not handle it in the traditional manner. The meeting of Abraham and Sarah with the three angels, who sat down to supper under a tree in the plains of Mamre (Genesis 18:1–15), was interpreted in Christian thought as a revelation of the Trinity. In Russian icons Abraham and Sarah had always been represented, and a lamb's head, symbolic of the sacrifice of Christ,

10-70

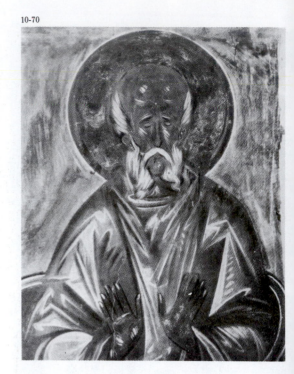

10-70. THEOPHANES THE GREEK. *Stylite*, detail of a fresco, Church of Our Savior of the Transfiguration, Novgorod. 1378

10-71

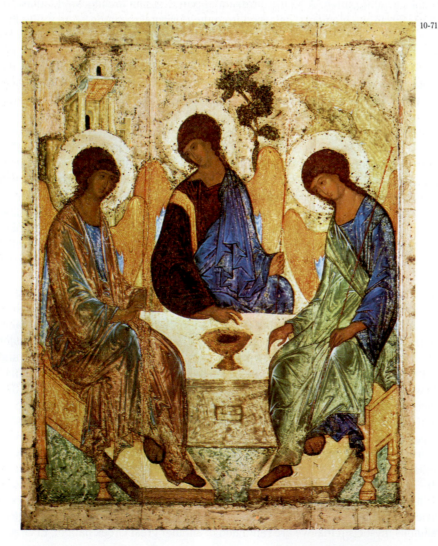

10-71. ANDREI RUBLEV. *Old Testament Trinity*. c. 1410–20. Panel painting, 55½ × 44½″ (1.41 × 1.13 m). Tretyakov Gallery, Moscow

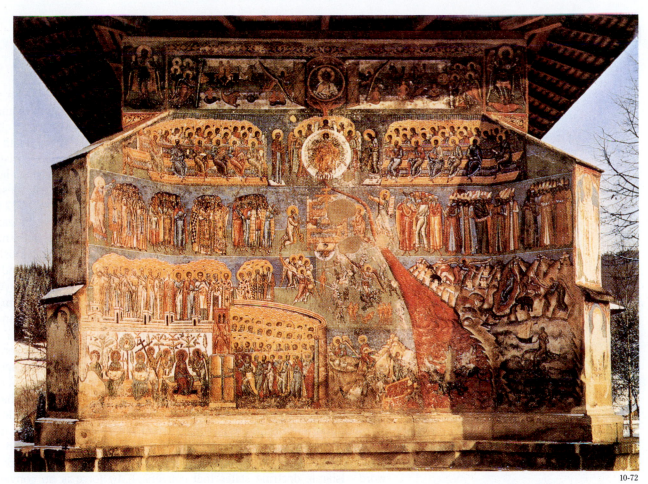

10-72

10-72. *Last Judgment,* fresco on the west wall of the narthex, Church of St. George, Voroneţ, Romania. c. 1550

substituted for the textual calf. Rublev goes to the heart of the mystery, showing us only the three angels as if we were Abraham and Sarah experiencing the vision. The relationships among the three angels are treated with the greatest poetic intensity and linear grace; the contours flow from body to body as the glances move from face to face.

Romania.   The region of Moldavia, the eastern portion of present-day Romania, preserves a handsome group of monastic churches erected in the late fifteenth and early sixteenth centuries and frescoed not only in the interior but also over all the outside walls, where the frescoes are protected only by wide, overhanging eaves. Unlikely though it may seem in view of the severe winters of this region in the foothills of the Carpathians, the exterior frescoes on all but the north walls are better preserved than those in the interiors; apparently, rain, sun, and wind are not as injurious to paintings as are candle smoke and incense.

Among the best of the Moldavian fresco cycles is that of the former Voroneţ monastery church. The *Last Judgment* (fig. 10–72), dating from about 1550, covers the entire west wall of the narthex above the entrance. At the top, angels roll up the heavens as a scroll (Isaiah 34:4; Revelation 6:14). In a circle in the center appears the bust image of God the Father; below him is the Deësis flanked by six Apostles enthroned on each side and angels behind them. In the next tier below, choirs of ecclesiastical saints are grouped on either side of the throne prepared for Christ's Second Coming. A river of fire pours from the throne of Christ and falls upon the damned in Hell to Christ's left, penetrating earth and sea, which give up their dead. On his right Heaven opens up in two tiers of the blessed, whose halos blend into an almost continuous surface of gold.

CHAPTER ELEVEN

The lightning expansion of Islam in the seventh century combined a speed approaching that of Alexander's conquests with a political tenacity rivaling that of Rome and at least as much religious unity as Christianity. Never before or since has a world religion appeared and spread in so short a time. At the death in 632 of Muhammad, its prophet, Islam ruled Arabia, though few in the Christian world were then aware of the existence of so dangerous a rival. Thirty years later Egypt, Syria, Palestine (including the Hebrew and Christian holy places), Mesopotamia, and Persia had fallen into Muslim hands (see Map 11, page 298). By 732 Islam had reached into Central Asia, Afghanistan, and the Indus Valley to the east, and its domains to the west, including Sicily, Spain, Portugal, southwestern France, and all of North Africa, stretched to the Atlantic Ocean. In France the Muslims were stopped—and eventually expelled—by the Franks. The Byzantines and Sasanian Persians crumbled before Islam; Constantinople soon controlled only Asia Minor and the Balkans. All the Asiatic and African regions conquered by Islam in its first century of life, with the sole exception of modern Israel and Lebanon, and many in eastern Europe, remain predominantly Islamic today.

The rapid spread of Islam was due in large part to the military genius of the Arabs as well as to their intense religious fervor. In contrast to the spontaneous diffusion of the initially gentle Christianity, which took place in spite of the official opposition of the Roman Empire, not until relatively modern times has a single country or region (outside of Central Asia, converted by missionary dervishes in the ninth and tenth centuries) adopted Islam before conquest; prior missionary attempts conspicuously failed. Muhammad himself led prayers and delivered sermons while leaning on a lance. Not that the new religion was enforced with the sword—Islamic doctrine states that conversion by force is no conversion. But Muhammad spread his *rule* with the sword, and his dazzling successes may well have been attributed by millions to divine favor. In assessing the expansion of Islam, it is hardly possible to overlook the material advantages, including decreased taxation, attending submission to a militarily and politically dominant Islamic culture. Perhaps the overwhelming factor, however, was that once the new religion could be witnessed by masses of people, the depth of its message could be understood. Throughout the history of Islam, determined pockets of Christianity remained—relatively unmolested, to be sure, but nonetheless unyielding—in Egypt, where the Coptic Church survives to this day, and in Syria, Lebanon, and Palestine. Jews, however, were often persecuted. It should be remembered that from the moment when Islam burst out of Arabia it was no longer purely an Arab movement. A vast array of Christianized peoples in the Middle East, North Africa, and Spain—Berbers, Carthaginians, Greeks, Moors, Romans, Syrians, Vandals, and Visigoths, to name only a few, as well as Zoroastrians in Persia—adopted the new religion, which then became multiracial and universal, and this it still is. Since God's message was given to Muhammad in Arabic, the Koran was not to be translated, and wherever the Muslim conquerors went, Arabic was adopted, save only in Persia. And wherever Islam went, the heritage of preexistent art was rapidly dissolved in a new art of astonishing creative originality, power, and beauty.

Compared with the increasing theological complexity of organized Christianity, in either its Roman or its Eastern Orthodox form, Islam (the word means "submission"—that is, to God) is a remarkably simple and clear-cut religion. It dispensed with priesthood, sacraments, and liturgy from its very start; every Muslim has direct access to God in prayers. But its *caliphs* (*khalifa:* "successors"), at first deriving authority from their degree of family relationship to Muhammad, exercised supreme political power in a theocratic state. Islam's sacred book, the

Koran, embodies divine revelation received by Muhammad in ecstatic, face-to-face confrontations with the angel Gabriel, as recalled by himself and set down by his companions on palm leaves. These teachings include the doctrine of one indivisible God, who has many Prophets (including those of the Old Testament and Jesus), of whom the greatest was Muhammad; Islam posits a Last Judgment, a Heaven, and a Hell, but it makes no clear division between the demands of the body and those of the soul. The good life on earth and the afterlife of Paradise can include many forms of self-indulgence, including a host of concubines, thus strengthening a tendency to view women solely as instruments of pleasure. In contrast to the celibacy eventually imposed upon Roman Catholic clergy of all ranks, and upon Orthodox bishops, no such sacrifice was required of the caliphs or the *imams* ("teachers"); Muhammad had six wives. The duties of a Muslim include circumcision, daily prayer at five stated hours, abstention from certain foods and from alcohol, fasting during the lunar month of Ramadan, acts of charity, and a pilgrimage to Mecca at least once in a lifetime. This pilgrimage brings visually to the experience of every pilgrim the transcendence of religious truths over racial and national differences, just as the five-times-daily prayers—wherever the believer happens to be—reinforce the conviction of the omnipresence of God and the lack of any intermediary between God and the worshiper.

It would be a mistake to assume that Islamic culture, at least in its developed stages, was in any way inferior to those it conquered, particularly in France and in Spain; in many respects it surpassed them. One of the most surprising aspects of the growth of Islam is the rapidity with which it assumed the role of conservator and continuator of the Helleno-Roman philosophical and scientific heritages preserved by Byzantine culture. We owe much of our knowledge of classical science, especially botany and medicine, and the invention of algebra (and the diffusion of the very numbers used in this book) to the Arabs. Although the Koran itself does not forbid representation of men and animals, later interpretations sometimes did, and religious images were resolutely opposed as inherently idolatrous. According to Islamic tradition, Muhammad personally cleaned all sculpture out of the Kaaba, the pre-Islamic sacred shrine in Mecca. Secular sculpture, generally in stucco, decorated the palaces of the caliphs. The Arabs had little artistic tradition of their own save for the legendary lost palaces of Yemen in the extreme south, but mosques large enough to embrace entire populations were needed in a hurry, and under Islam architecture and architectural decoration made gigantic progress, rapidly absorbing and transforming almost beyond recognition the Graeco-Roman heritage of columns, arches, vaults, domes, and mosaic decoration as preserved by the Byzantines. Doubtless the Islamic conquerors were also profoundly influenced by the architectural example of the Sasanians who controlled Mesopotamia, as witnessed by the stucco-faced rubble construction found in Islamic architecture from an early date. At this point it seems best to introduce one of the rare surviving fragments of Sasanian architecture, the palace of the Sasanian Persian monarch Shapur I at Ctesiphon in Mesopotamia, of 242–72, near the later site of Baghdad. Fig. 11–1 shows the great building as it stood in the late nineteenth century; since then the whole right-hand section of the façade has fallen, and the remainder was exposed to danger in the 1991 Gulf War. Aside from the syncopated, superimposed blind arcades of the façade, the most influential feature for Islam of this and other now-lost Sasanian palaces that can be ideally reconstructed was the almost pointed barrel vault of the great audience hall, open on one side, and providing at once easy access and shelter for large numbers of people. This grand form will be adopted as the *iwan,* an important feature of Islamic palace architecture from the beginning

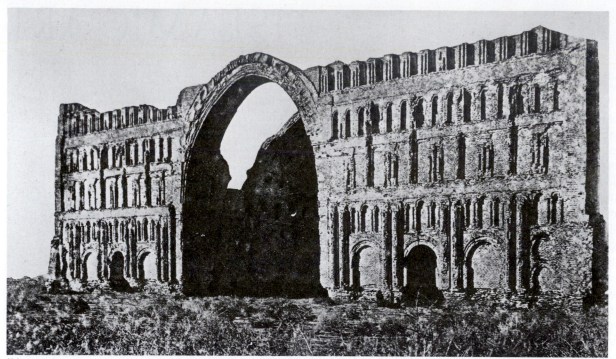

11-1

11-1. Palace of Shapur I, Ctesiphon, near present-day Baghdad, Iraq. 242–72

and of mosque design from the eleventh century onward, and later of tomb design as well.

In Islamic religious architecture the leading form of decoration was at first, and of necessity, *calligraphy* to carry the divine message of the Koran, and calligraphers were esteemed above all other artists. Islam fostered scientific and intellectual investigation, especially mathematics, and it is no accident that, out of the largely naturalistic Graeco-Roman sources, Islam eventually forged an art of abstract, mathematically based architectural decoration that is one of the artistic triumphs of humanity. In addition to this abstract tradition, later Islamic culture in Persia and in India also gave rise to a narrative pictorial art of the greatest originality and beauty.

Muhammad had no greater need of architecture than had Jesus; he could and did teach anywhere, but much of his discourse was carried on in his own house, which served as the model for the first mosques. His followers required only a simple enclosure, one wall of which, known as the *qibla,* at first faced Jerusalem, later Mecca, the focus of prayer. A portico of palm trunks on the qibla side was a practical necessity as a protection from the sun. Ablution before prayer was a requirement of the faith, and every mosque has a pool for ritual ablutions, known as the *sahn,* in the center of its courtyard. (Pools or fountains were standard features of Egyptian, Roman, and Near Eastern houses.) Soon the qibla was given a sacred niche, called the *mihrab* (see fig. 11–16), which represents the spot where Muhammad addressed the first Muslim congregation at his home in Medina. To the right of the mihrab stands the *minbar* (see fig. 11–16), a lofty pulpit from which the imams read the Koran to the assembled faithful and preach the Friday sermons. The simple early mosques always contained the qibla, the sahn, the mihrab, and the minbar, but unfortunately none of the first mosques have been preserved. As in the case of Christianity, and indeed following its example (see fig. 11–2 and page 358), the taste for splendor soon accompanied success. But the basic form of the mosque with its open arcades is in itself beautiful, as simple and direct in its appeal as the message of early Islam. The graceful shape of the minarets, from which the *muezzin* ("crier") intoned the call to prayer (now all-too-often a recording), made mosques even more so, lifting their visual message skyward. The history of these

11-2. Dome of the Rock, Jerusalem. Late 7th century (completed 691)

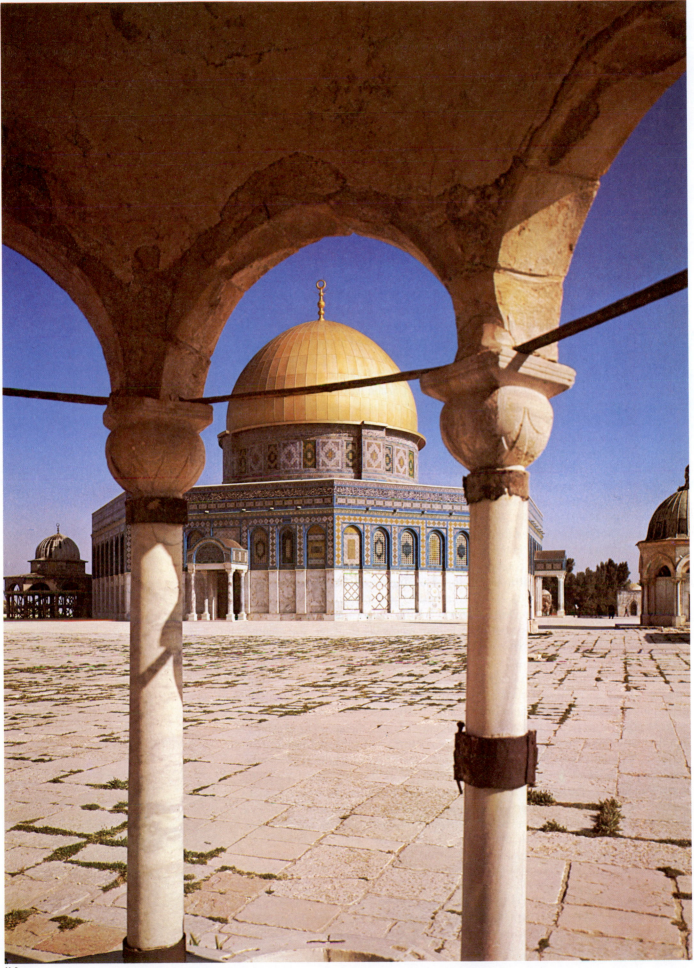

countless structures is as rich and complex as that of the turbulent civilization that produced them. To illustrate certain key aspects of this history let us examine eleven important structures over a span of a thousand years.

Early Architecture

THE DOME OF THE ROCK   As early as 670 the now-vanished mosque at Kufa in Mesopotamia (located in present-day Iraq) was rebuilt with a roof forty-nine feet high, supported by a colonnade in apparent imitation of the Hundred-Column Hall at Persepolis (see fig. 4–28). But the earliest still-extant Muslim structure—and one of the most beautiful—is not a mosque but a shrine, the celebrated Dome of the Rock, whose delicate profile and shining dome dominate Jerusalem. This shrine was built on the site of the Temple (which the emperor Titus had totally destroyed in A.D. 70) and encloses the rock on which, according to tradition, Abraham had attempted to sacrifice Isaac and from which, it was later believed, Muhammad had made an ascent to Heaven on a human-headed horse. But toward the end of the seventh century, the caliph Abd al-Malik, as a chronicler tells us, "noting the greatness of the Church of the Holy Sepulcher and its magnificence, was moved lest it should dazzle the minds of the Muslims, and hence erected above the Rock the dome which is now to be seen there." Abd al-Malik's new building, completed in 691, was magnificent from the start (fig. 11–2). The rich fabric of blue, white, yellow, and green tiles that now clothes the upper portion was added only in the sixteenth century under the Ottoman Turks, but it replaces decorative glass mosaics that emulated those in Christian churches, in which one may note the modest beginnings of the abstract, geometric ornament that became so dazzling in later Muslim architecture. The wooden dome (regilded in 1960, alas, in anodized aluminum!) was covered originally with gold leaf.

The plan derives from the central-plan Christian martyrium, so that pilgrims could walk around the sacred Rock just as the Christians did around a martyr's tomb (see figs. 10–11, 10–12). A simple octagon is surmounted by a graceful, slightly pointed dome, the idea for which may have been suggested by Sasanian arches. The shape is repeated in the delicately pointed arches used throughout the building, in the surrounding courtyard, in the blind arcade and windows of the exterior, and in the two concentric ambulatories around the Rock. The pointed arch offers great advantages over its round counterpart, since it can be designed in almost any proportion, thus freeing the architect from the tyranny of that inconvenient quantity *pi* (π) in working out his calculations. As we shall see, the pointed arch is only one of the many flexible features introduced by Muslim architects in the course of time. The pointed arch later found its way to the West, where it was employed in the late eleventh century in Romanesque architecture, as at Cluny (see fig. 14–7), and where it became the standard shape for arches in the Gothic period. As in most mosques, the windows of the Dome of the Rock are filled with a delicate grille of stone in order to temper the harsh rays of the sun. The Muslims, like the early Christians, pressed into service columns and capitals from Roman buildings, but their refined sensibility admitted none of the gross discrepancies— between juxtaposed Ionic and Corinthian capitals, let us say—which did not seem to bother the early Christians. The exterior capitals of the Dome came from Roman monuments of the fourth century. The interior, with two concentric arcades around the Rock, is sheathed with veined marble and decorated with glass mosaics that in a sense may be regarded as the final phase of late classical plant ornamentation. They feature inscriptions proclaiming the superiority of Islam, including all the major Koranic passages concerning Christianity.

THE GREAT MOSQUE AT DAMASCUS   The earliest Muslim building on a gigantic scale is the Great Mosque at Damascus (fig. 11–3), built from 705 to 711, inside the fortified outer enclosure of a Roman sanctuary, measuring 517 by 325

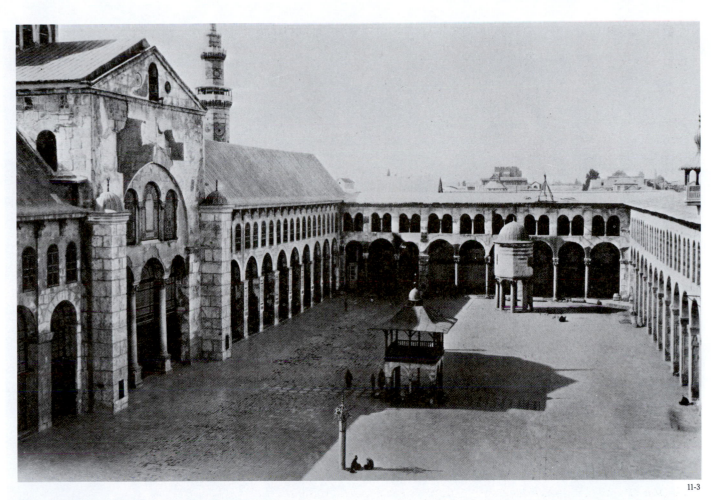

11-3

11-3. Courtyard and façade, Sanctuary of the Great Mosque, Damascus, Syria. c. 705–11

feet, originally containing a temple dedicated to Jupiter. The Christians had converted the temple into a church, and for decades after their conquest the Muslims left the Christians undisturbed. Then the caliph al-Walid I demolished everything inside the enclosure, utilizing the salvaged masonry blocks, columns, and Corinthian capitals, still in perfect condition, for a grand arcade, supported by columns and piers on the short sides, in a rhythm of two to one, and piers on the long; across the south arcade he ran a lofty transept leading to the central mihrab. The square corner towers, built for defense, were utilized as *minarets,* and they are the earliest known. Minarets, still in use today for the muezzin's call to prayer, were not strictly necessary; a rooftop or a lofty terrace could serve the same purpose. But henceforward they became a common if not indispensable feature of the mosque. The present minaret crowning the Roman tower of the Great Mosque is a much later addition. The building has been repeatedly burned and rebuilt; originally, its dome was slightly pointed like that of the Dome of the Rock. Some of the interior mosaic decoration still survives (fig. 11–4), consisting of dreamlike architectural fantasies in the tradition of Roman screen architecture as we have seen it in early Byzantine mosaics at Salonika (see fig. 10–17), interspersed with city views, like those of the mosaics at Santa Maria Maggiore in Rome (see fig. 10–18), feathery trees, and flowing streams, all on a gold background and, in keeping with their position in a mosque, devoid of any human or animal representations. As pointed out to the author by Scott Redford, the meaning of these mosaics—which once covered the walls of the courtyard as well—is obscure, but they may represent the Islamic paradise, or else (less persuasively) the world as conquered by the first caliphs. In their flat, uniform patterning these mosaics resemble a richly designed

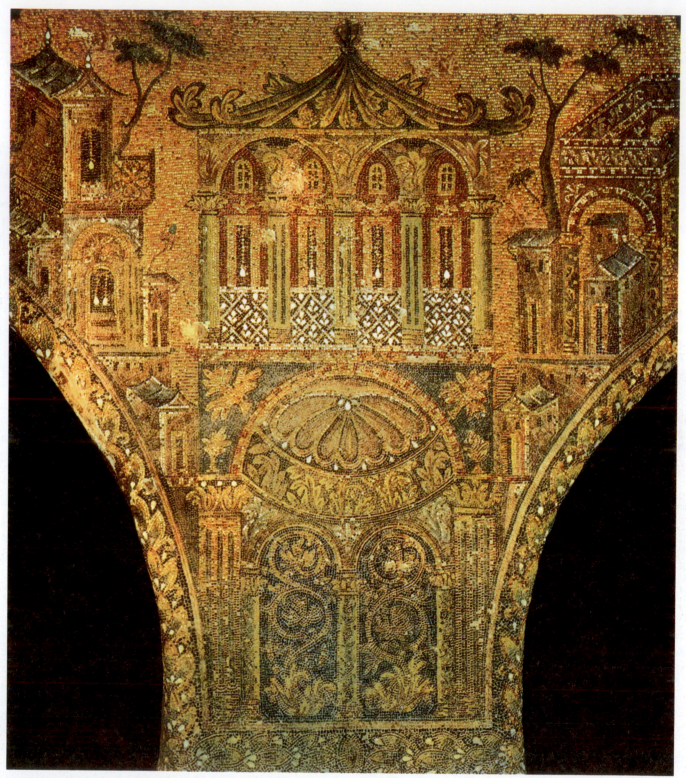

11-4. *Architectural View*, detail of a mosaic, Great Mosque, Damascus. c. 705–11

Islamic textile. The artists who made them were possibly Syrian Greeks, although this is by no means certain.

THE PALACE AT MSHATTA   Much of the ornamentation of early Islamic palace architecture gives a similar effect of textile design. For example, the façade of the square, fortified palace built about 743–44 in the desert at Mshatta, in what is now Jordan, on a plan derived, like that of the palace of Diocletian at Split (see fig. 9–78), from Roman camps had a lower zone of almost incredible richness (fig. 11–5). Here rosette forms and floral interlace derived from later Roman and Early Byzantine traditions mingle with confronted winged griffins of Mesopotamian derivation to clothe considerable areas of masonry with a flickering tissue of light and dark, which on inspection resolves into exquisitely skillful representation of interwining vegetation; from this living interlace peer birds and animals, significantly absent in front of the palace mosque. The resultant pattern, known as *arabesque,* is quite as bewildering in its complexity as that of Germanic ornament and Hiberno-Saxon manuscripts (see especially figs. 12–6, 12–8), but it is equally disciplined and organized into zones by broad zigzags. The ornamentation at Damascus and Mshatta foreshadowed the Islamic intoxication with the mysteries of pure geometric interlace, which often dominates Islamic interiors instead of wall paintings (see figs. 11–11, 11–20).

The original Umayyad dynasty of caliphs was succeeded by the Abbasids, whose great caliph al-Mansur (ruled 754–75) removed his capital from Damascus to

11-5. Façade, Palace at Mshatta, Jordan (detail). c. 743–44. Staatliche Museen zu Berlin—Preussischer Kulturbesitz

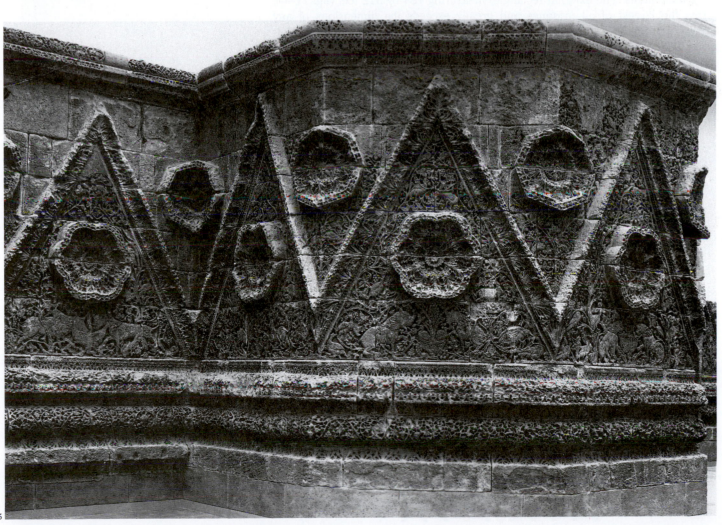

11-5

Baghdad on the upper Tigris in Mesopotamia. Here he built a round city about a mile and a quarter in diameter, symbolizing the cosmic domination of the Islamic empire. The plan was considered unique by Arab historians but actually derived from the circular camps of the Assyrians and from later Mesopotamian models, Parthian and Sasanian. It had two concentric circles of walls, four gateways, concentric circular avenues, and vaulted streets radiating outward from the center like the spokes of a wheel, and in the vast central area stood a great mosque and the caliph's palace. According to literary accounts the palace boasted a feature drawn directly from Sasanian palace architecture (see fig. 11–1), the barrel-vaulted hall open on one side, now known as the iwan. Unfortunately, al-Mansur's wonderful round city, immortalized by the stories of his great successor Harun al-Rashid, who developed an unlikely pen-palship with the emperor Charlemagne, was a victim of its own success. Within decades it had far outgrown its central plan and was eventually abandoned. Like most Mesopotamian monuments, it was made of mud brick, only faced with fired brick, and when the Mongols swept down in their second wave of conquest they murdered the last Abbasid caliph in 1258 and destroyed everything.

THE GREAT MOSQUE AT SAMARRA Caliph al-Mutasim built the city of Samarra on the Tigris River upstream from Baghdad after 836. It was twenty miles in length and counted a population of about a million, enjoying a rational plan and a complex drainage system; Caliph al-Mutawakkil built between 848 and 852 a mosque that could accommodate at any one time a considerable proportion of the city's inhabitants. The external rectangle, measuring 784 by 512 feet (fig. 11–6), forms the largest of all mosques and greatly exceeds the dimensions of any Christian house of worship. The fired-brick exterior walls still stand, but little is left of the 464 mud-brick piers that supported the wooden roof, and nothing of the mosaics that once ornamented the interior. The stupendous spiral minaret, of fired brick (fig. 11–7), towers to a height of 176 feet; it forcefully recalls the principle of the Mesopotamian ziggurat adapted to spiral form. This noble building also was exposed to great danger in the 1991 Gulf War.

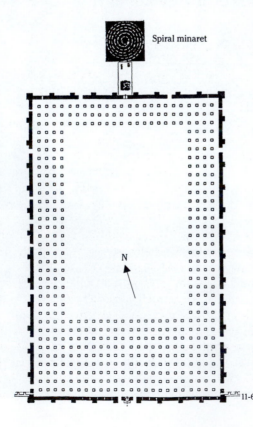

11-6. Plan of the Great Mosque of al-Mutawakkil, Samarra, Iraq (after Creswell). c. 848–52

11-7. Spiral minaret, Great Mosque of al-Mutawakkil, Samarra. Fired brick, height 176′ (53.64 m)

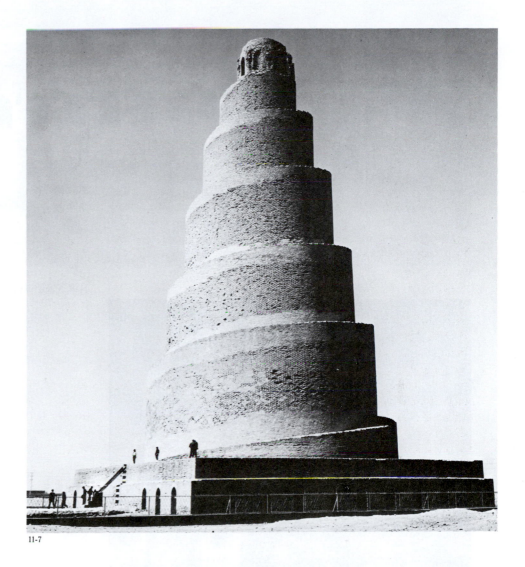

11-7

THE MOSQUE OF IBN TULUN AT CAIRO   Something of the grandeur of the Great Mosque at Samarra, and much of its original character, can be seen in the well-preserved mosque built at Cairo by a former inhabitant of Samarra, Ibn Tulun, from 877 to 879. This new Muslim city rose near the vanished Memphis of the pharaohs, and its surviving Islamic buildings rank second in quality in Egypt only to the nearby monuments of pharaonic antiquity. Many of these buildings were of great importance to the medieval architecture of Europe, and of these the Mosque of Ibn Tulun is the earliest (fig. 11–8). The rectangular structure, measuring 460 by 401 feet, was built on a slight eminence and enclosed by a crenellated outer wall. A double arcade lines the wall on three sides (fig. 11–9), and a five-aisled portico on the fourth contains, exceptionally, several mihrabs. As at Samarra the piers are of brick, but here they were protected with a thick coating of fine, hard stucco, which has survived almost intact and which makes the building appear monolithic. The sharply pointed arches, of noble simplicity, are supported by massive rectangular brick piers, into whose corners *colonnettes* (little columns) are set, an early example of a device to be used extensively in Christian architecture of the Middle Ages. The ceiling was originally coffered below the wooden beams; little of the coffering is intact, but the rich floral ornament, impressed into the plaster of the arches as if carved in stone, has survived in splendid condition. Especially remarkable are the smaller arches that pierce the spandrels between the larger ones to illuminate the aisles; they produce an impression of lightness and variety,

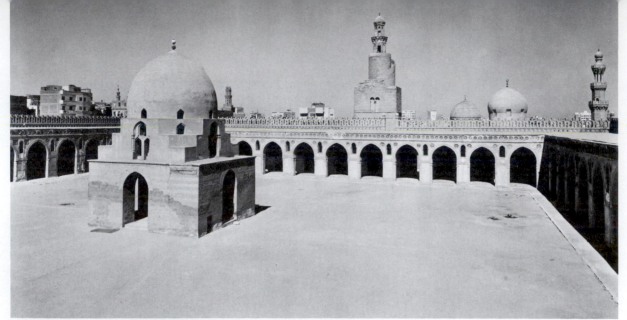

11-8. Courtyard, Mosque of Ibn Tulun, Cairo. c. 877–79

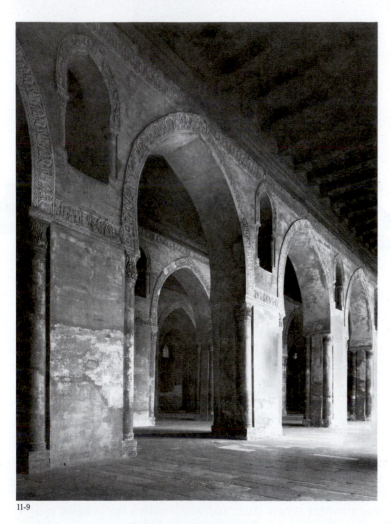

11-9. Arcades, Mosque of Ibn Tulun, Cairo

treating the arch—as often in Islamic architecture—as something that can be freely played with. The vast spaces of the courtyard and the arcades produce an effect of spiritual grandeur, impossible to experience adequately in photographs, and not to be rivaled in Western religious architecture before the Gothic cathedrals.

THE GREAT MOSQUE AT CÓRDOBA   One of the most brilliant achievements of Islamic architecture, the Great Mosque (now the Cathedral) of Córdoba (fig. 11–

11-10. Interior, Great Mosque, Córdoba. c. 786

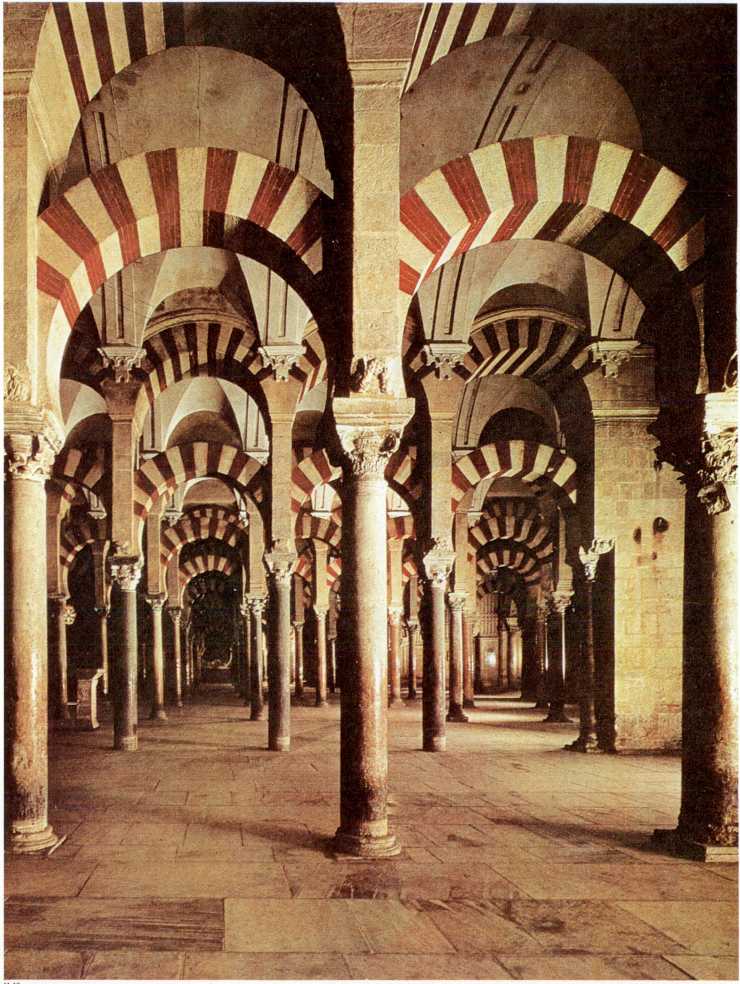

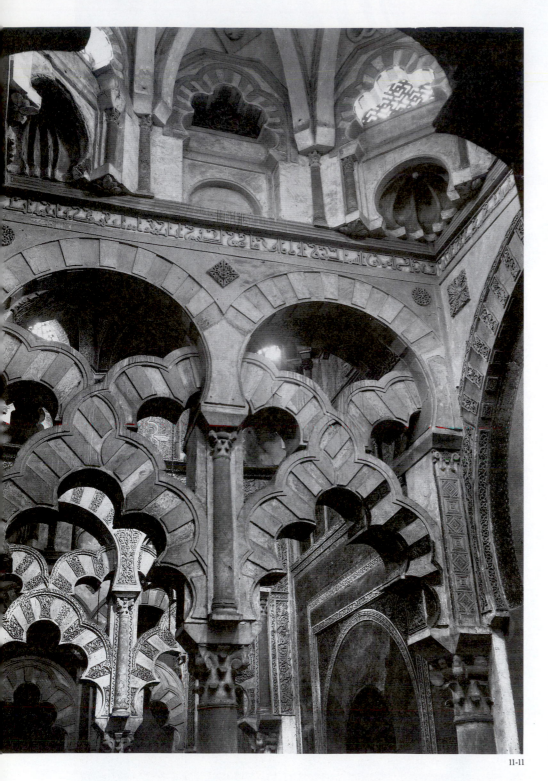

11-11

11-11. Vestibule of the mihrab, Great Mosque, Córdoba. c. 10th century

10), was built in Spain, where the only surviving member of the Umayyad dynasty had escaped after the Abbasids massacred eight hundred of his family at a peace banquet between the warring factions, and established the new Umayyad caliphate of Córdoba, thus splitting the Islamic world. Other splits would soon follow, and Islamic political unity became an unrealizable dream. The original mosque, erected in 786, had all its aisles on the qibla side of the sahn. As necessity required,

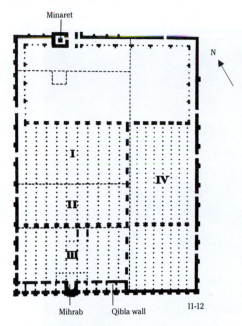

11-12. Plan of the Great Mosque, Córdoba, Spain, showing successive enlargements (after Marçais). c. 786–987

these aisles were repeatedly lengthened in the late eighth century and again in the tenth and the qibla moved back; eventually, the location of the Guadalquivir River forbade further lengthening in that direction, so the structure was extended on the east (fig. 11–12). Unfortunately, in the sixteenth century the canons of the Cathedral (the mosque had been converted into a Christian place of worship long since) built a choir inside it, greatly to the displeasure of the emperor Charles V, who rightly accused them of having ruined a monument unique in the world for the sake of something they could have built anywhere. They also installed Renaissance vaulting, visible in the illustration. But from most viewpoints the interior, now a hypostyle hall, still presents an enthralling spectacle of seemingly infinite extent in any direction—a forest of columns and arches with many aisles and no axis (see fig. 11–10). The hundreds of marble or granite columns were, of course, cribbed from Roman and Early Christian buildings (the Christians had also appropriated them), but visually they play second to the striped, horseshoe-shaped arches, unknown in architecture before Muslim builders employed them. The uniqueness of the Great Mosque of Córdoba demonstrates a principle common to many mosques—that Islamic space, originally at least, was not determined by the requirements of a set ritual as was that of Christian interiors. In the basilica the columns, like the worshipers, unite in obedience to the longitudinal vista extending toward the altar; in the mosque the columns are endless and uniform like the worshipers, who are united only in common prayer.

Another striking feature of the Great Mosque of Córdoba is the introduction of a second set of freestanding arches above the first. These spring from square piers that stand on the Roman columns as though on stilts. These flying arches, intended to uphold a wooden roof (the vaulting was added in the sixteenth century), ingenious as they are, are outdone by the inventions in the mihrab, which was built during the last southward extension of the mosque in the tenth century. The arches here are scalloped and intertwine freely in open space (fig. 11–11). Other arches soar from the upper corners to cross as ribs for the vault. Here and there, in the archivolts, in the inner surfaces of the arches, and in the vertical panels, appear passages of pure arabesque; the area that in classical architecture would constitute the frieze is decorated with passages from the Koran in richly ornamental Kufic writing (see page 374).

Later Architecture

THE GREAT MOSQUE AT ISFAHAN   In the eleventh century a Turkish people from Central Asia, a branch of the Seljuk dynasty, with a long and rich artistic tradition, invaded Persia and founded a monarchy; the king was granted the title of *sultan* (originally a noun meaning "power") by the Abbasid caliph. Eventually the Seljuks invaded Anatolia, defeating the Byzantines and founding a separate kingdom there. In their Persian capital at Isfahan the Seljuks constructed over the decades beginning in the late eleventh century a vast mosque, the Masjid-i Jama (Friday Mosque), changing and enormously enlarging the previous hypostyle mosque, centered on a courtyard (fig. 11–13). The most striking feature of the Seljuk mosque, which contains no less than 476 vaults, almost all domes, is that it is the first of a new type with four iwans, one in the center of each side of the sahn courtyard. Instead of colonnades the sides are made up of two superimposed arcades of pointed arches, the lower ones giving light to endless aisles. The south iwan admits the worshiper between two lofty minarets to a majestic domed space before the qibla instead of the usual mihrab. This four-iwan plan has not yet received an adequate explanation, but it was eventually put to a new use in Egypt (see below). Under the domination of the Timurid rulers (see page 375) in the fifteenth century, the towering iwans were enriched with *muqarnas* (interlocking honeycomb vaults) and with a marvelous ornament of blue and gold glazed tile, like some colossal Persian carpet, which by no means detracts from the noble

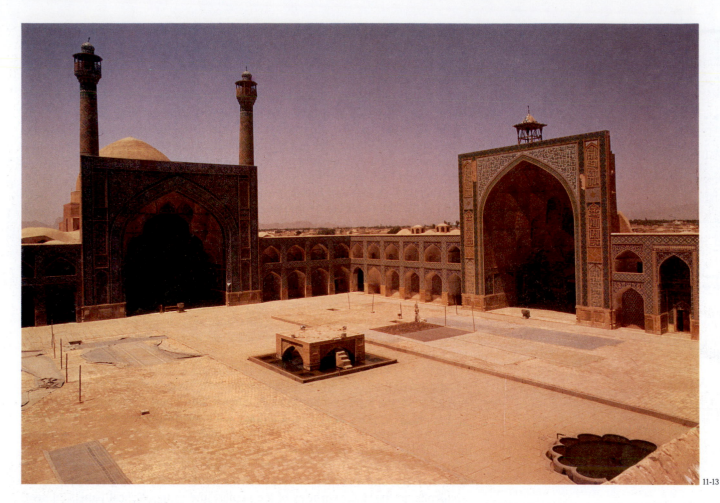

11-13

simplicity of the architectural forms. The ornament of the west iwan, to the right in our illustration, dates from the eighteenth century.

THE MADRASA OF SULTAN HASAN   Among the host of splendid religious structures that rose throughout the Islamic world, we must present a completely new type, the *madrasa,* a building intended for religious and legal instruction (because the two were fused in the Islamic theocracy). The first such combined theological seminary and law school seems to have been built in Persia about 1000 in an attempt to enforce Sunni Muslim orthodoxy against the competing Shiites. The architectural requirements were a customary central sahn and separate quarters for each of four schools of Islamic law. The solution was a series of cells for each school at one of the four corners of the sahn courtyard; in the center of each face of the courtyard a spacious iwan, used as a classroom, separated each school from its neighbors. The relation to the four-iwan plan of the Great Mosque at Isfahan is obvious, but the exact pattern of the derivation is not known; in fact, for madrasas, mosques, and palaces this plan was widespread throughout the medieval Islamic world.

   In fourteenth-century Egypt the Mamluk sultans (descendants of Turkish slaves who had seized power) built a number of madrasas in Cairo. The grandest example is the madrasa constructed by Sultan Hasan in 1356–63 (figs. 11–14, 11–15), whose towering iwans leave little room for windows in the four stories of student cells at the corners of the restricted sahn courtyard. With their pointed barrel vaults, the iwans give an overpowering impression of mass and space, increased by the chains of the seventy bronze lamps that still hang in the sanctuary (as once in Early Christian basilicas). The east iwan, richly paneled in veined marble, contains the usual mihrab and minbar (fig. 11–16), surmounted by a superb arabesque

11-13. Courtyard of the Masjid-i Jama (Friday Mosque), Isfahan, Iran (view from the northeast). c. 1475–18th century

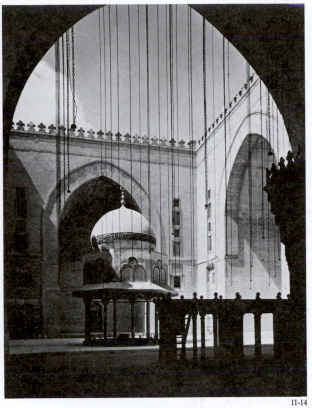

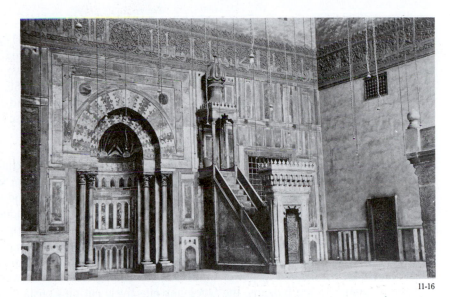

11-16. The east iwan, containing the mihrab and minbar, Madrasa of Sultan Hasan, Cairo

11-14. Courtyard of the Madrasa of Sultan Hasan, Cairo. c. 1356–63

11-17. Mausoleum of Sultan Hasan, Cairo (the south wall with minarets and the dome of the Madrasa are visible behind it)

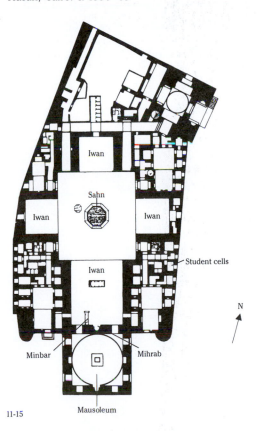

11-15. Plan of the Madrasa and Mausoleum of Sultan Hasan, Cairo

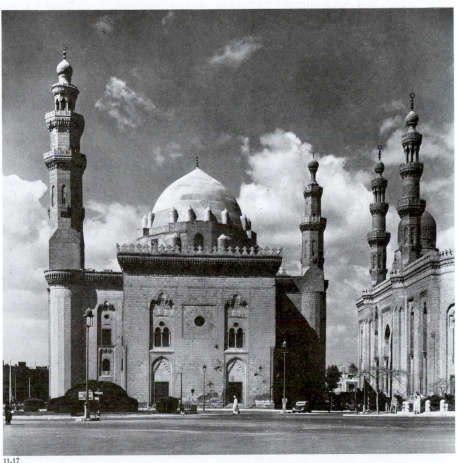

frieze. Behind the gate to the minbar can be seen the bronze grille that gives access to the domed interior of the sultan's tomb. From the exterior (fig. 11–17) the mausoleum dominates the entire structure, whose outer walls are pierced with pointed windows, some single, others paired with a round window above, in a grouping that recalls the tracery of French Gothic cathedrals (see pages 456, 460, and fig. 15–10). The tomb is crowned with a handsome pointed dome; the adjacent minaret, square in plan with several superimposed octagonal stories, rises to a height of nearly three hundred feet.

THE MOSQUE OF SELIM II   The achievements of Muslim religious architects, like those of Roman imperial builders, stand throughout North Africa, Spain, Sicily, the Balkans, and the Near East—and also in northern India, Pakistan, and even western China. When Persia was overwhelmed by Mongol conquerors under the ruthless Genghis Khan in the thirteenth century, a small Turkish tribe, originally from Khorasan in Central Asia, migrated to the Anatolian Seljuk kingdom, and in about 1300 their leader Osman seized power, founding the dynasty known as Ottoman, which remained in power until 1923. Extending their rule to western Anatolia, thence to the Balkans, the Ottomans effectively cut off Constantinople from its hinterland. Finally, in 1453, Constantine's great city, the center of Eastern Christendom, fell to the Ottoman Turks—an event considered a universal tragedy in a Europe now threatened constantly by Ottoman incursions, which reached to the gates of Vienna in the sixteenth century before being rolled back.

The new capital, which the Ottomans continued to call Kostantìnìyya (the name Istanbul, a corruption of the Greek word for "the city," became official only in the 1920s), does not offer the infinite surprises that delight the visitor bold enough to brave the dusty and tumultuous alleys of Cairo—every mosque utterly different! Although in the conquered sections of Anatolia, during the period while Constantinople still held out, the Ottomans at first constructed relatively modest rectangular mosques with pointed domes, once they had arrived in the metropolis they converted Hagia Sophia and all the other churches of the capital into mosques as apparently they worked very well for Muslim congregations and were not incompatible with the traditional Seljuk plan. Icons were easily removed and the required minbars and mihrabs installed, although the mosaics were not white-washed until the eighteenth century. As the Ottoman Empire grew, so did the capital, and the need for more religious buildings quite naturally prompted a revival in the early sixteenth century of the thousand-year-old model of Justinian's masterpiece in several sizes and many ingenious variations. It is thus difficult for the first-time visitor to pick out from a distance Hagia Sophia itself in Istanbul's romantic skyline of domes and minarets. Although the interiors of the Ottoman central-plan mosques sometimes seem heavy when compared with the seraphic lightness of Hagia Sophia, their exteriors, with their cascades of smaller domes and semidomes, often showed a considerable refinement and systematization of the free arrangements of similar features designed by Anthemius of Tralles and Isidorus of Miletus a thousand years earlier.

Most of the finest Ottoman structures in Istanbul are the work of a single extraordinary architect, SINAN, perhaps of Greek parentage (c. 1489/90–1588) and trained as a military engineer, during a lifetime that spanned nearly a century and according to contemporary records boasted some 304 monuments scattered throughout the Turkish Empire. The triumph of Sinan's long career was the gigantic Mosque of Selim II at Edirne (the former Adrianople), built between 1569 and 1575, when the eminent architect was already in his eighties (fig. 11–18). Characteristic of the Ottoman plan for mosque complexes was the inclusion of bathhouses and covered markets, the income from which was used for the maintenance of the mosque, as well as soup kitchens for the poor, a hospital, and educational buildings. The Selim complex was erected on a terrace on the edge of Edirne, dominating both the city and the surrounding landscape from any point of view. The

11-18. SINAN. Mosque of Selim II, Edirne (ancient Adrianople), Turkey. 1569–75

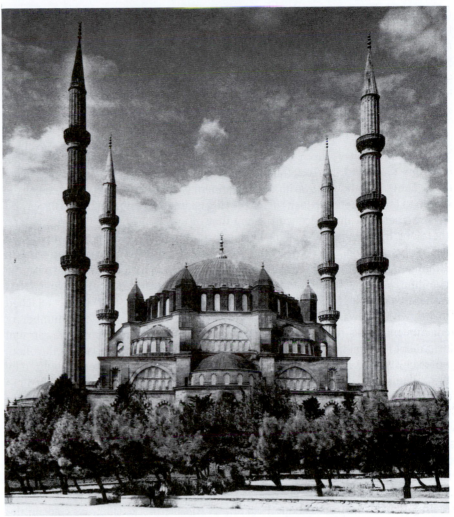

11-18

mosque was preceded by a rectangular *sahn* courtyard of the same area, surrounded by a dome-vaulted arcade.

While keeping the vast, shallow dome of Hagia Sophia, Sinan condensed its plan to a circle on a square, whose corners were cut at the second level into an octagon. From the exterior one sees on the lower level a semidome illuminated by windows between two arches, each embracing two rows of arched windows, and on the second a single, larger arch between two semidomes. The weight of the crowning dome is carried by eight colossal piers, which emerge on the exterior at the second level, each abutted by heavy flying buttresses, apparently an adaptation from Western Gothic architecture (see fig. 15–6). The piers appear on the dome level as octagonal, pointed turrets, in the manner of Gothic pinnacles, and apparently with a similar function, adding a totally new verticality to the profile, leading the eye to the lofty, fluted minarets, and cutting the drum of the dome into eight segments with four windows each. This break is masked with false windows in the interior, so as not to interrupt the movement of the mighty ring, but on the exterior the interdependence of dome and piers is emphasized by building both drum and turrets in a considerably darker stone than the rest of the building. As a result, the floating dome of Hagia Sophia is now anchored into a thoroughly Islamic structure of interlacing verticals and horizontals, transferred from the realm of ornament to that of engineering, though with even greater thoroughness than such early examples as the Great Mosque at Córdoba. This new structural density is expressed in the interior by a richly foliated blind arcade that locks in the windows of the drum.

Unlike the floating dome of Hagia Sophia, this one appears to be supported on a ring of powerful corbels. Thus vanishes the last element of the visionary, in favor of a vast, stone frame that allows, as in Gothic architecture, the multiple interior spaces to be flooded with light from a host of windows, in arches and semidomes, apparently countless yet actually controlled by mathematical ratios as rigorous as those that govern the structure. Like many definitive architectural solutions, this one was never exactly imitated.

THE TAJ MAHAL The conquest of India in the sixteenth century by the Moguls, a band of adventurers from Turkestan, claiming descent from both the Mongol Genghis Khan and the Turk Tamerlane, married to a Mongol princess (see page 375), brought to power over that subcontinent, with its own long and rich artistic tradition (see Chapter Sixteen), an art-loving Islamic dynasty that built palaces and entire cities of a magnificence rivaling that of imperial Rome. It is no accident, therefore, that the best-known of all Islamic monuments is the Taj Mahal at Agra in north-central India (fig. 11–19; and see Map 13, page 497), erected by the fifth Mogul emperor, Shah Jahan, from 1630 to 1643 as a tomb for his favorite wife, the beautiful Mumtaz Mahal, and later for himself. Much sentimental legend has gathered about the building. While the emperor was undoubtedly deeply attached to his wife, he was able to console himself for her loss with any number of concubines. It has recently been shown that the inscriptions from the Koran that ornament the building refer neither to the empress nor to Shah Jahan's devotion, but exclusively to the Last Judgment and to the Garden of Paradise, symbolized by the splendid surrounding formal gardens (the present Italianate planting is nine-teenth century). The entire park, enclosed by lofty red sandstone walls with ornamental gateways inlaid with black-and-white marble, covers an area larger than that of Saint Peter's in Rome and its entire piazza.

The central mausoleum is flanked by twin buildings, a mosque and a reception hall (not shown in the illustration), also in red sandstone and marble. But the mausoleum itself, including the lofty platform on which it stands and its four delicately tapering cylindrical minarets, immediately suggests a different spiritual realm. All are constructed entirely of snowy marble blocks (the rosy color in the illustration is due to sunset light), smooth but not polished, so that the crystals both absorb and radiate the intense Indian sunlight. While the basic principle—a central block surmounted by a pointed dome—derives eventually from Central Asian tombs of the tenth century, it was greatly refined in later tombs such as that of the conqueror Tamerlane himself at Samarkand in the early fifteenth century. The type appeared in India as early as the fourteenth century and reached new heights in the mausoleum of the second Mogul emperor, Humayun, at Delhi in the mid-sixteenth century. Every effort has been made to dissolve the sense of mass. As in Humayun's tomb, the four iwans, familiar to us from mosque courtyards, have been trans-ferred to the exterior, opening up the four faces of the block. The corners are cut to provide four new diagonal faces, each of which, as well as the spaces remaining between them and the central iwan, has been pierced by two superimposed smaller iwans—thus six for each corner, or a total of twenty-four, creating as much void as solid. The central dome, more than 250 feet high, slightly bulbous, and extremely graceful in its swelling curves, is flanked by four smaller domes, sur-mounting open octagonal pavilions, a favorite Indian motif. Similar structures crown the minarets. Thus domes in three sizes and openings in six repeat in solid and void with the utmost refinement the basic motif of the pointed arch with slight double curvature at the top.

The white marble surfaces are inlaid with floral ornament and Koranic inscrip-tions in black marble and colored, semiprecious stones, so calculated that every petal can be clearly distinguished with the naked eye from the platform below and every inscription, increasing in size in inverse proportion to perspective diminu-tion, read by anyone versed in this kind of highly ornamentalized Islamic script.

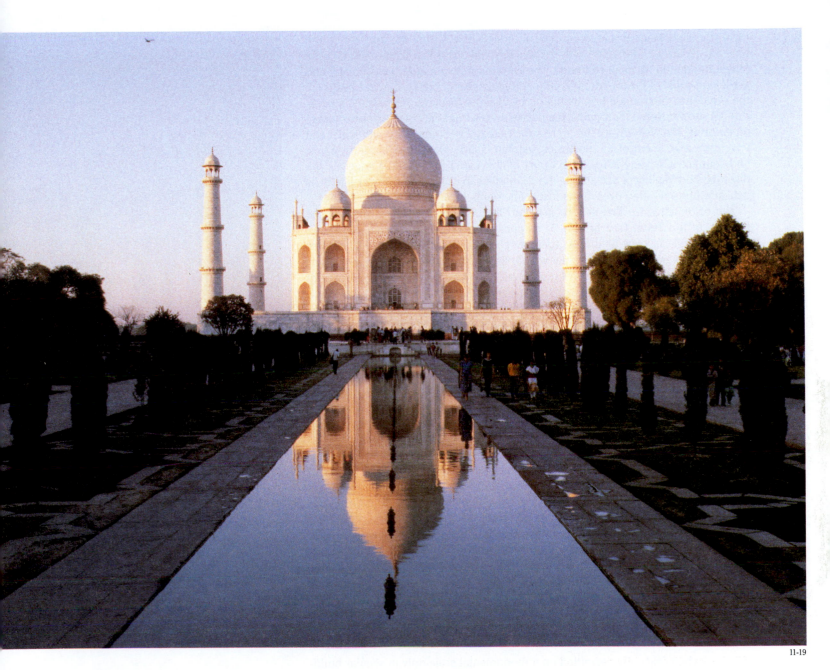

11-19. Taj Mahal, Agra, India. 1630–43

Even the joints between the white marble blocks composing the minarets are filled by delicate strips of black marble. The light is reflected upward with such intensity from the white marble terrace that shadows are greatly lightened, and the dome seems to float against the sky like a colossal pearl.

Shah Jahan was confined in his old age by his own usurping son Aurangzeb, but his prison was enviable—the splendid Red Fort of Agra. From an octagonal white marble pavilion set amid delicious gardens cooled by ingenious fountains and artificial waterfalls, the monarch could look out across a broad curve of the Jumna River to the Taj Mahal, where he was eventually to rejoin his departed wife.

THE ALHAMBRA   To many the supremely original creation of Islamic architecture will always be the Alhambra, the palace built by the Nasrid kings on a lofty rock above Granada in southern Spain in the fourteenth century, only a century and a half before all Moors were expelled from this last Iberian fortress by Queen Isabella and King Ferdinand. The rich valleys and fertile slopes that surround Granada made the final Moorish kingdom in Spain a paradise during the fourteenth and fifteenth centuries, darkened only by the internal strife that eventually laid the kingdom open to Spanish conquest. The extreme refinement of the scholarly and art-loving court of the kingdom of Granada finds its embodiment in the beauty of the Alhambra. Surrounded on its hilltop by towered fortifications, against a backdrop of snow-covered mountains, the palace seems from the outside to be colossal; on entering, the visitor is all the more surprised at the intimacy, human scale, and jewel-like refinement of the porticoes, vaulted chambers, courts, gardens, pools, and fountains. A view across the Court of the Lions (fig. 11–20) suggests the disembodied fragility of this architecture, cloudlike in its lightness, flower-like in its delicacy, but pervaded even in its last refinements by a rigorous sense of logic.

The colonnettes we first saw tucked into the corners of massive piers in the Mosque of Ibn Tulun (see fig. 11–8) reappear here freed from brute substance, standing singly in twos or threes, upholding vaults whose underlying bricks are covered with stucco into which fantastic shapes have been impressed, doubtless by the use of molds—a honeycomb of muqarnas, from which hang stalactites of pure ornament, framed by exquisitely ornamentalized Islamic inscriptions. The triumph of this abstract ornamental system—contrasting arches dissolved into countless muqarnas, with fields of pure arabesque interlace enclosing smaller and even more complex fields, and bands of Arabic and Persian inscriptions—is the so-called Queen's Chamber (see Introduction fig. 19). While the individual elements can all be found in structures in Egypt and throughout North Africa, and especially in Persian buildings of the fourteenth century, nothing like this brilliant combination of them had ever been executed before or ever would be again.

Caught in their last redoubt between the Mediterranean Sea and the Spanish sword, the Nasrid kings lived an existence in which luxury was refined to its ultimate distillation. One could contemplate the arabesques at the Alhambra for days on end and only begin to sample their delights. Such contemplation induces a passivity akin to transcendental meditation, freeing the intellect for the pursuit of the endless ramifications of pure logic. At first it may seem difficult to tarry over such complexities; the Western mind used to literal representation and clear-cut definition turns away frustrated—one has not quite been able to experience it all. But like contrapuntal music, or like the carvings at Mshatta or at Córdoba (or for that matter like the interlace of Hiberno-Saxon manuscripts; see Introduction fig. 23 and fig. 12–6), these arabesques of Granada are severely separated into parts and regions, each assigned its own duty in the final intellectual structure.

Painting

Painting, while originally permitted on a monumental scale only in secular buildings, was useful enough for manuscripts—though always secondary to the art of calligraphy. Islam was blessed with a singularly graceful form of writing. The earliest script, a massive style called Kufic, was especially appropriate to carving in stone. A page from a Koran written in the ninth century in either Syria or Iraq (fig. 11–21) shows how bold and harmonious this writing can be in manuscripts as well, with its noble black characters punctuated by red dots and adorned with a broad band of gold leaf used to emphasize an especially important passage. But there is more than at first meets the eye. One watches for a moment, and then the written characters come to life, transforming themselves into Muslims with red turbans, seated, prostrate, or kneeling in prayer, or lifting up their hands to God. This form of double imagery was not achieved in Western art until the sixteenth century.

By the thirteenth century lively explanatory or narrative illustrations were common in Islamic manuscripts, usually with paper made from cloth (no longer parchment) as the sole background and sometimes without borders. Only a summary indication of setting is given, such as curtains or a plant here and there. Under

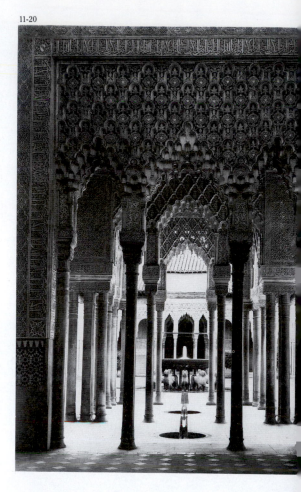

11-20

11-20. Court of the Lions, the Alhambra, Granada, Spain. c. 1354–91

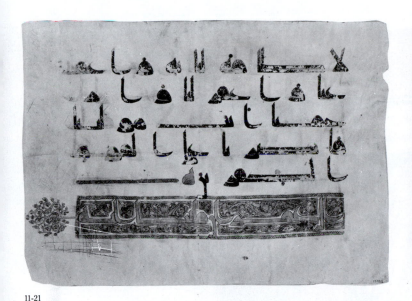

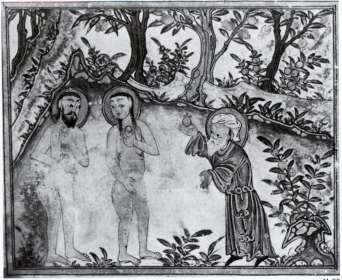

11-21

11-22

11-21. Page written in Kufic script, from a Koran. Syria or Iraq, c. 9th century. Illumination. The Metropolitan Museum of Art, New York. Rogers Fund, 1937

11-22. *Temptation of Adam and Eve,* illumination from a manuscript of the *Chronology of Ancient Peoples* by abu-al Rayhan Muhammad al-Biruni. Tabriz, Iran. Persian, 1307. Edinburgh University Library

the Mongol conquerors of Persia considerable changes appeared later in the century, partly due to the fact that Yuan (Mongol) dynasty artists (see pages 538–39) had been imported from China into Persia. These foreigners were employed side by side with natives for schemes of mural decoration, which has all perished; one tantalizing example was a prince's bathhouse completely decorated with mural paintings illustrating the art of love. An example of this pictorial blend is the disarming *Temptation of Adam and Eve* (fig. 11–22) from a manuscript of the *Chronology of Ancient Peoples* of al-Biruni, illustrated by different hands at Tabriz in Persia in 1307. The Garden of Eden is represented by fruit trees, rocks, and flowers, all ornamentalized in a style suggesting metalwork. A very Oriental-looking Adam and Eve appear naked (almost unparalleled in Islamic art), except for ineffectual bits of transparent drapery, and with halos, which to Christian eyes are undeserved. In fact, even Satan, garbed in a robe shaded in almost Chinese style and shown importuning a coy Eve with a golden fruit, has been provided with a halo.

Unexpectedly, the immense flowering of pictorial art in Persia took place under the fierce Turkish conqueror Tamerlane (Timur Lenk, meaning "Timur the Lame," 1335/6–1405) and his successors, the Timurids. Proclaiming himself the descendant by marriage of Genghis Khan, Tamerlane devastated Persia in the fourteenth century and added it to his shifting empire, which at times stretched from Asia Minor to the Indus Valley. Marking his battlefields with pyramids of enemy skulls, he was as cruel to his Islamic coreligionists as to infidels. Timurid mural paintings have perished, but the manuscripts in a totally new and unprecedented style remain, and they are dazzling. An especially beautiful example is the manuscript of the poems of Khwaju Kirmani by JUNAID, one of the leading Persian painters, illuminated in 1396 during Tamerlane's later years, for one of his grandsons. In *Bihzad in the Garden* (fig. 11–23), a dramatic scene presented in a style of almost unbelievable delicacy and elegance, a considerable expanse of landscape has been indicated by means of a division of the page into areas—the smallest being left for the text. Horizontal extent is indicated in Timurid illumination by a high horizon, which makes the ground seem to rise like a hillside; once this convention is accepted, the new sense of depth in this painting is striking. At the back, a wall encloses the garden from the outside world, and above it one sees only the blue sky dotted with gold stars and a gold crescent moon. Even with the exquisite grace of his representation of foliage, flowers, figures, and seemingly weightless draped figures in a style that seems utterly relaxed, Junaid was never unaware of the inner rhythmic relationships of motifs apparently strewn at random. Nor did he neglect

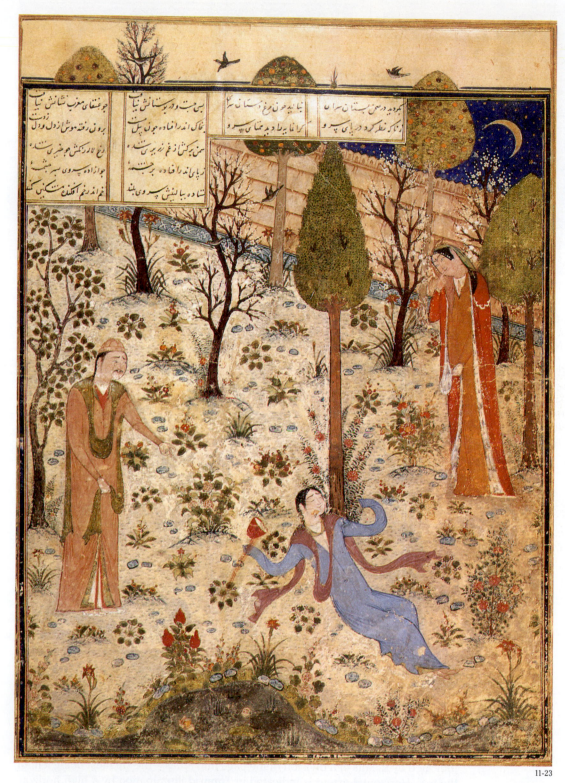

11-23

the harmonies of rose, soft green, soft red, pale blue, and gold that make his picture sing. The story is narrated in panels of script, which appear to hang from an elegant gilded molding running round the painting. One observes with delight how the trees arise beyond, even between, the upper moldings onto the blank page, against which the birds soar. Junaid's intense and wholly new attention to the beauties of the natural world came, significantly enough, in the same century as the rebirth of naturalism in the work of the Late Gothic European masters.

11-23. Junaid. *Bihzad in the Garden,* illumination from the manuscript of the poems of Khwaju Kirmani. Persian, 1396. British Museum, London

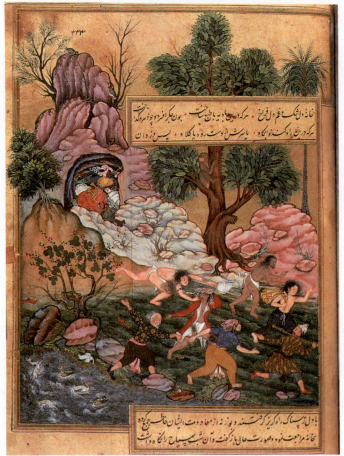

11-24. *The Ape Outsmarts Thieves,* illumination for *Anwar-i-Suhaili.* Delhi, India (Mogul dynasty), 1570. School of Oriental and African Studies, University of London

11-24

The art-loving Mogul emperors brought the new manuscript style to India, in a somewhat less refined but more dramatic form. A brilliant school of painting arose at Delhi under the third emperor, Akbar (ruled 1556–1605). Although he never learned to read, Akbar possessed a vast library and, not surprisingly, was especially fond of the illustrations. He is quoted as saying:

> *It appears to me as if a painter had quite peculiar means of recognizing God: for a painter in sketching everything that has life, and in devising its limbs one after the other, must come to feel that he cannot bestow individuality on his work, and is thus forced to think of God, the giver of life, and this will increase his knowledge.*

The vitality of the painting done under Akbar overflows from the pictures for the *Anwar-i-Suhaili* (The Lights of Canopus) of 1570. The illustration of *The Ape Outsmarts Thieves* (fig. 11–24) shows how a "clever and honorable ape," seeing that a band of thieves had set upon a traveler and robbed him of his belongings, hid the loot in a cave while the thieves slept. When they woke they thought the place was haunted and dashed off in terror, some still scantily dressed. The excited traveler is shown at the bottom, and the rest can be easily made out, including the self-satisfied ape in the tree. The richly modeled rocks and powerful tree trunk, against a gold background that shades off to blank paper toward the top—indeed all the vigorous forms and rhythms and strong colors—are worlds apart from the exquisite formal vocabulary of Junaid. Trees actually burst from the (much heavier) gilded frame, to which the equally framed narrative sections are attached like marble slabs. The painter, whose name is not known, observed not only the ducks chasing fish in the foaming river (one lies dead on the shore) but color distinctions among what is apparently a multiracial predatory expedition.

CHAPTER TWELVE

CHRISTIAN ART IN

Throughout the history of the ancient world and the early Middle Ages, preliterate and literate societies, which we tend to think of as separate stages in human development, were in fact, at almost any given moment, locked in endemic conflict with each other. Ever since the Mycenaean civilization succumbed to the Dorian invaders the patterns of European history in many ways repeated themselves from age to age. Settled, literate, urban cultures in the sunny Mediterranean basin were magnets for wave upon wave of preliterate barbarian tribes (*barbarian* from the Latin word for "beard"; throughout most of their history the Romans were clean-shaven), from the dark forests, cold mountains, and windy steppes of the unsettled world to the north and east of the Alps, the Carpathians, and the Urals (see Map 1, page 35, and Map 11, page 298).

Sometimes the attack was completely successful, as with the Dorians in the years before 1100 B.C., in which case the defeated culture was obliterated and the barbarians took over, eventually to bring forth their own civilization. With the later waves of Celtic, Germanic, Mongol, and Slavic invaders the story was more complex. The Gauls, a Celtic people, besieged Asia Minor unsuccessfully in the fourth century B.C., then wandered along the eastern and northern perimeter of the Hellenistic world, to settle in northern Italy and in modern France, both of which, along with part of western Germany, were known as Gaul. There they were conquered and annexed, like indigenous peoples elsewhere, by the Romans in the course of their expansion. So were the Celtic Britons who had invaded Britain. Such tribes were first converted to the Roman state religion, then after Constantine to Christianity, but in spite of physical differences they were soon indistinguishable in dress and behavior from other Roman provincial populations; in fact they became Roman citizens and soldiers, assuming their role in defending the perimeter of the empire against later waves of invaders.

By the fifth century A.D., in the third great wave of migrations, Germanic peoples, notably the Ostrogoths in Italy, the Visigoths in Spain, and the Vandals in North Africa, conquered both Romans and Romanized populations of whatever origin and again in turn became Romanized and Christianized. After the departure of the Romans from Britain in the early fifth century the Germanic Jutes, Angles (origin of the word *England*), and Saxons began their slow conquest of the island, driving the Britons into Wales. In the later fifth century another Germanic tribe, the Franks, took over Gaul and gave it their own name. In the sixth the Lombards entered Italy sometime after the expulsion of the Ostrogoths and divided the peninsula irregularly and unstably with the Byzantines, who retained most of the ports, and with the popes, who had assumed political as well as spiritual control over Rome and a considerable surrounding area. Both Lombards and Franks were soon Christianized and so, in the later sixth century A.D., were the Anglo-Saxons, although by now Roman culture had been diluted to such a degree that we could scarcely speak of Romanization. Under these last invaders the feudal system grew up as a method of holding society together with ties of tribal loyalty. And finally there were the never-civilized tribes, above all the fierce Huns, Mongols who pushed the others along before them in their westward and southward migrations. The mobility of the barbarians is astonishing in a world without roads or bridges—for example, the transcontinental trajectory of the Gauls or the even more spectacular zigzag of the

BARBARIAN AND NORTHERN EUROPE

Vandals from Asia Minor to central Europe to Spain to North Africa, before they disappeared entirely in Justinian's short-lived attempt to revive Western Roman power.

More important than the disappearance of the Roman imperial title in the West were the virtual collapse of Roman administration, economy, manufacture, agriculture, transportation, education, and art and the depopulation of the cities. Only in the Church—especially the monasteries—did learning remain alive. The destruction in the West in two centuries of much of what the ancient world had built up throughout three millennia was by no means compensated for by the Christianization of the invaders. The ensuing era, generally known as the Dark Ages, was not as protracted as historians once believed, as we shall see when we come to the extraordinary figure of the emperor Charlemagne at the end of the eighth century.

In contrast to the monumental architecture of the Early Christian and Byzantine world, on whose inner walls is figured forth in pictorial imagery the full complexity of Christian iconography, the barbarians, as long as they lived in the wilds, had no permanent buildings at all, only structures of timber and wattles. As far as we can discover, the art of painting was unknown to them. The surviving buildings and images created by the invaders once they had settled (with the exceptions of the partially Byzantinized Theodoric and the Visigoths in Spain) are for the most part small, rough, and unpretentious, giving little indication that the Germanic tribes had learned much from the culture they destroyed. Few of these examples are comparable in quality to the metalwork, an ancient and highly refined art, that the tribes brought with them and presumably continued to practice.

This metal art was generally foreign to Mediterranean culture but was especially relevant to the needs of nomadic peoples. Its practice was restricted to the manufacture of objects of daily life that the migrants could carry on their wanderings—weapons, personal adornments, and horse gear for the most part, often made of precious metals and studded with precious or semiprecious stones, but also objects of unknown ritual use. It is crucial to consider this barbarian art because both Celtic and Germanic ornament, generally free from all classical restraint, formed a countercurrent to the humanistic heritage of antiquity throughout European art in the Middle Ages up to the dawn of the Renaissance and was later to burst forth in certain aspects of the art of the twentieth century.

Celtic Art

The Celts, a race of great imaginative powers but, insofar as we know from classical sources, given to horrifying sacrificial and funerary rites, swept across Europe in the fourth century B.C. and appear to have picked up a number of elements and ideas from settled cultures with which they had already come in contact. Many splendid objects, of great historical as well as aesthetic importance, are identified with the richly productive La Tène culture, named after a site on Lake Neuchâtel in Switzerland, where immense numbers of such objects were found in peat bogs, which indicates that they were thrown into lakes, ponds, or rivers. Since many were useless from any practical standpoint (gold swords, let us say) it seems probable that they were made from the start as offerings to water gods. Appropriately, all La

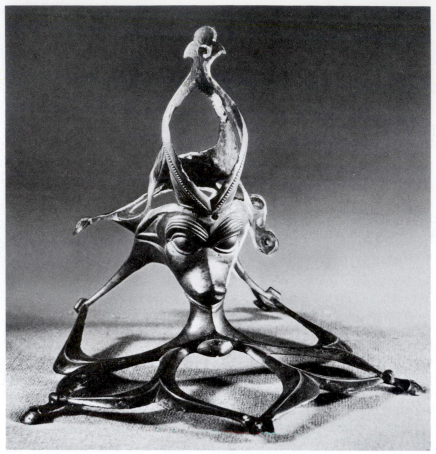

12-1. Openwork ornament, from Brno-Malomeřice, Czechoslovakia. c. 3d century B.C. Bronze, 4¾ × 5¾″ (12 × 15 cm). Moravian Museum, Brno, Czechoslovakia

12-1

Tène metalwork is characterized by a beautiful, sometimes bewildering, fluidity of style. One of the most complex is an openwork ornament in bronze of about the third century B.C., found at Brno-Malomeřice in Czechoslovakia (fig. 12–1). The organic shapes well outward and upward, expanding freely to enclose far more open space than solid form; a spatial pattern of surprising elegance and grace centers upon an antelope head with wide-open, staring eyes and upward-twisted horns, but ends in delicate hooves. La Tène motifs and shapes continue in Celtic art for the next thousand years or so, reappearing in some surprising places.

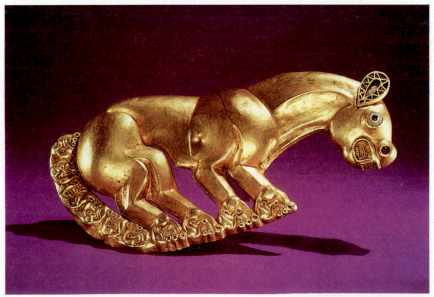

12-2. *Panther,* from Kelermes (near Rostov). Scythian, c. 6th century B.C. Gold, length 11⅝″ (30.5 cm). The State Hermitage Museum, St. Petersburg

12-2

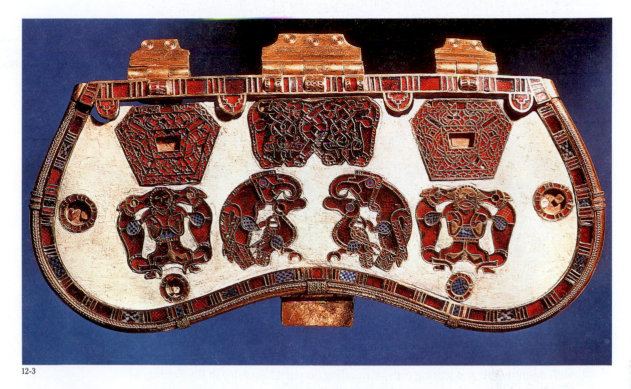

12-3

12-3. Purse lid, from a ship burial at Sutton Hoo (Suffolk), England. C. A.D. 655–56. Cloisonné plaques of gold and enamel with garnets and emeralds, originally set in ivory or bone (now lost), length 8″ (20.3 cm). British Museum, London

12-4

12-4. Animal head for a prow, from a ship burial at Oseberg, Norway. C. A.D. 825. Wood, height of head 5″ (12.7 cm). Institutt for Kunsthistorie og Klassisk Arkeologi, University of Oslo

The Animal Style

A further ingredient in the medieval mixture was the art of Slavic groups, who apparently never reached western Europe, although as we shall see, some of their products did make the journey and had a decisive effect on the arts of Scandinavia, Ireland, and the islands between Ireland and England. Unlike Celtic art, in which mere portions of animals are occasionally embedded, the very subject of this nomadic art was animals. For this reason the term "Animal Style" is often applied to it. To find its origin we have to go back to the Scythians, a people who lived on the steppes north and east of the Black Sea. They were regarded by the Greeks as arch-barbarians, but before they were Hellenized they produced gold objects of great beauty and frightening intensity, such as the crouching *Panther* (fig. 12–2) of the sixth century B.C., found in a burial mound at Kelermes. No work of twentieth-century sculpture has surpassed the power of the harsh masses and rhythms into which this animal is divided, nor the sheer ferocity of its snarling expression. The paws and the tail of the beast are beaten into the shapes of panthers, and the ears are executed in *cloisonné*. This technique consists of soldering small strips of metal to the underlying surface so that the small compartments they form may be filled with enamel, glass, or inlaid stones.

A more intricate example of cloisonné work is a purse lid (fig. 12–3) from an Anglo-Saxon royal ship burial at Sutton Hoo in Suffolk, England, dated A.D. 655–56, about 1,200 years later than the *Panther* but still unmistakably in the Animal Style. The lid, originally ivory or bone, is set with cloisonné plaques, of which those at upper right and left are ornamented with purely geometric patterns. The central panel is composed of fighting animals whose jaws are prolonged to form interlaced ribbons. Below are two plaques, each composed of an eagle capturing a duck, while at either side appears that rarest of animals in Migrations art, man, highly stylized and standing between two hostile wolves in a configuration that recalls the far-off days of the ancient Sumerians (see fig. 4–8); in fact the motif may have been derived from heraldic groupings in Mesopotamian art.

A final stage in the development of the animal interlace is seen in a fierce animal

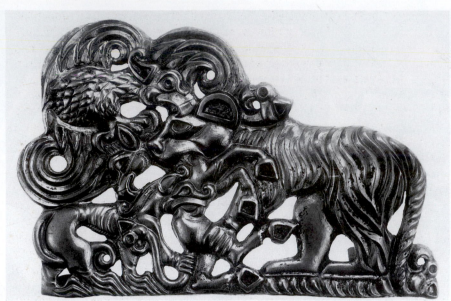

12-5

12-5. Scythian plaque with animal interlace, from the Altai Mountains, Siberia. Gold, 5⅛ × 7¾″ (13 × 20 cm). The State Hermitage Museum, St. Petersburg

head in the carved wood of a prow (fig. 12–4), from a ship burial of Viking seafarers at Oseberg, Norway, datable about A.D. 825. The animal itself is frightening enough, with open mouth and glaring eyes, reminding one of its ancestry in the *Panther* of Kelermes, but the wood-carver has embellished its head with a rich interlace of crisscrossing and entwined ribbon-like shapes that one would have difficulty tracing back to its probable origins in such an object as fig 12–5, another Scythian gold plaque, perhaps of the second century B.C., from the Altai Mountains in southern Siberia just above the border of Mongolia (see Map 14, page 523). This seething cauldron of destruction resolves itself relatively easily (after a moment's gaze) into a wolf and a tiger that are tearing a colt apart, while an eagle in turn attacks the tiger with beak and wings. The fighting animals have just begun to form an interlace, whose parallel striations are derived from the stripes of the tiger, the feathers of the eagle, and the shapes of the grasses below.

Hiberno-Saxon Art

The Anglo-Saxon pagan conquest of Britain in the fifth and sixth centuries A.D. left Christianized Ireland cut off from easy access to Continental Europe. Under such circumstances it is not surprising that a highly individual form of monasticism flourished in Ireland, a form adapted to the needs of an isolated country without urban centers. What was less to be expected was the rise of an intense Irish missionary activity, directed toward the Continent and toward England. From the sixth through the ninth centuries, Irish monks traveled through northern and central Europe, founding monasteries as far south as Switzerland and Italy. In 633, at the invitation of the king of Northumbria, one of the seven Anglo-Saxon kingdoms, an Irish monastery was established on the island of Lindisfarne, off the northeast coast of England. Quite independently, the Roman missionary Augustine (not to be confused with Saint Augustine, one of the four fathers of the Western Church) arrived in England in 597 to commence the conversion of the southern Anglo-Saxons to the Roman form of Christianity, from which the Irish by that time had deviated in a number of respects. At the Synod of Whitby in 664 the two missions met head-on, not without fireworks. Eventually, the Irish submitted to Rome but continued to maintain a certain independence.

An activity essential to the Irish missions was the copying of religious books, especially the Gospels. For the enrichment of their manuscripts, the Irish drew on established metalwork traditions, both Germanic and Celtic, as well as on examples of Early Christian illumination. The resultant art, carried out in all probability by Anglo-Saxon artists (although this is by no means certain) under Irish inspiration, is best known as Hiberno-Saxon. The transformations of Early Christian originals produced by these artists are interesting, but these pale in comparison with the marvels they turned out in a tradition they knew and understood. For example, one of the earliest of the Hiberno-Saxon manuscripts, the *Book of Durrow*, done in Northumbria in the second half of the seventh century, contains a brilliant decorative page (see Introduction fig. 23) whose ornamentation, surprisingly for a work of Christian art, can be traced directly to three of the four types seen in the purse lid from Sutton Hoo (see fig. 12–3): the animal interlace, the abstract interlace, and the pure geometric, translated from metal into painting. All of it is carried out in a style based on clear contours bounding flat areas of color obviously derived from the cloisonné technique. But a momentous change has taken place. Instead of being freely scattered across the area as in the purse lid, the three types of ornamentation are combined into a unified whole by powerful embracing shapes and movements. Two horizontal panels of animal interlace at the top and two at the bottom are united by smaller vertical panels to bound a square, in which floats a circle containing abstract interlace. Within this interlace are embedded three smaller circles of geometric ornament, arranged in an equilateral triangle. In the center a smaller circle surrounds a cross, composed of four equal triangular elements. This total grouping combines within itself the numbers of the Gospels and the Trinity, and by means of these numbers—the three outer circles, the four corners of the square, and the four horizontal bands, whose widths and lengths are related to each other as one to four—imposes its own proportional unity on the pagan magnificence of the ornament. The animals-biting-animals pattern now proceeds in a beautiful rhythmic motion, which also obeys distinct laws of repetition, alternation, and reversal as well as those of color and shape, all of which may be deduced if one is willing to look long enough.

An even more splendid book, the Gospels illuminated at Lindisfarne from 698 to 721, shows a more highly developed form of this harmony between Christian symbolism and pagan ornamental tradition in a symbolic structure of dizzying complexity and cosmic grandeur (fig. 12–6). Cross, circle, and square, extended at top and bottom to fit the oblong format, embrace the entire page in a manner recalling the heavenly Cross of the catacomb frescoes (see fig. 10–4). All three symbols are filled with abstract interlace, so divided into different color zones that at the ends of the crossbars four smaller crosses emerge. Between the crossbars the fields are filled with animal interlace of violent activity. The comparatively serene ornament in the central circle discloses one large and four smaller crosses. Tabs projecting from the four outer corners are formed by animal ornament; on the center of each side is another tab composed of facing birds whose beaks open to display sharp teeth. Most surprisingly, pure La Tène ornament, whose origins go back a thousand years, fills the corners of the extensions with active whorls.

If the Hiberno-Saxon artists had a Continental model before them, they translated its imagery recognizably enough into a geometrized equivalent, but when they invented their own figures, the result can be startling. The *imago hominis* ("image of man") page from the Gospels illuminated in the first half of the eighth century by a Northumbrian artist at Echternach in Luxembourg (fig. 12–7) is conveniently labeled, for otherwise we might not know a human being was intended. The little head, with its endearing cross-eyes, appears caught in the mechanism of the cruciform interlace that proceeds from all four sides of the border seemingly to form a vise. The artist, asked to paint the winged man symbolizing Matthew, treated him as a six-winged seraph. Locked in place by the four bars, he completes the form of the Cross.

The freest compositions of the Hiberno-Saxon manuscripts are those that display enormous letters engulfing the entire page. No pagan scribe would have thought of endowing initial letters with exceptional importance. But since the Bible

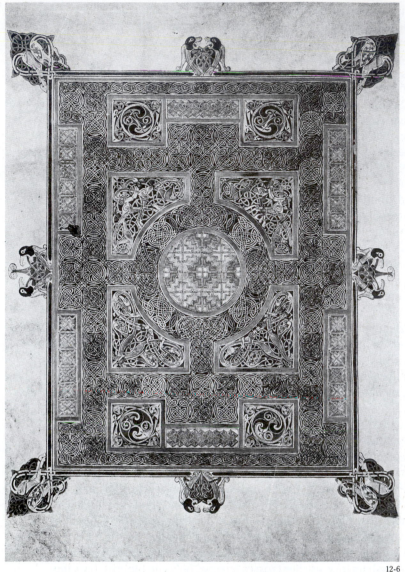

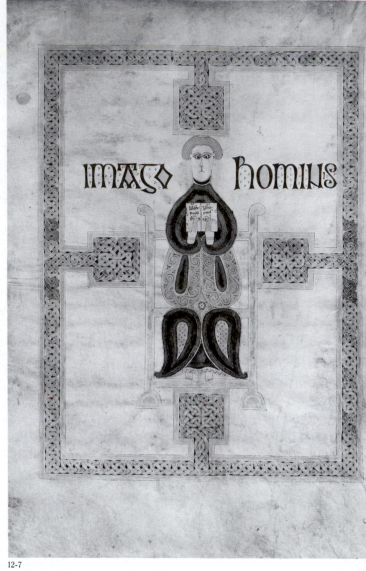

12-6   12-7

was divinely inspired and therefore sacred, its very letters—and most of all the initials—were regarded as exerting magical potency. What we might call the "Baroque" phase of the Hiberno-Saxon development is exemplified by the *Book of Kells* (fig. 12–8), a copy of the Four Gospels illuminated in southeastern Ireland between 760 and 820. The words *Christi liber generationis* ("the book of the generation of Christ"; Matthew 1:1) fill the entire page. The name of Christ, reduced to its Greek contraction *XPI,* becomes like the Cross an immense celestial apparition (divided neatly, of course, into successive areas of animal interlace, abstract interlace, and geometric ornament). The powerful diminishing curves, like comets, involve whole galaxies of La Tène circles-within-circles, large and small, filled with vibrant whorls—all going at once. After contemplating this revelation for a while, we are astonished to see emerging from its intricacies the faces and upper torsos of three angels, whose wings have become a part of the ornament along the clean outer edge of the mighty *X,* and a head on its side, gazing sadly outward as it terminates the inner curve of the *P.* Stranger yet, in the second spiral from the bottom of the page, at the tail of the same shape, two naturalistic mice appear in a heraldic grouping on either side of a small round object (a piece of cheese?), contemplated by two sleepy cats, each with a mouse on its back.

12-6. Cross page from the *Lindisfarne Gospels.* Northumberland, England, c. A.D. 698–721. Illumination. British Library, London

12-7. *Imago Hominis (Image of Man),* illumination from the *Echternach Gospels.* Luxembourg, c. first half of 8th century A.D. Bibliothèque Nationale, Paris

12-8. *XPI* page from the *Book of Kells.* Ireland, c. A.D. 760–820. Illumination. Trinity College, Dublin

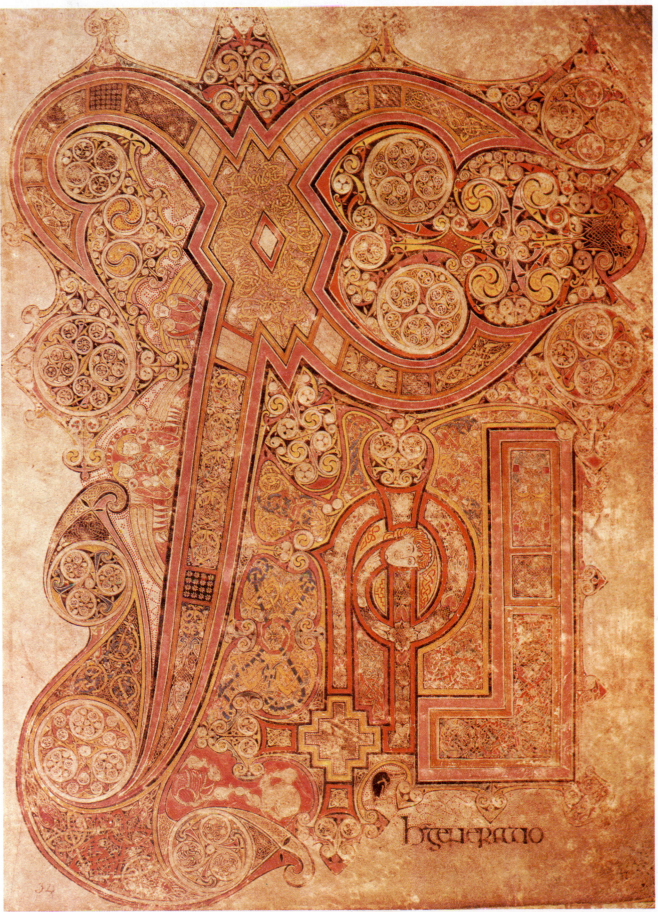

TIME LINE VI

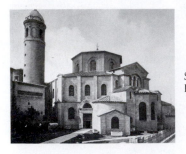

San Vitale,
Ravenna

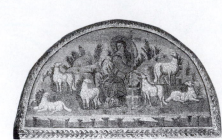

Good Shepherd,
Galla Placidia

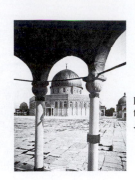

Dome of
the Rock,
Jerusalem

	HISTORY	CULTURE
200	Shapur I, Sassanian king of Persia, r. 242–72	Christian persecution in Roman Empire, 250
	Constantine the Great, r. 324–37	Emperor Gallienus grants Christians right to possess churches, 260
300	Constantinople (Byzantium) new imperial capital, 330	Great persecution, 303–5
	Theodosius divides Empire: East (Arcadius), West (Honorius), 395	Constantine proclaims toleration, Edict of Milan, 313
	Honorius makes Ravenna capital of West, 402	First Council of Nicea, 325
400	Alaric I, Visigothic king, sacks Rome, 410	St. Jerome translates Bible into Latin, 382
	Galla Placidia regent of West, 423–25	St. Augustine writes *City of God*, 412
	Vandals invade North Africa, 429	Council of Ephesus; Mary proclaimed *Theotokos* (Mother of God), 431
	Attila, king of Huns, destroys Milan, 450; Pope Leo persuades him to spare Rome	St. Patrick (d. 461) said to have founded Christian church in Celtic Ireland
	Odoacer takes Empire of West, Ravenna, 476; end of Western Roman Empire	
500	Theodoric founds Ostrogothic kingdom in Italy	
	Justinian Emperor of Byzantium	Justinian initiates "Golden Age," 527–65, codifies Roman laws
	Byzantine army reconquers Ravenna, 540	
	Lombards establish kingdom in Italy, 568	Silk cultivation brought from China, c. 550
600	Muslims conquer Byzantine provinces in Near East and North Africa, 637–40	Muhammad, prophet of Islam (c. 570–632), flees Medina (Hegira), 622
700	Omayyad caliphate, Damascus, 661–750	Text of Koran established, 651
	Muslims take Visigothic Spain, 711	Iconoclastic controversy, 726–843; Second Council of Nicea rejects iconoclasm, 787
	Abbasid caliphate, Baghdad, 750–1256	
800	Macedonian dynasty, 829–976	Macedonian "Renaissance" marks return to Hellenistic ideals
	Vládimir, grand prince of Kiev, r. 980–1015	Conversion of Russia to Orthodox Church, c. 990
1000–1600	Schism between Eastern and Western churches becomes final, 1054	

EARLY CHRISTIAN AND BYZANTINE/ISLAMIC/NORTHERN EUROPE

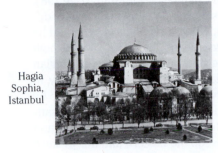

Hagia
Sophia,
Istanbul

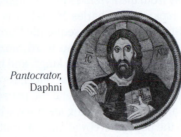

Pantocrator,
Daphni

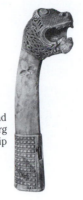

Animal-head
prow, Oseberg
Ship

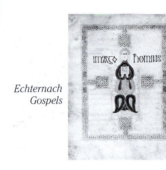

*Echternach
Gospels*

PAINTING, SCULPTURE, ARCHITECTURE

Ceiling fresco, Catacomb of Sta. Priscilla, Rome
Openwork ornament from Brno-Malomeřice
Christian community house and *Haman and Mordecai,* Dura-Europos
Palace of Shapur I, Ctesiphon
Ceiling fresco, Catacomb of Ss. Pietro e Marcellino, Rome
Sarcophagus of Junius Bassus; Vatican Virgil
Old St. Peter's and Sta. Costanza, Rome
Mosaics at Hagios Georgios, Salonika
Mausoleum of Galla Placidia, Ravenna, with mosaics
Mosaics at Sta. Maria Maggiore, Rome
St. Simeon Stylites, Qal'at Saman; *Colossus of Barletta*

San Vitale and S. Apollinare in Classe, Ravenna, with mosaics
Hagia Sophia, Constantinople; *Vienna Genesis; Rabula Gospels*

Dome of the Rock, Jerusalem
Purse lid, Sutton Hoo; *Book of Durrow*
Echternach and *Lindisfarne Gospels*
Frescoes, Sta. Maria Foris Portas, Castelseprio
Book of Kells
Oseberg Ship; Great Mosque, Samarra; Mosque of Ibn Tulun, Cairo
Virgin and Child mosaic, Hagia Sophia; *Paris Psalter*
Joshua Roll; Harbaville Triptych
Churches at Hosios Loukas; Hagia Sophia, Kiev
Alhambra; Madrasah of Sultan Hasan; *Bihzad in the Garden*
Last Judgment, Voroneţ; Taj Mahal, Agra; Mosque of Selim II, Edirne

PARALLEL SOCIETIES

Roman Empire	200
Celtic	
Early Christian	
	300
	400
Lombard	500
Byzantine	
Muslim	600
Viking	
Hiberno-Saxon	700
Carolingian	800
Ottonian	1000–
Romanesque and *Gothic*	1600
Mogul	

The victorious advance of the Muslims in Europe was stopped in 732 at Tours, two-thirds of the way from the Pyrenees to the English Channel (see Map 11, page 298), by Frankish forces under Charles Martel. It is sobering to contemplate how different European history, and consequently European art, might have been had he lost this battle. Charles Martel (the word *martel* means "hammer") was a high official under the weak Merovingian kings, and he gave his name to the Carolingian dynasty that, under his son Pepin the Short, replaced them. Pepin entered Italy, in answer to the pope's appeal, to defend the papacy against the Lombards; in 756 he gave Ravenna and the surrounding territory, which rightly belonged to the Byzantine Empire, to the pope, thereby at once strengthening the ties between Rome and the Frankish kingdom and weakening those between the Eastern and the Western Church.

Pepin's son, known to history as Charlemagne (Charles the Great), ruled as Frankish king from 768 to 814, a reign of forty-six years that transformed the cultural history of northern and central Europe. On Christmas Day in the year 800 he was crowned Roman emperor in Saint Peter's by Pope Leo III. While it appeared that Charlemagne revived the fifth-century division between East and West, in fact he ruled a region that included modern France, the Low Countries, Germany, much of central Europe, a small slice of northern Spain, and Italy down to a borderline not far south of Rome. He governed this territory from his court in the German city of Aachen (also known by its French name of Aix-la-Chapelle), near the modern border of Germany with Belgium and the Netherlands. In point of fact, Charlemagne founded a wholly new institution, a northern dominion known after the thirteenth century as the Holy Roman Empire. For a thousand years his successors exercised an often disputed and never clearly defined authority over much of Europe, until Napoleon dissolved the Holy Roman Empire in 1806. In the imagination of the Middle Ages, the emperor exercised in temporal affairs the sovereignty that in spiritual matters belonged to the pope. Since the latter was by now a temporal monarch as well, largely by courtesy of the Carolingian rulers, Pepin the Short had opened a Pandora's box, which none of his successors ever quite succeeded in closing.

Carolingian Art

Abbot Einhard, Charlemagne's biographer, said of him:

> He made his kingdom which was dark and almost blind when God committed it to him . . . radiant with the blaze of fresh learning hitherto altogether unknown to our barbarism.

If we discount courtly hyperbole, Einhard's claim still contains much truth. We must imagine the Roman cities of Charlemagne's realm as largely in ruins and very nearly depopulated, and there is no indication that he tried to rebuild them. To his court at Aachen, however, he brought Greek and Latin manuscripts, and foreign scholars, especially Alcuin of York, who supervised imperial campaigns aimed at the revival of Greek and Roman learning and the establishment of the correct text of the Bible, which, through constant recopying, had grown corrupt. Such concerns are remarkable in an emperor who retained Frankish dress and who, although he understood spoken Greek and could converse in Latin, never succeeded in learning to write. The emperor's architectural ambitions seem to have been limited to the embellishment of the imperial court and of the monasteries that, under the

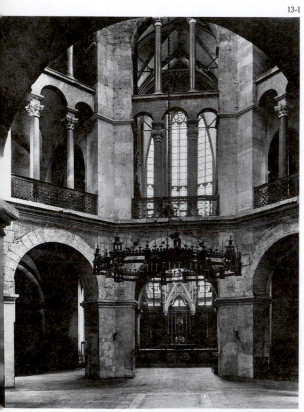

13-1

13-1. ODO OF METZ. Palatine Chapel of Charlemagne, Aachen, Germany. 792–805

Benedictines based at Monte Cassino in southern Italy and under the Irish monks who had founded monasteries in much of the territory to which Charlemagne fell heir, had established themselves as Western guardians of classical Christian culture.

ARCHITECTURE

Aachen. Little of what Charlemagne built is still standing in anything like its original condition; luckily, the chapel of his palace at Aachen is preserved, although it was extended by a Gothic choir in the late Middle Ages and stripped of its splendid mural decorations. The architect, ODO OF METZ, is the first builder known to us by name north of the Mediterranean. The Palatine Chapel of Aachen is an octagon (figs. 13–1, 13–2), and a first glance will show that Odo modeled it on San Vitale at Ravenna, a church that Charlemagne must have greatly admired. The next look, however, discloses crucial differences. The flexible, expanding plan of San Vitale (see figs. 10–27, 10–28) has been abandoned, possibly because it was unbuildable in stone, possibly because no one knew enough about architectural draftsmanship in 792 to reproduce it; Odo may never have visited Ravenna. Each of the seven transparent apses of San Vitale has been replaced by two superimposed round arches. The upper arch embraces two levels, the lower of which is a straight arcade formed by three round arches and the upper of which is sheer fantasy—two columns that support the crowning arch at just the point on either side of the keystone where it needs no support, as these lateral voussoirs tend to be pushed up, not down, by the pressure of the central keystone (see fig. 9–34). Such a use of Early Christian—in fact, Roman—motifs, shorn of their original function and deprived of their true spatial extension, was significant for Carolingian figurative art as well. Needless to say, many if not all of the colored marble and granite columns and white Corinthian capitals were imported from Roman buildings in Italy. Most of the heavy masonry is composed of massive blocks of stone, but the cores of the piers are rubble. Originally, the dome was resplendent with a mosaic representing Christ enthroned in Heaven among the four-and-twenty elders rising from their thrones to cast their crowns before his throne, according to the vision of John (Revelation 4:1–10), an appropriate subject for a patron who claimed divine authority for his own imperial rule. (Recently, it has been suggested that the enthroned Christ is a later interpolation, and that the original mosaic showed the Lamb upon the throne.)

Interestingly enough, the customary narthex, set at an angle at San Vitale, is replaced here by a central portal flanked by two circular towers and entered from the main court of the palace. The emperor could thus attend Mass in the gallery as though in a box at the theater, and he could appear at an opening above the portal to the populace in the courtyard outside. Here Charlemagne had set up a bronze equestrian statue of Theodoric (a worthy model, as a Romanized Germanic chieftain), which he had brought across the Alps from Ravenna. The courtyard could hold about seven thousand persons. The design of the Palatine Chapel was so successful that it was repeated several times in different parts of Germany.

Centula. In the still largely agricultural and patriarchal society of the Franks and their Germanic and Gallic subjects, there was no need for new urban churches, but monasteries were essential to Charlemagne's program, and he rebuilt them and founded new ones in great numbers. Only a few remain, largely remodeled, but plans exist that show how crucial these monasteries were for the late Middle Ages.

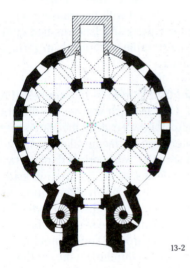

13-2

13-2. Plan of the Palatine Chapel of Charlemagne, Aachen

The plan of the now totally vanished Abbey Church of Saint-Riquier at Centula (fig. 13–3), near Abbeville in northern France, is basically that of a Constantinian basilica with a nave and two side aisles for the congregation, the whole structure roofed with timber. The extensive transept was necessary for processions from the *sacristies,* where the vestments, books, and vessels for the Mass were kept, to the altar, and became a fixture in all large churches, eventually developing side aisles of its own. The apse is separated from the transept by a rectangular space called the *choir,* intended for the use of the monastic community in chanting the complex music of the Mass and of the Divine Office (the prayers at the seven stated hours; in contrast to Islam, these were recommended for the faithful but not required). The choir, eventually supplied with elaborately carved seats rising in tiers on either side, also became a fixture in monastic and cathedral churches from then on. The church plan thus assumed, almost accidentally, the shape of a cross.

At the west end (churches where possible faced east, toward Jerusalem) is an important addition—a narthex running at right angles to the nave and projecting beyond it, forming in effect a second transept. This addition is known in German churches as the *westwork* (fine later examples are shown in figs. 13–13, 14–29). The westwork was divided into two or even three groin-vaulted stories; the upper levels could be used as chapels for smaller services. Before the westwork is a large atrium, as at Saint Peter's. In the corners of the atrium, on either side of the westwork, are two cylindrical staircase towers, and two more are visible flanking the choir in the angles of the transept. These towers apparently rose to a considerable height. It may fairly be asked what their use could have been. We do not know whether bells were employed in European churches at this time, but if they were, a single tower would have sufficed for this purpose, as was generally the case in Italy. Four clearly represent an attempt to assert the existence of the church and to render it visible from afar. To make its appearance still grander, Saint-Riquier also sported massive round towers above the crossing points of the nave with the westwork and with the transept. These towers culminated in round lanterns; both corner towers and lanterns had conical roofs. All at once the lofty skyline of the medieval cathedral appears in germ, replacing the low profile of the Early Christian basilica.

Saint Gall. In 816–17 a council at Aachen devised an ideal plan for a monastery (fig. 13–4), which was sent to the abbot of Saint Gall in Switzerland; although he did not follow it exactly, the plan is revealing in that it shows all the major features of a later Western medieval monastery. The plan is dominated by the church, whose semicircular westwork is flanked by two cylindrical towers. The customary nave and side aisles of the interior lead as usual to transept, choir, and apse. The buildings to the north of the church include a guest house, a school, and the abbot's house. Behind the apse and to the south is a building for novices. Adjacent to the novitiate and to the south lie the cemetery (frugally used also as an orchard), the vegetable gardens, and the poultry pens. In the position that became customary in all oriented churches, in the southwest corner of the transept—the warmest spot in the monastery—is the *cloister,* a courtyard surrounded by arcades, under which the monks could walk, write, and—when permitted—converse. Storerooms flank the cloister to the west, the monks' dormitory with connecting bath and latrine lies to the east, and a refectory for meals with a nearby kitchen is to the south. To the south of the refectory are workshops, brewhouse, bakehouse, and other work buildings. A hospice for the poor is adjacent to the southwest tower. The whole was laid out with the same sense of system and order that prevailed in a Hellenistic or Roman civic center, for the monastery was indeed a town in itself.

The Carolingian period is often characterized as a renaissance because Charlemagne made a deliberate effort to revive classical antiquity. But each renaissance (that of Augustus or of Hadrian, for example) picks and chooses among the treasures of the past only those it feels it needs. Charlemagne did not revive

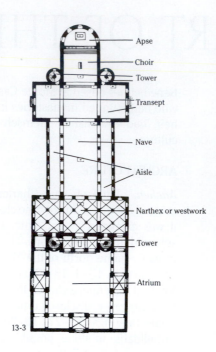

13-3. Plan of the Abbey Church of St.-Riquier, Centula, France (destroyed). Late 8th century

The labels on the monastery plan (fig. 13-4):

Guest house   School   Abbot's house

Tower

Public entrance

Tower

Parlor

Storerooms

Hospice for the poor

Barns and pens

Cloister court

Main altar

Raised gallery

Infirmary

Convent of the novices

Apples

Pears   [Figs]

Plums   Laurel

Chestnuts

Medlars

Orchard and cemetery

Garden

Kitchen   Bake house   Refectory   Baths   Latrine

Brew house

Limekiln   Mortars   Mills   Workrooms for artisans   Barn

Poultry pens

13-4

13-4. Drawing after a schematic plan for a monastery at St. Gall, Switzerland. c. 819. Original manuscript in red ink on parchment, 28 × 44⅛″ (71.1 × 112.1 cm). Stiftsbibliothek, St. Gall (inscriptions translated from Latin)

13-5

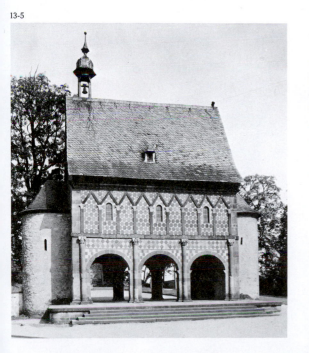

13-5. Gateway, Abbey of Lorsch (Hesse), Germany. 768–74

temples or nude statues; he was interested in establishing in the North a durable Christian society after an interregnum of tribal near-chaos. He went to considerable trouble to work out an administrative system for his empire, and widespread knowledge was necessary for the fulfillment of his purpose. For the acquisition and diffusion of knowledge, the monasteries, with their libraries and busy *scriptoria* (rooms for copying manuscripts), staffed by disciplined and devoted monks, were essential. As we have seen, the earliest extant copies of many ancient, even pagan, authors were made in these very scriptoria.

Lorsch. It is interesting, therefore, to see what dignity could be given to the gateway leading to the imperial Abbey of Lorsch, in the central Rhineland (fig. 13–5). This little building was imitated from the now-vanished triple gateway that gave access to the atrium before Saint Peter's (see fig. 10–9). Charlemagne has let his gateway stand free like a triple arch of triumph. Undoubtedly, the columns and capitals were culled from a Roman building. But the pilasters above the columns support colored marble zigzags that savor more of Germanic metalwork than of ancient Rome, and the overall effect of the monument, agreeable as it is, is anything but classical, with its flickering background of inlaid colored marble lozenges on the first story and octagons on the second, not to speak of its steep, Northern roof.

PAINTING AND LITURGICAL ARTS   From contemporary accounts we know that Charlemagne heard evidence on both sides of the iconoclastic controversy then raging in the East (see page 335); he rejected the views of those who would destroy religious images and would forbid the creation of new ones, yet even more firmly he opposed the worship of images. The emperor was deeply interested in the instructional value and the quality of the mural paintings and mosaics throughout his realm; he commissioned an inventory of their subjects (which still survives) and expected periodic reports on their condition. He ordered that paintings done during his reign were to depict Christ and the Apostles, narratives from the New Testament and to a lesser extent from the Old, and the lives of the saints. Military leaders from ancient history could be shown if paralleled with their Christian counterparts (for example, Alexander/Constantine), but classical deities and personifications were to be avoided in paintings visible to the public. Alas, little but the written accounts remains of the presumably splendid Carolingian art of mural painting, and what does survive is either so provincial or so fragmentary that we can gain no clear idea of how the murals once looked. But illuminated manuscripts from the period are preserved by the score, often in well-nigh perfect condition. They glow with color and gold and are so beautiful that we mourn the loss of the wall paintings all the more.

The manuscripts illuminated for the emperor himself were often written, like those commissioned by Justinian, in letters of gold on purple parchment. Although he could not write, Charlemagne laid great stress on legibility. He caused the disorderly and at times nearly indecipherable script of Merovingian times to be replaced by a new form of letters, more useful than the capitals that the Romans employed exclusively. (In fact, the capitals used on this page are based on those in inscriptions dating from the reign of Trajan, while the small letters descend from the script invented for Charlemagne and taught throughout his dominions.) Schools of illumination were set up at various centers, including the court at Aachen and the bishoprics of Reims, Metz, and Tours. Although the large initial letters often proudly display the complex interlaces of Hiberno-Saxon tradition, the illustrations are figurative, either copied from Early Christian originals (this is a hypothesis, since no such originals are known) or invented anew. Christ and the Evangelists were often given full-page illustrations—Christ as King, the Evangelists as authors. King David, naturally enough, was another favorite of the emperor and was often prominently depicted. Pages were also filled with *canon tables* (which show the correspondence of passages in the four Gospels), written in under illusionistic arcades.

13-6. *Saint Matthew*, illumination from the *Coronation Gospels (Gospel Book of Charlemagne)*. c. 795–810. Kunsthistorisches Museum, Vienna

13-7. *Portrait of Menander*, Fourth Style wall painting in the House of Menander, Pompeii, Italy. c. 70

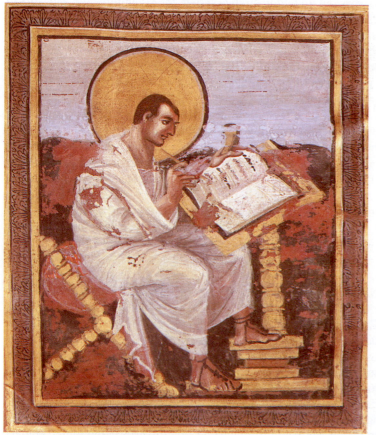

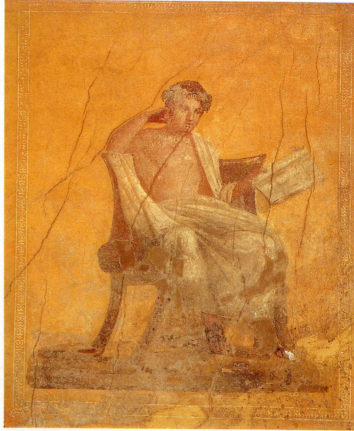

13-6   13-7

13-8. *Saint Matthew,* illumination from the *Ebbo Gospels (Gospel Book of Archbishop Ebbo).* Reims, France, 816–41. Bibliothèque Nationale, Paris

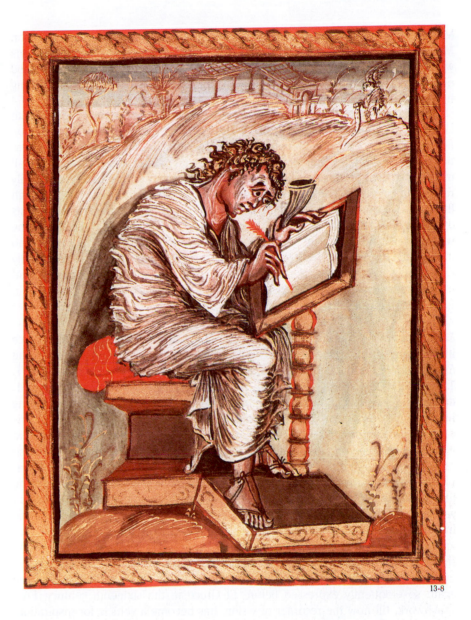

13-8

Coronation Gospels. One of the finest Carolingian manuscripts is the *Coronation Gospels,* said to have been found on Charlemagne's knees when his tomb was opened in the year 1000. Like most manuscripts of the Palace School, the *Coronation Gospels* are illuminated only with canon tables and with full-page portraits of the Evangelists. The Evangelist Matthew (fig. 13–6) is painted in a manner so classical that it is hard to realize we are looking at a work done between 795 and 810 rather than five hundred years earlier. The Evangelist, seated on a folding stool, is robed in snowy white and holds his inkhorn above the page with his left hand while his right, grasping a reed pen, is poised as if he were awaiting inspiration. The background landscape, with its rich blue-greens and with rose-and-white clouds streaking the sky, not to speak of the lights and shadows and the soft brushwork of the mantle, comes straight from the Helleno-Roman illusionistic tradition. This beautiful illustration has often been compared with Roman author representations, especially the *Portrait of Menander,* of the Fourth Style, dating from about A.D. 70, from the House of Menander at Pompeii (fig. 13–7). But as Meyer Schapiro has pointed out, there is a fundamental difference, which tells us much about the essential character of illuminated manuscripts. Like all authors in classical art,

Menander is shown reading from a rotulus, in a relaxed and patrician manner. Matthew is pictured *writing,* in a codex, of course. To the Greeks and Romans writing was a manual activity they relegated to slaves, and books were copied quasi-mechanically in shops, which were the ancestors of modern publishing houses.

Christians believe that "In the beginning was the Word, and the Word was with God, and the Word was God" (John 1:1). Thus, copying the Word was a sacred duty; how much more elevated, then, the activity of writing under direct divine inspiration! It is to this solemn moment that the Carolingian painter admits us. And, like all medieval artists, he was not really interested in an exact representation of earthly relationships. We look at the portrait through a classical acanthus frame as though through a window, but one leg of the stool is clearly inside the frame, the other rests on its edge, and the Evangelist's right foot is placed somewhere near the base of the writing desk, not really on it. The question of the homeland of the artist who illuminated the *Coronation Gospels,* at once so serenely classical and so profoundly Christian, has often been asked but never answered. He may have been an Italian trained in the Byzantine tradition, but in the absence of any paintings of this style in Italy itself, we cannot say.

Ebbo Gospels. A startling transformation of the calm, classical image takes place in the manuscripts of the Reims School, of which the outstanding example is the *Ebbo Gospels,* illuminated for Ebbo, archbishop of Reims between 816 and 841. The same Matthew (fig. 13–8), seen through the same acanthus frame, has suddenly been seized as if by the *furor divinus.* He bends over as he writes, clutching his quill pen, his eyes almost starting from their sockets with excitement, his drapery dashing madly about his form, the very locks of his hair on end and writhing like serpents. Both the figure and the quivering landscape have been so rapidly set down in quick, nervous strokes of the brush that they seem to participate in his emotion, recalling the words: "The mountains skipped like rams, and the little hills like lambs" (Psalm 114:4). The tiny structures in the background seem seriously endangered in this cosmic dance, and even the acanthus leaves of the frame run like flames about the edges—left and upper borders together, right and lower borders meeting. The angel, Matthew's symbol, is sketchily brushed in on the right horizon; he brandishes a scroll, the source of the Evangelist's inspiration. We are here confronted with a form of ecstatic mysticism that we shall seldom see again so eloquently expressed before El Greco in the sixteenth century. Free brushwork, till now the recorder of vision, has become a vehicle for inspiration.

Utrecht Psalter. One of the masterpieces of Carolingian art is the *Utrecht Psalter,* a book of psalms written and illustrated in the Reims School (which comprised several monasteries) at about the same moment the *Ebbo Gospels* were being illuminated and in a similar passionate style. While the psalter was written in reed pen, the illustrations were drawn with quill pen, and in the course of time the ink has turned a rich brown, running from quite dark brown to soft golden tones. The little drawings are frameless, scattered freely about the page between the psalms as if they were mental images, some invading the Latin text (still written, by the way, in traditional Roman capitals, without spaces between the words). The compositions may derive from earlier models, and the lively drawings in the psalter are the work of several different hands of varying degrees of quality. However, the style is so consistent that one major master must have inspired the unflagging freshness of the scenes and their rapidly moving and gesticulating figures. The illustrations are quite literal. Fig. 13–9 illustrates both Psalm 82 in the King James Version (81 in the Douay Version), which is written in the central register, and Psalm 83 (82 in the Douay Version), whose text appears on the following page of the psalter. Psalm 82 is pictured in the top register. The illustrations can best be read juxtaposed with the appropriate verses:

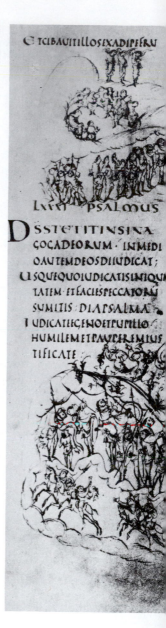

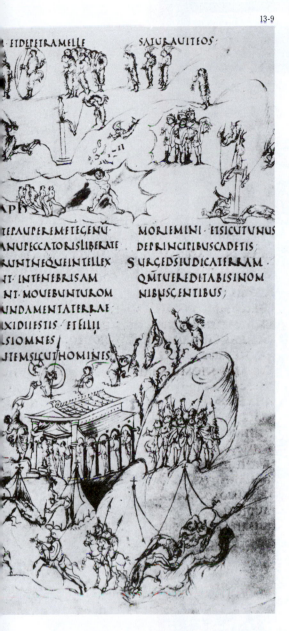

13-9

13-9. *Last Judgment* (above) and *Angels of the Lord Smiting the Enemies of the Israelites* (below), illuminations from the *Utrecht Psalter.* Reims, c. 820–32. University Library, Utrecht, the Netherlands

Verse 1	*God standeth in the congregation of the mighty; he judgeth among the gods.*	In the center the Lord, in a mandorla and holding a cross-staff, addresses crowds on either side of him; farther out three angels on each side keep a respectful distance.
Verse 4	*Deliver the poor and needy; rid them out of the hand of the wicked.*	At the lower left an angel with a sword welcomes the poor, while their tormentors slink away.
Verse 5	*... all the foundations of the earth are out of course.*	Toward the center a giant (Tellus, the Roman god of the earth) shakes the earth gleefully, and things fall to bits; five men flee.
Verse 7	*But ye shall die like men, and fall like one of the princes.*	At the lower right crowned figures watch an angel set fire to a statue on a column; two angels knock a statue down, and two men fall dead below it.

Psalm 83 (82 in the Douay Version) is illustrated in the bottom register:

Verse 2	*For, lo, thine enemies make a tumult: and they that hate thee have lifted up the head.*	At the left a crowd of armed men mill about in confusion, lifting up their heads.
Verse 12	*... let us take to ourselves the houses of God in possession.*	In the center people fill the arches of a pedimented house; one defies the Lord above, who bears spear and shield.
Verse 14	*... as the flame setteth the mountains on fire; ...*	Across the illustration, right and left of the Lord, angels set the mountains on fire.
Verse 17	*Let them be confounded and troubled for ever ...*	At the bottom an army of men on horseback retreats rapidly; three of the horsemen are trapped in rope snares.

The artist never loses either the compositional coherence of the entire image, made up of several moments in time with the Lord always pictured in the center, or the speed of a sprightly pen style, which fairly dashes across the page.

Bible of Charles the Bald. After Charlemagne's death his descendants partitioned his domains and proved incapable of continuing his great dream of a newly revived Roman Empire. Nonetheless, the lively narrative and expressive style of the Reims School continued to influence the development of manuscript painting under Charlemagne's grandson, Charles the Bald, who ruled over a region corresponding more or less to modern France. Charles briefly wore the imperial crown (875–77). The splendid *Bible of Charles the Bald* contains a rich series of succinct visual narrations, in brilliant colors, picturing scenes from both Old and New Testaments. One full-page illustration (fig. 13–10) gives incidents from the ninth chapter of Acts in three registers. At the left of the upper register Saul (not yet Paul) receives a scroll from the high priest on which are written letters for Damascus. At the right, on the way to Damascus, he falls to the ground before the Lord, who appears as the conventional Hand of God, to the astonishment of his companions, who hear a voice but see no one. At the left of the central register Saul is led blind into Damascus. At the right the aged Ananias, asleep on his bed, lifts his hand to the

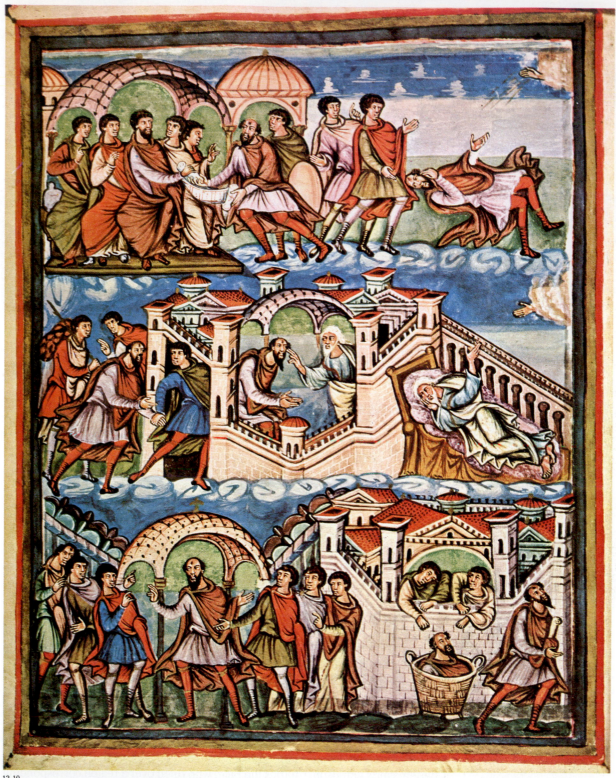

13-10

13-10. *Scenes from the Life of Saint Paul,* illumination from the *Bible of Charles the Bald.* Rome, c. 875–77. S. Paolo fuori le mura, Rome

Lord, from whom he receives the command to restore Saul's sight. The miracle, in which Ananias places his hand on Saul's eyes, has been moved out of order to the center of the register and also occupies the center of the page. At the lower left Saul confounds the incredulous Jews; at the right he is let down over the walls of Damascus in a basket.

The scenes unfold according to the continuous method we have seen in all manuscript narrations so far, a scheme derived ultimately from Roman historical reliefs. But the naturalistic concepts of support and of enclosure have been dis-

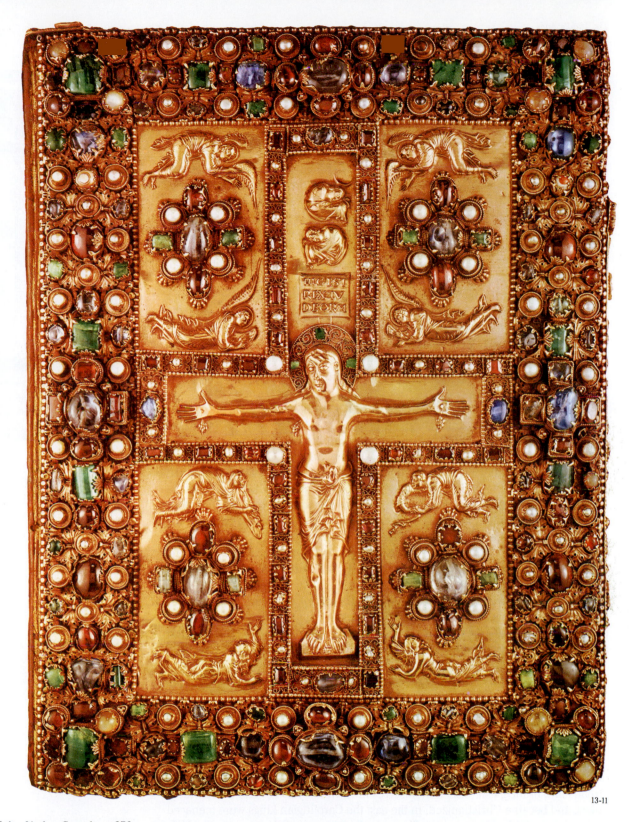

13-11. Front cover of the *Lindau Gospels*. c. 870. Gold with precious and semiprecious stones, 13¾ × 10½″ (34.9 × 26.7 cm). The Pierpont Morgan Library, New York

missed. Green earth runs under most of the scenes, with blue sky and white clouds above, but often the feet of the figures in one scene project beyond the ground strip into the clouds of the scene below. Likewise, the simple baldachin on four columns, which does triple duty for the Temple in the first scene, for the house of Judas in which Saul receives his sight in the fifth, and for the locale where Saul confounds the Jews in the sixth, does not enclose the figures, who stand or walk in front of columns they should be behind. The little cities of late Roman and Early Christian art are now toylike. The broad strips of energetic figures and ornamental architecture have been worked into a pattern uniting the whole page, enlivened and reinforced by the systematic distribution of blues, greens, red browns, rose tones, and lavenders.

How precious the illuminated Christian codex, the work of many months and even years, had become as compared with the utilitarian rotulus of antiquity may be seen in the magnificent covers that protected the painted pages. Most dazzling of all the covers are, of course, those made of gold and studded with precious and semiprecious stones, whose craftsmanship shows that the Germanic tradition of metalwork was by no means extinct. The front cover of the *Lindau Gospels* (fig. 13–11), made apparently in the third quarter of the ninth century for a Carolingian monarch, is almost unbelievable in its splendor. Not only the massive acanthus frame but also the interlaced border of the Cross are set with gems, not faceted, as is customary today, but smooth and lifted above the gold to receive light from all sides. Christ is represented calmly alive (a type known as the *Christus triumphans*), seeming to stand on the footrest and to extend his arms voluntarily. He is shown as one who has conquered death. Above his head little half figures representing the sun and the moon hide themselves, and in the upper panels four angels float in beautiful poses of grief. In the panels beneath the Cross, in the style of the flying angels, crouch the figures of Mary, John, and the other Marys. The still-Hellenic delicacy of the floating drapery contrasts strongly with the barbaric richness of the jeweled setting.

The back cover of the *Lorsch Gospels* (fig. 13–12), probably carved at the court of Aachen in the early ninth century, is made of ivory, as were the Early Christian and Byzantine diptychs from which the style derives. In the central relief a beardless Christ stands under an acanthus arch supported by modified Corinthian columns, as mentioned in Psalm 91 (90 in the Douay Version), Verse 13: "Thou shalt tread upon the lion and the adder: the young lion and the dragon shalt thou trample under feet." A rabbit appears at the right, a very wavy adder at the left, and under Christ's feet the lion and the dragon are being firmly trampled. The arches of the side panels shelter the angels who, in Verse 11, are given "charge over thee, to keep thee in all thy ways." In the upper strip two angels uphold a medallion containing the Cross; in the lower left the three Magi come before Herod and on the right they present their gifts to the Virgin and Child. Clearly, the style is directly imitated from Early Christian or Byzantine originals (see fig. 10–24, for example); the beardless Christ suggests a source in Ravenna. However, as in the manuscripts, the drapery patterns, still fluttering freely at the edges, are beginning to crystallize into ornamental motifs that do not derive from the actual performance of cloth over bodies.

Ottonian Art

Under the uncertain conditions prevailing in northern Europe in the ninth century, the continued maintenance of imperial administration throughout so great an area would have required a dynasty of rulers of Charlemagne's exceptional ability. Unfortunately, his successors divided his empire among themselves and were unequal to the task of repelling renewed waves of invasion. The Vikings made inroads into France, established themselves in Normandy as *de facto* independent dukes, and became Christianized. In the east the Carolingian kings were menaced by incursions from Magyars and Slavs. As the dynasty disintegrated, the Holy Roman Empire lapsed. Royal power in France passed to Hugh Capet, whose descendants ruled without interruption until the French Revolution. In Germany the duke of Saxony was elected king as Henry I but avoided ecclesiastical coronation. His extraordinary son, Otto I (ruled 936–73), was determined to revive imperial power on a Roman scale, but he succeeded only in reestablishing direct rule over Germany and Italy, often by installing members of his family in crucial positions. He set up relatives as dukes throughout Germany; married the widow of Lothair II, king of Italy; and arranged the marriage of his son, later Otto II, to

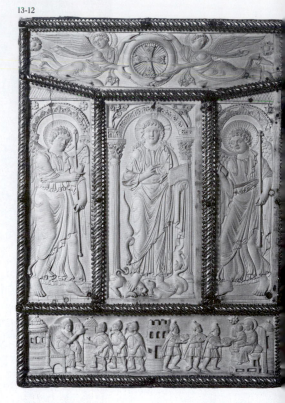

13-12. Back cover of the *Lorsch Gospels.* Probably Aachen, Germany, early 9th century. Ivory, 14¾ × 10¾″ (37 × 27 cm). Musei Vaticani, Rome

Theophano, daughter of the Byzantine emperor Romanus II, thereby laying claim to Byzantine southern Italy. Otto I also made three expeditions to Italy, had himself crowned king at Pavia, deposed two popes and nominated their successors, and reinforced the imperial claim to the right to approve papal elections. Before Saxon hegemony came to an end in the eleventh century, two descendants of Otto I had occupied the throne of Saint Peter. The five Ottonian rulers (919–1024) brought Germany to the artistic leadership of Europe in the construction of monastic buildings, in painting, and in the revived art of monumental sculpture.

ARCHITECTURE   Only a few Ottonian church buildings remain, including the westwork of the Benedictine Abbey Church of Saint Pantaleon at Cologne, consecrated in 980 (fig. 13–13); the church was especially favored by Archbishop Bruno of Cologne, the brother of Otto I. Although most of the church was transformed in the late Middle Ages, the surviving original fragment shows us something of the grandeur of Ottonian architecture. The two arms of the westwork and the western porch (the latter a modern addition) are of almost equal length, radiating from a square crossing tower with a pyramidal roof. In the angles stand tall towers, which begin square, continue octagonal, and end cylindrical. We are at once aware of two new traits of style. First, the powerful impression exerted by the exterior is achieved by block masses of heavy masonry rather than by the thin, flat walls used by Early Christian architects. The splaying of the windows, to admit more light, increases the apparent thickness of the walls. Second, the stories are separated by *corbel tables* (tiny blind arches without supports, upholding a continuous cornice). The establishment of a strong exterior view of the church building, begun in Carolingian architecture, thus culminates in a dramatic massing of clearly demarcated cubes, pyramids, octagons, and cylinders.

One of the most active patrons of the arts during the Ottonian period was Bishop Bernward of Hildesheim, who had been a tutor of Otto III and had traveled to Rome. The great Church of Saint Michael at Hildesheim (fig. 13–14), which Bernward rebuilt from 1001 to 1033, was considerably altered in later times and largely destroyed in World War II. It has since been reconstructed so as to reproduce as far as possible its eleventh-century appearance. The exterior view before the bombing (fig. 13–15) shows the westwork to the right, the choir and apse to the left, and identical square towers over the two crossings. The side-aisle windows are later Gothic additions. The transept towers have been moved from the inner corners to the ends. In the interior the westwork is raised above the level of

13-13

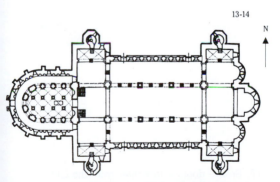

13-13. Westwork, Abbey Church of St. Pantaleon, Cologne, Germany. c. 980

13-14

N

13-14. Plan of St. Michael's, Hildesheim, Germany (after Beseler). 1001–33

13-15. St. Michael's, Hildesheim (before restoration)

13-15

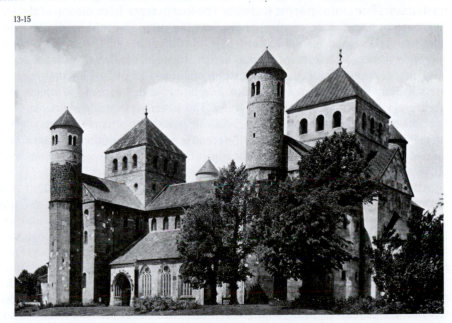

the rest of the church in order to provide an entrance to a crypt with an ambulatory. Especially original is the way in which the sometimes monotonous impression of the customary basilican interior is broken up (fig. 13–16). The massive masonry construction permitted a high clerestory, separated from the nave arcades by an expanse of unbroken wall surface, measured by the height of the side-aisle roof, doubtless intended for frescoes. The nave arcade itself, as in some Eastern basilicas, is broken by a pier after every second column into three groups of three arches on each side, there being twelve columns and four piers in all. It can scarcely have escaped Bernward's attention that he was founding this numerical arrangement on the number of persons in the Trinity, the number of the Twelve Apostles, and the number of the Four Evangelists.

SCULPTURE Bernward commissioned for the south portal of Saint Michael's a pair of bronze doors (fig. 13–17), completed by 1015 and probably before 1035 installed in Hildesheim Cathedral. Bronze doors were traditional in ancient times (the Pantheon had a splendid set), and plain bronze doors without sculpture had been made for the Palace Chapel at Aachen. Bernward is recorded to have been an amateur artist and is generally believed to have supervised not only the iconographic program but also the actual execution of the doors. These massive plates of bronze, about fifteen feet in height, appear each to have been cast in one piece. They begin a long succession of figured bronze doors created throughout the Middle Ages and the Renaissance in Germany, Italy, and Russia, culminating in Lorenzo Ghiberti's masterpieces for the Baptistery in Florence. In sixteen scenes (the number of the Gospels multiplied by itself), the story of man's Fall down through Cain's murder of Abel is told on the left door, reading from top to bottom, and that of man's Redemption through Christ is narrated, reading upward, on the right, a sort of *Paradise Lost* and *Paradise Regained*. Each of the eight scenes on either door is so matched with its counterpart on the other that they complement each other precisely. For instance, in the third pair from the top, the *Temptation of Adam and Eve* (man falls through eating the forbidden fruit of the Tree of the Knowledge of Good and Evil) is opposite the *Crucifixion* (man is redeemed through Christ's sacrifice on the Tree of the Cross). There is little indication of ground, and broad areas of background appear between the figures, so that each scene conveys a strong impression of enveloping space.

The individual narratives are intensely and spontaneously dramatic, and most of them give every sign of having been inspired by a direct reading of the text rather than drawn from iconographic tradition. The fourth scene from the top of the left door, *Adam and Eve Reproached by the Lord* (fig. 13–18), could hardly be more effective in its staging. A wrathful God (note that the triune God appears, as often in Creation scenes, in the form of the Son, with a cruciform halo) in a gesture of anger and dismay expostulates with the cowering Adam and Eve, who hide their nakedness with fig leaves. Adam blames Eve, Eve points to the serpent—a dragon-like creature, which in turn snarls back at her. The freely arranged little figures, with their heads almost in the round, contrast strongly with the ornamentalized vegetation, including the fateful tree. Below the scene is a Latin inscription in inlaid silver, added shortly after Bernward's death, which translates: "In the year of Our Lord 1015 Bernward the bishop of blessed memory cast these doors."

A less influential but equally original creation of Bernward's workshop is a bronze column, more than twelve feet in height, which he also gave to Saint Michael's (fig. 13–19). The crucifix it originally supported is now lost, and the present capital is a nineteenth-century reconstruction. The column itself, obviously derived from the imperial columns of Rome and Constantinople, shows the triumphant deeds of no earthly emperor but of the King of Kings—Christ's earthly ministry in twenty-four scenes, beginning at the bottom with the Baptism in the River Jordan and ending with the Entry into Jerusalem. Like each door, the hollow column was cast in one piece, a remarkable technical achievement. The scenes are

13-16

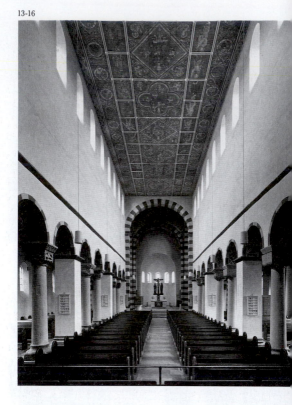

13-16. Interior, St. Michael's, Hildesheim (after restoration)

13-17. Bronze doors with scenes from the Old and New Testaments. c. 1015. Height approx. 15′ (4.57 m). Cathedral of Hildesheim

13-18. *Adam and Eve Reproached by the Lord,* detail of the doors of the Cathedral of Hildesheim. Bronze, 23 × 43″ (58.4 × 109.2 cm)

13-19. Column of Bishop Bernward. Early 11th century. Bronze, height approx. 12′ (3.66 m). Cathedral of Hildesheim

13-17

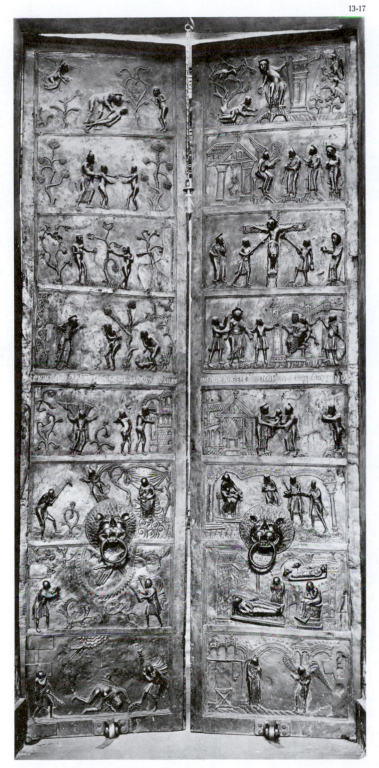

13-18

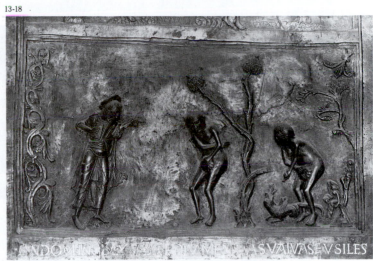

13-19

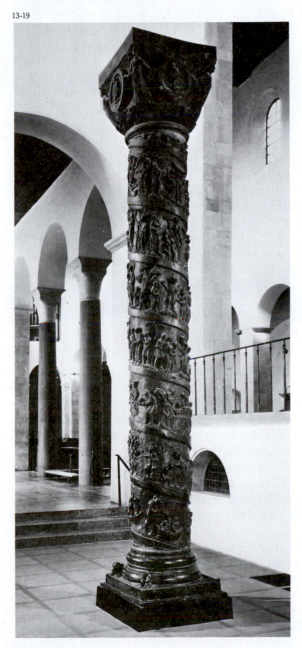

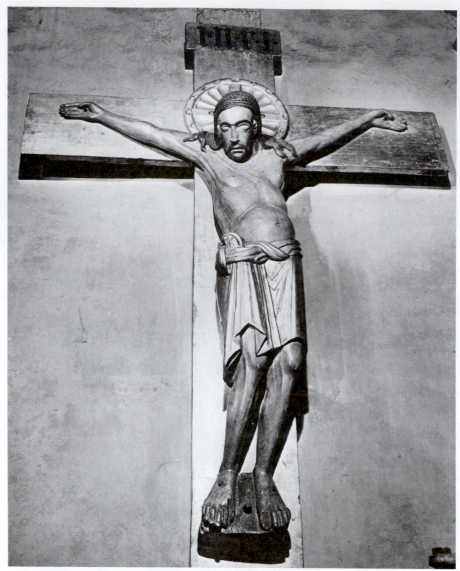

13-20. *Crucifix of Archbishop Gero.* c. 969–76. Wood, height 6′2″ (1.88 m). Cathedral of Cologne, Germany

13-20

more densely spaced than on the doors, but quite as dramatic, and may have been the work of the same team of sculptors. The column gains considerable architectural strength from the broad spiral bands that separate the levels.

An unexpectedly powerful example of the new Ottonian art of monumental sculpture is the life-size wooden crucifix (fig. 13–20), given to the Cathedral of Cologne by Archbishop Gero between 969 and 976. This is the oldest surviving large-scale crucifix. The Ottonian sculptor, doubtless under ecclesiastical direction, has represented a type not yet seen in the West and apparently adopted from Byzantine art—where, in fact, Christ was never depicted with such intense emotion or such emphasis on physical torment. Instead of the *Christus triumphans* of the *Lindau Gospels* (see fig. 13–11), the *Christus patiens* (Suffering Christ) is shown, and the viewer is spared little. The eyes are closed, the face is tense with pain, the body hangs from the crossbar, and the lines of tension in arms and legs are strongly indicated; the belly is swollen as if with gas. Christ's hair seems to writhe upon his shoulders. This kind of expressiveness, which achieves its end even by showing the most repulsive physical conditions, is characteristic of German art throughout its long history and reappears again and again at different moments.

A small ivory plaque representing *Doubting Thomas,* made about the year 1000

13-21. *Doubting Thomas.* c. 1000. Ivory panel, 9½ × 4″ (24 × 10.5 cm). Staatliche Museen zu Berlin—Preussischer Kulturbesitz

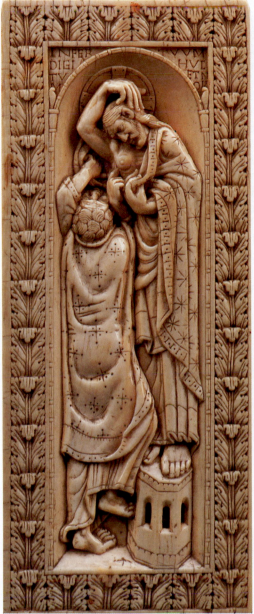

13-21

(fig. 13–21), raises Ottonian expressionism to the level of spiritual exaltation. The artist has made the relief look higher than it is through the illusion of a niche that encloses and compresses the two figures. In the spandrels appear Christ's words to Thomas, "Reach hither thy finger . . ." in Latin (John 20:27). Christ lifts his right arm, draws aside his mantle, and bends his head with a look of deep compassion, while Thomas inserts his finger into the wound. Every line of Christ's body and drapery is receptive, and every line of Thomas's pose and garments ascends; Thomas's head is turned backward so that we can see his expression. Master and disciple are bound together in a mystic union of faith and love, in which even the ascending shapes of the framing acanthus leaves seem to share.

PAINTING   As so often in the fragmented history of painting from antiquity through the early Middle Ages, we are left with nothing but tantalizing descriptions of the cycles of wall paintings that once brightened the interiors of Ottonian churches. Only in the Church of Saint George on the island of Reichenau in Lake Constance is a fairly complete cycle preserved, and that, like the fragmentary frescoes that survive elsewhere, is too badly faded for reproduction here. Again we must turn to manuscripts to assuage our loss, and again the consolation is great. The expressive and visionary qualities so evident in Ottonian architecture and sculpture are concentrated in Ottonian manuscripts.

Emperor Otto. In a detached leaf from an unknown volume, we behold a youthful crowned emperor (fig. 13–22), labeled *Otto Imperator Augustus,* probably Otto II, majestically enthroned under a baldachin. He holds his staff of office with his right hand and his golden orb of power in his left, while crowned women representing subject countries, optimistically entitled *Germania, Francia, Italia,* and *Alamannia* (he ruled only Germany), present him their orbs as well. In the awesome detachment of Ottonian art, naturalism of expression is unaccompanied by concern with real space. Any attempt to deduce the spatial relationships of the columns upholding the baldachin will leave the observer in a quandary. In order not to cut up the noble Latin inscription, barely visible behind the emperor's head, the artist represented only three columns; the throne levitates partly within and partly forward of the front columns, being even higher than their bases. But these unreal spatial relationships are part of the magic of Ottonian manuscripts, and if anything enhance their expressive and spiritual depth. Contours are smooth and unbroken,

13-22

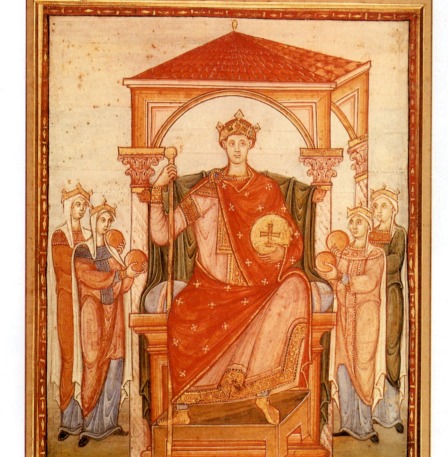

13-22. *Otto Imperator Augustus,* detached page from an unknown illuminated manuscript. c. 985. Musée Condé, Chantilly, France

13-23. *Annunciation to the Shepherds,* illumination from the *Gospel Lectionary of Henry II.* Reichenau (Lake Constance), Germany, c. 1002–24. Bayerische Staatsbibliothek, Munich

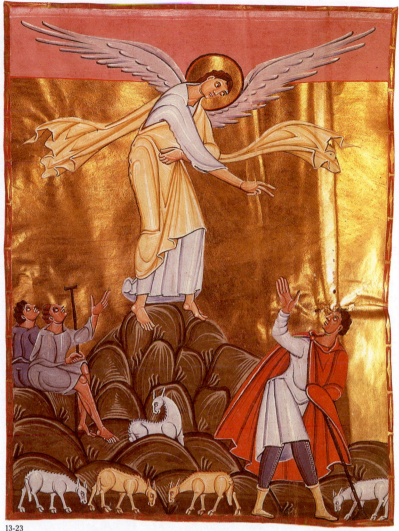

13-23

colors richly and subtly contrasted, surfaces strongly modeled, but the Helleno-Roman careful observation of light has now turned into a conventional pattern of strokes of graduated value.

Gospel Lectionary of Henry II. The half-real, half-unreal Ottonian style is very grand when turned to narrative purposes, as in the *Annunciation to the Shepherds* (fig. 13–23) from a *Gospel lectionary* (the Gospel texts arranged in the order in which they are read at Mass) given to the Cathedral of Bamberg by Henry II (ruled 1002–24). The background, partly gold and partly rose, is abstract. On a mountain formed of conventionalized rocks stands a colossal angel, his mantle floating against the gold, ready to announce to the awestruck shepherds the "good tidings of great joy." Yet all seem more overcome with the mystery of the message than by its gladness. The last traces of illusionism have given way to strongly ornamental and unbroken contours; only a few parallel stripes remain to suggest the origin of such strokes in reflections of light.

Bamberg Commentary. The highest attainment of Ottonian art is the series of visions from both Old and New Testaments, represented with an explosive power never seen before in figurative art. As if pervaded by something of the ornamental splendor that had flowered in Hiberno-Saxon art, these illuminations yet overflow with the expressiveness of Ottonian religiosity. The *Vision of Isaiah*, from a Com-

405

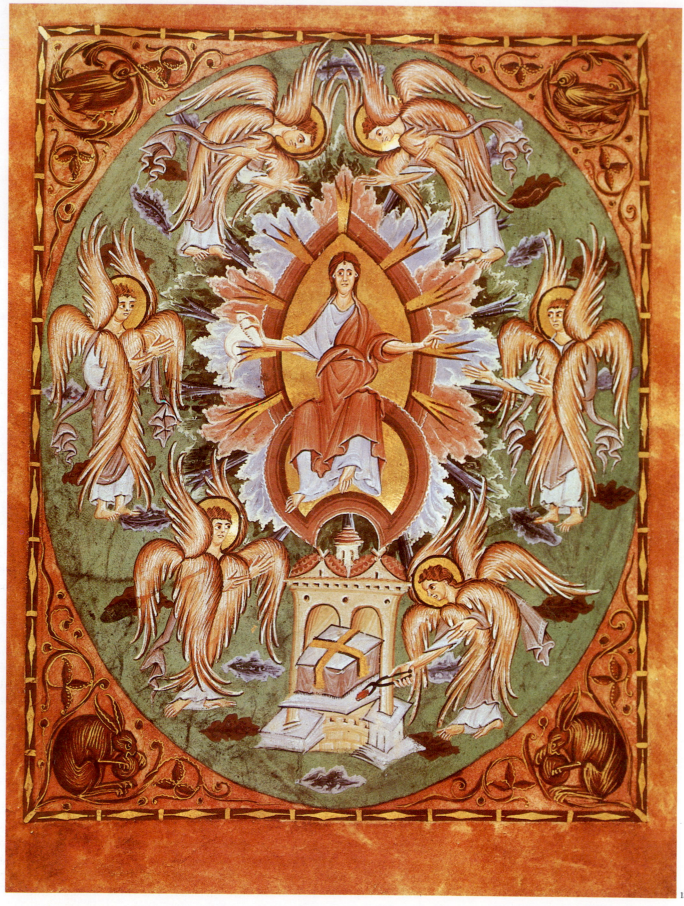

13-24

mentary illuminated in the late tenth or early eleventh century (fig. 13–24), should be contemplated along with the text it illustrates, Isaiah 6:1–4:

> *1 . . . I saw also the Lord sitting upon a throne, high and lifted up, and his train filled the temple.*
>
> *2 Above it stood the seraphims; each one had six wings; with twain he covered his face, and with twain he covered his feet and with twain he did fly.*
>
> *3 And one cried unto another, and said, Holy, holy, holy, is the Lord of hosts: the whole earth is full of his glory.*
>
> *4 And the posts of the door moved at the voice of him that cried, and the house was filled with smoke.*

The Ottonian artist was less literal and more imaginative than the masters who illustrated the *Utrecht Psalter* (see fig. 13–9). He has shown the beardless Lord sitting upon and within a fantastic shape composed of an overlapping golden disk and a golden mandorla, both with rainbow borders, with his arms outstretched and eyes gazing forward as if he were in a trance. Nine threefold tongues of gold flame spurt from the mandorla. The smoke, which the text tells us filled the house, is shown as concentric bursts of blue and violet with white edges, like the petals of a gigantic flower. In reciprocal and often double curves, the six-winged seraphim float about his throne, making wonderful patterns of feathers. Below the throne is an altar from which, as related in Verses 6 and 7, an angel takes with tongs the live coal he will place upon Isaiah's tongue. And yet with the same surprising disregard for the theme of the principal illustration we found in the *Book of Kells* (see fig. 12–8), two unconcerned rabbits in the lower corners gnaw on pieces of fruit. Perhaps a contrast between their blind greed and the beauty of revelation was intended.

Two of the most sumptuous manuscripts remaining from the Ottonian era were ordered by abbesses, who in both Carolingian and Ottonian society were often personages of considerable economic and political influence. In illustrations in both works a special attempt was made to dramatize pictorially the relation of the abbess and her community of nuns to the means of salvation. The two manuscripts, both Gospel books, also reveal strikingly different aspects of Ottonian style.

Hitda Codex.   Not dated, but probably executed shortly after the year 1000, the great *Hitda Codex* was ordered by Hitda, Abbess of Meschede, near Cologne in the Rhineland, in northwest Germany, and is considered the masterpiece of the Cologne school of illumination, characterized by a remarkably free and sketchy use of the brush. Among the many brilliant and often intensely expressive illustrations, the most interesting for us is the page that shows the donor herself, labeled *Hitda Abbatissa*, under a symbolic arch above which rises a jumble of monastic buildings—walls, clerestories, gabled roofs, and towers. With an expression of great fervor, the abbess presents the gold-covered book to Saint Walburga, female patron of the abbey (fig. 13–25). The soft, pictorial touch and the understanding of the play of light have been connected with the influence of the Macedonian renaissance.

Uta Codex.   Illuminated for the Abbess Uta of Niedermünster, near Regensburg on the Danube in south-central Germany, between 1002 and 1025, the *Uta Codex* shows in the density and mathematical complexity of its design the intellectuality of the extraordinary city of Regensburg, known for its philosophical and theological interest. Regensburg was especially devoted to the cult of Saint Denis, whose relics were believed to be enshrined there and who was identified with the mysterious Early Christian philosopher known today as Dionysius the Pseudo-Areopagite (who will reappear in Chapter Fifteen). Saint Erhard, bishop of Regensburg about 700, whose relics were venerated at Niedermünster, is shown celebrating Mass (fig.

13-24. *Vision of Isaiah,* illumination from a Commentary. Late 10th or early 11th century. Staatsbibliothek, Bamberg, Germany

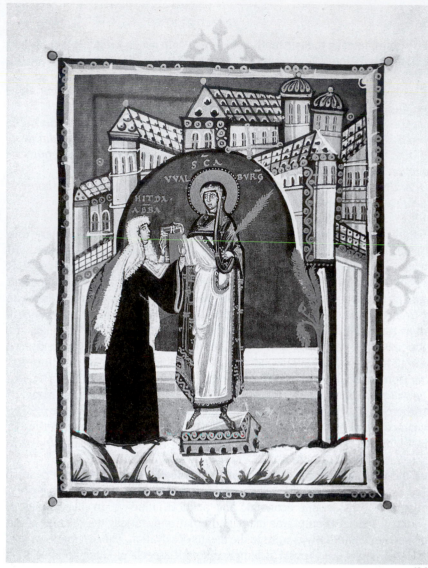

13-25. *Abbess Hitda Presenting Her Book to Saint Walburga,* illumination from the *Hitda Codex.* Cologne, Germany, first quarter of 11th century. Hessische Landes- und Hochschul-Bibliothek, Darmstadt, Germany

13–26) under a *ciborium*—usually a domical structure supported by four colonnettes—which generally covered altars in both East and West in the early Middle Ages. This time, however, there are distinct references to the Old Testament. It has been shown that the ciborium is constructed according to a linkage principle as directed for the Tabernacle in Exodus 36:18 and that the saint's vestments, while conforming in general to those still required for the celebrant at High Mass, contain elements drawn directly from those of the Hebrew High Priest. He stands with hands extended in orant posture, a deacon on the right as assistant and on the left an altar, of a movable type (*altare semifixum*), on which can be seen among other objects the missal, the chalice for the wine, and the paten, or plate for the Eucharist.

Above the ciborium the Lamb of God holds an open book before the Latin inscription "The Spouse of Virgins," obviously meaning the nuns. In the upper right corner of the frame sits Uta herself, labeled "Lady Abbess"; at upper left "Piety," hands crossed on breast; at lower right "Rigor of Discipline," a woman pointing to her closed lips; at lower left "Temperament of Discretion," a woman teaching two children. Below the altar rise the domes, towers, and battlemented walls of the abbey. Clearly the illustration is an allegory, demonstrating in visual terms the possibility of bringing Christ in the Mass, by means of portable altar and ciborium, into the lives of the community of women at any proper point in the monastery. The whole is converted into a design of brilliant complexity and geometrical rigor.

13-26. *Saint Erhard Celebrating Mass,* illumination from the *Uta Codex.* Regensburg, Germany, 1002–25. Bayerische Staatsbibliothek, Munich

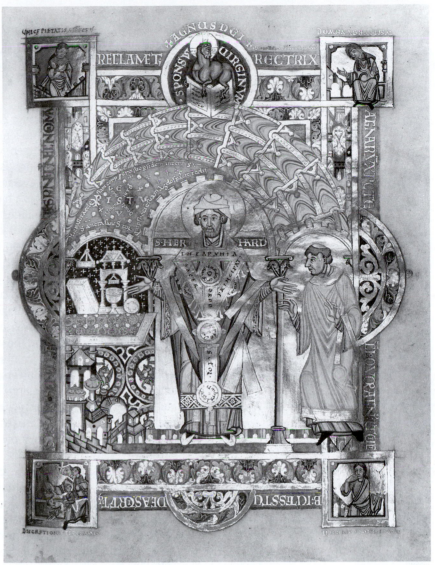

13-26

The least that can be said of these two powerful abbesses (among their many women contemporaries in similar positions of monastic leadership all over Christendom) is that they stood at the apex of the intellectual, spiritual, and artistic life of their times. Were the scribes and painters of these two magnificent works, whose illustrations correspond so closely to the ideas of Hitda and Uta, actually nuns in the convents of Meschede and Niedermünster? That the question seems never to have been raised is surprising in view of the host of texts recording the training, the achievements, and even the names of many women scribes and illuminators, beginning as early as the sixth century. The biographer of the two eighth-century women painters Harlinde and Relinde expressed wonder that they excelled in "writing and painting, a task laborious even for men." The burden of proof really rests on those who would maintain that Hitda and Uta had to turn to male scriptoria for their manuscripts.

The classical and Byzantine heritage of Carolingian manuscript painting and ivory sculpture was formalized in the brief Ottonian period and replaced the last remnants of classical illusionism with a grandly conceived art dominated by linear contours and patterned compositional structure. The innovations of Carolingian architecture were adopted and expanded. Except for Bishop Bernward's brilliant bronze sculpture, which had no immediate followers, Ottonian art formed a bridge to the Romanesque. Its greatest achievements are majestic in form and color, witness of an artistic creativity and a spirituality unmatched in the rest of Europe.

CHAPTER FOURTEEN

The name *Romanesque* was a catchall term coined in the nineteenth century to designate a style that was no longer Roman but not yet Gothic. But *Gothic* itself, as we shall see in Chapter Fifteen, was a misnomer from the start. The word *Romanesque* has other shortcomings as well: originally, it had to cover both Carolingian and Ottonian art, which have assumed distinct identities only in the last hundred years or so. Even worse, it is a term implying transition, inappropriate for a period that has strong positive qualities of its own. Today, the name is so deeply rooted in common usage that it cannot be eradicated. For want of a better term, then, *Romanesque* is now applied to the art of the eleventh and twelfth centuries in western Europe (in France, for special reasons, it is used for the arts only up to about the middle of the twelfth century).

For a rarity in this book since the chapter dealing with the Roman Republic, neither headings nor subheadings in the discussion of Romanesque art will contain the name of a single monarch or dynasty. After the year 1000, there were many competing monarchies, and the very institution of kingship had acquired a powerful competitor—a rising commercial and industrial class. No monarchy could any longer enforce claims to universal rule. In the eleventh and twelfth centuries the emperors were, in effect, kings of Germany only. The kings of France ruled as feudal lords a region in north-central France centering on Paris and had next to no control over the rest of the area that makes up modern France, which was governed by several dukes and counts owing shadowy allegiance to another king. Norman barons wrested Sicily from the Arabs in 1105 and set themselves up as kings, controlling most of formerly Byzantine southern Italy as well. In addition to the Muslims in the south, at least four Christian kingdoms divided Spain. Under the kings and dukes were feudal lords, ruling from their castles and acknowledging often conflicting feudal allegiances. The system was chaotic in the extreme and constantly shifting; the general disorder often involved the papacy, which found itself at times the football of rival monarchs.

But the towns were growing at a pace that exceeded even that of the monarchies. Cities were still small—medieval Rome and Renaissance Rome, for example, each occupied only a fraction of the center of the ancient city. Yet in France, England, Germany, and the Low Countries, cities devoted to manufacture, trade, and banking demanded and received clear-cut legal rights and charters as corporate persons equal to the feudal lords and sheltered by dukes and kings who depended on them in many respects. In Italy, with the collapse of the remnants of Lombard power in the eighth century and the infrequent visitations of emperors, northern cities became independent communes. At first they were ruled by their bishops but soon developed republican forms of government with administrations, often chosen by lot among the leading commercial families, succeeding each other for very brief terms. Venice (long a republic), Genoa, Naples, and Amalfi built merchant marines for trade throughout the Mediterranean and navies to protect their commerce from Arab pirates. Venice, in fact, established a commercial empire, with bases in islands and seaports throughout the eastern Mediterranean and a fixed extraterritorial seat in Constantinople, the capital of the Byzantine Empire. The capture of Sicily and the mass movements of the first three Crusades, the latter culminating in the institution of a Western kingdom of Jerusalem (1099–1187), also assisted in opening Western eyes to the worlds of Byzantine and Islamic cultures.

It is hard to find enough surviving Carolingian and Ottonian churches to illustrate the architectural styles of those periods; in contrast, so many hundreds of Romanesque churches, large and small, most in excellent condition, still stand in Europe that even a general treatment of Romanesque architecture would require a book as thick as this one. Even more would have been preserved if in the Gothic period many had not been replaced by more sumptuous edifices. An oft-quoted and generally misinterpreted passage, written in 1003 by the French monk Raoul Glaber, tells us about the new wave of church construction after the year 1000, when (so it was widely believed) the end of the world was to have taken place:

> *Therefore, after the above-mentioned year of the millennium, which is now about three years past, there occurred, throughout the world, especially in Italy and Gaul [France], a rebuilding of church basilicas. Notwithstanding the greater number were already well established and not in the least in need, nevertheless each Christian people strove against the others to erect nobler ones. It was as if the whole earth, having cast off the old by shaking itself, were clothing itself everywhere in the white mantle of churches. Then, at last, all the faithful altered completely most of the episcopal seats for the better, and likewise the monasteries of the various saints as well as the lesser places of prayer in the towns.*

Considering how many years it took to build a Romanesque church, Raoul Glaber's account should be read as a description of what was beginning to happen rather than of what had already taken place.

But the passing of the dreaded millennium and the new growth of cities were not the only factors that spurred the building of churches; the requirements of pilgrimages also had to be considered. Populations in the Middle Ages were surprisingly mobile. Pilgrimages, a feature of many religions, were ostensibly undertaken for religious reasons, but in the fourteenth century the wise Geoffrey Chaucer hinted at other motives as well, once April stirs the blood:

> *Than longen folk to goon on pilgrimages*
> *(And palmers for to seken straunge strondes)*
> *To ferne halwes, couthe in sondry londes; . . .*

Palmers were those who had been to the Holy Land and were entitled to wear palms (the travel stickers of the Middle Ages) on their garments. Among the "ferne halwes" (distant saints) was James, whose shrine at Santiago de Compostela in the far northwestern corner of Spain attracted pilgrims by the thousands, who had to be cared for along the way, thus encouraging the development of monasteries along the main routes. The pilgrimages, of course, could account only for the great *size* of the new churches—far larger than necessary for their monastic or urban communities—but not for their *style*. (Some scholars have doubted whether the pilgrimages really were an important factor in Romanesque art.)

Just as dramatic as the great new wave of church building in the Romanesque period was the revival of architectural sculpture. Save for a few scattered examples, monumental sculpture in stone very nearly died out in Europe after the collapse of the Roman Empire. Contemporary accounts relate that some Carolingian and Ottonian church façades were ornamented with sculptures, but no examples have survived; as far as we now know, sculpture connected with church buildings was mostly limited to doors, pulpits, baptismal fonts, and other interior features. But the new Romanesque churches demanded architectural sculpture just as the Greek temples had—not as additions to fill predetermined spaces, however, but as integral parts of the architecture (fig. 14–1). Romanesque church portals, especially, were enlivened with sculptures so as to present in vivid form essential elements of Christian doctrine in order to excite not only the piety but also the

14-1

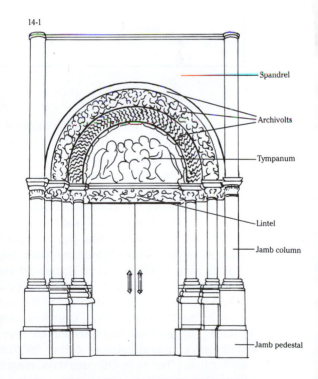

14-1. Diagram of a Romanesque church portal

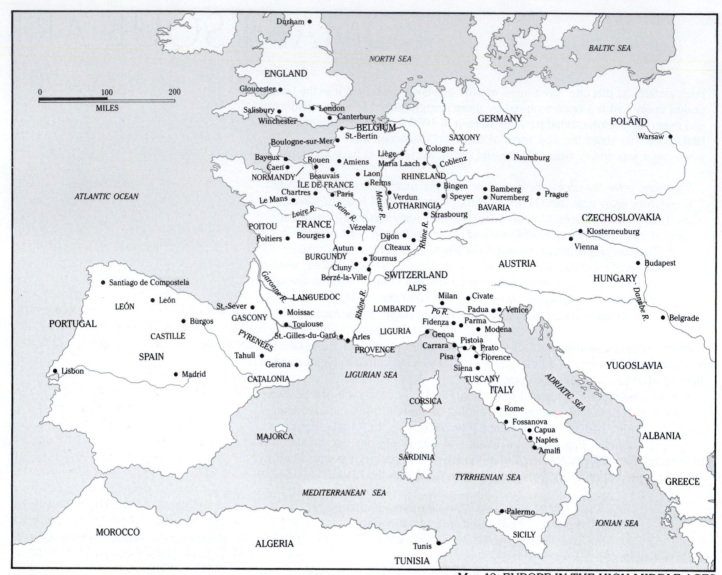

Map 12. EUROPE IN THE HIGH MIDDLE AGES

imagination of the worshiper at the moment of entry into the church. The typical Romanesque portal, which often included a number of reliefs and statues attached to supporting elements, was centered on a large-scale composition that filled the *tympanum* (the semicircular space bounded by the arch and the lintel). A Romanesque tympanum was not made up of separate statues or groups, as in Greek temple pediments, but was drawn on the surface of the component slabs, then cut deeply to form a kind of relief, and finally painted in brilliant colors. An unexpected field for sculpture was a new type of capital, which appeared at the end of the eleventh century, showing human figures and sometimes narrative scenes. *Figured capitals* were relatively rare in Roman art and were seldom used before the third century; Romanesque artists, however, produced them in enormous numbers before the taste for them died out in the Gothic period.

As in the Ottonian period, churches were often richly decorated with mural paintings of great size and splendor. We have no records of any women architects, sculptors, or mural painters during the Romanesque period any more than in earlier times, but as in Ottonian days, magnificent manuscripts were written and illustrated by women, whose special contribution seems to have been an unusual and very exciting freedom of imagination.

Architecture and Sculpture in France

Throughout the old Roman cities of northern Europe and of central and northern Italy (with the exception of Rome, whose basilicas were pilgrimage goals in themselves), many Early Christian, Carolingian, and Ottonian churches gave way to larger Romanesque ones. A prime requirement, based on bitter and oft-repeated experience, especially in France where cathedrals were in urban centers constantly subject to conflagrations, was that the new structures be fire-resistant, therefore vaulted in masonry. Although a manuscript of Vitruvius, in which he explained the Roman technique of vaulting with concrete, was in the monastic library at Cluny, the technique seems never to have been considered by Romanesque builders, possibly because the expense of the wooden forms would have been prohibitive. (Presumably the timber used in the erection of scaffolding in the interior could have been pressed into service a second time for the external roofs.) The new vaults of brick or stone masonry required massive systems of support. As long as the static problems were imperfectly understood—medieval engineering was unequal to the task of calculating stress scientifically—the massive supports for the vaulting could block out the light. A three-way balance among great church size, stable vaulting, and adequate illumination had somehow to be struck; the dramatic changes in the form and appearance of church buildings in the Romanesque and Gothic periods are bound up with many trial-and-error attempts to refine this balance.

TOURNUS But there was a fourth factor, seldom taken into consideration in modern studies of medieval architecture and yet doubtless the final determinant: the result had to be aesthetically satisfying. One striking instance should be considered, the Benedictine Abbey Church of Saint-Philibert at Tournus in central France. The church was rebuilt after a fire in the early eleventh century. During the late eleventh century and the early twelfth century the building was vaulted. The impressive interior (fig. 14–2) would seem to fulfill all practical requirements for a Romanesque church: it is capacious, stone vaulted, and well lighted due to an ingenious constructional system. The nave arcades are sustained by powerful cylindrical columns, without capitals. Engaged half columns are visible in the side aisles. The columns and the half columns provide excellent support for the groin vaults that cover the side aisles. In the nave above each column rises a shorter, engaged column, sustaining a massive arch that bridges the nave. These arches, in turn, support a series of small barrel vaults, which unexpectedly cross the nave at right angles. The weight of the transverse barrel vaults is adequately borne by the arches. But barrel vaults also thrust outward, and this thrust must be abutted. At Tournus this problem was settled by having the transverse vaults abut each other. The outer walls, relieved of all weight, were pierced by clerestory windows admitting ample light. This practical system was adopted in only two other major churches, later reconstructed; why not elsewhere? The answer seems to be that the effect of the heavy arches, cutting up the ceiling into a succession of separately barrel-vaulted compartments, was unacceptable aesthetically; architects and patrons wanted a more unified look. It is also possible that such a ceiling had a bad acoustical effect, creating multiple echoes that blurred the chanting of the services.

TOULOUSE The solution utilized on a grand scale for pilgrimage churches erected in the late eleventh century and early twelfth century may be seen in the Church of Saint-Sernin at Toulouse (fig. 14–3), the capital of the southern French region of Languedoc. Built about 1080–1120, this structure repeats in many respects the plan and disposition of elements at Santiago de Compostela, the goal of the pilgrimages, whose construction began in the 1070s. In contradistinction to Early Christian basilicas, the plan (fig. 14–4) is unmistakably a cross. The immense nave (eleven bays) is flanked by double side-aisles. The inner aisle is continuous,

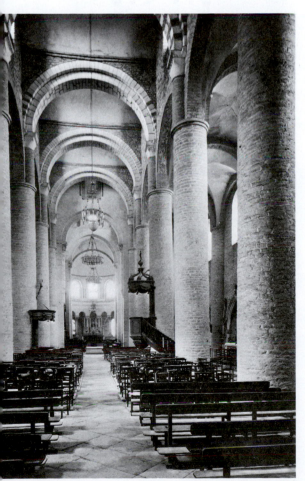

14-2. Interior, Abbey Church of St.-Philibert, Tournus, France. 11th century–early 12th century

14-2

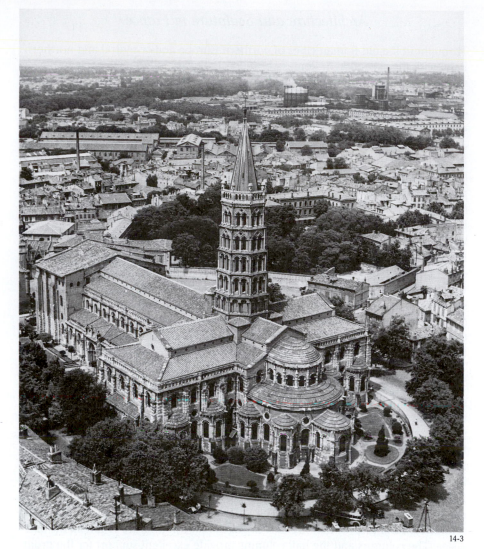

14-3

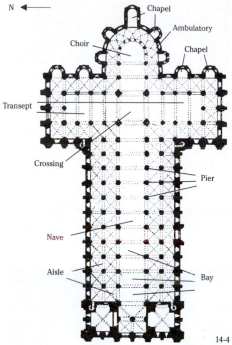

14-4

14-4. Plan of St.-Sernin, Toulouse (after Kenneth John Conant)

stretching around both ends of the transept and the apse—like the ambulatory in a martyrium—so that crowds of pilgrims could move along constantly and easily. (Medieval sources tell us about the difficulty and danger of handling large crowds in the old basilicas.) Along their way the pilgrims could stop and pray at small chapels, each containing the relics of a saint. The cult of relics was intense in the Romanesque period, and the need for relics to venerate was often satisfied by worse than dubious means. Two chapels open off the east side aisle of each arm of the transept, and five more radiate outward from the ambulatory around the apse. Ambulatory and *radiating chapels* became indispensable features of pilgrimage churches and were uniformly adopted for cathedral churches in the Gothic period, save only in England and Italy.

The nave, transept, and choir of Saint-Sernin are barrel vaulted (fig. 14–5); the triumphal arch has vanished, and the apse (now partly obscured by a much later altar) is a half dome at the same height as nave and choir. The downward pressure of this barrel vault, but not its outward thrust, could have been supported by the arches of the usual clerestory; without abutment, the vault would have collapsed. At Saint-Sernin a gallery (which doubtless also accommodated crowds of pilgrims) runs around the building above the side aisles, stopping only at the apse. This gallery is roofed by a half-barrel vault, which rests against the piers of the nave at the springing point of the nave vault and abuts the thrust, directing it back inside the piers to the ground. Unfortunately, the gallery windows light only the galleries;

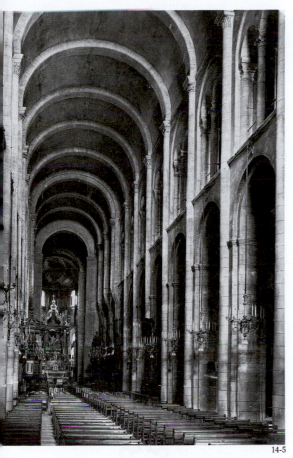

14-5. Nave and choir, St.-Sernin, Toulouse

little light filters into the nave. Churches roofed by barrel vaults are inevitably dark. The Abbey Church at Cluny, as we shall see, was an exception.

The continuous barrel vault, however, does have a grand effect. Like a great tunnel, it draws attention rapidly down the nave toward the altar. The barrel vault is crossed at every bay by transverse arches, which have an aesthetic rather than a functional purpose; they *seem* to support the barrel vault, and may have helped in its construction, but it would stand quite well without them. The arches spring from capitals, which belong to slender colonnettes of entirely unclassical nature, although their capitals preserve classical elements, looking like those in the Mosque of Ibn Tulun (see fig. 11–9). These colonnettes run two stories in height, from floor level, where they are engaged to the square piers that support the nave arcades, up to the transverse arches and down the other side. These piers are in turn subdivided into parallel vertical elements. At Saint-Sernin, therefore, we encounter a basic feature of most Romanesque and later all Gothic architecture, the *compound pier,* composed of several different elements, each with its own function in the complex fabric of the building. This compound pier replaces the Early Christian column (see fig. 10–10) and the square pier of Ottonian buildings (see fig. 13–16).

The plan shows that the side aisles, which are relatively low, are groin vaulted (see fig. 14–4; a groin vault is indicated on a plan by a dotted X). The outward thrust of the groin vaults was met by external buttresses. Each bay of the side aisles is square; the width of the nave corresponds to the width of two of the side-aisle bays, so that each nave bay is an oblong of one to two. This proportion between nave and side-aisle bays was generally maintained in later churches.

From the east end, the exterior (the west façade was never completed) shows a superb massing of clearly distinct elements, resembling that we saw in Ottonian churches but far richer and more complex. The transept chapels, radiating chapels, ambulatory roof, semidome over the apse, gallery windows in the transept, gallery roof, transept roof—all culminate in a grand octagonal *crossing tower*. This tower is Romanesque only in its first three stories; the last two were added in the Gothic period. The clear, rational articulation of the building is carried into smaller elements as well: each bay of the transept is demarcated by a buttress countering the thrust of the vaults within; below each roof runs a sculptured corbel table; each arched window is framed by a larger blind arch, supported in the gallery windows by engaged colonnettes.

CLUNY   The grandest of all Romanesque buildings was the third Abbey Church of Saint-Pierre at Cluny in Burgundy, in eastern France; it was the mother church of the Cluniac Order, which, in the eleventh and twelfth centuries, comprised hundreds of monasteries scattered throughout western Europe. Its greatest abbot, Saint Hugh, entrusted the building to an ecclesiastical architect, a retired abbot named GUNZO, known also as a musician. Until the rebuilding of Saint Peter's in Rome in the sixteenth and seventeenth centuries, Cluny was the largest church in Christendom (fig. 14–6). Construction began in 1085 or 1086 and was virtually completed by 1130. Cluny's dimensions were staggering: the total length was 531 feet, the height of the nave vaults above the floor was more than 100 feet (fig. 14–7), and the richly sculptured central portal was 62 feet high. The nave of eleven bays was preceded by a five-bay narthex; there were four side aisles, double transepts, and five large and two small towers (fig. 14–8). Only portions of one transept remain. The rest of the vast fabric was demolished by a group of real-estate speculators in the years following the French Revolution and the stone and other materials sold for profit; it took twenty-five years to blow the church up, section by section.

From the remaining fragment it is possible to gain a clear idea of what the church was once like (see fig. 14–7). The barrel vault was slightly pointed to reduce the outward thrust so that the supporting gallery could be eliminated. Unfortunately, this device proved insufficient, and external supports (flying buttresses, which will be discussed in Chapter Fifteen) had to be added later, although no one knows exactly when. Unexpectedly, the church's architectural details were derived partly from Roman, partly from Islamic sources. The compound piers were cruciform in plan. Engaged colonnettes supported the nave arcade and the transverse arches of the double side-aisles, which were groin vaulted, but fluted pilasters were attached to the inner faces of the piers, their long, parallel lines increasing the effect of height. All the capitals were imitated directly from Corinthian models. The arches, however, were strongly pointed, somewhat like those of the Mosque of Ibn Tulun (see figs. 11–8, 11–9).

Above the arcades, in a space measured by the height of the sloping side-aisle roof, was the *triforium* (so called because it generally has three openings in each bay). The triforium arches, barely visible in the reconstruction, were ornamented all around with little horseshoe-shaped lobes, patterned after Islamic examples. The arches were separated by fluted Corinthian pilasters. Above the triforium was the clerestory, with three windows to each bay, each window framed by a round arch connecting engaged columns. The apse was slightly lower than the three-bay section between the two transepts; its semidome was filled with a gigantic fresco of

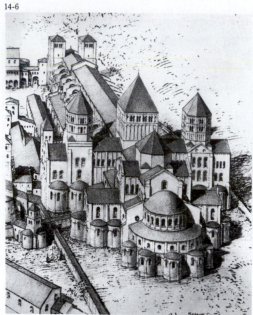

14-6

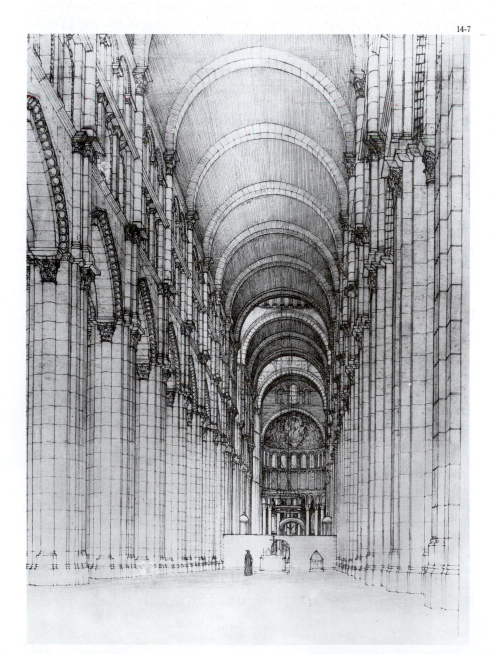

14-7

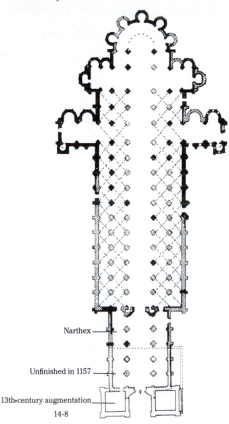

14-6. Reconstruction of the third Abbey Church of St.-Pierre, Cluny, France (after Kenneth John Conant). c. 1085–1130

14-7. Reconstructed view of the interior, third Abbey Church of St.-Pierre, Cluny (after Kenneth John Conant and Turpin Chambers Bannister)

Narthex

Unfinished in 1157

13th-century augmentation

14-8

14–8. Plan of the third Abbey Church of St.-Pierre, Cluny (after Kenneth John Conant)

14-9

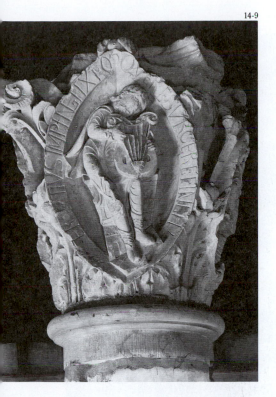

14-9. Capital with relief representing the Third Tone of Plainsong, from the choir, Abbey Church of St.-Pierre, Cluny. Musée Lapidaire du Farinier, Cluny

Christ enthroned in glory. Gunzo's colossal interior was proportioned throughout according to the intervals in medieval music, and contemporary accounts tell us that the barrel vaults carried the chanting beautifully throughout the entire length of the church. A *choir screen* stood before the crossing, supporting a little domed structure on either side from which the Epistle and the Gospel were read; an altar for the congregation was set before the gate in the choir screen. This system became customary in large medieval churches.

The sculpture of Cluny was of the highest quality. The destroyed tympanum was the largest of all such Romanesque reliefs, about twenty feet in width. Although Kenneth John Conant, to whom we owe our knowledge of the abbey in every stage of its history, identified and reassembled the fragments of the tympanum, so as to reconstruct its composition, even down to its original coloring, only a few small pieces have been exhibited. Luckily, the ten beautifully carved capitals of the tall, round columns that once stood in the apse are preserved. The Cluny capitals are in most architectural details quite correctly Corinthian. In one of them (fig. 14–9), against the acanthus leaves, as if suspended, is a graceful mandorla shape, hollowed out to contain a figure playing a lyre, the relief representing the Third Tone of Plainsong. The energetic pose recalls the tradition of Carolingian manuscripts, as does the floating cloak, but the sculpture already shows a complete mastery of high relief, being strongly undercut, in fact almost in the round. The drapery lines were treated like overlapping layers rather than folds of cloth and executed with crisp, clean curves.

VÉZELAY   A highly original plan and vaulting solution is seen in another Burgundian church, Sainte-Madeleine at Vézelay, constructed between about 1104 and 1132 (see Introduction fig. 21); this represents one of the earliest French attempts to roof an entire nave with groin vaults (the choir was rebuilt in the Gothic period). The church has the expected compound piers, almost all of which are enriched with figured capitals; the bays are separated by heavy transverse arches. The eye is immediately struck by a color contrast new to the North, and surely borrowed from such Islamic buildings as the Great Mosque at Córdoba (see fig. 11–10). The soft golden limestone of which most of the church is built alternates in the arches with blocks of pale pink granite, achieving a brilliant effect further enhanced by the white limestone used for the capitals. The unknown architect did not dare to carry his edifice to the height of Cluny, nor did he quite understand how to support his massive groin vaults. The illustration shows that they have pushed the walls slightly outward, and the vaults would have fallen if in the Gothic period the walls had not been strengthened by external flying buttresses.

The glory of Vézelay is its set of three sculptured portals, opening from the narthex into the nave and side aisles, carved between about 1120 and 1132; the sculpture of these portals is in such high relief that many of the figures are almost entirely in the round. The central portal represents the *Mission of the Apostles* (fig. 14–10). Romanesque artists reverted to the archaic system of scale, according to which the size of a figure indicates its importance. A gigantic Christ is enthroned in the center in a mandorla, his knees turned in a zigzag position, his arms outstretched. From his hands (the left one is missing) stream rays of light to the Apostles, who start from their seats to go forth and evangelize the world. On the archivolts, divided into separate compartments, and on the lintel are represented the peoples of many lands, as described in medieval travelers' tales. All of these people—some with heads of jackals, some with pig snouts, some covered with hair and shading themselves with enormous ears, some so small that one must mount a horse with a ladder—await Christian enlightenment. In spite of the heavy damage suffered by projecting portions, the entire scene radiates intense excitement. Partly this is due to the composition, in which each of the central figures breaks through into the area above it, partly to the use of wavy or swirling lines for the drapery, the clouds on either side of Christ, and the trembling floor below the Apostles' feet. The

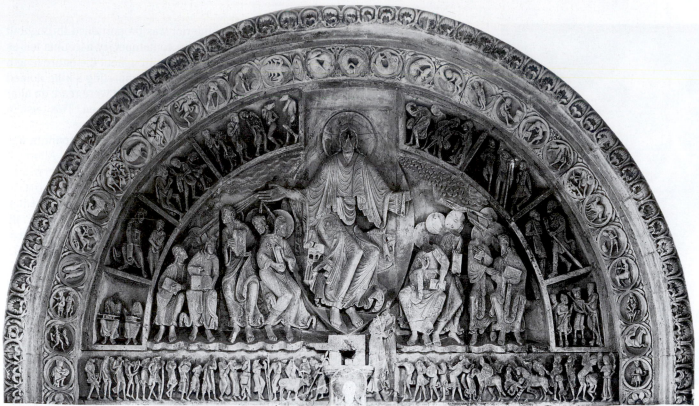

14-10

14-10. *Mission of the Apostles,* tympanum of the central portal of the narthex, Ste.-Madeleine, Vézelay. c. 1120–32

fantastic whorls of drapery on the right hip and knee of Christ take us back through Hiberno-Saxon manuscripts to La Tène (see fig. 12–1). When the original brilliant colors and gold were intact, the effect of the portal must have been electric. Scholars have shown that the meaning of this Vézelay portal was closely related to the Crusades, which were intended not only to redeem the holy places but also to carry the Gospel to the infidels, in effect a new Mission of the Apostles; the First Crusade was to have been preached from Vézelay in 1095, the Second actually was (by Saint Bernard) in 1146, and the Third Crusade started from Vézelay in 1190.

AUTUN   An equally awesome, if somewhat less energetic, Burgundian tympanum is that of the Cathedral of Autun (fig. 14–11), probably dating from about 1130 and representing the *Last Judgment*. This work is an early example among the many representations of the Last Judgment that later appeared in the portal sculptures of almost every Gothic cathedral. Their purpose was to remind Christians of their final destination before the throne of Christ. Again in a mandorla, the huge, impersonal figure of the Judge stares forward, his hands extended equally on either side. In the lintel the naked dead rise from their graves; on the left, souls grasp the arms of a friendly angel; in the center the archangel Michael, wielding a sword, sends the damned to their fate, and their little bodies quiver with terror. In the tympanum fantastically tall and slender Apostles, on Christ's right, superintend the process of salvation, and angels lift the blessed into Heaven, represented as a house with arched windows. On Christ's left a soul's sins are weighed against its virtues, as in the Egyptian Books of the Dead more than two thousand years earlier (see fig. 3–48). Monstrous demons grasp the damned and thrust them into the open mouth of Hell. The sculptor of this amazing work signed his name, GISLEBERTUS; with Renier de Huy (see fig. 14–18) and the Spanish illuminators Ende and Stephanus Garsia (see figs. 14–43, 14–44), he is one of the first artists of the Middle Ages whose name can be connected with a surviving work.

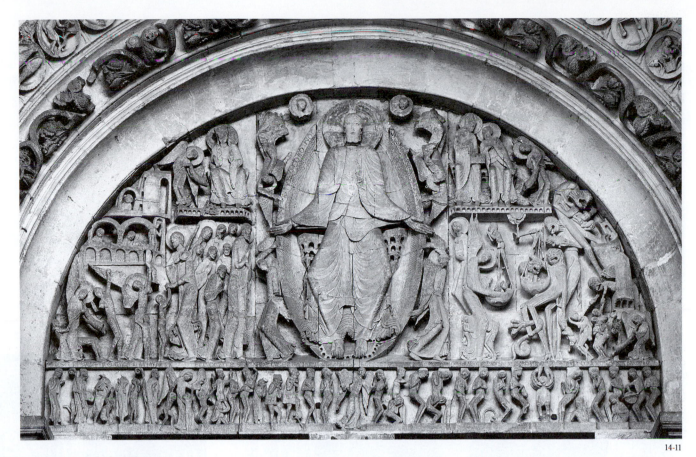

14-11. GISLEBERTUS. *Last Judgment,* west tympanum, Cathedral of Autun, France. c. 1130

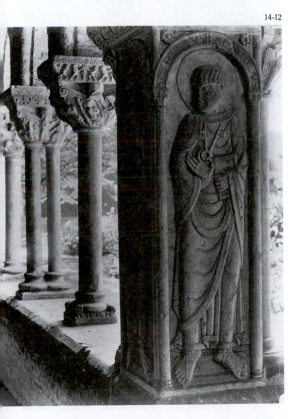

14-12. Corner pier with relief of *Saint Peter,* in the cloister, Abbey Church of St.-Pierre, Moissac, France. c. 1100

MOISSAC An extraordinary complex of Romanesque sculpture enriches the cloister and the portal of the Abbey Church of Saint-Pierre at Moissac in Languedoc, not far from Toulouse. The corner piers of the cloister were sculptured about 1100 with reliefs showing standing saints. In this relatively early phase of Romanesque sculptural style, the tradition of Byzantine, Carolingian, and Ottonian ivory carving is still evident. An arch supported by slender colonnettes frames a flattened niche, on whose sharply rising floor stands Saint Peter, to whom the church is dedicated (fig. 14–12). Save only for the head, turned sharply to the right, the figure is frontal; under the garment the legs appear cylindrical, and although the drapery lines are raised in welts from the surface and given an ornamental linear coherence, they flow about the figure sufficiently to suggest its existence in depth. The figure generally appears stable enough, but the right hand is not; in fact, it is turned violently against the forearm and displays the Keys to Heaven, as though they were weightless, by merely touching them with thumb and forefinger. The columns of the cloister, alternately single and double, are crowned with capitals of a radically new design, which taper sharply toward a small band above the column; each is a unique and brilliant work, some ornamented but the majority carved with scenes from Scripture.

The sculptural activity of Moissac flowered between about 1120 and 1125 to produce another masterpiece of portal sculpture. A deep porch with a pointed barrel vault, whose supporting walls are enlivened by splendid high reliefs, leads to the pointed tympanum in which the Heavens open to reveal the Lord upon his throne—the *Vision of Saint John* (fig. 14–13), the same scene that had been represented in the mosaic, now lost, of the Palace Chapel at Aachen (see page 389; for another treatment of this scene, see fig. 14–43). A colossal crowned Christ is flanked by the symbols of the Evangelists, twisting and turning in complex poses, and by tall and slender angels waving scrolls. The rest of the tympanum is filled by the four-and-twenty elders in three registers, all of whom turn to gaze at the majestic vision. The relative stability of the cloister relief has now given way to an

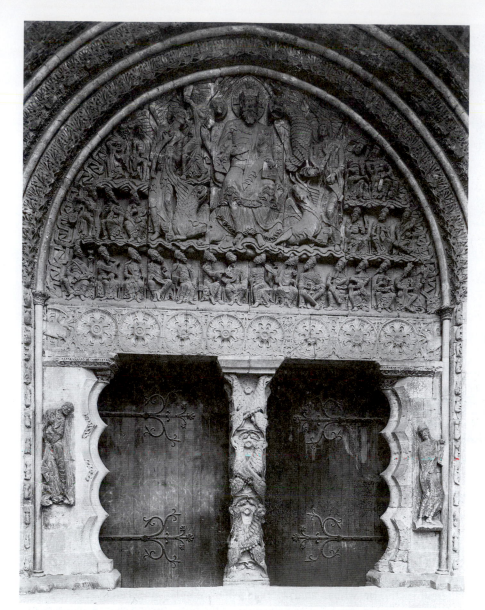

14-13

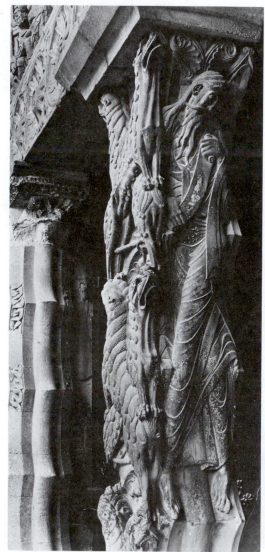

14-14

14-13. *Vision of Saint John,* tympanum of the south portal, Abbey Church of St.-Pierre, Moissac. c. 1120–25

excitement as intense as that of the later central portal at Vézelay although produced by subtler, linear means. Wavy lines representing clouds separate the registers; the border is formed by a Greek fret motif treated as if it were an infinitely folded ribbon. Three successive layers of rich foliate ornament of classical derivation, separated by the slenderest of colonnettes and pointed arches, frame the portal; this is the first example we have seen of splayed enframement, which became a constant feature of church architecture in the Gothic period.

The lintel is ornamented with recessed rosettes, strangely enough cut at each end by the colonnettes as if disappearing behind them. To our surprise the *jambs* are scalloped (an Islamic element), and so, as a close look shows, are the colonnettes that border them, as if they were collapsing with the earthquake effect of the vision. The *trumeau* (central support) is even more startling; it consists of lions and lionesses crossed so that the forepaws of each rest on the haunches of the other—an obvious reminiscence of the old tradition of the animal interlace. On the right side of the trumeau (fig. 14–14), wedged in against the quivering colonnette and the inner scalloped shape, is one of the strangest figures in the whole of Western art, a prophet (possibly Jeremiah) whose painfully slender legs are crossed as if in a ritual dance, which lifts the folds of his tunic and his cloak in complex linear patterns. He clutches nervously at his scroll of prophecy; his head turns languidly as the long locks of his hair and beard stream over his chest and shoulders, and his

14-14. *Prophet,* trumeau of the south portal, Abbey Church of St.-Pierre, Moissac

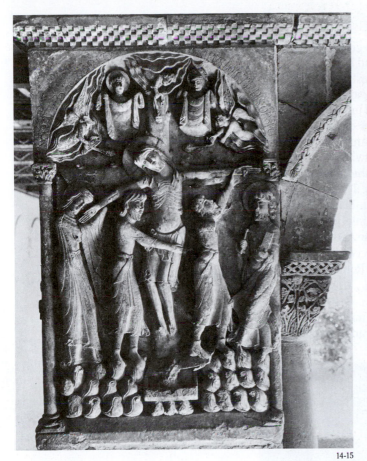

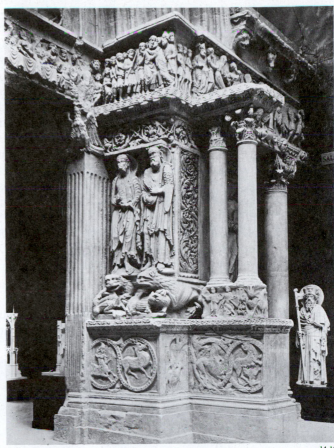

14-15. *Descent from the Cross*, relief in the cloister, Monastery of S. Domingo de Silos, near Burgos, Spain. c. 1085–1100

14-16. South jamb, central portal of the Priory Church of St.-Gilles-du-Gard, France. c. 1130–40

long mustaches flow across his cheeks. For all the fervor of his inspiration, the unknown prophet (doubtless his scroll once bore a painted inscription that identified him) seems trapped in the mechanism of this fantastic portal, a situation that would be completely baffling to us if we did not recall its forebears in Hiberno-Saxon illuminations (see figs. 12–7, 12–8).

SILOS   The mystical style of Languedoc was strongly related to an earlier northern Spanish work, probably dating from about 1085–1100, the cloister reliefs of the Monastery of Santo Domingo de Silos, near Burgos. Under the characteristic arch appears the *Descent from the Cross* (fig. 14–15), a subject that became popular during the Romanesque period on account of its direct appeal to the sympathies of the spectator. The expressions of the figures are quiet; the carrier of intense emotion is the line itself—the sad tilt of Christ's head, the stiff line of his right arm liberated from the Cross, the gentle line of Mary's head pressed to his right hand, the delicate lines of the drapery, and the looping folds of Christ's garments upheld by two angels. Three more angels emerge from swirling clouds to swing censers above the Cross.

SAINT-GILLES-DU-GARD   A more classical manner characterizes the sculpture of the region of Provence in southeastern France, rich in monuments of Roman architecture and sculpture. The triple portal of the Priory Church of Saint-Gilles-du-Gard (fig. 14–16), whose dating has varied enormously but should probably be set about 1130–40, has often been compared with the triumphal arches of the late Roman Empire. The general arrangement, superficially at least, looks Roman, and the details of vinescroll ornament, Corinthian capitals, fluted pilasters, and cascading drapery folds are often directly imitated from Roman originals. More important, when compared with the nervous undercutting of Burgundy and the linear style of Languedoc, the figures at Saint-Gilles do not look as if they had been first drawn on the surface and then cut in to a certain degree, but as if they had been fully three-dimensional in the artist's mind from the start. They show the gravity, weight, and richness of form and surface and the constant play of light and dark that betoken either a continuing classical tradition or an interest in Roman art, or perhaps both.

But the relationship between the various elements is unclassical in the extreme. Two small central columns shorter than those at the sides and jutting out from the jambs in tandem, eagles doing duty for capitals, fierce lions capturing men or sheep, figures moving freely around column bases—all these are unthinkable in a Roman monument. Characteristically Romanesque are the entwined circles on the high socles; these circles, with their enclosed animals, like the lintel rosettes at Moissac (see fig. 14–13), are not complete within their spaces. The frieze tells the story of the Passion of Christ (the incidents of the last week in his life, beginning with the Entry into Jerusalem) in great detail. Over the central lintel can be seen the richly draped table of the Last Supper, although the figures of the Apostles are badly damaged. Better preserved, in low relief to the right of the central lintel, is the Betrayal, the dramatic scene in which Judas indicates to the Roman soldiers the identity of Christ by an embrace.

POITIERS   In western France the tide of sculpture and sculptural ornament broke loose about 1150 and inundated portals, apses, and entire façades, mingling with

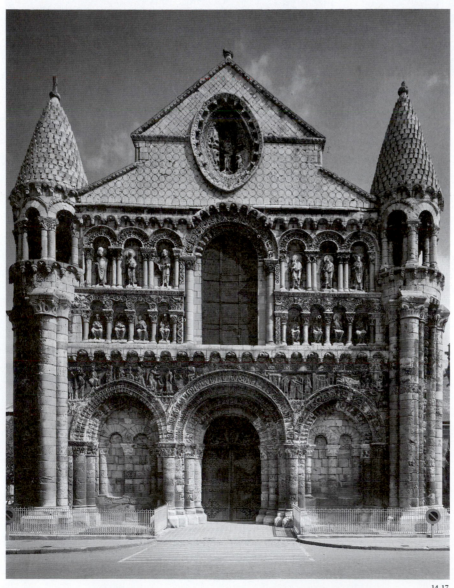

14-17

14-17. West façade, Notre-Dame-la-Grande, Poitiers, France. Middle 12th century and almost submerging the architecture, as in the mid-twelfth-century façade of the Church of Notre-Dame-la-Grande at Poitiers (fig. 14–17). The clustered columns of the lower story of each corner turret appear to—but do not—carry the arcaded second story, whose paired columns, oddly enough, are arranged side by side on the left, tandem on the right. Even more irresponsible are the conical caps, covered with scales imitating Roman tiles, which pointed downward to shed rainwater; these point up but are said to do the job just as well. In the central portion of the façade no register corresponds numerically to that below it, and the arch of the central window even moves upward into the irregularly shaped gable. Time has treated the porous stone unkindly, but the light-and-dark effect of the deeply cut ornament remains dazzling.

RENIER DE HUY   We conclude this brief survey with the consideration of a work in a totally opposite style—the bronze baptismal font (fig. 14–18) now in the Church of Saint-Barthélémy at Liège in modern Belgium, done between 1107 and 1118 and attributed in a fifteenth-century document to the master RENIER DE HUY. The Meuse Valley, in which Liège is situated, was known in the Middle Ages as Lotharingia, after Lothair II, one of Charlemagne's grandsons, and was now under the rule of French-speaking monarchs, now of German. The entire region preserved from the Carolingian period a strong classical tradition derived from the Palace School and the Reims School, and Renier's font is probably the most strongly classical work of Romanesque sculpture made outside Italy. The idea for the font, which appears to be supported on twelve half-length bronze oxen in the round (only ten survive), was drawn from the Old Testament account of Solomon's bronze basin in the forecourt of the Temple. The Baptism of Christ takes place against an impenetrable cylinder of bronze, quite the reverse of the almost atmospheric backgrounds of Bernward's doors (see fig. 13–17). The figures are modeled nearly

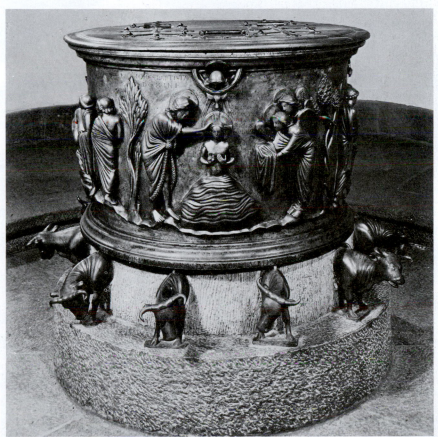

14-18. RENIER DE HUY. Baptismal font. 1107–18. Bronze, height 25″ (63.5 cm). St.-Barthélémy, Liège, Belgium

14-18

in the round, with no hint of the fantastic, visionary styles of Burgundy and Languedoc. The fullness and grace of the figures, their harmonious balance and spacing, and the sculptor's sensitive understanding of the play of drapery over bodies and limbs are unequaled in any French stone sculpture of the time. The lovely classical figure seen from the back at the left may well have derived from an ancient model; one very like it appears in Lorenzo Ghiberti's famous *Gates of Paradise* of the early Italian Renaissance. Renier's figures actually seem to move forward into our space; the head of God the Father (instead of the Hand of God we have seen up until now) leans downward from the arc of Heaven so strongly as to appear foreshortened from above.

Architecture and Sculpture in Italy

Throughout the eleventh and twelfth centuries, the prosperous communes of central and northern Italy and the cities of the kingdom of Naples and Sicily built Romanesque churches on a grand scale. The tradition of basilican architecture had never quite died out in Italy. In addition to the persistence of classical tradition and the presence of many Roman monuments—far more than are standing today—central Italy possessed an unlimited source of beautiful white marble in the

14-19. Baptistery of S. Giovanni, Florence. 11th century

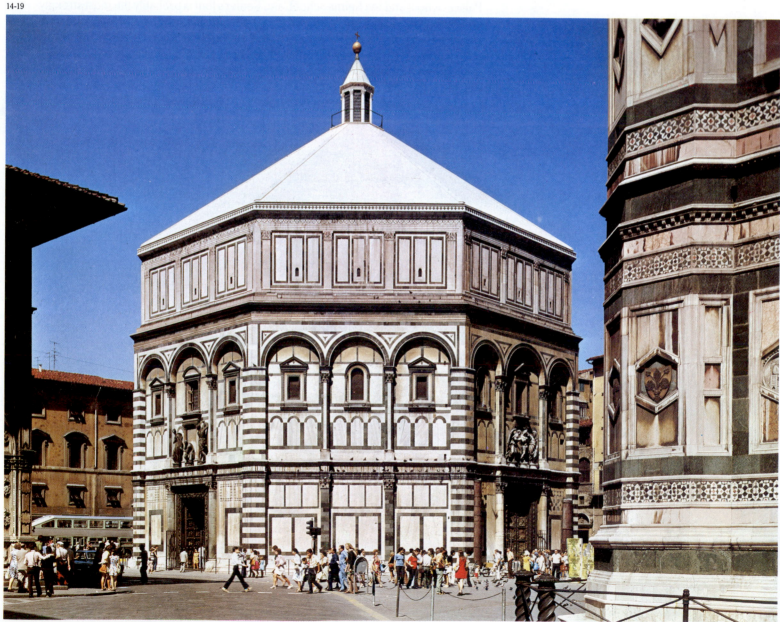

14-19

mountains of Carrara, to the north of Pisa, as well as green marble from quarries near Prato, just to the west of Florence. While the use and emulation of classical elements and classical details in the Romanesque architecture of Tuscany are so striking as to have caused art historians to speak of a Romanesque renaissance (like the Carolingian renaissance), these classical elements were generally played against an accompaniment of strongly unclassical Romanesque green-and-white marble paneling, in some cases very sprightly and witty in its combination of shapes and intervals.

BAPTISTERY OF FLORENCE   The most remarkable Tuscan Romanesque building is certainly the octagonal Baptistery of San Giovanni in Florence (fig. 14–19). In many communes in central and northern Italy, all children born in the commune were baptized in a centrally located building, which was separate from the cathedral and took on considerable civic importance. The Florentine Baptistery was consecrated in 1059, but it is so classical, in so many ways, that a controversy over the original date of its construction continued until quite recently. The Florentines of a later era believed that the building had once been a Roman temple dedicated to the god Mars; the foundations of the present edifice are certainly of Roman origin, but the weight of evidence indicates that the building itself dates from the eleventh century. The external decorative work on the Baptistery went on through the twelfth century, and the corners were not paneled in their zebra-striped marbles until after 1293. The interior is crowned by a pointed dome, masked on the outside by an octagonal pyramid of plain white marble.

The classical aspect of the exterior is limited to the blind arcades and pilasters, whose Corinthian capitals are carved with a precise understanding of Roman architectural detail. But nowhere in Roman architecture can one find anything like the vertically striped green-and-white engaged columns or the striped arches. The most vividly anticlassical feature is found in the second story, in the succession of tiny paneled arch shapes too small to connect with the pilaster strips that should support them. Such witty devices are in the tradition of irresponsible linear activity, which was strong in Romanesque ornament throughout Europe.

SAN MINIATO AL MONTE   Somewhat more accurately classical at first sight is the twelfth-century façade of the Abbey Church of San Miniato al Monte (fig. 14–20). The church was built between 1018 and 1062 high on a hill and commands a

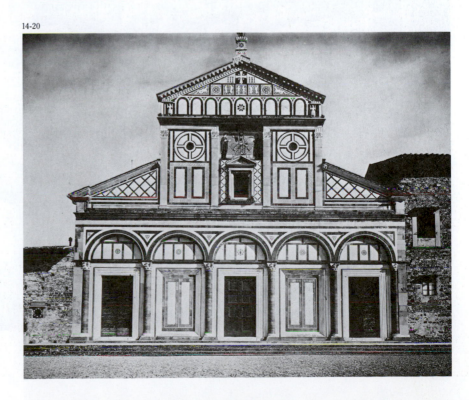

14-20

14-20. West façade, Abbey Church of S. Miniato al Monte, Florence. 1018–62 superb view of Florence. This building represents a quite successful attempt to integrate the inconvenient shape of a Christian basilica, with high nave and low side aisles, into a harmonious architectural façade by the ingenious device of setting a pedimented, pilastered temple front on a graceful arcade of Corinthian columns. But the triangles formed by the low roofs of the side aisles are paneled in a diagonal crisscross that again recalls the tradition of the interlace. Both the Baptistery and San Miniato were influential in establishing the style of Early Renaissance architecture in Florence, particularly in the work of the great innovators, Filippo Brunelleschi and Leonbattista Alberti. But it is instructive to note how these masters always strove to regularize the capricious shapes of the Romanesque marble paneling they imitated.

PISA   The grandest of the Tuscan Romanesque architectural complexes is that at Pisa (fig. 14–21). The Cathedral (begun in 1063), the Baptistery (begun in 1153), whose upper stories and dome were completed in the Gothic period, the Campanile or bell tower (begun in 1174), and the Campo Santo (an enclosed cemetery seen behind the Baptistery in the illustration, dating from 1279–83) form a snowy marble group set apart from the buildings of the town on a broad green lawn. The Campanile—the famous Leaning Tower—started to lean before construction was far advanced; the builder's efforts to straighten the tower by loading the upper stories and bending its shaft resulted in a noticeable curve. The earth beneath has continued to settle, and all efforts to stop the tower's increasing tilt have proved futile. The Cathedral was designed by a Greek architect named BUSKETUS on the plan of Hagios Demetrios at Salonika. As in all the Romanesque churches of Pisa and nearby Lucca, slender superimposed arcades divide the façade and are contin-

14-21. Left to right: Aerial view of the Baptistery (begun 1153), Cathedral (begun 1063), and Campanile (begun 1174), Pisa, Italy. Visible behind the Baptistery is the Campo Santo, or cemetery (1278–83)

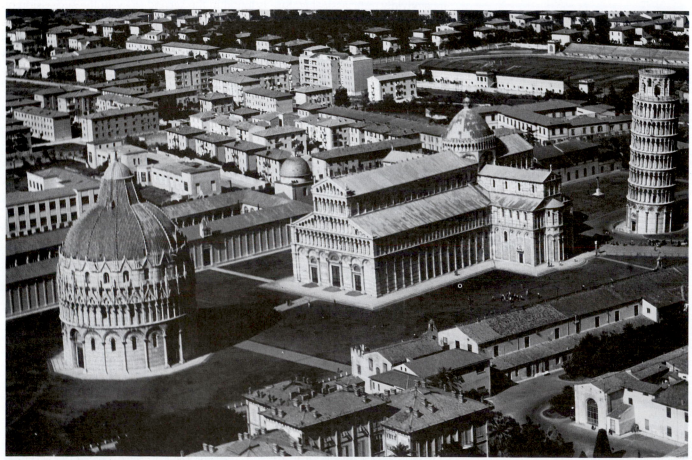

14-21

14-22

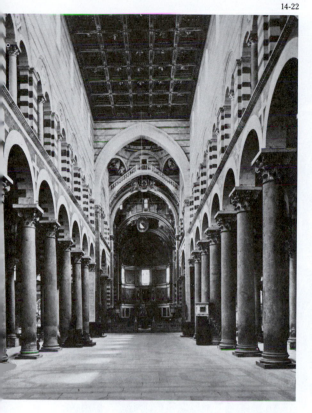

14-22. BUSKETUS. Interior, Cathedral of Pisa

ued in blind arcades that run around the entire building. Each arm of the transept ends in a small apse, and a pointed dome crowns the crossing. The total effect is serene and harmonious; so indeed is the grand interior of the Cathedral (fig. 14–22). The pointed arch at the crossing is Gothic, and the open, timber roof was masked by a flat, coffered ceiling during the Renaissance, but the rest of the interior is original. The steady march of freestanding columns upholding an arcade is familiar from Early Christian basilicas, as is the use of Roman gray granite columns. It is often difficult to tell at first glance which of the capitals are Roman and which are Romanesque imitations. The widely separated, narrow strips of black marble on the exterior have become an insistent zebra striping in the triforium.

MONREALE   The Pisan style strongly influenced church building in southern Italy, but Sicily in the eleventh and twelfth centuries was a special case. The local population was part Greek and part Muslim; the conquerors were French-speaking Normans. In this polyglot land, mixture resulted in unexpected architectural juxtapositions. One might have encountered in Palermo during this era Norman architects, sculptors from the Île-de-France (the territory ruled directly by the French kings), a bronze-caster from Pisa and another from southern Italy, Muslim craftsmen, and Byzantine mosaicists directing artisans of all these races.

The Cathedral of Monreale, founded in 1174 by King William II of Sicily on a mountainous slope above Palermo (fig. 14–23), is a spacious, three-aisled basilica, whose Roman gray granite columns support pointed Islamic arches. The floors and lower wall surfaces are paneled in Byzantine style in white-and-gray marbles; every inch of the timber roof is brilliantly painted in Islamic designs; and all the rest of the interior, including the arches and the impost blocks above the Roman capitals, is covered with a continuous fabric of Byzantine mosaics—the most extensive still in existence. Despite misguided restorations (the reason for the choice of Cefalù instead of Monreale to illustrate Sicilian mosaic art; see fig. 10–62), the total effect of the interior is overwhelming in its coloristic richness, in the completeness of its narrative sequences, and in the rhythmic movement of its elements, which reach a climax in the gigantic mosaic of the Pantocrator that fills the pointed semidome of the apse (for earlier Pantocrators, see figs. 10–43, 10–56).

14-23. Interior, Cathedral of Monreale, Sicily. Founded 1174

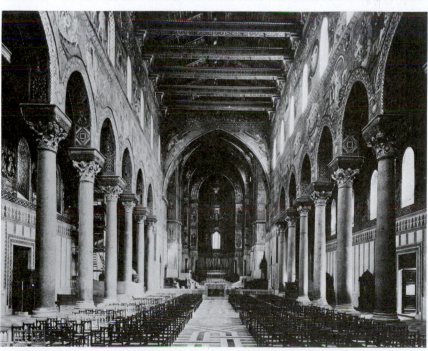

14-23

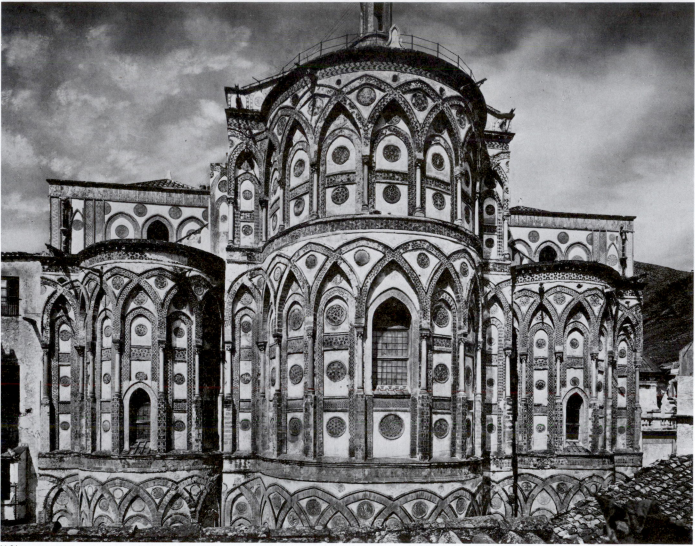

14-24

The exterior of the Cathedral is even more fantastic (fig. 14–24). Its three apses are clothed with blind arcades in the Pisan manner, but the imaginative Muslim craftsmen interlaced them (Norman architects had done this in England) as in the flying arches of the Great Mosque at Córdoba (see fig. 11–11) and enlivened both the arches and the intervening spaces with sparkling patterns in inlaid marbles that seem more appropriate to the decoration of a mihrab or a minbar.

WILIGELMO DA MODENA The most pronounced individual personalities among Italian Romanesque sculptors were two gifted masters both of whom we know by name. Both worked in a region of north-central Italy known today as Emilia-Romagna, at the southern edge of the Po Valley. The earlier of these was Wiligelmo da Modena, whose principal work is a signed series of reliefs, executed about 1100–1110, on the façade of the Cathedral of Modena. In one relief strip (fig. 14–25), the Lord is first shown half length at the left in a mandorla upheld by two angels, then placing one hand on the head of the still-strengthless Adam to "make him a living soul," then creating Eve from the rib of the sleeping Adam; finally, at the right, Adam is shown eating the apple with one hand and (anachronistically) keeping his fig leaf in place with the other, while Eve places her left hand in the serpent's mouth. Wiligelmo treated the enframing architecture with com-

14-25. WILIGELMO DA MODENA. Scenes from the Old Testament, reliefs on the façade, Cathedral of Modena, Italy. c. 1100–1110

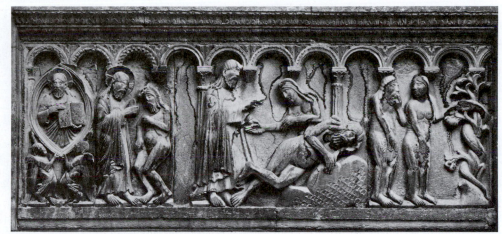

14-25

plete irreverence. Rarely do the figures correspond to the corbeled arches above; more often they move in front of the columns and corbels, and their feet overlap the edge of the groundline. At the extreme right a column has been transformed into the trunk of the Tree of Knowledge of Good and Evil, around which is wound the hissing serpent. These strange figures, with their heavy heads, hands, and feet, give the impression of clumsiness, but the block masses have great power, and the moments chosen for illustration bring out intense human feeling.

BENEDETTO ANTELAMI A more accomplished phase of northern Italian Romanesque style is seen in the work of Benedetto Antelami (c. 1150–c. 1230), an architect as well as a sculptor. His earliest known work is a *Descent from the Cross* (fig. 14–26) in the Cathedral of Parma and is signed and dated 1178 in an inscription in the background; the artist's name appears above the left arm of the Cross. Perhaps under the influence of such Provençal sculpture as that at Saint-Gilles-du-Gard (see fig. 14–16), certainly through study of Roman reliefs, but above all through his native genius, Antelami composed a beautiful melodic flow from one figure to the next, so that the lifting of Christ's right hand from the Cross becomes an act of ritual grace accomplished with the aid of an angel. Accents of grief ebb and rise, suggesting and then avoiding symmetry; the solemn chord progression of the figures at the left, with their clustered drapery folds, is contrasted with the huddle of oblivious soldiers at the right around the flowing, seamless robe.

14-26

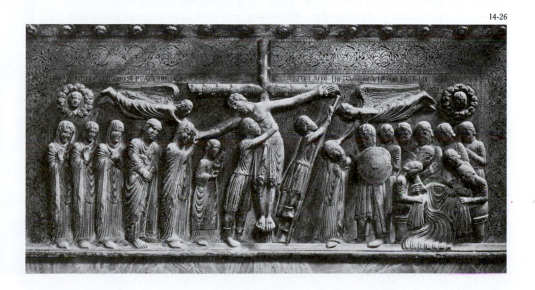

14-26. BENEDETTO ANTELAMI. *Descent from the Cross*, relief, Cathedral of Parma, Italy. 1178

The background is enriched with a delicate web of melodic lines in the vinescroll ornament and in the inscription, which forms an accompaniment to the foreground scene.

Probably during the following decade Antelami contributed some sculptures to the façade of the Cathedral of Fidenza; the town was then called Borgo San Donnino. His statues of *King David* (fig. 14–27) and *Ezekiel,* in which each Old Testament figure has been treated as if he were having a vision, appear in niches under scenes from the New Testament. The *Presentation of the Christ Child in the Temple* hovers in the niche over David's crowned head, on tiny patches of ground. He turns to look over his shoulder as if inspired, holding his long scroll of prophecy. The cadences of his flowing beard and of the folds of his garments are recognizable as permanent elements of Antelami's style. Although not entirely in the round, the figure—pedestal and all—seems to issue from its niche when compared with its direct ancestor, the low-relief *Saint Peter* at Moissac (see fig. 14–12). Antelami's *King David,* in turn, is a worthy precursor of such great niche statues of the Early Renaissance as those created by Donatello.

Vaulting in the Rhineland, Lombardy, Northumbria, and Normandy

Many more solutions to the insistent problem that concerned twelfth-century builders—how to construct a lofty, safe, well-lighted, yet aesthetically unified interior—were advanced than can possibly be treated here. It is a significant fact that the regions that produced the most elaborate sculpture and richest decoration did not contribute much toward solving the vaulting problem. This solution was brought close to its final form in several widely scattered churches that are notable rather for their austerity—in fact, for their virtual elimination of sculptural enrichment.

SPEYER   One of these churches is the immense Cathedral of Speyer, originally built in the early eleventh century as a timber-roofed basilica, in the Rhineland. Between 1082 and 1106 the interior was considerably remodeled in order to receive groin vaults, towering about 107 feet at the crown line, the highest of all Romanesque vaults (fig. 14–28).

A firm supporting structure was essential; to that end, every second pier of the nave arcade was reinforced by the addition of a massive colonnette sustaining a transverse arch. This is the earliest datable example of the alternating system of large and small piers, or piers and columns, which became a standard feature of vaulted churches by about the middle of the twelfth century. Longitudinal arches were built, each uniting two bays of the clerestory, and each intervening lunette was pierced by a window, thus forming a second series of small clerestory windows. Over each double bay bounded by transverse and longitudinal arches groin vaults were constructed. The method of building, starting from masonry arches supported on temporary wooden centering, was strikingly different from the Roman technique employing formed concrete, which resulted in groin vaults with horizontal crown lines (see fig. 9–49). At Speyer each double bay was treated almost like a separate dome, with its crown several feet above the keystones of the arches.

The heavy outward thrust of this construction was supposed to be absorbed by the thick walls and reinforced piers, but although the supports were better calculated than the somewhat later ones at Vézelay (see Introduction fig. 21), they tended to push the walls out, as can clearly be seen in the illustration. At a later period the springing points of the vaults had to be joined together by iron tie-rods in order to prevent collapse. The Cathedral, though provided with a western entrance, preserved the westwork of Carolingian and Ottonian churches. Later rebuilding has severely altered the west end; the church's original appearance, with octagonal crossing lantern, central western tower, and a smaller tower on each arm

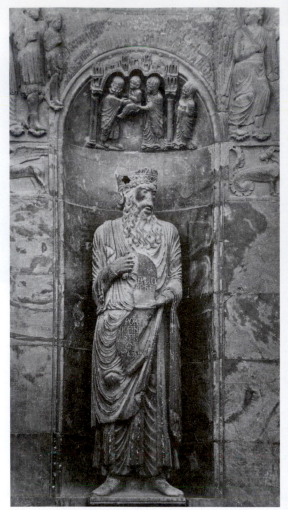

14-27

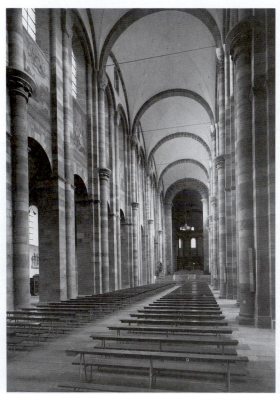

14-28

14-27. BENEDETTO ANTELAMI. *King David,* west façade, Cathedral of Fidenza (formerly Borgo San Donnino), Italy. c. 1180–90

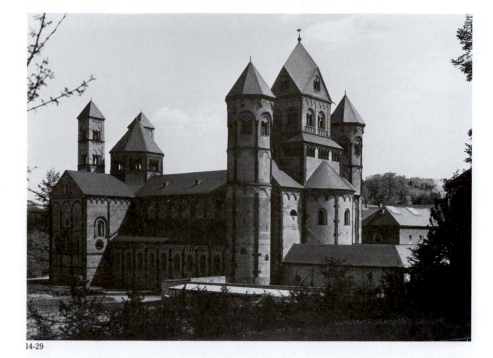

14-29

14-29. Abbey Church of Maria Laach, near Coblenz, Germany. c. 1156

14-30. Plan of the Abbey Church of Maria Laach

14-30

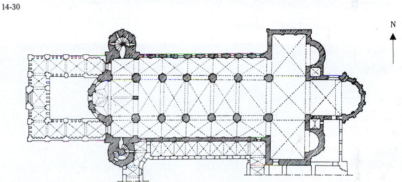

N

14-28. Interior, Cathedral of Speyer, Germany. c. 1082–1106

of the transept and westwork, can be imagined from a somewhat smaller version of this type, the Abbey Church of Maria Laach near Coblenz (figs. 14–29, 14–30), consecrated in 1156. The double-ended shape appears in several of the massive Romanesque cathedrals that dominate Rhenish cities.

SANT'AMBROGIO AT MILAN An important innovation was made in the Church of Sant'Ambrogio at Milan (fig. 14–31), the principal city of Lombardy, whose nominal subjection to the Holy Roman Empire kept it in relatively close touch with events in Germany. A glance at the plan (fig. 14–32) shows that vaulting must have been intended for the nave from the very start. Each double bay of the nave is square, exactly twice as long as one of the side-aisle bays. The alternating system was also built in from the beginning. Stone piers support brick arches and vaults; in the angle between each heavy pier and the nave arcade (fig. 14–33) was set an additional colonnette, which supports an entirely new feature—a diagonal arch intersecting its counterpart from the other side in the center of the bay. In other words the groin vault has now been provided with ribs along the groins, on the principle of the ribs of an umbrella. The account by Abbot Suger of the rebuilding of Saint-Denis in France in 1140 (see Chapter Fifteen) makes clear that the three pairs of arches, longitudinal, transverse, and diagonal, were customarily built first,

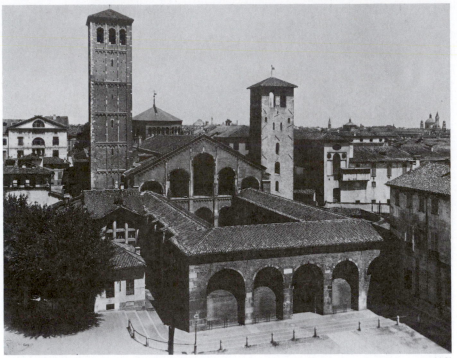

14-31. Sant'Ambrogio, Milan, Italy. Late 11th century–early 12th century

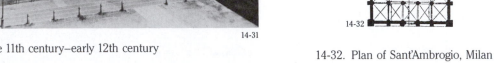

14-32. Plan of Sant'Ambrogio, Milan

14-33. Interior, Sant'Ambrogio, Milan

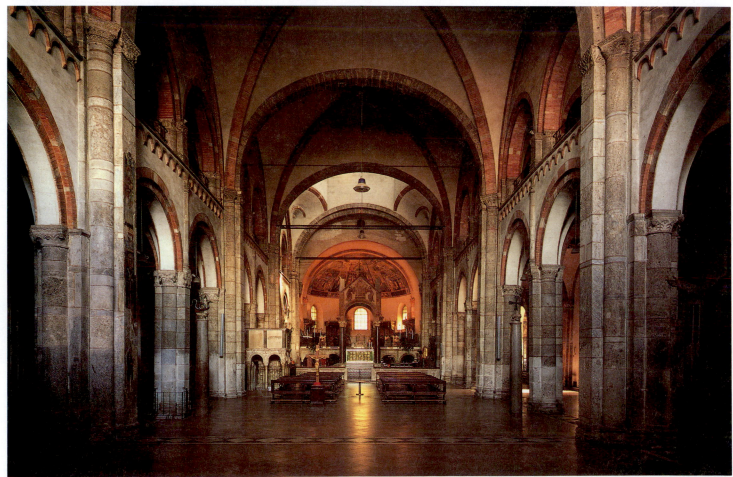

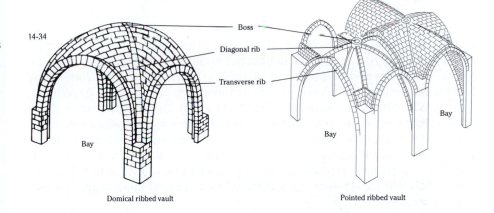

14-34. Diagram of ribbed vaults

14-34

Boss

Diagonal rib

Transverse rib

Bay

Bay

Bay

Domical ribbed vault

Pointed ribbed vault

the centering was then removed, and when the mortar was thoroughly dry, the intervening compartments were filled with a web of masonry.

This use in Sant'Ambrogio is possibly the earliest example of what has come to be known as the rib, or ribbed, vault (fig. 14–34, left). As we shall see, this invention was the absolute essential for the creation of Gothic architecture in northern Europe. Unfortunately, we do not know the date of the vaulting at Sant'Ambrogio, but it is generally agreed that this pioneer attempt must have been started about 1080 and that the church may not have been vaulted until after the earthquake of 1117. The outward thrust of the vault at Sant'Ambrogio was intended to be contained by a vaulted gallery, which not only darkens the interior badly but also appears not to have done its job, as the walls slant visibly outward. The ominous tie-rods have had to be installed.

14-35. Nave, Cathedral of Durham, England. c. 1093–1130

14-36. Plan of the Cathedral of Durham (after Webb)

DURHAM Norman architects built at Durham in northern England one of the most forceful interiors of the Middle Ages, a massive cathedral that was clearly intended for ribbed vaulting from the start (fig. 14–35). Construction began in 1093, and the choir had been vaulted by 1104 (the rose window is a Gothic addition). The building was completed about 1130. As may be seen in the plan (fig.

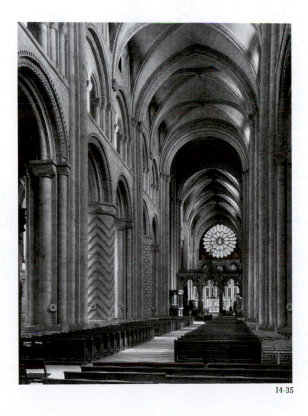

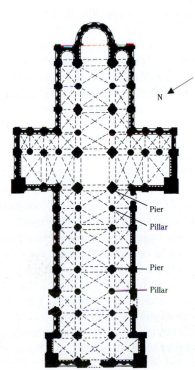

N

Pier

Pillar

Pier

Pillar

14-35

14-36

433

14–36), the double bays are oblong rather than square, and the diagonal ribs cross only a single bay. As a result each double bay is cut into seven vaulting compartments. This device may have been used in order to flatten out the crown line—thus creating greater unity in the vault—which was also partly accomplished by pointing the very heavy transverse arches (see fig. 14–34, right). The most dramatic feature of the interior is the use of powerful cylindrical pillars in alternation with compound piers; the pillars are boldly ornamented with enormous incised chevrons, lozenge patterns, and other designs in a style that recalls the geometric ornament of Hiberno-Saxon art. Originally, this decoration was even painted in bright colors. The capitals are plain blocks, each trimmed to a circle at the bottom, and are without ornament.

The alternating diagonal ribs rest only on small corbels above the capitals of the large triforium; this feature looks like a constructional gallery intended to abut the thrust of the vaulting but is actually covered only by the side-aisle roofs, which do, however, hide relieving arches. The architects seem to have relied on the immense mass of the piers, pillars, and walls to contain the thrust of the vaults, and their confidence was well placed. Tie-rods have never been required. A small, columned clerestory is let into the thickness of the walls at the level of the vaulting, and a catwalk runs behind the conoids of the vaults. These *conoids* (conelike shapes) are formed by the convergence of the triangular compartments of a groin or ribbed vault on the capital of a colonnette or on a corbel. As twelfth-century builders experimented with this form, they were to discover that they could shape the conoids so as to concentrate all weight on the compound piers or on pillars, thus freeing the walls entirely. The manipulation of the conoids will be one of the major goals of Gothic builders.

CAEN   The most influential building for early Gothic architecture, however, was the Abbey Church of Saint-Étienne at Caen in Normandy. Started in 1067 by William the Conqueror, it was completed by the time of his interment there in 1087. The nave does not seem to have been planned for vaulting, but the square double bays (as at Sant'Ambrogio) easily accommodated the daring and very refined system of ribbed vaulting built over the nave about 1115–20 (or perhaps later; the vaults were rebuilt in the seventeenth century). Its thrust is strongly abutted by the vaults of the gallery, which act as a gigantic girdle.

As at Durham a small clerestory was built at the level of the vaulting with a catwalk running behind the conoids (fig. 14–37). The alternating system was preserved only through the addition of two oblique colonnettes, much slenderer than their counterparts at Sant'Ambrogio, to every second compound pier. The striking innovation at Saint-Étienne was the introduction of a second transverse rib, cutting across the vault from side to side and splitting it into six compartments. The six-part vault may have been thought necessary to sustain the slender diagonal ribs before they could be anchored together by the masonry webs of the vault compartments; in any event, it was adopted in the first cathedrals of the Gothic style. The six-part vaults succeeded, at long last, in creating a far more unified interior appearance than had any earlier technique.

Another decisive feature of Saint-Étienne is the three-part, two-tower façade (fig. 14–38), which later became standard for all French Gothic cathedrals. The elaborate—and indeed very beautiful—spires were added in the Gothic period; they must be thought away in order to re-create the effect of austere simplicity intended by the original builders. Of crucial importance to our understanding of the symbolic basis of medieval architecture is the division of the façade of Saint-Étienne so as to embody in almost every reading the number of the Trinity. For example, the façade has three stories, each of which is divided into three parts; the church possesses three portals (those at the sides enter the towers); the second and third stories of the central part are each lighted by three windows; finally, the towers themselves are each divided into three stories.

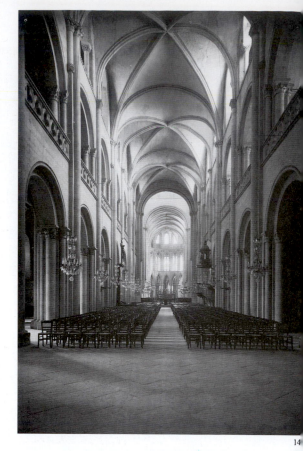

14-37. Interior, Abbey Church of St.-Étienne, Caen, France. 1067–87; vaults c. 1115–20; apse 13th–14th centuries

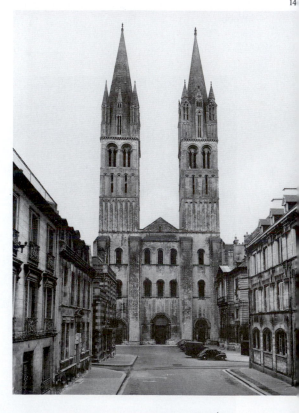

14-38. West façade, Abbey Church of St.-Étienne, Caen. 1067–87 (Gothic spires added later)

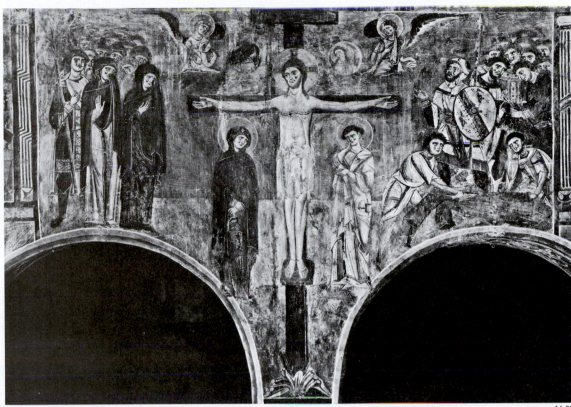

14-39. *Crucifixion,* nave fresco, Sant'Angelo in Formis, near Capua, Italy. Before 1087

Pictorial Arts

In contrast to Carolingian and Ottonian mural painting, a great deal of Romanesque painting survives, some in fairly legible condition, including complete cycles of high quality.

SANT'ANGELO IN FORMIS, CAPUA   We may, however, mourn the loss of the mosaics done by Greek artists who were brought to Monte Cassino by Abbot Desiderius in the eleventh century to reform painting, which—in contrast to its achievements in Carolingian France and Ottonian Germany—had sunk to a low ebb in Italy. Desiderius, according to a delightful contemporary account by his archivist and biographer, Leo of Ostia, made provision for the Greek artists to train Italian monks and craftsmen in the techniques of religious art. The most impressive example of the Monte Cassino style is the almost complete cycle of frescoes commissioned by Desiderius before 1087 for the interior of the Church of Sant'Angelo in Formis on a mountainside above Capua, north of Naples. As in all such cycles, the cumulative effect of the whole is far greater than the sum of its parts. Although the frescoes have faded sadly in recent years, the succession of biblical narratives and the great *Last Judgment* on the entrance wall still exert a profound emotional effect on the visitor. In spite of the teaching of Byzantine masters, the style of the Sant'Angelo frescoes seems somewhat rough in comparison with the extraordinary refinement achieved by the art of Constantinople. Yet their dramatic and decorative power depends in no small measure on their naïveté.

Especially beautiful among the Sant'Angelo frescoes is the *Crucifixion* (fig. 14–39), which fills most of the space above two arches of the nave. Christ is represented as alive, triumphant over suffering as in the *Lindau Gospels* (see fig. 13–11), his perfect serenity in sharp contrast to the grief of the Virgin and John and to the two mourning angels in midair. The forces of the architecture have been allowed to determine the disposition of the elements: the Cross is planted over one of the columns of the nave arcade; on the arch to the left stand weeping women and Apostles; on that to the right the Roman centurion, overcome by the revelation of Christ's divinity, detaches himself from the soldiers' dice game for the seamless robe. The coloring is limited to gray blue for the background and to terra-cotta red, tan, oranges, greens, and grays. As in Romanesque sculpture, the drapery is strongly compartmentalized.

CIVATE   A very nearly contemporary cycle of Italian Romanesque painting, dating from the late eleventh or early twelfth century, adorns the simple Romanesque church of San Pietro al Monte in Civate, a remote spot in the foothills of the Alps. The lunette above the triple arcade at the west end of the nave (fig. 14–40), framed by crisp acanthus ornament in stucco, is filled by the celestial drama related in Revelation 12. Christ is enthroned in a mandorla (unfortunately, his head is lost), and all about him angels led by the archangel Michael spear a magnificent dragon, who unfolds his scaly coils below the throne. On the left a woman "clothed with the sun" reclines upon a couch, while her newborn child is saved from the dragon. "And there was war in heaven: Michael and his angels fought against the dragon . . ." (Revelation 12:7). The scene floats toward the top of the arch in a mighty involvement of linear curves and stabbing spears, forming one of the most powerful pictorial compositions of the Middle Ages.

14-40. *Christ Enthroned, with the Archangel Michael Battling a Dragon,* wall painting, S. Pietro al Monte, Civate, Italy. Late 11th century–early 12th century

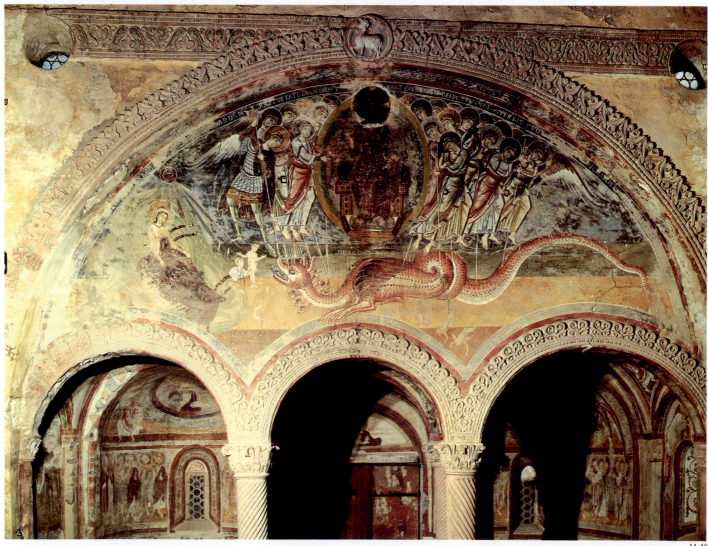

14-40

14-41. *Martyrdom of Saint Lawrence,* wall painting, Cluniac Priory Church, Berzé-la-Ville, France. Early 12th century

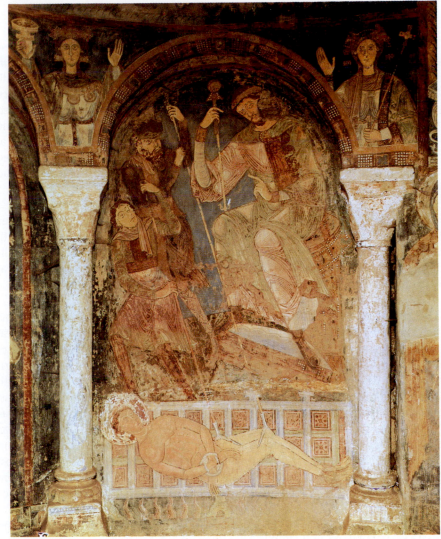

14-41

BERZÉ-LA-VILLE   A number of Romanesque fresco cycles survive in France in varying stages of preservation; most are very difficult to reproduce adequately. The small former Cluniac Priory of Berzé-la-Ville in Burgundy, whose apse shows a colossal *Christ in Majesty* imitated from the larger one at Cluny, has well-preserved wall frescoes that include the *Martyrdom of Saint Lawrence* (fig. 14–41), a work of immense power. From its coloring we may gain an idea of how the tympanum at Vézelay (see fig. 14–10) must have looked when its original painted surface was intact. Saint Lawrence lies upon the gridiron, which is arranged schematically parallel to the picture surface, and stylized flames rise from below it. The rest of the arched space is completely filled by the two executioners and the gigantic judge. The diagonal thrust of the two long rods ending in iron forks, which hold the victim on the gridiron, crosses the compartmentalized drapery masses, whose striations show the influence of Byzantine drapery conventions but whose folds move with a fierce energy totally alien to the elegant art of Constantinople — the pictorial equivalent, as it were, of the sculpture at Vézelay. Note also that the French limestone columns flanking the fresco have been painted to resemble the veined marble ones of Byzantine architecture.

TAHULL   The Romanesque frescoes that once decorated the great metropolitan churches of Europe have for the most part been replaced by later and more fashionable works of art; the best-preserved group of Romanesque frescoes originally adorned the mountain churches of Catalonia in the picturesque and produc-

437

tive northeast corner of Spain. Almost all of these have been detached from their original walls and are today in museums. A powerful example is the *Christ in Majesty* (fig. 14–42), painted about 1123 in the Church of San Clemente de Tahull. The style is somewhat less accomplished than that of the Burgundian masterpiece we have just seen, but it is by no means less expressive. Christ's mandorla is signed with the Alpha and Omega (the first and last letters of the Greek alphabet), and he holds a book inscribed (in Latin): "I am the light of the world" (John 8:12), as at Cefalù (see fig. 10–62). The drapery is rendered in broad, parallel folds, shaded arbitrarily with little elegance and much force. The delicacy of Christ's hands and feet and the portrait quality of his face are therefore the more surprising.

Romanesque manuscript illumination shows as rich a profusion of regional styles as do the churches, the sculptures, and the murals. England in the late tenth century produced a strongly independent style characterized by a freedom recalling that of the Reims School. This energetic art, which flourished especially at Winchester in southern England, was carried across the Channel to France.

THE BEATUS MANUSCRIPTS A rich treasury of fantasy and imagination was unlocked for artists of the Middle Ages in Spain and later in France by a theological work, the *Commentary on the Apocalypse*, written by the Spanish monk Beatus of Liebana in 786, during the period when the Moors ruled central and southern Spain and when Christian communities were in a state of constant struggle with Islam. The second earliest of the many surviving manuscript copies of Beatus' work, and also one of the finest, was written in 975 in Visigothic script by two priests at the monastery of Távara, in the north Spanish kingdom of León, and was illustrated largely, if not entirely, by a woman painter called ENDE, characterized in the text as *pictrix et adiutrix Dei* (woman painter and helper of God). Like most manuscript illuminations Ende's compositions were probably based to some extent on those of earlier illustrations, but their special qualities of freedom and buoyancy are her own.

The visions of Saint John, of course, provide exciting material for artists, and Ende exploited them to the full in page after splendid page. In one of the grandest (fig. 14–43) she depicts a vision that was to reappear in the sculpture of the Romanesque portal at Moissac (see fig. 14–13)—the heavens opening before Saint John to disclose the Lord upon his throne among the four-and-twenty elders (Revelation 4:2–5). Ende shows the sleeping visionary at the bottom of the page, and his spirit as a white bird whose wavy path can be followed all the way from the saint's mouth to the throne on which the Lord sits, surrounded by "a rainbow . . . in sight like unto an emerald," holding the usual book in his left hand and blessing with his right. The elders sit in freely distributed groups of six on either side of the throne, against the upper and lower stripes into which the background is divided. Surprisingly they are beardless, and their "golden crowns" become curious bloops, each with three vertical grooves and three groups of vertical marks. The rainbow is translated as a circular glory, intersecting the lower stripe and floating against the central one, but not quite touching the upper. Seven lamps, "the seven spirits of God," float at the top of the central stripe, and the "lightnings and voices" (labeled in Latin) proceeding from the throne are rendered as showers of alternating arrows and spears. The four beasts, indispensable in later renderings of the vision, are unaccountably omitted. The astonishingly simple facial drawing increases the power of the composition.

Another magnificent Beatus manuscript was illuminated at Saint-Sever in Gascony, in southern France, by STEPHANUS GARSIA, probably also Spanish. An especially powerful illustration (fig. 14–44) shows the plague of locusts loosened upon the earth to strike men with their scorpions' tails so that they "seek death and shall not find it." So vividly is the passage (Revelation 9:7–11) illustrated that it demands quotation:

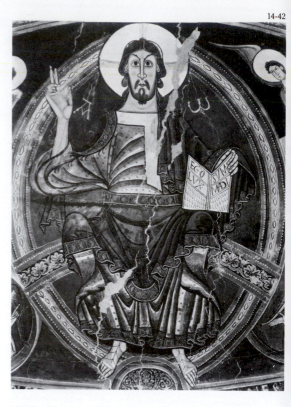

14-42

14-42. *Christ in Majesty,* fresco from S. Clemente de Tahull, Spain. c. 1123. Museo de Bellas Artes de Cataluña, Barcelona

14-43

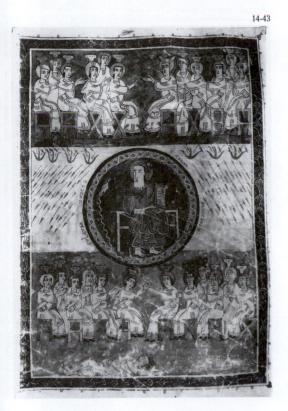

14-43. ENDE. *Vision of Saint John*, illumination from the *Commentary on the Apocalypse* by Beatus of Liebana. Monastery of Távara (León), Spain, 975. Cathedral of Gerona, Spain

And the shapes of the locusts were like unto horses prepared unto battle; and on their heads were as it were crowns like gold, and their faces were as the faces of men.

And they had hair as the hair of women, and their teeth were as the teeth of lions.

And they had breastplates, as it were breastplates of iron; and the sound of their wings was as the sound of chariots of many horses running to battle.

And they had tails like unto scorpions, and there were stings in their tails: and their power was to hurt men five months.

And they had a king over them, which is the angel of the bottomless pit, whose name in the Hebrew tongue is Abaddon, but in the Greek tongue hath his name Apollyon.

The ferocity of the linear style in which these terrible beasts are drawn is intensified by the harsh coloring of the background rectangles: red ocher, brown, green, yellow, and blue.

CÎTEAUX   Still another possibility for the Romanesque manuscript style is seen in a highly imaginative illumination from the *Moralia in Job* by Saint Gregory (fig. 14–45), painted at the very beginning of the twelfth century at the Burgundian monastery of Cîteaux, the mother church of the reforming Cistercian Order. A border of floral ornament at the sides and of zigzag at top and bottom, in delicate tones of orange, lavender, green, and blue, surrounds the initial letters of Gregory's dedication of the book to Bishop Leander. The *R* (beginning the word *Reverentissimo*) is partly formed by a standing knight, possibly Saint George, whose left leg in blue hose emerges elegantly from his orange tunic. He holds a green shield and brandishes a blue sword high above a delightful dragon, which makes up the rest of the *R* and which has two heads and green, blue, orange, and gold wings. The knight's pose is actually an unnecessary ritual because the hapless squire on whose back the knight stands has already taken the precaution of running the dragon through with a spear. Here again are the linear energy and brilliance of design we have seen in Burgundian architecture, sculpture, and painting, accompanied by a wit that could be given free rein only in manuscripts intended for the few. At this point it is interesting to quote from Saint Bernard's famous letter of 1127 on the subject of the impieties of Romanesque art:

. . . what profit is there in those ridiculous monsters, in that marvelous and deformed comeliness, that comely deformity? To what purpose are those unclean apes, those fierce lions, those monstrous centaurs, those half men, those striped tigers, those fighting knights, those hunters winding their horns? Many bodies are there seen under one head, or again, many heads to a single body. . . .

In fact, Saint Bernard, who clearly enjoyed and understood what he was condemning, put an end to all figurative art not only at Cîteaux but also throughout the Cistercian Order—luckily not before the illumination of this and other beautiful manuscripts. It almost seems as if he had correctly traced, whether consciously or not, such animal fantasies back to their ultimate source in the art of the pagan barbarians.

GOSPELS OF SAINT-BERTIN   An English painter was surely responsible for the illustrations in the *Gospel Book* illuminated at Saint-Bertin, near Boulogne-sur-Mer on the Channel coast, at the end of the tenth century. The first page of the Gospel of Matthew (fig. 14–46) is divided in two vertically; on the right a large initial *L* (for *Liber generationis*) preserves echoes of the old Hiberno-Saxon interlace, but carried out with little interest and already invaded by acanthus ornament. What really fascinated the artist was the narrative side of the page. On a little plot of ground at

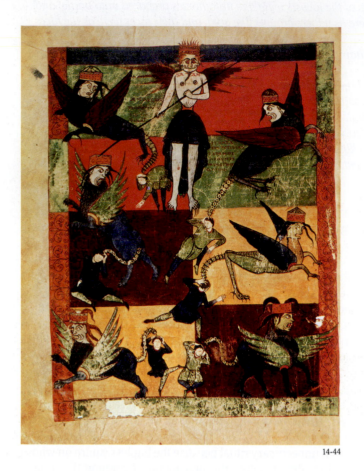

14-44

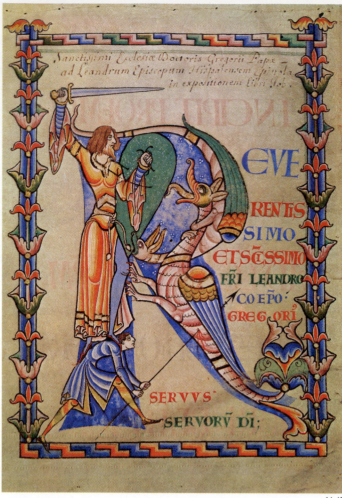

14-45

the top a benign angel gives the glad tidings to two astonished shepherds (the scene is very different from the solemn apparition in the *Gospel Lectionary of Henry II;* see fig. 13–23). Directly below, Mary is stretched out on a couch, apparently already missing her Child, after whom she reaches out her hands. A midwife bends over to comfort her, while Joseph admonishes her vehemently from his seat at the right. At the bottom of the page Joseph bends affectionately over the Christ Child, wrapped in swaddling clothes and lying in a manger, as the ox and ass look on wide-eyed. Above the initial letter the arc of Heaven discloses five delighted angels. The human, narrative style is matched by the sprightly drawing, the delicate and transparent colors, and the rippling drapery folds.

BIBLE OF BURY SAINT EDMUNDS   The apex of skill in Romanesque illumination is achieved in the lavishly illustrated *Bible of Bury Saint Edmunds,* illuminated in England probably just before the middle of the twelfth century. At the top of an illustration to Deuteronomy (fig. 14–47), Moses and Aaron reveal the Law to the assembled Hebrews, delightfully individualized in their faces and in their reactions. Moses is pictured with the horns he was given in art according to Saint Jerome's translation of the Hebrew word that also means "rays," but that, it has been shown recently, is also connected with a long tradition of horned deities and even with the shape of the Christian miter. In the lower illustration Moses points out the clean and the unclean beasts; two defiant red pigs rejoice in their uncleanness. This style is a very elegant one, with its enamel-like depth and brilliance of color and high degree of technical finish. The perfection of the ornament, the smooth linear flow of poses and draperies, and the minute gradations of value have brought the art of painting about as far as it could go within the conventions of Romanesque style. Marion Roberts Sargent says, referring to this illustration, "The real achievement of

14-44. STEPHANUS GARSIA. *Plague of Locusts,* illumination from the *Commentary on the Apocalypse* by Beatus of Liebana. St.-Sever (Gascony), France, middle 11th century. Bibliothèque Nationale, Paris

14-45. Initial *R* with *Saint George and the Dragon* (?), illumination from the *Moralia in Job.* Cîteaux, France, early 12th century. Bibliothèque Municipale, Dijon

14-46. Initial *L* and *Scenes of the Nativity,* illumination from a Gospel Book. St.-Bertin, France, late 10th century. Bibliothèque Municipale, Boulogne-sur-Mer, France

14-47. Frontispiece, Book of Deuteronomy, *Bible of Bury St. Edmunds.* Abbey of Bury St. Edmunds, England, first half of 12th century. Illumination. Corpus Christi College, Cambridge, England

14-48. *Landing of Horses from Boats,* detail of the *Bayeux Tapestry.* c. 1073–83. Wool embroidery on linen, height 20″ (50.8 cm). Courtesy Centre Guillaume le Conquérant, Bayeux, France

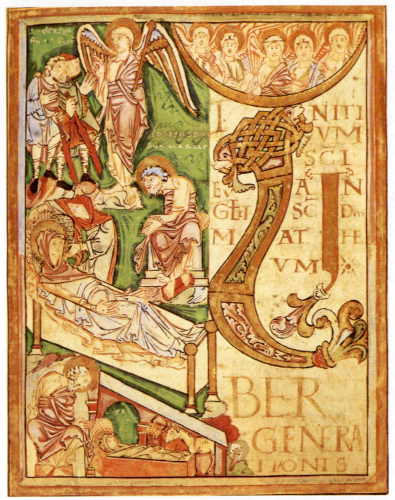

14-46

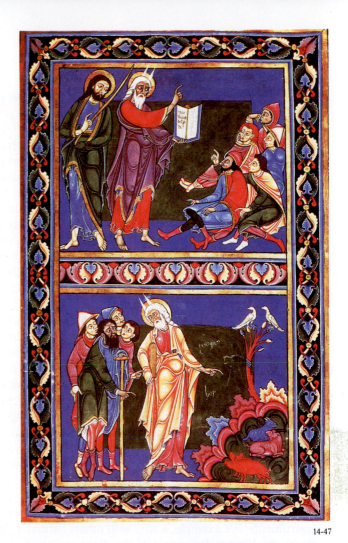

14-47

14-48

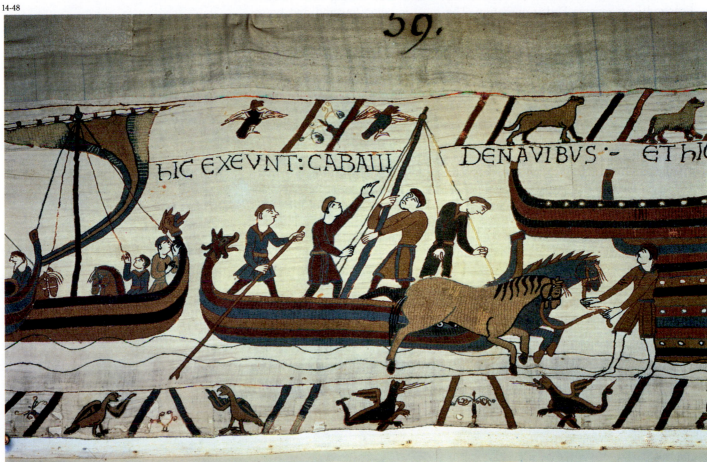

Romanesque illumination is the complete domination of two-dimensional space. Figures, border, ornament, architecture, and landscape, even the text, are treated equally in brilliant color, resulting in total mastery of surface design."

We may conclude our survey of Romanesque pictorial arts with two works executed and, to a significant though indeterminate extent, conceived by women. One is entirely temporal; one lies beyond the compass of ordinary experience.

THE BAYEUX TAPESTRY   One of the largest and also best-preserved pictorial efforts of the Romanesque period is the so-called *Bayeux Tapestry*. (In point of fact, this is an embroidery, done on eight bolts of natural-colored linen with only two different stitches of wool; in tapestry the design is woven along with the fabric.) Originally somewhat longer, the work now measures 230 feet in length by only 20 inches in height. It was designed and executed to run clockwise around the entire nave of the Cathedral of Bayeux in Normandy, from pier to pier. Especially interesting since Romanesque secular works are rare, the hanging narrates for the populace the detailed story of the invasion of England by William the Conqueror, including the background of political intrigue, from the official Norman point of view and complete with titles in Latin for the benefit of those who could read.

Traditionally the immense project is supposed to have been embroidered by the ladies of Queen Matilda's court. There seems little reason to doubt that the needlework was done by women, who in the Middle Ages made all the embroideries for church vestments, altar cloths, and altar frontals. One of the women seems to have been an Anglo-Saxon, judging from the forms of some of the letters. The hanging was probably ordered by William's brother Odon, bishop of Bayeux, for the consecration of his cathedral in 1077. But were the designers of the splendid narrative also women? This has been doubted, since the actors are exclusively male and the scenes are depicted with close knowledge of military operations and instruments. For example, a ship with others behind it (fig. 14–48), strikingly like those the Vikings (ancestors of the Normans) had used during their raids, is beached in a reverse D-day operation. The mast is being lowered and horses disembarked upon the English beach. Still, the women artists could have been provided with a detailed scenario, informed by veterans of the battle as to exactly how these things were done. Almost certainly the needlewomen were left free to add their own creatures in the margins.

Space was required for this continuous method of narration, descending of course directly from Greek and Hellenistic friezes and Roman historical columns — doubtless scattered here and there throughout the Empire — and emulated in Bishop Bernward's column (see fig. 13–19) and in such rotuli as the *Joshua Roll* (see fig. 10–50). No excerpt can convey the cumulative force of the *Bayeux Tapestry*. Exhibited today around a single long room, the typically Romanesque figures move with such vivacity that every aspect of the Norman Conquest seems to take place before our eyes, and we easily accept the Romanesque convention of flatness.

SAINT HILDEGARDE OF BINGEN   Among all the visionaries of the Romanesque period the most original and unpredictable was Hildegarde of Bingen (1098–1179), the first of a long line of influential women mystics throughout the Middle Ages, the Renaissance, and the Baroque. Notwithstanding his declared attitude toward the fantastic strain in Romanesque art, Saint Bernard firmly championed the validity and importance of Hildegarde's visions. Although the procedures for her canonization were never completed, Hildegarde's name is today officially inscribed among the saints because of her long life divided between mystical revelations of otherworldly powers of light and darkness, which began during her childhood, and intense scholarly activity. In 1136 Saint Hildegarde was elected prioress of her convent, which she then transferred to Rupertsberg near Bingen, on the Rhine. There she wrote books on medicine and history, allegorical sermons, and both the words and the music of canticles and hymns. Her most important work for our purposes is the *Liber Scivias* (abbreviation of *Scite vias lucis*, "know ye the ways of light"). Whether or not she painted any of the illuminations with her own hand, she certainly directed the work, which was lettered and illustrated by her nuns. Among the twenty-six visions we may choose that of the ball of fire (fig. 14–49):

> *Then I saw a huge image, round and shadowy. It was pointed at the top, like an egg. . . . Its outermost layer was of bright fire. Within lay a dark membrane. Suspended in the bright flames was a burning ball of fire, so large that the entire image received its light. Three more lights burned in a row above it. They gave it support through their glow, so that the light would never be extinguished.*

Whatever the wonderful visions may have been in the transfigured mind of the saint, it is significant that her nuns set them down in the visual language of the Romanesque—two-dimensional surfaces and ornamental line. It is tragic to have to record the destruction of the original manuscript in World War II.

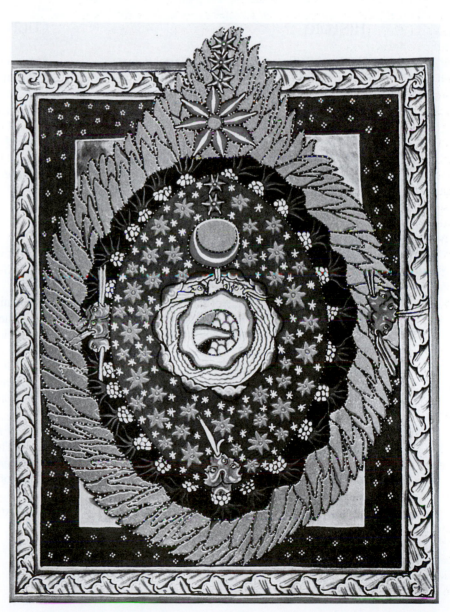

14-49. HILDEGARDE OF BINGEN. *Vision of the Ball of Fire*, illumination from the *Liber Scivias*. Rupertsberg, Germany, 12th century (original destroyed)

14-49

TIME LINE VII

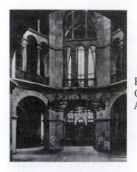

Palatine
Chapel,
Aachen

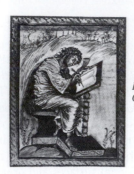

*Ebbo
Gospels*

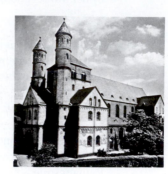

St. Pantaleon,
Cologne

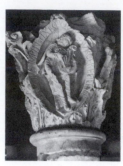

Capital,
Cluny

HISTORY	CULTURE
700 Battle of Poitiers, 732; Charles Martel defeats Muslims	Alcuin (735–804) begins revision of the Vulgate (Latin Bible)
800 Charlemagne crowned Emperor at Rome, 800	Ebbo, archbishop of Reims, r. 816–35
	Carolingian revival of Latin classics
Vikings begin raids on England, 835	Earliest documented church organ, Aachen, 822
Charles the Bald, Carolingian king, r. 840–77	Einhard writes *Life of Charlemagne,* 821
900 Carolingian Empire divided among sons of Louis the Pious at Treaty of Verdun, 843	Cluniac Order founded, 910
Charles the Simple cedes Normandy to Vikings, 911	Gero, archbishop of Cologne, r. 969–76
Otto I, German king, crowned Holy Roman emperor, 962	
1000 Hugh Capet, French king, r. 987–96, founds Capetian dynasty	St. Bernward, archbishop of Hildesheim, r. 993–1033
Leif Ericson sails to North America, 1002	
1025 William the Conqueror, Norman duke, r. 1035–87	St. Dominic of Silos (d. 1037)
Normans begin conquest of Sicily, 1043	Avicenna (980–1037), chief medical authority of Middle Ages
Battle of Hastings, 1066; William the Conqueror wins England	College of Cardinals formed to elect popes, 1059
First Crusade, 1095–99	Pope Gregory VII, r. 1073–83
Crusaders found Latin kingdom of Jerusalem, 1099	St. Bruno founds Carthusian Order, 1084
	Cistercian Order founded, 1098
1100 Louis IV the Fat of France, r. 1108–37, strengthens monarchy	*Song of Roland* composed, c. 1098
Roger II, Sicilian king, r. 1130–54	Monk Theophilus' *De diversis artibus,* c. 1100
Second Crusade initiated by St. Bernard, 1147	St. Bernard, abbot of Clairvaux, r. 1115–53
Saladin captures Jerusalem, 1187	Order of Knights Templars founded in Jerusalem, 1119
	Hildegarde of Bingen (1098–1179)

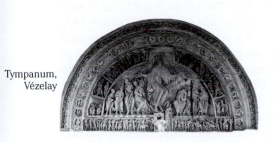

Tympanum,
Vézelay

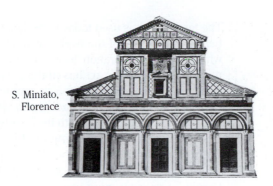

S. Miniato,
Florence

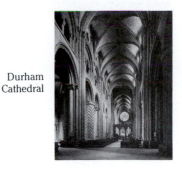

Durham
Cathedral

PAINTING, SCULPTURE, ARCHITECTURE

Abbey Church of St.-Riquier; Abbey of Lorsch and gateway

Palatine Chapel, Aachen; plan for monastery at St. Gall
Coronation Gospels; Lorsch Gospels; Ebbo Gospels; Utrecht Psalter; Lindau
   Gospels; Bible of Charles the Bald

Crucifix of Archbishop Gero
Vision of St. John, by Ende
Otto Imperator Augustus

St. Pantaleon, Cologne

Doubting Thomas; Lectionary of Henry II; St. Michael's Hildesheim
Hitda Codex; Uta Codex

Baptistery, Florence; Cathedrals of Pisa, Speyer
Plague of Locusts, by Stephanus Garcia
St.-Étienne, Caen; Cathedral, Durham
St.-Sernin, Toulouse; Abbey Church, Cluny
Sculpture, S. Domingo de Silos
Fresco cycle, S. Angelo in Formis; *Bayeux Tapestry*
Frescoes, Civate

Moralia in Job; Christ, S. Clemente de Tahull; *Bible of Bury St. Edmunds*
Reliefs by Wiligelmo da Modena; baptismal font by Renier de Huy
St.-Madeleine, Vézelay, with sculpture; *Last Judgment,* by Gislebertus,
   Autun; tympanum, portal, and cloister sculpture, Moissac; portal
   sculpture, St.-Gilles-du-Gard; Notre-Dame-la-Grande, Poitiers
Cathedral, Monreale; *King David,* by Antelami
Liber Scivias, by Hildegarde of Bingen

PARALLEL SOCIETIES

Frankish	700
Byzantine	
Carolingian	800
Viking	
Muslim	
Ottonian	900
	1000
Norman	1025
Italian city-states	
French Monarchy	
German Monarchy	
	1100
English Monarchy	

CHAPTER FIFTEEN

The term *Gothic* is used today to designate the style that began in northern France before the middle of the twelfth century and in the rest of western Europe anywhere from a generation to a century later. We now know that the name is a misnomer, for Gothic art has nothing whatever to do with the Goths, who swept down on Roman Italy in the fifth century (see page 378). But the Italians of the Renaissance thought that it had. The medieval buildings surrounding them seemed so barbaric in comparison with the beauty of Roman architecture that they believed this style could have been imported into classical Italy only by the Vandals, the Goths, the Lombards, and the Huns. Giorgio Vasari, the Renaissance artist and writer who characterized Byzantine pictorial style as "the rude manner of the Greeks," was even more caustic about medieval architecture, which he claimed "was invented by the Goths." The disparaging term *Gothic* took root; by the seventeenth century the great French dramatist Molière was referring to the "torrent of odious Gothic monsters" that had been unleashed on France. Not until the beginnings of Romanticism in the late eighteenth century did Gothic art begin to catch hold of the imagination of a cultivated elite as a welcome escape from the rules of classical art into a past that seemed both natural and intriguingly remote. And only with the historical studies of the early nineteenth century did it become clear that so-called Gothic art was really a phenomenon separated from the Gothic invasions by at least seven centuries. Soon Gothic art became recognized as the refined intellectual, aesthetic, and spiritual achievement of a highly developed urban society, but there was no longer any possibility of changing the name.

Non-French European regions in the late twelfth and early thirteenth centuries, however, were well aware of the origin of the Gothic style. They referred to it as *opus francigenum* ("French work"), and they were right—in the narrow and restricted sense denoted by the term *French* at the time. The Gothic style was born in that region of north-central France centering around Paris, known as the Île-de-France, which as we have seen (see page 410) was the personal domain of the French kings. Today art historians are in a position to add the birthdate of the Gothic style: shortly before the year 1140, when the first stage of the reconstruction of the royal Abbey Church at Saint-Denis was completed. From the Île-de-France (see Map 12, page 412) the style radiated outward, winning acceptance in region after region, first throughout northern France and almost immediately in England, then in Germany, the Low Countries, central Europe, Spain, and Portugal, and finally in a reluctant Italy—which never fully understood or accepted it and was, as we have noted, the first to brand it barbarous and to rebel against it. Eventually the style was carried to regions as remote as Mexico and Palestine. The Gothic revival of the eighteenth century meant that Gothic-revival buildings have continued to appear in most parts of the world. In England, it has been claimed, there is no century since the eleventh when Gothic structures have not been built.

In contrast to the individuality of the local Romanesque schools, their wide diversity of styles and technical methods, and the extreme brevity of their period of full bloom, five outstanding phenomena characterize the Gothic.

First, the Gothic is remarkably consistent throughout wide areas of central and northern France; it was carried almost unaltered into the rest of western Europe and was only somewhat modified by local requirements in England. So well did it satisfy the needs of urban populations throughout its vast geographical extent that an extremely large proportion of Gothic religious buildings survive today, in spite of innumerable social upheavals and two world wars, with their cycles of sculptural and pictorial decorations (in Catholic countries at least) largely intact, and are still quite practical for daily use.

Second, the Gothic developed a competitive momentum; architects, sculptors, and painters were well aware of what was being done elsewhere and were constantly trying to beat their rivals at their own game. The excitement of this momentum may be partly responsible for our enjoyment of Gothic art. We get to understand the system, we know what can be expected, and we rejoice when Gothic artists surpass each other and themselves in fulfilling its demands.

Third, the Gothic lasted for four hundred years, although transformed and expanded by regional tastes and requirements, from the mid-twelfth well into the sixteenth century (everywhere except Italy, of course), constituting a unifying force throughout western Europe.

Fourth, the Gothic created structures completely without precedent in the history of art, surpassing in technical daring anything imagined in the ancient world.

Finally, after the long interregnum of the early Middle Ages, the Gothic was the first Western art to present a believable image of a complete human being including, for the first time since antiquity, a repertory of facial expressions answering to inner emotional states.

We tend to think of Romanesque as the architecture of the monasteries, and to a great extent this is true, but largely because in most Western cities, even some very small ones, the Romanesque cathedrals of the eleventh and early twelfth centuries became inadequate and were replaced in the late twelfth and thirteenth centuries by far larger Gothic structures. By the beginning of the Gothic period, the great cultural and economic mission of the monasteries had largely come to an end. Their role as conservators of learning was being assumed by the universities, and their economic importance had been superseded by that of the towns. The growing kingdoms of northern and western Europe, the Holy Roman Empire in central Europe, and the papacy with its worldwide claims emanating from Rome were earthly counterparts of an intricate cosmic order of being, under the monarchical rule of the Christian Deity. In this encyclopedic universal structure, whose towering symbol was the cathedral, every smallest human or natural phenomenon—however imperfectly understood—found its preordained niche. In contrast to the visionary withdrawal of the monastic Romanesque, the urban Gothic may have had its head in the stars but its feet were firmly planted on earth, and every intervening connection was thought out. It was pointed out by Meyer Schapiro that the Gothic cathedrals were the largest economic enterprises of the Middle Ages. The cathedrals absorbed the activities of architects, builders, masons, sculptors, stonecutters, painters, stained-glass makers, carpenters, metalworkers, jewelers—utilizing materials brought sometimes from great distances—and gave back nothing in a material sense.

Monasteries were generally located in the country; a cathedral, by definition the seat of a bishop, was in a town, and it became a symbol of the town's corporate existence. To a great extent this is still true. A contemporary Florentine will boast of being *fiorentino di cupolone* ("Florentine from the great dome [of the Cathedral]"); during the air attacks of World War II, Londoners kept watch nightly, risking their lives, on the roofs and towers of Saint Paul's Cathedral in order to extinguish firebombs as they fell. In the Gothic period communal devotion to the construction of the cathedrals was so great that, according to contemporary chroniclers, not only did the rich contribute financially to the limit of their ability to the building and decoration of the cathedrals, but also rich and poor alike joined with laborers and oxen to pull the carts laden with building materials.

With their soaring height, their immense interiors, their pinnacles, towers, and spires, their innumerable images and narratives in stone, paint, and glass, the

447

cathedrals summed up the knowledge and experience of humanity's brief earthly tenancy in artistic forms and iconographic cycles of astonishing completeness, united in a structure that constituted a comprehensive medieval picture of the universe from the heights of Heaven to the depths of Hell. But we have not defined the Gothic style, and that will not be easy. It is best to illustrate its nature and main lines of development with a few selected works.

The Beginnings of Gothic Style

SAINT-DENIS AT PARIS   On June 9, 1140, in the presence of King Louis VII of France and his queen, Abbot Suger consecrated a new façade, with a triple, sculptured portal and two square towers (of which only one was ever completed), on the Carolingian church of his Abbey of Saint-Denis, just north of Paris; on June 11, 1144, the same abbot brought to completion a new choir with ambulatory and radiating chapels that replaced the Carolingian apse. Both additions were necessary to accommodate the crowds of pilgrims who came to venerate the relics of Saint Denis and other saints preserved in the apse. Saint-Denis was not only a pilgrimage monastery but also a royal foundation in which French monarchs were buried. As its abbot, Suger was a person of great political importance, the power behind the thrones of two kings and regent of France (1147–49) during the absence of one king on the Second Crusade.

Suger intended eventually to replace the Carolingian nave of his church as well. Ironically, when this nave was replaced in the thirteenth century by a Gothic one, Suger's choir was also demolished, except for the ambulatory, which is an extraordinary achievement (figs. 15–1, 15–2). At first sight the ambulatory with its radiating chapels recalls Saint-Sernin at Toulouse (see fig. 14–4), but the ambulatory of Saint-Denis is doubled at the expense of the chapels, which are reduced to hardly more than bay windows, expanding and contracting at regular intervals so as to carry the crowds easily around the high altar with its reliquary shrine.

Suger left a written account, unique in the annals of patronage, explaining his feelings about the work and his reasons for doing as he did, recounting its history (not without miracles), and preserving valuable information about architectural practices in the twelfth century. According to a famous study by Erwin Panofsky (see Bibliography), Suger believed that the writings of the fifth-century Syrian mystic known as Dionysius the Pseudo-Areopagite, preserved at Saint-Denis, were in fact those of Saint Denis, the patron saint of France and of the abbey (*Denis* is French for "Dionysius"). The complex Neoplatonic system according to which Dionysius identified light with divinity was seen by Panofsky as the justification for Suger's enthusiasm for the light from the "circular string of chapels, by virtue of which the whole [church] would shine with the wonderful and uninterrupted light of most luminous windows. . . ."

One is tempted to ask why such a theological explanation of light would not refer just as easily to Hagia Sophia, for example, with its rows on rows of windows under and around the floating dome. One notices also that Suger reserved his special raptures for the beauty of the gold used to cover the new doors and for the gold and jewels of the reliquary shrine, without mentioning the design of either. He was so unresponsive, in fact, to the style of his time that he caused a gold mosaic instead of sculpture to be set up in the tympanum of the left portal, although he admitted it was contrary to "modern" practice. One is almost more impressed by what Suger omitted from his account, such as the name of the architect, than by what he mentioned. Suger was also silent about the master's technical and stylistic innovations, but he recounted with admiration the architect's ability to measure the Gothic choir so accurately that when the Carolingian apse left standing inside it was finally taken down, the new choir was found to be in perfect alignment with the old nave. About the columns Suger said no more than that their number corresponds to the numbers of the Apostles and the minor prophets.

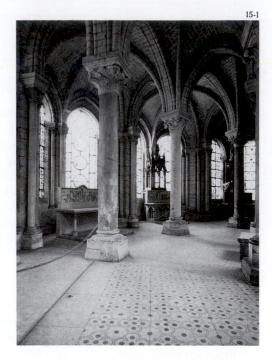

15-1

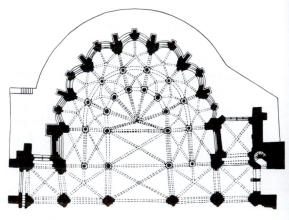

15-1. Ambulatory, Abbey Church of St.-Denis, Paris. 1140–44

15-2

15-2. Plan of the ambulatory, Abbey Church of St.-Denis, Paris (after Sumner Crosby)

So far from being in any way responsible for the new style evolving around him, Suger in his account reveals himself to have been unaware that it was new. Modern studies of the development of ribbed vaults have shown that for a decade or so before the rebuilding of Saint-Denis, architects—under probable Norman influence—had been experimenting with ribbed vaults in the parish churches of the Île-de-France. Whoever he was, the architect of Saint-Denis was probably of local origin (only the stained-glass makers, Suger tells us, were brought from throughout France). A glance at the illustration (see fig. 15–1) makes clear what is really new: for the first time we have an architecture not of walls but of supports. Columns or compound piers including colonnettes support the ribs, between which the concave vault surfaces are constructed. Walls tend to be replaced by windows. From this moment walls in French cathedral architecture are residual, and architects will vie with one another to reduce them to a minimum, while at the same time they refine the connection between the supports and slim down the supports to the ultimate. In each of the trapezoidal bays and pentagonal chapels of the ambulatory at Saint-Denis, the transverse ribs are pointed so as to lift the inner side of each bay as high as possible, thereby concentrating the outward thrust of the vaults on the columns and piers. The plan shows that this thrust is carried to the exterior of the church where it is met by the buttresses, which appear as black, rectangular projections between the windows.

Architecture at Saint-Denis has become an organic system of interacting supports (columns, colonnettes, ribs, buttresses), both inside the church and outside, enclosing vaulting surfaces above and windows on the sides. Four thousand years of post-and-lintel construction and at least a thousand years of massive vault design have suddenly become obsolete. The only derivation of early Gothic architecture from the past can be found in the ribbed domes of Byzantine architecture, such as that of Hagia Sophia (see fig. 10–39), but even Byzantine ribs stop at the pendentives and walls remained necessary. Suger recorded his gratitude for divine intervention when the bare ribs of the incomplete choir vaults of Saint-Denis, protected by the outer roof but still without the stabilizing factor of the inner triangles of the vaulting, were shaken by a terrible storm; they vibrated visibly but remained standing. It would have been more to the point for Suger to congratulate the architect on his extraordinary knowledge and skill.

Like many medieval patrons before him, Suger thought of plundering Rome for marble columns and even worked out the route by which they could be transported. Luckily (again, according to Suger, by miracle) he found an inexhaustible quarry of local limestone. But it was not by accident that in this new organic architecture not only Roman columns but also Roman, Byzantine, and Romanesque capitals have been abandoned. The new capital shapes are based, however schematically, on the growth of actual foliage that the architects had seen rather than on Greek acanthus leaves that they had not. It is worth remembering that several Renaissance writers felt that Gothic architecture had originally been suggested by primitive shelters formed by tying trees together. Such was the beauty and utility of the style invented by the unknown genius who designed the new work at Saint-Denis in the 1140s that Romanesque building stopped at once in northern France, and long before the end of the twelfth century the Romanesque was relegated to a few remote, provincial centers.

THE FAÇADE AT CHARTRES   One masterpiece of transitional Gothic architecture, sculpture, and stained glass survives intact: the façade of the Cathedral of Chartres (fig. 15–3), to the southwest of Paris. In 1134 the façade of the eleventh-century cathedral was damaged by fire, necessitating its replacement. The north tower was built first, without a spire. Then about 1142 the south tower was erected to its full height, culminating in one of the most beautiful spires of the Gothic period. The simple addition of one element to the next, visible throughout Romanesque structures (see figs. 14–3, 14–4), has here given way to a delicately adjusted

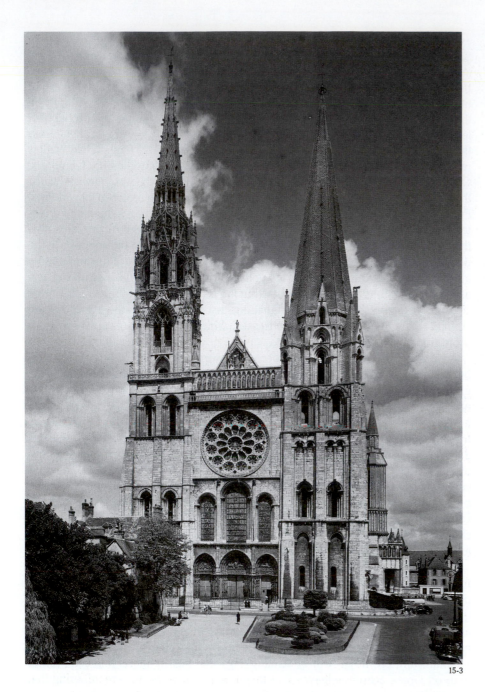

15-3

15-3. West façade, Cathedral of Chartres, France. 1140–50

interconnection. The transition from the square to the octagon, for instance, is prepared as early as the second story by placing the colonnettes of the blind arcade directly on the keystones of the arched windows and by the splaying of the corner buttresses. By the time the eye rises to the fourth story, which is clearly octagonal, the transition has been accomplished almost unnoticeably. The tower rose high above the roof of the Romanesque cathedral at the beginning of the third story; its effect was somewhat diminished by the taller Gothic structure commenced in 1194 (see page 455).

The façade was built to connect the towers at their eastern flanks, so that they would project on either side and appear partly to enclose it. At some undetermined time these plans were changed, and the Royal Portal (fig. 15–4), dating from about 1140–50, was set up in its present position flush with the towers. The splayed triple portal is completely sculptured and devoted to a unified theme: the Nativity and scenes from the Infancy of Christ on the right, the Ascension on the left, scenes from

15-4. Royal Portal, west façade, Cathedral of Chartres. c. 1140–50

15-5. Jamb statues, Royal Portal, Cathedral of Chartres

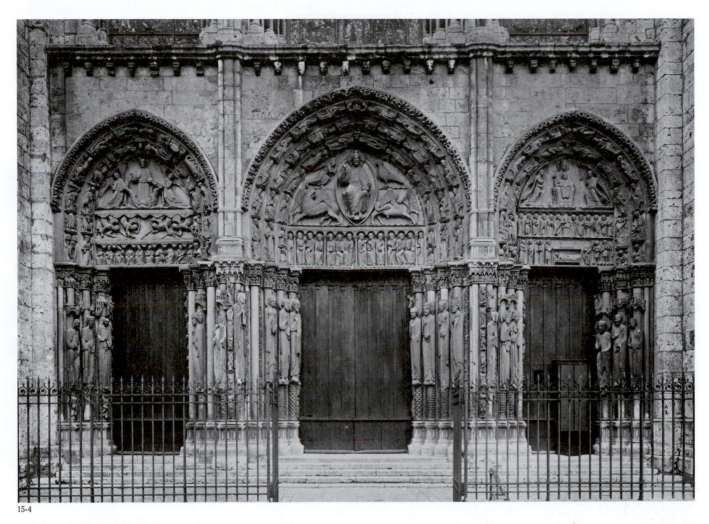

15-4

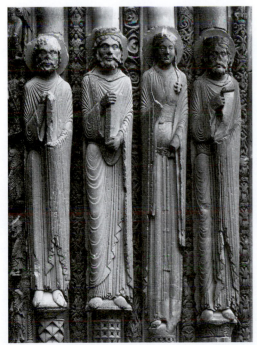

15-5

Christ's life in the capitals of the colonnettes, and in the center his heavenly apparition according to the Vision of John, as at Moissac (see fig. 14–13), but including the Twelve Apostles. The freedom of Romanesque sculpture has been abandoned here in favor of a disciplined structure that embraces every element in the portal and of which Christ himself is the center. In contrast to the rich confusion of the Moissac tympanum, the central lunette at Chartres is immediately legible. Each of the symbols of the Evangelists occupies its predetermined position. Each of the four-and-twenty elders of the Apocalypse in the outer archivolts and the twelve angels in the inner archivolts moves in conformity with the motion of the arch, even though that involves tilting over, until they converge at the keystone, where two other angels uphold a royal crown.

The infinitely tall and slender figures on the jambs of the doors (fig. 15–5) represent in all probability kings, queens, and prophets from the Old Testament. They, too, obey the forces of the architecture to the extent of assuming the shapes of the colonnettes of which they form a part. They stand upon firm pedestals, and the long, taut drapery lines contrast in their severity with the luxuriance of the interlaced vinescroll ornament between the colonnettes. Paradoxically, the columnar figures support nothing; each usurps the shape of a column, but not its function, in contrast to the maidens of the Erechtheion (see fig. 7–65), for example, who took over the function of columns without relinquishing their own shapes. Calm has settled over the scene after the wildness of Vézelay and Moissac less than twenty years before. The figures seem to enjoy their role in a perfect system, which, incidentally, includes among its minor sculptures the seven liberal arts, the signs of the zodiac, and the labors of the months. The figures assume a cylindrical existence in depth, which in Romanesque sculpture had been seen only in Provence (see fig. 14–16). So rapid, in fact, is the development of early Gothic style that some of the sculptors at Chartres appear also to have worked at Saint-Gilles-du-Gard. The delicacy of the parallel drapery lines, recalling those of Archaic kore figures (see figs. 7–10, 7–12), is surpassed only by the sensitive delineation of the quiet faces. The serenity of this royal allegory was never again achieved, but the decisive step in the creation of a new architectural sculpture had been taken. Henceforward, the figure could assert its individual existence in harmony with the forces of an all-embracing architecture.

The French Cathedral

The story of French cathedral building in the late twelfth and thirteenth centuries is made more exciting by the element of intense competition. No sooner was a new form or a new device established in one cathedral than it was outdone in another. One architect and sculptor, VILLARD DE HONNECOURT, went from cathedral to cathedral drawing the latest architectural and sculptural achievements (fig. 15–6), in this case the *flying-buttress* system in the choir of the cathedral at Reims, making clear exactly how the flying buttresses start from lofty, freestanding buttresses counterweighted by *pinnacles* (tiny steeples) and leap in a flattened arch over the radiating chapels to the next freestanding buttresses and then in a final flight over the ambulatory to the wall of the clerestory. (Compare fig. 15–6 with fig. 15–27, a modern diagram of the flying buttresses of the nave at Amiens; for the function and nature of the flying buttress, see page 456). It will be noted that only the lower flight supports the vault, a segment of whose converging ribs can be seen in Villard's sketch.

There was no practical reason for the immense and constantly increasing height of the cathedrals; vast congregations could have been accommodated by much lower structures. The height was surely symbolic of humanity's heavenward aspiration, and as we move from cathedral to cathedral we can share the excitement of the builders as they embodied in their soaring structures the ascent from earth to God.

LAON The earliest Gothic cathedral is that at Laon, to the northeast of Paris. The situation is spectacular because Laon itself is a hill town lifted high above an almost flat plain; the cathedral with all its towers may thus be seen for many miles (fig. 15–7). It was to have had seven towers, one over the crossing between nave and transept, two on the nave façade, and two on each transept. Although even some specialists do not know this, all save the crossing tower—a total of six—were actually completed. During the French Revolution one tower on each transept façade was torn down for its stone, to the dismay of the local population; only four now remain. The number seven had mystical significance, since it was the sum of the Trinity and the Gospels, the number of the Virtues (and the Vices), the number of the gifts of the Holy Spirit, the number of the liberal arts, and the number of the candlesticks in Heaven. No Gothic cathedral ever boasted all seven towers, but many were planned for that number (Chartres was to have had eight). Whether the towers at Laon were also intended to receive spires is uncertain but unlikely; the tiny steeple on one of the transept towers is a much later addition.

The façade, begun about 1190, is unexpectedly dramatic. The triple portal is protected by three porches; above the central porch is an early example of a *rose window*. Radiating from the center of this circular window is an elaborate network made of separate pieces of stone, known as *tracery*, one of the great inventions of the Gothic period. Pierced slabs of stone, or grilles, had been used in Byzantine and Islamic windows, and the Gothic rose window derives from this tradition. However, the tracery intended to hold stained glass obeys precise geometrical laws. Above the rose and its flanking arched windows runs an open arcade, broken to indicate on the exterior the relation of the clerestory and side aisles within. The façade

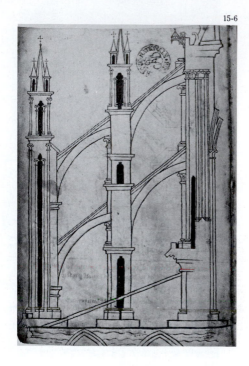

15-6. VILLARD DE HONNECOURT. *Flying Buttresses at Reims Cathedral.* c. 1230–35. Pen and ink. Bibliothèque Nationale, Paris

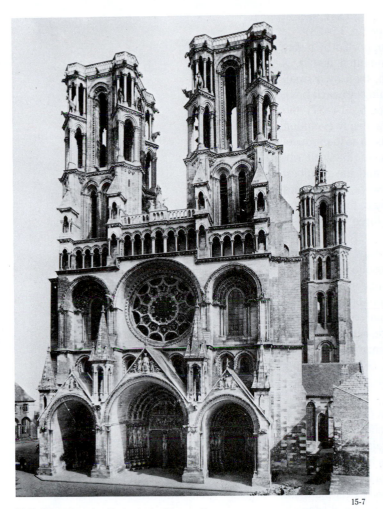

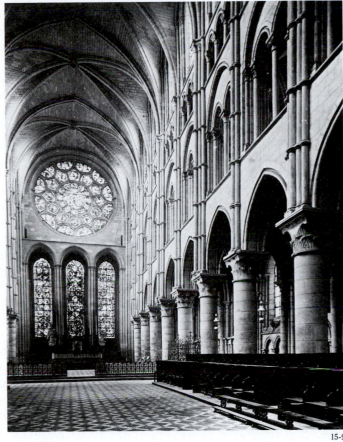

15-7

15-9

15-7. West façade, Cathedral of Laon, France. c. 1190

15-8. Plan of the Cathedral of Laon (after G. Dehio). Begun c. 1160

15-9. Choir, Cathedral of Laon

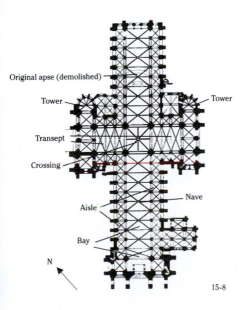

Original apse (demolished)

Tower

Tower

Transept

Crossing

Nave

Aisle

Bay

N

15-8

towers are flanked by superimposed aediculae with pointed arches, square on the first two stories and octagonal on the third. In contrast to the lofty pointed central windows these aediculae create a broken and irregular silhouette. The towers are transparent, skeletal structures, through which the wind blows easily. From the uppermost aediculae protrude statues of oxen, popularly believed to be those that dragged the stones for the cathedral up the steep hill of Laon. For some as-yet-unexplained reason, the round apse at Laon, begun about 1160, was replaced only a few years after completion by a much longer, square east end on the English model (figs. 15–8, 15–9), leaving intact the flanking round chapels on the east corners of the transepts. The present great length of the noble interior—eleven bays for the nave, ten for the choir—is as dramatic as the towers.

In looking at the interiors of Gothic cathedrals throughout Europe we should remember, however, that the vista was originally broken in almost every one by a monumental stone screen running across the entrance to the choir. This screen was provided with a central Crucifixion group, twin pulpits from which the Epistle and Gospel were read at Mass, and sometimes even small chapels. The purpose of these choir screens was to separate the laity's Masses and preaching services, held in the nave, from the Divine Office (prayers at seven stated times) and other liturgical functions, which had to be chanted in the choir by the clergy of the cathedral whether or not there was a congregation. An altar for congregational Masses stood before the gate into the choir. These choir screens, with all their precious sculpture, were systematically destroyed during the Counter-Reformation in order to unify the interiors for enormous congregations and provide a clear view of the high altar. Their original effect can be judged by surviving examples at Durham in England (see fig. 14–35) and Amiens in France (see fig. 15–28).

The interior at Laon is four stories high. The nave arcade, supported by heavy cylindrical pillars instead of compound square piers, is surmounted first by a vaulted gallery with coupled arches under an embracing arch, then by a small triforium (a gallery in the thickness of the wall with three openings in each bay), and finally by a clerestory tucked into the vaults. As at Caen (see fig. 14–37), the vaults are six-part, but somewhat less domical. From here on, a steady evolution will be observed in the flattening of the vaults of Gothic cathedrals so as to produce, eventually, a level crown line. At Laon, for the first time, each rib—wall rib, transverse rib, diagonal rib—is represented by a colonnette, and the resultant bundle declares at any point the nature of the entire living framework. Since round pillars are used throughout, the alternating system survives only in these clusters that spring from the capitals—five where all ribs are included, three where there are only wall and transverse ribs.

There is an even more significant difference, too often overlooked by art historians, in which resides the secret of Gothic as opposed to Romanesque vaulting: the *conoids* (the conelike shapes formed by the convergence of ribs and vault surfaces on the capitals of the colonnettes) are sharply pinched together on the side next to the clerestory. This pinching of the conoids frees the diagonal ribs from the clerestory, allowing them to establish their own positions in space, actually passing slightly in front of the clerestory. The thrust of the vaults seems to have been contained by the girdle of the gallery, but in the thirteenth century cautious architects added flying buttresses on the exterior.

NOTRE-DAME AT PARIS The façade of Notre-Dame at Paris (fig. 15–10) was planned about 1200 and completed about 1250. The dramatic effects of Laon are avoided; the elements are brought under the control of a majestic, four-story, rectilinear design, which has won universal admiration. The porches are retracted into the mass of the building, and the towers rise only a single story above the nave roof, which can be seen through the screen of tracery; only two were ever planned. The nave is lighted by a magnificent rose window inserted in the thirteenth century; the two arched windows on either side admit light only to chambers in the lowest story of the tower. The coupled windows that admit light to the upper story were widely imitated. The plan of the church (fig. 15–11), laid out about 1163, is much more regular than that of Laon. The nave is ten bays long, the choir before the apse exactly half that; the apse vault is divided into five compartments. Instead of the wide transepts of Laon, those of Notre-Dame are retracted like the porches so that they hardly project beyond the church. Intended for a larger city, Notre-Dame has four side aisles rather than the customary two (an outer line of chapels was added between the buttresses in the thirteenth century, thereby darkening the interior; only those on the north side of the church are shown in the plan).

But the interior design of Notre-Dame proved obsolete within sixty years. Only the last bay on the right (fig. 15–12), next to the crossing, shows the original four-story design of the nave, with an arcade supported by round pillars as at Laon, a gallery lighted by triangular windows, and a double clerestory made up of small windows without tracery surmounting tiny rose windows (the remaining one has been much restored). About the middle of the thirteenth century, the original row of flying buttresses against the nave (required to supplement the containing action of the gallery) was replaced by the present ones, and the clerestory was greatly enlarged into tall windows filled with tracery extending well below the springing points of the vaults, influenced by developments at Chartres, Reims, and Amiens. The photograph renders it clear that the pinching of the conoids by the original architect made this "modernization" possible, as it allowed the diagonal ribs to pass freely across the upper edge of the clerestory windows. Each rib, incidentally, is channeled so that the appearance of a cluster is maintained at all points from the

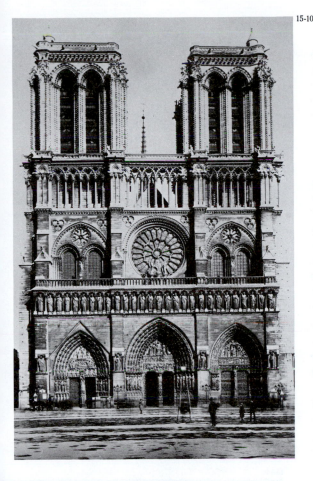

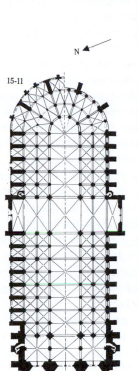

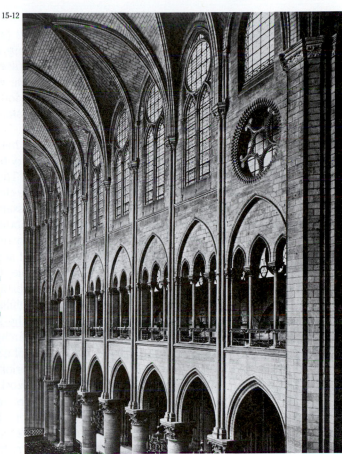

15-10. West façade, Notre-Dame, Paris. c. 1200–1250

15-11. Plan of Notre-Dame, Paris. 1163–c. 1250

15-12. Nave, Notre-Dame, Paris. 1163–c. 1200

capitals to the crown of the vault. The vaults are still slightly domical but have been carried to a height of 107 feet, 27 feet higher than those at Laon and higher than any Romanesque vaults except those of Speyer Cathedral.

CHARTRES The fire of 1194, which consumed the town and the Romanesque Cathedral of Chartres, except for the two towers and the Royal Portal, gave Gothic architects the opportunity to take the next and definitive step, which ushered in the phase known as High Gothic. After the conflagration at Chartres, a suspicious number of other old cathedrals caught fire. The Cathedral of Chartres is the most nearly complete of all in architecture, sculpture, and stained glass, and it demands study as an integrated whole. Smaller than Paris, the town of Chartres needed a cathedral with a nave of only seven bays and a choir of four, and two side aisles (fig. 15–13). Nonetheless, the vaults rise to a height of 118 feet in one unbroken ascent.

The architect eliminated the gallery, since flying buttresses were, for the first time, planned from the start. Only a small triforium separates the clerestory from the nave arcade (fig. 15–14). Liberated from the vaults, the clerestory has become almost equal in height to the nave arcade (see fig. 15–16) and now dominates the interior. The cylindrical piers, still inviolate at Laon and at Notre-Dame in Paris, have now been absorbed into the skeletal system; the colonnettes supporting the transverse ribs are coupled to the piers and run straight to the floor. The resulting new type of compound pier became universal. A subtle change took place in the course of construction; the piers nearest the crossing consist of octagonal colonnettes clustered about a central round pillar; from there westward, the central pillars also are octagonal, producing a smoother succession of surfaces. The six-part vault is given up as unwieldy and is replaced by a four-part vault, dividing each double bay into two single, equal ones, of necessity oblong. With this final demise of the alternating system the interior presents a more unified appearance. In the choir the enlarged clerestory is composed of simple *lancets* (single pointed-arch windows), but in the nave the windows are filled with tracery, achieved by piercing the wall of each bay with two lancets under a small rose (see drawing in fig. 15–16); this form is known as *plate tracery* (a more elaborate example from the north transept is shown in fig. 15–18). At the crossing the four supporting piers have been enriched with colonnettes, in the manner of clustered organ pipes, to great effect.

The massive buttresses (fig. 15–16) rise in steps to a height far above the sloping roof of the side aisle, to be connected with the clerestory by means of two slanting, superimposed arches joined together by a tiny arcade. These are flying buttresses, which "fly" from the buttresses to make contact with the clerestory at the two points where, so the architects believed, pressure was necessary to counteract the outward thrust of the nave vaults. A third flying buttress, above the other two, added a few years later, was probably intended to help the heavy timber-and-lead roof over the vaults resist the action of the wind; an upper flight appears in all later French and German flying-buttress systems (see, for example, fig. 15–6, for Villard de Honnecourt's diagram). The flying buttress simply substitutes for the vault of the gallery, which in Norman and Early Gothic churches fulfilled the same function. Its quarter-arc shape is that of the transverse ribs of the gallery vaults. With the adoption of flying buttresses the concept of skeletal architecture began to determine the exterior as well as the interior appearance of a building; every exterior member corresponds to a necessity created by an interior pressure. The resultant Gothic structural system has been aptly termed an exoskeleton.

Chartres was planned for two western façade towers, two flanking each arm of the transept, and one flanking each side of the choir, or a total of eight; all but the western towers were left unfinished at the height of the vaults. The south transept façade (fig. 15–15), built about 1215–20, shows a richness of articulation far beyond that of the main façade of Notre-Dame, designed only a few years earlier; slender colonnettes, like those at the crossing, screen the buttresses. The projecting triple porch was an afterthought, added to the portal after the sculpture.

The three portal statues of standing saints to the right (fig. 15–17) are still columnar, but when compared with those of the Royal Portal, they are partially liberated from the architecture and stand on pedestals more nearly suited to their function; on these pedestals are figures or images alluding to the legend of each saint. The wealth of tiny sculptures above the statues of the Royal Portal has been replaced here by naturalistic foliate capitals, enshadowed by greatly enlarged canopies, which resemble little city views with arches, windows, pinnacles, and towers. The portrait-like heads are thrown into stronger light against the shadow, and the figures, far more strongly projected than those of the Royal Portal and largely free from their architectural backgrounds, are wrapped in complete cylindrical envelopes of drapery whose folds also move in greater depth.

The statue at the left, probably representing Saint Theodore, was added at the same time as the porch and shows an increased freedom of style. For the first time since Roman art a figure is balanced with the weight largely on the right foot and the left leg at least partially free. Gothic sculpture seems in a way to recapitulate the development of sculpture in Greece from the late Archaic to the Severe Style (see figs. 7–7, 7–31), with the crucial difference that in Christian art the movement of the figure must be carried out under voluminous clothing. Once established in the portal figures of Chartres, the freedom of the figure from the architecture increased, as did the freedom of the architectural members themselves from the obsolete concept of the wall. With his knightly attitude, his spear at the ready, and his calm, handsome face, Saint Theodore seems the very ideal of the Christian warrior fostered by the Crusades.

The lightening and heightening of Gothic cathedrals cannot be adequately explained by the desire for illumination—that, as we have seen, could have been handled by a system along the lines of Saint-Philibert at Tournus (see fig. 14–2).

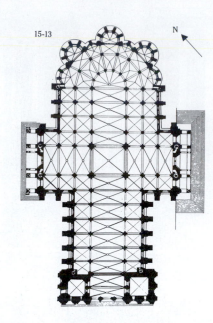

15-13. Plan of the Cathedral of Chartres (after G. Dehio). 1194–1220

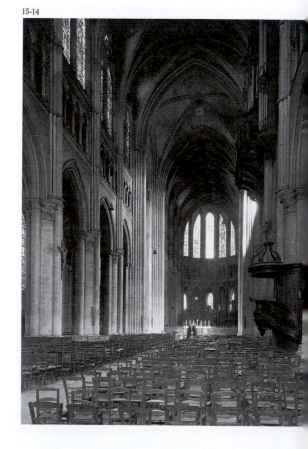

15-14. Nave, Cathedral of Chartres. 1194–1220

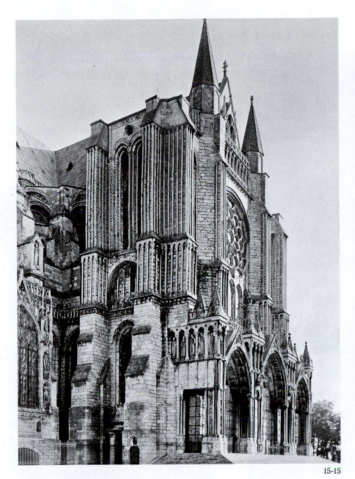

15-15. Façade of the south transept, Cathedral of Chartres. c. 1215–20

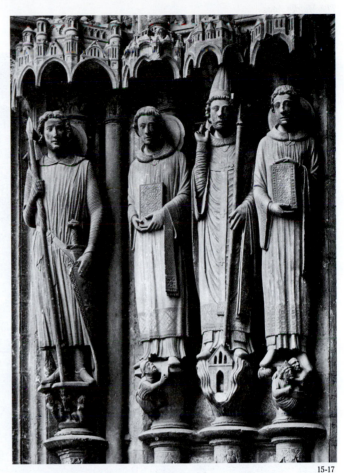

15-17. Jamb statues, south transept portal, Cathedral of Chartres. c. 1215–20

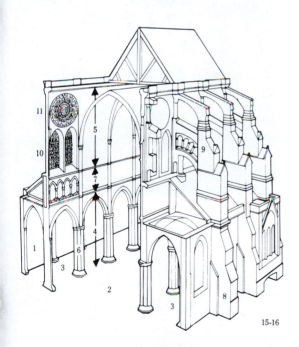

15-16. Isometric projection and cross section showing the structure and parts of the Cathedral of Chartres (after Wilkins and Schultz)   1. Bay   2. Nave   3. Aisle   4. Nave arcade   5. Clerestory   6. Pier   7. Triforium   8. Buttress   9. Flying buttress   10. Lancet window   11. Rose window

The entire cathedral in the twelfth and thirteenth centuries became a framework to hold *stained glass,* which inevitably darkened the interior but had its own indescribable beauty of color and pattern. Much Gothic stained glass has perished, some deliberately destroyed in later times either by Protestant reformers or simply in order to lighten cathedral interiors. Chartres contains the most nearly complete cycle of medieval stained glass, much of it in good condition, from the twelfth-century lancets above the Royal Portal to the thirteenth-century windows girdling the rest of the church. Between the windows, some of which have scores of separate, carefully organized subjects, and the innumerable sculptures on the three triple portals, it takes a studious visitor several days, guidebook in hand, just to identify all the images. One comes away from such an experience with a deep respect for the Middle Ages because the representations encompass the entire range of medieval knowledge—Old and New Testaments, lives of the saints, fundamentals of Christian doctrine, labors of the months, signs of the zodiac, Virtues and Vices, and the activities of the guilds that contributed to the building of the cathedral.

The gigantic window of the north arm of the transept (fig. 15–18) is a rose, still in the form of plate tracery, above five lancets. In the central lancet Saint Anne, mother of the Virgin, holds her child; she is flanked by two kings, David to the left and Solomon to the right. Two high priests, Melchizedek to the left and Aaron to the right, flank the kings. The rose above, more than forty-two feet in diameter, shows Mary in the center enthroned as Queen of Heaven holding the Christ Child. With the growth of the cult of the Virgin, under the direct influence of Saint Bernard, Mary has now displaced the Romanesque Christ in Majesty and the Byzantine Pantocrator. In the next circle four doves indicating the Gospels proceed toward Mary, and below them eight angels kneel or stand in adoration. Twelve kings from

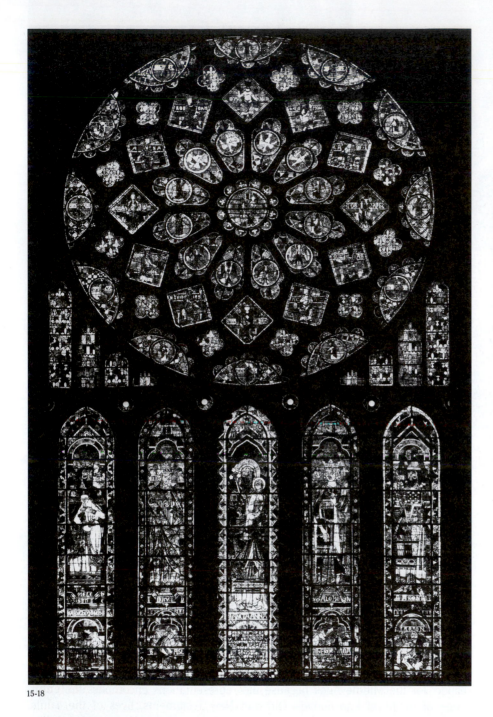

15-18

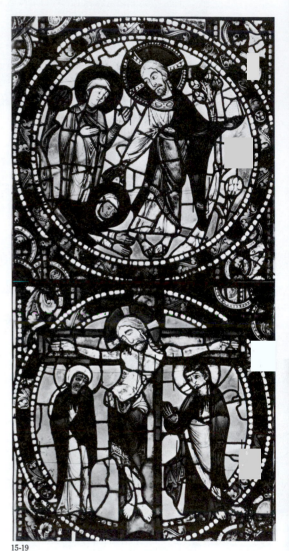

15-19

15-18. Rose window and lancet windows, north transept, Cathedral of Chartres. Stained glass. 13th century

15-19. *Noli me tangere* and *Crucifixion,* details of a stained-glass window, Cathedral of Chartres. 12th century

the Old Testament, clearly labeled, all ancestors of Christ, sit in the next circle of twelve lozenges. Finally, in the twelve semicircles around the rim stand prophets. Significantly enough, the twelve quatrefoil (four-leaf) shapes between the kings and the prophets are filled with the golden lilies of the kings of France on a blue field.

Stained glass achieves its effect by the passage of sunlight through it rather than by the reflection of light from it, as in mosaics. Stained glass is, therefore, the most brilliant coloristic medium invented by man before the light-sculpture of the twentieth century. It is best to experience the stained-glass windows of Chartres (or any other Gothic church) in the gray weather common in northern France, for which this glass was planned; otherwise, the glitter from the south windows not only destroys their unity but also cancels out the glow from the north. In the early morning or in the late afternoon the colored windows float like immense jewels in the dim interior. Medieval theologians saw in the beauty of stained glass a symbol of the sacred mystery of the Incarnation, for as Divine Light, which is Christ (see fig. 10–42), entered the human body of Mary without violating her virginity and took on mortal flesh, so the light of the sun passes through colored glass without breaking it and assumes its color.

In thirteenth-century glass the predominant colors are red and blue; white, yellow, and green appear, but the red and blue contrast is what one remembers. Unlike mosaics, which are made up of uniform tesserae, stained glass is fabricated from pieces shaped as closely as possible to the contour of a section of face, figure, drapery, or background. First, a full-scale model is made, drawn on wood or later on paper, and the pieces of colored glass are cut to fit. The lines are then painted on the glass with a dark pigment. After this paint dries, a coating of pigment is sometimes applied and scraped away with a stiff brush while still wet, so that what remains in the hollows will increase the sparkle of the underlying color. The pieces are then fired (baked) in a kiln, so that the pigment will harden and at least partially amalgamate with the glass. Finally, the pieces are arranged on the model and joined together by lead soldering strips. Each scene is enclosed in an iron frame and the frames bolted together within the tracery so that they can easily be taken down for repairs. In France cathedral windows were removed twice in the present century, to protect them from damage in the two world wars.

In two panels from a twelfth-century window in the façade at Chartres (fig. 15–19), a *Noli me tangere* ("Do not touch me," the words spoken by the resurrected Christ to Mary Magdalen in the garden) and a *Crucifixion,* the technique can be clearly seen. The lines of the pigment closely resemble those of the drapery and hair of the sculpture in the Royal Portal below (see fig. 15–5). The lead contours, a bit disturbing in black-and-white reproductions, serve in the colored original to reinforce by contrast the glowing splendor of the glass. The iron frames were often set into an elaborate master design built up of lozenges and circles. Panels of colored glass were known from Early Christian times and were certainly used in Constantinian basilicas, as well as later in Hagia Sophia and in other Byzantine churches. They also appeared commonly in mosques. But glass treated in this manner does not seem to have been known before Carolingian times, and only a few fragments that date before the Romanesque period remain. Only in Gothic architecture does such stained glass become universal.

BOURGES   The architectural arrangement established at Chartres became the model for most High Gothic cathedrals, but there is a beautiful variant at Bourges in central France, where the Cathedral has four side aisles (fig. 15–20) as at Notre-Dame in Paris. So that the inner side aisles would not be dark, the architect raised them above the outer side aisles, giving them triforia and clerestories of their own and thereby making them look like complete three-story naves. The nave arcade in turn rises above the inner side aisles, supporting still another triforium and another clerestory. The spatial effect is very open, with views out on every side. The absence of a transept at Bourges affords the eye a clean sweep of arches from façade to apse.

LE MANS   The brilliant device at Bourges was seldom repeated in France. In the artistic vocabulary of the High Gothic, the façade with its two towers soon came to compete in interest with the *chevet* — the apse, with its radiating chapels and flying buttresses, crowned by a conical roof. Le Mans Cathedral has the most spectacular chevet in France (fig. 15–21), in compensation, perhaps, for its low and unobtrusive Early Gothic nave, contrasting with the High Gothic choir, built between 1217 and 1254. As at Bourges, the inner ambulatory has its own clerestory above the radiating chapels, and the windows pile up in three stories. Two flights of flying buttresses carry the thrust of the choir vaults across the intervening ambulatory,

15-20. Nave and aisles, Cathedral of Bourges, France. 12th–13th centuries

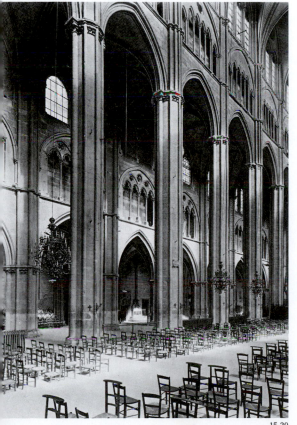

15-20

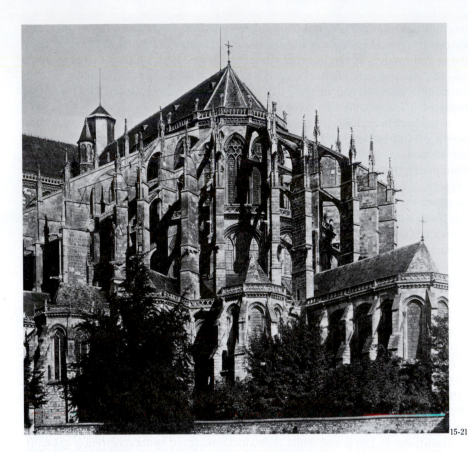

15-21. Exterior of the chevet, Cathedral of Le Mans, France. 1217–54

and to abut the thrust of the ambulatory vaults they divide in a Y-shape. At the point where each flying buttress springs from a buttress or alights against another or against the outer wall of the structure is placed a pinnacle. These pinnacles are not purely ornamental; they establish a counterweight that abuts the thrust of the flying buttress and sends that of the vaults harmlessly to the ground. Nonetheless, their contours are enriched with *crockets* and culminate in *finials,* composed of foliate ornament. The lines have been kept as clean and orderly as those of a flight of wild geese, massing in perfect harmony buttresses, flying buttresses, pinnacles, windows, and conical roof.

REIMS   The Cathedral of Reims, in Champagne in northeastern France, was traditionally the coronation church of the French kings. Designed in 1210 (after a fire), probably by Jean d'Orbais, Reims was intended for six towers and a central spire; only the façade towers rise above the roof. At first sight the interior (fig. 15–22) resembles that of Chartres, with four-part vaults, cylindrical compound piers, three stories, lofty clerestory, and colonnettes rising from floor to vault interrupted only by capitals and moldings to mark the stories. The height of the vault has risen to 127 feet, and three additional differences are visible in the illustration. First, the arches are more sharply pointed than those at Chartres, which increases the feeling of verticality. Second, the richly sculptured capitals are composed of naturalistic foliage that seems to follow no predetermined scheme but to grow in place. Finally, a new kind of tracery appears—*bar tracery,* erected as a linear fabric of slender pieces of stone inside the window opening, preserving only in line the arrangement of lancets and rose as a framework for the glass (compare figs. 15–22 and 15–18).

   It will be noticed that in the apse the ribs move so freely and in so sharply pointed an arch that they cut sharply into the clerestory windows. During World War I some of the ribs fell under German bombardment (the cathedral was attacked deliberately as an attempt to undermine French morale), but the vaults stood, a tribute to the medieval masons. Villard de Honnecourt, as we have seen, made a careful drawing of the flying buttresses at Reims (see fig. 15–6), in two flights over the ambulatory as at Le Mans, and indicated the points at which they sustain the vaults.

The façade of Reims Cathedral (fig. 15–23) may have been started as early as 1225 but was under construction until late in the thirteenth century. The general arrangement repeats that of Notre-Dame in Paris, but the differences disclose both the rapid growth of the Gothic style and its organic character. Solid matter has been dissolved into lines moving through air, with the sole exception of the gallery in the third story, which had to be solid in order to hold statues of the French kings (added in the fourteenth century). The very tympana of the portals have given way to windows filled with bar tracery. The porches culminate in gables that move into the second story. The second story is transparent, and one looks through the open tracery of the *paired* windows (they have no glass) to see the flying buttresses of the nave. The nave roof appears as a gable above the gallery. Finally, the towers, among the most beautiful creations of Gothic architecture, are entirely made of tracery with no wall surface whatever. The corner turrets, constructed completely of tracery, were intended to support octagonal corner pinnacles, just as each central section, with its window of bar tracery and its pointed gable, was designed to support an octagonal spire; the octagonal bases of both pinnacles and spires can barely be distinguished above the tracery gables.

15-22. Nave, Cathedral of Reims, France. Begun 1210

15-23. West façade, Cathedral of Reims. c. 1225–99

15-22

15-23

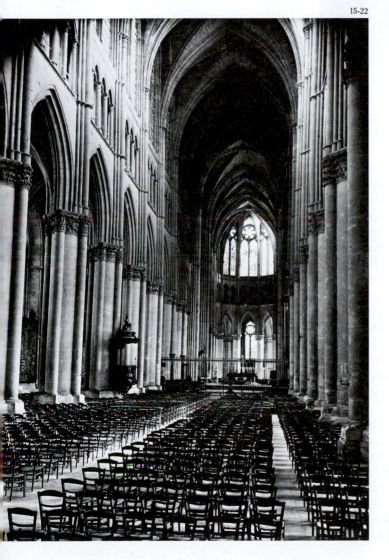

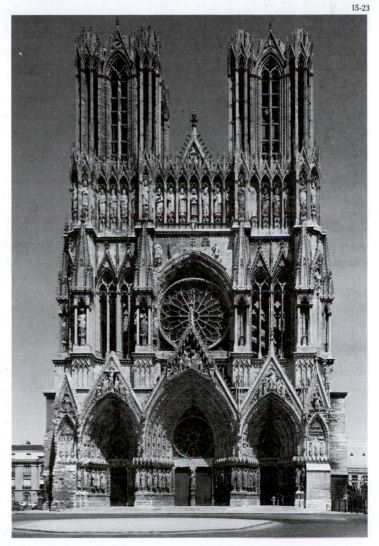

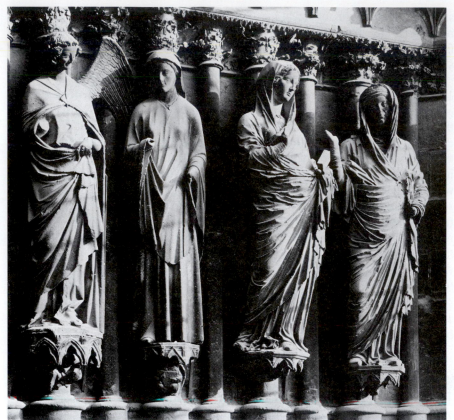

15-24

The façade sculpture at Reims, dating from about 1225–45, continues the tendency toward free volumes in space and independence from architecture that had begun in the transept sculpture of Chartres, and the humanism of the figures is even more pronounced. Not a trace of the Romanesque incised forms remains. Two groups side by side (fig. 15–24) were obviously made by two sculptors working in strongly individual styles and probably at slightly different times. The group to the right, done about 1225–30, depicts the *Visitation,* the visit of Mary to the house of her cousin Elizabeth, when the two women rejoiced in each other's pregnancy. The sculptor, while strongly aware of the call of visual reality, responds to it in a classical style. He must have seen and studied Roman sculpture during his travels, almost certainly Gallo-Roman sculpture in France. The mantles of Mary and Elizabeth sweep about their bodies and over their heads like Roman togas. Mary stands with the grace of a Roman virgin, Elizabeth with the dignity of a Roman matron. Even their faces recall classical types. But there are differences; the poses do not entirely achieve the balance between the reciprocally tilted masses of the body that was instinctive for all ancient sculptors after about 400 B.C. The faces are only superficially classical. The folds break into more tiny facets than can be explained by the fall of the cloth. Nonetheless, we are clearly confronted with evidence of yet another renaissance of interest in ancient art, of which this is by no means the only Northern example in the thirteenth century (see fig. 15–44).

In the *Annunciation,* dating from the 1230s or 1240s, a very different style appears, made more apparent by the unfortunate inclusion, in a seventeenth-century restoration, of the wrong angel; he smiles a bit too broadly—though for the first time since classical antiquity—for his religious function. His figure bends and sways in an accentuated S-curve, and his cloak is a complete and continuous fabric, which can move about his body as cloth will, responding to pressures and tugs and breaking into real folds. In the figure of Mary, shyly waiting, the change in style is even more surprising because for the first time since antiquity (again) a body really

15-25. *The Knight's Communion*, west interior wall, Cathedral of Reims. After 1251

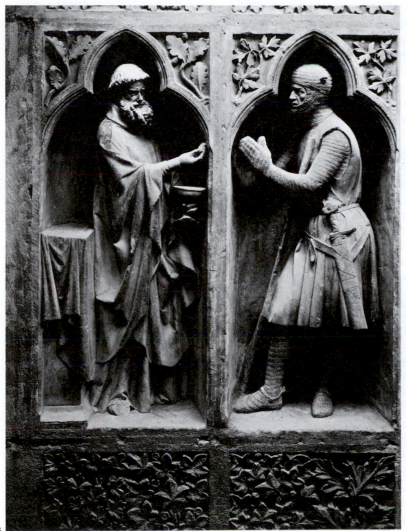

15-25

shows through drapery—not just a volume of some undetermined substance, but a warm, human body. Mary's bosom can be clearly seen swelling through the soft garment that enfolds her, much as the bosom of Athena is visible through her peplos in the metope from Olympia (see fig. 7–44).

Another significant step was taken at Reims by the sculptor who carved, after 1251, the statues in the niches that fill the inside of the west façade. In spite of the fact that the two figures inhabit separate niches, *The Knight's Communion* (fig. 15–25; long misnamed *Melchizedek and Abraham*) forms a unified dramatic and compositional group. The knight, in complete chain mail, spurred, and girt with his sword (the tip has broken off), with mailed hands folded in prayer, looks from his niche toward the Eucharist extended to him from the ciborium (the appropriate vessel) by a priest who has turned toward him from a small altar. The priest, apparently a monk since secular clergy were not permitted to wear beards until the sixteenth century, is robed in a magnificent chasuble (a vestment worn by the celebrant at Mass in commemoration of the seamless robe of Christ) whose billowing folds, obscuring his body, contrast with the severe military dress of the knight. However, the artist was well aware of the proportions and movements of the masses of the body, as can be seen in the way he has handled the figure of the knight, in spite of chain mail and tunic. We have reached a classic moment in Gothic sculpture, in which figures, fully in the round, are endowed with the capability of movement in space. The sculptor has set forth eloquently the contrast between the earnest, slightly frowning glance of the priest, with his richly curling beard, and the intense expectancy of the knight, receiving Communion presumably just before battle. The foliage of the frame is typical of High Gothic ornament, in its combination of crisp naturalism with easy rhythmic flow.

AMIENS   The climax of the High Gothic architectural style was achieved at the Cathedral of Amiens (figs. 15–26, 15–27), begun in 1220 by the architect Robert de Luzarches, in Picardy, due north of Paris. The soaring effect of the Amiens interior (fig. 15–28) surpasses that of any other Gothic cathedral; the vaults leap to the height of 144 feet. (A fourteen-story office building could be constructed in the nave.) The proportions of all the elements are even more slender than at Reims. The last trace of doming is gone from the vaults, whose crown line is now level. The triforium openings are filled with bar tracery rather than the continuous arcade of Reims. In the clerestory a momentous step has been taken: the same molding serves as wall rib and window frame, thus canceling out the wall. The nave of Amiens was built first; the two upper stories of the choir show still another step in the direction of dematerialization, probably taken by Robert de Luzarches' successor, Thomas de Cormont, after 1258. The roof covering the ambulatory vaults is no longer sloping but converted into a succession of pyramidal caps, one over each bay. This change permitted the architect to turn the triforium into a second row of windows, greatly lightening the interior, which now looks bare without its stained glass. As the photograph of the choir vaults from below clearly shows (fig. 15–29), the entire cathedral has become a cage of delicate stone members—colonnettes, ribs, tracery—to hold the vault surfaces above and the stained glass on the sides. Mass has been almost totally replaced by linear fabric. This ultimate phase of the High Gothic style in France is called the Rayonnant ("Radiant") on account of the tracery patterns that in the rose windows expand like rays.

That the vaulting of Amiens suggests the quality of flight and the outstretched wings of birds has often been commented on. It is noteworthy that Amiens Cathedral received special dispensation to keep the Blessed Sacrament (the consecrated host) in a silver dove of the Holy Spirit with outstretched wings hanging on a silver chain from the apex of the star-vault of the choir, a descendant of the doves that used to float down from the marble canopies over the altars of Early Christian churches at the moment of the consecration. The parallel between the constructional logic of High Gothic architecture and the rational structure of medieval Scholastic philosophy justly observed by Erwin Panofsky seems of less importance than the mystical effect of this interior, which in its wonderful heights embodies the aspiration of the worshiper to God, as God descends to the faithful in the Eucharist, borne by the wings of a dove.

The flying buttresses of the nave at Amiens resemble those at Reims, but those of the transept and choir show a transformation, again probably due to Thomas de Cormont, and teach a striking lesson in the combined imaginative daring and structural logic of Gothic building. The architect has largely dematerialized the very device on which he depends for the support of the building: the flying buttress itself (fig. 15–30) is composed of bar tracery, connecting an upper strut and a lower arch, which were clearly sufficient to sustain the thrust of the slender vaults. Even the buttresses and their pinnacles have been decorated by a fabric of applied colonnettes and arches, which have no structural function but make the solid masses appear lighter and more vertical. As a final touch, the choir windows, one of which is to be seen at the right of the illustration, are surmounted by false gables made of tracery in order to dissolve the last remaining strip of wall above the window and to break the horizontal line of the cornice molding.

As compared with those of Laon, Paris, and Reims, the façade of Amiens (fig. 15–31), probably begun in 1220, is not a complete success. The center pinnacle marks the height of the nave roof, almost level with the south tower. From the side view the height of the church is so great as to render towers superfluous, and these are

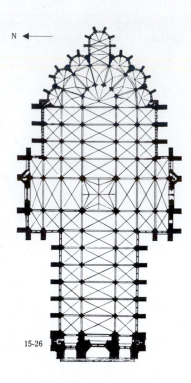

15-26

15-26, 15-27. Robert de Luzarches. Plan and transverse section of the Cathedral of Amiens, France. Begun 1220

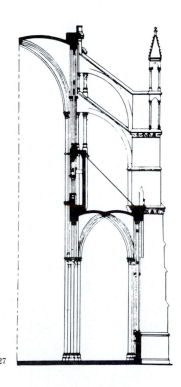

15-27

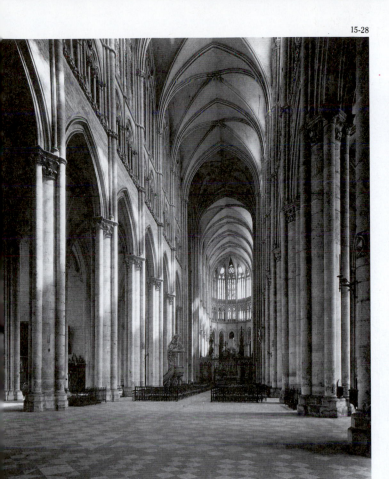

15-28. Robert de Luzarches. Nave, Cathedral of Amiens

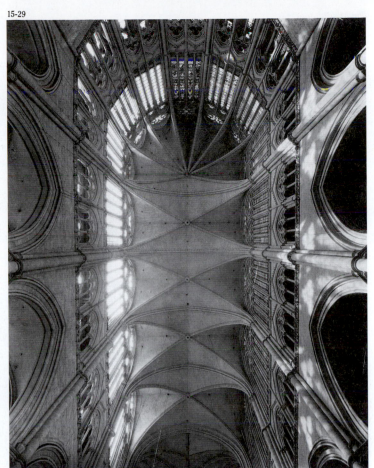

15-29. Thomas de Cormont. Choir vaults, Cathedral of Amiens (view from below). After 1258

15-30. View of choir and south transept, Cathedral of Amiens, showing flying buttresses

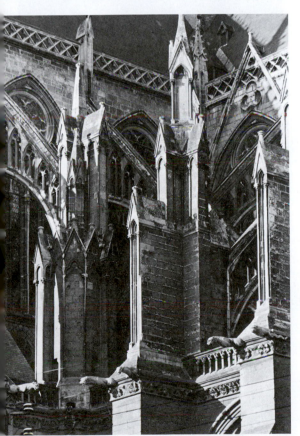

15-30

only one window deep. The unity of the façade at Amiens is also disturbed by the much later—and in themselves very fine—rose window and details crowning the towers and the screen, belonging to the Flamboyant phase (see page 470). However, the Amiens portals contain sculpture of great dignity and beauty, especially the statue of *Christ Treading on the Lion and the Basilisk* (fig. 15–32; compare with an earlier version of the same theme in fig. 13–12), which stands against the trumeau of the central portal. Stylistically the figure, with its firm stance and flowing but controlled drapery folds, represents a stage between that of the transept sculpture at Chartres and the highly developed naturalistic and classicistic statues at Reims. Nicknamed locally "le beau Dieu," the image is that of a man in early maturity, with straight nose, broad brow, calm expression, short beard, and flowing hair. With a few striking exceptions, this is the Christ-type that has replaced in Western imagination both the Apollonian youth of the Ravenna mosaics and the awesome Pantocrator of Byzantine art. The emphasis is all on the nobility of the figure and the beauty of the drapery folds, so much so that the lion and basilisk tend to get overlooked. It is a remarkable paradox that Gothic artists should have populated their dematerialized, linear cathedrals with believable, many-faceted, and very solid images of complete human beings, even when it was necessary to portray the Second Person of the Trinity. The canopy over Christ's head, instead of showing the usual generalized array of domes and towers, is a tiny model of a

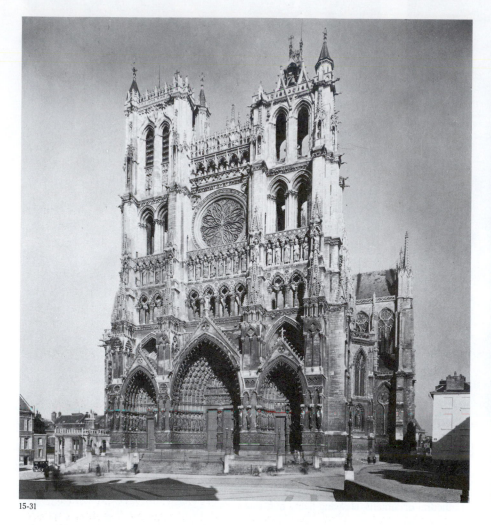

15-31

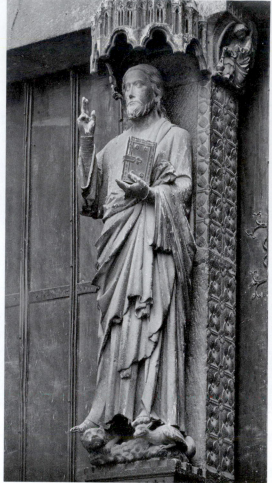

15-32

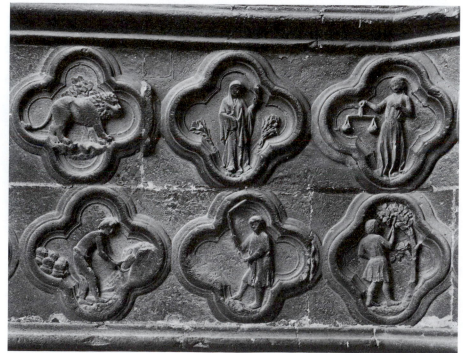

15-33

15-31. West façade, Cathedral of Amiens. Probably begun 1220

15-32. *Christ Treading on the Lion and the Basilisk*, trumeau of the central portal of the west façade, Cathedral of Amiens. c. 1230

15-33. *Signs of the Zodiac* and *Labors of the Months*, detail of reliefs on the jambs of the west portal, Cathedral of Amiens. c. 1220–30

Gothic chevet, with radiating chapels, possibly a reminder that the apse of this cathedral enshrines the Christ of the Sacrament. The dignity of the Amiens statues contrasts with the vivid naturalism of the little scenes from the Old and New Testaments and from such allegorical cycles as the Virtues and Vices, the signs of the zodiac, and the labors of the months, which appear in low relief in the quatrefoils on the bases of the portal jambs (fig. 15–33).

BEAUVAIS   The practical limit of the Gothic dream was reached at Amiens. About 1225 the architect who designed the Cathedral of Beauvais (fig. 15–34), located between Paris and Amiens, tried to surpass it. By 1272 the lofty skeleton of stone, with a glazed triforium as at Amiens, had reached the unbelievable height of 157 feet above the floor. Then in 1284, before the transept could be completed, the choir vault fell, leaving only the apse vault standing. Collapses like this, frequent in the Romanesque period, were rare in the thirteenth century, when architects had, through trial and error, arrived at a system that generally worked. The reason for the disaster at Beauvais is not entirely understood; it may have been a matter of inadequate foundations. In any event the choir was rebuilt with a doubled number of supports and flying buttresses, and old-fashioned six-part vaults were revived for the last time. The building of the transept lagged on into the fourteenth century, with yet another calamity, the fall of a tower, and then the money ran out. From the outside the truncated choir, towering sadly above the Carolingian nave, is a monument to the unattainable, but the effect of the interior, catapulting in one leap from floor to lofty vault, is exhilarating.

THE SAINTE-CHAPELLE AT PARIS   In contrast to the Beauvais catastrophe, the small-scale Sainte-Chapelle in Paris is a brilliant achievement of the Rayonnant style. The chapel was built from 1243 to 1248 by Louis IX of France, later canonized as Saint Louis, to enshrine relics of the Crucifixion. Louis met these relics, which were brought to France from Syria and Constantinople, at the gates of Paris and walked barefoot behind them in solemn procession. Although deprived of its surrounding royal palace, and badly repainted in the nineteenth century, the chapel is structurally intact. It consists of a lower and rather modest story supporting an upper chapel that represents the utter perfection of the High Gothic (fig. 15–35), a delicate framework of slender stone elements enclosing stained-glass windows. As there are no side aisles, flying buttresses were not required. Only a small strip of wall remains below the windows, and even this is relieved by a tracery of arches, broken at the left and right by niches for the king and queen. Behind and above the usual location of the altar stands a Gothic shrine in which the relics were kept and from which they could be displayed. For completeness and for quality the stained-glass windows of the Sainte-Chapelle compete only with those at Chartres. Their innumerable scenes organized as comparisons between Old and New Testaments are small, and the upper ones are not easy to read from the floor—a problem we have encountered before in the sculpture of the Column of Trajan (see fig. 9–47). From a slight distance the windows fuse into an indescribable radiance of red and blue.

French Manuscripts

Never before or again in the history of art was architecture so completely dominant as in the Gothic period in France. Pictorial imagination was directed toward stained glass rather than mural painting, for which few wall surfaces remained in Gothic churches outside Italy. Even illuminated manuscripts, which survive in great numbers from this period, are dominated on every page by architectural concepts. One of the finest is a *Bible Moralisée* (moralized Bible—a collection of biblical passages and illustrations arranged as parallels between Old and New Testaments, as, for example, in the manner of the windows of the Sainte-Chapelle), probably

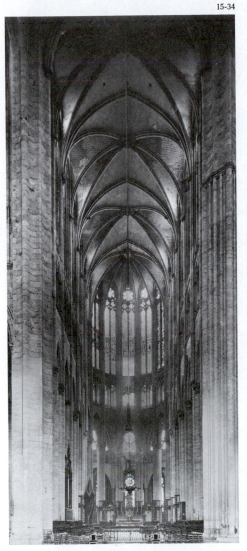

15-34. Interior, Cathedral of Beauvais, France. c. 1225

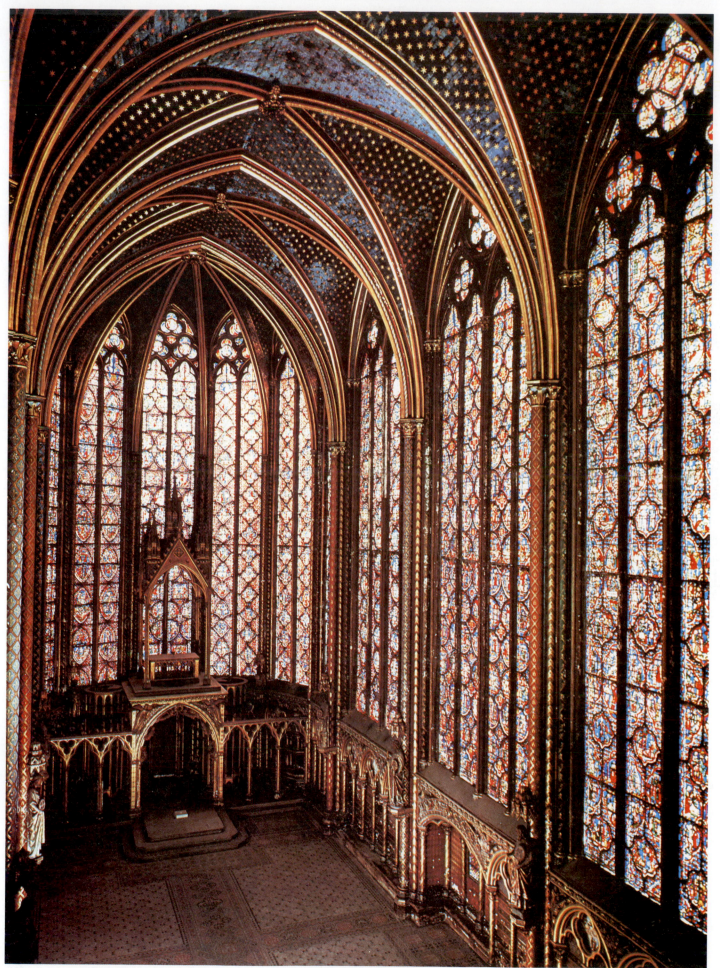

15-35. Interior, Ste.-Chapelle, Paris. 1243–48

15-36. *Abraham and the Three Angels,*
illumination from the *Psalter of Saint Louis.*
Paris, 1253–70. Bibliothèque Nationale, Paris

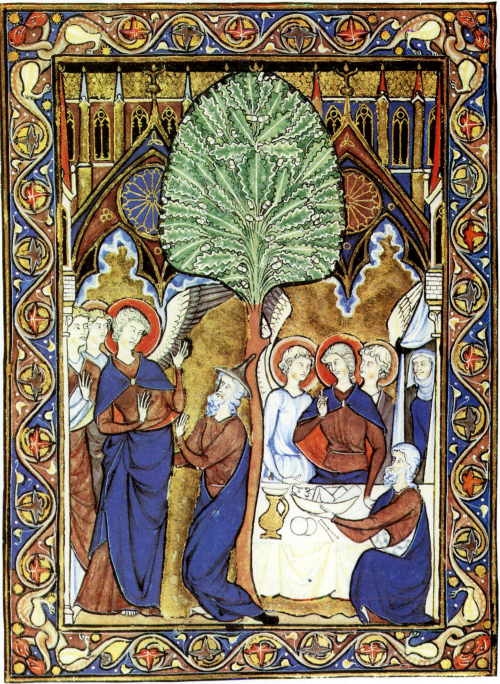

15-36

written and illustrated in the mid-thirteenth century at Reims for Thibaut V, count
of Champagne and king of Navarre, and his wife Isabelle, daughter of Louis IX. On
one magnificent page God himself is shown as an architect, using that indispensable tool of architectural draftsmanship, the compass, to create heaven and earth,
which "was without form, and void" (see Introduction fig. 24). The artist has
imagined the Deity on such a cosmic scale that the universe is literally in his hand.
The border, brilliant in its flashing alternation of patterned red and blue, is insufficient to contain him as he strides through space. The folds of his blue tunic and
rose mantle, lined respectively with orange and yellow, are depicted in a free
pictorial approximation of the parallel folds of the classicistic sculpture of Reims
Cathedral. The artist has imagined the Creation as a moment of intense artistic
inspiration; the Lord's eyes are dilated, his mouth slightly open, as he measures the
circle containing green and blue waters, dark blue sky with stars, sun, and moon,

and a still-formless earth, giving it form by a supreme act of creative will. As often in Gothic art, the Lord's appearance is youthful and his halo contains the Cross of Christ, intended to show that not just God the Father but all three persons of the Trinity, under the guise of God the Son, were present at Creation. This unforgettable image should be compared with the totally different view of Creation in the Renaissance.

A dazzling page in the *Psalter of Saint Louis* (fig. 15–36), made for Louis IX and datable between 1253 and 1270, represents the appearance of the three angels to Abraham and the supper served them by Abraham and Sarah, the two incidents separated by the beautifully ornamentalized oak at Mamre. The excitement of the painting, which vibrates with brilliant color and tense, incisive line, could hardly be more different from the serene icon by Andrei Rublev dedicated to a synthesis of the same subject (see fig. 10–71). The elegant, swaying figures with tiny hands and feet are embraced, as often in Gothic illumination, by shapes derived from cathedral architecture. The gables and tracery are recognizable as belonging to the period of the choir of Amiens (see fig. 15–30), and a clerestory can be seen, too. As in stained glass, red and blue, white and green predominate. The border, which Saint Bernard would have hated, repeats the theme of animal interlace, whose origin we have traced to barbarian art.

The Later Gothic in France

After the thirteenth century, the pace of church building slowed in the domain of the French kings; almost every town that could afford a Gothic cathedral had built one. But in spite of constant warfare with the English, who controlled Normandy and much of western France, the elaborate and expensive process of finishing towers, façades, and gables continued in an always more imaginative style. The latest phase, beginning in the middle of the fourteenth century, is known as the Flamboyant because of the characteristic flamelike shapes of the tracery, based on double curvature rather than on the logical mullions, pointed arches, and circles of the High Gothic. A striking example is the rose window of Amiens Cathedral, done about 1500 (see fig. 15–31).

SAINT-MACLOU AT ROUEN   The climax of the Flamboyant style is represented by the façade of the Church of Saint-Maclou (fig. 15–37) at Rouen, the capital of Normandy, built in the early sixteenth century, the moment of the High Renaissance in Florence and Rome. The lower portion of the façade bows sharply outward. Of the five apparent portals, those at far left and right are blind. No inert surfaces remain; transparent, linear shapes of stone merge with each other as they flicker upward, the transparent central gable even passing in front of the rose window. Only the main contours of the flying buttresses, gables, and arches are still apparent, drawn in thin air with lines of stone; the rest is sheer fantasy.

THE HOUSE OF JACQUES COEUR   The finest surviving monument of Late Gothic domestic architecture is the mansion (fig. 15–38) built at Bourges from 1443 to 1451 by the wealthy merchant Jacques Coeur, treasurer to Charles VIII of France during and after the unhappy period when this weak monarch, driven out of Paris by the English, was known disparagingly as the king of Bourges. The house is a freely arranged succession of blocks, with steeply pitched roofs of different heights, the highest being reserved for the owner's private chapel, with a Flamboyant window located over the main entrance. Flamboyant ornament is restricted to the balustrades at the eaves, to the panels under the windows, and to the rich staircase tower, ending in an openwork octagonal cap. This delightful, asymmetrical structure, with its inviting appearance of improvisation, should be compared with the rigidly symmetrical palaces being built by the same merchant class in Italy at the same moment. Alas, Jacques Coeur had only two years to enjoy his gorgeous

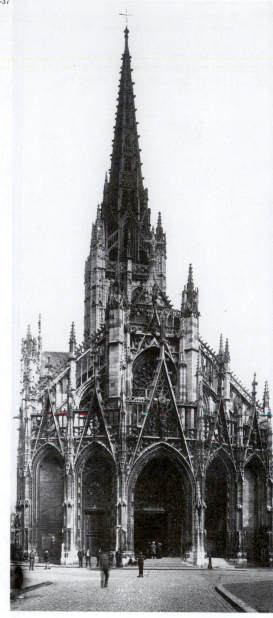

15-37. West façade, St.-Maclou, Rouen, France. Early 16th century

15-38. House of Jacques Coeur, Bourges, France. 1443–51

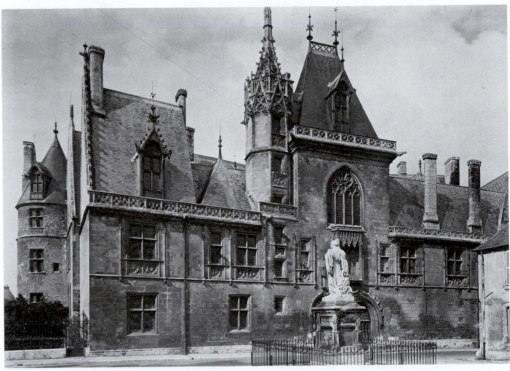

15-38

house before he was falsely accused of attempting to poison the king's mistress and had to flee France.

SCULPTURE AND PAINTING   The sculptural style of the fourteenth century does not continue either the classicistic or the naturalistic tendencies we have seen in the sculpture of the great cathedrals. A typical early-fourteenth-century example, the *Virgin of Paris* (see Introduction fig. 12; originally from the Church of Saint-Aignan), moves with an elegant lassitude that embodies the ultimate in courtly aloofness. The face looks almost Far Eastern in its soft contours and slightly slanting eyes. The folds, despite the sculptor's exact observation of the behavior of cloth, are so voluminous that they give little hint of the Virgin's body beneath them. She wears her heavy crown with languid grace, but her pose, one hip sharply moved to the left to support the Child, shows a distinct element of exaggeration. Nonetheless, the sculptor has observed a delicate and affectionate byplay between mother and Child as the babe holds the orb of power in his left hand and toys with her mantle with his right.

Fourteenth-century painting in France, luxurious and worldly, may be represented by an entrancing page from the *Belleville Breviary* (fig. 15–39), illuminated at Paris about 1323–26 and attributed to JEAN PUCELLE, a still-undefined artistic personality. The architectural frame of the thirteenth century has been replaced by a delicate border of gold and blue; at the upper left a painting of *David before Saul* was either executed under direct Italian influence or painted by an Italian artist. At the bottom of the page the French style reappears, in the tiny strip representing at the left Cain killing Abel, in the center the Eucharist offered by a priest to the dove of the Holy Spirit, and on the right Charity as a queen, assisted in her almsgiving by the Hand of God. A breviary is a book containing the readings for the Divine Offices; yet the patron who ordered the manuscript and the artists who illuminated it had other concerns as well as the strictly religious, as a glance at the border will reveal. The animal interlace has disappeared, but animals, birds, and insects have been revived in very lifelike terms—a beautifully painted pheasant, a dragonfly, a butterfly, a monkey, a snail, a dragon, among which three musicians play a lute, a bagpipe, and a flute. What we witness in these caprices of sculpture and painting,

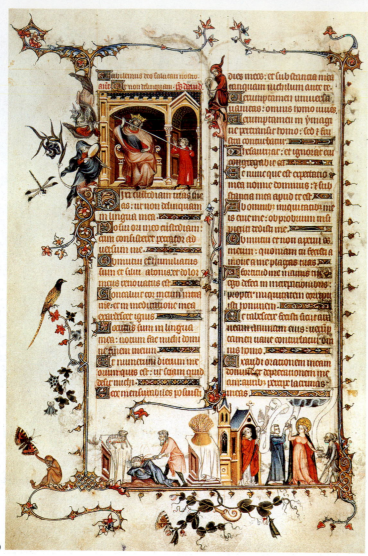

15-39

15-39. JEAN PUCELLE. Page of the *Belleville Breviary.* Paris, c. 1323–26. Illumination. Bibliothèque Nationale, Paris

which lingered into the fifteenth century, is the first glimmer of a new and exciting naturalistic worldview, in which the religious subjects seem embedded.

Germany

COLOGNE CATHEDRAL   At first French Gothic was imported directly into the Rhineland, which was already amply provided with massive, apparently fireproof, double-ended Romanesque cathedrals. When the Carolingian Cathedral of Cologne burned down in 1248, Bishop Gerhard was ready with complete plans for a Gothic replacement; work started within three and a half months. Building continued into the fourteenth century, then languished. Only the choir and the lower story of the south tower had been built; unexpectedly, in the nineteenth century a large and detailed drawing for the façade and the towers, dating from about 1320, came to light, and the rest of the Cathedral was then completed with remarkable accuracy.

While the details of the nave and façade betray nineteenth-century handling, the general appearance of the Cathedral (fig. 15–40) is correct, and overwhelming. The interior (fig. 15–41) is only slightly less daring than Beauvais in its verticality and slenderness, and the glazed triforium may even have been designed earlier than the one by Thomas de Cormont at Amiens. The French would probably never have countenanced the profusion of heavy foliate ornament around the arches of the arcade, but otherwise the interior is French. So indeed are the tracery flying buttresses and the pinnacles veiled in tracery, as well as the gables over the

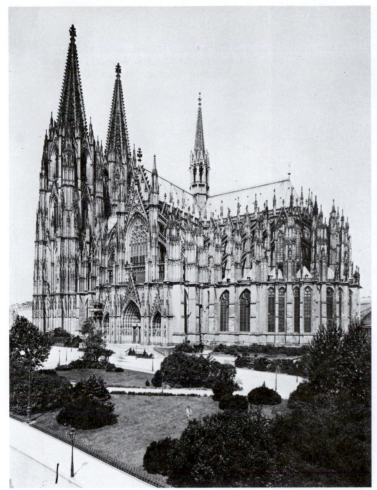

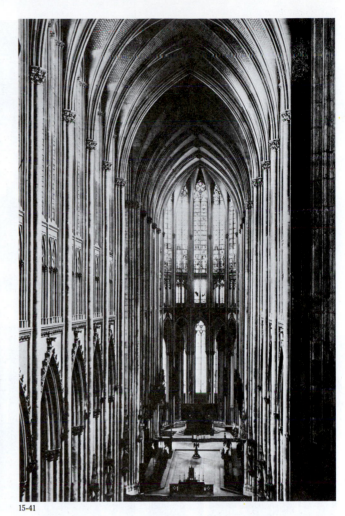

15-40   15-41

15-40. Cathedral of Cologne, Germany. 1248–1322 (completed in the 19th century)

15-41. Choir, Cathedral of Cologne

clerestory windows. But as we have seen at Amiens French architects had never solved the problem posed by the effect of a lofty church on the design of the towers. The fourteenth-century architect at Cologne made a fresh start, treating the second stories of his towers as extensions of the clerestory, imposing majestic third and fourth stories, and bringing the towers to a brilliant climax in two pointed tracery spires.

SAINT LAWRENCE AT NUREMBERG   The basically French plan at Cologne was not popular in Germany; almost contemporary with it appeared a more influential design, the *Hallenkirche* ("hall-church"). In this type, widely followed throughout central Europe, the nave and side aisles are the same height, eliminating the necessity for flying buttresses. Although exterior forms and interior spaces are inevitably less dramatic, space does flow more freely throughout the church, rendering it especially suitable for preaching. A remarkable late example of the Hallenkirche type is the choir of the Church of Saint Lawrence at Nuremberg (fig. 15–42), built by KONRAD HEINZELMANN beginning in 1439 and vaulted by KONRAD RORICZER after Heinzelmann's death in 1454. Octagonal piers support the arches and vaults; as in many churches from the beginning of the fifteenth century, these piers have bases but no capitals. Ribs grow like branches directly from the piers or from the applied colonnettes, and move into the vaults to lose themselves in a crisscross of merging elements like intertwined branches in a forest. Transverse ribs have vanished, and the only vestige of High Gothic vaulting is the diagonal rib; the result, inexplicably, is what Paul Frankl has called the "supreme harmony" of the Late Gothic style. German Gothic architecture pursues a course similar to that of the Flamboyant phase of French Gothic, concentrating, however, on more and more individual and fantastic solutions to vaulting problems, sometimes reinforc-

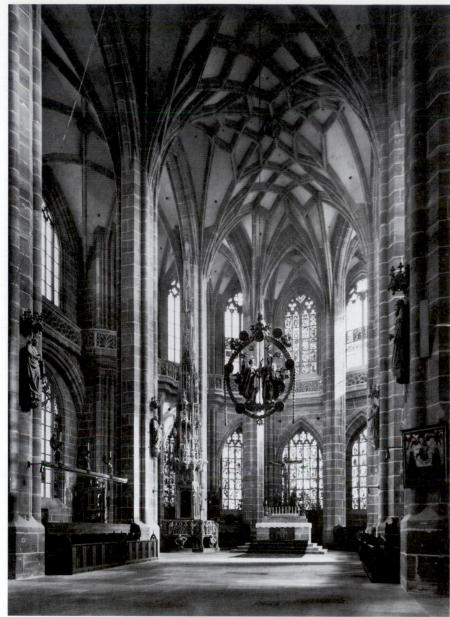

15-42. KONRAD HEINZELMANN and KONRAD RORICZER. Choir, Church of St. Lawrence, Nuremberg, Germany. Begun 1439

15-42

ing the similarity to forests by sprouting richly carved foliage, in buildings through-out not only southern Germany but Austria and Bohemia.

NICHOLAS OF VERDUN   German thirteenth-century sculpture can scarcely be understood without a consideration of the art of metalwork, highly regarded in the Middle Ages, and without a return to the valley of the Meuse, where in the twelfth century the classicism of Renier de Huy (see fig. 14–18) held sway at Liège. Another master from the same region, Nicholas of Verdun, had great success in Germany. In 1181 he completed an extensive cycle of gold and enamel scenes for a pulpit at the Abbey of Klosterneuburg, not far from Vienna; these were later remounted to form an altarpiece. The persistent debate as to whether Nicholas's style should be considered Romanesque or Early Gothic should be settled by the characteristically Gothic trefoil (three-lobed) arches of the borders. Nicholas's strong classicism is also Gothic in the sense that all his figures stand or move firmly on the ground, and though the drapery lines still retain some Romanesque orna-mental character, the convincing action poses and the thoroughly consistent drap-ery folds are Gothic. The *Sacrifice of Isaac* (fig. 15–43) is presented in terms of

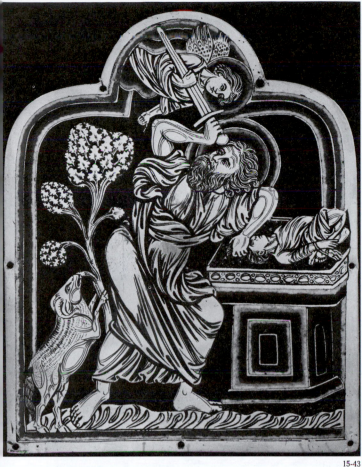
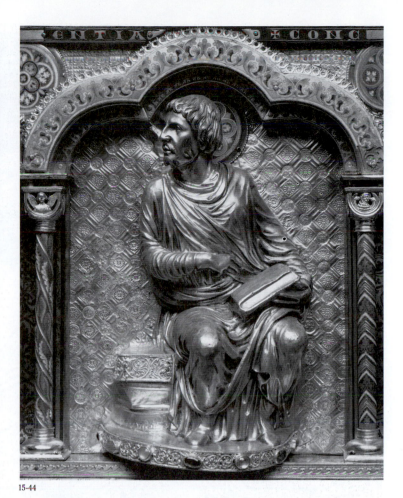

15-43   15-44

15-43. NICHOLAS OF VERDUN. *Sacrifice of Isaac.* 1181. Gold and enamel plaque, height 5½" (14 cm). Abbey of Klosterneuburg, Austria

15-44. NICHOLAS OF VERDUN. *Prophet Habakkuk*, detail of the *Shrine of the Three Kings*, Cathedral of Cologne, Germany. c. 1182–90. Gold, enamel, and precious stones, height of shrine 67" (1.7 m)

physical action; the angel swoops down to draw back Abraham's sword, as he holds Isaac bound upon the altar. The stormy movement brings back memories of Hellenistic sculpture, and perhaps more relevant echoes of Nerezi (see fig. 10–63). This scene should be compared with Lorenzo Ghiberti's rendering of the same incident at the beginning of the Italian Renaissance.

The Klosterneuburg plaques were followed by the gold figures of the rich *Shrine of the Three Kings,* made by Nicholas about 1182–90 for the Cathedral of Cologne. The *Prophet Habakkuk* (fig. 15–44) is surely one of the most classicistic figures of the entire Middle Ages—even more so than the *Visitation* group at Reims (see fig. 15–24). The prophet is seated in a strongly Hellenistic pose, his mantle sweeping around him in folds that recall fifth-century Greek sculpture (see fig. 7–30) as much as they do the togas of Roman sculpture (see fig. 9–1). His head is turned in an attitude of tense alertness, as if he were attending divine inspiration. The movement of surfaces has surpassed even that of the work of Renier de Huy, with which it appears in a continuous tradition.

STRASBOURG CATHEDRAL   German Gothic sculpture reflects also at the start the classicism of Nicholas of Verdun. Especially impressive is the *Death of the Virgin* tympanum (fig. 15–45), of about 1220, in the Cathedral of Strasbourg. Today in France, Strasbourg has been throughout most of its history a German city called Strassburg. The ornament of the preexistent arch is Romanesque, and the heads of the Apostles radiate outward from the center as at Vézelay but the sweep and flow of the drapery and the deep undercutting are strongly Gothic, as are the delicacy of psychological observation and the intensity of the emotion displayed by the grieving Apostles.

A legend, given wide circulation in recent years, attributes some of the finest sculpture at Strasbourg to a woman sculptor called Sabina, supposedly the daugh-

475

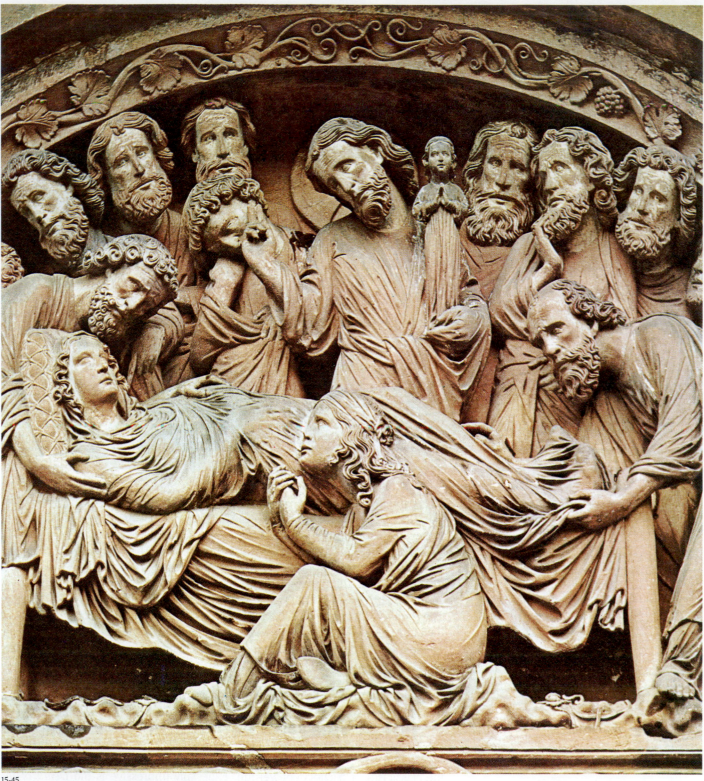

15-45.

ter of Master Erwin von Steinbach. Master Erwin (the name Steinbach is also legendary), a brilliant architect in a later, wholly different phase of German Gothic, was actually not recorded at Strasbourg until 1284, sixty years after the date of the sculptural masterpieces, and survived until 1318. Sabina, no relation, whose name does indeed appear in an inscription, was a patron of the work, not a sculptor. There are no records suggesting that women in the Middle Ages were permitted to engage in the arduous work of cutting stone.

15-45. *Death of the Virgin,* tympanum of the south transept portal, Cathedral of Strasbourg, France. c. 1220

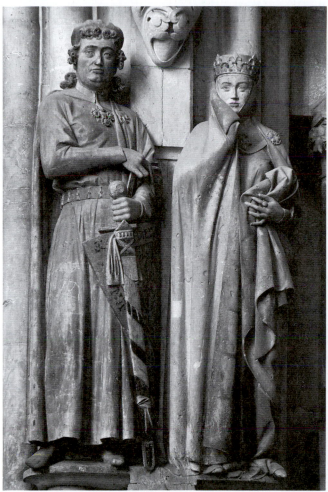

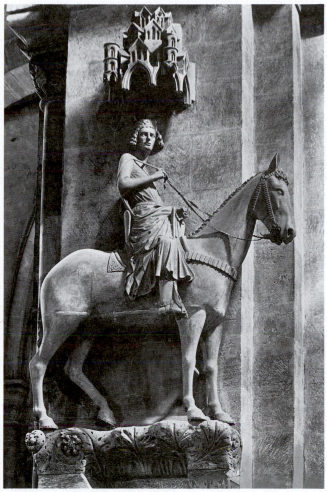

15-46

15-47

15-46. *Ekkehard and Uta,* choir responds, Cathedral of Naumburg, Germany. c. 1250–60

15-47. *Rider.* Middle 13th century. Sandstone, height 7′6″ (2.3 m). Cathedral of Bamberg, Germany

THE NAUMBURG MASTER Massive sculptural cycles like those of the French cathedral portals were apparently not needed in Germany. German thirteenth-century masters, with less compulsion to conform to a "corporate" style, are impressive in their directness. The best of these is an anonymous artist known for his work in the Gothic Cathedral of Naumburg in Saxony. This powerful sculptor carved a series of statues of nobles from local history who were believed to have been founders of the Cathedral and brought these subjects—about whose actual appearance he knew nothing—to convincing life. The heavyset, pouting Ekkehard (fig. 15–46), with his hand resting from habit on his sword hilt, is contrasted with his wife Uta, an aloof beauty who gathers up her cloak with her left hand while with her right she draws it closer about her neck.

THE BAMBERG RIDER Perhaps the most memorable achievement of German Gothic sculpture is the mid-thirteenth-century *Rider* (fig. 15–47), who stands against one of the Romanesque piers of Bamberg Cathedral in Bavaria, under a French-style canopy that seems both inappropriate to Germany and inadequate for a man on horseback. The earliest monumental equestrian group to survive since the days of Marcus Aurelius (see fig. 9–58), this work may preserve some memory of the vanished bronze *Theodoric* that once stood in front of Charlemagne's Palace Chapel at Aachen, but it is in every way unclassical. The horse is hardly to be compared with the fiery steed of Marcus Aurelius; his forefeet are planted side by side, his left hind hoof is lifted to paw the ground. He looks nervous and tense. In contrast to classical equestrian figures, it should be noted, the Bamberg rider is represented to the same scale as his mount. We do not know the identity of the subject—he may be the emperor Conrad III—but in its calm, dignity, and apparent courage, the statue sums up as nobly as does the *Saint Theodore* at Chartres the qualities essential to the knightly idea.

HERRAD OF LANDSBERG   If Sabina von Steinbach turns out to have been a myth, HERRAD OF LANDSBERG (1125/30–1195) was a magnificent reality. Abbess of Hohenburg, near Strasbourg, in Alsace, then considered German, Herrad composed between 1159 and 1180 a treatise called the *Hortus Deliciarum* (Garden of Delights) for the instruction of her nuns, who illustrated it under her direction. Some, perhaps many, of the illustrations were drawn and painted by Herrad's own hand. The book, one of the highest achievements of Gothic manuscript painting, was a compendium of medieval knowledge that was based largely on Scripture but contained many passages drawn from classical learning and from contemporary science, especially the medieval cosmogony, as well as an explication of the seven liberal arts (which, as always in the Middle Ages, included music but none of the visual arts). The author tells us her purpose in touching words:

This book, entitled Garden of Delights, *I myself, the little bee, composed inspired by God from the sap of diverse flowers from Holy Scripture and from philosophical works, and I constructed it by my love for you [that is, her nuns] in the manner of a honeycomb full of honey for the honor and the glory of Jesus Christ and the Church.*

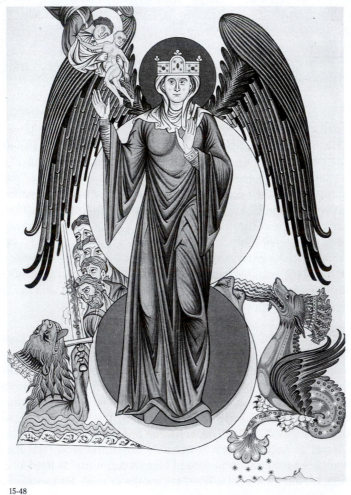

15-48

15-48. HERRAD OF LANDSBERG. *Woman of the Apocalypse,* illumination from *Hortus Deliciarum* (original destroyed). 1159–80

The last page was a gallery of bust-portraits of the nuns of Hohenburg, sixty all told, each one labeled like a photograph in a high-school yearbook, all listening intently to an address by Herrad herself—shown full length.

Tragically, the original manuscript was destroyed by fire in the German artillery bombardment of Strasbourg in 1870, before the photography of illuminated manuscripts had begun in earnest. Outline tracings of most of the illustrations had nonetheless been made, and from these we can now reconstruct the original compositions, although the details, of course, are seen through nineteenth-century eyes. Only one, the *Woman of the Apocalypse* (fig. 15–48), was copied in color. The complex text of Revelation (Apocalypse), Chapters 12 and 13, has been condensed into a single majestic image, the vision of the Woman "clothed with the sun and with the moon under her feet, and on her head a crown of twelve stars." She is attacked at the lower right by the red dragon "having seven heads and ten horns and on his heads seven diadems," his tail drawing "the third part of the stars of heaven," a river coming out of his mouth to carry her away, and the earth opening up *its* mouth to swallow the river; at the lower left the beast from the sea, also with seven heads, ten horns, and seven diadems, with the mouth of a lion and the feet of a bear, makes war with the saints. The Woman, given "two wings of a great eagle," has brought forth her "man child to rule all nations," and an angel appears to take him up to God, safe from the two ferocious enemies. In her commentary Abbess Herrad interprets the Woman as the Church, bearing the name of Woman because she is always giving birth to a spiritual race, and goes on to find a symbolic significance in every aspect of the vision. Most important of all, she has succeeded in endowing her vision of Woman with a universal grandeur that survives even the destruction of the original. As artists, Herrad and her nuns control absolutely the sure sense of proportion and the classical flow of surface that are typical of their slightly later contemporary Nicholas of Verdun and that eventually ennobled the sculpture of Strasbourg Cathedral.

Spain

French Gothic architecture was also imported into Spain, and the interiors of three major Spanish cathedrals, those at Burgos, Toledo, and León, derive in detail from their French models (their exteriors have been much reworked in a later phase of Gothic). Nonetheless French Gothic motifs were brilliantly reinterpreted in Catalonia in northeastern Spain, especially in the Cathedral of Gerona, whose apse, ambulatory, and accompanying side aisles had already been constructed between 1312 and 1347 in a somewhat simplified version of French thirteenth-century style. In 1369, apparently (roughly contemporary with the Alhambra in Muslim Spain), a daring architect, PEDRO ÇA COMA, proposed continuing the building with a single gigantic nave consisting of four bays, with no transept and no side aisles, only lateral chapels, an obvious gesture in favor of improved visibility and audibility for the congregation. The resultant immense width of the nave vault excited the doubts of the authorities and of two successive commissions of architects, a record of whose vehement discussions has luckily been preserved. Not until 1417 did the various councils summon up the courage to proceed with Pedro's grand design, under a later architect, JAIME BOFILL. The last stone of the giant vault was set in place, still in perfect Gothic style, nearly two centuries later, in 1604!

Although by French standards the height of the Gerona vault (fig. 15–49), approximately 110 feet, is not exceptional, its 75-foot span makes it by far the largest Gothic vault ever constructed. In comparison the naves at Cologne (see fig. 15–41) and Milan (see fig. 15–62) measure respectively 49 and 59 feet in width. In fact among all masonry vaults in history only that of Saint Peter's in Rome exceeds Gerona in width, by a mere ten feet. Relatively narrow windows, for the intense Mediterranean light, and heavy intervening walls, unthinkable in France, have ensured the stability of the vault without flying buttresses. The placing of the

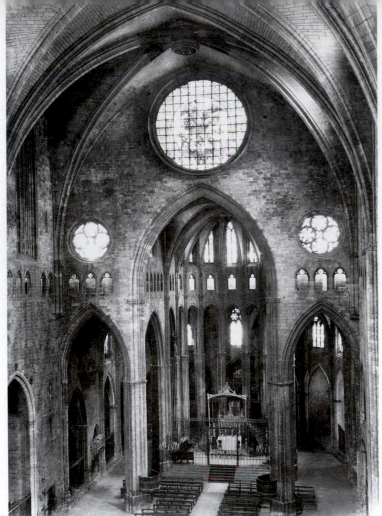

15-49. PEDRO ÇA COMA and JAIME BOFILL. Interior, Cathedral of Gerona, Spain. 1312–47, 1417–1604

15-49

Cathedral at the highest point of the city, accessible from the front only by a flight of no less than ninety steps, leaves the visitor breathless even before encountering the overwhelming experience of the unified interior space. The sweep of the colossal vault cradles as with a giant arm the three-aisled fourteenth-century sanctuary, suggesting the toylike structures in Italian fourteenth-century painting (see fig. 19–13) and further dwarfed by the insertion of a simplified rose window over each side aisle and an *oculus* ("circular opening") just twice the diameter of the roses in the impressively blank wall above the sanctuary arch. Certainly the Gerona vault is one of the great triumphs of Gothic architecture. As in Germany and central Europe, later Spanish and particularly Portuguese Gothic enjoys a luxuriant final phase comparable to the Flamboyant in France.

England

Gothic architectural principles were adopted immediately and enthusiastically in England, already prepared to a certain extent by the structural innovations of the Norman Romanesque. It has been claimed by Paul Frankl—and quite correctly—that in no century since the twelfth has Gothic architecture not been built in England. In the last quarter of the twelfth century, the French Gothic architect William of Sens brought the latest French techniques to the rebuilding of the cathedral at Canterbury, and from there they spread.

SALISBURY CATHEDRAL   But the minute French ideas crossed the English Channel they became distinctly English. First of all, the English neither shared the French enthusiasm for height nor renounced their preference for the extreme

15-50. Plan of Salisbury Cathedral, England. Begun 1220

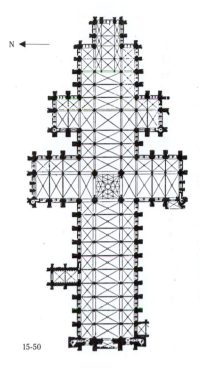

N ←

15-50

15-51. Nave and choir, Salisbury Cathedral. 1220–58

15-52. Salisbury Cathedral (view from the northeast)

length of Romanesque churches. The plan of Salisbury Cathedral (fig. 15–50), begun in 1220 and consecrated in 1258, with its double transept, recalls in that respect the arrangement at Cluny and resembles the layout of no French Gothic building, except that its characteristic square east end recalls that at Laon (see fig. 15–8). The square east end and lengthy choir of English cathedrals probably correspond to the need to accommodate a larger number of clergy than was customary in France; English cathedrals also have cloisters like those of monasteries (many, in fact, were served by Benedictine monks). Second, the majority of English cathedrals are situated not in the centers of towns but in the midst of broad lawns (originally graveyards) and massive shade trees.

In the interior of Salisbury Cathedral (fig. 15–51) every effort was made to increase the appearance of length and to diminish what to the French would seem a very modest height. No colonnettes rise from floor to ceiling; those attached to the compound pillars support only the ribs that make up the arches of the nave arcade. The triforium is large and the clerestory small—tucked away under the vaults as in French Early Gothic cathedrals. Characteristically English is the use of dark Purbeck marble for the colonnettes and capitals, establishing a color contrast similar to that of Romanesque interiors. In this chaste, unpretentious thirteenth-century style known as Early English, there is no tracery; lancet windows are grouped in threes and fives. The appearance of the interior was doubtless far richer when the stained glass (partly destroyed during the Reformation and partly removed in the eighteenth century) was intact and when the original choir screen and its sculpture were in place.

Compared with the soaring lines of French or German cathedrals, the exterior of Salisbury (fig. 15–52) looks earthbound. There is no true façade with flanking towers (although these are present in a number of English cathedrals), but a mere screen that extends without supports to mask the angle of the side-aisle roof. In few English cathedrals are there massive sculptural programs in the French manner; statues and reliefs were scattered over the screen façades, but few have escaped the axes of the reformers. Flying buttresses, in so low a building, did not seem

15-51

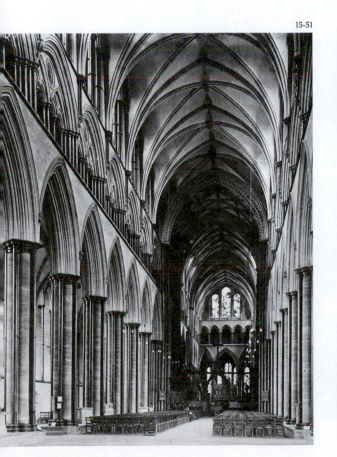

15-52

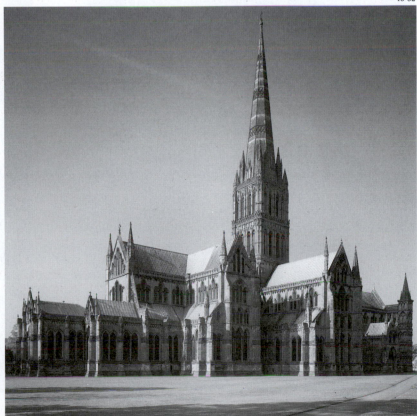

necessary; nonetheless, some had to be added here and there. There is no dramatic chevet; the effects at Salisbury are obtained by the sensitive balancing of elements kept deliberately simple. The square east end is prolonged by the Lady Chapel (a chapel dedicated to the Virgin). The glorious distinguishing feature of Salisbury is the spire over the crossing, a fourteenth-century addition in the second phase of English Gothic, known as Decorated. Although the building was not originally intended for so tall a central tower, the spire, rising to a height of 404 feet, was designed so as to complete the diagonal massing of the exterior composition, and its ornamentation is restrained in order not to conflict with the purity of the Early English building. The effect of this immense weight on the interior was less happy; it required elaborate new supports.

GLOUCESTER CATHEDRAL   The most original invention in English architectural history is the style appropriately known as the Perpendicular, which began to appear in the fourteenth century. The choir of the massive Romanesque Cathedral of Gloucester (fig. 15–53) was remodeled from 1332 to 1357 to enshrine the tomb of Edward II, murdered at the order of his estranged wife, and is a pioneer example of the new style (the Romanesque nave was left intact). The original round arches of the arcade and the gallery may still be made out under the covering screen of Perpendicular tracery, with its infinity of dominant vertical elements. If the English were slow in adopting the idea of tracery, they soon went at it with a will; in this respect the Perpendicular may be considered the English answer to the Flamboyant, whose caprices are countered with brilliant and inexorable logic. The entire interior of the choir is transformed into a basketwork of tracery, with predominantly vertical members, which form the windows and dissolve into the vault. In this refined stage the ribs have lost any constructional function they may once have had. The triangular compartments are subdivided by additional diagonal ribs, and all the ribs are connected by an intricate system of crisscrossing

15-53. Choir, Cathedral of Gloucester, England. Remodeled 1332–57

15-54. Fan vaults, Chapel of Henry VII, Westminster Abbey, London. 1503–19

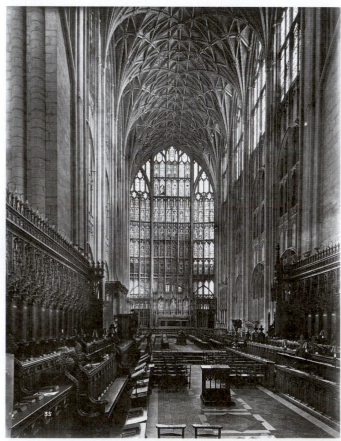

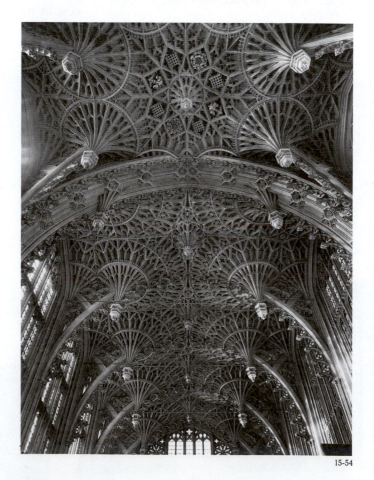

15-53

15-54

diagonals. The original Romanesque apse is replaced by an east window seventy-two feet in height, which not only extends from wall to wall but also even bows slightly outward, doubtless in order to increase resistance to wind.

THE CHAPEL OF HENRY VII The final development of Perpendicular flowered in the *fan vaults* of the late fifteenth and early sixteenth centuries, the richest of which are those in King Henry VII's Chapel in Westminster Abbey in London (fig. 15–54), dating from the first quarter of the sixteenth century, nearly contemporary with Saint-Maclou at Rouen (see fig. 15–37). The complex shapes are as bewildering at first sight as those of Hiberno-Saxon interlace (see Introduction fig. 23) and as open to logical analysis. The vault is made up of tangent cones of tracery, each composed of tiny coupled trefoil arches, surmounted by quatrefoils and enclosed by gables—the standard repertory of High Gothic tracery, as compared to the flickering shapes of the Flamboyant. The cones radiate from central pendants; in the interstices between the cones, down the center of the vault, are smaller ones, also culminating in pendants. The larger cones are held in position by cusped tracery arches, springing from between the windows and continuing the line of the old transverse ribs. Tie-rods added later indicate that on this occasion the imagination of the Perpendicular architects may have been carried a bit far for structural safety.

THE WILTON DIPTYCH Among the rare panel paintings surviving from the Gothic period in England is the *Wilton Diptych* (fig. 15–55), a small masterpiece

15-55. *Wilton Diptych*. c. 1377–1413. Each panel 18 × 11½″ (46 × 29 cm). National Gallery, London. Reproduced by Courtesy of the Trustees

15-55

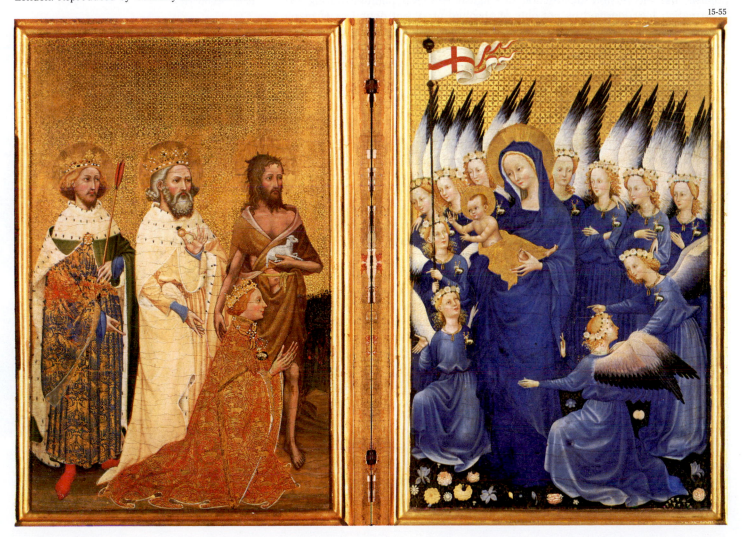

painted in the tempera technique. On rocky ground to the left kneels Richard II, represented as a youth and accompanied by his patron saints, John the Baptist and kings Edward the Confessor and Edmund. Most of the background is gold, tooled in a neat, regular pattern to increase its sparkle, but beside the figure of John the Baptist we look into a deep wilderness. The young king's hands are extended less in prayer than in astonishment at the apparition in the facing panel of the Virgin Mary, holding the Christ Child and attended by eleven rose-crowned blond angels, each wearing the same badge of the white hart as the king wears (he was eleven years old at the time of his coronation in 1377). The sacred figures stand or kneel on a carpet of rich foliage, on which plucked roses and irises are strewn. The rich crimsons of Richard's damasks and the white of the ermines contrast with the sky-blues that dominate the right panel, ranging from the deep tones of the tunics in the upper row of angels through the medium value of Mary's mantle and tunic to the pale blues in the foreground; even the angels' white wings are tipped with blue.

The faces, hands, arms, and feet show an unprecedented delicacy of drawing and shading and accuracy of anatomical observation, held in check by an extreme refinement of taste. This exquisite style is the more mysterious since so little panel painting of the period survives in England. There are many theories regarding the diptych's date (anywhere from 1377 to 1413) and authorship, but no sure conclusions. The painter was certainly trained in the Italian tradition and knew Sienese art, especially the work of Duccio and Simone Martini and even more intimately that of Giovanni da Milano (see figs. 19–12, 19–15, 19–21). He was also one of the most accomplished painters of the fourteenth century in Europe. Prolonged discussion of the nationality of the painter has resulted in wide agreement that he was English, but the terrible destruction of English medieval painting during the Reformation has deprived us not only of absolute proof but doubtless of many other such beautiful works. In its extraordinary grace and refinement the painting corresponds to the rarefied taste of the court of Richard II; since his reign was destined for an unhappy end, it is comforting to hope that the unknown painter of the *Wilton Diptych* gave it a beautiful beginning.

Architecture in Italy

France's neighbors, in general, welcomed the new Gothic style and imported French architects and architecture, subject only to modifications in accordance with local taste and customs. In the kingdom of Naples, ruled by French descendants of Louis IX, the existence of French Gothic churches is not surprising. Elsewhere in Italy, however, the only churches in French style are those of the Cistercian Order, itself French and governed from Cîteaux in Burgundy. The austerity decreed by Saint Bernard forbade anything like the splendors of the cathedrals.

ABBEY OF FOSSANOVA   The Cistercian Abbey of Fossanova (fig. 15–56), south of Rome, was commenced in 1187 and consecrated in 1208. Its essentials might as easily be found in Cistercian buildings in France or in England and clearly reflect the austerity of Saint Bernard's tradition. The east end is square. Massive compound piers support pointed transverse arches and groin vaults over nave and choir. Only the crossing is rib vaulted. The capitals are French transplants, close to those at Laon and Paris. As there was to be no stained glass, there was no need for the structural refinements of the Early Gothic. The total lack of ornamentation or of painting forces the observer to concentrate on the grand masses and spaces of the noble structure.

SANTA CROCE AT FLORENCE   In the independent republics of central and northern Italy, the Romanesque often continued into the thirteenth century, although many Gothic details were adapted. The major influence on church building emanated from two remarkably different religious figures, Saint Francis of Assisi

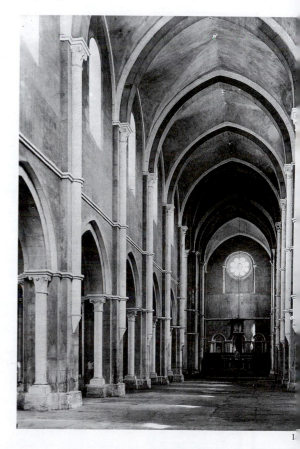

15-56. Interior, Abbey Church of Fossanova, Italy. Begun 1187

15-57. Nave and choir, Sta. Croce, Florence. Begun c. 1294

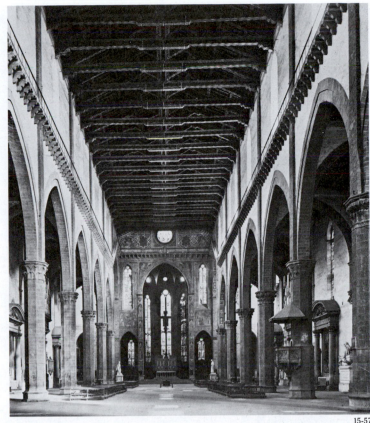

15-57

(1182–1226) and Saint Dominic (1170–1221), both of whom founded orders with innumerable branches, devoted not to a life of work and study apart from the people but to direct preaching before urban masses and to missionary endeavors. The preaching orders revolutionized traditional Italian basilican architecture, for they required simple but very large interiors, usually timber-roofed both for economy and for speed in construction. French Gothic, with its intricacy of structure and decoration, was simply inappropriate. Santa Croce in Florence (fig. 15–57), started in 1294, is one of the most imposing of these basilicas. Its octagonal columns, pointed arches, and foliate capitals and its impression of lightness and openness mark the church as Gothic, although at first sight it resembles nothing we have seen elsewhere. As the church was not planned for vaulting, there was no need for the usual French system of colonnettes rising two or more stories. The light and heat of Italian summers would have made large French windows intolerable. The windows at Santa Croce were, however, designed for stained glass, much of which is still in place, although it is very different from French stained glass.

When we look at the choir of Santa Croce, beyond the triumphal arch, we see that the unknown architect (perhaps Arnolfo di Cambio, c. 1245–before 1310) did indeed understand French Gothic principles and adapted them intelligently to Italian requirements. The choir and the five chapels on either side of it, entered from the west side of the transept (two may be seen in the illustration), show a familiarity with the refinements of ribbed vaulting. The tall windows with their bar tracery resemble those inserted into the clerestory of Notre-Dame in Paris in the thirteenth century (see fig. 15–12). Large wall surfaces were needed in Italy, especially in Tuscany, for the highly respected art of fresco painting; the two chapels to the right of the choir were frescoed entirely by Giotto, and two others by his pupils, while the nave was under construction. The timber roof, recalling that at Monreale (see fig. 14–23), retains its original Gothic painted decoration.

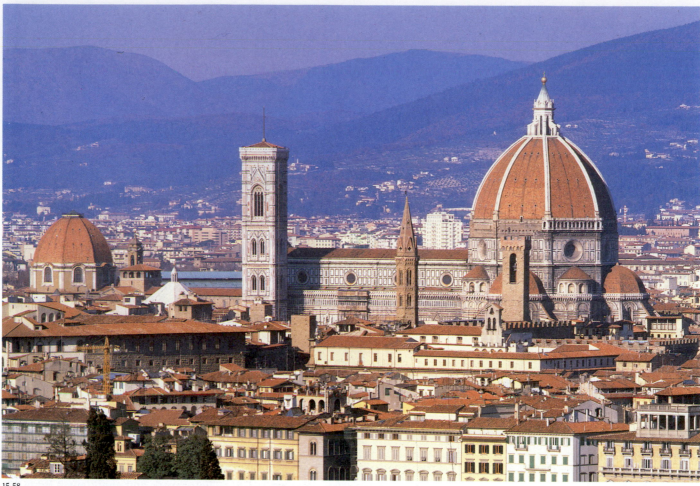

15-58

15-58. Cathedral of Florence. Begun 1368 by FRANCESCO TALENTI and others

15-59. Plan of the Cathedral of Florence (after ARNOLFO DI CAMBIO, 1296)

FLORENCE CATHEDRAL

FLORENCE CATHEDRAL   An entirely different problem was presented by the Cathedral of Florence (fig. 15–58), which has so long and so complex a building history that its final appearance can be attributed to no single architect. A fairly large structure was planned by the architect ARNOLFO DI CAMBIO in 1296, with identically shaped apsidal choir and transept arms radiating outward from a central octagonal dome (fig. 15–59). In the main Arnolfo's plan was followed but much expanded by the architects, chief among them FRANCESCO TALENTI, who, under the close supervision of a commission, commenced building from the final design in 1368. The colossal interior (fig. 15–60) is only four bays long and the impression so simple and bare in comparison with the complexity and mystery of French interiors that it is a surprise to discover that the height of the vaults is approximately the same as at Amiens, although each bay of the nave is almost three times as wide. The compound piers are cubic rather than cylindrical as in France, and their foliate capitals are treated as cubes of ornament. Pilasters continue above the giant arches to the catwalk supported on brackets required by the commission of 1368, which also insisted that the vaults spring directly from the level of the catwalk, thus canceling out any considerable clerestory. The interior, therefore, appears as one enormous story, lighted by oculi in the lunettes under the vaults. Walking through the building, one experiences immense cubes of space, which, as soon as their size becomes apparent, are dwarfed by the grandeur of the octagonal central space under the dome, from which the three half-octagonal apses radiate. The vaults are heavily domed and exert strong outward thrust. In the absence of flying buttresses, tie-rods had to be installed.

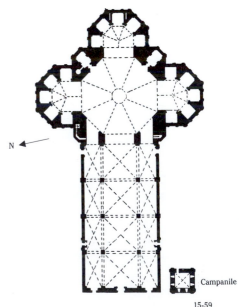

N

Campanile

15-59

15-60. Interior, Cathedral of Florence

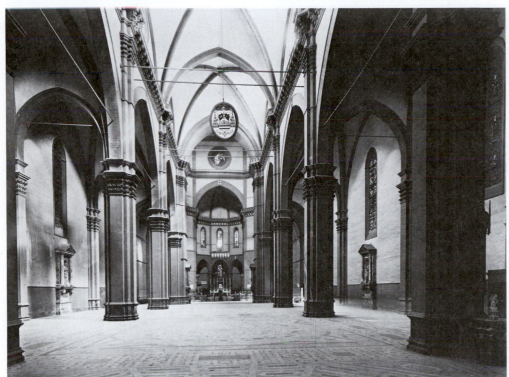

15-60

The simple, cubic exterior masses of the nave and the more complex forms of the semidomes surrounding the central octagon were paneled in white, green, and rose marbles to harmonize with the Baptistery. The campanile, separate like that of Pisa and also paneled in marbles, was commenced by Giotto, who designed only the lower two stories; the much richer upper five stories (three are visible in fig. 15–58) are the work of Talenti in the middle of the fourteenth century. At the opening of the fifteenth century (so uncertain was the art of building), no one in Florence had the faintest idea how the octagonal central space of the cathedral could be covered. How *that* problem was solved is one of the dramas of the Early Renaissance.

SIENA CATHEDRAL Perhaps because of the long tradition of Early Christian basilicas in Italy, the two-tower façade, universal in France and common throughout England, Spain, and Germany, was almost never adopted in Italy. In fact, the building of any sort of façade often lagged behind the construction of the rest of the church. Only one of the major churches of Florence received its façade during the period of its original construction; those of the Cathedral and Santa Croce were added only in the nineteenth century. But the Cathedral of Siena, the independent patrician republic forty miles to the south of Florence, was given a dazzling marble façade (fig. 15–61) in Gothic style that shows certain standard features of Gothic façades in other Italian cities and gives some notion of what that of the Cathedral of Florence might have looked like had it been completed in the Gothic period. The lower half of the façade was designed—probably in the late 1280s—by GIOVANNI PISANO, a leading master of Italian Gothic sculpture (see figs. 19–3 to 19–5).

Giovanni flanked his three gabled portals with rich tracery turrets, whose black-and-white marble bases incorporate the striping of the body of the Cathedral. The splayed jambs, with their alternating white and rose colonnettes, lack the statues one would have expected by French standards. Giovanni has transferred his figures to more independent positions on the turrets, where they appear to issue from

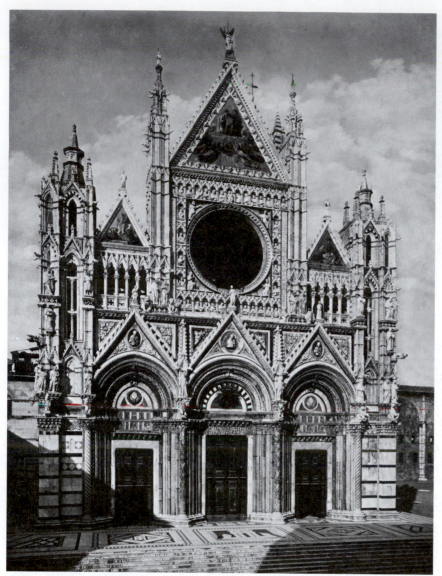

15-61. GIOVANNI PISANO. West façade, Cathedral of Siena, Italy. Begun late 1280s

15-61

shallow niches, in lively attitudes and even in conversation. This new freedom of the human figure from its architectural bonds is not only symptomatic of the role of the individual in the Italian city-republics but also indicative of the emergence of independent personalities among the artists themselves. From time to time we have encountered artists whose names we know and can associate with specific works outside Italy, and a few have even assumed a certain individuality in our minds, but they are exceptions. In Italy such instances become the rule.

MILAN CATHEDRAL   In northern Italy the severe architecture of the Lombard Romanesque was replaced in the later fourteenth century by an especially florid phase of Gothic under the domination of the Visconti family, who had made themselves dukes of Milan and had absorbed into a powerful monarchy most of the independent north Italian communes, with the notable exception of the Venetian Republic. The construction of the Cathedral of Milan, one of the largest of all Christian churches, was subject to the committee procedure we have already seen in Florence, carried on, however, not only by north Italian masters but also by builders imported from France and Germany, each of whom brought to bear arguments based on his own national architectural tradition and theory. As in Florence, the colossal project had been commenced (probably in 1386) and the

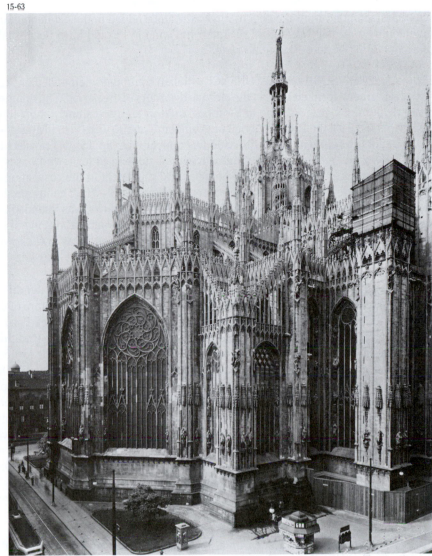

15-63

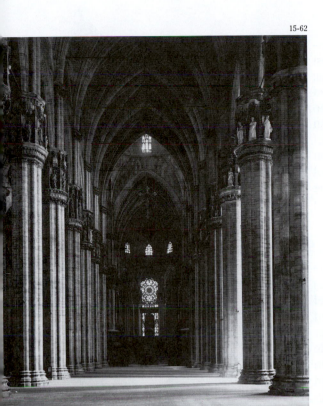

15-62

15-62. Interior, Cathedral of Milan. Begun 1386

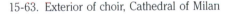

15-63. Exterior of choir, Cathedral of Milan

columns partly erected before anyone was certain how high they were going to go or what shape of arches and vaults they would support. The often acrimonious discussions continued, off and on, from 1392 to 1401. An Italian mathematician, Gabriele Stornaloco, subjected the fabric to the governance of an abstract system of expanding equilateral triangles, and one of the French architects, Jean Mignot, summarized his bitter denunciation of Italian methods with the oft-quoted remark, "Ars sine scientia nihil est." This should not be taken to mean literally that art is nothing without science, but rather that practice is meaningless without theory. But that Mignot's theory should include appeals to God on his throne surrounded by the Evangelists demonstrates how far medieval builders were from being able to calculate static problems by what we would recognize as engineering science. The resultant interior (fig. 15–62) resembles partly the arrangement at Bourges (see fig. 15–20) with its four side aisles of diminishing heights and partly that at Florence (see fig. 15–60) with its single colossal story dwarfing a tiny clerestory under the vaults. The clustered columns are surmounted by outsize capitals intended for a host of statues—eight to a column—in the gathering gloom of the arches. The four-part vaulting is based on French High Gothic examples. The exterior (fig. 15–63) shows the characteristic Italian desire to keep the whole structure within the limits of a block, so that the flying buttresses are invisible from street level. That they were also insufficient is betrayed by the telltale tie-rods in the interior. The forest of pinnacles, intended from the beginning, was actually added in the eighteenth and nineteenth centuries. The gigantic Flamboyant windows would have been totally unacceptable to severe Florentine taste.

THE PALAZZO VECCHIO AT FLORENCE   Italian communes demanded impressive civic centers, fortified against the chronic disorders of the period. The grandest example is the Palazzo Vecchio at Florence, built in an astonishingly short time, from 1299 to 1310; the Priori (council or cabinet members) were actually installed in the building as early as 1302. Its castle-like appearance (fig. 15–64) carries into large-scale civic architecture the roughly trimmed stone used for town houses in medieval Florence. This technique had a classical precedent in the rustication of such Roman civic buildings as the Porta Maggiore (see fig. 9–31). The impression of block mass, relieved only by relatively small Gothic windows, was intended not only for defense but also for psychological effect. The asymmetrical placing of the mighty bell tower was due to the requirements of the site and was not followed elsewhere; yet to modern eyes the result is extremely powerful.

THE PALAZZO DUCALE AT VENICE   One could hardly imagine a greater difference in appearance than that which distinguishes the mountainous structure of the Palazzo Vecchio from the elegant and largely open Palazzo Ducale (Doges' Palace) in Venice, built for a similar purpose, as the official residence of the *doge* (the chief magistrate of the Venetian Republic) and the grand council of a republic fortified only by water. In spite of the fact that construction continued from 1340 until after 1424, the appearance of the building is remarkably unified (fig. 15–65). A simple arcade of pointed arches on low columns supports a more elaborate *loggia* (open gallery) on the second story, with twice as many columns under trefoil arches, and quatrefoil tracery drawn from the standard High Gothic repertory. The massiveness of the upper story, broken only by pointed-arch windows, is relieved by an allover lozenge pattern of white-and-rose marble facing. The distinction between Florentine mass on the one hand and Venetian interest in color, texture, and light effects on the other is one we shall see maintained throughout the long history of these two leading Italian schools, especially in painting.

THE CA' D'ORO AT VENICE   Through the first half of the fifteenth century (the Early Renaissance in Florence), Venetian architecture remained Gothic. The most sumptuous dwelling from this period is the Ca' d'Oro ("Golden House"), built between 1422 and about 1440 on the Grand Canal. The façade (fig. 15–66) was designed for the effect of glittering white arcades and interlaced arches against dark openings and of walls paneled in softly veined marbles in the Byzantine manner, rather than the hard contrast of white and green used in Tuscany; probably neither the architect nor the patron was oblivious to the beauty of the reflections of all this light and color in the blue-green water below, and the very existence of the open loggias reveals the Venetian delight in observing from such vantage points the passing spectacle of traffic on the Grand Canal. Insubstantial as such architecture may seem in comparison with the severity of the Florentine palaces built at the same time for the same class of wealthy merchants, it looks compact and unified, and thus thoroughly Italian, in contrast to the free improvisation of shapes in the almost contemporary house of Jacques Coeur at Bourges (see fig. 15–38).

Despite its special regional variations from the European norm, Italian Gothic architecture can be considered as a part of European Gothic in general. But Italian sculpture and painting of the thirteenth and fourteenth centuries are another story. Unlike medieval artists elsewhere, about whom we know little, the great Italian sculptors and painters of the Late Gothic period are fully rounded human beings. Their styles and achievements are so strongly individual that they demand separate consideration, not just as a prelude to the Renaissance but as an independent and impressive artistic group (see Chapter Nineteen).

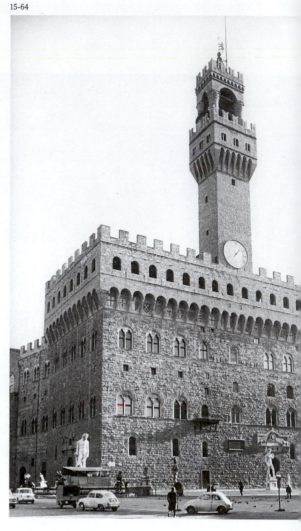

15-64. Palazzo Vecchio, Florence. 1299–1310

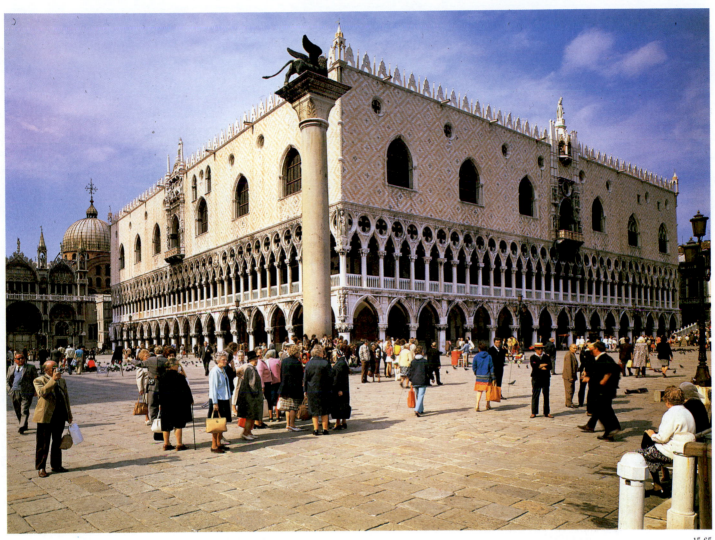

15-65

15-65. Palazzo Ducale (Doges' Palace), Venice. 1340–after 1424

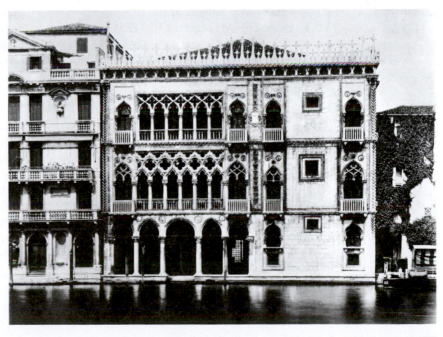

15-66. Ca' d'Oro, Venice. 1422–c. 1440

15-66

TIME LINE VIII

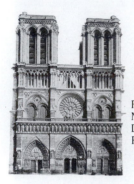

Façade, Notre-Dame, Paris

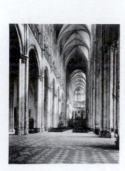

Interior, Amiens Cathedral

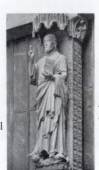

Beau Dieu, Amiens

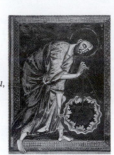

Bible Moralisée

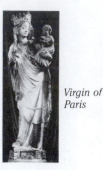

Virgin of Paris

HISTORY

1140	Christian border states begin to wrest Spain from Arabs, 1085–1492
	Pope Innocent III recognizes Frederick Hohenstaufen as king of Sicily, 1198, later Frederick II, HRE, r. 1215–50
	Third Crusade, to rescue Jerusalem, succeeds, 1189–92
1200	In Fourth Crusade, 1202–4, Crusaders sack Constantinople and found Latin Empire of the East (1204–61)
	Magna Carta signed in England, 1215
	St. Louis IX, French king, r. 1226–70
	Sixth Crusade led by Frederick II, 1228–29
	Seventh Crusade led by Louis IX, 1248–54
1250	Greeks retake Constantinople from Latins, 1261
	Eighth Crusade, 1270
	Marco Polo travels to China and India, c. 1275–95
	Turks take Acre, last Christian holding in Holy Land, 1291
	Papacy moved to Avignon, 1309
	Hundred Years' War between France and England, 1337–1453
1350	Black Death epidemic in Europe, 1347–50
	Philip the Bold, Burg. duke, r. 1363–1404
	G. Visconti, Milanese duke, r. 1378–1402
	Papacy returns to Rome, 1378
	Ivan the Great (1462–1505) shapes Muscovite duchy into a national state

CULTURE

Rise of universities: Paris, c. 1150–60; Oxford, 1167

Flowering of vernacular literature; Age of Troubadours

Earliest use of compass for navigation

Albertus Magnus (1193–1280)

Age of minnesingers in Germany

Nibelung epic, 1205

St. Dominic founds Dominican Order, 1206

Albigensian Crusade against heretics in southern France, 1208

Inquisition established (1215–31) to combat heresy

St. Francis (1182–1226) founds Franciscan Order, 1209

Roger Bacon (1214–92)

Dante Alighieri (1265–1321)

Jacobus de Voragine (1266–83)

St. Thomas Aquinas' *Summa Theologica,* 1266–73

Master Eckhart, German theologian and mystic (d. 1327)

Spectacles invented, c. 1286

William of Occam (c. 1300–1349)

First large-scale production of paper

Earliest known use of cannon, 1326

Earliest cast iron in Europe

Boccaccio writes *Decameron,* 1353

John Wycliffe (d. 1384)

Canterbury Tales, by Chaucer, c. 1387

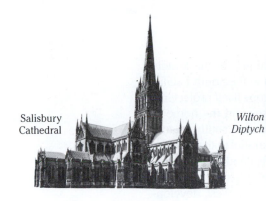

Salisbury
Cathedral

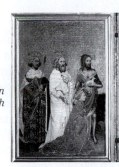

Wilton
Diptych

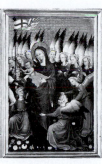

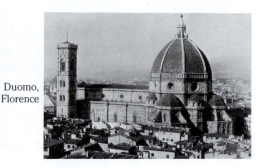

Duomo,
Florence

PAINTING, SCULPTURE, ARCHITECTURE	PARALLEL SOCIETIES	
Ambulatory, Abbey Church of St.-Denis; south tower and Royal Portal, Cathedral of Chartres; Abbey of Fossanova *Hortus Deliciarum,* by Herrad of Landsberg *Sacrifice of Isaac* and *Shrine of the Three Kings,* by Nicholas of Verdun	French Monarchy *Byzantine Empire* Holy Roman Empire in Central Europe *Muslim*	1140
Cathedrals of Laon, Notre-Dame (Paris), Chartres, Bourges, Le Mans, Reims, Amiens, Beauvais; Ste.-Chapelle, Paris Cathedral, Salisbury Sculpture, Cathedrals of Strasbourg, Bamberg, and Naumburg Cathedral, Cologne	English Monarchy Italian city-states	1200
Bible Moralisée; Psalter of St. Louis Giovanni Pisano, façade of Siena Cathedral; Sta. Croce, Florence Palazzo Vecchio, Florence Cathedral, Gerona *Virgin of Paris; Belleville Breviary,* by Jean Pucelle Choir, Cathedral of Gloucester Palazzo Ducale, Venice	Spanish kingdoms: Navarre, Castille, Aragón *Yuan dynasty, China*	1250
Duomo (Cathedral), Florence *Wilton Diptych* Cathedral, Milan Choir, St. Lawrence, Nuremberg St.-Maclou, Rouen; Chapel of Henry VII, Westminster	 Russian Empire	1350

PART FOUR

Up to this point, we have followed the development of visual arts in the Middle East, Africa, Europe, and the Americas, with a brief excursion to the South Pacific. Not only the Middle East, geographically a part of Asia, but Europe itself project like dependencies from Asia, the largest of the world's landmasses and the home of more than half of the world's population. The civilizations of central, southern, and eastern Asia, known collectively as the Far East, run roughly parallel to those of the West and the Middle East. Historical contacts between the West and the Far East, however, were remarkably few and generally limited to trade in luxury goods. In most eras, Far Eastern civilizations were totally independent of the West, developing according to their own necessities, but succumbing to Western influence usually at quite late periods in their development. There is, therefore, no chronological point in this book at which Far Eastern art can be easily introduced, and to consider it we must first backtrack in time and then move forward far beyond the chronological limits of Part Three. According to any standards, the achievements of Far Eastern civilizations are comparable to those of the richest Western cultures. If our study could be organized in terms of quality alone, Far Eastern art would take up almost half of our space. No matter how hard we try, our Western view is sure to be myopic, but even this brief survey will succeed in its purpose if it persuades the reader to go deeper into the study of the endless beauties of Far Eastern art.

All the world's great religions originated in Asia. Judaism, Christianity, and Islam, in chronological order, eventually spread worldwide in varying degrees of strength. Buddhism, a truly international religion, Hinduism and Jain in India, Confucianism and Daoism in China, and Shinto in Japan remained almost exclusively Asian, and—with Islam—are still powerful.

Until the beginning of the Renaissance in Europe, the art of the Far East follows a pattern of development in many ways comparable to that of Europe, and the two are even linked at times through the spread of Roman style to western India. With few exceptions, buildings and works of sculpture and painting were produced, as generally in ancient and medieval Europe, to satisfy religious and civic needs. Then the ways part. In Asia no Renaissance ever took place. There were reasons. The Renaissance, as we will see in Part Five, owed its origin to a new kind of individualism, which in turn was closely linked to the rise of a trading class. Science and technology, philosophy and the arts—already to a great degree independent of religion in European antiquity but resubjected to it in the Middle Ages—eventually became autonomous. But in Asia no merchant republics like those of Greece in ancient times or Italy in the late Middle Ages ever arose. Dynastic monarchies held sway until the Europeans invaded India and Southeast Asia in the eighteenth and nineteenth centuries, and even afterward survived in name and in political forms. In certain Asian countries, notably Japan, Nepal, and Thailand, such monarchies are still very much alive, even if at times they are sharply limited by democratic

THE FAR EAST

institutions imported from Europe or America. Although Asian art often and early developed a high degree of naturalism in the representation of the visible world—as did that of Europe in Greek times and in the late Middle Ages—essentially it embodied the thoughts and feelings of collective societies, which imposed their own categories of artistic production, even when, as in China and Japan, strongly individual artists made their appearance. In the Far East the natural environment is fitted into generally accepted patterns of thought and creation. The differences between major Far Eastern artistic traditions are, if anything, even greater than those that separate their European counterparts, all of which ultimately derive from the heritage of Egypt, Greece, and Rome. The multitude of Far Eastern arts can, however, be grouped into two major divisions, roughly but not entirely corresponding to their ethnic origins. A collection of supremely gifted ethnic groups ranging from pale-skinned Iranians to dark-skinned Dravidians eventually filled the entire Indian subcontinent and adjacent islands. A second and equally talented collection of ethnic groups characterized by "Mongolian" appearance inhabit China, Korea, Tibet, Japan, and much of Southeast Asia. These two major populations have little in common physically beyond their black hair and brown eyes. The artistic culture of Indian groups dominates not only the Indian subcontinent but ethnically diverse Southeast Asia as well. A generally unrelated artistic tradition sprang from the peoples of China, Korea, and Japan.

The differences between these cultures may be illustrated by their contrasting conceptions of the nature and purpose of temple architecture. On the Indian subcontinent, architecture is synonymous with mass. An Indian temple is either carved out of living rock (see figs. 16–6, 16–10) or so built that it seems to be (see figs. 16–28, 16–30). The necessities of support are seldom visible on the exterior. A Chinese or Japanese temple—or dwelling, for that matter—is essentially a roof. It is the roof that receives the richest treatment, and its exquisitely calibrated support system, always wooden, belongs visually to the roof (see fig. 18–3). Walls are screens, without bearing function.

As a natural consequence, in the Indian tradition sculpture is the leading art, employed not only for a temple's central images but for the enrichment of enormous masses of stone with statues and reliefs. Painting, however high in quality, is an adjunct. In the Chinese-Japanese tradition, the central and accompanying images provide the only demand for sculpture; there are no building masses to shape into sculpture but limitless views of the world between the supporting posts. Thus, painting—decorating screen-walls—becomes automatically the leading art. It is not surprising that the Indian sculptural tradition takes its place with the greatest that pre-Renaissance Europe can offer (with the sole, unapproachable exception of Greece) and that Chinese and Japanese painting ranks with the finest in the world.

CHAPTER SIXTEEN

The Indian subcontinent, a triangular landmass more than fifteen hundred miles in maximum length and maximum width, stretches from the Indus River on the west to the borders of Myanmar (formerly Burma) on the east. It embraces landscapes as dissimilar as the eternal snows of the Himalayas, by far the highest mountain range on earth, bordering magnificent green valleys; the semiarid region of Rajasthan to the west; the fertile Ganges Valley to the northeast; and the steaming farms and palm glades of Tamil Nadu to the extreme south. About half of the area lies within the tropical zone, but only the mountainous regions escape tropical heat. The sphere of Indian artistic influence includes Nepal, Sri Lanka (formerly Ceylon), Myanmar, Thailand, Cambodia, and even Indonesia.

Only under British rule was the entire subcontinent ever united. At Independence, in 1947, the western and extreme eastern regions were removed, under tragic circumstances, to create the new republic of Pakistan, later subdivided into Pakistan on the west and Bangladesh on the east. Ethnic, linguistic, and religious barriers imperil the unity of the remaining republic of India. Fourteen Indian languages spoken today are recognized as official—some not of Indo-European origin—and these are subdivided into more than two hundred dialects. To an extent these languages reflect ethnic and historical divisions. About 1500 B.C. an indigenous population was overrun by Indo-European–speaking invaders from the northwest. The religion of these Aryans (who must not be confused with the "race" of that name invented by the German Nazis) survives in Hinduism, Buddhism, and Jain. A third major group, the Arabs, conquered much of northern India at the end of the twelfth century A.D., bringing Islam with them. A fourth group, the Moguls, also Muslims and related to the Persians and the Afghans, invaded India in the late fifteenth century and conquered much of the subcontinent (see Chapter Eleven). A fifth Indian religion, Sikhism, arose in northern India in the sixteenth century.

Despite differences and antagonisms between its component groups, India is still India. It is the only ancient civilization that has survived to the present day relatively intact. Although forbidden by law the caste system, at the bottom of which live tens of millions of Untouchables, is still observed. In most portions of the country the extended family of at least three generations lives under a single roof. All women, and in the villages all men as well, dress in local draped rather than Western tailored costume. However crushing may be the burden of poverty for the lower economic classes, the Hindu women in their gorgeous saris (surely the most graceful garment ever devised) know how to walk like empresses.

In the villages little has changed since ancient times, and the automobile is an interloper. Except in the Himalayan region, where chalet-like mountain architecture is common, and whether dominated by temples or mosques, the cities with their tall apartment houses next to appalling slums, the streets in which bullocks and camels mingle with motor vehicles, look and feel similar. Enchanting gardens surround palaces and shrines. Everywhere the magic of India is inescapable and unforgettable.

The Indus Valley Civilization

In the 1920s and 1930s, a previously unsuspected ancient civilization came to light in the valley of the Indus River, in what is today Pakistan. At Mohenjo-daro an entire city was excavated, whose rectilinear blocks of houses, built over earlier haphazard constructions, were grouped according to two major thoroughfares also intersecting at right angles and oriented north and south. Almost all the structures,

INDIAN ART

built of mud and fired brick, were more than one story in height. Surprisingly, none can be shown to have any religious purpose. The largest and most impressive structure, with a central tank surrounded by cells, was a bath. This was provided with an efficient water system, and so were the dwellings—even sewers of sorts exist. Seals of the type found at Mohenjo-daro have also been unearthed at sites in Mesopotamia, thereby rewarding us with a dating of 2350–1500 B.C., or even earlier. The Indus Valley civilization, therefore, while later than the earliest cultures

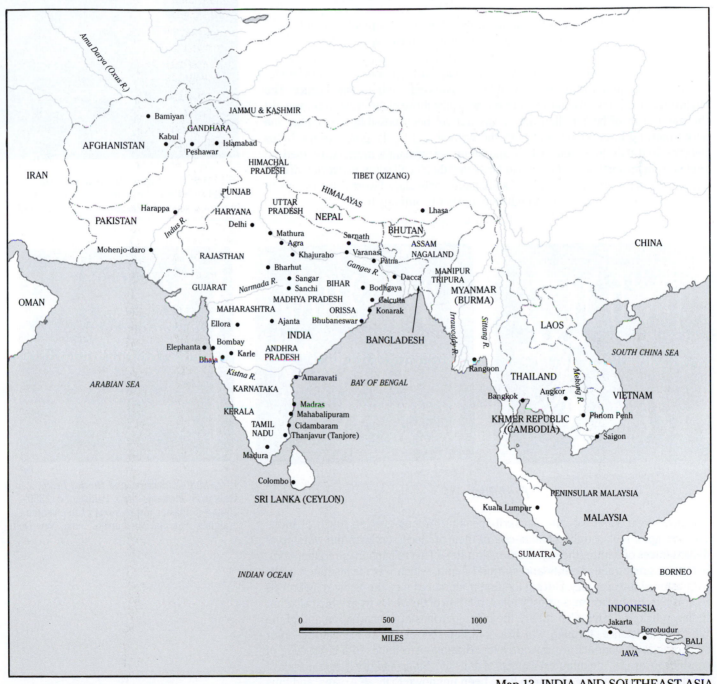

Map 13. INDIA AND SOUTHEAST ASIA

16-1

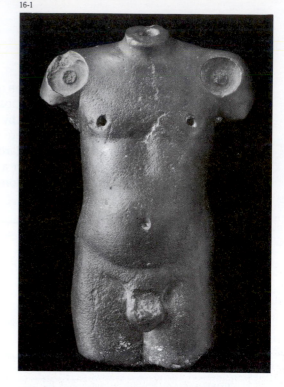

of the Nile Valley and Mesopotamia, is one of the oldest known. Archaeological finds show that the Indus culture stretched along the coast of the Arabian Sea as far south as Bombay.

Among the astonishing variety of objects of daily use found in the Indus cities is a tiny *Male Torso* in red sandstone excavated at Harappa, a fortified city north of Mohenjo-daro on the Indus (fig. 16–1). The great beauty of the object is due to its sensuous softness, in striking contrast to the athletic and military male ideals of Egypt and Greece. The relaxed muscles and rounded belly show little interest in muscular construction. But the surfaces are so handled that light glides across them in a manner that—perhaps deceptively—seems to foretell the sensuous richness of later Indian sculpture. It has so far been impossible to explain the holes drilled into the nipples and the saucer-shaped depressions in the shoulders and neck. Perhaps these were intended for the insertion of ornaments and a head in more precious materials.

Of equally high quality are the stamp seals carved with exquisite skill into hard white steatite, best visible in modern plaster impressions (fig. 16–2), which turn the deep incisions into relief. A lordly bull, a less than convincing rhinoceros, and a fantastic, seated horned being (a god?) surrounded by properly submissive elephants, a tiger, and a rhinoceros, doubtless possessed symbolic significance. The rhythmic smoothness of contours and surfaces, like those of the *Male Torso*, suggest the naturalism of later Indian art. It has not yet been possible to decipher the accompanying inscriptions, and both the writing and the language of the Indus peoples, and therefore their history and literature, remain a mystery. Heaped-up skeletons in the fortress at Harappa indicate that their civilization met a violent end. Probably, but not certainly, those not slaughtered or enslaved were driven south, to become the ancestors of the Dravidian peoples of southern India.

16-1. *Male Torso*, from Harappa, Pakistan. c. 2350–1500 B.C. Red sandstone, height 3¾" (9.5 cm). National Museum of India, New Delhi

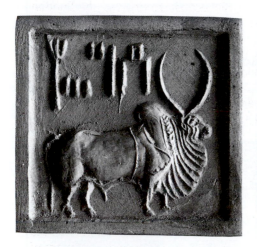
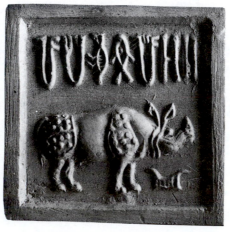
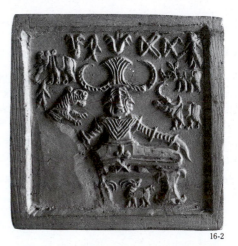

16-2

16-2. *Bull, Rhinoceros, and Horned Being,* stamp seals from Mohenjo-daro, Pakistan. c. 2350–1500 B.C. Plaster impressions of the steatite originals. National Museum of India, New Delhi

Buddhist Art

About the year 1500 B.C., the Sanskrit-speaking Aryans overran much of India. Their religion replaced the phallus-cult of their predecessors with the worship of deified forces of nature (the sky, the sun, thunder). This religion inspired the *Vedas*, hymns of great poetic beauty and spiritual depth, which were transmitted orally with astonishing accuracy. During the first millennium B.C., the Vedic religion was replaced by Brahmanism, a priestly interpretation of the Vedas from which all other Indian religions derive. Central are the twin doctrines of reincarnation and of the Wheel of Existence, through which a soul can rise or fall in the natural order according to its conduct in previous lives. Brahmanism imposed a strict code of conduct governing the minutest aspects of daily life. Stone and brick as materials of construction and carving appear to have been unknown to these Aryans, and thus only pottery and some utilitarian metal objects survive from the next twelve hundred years of Indian history.

Far-reaching changes were brought about by the Buddha (Enlightened, or Holy One), a title conferred upon a north Indian royal prince called Siddhartha who (traditionally) lived between 563 and 483 B.C. The Buddha never considered himself to be other than a reformer and ethical teacher yet was in effect one of the earliest great religious leaders. Confusingly, he is also known as Gautama, the name of his subcaste, and as Sakyamuni, "sage of the Sakya clan." Distressed by the seemingly inevitable misery of humanity, he left his palace and his family for a life of asceticism, wandering from teacher to teacher without achieving a solution. While meditating under a pipal tree in the city of Bodhgaya near the border of Nepal, he experienced Enlightenment: suffering arises only from desire, and the elimination of suffering can be achieved only through renunciation of all desire, resulting in release from the Wheel of Existence and any further reincarnations and culminating in blissful nonbeing, or Nirvana. The Buddha announced his ethical doctrines in the First Sermon, in the Deer Park at Sarnath, north of Varanasi (Benares), formulating the simple eightfold path of righteousness, from which—for Judeo-Christian observers—the love of God is notably absent.

After the Buddha's death (to believers, his Parinirvana, or final release) his ideas spread rapidly, and monastic orders of men and, eventually, of women were formed, in many ways resembling the later religious orders of Christianity. Although the facts of Siddhartha's life were well known, a legend was soon spun about them, including miraculous episodes. The relatively simple early faith, in which Buddha appears as teacher and model (later known as Hinayana, or Lesser Vehicle), soon spread throughout India, Sri Lanka, and Myanmar. A far more elaborate version of Buddhism termed Mahayana (Greater Vehicle), complete with philosophical systems, a deified Buddha, and a heavenly hierarchy, took root and spread over most of east Asia. Before the late second century A.D., the Buddha himself is never directly represented. But in the art of the Hinayana sanctuaries and from the great later Buddha images radiates a feeling of celestial peace not to be encountered in the art of any other religion.

MAURYA PERIOD   Just before the rule of the Maurya dynasty in northern India (322–185 B.C.), the subcontinent was invaded by Alexander the Great at the head of his armies. In 327–326 B.C. Alexander descended through Gandhara as far as the Punjab. Astonishingly, no significant trace of Greek influence has been found. Fragments of a Maurya columned hall at Patna in the Ganges Valley suggest, however, a familiarity with the Palace of Darius and Xerxes at Persepolis (see figs. 4–25, 4–26). After long and bloody wars, the Maurya king Asoka (ruled c. 269–232 B.C.) established imperial rule over most of the subcontinent. On his conversion to Buddhism, Asoka repented of his violence but not of his conquests and set up throughout his territories edicts, legible today, based on the doctrines of the Buddha but having the force of law on tablets, columns, and even outcroppings of rock. Probably on the model of earlier wooden columns with copper capitals, he also erected stone columns some forty to fifty feet high with splendid capitals of smoothly polished sandstone bearing imperial symbols. One of the finest (fig. 16–3), now adopted as the symbol of the Republic of India, shows the forequarters of four snarling royal lions, issuing from a central cylinder, over a circular abacus supported by an inverted lotus flower. The geometrical purity of the design, especially the ornamentalized manes of the lions treated as innumerable flamelike curls, and the stylized lotus, not to speak of the crispness of the carving, have often been considered evidence of contact between Asoka's sculptors and those of Persia. The wheel on the abacus, with its twenty-four spokes, is generally considered a symbol of the Buddha's Law but the animals on either side, treated with a gentle naturalism typical of later Indian art, may symbolize the gods in the service of the Buddha. The humpbacked Brahman bull, for instance, reappears later as Nandi,

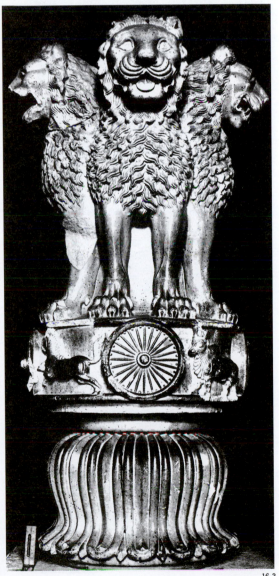

16-3. *Lion Capital*, from a column erected by King Asoka at Pataliputra (present-day Patna), India. c. 261–232 B.C. Polished sandstone, height 7′ (21.34 m). Museum of Archaeology, Sarnath

16-3

499

the bull on which rode Siva, favorite among the Hindu gods, in images all over India. Judging by the surviving remnants of Maurya architecture and sculpture, it was certainly an art of great elegance and sophistication.

Buddhism had simple structural requirements, chief among which was the *stupa* (see figs. 16–7, 16–8), a solid, hemispherical mound, originally of earth and later of masonry, probably once enclosing relics of the Buddha, erected in sacred places, like hills and the confluence of rivers, and especially at sites associated with the Buddha's life. Many such stupas were built under Asoka, but all have been destroyed. Within the Maurya period, also, appear the earliest known examples of Buddhist cave-temples. Warm in winter, cool in summer, excavated caves provided an ideal setting for Buddhist congregational worship. They were served by communities of monks and nuns living in adjacent groups of cells also carved from living rock. More than a thousand of these caves remain, some securely dated, executed from the late second century B.C. to the sixth century A.D. All were strategically situated accessible to cities and along the great trade routes, and their inscriptions record the names of donors, whose widely scattered hometowns reveal the enormous spread of the new religion. The *chaitya* (congregational) caves are designed so as to accommodate processions around a stupa contained in the apse (see fig. 16–10) and their component elements are directly derived from wooden constructions once, presumably, existing in vast numbers. To modern observers, tramping along paths cut from precipices, the experience of these caves is overwhelming.

SHUNGA AND ANDHRA PERIODS   The imperial state of the Mauryas disintegrated in a period of invasions and civil war under the short-lived Shunga dynasty (185–72 B.C.) in north-central India and the Satavahana family, who ruled in the Andhra region of central and southern India (220 B.C.–A.D. 320). Although the great stupa at Bharhut in north-central India, dating from the late second century or early first century B.C., has perished, its magnificent sculptured fence, whose forms are based on wood construction, intended to embrace processions around the stupa enclosure, has been preserved and remounted in the Indian Museum in Calcutta (fig. 16–4). Throughout this complex the quality of the soft red sandstone

16-4. Gateway and railing from the stupa, Bharhut, India. Late 2d century B.C. Stone, height of gateway approx. 20′ (61 m). Indian Museum, Calcutta

16-5. *Female Deity (Yakshi)*, pillar relief from the stupa, Bharhut. Late 2d century B.C. Red sandstone, height 7′ (21.34 m). Indian Museum, Calcutta

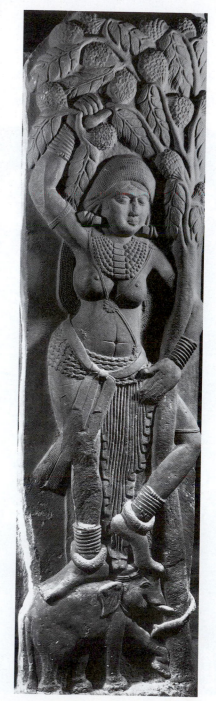

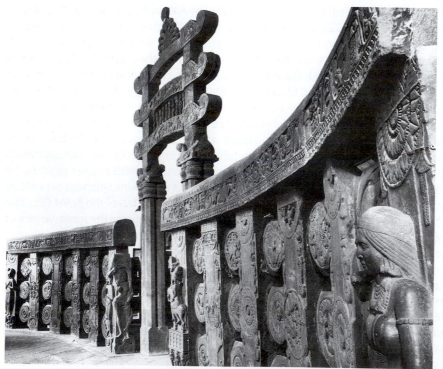

16-4

16-5

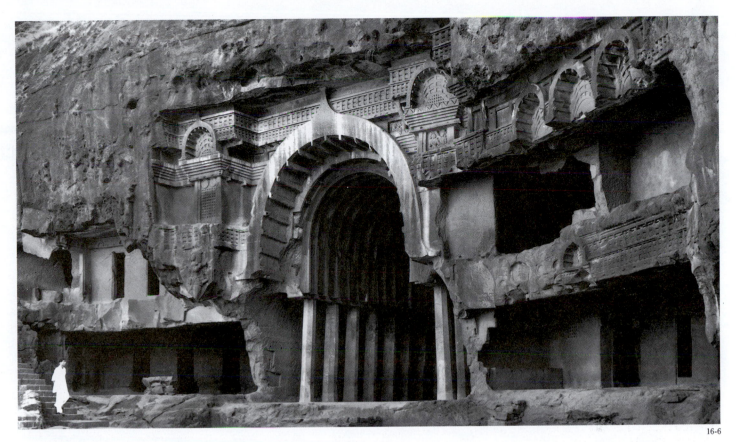
16-6

16-6. Entrance, chaitya hall, Bhaja, India. c. 1st century B.C.

from which it is carved is respected, in the breadth of surfaces and absence of undercutting. The surmounting beam is ornamented with lotus flowers (central to Buddhist symbolism as a perfect creation growing from slime), and its supporting shafts are punctuated by medallions. The connecting medallions, suggesting the original wooden bars of the fence, are in three rows, the lowest filled with lotus ornament, the next with bust-portraits, and the uppermost with scenes from the life of the Buddha or from the *jataka* tales—pre-Buddhist folk-legends retold to star the Buddha in some previous reincarnation. The four majestic *toranas* (entrance gates) are supported by clusters of four polygonal columns, with inverted lotus capitals surmounted by lions in the manner of the Asoka column. As in subsequent stupas, the toranas are connected by three superimposed curved beams, whose shapes obviously derive from wooden architecture, carved into lively reliefs representing scenes from the Buddha's life or from the jatakas. Of another order of being are the almost nude *yakshas* and *yakshis,* male and female nature deities flanking the toranas, which combine a simple nobility of form with a beguiling idiosyncrasy of pose (fig. 16–5). Obviously drawn on the surface, then carved inward to create a continuous flat background, these delightful figures preserve the monumentality and even the surface of their sandstone shafts. Wide, bulging eyes stare calmly outward from blocky faces, while hands are twisted, knees bent, and heels rub against ankles as these beings trample upon animals or demons.

From the late Shunga period, about the first century A.D., dates the impressive cave at Bhaja, south of Bombay (fig. 16–6). One looks directly into the chaitya hall, through a huge pointed arch running the full height of the interior and continued in the arched form of the rib. Although these shapes seem to suggest Gothic pointed arches and ribbed vaults, in reality they are derived from stripped branches bent as a support for thatch, and the polygonal columns, leaning sharply inward, imitate wooden posts. Side aisles, like those of Roman basilicas, and ambulatories continue around the stupa in the apse (not visible in the illustration), in the manner of

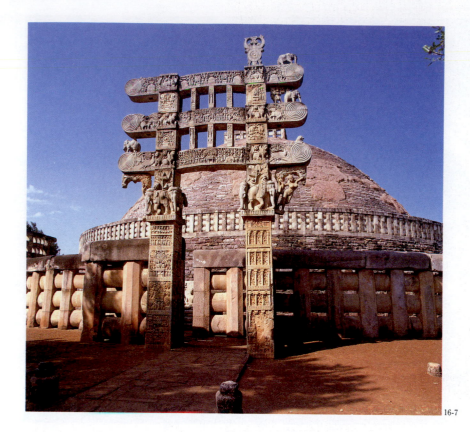

16-7

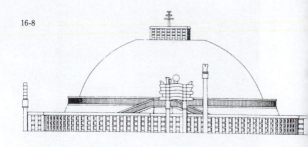

16-8

16-7. Great Stupa, Sanchi, India. Middle 2d century B.C.

16-8. Elevation of the Great Stupa, Sanchi

Christian ambulatories, and for much the same reason. The outer chaitya arch, although carved from the cliff, is made to look as if supported by rafters, and is flanked by rows of smaller arches surrounding illusionistic views of interior arched ceilings and by grilled balconies, all in relief, as if by a whole city of temples and palaces. Barely visible above a destroyed section, just to our left of the chaitya arch, is a nude yakshi.

The grandest of all surviving stupas, the Great Stupa of Sanchi (figs. 16–7, 16–8), was built of local golden sandstone in the Shunga period, about the middle of the second century B.C., to encase a much smaller Mauryan stupa of brick attributed to Asoka. The hilltop site looks out upon a landscape of perfect peace, serenity, and beauty. The Great Stupa (accompanied by two smaller ones and several rectangular temples of later date) stands on a platform with its own simple stone fence around a narrow terrace, imitating trimmed logs in its coping and its connecting rails, mortised into polygonal shafts. A second, much higher rail (10 feet 7 inches tall), enclosing a paved processional path around the structure, is joined by a staircase to the upper terrace. The great hemisphere, coated with concrete of which some remains, and probably finished in white stucco, is crowned by a square balustrade similar to the two below enclosing the triple umbrella of stone, symbolic of the Buddha, the Law, and the monastic order.

So far all is of noble simplicity. Then in the Andhra period, the early first century A.D., four great toranas were added, similar to those at Bharhut but enriched—pillars, beams, and all—with sculpture of far greater complexity, which has been attributed to ivory carvers since one gate was actually given by these craftsmen. Here the incidents of the Buddha's life, including only five jataka scenes, are depicted with unprecedented delicacy. The Buddha is never represented but is symbolized by his footprints, a throne, and the sacred tree. The reliefs, expanding to represent cities, forests, and rivers, have all of the detailed richness that in almost any major Indian monument from here on will reward weeks of careful study. The capitals are freestanding elephants in profile, and the brackets are

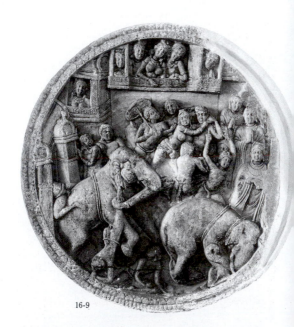

16-9

16-9. *The Buddha Taming the Mad Elephant,* railing medallion from the stupa, Amaravati, India. Late 2d century A.D. Marble, height 35″ (89 cm). Government Museum, Madras

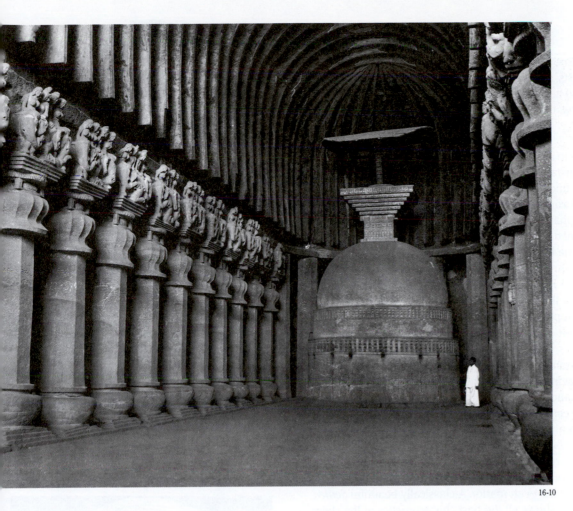

16-10

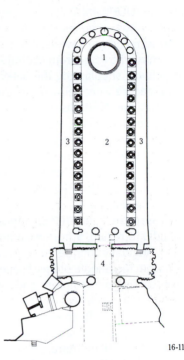

16-11

16-10. Nave, chaitya hall, Karle, India. Early 2d century A.D.

16-11. Plan of the chaitya hall, Karle 1. Stupa 2. Nave 3. Side aisle 4. Vestibule

16-12. *Couple,* stone relief, façade of the chaitya hall, Karle. Early 2d century A.D.

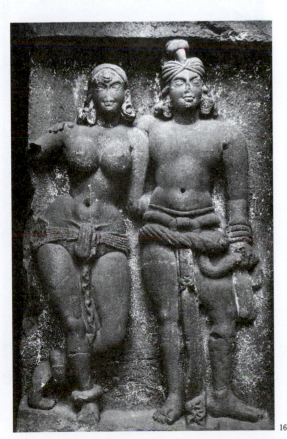

16-12

formed by voluptuous nude yakshis, with the large, full breasts typical of Indian sculpture and sharply accented genitals. Even the intervals between the beams contain cutout riders on horses or on elephants. The probably painted sculpture must have contrasted brilliantly with the purity of the white hemisphere.

An even more magnificent stupa, of white stone relieved by color, was erected at Amaravati in east-central India in the late second century A.D.; among the many stupas attributable to the Andhra period it was, alas, demolished in fairly recent times. Much of the sculpture has been rescued, however, and shows a style more accomplished than any we have yet seen. Although symbols of the Buddha are often used, the Buddha himself at last appears. In a medallion depicting *The Buddha Taming the Mad Elephant* (fig. 16–9) the use of marble permits deep undercutting, thus giving a more forceful illusion of form and space than was possible in sandstone. Issuing from a city gate at the left, the rearing elephant is about to trample one victim with his forefeet while he picks up another by the leg with his trunk. At the right he kneels in gentle submission before the serene standing Buddha, while excited crowds flee the event or watch safely from palace balconies—an astonishing action scene for a relief less than a yard in diameter.

At Karle, not far from Bhaja, is one of the most majestic of all chaitya halls, dating from the early second century A.D. (figs. 16–10, 16–11). The columns of the apse surrounding the stupa are still simple polygonal posts, but those of the nave have richly swelling bases and bell-shaped capitals surmounted by elephants with riders. Their mass and the dense clustering of the ribs over the nave and lining the apse produce in the dimness an effect of awesome grandeur. On the stone screen before the entrance, among many later additions, is an over-life-size, smiling male and female couple, their arms about each other and nude, save for complex twisted and knotted sashes about the waist (fig. 16–12), sometimes identified as donors, although their real purpose is unknown. Their sensuous beauty, of the soft Indian type, with narrow waists, full breasts, and rounded limbs, is irresistible. The archaic stiffness and blockiness of Bharhut have vanished, and the whole is carved in such high relief, with some undercutting, that the figures look almost like statues in the round.

THE BUDDHA IMAGE   As often in attempting to summarize the art of a subcontinent whose regimes were in constant fluctuation, we must backtrack a little, to northern and northwestern India under another invading dynasty, the Kushans—Iranians who came from central Asia. During their rule, from about A.D. 50 to 320, eventually supplanting the Satavahanas in the Andhra region, Buddhist thought and practice were being transformed, probably in response to the rapidly growing rival religion of Hinduism. Hinayana Buddhism had a great intellectual appeal, but pure meditation is no match for anthropomorphic imagery in popular imagination; indeed, as we have seen, even the Hinayana shrines were soon inundated with narrative sculpture, not to speak of the yakshis and yakshas. In Kushan times the image of the Buddha himself first appeared; there is a seated example dated A.D. 32 and many standing figures as well—all upholding the right hand in a gesture meaning "Fear not!"

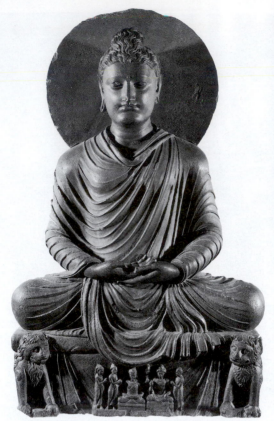

16-13

A surprise is the sudden appearance of Western classical style in the art of the Gandhara region, a northwest province including much of Pakistan and Afghanistan, originally conquered by Alexander in the fourth century B.C. But all the dates are from the middle of the second century A.D. onward, and the influence is that of Roman Trajanic sculpture and even architecture (see pages 259–67). Stupas are raised on bases articulated by pilasters, and Corinthian capitals turn up, along with motifs from Scythian sources. There is no way of telling whether the Buddha images appeared first in Gandhara or in Mathura, 750 miles or so to the southeast, between Delhi and Agra, and it may not even matter. A classically beautiful *Seated Buddha* from Gandhara (fig. 16–13) shows all the best characteristics of the style. The blue-gray schist from which it is carved is handled so as to produce a velvety effect. A huge disklike halo surrounds the head and shoulders. The open pose of the hands, one of the four characteristic positions for Buddha images, is that of meditation, and the eyes are downcast as all attention is turned inward. The prolonged earlobes are typical of all representations of the Buddha. The knotted hair is treated like Greek wavy locks and the full features are dominated by a typical Hellenic nose, but most classical of all is the drapery, apparently a single piece of cloth falling over torso, arms, and legs, in modeled if simplified folds whose liquid melody enhances the rapt contemplation of the figure. Two scenes from the life of the Buddha appear below reminding one, in their strong projection, of late Roman and Early Christian sarcophagus reliefs (see fig. 10–23).

GUPTA PERIOD   After the dissolution of the Kushan state, an Indian dynasty, that of the Guptas (A.D. 320–647), unified the whole of northern India under an unusually intelligent, progressive, and prosperous rule. The Guptas were Hindus but also supported both Buddhism and Jain (see pages 508–10 for a discussion of Hindu art under the Guptas), creating a balanced and harmonious style considered classic in the history of Indian art. Typical of the dignity, restraint, and beauty of Gupta art is *The Seated Buddha Preaching the First Sermon* from Sarnath (fig. 16–14), datable in the fifth century A.D. The classical serenity of Gandhara has given way to a typically Indian sensuous mysticism. The feet, veiled in drapery in the *Seated Buddha* from Gandhara, are here shown with upturned soles in the pose of the Yogi ascetic. The body is everywhere visible through transparent garments, completely smooth until a single passage of folds appears on the cushion below the legs, so displayed as to suggest the petals of a great lotus. The hands, somewhat damaged, are arranged in a teaching pose, ticking off on the fingers the eightfold path of righteousness. As is characteristic of most Indian Buddha representations,

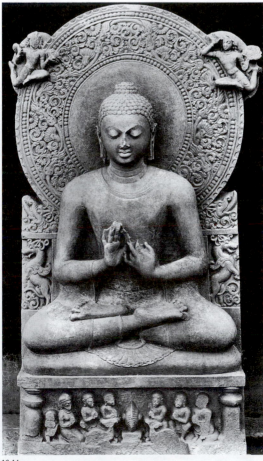

16-14

16-13. *Seated Buddha,* from Gandhara. 2d century A.D. Gray schist, height 43″ (1.09 m). National Museums of Scotland, Edinburgh

the hair is ornamentalized into a series of identical snail-shell curls and the halo surrounded by a rich border of lotus ornament. Two winged *apsaras* (heavenly musicians) soar above, half within the halo, half projecting from it. Rampant winged lions in low relief, suggesting Gautama's royal lineage, guard the throne. The relief below shows six disciples turning the Wheel of the Law, represented foreshortened from the side; two now badly damaged deer suggest the setting in the Deer Park.

A spectacular series of caves from Gupta and immediately post-Gupta times are carved from the rocky cliffs of Ajanta, in central India, including chaitya halls, far more elaborate sculpture than at Bhaja and Karle, monks' cells, and shrines. The columns before the central shrine of Cave 17 at Ajanta, of about A.D. 470–80 (fig. 16–15), give an idea of the richness of the new style. The heavy bases are carved into addorsed (back-to-back) lions in relief, the capitals into floating apsaras at the corners upholding the abaci, separated by panels of foliate ornament. The short, massive shafts contrast sharply with the simplicity of Maurya and Shunga columns; they are broken into seven sections differing in both height and plan; the first is square, the second octagonal, the third sixteen-sided, the fifth round, the others fluted in mutually incompatible numbers, to produce an effect clearly intended to elude analysis. Like the columns in the chaitya halls at Ajanta, they were certainly painted, for painting is the great art of this amazing site. Painting was highly regarded in the Gupta period and its precepts and techniques discussed in learned treatises. Gupta murals are not frescoes; color in a glue or gum vehicle was applied to dry plaster over a mud ground on the rock walls. Considering their fifth- and sixth-century dates, these are well preserved, and the ceiling paintings are still fresh in color; unfortunately, Italian restorers in the 1930s coated the wall paintings with shellac, which eventually turned brown. Comparisons have often been made with Pompeiian painting (see Chapter Nine) in regard to their method of modeling in light and their spatial complexity, but no direct influence can be shown.

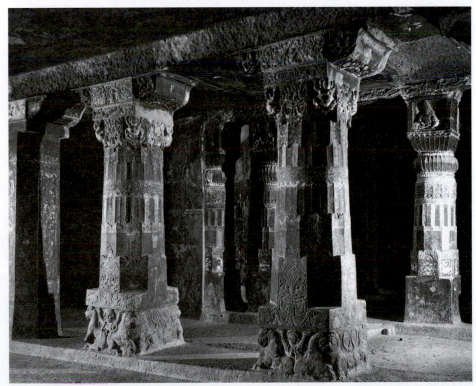

16-14. *The Seated Buddha Preaching the First Sermon,* stela from Sarnath, India. 5th century A.D. Sandstone, height 63″ (1.6 m). Museum of Archaeology, Sarnath

16-15. Columns before the central shrine, Cave 17, Ajanta, India. c. A.D. 470–80

16-15

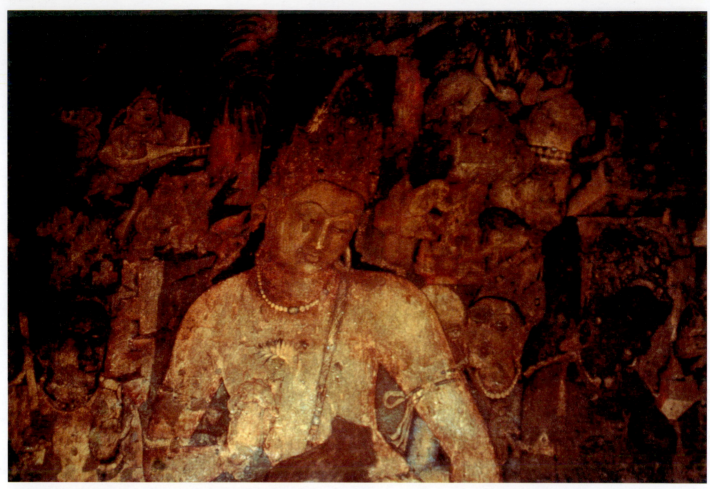

16-16

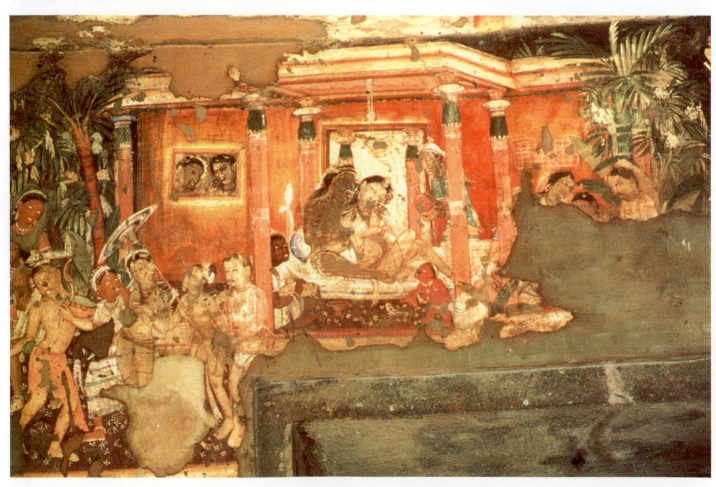

16-17

16-16. *Seated Bodhisattva,* detail of a wall painting, Cave 1, Ajanta, India. c. A.D. 600

16-17. *Palace Scene,* detail of a wall painting, porch of Cave 17, Ajanta. c. A.D. 500

A *Seated Bodhisattva* (fig. 16–16; a potential buddha, who gives up buddhahood temporarily to guide others) shows the style at its most refined. The exquisite features—narrowed and prolonged eyes, delicately curving brows, long, straight nose, full yet unsmiling lips—correspond closely to those of the *Seated Buddha* from Gandhara but are of even more striking beauty, due to the characteristic flexibility of Gupta pictorial style. The porch to Cave 17 is decorated with delightful paintings. The luscious *Palace Scene* (fig. 16–17) illustrates a jataka tale in which a brown prince, seated on cushions in the projecting central bay of a columned portico, embraces a pale-skinned and coyly reluctant princess, her hand nonetheless over his leg, while further incidents take place, at right and left, before a park on whose flowering palm trees perch white cockatoos.

These magnificent works mark the beginning of the end of Buddhism in India. Hinduism, already its equal competitor in Gupta times, soon absorbed the loyalty of the Indian peoples but spread only to Cambodia. Buddhism, however, survived and expanded in Afghanistan, in Myanmar, in central and southeastern Asia, in China, and in the island civilizations of Sri Lanka and Japan. Stupas of varying shapes, and seated, standing, and recumbent (Paranirvana) Buddha images, deriving directly from Indian prototypes, appear throughout these regions, often of colossal size; the badly damaged standing Buddha at Bamiyan in Afghanistan is 175 feet high! So in Sri Lanka do murals of basically Indian style. But the most striking new developments of Buddhist art are those of Indonesia. The Great Stupa of Borobudur in central Java, finished in a few years about the year A.D. 800 (fig. 16–18), is the most extensive of the Indonesian monuments, 408 feet square and 105 feet high. Hemispherical in profile, it rises in six rectangular levels, each divided into five splayed sections adorned with more than ten miles of relief sculpture, and three superimposed circular platforms, adorned with seventy-two perforated stupas each containing a seated Buddha statue of great beauty, and culminating in a final stupa. The sculpture, accompanying the procession of the faithful as they ascended from level to level in corridors open to the sky, unfolds an entire Mahayana view of the universe, from the jataka tales of the Buddha's previous lives to his actual life and then through all the degrees of the celestial hierarchy. The extraordinary precision and delicacy of Indonesian sculpture continues into the thirteenth century, as can be seen in a beautiful detail from the statue of *Queen Dedes as Prajnaparamita* (goddess of transcendental wisdom; fig. 16–19), with eyelids, eyebrows, and lips indicated with double incised outlines.

16-18. Aerial view of the Great Stupa, Borobudur, Java. c. A.D. 800

16-19. *Queen Dedes as Prajnaparamita,* detail of an andesite statue from Chandi Singasari, Java. Early 13th century A.D. Rijksmuseum voor Volkerkunde, Leiden

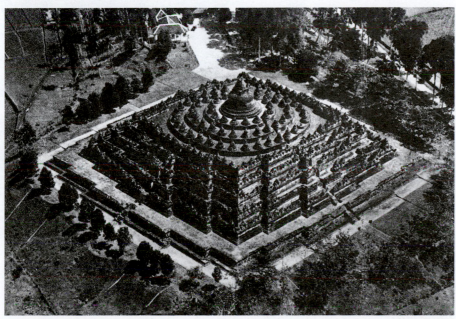

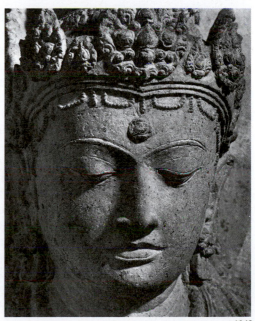

16-18

16-19

Hindu Art

Hinduism, Buddhism's triumphant competitor, still today one of the two largest religious groups on earth, is difficult to summarize because of its extreme complexity enhanced by time, geography, and intellectual level. There is no single sacred Hindu text, but the *Brahmanas* and *Upanishads* were inherited from Brahmanism, enriched by a great poem, the *Bhagavad-Gita,* and codified by the *Tantras,* prescriptions for propitiating various deities, and the *Puranas,* poems of praise to those deities who assumed human form. Essentially, Hinduism holds that Divine Being is One and that we can be united with it after the illusion of time and space have disappeared. But divinity is manifest chiefly in the persons of a trinity of gods: Brahma the Creator, Vishnu the Preserver, and Siva the Destroyer. Often, however, it is Siva who assumes all three functions. Brahma, remote and impersonal, is seldom separately worshiped or represented. Vishnu, who has a wife called Lakhsmi, has shown himself in nine different *avatars* (incarnations), the most popular of which is the great lover Krishna. Siva, the most universally revered of the three, rode a bull called Nandi (therefore no cows may be eaten) and is revered as the *lingam* (phallus), doubtless inherited from the Indus civilization but transfigured into a symbol of creativity. He, too, has a lovely wife, called Parvati, manifested also as Durga, goddess of virtue striving against evil, and as Kali, goddess of death, who wears necklaces of skulls and whose mouth drips blood. There are also nature deities persisting from Vedic religion, often identified also with Vishnu or with Siva, and a host of minor and local gods. Deities are propitiated by sacrifices—Kali gets bloody ones. They are considered to dwell in their images; therefore, these are reverently tended, decked with garlands of flowers, even oiled or buttered. Temples are their homes, not places for congregational worship but for individual or family prayer, solemnized by ashes applied to the forehead by a generally hereditary priest, sometimes surprisingly youthful. Images of the deities and the vast mythology surrounding them provide rich material for art. Pilgrims to sacred sites come from all over India, usually in large groups. To protect them and the regular worshipers as they come and go, and to house the holy men who meditate in the temple, an arcaded courtyard is essential. So is a tank—in large temples the size of a football field—for ritual ablutions. Burial is forbidden; the dead are burned on pyres of costly sandalwood and their ashes, when possible, strewn upon the river Ganges. Thus neither tombs nor shrines for the veneration of relics exist.

GUPTA AND POST-GUPTA ART   The Gupta period (A.D. 320–647) created not only the great Buddhist monuments we have seen but equally splendid works to celebrate Hindu worship. The larger Gupta temple buildings have all been extensively altered; those intact are small. It is best, therefore, to defer the discussion of the Hindu temple structure to later monuments at Khajuraho and Bhubaneswar. But the Guptas and their immediate contemporaries the Chalukyas were responsible for two masterpieces not only of Indian but of world sculpture. From Eran in central India, now a village but once an important Gupta center, comes the overpowering *Boar Avatar of Vishnu* (fig. 16–20), shown triumphantly lifting the helpless Bhu Devi (goddess of earth) from the dominion of the seas. The incident is often represented, usually as a relief sculpture in which the colossal god is attended by hosts of tiny deities. Here he is triumphant and virtually alone, his right hand on his hip, his left on his raised knee, as he strides from the water with the helpless Bhu Devi hanging onto one tusk, reminding modern eyes of a figure from a science-fiction film. Although the avatar has only the head of a boar, its swinish nature bloats the body and limbs, simplified into spherical and cylindrical shapes and contrasted with the loops of the necklace and the belt with a force and authority that twentieth-century abstract sculptors might well envy.

The ultimate mystical polarity of Hindu sculpture is represented by the *Siva*

16-20

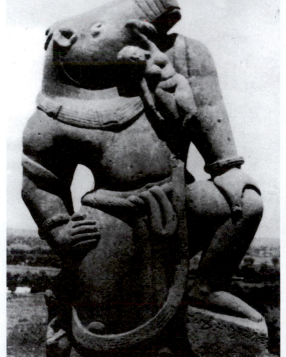

16-20. *Boar Avatar of Vishnu,* from Eran, India. Gupta period, late 5th century A.D. Sandstone, life size. University Museum, Sagar

16-21. *Siva Mahadeva (Siva the Great Lord).* 7th century A.D. Stone, height 10'10" (3.3 m). Elephanta, India

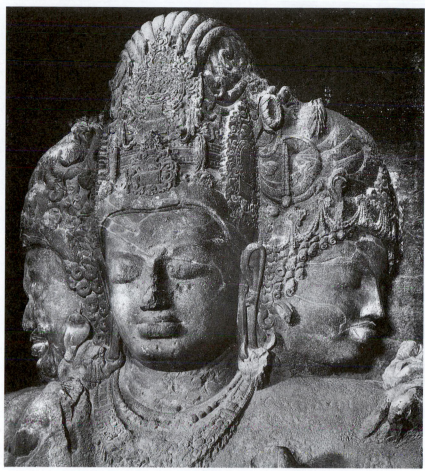

16-21

Mahadeva (Siva the Great Lord) on the island of Elephanta—so called because of an elephant sculpture that stands there—some seven miles out in Bombay harbor (fig. 16–21). One climbs a long stairway up most of a rocky hill and enters a temple originally carved from dark gray sandstone for a Buddhist shrine, but converted to Hindu use at a still-controversial date, probably the middle of the sixth century A.D. The larger *mandapa* (columned chamber) enshrines several large and splendid relief sculptures representing scenes from the Siva legend; all the sculptures, inevitably blurred by the seepage of water, were hideously damaged by a sixteenth-century Portuguese artillery captain who enjoyed hearing his shells burst inside the cave. To the left, off the axis of the mandapa, one moves from a sunlit courtyard into the dimness of the awesome presence. Dwarfing colossal images on either side, the bust of the triple aspect of Siva rises more than ten feet above its three-foot base—a complete figure on such a scale would stand thirty feet high. But the idea of a bust length is more compelling: the god seems to rise from the heart of the mountain, and, seeing the triple countenance closer than a full figure would allow, we are able to contemplate the contrasts within his godhead. On the left, facing east, he is the wrathful Aghora, holding a cobra, and crowned with intertwined snakes held together by the skull of Brahma's fifth head, which Siva cut off in fury and was condemned to wear in penance. In the center, facing north, he is Tatpurusha, serene and calm, broad-chested and tall-crowned, his right hand (now broken) lifted, his left holding a citron. On the right, facing west, he is Vamadeva, blissful and lovable, almost feminine (often Siva is represented as half male, half female), with full lips, heavy earrings, and headdress draped with pearls. In all three aspects, his eyes are downcast, almost closed, as if the triune apparition from another realm were rapt in his own divinity, unconscious of our existence. The

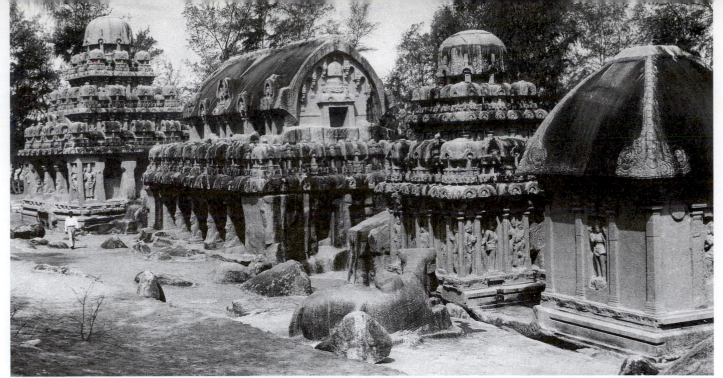

16-22

sculptors of this majestic work may well have been trained on Gupta monuments, whose broad, noble style they continued, and the shop may conceivably have flourished for generations, to work at Ellora (see pages 512–13).

MAHABALIPURAM   South of Madras, on the palm-fringed strand of the sparkling Indian Ocean, lies one of India's most alluring sites, Mahabalipuram (also transliterated as Mahamallapuram and Mamallapuram), filled with wonderful monuments of the Pallava dynasty, which from about A.D. 500 to about 750 controlled a large region in what is today the state of Tamil Nadu, inhabited largely by Dravidians. Only a modest village remains of what was once a flourishing port. The magnificent seventh-century monuments are all carved from outcroppings of granite that rise through the white sands. The five *rathas* (freestanding rock-cut shrines), of which four are shown (fig. 16–22), are in part models of earlier wooden constructions. At the right is a square shrine of Durga, whose image appears in the niches articulated with pilasters and roofed with a direct imitation of thatch. Next comes the ratha of the warrior-king Arjuna, still imitating post-and-lintel construction in the lower block, but continuing in the characteristic sharply stepped, two-story *sikhara,* or pyramidal tower—to reach for the stars in later south Indian temple architecture (see fig. 16–33)—of such huge mass and weight that the tiny colonnettes could never have supported it, culminating in an octagonal cupola. Arjuna's shrine is ornamented, as throughout the history of Dravidian architecture, with chaitya roofs and chaitya arches (the chaitya was initially used by Hindus as well as Buddhists), so as to look like an entire city in the illusionistic manner of the Bhaja façade (see fig. 16–6). The third, the Bhima Ratha, is an obvious chaitya, between whose by-now-residual square piers one can enter with ease. The fourth, or Dharmaraja Ratha, is crowned with a three-story sikhara and cupola, supported on a peristyle of square piers, unfinished like much of the work at Mahabalipuram, through which one enters the dark interior.

A number of mandapas carved from the cliff contain sculpture of the highest quality, including reliefs gently illuminated from the side by the light from the wide, columned entrances. Among the finest of these is a relatively early appearance of a scene repeated in Indian art to this day, *Durga Slaying the Bull Demon* (fig. 16–23). Provided with eight arms for the purpose, the mighty goddess brandishes a mace, a dagger, and a sword, and draws her bow as she charges forward on her lion. She is accompanied by dwarf-warriors, who not only wield weapons and shields but

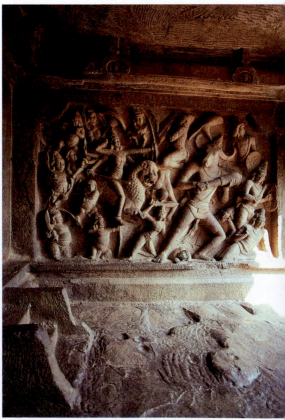

16-23

510

manage to carry a parasol over Durga in the midst of battle. Also shaded by a parasol, the bull-demon Mahisha, his club now powerless, rushes off in the midst of his collapsing henchmen. The powerful diagonals create a composition of immense energy, uncluttered by detail. In fact, the surface of the granite is left unpolished as throughout the work at this site, possibly intended to be stuccoed and painted.

The greatest of all the carvings at Mahabalipuram, certainly one of the greatest sculptures of all time, is the colossal *Descent of the Ganges* (fig. 16–24), which also enjoys the distinction of being the largest single scene ever carved in relief. Approximately 29 feet high by 89 feet long, it covers the face of a granite cliff (often misidentified as boulders) split acentrally by a natural crevice, at the top of which may be seen the masonry of a recently and badly built dam. The relief is also believed to represent the penance of Arjuna, a monarch celebrated in Indian epic poetry, identified as the ascetic seated in a penitential pose before the shrine of Siva, just to the left of the crevice. More probably the relief depicts the descent of the heavenly river Ganges to earth as a reward for the piety of the saintly king Bhahagiratha, and indeed a crowned figure can be seen, his hands raised, looking upward in the lowest row just next to the cleft. Due to its size and to its innumerable figures, a satisfactory illustration of the relief is hard to obtain; the present angled view brings out the force of the individual figures and groups. Serpent deities can just be made out in the cleft. Apparently a cistern at the top, part of a now-destroyed royal residence, provided a flow of real water to illustrate the myth, suggesting the great fountains of seventeenth- and eighteenth-century Europe.

The face of the cliff is filled with humans and animals arranged in four superimposed levels, but avoiding the straight rows one might have expected in order to convey the idea that they are crowding to the miracle through a mountainous landscape. Nevertheless, each figure is complete, and there are no overlappings. All are created with an astonishing mastery of anatomy and of movement but, in

16-24. *Descent of the Ganges,* relief cut in a cliff, Mahabalipuram. 7th century A.D. Height approx. 29′ (8.84 m)

16-24

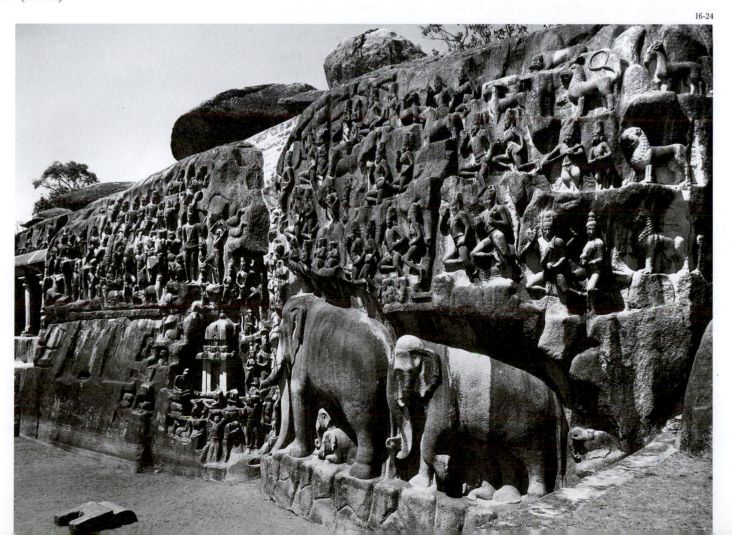

keeping with the monumentality of the work and with the character of the granite, surfaces are kept broad and detail is held to a minimum. The scale is unexpected; while the humans and most animals are represented slightly under life size, the wonderful elephants are possibly larger than life. The typical Asiatic bull elephant today attains a height of about 9 feet; the majestic creature at the river's brink stands about 11 feet 6 inches tall. Much has been said about the affectionate naturalism of the animals, especially the deer and the baby elephants, but the lions are traditional and ornamentalized, while the curly-maned, ring-tailed creature near the upper right is surely legendary. The combination of surface restraint, even severity, with flexibility of movement renders this work unique in monumental sculpture anywhere. Unfortunately, the lower left quarter of the relief was interrupted in mid-career; only an animal and four heads emerge from the roughed-out mass of granite, suggesting that one sculptor executed the human heads and the animals, another the human bodies.

Later Hindu Art

The breakup of the Gupta Empire opened the field for a fluctuating number of local dynasties, under whose rule Hindu monumental art flourished until well into the eighteenth century. Eventually, the Muslims made a clean sweep of temples in most major cities under their domination, but literally thousands of richly sculptured monuments of later Hindu art remain, chiefly along the east and southeast coasts. Most of this inestimable treasure is in surprisingly good condition today, even when neglected and abandoned. The larger, later temples still in use have all too often been recently stuccoed and painted in garish colors, probably to replace original stucco and polychromy now lost.

ELLORA   In territory devastated by the Moguls the few remaining Hindu monuments are the rock-cut temples of pure Dravidian (south Indian) style, which compete with Buddhist temples, at Ellora in the Deccan plateau of west-central India. The Kailasanatha Temple (fig. 16–25) at Ellora, begun in the late eighth century A.D. under the Rashtrakutan dynasty, in the reign of King Krishna I (ruled A.D. 756–73), is the largest and most richly sculptured rock-cut temple anywhere in the world. Quarried and carved from the surface downward, the central shrine, dedicated to Siva, stands 96 feet high, in a man-made courtyard extending 276 by 154 feet. The manual labor of removing so many thousands of tons of rock compares with that expended on the pyramids of Egypt. Seen silhouetted against the cliff in the illustration, the shape of the sikhara is related to those of the masonry temples constructed in southern India after the rock-cut temples of Mahabalipuram. In spite of its apparent complexity, giving the impression of a gigantic, quivering mass of soft material permeated by waves of energy, the composition of the temple can be clearly analyzed. For, as at Mahabalipuram, the vertical shaft is composed of a base—here quite lofty and enriched by sculptured friezes— separated by cornices from a principal story organized in terms of niches containing statues, alternating with openings either into the mandapa or into the ambulatory surrounding the sanctuary. Above these levels rise the four superimposed tiers of the pyramidal sikhara, separated by double and triple cornices and ornamented with the familiar chaitya arches, imitated from masonry architecture, itself derived from rock-cut temples, and eventually, as we have seen, from wood—a significant illustration of the interchangeability of traditional forms between the three methods of temple construction. In the foreground of the illustration rises one of two rock-cut square columns, a special feature of the Kailasanatha Temple, each 60 feet high. A magnificent rock-cut elephant, one of many at the site, stands at the lower left facing the temple dedicated to Nandi, Siva's bull. The man-made cliffs, towering 120 feet above the floor of the courtyard, cast the temple into shadow in early morning and late afternoon. But at midday—in contrast with the mysterious

16-25. Kailasanatha Temple, Ellora, India. c. A.D. 760–800, with later additions

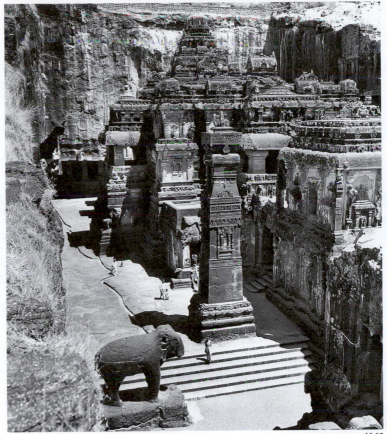

16-25

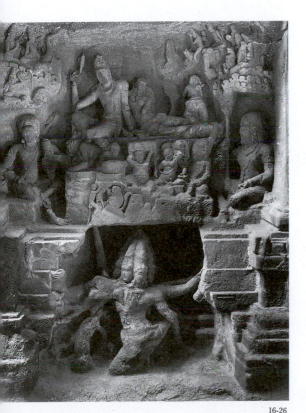

16-26

16-26. *Siva and Parvati on Mount Kailasa*, rock-cut sculpture, Kailasanatha Temple, Ellora. c. A.D. 750–800. Height approx. 12′ (3.65 m).

dimness of the adjacent Buddhist chaitya halls—the strong Indian sunlight, with its consequent dark shadows and reflected lights, throws the sculptured statues, ornament, and reliefs illustrating scenes from Hindu mythology and fighting animals into intense projection against the raw stone of the excavation. Like many works of Indian sculpture, the reliefs and statues may have been stuccoed and painted. As in certain other Indian temples, here and there patches of stucco still remain, and the Muslim conquerors of the sixteenth century referred to the temple as the "painted palace."

On a par with the sculptures at Mahabalipuram is the magnificent *Siva and Parvati on Mount Kailasa* (fig. 16–26), partly in relief but with the principal figures—life-size—in the round. The four-headed demon Ravana, who was incarcerated under Mount Kailasa (after which the temple is named), tried to shake the mountain and destroy Siva's power; restoring mentally his many now-damaged arms, we can see the crouching Ravana grasping the cliffs in murderous rage. On the summit of the mountain, between seated deities and celestial figures on parting clouds, the slender Siva, next to his recumbent wife Parvati, needs merely to advance the toe of his left foot (the lower leg is broken) to crush the demon and save our planet. In the thunderclap action of the scene even the cliffs of the surrounding courtyard play a role, situating the observer in the heart of the threatened mountain.

ORISSA   In the state of Orissa, on the low-lying northeast coast of India south of Bengal, under a succession of short-lived dynasties rose a splendid series of Hindu temples, including the major pilgrimage site of Puri, dating from the eighth through the thirteenth centuries A.D. The characteristic Orissan temple form, established as early as the eighth century, bears little relation to the Dravidian type and relegates motifs derived from wooden architecture to the realm of tiny ornamental themes, infinitely repeated like musical subjects, so as to cover the entire temple structure. As in all masonry Hindu temples, the entire structure is as solid as if carved from stone, save for the interiors of mandapa and image chamber, which are both

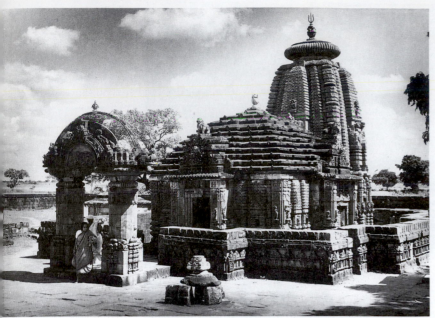
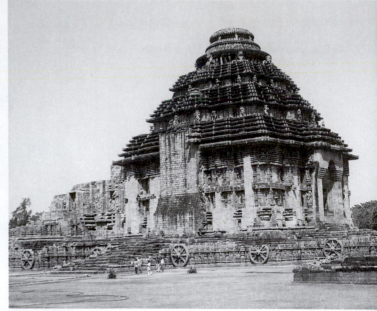

16-27   16-28

covered with continuous stone slabs from wall to wall, and small, unlit chambers above. All accents in the mandapa are horizontal. The sikhara rises from the surrounding terrace in eight verticals like the ribs of a partly closed umbrella, flat on the sides, rounded at the corners, joined by a huge capstone in the shape of a flattened bell, culminating in a small knob and a symbolic metal ornament. These verticals are corded horizontally for their entire distance with bands of ornament. Carved from chlorite, a warm, brown stone with purplish overtones, Orissan temples blend form and color in a rich texture totally unlike the strong contrasts of the south.

The small city of Bhubaneswar and its surroundings contain some of the finest of these monuments; indeed, the Muktesvara Temple (fig. 16–27), situated among companion temples beside its own tank in a lovely mango grove, is often character-ized as the jewel of Orissan architecture. One enters through a low torana onto a low-walled terrace, from whose slabs rise the mandapa and the sikhara. The glory of the Muktesvara Temple is its carving, which covers every inch of the surface, torana, parapet and all, as with a marvelous embroidery; chlorite is susceptible to extreme detail, and the deep undercutting creates continuous threads of ornament, shimmering in sun and shade, within which one enjoys humans, animals, birds, flowers, all in refreshingly miniature scale.

At the opposite extreme of Orissan style, but just as elaborate in detail, is the colossal ruin of the temple at Konarak, on the coast of the Bay of Bengal south of Bhubaneswar. Built in the mid-thirteenth century A.D. by King Narasimhadeva I in honor of Surya, the sun-god, with whom the king seems to have identified himself, the temple represents the climax of Orissan style (fig. 16–28). Subject to salt air and actual inundations, the sikhara, once more than two hundred feet high and a landmark to seafarers, long ago collapsed, but the mandapa was rescued from destruction early in the twentieth century by the crude expedient of filling it in with rubble and masonry. Surrounded by an immense walled enclosure, it still stands on its high stone terrace representing the chariot of the sun-god, supplied with stone wheels some twelve feet in diameter and drawn by six stone horses of ordinary size (not visible in the illustration). In spite of all the damage, the Sun Temple, now under more accurate restoration, contains some of the finest sculpture of the Orissan school, much of it of astonishing erotic frankness, possibly reflecting the doctrines of Tantrism (see below). The wheels, carved with foliate ornament of extreme delicacy, roll above a frieze of tiny elephants—every one different—stomping, prancing, trumpeting, as often in central and northern Indian temples. Above are two tiers of joyfully embracing nude couples.

16-27. Muktesvara Temple, Bhubaneswar, India. C. A.D. 950

16-28. Sun Temple (Surya Deul) Konarak, India. C. A.D. 1240

16-30. Kandarya Mahadeva Temple, Khajuraho. C. A.D. 1000

514

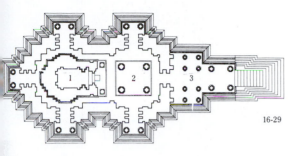

16-29

16-29. Plan of the Kandarya Mahadeva Temple, Khajuraho, India 1. Sanctuary 2. Closed mandapa 3. Open mandapa

KHAJURAHO A long-lived local dynasty, the Chandellas, who ruled a region where the Deccan plateau meets the valley of the Ganges in north-central India between the seventh and the early fourteenth centuries A.D., established their capital at Khajuraho, today a tiny village amid forest and farmland, difficult of access save by air. Legend has it that they built eighty-five temples there; twenty-two survive, mostly in excellent condition, rendering this the most spectacular of all temple sites in India. The Hindu Chandellas were known for their religious tolerance, extending not only to Jain but to the worship of the Vedic sun-god and to Tantrism, a cult that exalted the sexual relationship as a means of approach to Siva. The resultant relief sculpture, explicit in detail, has played its part in making little Khajuraho one of the major tourist sites in India.

The most splendid of the thirteen soaring temples of the central group, scattered across what is today a broad lawn, and indeed one of the most beautifully devel-

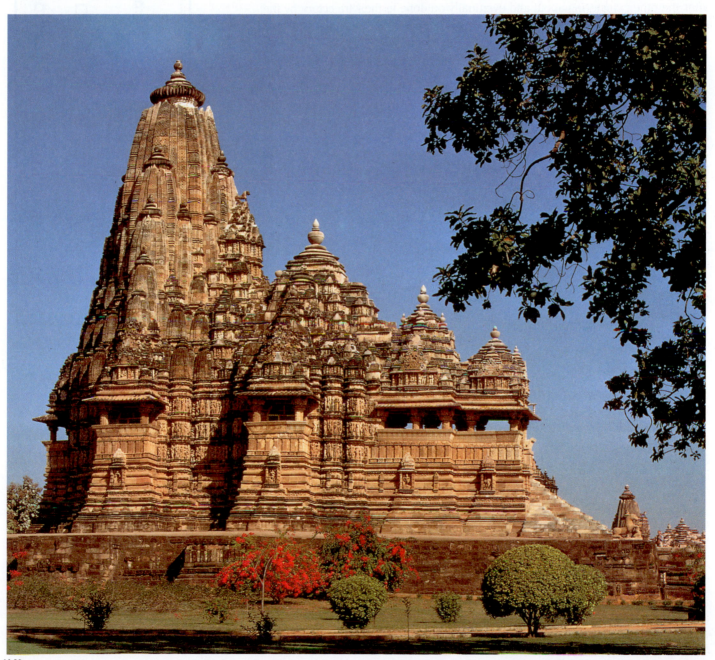

16-30

oped temples in India, is the Kandarya Mahadeva Temple, built about the year 1000 A.D. (figs. 16–29, 16–30). The impression of competing fountains of stone, each of different height and apparent speed, veils the rationality of the plan. The temple stands on a high ashlar masonry platform, from which a steep flight of steps ascending a lofty carved base gives access to a first, open, mandapa, in reality a cluster of porches. From this one enters the second, enclosed, mandapa, and thence the sanctuary, containing a chamber for the statue of Siva, surrounded by an ambulatory lighted by porches. The sanctuary and the closed mandapa are in plan a doubled cross, with staggered buttresses lining the reentrant angles, reflecting the influence of the Orissan temple type, but more freely organized.

On the exterior, the infinitely multiplied horizontal moldings and three superimposed bands of moldings of the base supporting the porches act like a taut bowstring, from which are launched the astonishing array of leaping verticals. Two of these are grouped in each reentrant angle of the closed mandapa, to which they are tied by moldings and reliefs. Those around the sanctuary are shot upward, one after the other, clustering about and eventually outdone in their trajectory by the final burst of the central sikhara, crowned as in Orissa by a gigantic capstone ending in a finial. As compared with the clarity of Orissan architectural compositions, the host of finials crowning the buttresses create an effect of bewildering richness and splendor.

Despite their vivid narrative quality, the reliefs do not reach the heights of earlier Indian sculpture; neither does the perfunctory incised ornament. But many individual figures do show a new and startling understanding of contrapposto, especially the *Celestial Beauty* in a corner position on the Parsvanatha Temple (fig. 16–31). With a combination of seductive languor and athletic prowess, the figure moves forward on her right foot while twisting in the other direction. Stylized and flattened both in form and in detail, she nonetheless shows the sculptor's astonishing ability in the realm of figural movement, twists, and turns.

16-32. Plan of the Brihadesvara Temple
1. Shrine and sanctuary   2. Mandapa
3. Shrine of Nandi   4. Gopura

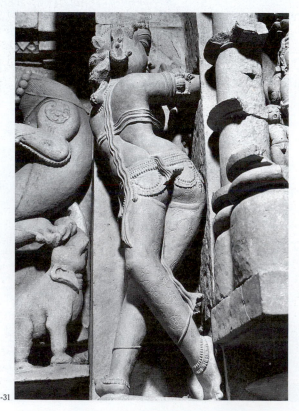

16-31. *Celestial Beauty*, relief, Parsvanatha Temple, Khajuraho. C. A.D. 1000. Stone, height approx. 48″ (1.22 m)

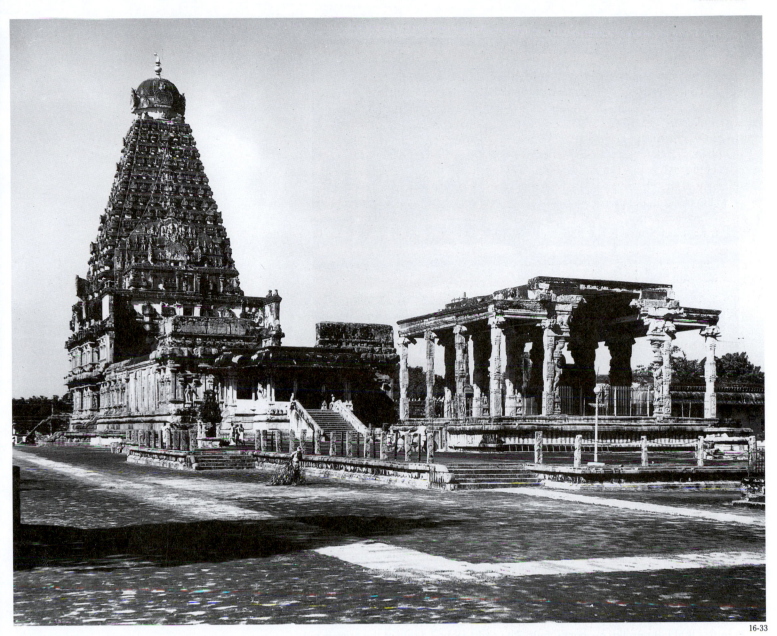

16-33

16-33. Brihadesvara Temple, Thanjavur
(Tanjore), India. c. A.D. 1000

THANJAVUR   We return to Tamil Nadu in the south, during the long and prosperous reign of the Chola dynasty (c. A.D. 850–c. 1310), for one of the most
breathtaking experiences in Asian architecture, the mighty Brihadesvara Temple,
dedicated to Siva in his fearsome aspect (figs. 16–32, 16–33), built in an astonishingly brief period by Rajaraja I (his name means "king of kings"), and consecrated
in 1009–10. The dimensions are daunting. The outer precinct measures 877 by
455 feet. This and the inner courtyard are entered through two aligned towers of
the *gopura* (monumental pyramidal gateway), characteristic of all Dravidian
temples from this time on. Unlike most large temple complexes, the courtyard
contains few later structures, and even these are so placed as not to disturb the
grand harmony of form and space.

   The principal shrine, situated at the exact center of the inner half of the courtyard, rises to a height of about 216 feet. We approach the temple, past the shrine of
Nandi—whose image is so impregnated with oil that he looks like bronze—by
means of steps rising to a colonnaded porch, and then enter the mandapa, a hall of
thirty-six columns, lighted only from the entrance. Beyond the mandapa lies the

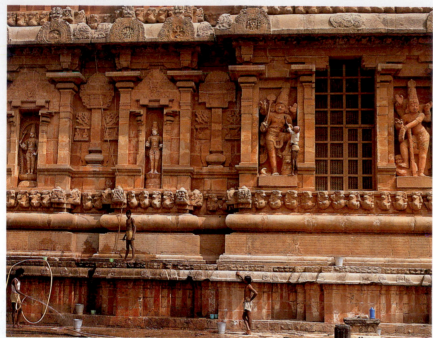

16-34. Exterior wall of the sanctuary, Brihadesvara Temple, Thanjavur (Tanjore)

16-34

two-storied square shrine, consisting of an ambulatory surrounding a sanctuary housing a colossal lingam. The outer height of the sanctuary is one half its width—that of the entire shrine eight times its width; the human body was considered to be eight palms tall. The architectural and sculptural elements of the temple are from standard Chola repertory (proportions vary widely from site to site). Each of the three outer faces of the Brihadesvara Temple is articulated by twelve niches—six on each story—with a window opening in the center of each story to light the ambulatory, a total of thirty-six niches. Each contains a statue, representing Siva in various aspects, or other Hindu deities (fig. 16–34). The rationality of the design is matched by the breadth and dignity of the pilasters and blank walls and the monumentality of the sculptured bodies and their poses, as compared with the flexibility of the usual Indian figure sculpture. The thirteen stories of the steep, hollow sikhara are ornamented with bulbous, four-ribbed domes alternating with chaityas in side view and punctuated at key points with arrangements of clouds and divinities that fan out like peacocks' tails. The eight-ribbed dome at the apex is cut from a single piece of stone, weighing approximately twenty tons, surmounted by a copper finial plated with gold. The engineering problems involved were immense; probably a two-mile ramp of earth was required to raise it.

The temple base is covered with inscriptions recording ceremonies and gifts, including many metal statues cast by the lost-wax process (see page 49). Although of unknown provenance, a magnificent bronze statue of *Nataraja (Siva as Lord of the Dance)* in the collection of the Cleveland Museum of Art (fig. 16–35) closely resembles in its breadth of form and austere smoothness of surface the stone statues at Thanjavur. This aspect of the great god, repeated countless times in Hindu art, shows the heavens and their fires as reflections of his harmoniously moving body.

By the thirteenth century the great creative period of Hindu art was over. Temples continued to be built and decorated on a vast scale, but the same symbolic and figural motifs were infinitely repeated, with increasing stiffness, in spite of imaginative variations in plan, including star shapes and, eventually, endless dim "halls of a thousand pillars." These later temple complexes were dramatized by the addition of soaring gopuras, sometimes reaching the height of a modern eighteen-story office building and seen for miles over cities and plains. They are pyramidal

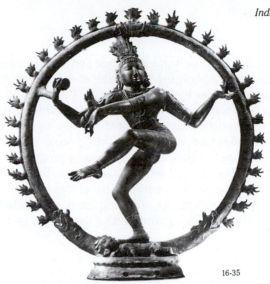

16-35. *Nataraja (Siva as Lord of the Dance).* 11th century A.D. Copper, height 43⅞″ (1.11 m). Cleveland Museum of Art

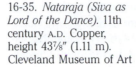

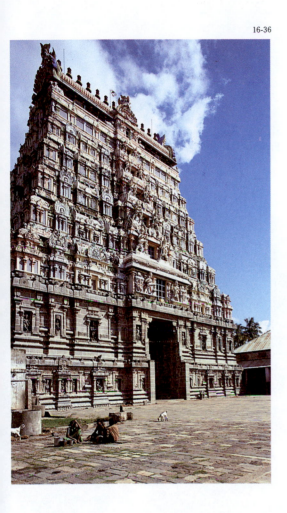

16-36. Inner façade, east gopura, Nataraja Temple, Cidambaram, India. c. A.D. 1200

like the sikharas, but oblong in plan and concave in profile. Although entirely accidental, the similarity to the Mayan temple complexes with their towering stepped pyramids (see fig. 5–6) is striking, especially in effect from a distance. Differences, however, are essential, especially the fact that neither gopuras nor sikharas are provided with exterior flights of steps. An early and dramatic example is the gopura of the Nataraja Temple at Cidambaram in Tamil Nadu (fig. 16–36), of about 1200. All the motifs used at Thanjavur can be seen here, but like most gopuras this one is topped by a chaitya running the entire width of the upper story and crowned with a line of urns.

The later history of Indian art is dominated by the tastes and desires of the Muslim conquerors and belongs to the sphere of Islamic culture (see Chapter Eleven).

CAMBODIA   During the Gupta period the influence of Hindu art passed to Thailand and especially to Cambodia, where an art of great originality and beauty developed. Two concepts determined the layout and appearance of the Cambodian

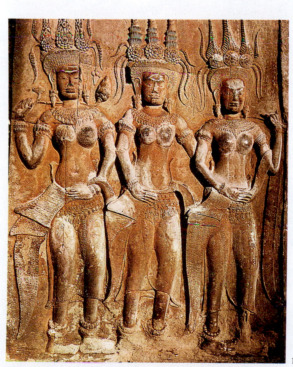

16-37. *Apsaras* or *Celestial Dancers,* relief sculptures, Temple of Angkor Wat. First half of 12th century A.D. Sandstone

temple complex—the world-mountain and the god-king. The earliest temples were built on hills symbolizing the world at the center of Hindu cosmogony; later, towering structures took over this duty. The Khmer (Cambodian) monarchs, assuming both political and religious power, deified themselves during their lifetimes. While Cambodian temples adopted the stepped towers of India, they moved in their own direction, assuming fantastic scale in the temples surrounding the vanished Khmer capital at Angkor, today a jungle. The most extensive of these is Angkor Wat (fig. 16–38), dedicated to Vishnu. Built by King Suryavarman II in the first half of the twelfth century A.D., at the peak of the rapid development of Cambodian temple design, the complex is approached by a bridge over a wide moat. The long galleries surrounding the temple grounds are entered through a

16-38. Aerial view of Angkor Wat, Cambodia. First half of 12th century A.D.

16-38

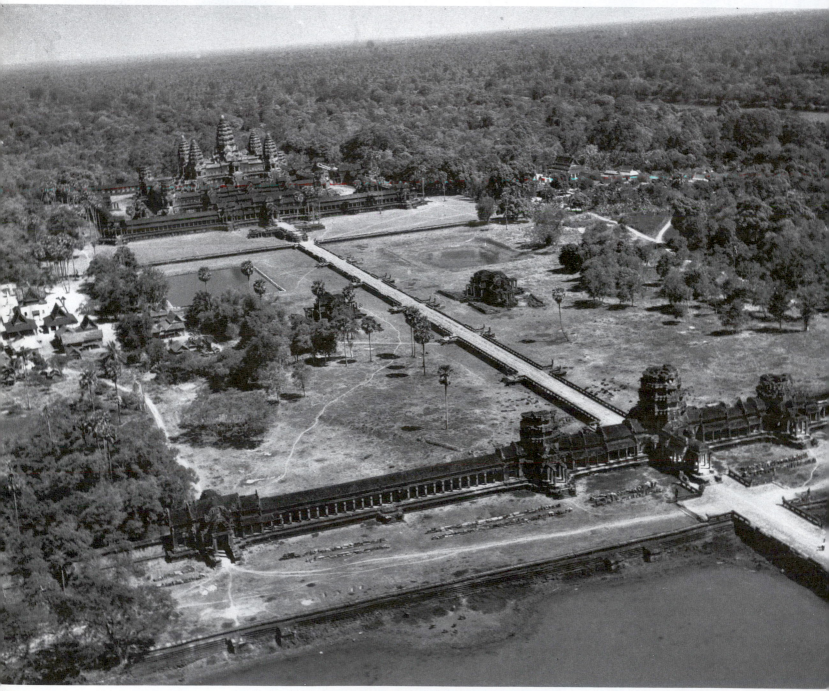

16-39. Bayon, Angkor Thom, Cambodia (detail of the central towers). Late 12th century–early 13th century A.D.

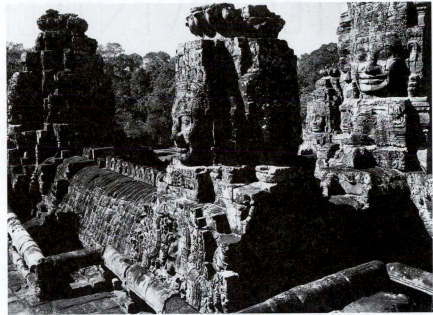

16-39

triple-towered gateway, recalling the function of the Indian gopura. A causeway punctuated by shrines continues to the temple proper, itself surrounded by galleries. The world-mountain of the central pyramid rises to a final platform, towered at each corner, and a central tower, all stepped in the Indian manner. The entire structure is enriched by low reliefs, sharply different in basic principle from their Indian counterparts in that all surrounding stone is cut away from the carved blocks, so that their background is flush with the masonry of the building, against which the figures float freely. A relief carving of *Apsaras* (fig. 16–37) shows at once the fluidity of Cambodian composition and the rigidity of the frontal figures, striking after the flexibility of Indian deities.

The most surprising of the Cambodian monuments is the Bayon at Angkor Thom (fig. 16–39), built by King Jayavarman II in the late twelfth or early thirteenth century. Although a Buddhist shrine, dedicated to the deity Lokesvara, with whom the king identified himself, the Bayon belongs to the Hindu architectural tradition, and many Hindu subjects are represented in the sculpture. The five towers of the central world-mountain, connected by stone chaitya roofs common to both religions, are carved on all four sides into colossal smiling faces of Lokesvara, actually symbolic portraits of the king, looking out serenely to all four points of the compass over his domain.

The tradition of Indian and Southeast Asian artistic culture, spanning four millennia, is one of the richest in human history. Architecture, sculpture, and painting (although little is left before Mogul times—see Chapter Eleven) rank with the very greatest. India, with mixed effect upon its population and disaster to its creative tradition, was subject to progressive European colonization as early as the sixteenth century. It is surprising, therefore, that Indian influence upon Western art has been almost negligible compared with that of China and Japan. At first Europeans even confused the radically different cultures of East Asia and South Asia, even supplying "Indian" stage spectacles with scenery based on Chinese architecture. Indian sculpture, some of it excavated, some torn from its architectural settings, found its way into European collections, but even today an effort is necessary to appreciate the opulence of the Indian conception of the human body. And only when we realize that the apparent jungle of Indian temple architecture is based on a rational system of proportion and of repeated religious symbols can we begin to understand its beauties.

CHAPTER SEVENTEEN

The vast area of modern China supports one-quarter of the human race. Today approximately the size of the United States, the lands under Chinese rule at times expanded to include much of Central Asia. Under such circumstances the traditional Chinese term for their country—the Middle Kingdom—is justifiable. Although it is not yet conclusively proven, recorded Chinese culture probably began with the legendary Xia dynasty (traditionally 2205–1766 B.C.), slightly later than the Indus Valley civilization. But in contrast to that of India, Chinese history continued without any substantial break. Ethnically and linguistically, Chinese civilization is also more consistent than that of the Indian subcontinent. Often at war with each other, Chinese ethnic groups are nevertheless closely related; the Sino-Tibetan language group extends from Southeast Asia to remote Tibet. Although the various spoken dialects of Chinese are so sharply different from each other as to be mutually incomprehensible, written Chinese is everywhere legible. There is no alphabet, rather thousands of separate characters, often ideographic in origin, each standing for a word. Through their descendants in modern Chinese, the oldest inscriptions found can be accurately deciphered.

Ancient Chinese religion was animistic, with a component of shamanism (cult of the priest-healer) and a strong component of ancestor worship, but was gradually dominated by the teachings of Confucius (the latinized form of the name of Kong Fu Zi; c. 551–479 B.C.) who—like the Buddha—concerned himself not at all with divinity. However, he did not renounce the material world; his firm ethical system of family and societal relationships, founded on a principle called *li* (ritual, decorum, propriety), was devised for the purpose of governing human life on earth, which he regarded as eventually perfectible, from the peasant to the emperor. *Li* was energized by a quality called *jen,* often translated as "sympathy"; these and other Confucian principles were recorded in the *Analects.* Many found Confucianism not only emotionally unappealing but in essence conservative, in its support of the status quo. They turned in large numbers to mystical Daoism, embodied in the *Dao de jing* (Book of the Way), whose probably mythical author, Lao Zi, was believed to have been born in 604 B.C., thus an older contemporary of Confucius. Daoism taught that the *Dao* ("Way") was at the heart of the universe, activating natural phenomena. The Daoist must live in inner harmony with the Way, attainable through contemplation. Mahayana Buddhism got an early but slow start in China; its ascendancy over native religions, which continued to be believed in and practiced, was imposed under the Tatar Northern Wei dynasty in the fourth century A.D.

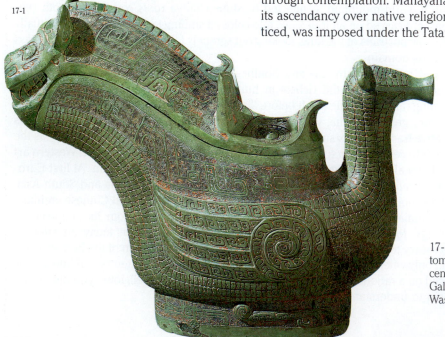

17-1

17-1. Ceremonial vessel (*guang*), from a royal tomb at Anyang, Henan. Shang dynasty, 12th century B.C. Bronze, length 12¼″ (31 cm). Freer Gallery of Art, Smithsonian Institution, Washington, D.C.

CHINESE ART

Eventually it achieved a sort of fusion with indigenous Daoism in the mystical Chan Buddhist movement (called Zen in Japan), which arose as early as the ninth century but reached its height in the twelfth and thirteenth.

As we have seen, Indian creativity is founded on the pleasure of physical existence including sensuality, expressed in sculpture, painting, and basically anthropomorphic architecture. In Chinese art the nude human body appears only in those rare instances when illustration demands it, and it is never found to be beautiful. Confucian ethics require representations of clothed humans in their relation to each other, including superb portraits at a very early date. Daoist

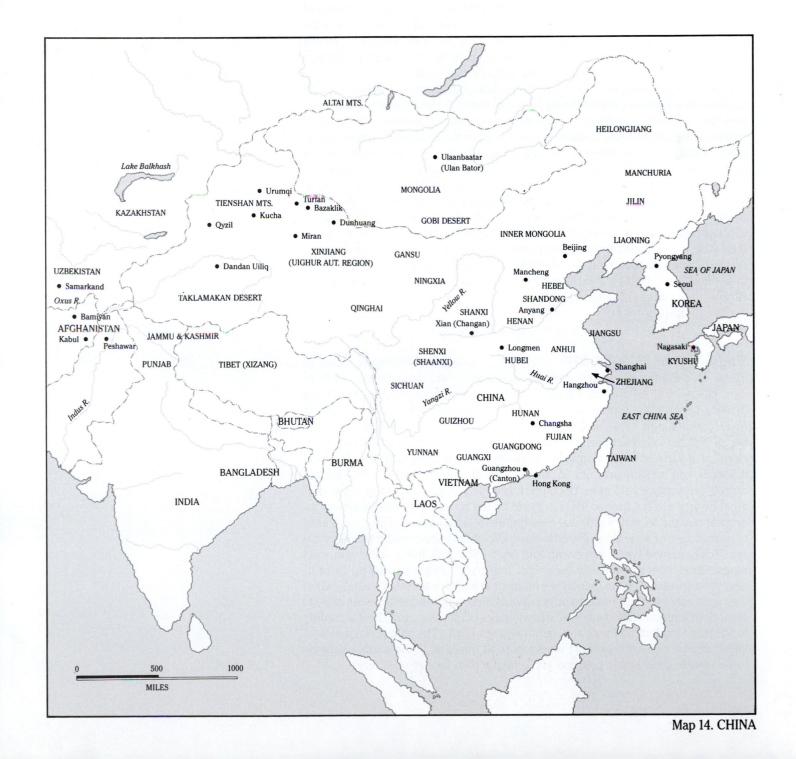

Map 14. CHINA

mysticism inspires rapt contemplation of the natural world, thus fostering one of the greatest landscape arts of all time. Chinese landscape painting differs from that of the West chiefly in its lack of focus on human vision and anthropocentric space; it is concerned rather with the endlessness of nature. For all Chinese painting, therefore, the Western—and Indian—necessity of an enclosing frame is a contradiction in terms.

Except for fortifications and a few surviving masonry structures, Chinese buildings are essentially roofs to provide cover from the weather, upheld by posts, the distance between which is governed by the length of available logs for beams. Walls have no structural function, and windows are essentially open spaces in walls, without enframing purpose. Wooden architecture rarely withstands the passage of centuries. Successive invasions destroyed all ancient Chinese wooden buildings, which can be reconstructed mentally only by study of their imitations in Japanese architecture, reverently preserved and renewed piece by rotted piece, or of their representations in painting. Most Chinese cities, therefore, are agglomerations of modest and relatively recent houses, with little architectural interest beyond the occasional majestic gateway or tower. After our discussion of ancient China, we will be chiefly concerned with the sublime art of painting, in which the Chinese achieved previously unimaginable poetic and spiritual depth.

Despite tragic losses, the art of China presents an extraordinary historic unity. All the basic elements are present almost from the start of the long tradition, which was developed, enriched, explored in every implication, and at last endlessly copied. If India may be said to have attained its spiritual goals through concentration on the physical body and inner life of the human being projected into the Infinite, those of China were reached through contemplation of Infinity in nature. Not in the whole of Western art before the Renaissance did artists pay anything like the Chinese attention to nature; rarely were they so deeply in tune with nature; never were they wholly submerged in nature. Westerners, indeed, whether within or outside the Chinese tradition, have no way of establishing a comparable harmony with nature; their view is inevitably objective and personal rather than symbolic. For this very reason, Chinese influence on the West has been largely literary and critical rather than directly artistic. The great Chinese achievements, however, are accessible to all who are willing to contemplate them.

Ancient Chinese Art

SHANG DYNASTY (1766–1045 B.C.) The earliest archaeological finds in China—handsome pottery and small jade sculptures—are characteristic of a Neolithic culture. But the first art of great importance was produced during the Shang dynasty, apparently Chinese in origin. The finest works are the bronzes found in royal tombs datable between 1300 and 1045 B.C. at Anyang in northeast China, the site of Yin, the last Shang capital. The contents of these sepulchers include skeletons of horses and of decapitated humans, slain to propitiate the deceased monarch and accompany him in another world. Among the splendid bronze objects are ornamented axes, doubtless used for beheading. Less grisly, and of great beauty, are the bronze vessels, made by the means of piece molds over an original clay model with a skill that presupposes a long tradition. These were used to contain food or wine to be offered to the spirits of the ancestors and are of several specifically named types, some with four legs, some with three, some with solid bases. Many were scientifically excavated, but many more were dug up by profiteers and appeared on the market at a moment in the early twentieth century when they were especially appreciated on account of their supposed affinity with aspects of modern sculpture. (Nowadays all excavations in China are carried out according to advanced modern methods and rigorously controlled.) The blue-green patina so highly prized today is a product of exposure to minerals in the earth; originally these vessels were highly polished and either golden bronze or silvery.

A majestic example of the *guang* type (fig. 17–1) is provided with a large lid ending in a grinning tiger face, with an owl mask at the right (one eye and the beak can be seen in profile). The vessel itself is a plump bird (a duck?) with a handsome folded wing; the head and neck become a handle, used for pouring, while the tail flares upward to form the throat of the tiger. On the base can be seen a stylized dragon. These four beasts blend with cheerful ferocity into a shape of astonishing compression and simple beauty. The major forms vibrate with the surface ornamentation typical of Shang and Zhou bronzes, probably derived from wood carving, and executed with almost microscopic precision. The motifs are traditional, in this case a squared spiral—the "thunder pattern"—infinitely repeated but never identical, in two different projections. Sharply raised elements continue along the bird's wing-feathers to form a large spiral over the shoulder, while a second, much smaller, incised pattern covers almost everything else. Constantly changing, the primary pattern at times clusters in shapes misnamed the *tao tie* ("ogre mask") and probably of religious significance; these grinning faces have often been compared to the masks common in Northwest Coast American Indian wood carving (see fig. 2–16) but no connection can be established.

ZHOU DYNASTY (1045–256 B.C.)

According to an inscription on a bronze vessel, the Shang kingdom was defeated by the Zhou invaders from western China on the morning of January 15, 1045 B.C. The new rulers seem to have phased out Shang animism and to have adopted and reinforced ancestor worship, eventually incorporating it in a basically Confucian system of family and social organization recorded in the canonical books called the *Classics*. The Zhou also continued Shang bronze manufacture, with some changes in shapes and a notable transformation of style. Already in later Shang the basically planar surface had come to be punctuated here and there by explosions of three-dimensional forms. These are characteristic of Zhou bronzes from the outset, as seen in a powerful *fang ding*, or four-legged open food vessel (fig. 17–2), each of whose faces bristles with five rows of projecting cones, while silhouetted tigers jut from the four corners and from the center of each face and confronted horned animals climb up the handles. Eventually the forms of bronzes were sharply altered and the patterns inlaid with silver; ceremonial significance seems to have been replaced by love of ornament. Many objects show the influence of the Animal Style (see pages 381–82), which extended from northern Europe, across European Russia and Siberia, into China. The earliest examples of the great Chinese art of painting—horsemen and carriages on lacquer bowls—appear in late Zhou. By the early fifth century B.C. Zhou rule had disintegrated into a group of warring states.

QIN DYNASTY (221–206 B.C.)

For a mere eleven years a single ruler, King Zheng of the state of Qin, in present-day Shenxi province, took over the entire country, slaughtering all opponents, persecuting the Confucians, and burning the *Classics*. Calling himself Shi Huang Di, this ruthless monarch established the empire of China (the name derives from the Qin dynasty), founding a system of government that lasted through all subsequent dynasties into the twentieth century, standardizing script and coinage, building a network of roads, and beginning work on the Great Wall, which stands to this day. The emperor was buried in a mound originally some six hundred feet high (the height of a sixty-story skyscraper). Although literary accounts describe a treasure of thousands of objects buried with Shi Huang Di, including a map of the universe as then known with rivers in mercury, the first discoveries near the mound were made accidentally by well-diggers. A hall approximately 100 by 300 feet was partially unearthed about a mile from the funeral mound. The original roof was upheld by wooden posts, then covered with earth and turf so as not to be visible on the surface. Within were sheltered at least six thousand life-size terra-cotta statues of soldiers and two thousand horses in formation, guarding the approach to the tomb (fig. 17–3). Only

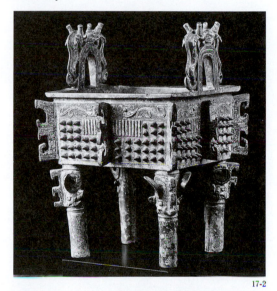

17-2. Ceremonial food vessel (*fang ding*). Early Zhou period, c. 1000 B.C. Bronze, height 11" (28 cm). The Nelson-Atkins Museum of Art, Kansas City

17-2

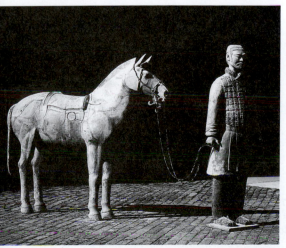

17-3. *Cavalryman and Saddle Horse*, from the Tomb of Emperor Shi Huang Di, Lintong, Shenxi. Qin dynasty, c. 210 B.C. Terra-cotta, height 70½" (1.79 m). Shenxi Provincial Museum

17-3

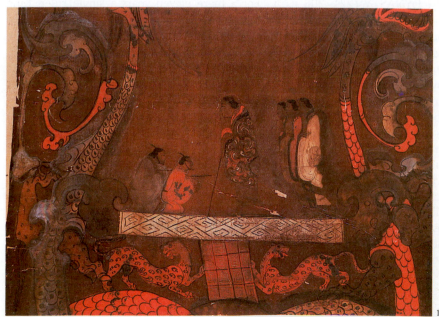

four years after Shi's death, the Han invaders set fire to the posts and the roof collapsed, burying the statues as conveniently for posterity as Vesuvius buried Pompeii and Herculaneum, and causing only minor damage to the statues. Enough traces of their original polychromy remain so their original appearance can be reconstructed. Each statue is an individual portrait—the horsemen at attention, the archers kneeling—and vibrant with life. The artistic quality of the tall soldiers and their small horses differs from one statue to the next, but is at times astonishingly high; there were apparently masters and assistant artisans at work. Heads and bodies were made separately, and each could have been done in a day—which makes sixteen thousand man-days or, to put it differently, forty-four sculptors working seven days a week for a year. Add the clay-diggers, clay-mixers, woodcutters, carpenters, kiln attendants, carters, porters, and painters, not to speak of the excavators, cooks, and other service personnel, and one arrives at a team of hundreds, all working at top speed, just for the military statues. Recently, hundreds of life-size scribes have been found, although not yet published, and also smaller bronze chariots inlaid with gold and silver, suggesting that the entire imperial court accompanied the deceased in effigy. For the rest of the contents of the once-lofty burial mound we must await continuing excavations.

HAN DYNASTY (206 B.C.–A.D. 220)   After four years of civil war, a peasant became the first emperor of the Han dynasty. He reinstated Confucianism but reinforced the centralized system founded by Emperor Shi without his excesses. Cities were founded, duly oriented to the four cardinal points of the compass, with a spot at the north reserved for the palace of the emperor or his representative. Indeed, magnificent palaces ornamented with splendid mural paintings are recorded in literary sources. Imperial control was extended over vast areas of western China and trade routes established with both India and the Near East.

While very little remains of Han painting, we possess just enough to give us an insight into the probable splendor and surprising freedom of the vanished art. In 1971 the tomb of a great lady, the marchioness (to give her a Western equivalent) of Dai, was found in Hunan province. Among the treasury of objects it contained was a T-shaped silk banner covering the inner coffin of the intact marchioness, painted with a formal hierarchy of three regions, sky, earth, and netherworld, each populated with appropriate figures and united by an intricate design of interlaced dragons. Earth contains a delightful full-length portrait of the great lady herself (fig. 17–4), clothed in a wonderful robe apparently painted in free spiral designs like those that appear on painted lacquer objects from the same tomb. Supported on a

17-4. *Marchioness of Dai with Attendants,* detail of a painted silk banner from the Tomb of Dai Hou Fu-ren, Mawangdui, Hunan. Han dynasty, c. 180 B.C. Formerly Historical Museum, Beijing

17-4

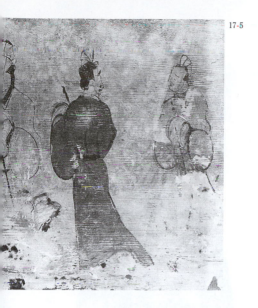

17-5. *Five Men Conversing*, detail of a painted terra-cotta tile. Han dynasty, 1st century A.D. Height 7½″ (19 cm). Courtesy, Museum of Fine Arts, Boston

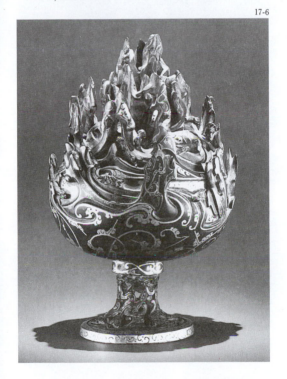

17-6. Incense burner, from the Tomb of Liu Sheng, Mancheng, Hebei. Han dynasty, c. 113 B.C. Bronze with gold inlay, height 10¼″ (26 cm). Hebei Provincial Museum

17-7. *Instructress Writing Down Her Admonitions for the Benefit of Two Young Ladies*, portion of the handscroll *Admonitions of the Instructress to the Ladies of the Palace*. Attributed to GU KAIZHI (c. A.D. 344– 406). Six Dynasties period. Ink and color on silk, height 9¾″ (24.8 cm). British Museum, London

cane, and accompanied by three serving maids who have nothing to stand on, she receives the tribute of two kneeling men. The delicacy of the rhythmic line is typical of Han art and reappears in the somewhat more pungent male portraits in animated conversation, briskly painted on a hollow tile from the Han period (fig. 17–5). In connection with the strikingly free brushwork of these figures of the first century A.D., James Cahill has quoted a significant remark made by the Qing painter Dao-Ji that the single brushstroke was "the origin of all existence, the root of the myriad phenomena." Nothing could be more important for the understanding of Chinese painting. From all that we can tell, the discovery of the primal importance of the brush seems to have been made during the Han dynasty.

In some ways the most prophetic of the Han tomb finds are the bronze incense burners inlaid with gold that are modeled into three-dimensional landscapes, such as that found in the tomb of Liu Sheng at Mancheng in Hebei, in northeast China (fig. 17–6). Tall mountains, depicting the Daoist Isles of the Immortals, rise above flowing water depicted in graceful curves, while a hunter strides along the shore. Here we have the basic elements of the great Chinese art of landscape painting— mountains and water. (Incense escaping from tiny holes supplied the mist essential to most Chinese landscapes.) In fact, the Chinese expression for landscape is "mountain-water picture." At times deeply imbued with philosophical and religious significance, at times hardly more than decorative, mountain-water pictures continue throughout Chinese history and are still being painted in China today.

SIX DYNASTIES (A.D. 220–589)   Dynasties last only so long before they either fall of their own weight or open themselves to attack. With the Tatar invasions of the third century, imposing on the population the Buddhist religion (which spread rapidly beyond Tatar dominions), educated classes fled to the south, taking Confucianism and Daoism with them and setting up local rule. During this period of chaos we begin for the first time to be able to associate works of art with specific artists.

A major early treatise by Xie He includes the *Six Canons of Painting:*

1. Sympathetic responsiveness of the vital spirit
2. Structural method in the use of the brush
3. Fidelity to the object in portraying forms
4. Conformity to kind in applying colors
5. Proper planning in the placing of elements
6. Transmission of the experience of the past in making copies

The first of these canons is the soul of Chinese painting, and the varying degrees of its presence or absence are what distinguish masterpieces from mediocrities, and mediocrities from failures. How can we as twentieth-century observers distinguish sympathetic responsiveness of the vital spirit (there has to be a shorter version— perhaps "spiritual response")? One can only answer "Just look!" We can, indeed,

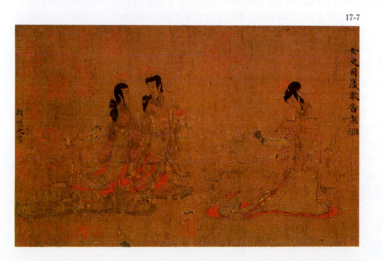

look at any work of art in the entire history of humanity and test it for this very quality. The great ones will always pass with flying colors, and the others will fall into their proper categories. Xie He's first canon, therefore, is truly universal.

How about the second? As we have seen, emphasis on the brush is especially Chinese. Brush had little importance in Western painting before the illusionist work at Pompeii (see pages 235–40). In China the actual touch was essential from the start—but not just as a slapdash expression of emotion. There had to be some consistency—structure—in the use of the brush. Difficult for Westerners to understand before the twentieth century is that the Chinese have always rated calligraphy as highly as painting, and those grand characters do lend themselves to powerful statements with the brush. The great murals of Han and Tang have disappeared, leaving the characteristic Chinese portable paintings. These were chiefly scrolls, at first on silk, generally mounted on paper and often bordered at a later date with brocade to protect the edges. By the ninth century A.D., paper was introduced for leaves mounted in albums, screens, and fans, then also for scrolls. These were of two types: the hanging scroll to be hung on a wall, and the handscroll, too long for such exhibition and intended rather to be unrolled like a Western papyrus, one section at a time. There were also single leaves of silk or paper, mounted in albums for delighted perusal.

Basically all Chinese scrolls are ink paintings, even when color was applied quite liberally to details. In the absence of color, the power of the brush takes over. Ink was a careful preparation of lampblack mixed with various gums, compressed to blocks or sticks of porcelain hardness and smoothness, and often carved. The painter crouched on the floor or stood at a table, his silk or paper spread before him, dipped his brush in water, mixed the ink on the ink tablet, and began to work. His very position left the arm free of tension and allowed the hand to perform its own untrammeled choreography with the brush.

The third canon of Xie He implies at least that objects should be recognizable, and before abstract art this has been universally the case. The fourth meant that horses should not be green or grass red, although in practice the artist was allowed some license according to the necessities of his picture. This also holds generally true throughout the history of art.

We might be tempted to translate the fifth as composition, with one crucial proviso: the absence of any enframement in Chinese painting means that figures and objects must succeed each other in free space on the basis of their own interior logic. Every now and then Western art is panoramic, as for example the Column of Trajan, which unrolls a cinematic experience of successive episodes in a developing narration (see fig. 9–47); Chinese painting is, more often than not, an endless experience in time, inevitably so in the case of large-size hanging scrolls and all handscrolls.

The final canon, although often respected in Western art (and often not!), is quintessentially Chinese in its application. Works of art by the masters of the past were so universally copied, and not always by students, that a continuity of tradition for many centuries is to be taken for granted. But there is a minus side. Without any wish to produce a forgery, the copyist often supplied the original master's name. It has taken scholars a while to sort out the resulting confusion, but in most cases it has not been too difficult; copies almost always betray the date of their execution by devices of style that can be clocked by means of known examples. Sometimes they are a mere bow to the so-called original, which the copyists may have seen only briefly or not at all.

The beautiful handscroll of a typically Confucian subject, *Admonitions of the Instructress to the Ladies of the Palace* (fig. 17–7), has always been attributed to the great painter GU KAIZHI (C. A.D. 344–406), the author of an informative "how to" treatise on the art of painting. The quality is so much higher than that of most copies that all scholars believe it may be close to the master. Certainly the first scene, showing the instructress writing down her counsel for the benefit of two

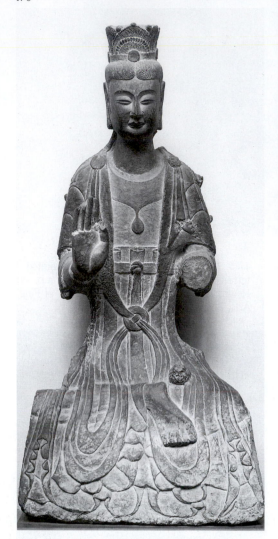

17-8

17-8. *Bodhisattva Maitreya.* Northern Wei dynasty, A.D. 386–535. Gray limestone, height 6′5⅛″ (1.96 m). Courtesy, Museum of Fine Arts, Boston. Gift of Denman Ross in memory of Okakura Kakuzo

young ladies, fulfills the Six Canons admirably, especially the first. A wonderful airy rhythm flows through the graceful poses and apparently breeze-swept garments of the ladies as they move, twist, and turn in totally undefined yet very convincing space. Apparently the Chinese were not bothered by the collectors' seals, which to Western eyes disfigure the background; only the exquisitely placed vertical inscription is of the period. The style of the witty faces and linear drapery derives directly from Han painting as seen in the few surviving examples, and one scene in the scroll is almost a translation into painting of the mountain-water-hunter combination we saw in a Han incense burner (see fig. 17–6).

Buddhism made its first appearance in China as early as the first century A.D., but under the Tatar dynasty ruling in the north as Northern Wei (A.D. 386–535), the new faith assumed rapid supremacy, from which it was not to slip during the great succeeding periods of Chinese culture. Beginning with the very earliest examples of Buddhist sculpture in China—innumerable images ranging from perfunctory to sublime—along the trade routes to Central Asia and in cave-temples reminding one in some ways of their Indian counterparts, elements imported from India are partially, soon thoroughly, converted to Chinese style. A beautiful example is the over-life-size statue of the *Bodhisattva Maitreya*, the Buddha of the Future (fig. 17–8), of unknown provenance. While the pose of the figure is derived from that of Indian seated Buddhas and Bodhisattvas, every element of style has undergone an immense transformation. The sensuality indispensable to Indian art has vanished. There is no interest whatsoever in the body; a kind of hypnotic delight is derived from the cascading rhythms of the folds, perfectly exemplifying the spiritual vitality of the first canon. The drapery might be falling over anything; not even the position of the legs can be securely determined, although one flattened foot appears. And above the lines, loops, and wavelets of the drapery folds, recalling the floating rhythms of Gu Kaizhi, the gently smiling head seems miraculously poised on a cylinder rather than a neck, its half-closed eyes gazing inward on a world of the spirit.

The great temple complexes of the Six Dynasties were constructed of wood and were destroyed in the tragic persecution of Buddhism in the years A.D. 842–45. An idea of their probable appearance can be gained from their reflection in the contemporary Horyu-ji shrine at Nara, in Japan (see fig. 18–3).

The Classic Periods of Chinese Art

TANG DYNASTY (A.D. 618–907)   After the divided period of the Six Dynasties, the Sui dynasty briefly reestablished control over the entire country. But under the succeeding Tang emperors, China entered one of the greatest periods in her history, holding sway over a territory surpassing that of the Roman Empire at the greatest extent. From the Caspian Sea at the extreme west, imperial rule extended down into the Indus Valley and embraced all of Central Asia as well as Korea, Manchuria, and even part of Vietnam. Changan, the Tang capital (modern Xi-an), was probably the largest city on earth at the time, with a population and splendor not remotely approached by any contemporary European center. Tang trade routes maintained peaceful commerce between East and West. Politically unified, the Tang Empire could at the outset afford to be tolerant; not only Confucianism but the newly imported Mahayana Buddhism, Nestorian Christianity, Hebraism, Islam, and Zoroastrianism flourished under its enlightened rule. So did culture and the arts. A treasury of Tang writings exists, but only copies and provincial imitations remain to assist us in reconstructing the grandeur of Tang art, which must have been in keeping with that of classic periods anywhere, from fifth-century-B.C. Greece to the High Renaissance in Italy.

Imperial dignity, dependent not on trappings but on sheer force of character, radiates from the *Scroll of the Emperors* (fig. 17–9), attributed to YAN LIBEN (died before A.D. 673)—the only plausible attribution to this artist, who was also, like so

17-9

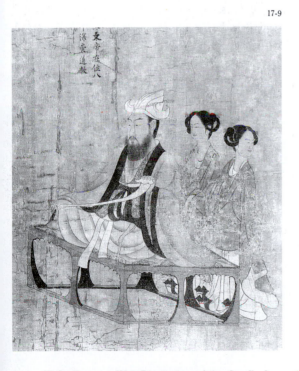

17-9. *Emperor Wen Di*, portion of the *Scroll of the Emperors*. Attributed to YAN LIBEN (died before A.D. 673). Tang dynasty. Handscroll; ink, gold, and color on silk, height 20⅛″ (51 cm). Courtesy, Museum of Fine Arts, Boston. Denman Waldo Ross Collection

many painters of later periods, an important imperial official. Imperial seals dating back to the twelfth century, with which it is stamped but with whose style this scroll is incompatible, strengthen its claim to authenticity. In fig. 17–9 Wen Di, emperor of the southern Chen dynasty during the Six Dynasties period, sits cross-legged and bolt upright on a simple eight-legged, square, backless, lacquered seat, of a variety visible in countless other portraits, gazing impassively outward while he holds up a ceremonial object with both hands. Delineated with close attention to individual character, the face is formidable. A special concession to exalted rank is the emperor's scale. If he stood up he would be twice the height of the two graceful ladies who attend him. In the undefined space and in the linear method of indicating drapery folds we are reminded of Gu Kaizhi. But the forms are fuller, the linear melody graver and slower, and Han wit has yielded to Tang majesty.

According to literary accounts, Tang temples were of enormous extent and splendor, built of wood and richly painted and containing murals by the greatest masters and sculptures in bronze. Like the temples of the Six Dynasties, all were destroyed by fire in A.D. 842–45. The Great Gander Pagoda (fig. 17–10) remains at Xi-an. Pagodas were probably derived from the Indian stupas. This one, built of brick and dating from A.D. 652, was part of a wooden Buddhist temple and is one of the earliest surviving Chinese masonry constructions. The seven stories (the last two were added before the middle of the tenth century) are almost square in plan and diminish progressively upward. Their severity is no more surprising than is the fact that they are articulated by slender pilasters similar to those in certain Buddhist temples in faraway Gandhara. Later pagodas adopt typical Chinese tiled roofs jutting outward at every story.

The classic ideal of Tang art may be seen in two extremes. The cave sculptures at Longmen, in central China near the Tang city of Luoyang, show the calm and balance of Tang, often on the grandest scale. The rock-cut, 46-foot-tall *Buddha Vairocana* (fig. 17–11) towers in utter serenity, the narrowed eyes concentrating on the world within, and the full cheeks showing only a hint of Gupta-style interest in the physical being. Every form is broad, every drapery line flows slowly, compared with the rapid course of Gu Kaizhi's folds, or those of Northern Wei sculpture (see figs. 17–7, 17–8). The broad apselike niche in which the figure sits is filled with

17-10

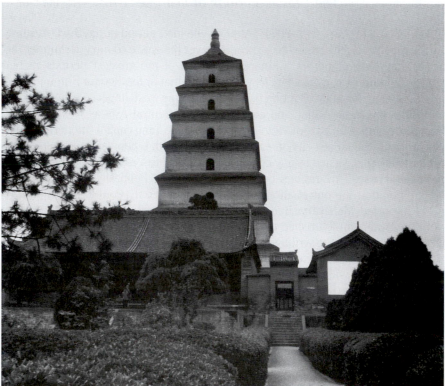

17-10. Great Gander Pagoda, Xi-an. Tang dynasty, A.D. 652, with later additions

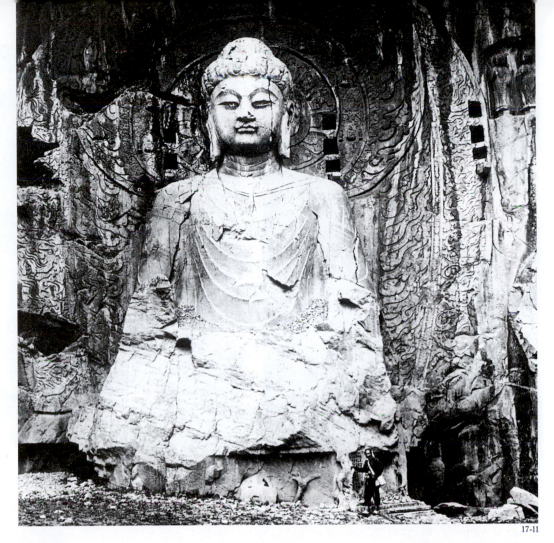

17-11. *The Buddha Vairocana,* Longmen, Henan. Tang dynasty, c. A.D. 672–76. Rock-cut stone, height 46′ (14.02 m)

halo upon halo and flame and cloud patterns all vibrating in celestial harmony with the calm Buddha.

At the opposite extreme in size and significance are the terra-cotta figurines, some glazed, some painted, that populate Tang tombs in enormous numbers. The chunky, muscular horses are particularly attractive (fig. 17–12), with their firm chests and hindquarters, their alert heads, and their saddles at the ready. These animals were indeed the foundation of Tang economic and military power, holding the vast empire together; one Tang painter, Han Gan, specialized in painting horses for the imperial court.

Literary accounts tell us of a Tang painter called Wu Daozi, greatest of the great, whose wall paintings adorned the temples of Changan and Luoyang. These, too, were destroyed in A.D. 842–45, and not even credible or enjoyable copies survive. His style was marked by great force and freedom, in conception and in brush, and people gathered round to watch him bring figures and animals into abundant life. Only the iconography of his paintings may be distantly glimpsed through the murals at Dunhuang, the western pilgrimage center along the famous Silk Road. A huge, damaged fresco of the *Western Paradise* (fig. 17–13) depicts the Amitabha Buddha (Buddha of the West), seated on his lotus throne, accompanied on either side by the two major Bodhisattvas equally enthroned, in a marvelous garden between pavilions, whose roofs with their turned-up corners give us an idea of the vanished temple and palace architecture of the period. Flames rise from the aureoles of light surrounding the Buddha and his companions; smaller images of Bodhisattvas appear in vast numbers on lotus flowers; and swans float through the air above devotees arranged in the foreground on either side of a gorgeous carpet. All this corresponds to the literary texts, which describe in detail the material joys of the Western Paradise, including trees whose flowers are jewels, and jewels that can

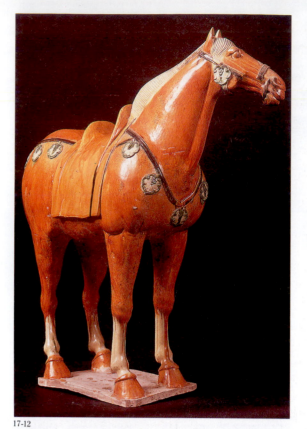

17-12

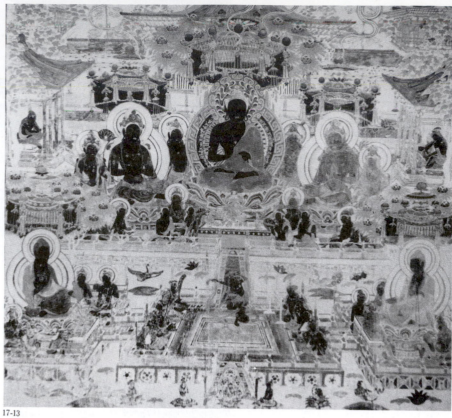

17-13

17-14

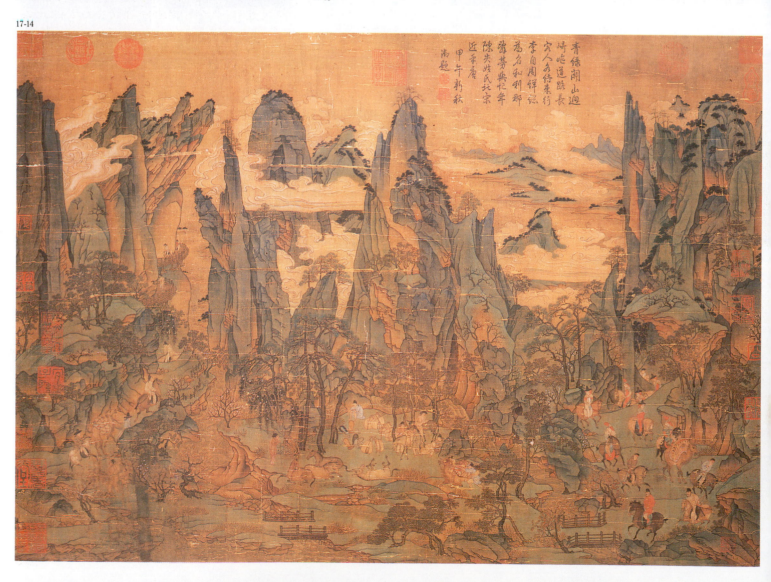

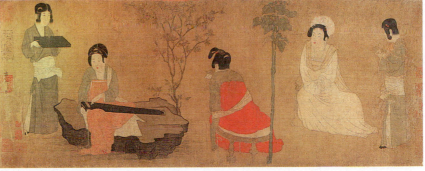

17-15.

17-15. *Palace Ladies Tuning the Lute.* Attributed to ZHOU FANG (active c. A.D. 780–810). Tang dynasty. Handscroll; ink and color on silk, height 11″ (28 cm). The Nelson-Atkins Museum of Art, Kansas City. Nelson Fund

17-12. *Horse.* Tang dynasty, A.D. 618–907. Glazed terra-cotta tomb figurine, height 30¼″ (76.8 cm). Cleveland Museum of Art. Anonymous Gift

17-13. *Western Paradise,* section of a wall painting, Dunhuang, Gansu. Tang dynasty, second half of 8th century A.D.

17-14. *Emperor Ming Huang's Journey to Shu.* Copy of a painting by LI ZHAODAO (c. A.D. 670–730). Tang dynasty. Ink and color on silk, height 21¼″ (54 cm). National Palace Museum, Taibei

17-16. *Guan Yin.* Song dynasty, A.D. 960–1279. Polychromed wood, height 42⅛″ (1.07 m). Rijksmuseum, Amsterdam

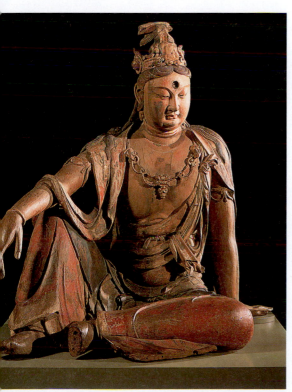

17-16

be scooped up from the lawns—a far cry from the blissful nonexistence that was the goal of Siddhartha.

Few paintings on silk can lay claim to Tang date, but some much later copies remain to illustrate the ideas of the famous Tang master Wang Wei (A.D. 699–759), credited with the invention of monochrome landscape painting. Better than through any of the late copies after Wang Wei's landscape scrolls we can recapitulate Tang landscape through a fine painting on silk in line, with areas of color, in the style of (though not by) LI ZHAODAO (active c. A.D. 670–730), entitled *Emperor Ming Huang's Journey to Shu* (fig. 17-14). As often in Chinese landscape painting, we are struck by the fantastic mountain crags, four or five times as high as they are wide. However, just such crags did and still do exist in the gorge of the Yangzi River. The painter obviously loved them, perched clumps of trees on the wildest points, and let clouds—still echoing the cloud patterns of Shang and Zhou (see fig. 17-2)—swirl among them the way the mountain mists can be seen to drift today. Although distances between mountains, and therefore space itself, are as yet indicated only by overlapping, between the peaks one looks out to distant hills surrounded by their own swirling clouds, separated by unaltered silk doing duty for water. The figures establish the vast scale achieved in Asian landscape art by no one before the Chinese. More important, however, they ask us to identify with them as they move through landscape, which is what the literary sources also invite us to do. We labor up the hill with the travelers at the right, then rest with them in a forest glade, while the horses frolic by a stream. Then we set off again at the left, through a narrow defile and out on a road that is eventually built out on struts from the side of a terrifying cliff. In this painting, or rather in its vanished original, we note that a large-scale Chinese landscape painting is an experience in time, like a book, and not intended to be seen all at once. Chinese traditionalism ensures that the basic repertory of rock, tree, and cloud forms, begun in Han and enriched by observation in Tang, persists in spite of extensive alterations through all the dynastic changes into the twentieth century.

The amplitude, grace, and balance of the classic Tang period are fully manifest in a handscroll, *Palace Ladies Tuning the Lute* (fig. 17-15), attributed to ZHOU FANG (active c. A.D. 780–810). Despite the similarity of the courtly subject, there could scarcely be a greater difference between this and Gu Kaizhi's *Admonitions of the Instructress* (see fig. 17-7). A good deal of color is preserved and was once doubtless quite bright, especially the pink and the red. Space, still not defined, is indicated by subtle overlappings in depth. The locale—a palace garden—is suggested by horizontal strokes to indicate the ground, a rock on which the musician is seated, and two trees, one in flower. Figures and faces are proportioned more fully, and the waistlines have moved strikingly low. Rather than flowing freely in extravagant folds, the lines of the drapery fall calmly to the ground. The broad serenity of the composition, the dignity of the proportions, the slow melody of the linear flow all embody the ideals of the waning Tang culture.

FIVE DYNASTIES AND SONG DYNASTY (A.D. 907–1279) The fall of the Tang dynasty in 907 provoked a period of extreme disorder from which China never wholly recovered. Five dynasties were soon competing for imperial control in the north—there were others in the south and west. Centralized control was not reestablished until a general sent to expel Tatar invaders proclaimed himself emperor, and even then the outlying territories were lost. The new Song dynasty, beginning in 960, marked inevitable political retreat. In 1127 the Tatars took over all northern China, including Changan, and carried into captivity the art-loving Emperor Hui Zong, himself a painter to whom many works are attributed. The court fled to the south, founding a new capital at Hangzhou. The Song policy of using barbarians to fight barbarians eventually backfired, and in 1279 their Mongol allies, the Yuan, took over the entire nation, north and south. Despite this dismal political history the Song period is considered a kind of golden age for Chinese culture, poetry, and art. A glorious polychromed wooden statue of *Guan Yin* (fig. 17–16) may serve us as an introduction to the relaxed and luxury-loving atmosphere of the Song era. The great Indian Bodhisattva Avalokitesvara was known as Guan Yin in China. Represented as standing or seated in a Buddha-like pose in earlier periods, he becomes partially feminized in Song art—in later periods, indeed, is transformed into a goddess of mercy—and is here seated in what to us seems a highly informal pose (the "pose of the great king" in Indian art). He rests asymmetrically on his left leg and hand, his right leg drawn up to support his outstretched right arm. The fullness and softness of the forms, especially the fatty cheeks, the gentle melody of the curves of the drapery, and the languid grace of the dangling right hand admit us to a world of elegance and beauty totally removed from the majesty and power of the Tang period.

Under the Song a painting academy was founded, and literary records preserve the names of hundreds of painters as well as detailed accounts of their styles. Large numbers of paintings survive claiming to be Song, but in spite of the signatures of known masters, many are school works and many more later copies. There are still enough genuine works to give us a far clearer idea of Song painting, even of the individual styles of some of the most celebrated masters, than we have had in any earlier era. The best of Song painting takes its place among the great pictorial styles in world history, and for their special achievements the major Song masters are unmatched. Traditional techniques of painting, especially line and color—always the conservative current in Chinese art—persist from period to period, but the heritage of Wu Daozi with his powerful brush gave rise to a new and much freer calligraphic method, known graphically as *po-mo* ("ink splashing"), especially useful as a vehicle for a new form of personal, meditative, and mystical Buddhism called Chan (see pages 523 and 537–38). Traditional Confucian painters became less literal; their principle of order seemed to fuse with Dao, as the artist sought identification with the inner mystery of nature.

A majestic hanging scroll, nearly seven feet high, entitled *Travelers amid Mountains and Streams* (fig. 17–17), attributed to the Northern Song master FAN KUAN (active c. A.D. 990–1030), exemplifies the Song attitude toward nature. It can be safely said that no painters anywhere expressed the very soul of mountains as have the Chinese. In the West mountains appear as backgrounds for human action or objects of aesthetic enjoyment, seen from a single point of view. In Chinese art the mountain is the sole and final subject of the painting, and—as we have seen with Li Zhaodao—is experienced in time. Humanity is almost lost. Fan Kuan's mountain rises as if by some inner energy to fill almost the whole background. Trees soften its summits. From a cleft at the right pours a slender waterfall, deflected by rocks; a second waterfall seems to split from the first and runs parallel to it in a dizzying descent. Mists, indicated by bare silk against the glowing black, brown, and gray ink, separate the barren cliffs from the rocky, forested middle distance, and below them an almost microscopic line of horsemen makes its way along the riverbank, the only sign of humanity save for the roofs of a temple barely visible at the right along the silhouette of the trees, diminished still further by the foreground rocks. The solemnity of the mountain, the power of the rocks, the density of the forests, the

17-17. FAN KUAN. *Travelers amid Mountains and Streams*. Northern Song dynasty, c. A.D. 990–1030. Hanging scroll; ink on silk, height 6′9¼″ (2.06 m). National Palace Museum, Taibei

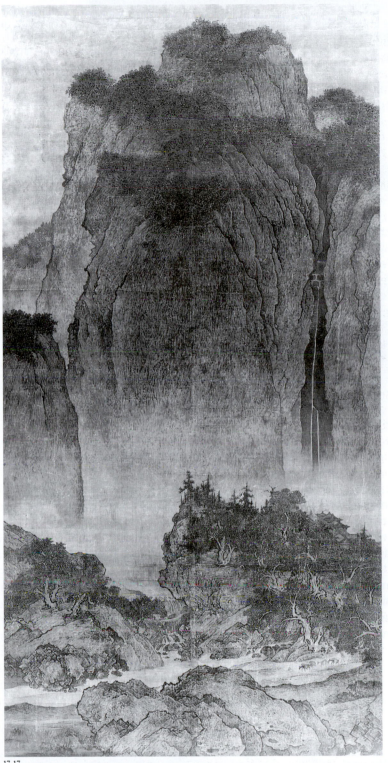

17-17

softness of the mists dwarf the patient progress of microscopic humans caught up in the forces of enveloping nature.

A very different scroll, *Early Spring* (fig. 17–18), dated 1072, is attributed to another celebrated Song master, GUO XI (c. A.D. 1020–90). Less interested in the remoteness and majesty of nature than in its wildness, Guo makes us climb the mountain, from patches of water at either side, on which people venture in tiny boats, up knolls and hummocks, past gnarled and twisted pines, from one scene to

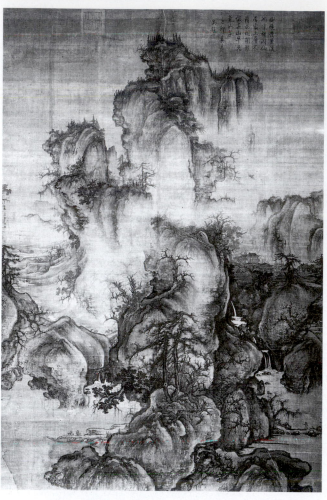

17-18

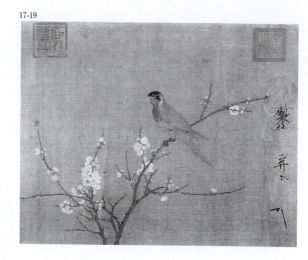

17-19

17-18. GUO XI. *Early Spring*. Northern Song dynasty, A.D. 1072. Hanging scroll; ink and slight color on silk, height 62½″ (1.59 m). National Palace Museum, Taibei

17-19. *Five-Colored Parakeet*. Northern Song dynasty, before A.D. 1127. Handscroll; ink and color on silk, height 20⅞″ (53 cm). Courtesy, Museum of Fine Arts, Boston

the next separated by patches of mist, always wilder and higher, until we look up to the unapproachable tangle of forest at the summit of the last crag.

The opposite pole from these vast landscapes might seem to be such exquisite paintings of the Song court as the handscroll entitled *Five-Colored Parakeet* (fig. 17–19), bearing the signature of the last Northern Song emperor, Hui Zong, but generally believed to have been painted by a court academician. For botanical and ornithological accuracy the painting is astonishing—every bud, every petal, every feather is treated in painstaking detail. Moreover, the composition fulfills the fifth canon of Xie He (see page 527): no placing of the elements could be more subtly perfect. Yet for all its delicacy of line, color, and composition, this is not just an example of courtly refinement; both li and Dao are manifest in these blossoms and birds as truly as in Fan Kuan's mountains and forests. Both extremes are equally pantheistic; both achieve the highest goals of Song poetic painting.

17-21. XIA GUI. Right to left: *Flying Geese over Distant Mountains; Returning to the Village in Mist from the Ferry; The Clear and Sonorous Air of the Fisherman's Flute; Boats Moored at Night in a Misty Bay* (four scenes from the fragmentary handscroll *Twelve Views from a Thatched Hut*). Southern Song dynasty, late 12th century–early 13th century A.D. Ink on silk, height 11″ (28 cm). The Nelson-Atkins Museum of Art, Kansas City

17-21

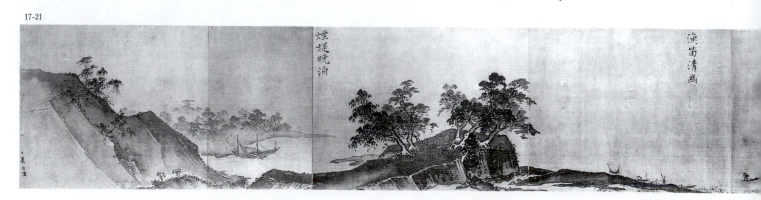

17-20

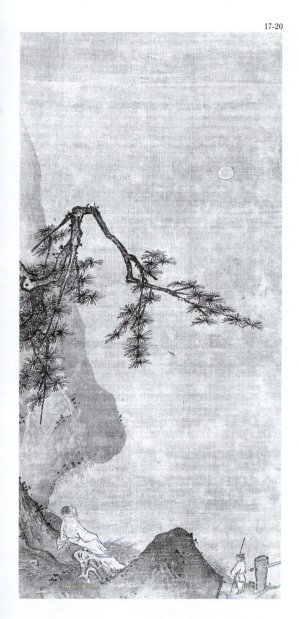

During its threatened life of a century and a half at the southern capital of Hangzhou, Song culture explored ever deeper realms of the spirit. Although scholar-painters of later centuries regarded him and his pupils with little sympathy, MA YUAN (active C. A.D. 1190–1225) was surely one of the greatest painters of any era. His hanging scroll *Scholar Contemplating the Moon* (fig. 17–20) strikes a responsive chord today, but we should not confuse the spirit of such pictures with the modern attitude toward nature. In addition to enjoyment, such pictures symbolize identification with the infinite and the ultimate. Hardly more than a fragment of some cosmic Northern Song landscape, the profile of a precipice appears, from which struggles a jagged pine tree. While a servant boy stands unseeing next to a fence post at the edge of the chasm that we *feel* rather than see, an aged scholar rests by himself on a patch of grass, gazing past a tiny bird gliding below the branch—upward and upward to the cold moon hanging in the mist. Ma knows all about naturalistic painting Chinese-style. In melodious line the drapery flows as it should; in dark blobs of ink the tiny rock plants cluster; in soft wash the grass bends in the evening breeze; in deep and masterful strokes of black the pine branches and needles bristle fiercely, like the most splendid Chinese calligraphy; the very moon is flattened by the distorting mist. But Ma has gone beyond observation and technique. The most important element in the picture is emptiness, mist suffused with moonlight, a triumph of suggestion but also of poetry and, above all, pantheism. All Xie He's canons are abundantly fulfilled save the last; even though in the final analysis man and nature in this picture derive from their depiction in a tradition going back to such representations as the little Han incense burner, man hunts no longer with bow and arrow but with the concentrated forces of the mind, and his quarry is not a bird but harmony of the spirit.

Ma's contemporary XIA GUI (active c. A.D. 1180–1230) shares artistic if not poetic honors with him. *Twelve Views from a Thatched Hut* is a scroll from which we see in this composite photograph—reading from right to left, as one would unroll the scroll—the four remaining scenes: *Flying Geese over Distant Mountains, Returning to the Village in Mist from the Ferry, The Clear and Sonorous Air of the Fisherman's Flute,* and *Boats Moored at Night in a Misty Bay* (fig. 17–21). The touches of the brush and the gradations of the ink are just as masterful as those of Ma, but both setting and personnel have changed; harmony is sought and found not in mountain fastnesses, but in daily life. Fishermen, their boats, and their villages replace the scholar. As we were intended to, we search in vain for the flute-playing fisherman. Such horizontal scrolls are truly cinematographic; although they are at times exhibited fully unrolled, we were not intended to experience at one time more than can be unrolled—with extreme care!—as the rolls are held in both hands. They are also in the highest degree personal, for under such conditions they were intended to be seen by only one person, at the most two, at one time.

New in Southern Song culture is the importance of the mystical sect of Chan (Japanese Zen) Buddhism already established during the Five Dynasties. In addition to monastic communities, Chan sages lived, hermit-like, in meditative isola-

17-20. MA YUAN. *Scholar Contemplating the Moon.* Southern Song dynasty, late 12th century–early 13th century A.D. Hanging scroll; ink and faint color on silk, height 22¾″ (57.8 cm). MOA Museum of Art, Atami

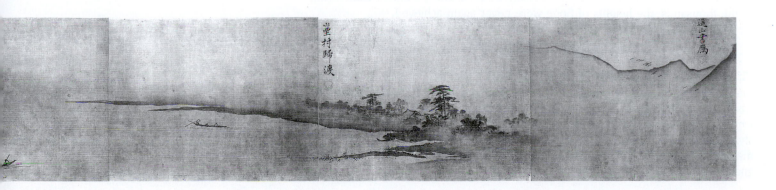

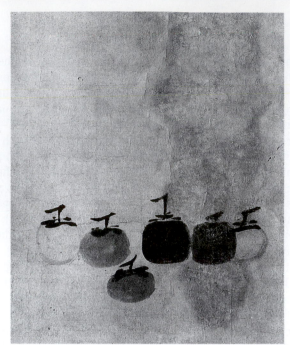

17-22. Mu-Qi. *Six Persimmons*. Southern Song dynasty, 13th century A.D. Ink on paper, width 14¼″ (36.2 cm). Daitoku-ji, Kyoto

17-22

tion, preferably in mountain retreats where they could seek and find unity with the spiritual forces of the universe. Aspiring pupils who sought them out were greeted with riddles whose seeming irrationality embodied profound lessons, in an attempt to guide them to sudden Enlightenment. Many of these sages were painters; among the greatest was Liang Kai (later twelfth century A.D.–c. 1246). The free, new style of Liang Kai is seen in an extraordinary hanging scroll, *Hui Neng, the Sixth Chan Patriarch, Chopping Bamboo at the Moment of Enlightenment* (see Introduction fig. 14). We are permitted to participate in the flash of ultimate realization through a humble, daily act, depicted with sparing washes and dark, hooklike strokes of tremendous intensity.

Enlightenment, beyond reason yet profoundly convincing, is achieved, by what seem the simplest of means that yet presuppose immense technical knowledge and experience, in *Six Persimmons* (fig. 17–22) by another Chan painter, Mu-Qi (early thirteenth century A.D.–after 1279). Blue-black ink on paper sets down with powerful brush and in subtle spacing and overlapping six identical yet different pieces of fruit, in a space that eludes all definition. In throbbing intensity a Chan riddle is at once asked and answered.

The Mongol conquest opened a new and difficult era, in which the representatives of an ancient and sophisticated culture were forced to serve masters whom they regarded as barbarians. Endlessly during the Yuan and succeeding dynasties the stylistic achievements of Song were emulated, sometimes with deep understanding but more often with more dexterity than sensitivity—and there is no doubt that completely new problems, chiefly of personal expression, were posed and solved. Yet despite the brilliance and skill of later Chinese painters, numbering in the thousands, the heights of Song were never again achieved.

Later Chinese Art

YUAN DYNASTY (A.D. 1279–1368)   The Mongols who assumed by violence and maintained by repression control of all of China eventually attempted to absorb Chinese culture. Nonetheless, the conquerors were shunned by most artists, who were not professionals but *wen-ren*, scholarly painters. They were masters of all the styles and techniques of earlier periods in ink and in line and color, and devised many of their own; they also continued to paint lofty mountains, waterfalls, forests, gnarled pine trees, water, and micro-people, portraits of men and horses, birds and

17-23. LI KAN. *Bamboo* (section of a handscroll). Yuan dynasty, A.D. 1308. Ink on paper, height 14¾″ (37.5 cm). The Nelson-Atkins Museum of Art, Kansas City. Nelson Fund

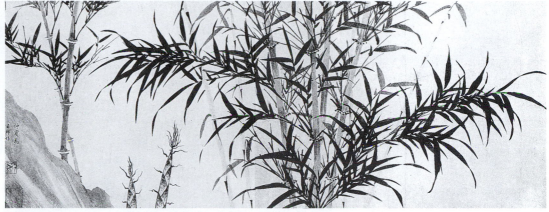

17-23

17-24

17-24. NI ZAN. *Rongxi Studio*. Late Yuan dynasty/early Ming dynasty, A.D. 1372. Hanging scroll; ink on paper, height 29¾″ (75.6 cm). National Palace Museum, Taibei

flowers. But despite their virtuosity none of the Yuan painters were able to reach the intensity of the great Song masters. It is difficult for Westerners to understand that Chinese critical tradition preferred these gentlemen-amateurs to the Song academy. Professional painters were disparaged as "commercial." The mists vanished, and with them the mystery. Most of these scholar-painters worked on paper rather than silk, which deprives their ink of a certain resonance. There is no parallel elsewhere in the history of world art to this truly unique phenomenon of the scholar-painter.

A special favorite of Yuan is the painting of bamboo, chosen from Song through Qing as a symbolic subject because the apparent fragility of stems and leaves is belied by the plant's virtual indestructibility. LI KAN (A.D. 1245–1320) was a master of bamboo painting (fig. 17–23), in which he was able to communicate in brushed nuances of unprecedented flexibility and sureness the inner rhythm of the plant's growth—even the air between the branches—while softening the stems.

Among the host of wen-ren master painters, four have been considered especially great by the Chinese. One of these, NI ZAN (A.D. 1301–74), is the epitome of wen-ren, brought up as he was in the tradition of the scholar-poet-painter. *Rongxi Studio* (fig. 17–24), dated 1372, whose distant landscape seems almost buried under a lengthy text, seems truly written rather than painted. Deft calligraphic touches, often hook-shaped, establish rocks, pine trees, islands, and mountains. Mysteriously the thatched pavilion, as always with Ni, is empty. Dao Qi, a painter of the Ming dynasty, declared:

The paintings by master Ni are like waves on the sandy beach, or streams between the stones which roll and flow and issue by their own force. Their air of supreme refinement and purity is so cold that it overawes men.

MING DYNASTY (A.D. 1368–1644)   A true upheaval in the Middle Kingdom replaced the Yuan in north and south with native rulers by 1382. At first as tyrannical as the Mongols, soon the Ming dynasty encouraged the arts, especially that of porcelain, and their interest produced in the imperial factories an endless stream of splendid ornamental works. As their capital the emperors laid out Beijing (then known as Peking) in a rectilinear plan oriented toward the cardinal points, based on prototypes in earlier Chinese history, that has survived to the present, save only for alterations made by the People's Republic. Beijing's nerve center was the Forbidden City, the only imperial palace in Chinese history that remains intact. This rectangular compound surrounded by high walls enclosed the entire imperial administration, whose bureau, in intricately organized one-story structures, flanks the palace proper. Towering gateways of brick provide entry to vast courtyards. Bridges across waterways lead to stairs guarded by lions, giving access to

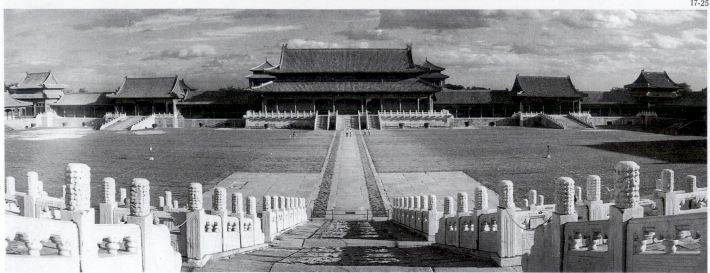

17-25. Gate of Heavenly Purity and (foreground) stairway before the Hall of Supreme Harmony, Forbidden City, Beijing. Ming dynasty, 17th century A.D. and later

17-26. DONG QICHANG. *Qingbian Mountains.* Ming dynasty, A.D. 1617. Hanging scroll; ink on paper, height 7'4⅜" (2.24 m). Cleveland Museum of Art

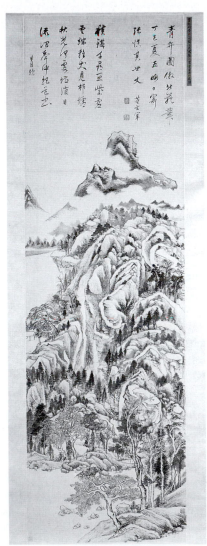

terraces—all in white marble (fig. 17–25). On the terraces stand enormous halls with symbolic names, for the official functions of the emperor; deeper within the compound are the private quarters of emperor and empress, with splendid gardens composed not of flowers or formalized plants as in the West but of miniatures of natural landscape, in a manner epitomized by the gardens of Japan (see fig. 18–13). All structures are built according to the ancient post-and-lintel system governing the height and width of bays, and supporting intricate brackets to receive the weight of the roofs with their upward-tilted corners. The colors are eye-smiting: posts are bright red, brackets red, yellow, blue, and green, and all roofs are covered with glazed tiles in imperial yellow. But in the immensity of the spaces the massive roofs and terraces are majestic.

Chinese cultural history is in a sense cumulative; all the styles of preceding dynasties including Yuan were emulated under Ming, and vast numbers of more or less accurate copies were made of masterpieces of the past—often mere re-creations from literary accounts. New is a taste for rich ornament, covering architecture, porcelains, fabrics, and furniture, all carried out with elegance and grace. Much Ming painting, of the type produced by the "blue and green" landscape school, was as ornamental as the crafts. Wen-ren painting continued in the works of scores of gifted scholar-painters who expressed contempt for professional artists, and especially for the Song academy. An unexpected combination of Song-admirer and startling innovator was DONG QICHANG (A.D. 1555–1636), himself a scholar and a high government official. His work, combining subjects and brushwork based on Song and Yuan models with a wholly arbitrary delineation of space, transformed painting into an art of personal expression rather than absorption in nature. Powerful masses of rocks, trees, and water are composed in an often dissonant manner, as in his *Qingbian Mountains* (fig. 17–26), dated 1617, and supplied with his own inscriptions expressing dogmatic opinions, which had enormous influence not only on his contemporaries but on subsequent scholar-painters.

WOMEN PAINTERS   Recent research by Marsha Weidner has reintegrated the work of scores of women painters in China after the year A.D. 1300 (before that approximate date, no works can be connected with the names in the records). In general, Chinese women painters seem to have been the daughters, wives, or concubines (a respected social position in imperial China) of painters. They were never as highly regarded as their male counterparts, although they painted most of the same subjects, and some of them to Western eyes, particularly the vigorous paintings of rocks and bamboo, are difficult to tell from those of men. To their

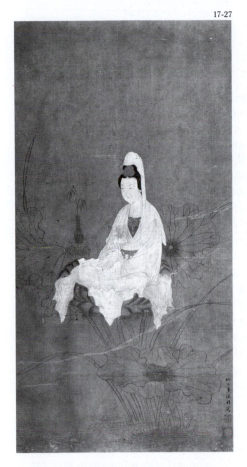

17-27

17-27. "MISS QIU" (QIU ZHU?). *White-Robed Guan Yin.* Ming dynasty, 16th century A.D. Hanging scroll; ink and color on silk, height 21¼" (54 cm). National Palace Museum, Taibei

contemporaries the achievements of the women painters were valued often in direct relationship to the degree of their femininity; thus, bird and flower paintings, representations of lovely ladies on terraces, exquisite fans, and so on, are typical. An especially accomplished woman painter of the Ming dynasty was Miss QIU, daughter of a well-known sixteenth-century painter—a stopgap name since we are not sure of her personal name, which may have been Qiu Zhu. She was at one time married but preferred to live alone "burning incense, playing the *qin,* cleaning the inkstone, and wielding the brush." A magically beautiful painting identified with Miss Qiu is the *White-Robed Guan Yin* (fig. 17–27). Now fully feminine, the goddess has descended with infinite grace to sit upon a colossal lotus flower, a descendant of the ornamentalized lotuses of early Buddha images. Leaves and petals are drawn in clear, soft line, so delicately that at first sight the divine figure, whose face is as white as her robe, seems to float in space.

QING DYNASTY (A.D. 1644–1912)   The decaying Ming dynasty gave way to new rulers from neighboring Manchuria, who fitted themselves into the traditional Chinese social and cultural structure without experiencing much opposition until replaced by a nationalist republic; descendants of the Qing rulers are still alive. As could be expected under such circumstances, all the tendencies of Ming art continued to flourish under the new dynasty, and not until the nineteenth century did both inventiveness and quality decline sharply. The imperial reign (A.D. 1736–95) of Qian Long (better known in the Wade-Giles romanization of his reign: Ch'ien-lung) was counted a new golden age. During the eighteenth century, works of art, mostly ornamental, were imported into Europe, and Chinese elements became a part of the Rococo decorative style. Among the host of Qing artists working in older traditions, a number of individualists stand out, particularly DAO-JI (A.D. 1641–1707), whose hanging scroll *Spring on the Min River,* dated 1697, while repeating traditional subjects—pavilion, gnarled pines, water, distant boat, mountains—is brilliantly original in treatment (fig. 17–28). The whole painting glows with strokes of fairly dense black ink, further enriched by touches of color. Rather than soaring in the distance above the mist as was traditional, the drastically simplified, repeated lines of the rocks and rugged peaks at upper right, independent of any notion of distance, burst upon the mind like a thunderclap.

17-28

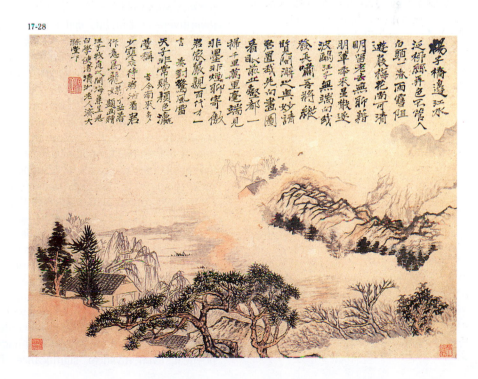

17-28. DAO-JI. *Spring on the Min River.* Qing dynasty, A.D. 1697. Hanging scroll; ink and color on paper, height 15⅜" (39 cm). Cleveland Museum of Art

CHAPTER EIGHTEEN

The long chain of volcanic islands numbering in the hundreds that forms the present-day empire of Japan stretches from nearly subarctic to virtually subtropical climatic zones. Of the four principal islands only Honshu, supporting all the major cities, boasts any considerable size. The islands are subject to frequent and violent earthquakes and to oceanic storms of frightful intensity. Largely mountainous and heavily forested, the islands offer no more than 20 percent of habitable land, within which an enormous population must exist under the most crowded conditions of any nation on the planet. Ethnically they are of several different origins, now largely mixed. Japanese history is distinct from that of China and India in that the islands, defended by the Sea of Japan, were never governed by invaders; concerted Mongol attacks in the thirteenth century were definitively repelled.

Only since World War II has Japanese history begun to be accessible in great detail to foreigners who have not mastered the Japanese language. According to prewar Japanese belief, doubtless still accepted in rural regions, the emperor is a direct descendant of the sun-goddess Amaterasu, and there is indeed a possibility that the imperial family line may have continued unbroken since prehistoric times. But the division of the territory by water and by mountain chains made centralized imperial government on the Maurya or Tang models no more than a pious hope. For most of Japanese history, real power lay in the hands of local nobility, more or less controlled from the twelfth into the nineteenth century by military dictators called *shogun*s. Civil war was the rule rather than the exception, and the Japanese ideal was not the Indian sage or the Chinese scholar but the warrior, especially the independent swordsman, or *samurai*. Notwithstanding its basic militarism, Japanese culture has always laid stress on poetic and artistic refinement and on apparently simple but in reality extremely complex ceremonial patterns, still governing polite behavior to an extraordinary degree. In no other way, perhaps, could civilization be maintained under the conditions imposed upon Japan by geography.

The Westerner is struck by the almost incredible Japanese capacity for hard, patient, and precise work, and at the same time by an apparent Japanese lack of inventiveness. But this last is often exaggerated. True, most leading religious, philosophical, scientific, and artistic ideas, including even script, were imported. But the Japanese desire for infinite, even drastic, simplification tends to strip the implications of an idea or a form down to their perfect essence, in the statement of which the artist or writer often exploits the surprise due to the sudden interpenetration of opposites. This process often culminates in literary and artistic statements of astonishing finality, and renders cultural imports in the last analysis peculiarly Japanese. Even more important is the Japanese reverence for the inner quality of the object, whether natural or man-made, as the subject, the material, or the result of artistic creation. A single painting or writing, a bowl, a flower, a tree, a rock, a waterfall, deserves and receives careful and prolonged contemplation. From such contemplation springs the special and inimitable beauty of Japanese art.

In attempting to understand the Japanese catalyst of symbolic simplification, one should bear in mind three quintessentially Japanese cultural phenomena: the tea ceremony, in which the slightest glance or movement in preparing, contemplating, and consuming a simple beverage is refined to the ultimate and fraught with symbolic significance; the No drama, in which traditional stories, which everyone can follow in books, are performed with enormous tension and terrifying slowness on prescribed stage sets; and the seventeen-syllable *haiku*—five, seven, and five—which record a simple action or image in what is instantly felt as its ultimate poetical, even mystical, significance. Totally Japanese in their definitive form, although based on Chinese models, are the many-paneled standing screens, often painted by the greatest artists, and, although they, too, owe something to earlier Chinese examples, so also are the *ukiyo-e,* the popular woodblock prints, which became works of art of high quality. Both have had enormous influence on Western art and society.

Early Japanese Art

Japan got off to a late start. While India and China nurtured magnificent imperial civilizations, the central Japanese islands were inhabited by apparently indigenous Neolithic peoples who were able to make strikingly original pottery and clay figurines, then by immigrants—apparently from Korea—who brought with them bronze mirrors from China and iron objects. During the Yayoi period (c. 200 B.C.—

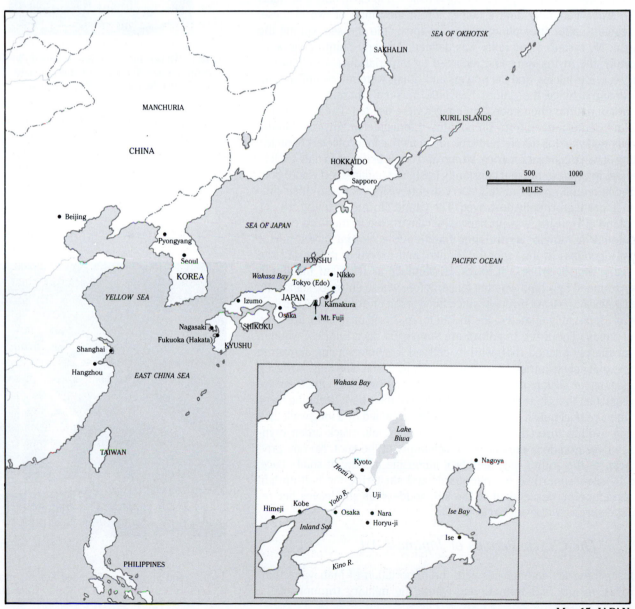

Map 15. JAPAN

A.D. 200), the inhabitants of Japan learned to cast bronze themselves. Later waves of immigration, also probably from Korea, brought the horse.

KOFUN PERIOD (c. A.D. 200–552)   According to contemporary Chinese chronicles, which speak of the Japanese as barbarians, the settled portions of the islands were ruled by more than a hundred petty priest-kings. Between the third and the sixth centuries one such monarchy, under the Yamato clan, succeeded in consolidating its power over much of the area, laying the foundations for the later imperial state. A number of large mound-tombs called *kofun* survive, from which the period has received its name; a very large mound-tomb of the emperor Nintoku near Osaka dates from the fifth century. Rows of small clay cylinders called *haniwa*, placed on such tombs for a purpose not yet entirely understood, were often formed into the shapes of warriors and horses. The illustrated haniwa, *Warrior in Armor* (fig. 18–1), impressive in its almost abstract rigidity and devoid of any outside influence, might be compared with the life-size Qin tomb figures from Xi-an (see fig. 17–3) to show the totally different approach to figural art between ancient Chinese civilization and the protohistoric culture of Japan.

The native religion of Japan is Shinto, still official today. Not only its origins but its very nature are mysterious. No supreme being is believed to exist, only a fluctuating number of *kami*, generally nature deities. From the union of two of these, Izanagi and Izanami, after they plunged a jewel-spear into the sea, sprang the islands of Japan. No system of morality was defined. All early Shinto texts were transmitted orally; the myths were first recorded by imperial decree only in two eighth-century-A.D. chronicles, and the prayers and rituals were not compiled until the eleventh century. Since the deities had little personal character and were already manifest in natural phenomena, no images were needed. The importation of Buddhism and Confucianism from China infused foreign elements into Shinto, which also venerated warrior-heroes and took on an increasingly official character.

The founding of two major sanctuaries, Izumo and Ise, is believed to date back to the Kofun period; in order to present constantly fresh and undamaged wood, both have been exactly rebuilt approximately every twenty years, alongside their predecessors, which are then ritually destroyed. The Grand Shrine at Ise (fig. 18–2), on the main island of Honshu, was probably first constructed in the third century A.D. at Kasamimura in Yamato, according to tradition to enclose a sacred mirror given by the sun-goddess to the emperor Himiko, and moved to its present site twenty-four years later. Doubtless it looks substantially as it did in the Kofun period. It is surrounded by a high wooden fence, before whose entrance stands the *torii*, or sacred gateway, passing through which the worshiper experiences spiritual rebirth. Such toriis, possibly related to the Indian toranas (see page 501), are to be found all over Japan. The three buildings are supported on cylindrical wooden posts; so is the sharply pitched roof, with its crossed logs intersecting above the woven thatch, exquisitely trimmed to resemble two huge slabs. The logs, however, are not trimmed; as for all Japanese buildings employing such logs, the trees are cut in the spring when the sap is rising, then stripped of their bark. Rubbing turns the sap itself into a perfect polish. Access to the shrine is gained by a long walk up a sharply curving avenue through a forest of immensely tall, black-green cryptomeria trees, whose grandeur enhances the solemnity of the spot. No one privileged to witness, as the author has, the black limousine moving at snail's pace, accompanied by silent, unarmed temple guards and sheltering the bolt-upright daughter of the emperor, descendant of the sun-goddess, as she leaves her re-dedication of the shrine, will ever forget it.

The Classic Periods of Japanese Art

A new era in Japanese art commences with the importation of Mahayana Buddhism into Japan in A.D. 552 from Korea, where the military triumph of the

18-1

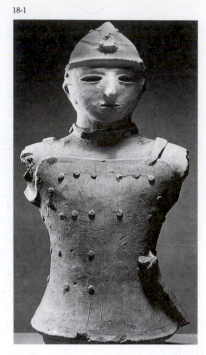

18-1. *Warrior in Armor.* Kofun period, 3d–6th centuries A.D. Terra-cotta haniwa, height 25″ (63.5 cm). Negishi Collection, Saitama

18-2

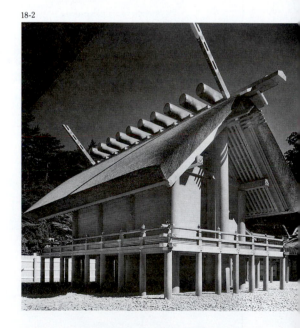

18-2. Grand Shrine, Ise. Founded Kofun period, 3d century A.D. Photograph © Yoshio Wanatabe

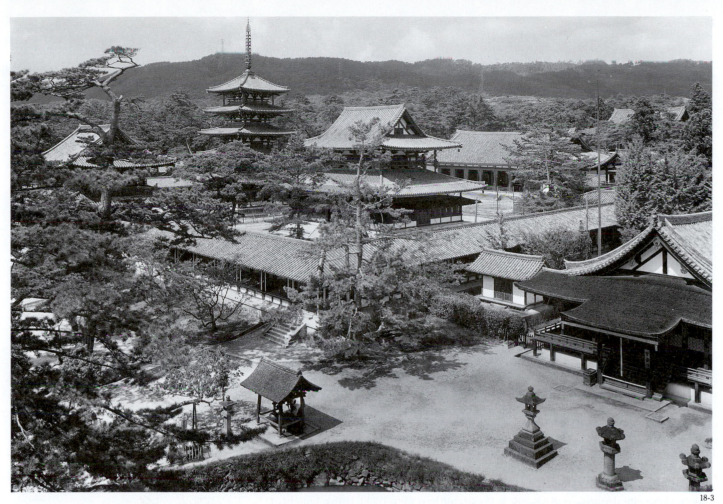

18-3. Horyu-ji, Nara. Founded Asuka period,
c. A.D. 610

18-3

Buddhist faction rendered their religion enticing to the Japanese court. After a period of clan warfare and assassinations, the Shoga clan placed in power the devout Buddhist Shotoku (A.D. 572–622), as crown prince and regent for the empress Suiko. Shotoku's *Constitution in Seventeen Articles* is in some respects reminiscent of the edicts proclaimed by the Indian Buddhist emperor Asoka (see page 499). Chinese ideographs were adopted for writing and temples were built, decorated, and manned with priests throughout the empire, in an astonishingly short time. Such a cultural phenomenon might be compared, in the present materialistic age, with the Soviet importation of Fiat plants from Italy, complete with architects, engineers, and foremen. While the new official religion heavily infiltrated Shinto, the old beliefs continued to flourish; many Japanese professed both.

ASUKA PERIOD (A.D. 552–645)   The greatest temple complex of the Asuka period, so called from one of its capitals (now a mere village south of Nara), is the magnificent Horyu-ji shrine (*ji* is the Japanese suffix indicating "temple"), built by Korean architects at Nara about 610 (fig. 18–3). The present buildings are the result of reconstruction after a fire at the close of the seventh century. Thereafter they were jealously preserved and are probably the oldest wooden structures anywhere. But in 1949 a tragic fire burned the Kondo ("Golden Hall"), the two-story building visible at the center of the illustration. Luckily, considerable portions had been removed for repair and were incorporated in the painstaking reconstruction. Horyu-ji is generally considered a faithful reflection of the vanished Chinese architecture of the Six Dynasties (see page 529) in its superimposed tiled roofs, with slight upward tilt at the corners, supported on relatively slender posts carved

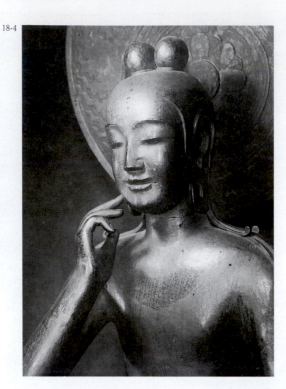

18-4

into animal shapes, to which the weight is transferred by the usual flexible system of multiple interlocking corbels, which allows for contraction and expansion of the wood under atmospheric change. Later these brackets become more intricate from temple to temple. Japanese woodwork is always left unsanded. The silken beauty of the surfaces is produced by razor-sharp planes, which part wood fibers from one another without violating their integrity. The porch added around the lower story of the Kondo is a wholly Japanese feature. The Kondo contains not only important mural paintings, reduced to fragments in the fire, but splendid bronze sculptures of pure Longmen style (but earlier than that illustrated in fig. 17–11), by a sculptor of Chinese descent, which escaped. A strikingly Japanese work in spite of such imported iconographic elements as the designs on the halo is the famous wooden statue of *Miroku,* the Maitreya (a detail is shown in fig. 18–4), in the nunnery of Chugu-ji attached to Horyu-ji. Instead of the imperturbable calm of Indian and Chinese Buddha types, we witness a peculiarly Japanese resolution of extreme tension by means of lyric beauty and deliberate understatement. Detail is omitted in the interest of continuous flow of all the surfaces into each other in a moment of exquisite poise.

NARA PERIOD (A.D. 645–794)   After several changes of site, the imperial capital was established at Nara, south of Kyoto in western Honshu, and completed in 710, when the empress Gommei took up residence. It was an oriented, quadrilateral grid on the model of Changan, the Tang capital, three miles by two and one-half, with artists and artisans housed in a place of extraordinary favor near the imperial palace—priests, nuns, and nobles in the center and common people in the outskirts. However, despite determined measures taken to centralize all authority under imperial control and to allocate land to the peasants, it became increasingly difficult for them to pay their taxes. Land rapidly reverted to the great nobles and the powerful monasteries, resulting in the growth of a feudal society. This very period of tension saw the development of a Buddhist art based on Tang examples but in the long run intensely Japanese.

The interiors of Nara shrines are believed to present a faithful picture of their often contemporary Tang models. Large, sometimes over-life-size, statues of the

18-5

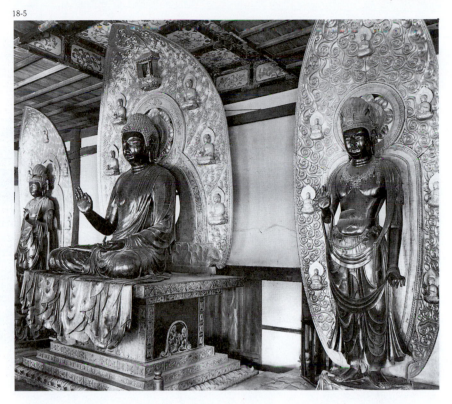

18-5. *Yakushi Trinity.* Nara period, A.D. 726. Bronze, height of central figure 8′4″ (2.54 m). Yakushi-ji, Nara

Buddha seated between Bodhisattvas and flanked by armed and angry guardians, in painted wood, painted clay, or lacquer, are lined up abreast on a raised platform, under the richly painted, coffered wooden ceiling. Intended to be seen from only a slight distance and from below, the statues are illuminated by the low light coming through the grills that cover the spaces between the wooden columns, with overpowering effect. The *Yakushi Trinity* in the Yakushi-ji at Nara (fig. 18–5), dated 726, consists of three bronze figures, the side ones about ten feet tall. The central seated figure, the Healing Buddha, or Yakushi, is flanked by Bodhisattvas, reflecting the classic dignity, amplitude, and beauty of vanished Tang models in the grace of their relaxed poses with the weight on one foot, reminding one of fourth-century-B.C. Greece, their freely gesturing hands, and the broad flow of their drapery.

HEIAN PERIOD (A.D. 794–1185)   The emperor Kammu, dissatisfied with his situation at Nara, decided to move his capital to the northern end of the same plain, at a place called Heian-kyo, the modern Kyoto. In 794 the imperial government was transferred there, and remained at Kyoto until 1868, when the emperor Meiji moved it to Edo, the modern Tokyo. Significantly, Kammu forbade the monasteries to move from Nara to Heian-kyo. Buddhism, previously a religion solely for the Japanese aristocracy, was widened to the general populace by the introduction from China of Amitabha (Amida Butsu in Japanese), a deified Bodhisattva and great savior. The ability to read Chinese became essential for governmental office. The powerful Fujiwara clan founded schools for the children of the nobility alone; commoners were thus effectively excluded from power. In the ninth century, however, a method was devised to transcribe the monosyllables of the Japanese language and those imported from China and elsewhere by means of 152 characters, thus bypassing the vastly complicated Chinese system of ideograms, and favoring the development of an essentially Japanese literature. But Chinese influence soon decreased when, for a variety of reasons, ambassadorial contact with China came to a virtual close after 838.

The Late Heian period (A.D. 897–1185) is also known as the Fujiwara period from the clan that initiated the basic phenomenon of Japanese political history for the next thousand years—the removal of the emperor from active government.

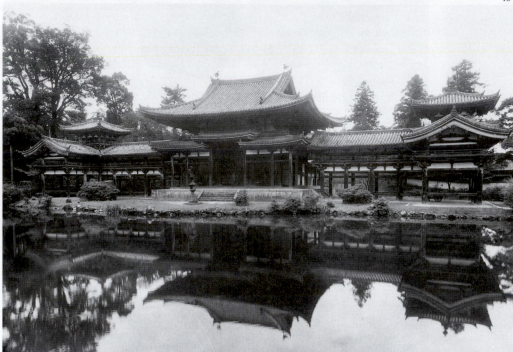

18-6. Ho-o-do (Phoenix Hall), Byodo-in, Uji. Late Heian period, 11th century A.D.

Real power was held by any group strong enough to seize it, by whatever means. The Fujiwara governed at first as regents, ostensibly for underage sovereigns, but the regency soon became permanent, and the imperial family was relegated to a largely ceremonial existence.

The supreme Late Heian structure is the Phoenix Hall (Ho-o-do), so called on account of its resemblance to a great bird in flight, of the Byodo-in temple complex at Uji (fig. 18–6), which had once been a Fujiwara country house. Poetically situated in the center of a large pond so as to exploit the reflections of its upturned roofs, the building is shown to derive from Chinese temple ancestors, such as that depicted in the *Western Paradise* at Dunhuang (see fig. 17–13). The two-story central structure is built on a stone platform and connected to lateral pavilions by means of open galleries on posts.

Two opposed polarities of the period are represented by sacred and secular paintings. *Paranirvana of the Buddha* (fig. 18–7), dated 1086, a picture of magical beauty more than eight feet square, represents in a style derived from Tang line-and-color painting the traditional moment in Buddhist iconography when bodily death has released the Buddha to Nirvana, the state of blissful nonbeing. The colossal figure of the Buddha is extended in utter calm on a lacquered bed among flowering trees, while his mother, Queen Maya, appears in the heavens at the upper right. Bodhisattvas at his head accept the Buddha's passing with due serenity, but less enlightened mortals grieve, weep, even scream, while a distraught lion rolls on the ground in agony. Every extreme can be encompassed within this epitome of artistic, intellectual, and spiritual control.

The *Tale of Genji,* a long novel by Lady Murasaki recounting the amorous intrigues of the Heian court, was illustrated in the twelfth century in handscrolls usually attributed to the painter TAKAYOSHI—of which only sections survive—to form the most striking example of the purely Japanese decorative-narrative pictorial style, known as *yamato-e,* from Yamato, the central region of Honshu, cradle of Japanese culture, to distinguish it from the imported Chinese manner. Episodes in the story are delayed by the separate savoring of each passing manifestation of human or natural beauty, even of a costume or of a single flower. The painter utilizes the characteristic Japanese device of representing episodes from above by removing the roof. Ground and background thus become almost identical. In fig. 18–8 we look into the apartment in which a maidservant is combing the long black hair of Lady Naka no Kimi after a wash, while her sister Ukifune gazes at pictures in a handscroll and another attendant reads aloud the text they illustrate. In early examples of pictures within pictures, a landscape screen occupies the upper right-hand corner of the scene, and a hanging is lowered to show Naka no Kimi in further conversation with her maid. Delicate outlines in black ink, especially visible in the kimono of the kneeling Naka no Kimi, where the colors have peeled off, define the angular folds of stiffened costumes, which betray no memories of the flowing drapery of Indian-Chinese religious art. The flattened figures against the rising floor are early examples of the interest in broad, angular, geometric design that is typical of later Japanese pictorial art. Thick layers of pigment are applied in sometimes startling color. The *tatami* (floor mats) are bright green, and the kimonos vary from cream to violet, with here and there a touch of dark, or even bright, red. The brilliant green hilltops in the landscape screen emerge from surrounding violet mists. Against this vibrant color, the white (powdered) faces and straight black hair of the women form startling accents. The yamato-e style continued to produce a multitude of Japanese narratives.

KAMAKURA PERIOD (A.D. 1185–1333)   Increasingly, emperors retired to monasteries, where they could exercise residual authority free from court ritual; sometimes there were two cloistered emperors at once. The decline of the Fujiwara, despite their blood relationship to the emperor, led to open and prolonged warfare between two rival clans, which devastated much of the country during the twelfth century and partially depopulated Kyoto. In 1185 the leader of the Minamoto family, Yoritomo, who had already established a military government at Kamakura, became undisputed master of most of Japan. Not until 1192, however, was he awarded the title of *shogun* ("Military Pacifier of the East"), thus founding an institution, the shogunate, that lasted until 1868. The shogun's headquarters at Kamakura became the seat of power, leaving Kyoto no more than ceremonial status. Although a Shintoist, especially dedicated to the Shinto god of war, Yoritomo favored Buddhism, and he undertook the construction and decoration of new temples, along with a wide variety of social and political reforms necessary after the tumultuous period the country had undergone. Alas, the Kamakura government acquired a new and terrible enemy in the person of Kublai Khan, the first Mongol emperor of China, who for nearly thirty years plotted the addition of Japan to his empire and attempted two actual invasions in great force, in 1274 and 1281. Although both were beaten back, the second with the aid of a providential typhoon, the necessity of supporting an enormous standing army, added to the devastation of war, proved disastrous to the Kamakura regime. A period of great internal dissension ensued, resulting in the establishment of two rival imperial courts, prolonged and destructive civil war, and the rise of the samurai and their code of honor, *bushido,* which owned no ethics higher than loyalty to the sovereign. Chan Buddhism (see pages 537–38) was imported from China, renamed Zen, and in its reliance on enlightenment through nonrational, individual experience encouraged not only sages in their hermit-like existence but, paradoxically, unhermit-like samurai as well.

The disorder of the Kamakura period is reflected in the numerous realistic scrolls, whose everyday subject matter, embracing in minute detail every aspect of life from birth to death, is couched in yamato-e style. The greatest are the *Heiji-Monogatari* handscrolls, illustrating a novel concerning one of the frequent insurrections of the period. In the *Night Attack on the Sanjo Palace* (fig. 18–9), armored horsemen, brilliantly depicted in action poses, attempt to flee, often unsuccessfully, the blazing timbers of the palace that crash around them and the ensuing firestorm. Vivid, accurate outline in ink is reinforced by small areas of solid color and by the red streaks of the advancing flames.

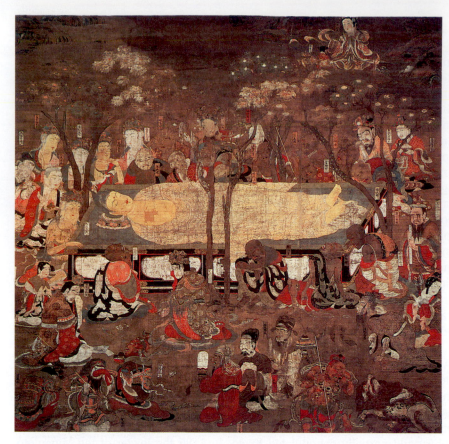

18-7. *Parinirvana of the Buddha.* Late Heian period, A.D. 1086. Color on silk, height 8′10″ (2.69 m). Kongobu-ji, Koyasan, Wakayama

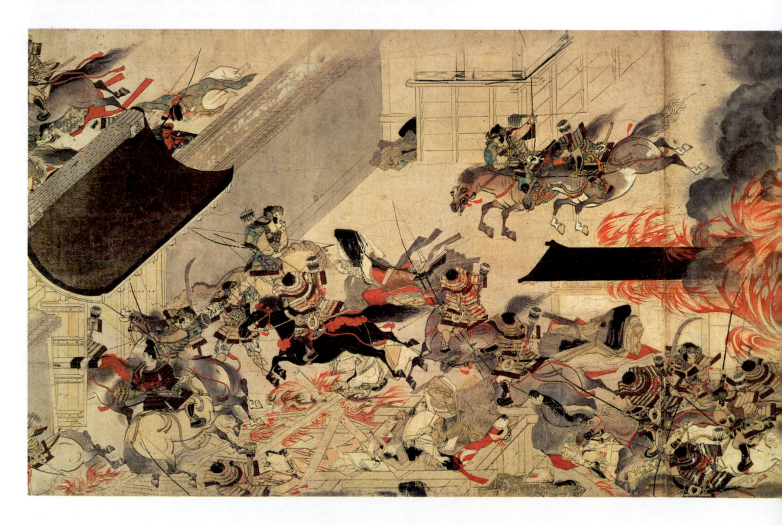

18-8. First illustration to the *Azumaya* chapter of the *Tale of Genji*. Attributed to TAKAYOSHI. Late Heian period, 12th century A.D. Handscroll; ink and color on paper, height 8½″ (21.6 cm). Tokugawa Art Museum, Nagoya

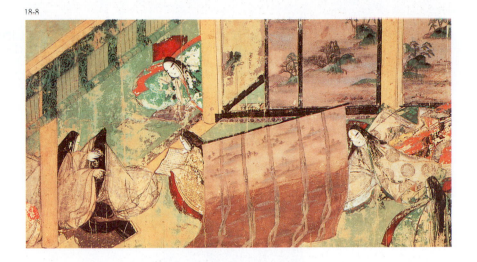

18-9. *Night Attack on the Sanjo Palace* (section of the *Heiji-Monogatari* handscroll). Kamakura period, second half of 13th century A.D. Ink and color on paper, height 16¼″ (42.5 cm). Courtesy, Museum of Fine Arts, Boston. Fenollosa-Weld Collection

Not unexpectedly, a vivid realist art flourished during this period of violence, alongside inherited Buddhist iconographic tradition. Especially powerful are the large temple statues of polychromed wood made on a new principle, not unrelated to that of the temple corbels, involving several interlocking pieces to allow for expansion and contraction and thus prevent cracking. The leader of the Kamakura sculptors was UNKEI (active A.D. 1163–1223), to whom a number of statues have been attributed. The psychological intensity of the school is fully evident in the *Priest Muchaku,* of about 1208, one of a pair of polychromed wood sculptures by

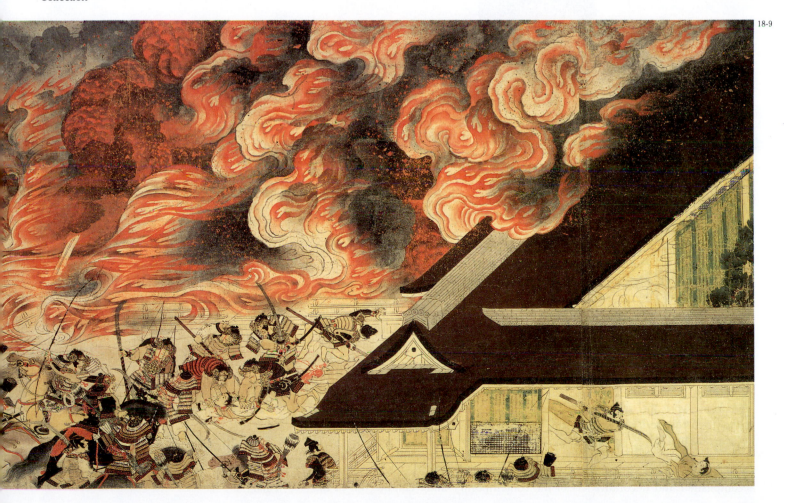

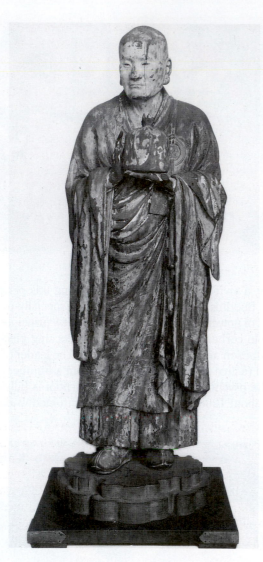

18-10. Unkei. *Priest Muchaku.* Kamakura period, c. A.D. 1208. Painted wood, height approx. 6′2″ (1.88 m). Hokuen-do, Kofuku-ji, Nara

18-10

Unkei (fig. 18–10). The stern, shaven-headed ascetic stands quietly, holding a lacquer box with both hands, his weight resting slightly more on his left foot, his garments falling in naturalistic folds without a trace of traditional drapery patterns. Nothing like the extreme realism of the head had been seen since the days of Roman portraiture (no connection, of course). The searching vision of the sculptor has picked up every wrinkle on the aged face, and the eyes are crystal. Even more than sculptor's devotion to fact, however, the effect of the work depends on its projection of the intensity of the priest's Buddhist faith.

ASHIKAGA PERIOD (A.D. 1392–1573)   Under the succeeding Ashikaga shogunate the worst was yet to come. With the transfer of the military government back to the imperial capital at Kyoto, the shogun soon became as powerless as the emperor. Japan entered a period of deepening terror and appalling bloodshed, in which even Kyoto was devastated, and, as Sherman Lee puts it, "The house laws of the feudatories were the only law in Japan." Finally the long-suffering peasants revolted, firearms were introduced, and the old Japan came to a terrible end but a new beginning.

Yamato-e continued in weakened form. However, the ascendancy of individualistic Zen involved a sudden transfer of artistic interest to China, not to the accomplished and decorative art of the contemporary Ming culture, but to the

18-11. Sesshu. *Winter Landscape.* Ashikaga period, 15th century A.D. Hanging scroll; ink and slight color on paper, height 18¼″ (46.4 cm). National Museum, Tokyo

18-12. Sesson. *Dragon* (one of a pair of six-fold screens). Ashikaga period, 16th century A.D. Ink on paper, length 12′ (3.66 m). Cleveland Museum of Art. Purchase from the J. H. Wade Fund

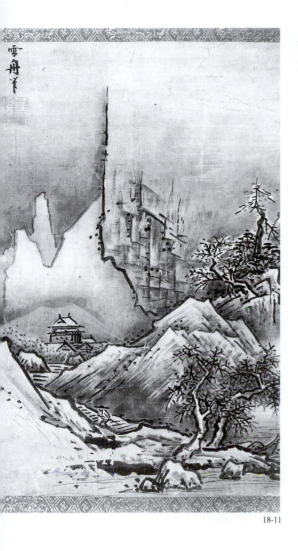

mystical monochrome Southern Song painting of two and a half centuries earlier, which was imported in quantity. The greatest Japanese painter of the period, perhaps the greatest of all Japanese painters, the Zen monk SESSHU (A.D. 1420–1506), traveled extensively in China, where he was influenced by the Ming version of Song style, but also made and signed loving copies of Ma Yuan, Xia Gui, and Liang Kai. The familiar landscape of Japan became suddenly unfashionable; Chinese crags and pinnacles (not to be seen in Japan) were imported along with Chinese ink techniques. But there is an essential difference: seldom does man seek harmony in nature—he fights it. In Sesshu's magical *Winter Landscape,* a tiny figure makes his painful way along a riverbank toward safety and warmth in a seemingly inaccessible distant temple surrounded by thatched roofs (fig. 18–11). Far from the smooth, perfect brushstrokes of Ma Yuan and Xia Gui, jagged touches like exploding firecrackers outline the wintry trees and the threatening cliff. Is there a lesson? Is safety unattainable, save in a flash of enlightenment?

Master of every stylistic implication of the monochrome technique, from elaborate description of landscape, birds, and flowers to the Japanese equivalent of po-mo (see page 534), Sesshu was the founder of a fifteenth-century school of ink painters that continued into the sixteenth century, culminating in the art of another great Zen master, SESSON (A.D. 1504–after 1589), whose immensely long life was lived in northeastern Honshu, far from the court and even from Zen centers. His magnificent six-fold dragon screen (fig. 18–12), one of a pair done in ink on paper—the other is a tiger—shows the mythical being, often celebrated in Song, appearing through concentric circles of whirlwind only in glimpses of a scaly tail, a claw, an agonized face, in a world of scudding waves and whirling storm.

A special contribution of both Chinese and Japanese culture is the apparently informal garden, in reality planned with even greater care and sensitivity than the elaborate patterns of Western formal gardens. Nowhere did the Far Eastern garden reach greater heights of subtlety and refinement than in the temple gardens of Japan, which no foot is permitted to tread, and only the spirit may enter. Sand gardens, with the sand raked in patterns to represent water, were meant for meditation only. Most refined of all are the intimate Zen gardens that are in a sense

18-11

18-12

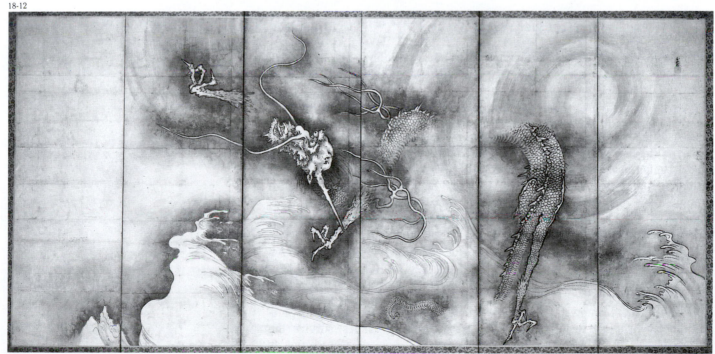

1404

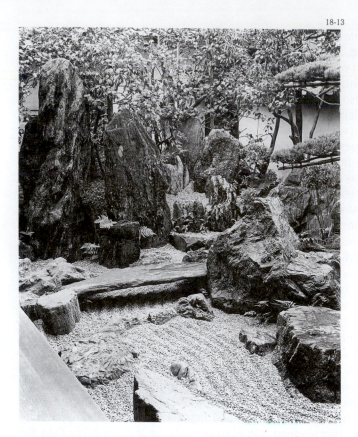

18-13

18-13. Garden of the Daisen-in of Daitoku-ji, Kyoto. Attributed to SOAMI (died A.D. 1525). Ashikaga period

models of painted landscapes and were often designed by major Zen painters. The tiny garden of the Daisen-in of the Daitoku-ji at Kyoto (fig. 18–13) represents the epitome of the Japanese landscape garden, and is indeed attributed to the painter SOAMI (died A.D. 1525). From one of two vantage points one watches the light play across the sand-water, the rock-mountains, and the shrub forests according to the times of day, as if one had entered in spirit a mystical landscape by Sesshu.

Later Japanese Art

MOMOYAMA AND TOKUGAWA PERIODS (A.D. 1573–1868) The intolerable civil war of the Ashikaga period was brought to a close by the exhaustion or extinction of most of the clans. The assumption of the shogunate of 1573 by Oda Nobunaga, and the brief subsequent rule of his family, was followed by that of an amazing upstart called Hideyoshi, who brought the barons to heel and enriched himself to such an extent that he was able to lend the impoverished emperor money to repair his palace. He even made two determined attempts to conquer China, beaten back each time in Korea. His favorite son and successor together with all the family were slaughtered in 1615 and their legendary castle at Osaka destroyed by their former ally Tokugawa Ieyasu; the period is known as Momoyama ("Peach Hill") from the orchard planted on the site of Nobunaga's demolished castle south of Kyoto. Ieyasu and his successors ruled a unified Japan from a new capital at Edo, the modern Tokyo, until the emperor Meiji abolished the shogunate in 1868. Under the Tokugawa regime, contact with the outer world almost ceased; Christianity, which had gained a foothold, was persecuted; Japan retreated into itself.

Artistically there is no separation between the Momoyama and Tokugawa periods. A necessity for the dictatorship was the castle; only a few of these survive (the feudal barons were forbidden to repair theirs!), but they are magnificent examples

18-14. Himeji Castle, Hyogo Prefecture.
Momoyama period, A.D. 1581; enlarged 1609

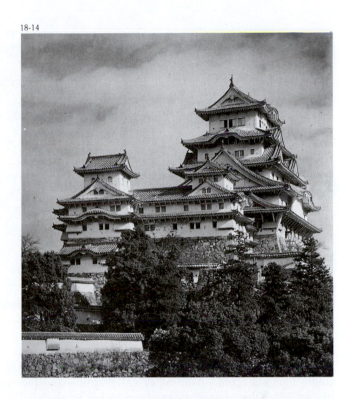

18-14

of combined military and residential architecture. One of the most imposing is Himeji Castle (fig. 18–14), another of Hideyoshi's residences, built in 1581 and enlarged in 1609. Typically, the castle is surrounded by a moat, from which massive stone walls, battered to repel artillery, rise to fifty or sixty feet. Within are court-yards, outbuildings, housing for servants and guards, and opulent gardens. In the center, a square tower supports a five-story wooden palace that resembles a more massive pagoda, whose small windows are the only sign of its defensive purpose. Upturned roofs, punctuated by gables in different positions on each story, enrich the silhouette. Against the gray stone and the dark surrounding pines, the walls and gables of Himeji glisten white.

The conservative Kano school of monochrome painting, founded in Ashikaga times by Kano Masanobu (A.D. 1434–1530), continued for two centuries in the more decorative work of the extended Kano family, often intended for the splendid interiors of castles or residences. Some fine sliding screens, notably *Plum Tree by Water* (fig. 18–15), attributed to KANO EITOKU (A.D. 1543–90), convert the "ax-cut" rocks, gnarled trunks, blossoming boughs, and bamboo of the standard Sino-Japanese repertory to effective ornamental purpose through patterns based on repeated rhythms in varying sizes, delicately indicated in ink and soft washes of color, including gold. Screens such as this acted as partitions in Momoyama and Tokugawa interiors, and their frequent backgrounds of gold leaf were relied upon to reflect the light from small castle windows.

An antidote to the magnificence of the castles is the austerity of the teahouses, often situated in their gardens. These structures, sometimes tiny, were built to house the tea ceremony founded in Ashikaga times, codified by Sen no Rikyu (A.D. 1521–91), tea master to Hideyoshi, and handed down by generations of hereditary tea masters. As in much Japanese cuisine, taste is subordinate to idea. Nothing could be further from the tea ceremony than the mere enjoyment of tea. The strict ritual was and is to this day intended to inculcate the basically Zen ideals of simplicity and purity and to foster the understanding of natural and artistic beauty. Five guests arrive through the garden after stopping to purify hands and mouth.

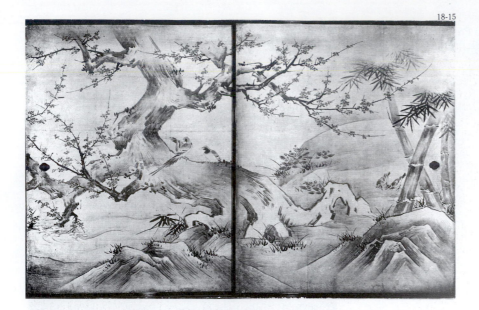

18-15. *Plum Tree by Water* (one of a pair of sliding screens). Attributed to KANO EITOKU (A.D. 1543–90). Momoyama period. Ink and slight color washes on paper, height 69⅛″ (1.77 m). Juko-in, Kyoto

They are taught humility by crouching to enter a low door, quietly contemplate the single hanging scroll—painting or calligraphy—and the single flower in a vase placed within the *tokonoma,* or niche, which is an essential feature of the traditional Japanese house, and kneel-sit in strict order on the tatami to await the arrival of the host. Silently, he or she prepares each cup of tea with the simplest of traditional instruments, according to a ritual that prescribes even the way in which host and guest turn the bowl, the number of sips, and the later inspection of the instruments. The guests leave as silently as they came. The interior (fig. 18–16) is made of rustic materials such as those of the typical Japanese farmhouse, or, indeed, of the Grand Shrine at Ise. These include untrimmed—but carefully polished—post-and-paper walls, of typically Japanese rightness in their asymmetrical disposition, the like of

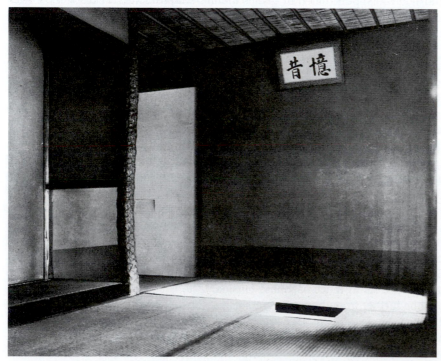

18-16. Interior of the teahouse named *Taigra.* Momoyama period, A.D. 1573–1615. Hara Collection, Yokohama

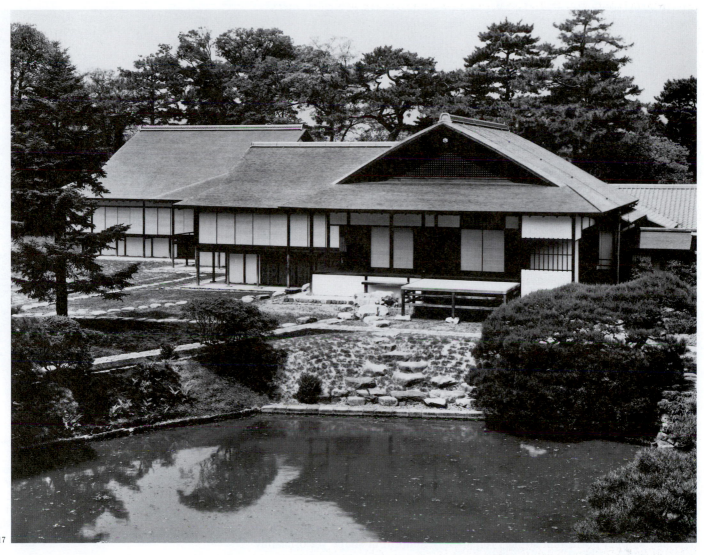

18-17. Katsura Palace, near Kyoto (view from the east). C. A.D. 1615–63

which was not achieved in the West until Le Corbusier and Piet Mondrian in the early twentieth century.

The epitome of domestic architecture based on the tradition of the teahouse, and the opposite pole to the grandeur of the Himeji Castle, is the imperial villa at Katsura near Kyoto, a seventeenth-century structure in which total simplicity becomes perfect beauty (figs. 18–17, 18–18). The Chinese upturned roofs are abandoned in favor of the straight roofline of ancient Japan, as at Ife, upheld by exquisitely planed and polished wooden posts. Openings are filled with removable paper screens so that interior and exterior, building and garden, human life and nature, are perfectly coordinated through an inimitable sense of universal harmony.

The most characteristic Tokugawa contributions were the decorative screen, new forms of ink painting, and the woodblock print. OGATA KORIN (A.D. 1658–1716), one of the most successful of the decorative painters, raised the screen to the level of great art, exploiting the possibilities of gold leaf on paper, as in his two-fold screen *White Prunus in the Spring* (fig. 18–21). The branch plunges in a drastic diagonal, fixed in utter perfection of line and color. The gold ground (is it earth, is it snow?) leads us to the black waters, swirling with touches of gold. In this stark world, the many buds and few blossoms sparkle like tiny diamonds.

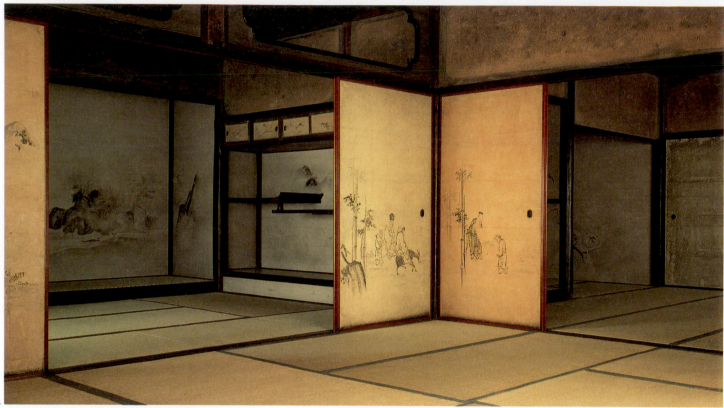

18-18

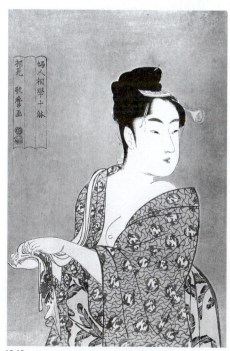

18-19

18-18. Interior, Katsura Palace, near Kyoto

18-19. KITAGAWA UTAMARO. *Bust of a Beautiful Lady Dressed in a Kimono* (from *Types of Physiognomic Beauty*). Tokugawa period, A.D. 1794. Full-color wood-block print, height 14¾″ (37.5 cm). Cleveland Museum of Art. Bequest of Edward L. Whittemore

Among the Tokugawa ink styles derived from Chinese painting the *nanga* ("southern") manner, based on careful study of wen-ren, is in the last analysis the most thoroughly Japanese. URAGAMI GYOKUDO (A.D. 1745–1820) was one of the most powerful painters of this group. His *Forbidden to the Vulgar* (fig. 18–20) astonishes the observer by its calligraphic dexterity, poetry, and wit. Dry brush in vigorous, parallel horizontal strokes remarkably uniform in shape yet brilliantly various in tone sets forth a deliberately nonnaturalistic landscape of floating crags and forests with a scholar-painter's delicate disdain for those not educated to his recondite standards. These standards are indeed high. The at times almost abstract brushwork runs the gamut from pearly gray to velvety black. Deep among the swimming strokes, which suggest the forest of a scholar's meditation rather than any to be found in the natural world, nestles the pavilion of his refuge from the vulgar.

It fell to the most popular and cheapest of the arts, woodblock printing, to exert the greatest influence over the West, perhaps because it was the easiest to transport once Japan had been reopened to foreign trade in 1854 by the high-handed but productive naval presence of Commodore Matthew Perry. *Ukiyo-e,* the "pictures of the floating [passing] world," was the name applied to the art that arose not in the court or the houses of the wealthy but in the entertainment district of Edo and that dealt not with an ideal world of grace and beauty but a very real one of street scenes, actors in the vivid, popular Kabuki plays (running counter to the stylized aristocratic No drama), peddlers, and courtesans. In the seventeenth century, the already well-known technique of block printing began to be used for the illustration of books; what color was used was applied by hand. In the eighteenth century, color blocks, restricted to two hues, were devised. In 1765 multiple color blocks were introduced to produce the so-called brocade prints, resulting in much richer and more delicate color effects, with enormous popular success. The artist made his line drawing indicating the color, but all depended on the skill with which the

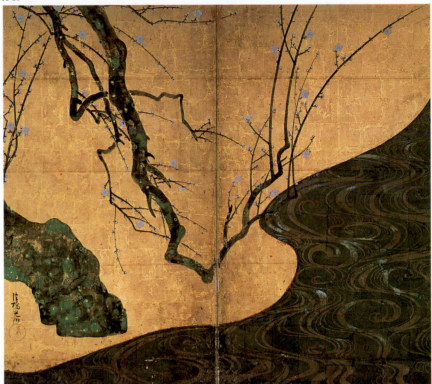

18-20. URAGAMI GYOKUDO. *Forbidden to the Vulgar.* Tokugawa period, late 18th century–early 19th century A.D. Ink on paper, 53 × 20½″ (134.6 × 52 cm). Cleveland Museum of Art. Mr. and Mrs. William H. Marlatt Fund

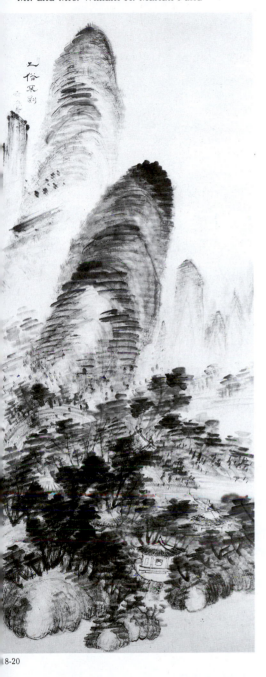

18-20

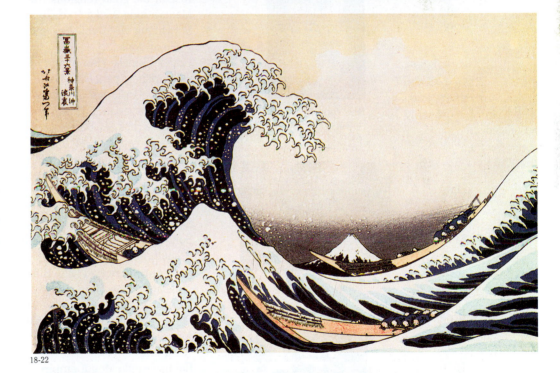

18-22

18-21. OGATA KORIN. *White Prunus in the Spring* (two-fold screen). Tokugawa period, c. 1680–1715. Color and gold leaf on paper, height 62″ (1.58 m). MOA Museum of Art, Atami

18-22. KATSUSHIKA HOKUSAI. *Great Wave off Kanagawa* (from *Thirty-six Views of Mount Fuji*). Tokugawa period, c. A.D. 1823–39. Full-color wood-block print, 10⅛ × 14¾″ (25.7 × 37.5 cm). The Metropolitan Museum of Art, New York. Bequest of Mrs. H. O. Havemeyer, 1929

woodcutter transferred the drawing to the separate blocks and the artistry of the color printer in producing the final multicolor print with its subtle gradations of tone, depending on precise "registration" (coordination of the blocks).

One of the most brilliant ukiyo-e figure artists was KITAGAWA UTAMARO (A.D. 1753–1806), whose prints were very influential in Europe in the mid-nineteenth century. His *Bust of a Beautiful Lady Dressed in a Kimono,* from a series entitled *Types of Physiognomic Beauty* (fig. 18–19), of 1794, shows the combined resiliency and incisiveness of the style. With resounding effect Utamaro contrasts the soft white of the lady's face, neck, and artfully revealed breast, modeled only by contour, with the deep black of her hair and the two rich and contrasting patterns of the kimono and the obi.

In the early nineteenth century, subject matter shifted to landscape, in which one of the leaders was KATSUSHIKA HOKUSAI (A.D. 1760–1849). One of the finest, as well as one of the best known of Japanese full-color wood-block prints is Hokusai's *Great Wave off Kanagawa* (fig. 18–22), from a series of thirty-six views of the mystic Mount Fuji. All of the traditional Japanese tendencies—natural violence, fatalism,

TIME LINE IX

HISTORY, CULTURE

2350 B.C.	Neolithic culture develops in China, India
1300	Feudal government is established in China
1000	Vedic period in India; *Rig-Veda* is composed
600	Rise of the great religions: Taoism, Buddhism, Confucianism
300	Maurya king Asoka (r. c. 269–232) is founder of first Indian empire
200	Shi Huang Di establishes first centralized state in China, builds Great Wall
	Under Chinese Han dynasty (206 B.C.–A.D. 200) trade with West flourishes; paper is invented
A.D. 200	Yamato clan lays foundations of imperial state in Japan; Buddhism reaches Japan, 552
500	Xia He writes *Six Canons of Painting* (c. 525–50)
600	Japanese capital is established at Nara, 645
	Under Tang dynasty (619–907) Chinese empire surpasses Roman empire in area and population
800	Japanese capital moves to Kyoto: Heian period (794–1185)
900	Song dynasty rules China (960–1279)
1100	Song dynasty is forced out of northern China; establishes capital in south at Hangzhou, 1127
1200	Kamakura period (1185–1333) marks triumph of feudalism in Japan
	Mongol Yuan dynasty rules China (1279–1368)
1300	Ming dynasty rules China (1368–1644)
1400	Ashikaga period (1392–1573) in Japan is one of continual civil warfare
1500	Babur founds Mogul empire in India (1526–1756)
	During Momoyama period (1573–1615) in Japan three warlords struggle for supreme rule
1600	Tokugawa shogunate is established by Japanese warlord Ieyasu, 1615
	Qing dynasty rules China (1644–1912)
1700	East India Company carries out British colonial policies in India, 1600–1858
1800	China and Japan open to foreign trade (1842, 1854)

Male Torso, from Harappa, Pakistan

Bayon, Angkor Thom, Cambodia

Celestial Beauty

drastic tension, extreme aestheticism—are embodied in this daring composition. With a boldness and geometrical brilliance going back to the yamato-e tradition of the *Genji* scrolls, Hokusai has shown us three fishing boats caught by the forces of the sea, one gliding down a wave, one wallowing in the trough, one struggling up the next slope, and all three menaced by the towering ferocity of a giant breaker that claws down upon them as it shoulders out the sky. Like the fragile islands constantly menaced by typhoons and tidal waves, even the perfect cone of Fuji seems powerless against the hostile waters.

THE FAR EAST

PAINTING, SCULPTURE, ARCHITECTURE

Early Spring, by Guo Xi

Ho-o-do, Uji

Bust of a Beautiful Lady, by Utamaro

Male Torso from Harappa	2350 B.C.
Bronze vessels from Shang royal tombs, Anyang	1300
Bronze Zhou vessel (*fang ding*)	1000
	600
Lion Capital from Asoka's column at Pataliputra	300
Stupas at Sanchi, Bharhut, Bhaja	200
Incense burner from Tomb of Liu Sheng	
Five Men Conversing, painted Han tile	
Izumo and Ise shrines, Honshu	A.D. 200
Palace Scene, Cave 17, Ajanta	500
Rock-cut rathas, Mahabalipuram	600
Horyu-ji, Nara	
Buddha Vairocana, Longmen	
Kailasanatha temple, Ellora	800
Great Stupa, Borobudur	
Muktesvara Temple, Bhubaneswar	900
Angkor Wat, Cambodia	1100
Tale of Genji illustrations	
Ma Yuan, *Scholar Contemplating the Moon*	1200
Unkei, *Priest Muchaku*	
Sun Temple, Konarak	
Ni Zan, *Rongxi Studio*	1300
Sesshu, *Winter Landscape*	1400
Garden of the Daisen-in, Kyoto	1500
Kano Eitoku, *Plum Tree by Water*	
Himeji Castle, Hyogo Prefecture	
Katsura Palace, near Kyoto	
Stairway, Hall of Supreme Harmony, Beijing	1600
Taj Mahal, Agra	
Ogata Korin, *White Prunus in the Spring*	1700
Utamaro, *Bust of a Beautiful Lady*	
Hokusai, *Great Wave off Kanagawa*	1800

While Italian Gothic architecture, for all its grandeur, remains essentially a late adaptation to local needs of forms and ideas imported from France and Germany (and is therefore treated in an earlier chapter), Italian painting and sculpture of this same period owe relatively little to the North. They seem to emerge from the Middle Ages into a wholly new era, with such striking force and originality that they are often and with good reason considered separately from the Gothic as forerunners of the Renaissance. For, beginning in the late thirteenth century, Italian artists are, above all, individuals, often intensely so. They are, of course, not the first artists since antiquity whose names we know. But the personalities and ideas of medieval artists can be deduced only from their work and occasionally their theological writings, which tell us little about their art. In most cases we have only their signatures. In contrast the Italians have left us mountains of verbal information—contracts, payment records, letters, legal documents, sometimes vividly personal inscriptions. Eventually, in the fifteenth and sixteenth centuries, they were to expound their professional traditions and theoretical ideas at great length in magnificent treatises, read avidly today. We possess precious, if scattered, accounts of Italian artists' lives and achievements by their contemporaries, and they are also mentioned glowingly by contemporary chroniclers and poets as great men of their communities. Their personalities live on in popular tradition and in the works of later writers, such as Lorenzo Ghiberti in the fifteenth century and Giorgio Vasari in the sixteenth, both artists in their own right with strong critical opinions and historical ideas.

The individuality of Italian artists arose from the very nature of Italian political and social life. In the later Middle Ages, with the sole exception of a few scattered independent or semi-independent city-states, all of Europe outside Italy was ruled by monarchies of one sort or another still under the feudal system. The princes of central Europe, moreover, all owed allegiance to the Holy Roman Empire, which, by historic right, also claimed control over Italy. But during the eleventh and twelfth centuries the rapidly growing Italian city-states, whose trade and banking connections spanned Europe from England to the Middle East, formalized their communal governments as republics (Venice, owing to special geographical and historical circumstances, had been a republic since the eighth century). Fortified by their immense commercial power, the new republics defied imperial authority. Ruled by members of guilds (associations of merchants, professionals, and artisans), the republics often went so far as to expropriate neighboring feudal domains, forcing the nobles to become burghers if they wished to enjoy the rights of citizenship. The artists, as guild members, participated fully in the vigorous activities of the aggressive and expanding republics, working for the leading citizens as well as for the church and the state. Under such circumstances their new individualism is easy to understand, in contrast to the relative docility and anonymity of the subjects of medieval monarchies. Like the burgher-artisans they were, the artists kept shops in which they produced works on commission and trained apprentices, some of whom were family members. With its strenuous manual activities, however, the Italian late-medieval shop was by custom and law a man's world. No women artistic figures have been identified.

NICOLA AND GIOVANNI PISANO Two extremely original sculptors, Nicola Pisano (active 1258–78) and his son Giovanni (c. 1250–c. 1314), whom we have already encountered as the principal architect of the façade of Siena Cathedral, embody sharply different phases of the rather tardy change from Romanesque to Gothic style in Italian sculpture. Although Nicola's surname indicates his Pisan citizenship, he came to Tuscany from southern Italy, where, since the days of Frederick II (ruled 1215–50)—more Italian king than German emperor—there had flourished a strong current of interest in ancient art. More to the point, perhaps, as the studies of Eloise M. Angiola have shown, is the classicism of Pisa, which considered itself a second Rome. Once capital of the ancient Roman province of Tuscany, Pisa, with its vast merchant marine and formidable navy, was favored by the Holy Roman Empire in the Middle Ages and was given sway over a wide territory along the Mediterranean and the entire island of Sardinia. In 1133, in fact, Pisa found itself briefly capital of Western Christendom, chosen as temporary residence by Pope Innocent II, who was excluded from Rome by an antipope.

Nicola's first great work was the hexagonal marble pulpit in the Baptistery at Pisa (fig. 19–1) that he signed with a long, self-laudatory inscription in 1260. Scuptured pulpits were traditional in Italy; that one could be needed in a baptistery may indicate the special importance of the sacrament of Baptism in the Italian republics as the moment in which a child took his place in the Christian community, and of course in the individual Italian commune. Nicola's handsome creation combines elements already familiar from central Italian medieval art, such as columns of red porphyry, red-and-gray granite, and richly veined brown marble, with Gothic trefoil arches. The capitals, partly Corinthian, partly Gothic, seem to partake of both styles. Like his earlier namesake Nicholas of Verdun and like the Visitation Master at Reims, Nicola had a strong interest in ancient art. Luckily, he had no dearth of models in Pisa. The close packing of forms filling the entire frame of the *Adoration of the Magi* (fig. 19–2) recalls the density of Roman sarcophagus relief, and in fact Nicola repeated almost exactly the pose of a seated figure in a sarcophagus still in the Campo Santo in Pisa for his Virgin, who has become a Roman Juno, impassive and grand. The carving of the beards of the Magi and the parallel drapery folds of all the figures also recall Roman examples, but the angular breaking of the folds betrays Nicola's familiarity with Byzantine mosaic art.

Giovanni, who claims in inscriptions to have outdone his father, was responsible for a sharply different octagonal pulpit at Pistoia (fig. 19–3). Dated 1298–1301, it is distinguished by its greater Gothicism in the sharp pointing of the arches as well as in the freer shapes of the foliate capitals, which only here and there disclose classical derivations. As we would expect from the unconventional shapes and animated statuary of the Siena façade, Giovanni's sculptural style is far more dramatic than his father's serene manner and shows almost no interest in classical art. Instead, the relaxed poses and free, full drapery folds of the corner statues suggest a familiarity with the portal sculptures of Amiens and Reims; Giovanni's inscriptions proclaim him as a traveler, and in all probability he visited the great French cathedrals. In the *Slaughter of the Innocents* (fig. 19–4), a panel of the Pistoia pulpit, he shows himself the master of a free narrative style, depending for

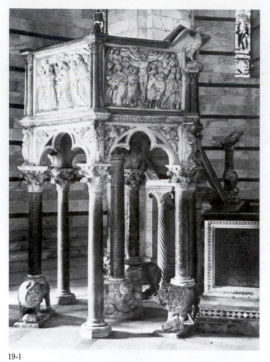

19-1

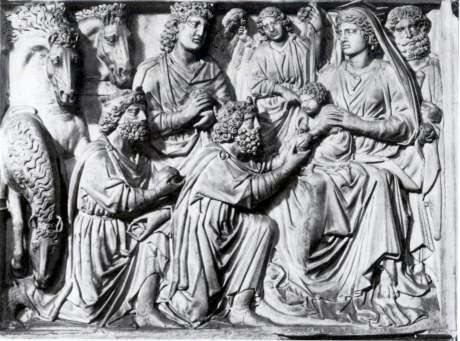

19-2

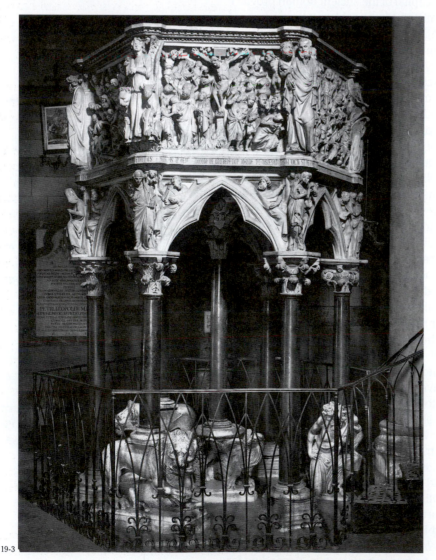

19-3

19-1. NICOLA PISANO. Pulpit. 1259–60. Marble, height approx. 15′ (4.57 m). Baptistery, Pisa

19-2. NICOLA PISANO. *Adoration of the Magi*, detail of the pulpit, Baptistery, Pisa. Marble relief, height approx. 34″ (86 cm)

19-3. GIOVANNI PISANO. Pulpit. 1298–1301. Marble. Sant'Andrea, Pistoia

19-4. Giovanni Pisano. *Slaughter of the Innocents*, detail of the pulpit, Sant'Andrea, Pistoia. Marble relief, 33 × 40″ (84 × 102 cm)

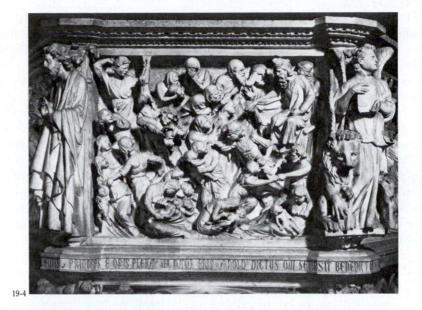

19-4

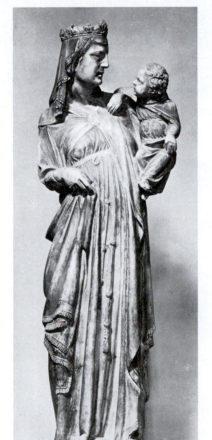

19-5

19-5. Giovanni Pisano. *Virgin and Child*. c. 1305. Marble. Arena Chapel, Padua

its effect on rapid, even violent movement of ferocious soldiers and screaming mothers and on considerable undercutting, which produces sharp contrasts of light and dark. The expressive power of Giovanni's style is brought under firm control, possibly in emulation of the great painter Giotto, in the marble statue of the *Virgin and Child* (fig. 19–5), which Giovanni carved about 1305 for the altar of the Arena Chapel in Padua, whose walls and ceiling were being frescoed by Giotto (see Introduction fig. 6 and figs. 19–9, 19–10). The boldness of the masses, the clarity of the contours, and the firmness of the pose of Giovanni's *Madonna* contrast strikingly with the elegance and lassitude of earlier examples.

Changes in thirteenth-century religious ritual gave rise to the demand for a new kind of image—of immense importance for the development of art, especially painting—the *altarpiece*. Until now the Mass had been celebrated, as again in the Roman Catholic Church since Vatican II, behind the altar, with the priest facing the congregation. This practice precluded the placing of anything more than the required crucifix, candlesticks, and sacred vessels upon the altar. In the course of the century, the celebrant's position was moved to the front of the altar, thus freeing the back of the altar for the development of imagery, both sculptural and pictorial. Although the icon, that all-important focus of Byzantine devotion, had been imported into the West in the early Middle Ages, it had not taken root. But in the thirteenth century, large-scale painted crucifixes, which had already been used in other positions in Italian churches, began to appear on altars. Soon the Madonna and Child competed for this prominent place, and eventually won. The altarpieces, which rapidly grew to considerable size so as to be visible to the congregation, were painted in a technique known as *tempera,* with egg yolk used as the vehicle. The procedure was slow and exacting. A wooden panel had to be carefully prepared and coated with *gesso* (fine plaster mixed with glue) as a ground for the underdrawing. Gold leaf was applied to the entire background, and then the figures and accessories were painted with a fine brush. As egg dries fast and does not permit corrections, the painter's craft called for accurate and final decisions at every stage. Under the impulse of this new demand, and spurred by the intense political and economic life of the Tuscan republics, painting rapidly developed in a direction that had no Northern counterparts until the fifteenth century.

CIMABUE Although at least two generations of Tuscan painters had preceded him in the thirteenth century, the first Italian painter known to Vasari by name was the Florentine Cenni di Pepi, called Cimabue (active c. 1272–1302). About 1280 Cimabue painted the *Madonna Enthroned* (fig. 19–6), an altarpiece more than twelve feet high, which in Vasari's day stood on the high altar of the church of Santa Trinita in Florence. The derivation of Cimabue's style from that of the Greek painters with whom Vasari said he worked is clear enough in the poses of the Virgin and the Child and also in the gold-striated patterns of their drapery folds. But in the delicate modeling of the faces and drapery of the angels, Cimabue also shows his familiarity with the refined Constantinopolitan style of his own time. Clearly, Cimabue was trying to rival in paint the monumental effects of Byzantine mosaics, but the gabled shape of his huge altarpiece is unknown in the East, as is the complex construction of the carved and inlaid throne; the effect is that of strong verticality, increased by the constant flicker of color in the angels' rainbow wings. Cimabue's insistent linear tension, maintained throughout the gigantic altarpiece, is also alien to the harmony of Byzantine art: it is thoroughly Tuscan, recalling the sculpture of the Pisani.

CAVALLINI   An exception to the dominance of the republics in Italian art was the school of Rome. After centuries of repetition of Early Christian models without major innovations, in the last decades of the thirteenth century Roman painting rose to a brief period of splendor, brought to a sudden end in 1305 when its chief patron, the papacy, unable to resist the power of the French monarchy, allowed itself to be carried off to Avignon in southern France, leaving Rome in a state of political and economic decline. The leader among all the gifted Roman painters was Pietro Cavallini, whose documented activities run from 1273 to 1308 but who was said by his own son to have lived nearly a hundred years. Vast fresco cycles by

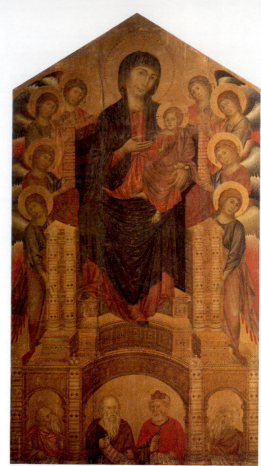

19-6

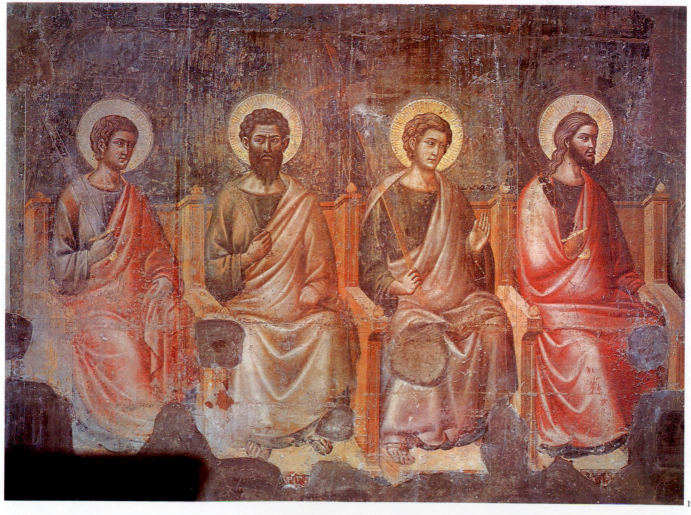

19-7

19-6. CIMABUE. *Madonna Enthroned,* from Sta. Trinita, Florence. c. 1280. Tempera on panel, 12′7½″ × 7′4″ (3.85 × 2.24 m). Galleria degli Uffizi, Florence

Cavallini, in part renewing, in part replacing damaged Early Christian works, once lined the nave walls of two great Roman basilicas, San Giovanni in Laterano (then the seat of the papacy and still today the Cathedral of Rome) and San Paolo fuori le mura (Saint Paul's Outside the Walls), as well as other churches. Almost all of these frescoes are now lost, but in his own time and well into the Renaissance Cavallini enjoyed a towering reputation. Certainly he had a tremendous influence on the art of the more famous Giotto, who surely saw Cavallini's work with a sense of discovery when he came to the Jubilee of 1300 called by Pope Boniface VIII.

Cavallini's major surviving work in fresco is the fragmentary *Last Judgment* of about 1290 in Santa Cecilia in Trastevere in Rome (fig. 19–7). This painting, impossible to photograph as a whole because of a gallery later built in front of it, carries the knowledge of the effects of light to a point inaccessible to Cimabue. Light and light alone brings out the fullness and sweep of the mantles that envelop these majestic figures. Their heads, however, especially those of the beardless Apostle second from the right and the bearded James (?) on the right, show a familiarity with French Gothic sculpture. Surely Cavallini had also studied such advanced Byzantine works as the frescoes at Sopoćani, which show an extraordinary advance in the interrelationship of light and volume. But the final result, endowing the art of painting with a grandeur and nobility of form previously exercised only by sculpture, and with a hitherto unknown beauty and softness of color gradations, is his own achievement.

GIOTTO   The final break with Byzantine tradition was accomplished by the Florentine master Giotto di Bondone (c. 1267–1337), the first giant in the long history of Italian painting. Even in his own day Giotto's greatness was recognized by his contemporaries. Dante puts in the mouth of a painter in Purgatory (*Purgatorio* XI, 94–96) his famous remark:

19-7. PIETRO CAVALLINI. *Last Judgment* (detail of a fresco), Sta. Cecilia in Trastevere, Rome. c. 1290

Cimabue believed that he held the field
In painting, and now Giotto has the cry,
So that the fame of the former is obscure.

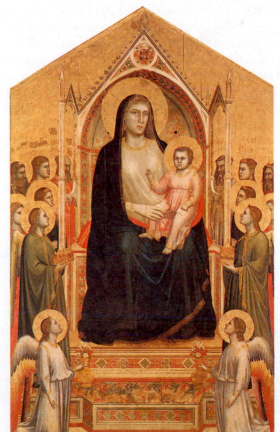

19-8. GIOTTO. *Madonna and Child Enthroned,* from the Church of Ognissanti, Florence. c. 1310. Tempera on panel, 10′8″ × 6′8¼″ (3.25 × 2.04 m). Galleria degli Uffizi, Florence

19-8

The *Chronicles* of the historian Giovanni Villani (died 1348) list Giotto as one of the great men of the Florentine Republic, a position such as had been accorded to no other artist since the days of ancient Greece. The sources also indicate wherein Giotto's greatness was thought to lie. Vasari summed up Italian estimates when he said that Giotto revived the art of painting, which had declined in Italy because of many invasions, and that since Giotto continued to "derive from Nature, he deserves to be called the pupil of Nature and no other." Cennino Cennini, a third-generation follower of Giotto, wrote in his *Book on Art,* a manual on technical methods, that Giotto had translated painting from Greek into Latin.

A comparison of Giotto's *Madonna and Child Enthroned* (fig. 19–8) of about 1310 with its counterpart by Cimabue (see fig. 19–6) will test these traditional observations. Nature, in the modern sense of the word, would hardly enter our minds in connection with Giotto's picture any more than with Cimabue's. Both are ceremonial images of the Virgin as Queen of Heaven, remote from ordinary experience, and both rule out distant space by the use of a traditional gold background. But in contemporary Italian eyes the step from Cimabue to Giotto was immense in that weight and mass, light and inward extension were suddenly introduced in a direct and convincing manner. In contrast to Cimabue's fantastic throne, which needs a steadying hand from the attendant angels, Giotto's structure is firmly placed above a marble step, which can be climbed, and the Virgin sits firmly within it. The poses of the angels kneeling in the foreground are so solid, in comparison to the uncertain placing of Cimabue's angels, that we are willing to believe that the angels and saints behind them, on either side of the throne, stand just as securely. Light, still diffused and without indication of source, models the forms so strongly that they resemble sculptural masses. By "translating painting from Greek into Latin," Cennini meant that Giotto had abandoned Byzantine models in favor of Western ones, and in the early fourteenth century those could only have been French cathedral statues. Not only do Giotto's facial types and drapery motifs recall Gothic sculptures of the preceding century, but also the Virgin's throne is set in an aedicula whose pointed central arch, trefoil side arches, and culminating pinnacles are taken directly from the French architectural repertory. Giotto's miracle lay in being able to produce for the first time on a flat surface three-dimensional forms, which the French could achieve only in sculpture. Whether or not the Florentines would have admitted this, Giotto also owed a debt to Cavallini, but here he has gone well beyond the Roman master. Effects of shoulders and knees showing through drapery masses, of the Child's body and legs, and of the Virgin's hand holding his thigh are at every point convincing. For the first time since antiquity a painter has truly conquered solid form. Giotto did not, however, adopt as yet a naturalistic scale. The Virgin and Child are represented as almost twice the size of the attendant figures.

Cennini tells us that the painting of frescoes was the most agreeable of all pictorial activities. The technique he describes was probably based on that of Roman painting as handed down through the Middle Ages. The painter first prepared the wall with a layer of rough plaster, on which he proceeded to draw with the brush (probably on the basis of preliminary sketches) the figures and background in a mixture of red earth and water known as *sinopia* (see fig. 19–20). Over this preparatory drawing he laid on as much smooth plaster as he could paint in a day, and painted it while wet so that the color in its water vehicle would amalgamate with the plaster. The following day he added another section, covering up the sinopia as he went. This procedure meant that the fresco was literally built section by section and acquired a solidity of composition and surface handling that would preclude any spontaneous painting technique such as that of the Byzantine artists.

Giotto's masterpiece is the cycle of frescoes dating from 1305–6 that lines the entire interior of the Arena Chapel in Padua in northern Italy, not far from Venice. Here he shows the full range of his naturalism in a new kind of pictorial drama for which nothing we have seen in the history of art could prepare us. The entire interior walls of the chapel, except for windows, is organized in three tiers, showing

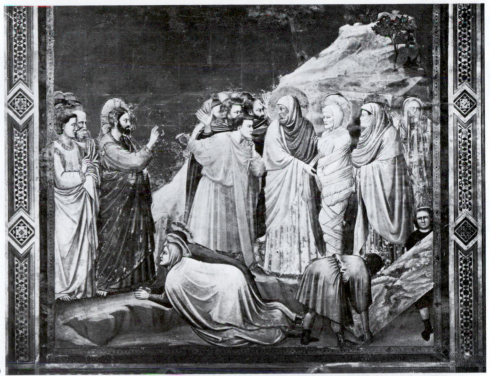

19-9. GIOTTO. *Raising of Lazarus,* fresco, Arena Chapel, Padua. 1305–6

19-9

scenes from the life of the Virgin, the life and mission of Christ, and the Passion and Resurrection. In a scene from the lowest tier Joachim, father of the Virgin, takes refuge with shepherds in the wilderness after his expulsion from the Temple because of his childlessness (see Introduction fig. 6). Humiliated, his head bowed, he stands before two shepherds, one of whom scans his companion's face to see whether they dare receive the outcast. The subtlety of the psychological interplay is enriched by Giotto's delicate observation of the sheep crowding out of the sheepfold and of the dog, symbol of fidelity in the Middle Ages as today, who leaps in joyful greeting.

As in the *Madonna,* Giotto recognizes one scale for the figures, another for the surroundings, including the animals and the sheepfold. Cennini recounts that to paint a mountainous landscape one need only bring a rock into the studio, and that a branch could do duty for a tree. The results of this principle show that Giotto, for all his ability to project three-dimensional form, is far from accepting the notion of visual unity. His landscape, however, has an expressive purpose; the rock behind Joachim bends along with his head, and the jagged edges toward the center underscore the division between him and the shepherds. The cubic rocks form a definite stage in space, limited by the blue background, which does not represent the sky—there are no clouds—but is an ideal, heavenly color continuing behind all the scenes in the same manner as the gold backgrounds for altarpieces, and covering the barrel vault above. In order to emphasize the three-dimensionality of the columnar figure of Joachim, Giotto has designed his halo foreshortened in perspective. The simplicity of the masses, the compact organization, and the noble clarity of the drawing and color create a composition of the greatest beauty.

In the *Raising of Lazarus* in the second tier (fig. 19–9) the composition divides into two groups: one centered around Lazarus, who has just risen from the tomb and is still wrapped in graveclothes, is read together with the rock; the other, beginning with the prostrate Mary and Martha, culminates in Christ, who calls the dead man forth by a single gesture of his right hand against the blue, in a pose and gesture recalling the teaching Christ from the portal of Amiens Cathedral in thirteenth-century France. The calm authority of Giotto's Christ is contrasted with the astonishment of the surrounding figures. Though in the *Lamentation* in the third tier (fig. 19–10) the Byzantine tradition is by no means forgotten, Giotto has

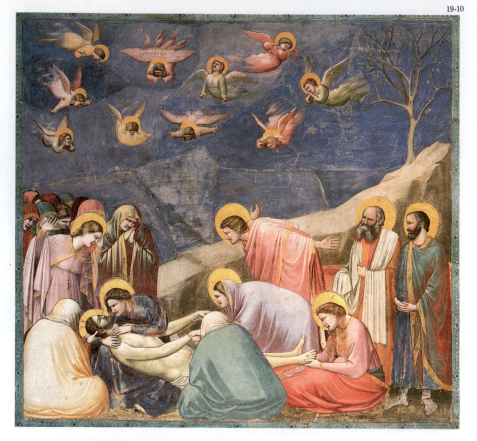

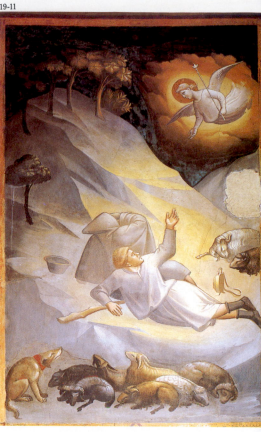

19-10. GIOTTO. *Lamentation,* fresco, Arena Chapel, Padua. 1305–6

19-11. TADDEO GADDI. *Annunciation to the Shepherds,* fresco, Baroncelli Chapel, Sta. Croce, Florence. Begun shortly after 1328

19-12. DUCCIO. *Virgin as Queen of Heaven,* center panel of the *Maestà* altarpiece (now divided), from the Cathedral of Siena. 1308–11. Tempera on panel, 7′ × 13′6¼″ (2.13 × 4.12 m). Museo dell'Opera del Duomo, Siena

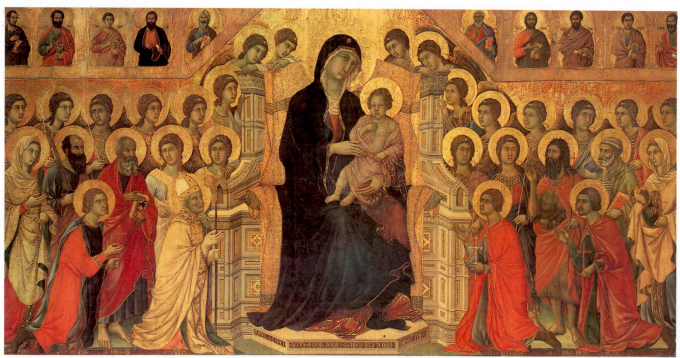

enriched the dialogue between life and death with all the subtlety of his psychological observation. Instead of an explosion of grief, he has staged a flawlessly organized tragedy, the equal of Sophocles or Shakespeare in its many-faceted analysis of a human situation. The figures grieve in the manner possible to their individual personalities—John, the beloved disciple, most deeply of all. Giotto has added to the scene anonymous mourners who turn their eloquent backs to us; one upholds Christ's head, the other his right hand. Mary, with one arm around Christ's shoulder, searches his countenance, conscious of the widening gulf between life and death. Only the angels are released to cry in pure grief, each half-hidden in clouds to show that he is supernatural. (Significantly, with Giotto clouds appear only as accompaniments to heavenly figures.)

Giotto's brushwork remains as calm in this scene as in any other. He achieved his effect not only by the grouping of the figures but also by the inexorable diagonal line of the rock, descending toward the faces of Mary and Christ, its course weighted by the downward tug of the drapery folds. At the upper right, as if to typify the desolation of the scene, a leafless tree stands against the blue. Giotto surely expected his audience to remember that, according to medieval legend, the Tree of Knowledge was withered after the sin of Adam and Eve and made fruitful again after the sacrifice of Christ, and that Christ himself was believed to have alluded to this doctrine on his way to Calvary: "For if they do these things in a green tree, what shall be done in the dry?" (Luke 23:31).

Giotto indeed had the cry; within a decade after his great works made their appearance, the style of Cimabue had been relegated to country churches, and Giotto, his many pupils, and still more numerous followers dominated the Florentine scene. For Giotto had transformed the whole purpose and nature of painting, in a revolution whose effects are felt to this day.

TADDEO GADDI One of the closest of Giotto's pupils, Taddeo Gaddi (active c. 1328–c. 1366), although he could never approach the heights of his master's achievements, continued some aspects of his style, in the depiction of solid figural volumes and landscape masses but especially in the representation of light. Shortly after 1328 Taddeo painted a series of frescoes in the Baroncelli Chapel of Santa Croce in Florence, almost adjoining two chapels painted by Giotto only a few years earlier. In the fourteenth century natural light was always diffused and generalized, without indication of a specific source. But Taddeo has shown the traditional scene of the *Annunciation to the Shepherds* (fig. 19–11) as a revelation of light, which in a long Christian tradition symbolizes the second person of the Trinity. After all, every Christian knew the sublime words of John 1:4–5, repeated, until Vatican II, at the close of every Mass:

In him was life; and the life was the light of men. And the light shineth in darkness; and the darkness comprehended it not.

As a devoted follower of Giotto, Taddeo never represents natural light, but he presents the announcing angel in the midst of a wonderful display of light, which descends upon the shepherds who have fallen to the ground in amazement and lights the whole dark landscape with its radiance. We are here experiencing the reversal of the process by which, at the beginning of the Middle Ages, the illusionistic art of the Helleno-Roman tradition was transformed into the otherworldly art of Byzantium. Techniques derived from naturalistic painting were used in the early Middle Ages to represent supernatural light. Now at the end of the Middle Ages, that same spiritual light is used to aid the artist in the rediscovery of material reality.

DUCCIO In Siena the Byzantine tradition continued into the fourteenth century and was refined to the ultimate in the work of Duccio di Buoninsegna (active 1278–

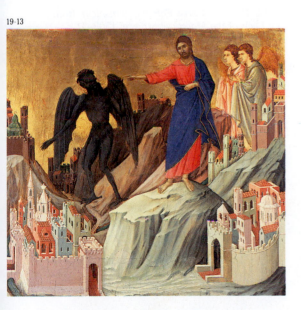

19-13

19-13. DUCCIO. *Temptation of Christ on the Mountain,* from the back of the predella of the *Maestà* altarpiece. 1308–11. Tempera on panel, 17 × 18⅛″ (43 × 46 cm). The Frick Collection, New York

1318). His great altarpiece, the *Maestà (Madonna in Majesty),* more than thirteen feet in width, was started in 1308 for the high altar of the Cathedral of Siena. It was considered such a triumph for the artist and such an important contribution to the welfare of the Sienese Republic (whose patron saint was the Virgin) that on its completion in 1311 it was carried at the head of a procession of dignitaries and townspeople from Duccio's studio to the Cathedral, to the ringing of church bells and the sound of trumpets. The high altar was freestanding, so that the back of the altarpiece and even its pinnacles were covered with a cycle of scenes from the life of Christ somewhat more detailed than that Giotto had just painted for the Arena Chapel. In the sixteenth century the altarpiece was taken down and partially dismembered; panels from the pinnacles at the top and from the *predella* (the lower strip at the base of an altarpiece) are scattered through many museums, but most remain in Siena. The central panel shows the Virgin as Queen of Heaven (fig. 19–12), adored by her court of kneeling and standing saints and angels and half-length prophets in the arches above—a sort of cathedral façade in paint. And, though the pose of the Virgin and Child shows that Duccio is still working in the Byzantine tradition, he has nonetheless learned from the works of Giovanni Pisano new and Gothic ways to handle flowing masses of drapery and dense crowds of figures. While the oval shapes of the faces are Byzantine, their small almond eyes bear no relation to the lustrous orbs of the saints in most Byzantine mosaics, frescoes, and icons.

Although Duccio accepted neither Giotto's cubic rocks nor his columnar figures, and although he could not achieve Giotto's subtlety of psychological observation, he was an artist of great individuality especially in the handling of landscape elements, as can be seen in the *Temptation of Christ on the Mountain* (fig. 19–13), once a part of the *Maestà.* The kingdoms of the world, shown to Christ by Satan, were depicted by Duccio, a good republican Sienese, as seven little city-states crowded into a panel not quite eighteen inches square. Obviously, they derive from the late Roman and Early Christian depiction of little nugget-cities, but each one is different, with its own houses, public buildings, city gates, and towers, all modeled in a consistent light. If we are willing to accept the medieval convention of the double scale for figures and setting, we must admit that within it Duccio was very successful in suggesting the scope and sweep of landscape, which soon became Siena's great contribution to the history of art.

In one of the larger panels of the *Maestà,* Duccio set the stage, as it were, for *Christ Entering Jerusalem* (fig. 19–14) in the suburban orchards outside the walls of Siena. We look over trees, garden walls, and a gate in the foreground to the road moving uphill, more garden walls on the other side, the city gates, and houses fronting a street. The towering octagonal building is the Temple, combining travelers' tales of the Dome of the Rock, built on the site of the Temple, with the familiar outlines of the Baptistery of Florence. This setting, of a spatial complexity unprecedented in medieval art, Duccio filled with more than fifty people, all sharply individualized (within the range of Byzantine-Sienese facial types), from the solemn Christ mounted on an ass to the excited populace and children climbing trees, including some inhabitants looking out of windows and over the city wall.

SIMONE MARTINI Duccio's pupil Simone Martini (active 1315–44), while fully abreast of all his master could achieve in the realm of landscape and urban settings, finally broke with the Byzantine tradition in favor of the more fashionable courtly French Gothic manner of the early fourteenth century. He blended these two separate sources into a unified, and in the long run highly original, style of great lyric beauty and material splendor. Simone worked for the French king Robert of Anjou at Naples and brought back to Siena the latest French imports. Even more than the *Maestà* of Duccio, his *Annunciation,* also for Siena Cathedral (fig. 19–15), is a condensed cathedral façade, Gothic this time, with all the richness of Flamboyant double curvature (which had not as yet made its appearance in the architecture

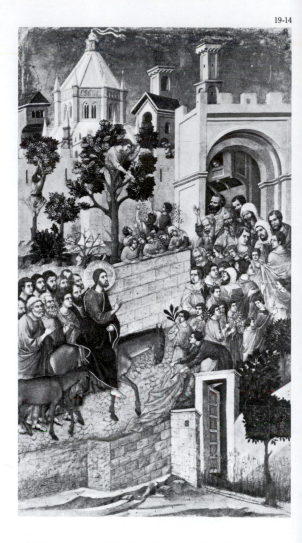

19-14

19-14. Duccio. *Christ Entering Jerusalem,* from the back of the *Maestà* altarpiece. 1308–11. Tempera on panel, 40½ × 21⅛″ (102.9 × 53.7 cm). Museo dell'Opera del Duomo, Siena

of Giovanni Pisano). The elaborate frame, glittering with Gothic gables, pinnacles, and foliate ornament, all richly gilded, encloses the most sacred of all scenes in Christian art. For according to theological teaching and tradition, the Incarnation of Christ, the second person of the Trinity, in human form occurred at the precise moment when the words of the Angel Gabriel struck the ear of the Virgin Mary.

Simone has enhanced the dramatic impact of the event by a veritable explosion of forms and colors. The center of the altarpiece is occupied only by a great vase containing lilies, symbols of Mary's virginity; there are four of them, the number of the Gospels. Everything else seems to have been blown away from the gold background by the force of the angel's message, "Ave gratia plena dominus tecum" ("Hail thou that art highly favored, the Lord is with thee," Luke 1:28), embossed so as to catch and reflect light. Even the expected two colonnettes, presumably needed to support the central arch, have been omitted, so that the capitals seem to hang in the breeze. The dove of the Holy Spirit ("The Holy Spirit shall come upon thee, and the power of the most High shall overshadow thee," Luke 1:35) flies downward toward Mary and is surrounded by tiny seraphim, whose crossed swallow-wings echo in reverse the cusps of the frame. Unexpectedly, the slender and elegant Mary, "troubled at his saying" (Luke 1:29), recoils almost in terror at her fate, her face clouded with apprehension. The angel is dressed magnificently in white and gold brocade with a floating, plaid-lined mantle, and the Virgin's blue mantle is edged with a deep gold border. The swirling drapery rhythms in their curvilinear exaggerations contrast strongly with the controlled shapes of Giotto and Duccio. This is an extraordinary and unexpected style, graceful in the extreme yet intensely dramatic, with all the characteristic Sienese fluency of line translated from Byzantine Greek into Flamboyant French Gothic.

THE LORENZETTI   Giotto's new devices reached Sienese painting in the work of two brothers, Pietro (c. 1280–1348?) and Ambrogio (c. 1285–1348?) Lorenzetti, who, nonetheless, continued independently the Sienese tradition of the exploration of landscape and architectural settings. The Lorenzetti brought Sienese painting to a position of absolute leadership in Europe during the decade following Giotto's death. In Pietro's *Birth of the Virgin* of 1342 (fig. 19–16), another in the cycle of Marian altarpieces for the Cathedral of Siena, we are aware of Giotto's cubic space and columnar figures, but Pietro has taken a significant step in the direction of illusionism. The gold background is eliminated except where it peeks through a tiny window at the left. The architectural setting has been identified with the actual carved shape of the frame, which it was customary for the artist himself to design and which was usually built and attached to the panel before the process of painting was begun. The picture thus becomes a little stage into which we can look, so that we cannot help wondering from the illustration what is carved and what is painted. (This requires a mental effort because, in a misguided devotion to historical "purity" the authorities have removed the later colonnettes substituted for the rotted originals.) Pietro's altarpiece is a pioneer attempt to build up the consistent interior space that never seems to have occurred to the Romans. His perspective is not entirely consistent, but the upper and lower portions of the interior are drawn so that the parallel lines in each converge to a single separate vanishing point. An enormous step has been taken in the direction of the unified perspective space of the Renaissance.

Not even Pietro's formulation of interior space is quite as startling as what Ambrogio had already achieved in the fresco representing the effects of good government in city and country. This panorama fills one entire wall of a council chamber in the Palazzo Pubblico (the Sienese counterpart of the Florentine Palazzo Vecchio) and is in fact so extensive that it requires two photographs to show it in its entirety (figs. 19–17, 19–18). Ambrogio has assumed the high point of view taken by Duccio for his exterior scenes, but he has immensely expanded it. On the right in fig. 19–17 we look over the zigzag line of the city wall into open squares and

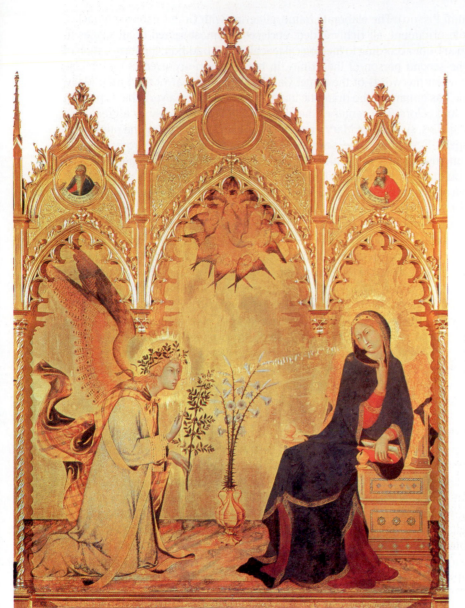

19-15

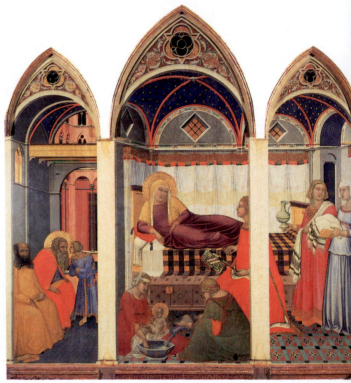

19-16

19-15. SIMONE MARTINI. *Annunciation.* 1333 (frame reconstructed in the 19th century). Panel painting, 10′ × 8′9″ (3.05 × 2.67 m). Galleria degli Uffizi, Florence

19-16. PIETRO LORENZETTI. *Birth of the Virgin.* 1342. Tempera on panel, 73½ × 71½″ (1.88 × 1.82 m). Museo dell'Opera del Duomo, Siena

19-17. AMBROGIO LORENZETTI. *Allegory of Good Government: The Effects of Good Government in the City,* detail of a fresco, Sala della Pace, Palazzo Pubblico, Siena. 1338–39

19-18. AMBROGIO LORENZETTI. *Allegory of Good Government: The Effects of Good Government in the Country,* detail of a fresco, Sala della Pace, Palazzo Pubblico, Siena. 1338–39

streets lined with houses, palaces, and towers, some still under construction (note the masons at work under the center beam). At the upper left can barely be made out the campanile and dome of the Cathedral. Richly dressed Sienese burghers and their wives ride by on horseback; one horse has already half-disappeared down a street in the center. The three arches of the building in the foreground contain (from left to right) a shoe shop, a school with a teacher at a desk on a platform and a row of pupils, and a wineshop with a little bar in front. Groups of happy citizens dance in the street.

To the right of the city wall (see fig. 19–18), under a friendly floating near-nude labeled *Securitas,* who brandishes a scroll with one hand and a loaded gallows with the other, the city people ride downhill into the country and the country people walk uphill into the city. The view of the countryside is amazing: roads, hills, farms and orchards with peasants hard at work, a lake, a country chapel, villas and castles, hills beyond hills, stretching to the horizon. But just where we would expect a blue sky with clouds, Ambrogio drops the iron curtain and reminds us that we are

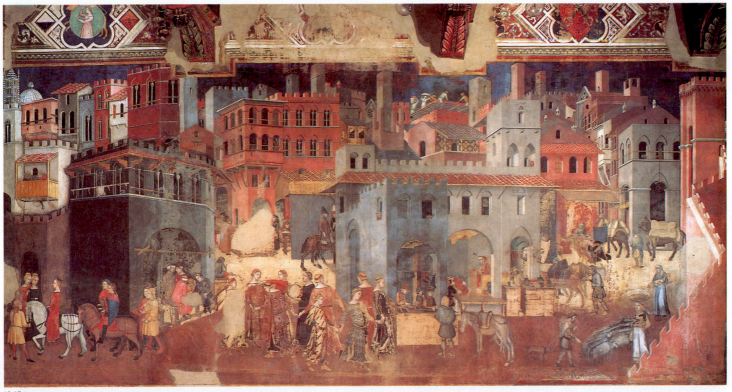

19-17

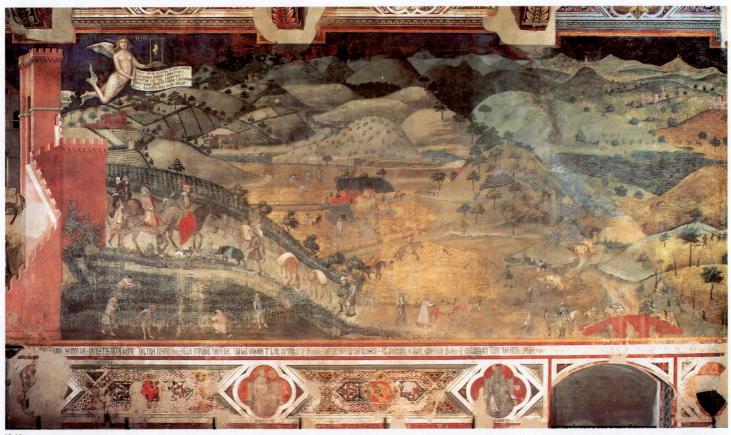

19-18

still in the Middle Ages. The background is a uniform gray black. This encyclopedic view of the Sienese world and everything in it is an exciting preview of the Renaissance, but there it stops. The Black Death, an epidemic of the bubonic plague that swept Europe in 1348, killed from half to two-thirds of the populations of Florence and Siena, probably including Ambrogio and Pietro Lorenzetti, and put an end to such explorations.

TRAINI   The fresco representing the *Triumph of Death* in the Campo Santo, or walled cemetery, at Pisa is probably the work of a local master named Francesco Traini (active c. 1321–63) and has been interpreted as reflecting the universal gloom following the Black Death. Recent research suggests that the fresco may have been painted a year or two earlier, but the plague had already appeared in Tuscany well before the devastating attack in 1348. In this panorama (fig. 19–19), very different from the carefree world of Ambrogio Lorenzetti, no one escapes. At the left three richly dressed couples on horseback, out hunting, come upon three open coffins containing corpses in varying stages of putrefaction, a common enough sight in plague times; they draw back in consternation, one rider holding

19-19. FRANCESCO TRAINI. *Triumph of Death*, fresco, Campo Santo, Pisa. Middle 14th century

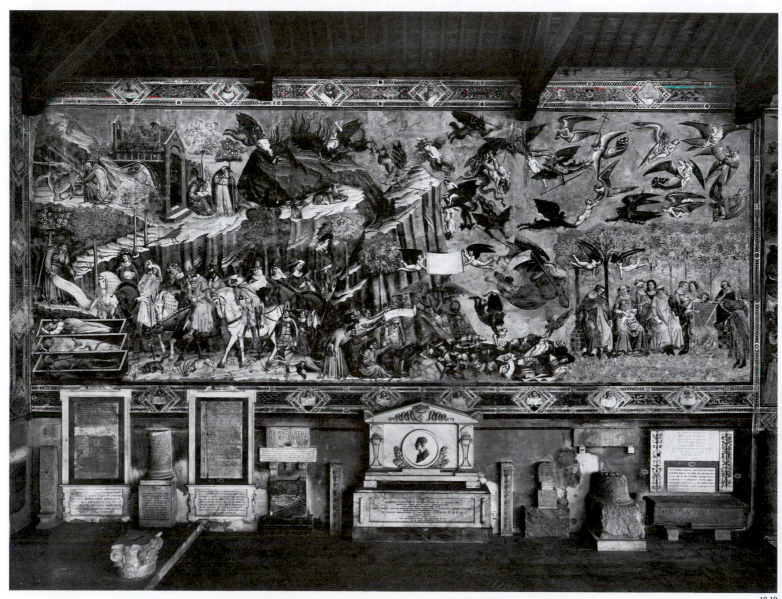

19-19

19-20. Detail of the preliminary brush drawing (*sinopia*) for *Triumph of Death*

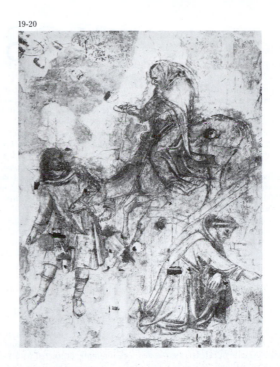

19-20

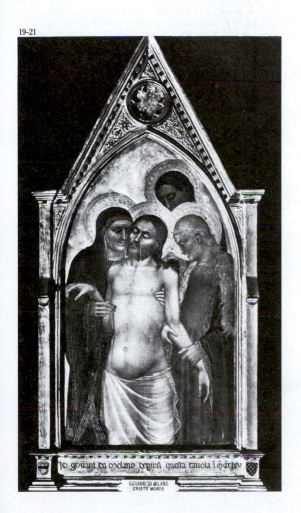

19-21. GIOVANNI DA MILANO. *Pietà*. 1365. Tempera on panel, 48 × 22¾″ (122 × 58 cm). Galleria dell'Accademia, Florence

his nose. At the right in a grove of orange trees sits a happy group of gentlemen and ladies, engaged in music and conversation, reminding us of Giovanni Boccaccio's *Decameron,* written at the time of the Black Death. They seem not to see Death, a winged, white-haired hag, sweeping down on them with a scythe. In the air above, angels and demons fight over human souls. The rocky path at the upper left leads to hermits' cells, as if to demonstrate that the only road to salvation is retreat from the world. The severe damage suffered by these frescoes in the fire following the fall of random American shells in World War II necessitated the detachment from the wall of all those that still adhered; underneath was found the most extensive series of sinopias then known (fig. 19–20). These sinopias reveal the boldness and freedom of brushwork, recalling Byzantine painting, that underlie the meticulous finish of fourteenth-century frescoes.

GIOVANNI DA MILANO   In the wake of the Black Death, no new figures emerged of the stature of the great masters of the early fourteenth century, but many painters showed new observations and insights. One of the most gifted of these was Giovanni da Milano (active 1346–66), a Lombard working in Florence, where in 1365 he signed a new kind of image, a *Pietà* (fig. 19–21), from the Italian word for both "pity" and "piety," both of which it was intended to excite. The intensified religious life of Italy after the catastrophe required new images, which would draw from biblical sources figures, situations, and emotions rather than narrative incidents and recombine them in timeless configurations designed to strengthen the reciprocal emotional bond between sacred figures and the individual worshiper. In an attempt at once to arouse the sympathies of observers and to demonstrate to them that for their salvation Christ had shared the sufferings of all humanity, Giovanni has depicted him after death, being lifted in the arms of Mary, Mary Magdalene, and John. The emotional intensity of the painting has reached fever pitch, but it is no longer expressed in outbursts; it is felt within, rather, like a self-inflicted wound. As impressive as the content of Giovanni's painting is his new attention to muscles, bones, and tendons—not only where they affect the texture of an anatomical surface but also where they appear in profile along the sensitive contour. His art prepares the way for the great discoveries of the approaching Renaissance, in both Italy and the North.

GLOSSARY

ABACUS (pl. ABACI). In architecture, the slab that forms the uppermost member of a CAPITAL and supports the ARCHITRAVE.

ABBEY. The religious body governed by an abbot or an abbess, or the monastic buildings themselves. The abbey church frequently has special features such as a particularly large CHOIR to accommodate the monks or nuns.

ACANTHUS. A plant having large toothed and scalloped leaves whose forms were imitated on CAPITALS and used to ornament MOLDINGS, BRACKETS, and FRIEZES.

ACROTERIUM (pl. ACROTERIA). A sculpture or other ornament placed at the lower angles and the apex of a PEDIMENT, or the PEDESTAL, often without a BASE, on which it stands.

ADOBE. A sun-dried brick used by the Indians of the western United States and Mesoamerica. A structure made of the same.

AEDICULA (pl. AEDICULAE). Latin word for *niche* or *small shrine.*

AGORA. Greek word for *assembly,* thus denoting the square or marketplace that was the center of public life in every ancient Greek city.

AISLE. See SIDE AISLE.

ALABASTER. A fine-grained gypsum or calcite, often white and translucent, though sometimes delicately tinted.

ALTARPIECE. A painted and/or sculptured work of art that stands as a religious image upon and at the back of an altar, either representing in visual symbols the underlying doctrine of the MASS or depicting the saint to whom a particular church or chapel is dedicated, together with scenes from his or her life. Examples from certain periods include decorated GABLES and PINNACLES, as well as a PREDELLA. See MAESTA.

AMBULATORY. A place for walking, usually covered, as in an ARCADE around a CLOISTER, or a semicircular passageway around the APSE behind the main altar. In a church or mosque with a centralized PLAN, the passageway around the central space that corresponds to a SIDE AISLE and that is used for ceremonial processions.

AMPHIPROSTYLE. Having a PORTICO in the rear as well as in the front, but not on the sides.

AMPHITHEATER. A double THEATER. A building of elliptical shape with tiers of seats rising one behind another about a central open space or arena.

AMPHORA (pl. AMPHORAE). A storage jar used in ancient Greece having an egg-shaped body, a foot, and two handles, each attached at the neck and shoulder of the jar.

APOCALYPSE. The Book of Revelation, the last book of the New Testament, in which are narrated the visions of the future experienced by Saint John the Evangelist on the island of Patmos.

APOCRYPHA. A group of books included at one time in authorized Christian versions of the BIBLE (now generally omitted from Protestant versions).

APOSTLES. In Christian usage the word commonly denotes the twelve followers or disciples chosen by Christ to preach his GOSPEL, though the term is sometimes used loosely. Those listed in the Gospels are: Andrew; James, the son of Zebedee, called James the Major; James, the son of Alphaeus, called James the Minor; Bartholomew; John; Judas Iscariot; Matthew; Philip; Peter; Simon the Canaanite; Thaddeus; and Thomas (Matthew 10:1–4; Mark 3:13–19).

APSARAS (sing. APSARA). Sanskrit word for *female celestial nymphs.* In Hindu art these seductive dancers and musicians of the gods are usually represented standing in trees; in Buddhist art they are angelic beings, often winged.

APSE. A large semicircular or polygonal niche. In a Roman BASILICA it was frequently found at both ends of the NAVE; in a Christian church it is usually placed at one end of the nave after the CHOIR; it may also appear at the ends of the TRANSEPT and the ends of chapels.

AQUEDUCT. From the Latin for *duct of water.* An artificial channel for conducting water from a distance, which, in Roman times, was usually built overground and supported on ARCHES.

ARCADE. A series of ARCHES and their supports. Called a *blind arcade* when placed against a wall and used primarily as surface decoration.

ARCH. An architectural construction, often semicircular, built of wedge-shaped blocks (called *voussoirs*) to span an opening. The center stone is called the *keystone.* The weight of this structure requires support from walls, PIERS, or COLUMNS, and the THRUST requires BUTTRESSING at the sides. When an arch is made of overlapping courses of stone, each block projecting slightly farther over the opening than the block beneath it, it is called a CORBELED arch.

ARCHBISHOP. The chief BISHOP of an ecclesiastical province or archbishopric.

ARCHITRAVE. The main horizontal beam and the lowest member of an ENTABLATURE; it may be a series of LINTELS, each spanning the space from the top of one support to the next.

ARCHIVOLT. The MOLDING or moldings above an arched opening; in Romanesque and Gothic churches, frequently decorated with sculpture.

ARK OF THE COVENANT. The wooden chest containing a handwritten scroll of the TORAH. It is kept in the holiest place in the TABERNACLE, which, in Western countries, is usually against the east wall, the direction of the Holy Land.

ARRICCIO, ARRICCIATO. The rough coat of coarse plaster that is the first layer to be spread on a wall when making a FRESCO.

A SECCO. See FRESCO.

ATRIUM. The open entrance hall or central hall of an ancient Roman house. A court in front of the principal doors of a church.

ATTIC. The upper story, usually low in height, placed above an ENTABLATURE or main CORNICE of a building and frequently decorated with PILASTERS.

AVATAR. An incarnation of the divine. In Hinduism, only the god Vishnu is incarnated, traditionally taking ten forms including Krishna, Rama, Varaha the boar, and Kalki, the tenth, who has not yet appeared.

BACCHANTE. See MAENAD.

BALDACHIN. From the Italian *baldacchino,* a rich silk fabric from Baghdad. A canopy of such material, or of wood, stone, etc., either permanently installed over an altar, throne, or doorway, or constructed in portable form to be carried in religious processions.

BALUSTRADE. A row of short pillars, called *balusters,* surmounted by a railing.

BAPTISTERY. Either a separate building or a part of a church in which the SACRAMENT of Baptism is administered.

BARREL VAULT. A semicylindrical VAULT that normally requires continuous support and BUTTRESSING.

BAR TRACERY. See TRACERY.

BASALT. A fine-grained volcanic rock of high density and dark color.

BASE. The lowest element of a COLUMN, PIER, PILASTER, temple, wall, or DOME, occasionally of a statue.

BASILICA. In ancient Roman architecture, a rectangular building whose ground PLAN was generally divided into NAVE, SIDE AISLES, and one or more APSES, and whose elevation sometimes included a CLERESTORY and GALLERIES, though there was no strict uniformity. It was used as a hall of justice and as a public meeting place. In Christian architecture, the term is applied to any church that has a longitudinal nave terminated by an apse and flanked by lower side aisles.

BAY. A compartment into which a building may be subdivided, usually formed by the space bounded by consecutive architectural supports.

BEMA. The SANCTUARY of an Early Christian or modern Eastern Orthodox church. See PROTHESIS.

BENEDICTINE ORDER. Founded in 529 by Saint Benedict of Nursia (c. 480–543), at Subiaco, near Rome, the Benedictine ORDER spread to England and much of western Europe in the next two centuries. Less austere than other early orders, the Benedictines divided their time into periods of religious worship, reading, and work, the last generally either educational or agricultural.

BIBLE. The collection of sacred writings of the Christian religion that includes the Old and the New Testaments, or that of the Jewish religion, which includes the Old Testament only. The versions commonly used in the Roman Catholic Church are based on the Vulgate, a Latin translation made by Saint Jerome in the fourth century A.D. An English translation, made by members of the English College at Douai, France, between 1582 and 1610, is called the Douay. Widely used Protestant translations include Martin Luther's German translation from the first half of the sixteenth century, and the English King James Version, first published in 1611.

BISHOP. A spiritual overseer of a number of churches or a DIOCESE; in the Greek, Roman Catholic, Anglican, and other churches, a member of the highest order in the ministry. See CATHEDRAL.

BLIND ARCADE. See ARCADE.

BODHISATTVA. In Buddhism, an enlightenment being; a person or a cosmic figure who is dedicated to saving all beings from suffering and bringing them to perfect enlightenment.

BRACKET. A piece of stone, wood, or metal projecting from a wall and having a flat upper surface that serves to support a statue, beam, or other weight.

BREVIARY. A book containing the daily offices or prayers and the necessary psalms and hymns for daily devotions. Frequently illustrated and generally intended for use by the clergy.

BROKEN PEDIMENT. See PEDIMENT.

BRONZE and IRON AGES. The period from approximately 3000 B.C. to the first century B.C., characterized in general by the use of metal and the smelting of metal. Farming communities were settled, and the making and use of pottery became widespread.

BUDDHA. One who has attained complete enlightenment and thus is liberated from ignorance, suffering, and desire. Also used to refer to a particular Buddha, the historical founder of Buddhism, whose given name was Siddhartha Gautama and who has long been referred to as Sakyamuni Buddha, or "Sage of the Sakya clan."

BUTTRESS. A masonry support that counteracts the lateral pressure, or THRUST, exerted by an ARCH or VAULT. See FLYING BUTTRESS and PIER BUTTRESS.

CALIPH. A leader of Muslims in both a spiritual and political sense; in theory, there should be only one, but in fact, after the loss of power by the Abbasid caliph in the tenth century, a Sunni caliphate was established at Córdoba (925–1030) and a Shia caliphate was established by the Fatimids (915–1171). With the murder of the last Abbasid caliph at Baghdad in 1258, a shadow caliphate survived in Egypt until the Turkish conquest of 1517. The claim of the later Turkish sultans to the caliphate was not legitimate.

CALLIGRAPHY. In a loose sense, handwriting, but the word usually refers to beautiful handwriting or fine penmanship.

CALVARY. See GOLGOTHA.

CAMEO. A carving in RELIEF upon a gem, stone, or shell, especially when differently colored layers of the material are revealed to produce a design of lighter color against a darker background. A gem, stone, or shell so carved.

CAMPANILE. From the Italian word for *bell* (*campana*). A bell tower, either attached to a church or freestanding nearby.

CAMPO. Italian word for *field;* used in Siena, Venice, and other Italian cities to denote certain public squares. See PIAZZA.

CAMPO SANTO. Italian phrase for *holy field;* thus, a cemetery.

CANON. A clergyman who serves in a CATHEDRAL or a collegiate church.

CANON OF THE MASS. The part of the Christian MASS between the Sanctus, a hymn, and the Lord's Prayer; the actual EUCHARIST, or sacrifice of bread and wine, to which only the baptized are admitted.

CANOPY. An ornamental rooflike projection or covering placed over a niche, statue, tomb, altar, or the like.

CAPITAL. The crowning member of a COLUMN, PIER, or PILASTER on which rests the lowest element of the ENTABLATURE. See ORDER.

CARDINAL VIRTUES. See VIRTUES.

CARTOUCHE. An ornamental SCROLL-shaped tablet with an inscription or decoration, either sculptured or drawn.

CARVING. The shaping of an image by cutting or chiseling it out from a hard substance, such as stone or wood, in contrast to the additive process of MODELING.

CARYATID. A figure, generally female, used as a COLUMN.

CASTING. A method of reproducing a three-dimensional object or RELIEF by pouring a hardening liquid or molten metal into a mold bearing its impression.

CATACOMBS. Subterranean burial places consisting of GALLERIES with niches for SARCOPHAGI and small chapels for funeral feasts and commemorative services.

CATECHUMEN. One under instruction in the rudiments of Christian doctrine, usually a new convert.

CATHEDRAL. The principal church of a DIOCESE, containing the bishop's throne, or cathedra.

CATWALK. A narrow footway at the side of a bridge or near the ceiling of a building.

CELLA. The body of a temple as distinct from the PORTICO and other external elements, or an interior structure built to house an image.

CENOTAPH. An empty tomb; a commemorative sepulchral monument not intended for burial.

CENTAUR. In Greek mythology, a creature with the head and torso of a man and the body and legs of a horse.

CENTERING. A wooden framework used as support during the construction of a stone ARCH or VAULT.

CHAITYA. Originally meaning *sanctuary* in Sanskrit, the assembly hall of early Indian Buddhism. It was a rectangular building or cave with a central nave and two aisles, or additional naves, and a STUPA at the end of the nave.

CHANCEL. In a church, the space reserved for the clergy and the CHOIR, between the APSE and the NAVE and TRANSEPT, usually separated from the latter two by steps and a railing or a screen.

CHASUBLE. A long, oval, sleeveless mantle with an opening for the head; it is worn over all other vestments by a priest when celebrating MASS and it is used in commemoration of Christ's seamless robe.

CHERUB (pl. CHERUBIM). One of an order of angelic beings ranking second to the SERAPH in the celestial hierarchy, often represented as a winged child or as the winged head of a child.

CHEVET. The eastern end of a church or CATHEDRAL, consisting of the AMBULATORY and a main APSE with secondary apses or chapels radiating from it.

CHEVRON. A zigzag or V-shaped pattern used decoratively, especially in Romanesque architecture.

CHITON. A sleeveless Greek TUNIC, the basic garment worn by both men and women in ancient times.

CHOIR. A body of trained singers, or that part of a church occupied by them. See CHANCEL.

CHOIR SCREEN. A partition of wood or stone, often elaborately carved, that separates the CHOIR from the NAVE and TRANSEPT of a church. In Byzantine churches, the choir screen, called an ICONOSTASIS, is decorated with ICONS.

CHRISTUS MORTUUS. Latin phrase for *dead Christ.*

CHRISTUS PATIENS. Latin phrase for *suffering Christ.* A cross with a representation of the dead Christ, which in general superseded representations of the CHRISTUS TRIUMPHANS type.

CHRISTUS TRIUMPHANS. Latin phrase for *triumphant Christ.* A cross with a representation of the living Christ, eyes open and triumphant over death. Scenes of the PASSION are usually depicted at the sides of the cross, below the crossarms.

CISTERCIAN ORDER. A reform movement in the BENEDICTINE ORDER started in France in 1098 by Saint Robert of Molesme for the purpose of reasserting the original Benedictine ideals of fieldwork and a life of severe simplicity.

CLAUSURA. Latin word for *closure.* In the Roman Catholic Church the word is used to signify the restriction of certain classes of nuns and monks prohibited from communication with outsiders to sections of their convents or monasteries. Those living within these restrictions are said to be *in clausura* or CLOISTERED.

CLERESTORY. The section of an interior wall that rises above adjacent rooftops, having a row of windows that admit daylight. Used in Egyptian temples, Roman BASILICAS, and Christian basilican churches; in Christian churches, the wall that rises above the nave ARCADE or the TRIFORIUM to the VAULTING or roof.

CLOISTER. Generally, a place of religious seclusion; a monastery, nunnery, or convent. Specifically, a covered walk or AMBULATORY around an open court having a plain wall on one side and an open ARCADE or COLONNADE on the other. It is commonly connected with a church, monastery, or other building and is used for exercise and study. See CLAUSURA.

CLOSED DOOR or CLOSED GATE. Ezekiel's vision of the door or gate of the SANCTUARY in the temple that was closed because only the Lord could enter it (Ezekiel 44:1–4). Interpreted as a prophecy and used as a symbol of Mary's virginity.

CLOSED GARDEN. "A garden enclosed is my sister, my spouse; a spring shut up, a fountain sealed" (Song of Solomon 4:12). Used like CLOSED DOOR as a symbol of Mary's virginity.

CLUNIAC ORDER. A reformed ORDER of BENEDICTINE monks founded in 910 by William I the Pious at the monastery of Cluny in eastern France. For about 250 years it was headed by a succession of remarkable abbots who extended its rule over hundreds of monasteries in western Europe and exerted great influence in ecclesiastical and temporal affairs. With the rise of the CISTERCIAN and the MENDICANT ORDERS, its strength declined, and it became merely a group of French religious houses. The order was dissolved in 1790.

CODEX (pl. CODICES). A manuscript in book form as distinguished from a SCROLL. From the first to the fourth century A.D., the codex gradually replaced the scroll.

COFFER. A casket or box. In architecture, a recessed panel in a ceiling.

COLONNADE. A series of COLUMNS spanned by LINTELS.

COLONNETTE. A small COLUMN.

COLOR. See HUE, SATURATION, and VALUE.

COLUMN. A vertical architectural support, usually consisting of a BASE, a rounded SHAFT, and a CAPITAL. When half or more of it is attached to a wall, it is called an *engaged column.* Columns are occasionally used singly for a decorative or commemorative reason. See also ORDER.

COMPOUND PIER. A PIER with COLUMNS, PILASTERS, or SHAFTS attached to it, which members usually support or respond to ARCHES or RIBS above them.

CORBEL. An overlapping arrangement of stones, each course projecting beyond the one below, used in the construction of an ARCH or VAULT, or as a support projecting from the face of a wall.

CORBEL TABLE. A horizontal piece of masonry used as a CORNICE or part of a wall and supported by CORBELS.

CORBEL VAULT. An arched roof constructed of corbeled masonry.

CORNICE. The crowning, projecting architectural feature, especially the uppermost part of an ENTABLATURE. It is frequently decorated. When it is not horizontal, as above a PEDIMENT, it is called a *raking cornice.*

COURSED MASONRY. Masonry in which stones or bricks of equal height are placed in continuous horizontal layers.

CRENELLATED. Fortified or decorated with battlements (notched or indented parapets).

CRO-MAGNON. A race of PALEOLITHIC humans, ancestors of modern Europeans, whose remains were discovered in the Cro-Magnon cave in the Dordogne region of France.

CROMLECH. A circle of standing unhewn stones; the term is sometimes used interchangeably with DOLMEN.

CROSSING. That part of a church where the TRANSEPT crosses the NAVE; it is sometimes emphasized by a DOME or by a tower.

CROSS SECTION. See SECTION.

CRUCIFIX. From the Latin word *crucifixus.* A representation of a cross with the figure of Christ crucified upon it. See CHRISTUS MORTUUS, CHRISTUS PATIENS, and CHRISTUS TRIUMPHANS.

CRYPT. A VAULTED chamber, usually beneath the raised CHOIR of a church, housing a tomb and/or a chapel. Also, a vaulted underground chamber used for burial, as in the CATACOMBS.

CUFIC. See KUFIC.

CUNEIFORM. From the Latin for *wedge-shaped.* Used to describe Mesopotamian scripts, which were written in soft clay with the wedge-shaped end of a reed.

CUPOLA. A rounded, convex roof or VAULTED ceiling, usually hemispherical, on a circular BASE and requiring BUTTRESSING. See DOME.

CUSP. The pointed projection where two curves meet.

CYCLOPEAN MASONRY. Walls constructed with massive stones more or less irregular in shape, once thought to be the work of the mythical race of giants called CYCLOPES.

CYCLOPS. In ancient Greek and Roman mythology, a member of a race of giants with one round eye in the center of the forehead. The Cyclopes were believed to have forged thunderbolts for the king of the gods and to have built massive prehistoric walls.

DAO. The core of the Chinese philosophy of Daoism, the Way that is the guiding principle of the universe, the indescribable source of all phenomena, and the unifying resolution of all contradictions. To live in accord with the Dao is to be spontaneous, nonactive, and effortlessly yielding.

DEËSIS. The Greek word for *supplication.* A representation of Christ Enthroned between the Virgin Mary and Saint John the Baptist, who act as intercessors for mankind, which appears frequently in Byzantine MOSAICS and in later depictions of the Last Judgment.

DENTILS. A series of small, ornamental, projecting, teethlike blocks found on Ionic and Corinthian CORNICES.

DIAKONIKON. In an Eastern Orthodox church, the area where vessels and vestments are stored; similar to the VESTRY in a Roman Catholic church.

DIOCESE. The district, or see, in which a BISHOP has authority.

DIPTERAL. Having a double COLONNADE or PERISTYLE.

DIPTYCH. A pair of wood, ivory, or metal plaques usually hinged together, with the interior surfaces either painted or CARVED with a religious or memorial subject, or covered with wax for writing.

DOGE. Italian word for the chief magistrate in the former republics of Venice and Genoa.

DOLMEN. A structure of large unhewn stones set on end and covered with a single stone or several stones.

DOME. A large CUPOLA supported by a circular wall or DRUM or, over a noncircular space, by corner structures. See PENDENTIVE and SQUINCH.

DOMINICAN ORDER. A preaching ORDER of the Roman Catholic Church founded by Saint Dominic in 1216 in Toulouse. The Dominicans live austerely, believe in having no possessions, and subsist on charity. It is the second great MENDICANT ORDER, after the FRANCISCAN.

DOUAY VERSION. See BIBLE.

DRUM. One of several sections composing the SHAFT of a COLUMN. Also, a cylindrical wall supporting a DOME.

ECHINUS. In architecture, the rounded cushion-shaped MOLDING below the ABACUS of a Doric CAPITAL.

ELEVATION. One side of a building or a drawing of the same.

ENAMEL. Powdered colored glass thermally fused to a metal ground. *Champlevé* is a method by which the areas to be filled with enamel are dug out of the ground with a cutting tool. *Cloisonné* is a method in which the surface to be decorated is divided into compartments or *cloisons* by strips of metal attached to the ground. The compartments are filled with enamel powder and the piece is fused.

ENCAUSTIC. A method of painting on wood panels and walls with colors dissolved in hot wax.

ENGAGED COLUMN. See COLUMN.

ENTABLATURE. The upper part of an architectural ORDER, usually divided into three major parts: ARCHITRAVE, FRIEZE, and CORNICE.

ENTASIS. The subtle convex curvature swelling along the line of taper of classical COLUMNS.

EPISTLE. In Christian usage, one of the apostolic letters that constitute twenty-one books of the New Testament. See also MASS.

EUCHARIST. From the Greek word for *thanksgiving* or *gratitude*. The SACRAMENT of the Lord's Supper, the consecrated bread and wine used in the rite of Communion, or the rite itself.

EVANGELISTS, FOUR. Matthew, Mark, Luke, and John, generally assumed to be the authors of the GOSPELS in the New Testament. They are usually represented with their symbols, which are derived either from the four mysterious creatures in the vision of Ezekiel (1:5) or from the four beasts surrounding the throne of the Lamb in Revelation (4:7). Frequently, they are referred to by the symbols alone—an angel for Matthew, a lion for Mark, a bull for Luke, and an eagle for John—or by a representation of the four rivers of Paradise.

EXARCHATE. A province of the Byzantine Empire ruled by a provincial governor called an *exarch*.

EXEDRA (pl. EXEDRAE). A semicircular PORCH, chapel, or recess in a wall.

EXOSKELETON. By extension from zoology, the system of supports in a French Gothic church, including the RIBBED VAULTS, FLYING BUTTRESSES, and PIER BUTTRESSES.

FAÇADE. The front or principal face of a building; sometimes loosely used to indicate the entire outer surface of any side.

FAIENCE. Glazed earthenware or pottery used for sculpture, tiles, and decorative objects.

FAN VAULT. A complex VAULT, characteristic of late English Gothic architecture, in which radiating RIBS form a fanlike pattern.

FASCES. Latin plural of *fascis* (bundle). A bundle of rods containing an ax with the blade projecting, borne before Roman magistrates as a symbol of power.

FASCIA (pl. FASCIAE). Any long, flat surface of wood or stone. In the Ionic and Corinthian ORDERS, the three surfaces, the top two of which project slightly over the one below, that make up the ARCHITRAVE.

FLUTING. The shallow vertical grooves in the SHAFT of a COLUMN that either meet in a sharp edge as in Doric columns or are separated by a narrow strip as in Ionic columns.

FLYING BUTTRESS. An ARCH that springs from the upper part of the PIER BUTTRESS of a Gothic church, spans the SIDE AISLE roof, and abuts the upper NAVE wall to receive the THRUST from the nave VAULTS; it transmits this thrust to the solid pier buttress.

FONT. A receptacle in a BAPTISTERY or church for the water used in BAPTISM; it is usually of stone and frequently decorated with sculpture.

FORESHORTENING. In drawing, painting, etc., a method of reproducing the forms of an object not parallel to the PICTURE PLANE so that the object seems to recede in space and to convey the illusion of three dimensions as perceived by the human eye.

FORUM (pl. FORA). In ancient Rome, the center of assembly for judicial and other public business, and a gathering place for the people.

FOUR RIVERS OF PARADISE. See EVANGELISTS, FOUR.

FRANCISCAN ORDER. The first great MENDICANT ORDER. Founded by Saint Francis of Assisi (Giovanni de Bernardone, 1182?–1226) for the purpose of ministering to the spiritual needs of the poor and imitating as closely as possible the life of Christ, especially in its poverty; the monks depended solely on alms for subsistence.

FRESCO. Italian word for *fresh*. A painting executed on wet plaster with pigments suspended in water so that the plaster absorbs the colors and the painting becomes part of the wall. *Fresco a secco*, or painting on dry plaster (*secco* is the Italian word for *dry*), is a much less durable technique; the paint tends to flake off with time. The *secco su fresco* method involves the application of color in a vehicle containing some organic binding material (such as oil, egg, or wax) over the still-damp plaster.

FRIEZE. The architectural element that rests upon the ARCHITRAVE and is immediately below the CORNICE; also, any horizontal band decorated with MOLDINGS, RELIEF sculpture, or painting.

GABLE. The vertical, triangular piece of wall at the end of a ridged roof, from the level of the eaves or CORNICE to the summit; called a PEDIMENT in classical architecture. It is sometimes used with no roof, as over the PORTALS of Gothic cathedrals, and as a decorative element on ALTARPIECES.

GALLERY. An elevated floor projecting from the interior wall of a building. In a BASILICAN church it is placed over the SIDE AISLES and supported by the COLUMNS or PIERS that separate the NAVE and the side aisles; in a church with a central PLAN, it is placed over the AMBULATORY; in an ancient Roman basilica, it was generally built over each end as well as over the side aisles.

GESSO. A mixture of finely ground plaster and glue spread on wooden panels in preparation for TEMPERA painting.

GILDING. Coating paintings, sculptures, and architectural ornament with gold, gold leaf, or some gold-colored substance, by either mechanical or chemical means. In panel painting and wood sculpture, the gold leaf is attached with a glue sizing that is usually a dull red in color.

GLAZE. In pottery, a superficial layer of molten material used to coat a finished piece before it is fired in a kiln.

GLORY. The circle of light represented around the head or figure of the Savior, the Virgin Mary, or a saint. When the circle surrounds the head only, it is called a *halo*. See MANDORLA.

GOLGOTHA. From the Aramaic word for *skull*; thus, *the Place of the Skull*. The name of the place outside Jerusalem where Christ was crucified (Matthew 27:33). *Calvary*, from *calvaria*, meaning *skull* (Luke 23:33), is the Latin translation of the Aramaic word.

GOPURA. Sanskrit word for the gatehouse of south Indian building complexes, especially Hindu temples, often multistoried and elaborately carved.

GORGON. In ancient Greece, one of three mythological sisters, having snakes for hair, whose hideous appearance turned every beholder to stone. Of the three, Medusa is represented most frequently.

GOSPEL. In Christian usage, the story of Christ's life and teaching, as related in the first four books of the New Testament, traditionally ascribed to the Evangelists Matthew, Mark, Luke, and John. Also used to designate an ILLUMINATED copy of the same; sometimes called a Gospel LECTIONARY. See MASS.

GREEK CROSS. A cross with four equal arms.

GRIFFIN. A fabulous animal usually having the head and wings of an eagle and the body of a lion.

GROIN. The sharp edge formed by two intersecting VAULTS.

GROIN VAULT. A VAULT formed by the intersection at right angles of two BARREL VAULTS of equal height and diameter so that the GROINS form a diagonal cross.

GROUND PLAN. See PLAN.

GUILDS. *Arti* (sing. *Arte*) in Italian. Independent associations of bankers and of artisan-manufacturers.

HALLENKIRCHE. German word for *hall-church*. A church in which the AISLES are as high, or almost as high, as the NAVE; especially popular in the German Gothic style.

HALO. See GLORY.

HANIWA. Japanese word for the clay cylinders placed on the earth of burial mounds in Japan in the Kofun period (c. A.D. 200–552), variously shaped like houses, helmets, parasols, people, and animals.

HIEROGLYPHS. Characters (pictures or symbols representing or standing for sounds, words, ideas, etc.) in the picture-writing systems of the ancient Egyptians and the Maya of Mesoamerica.

HIMATION. A mantle worn in ancient times by Greek men and women and draped in a variety of styles over the CHITON.

HOST. From the Latin word for *sacrificial victim* (*hostia*). In the Roman Catholic Church it is used to designate the bread or wafer, regarded as the body of Christ, consecrated in the EUCHARIST.

HUE. The name of a color. The spectrum is usually divided into six basic hues: the three primary colors of red, yellow, and blue, and the secondary colors of green, orange, and violet.

HYPOSTYLE HALL. A building whose roof is supported on COLUMNS.

ICON. Literally, any image or likeness, but commonly used to designate a panel representing Christ, the Virgin Mary, or a saint and venerated by Orthodox (Eastern) Catholics.

ICONOCLASM. Breaking or destroying of images, particularly those set up for religious veneration. Many paintings and statues were destroyed in the Eastern Christian church in the eighth and ninth centuries as a result of the Iconoclastic Controversy. In the sixteenth and seventeenth centuries, especially in the Netherlands, the Protestants also destroyed many religious images.

ICONOSTASIS. In Eastern Christian churches, a screen separating the main body of the church from the SANCTUARY; it is usually decorated with ICONS whose subject matter and order were largely predetermined.

ILLUMINATED MANUSCRIPTS. CODICES or SCROLLS decorated with illustrations or designs in gold, silver, and bright colors.

IMAM. Muslim teacher serving as a priest in a mosque, who recites the prayers and leads the devotions of the faithful.

IMPERATOR. Freely translated from the Latin as *emperor*, but in Roman times it literally meant *army commander*.

IMPOST BLOCK. A block placed between the CAPITAL of a COLUMN and the ARCHES or VAULTS it supports.

INSULA (pl. INSULAE). Latin word for *island*. In Roman antiquity, a mapped-out space or a city block. Also, a group of buildings or a large building similar to a modern apartment house.

IRON AGE. See BRONZE and IRON AGES.

IWAN. In Muslim buildings, a vaulted chamber with three walls, open on the fourth side; the latter often flanks a quadrangular court.

JAMB. The vertical piece or pieces forming the side of a doorway or window. In Romanesque and Gothic churches, these supports were slanted or splayed outward to increase the impression of thickness in the walls and to provide space for sculptural decoration.

JATAKA. Word in the sacred Indian language Pali for a large set of stories of the previous lives of the BUDDHA, when he was a BODHISATTVA, variously presented as an animal or as a person; they describe the consequences of actions and the selfless compassion of the central figure.

KAABA. The most sacred shrine of the Muslims. A small cube-shaped building in the great mosque at Mecca toward which Muslims face when praying. It contains a sacred stone said to have been turned black by the tears of repentant pilgrims or, according to another tradition, by the sins of those who have touched it.

KEEP. The innermost central tower of a medieval castle, which served both as a last defense and as a dungeon and which contained living quarters, a prison, and sometimes a chapel; or a tower-like fortress, square, polygonal, or round, generally built on a mound as a military outpost.

KEYSTONE. See ARCH.

KING JAMES VERSION. See BIBLE.

KORAN. The sacred Muslim writings as revealed by God to Muhammad and taken down by him or his companions.

KORE (pl. KORAI). Greek for *maiden*. An archaic Greek statue of a standing clothed young woman.

KOUROS (pl. KOUROI). Greek for *youth*. An archaic Greek statue of a standing nude young man.

KRATER. A Greek or Roman bowl with a wide neck, used for mixing wine and water. The body has two handles projecting vertically from the juncture of the neck and body.

KUFIC or CUFIC. The earliest Arabic script used on CARVINGS and manuscripts, and, in the West, sometimes as pure ornament.

KYLIX. In Greek and Roman antiquity, a drinking vessel shaped like a shallow bowl with two horizontal handles projecting from the sides; often set upon a stem with a foot.

LABORS OF THE MONTHS. Representations of occupations suitable to the twelve months of the year; frequently CARVED around the PORTALS of Romanesque and Gothic churches, together with the signs of the ZODIAC, or represented in the calendar scenes of ILLUMINATED MANUSCRIPTS.

LANCET WINDOW. A high, narrow window with a pointed arch at the top.

LANTERN. In architecture, a tall, more or less open structure crowning a roof, DOME, tower, etc., and admitting light to an enclosed area below.

LAPIS LAZULI. A deep blue stone or complex mixture of minerals used for ornamentation and in the making of pigments.

LECTIONARY. A book containing portions of the Scriptures arranged in the order in which they are read at Christian services.

LEKYTHOS. In ancient Greece, a tall vase with an ellipsoidal body, a narrow neck, and a flanged mouth. The curved handle extends from below the lip to the shoulder, and the narrow base ends in a foot. It was used to contain oil or perfumes.

LI. Chinese term meaning *rites;* in Confucianism, all the traditional formal acts and observances that represent the moral order of society and also the ethical behavior and decorum that the rites symbolize.

LIBERAL ARTS, SEVEN. Derived from the standard medieval prephilosophical education, they consisted of the trivium of Grammar, Rhetoric, and Logic, and the quadrivium of Arithmetic, Music, Geometry, and Astronomy. During the Middle Ages and the Renaissance, they were frequently represented allegorically.

LINGAM. A stone pillar shaped like a phallus, considered in Hinduism to symbolize Siva, the god of destruction and creation.

LINTEL. See POST AND LINTEL.

LITURGY. A collection of prescribed prayers and ceremonies for public worship; specifically, in the Roman Catholic, Orthodox, and Anglican churches, those used in the celebration of the MASS.

LOGGIA (pl. LOGGIE). A GALLERY or ARCADE open on at least one side.

LUNETTE. A semicircular opening or surface, as on the wall of a VAULTED room or over a door, niche, or window. When it is over the PORTAL of a church, it is called a TYMPANUM.

MADRASA. Arabic word meaning *place of study*. An Islamic theological college providing student lodgings, a prayer hall, lecture halls, and a library. Perhaps first established in the tenth century by the Ghaznavids to combat the influence of dissenting sects, such as the Shiites; by the fourteenth century madrasas were located in all great cities of the Muslim world. Usually consists of an open quadrangle bordered by VAULTED CLOISTERS called IWANS.

MAENAD. An ecstatic female follower of the wine-god Dionysos (Greek) or Bacchus (Roman); hence, also called a *bacchante* (pl. *bacchae*).

MAESTÀ. Italian word for *majesty*, and in religion signifying the Virgin in Majesty. A large ALTARPIECE with a central panel representing the Virgin Enthroned, adored by saints and angels.

MAGUS (pl. MAGI). A member of the priestly caste in ancient Media and Persia traditionally reputed to have practiced supernatural arts. In Christian art, the Three Wise Men who came from the East to pay homage to the Infant Jesus are called the *Magi*.

MANDAPA. Sanskrit word for *pillared temple-hall;* in some cases an open structure with many columns supporting a roof, but lacking walls.

MANDORLA. The Italian word for *almond*. A large oval surrounding the figure of God, Christ, the Virgin Mary, or occasionally a saint, indicating divinity or holiness.

MARTYRIUM. A shrine or chapel erected in honor of or over the grave of a martyr.

MASS. The celebration of the EUCHARIST to perpetuate the sacrifice of Christ upon the Cross, plus readings from one of the GOSPELS and an EPISTLE; also, the form of LITURGY used in this celebration. See CANON OF THE MASS and ORDINARY AND PROPER OF THE MASS.

MASTABA. Arabic for *bench*. In Egyptian times, a tomb constructed of masonry and mud brick, rectangular in plan, with sloping sides and a flat roof. It covered a burial chamber and a chapel for offerings.

MAUSOLEUM. The magnificent tomb of Mausolus, erected by his wife at Halikarnassos in the middle of the fourth century B.C. Hence, any stately building erected as a burial place.

MEANDER. From the name of a winding river in Asia Minor. In Greek decoration, an ornamental pattern of lines that wind in and out or cross one another.

MEGARON. Principal hall in the Mycenaean palace or house.

MENDICANT ORDERS. Religious societies or confraternities whose members are required to subsist on alms. See DOMINICAN ORDER and FRANCISCAN ORDER.

MENHIR. A prehistoric monument consisting of an upright monumental stone, left rough or sometimes partly shaped, and either standing alone or grouped with others.

MESOLITHIC ERA. The Middle Stone Age, approximately 19,000–18,000 to 9000–8000 B.C. An intermediate period characterized by food-gathering activities and the beginnings of agriculture.

METOPE. A square slab, sometimes decorated, between the TRIGLYPHS in the FRIEZE of the ENTABLATURE of the Doric ORDER. Originally, the openings left by Greek builders between the ends of ceiling beams.

MIHRAB. Arabic word for a niche in the QIBLA wall of a mosque, pointing in the direction of Mecca. Perhaps of Egypto-Christian origin, it was first installed in the early eighth-century-A.D. rebuilding of the mosque at Medina.

MINARET. A tall, slender tower attached to a mosque and surrounded by one or more balconies from which the MUEZZIN calls the people to prayer.

MINBAR. Arabic word initially referring to the pulpit used in Medina by Muhammad, and later referring to the pulpit installed in each mosque to the right of the MIHRAB for the reading of the KORAN and prayers by the IMAM.

MINOTAUR. In Greek mythology, a monster with the body of a man and the head of a bull, who, confined in the labyrinth built for Minos, king of Crete, in his palace at Knossos, fed on human flesh and who was killed by the Athenian hero Theseus.

MITER. A tall cap terminating in two peaks, one in front and one in back, that is the distinctive headdress of BISHOPS (including the pope as bishop of Rome) and abbots of the Western Church.

MOAT. A deep defensive ditch that surrounds the wall of a fortified town or castle and is usually filled with water.

MODELING. The building up of three-dimensional form in a soft substance, such as clay or wax; the CARVING of surfaces into proper RELIEF; the rendering of the appearance of three-dimensional form in painting.

MOLDING. An ornamental strip, either depressed or projecting, that gives variety to the surface of a building by creating contrasts of light and shadow.

MOSAIC. A type of surface decoration (used on pavements, walls, and VAULTS) in which bits of colored stone or glass (*tesserae*) are laid in cement in a figurative design or decorative pattern. In Roman examples, colored stones, set regularly, are most frequently used; in Byzantine work, bits of glass, many with gold baked into them, are set irregularly.

MUEZZIN. In Muslim countries, a crier who calls the people to prayer at stated hours, either from a MINARET or from another part of a mosque or high building.

MULLION. A vertical element that divides a window or a screen into partitions.

MURAL. A painting executed directly on a wall or done separately for a specific wall and attached to it.

MUSES. The nine sister goddesses of classical mythology who presided over learning and the arts. They came to be known as Calliope, muse of epic poetry; Clio, muse of history; Erato, muse of love poetry; Euterpe, muse of music; Melpomene, muse of tragedy; Polyhymnia, muse of sacred song; Terpsichore, muse of dancing; Thalia, muse of comedy; and Urania, muse of astronomy.

NAOS. The principal room, or SANCTUARY, in a Greek or Roman PERIPTERAL temple.

NARTHEX. A PORCH or vestibule, sometimes enclosed, preceding the main entrance of a church; frequently, in churches preceded by an ATRIUM, the narthex is one side of the open AMBULATORY.

NAVE. From the Latin word for *ship*. The central aisle of an ancient Roman BASILICA or a Christian basilican church, as distinguished from the SIDE AISLES; the part of a church, between the main entrance and the CHANCEL, used by the congregation.

NEOLITHIC ERA. The New Stone Age, from about 9000–8000 to 3000 B.C. Characterized by fixed settlements and farming and the beginnings of architecture and organized religion.

NIKE. See VICTORY.

NIRVANA. Literally, *extinction*, in Sanskrit, the highest enlightenment, that of the BUDDHA; also understood as transcendence by means of wisdom and compassion of suffering, birth, and death.

OCULUS (pl. OCULI). Latin word for *eye*. A circular opening in a wall or at the apex of a DOME.

OINOCHOE. A Greek pitcher with a three-lobed rim for dipping wine from a bowl and pouring it into wine cups.

ORANT. From the Latin word for *praying*. Used to describe figures standing with arms outstretched in an attitude of prayer.

ORDER (architectural). An architectural system based on the COLUMN (including BASE, SHAFT, and CAPITAL) and its ENTABLATURE (including ARCHITRAVE, FRIEZE, and CORNICE). The five classical orders are the Doric, Ionic, Corinthian, Tuscan, and Composite.

ORDER (monastic). A religious society or confraternity whose members live under a strict set of rules and regulations, such as the BENEDICTINE, CISTERCIAN, DOMINICAN, FRANCISCAN, Carthusian, CLUNIAC, Jesuit, and Theatine.

ORDINARY AND PROPER OF THE MASS. The service of the MASS exclusive of the CANON. It includes prayers, hymns, and readings from the EPISTLES and the GOSPELS.

ORTHOGONALS. Lines that are at right angles to the plane of the picture surface but that, in a representation using one-point PERSPECTIVE, converge toward a common vanishing point in the distance.

PALAESTRA (pl. PALAESTRAE). In Greek antiquity, a public place for training in wrestling or athletics. A gymnasium.

PALAZZO (pl. PALAZZI). Italian word for a *large town house;* used freely to refer to large civic or religious buildings as well as relatively modest town houses.

PALEOLITHIC ERA. The Old Stone Age, which began approximately two million years ago. During the last period of glaciation, about 30,000 B.C., modern hunters emerged and their remains have been found in many sites in Europe and the Middle East. Settlement of the Americas may have begun about this time, via the Bering Strait. In Europe these hunters, who used stone weapons and implements, lived largely in caves that they decorated with paintings. The period ended about 19,000 B.C.

PALETTE. A thin, usually oval or oblong tablet, with a hole for the thumb, upon which painters place and mix their colors.

PANTHEON. From the Greek words meaning *all the gods;* hence, a temple dedicated to all the gods. Specifically, the famous temple built about 25 B.C. in Rome and so dedicated.

PANTOCRATOR. A representation of Christ as the Almighty Ruler of the Universe (from the Greek) in which the attributes of God the Father are combined with those of the Son; an image frequently found in the apse or dome MOSAICS of Byzantine churches.

PAPYRUS. A tall aquatic plant formerly very abundant in Egypt. Also, the material used for writing or painting upon by the ancient Egyptians, Greeks, and Romans. It was made by soaking, pressing, and drying thin strips of the pith of the plant laid together. Also, a manuscript or document of this material.

PARAPET. A low protective wall or barrier at the edge of a balcony, roof, bridge, or the like.

PARCHMENT. A paper-like material made from animal skins that have been carefully scraped, stretched, and dried to whiteness. The name is a corruption of *Pergamon*, the city in Asia Minor where parchment was invented in the second century B.C. Also, a manuscript or document of such material.

PARECCLESION. A funeral chapel.

PASSION. In the Christian Church, used specifically to describe the sufferings of Christ during his last week of earthly life; the representation of his sufferings in narrative or pictorial form.

PEDESTAL. An architectural support for a COLUMN, statue, vase, etc.; also, a foundation or BASE.

PEDIMENT. A low-pitched triangular area, resembling a GABLE, formed by the two slopes of a roof of a building (over a PORTICO, door, niche, or window), framed by a raking CORNICE, and frequently decorated with sculpture. When pieces of the cornice are either omitted or jut out from the main axis, as in some late Roman and Baroque buildings, it is called a *broken pediment*. See TYMPANUM.

PENDENTIVE. An architectural feature, having the shape of a spherical triangle, used as a transition from a square ground PLAN to a circular plan that will support a DOME. The dome may rest directly on the pendentives or on an intermediate DRUM.

PENTATEUCH. See TORAH.

PEPLOS. A simple, loose outer garment worn by women in ancient Greece.

PERICOPE. Extracts or passages from the BIBLE selected for use in public worship.

PERIPTERAL. Having a COLONNADE or PERISTYLE on all four sides.

PERISTYLE. A COLONNADE or ARCADE around a building or open court.

PERSPECTIVE. The representation of three-dimensional objects on a flat surface so as to produce the same impression of distance and relative size as that received by the human eye. In one-point *linear perspective,* developed during the fifteenth century A.D., all parallel lines in a given visual field converge at a single vanishing point on the horizon. In *aerial* or *atmospheric perspective* the relative distance of objects is indicated by gradations of tone and color and by variations in the clarity of outlines. See ORTHOGONALS and TRANSVERSALS.

PHARAOH. From the Egyptian word meaning *great house.* A title of the sovereigns of ancient Egypt; used in the Old Testament as a proper name.

PIAZZA (pl. PIAZZE). Italian word for *public square.* See also CAMPO.

PICTURE PLANE. The actual surface on which a picture is painted.

PIER. An independent architectural element, usually rectangular in section, used to support a vertical load; if used with an ORDER, it often has a BASE and CAPITAL of the same design. See COMPOUND PIER.

PIER BUTTRESS. An exterior PIER in Romanesque and Gothic architecture, BUTTRESSING the THRUST of the VAULTS within.

PIETÀ. Italian word meaning both *pity* and *piety.* Used to designate a representation of the dead Christ mourned by the Virgin, with or without saints and angels. When the representation is intended to show a specific event prior to Christ's burial, it is usually called a *Lamentation.*

PILASTER. A flat vertical element, having a CAPITAL and BASE, engaged in a wall from which it projects. It has a decorative rather than a structural purpose.

PINNACLE. A small ornamental turret on top of BUTTRESSES, PIERS, or elsewhere; mainly decorative, it may also have a structural purpose, as in Reims Cathedral.

PLAN. The general arrangement of the parts of a building or group of buildings, or a drawing of these as they would appear on a plane cut horizontally above the ground or floor.

PODIUM (pl. PODIA). In architecture, a continuous projecting BASE or PEDESTAL used to support COLUMNS, sculptures, or a wall. Also, the raised platform surrounding the arena of an ancient AMPHITHEATER.

PO-MO. Chinese word literally meaning *broken ink* or *splashed ink.* As "broken ink," it refers to painting with ink alone to achieve modeling and texture, but without emphasizing line; as "splashed ink," it is a technique of freely applied ink.

PORCH. An exterior structure forming a covered approach to the entrance of a building.

PORPHYRY. A very hard rock having a dark purplish-red base. The room in the Imperial Palace in Constantinople reserved for the confinement of the reigning empress was decorated with porphyry so that the child would be "born to the purple," or "Porphyrogenitus."

PORTA. Latin and Italian word for *gate.*

PORTA CLAUSA. Latin phrase for CLOSED DOOR or CLOSED GATE.

PORTAL. A door or gate, especially one of imposing appearance, as in the entrances and PORCHES of a large church or other building. In Gothic churches the FAÇADES frequently include three large portals with elaborate sculptural decoration.

PORTICO. A structure consisting of a roof, or an ENTABLATURE and PEDIMENT, supported by COLUMNS, sometimes attached to a building as a PORCH.

POST AND LINTEL. The ancient but still widely used system of construction in which the basic unit consists of two or more upright posts supporting a horizontal beam, or lintel, which spans the opening between them.

POTSHERD. A fragment or broken piece of earthenware.

PREDELLA. PEDESTAL of an ALTARPIECE, usually decorated with small narrative scenes that expand the theme of the major work above it.

PRIORI. Italian word for *priors.* The council or principal governing body of a town.

PRIORY. A monastic house presided over by a prior or prioress; a dependency of an ABBEY.

PRONAOS. The vestibule in front of the doorway to the NAOS in a Greek or Roman PERIPTERAL temple.

PROPYLAION (pl. PROPYLAIA). Generally, the entrance to a temple or other sacred enclosure. Specifically, the entrance gate to the Acropolis in Athens.

PROSTYLE. Used to describe a temple having a PORTICO across the entire front.

PROTHESIS. In an Early Christian or modern Eastern Orthodox church, a space or chamber next to the SANCTUARY for the preparation and safekeeping of the EUCHARIST. See BEMA.

PSALTER. The Book of Psalms in the Old Testament, or a copy of it, used for liturgical or devotional purposes; many psalters illuminated in the Middle Ages have survived. See ILLUMINATED MANUSCRIPTS.

PUEBLO. Communal houses or groups of houses built of stone or ADOBE by the Indians of the southwestern United States.

PYLON. Greek word for *gateway.* In Egyptian architecture, the monumental entrance to a temple or other large edifice, consisting of two truncated pyramidal towers flanking a central gateway. Also applied to either of the flanking towers.

QIBLA. The direction of Mecca, which Muslims face when praying, indicated by the MIHRAB in the qibla wall of a mosque.

QUATREFOIL. A four-lobed form used as ornamentation.

RAKING CORNICE. See CORNICE.

RATHA. Sanskrit word for *chariot,* especially for the ceremonial conveyance of Hindu gods; also a small shrine at a temple complex, often a detached structure, possibly derived from the chariot.

REFECTORY. From the Latin verb meaning to *renew* or *restore.* A room for eating; in particular, the dining hall in a monastery, college, or other institution.

REGISTER. One of a series of horizontal bands used to differentiate areas of decoration when the bands are placed one above the other, as in Egyptian tombs, medieval church sculpture, and the pages of a manuscript.

RELIEF. Sculpture that is not freestanding but projects from the background of which it is a part. *High relief* or *low relief* describes the amount of projection; when the background is not cut out, as in some Egyptian sculpture, the work is called *incised relief.*

RELIQUARY. A casket, COFFER, or other small receptacle for a sacred relic, usually made of precious materials and richly decorated.

RHYTON. An ancient Greek drinking vessel having one handle and, frequently, the shape of an animal.

RIB. A slender projecting ARCH used primarily as support in Romanesque and Gothic VAULTS; in late Gothic architecture, the ribs are frequently ornamental as well as structural.

RIBBED (or RIB) VAULT. A compound masonry VAULT, the GROINS of which are marked by projecting stone RIBS.

ROSE WINDOW. A circular window with stone TRACERY radiating from the center; a feature characteristic of Gothic church architecture.

ROSTRUM (pl. ROSTRA). A pulpit or platform for public speakers. In the Roman Republican FORUM, the orator's platform that was decorated with the beaks of warships captured in 338 B.C.

ROTULUS (pl. ROTULI). Latin word for SCROLL.

RUSTICATION. Masonry having indented joinings and, frequently, a roughened surface.

SACRAMENT. A rite regarded as an outward and visible sign of an inward and spiritual grace. Specifically, in the Roman Catholic Church, any one of the seven rites recognized as having been instituted by Christ: Baptism, Confirmation, the EUCHARIST, Penance, Matrimony, Holy Orders, and Extreme Unction.

SACRISTY. See VESTRY.

SAHN. Arabic name for the open interior courtyard of a mosque; it usually has a pool in the center.

SANCTUARY. A sacred or holy place. In architecture, the term is generally used to designate the most sacred part of a building.

SARCOPHAGUS (pl. SARCOPHAGI). From the Greek words meaning *flesh-eating.* In ancient Greece, a kind of limestone said to reduce flesh to dust; thus, the term was used for coffins. A general term for a stone coffin often decorated with sculpture or bearing inscriptions.

SATURATION. The degree of intensity of a HUE and its relative freedom from an admixture with white.

SATYR. In classical mythology, one of the woodland creatures thought to be the companions of Dionysos and noted for lasciviousness, represented with the body of a man, pointed ears, two horns, a tail, and the legs of a goat.

SCRIPTURE. See BIBLE and KORAN.

SCROLL. A roll of paper, PARCHMENT, or the like intended for writing upon. In architecture, an ornament resembling a partly unrolled sheet of paper or having a spiral or coiled form, as in the VOLUTES of Ionic and Corinthian COLUMNS.

SECTION. A drawing or diagram of a building showing its various parts as they would appear if the building were cut on a vertical plane.

SERAPH (pl. SERAPHIM). A celestial being or angel of the highest order, usually represented with six wings.

SHAFT. A spire-shaped or cylindrical form; in architecture, the part of a COLUMN or PIER between the BASE and the CAPITAL.

SIBYL. Any of various women of Greek and Roman mythology who were reputed to possess powers of prophecy and divination. In time, as many as twelve came to be recognized.

SIDE AISLE. One of the corridors parallel to the NAVE of a church or BASILICA, separated from it by an ARCADE or COLONNADE.

SIKHARA. Sanskrit word for a tower or a spire topping a Hindu temple-hall.

SINOPIA (pl. SINOPIE). An Italian term taken from *Sinope,* the name of a city in Asia Minor famous for its red earth. Used to designate the preliminary brush drawing, executed in red earth mixed with water, for a painting in FRESCO; usually done on the ARRICCIO.

SINS, SEVEN DEADLY. See VICES.

SIREN. In classical mythology, one of several fabulous creatures, half woman and half bird, who were reputed to lure sailors to destruction by their seductive singing.

SLIP. Potter's clay reduced with water to a semiliquid state and used for coating or decorating pottery, cementing handles, etc.

SOCLE. A square block supporting a COLUMN, statue, vase, or other work of art, or a low BASE supporting a wall.

SPANDREL. An area between the exterior curves of two adjoining ARCHES; or an area enclosed by the exterior curve of an arch, a perpendicular from its springing, and a horizontal through its apex.

SPHINX. In Egyptian mythology, a creature with the body of a lion and the head of a man, a bird, or a beast; the monumental sculpture of the same. In Greek mythology, a monster usually having the winged body of a lion and the head of a woman.

SQUINCH. An architectural device that uses ARCHES, LINTELS, or CORBELS across the corners of a square space to support a DOME and to make the transition from the square space to a polygonal or round one.

STEATITE. A variety of talc or soapstone.

STELA (pl. STELAE). From a Greek word meaning *standing block*. An upright slab bearing sculptured or painted designs or inscriptions.

STOA. In Greek architecture, a PORTICO or covered COLONNADE, usually of considerable length, used as a promenade or meeting place.

STONE AGE. See MESOLITHIC, NEOLITHIC, and PALEOLITHIC.

STUCCO. Any of various plasters used for CORNICES, MOLDINGS, and other wall decorations. A cement or concrete for coating exterior walls in imitation of stone.

STUPA. Originally a memorial reliquary of the BUDDHA, later containing other sacred relics. The traditional shape in India was a hemisphere on a circular base, topped by a post or spire often set on latticework or rings; in Southeast Asia, the hemisphere became elongated and often bell-shaped, capped by a tall, slender spire; the pagoda of East Asia developed out of the stupa.

STYLOBATE. The top step of a stepped BASE of a Greek temple, on which COLUMNS rest.

STYLUS. A pointed instrument used in ancient times for writing on tablets of a soft material, such as clay.

SUPERIMPOSED ORDERS. One ORDER on top of another on the face of a building of more than one story. The upper order is usually lighter in form than the lower.

TABERNACLE. The portable SANCTUARY used by the Israelites in the wilderness before the building of the Temple. Generally, any place or house of worship. In architecture, a canopied niche or recess, in a wall or a pillar, built to contain an image.

TEMPERA. Ground colors mixed with yolk of egg, instead of oil, as a vehicle; a medium widely used for Italian panel painting before the sixteenth century.

TERRA-COTTA. Italian words for *baked earth*. A hard glazed or unglazed earthenware used for sculpture and pottery or as a building material. The word can also mean something made of this material or the color of it, a dull brownish red.

TESSERA (pl. TESSERAE). See MOSAIC.

THEATER. In ancient Greece and Rome, an open-air structure in the form of a segment of a circle, frequently excavated from a hillside, with the seats arranged in tiers behind and above one another.

THEOLOGICAL VIRTUES. See VIRTUES.

THEOTOKOS. The Virgin Mary as the Mother of God.

THOLOS. In Greek and Roman architecture, a circular building derived from early Greek tombs and used for a variety of purposes.

THRUST. The outward force exerted by an ARCH or VAULT that must be counterbalanced by BUTTRESSING.

TIE-ROD. An iron rod used as a structural element to keep the lower ends of a roof or ARCH from spreading.

TOGA. A loose outer garment consisting of a single piece of material, without sleeves or armholes, which covered nearly the whole body, worn by the citizens of ancient Rome when appearing in public in times of peace.

TOKONOMA. Japanese word for the shallow alcove in a traditional Japanese room, its floor elevated slightly above that of the room. It serves as a focal point for the display of art, usually a hanging scroll or ceramic object, and flower arrangements.

TORAH. The Jewish books of the law or the first five books of the Old Testament. Also called the *Pentateuch* in both Jewish and Christian usage.

TORANA. Sanskrit word for the *arch*, both structural and ornamental; a common feature of Hindu temple architecture, where it serves as an entrance gate and is often elaborately decorated with carvings.

TORII. Japanese word for the gateway to a Shinto shrine that marks the entrance to the sacred precincts, consisting of two upright posts capped by two horizontal beams that extend past the posts.

TOTEM POLE. A wooden post carved and painted with the emblem (totem) of a clan or family, and erected in front of the homes of the Indians of coastal northwestern America.

TRACERY. Ornamental stonework in geometric patterns used primarily in Gothic windows as support and decoration, but also used on panels, screens, etc. When the window appears to be cut through the solid stone, the style is called *plate tracery;* when slender pieces of stone are erected within the window opening, the style is called *bar tracery.*

TRANSEPT. In a BASILICAN church, the crossarm, placed at right angles to the NAVE, usually separating the latter from the CHANCEL or the APSE.

TRANSVERSALS. Horizontal lines running parallel to the PICTURE PLANE and intersecting the ORTHOGONALS.

TRAVERTINE. A tan or light-colored limestone used in Italy, and elsewhere, for building. The surface is characterized by alternating smooth and porous areas.

TREE OF THE KNOWLEDGE OF GOOD AND EVIL. A tree in the Garden of Eden bearing the forbidden fruit, the eating of which destroyed Adam's and Eve's innocence (Genesis 2:9, 3:17).

TREFOIL. A three-lobed form used as ornamentation or as the basis for a ground PLAN.

TRICLINIUM. The dining room in a Roman house.

TRIFORIUM. The section of the wall in the NAVE, CHOIR, and sometimes in the TRANSEPT above the ARCHES and below the CLERESTORY. It usually consists of a blind ARCADE or a GALLERY.

TRIGLYPH. From the Greek for *three grooves*. An ornamental member of a Doric FRIEZE, placed between two METOPES and consisting of a rectangular slab with two complete grooves in the center and a half groove at either side. Originally the end of a ceiling beam.

TRILITHON. Greek for *three stones*. A structure consisting of large unhewn stones, two upright and one resting on them like a LINTEL.

TRIUMPHAL ARCH. In ancient Rome, a freestanding monumental ARCH or series of three arches erected to commemorate a military victory; usually decorated with sculptured scenes of a war and its subsequent triumphal procession. In a Christian church, the transverse wall with a large arched opening that separates the CHANCEL and the APSE from the main body of the church, and that is frequently decorated with religious scenes executed in MOSAIC or FRESCO.

TRUMEAU (pl. TRUMEAUX). A central PIER dividing a wide doorway, used to support the LINTEL; in medieval churches, trumeaux were frequently decorated with sculpture.

TUFA. Any of various porous rocks composed of calcium deposited by springs or streams; or a volcanic stone.

TUMULUS (pl. TUMULI). An artificially constructed mound of earth raised over a tomb or sepulchral chamber.

TUNIC. In ancient Greece and Rome, a knee-length garment with or without sleeves usually worn without a girdle by both sexes.

TYMPANUM (pl. TYMPANA). In classical architecture, the vertical recessed face of a PEDIMENT; in medieval architecture, the space between the ARCH and the LINTEL over a door or window, which was often decorated with sculpture.

UKIYO-E. Japanese word for the art of the Japanese "floating world" of pleasure—the theater, entertainment, and the brothel. Characteristically, scenes from daily life and portraits, in wood-block prints and paintings.

VALUE. The degree of lightness or darkness of a HUE.

VAULT. An ARCHED roof or covering made of brick, stone, or concrete. See BARREL VAULT, GROIN VAULT, RIBBED VAULT, and CORBEL VAULT.

VELLUM. A fine kind of PARCHMENT made from calfskin and used for the writing, ILLUMINATING, and binding of medieval manuscripts.

VESTRY. A room in or a building attached to a church where the vestments and sacred vessels are kept; also called a *sacristy.* Used, in some churches, as a chapel or a meeting room.

VICAR. An ecclesiastic of the Roman Catholic Church who represents a pope or BISHOP; the pope himself as the vicar of Christ.

VICES. Coming from the same tradition as the VIRTUES, and frequently paired with them, they are more variable but usually include Pride, Avarice, Wrath, Gluttony, and Unchastity. Others such as Sloth, Folly, Inconstancy, or Injustice may be selected to make a total of seven.

VICTORY. A female deity of the ancient Romans, or the corresponding deity the ancient Greeks called NIKE. The representation of the deity, usually as a winged woman in windblown draperies and holding a laurel wreath, palm branch, or other symbolic object.

VIRTUES. Divided into the three Theological Virtues of Faith, Hope, and Charity (Love) and the four Cardinal Virtues of Prudence, Justice, Fortitude, and Temperance. As with the VICES, the allegorical representation of the Virtues derives from a long medieval tradition in manuscripts and sculpture, and from such literary sources as the *Psychomachia* of Prudentius and the writings of Saint Augustine.

VOLUTE. An ornament resembling a rolled SCROLL. Especially prominent on CAPITALS of the Ionic and Composite ORDERS.

VOUSSOIR. See ARCH.

VULGATE. See BIBLE.

WEN-REN. Chinese word for the Chinese literati who were scholars and painters, gentlemen who painted for expression rather than as a profession.

WESTWORK. The multistoried, towered western end of a Carolingian church that usually included a second TRANSEPT below and a chapel and GALLERIES above.

YAKSHA (-SHI). Sanskrit word for a class of male and female minor deities of forests and fields, usually depicted as powerful and plump, and associated with prosperity, well-being, and fertility in Hindu mythology. In Buddhism, they became fierce guardian deities, sometimes demonic.

YAMATO-E. Japanese word meaning *Japanese-style painting,* in contradistinction to Chinese painting styles; primarily, colorful narrative art focusing on native secular themes.

ZIGGURAT. From the Assyrian-Babylonian word for *mountaintop* (*ziqquratu*). A staged, truncated pyramid of mud brick, built by the Sumerians and later by the Assyrians as a support for a shrine.

ZODIAC. An imaginary belt encircling the heavens within which lie the paths of the sun, moon, and principal planets. It is divided into twelve equal parts called *signs,* which are named after twelve constellations: Aries, the ram; Taurus, the bull; Gemini, the twins; Cancer, the crab; Leo, the lion; Virgo, the virgin; Libra, the balance; Scorpio, the scorpion; Sagittarius, the archer; Capricorn, the goat; Aquarius, the water-bearer; and Pisces, the fishes. Also, a circular or elliptical diagram representing this belt with pictures of the symbols associated with the constellations.

BOOKS FOR FURTHER READING

The following list of suggested works for further reading was prepared for this edition by Carol Anne Dickson, assistant to Frederick Hartt. Citations include classic works of art-historical writing as well as recent publications that reflect new approaches to the discipline. For a comprehensive listing of art books (excluding monographs) published prior to 1980, see *Guide to the Literature of Art History* by Etta Arntzen and Robert Rainwater (American Library Association, Chicago, 1980). *Art Books: A Basic Bibliography of Monographs on Artists* by Wolfgang Freitag (Garland, New York, 1985) provides citations on individual artists from all periods and cultures. An excellent research guidebook for students is *Art Information: Research Methods and Resources* by Lois Swan Jones (3d ed., Kendall/Hunt, Dubuque, Iowa, 1990). It provides detailed information on indices, general bibliographies, and databases pertaining to the history of art. *A Short Guide to Writing about Art* by Sylvan Barnet (3d ed., Scott, Foresman, Glenview, Illinois, 1989) and *The Artist's Handbook of Materials and Techniques* by Ralph Mayer (5th ed., Viking, New York, 1991) are other valuable resources.

INTRODUCTION

ARNHEIM, RUDOLF, *New Essays on the Psychology of Art*, University of California Press, Berkeley, 1986

BROUDE, NORMA, and GARRARD, MARY, eds., *The Expanding Discourse: Feminism and Art History*, Harper-Collins, New York, 1992

———, eds., *Feminism and Art History: Questioning the Litany*, Harper & Row, New York, 1982

BRYSON, NORMAN, *Vision and Painting: The Logic of the Gaze*, Yale University Press, New Haven and London, 1988

FOCILLON, HENRI, *The Life of Forms in Art*, 2d ed., Wittenborn, New York, 1958; repr. ed., Zone Books, New York, 1989

GOMBRICH, ERNST H., *Art and Illusion*, 4th ed., Phaidon, London, 1972

———, *Art, Perception and Reality*, Johns Hopkins University Press, Baltimore, 1972

HAUSER, ARNOLD, *The Social History of Art* (tr. S. Goodman, in collaboration with the author), Knopf, New York, 1951; repr. ed., Vintage Books, New York, 1985

HOLT, ELIZABETH B., *A Documentary History of Art*, 2d ed., 2 vols., Doubleday, Garden City, N.Y., 1981

KLEINBAUER, W. EUGENE, *Modern Perspectives in Western Art History*, University of Toronto Press and Medieval Academy of America, 1989

KOSTOF, SPIRO, *The City Shaped: Urban Patterns and Meanings Through History*, Thames & Hudson, London, and Little, Brown, Boston, 1991

———, *A History of Architecture: Settings and Rituals*, Oxford University Press, New York and Oxford, 1985

PETERSEN, KAREN, and WILSON, J. J., *Women Artists: Recognition and Reappraisal from the Early Middle Ages to the Twentieth Century*, New York University Press, 1976

ROSKILL, MARK, *What Is Art History?*, University of Massachusetts Press, Amherst, 1989

Part One: Art Before Writing

MARSHACK, ALEXANDER, *The Roots of Civilization: The Cognitive Beginnings of Man's First Art, Symbol and Notation*, McGraw-Hill, New York, 1971

CHAPTER ONE: ART IN THE STONE AGE

Paleolithic and Mesolithic Art

BREUIL, HENRI, *Four Hundred Centuries of Cave Art*, Centre d'Études et de Documentation Préhistorique, Montignac, France, 1952; repr. ed., Hacker, New York, 1979

———, and LANTIER, R., *The Men of the Old Stone Age*, 2d ed., St. Martin's Press, New York, 1965; repr. ed., Greenwood Press, Westport, Conn., 1980

GIEDION, SIGFRIED, *The Eternal Present*, 2 vols., Bollingen Foundation, New York, 1962–64 (Vol. 1, *The Beginnings of Art*; Vol. 2, *The Beginnings of Architecture*); Princeton University Press, 1981

LEROI-GOURHAN, ANDRÉ, *The Dawn of European Art: An Introduction to Palaeolithic Cave Painting*, Cambridge University Press, New York, 1982

MELLARS, PAUL, *The Emergence of Modern Humans: An Archaeological Perspective*, Cornell University Press, Ithaca, 1990

WHITE, RANDALL K., *Dark Caves, Bright Visions: Life in Ice Age Europe*, American Museum of Natural History, Washington, D.C., and Norton, New York, 1986

Neolithic Art

DANIEL, GLYN E., *The Megalith Builders of Western Europe*, Hutchinson, London and New York, 1958; repr. ed., Greenwood Press, Westport, Conn., 1985

GIMBUTAS, MARIJA, *The Civilization of the Goddess: The World of Old Europe*, Harper, San Francisco, 1991

MELLAART, JAMES, *The Neolithic of the Near East*, Scribner, New York, 1975

PIGGOTT, STUART, *Ancient Europe*, Aldine, Chicago, 1966

CHAPTER TWO: TRIBAL ART

ANTON, FERDINAND, and TROWELL, KATHLEEN, *Primitive Art: Pre-Columbian, North American Indian, African, Oceanic*, Abrams, New York, 1979

Black African Art

BASCOM, WILLIAM R., *African Art in Cultural Perspective: An Introduction*, Norton, New York, 1973

BRENTJES, BURCHARD, *African Rock Art*, C. N. Potter, New York, 1970

COURTNEY-CLARKE, MARGARET, *Ndebele: The Art of an African Tribe*, Rizzoli, New York, 1986

D'AZEVEDO, WARREN L., ed., *The Traditional Artist in African Society*, Indiana University Press, Bloomington, 1975

DREWAL, HENRY JOHN, *Yoruba: Nine Centuries of African Art and Thought*, Center for African Art and Abrams, New York, 1989

GILLON, WERNER, *A Short History of African Art*, Penguin, New York, 1984

SIEBER, ROY, and WALKER, ROSLYN ADELE, *African Art in the Cycle of Life*, National Museum of African Art, Washington, D.C., and London, 1988

VOGEL, SUSAN M., *African Masterpieces from the Musée de l'Homme*, Center for African Art and Abrams, New York, 1985

WASSING, RENÉ S., *African Art: Its Background and Traditions*, Abrams, New York, 1968

Oceanic Art

HANSON, F. ALLAN, and HANSON, LOUISE, *Art and Identity in Oceania*, University of Hawaii Press, Honolulu, 1990

MEAD, SIDNEY MOKO, *Te Maori: Maori Art from New Zealand Collections*, Abrams, New York, 1985

SCHMITZ, CARL A., *Oceanic Art: Myth, Man, and Image in the South Seas*, Abrams, New York, 1971

North American Indian Art

EWERS, JOHN C., *Plains Indian Sculpture: A Tradition from America's Heartland*, Smithsonian Press, Washington, D.C., 1986

FENTON, WILLIAM N., *The False Faces of the Iroquois*, University of Oklahoma Press, Norman, 1987

FURST, PETER T., and FURST, JILL LESLIE, *North American Indian Art*, 3d ed., Rizzoli, New York, 1992

JONAITIS, ALDONA, *From the Land of the Totem Poles: The Northwest Coast Indian Art Collection at the American Museum of Natural History*, American Museum of Natural History, New York, 1988

PATTERSON, NANCY-LOU, *Canadian Native Art*, Collier-Macmillan Canada, Don Mills, Ontario, 1973

WADE, EDWIN, and HARALSON, CAROL, *The Arts of the North American Indian: Native Traditions in Evolution*, Philbrook Art Center, Tulsa, and Hudson Hills Press, New York, 1986

Part Two: The Ancient World

AMIET, PIERRE, *Art in the Ancient World: A Handbook of Styles and Forms*, Rizzoli, New York, 1981

DIAKONOFF, I. M., ed., *Early Antiquity* (tr. Alexander Kirjanov), University of Chicago Press, Chicago and London, 1991

GREEN, PETER, *Classical Bearings: Interpreting Ancient History and Culture*, Thames & Hudson, London, 1989

GROENEWEGEN-FRANKFORT, HENRIETTE A., and ASHMOLE, BERNARD, *Art of the Ancient World*, Abrams, New York, and Prentice-Hall, Englewood Cliffs, N.J., 1984

LLOYD, SETON, et al., *Ancient Architecture*, Electa/Rizzoli, New York, 1986

WOLFF, WALTHER, *The Origins of Western Art: Egypt, Mesopotamia, the Aegean*, Universe Books, New York, 1989

CHAPTER THREE: EGYPTIAN ART

ALDRED, CYRIL, *The Development of Ancient Egyptian Art from 3200 to 1315 B.C.*, 3 vols., Academy Editions, London, 1973

ARNOLD, DIETER, *Building in Egypt: Pharaonic Stone Masonry*, Oxford University Press, New York, 1991

DAVIS, WHITNEY, *The Canonical Tradition in Ancient Egyptian Art*, Cambridge University Press, Cambridge, 1989

PORTER, BERTHA, and MOSS, R., *Topographical Bibliography of Ancient Egyptian Hieroglyphic Texts, Reliefs, and Paintings*, 2d rev. ed., 7 vols., Griffith Institute, Ashmolean Museum, Oxford, 1970

RICE, MICHAEL, *Egypt's Making: The Origins of Ancient Egypt, 5000–2000 B.C.*, Routledge, London and New York, 1990

SMITH, WILLIAM STEVENSON, *The Art and Architecture of Ancient Egypt*, rev. ed., Penguin, New York, 1981

CHAPTER FOUR: MESOPOTAMIAN ART

AKURGAL, EKREM, *Art of the Hittites*, Abrams, New York, 1962

ALBRIGHT, WILLIAM F., *The Archaeology of Palestine*, rev. ed., Penguin, Harmondsworth, 1960; repr. ed., Peter Smith, Gloucester, Mass., 1971

AMIET, PIERRE, *Art of the Ancient Near East*, Abrams, New York, 1980

CRAWFORD, HARRIET, *Sumer and the Sumerians*, Cambridge University Press, Cambridge and New York, 1991

DOWNEY, SUSAN B., *Mesopotamian Religious Architecture: Alexander Through the Parthians*, Princeton University Press, 1988

FRANKFORT, HENRI, *The Art and Architecture of the Ancient Orient*, Penguin, Harmondsworth, 1985

GHIRSHMAN, ROMAN, *Iran from the Earliest Times to the Islamic Conquest*, Penguin, New York, 1978

GOFF, BEATRICE L., *Symbols of Prehistoric Mesopotamia*, Yale University Press, New Haven, Conn., 1963

KRAMER, SAMUEL N., *The Sumerians: Their History, Culture, and Character*, University of Chicago Press, 1963

LLOYD, SETON, *The Archaeology of Mesopotamia: From the Old Stone Age to the Persian Conquest*, rev. ed., Thames & Hudson, London, 1984

————, *The Art of the Ancient Near East,* Thames & Hudson, London, and Praeger, New York, 1961

MELLAART, JAMES, *Earliest Civilizations of the Near East,* McGraw-Hill, New York, 1965

MOOREY, P. R. S., *Ancient Iraq: Assyria and Babylonia,* Ashmolean Museum, Oxford, 1976

————, *Materials and Manufacture in Ancient Mesopotamia: The Evidence of Archaeology and Art,* B.A.R., Oxford, 1985

PARROT, ANDRÉ, *The Arts of Assyria,* Golden Press, New York, 1961

————, *Nineveh and Babylon,* Thames & Hudson, London, 1960

————, *Sumer: The Dawn of Art,* Golden Press, New York, 1961

PORADA, EDITH, *The Art of Ancient Iran: Pre-Islamic Cultures,* rev. ed., Greystone Press, New York, 1969

READE, JULIAN, *Mesopotamia,* Harvard University Press, Cambridge, Mass., 1991

SMITH, WILLIAM STEVENSON, *Interconnections in the Ancient Near East,* Yale University Press, New Haven, Conn., 1965

WOOLLEY, SIR CHARLES LEONARD, *Ur of the Chaldees,* Cornell University Press, Ithaca, 1982

CHAPTER FIVE: PRE-COLUMBIAN ART IN MEXICO, CENTRAL AMERICA, AND SOUTH AMERICA

COE, MICHAEL, *The Maya,* Thames & Hudson, London, 1980

FURST, PETER T., "House of Darkness and House of Light: Sacred Functions of West Mexican Funerary Art," in E. P. Benson, ed., *Death and the Afterlife in Pre-Columbian America,* Dumbarton Oaks, Washington, D.C., 1975

GALLAGHER, JACKIE, *Companions of the Dead: Ceramic Tomb Sculpture from Ancient West Mexico,* Museum of Cultural History, University of California, Los Angeles, 1983

HEMMINGS, JOHN, and RANNEY, EDWARD, *Monuments of the Incas,* Little, Brown, Boston, 1982

HEYDEN, DORIS, and GENDROP, PAUL, *Pre-Columbian Architecture of Mesoamerica,* Rizzoli and Abrams, New York, 1980

KUBLER, GEORGE, *The Art and Architecture of Ancient America,* rev. ed., Penguin, Harmondsworth and Baltimore, 1975

LAPINER, ALAN C., *Pre-Columbian Art of South America,* Abrams, New York, 1976

MATTOS MOCTEZUMA, EDUARDO, *Teotihuacán, the City of the Gods,* Rizzoli, Milan, 1990

MILLER, MARY ELLEN, *The Art of Mesoamerica: From Olmec to Aztec,* Thames & Hudson, New York, 1986

————, *The Murals of Bonampak,* Princeton University Press, 1986

MORLEY, SYLVANUS, and BRAINERD, GEORGE W., *The Ancient Maya,* 4th ed., Stanford University Press, 1983

PASZTORY, ESTHER, *Aztec Art,* Abrams, New York, 1983

PROSKOURIAKOFF, TATIANA, *A Study of Classic Maya Sculpture,* Carnegie Institute, Washington, D.C., 1950

SABLOFF, JEREMY A., *The Cities of Ancient Mexico: Reconstructing a Lost World,* Thames & Hudson, New York, 1989

SCHELE, LINDA, and FREIDEL, DAVID, *A Forest of Kings: The Untold Story of the Ancient Maya,* Morrow, New York, 1990

SOUSTELLE, JACQUES, *The Olmecs: The Oldest Civilization in Mexico* (tr. H. R. Lane), University of Oklahoma Press, Norman, 1985

CHAPTER SIX: AEGEAN ART, c. 3000–1100 B.C.

BETANCOURT, PHILIP P., *The History of Minoan Pottery,* Princeton University Press, 1985

BLEGEN, CARL W., and RAWSON, M., *The Palace of Nestor at Pylos in Western Messenia,* 3 vols., Princeton University Press, 1966–73

BOARDMAN, JOHN, *Pre-Classical: From Crete to Archaic Greece,* Penguin, Harmondsworth, 1978

BRANIGAN, KEITH, *Aegean Metalwork of the Early and Middle Bronze Age,* Clarendon Press, Oxford, 1974

CASTLEDEN, RODNEY, *Minoans: Life in Bronze Age Crete,* Routledge, London and New York, 1990

EVANS, SIR ARTHUR JOHN, *The Palace of Minos,* 4 vols., Macmillan, New York, 1921–35; repr. ed., Biblo and Tannen, New York, 1964

FITTON, J. LESLEY, *Cycladic Art,* Harvard University Press, Cambridge, Mass., 1990

GRAHAM, JAMES WALTER, *The Palaces of Crete,* rev. ed., Princeton University Press, 1987

HAMPE, ROLAND, and SIMON, ERIKA, *The Birth of Greek Art, from the Mycenaeans to the Archaic Period,* Oxford University Press, New York, 1981

HIGGINS, REYNOLD, *Minoan and Mycenaean Art,* rev. ed., Thames & Hudson, New York, 1985

HOOD, SINCLAIR, *The Arts in Prehistoric Greece,* Penguin, New York, 1978

RENFREW, COLIN, *The Cycladic Spirit,* Abrams, New York, 1991

TAYLOUR, LORD WILLIAM, *The Mycenaeans,* rev. ed., Thames & Hudson, London, 1990

VERMEULE, EMILY, *Greece in the Bronze Age,* University of Chicago Press, 1972

WACE, ALAN J. B., *Mycenae: An Archaeological History and Guide,* Princeton University Press, 1949; repr. ed., Biblo and Tannen, New York, 1964

CHAPTER SEVEN: GREEK ART

ARCHIBALD, ZOFIA, *Discovering the World of the Ancient Greeks,* Quarto, London, 1991

ASHMOLE, BERNARD, *Architect and Sculptor in Classical Greece,* New York University Press, 1972

————, and YALOURIS, N., *Olympia: The Sculptures of the Temple of Zeus,* Phaidon, London, 1967

BEAZLEY, SIR JOHN D., *Attic Black-Figure Vase-Painters,* Clarendon Press, Oxford, 1956; repr. ed., Hacker, New York, 1978

————, *Attic Red-Figure Vase-Painters,* 2d ed., 3 vols., Clarendon Press, Oxford, 1971

————, and ASHMOLE, B., *Greek Sculpture and Painting to the End of the Hellenistic Period,* Cambridge University Press, Cambridge, 1966

BERVE, HELMUT; GRUBEN, G.; and HIRMER, M., *Greek Temples, Theatres, and Shrines,* Abrams, New York, 1963

BIEBER, MARGARETE, *The History of the Greek and Roman Theater,* 2d ed., Princeton University Press, 1961

BOARDMAN, JOHN, *Athenian Black Figure Vases,* Oxford University Press, New York, 1975

————, *Athenian Red Figure Vases: The Archaic Period,* Oxford University Press, New York, 1979

————, *Athenian Red Figure Vases: The Classical Period,* Thames & Hudson, New York, 1989

————, *Greek Gems and Finger Rings,* Abrams, New York, and Thames & Hudson, London, 1972

————, *Greek Sculpture: The Archaic Period,* Oxford University Press, New York, 1978

————, et al., *Greek Art and Architecture,* Abrams, New York, 1967

CARPENTER, RHYS, *Greek Sculpture: A Critical Review,* University of Chicago Press, 1971

CARPENTER, THOMAS H., *Art and Myth in Ancient Greece,* Thames & Hudson, New York, 1991

CHARBONNEAUX, JEAN, *Classical Greek Art,* Braziller, New York, 1972

————, *Greek Bronzes,* Viking, New York, 1962

————, *Hellenistic Art, 330–50 B.C.,* Braziller, New York, 1973

————, et al., *Archaic Greek Art,* Braziller, New York, 1971

COOK, ROBERT M., *Greek Art: Its Development, Character, and Influence,* Farrar, Straus & Giroux, New York, 1973

HIGGINS, REYNOLD A., *Greek and Roman Jewelry,* 2d ed., University of California Press, Berkeley, 1980

————, *Greek Terracottas,* Methuen, London, 1967

KRAAY, COLIN M., and HIRMER, M., *Greek Coins,* Abrams, New York, and Thames & Hudson, London, 1966

LANGLOTZ, ERNST, and HIRMER, M., *The Art of Magna Graecia: Greek Art in Southern Italy and Sicily,* Thames & Hudson, London, 1965

LAWRENCE, ARNOLD W., *Greek Architecture,* 4th ed., Penguin, New York, 1983

PAPAIOANNOU, KOSTAS, *The Art of Greece,* Abrams, New York, 1989

POLLITT, J. J., *The Ancient View of Greek Art,* Yale University Press, New Haven, Conn., 1974

————, *Art and Experience in Classical Greece,* Cambridge University Press, Cambridge, 1972

————, *The Art of Greece (1400–31 B.C.): Sources and Documents,* rev. ed., Cambridge University Press, Cambridge and New York, 1990

RICHTER, GISELA M. A., *A Handbook of Greek Art,* 9th ed., Phaidon, New York, 1969

————, *Perspective in Greek and Roman Art,* Phaidon, London and New York, 1970

————, *The Portraits of the Greeks,* 3 vols., Cornell University Press, Ithaca, 1984

————, *The Sculpture and Sculptors of the Greeks,* 4th ed., Yale University Press, New Haven, Conn., 1970

RIDGWAY, B. S., *The Archaic Style in Greek Sculpture,* Princeton University Press, 1977

————, *Fifth Century Styles in Greek Sculpture,* Princeton University Press, 1981

————, *Hellenistic Sculpture,* 2 vols., University of Wisconsin Press, Madison, 1990

————, *The Severe Style in Greek Sculpture,* Princeton University Press, 1970

ROBERTSON, DONALD S., *Greek and Roman Architecture,* 2d ed., Cambridge University Press, Cambridge, 1969

ROBERTSON, MARTIN, *Greek Painting,* Rizzoli, New York, 1979

WARD-PERKINS, JOHN B., *The Cities of Ancient Greece and Italy: Planning in Classical Antiquity,* Braziller, New York, 1974

WOODFORD, SUSAN, *An Introduction to Greek Art,* Cornell University Press, Ithaca, 1988

CHAPTER EIGHT: ETRUSCAN ART

BANTI, LUISA, *Etruscan Cities and Their Culture,* University of California Press, Berkeley, 1973

BOETHIUS, AXEL, and WARD-PERKINS, J. B., *Etruscan and Early Roman Architecture,* 2d integrated ed., rev., Penguin, New York, 1978

BRILLIANT, RICHARD, *Visual Narratives: Storytelling in Etruscan and Roman Art,* Cornell University Press, Ithaca, 1984

MANSUELLI, G. A., *The Art of Etruria and Early Rome,* rev. ed., Greystone Press, New York, 1967

RICHARDSON, EMELINE, *The Etruscans: Their Art and Civilization,* University of Chicago Press, 1976

SPRENGER, MAJA, et al., *The Etruscans: Their History, Art, and Architecture,* Abrams, New York, 1983

CHAPTER NINE: ROMAN ART

ANDREAE, BERNARD, *The Art of Rome,* Abrams, New York, 1977

BIEBER, MARGARETE, *The History of the Greek and Roman Theater,* 2d ed., Princeton University Press, 1961

BLAKE, MARION E., *Roman Construction in Italy from Nerva Through the Antonines,* American Philosophical Society, Philadelphia, 1973

BOATWRIGHT, MARY TALIAFERRO, *Hadrian and the City of Rome,* Princeton University Press, 1987

BOETHIUS, AXEL, *The Golden House of Nero,* University of Michigan Press, Ann Arbor, 1960

BRENDEL, OTTO, *Prolegomena to the Study of Roman Art,* Yale University Press, New Haven, Conn., 1979

BRILLIANT, RICHARD, *Roman Art from the Republic to Constantine,* Phaidon, New York, 1974

GUILLAUD, MAURICE, and GUILLAUD, JACQUELINE, *Frescoes in the Time of Pompeii* (tr. Ian Robson and Alphabyte SAS, Rome), C. N. Potter, New York, 1990

HANFMANN, GEORGE M. A., *Roman Art,* Norton, New York, 1975

————, *The Seasons Sarcophagus in Dumbarton Oaks,* 2 vols., Harvard University Press, Cambridge, Mass., 1952

HODDINOTT, RALPH F., *The Thracians,* Thames & Hudson, London, 1981

LEACH, ELEANOR WINSOR, *The Rhetoric of Space: Literary and Artistic Representations of Landscape in Republican and Augustan Rome,* Princeton University Press, 1988

LEHMANN, PHYLLIS W., *Roman Wall Paintings from Boscoreale in the Metropolitan Museum of Art,* Metropolitan Museum of Art, New York, 1953

MACCORMACK, SABINE G., *Art and Ceremony in Late Antiquity,* University of California Press, Berkeley, 1990

MACDONALD, WILLIAM L., *The Architecture of the Roman Empire,* Vol. 1, rev. ed., Yale University Press, New Haven, Conn., 1982

————, *The Pantheon: Design, Meaning and Progeny,* Harvard University Press, Cambridge, Mass., 1976

MCKAY, ALEXANDER G., *Houses, Villas and Palaces in the Roman World,* Cornell University Press, Ithaca, 1975

NASH, ERNEST, *Pictorial Dictionary of Ancient Rome,* 2d ed., 2 vols., Praeger, New York, 1968; repr. ed., Hacker, New York, 1981

PERCIVAL, JOHN, *The Roman Villa: An Historical Introduction,* University of California Press, Berkeley, 1976

POLLITT, J. J., *The Art of Rome and Late Antiquity: Sources and Documents in the History of Art,* Prentice-Hall, Englewood Cliffs, N.J., 1966; repr. ed., Cambridge University Press, Cambridge and New York, 1983

RAMAGE, NANCY, and RAMAGE, ANDREW, *Roman Art: Romulus to Constantine,* Abrams, New York, 1991

ROBERTSON, DONALD S., *Greek and Roman Architecture,* 2d ed., Cambridge University Press, Cambridge, 1980

ROULLET, ANNE, *The Egyptian and Egyptianizing Monuments of Imperial Rome,* Brill, Leiden, 1972

SEAR, FRANK, *Roman Architecture,* rev. ed., Cornell University Press, Ithaca, 1989

STRONG, DONALD E., *Roman Art,* 2d ed., rev., Penguin, New York, 1988

————, *Roman Imperial Sculpture: An Introduction to the Commemorative and Decorative Sculpture of the Roman Empire Down to the Death of Constantine,* A. Tiranti, London, 1961

TOYNBEE, JOCELYN M. C., *The Art of the Romans,* Praeger, New York, 1965

————, *Roman Historical Portraits,* Thames & Hudson, London, 1978

VERMEULE, CORNELIUS C., III, *Roman Imperial Art in Greece and Asia Minor,* Belknap Press, Cambridge, Mass., 1968

WARD-PERKINS, JOHN B., *Roman Architecture,* Electa/Rizzoli, New York, 1988

————, *Roman Imperial Architecture,* Penguin, New York, 1981

————, and BOETHIUS, AXEL, *Etruscan and Roman Architecture,* 2d integrated ed., Penguin, New York, 1978

WHEELER, MORTIMER, *Roman Art and Architecture,* Thames & Hudson, New York, 1985

Part Three: The Middle Ages

DAVIS-WEYER, CAECILIA, *Early Medieval Art, 300–1150: Sources and Documents,* Prentice-Hall, Englewood Cliffs, N.J., 1971; repr. ed., University of Toronto Press and Medieval Academy of America, 1986

ECO, UMBERTO, *Art and Beauty in the Middle Ages* (tr. Hugh Bredin), Yale University Press, New Haven, Conn., and London, 1986

KLINGENDER, FRANCIS D., *Animals in Art and Thought to the End of the Middle Ages,* MIT Press, Cambridge, Mass., 1971

MARTINDALE, ANDREW, *The Rise of the Artist in the Middle Ages and Early Renaissance,* McGraw-Hill, New York, 1972

OAKESHOTT, WALTER F., *Classical Inspiration in Medieval Art,* Chapman & Hall, London, 1959

SAALMAN, HOWARD, *Medieval Architecture: European Architecture, 600–1200,* Braziller, New York, 1967

SMITH, EARL BALDWIN, *Architectural Symbolism of Imperial Rome and the Middle Ages,* Princeton University Press, 1956; repr. ed., Hacker, New York, 1978

SNYDER, JAMES, *Medieval Art,* Abrams, New York, 1989

STOKSTAD, MARILYN, *Medieval Art,* Harper & Row, New York, 1986

CHAPTER TEN: EARLY CHRISTIAN AND BYZANTINE ART

BECKWITH, JOHN, *Coptic Sculpture, 300–1300,* A. Tiranti, London, 1963

————, *Early Christian and Byzantine Art,* 2d integrated ed., Penguin, Baltimore, 1979

BEZA, MARCU, *Byzantine Art in Roumania,* Batsford, London, 1940

BIHALJI-MERIN, OTO, *Byzantine Frescoes and Icons in Yugoslavia,* Abrams, New York, 1960

CONNOR, CAROLYN L., *Art and Miracles in Medieval Byzantium: The Crypt at Hosios Loukas and Its Frescoes,* Princeton University Press, 1991

CREMA DE IONGH, DANIEL, *Byzantine Aspects of Italy,* Norton, New York, 1967

DEMUS, OTTO, *Byzantine Art and the West,* New York University Press, 1970

————, *Byzantine Mosaic Decoration,* Paul, Trench, Trubner, London; repr. ed., Caratzas Brothers, New Rochelle, N.Y., 1976

————, *The Mosaics of Norman Sicily,* Routledge & Kegan Paul, London, 1950

DER NERSESSIAN, SIRARPIE, *Armenia and the Byzantine Empire,* Harvard University Press, Cambridge, Mass., 1945

FORSYTH, GEORGE H., and WEITZMANN, K., *The Church and Fortress of Justinian,* University of Michigan Press, Ann Arbor, 1973

FRAZER, MARGARET E., *Age of Spirituality: Late Antique and Early Christian Art, Third to Seventh Century,* Metropolitan Museum of Art, New York, 1977

GALAVARIS, GEORGE, *The Icon in the Life of the Church: Doctrine, Liturgy, Devotion,* Brill, Leiden, 1981

GILLES, PIERRE, *The Antiquities of Constantinople* (tr. John Ball), 2d ed., Italica Press, New York, 1988

GRABAR, ANDRÉ, *Byzantine Painting,* Rizzoli, New York, 1979

————, *The Golden Age of Justinian: From the Death of Theodosius to the Rise of Islam,* Odyssey Press, New York, 1967

HAMILTON, GEORGE H., *Art and Architecture of Russia,* 3d integrated ed., Penguin, New York, 1983

HAMILTON, JOHN A., *Byzantine Architecture and Decoration,* 2d ed., Batsford, London, 1956; repr. ed., Books for Libraries/Arno, Freeport, N.Y., 1972

KAZHDAN, ALEXANDER P., ed., *The Oxford Dictionary of Byzantium,* Oxford University Press, New York, 1991

KITZINGER, ERNST, *The Art of Byzantium and the Medieval West: Selected Studies,* Indiana University Press, Bloomington, 1976

KOSTOF, SPIRO K., *Caves of God: The Monastic Environment of Byzantine Cappadocia,* MIT Press, Cambridge, Mass., 1972

KRAUTHEIMER, RICHARD, *Early Christian and Byzantine Architecture,* 4th ed., rev., Penguin, Baltimore, 1965

————, *Studies in Early Christian, Medieval and Renaissance Art,* New York University Press, 1969

MAGUIRE, HENRY, *Art and Eloquence in Byzantium,* Princeton University Press, 1981

MAINSTONE, R. J., *Hagia Sophia: Architecture, Structure, and Liturgy of Justinian's Great Church,* Thames & Hudson, London, 1988

MANGO, CYRIL, *The Art of the Byzantine Empire, 312–1453: Sources and Documents,* Prentice-Hall, Englewood Cliffs, N.J., 1972; University of Toronto Press and Medieval Academy of America, 1986

————, *Byzantine Architecture,* Rizzoli, New York, 1985

MATHEWS, THOMAS S., *The Byzantine Churches of Istanbul: A Photographic Survey,* Pennsylvania State University Press, University Park, 1976

MILBURN, ROBERT, *Early Christian Art and Architecture,* University of California Press, Berkeley and Los Angeles, 1988

MILLET, GABRIEL, and RICE, D. T., *Byzantine Painting at Trebizond,* G. Allen & Unwin, London, 1936

PALOL SALELLAS, PEDRO DE, and HIRMER, M., *Early Medieval Art in Spain,* Thames & Hudson, London, and Abrams, New York, 1967

PAPAGEORGIOU, ATHANASIOS, *Icons of Cyprus,* Cowles, New York, 1970

RICE, DAVID TALBOT, *The Appreciation of Byzantine Art,* Oxford University Press, London, 1972

————, *Byzantine Art,* rev. ed., Penguin, Harmondsworth, 1968

————, and RADOJCIC, S., *Yugoslavia: Mediaeval Frescoes,* New York Graphic Society, Greenwich, Conn., 1955

ROSTOVTSEV, MIKHAIL I., *Dura-Europos and Its Art,* Clarendon Press, Oxford, 1938; repr. ed., AMS Press, New York, 1978

RUNCIMAN, SIR STEVEN, *Byzantine Style and Civilization,* Penguin, Baltimore, 1975

SIMSON, OTTO VON, *The Sacred Fortress,* University of Chicago Press, 1948; repr. ed., Princeton University Press, 1987

STYLIANOU, ANDREAS and JUDITH, *The Painted Churches of Cyprus: Treasures of Byzantine Art,* Trigraph for the A. G. Leventis Foundation, London, 1985

UNDERWOOD, PAUL A., *The Kariye Djami,* 4 vols., Bollingen Foundation, New York, 1966–75

VOYCE, ARTHUR, *The Art and Architecture of Medieval Russia,* University of Oklahoma Press, Norman, 1967

WALTER, CHRISTOPHER, *Art and Ritual of the Byzantine Church,* Variorum Reprints, London, 1982

————, *Studies in Byzantine Iconography,* Variorum Reprints, London, 1977

WEITZMANN, KURT, *Byzantine Book Illumination and Ivories,* Variorum Reprints, London, 1980

————, *Late Antique and Early Christian Book Illumination,* Braziller, New York, 1977

————, *The Monastery of Saint Catherine at Mount Sinai: The Icons,* Princeton University Press, 1976

————, et al., *The Icon,* Knopf, New York, 1982

CHAPTER ELEVEN: ISLAMIC ART

ASLANAPA, OKTAY, *Turkish Art and Architecture,* Praeger, New York, and Faber & Faber, London, 1971

ATIL, ESIN, ed., *Islamic Art and Patronage: Treasures from Kuwait,* Rizzoli, New York, 1990

BREND, BARBARA, *Islamic Art,* Harvard University Press, Cambridge, Mass., 1991

BRICE, WILLIAM C., ed., *An Historical Atlas of Islam,* Brill, Leiden, 1981

CRESWELL, K. A. C., *Early Muslim Architecture,* 2d ed., with Van Berchem, Marguerite, Clarendon Press, Oxford, 1969; repr. ed., Hacker, New York, 1979

————, *The Muslim Architecture of Egypt,* 2 vols., Clarendon Press, Oxford, 1952–59; repr. ed., Hacker, New York, 1978

ETTINGHAUSEN, RICHARD, *Arab Painting,* Skira, New York, 1962

GRABAR, OLEG, *The Formation of Islamic Art,* rev. ed., Yale University Press, New Haven, Conn., 1987

HILL, DEREK, *Islamic Architecture and Its Decoration:* A.D. *800–1500,* University of Chicago Press, 1964

HOAG, JOHN D., *Islamic Architecture,* Abrams, 1977; Rizzoli, New York, 1987

KOCH, EBBA, *Mughal Architecture: An Outline of Its History and Development, 1526–1858,* Prestel-Verlag, Munich, 1991

NASR, SEYYED HOSSEIN, *Islamic Art and Spirituality,* State University of New York Press, Albany, 1987

POPE, ARTHUR UPHAM, and ACKERMAN, P., eds., *A Survey of Persian Art from Prehistoric Times to the Present,* 7 vols., Oxford University Press, New York and London, 1977; repr. ed., Maxwell Aley Literary Association, New York, 1981

SCHIMMEL, ANNEMARIE, *Calligraphy and Islamic Culture,* New York University Press, 1990

TITLEY, NORAH M., *Persian Miniature Painting and Its Influence on the Art of Turkey and India,* University of Texas Press, Austin, 1984

CHAPTER TWELVE: BARBARIAN AND CHRISTIAN ART IN NORTHERN EUROPE

Barbarian Art

COLES, J. M., *The Bronze Age in Europe,* St. Martin's Press, New York, 1979

HUBERT, JEAN; PORCHER, J.; and VOLBACH, W. F., *Europe of the Invasions,* Braziller, New York, 1969

JETTMAR, KARL, *Art of the Steppes: The Eurasian Animal Style,* Methuen, London, 1967

KNOBLOCH, EDGAR, *Beyond the Oxus: Archaeology, Art and Architecture of Central Asia,* Benn, London, 1972

MEGAW, J. V. S., *Art of the European Iron Age,* Harper & Row, New York, 1970

MELLAART, JAMES, *The Chalcolithic and Early Bronze Age in the Near East and Anatolia,* Khayats, Beirut, 1966

MOSCATI, SABATINO, et al., *The Celts,* Palazzo Grassi, Venice, and Rizzoli, New York, 1991

Christian (Hiberno-Saxon) Art

ARNOLD, BRUCE, *A Concise History of Irish Art,* rev. ed., Thames & Hudson, London, 1977

BECKWITH, JOHN, *Early Medieval Art: Carolingian, Ottonian, Romanesque,* Thames & Hudson, London, 1985

HARBISON, PETER, et al., *Irish Art and Architecture from Prehistory to the Present,* Thames & Hudson, London, 1978

HENRY, FRANÇOISE, ed., *The Book of Kells,* Knopf, New York, 1974

MEGAW, RUTH, and MEGAW, VINCENT, *Celtic Art: From Its Beginnings to the Book of Kells,* Thames & Hudson, New York, 1989

STOLL, ROBERT, *Architecture and Sculpture in Early Britain,* Thames & Hudson, London, 1967

YOUNGS, SUSAN, ed., *The Work of Angels: Masterpieces of Celtic Metalwork, 6th–9th Centuries A.D.,* University of Texas Press, Austin, and British Museum Publications, 1989

CHAPTER THIRTEEN: THE ART OF THE HOLY ROMAN EMPIRE

BACKES, MAGNUS, and DÖLLING, R., *Art of the Dark Ages,* Abrams, New York, 1971

BECKWITH, JOHN, *Early Medieval Art: Carolingian, Ottonian, Romanesque,* Thames & Hudson, New York, 1985

CONANT, KENNETH J., *Carolingian and Romanesque Architecture, 800–1200,* 2d integrated ed., Penguin, New York, 1990

DODWELL, C. R., *Painting in Europe, 800–1200,* Penguin, Baltimore, 1971

HENDERSON, GEORGE, *Early Medieval,* Penguin, Baltimore, 1972

HENRY, FRANÇOISE, *Irish Art During the Viking Invasions, 800–1200 A.D.,* Cornell University Press, Ithaca, 1967

HINKS, ROGER P., *Carolingian Art,* University of Michigan Press, Ann Arbor, 1966

METROPOLITAN MUSEUM OF ART, *The Secular Spirit: Life and Art at the End of the Middle Ages,* Dutton, New York, 1975

MUTHERICH, FLORENTINE, and GAEHDE, J. E., *Carolingian Painting,* Braziller, New York, 1976

RICE, DAVID TALBOT, *The Dawn of European Civilization: The Dark Ages,* McGraw-Hill, New York, 1965

CHAPTER FOURTEEN: ROMANESQUE ART

AINAUD DE LASARTE, JUAN, *Catalan Painting,* Rizzoli, New York, 1990

ALLSOPP, BRUCE, *Romanesque Architecture: The Romanesque Achievement,* John Day, New York, 1971

ANTHONY, EDGAR W., *Romanesque Frescoes,* Greenwood Press, Westport, Conn., 1971

ARMI, C. EDSON, *Masons and Sculptors in Romanesque Burgundy,* Pennsylvania State University Press, University Park, 1983

AUBERT, MARCEL, *Romanesque Cathedrals and Abbeys of France,* N. Vane, London, 1966

BOASE, T. S. R., *English Art 1100–1216,* 2d ed., Clarendon Press, Oxford, 1968

BOLOGNA, FERDINANDO, *Early Italian Painting,* Van Nostrand, Princeton, N.J., 1964

BRAUN, HUGH, *English Abbeys,* Faber & Faber, London, 1971

CAHN, WALTER, *Romanesque Bible Illumination,* Cornell University Press, Ithaca, 1982

CLAPHAM, SIR ALFRED WILLIAM, *English Romanesque Architecture,* 2 vols., Clarendon Press, Oxford, 1964

CONANT, KENNETH J., *Carolingian and Romanesque Architecture, 800–1200,* 2d integrated ed., Penguin, New York, 1990

COURTENS, ANDRÉ, *Romanesque Art in Belgium,* M. Vokaer, Brussels, 1969

DEMUS, OTTO, *Romanesque Mural Painting,* Abrams, New York, 1970

DERCSÉNYI, DEZSÖ, *Romanesque Architecture in Hungary,* Kossuth, Budapest, 1975

DUBY, GEORGES, *The Age of the Cathedrals: Art and Society 980–1420,* University of Chicago Press, 1981

EVANS, JOAN, *Art in Medieval France 987–1498,* Clarendon Press, Oxford, 1948

————, *The Romanesque Architecture of the Order of Cluny,* 2d ed., AMS Press, New York, 1972

FOCILLON, HENRI, *The Art of the West in the Middle Ages,* Vol. 1, Phaidon, London, 1963; Cornell University Press, Ithaca, 1980

GRIVOT, DENIS, and ZARNECKI, GEORGE, *Gislebertus: Sculptor of Autun,* Orion, New York, 1961; repr. ed., Hacker, New York, 1985

HAZARD, HENRY, ed., *The Art and Architecture of the Crusader States,* University of Wisconsin Press, Madison, 1977

HELL, VERA, and HELL, HELLMUT, *The Great Pilgrimage of the Middle Ages,* Barrie & Rockliff, London, 1966

KIDSON, PETER, *The Medieval World,* McGraw-Hill, New York, 1967

KRAUS, HENRY, *The Living Theatre of Medieval Art,* University of Pennsylvania Press, Philadelphia, 1972

KUBACH, HANS E., *Romanesque Architecture,* Electa/Rizzoli, New York, 1988

KÜNSTLER, GUSTAV, comp., *Romanesque Art in Europe,* Norton, New York, 1973

MORRIS, RICHARD, *Cathedrals and Abbeys of England and Wales: The Building Church, 600–1540,* Dent, London, 1979

NICHOLAS, STEPHEN G., JR., *Romanesque Signs: Early Medieval Narrative and Iconography,* Yale University Press, New Haven, Conn., and London, 1986

PÄCHT, OTTO, *The Rise of Pictorial Narrative in Twelfth Century England,* Clarendon Press, Oxford, 1962

PLATT, COLIN, *The English Medieval Town,* Secker & Warburg, London, 1976

PORTER, ARTHUR KINGSLEY, *Lombard Architecture,* 4 vols., Yale University Press, New Haven, Conn., 1915–17; repr. ed., Hacker, New York, 1967

————, *Romanesque Sculpture of the Pilgrimage Roads,* 10 vols., Marshall Jones, Boston, 1923; repr. ed., Hacker, New York, 1969

SAALMAN, HOWARD, *Medieval Cities,* Braziller, New York, 1968

SCHAPIRO, MEYER, *Romanesque Art,* Braziller, New York, and Chatto & Windus, London, 1977

SMITH, J. T.; FAULKNER, P. A.; and EMERY, A., *Studies in Medieval Domestic Architecture,* Royal Archaeological Institute, London, 1975

STODDARD, WHITNEY S., *Art and Architecture in Medieval France,* Harper & Row, New York, 1972

STONE, LAWRENCE, *Sculpture in Britain: The Middle Ages,* 2d ed., Penguin, Baltimore, 1972

SWARZENSKI, HANNS, *Monuments of Romanesque Art,* University of Chicago Press, 1974

TIMMERS, J. J. M., *A Handbook of Romanesque Art,* Harper & Row, New York, 1976

WHITEHILL, WALTER M., *Spanish Romanesque Architecture of the Eleventh Century,* repr. ed., Oxford University Press, London, 1968

ZARNECKI, GEORGE, *Romanesque Art,* Universe Books, New York, 1989

CHAPTER FIFTEEN: GOTHIC ART

ACLAND, JAMES H., *Medieval Structure: The Gothic Vault,* University of Toronto Press, 1972

ARNOLD, HUGH, *Stained Glass of the Middle Ages in England and France,* 2d ed., Macmillan, New York, 1940

ARSLAN, EDOARDO, *Gothic Architecture in Venice,* Phaidon, London, 1972

AUBERT, MARCEL, *The Art of the High Gothic Era,* rev. ed., Greystone Press, New York, 1966

AVRIL, FRANÇOIS, *Manuscript Painting at the Court of France: The Fourteenth Century, 1310–1380,* Braziller, New York, 1978

BONY, JEAN, *The English Decorated Style: Gothic Architecture Transformed, 1250–1350,* Cornell University Press, Ithaca, 1979

————, *French Gothic Architecture of the 12th and 13th Centuries,* University of California Press, Berkeley, 1983

BRIEGER, PETER, *English Art 1216–1307,* Clarendon Press, Oxford, 1968

BUSCH, HARALD, and LOHSE, B., *Gothic Sculpture,* Macmillan, New York, 1963

CALKINS, ROBERT G., *Illuminated Books of the Middle Ages,* Cornell University Press, Ithaca, 1986

DEUCHLER, FLORENS, *Gothic Art,* Universe Books, New York, 1973

DUPONT, J., *Gothic Painting,* Rizzoli, New York, 1979

FOCILLON, HENRI, *The Art of the West in the Middle Ages,* Vol. 2, Phaidon, London, 1963; repr. ed., Cornell University Press, Ithaca, 1980

FRISCH, TERESA GRACE, *Gothic Art 1140–c. 1450: Sources and Documents,* Prentice-Hall, Englewood Cliffs, N.J., 1971; repr. ed., University of Toronto Press and Medieval Academy of America, 1987

GIMPEL, JEAN, *The Cathedral Builders,* Grove Press, New York, 1983

HARVEY, JOHN H., *The Gothic World,* Harper & Row, New York, 1969

————, *The Master Builders: Architecture in the Middle Ages,* McGraw-Hill, New York, 1971

————, *Mediaeval Craftsmen,* Batsford, London, 1975

JANTZEN, HANS, *The High Gothic: The Classic Cathedrals of Chartres, Reims, and Amiens,* Pantheon, New York, 1962

KATZENELLENBOGEN, ADOLF, *The Sculptural Programs of Chartres Cathedral,* Johns Hopkins University Press, Baltimore, 1959

MACAULAY, DAVID, *Cathedral: The Story of Its Construction,* Houghton, Mifflin, Boston, 1973

MÂLE, ÉMILE, *Religious Art in France: The Thirteenth Century* (English ed. of *L'Art religieux du XIIIe siècle en France,* H. Bober, ed.), Princeton University Press, 1984

MARTINDALE, ANDREW, *Gothic Art,* Praeger, New York, and Thames & Hudson, London, 1967

————, *The Rise of the Artist in the Middle Ages and Early Renaissance,* McGraw-Hill, New York, 1972

MEISS, MILLARD, *French Painting in the Time of Jean de Berry: The Limbourgs and Their Contemporaries,* 2 vols., Braziller, New York, 1974

PÄCHT, OTTO, *Book Illumination in the Middle Ages: An Introduction* (tr. Kay Davenport), Oxford University Press, New York, 1986

PANOFSKY, ERWIN, *Abbot Suger on the Abbey Church of St.-Denis and Its Art Treasures,* 2d ed., Princeton University Press, 1979

————, *Gothic Architecture and Scholasticism,* Meridian Books, New York, 1976

RUDOLPH, CONRAD, *Artistic Change at St.-Denis: Abbot Suger's Program and the Early Twelfth-Century Controversy over Art,* Princeton University Press, 1990

SAUERLÄNDER, WILLIBALD, and HIRMER, M., *Gothic Sculpture in France 1140–1270,* Abrams, New York, 1973

SIMSON, OTTO G. VON, *The Gothic Cathedral,* 3d ed., Princeton University Press, 1988

SPENCE, KEITH, *Cathedrals and Abbeys of England and Wales,* Norton, New York, 1984

WILSON, CHRISTOPHER, *The Gothic Cathedral: The Architecture of the Great Church, 1130–1530,* Thames & Hudson, New York, 1990

Part Four: The Far East

HUTT, JULIA, *Understanding Far Eastern Art,* Dutton, New York, 1987

LEE, SHERMAN E., *A History of Far Eastern Art,* 4th ed., Abrams, New York, 1982

CHAPTER SIXTEEN: INDIAN ART

BARRETT, DOUGLAS E., and GRAY, BASIL, *Painting of India,* Skira, Geneva, 1963; repr. ed., Rizzoli, New York, 1978

DEHEJIA, VIDYA, *Art of the Imperial Cholas,* Columbia University Press, New York, 1990

———, *Early Buddhist Rock Temples: A Chronological Study,* Cornell University Press, Ithaca, 1972

FONTEIN, JAN, et al., *The Sculpture of Indonesia,* National Gallery of Art, Washington, D.C., and Abrams, New York, 1990

HARLE, JAMES C., *The Art and Architecture of the Indian Subcontinent,* Penguin, New York, 1986

HUNTINGTON, SUSAN L., and HUNTINGTON, JOHN, *The Art of Ancient India: Buddhist, Hindu, and Jain,* Weatherhill, New York, 1985

RAMANAIAH, J., *Temples of South India: A Study of Hindu, Jain, and Buddhist Monuments of the Deccan,* Concept, New Delhi, 1989

WILLIAMS, JOANNA GOTTFRIED, *The Art of Gupta India, Empire and Province,* Princeton University Press, 1982

CHAPTER SEVENTEEN: CHINESE ART

CAHILL, JAMES, *Chinese Painting,* Rizzoli, New York, 1985

QIAN, HAO, et al., *Out of China's Earth: Archeological Discoveries in the People's Republic of China,* China Pictorial, Beijing, and Abrams, New York, 1981

RAWSON, JESSICA, *Ancient China: Art and Archaeology,* Harper & Row, New York, 1980

SICKMAN, LAWRENCE C., and SOPER, ALEXANDER, *The Art and Architecture of China,* 3d ed., Penguin, Baltimore, 1968

SIRÉN, OSVALD, *Chinese Painting: Leading Masters and Principles,* 7 vols., Ronald Press, New York, 1956–58; repr. ed., Hacker, New York, 1973

SULLIVAN, MICHAEL, *The Arts of China,* 3d ed., University of California Press, Berkeley, 1984

TING, FRANCISCA, *Chinese Painting,* Dover, New York, 1991

CHAPTER EIGHTEEN: JAPANESE ART

AKIYAMA, TERUKAZU, *Japanese Painting* (tr. J. Emmons), Skira, Geneva, 1971; repr. ed., Rizzoli, New York, 1977

KIDDER, J. E., *Japanese Temples: Sculpture, Paintings, Gardens, and Architecture,* Abrams, New York, 1964

MINO, YUTAKA, and ROSENFIELD, JOHN M., *The Great Eastern Temple: Treasures of Japanese Buddhist Art from Todai-ji,* Art Institute of Chicago and Indiana University Press, Bloomington, 1986

NOMA, SEIROKU, *The Arts of Japan* (tr. J. Rosenfield and G. T. Webb), 2 vols., Kodansha, Tokyo, 1978; distr. by Harper & Row, New York

PAINE, ROBERT, and SOPER, ALEXANDER, *The Art and Architecture of Japan,* 3d ed., Penguin, New York, 1981

STANLEY-BAKER, JOAN, *Japanese Art,* Thames & Hudson, New York, 1984

STERN, HAROLD P., *Master Prints of Japan: Ukiyo-e Hanga,* Abrams, New York, 1969

CHAPTER NINETEEN
EPILOGUE: THE DAWN OF INDIVIDUALISM IN ITALIAN ART — THE THIRTEENTH AND FOURTEENTH CENTURIES

BAXANDALL, MICHAEL, *Giotto and the Orators (1350–1450),* Clarendon Press, Oxford, 1971

CHIELLINI, MONICA, *Cimabue,* Scala Books, Florence, 1988; distr. by Harper & Row, New York

COLE, BRUCE, *Sienese Painting: From Its Origin to the Fifteenth Century,* Indiana University Press, Bloomington, 1985

CRICHTON, GEORGE H., and CRICHTON, SYLVIA R., *Nicolo Pisano and the Revival of Sculpture in Italy,* Cambridge University Press, Cambridge, 1938

FREMANTLE, RICHARD, *Florentine Gothic Painters from Giotto to Masaccio: A Guide to Painting in and near Florence,* Secker & Warburg, London, 1975

FRUGONI, CHIARA, *Pietro and Ambrogio Lorenzetti,* Scala Books, Florence, 1988; distr. by Harper & Row, New York

GILBERT, CREIGHTON, *Italian Art 1400–1500: Sources and Documents,* Prentice-Hall, Englewood Cliffs, N.J., 1980

MEISS, MILLARD, *Painting in Florence and Siena After the Black Death,* Princeton University Press, 1978

POPE-HENNESSY, SIR JOHN, *Italian Gothic Sculpture,* Vintage Books, New York, 1985

STUBBLEBINE, JAMES H., ed., *Giotto: The Arena Chapel Frescoes,* Norton, New York, 1969

INDEX

Pages on which illustrations appear are in *italics*. Names of artists and architects whose work is illustrated are in CAPITALS.

CREDITS

Photograph Credits

The author and publisher wish to thank the libraries, museums, galleries, and private collectors named in the picture captions for permitting the reproduction of works of art in their collections and for supplying the necessary photographs. Photographs from other sources are gratefully acknowledged below.

Harry N. Abrams Archives, New York, I-22, I-25, 1-14, 3-30, 3-31, 4-11, 9-17, 10-35/36/37, 16-8, 16-11, 16-29, 16-32; A.C.I., Brussels, I-7, 14-18; ACSAA Color Slide Project, Department of the History of Art, University of Michigan, Ann Arbor (Dr. Walter Spink), 16-16, 16-17; Alinari, Florence, I-6, I-26, 7-34, 7-36, 7-43, 7-100, 8-3, 9-6, 9-12, 9-16, 9-20, 9-29, 9-31, 9-36, 9-37, 9-40, 9-47, 9-48, 9-50, 9-51, 9-52, 9-55, 9-58, 9-63, 9-67, 9-70, 9-78, 10-6, 10-10, 10-18, 10-21, 10-26, 10-27, 10-30, 10-46, 10-59, 10-60, 10-61, 10-62, 14-20, 14-22, 14-24, 14-25, 14-26, 14-31, 14-33, 14-39, 15-57, 15-60/61/62/63/64, 15-66, 19-1/2/3/4/5/6, 19-9, 19-10, 19-19, 19-21; Jörg P. Anders (courtesy Bildarchiv Preussischer Kulturbesitz, Berlin), 13-21; Bernard Andreae, *The Art of Rome,* Harry N. Abrams, Inc., New York, 1977, Pl. 148, I-25; Antiken-Sammlung, Staatliche Museen zu Berlin, Hauptstadt der DDR, 7-101; Archaeological Survey of India, Janpath, New Delhi, 16-20; Archivio Fotografico dei Musei e Gallerie Pontificie, Vatican City, Rome, 10-15, 10-16; Courtesy The Art Institute of Chicago, All Rights Reserved, I-27; Arxiu MAS (A.y.R. MAS Barcelona), I-19, 11-10, 11-20, 14-15, 14-43, 14-46, 15-49; Asuka-En, Nara, 18-4, 18-10; The Athlone Press, University of London, 1-19; Esin Atil, *Turkish Art,* p. 121, copublished Smithsonian Institution Press, Washington, D.C., and Harry N. Abrams, Inc., New York, 1980, 11-18; James Austin, Cambridge, England, 14-11, 15-23; Avery Library, Columbia University, New York, 9-46; Maurice Babey, Basel, 3-25, 3-48; Bruno Balestrini, Electa Editrice, Milan, 3-47; Donald Bell-Scott, 7-102; Jacques Bendien, Naples, 9-42; Benri-Do, Japan, 18-5; Biblioteca Apostolica Vaticana, Rome, 13-12; Bibliothèque Nationale, Paris, 7-52, 10-51, 12-7, 13-8, 13-22, 14-44, 15-36, 15-39; Bildarchiv Foto Marburg, Marburg/Lahn, Germany, 3-18, 3-26, 7-72, 9-1, 13-5, 13-6, 14-10, 14-28, 14-37, 15-4, 15-5, 15-16, 15-20, 15-21, 15-25, 15-30, 15-34, 15-38, 15-40, 15-41, 15-47; Erwin Böhm, Mainz, 4-4, 14-23, 14-28, 14-29; Lee Boltin, New York, front cover, 3-43, 3-46, 7-109, 12-2; Buch- und Kunstsammlung St. Hildegarde, Rhein-Eibingen, 14-49; Bulloz, Paris, 7-5; Bundesdenkmalamt, Vienna, 15-43; Caisse Nationale des Monuments Historiques, Paris, 1-2, 1-3, 1-7, 1-8, 14-2, 14-9, 14-12, 14-13, 14-14, 14-16, 15-3, 15-8, 15-10, 15-19, 15-22, 15-37; Cameraphoto, Venice, 15-65; Ludovico Canali, Rome, I-13, 8-5, 8-6, 9-9, 9-18, 9-33, 9-44, 10-19, 10-31, 10-32, 10-33, 10-59, 10-60, 14-33, 19-8, 19-10, 19-16, 19-17, 19-18; The Chinese Embassy, Washington, D.C., 17-6; Geoffrey Clements, New York, 10-42 (from a color proof supplied by Kurt Weitzmann, Princeton); The Cleveland Museum of Art, 17-17; Fred R. Cohen, New York, 11-19, 16-30; Joan Lebold Cohen, New York, 17-10; Compania Mexicana Aerofoto, Mexico City, 5-3; Kenneth John Conant, Wellesley, 14-6, 14-8, (courtesy the Country Medieval Academy of America), 14-7; Courtauld Institute, 15-56; De Antonis Fotografico, Rome, 6-12, 9-77; Department of Antiquities, Algeria, 9-59; Deutsche Fotothek, Dresden, 10-68; Deutscher Kunstverlag, Munich, 13-1; Deutsches Archäologisches Institut, Athens, 7-18, 7-32; Deutsches Archäologisches Institut, Istanbul, 7-85; Deutsches Archäologisches Institut, Rome, 7-79, 7-105, 8-8, 9-21, 9-31, 9-38, 9-39, 9-56, 9-65, 9-76; Jean Dieuzade, (Yan) Toulouse, 1-9, 14-3; Directorate General of Antiquities and Museums, Damascus, 9-69; Dumbarton Oaks Center for Byzantine Studies, Washington, D.C., 10-49, 10-55, 10-56; Editions Cercle d'Art, Paris, 10-67; Editions d'Art Skira, Geneva, 11-4; Eliot Elisofon, 16-15, 16-19, 16-21, 16-24, 16-25, 16-38, 16-39; © Her Majesty Queen Elizabeth II, 2-3; Fotocielo, Rome, 14-21; Foto Grassi, Siena, 19-14; Fotostudio Rapuzzi, Brescia, 9-68; Fototeca Unione, Rome, 7-104, 8-2, 9-4, 9-8, 9-9, 9-10, 9-22, 9-23, 9-32, 9-49, 9-61, 9-72, 9-73, 9-80; Foto Vaghi, Parma, 14-27; Alison Frantz, Princeton, 6-16, 7-50, 7-62, 7-64, 10-52; Fraser, 10-9; Gabinetto Fotografico, Galleria degli Uffizi, Florence, 8-7; Gabinetto Fotografico, Nazionale, Rome, I-2, 8-4, 10-48; GAI, Baghdad, 4-1; Ewing Galloway, New York, 3-14; G.E.K.S., New York, 9-48, 9-60, 9-81, 10-40, 11-14; Giraudon, Paris, 9-25, 11-1, 15-12, 15-18, 15-35, back cover; Government of India, Department of Archeology, 16-2/3/4/5/6, 16-10, 16-12, 16-14, 16-22, 16-27; The Green Studio, Ltd., Dublin, I-23, 12-8; Irmgard Groth (reproduced with permission of Merle Green Robertson, Pre-Columbian Art Research Institute), 5-8; Hans G. Guterbock (the Anatolian Reconnaissance Expedition of The Oriental Institute of The University of Chicago, 1954), 4-16; Hara Collection, Yokohama, 18-16; Hauptamt für Hochbauwesen Bildstelle U. Denkmalsarchiv, Nürnberg, 15-42; André Held, Ecublens, Switzerland, 3-22, 7-107, 10-66; Dr. Hellmut Hell, Reutlingen, 10-13; Hickey & Robertson, Houston, I-28; Hirmerfotoarchiv, Munich, I-10, I-18, 3-2, 3-10, 3-15, 3-16, 3-20, 3-30, 3-31, 3-34, 3-40, 3-44, 4-5, 4-20, 6-3, 6-4, 6-6, 6-7, 6-9, 6-11, 6-13, 6-18, 6-19, 6-20, 7-1, 7-2, 7-8, 7-9, 7-10, 7-12, 7-16, 7-20, 7-24, 7-29, 7-40, 7-41, 7-44, 7-45, 7-54, 7-55, 7-57, 7-60, 7-61, 7-63, 7-65, 7-66, 7-67, 7-68, 7-74, 7-77, 7-78, 7-91, 7-93, 7-95, 7-96, 7-99, 8-13, 10-20, 10-23, 10-29, 10-41, 10-65, 13-16, 14-40, 15-32, 15-44; George Holton, New York, I-3; Rod Hook, 2-15; Professor Erik Hornung, Basel, 3-23; Martin Hurliman, Zurich, 10-69; The Institute for Art Research, Tokyo, I-14, 17-22; The Institute of Fine Arts, New York University (courtesy Professor Alfred Salmony), 16-9; Istituto Centrale del Restauro, Rome, 19-14; Istituto di Etruscologia e Antichita Italiche, Universita di Roma, 8-1; Istituto per la Collaborazione Culturale, Rome, 4-25; Bruno Jarrett, ARS/ADAGP, I-16; Bela Kalman, 16-37; Pal Keleman, 5-13; The Kern Institute, Leiden (courtesy N. J. Krom), 16-18; Justin Kerr, 5-6, 5-7; A. F. Kersting, London, 11-8, 11-17, 14-35, 15-14, 15-52, 15-54; Dimitri Kessel, Paris, I-5, 6-10; Nikos Kontos, Athens, 6-21, 6-22, 6-23, 7-4, 7-7, 7-11, 7-30, 7-31, 7-33, 7-81; Studio Koppermann, Gauting, Germany, 7-21, 7-22, 7-26, 7-35; Lampl (adapted from J. W. Crowfoot), 10-1, (adapted from J. M. C. Toynbee and J. B. Ward-Perkins), 10-2; Sherman Lee, *A History of Far Eastern Art,* 4th ed., Harry N. Abrams, Inc., New York, 1982, p. 163, 17-13; Tony Linck, Fort Lee, New Jersey, 2-13; Giovanni Mannino, Rome, 1-11; Eugene D. Markowski, Washington, D.C., 9-62, 16-7, 16-23, 16-34, 16-36; Leonard von Matt, Buochs, Switzerland, 6-14, 8-11, 9-14, 13-7; Mayuyama, Junkichi, 18-3, 18-6, 18-11, 18-14, 18-15; Mazenod, 7-53; James Mellaart, London, 1-15, 1-16, 1-17, 1-18; Metropolitan Museum of Art, New York (Egyptian Expedition), 3-41 (on loan from the People's Republic of China, photo Seth Joel), 17-3; Erwin Meyer, Vienna, 9-24; Courtesy of the Regents of the University of Michigan, 10-43; Ministry of Public Buildings and Works, London, 1-20, 1-21; MOA Museum, Atami, Japan, 18-21; Musée de l'Homme, Paris, 2-5; Musées de la Ville de Strasbourg, France, 15-48; Museum of Fine Arts, Boston, Harvard-Boston Expedition, 3-27; National Monuments Record, London, 15-51, 15-53; National Museum, Stockholm (Professor Gustav Siren), 17-11; Ohio Historical Society, 2-14; Ohmichi, Jiichi, 18-13; Okamoto, Shigeo, Tokyo, 18-17, 18-18; The Oriental Institute, University of Chicago, 4-7, 4-16, 4-17, 4-19, 4-26, 4-27; Kostas Papaioannou, *The Art of Greece,* Harry N. Abrams, Inc., New York, 1989 (pp. 400–401), 7-53, (p. 551), 7-86; Thomas Pedersen, Paul Pedersen, Aarhus, Denmark, 7-76; Courtesy People's Republic of China, 17-4; René Percheron, Puteaux, France, 11-16; Pericot-Garcia, Galloway, and Lommel, *Prehistoric and Primitive Art,* Sansoni Editore, Florence, © 1967, 1-4; Pickard, *Theatre of Dionysus in Athens,* Cambridge, 7-75; Pontificia Commissione di Architettura Sacra, Vatican City, Rome, 10-3, 10-4; Josephine Powell, Rome, 7-46, 7-47, 10-63; Tatiana Proskouriakoff, *An Album of Maya Architecture,* 1946, The Carnegie Institution of Washington, D.C., 5-5; Mario Quattrone Fotostudio, Florence, 15-58, 19-6, 19-11; Rémy, Dijon, 14-45; Michel Renaudeau, HOA-QUI Agency, Paris, 2-9; Rheinisches Bildarchiv, Cologne, 13-13, 13-20, 15-44; Rheinisches Landesmuseum, Trier, 9-83, 9-84; R.M.N., Paris, I-4, 3-19, 4-11, 4-12, 4-15, 4-30, 10-57; George Roos, New York, 9-85; Jean Roubier, Paris, 9-30, 14-38, 15-28; Sansoni Editore, Florence, 1-10; Scala/Art Resource, New York, 3-9, 7-37, 7-38, 14-19; Helga Schmidt-Glassner, Stuttgart, 15-46; Ronald Sheridan/Ancient Art & Architecture Collection, U.K., 11-13; Shogaku-Kan, Japan, 18-7; Edwin Smith, Essex, England, 4-22; Soprintendenza alle Antichita, Rome, 7-97; Sovfoto/Eastfoto, New York, 10-71, 17-25; Staatsbibliothek Preussischer Kulturbesitz, Berlin, 9-64; Henri Stierlin, Geneva, 3-5, 5-10; Dr. Franz Stoedtner, Düsseldorf, 7-19; M. Subramanian (courtesy Stephen Huyler), 16-28; Wim Swaan, New York, 3-11, 3-24, 3-29, 3-35, 11-9; T.A.P., Athens, 7-6; D. Tasic, Belgrade, 10-64; Taylor & Dull, Inc., New York, 2-10; Jerry L. Thompson, New York, 2-7; Marvin Trachtenberg, I-21, 9-25, 9-53, 10-39, 10-54, 15-1, 15-23, 15-64; United States Department of the Interior, 2-19; Jean Vertut, Issy-les-Moulineaux, 1-6, 3-36; Villani e Figli, Bologna, 7-57; Wanatabe, Yoshio, Japan, 18-2; Clarence Ward, Oberlin, 15-31; J.-B. Ward-Perkins, 9-11, 9-13, 9-28, 9-71; John Webb, London, 15-55; Yugoslav Tourist Office, New York, 9-79; ZEFA, London, 5-15.

Diagram Copyrights

John Fleming and Hugh Honour, *The Visual Arts: A History,* 3d ed., © 1991, Harry N. Abrams, Inc., New York: 10-38; Banister Fletcher, *A History of Architecture,* © 1961, Charles Scribner's Sons, New York: 10-58; Helen Gardner, *Art Through the Ages,* 5th ed., © 1970, Harcourt Brace Jovanovich, New York: 13-4; Irmgard Hutter, *Early Christian and Byzantine Art,* © 1971, Universe Books, New York: 10-4; A. W. Lawrence, *Greek Architecture,* © 1957, Penguin Books Ltd: 7-89.

Text Credit

The lines on pages 54–55 from Olowe's *oriki,* from *Yoruba: Nine Centuries of African Art and Thought,* by Henry John Drewal and John Pemberton III with Rowland Abiodun, are reprinted with the permission of the Center for African Art, New York. Copyright © 1989, The Center for African Art, New York.